International Handbook of Migration, Minorities and Education

Zvi Bekerman • Thomas Geisen
Editors

International Handbook of Migration, Minorities and Education

Understanding Cultural and Social Differences in Processes of Learning

Springer

Editors
Dr. Zvi Bekerman
School of Education, Melton Center
Hebrew University
91905 Jerusalem
Israel
mszviman@mscc.huji.ac.il

Dr. Thomas Geisen
School of Social Work
University of Applied Sciences
Northwestern Switzerland
Riggenbachstrasse 16
4600 Olten
Switzerland
thomas.geisen@fhnw.ch

ISBN 978-94-007-1465-6   e-ISBN 978-94-007-1466-3
DOI 10.1007/978-94-007-1466-3
Springer Dordrecht Heidelberg London New York

Library of Congress Control Number: 2011937702

© Springer Science+Business Media B.V. 2012
No part of this work may be reproduced, stored in a retrieval system, or transmitted in any form or by any means, electronic, mechanical, photocopying, microfilming, recording or otherwise, without written permission from the Publisher, with the exception of any material supplied specifically for the purpose of being entered and executed on a computer system, for exclusive use by the purchaser of the work.

Printed on acid-free paper

Springer is part of Springer Science+Business Media (www.springer.com)

Contents

1 **Migration, Minorities, and Learning—Understanding Cultural and Social Differences in Education** 1
Thomas Geisen and Zvi Bekerman

Part I Culture, Difference and Learning

2 **Movements and Migratory Processes: Roles and Responsibilities of Education and Learning** 9
Pat Cox

3 **Understanding Cultural Differences as Social Limits to Learning: Migration Theory, Culture and Young Migrants** 19
Thomas Geisen

4 **Beyond Limits and Limitations: Reflections on Learning Processes in Contexts of Migration and Young People** 35
Pat Cox

5 **The Concept of Ethnicity and its Relevance for Biographical Learning** 53
Ursula Apitzsch

6 **"No Place. Nowhere" for Migrants' Subjectivity!?** 67
Athanasios Marvakis

7 **Learning to Live Together—Towards a New Integration Society** 85
Esteban Piñeiro and Jane Haller

8 **Opportunities of Managing Diversity in Local Educational Programs** 101
Andreas Thiesen

v

9 Family Child-Raising and Educational Strategies Among European Mixed Couples 117
Sofia Gaspar

10 Opening a Gate to Citizenship: Media for Migrants 135
Esther Schely-Newman

11 Living in Different Worlds and Learning All About It: Migration Narratives in Perspective 153
Joanne Cassar

12 Early Childhood Education in Multilingual Settings 169
Drorit Lengyel

Part II Education in Multilingual Societies

13 Migration, Minorities, and Learning: Understanding Cultural and Social Differences in Education 189
M. Lynn Aylward

14 The State, Official-Language Education, and Minorities: Estonian-Language Instruction for Estonia's Russian-Speakers and the Võro 195
Kara D. Brown

15 *The Inuit Qaujimajatuqangit* Conversation: The Language and Culture of Schooling in the Nunavut Territory of Canada 213
M. Lynn Aylward

16 Ambivalence: Minority Parents Positioning When Facing School Choices 231
Zvi Bekerman and Moshe Tatar

17 Social Change and Minority Education: A Sociological and Social Historical View on Minority Education in Croatia 249
Jadranka Čačić-Kumpes

18 Reimagining Home in Alberta's Francophone Communities 265
Laura A. Thompson

19 New School, New System: The Experiences of Immigrant Students in Irish Schools 283
Merike Darmody, Emer Smyth, Delma Byrne and Frances McGinnity

Contents

20 Beyond Cultural Differences: Understanding and Negotiating the Conflict Between Chinese Immigrant Parents and Canadian Teachers 301
Yan Guo and Bernard Mohan

Part III Heterogeneity and Learning in Schools

21 Introduction: Heterogeneity, Belonging and Learning in Schools 321
Irina Schmitt

22 Dealing with Diversity and Social Heterogeneity: Ambivalences, Challenges and Pitfalls for Pedagogical Activity 331
Christine Riegel

23 A Learning Curve: The Education of Immigrants in Newcastle-upon-Tyne and Bremen from the 1960s to the 1980s 349
Sarah E. Hackett

24 School Policies, Gender-Sex-Sexuality and Ethnocultural Re-production in Sweden, Canada, and Germany 365
Irina Schmitt

25 Effects of the Head Start Program in the USA as Indicators of Ethnic Inequalities 383
Claudia Koehler

26 Project-Based Learning to Enhance Recognition and Acceptance of Cultural Diversity in the Elementary School 403
Christos Govaris and Stavroula Kaldi

27 School Performance of Children of Indian and Cape Verdean Immigrants in Basic Schooling in Portugal 419
Teresa Seabra

28 Migration, Educational Policies, and Practices: Constructing Difference in Buenos Aires and in Madrid 435
Ana Bravo-Moreno and Jason Beech

Part IV Higher Education

29 Introduction: Higher Education 455
Marisol Clark-Ibáñez

30	Encountering An-Other: The Culture of Curriculum and Inclusive Pedagogies 461
	Ruth Arber

31	Possible Selves and Goal Orientations of East-African Undergraduate Students in the United States 479
	Joash M. Wambua and Cecil Robinson

32	A Passport to Education: Undocumented Latino University Students Navigating Their Invisible Status 497
	Marisol Clark-Ibáñez, Fredi Garcia-Alverdín and Gricelda Alva

Part V Religion and Learning

33	Introduction Part 5: Religion and Learning 517
	Eoin Daly

34	Integration by Other Means: Hindu Schooling in the Netherlands 523
	Michael S. Merry and Geert Driessen

35	Negotiating the School Curriculum for the Malay Muslims in Singapore 543
	Charlene Tan and Salleh Hairon

36	Precarious Religious Liberties in Education: The Salience of Demographic and Social Contingencies Under a Formally Pluralist Public Philosophy 559
	Eoin Daly

37	Educational Processes and Ethnicity Among Hindu Migrants 577
	Helena Sant'ana

Part VI Community, Work and Learning 595

38	Community, Work and Learning 597
	Georgina Tsolidis

39	Multiculturalism in a Deeply Divided Society: The Case of Cyprus 605
	Michalinos Zembylas

40	Learning Who They "Really" Are: From Stigmatization to Opportunities to Learn in Greek Romani Education 623
	William New and Michael S. Merry

41	**Learning Difference in the Diaspora—Sharing Sacred Spaces** .... 641 Georgina Tsolidis	
42	**Deciphering Somali Immigrant Adolescents' Navigation and Interpretation of Resources Embedded in Social Relationships** .... 659 Moosung Lee and Na'im Madyun	
43	**Agency and Everyday Knowledge of Filipina Migrants in Dubai, United Arab Emirates** .... 677 Simone Christ	
44	**Ethnicized Youth Subcultures and "Informal Learning" in Transitions to Work** .... 695 Vitor Sérgio Ferreira and Axel Pohl	
45	**"I Am Illiterate. But I Am a Doctor of Capoeira": Integration of Marginalized Youth in Brazil** .... 711 Karin E. Sauer	
46	**Learning Insularity: Social Capital, Social Learning and Staying at Home Among European Youth** .... 729 David Cairns and Katarzyna Growiec	
47	**Concluding Remarks** .... 743 Zvi Bekerman and Thomas Geisen	

Index 747

Contributors

Gricelda Alva Department of Sociology, California State University, 333 S. Twin Oaks Valley Road, San Marcos, CA, 92096 USA

Ursula Apitzsch FB 03 Gesellschaftswissenschaften, J.W. Goethe-Universität Frankfurt, Robert-Mayer-Straße 5, 60054 Frankfurt am Main, Germany
e-mail: apitzsch@soz.uni-frankfurt.de

Ruth Arber Faculty of Arts and Education, School of Education, 221 Burwood Highway, Burwood 3121, VIC, Australia
e-mail: ruth.arber@deakin.edu.au

M. Lynn Aylward School of Education, Acadia University, Wolfville, NS, Canada
e-mail: Lynn.aylward@acadiau.ca

Zvi Bekerman School of Education, Melton Center, Hebrew University, 91905 Jerusalem, Israel
e-mail: mszviman@mscc.huji.ac.il

Jason Beech Escuela de Educación, Universidad de San Andrés, Vito Dumas 284, Victoria, Argentina
e-mail: jbeech@udesa.edu.ar

Ana Bravo-Moreno Facultad de Ciencias de la Educación, Universidad de Granada, Campus de Cartuja, 18071 Granada, Spain
e-mail: abravo@ugr.es

Kara D. Brown College of Education, University of South Carolina, Wardlaw Hall 136, Columbia, SC 29208, USA
e-mail: brownk25@mailbox.sc.edu

Delma Byrne The Economic and Social Research Institute, Whitaker Square, Dublin 2, Ireland
e-mail: Delma.Byrne@esri.ie

Jadranka Čačić-Kumpes Department of Sociology, University of Zadar, Zadar, Croatia
e-mail: jcacic@unizd.hr

David Cairns Centre for Research and Studies in Sociology, ISCTE-Lisbon University Institute, Edifício ISCTE, Av. das Forças Armadas, 1649-026 Lisboa, Portugal
e-mail: david.cairns@iscte.pt

Joanne Cassar Department of Youth and Community Studies, University of Malta, Msida, Malta
e-mail: joanne.cassar@um.edu.mt

Simone Christ Institute of Oriental and Asian Studies, Department of Southeast Asian Studies, University of Bonn, Nassestr. 2, 53113 Bonn, Germany
e-mail: simone.christ@uni-bonn.de

Marisol Clark-Ibáñez, Ph.D. Department of Sociology, California State University San Marcos, 333 S. Twin Oaks Valley Road, San Marcos, CA 92096, USA
e-mail: mibanez@csusm.edu

Pat Cox School of Social Work, University of Central Lancashire, Lancashire, PR1 2HE, UK
e-mail: pcox2@uclan.ac.uk

Eoin Daly School of Law and Government, Dublin City University, Glasnevin, Dublin 9, Ireland
e-mail: eoin.daly@dcu.ie

Merike Darmody The Economic and Social Research Institute, Whitaker Square, Dublin 2, Ireland
e-mail: Merike.Darmody@esri.ie

Geert Driessen ITS—Institute for Applied Social Sciences, Radboud University Nijmegen, PO Box 9048, 6500 KJ Nijmegen, The Netherlands
e-mail: G.Driessen@its.ru.nl

Vitor Sérgio Ferreira, Ph.D. Instituto de Ciências Sociais, Lisboa, Portugal
e-mail: vitor.ferreira@ics.ul.pt

Fredi García-Alverdín Department of Sociology, California State University, 333 S. Twin Oaks Valley Road, San Marcos, CA 92096, USA
e-mail: mibanez@csusm.edu

Sofia Gaspar CIES-ISCTE-IUL, Ed. ISCTE, Av. das Forças Armadas, 1649-026, Lisbon, Portugal
e-mail: sofia.gaspar@iscte.pt

Thomas Geisen School of Social Work, University of Applied Sciences, Northwestern Switzerland, Riggenbachstrasse 16, 4600 Olten, Switzerland
e-mail: thomas.geisen@fhnw.ch

Christos Govaris Department of Primary Education, School of Humanities, University of Thessaly, Argonafton & Filellinon, 38221 Volos, Greece
e-mail: govaris@uth.gr

Katarzyna Growiec Faculty of Psychology, Warsaw School of Social Sciences and Humanities, ul. Chodakowska 19/31, 03-815 Warsaw, Poland

Yan Guo Faculty of Education, University of Calgary, 2500 University Drive NW, Calgary, AB, Canada
e-mail: yanguo@ucalgary.ca

Sarah E. Hackett Faculty of Education & Society, University of Sunderland, Sunderland, SR1 3PZ, UK
e-mail: sarah.hackett-1@sunderland.ac.uk

Jane Haller Hochschule für Soziale Arbeit, Fachhochschule Nordwestschweiz, Unterer Batterieweg 39, 4053 Basel, Switzerland
e-mail: janehaller@gmx.net

Stavroula Kaldi Department of Primary Education, School of Humanities, University of Thessaly, Argonafton & Filellinon, 38221 Volos, Greece
e-mail: govaris@uth.gr

Claudia Koehler European Forum for Migration Studies (EFMS), Schuetzenstrasse 51, 96047 Bamberg, Germany
e-mail: claudia.koehler@uni-bamberg.de

MooSung Lee Educational Policy and Leadership, Hong Kong Institute of Education, 42-1F-D4, 10 Lo Ping Rd, Tai Po, Hong Kong
e-mail: mslee@ied.edu.hk

Drorit Lengyel Center for Assessment and Support, Faculty of Human Sciences, School of Education, University of Cologne, Gronewaldstr. 2, 50931 Cologne, Germany
e-mail: dlengyel@uni-koeln.de

Na'im Madyun Postsecondary Teaching and Learning, University of Minnesota-Twin Cities, 206 Burton Hall, Minneapolis, MN, USA
e-mail: madyu002@umn.edu

Athanasios Marvakis Department of Primary Education, University Campus—Building "Tower," Aristotle University of Thessalonica, 54124 Thessalonica, Greece
e-mail: marvakis@eled.auth.gr

Frances McGinnity The Economic and Social Research Institute, Whitaker Square, Dublin 2, Ireland
e-mail: Merike.Darmody@esri.ie

Michael S. Merry Faculty of Social and Behavioural Sciences, University of Amsterdam, Nieuwe Prinsengracht 130, 1018 VZ Amsterdam, The Netherlands
e-mail: m.s.merry@uva.nl

Bernard Mohan Faculty of Education, University of Calgary, 2500 University Drive NW, Calgary, AB, Canada
e-mail: yanguo@ucalgary.ca

William New Beloit College, Beloit, 53511, USA
e-mail: newb@beloit.edu

Esteban Piñeiro Institut Sozialplanung und Stadtentwicklung, Thiersteinerallee 57, 4053 Basel, Switzerland
e-mail: esteban.pineiro@fhnw.ch

Axel Pohl Institute for Regional Innovation and Social Research (IRIS), Tübingen, IRIS e.V., Fürststr. 3, D-72072 Tübingen, Germany

Christine Riegel Institute of Education, Social Pedagogy, Freiburg University of Education, Kunzenweg 21, 79117 Freiburg, Germany
e-mail: christine.riegel@ph-freiburg.de

Cecil Robinson University of Alabama, 308 Carmichael Hall, Campus Box 870231, Tuscaloosa, AL 35487-0231, USA

Hairon Salleh Policy & Leadership Studies, National Institute of Education, NIE2-03-64, 1 Nanyang Technological University, Singapore, Singapore
e-mail: charlene.tan@nie.edu.sg

Helena Sant'ana Universidade Técnica de Lisboa—ISCSP, Rua Almerindo Lessa—Polo Universitário do Alto da Ajuda, 1349-055, Lisboa, Portugal
e-mail: hsantana@iscsp.utl.pt

Karin E. Sauer Fakultät für Sozialwesen, Baden-Wuerttemberg Cooperative State University, Duale Hochschule Baden-Württemberg, Schramberger Str. 26, 78054 Villingen-Schwenningen, Germany
e-mail: karin.sauer@dhbw-vs.de

Teresa Seabra Department of Sociology, ISCTE–Instituto Universitário de Lisboa, 1500 2 Lisbon, Portugal
e-mail: teresa.seabra@iscte.pt

Esther Schely-Newman Noah Mozes Department of Communication and Journalism, The Hebrew University, Mount Scopus, Jerusalem
e-mail: msetti@mscc.huji.ac.il

Irina Schmitt Centre for Gender Studies, Lund University, PO Box 117, 221 00 Lund, Sweden
e-mail: irina.schmitt@genus.lu.se

Emer Smyth The Economic and Social Research Institute, Whitaker Square, Dublin 2, Ireland
e-mail: Emer.Smyth@esri.ie

Charlene Tan Policy & Leadership Studies, National Institute of Education, NIE2-03-64, 1 Nanyang Technological University, Singapore
e-mail: charlene.tan@nie.edu.sg

Moshe Tatar School of Education, Hebrew University, Jerusalem, Israel

Contributors

Andreas Thiesen Simrockstraße 26, 30171 Hannover, Germany
e-mail: A_Thiesen@web.de

Laura A. Thompson School of Education, Box 57, Acadia University, Wolfville, Nova Scotia, Canada, B4P 2R6
e-mail: laura.thompson@acadiau.ca

Georgina Tsolidis Open University of Cyprus, 5 Ayios Antonios St., 2002 Strovolos, Nicosia, Cyprus
e-mail: m.zembylas@ouc.ac.cy

Joash M. Wambua Miles College, 1652 Heritage Place, Birmingham, AL 35210, USA
e-mail: wambua@juno.com

Michalinos Zembylas Open University of Cyprus, 5 Ayios Antonios St., 2002 Strovolos, Nicosia, Cyprus
e-mail: m.zembylas@ouc.ac.cy; zembylas@msu.edu

About the Editors and Authors

Gricelda Alva graduated with Summa Cum Laude Honors from CSUSM in the field of Human Development with an emphasis in Counseling Services. She hopes to pursue a masters in Art Therapy. She is co-founder of a student support group for undocumented college students, has participated in outreach efforts to raise awareness about the experiences of undocumented students, and works to inform students and educators of the few resources available to undocumented students to pursue a higher education.

Ursula Apitzsch is Professor of Political Science and Sociology in the field of "Culture and Development" at the Goethe-University of Frankfurt/Main. She is Director of the Cornelia Goethe Centre for Women's and Gender Studies (CGC). Since 1998, she is board member of the RC 38 "Biography and Society" within the International Sociological Association (ISA). Since 2007, she is a member of the Executive Committee of the European Sociological Association (ESA). She has published broadly in the fields of migration, culture, and biography with special regard to the analysis of gender and ethnicity.

Ruth Arber is Senior Lecturer (TESOL) at Deakin University, Australia. Her research extends her interest in identity and difference in education, its implications for understanding how discourses of race and ethnicity are played out in schools and its consequences for critical and inclusive education. Her most recent application of this work focuses on the study of internationalization and cosmopolitanism in education systems which are becoming increasingly globalized. Her long experience as a teacher and lecturer of English as a second and foreign language is concerned with the application of this work for education in diverse contexts worldwide. Recent publications include articles in *Discourse, Journal of Intercultural Education, Race, ethnicity and Education, Globalisation, Societies and Education. Journal of Inclusive Education, Journal of Curriculum Studies, Journal of Educational Change,* book chapters and a book *Race, ethnicity and education globalised times (Springer: Netherlands).*

Lynn Aylward's research and teaching interests include the areas of community-based schooling, inclusive education, and teacher development. Her career in education has involved research, curriculum development, teacher education and public school teaching with diverse groups of learners from kindergarten to graduate school level in a wide variety of settings. She is currently a faculty member in the School of Education at Acadia University in Wolfville, Nova Scotia, Canada.

Jason Beech is Director of the School of Education at the Universidad de San Andrés in Buenos Aires, Argentina, where he also teaches Comparative Education. He is a Researcher of the National Council of Scientific and Technical Research of Argentina (CONICET). He is co-editor of the Journal *Revista de Política Educativa*. He recently published the book *Going to School in Latin America* (with Silvina Gvirtz, Westport, Greenwood Publishing Group, 2008).

Zvi Bekerman teaches Anthropology of education at the School of Education and the Melton Center, at the Hebrew University of Jerusalem. From 2003 to 2007 he was a Research Fellow at the Truman Institute for the Advancement of Peace, Hebrew University. His main interests are in the study of cultural, ethnic and national identity, including identity processes and negotiation during intercultural encounters and in formal/informal learning contexts. Since 1999 he has been conducting, with the support of the Ford, Spencer and Bernard Van Leer Foundations, a long term ethnographic research project on the integrated/bilingual Palestinian-Jewish schools in Israel. He has also recently become involved in the study of identity construction and development in educational computer-mediated environments. In brief, his interests lie in human learning processes, their development and practice, both in formal/informal and real/virtual environments; processes which, from the socio-historical perspectives within which he has been raised and from which he continues to learn, comprise a large portion of human activity. He has published numerous papers in these fields of study and is the editor (with Seonaigh MacPherson) of the referred journal *Diaspora, Indigenous, and Minority Education: An International Journal* (Taylor and Francis 2007). His recently published books include (edited with Nicholas Burbules and Diana Keller Silverman) *Learning in Places: The Informal Education Reader* (Peter Lang 2006); (with Claire McGlynn) *Addressing Ethnic Conflict through Peace Education: International Perspectives* (Palgrave McMillan 2007); (with Ezra Kopelowitz) *Cultural Education-Cultural Sustainability: Minority, Diaspora, Indigenous and Ethno-Religious Groups in Multicultural Societies* (Routledge Education—LEA, 2008) and (with Diana Silberman-Keller, Henry A. Giroux, and Nicholas Burbules) *Mirror Images: Popular Culture and Education* (Peter Lang—2008).

Ana Bravo-Moreno is an Associate Professor at the Department of Social Anthropology, University of Granada, Spain. Her most recent publications are (2010) "Access and Transitions in Education", in D. Mattheou (Ed.) *Changing Educational Landscapes*, and (2009) "Transnational mobilities: migrants and education". *Comparative Education Journal*. She is also the author of the book (2006) *Migration, Gender and National Identity,* Peter Lang.

Kara Brown is an Assistant Professor in the Department of Educational Studies at University of South Carolina. She teaches undergraduate and graduate courses in social foundations, comparative education and qualitative research methods. Brown's research focuses on language policy, minority schooling and teacher migration. Brown's work appears in *Anthropology of Education Quarterly, European Education, European Journal of Language Policy*, as well as chapters in edited volumes. Her research has been funded by the Spencer Foundation, Fulbright, the International Research and Exchange Board (IREX), the Association for the Advancement of Baltic Studies, and the University of South Carolina.

Delma Byrne is a Lecturer at the Departments of Sociology and Education at National University of Ireland Maynooth (NUIM). Her key areas of interest lie in sociology of education and social stratification in education and the labor market. She is current a co-ordinator of an international study that explores how inequality is maintained through the structure of schooling.

Jadranka Čačić-Kumpes is an Assistant Professor at the Department of Sociology, University of Zadar. She received her Ph.D. in sociology at the Faculty of Humanities and Social Sciences of the University of Zagreb. Her main fields of research include the sociology of education, the sociology of culture and the sociology of ethnic relations, especially the cultural and ethnic identity, ethnic minorities, interculturalism, multiculturalism and migration. She is Editor-in-Chief of the academic journal *Revija za sociologiju*.

David Cairns is a Senior Researcher at the Centre for Research and Studies in Sociology, ISCTE-Lisbon University Institute (CIES-IUL), Portugal. His main research interests are in the areas of youth and migration, particularly from comparative European perspectives, with over twenty publications to date, including articles in *International Migration, Journal of the Royal Anthropological Institute and Young*.

Joanne Cassar is Lecturer at the Department of Youth and Community Studies, University of Malta. Dr. Cassar's research interests comprise youth studies; in particular young people's construction of identities in multicultural contexts embedded in educational institutions, popular culture and policymaking bodies. She has presented papers in numerous international conferences and is also an author of children's books.

Simone Christ received an M.A. (Magister Artium) in Sociology, Cultural Anthropology and Political Science at the University of Trier in 2008, writing her thesis on Filipina migrant workers in Dubai, United Arab Emirates. Since 2008, she works as a lecturer at the Department of Southeast Asian Studies at the University of Bonn. She conducted fieldwork in the Philippines in 2009–2010 for her Ph.D. thesis on the Philippine culture of migration.

Marisol Clark-Ibáñez Ph.D. is an Associate Professor in the Department of Sociology at California State University San Marcos. She earned her doctorate in Sociology at University of California, Davis. Her areas of expertise include Sociology of Education, Qualitative/Visual Methods, and Latino Communities. She plans to expand the project on undocumented Latino college students to encompass the educational pipeline. Other current projects include the Scholarship of Teaching &

Learning and Sociology of Childhood. Her passion is teaching undergraduate and graduate courses. Professor Clark-Ibáñez enjoys working with students and is a recipient of the Latino Faculty Role Model Award and the Faculty Advocate Award.

Pat Cox is Senior Lecturer and Researcher in the School of Social Work, University of Central Lancashire UK. Her research and publications focus on issues in the lives of children and young people, including their experiences of migration. She has researched into the provision of community-based fostering care in Moldova as an alternative to institutional care and publications include 'Qualitative Research and Social Change' (2008, co-edited with T. Geisen and R. Green).

Eoin Daly is a Government of Ireland research scholar in the humanities and social sciences, and a doctoral student in the Faculty of Law at University College Cork. His research interests lie in the area of freedom of conscience and religion guarantees in the public education context, in Ireland, France the United States in particular. His work addresses competing claims on religious liberty from the standpoint of Rawls's justice as fairness.

Merike Darmody is a Research Officer at the Economic and Social Research Institute (ESRI). She mainly works in the area of education but is also interested in broader issues of the relationship between an individual and society. Her more recent work includes a study focusing on the integration of immigrant students in Irish primary and secondary schools. She is also involved in a European comparative study on the provision of religious education in a multicultural society.

Geert Driessen received a teacher's degree before continuing on to study educational theory. His Ph.D. thesis focused on the position of ethnic minority students in primary education. Currently he is a senior educational researcher at ITS (Institute for Applied Social Scienccs) of the Radboud University Nijmegen, the Netherlands. At ITS, he also served as a member of the Works Council, Head of the Department of Education, and member of the Management Team. He was involved in several large-scale cohort studies in primary and secondary education (VOCL: 400 schools, 20,000 students; PRIMA: 600 schools, 60,000 students; COOL: 550 schools, 38,000 students). Those studies were initiated to monitor the Dutch education system in general and to evaluate policies such as the Educational Priority Policy. He also performed policy evaluations with regard to Bilingual Education Programs, Early Childhood Education Programs, and Community Schools). In addition, he has served as a project manager of dozens of research projects. His major research interests include education in relation to ethnicity, social milieu and gender; other themes are parental participation; school choice; denominational schools; Islamic schools; integration and segregation; citizenship; preschool and early school education; bilingual education; dialects and regional languages; educational policy; compositional and peer group effects.

Vitor Sergio Ferreira Ph.D. born 1970, is a Researcher at the Institute of Social Sciences of University of Lisbon (ICS-UL), since 1993. His fields of expertise are youth cultures and transitions. He has been working at the Permanent Portuguese

Youth Observatory since 1996, a research program on Portuguese youth funded by the Portuguese government coordinated by ICS-UL. Recent work includes an empirical study on body modification techniques among young people like piercing, tattoos and others.

Fredi García-Alverdín is an M.A. candidate in Sociological Practice, under the Department of Sociology, at California State University-San Marcos (USA). His primary research interest is immigration, which he explores through race and ethnicity, race relations, identity, citizenship, education, labor, politics and community activism. His current research examines first-generation immigrants in North San Diego County (USA).

Sofia Gaspar holds a degree (IUL, Lisbon) and a Ph.D. (Universidad Complutense Madrid) in sociology. She was a lecturer in General Sociology and Sociological Theory at the Universidad Complutense de Madrid for two years. She is currently a post-doctoral research fellow at CIES-ISCTE, IUL (Lisbon, Portugal), where she is investigating European intra-marriage in Portugal, under the supervision of Professor Anália Torres. This project is financed by FCT of the Portuguese Ministry of Science, Technology and Higher Education (Ref: SFRH/BPD/38151/2007). Her main research interests are the sociology of the family, the sociology of migrations and European identity.

Thomas Geisen is Senior Lecturer and Researcher at the School of Social Work at the University of Applied Sciences Northwestern Switzerland. His main interests are in the study of migration, ethnicity and cultural issues as well as in questions of identity and belonging. Other fields of interest and research are work/labor relations and violence. His research encompasses racism, migrant families, family relations of right-wing youth and disability management. He has published numerous books and papers in these fields; among his recent publications are: *Arbeit in der Moderne. Ein dialogue imaginaire zwischen Karl Marx und Hannah Arendt* (VS Verlag, 2011); (edited with Henry Harder) *Disability Management and Workplace Integration* (Gower, 2011); (edited with Pat Cox and Roger Green) *Qualitative Research and Social Change. European Contexts* (Palgrave Macmillan, 2008); (edited with Anthony Andrew Hickey and Allen Karcher) *Migration, Mobility and Borders. Issues of Theory and Policy* (IKO Verlag, 2004); (edited with Christine Riegel) *Jugend, Partizipation und Migration. Orientierungen im Kontext von Integration und Ausgrenzung* (VS Verlag, 2007) and *Jugend, Zugehörigkeit und Migration. Subjektpositionierungen im Kontext von Jugendkultur, Ethnizitäts- und Geschlechterkonstruktionen* (VS Verlag, 2007); edited *Arbeitsmigration. WanderarbeiterInnen auf dem Weltmarkt für Arbeitskraft* (IKO Verlag, 2005).

Christos Govaris is an Associate Professor in the Department of Primary Education, University of Thessaly, Greece. He has carried out undergraduate studies in Pedagogics and postgraduate in Political Science (M.A.) at the University of Stuttgart and in Education (Ph.D.) at the University of Tübingen, Germany. His research interests include multicultural society and school inequalities, intercultural education and learning, and school development in a multicultural social environment.

Katarzyna Growiec is an Assistant Professor at the Faculty of Psychology, Warsaw School of Social Sciences and Humanities, Poland. Her main research interests are in social capital, social trust, subjective well-being, intergroup relations and social change during the economic crisis, with funded projects in Central and Eastern Europe (Global Development Network) and Iceland (EEA & Norway Grants), and recent articles published in journals including *European Societies*.

Yan Guo is Associate Professor in the Faculty of Education at the University of Calgary and an affiliated researcher with the Prairie Metropolis Centre of Excellence for Research on Immigration, Integration and Diversity (PMC). Her research interests include second language acquisition, immigrant parent knowledge, intercultural communication, second language acquisition and identity, content-based ESL instruction, discourse analysis, and diversity in teaching and learning.

Sarah Hackett holds a Ph.D. from the University of Durham and is a Lecturer in European History at the University of Sunderland. Her research interests include diaspora, migration and religion, place and space, and ethnic minorities in Europe. She is currently publishing the findings from recent research on the Muslim immigrant communities of Newcastle-upon-Tyne and Bremen, including a monograph that will be published by Manchester University Press.

Jane Haller cand. lic. phil. is studying sociology, cultural anthropology and psychology. She worked as a student assistant at the institute of cultural anthropology and for the institute of sociology at the university of Basel. Piñeiro and Haller have already co-written a theoretical article on the integration law in Basel: *Neue Migranten für die Integrationsgesellschaft. Versuch einer gouvernementalen Gegenlektüre des Prinzips "Fördern und Fordern"* (2009).

Stavroula Kaldi is an Assistant Professor in the Department of Primary Education, University of Thessaly, Greece. She has conducted undergraduate studies in Early Childhood Education (BA) at the Aristotle University of Thessaloniki, Greece and postgraduate studies on Teacher Education (MA) and in Education (PhD) at Sussex University, UK. Her research interests include project-based learning, co-operative teaching and learning and teacher education.

Claudia Koehler was born in 1974 in Dresden. She studied English and Spanish at the Institute for the Study of Foreign Languages in Erlangen. In 2008 she graduated from the University of Bamberg as a Diploma Sociologist. As a researcher at the European Forum for Migration Studies in Bamberg she is conducting a study on the integration of Muslim groups in Germany and evaluations of educational programs.

MooSung Lee is Assistant Professor in Educational Policy and Leadership at the Hong Kong Institute of Education. He earned his Ph.D. in Educational Policy and Administration at the University of Minnesota in 2009, funded by a Fulbright Scholarship. He is enthusiastic about studying contemporary educational issues facing socially-marginalized groups such as immigrants.

Drorit Lengyel is Assistant Professor at the University of Cologne, in the school of education and the Center for Assessment and Promotion. She was part of the research team for the German model program "Support for immigrant minority children and youth" (FörMig) at the Institute for International and Intercultural Comparative Education, University of Hamburg, 2005–2009. Her chief research interests are language socialization and early childhood education in multilingual settings, assessment and support in multilingual educational contexts, and classroom interaction in linguistically diverse settings.

Na'im Madyun is Assistant Professor in Postsecondary Teaching and Learning at the University of Minnesota. His research focuses on social factors (i.e., social capital, social disorganization theory) that explain the academic outcomes and experiences of students and faculty of color.

Athanasios Marvakis Psychologist (Dipl.-Psych., Dr. rer. soc., both University of Tübingen/Germany) is Associate Professor in Clinical Social Psychology at the School of Primary Education of the Aristotle University of Thessaloniki/Greece. His interests revolve around psychology and its relations with the various forms of social inequalities and social exclusion (e.g., racism, nationalism, ethnicism, multiculturalism), including youth as a social group (political orientations, youth and racism in Europe) and migrants in Greece. The last years he has started to be engaged in the critical psychology of the 'schooling-complex'.

Frances McGinnity has been a researcher at the Economic and Social Research Institute since 2004. She previously worked at the Max Planck Institute for Human Development in Berlin, and received her doctorate in sociology from Nuffield College Oxford in 2001. More recently her research has focused on equality and discrimination, both between men and women, and between different ethnic/national groups in Irish society.

Michael S. Merry is Professor of Philosophy of education in the Faculty of Social and Behavioral sciences. He earned his doctorate in educational policy studies with an emphasis in philosophy of education from the University of Wisconsin-Madison. He has published numerous articles in philosophy of education and comparative education and is the author of *Culture, Identity and Islamic Schooling: a philosophical approach* (Palgrave 2007) and is co-editor of *Citizenship, Identity and Education in Muslim Communities: essays on attachment and obligation* (Palgrave 2010). His philosophical and research interests include educational ethics, political and social philosophy, minority education and alternative pedagogies.

Bernard Mohan Emeritus Professor, Language and Literacy Education, University of British Columbia and Research Fellow at King's College London, and former Chair of the North American Systemic Functional Linguistics Association, finds that systemic functional models of language and linguistic analysis provide deep insights into both the research problems we study and the contemporary issues that face applied linguistics.

William New is Professor of Education and Youth Studies at Beloit College in Beloit, WI. He earned his doctorate in educational and applied developmental psychology from Teachers College, Columbia University. He has published a variety of articles on minority education, education policy and law, and student development.

Esteban Piñeiro lic. phil, studied sociology, cultural anthropology and media studies at the University of Basel and social work at the University of Applied Sciences Bern. He teaches and does research at the School of Social work, University of Applied Sciences Northwestern Switzerland. Currently he is co-directing a study on migration and representational administration. Together with Isabelle Bopp and Georg Kreis he edited the anthology *Fördern und Fordern im Fokus. Leerstellen des schweizerischen Integrationsdiskurses* (2009 Seismo, Zürich), reflections on current developments in migration and integration in Switzerland.

Axel Pohl born 1968, holds a university diploma in educational science and works as a researcher with the Institute for Regional Innovation and Social Research (IRIS), Tübingen/Germany, since 1994. His research is centered around the themes of education and social policies for immigrant youth, youth transitions and informal learning. He has been coordinating the UP2YOUTH project at IRIS from 2006 to 2009.

Christine Riegel Institute of Education at University of Tübingen/Germany. Previously she did research at the University of Fribourg/Switzerland, among others in an intervention study on the topic of preventing racism and exclusion in schools, founded by the Swiss National Found. 2003, she did her Ph.D. with a socio-biographic study on orientations of young immigrant women in Germany. Her field of research is on youth, migration, gender, racism, intersectional analysis, diversity and education.

Cecil Robinson is an Associate Professor of Educational Psychology at The University of Alabama. His research focuses on hope, well-being, and motivation of diverse student populations.

Hairon Salleh is an Assistant Professor at the National Institute of Education, Nanyang Technological University, Singapore. His research interests are in the fields of teacher professional development, critical theory, action research and education reform.

Helena Sant'ana is a Professor of Sociology at The Higher Institute of Social Sciences (ISCSP), Technical University of Lisbon, and belongs to the research team of CAPP Center of Administration and Public Policies. She specializes in social class and gender relations, ethnicity, colonialism in Africa and India, and identity formation of Indian Diaspora in Portugal. Universidade Técnica de Lisboa—ISCSP.

Karin E. Sauer Ph.D. in Social Sciences, Dipl.-Päd. (university degree in Education). Professor for Social Science at the Baden-Wuerttemberg Cooperative State University Villingen-Schwenningen since 2008. Research projects on *marginalized youth with successful trajectories of integration* in *Brazil* in 2006/2007 (supported by FAPERGS and Baden-Württembergisches Brasilien-Zentrum) and on *integration processes of children in multicultural societies* (Baden-Württemberg and California) from 2003 to 2006.

Teresa Seabra is Professor of Sociology of Education and researcher at the CIES/ISCTE-IUL. Main interests include children of immigrants, school achievement, social class and ethnicity. Has published two main books: *Families' education: ethnicity and social class* (1999) and *Adaptation and Adversity: school performance of children of Indian and Cape Verdian immigrants* (2010).

Esther Schely-Newman is an Assistant Professor in the Noah Mozes Department of Communication and Journalism at the Hebrew University of Jerusalem. Her research interests are language and society, discourse, life stories, and folklore. Her recent research appeared in *Discourse Studies, Western Folklore, Narrative Inquiry,* and *Research on Language and Social Interaction*. Her book, *Our Lives are but Stories: Narratives of Tunisian Israeli Women* was published by Wayne State University Press in 2002.

Irina Schmitt is a Teacher and Researcher at the Centre for Gender Studies, Lund University, Sweden. In her research and teaching, Irina draws on queer-feminist, anti-racist and post-colonial thinking to make sense of the power hierarchies in the world. Recently, Irina has focused her research on young people and schools – interesting spaces, where people negotiate belongings and norms in many ways, and where nationally specific notions of 'who we are' are re-created.

Emer Smyth is a Research Professor and program coordinator of Education Research at the ESRI. Her areas of interest include education, school to work transitions, and women's employment. She has a strong interest in comparative research on education and labor market issues. Currently she is a co-ordinator of a study that explores the transmission of religious beliefs and values through the education system and the family across different EU country contexts.

Charlene Tan is an Associate Professor at the national institute of education, Nanyang Technological University, Singapore. She has been a visiting research associate at the Oxford Centre for Islamic Studies and a visiting scholar at the Prince Alwaleed Bin Talal Centre of Islamic Studies, University of Cambridge. Her research and teaching areas are located in the fields of islamic/muslim education, philosophy of education, education policy, and comparative education.

Moshe Tatar Associate Professor, former Chair of the Department of Education and former Head of the Division of Educational Counseling, School of Education, The Hebrew University of Jerusalem. His teaching and research areas include: school counseling and psychology, multicultural education and counseling, adolescent's and teacher's help-seeking behaviors and attitudes, and parental perceptions of schools.

Andreas Thiesen M.A. fellow of the Hans-Böckler-Foundation; currently persuing PhD at the Leibniz University in Hannover/Germany. Research focus: European

Policy, Diversity Studies, Urban Development, Qualitative Social Research; Selected Publication: Thiesen, Andreas (2009): Vielfalt als Humanressource? Diversity als neues Paradigma in der Jugendberufshilfe. In: Finkeldey, Lutz/Thiesen, Andreas (Hrsg.): Case Management in der Jugendberufshilfe. Materialien für Theorie, Praxis und Studium der Sozialen Arbeit, Hildesheim: Olms-Verlag, S. 143–156.

Laura A. Thompson a French-Canadian Francophone from Ontario, is an Assistant Professor in the School of Education at Acadia University in Nova Scotia, Canada. Her research interests include (Francophone) Canadian curriculum perspectives, communities and identity formation. Her dissertation, entitled *A Geography of the Imaginary: Mapping Francophone Identities and Curriculum Perspectives in the Postcolonial Present*, won the 2008 National Doctoral Dissertation Award, sponsored by the Canadian Association for Curriculum Studies.

Georgina Tsolidis worked as a teacher, educational consultant and policy advisor for the Victorian Education Department before taking up academic positions at Monash University and the University of Ballarat. Her research interests include diasporic identification and how this is shaped through schooling and family. She has a long-standing interest in feminist theory with a focus on cultural difference.

Joash Mutua Wambua is an Associate Professor of Psychology at Miles College in Birmingham, Alabama. He was born and raised in Kenya, and has lived and been educated in the United States since 1988. His research focuses on motivation and academic achievement of East African students and immigrants in the United States.

Michalinos Zembylas is Assistant Professor of Education at the Open University of Cyprus. His research interests are in the areas educational philosophy and curriculum theory, and his work focuses on exploring the role of emotion and affect in curriculum and pedagogy. He is particularly interested in how affective politics intersect with issues of social justice pedagogies, intercultural and peace education, and citizenship education.

Chapter 1
Migration, Minorities, and Learning— Understanding Cultural and Social Differences in Education

Thomas Geisen and Zvi Bekerman

General Introduction

The debate over the relevance of culture and its potential influence on the learning processes of minority and migrant groups is a long-standing tradition: On the one hand culture is seen as crucial for an understanding of migration and minority issues, while on the other, the focus on culture is seen as a hindrance which leads to processes of 'culturalization' and 'ethnization' through which social inequalities are made invisible. Most prominent is the high relevance which 'culture' is awarded in discussions of the so-called 'clash of cultures' thesis (Huntington 1997) or the 'war of civilizations' (Tibi 1995), which has been highly influential in social and political debates on migration and minorities, especially after the events of 9/11 in the USA. The relevance of culture for an understanding of migration and minority issues is under review because when critically approached it is shown to support essentializing processes. A call has also been made to instead focus upon 'cultural' differences, and to turn our attention towards structures of social inequality (cf. Dittrich and Radtke 1990; Juhasz and Mey 2003). Within this line of research 'culture' has been predominantly understood as being less relevant in the social sphere; an impression or result of social inequality but not its cause. Such perspectives promote an understanding of culture from a structuralist perspective, which is also directed against the politics and practices of multiculturalism as established since the late 1970s (Bekerman 2003) in different Western countries such as Australia, Canada, the United Kingdom, and the Netherlands (cf. Guibernau and Rex 1999). This critique focuses on the essentializing effects of multiculturalism on so-called cultural groups, which are perceived as fixed and unchangeable. Anne Phillips, in her critic on multiculturalism, recommends avoiding the term 'culture' and suggests instead a 'Multiculturalism *without* Culture' (Phillips 2007). "When multiculturalism is represented as the accommodation of or negotiation with cultural communities or groups, this encourages us to view the world through the prism of separate

---

Z. Bekerman (✉)
School of Education, Melton Center, Hebrew University, 91905, Jerusalem, Israel
e-mail: mszviman@mscc.huji.ac.il

and distinct cultures. (...) The individuals, in all their complexity, disappear from view" (Phillips 2007, p. 179). Instead, Phillips argues for a multiculturalism which does not support processes of reification and homogenization while being able to address cultural inequalities (Phillips 2007, p. 179).

And yet, new theoretical approaches in migration/minority theory have shown 'culture' to be a highly relevant factor. These approaches—'transnationalism' (Pries 2008), 'transmigration' (Glick-Schiller et al. 1997), and 'transculturality' (cf. Hoerder et al. 2005)—consider not only the relevance of but also the transcending and dissolving capacities of (national) cultures. Moreover, the centrality of culture has been underlined when considering the demands of marginalized minority members for 'recognition' (cf. Fraser and Honneth 2003; Honneth 1994, 2004) and 'respect' (Sennett 2004). Both have been posited in social theory and practice as highly relevant concepts which in turn are in need of critical approaches. All in all, 'culture' has become a predominant factor for the explanation and understanding of social dilemmas and conflicts.

Migrants and minorities are affected by these theoretical directions as they are always at risk of becoming imprisoned in essentialized cultural definitions and/or of having their cultural preferences denied because they are perceived and qualified as standing in opposition to social solidarity. Migrants and minorities respond to these challenges in multiple ways; they are active agents in the pedagogical, political, and social processes that position and attribute them to this or that cultural sphere (cf. Geisen 2009). Often they get caught up in the ambivalence of cultural and ethnic self-attribution and cultural and ethnic attribution by others. Such a two-fold inscription into culture and ethnicity, by others and by themselves, offers the opportunity to develop a strong sense of belonging and participation in a community—even if often in an 'imagined' one (cf. Anderson 1993)—which does help the individuals to gain and keep self-esteem. However, members of migrant and minority groups, as individuals, reject ascribed cultural attributes while striving towards integration in a variety of social spheres, e.g. at school and in the workplace, in order to realize their social mobility while articulating a demand for individual and collective self-determination (not only cultural but also social and political). This striving of migrants and minority members for an all-embracing self-determination is not only the result of a desire to overcome the experienced heteronomy in society which confronts them with highly significant limitations for individual and social life; it is also fed by the strong desire for equal rights, freedom, and justice.

Questions related to the meaning of cultural heterogeneity and the social/cultural limits of learning and communication (e.g. migration, education, or critical multiculturalism) are highly important for the development of educational strategies and practices in societies with a high number of migration/minority groups. It is precisely here, where the chances for new beginnings and new trials are of utmost importance for educational theorizing, that answers are urgently needed to questions related to individual freedom, community/cultural affiliations, and societal democratic cohesion; answers which need to account for both 'political' and 'learning' perspectives in all macro, mezzo, and micro contexts.

This book is one of the first international efforts to gather knowledge across multiple socio-political contexts about the potential challenges presented by the discourses of culture for the development of educational processes with minority and migrant groups in mind. It considers critically modern cultural discourses that regard difference/alterity as potentially endangering social cohesion, while considering how migrants and minorities deal with these perceptions and their own expectations of educational settings. It hopes to contribute to a critical educational theory that avoids methodological individualism in educational research and practice, thus making its main focus 'culture' and 'the social' itself.

Moreover, while educational research, for the most part, has focused on teacher–learner relationships, conditions and processes, and educational and institutional politics, this volume points to the relevance and effects of the social in complex learning processes which have been seldom discussed in educational research. The chapters cover a wide variety of studies undertaken from diverse theoretical perspectives and conducted within multiple methodological traditions, both qualitative and quantitative, and focuses on a multiplicity of sites covering more than 20 locations in Europe, America, Australia, and Asia.

The book is divided into six sections each with its own introductory note.

Section 1 entitled 'Culture, Difference and Learning' addresses the complex and multifaceted relations between culture and education as these intersect in the development of migratory processes. The chapters critically engage the concept of culture as this is reified within the host context and uncovers the implications of such fixed understanding and conceptions of culture in multiple educational settings which incorporate a wide range of populations varying from early childhood to adulthood.

'Education in Multilingual Societies' is the title of Sect. 2 in this volume. This section focuses on struggles around issues related to identity and language in formal educational settings serving a variety of minoritized populations. The question of multilingual societies seems highly relevant and demanding for current societies, especially if they understand themselves as 'nation-states'.

Whereas the first two sections present and discuss more general subjects—theoretical questions, and language issues—Sect. 3—'Heterogeneity and Learning in Schools' focuses on formal educational systems. It discusses from diverse theoretical and methodological perspectives the interrelations of ethnification and education offering an understanding of both the transnational interconnectedness of politics and ideologies, and the limitations of national policy-making and practice in regard to the most important educational system, the school system. The contributions in Sect. 3 show not only the plurality of approaches, questions, and difficulties, relevant for an understanding of educational processes in multilingual societies, but as well the urgent need for new conceptualizations with which to improve schooling for minority migratory groups.

'Higher Education' is addressed in Sect. 4. It reflects on the experiences of minorities in tertiary educational settings while focusing on the methodological, theoretical, and practical implications of how culture, class, community, and dominant discourses shape the experiences of minority students.

Section 5 'Religion and Learning' offers insights into the intricate and delicate negotiations that take place between religious minorities and educational structures within dominant structures. The chapters in this section consider the evolving discursive concepts of national belonging and identity, in a context where the processes of belief formation and reproduction are also particularly sensitive to the exercise of state power. Moreover, they point towards the importance of considering the nature and structure of the social inequalities that affect religious minorities.

Section 6 entitled 'Community, Work and Learning', adopts a very wide educational perspective which encompasses both formal and informal settings. It focuses on cultural difference and points at the complex relations between power and education. The chapters in this section take into account how learning is enacted through dynamic social relations, including those concerned with work and cultural practices and illustrate how learning for transformation can occur across a wide spectrum of activities.

All in all the book has been devised to account for and expand upon our knowledge on processes of (social) learning under conditions of cultural heterogeneity while considering the outer and inner limits of social/cultural learning and emancipatory educational practices within heterogeneous cultural settings.

The contributions to this volume are an invitation to focus our attention on all—the individual, social relations, and cultural affiliations—if we want to better understand the complexities encountered by migrant and minority populations involved in educational processes guided by the majoriterian host society's practices and values. Learning in education is not an individual act but an activity which involves individuals, peers, families, and caretakers in complex socio-political contexts. Participants building and negotiating past events/activities sustain a present with a future in view. These past events often set the limits for present and future social activities and options. It is the task of all to try to widen the dialogue; in education it is also educators who are the ones that should try to widen and push forward the 'social limits of learning' (Mergner 1999) so as to open new spaces for freedom and action. Doing so might be beneficial not only to improve the chances of migrant and minority groups but also to advance freedom and justice in our societies.

References

Anderson, B. (1993). *Die Erfindung der Nation: Zur Karriere eines erfolgreichen Konzepts.* Frankfurt a. M.: Campus.

Bekerman, Z. (2003). Hidden dangers in multicultural discourse. *Race Equality and Teaching (formerly MCT-Multicultural Teaching)*, *21*(3), 36–42.

Dittrich, E. J., & Radtke, F.-O. (1990). *Ethnizität: Wissenschaft und Minderheiten*. Wiesbaden: Westdeutscher Verlag.

Fraser, N., & Honneth, A. (2003). *Umverteilung oder Anerkennung? Eine politisch-philosophische Kontroverse*. Frankfurt am Main: Suhrkamp.

Geisen, T. (2009). Vergesellschaftung statt Integration: Zur Kritik des Integrations-Paradigmas. In N.N. (Ed.), *N.N.* Wiesbaden: VS Verlag.

Glick-Schiller, N., Basch, L., & Szanton Blanc, C. (1997). From immigrant to transmigrant: Theorizing transnational migration. In L. Pries (Ed.), *Transnationale migration* (pp. 121–140). Baden-Baden: Nomos Verlagsgesellschaft.

Guibernau, M., & Rex, J. (Eds.). (1999). *The ethnicity reader: Nationalism, multiculturalism, and migration*. Cambridge: Polity Press.

Hoerder, D., Hébert, Y., & Schmitt, I. (2005). Transculturation and the accumulation of social capital: Understanding histories and decoding the present of young people. In D. Hoerder, Y. Hébert, & I. Schmitt (Eds.), *Negotiating transcultural lives: Belongings and social capital among youth in comparative perspective* (pp. 11–38). Göttingen: V & R Unipress.

Honneth, A. (1994). *Kampf um Anerkennung*. Frankfurt am Main: Suhrkamp.

Honneth, A. (2004). Anerkennung als Ideoogie. *WestEnd, 1. Jg.* (Heft 1), 51–70.

Huntington, S. P. (1997). *Kampf der Kulturen: Die Neugestaltung der Weltpolitik im 21. Jahrhundert*. München: Europaverlag.

Juhasz, A., & Mey, E. (2003). *Die zweite Generation: Etablierte oder Außenseiter?* Opladen: Leske + Budrich.

Mergner, G. (1999). *Lernfähigkeit der Subjekte und gesellschaftliche Anpassungsgewalt*. Hamburg: Argument Verlag.

Phillips, A. (2007). *Multiculturalism without culture*. Princeton: Princeton University Press.

Pries, L. (2008). *Die Transnationalisierung der sozialen Welt*. Frankfurt a. M.: Suhrkamp.

Sennett, R. (2004). *Respekt im Zeitalter der Ungleichheit*. Berlin: Berliner Taschenbuchverlag.

Tibi, B. (1995). *Krieg der Zivilisationen: Politik und Religion zwischen Vernunft und Fundamentalismus*. Hamburg: Hoffmann und Campe.

Part I
Culture, Difference and Learning

Chapter 2
Movements and Migratory Processes: Roles and Responsibilities of Education and Learning

Pat Cox

The English philosopher and mathematician Bertrand Russell wrote: 'No political theory is adequate, unless it is applicable to children, as well as to men and women' (Russell 1916/1997, p. 100). In this section, research and theorizing about migration, cultures, languages and difference is applied to the situations of children, young people, women and men within and following migratory processes and to the contributions of education and learning. This introduction opens with a brief summary of the contexts of migration and of culture early in the twenty-first century; these are followed by discussion of the contexts of education and of learning; a summary of the subject matter and key points within each chapter, with some closing remarks.

Contexts of Migration and of Culture

In the twenty-first century, migration is arguably a global phenomenon (Harzig and Hoerder 2009). Migration encompasses large social issues such as justice, equality, human flourishing, human suffering, human endeavour and mutual respect, in addition to questions of politics, economics, culture and education. Migration may be freely chosen or forced; it includes movements of groups, communities or people and of individual women, men, children, young people and families (Castles and Miller 2009; Giugni and Passy 2006).

Despite world-wide economic difficulties and financial crises, capitalism does not falter. As noted by Bauman (2003) when writing about the consequences of modernity, raw materials and goods flow generally without let or hindrance in pursuit of 'globalization', but the movements of people, whether groups or individuals, are more circumscribed. Migration is constructed as positive when required by receiving nations for their own purposes; negative when it is not required or when refuge is being sought. Media stories position migrant people themselves as the causes of

P. Cox (✉)
School of Social Work, University of Central Lancashire, PR1 2HE, Preston, UK
e-mail: pcox2@uclan.ac.uk

problems; however, the demands of capital lead not only to extremes of poverty and wealth (Bauman 2007, 2009) but also to natural disasters of flood, famine and disease which can be attributed in part to nations of the western world meeting their own needs at the expense of others (de Wet 2006; Ward 2010) and refusing to admit their contribution to some forced migrations: "…only rarely do we see that 'their' problems cannot be disentangled from our conduct." (Smail 1987, p. 35).

Works on migration such as Castles and Miller (2009) and others mentioned in this introduction and section chapters were published before recession in the western world became established. However, decisions concerning migration are influenced by numerous issues (which may or may not include economic factors) and migrant people who have established family and community ties in receiving nations may choose to stay rather than return to countries of origin, despite challenges ahead (Somerville and Sumption 2009). While the rate of migration to a number of current receiving nations has slowed, it is estimated that migration will not completely cease (Papademitriou et al. 2010) and despite cuts to public services, including education, and uncertainties about future demand, educators will continue to need to provide learning opportunities; will need to include migrant children, young people and adults in educational settings and to ensure that education provides learning for people of the receiving nation and migrant people together (Papademitriou et al. 2009).

Culture is an integral aspect of migration; migrant people have their own shared cultural understanding and practices, which are as valuable to them as the cultural understandings and practices are valuable to members of receiving nations. Multiculturalist endeavours in receiving nations have their supporters and their critics, for example: Modood and Ahmad (2007) and arguments for the need for more critical approaches are mounted (Dhaliwal and Patel 2006; Johnson 2008). Cultural 'differences' and the apparent impossibility of belonging within more than one cultural domain may be used to justify social differences and to exclude (Bekerman and Kopelowitz 2008).

Contexts of Education and of Learning

Arendt (1977) notes that in north America following the war of 1939–1945, school education was being used to inculcate migrant children and children of migrant parents into the cultural practices and prevailing language of the receiving nation. Due to education's accepted place in the structures of many societies, all levels of education systems may be thought able to reinforce cultural ideologies, norms and expectations and address concerns about the education of migrants and the impact of immigration upon education (House of Lords 2008; OECD 2006).

Such educational praxes reflect the assumption of a linear relationship between what migrant people—children, young people and adults—need to learn and how they need to learn it, and the existing education systems of the receiving nation. Expressed simply it is: here is a need and there is a resource; educators are 'specialized technicians' (Ibsen 1882/1997). However, monolithic educational institutions which have accreted indigenous values, ideologies, norms and cultural reference points and which operate with fixed internal systems are not always best placed to respond to the range of learning and social and psycho-social needs (Rose 2006; Scheifele 2008) which migrant people of all ages may experience at different stages during and following migration processes. When educational provision is unable to respond effectively to such needs, education may or may not lead to learning. Meintjes (1997) observes that education is not neutral, as it leads either to conformity or to transformation. Thus while upholding traditional cultural praxes, education may also incorporate possibilities for personal and societal change.

Content of This Section

While the relevance of social sciences such as sociology, social policy and politics in analysing and researching migration and migratory experiences are well-established, chapters in this section each provide a timely reminder of the significance of culture, education and learning during and following migratory processes. Relationships between migration, learning, culture and difference are multi-faceted and complex; some of these complexities are addressed in this themed section.

The chapters are informed by theoretical explorations and research studies and analyses and critique of these, establishing a body of understanding and knowledge around multi-faceted and inter-related issues. The authors of each chapter seek critical engagement with the unthinking acceptance of culture as given or fixed, with the varieties of culture's meanings and with its roles. Chapters here range across the life course, from learning issues and education for young children in migrant families to those who have migrated as adults. For example, Gaspar and Lengyel focus on early childhood and families; Geisen, Cox, Apitzsch and Thiesen focus on young people; while Cassar, Marvakis, Piñiero and Haller, Schely-Newman address issues for adults.

In the opening chapter of this section, Thomas Geisen analyses recent research studies on belonging, respect and recognition, in order to address core concepts of young migrant people's belonging, cultural positioning and social mobility. He emphasizes young people's agency and young migrant people as social actors. Feelings and experiences of young migrant people are located within recent research and theorizing on migration, which moves away from monocausal or binary explanations for migration and centralizes multiples causes and manifestations.

The chapter's core consists of secondary analysis of three qualitative studies—each with slightly different findings and analyses—into young migrant people's feelings of 'lack of belonging' and their relationships with and within the majority society. However, agency and ingenuity result in young people making spaces for themselves, resisting pressures and expectations and creating individual biographies. Secondary analysis of two additional studies concerned with the role of education in facilitating cultural integration and success demonstrates how young people use education to improve their situations in their new national settings.

In the studies' findings, feelings and experiences are expressed and strategies (including education) for managing emotions and experiences and succeeding are discussed; the regular psychological tasks of adolescence also impact upon young migrant people. Thomas Geisen reveals the multiple positionings of migrant adolescents within and between their parents' cultures of origin and the cultures and structures of the receiving nations; he argues both for moving away from 'essentializing' concepts of culture and for addressing culture *and* structure in analyses of migratory experiences.

Pat Cox, author of the second chapter, also focuses on specific issues for young migrant people in receiving nations, including young people who arrive with their families in a planned way or those who are 'forced migrants'. She links the subject of young migrant people's experiences and concerns with exploration and discussion of how educators in higher (university) education who research into and who teach about issues of migration might exercise their roles and responsibilities in influencing social and civic issues (including contributing to public knowledge and debates about migration), which universities once had and which, she argues, they could have again. In her analysis and discussion Pat Cox draws from the theories of Mergner and of Arendt, in order to explore learning processes (including learning limitations); education; ambivalence in human thought and action; the drawbacks of abstract equalizing; identity; cultural patterning and cultural 'othering'; relationships of solidarity with others and thinking for oneself rather than unquestioningly following rules. In particular, she addresses the (frequently unacknowledged) influences of cultural understandings and expectations on learning processes and learning experiences within higher education, for migrant and non-migrant students and for educators. Throughout the chapter there is an emphasis on learning, rather than on knowledge acquisition. In considering the public role and responsibilities of educators in university settings, the author examines an array of recent and current academic writings from within universities and about universities from across mainland Europe, North America and the UK. She concludes by asserting that the public role of universities needs to be resurrected and that alliances within and without universities are required to ensure that knowledge of, and research-informed debates about, young people's migration and migratory experiences reach the widest possible audience.

In her consideration of the inter-connections between migration and learning, Ursula Apitzsch begins by addressing the concept of ethnicity—which is now established as a social construction not a 'natural' one—demonstrating that a social-constructivist analysis of ethnicity is not unproblematic. The emphasis in this chapter is how the dynamics of ethnicity operate within social and cultural life and the identification, analysis and discussion and regular re-examination of the implications of such construction, for both social inclusion and social exclusion. The chapter includes some analysis of Kant's theorizing from the vantage point of current understandings and knowledge of 'race', ethnicity and culture in order to illustrate some of the hidden dangers which can be discerned in unthinking ascriptions. Apitzsch draws from Weber's early understanding and identification of the application of social-constructivism to 'ethnic groups' and from more recent scholarship such as that by Brubaker and by Hall. In her discussion she includes consideration of collective and gender dynamics, which frequently are overlooked in analyses of ethnicity and her reasoning is illustrated by reference to research about, and first person narratives from, young migrant people. She asserts the necessity for constant interrogation of definitions and ascriptions of ethnicity to assess their intent and their effects. While retaining awareness that for many, ethnic belonging may not be chosen freely, the author argues that there are examples of positive appropriation, perhaps re-appropriation, of ethnicity by some, imbuing ethnicity with their own particular meaning/s as one aspect of each individual's biographical whole, in addition to examples of collective positioning. She demonstrates a critical engagement with the possible multiplicities of ethnic belonging and with the significance of ethnicity and ethnic identification for individuals and collectives in contexts of education and learning.

Athanasios Marvakis examines how the subjectivity of migrant people is being denied in discourses of assimilation and integration, where lack of choice obtains widely. The significance of this is that such denial results in the submission of migrant people to the demands of prevailing cultures and powers. The concept and term 'integration' is, the author argues, far from neutral and he explores critical social science in order to begin developing alternative praxes, which would take account of the subjectivity of all.

Marvakis draws from his own research into migration and provides evidence that integration is a popular term across political divides, across academic disciplines and within the media. He argues that it is incorrect to subtract the subjectivity and agency of social actors from social phenomena and that the ways in which the term and concept 'integration' is applied, focuses understanding and debate in particular directions; the term itself is 'deficient'. He provides a range of examples of how integration is freighted with different meanings in various national and international settings, demonstrating that it is frequently a mechanism used by those with power against those without power.

Using guest workers (Gastarbeiter) as a specific example, the author traces the neo-liberal transformation of Germany and the mechanisms by which groups of migrant people have become divided from one another; examples of mechanisms described here also may be occurring among migrant people in other nations. He emphasizes the importance of reflection upon learning and associated praxes of talking and writing and concludes by re-affirming the responsibility of the critical social sciences—and critical social scientists—to develop social self-understanding, political consciousness and recognize and challenge the current conceptualizations of integration, their functions and their myriad effects.

For Esteban Piñeiro and Jane Haller, education is regarded as significant in operationalizing particular constructions of social and cultural differences within the context of recent policy developments in Switzerland in relation to migrant people from other nations. The main focus of the chapter is analysis of the discourse of integration in Switzerland; analysis is undertaken drawing on theories developed by Laclau and Mouffe on hegemony and by Foucault on different forms of power. The starting point for the chapter is close reading by the authors of major law and policy documents revealing the internal 'logic' according to which particular discourse(s) operate and are made intelligible to others. They then establish how the forces of social order are shaped in specific ways through discourse, and how education is similarly (and deliberately) manoeuvred to become an important factor in the achievement of this particular model of integration. Through their detailed analysis and discussion, the authors lay the foundations for, and then build a critique of, this particular form of integration. Their conclusions include analysis of differences encoded within the discourses of integration and education, and analysis of hidden assumptions being made about, certain national groups fitting more closely and appropriately with member of the host nation than other national groups. They present convincing arguments for integration as both concept and as praxis being a 'hegemonic project', which has been developed and deployed to manage not only migrant people, but also the Swiss population as a whole. Questions are raised as to the implications of all of the foregoing for what the authors describe as an imaginary community which they name the 'integration society'.

EU policies on integration emphasize social cohesion and employment and many educational programmes are designed to fit these imperatives, receiving money from EU Social Funds. As noted by Andreas Thiesen, the concept and term 'diversity' are used frequently in educational settings, where the effects of migration and integration policies at the macro level are enacted and experienced. The author argues that the different uses to which 'diversity' has been put in educational settings require thorough study. Analysis is undertaken using sociologist Albert Scherr's conceptualizations of diversity as functional understanding; as anti-discrimination discourse and as a critique of power and dominance. Andreas Thiesen argues that adoption of 'diversity' for political purposes is about the achievement of normative objectives, not necessarily about valuing and appreciating differences, and not about acknowledging minority people's particular needs arising from those differences. In addition to including Scherr's thinking in his analysis, Andreas Thiesen also draws upon Bourdieu's three forms of cultural capital in discussions of culture and of the complex inter-relationships between culture and diversity, deploying Bhabha's concept of hybridity to discuss how young migrant people communicate in more than one language and across and between languages, and the intelligence, creativity and skills required to do this. He devises a conceptual framework for diversity-focussed input within locally based education programmes, with categories of Content, Space, Institution, Everyday Culture and Politics/Justice; each of these has a set of sub-categories. He argues that the multi-lingualism and creativity of migrant people should be encouraged and celebrated, instead of their being constrained and constricted by requirements of integration. He also argues for educational institutions to train staff in diversity, rather than insisting that this is unnecessary.

The subject of the following chapter is the analysis, findings and discussion of the implications of, an original research study undertaken by the author, Sofia Gaspar. The research was undertaken with members of an 'under-examined group'; that is, adults from different EU states who marry one another and have families. Both partners have legal security and future decisions about mobility can be freely made; they are thus members of a 'privileged migrant group'. Most existing research on bi-national families has focussed on unions between a member of an EU state and a partner who is from a non-EU state or who is a migrant worker. The research described here explores how values and meanings are expressed in choices and decisions about marriage and the bringing up and education of children within settings which may be familiar to only one parent or to neither parent. The chapter opens with a detailed exposition of the existing research context, following which the author describes, discusses and analyses findings from qualitative research interviews with both parents. Subjects addressed in interviews include the transmission of language/s; school educational systems; selection of school or nursery; reasons for selection and the nature of social and relational ties and networks. Data analysis establishes three main strategies adopted by parents of young children in this situation: family assimilation strategy; bi-national family strategy and peripatetic family strategy and the author provides examples of each strategy, the likelihood of which strategy might be chosen by which family and its impact on the families themselves. The research analysed here expands existing knowledge both of migration and how one particular group of migrants interact with educational institutions; also discussed are the implications more generally of the study's findings for integration.

An adult literacy campaign and programme which was undertaken 40 years ago among migrant women in Israel is the starting point for the next chapter. Esther Schely-Newman connects with the programme's participants, both the migrant women and the young women—former soldiers who became community teachers—who were involved in their literacy education at that time. Using qualitative interviews the author has undertaken research with members of both groups; this research contributes to understanding and knowledge about the development of migration policies and practices and cultural and social integration across time in the national context of Israel. In this chapter research findings are discussed and from the data the author expands upon a range of subjects which are relevant to migration, culture and learning. The first such subject is gender in all its complexity, with accompanying issues of perceived and actual power: the community teachers had power of their role, but the women students—and often their husbands—exercised power within the home. For both groups of women, different cultural traditions and cultural ideologies had to be learned, understood, negotiated and re-negotiated. Esther Schely-Newman deploys the data to make comparisons with present-day political and policy approaches and attitudes to migrant people in Israel, revealing policy changes in relation to migrant people across time (and associated changes of attitude and language use) and differing perceptions about the deployment of education in the integration of migrant people. Through the programme, learning to read and write occurred despite cultural differences and expectations and the author demonstrates how the apparently straightforward task of learning to read and write in a language which is not the language of origin, becomes freighted with meaning and symbolism for learners and educators alike.

The possibility of migration being a learning experience in and of itself, irrespective of prior formal education experiences, is explored by Joanne Cassar. She argues that knowledge of the strengths and resilience within the self engendered by both the planning and the execution of the migratory journey and the engagement with opportunities in the receiving nations comprise a learning experience. She posits that the other side of learning experiences in relation to migration is that members of the receiving nations need to learn about and value the growth of a more culturally diverse population and its more recently arrived members. The author establishes that the prevailing public discourses in Malta regarding migrant people (especially migrant people who are refugees or asylum-seekers) are frequently hostile, racist and xenophobic, arguing that these discourses serve neither the Maltese people nor asylum-seekers and refugees. Research undertaken by the author and described in this chapter is documentary analysis of two personal narratives of Somali migrants (young men seeking asylum in Malta) whose accounts are already in the public domain (cyberspace). The author writes reflexively about how her approach may compound the meaning of the young men's accounts; there is the original 'filter' of the 'documents' in cyberspace and then her readings of them. Her readings are underpinned by awareness that there is learning to be gained and that there is value, worth and power within subordinated accounts and that while particular, these speak to the general. The author deploys Foucault's work to interrogate the young men's accounts and develop insights into migratory experiences. She analyses the weaknesses and potential strengths of school education and applies Foucauldian theory to envisage a less discriminatory and more culturally aware school education which problematizes hegemonic beliefs and discourses and establishes different forms of social relationships.

Drorit Lengyel gathers together research into and theories of language acquisition in order to explore language acquisition and children's learning in migrant families, and socialization. She analyses existing research and socio-cultural theories to reveal how thinking and practice about language acquisition in early childhood and early childhood education is perfused by the monolinguistic and cultural assumptions and ideologies of members of the receiving nation and by covert prejudices against multi-language learning and use. She makes visible the influence of the nation-state and associated requirement for heterogeneity of speech, and the influence of these two factors on language acquisition and education. She demonstrates the limitations of much research into children's language learning. Drorit Lengyel questions the meaning of being bilingual. She re-configures being bilingual as different *and* unique: bilingual children should not be assessed educationally as not competent in either language, as happens frequently. She argues that bilingual children take holistic approaches to conceptualizing and communicating; their language use is dynamic not static. Bilingualism results in mixing vocabularies, sentence structure and expression; this should be regarded as evidence of creativity and intelligence and such linguistic explorations should be encouraged. She considers how children growing up knowing two languages can be best supported. Using emergent findings from her own ethnographic research, the author demonstrates that existing patterns of language acquisition in education marginalize and exclude migrant children; many educators themselves know and speak only one language. She notes a contradiction between national imperatives for monolingualism and monoculturalism and educational requirements to focus upon children's needs. Having established correlation between language status and social and political status, especially in relation to migrant people, she argues for a developing a 'multilingual habitus' and moving towards more inclusive educational praxes which centralize 'plurilingualism'.

As Young (2002, p. 75) notes, theory is about connection with others, and the application of theories and research in this section establishes that calls to develop better theoretical understandings of migratory issues (Geisen 2004; Kofman 2010), are being responded to. All chapter authors demonstrate how education and learning might assist in moving from present conditions, understandings and knowledge of migratory experiences and processes and cultural and social differences to other (and better) understandings and knowledge and to action for change where it is required. Commenting upon research in educational contexts more broadly, Bekerman writes that it should:

> …allow readers, participants and others to identify the world described as the world they inhabit and experience…presenting a richness of details which otherwise would go unnoticed, and should allow participants to learn what needs to be done next if they want to continue or change their present situation. (Bekerman 2008, p. 160)

Individually and together, the chapters in this section illuminate the situations of migrant people, facilitate readers' recognition of the complex inter-relationships between migration, culture, difference and learning and indicate directions for actions to be taken.

References

Arendt, H. (1977). *Between past and future*. New York: Penguin.
Bauman, Z. (2003). *Wasted lives: The outcasts of modernity*. Cambridge: Polity Press.
Bauman, Z. (2007). *Consuming life*. Cambridge: Polity Press.
Bauman, Z. (2009). *Living on borrowed time: Conversations with Citali Rovirosa-Madrazo*. Cambridge: Polity Press.
Bekerman, Z. (2008). Educational research need not be irrelevant. In P. Cox, T. Geisen, & R. Green (Eds.), *Qualitative research and social change: European contexts* (pp. 153–166). Basingstoke: Palgrave Macmillan.
Bekerman, Z., & Kopelwitz, E. (Eds.). (2008). *Cultural education - cultural sustainability: Minority, diaspora, indigenous and ethno-religious groups in multi-cultural societies*. New York: Routledge.
Castles, S., & Miller, M. J. (2009). *The age of migration: International population movements in the Modern World* (4th ed.). Basingstoke: Palgrave Macmillan.
de Wet, C. (Ed.). (2006). *Development-induced displacement: Problems, policies and people*. New York: Berghahn Books.
Dhaliwal, S., & Patel, P. (2006). *Multiculturalism in secondary schools: Managing conflicting demands. Report on a pilot project*. London: Working Lives Research Institute and Southall Black Sisters.
Geisen, T. (2004). People on the move: The inclusion of migrants in 'Labor Transfer Systems' - The European Case. In T. Geisen, A. A. Hickey, & A. Karcher (Eds.), *Migration, mobility and borders* (pp. 35–79). Frankfurt am Main: IKO Verlag.
Giugni, M., & Passy, F. (Eds.). (2006). *Dialogues on migration policy*. Maryland: Lexington Books.

Harzig, C., & Hoerder, D. (2009). *What is migration history?* Cambridge: Polity Press.
House of Lords. (2008). *Select Committee on Economic Affairs First Report of Session 2007–2008: The economic impact of immigration.* London: The Stationery Office.
Ibsen, H., & Hampton, C. (1882/1997). *An enemy of the people.* London: Faber and Faber.
Johnson, N. (2008). *Citizenship, cohesion and solidarity.* London: The Smith Institute.
Kofman, E. (2010). Managing migration and citizenship in Europe: Towards an overarching framework. In C. Gabriel & H. Pellerin (Eds.), *Governing international labour migration: Current issues, challenges and dilemmas* (pp. 13–26). London: Routledge.
Meintjes, G. (1997). Human rights education as empowerment: Reflections on pedagogy. In G. J. Andreopoulos & R. P. Claude (Eds.), *Human rights education for the twenty-first century* (pp. 64–79). Philadelphia: Philadelphia University Press.
Modood, T., & Ahmad, F. (2007). British Muslim perspectives on multiculturalism. *Theory, Culture and Society, 24*(2), 187–213.
OECD. (2006). *Where immigrant students succeed - a comparative review of performances and engagement (PISA 2003).* Paris: OECD.
Papademitriou, D. G., Sumption, M., & Somerville, W. (2009). *Migration and the economic downturn: What to expect in the European Union.* Washington: Migration Policy Institute.
Papademtriou, D. G., Sumption, M., Terrazas, A., Burkert, C., Loyal, S., & Ferrero-Turrión, R. (2010). *Migration and immigrants two years after the financial collapse: Where do we stand?* Washington, DC : Migration Policy Institute.
Rose, J. (2006). Displacement in Zion. In K. E. Tunstall (Ed.), *Displacement, asylum, migration: Oxford Amnesty International lectures* (pp. 264–290). Oxford: Oxford University Press.
Russell, B. (1916/1997). *Principles of social reconstruction.* London: George Allen and Unwin1916/Routledge 1997.
Scheifele, S. (Ed.). (2008). *Migration und Psyche: Aufbrüche und Erschütterungen.* Giessen: Psychosozial Verlag.
Smail, D. (1987). *Taking care: An alternative to therapy.* London: J.M. Dent.
Somerville, W., & Sumption, M. (2009). *Immigration in the United Kingdom: The recession and beyond.* London: Equality and Human Rights Commission.
Ward, P. D. (2010). *The flooded earth: Our future in a world without ice caps.* New York: Basic Books.
Young, R. (2002). The sociology of education: A personal view. *Change: Transformations in Education, 5*(1), 65–77.

Chapter 3
Understanding Cultural Differences as Social Limits to Learning: Migration Theory, Culture and Young Migrants

Thomas Geisen

Migration research has at worst ignored the significance and the situations of young migrants almost completely, while at best, only viewed them as the relatives of migrating adults. However since the 1990s, young migrants have been included more often in migration studies (cf. Cox 2007; Geisen 2007; Hoerder et al. 2005b). This development can be considered as part of the overall progress in youth research that began as a field of research in the 1960s and became more established among social sciences as a systematic research approach from the 1970s (cf. Cox 2007). The increased interest in such research mirrors a growing public interest in migrant youth.

Changes discussed in the context of demographic changes, such as the lack of qualified labour in all economic sectors, particularly in care and services (cf. Anderson 2006; Apitzsch and Schmidbaur 2010; Lutz 2008; Metz-Göckel et al. 2008), have led, among other things, to more attention being paid to the available labour potential of migrants, especially in regards to their education and qualifications (cf. Hamburger et al. 2005; OECD 2006). However, while current social and political trends raise the question of young migrants' education and learning, it must be acknowledged that their long absence in research has had a negative impact on our understanding in this area. To address this situation, this chapter focuses on migration theory, culture and empirical research on migrant youth.

The advances in migration theory and the relevance of culture are crucial to improving our understanding of young migrants, and allow us to pay more attention to their life situations and needs. For instance, in the context of migration, 'culture' is often seen as a crucial factor in social life, but for migrants, it is often seen as more of a hindrance than a valuable social practice through which innovation can occur (cf. Erdheim 1992). This is especially so among young migrants, who are often regarded as being in danger of becoming entrenched in their culture of origin and thereby losing the capacity to become oriented towards the new cultural context in which they are now living. In this perspective young migrants are often seen as mere objects bounded by cultural norms and values. Recent research has empha-

T. Geisen (✉)
School of Social Work, University of Applied Sciences, Northwestern Switzerland
e-mail: thomas.geisen@fhnw.ch

sised the individuality of young migrants who seek to find their place in society by processes of self-positioning (cf. Geisen 2007; Geisen and Riegel 2009; Hamburger et al. 2005; Riegel and Geisen 2007). For young migrants the loss of culture is elegised, yet there is a tendency to devalue migrant cultural practices. This ambiguity is highly significant for education and learning. Such perceptions of the relevance of culture for migration also depend on our understanding of migration itself. In this process of devaluation of migrant cultural practices, migration is understood as an exception and migrants as merely objects driven by poverty and other emergencies (cf. Geisen 2005). This seems to be so for Western societies that have not yet fully developed a self-understanding as 'migrant societies'; cultural transformation driven by migration still takes place in a social context structured by nationalism. Recent developments in migration theory and history underline the fact that the modern nation–state has, from its beginning, experienced migration, but this is often neglected in social and political practice, or treated as marginal (cf. Bade 2004; Geisen 2009; Hoerder 2002a; Hoerder and Moch 1996; Husa et al. 2000).

With this in mind, this chapter refers *first* to the development of migration theory, in order to show what substantial changes have been made in the last two decades regarding cultural issues and young migrants. From an educational perspective, the special interest here is how migration theories deal with the complexity of migration processes, how intergenerational perspectives are taken up in migration theory and how their increasing relevance is discussed.

Second, this chapter looks at the processes in which cultural strategies and practices are transferred from one generation to another. This intergenerational transfer of culture is a crucial aspect of social reproduction. It is the transfer and creation of meaning and value to the things existing in a world, and to the acts performed anew by people in order to produce and reproduce the world, and to live together with others. Culture focuses on how individuals become situated in communities and in society, and how they position themselves in communities and societies (cf. Geisen 2008). The question of culture is closely related to education because it is via education that cultures are transferred from one generation to another and also maintain continuity as cultures adapt to new conditions.

The *third* part of this chapter discusses recent research findings from research into migrant youth in Germany and Switzerland. New paradigms have developed wherein the processes of cultural adaption and innovation are described, the key feature of which is the fact that young migrants are now perceived as active individuals. The chapter concludes with an outline of the current challenges for research into young migrants.

Migration, Migration Theory and Learning Migration is still often regarded as an exception or special case compared with the sedentary life that is considered to be the rule (Geisen 2005). One reason for this is that migration as a social fact is still not perceived as socially normal, omnipresent in everyday life. In many cases, however, it receives attention when social situations are perceived as problematic and a society has to deal with migration in connection with poverty, addiction, delinquency, internal security, unemployment, political persecution and the like. Poverty is offered as the cause of migration, and other social problem situations and conflicts are regarded as side-effects of migration. Insufficient cultural bonding, lack of integration or willingness to integrate, and a tendency towards withdrawal into the ethnic community are cited as reasons for the formation of such problematic situations, which are perceived as specific to migration. There is much disagreement in the literature as to whether these are general problems or are specifically related to migration. Consequently, the subject of migration is often integrated into discourses that situate migrants in social conflicts in various ways. To a great extent, migration is treated as a problem. It is only recently that an understanding of migration as a crucial part of modern society has gained increasing ground. Indeed, modern societies are migrant societies. This altered understanding of migration is reflected in the development of migration theories as well (cf. Geisen 2009).

Unilinear and monocausal theories of migration, including for example, approaches of (neo-) classical economics or of dual labour markets (cf. Borjas 1989; Piore 1979; Todaro 1969), have been increasingly replaced by more complex theories in which migration is no longer regarded primarily as the result of diverging social, political and economic relationships, whose effects are the so-called push and pull factors. Moreover, migrants are now considered to be the *agents* for whom migration is not only a means for the individual-biographic but also the collective-social creation of the life context.

This altered understanding was first represented in network theory (cf. Boyd 1989; Fawcett 1989; Massey 2000), which assumes that decisions to migrate are not taken on an individual level but are created and substantiated in a social environment. The theory clarifies how the economic and social resources necessary for migrating can be raised and applied. Apart from family, friends and colleagues, the broader social environment is of importance here, especially when there is already a background of migration and relationships with migrants living in the target region can be activated. Thus, network theory centres on the complexity of decision-making and the significance of social relationships for migration. Cultural matters and intergenerational relations are central to this approach, since family and network relations represent shared values and relationships of mutuality. This also means that questions of education and learning are relevant, yet these questions have rarely been reflected in migration theory and research, though in an exemplary study, Portes and Rumbaut (2001) did research into second-generation immigrants in the United States, focusing on issues of education and employment. It is only recently that migrants and their dependents have become of interest to educational research. In the last decade, particularly, there have been several studies on the performance and achievements (or lack of them) of pupils of migrant descent in schools (Baumert et al. 2006; Diefenbach 2010; Fürstenau and Gomolla 2009a, 2009b, 2011). It must be emphasised that those studies are not only of migrants, but since they focus on second and older generations, they focus on 'new ethnicities' or 'new minorities', signalling a shift not only in categories but also in the understanding and relevance of the social context for migrants and minorities. However, the network theory does not help us to understand much about these developments because migration analysis tends to focus primarily on migration as a process, not as a context. Migration as a process is concerned with migrants' motives and actions. Migration as a context looks at the effects of migration in a given social context and how it becomes the new centre of life for the immigrants, as well as the consequences of emigration on the social context which the migrants have left.

Focusing on migration as a process give us important hints about the relevance of ongoing and stable relations between the 'sending' and 'receiving' countries, with which migrants maintain relations. This aspect has been taken up by 'transnationalism' studies. Approaches of 'transnationalism' and 'transculturality' have been developing since the 1990s (Faist 2004; Glick-Schiller et al. 1997; Hoerder et al. 2005a; Pries 2008, 1997). Here, migration is perceived as an unfolding event that occurs beyond distinct nation--state attributions. As with network theory, migration is seen here as a process in which various parties are involved: close family members, relatives, friends and colleagues, among others. Furthermore, family members constitute a new form of community in a broader sense that is shared beyond nation--state borders. Migration itself is no longer seen as a unique and completed event, but is rather something that takes place continuously, perhaps within the framework of commuting migrations that extend over a specific phase of life and might lead to permanent migration, for example. This cancels the spatial and temporal limitations of migration, which remains incomplete both as a concrete individual-biographic and a familiar-collective undertaking. To single intermediate stages or periods, new and altered possibilities can be attached. Among other things, transnational households evolve as a social form because of migration. Members of such households are often dispersed across several states on several continents, not just temporarily but also permanently. What is crucial here is the formation of a social network, which spatially orients itself towards not just one but several societies.

Transnational migration, therefore, can be seen as a phenomenon which involves multiple institutional and non-institutional agents other than the migrants themselves. Transnational contextualisation patterns thus contain multilocalised forms of orientation within a world society and are supported by the perspectives of multiple agents. The notion of migration as a process is hence cemented in transnationalism, with regard to the diversity of places and regions it involves, and in view of the applied and exercised forms of migration, for instance in their differentiation between 'permanent' and 'temporary'. Participating in different societies also means participating in different cultures, by which the local or regional situatedness of cultures is transcended and 'transculturality' comes into existence (Hoerder et al. 2005a). So far, educational and learning processes have not been a focus of transnational migration research, which concentrates rather on transnational family relations and mainly from the perspective of the feminisation of migration. However, questions of education and learning are relevant for people living in transnational and transcultural contexts. The transnational perspective widens our perspective on migration in the sense that its focus is not only on one individual migrant but on the complexity of the migrant situation, characterised as a net of social relations built and sustained by family members and other dependents, involving two and more countries.

3 Understanding Cultural Differences as Social Limits to Learning 23

Thus the understanding of migration has shifted from a narrow to a multifaceted, plural one, which is reflected in Hoerder's work on migration as a 'balancing process' (Ausgleichsprozess) (2002b) between various global and local regions. While the 'balancing process' refers to the process aspect of migration and concentrates on its meaning and results, this can be supplemented by also seeing migration as a 'process of socialisation' (Vergesellschaftung) (Geisen 2005), which refers to the *context* of migration. This complex and multifaceted perspective sees migration as a process that starts in local and regional contexts, and grows to span several nation–states and continents. It also represents a temporal delimitation, since here, migration is no longer regarded predominantly as a unique biographical event, but as a structural process that shapes biographical development in distinct periods. Any such concept of migration goes against the grain of popular typologies that try to categorise it according to geography (international and internal migration), time (temporary, short- and long-term as well as permanent migration), and causal attributes (poverty-, work- and refugee-related migration) (cf. Lucassen and Lucassen 1997). The understanding of 'migration as a process' underlies the conception of it as a specific form of mobility, in which a relocation or a 'multilocalisation' of the centre of life is taking place. This relocation takes place independently of the initial intentions of the migrants. Any such understanding of migration brings into focus *mobility* as it is realised in local, regional and international contexts, and connects it with the socio-spatial and biographical situatedness of individuals, which are increasingly transnational.

The socialisation of migrants is addressed in the socio-spatial paradigm which accords importance to both how migrants position themselves and how they perceive they are positioned by others. In the local conditions, adaptation to social facts and the maintenance of social and cultural experiences, take place in equal measure; as a rule, however, this adaptation only lasts if it contributes to meeting the new social and cultural challenges. At the same time, the individual and collective competences that have been acquired represent an important resource. When it comes to dealing with altered social, cultural and political terms and conditions, these are the result of learning processes. Hence, learning in these circumstances means adapting to new social relations, as well as transferring socio-cultural capacities hitherto acquired in life. 'Learning' is understood here in a broad, multilayered sense, referring not only to the individual and her learning processes but also to the individual as a member of different communities and the world. Here, individual and collective learning processes are interwoven and are at the same time requisites and conditions for each other (cf. Jouhy 1996; Mergner 1999). For migrants' education and learning, this means that the layers—individual, community, national society and world society—affect and influence each other in such a way that create both options and limitations. Conflicting judgments in a given situation produce not only contradictions but also ambivalences. In general, processes and success of education and learning depend on people's aspirations. Therefore, we need to look at migration as a process and as a context at the same time. Questions of culture are as relevant as others, since it is a cultural matter to think that the promise of future gains can be realised in the near future. Culture is the result of the ongoing effort of communities and societies to deal with the uncertainties created by social conditions in which future events are not fully predictable. The dynamics are different in modern and traditional societies: the former can be understood as 'hot' cultures, characterised by ongoing change, whereas traditional societies are 'cold' cultures, characterised by stable social relations and conditions (cf. Erdheim 1992). But how are migration and culture related to each other?

Migration, Culture and Learning Understood as a 'balancing process' or a 'process of socialisation', migration refers to contexts and situations in which it is seen as a reaction to and part of social change, which places new demands on individuals, communities and societies. For individuals and communities, migration can be an answer to these demands, by which people actively make their 'own' decisions and plans. Therefore, migration research must focus on agency, must understand what migrants are doing, for what reasons and how they deal with the consequences. One of these consequences is cultural change, because migrants bring manifold cultural experiences and practices to the new location that they want to make their new centre of life. In the new place they try to keep and preserve cultural practices, but also change them as they try to invent new ways while simultaneously acquiring new cultural practices from the host society. Meanwhile, people who live in the location into migrants arrive also experience new cultural practices, which may not fit in easily into their established norms, values and cultural practices. It is precisely at this point, where processes of socialisation start, that is, when differences are perceived and/or constructed between individuals and social groups, and differences are accentuated. Senses of meaning and belonging, and social and cultural practices are questioned. Social change initiated by migration creates complexities in the system which must be surmounted by individuals, communities and the society as a whole. Social and political developments occur in such situations, where social change places new demands on the society.

Taking this complex understanding of migration into account, the question of culture comes into the centre of debate. In modern societies, 'culture' is used to describe a coherent individual and social pattern of action. 'Culture' is a hotly debated term, especially in the context of migration processes of 'culturalisation', which are often used to keep migrants in marginal positions. In this chapter, the term has a different meaning. Here, culture is not defined as a fixed set of norms, values and orientations acquired during socialisation in a certain local or national context. It is understood, following Clifford Geertz, as a tissue of meanings into which the individual is interwoven (Geertz 1987). This understanding sees culture not as a fixed set of variables but as a process (Wimmer 2005), and as such, it is a product of history, resulting in a 'system of forces' (Eagleton 2001).

An important criterion for culture is its continuity. Obviously, continuity of culture is stronger where culture is described as tradition. The central aspect of tradition is its invariance, as Hobsbawm explains: 'The object and characteristic of "traditions", including invented ones, is invariance. The past, real or invented, to which they refer imposes fixed (normally formalised) practices, such as repetition' (Hobsbawm 2003, p. 2). So, cultural traditions are solidified cultural practices that influence current patterns of action and interpretation. But how do social practices become significant and what is the relevance of different and competing expressions and understandings of culture?

The historical dimension of culture can be characterised as diachronic. In this dimension, culture can be seen as the result of a process in which a social group, for example, a community or a society, develops different patterns that follow each other in the course of time, in order to maintain the life-courses of both the social group and its members. Different groups in society command different social and economic resources, and are endowed with unequal power relations. Thus, they develop different cultural practices by which they become distinct from each other and create their own cultures. This cultural practice occurs not on a vertical level, as in the diachronic perspective, but on a horizontal level. From this perspective, culture can be seen as an ambivalent element in which cultural solutions, carried over from the past and therefore registered in a diachronic perspective, are not only a necessary condition for individuals and collectives but also can become a hindrance or obstacle to new tasks both individual and social (cf. Geisen 2008; Jouhy 1996; Mergner 1998, 1999). At the crossroads of diachronic and synchronic cultures, ambivalence arises. Migration adds a new dimension to the cultural texture of a society, so social conditions must be renegotiated between those affected by migration. The diachronic dimension of culture forces individuals into repetition of existing, dominant solutions, and thus, circular processes of thinking and action (Mergner 1999, p. 57). Starting something anew, finding solutions for current problems without being trapped in the vicious cycle of diachronic repetition is the characteristic of the synchronic dimension of culture.

The extension of theoretical perspectives on migration through the understanding of migration as a process of socialisation does emphasise the relevance of culture in migration. Migrant agency is at the centre of such an approach. Given the distinction between diachronic and synchronic cultures, we can propose an analytical framework in which the individual and social action of migrants can be better understood. This can be shown in recent research on migrant youth in Germany and Switzerland, which has brought into the debate new paradigms for a better understanding of migrant youth. These can be understood as a practice for developing new synchronic cultures against the diachronic cultural dominance of devaluation and exclusion of migrant youth.

New Paradigms: Belonging, Cultural Repositionings and Social Mobility The new approaches established in migrant youth research in Germany and Switzerland use concepts of belonging, cultural repositioning and social mobility. Common to these approaches is their interest in the individual strategies of adolescent migrants and their focus on the relevance of the synchronic dimension of culture for young migrants. These new paradigms are centred on agency. At the same time, however, they prompt new questions about the meaning of these concepts. We present these new paradigms of migration research here to underline not only their potential and limitations, but also to show how adolescents with migrant backgrounds are constructed in research.

At the heart of the social and political claim that migrants must integrate lies the idea of the national-cultural collective of the majority society. The 'belonging' discussed in qualitative migration research on adolescents and young adults (Mecheril 2003; Riegel 2004; Schramkowski 2007) represents the 'other side' of the discourse on integration as such. In empirical research on adolescent migrants, 'belonging' often figures as a particular problem. It describes a specific relationship between the majority and the migrants as members of old or new minorities. Barbara Schramkowski describes this interrelation as follows:

> *The recognition of their social belonging* is most crucial. This is the designated basis for the development of positive perceptions of integration that comes along with sentiments of identification with the adopting society. They make these assertions because of their experience with established definitions of belonging or extraneousness. These in turn are often based on the presumption that immigrants, because of their 'foreign' origin, are not able to be members of 'German' society, leading to their quasi 'self-evident' exclusion from the social 'we'. (Schramkowski 2007, p. 368 TRANS)

The interrelation described here rests on a double process of attribution. On the one hand, abstract demands for integration, together with likewise abstract, actual, or alleged integration deficits, are established by the majority society. Therefore, a social process of attribution takes place in the social discourse on integration, which is not directed at specific individuals, but at socially and culturally homogenised, abstract collectives. Thus the discourse on integration represents a social practice in which individuals are attached to certain collectives. On the other hand, belonging is regarded as precarious for individuals. According to social and political discourses on integration, it is not only migrants' individual feelings about their (social, cultural and political) belonging, that is, their relationship to the majority that is challenged, implicitly or explicitly; also discussed in the integration discourse is the relationship of the migrants to the incriminated minority. The demand for integration is directed towards the migrants indiscriminately and is at the same time a demand for alienation from their original culture.

Paul Mecheril attributes the challenge for young migrants to the legitimacy of multiple belongings to the social demand for 'exclusive denominations and pure identities' (Mecheril 2003, p. 388) vis-à-vis the national society. Concrete experiences of belonging are thus predispositioned in two ways: Belonging is based on notions that figure predominantly in the interrelation of the individual with the society yet, the individual has a subjective understanding of belonging (Mecheril 2003, p. 127). 'Understandings of belonging' are the result of an 'experience of belonging' in heterogeneous 'contexts of belonging', which are realised by subjective positioning. For adolescent migrants, an active process of forming subjective belonging occurs, which Mecheril describes as 'belonging work' (Zugehörigkeitsarbeit) (Mecheril 2003, p. 335).

For Christine Riegel, the 'struggle of belonging' (Kampf um Zugehörigkeit) (Riegel 2004, p. 352) is a structural element of the biographical narrative as well. The experience of lack of recognition and segregation 'as strangers' within communities that are nationally and ethnically connoted in their country of origin as well as in Germany form the basis of these needs for belonging and recognition

3   Understanding Cultural Differences as Social Limits to Learning   27

(Riegel 2004, p. 353). According to Riegel, however, the experience of a dual segregation as 'others' exists in contrast to their emotional connection and loyalty with both societies, as well as to their endeavours for integration (Riegel 2004, p. 353). The creation of 'cultures in-between' (Bhabha 1997, 1996) or 'third spaces' (Riegel 2004, p. 353), transnational spaces and cultures, is of crucial importance for adolescent migrants, since they offer the possibility of retreat if recognition is refused.

However, there is not only integration but also resistance or 'new social identifications', as Mannitz (2006) argues. Young migrants are not only driven by society and circumstances but are also active agents who develop new social identifications and are able to offer resistance to institutionally effective forms of devaluation and segregation in school. Success in education is considered by Mannitz as the 'expression of a remarkable independent achievement under unfavourable circumstances' (Mannitz 2006, p. 297). These strategies and achievements through which the process of socialisation takes place are actively co-determined by the adolescent migrants. Necessary processes of adaptation to society are realised as well as acts of resistance to devaluation and segregation. In these studies, adolescents who actively engage with and try to 'shape' their life-environment according to their needs are seen as able to shape their own biographical development.

In the 'struggle for belonging' and the 'new social identifications', education and training are very important (cf. Mannitz 2006; Riegel 2004). Young migrants can realise for themselves individual strategies of self-authorisation and self-positioning on the basis of success in education and training, which allows them a greater degree of autonomy and independence from their parents and families as well as from restrictive social conditions. Educational success can lead to economic independence from parents, which allows new individual and social possibilities. Tarek Badawia's study 'The Third Chair' (Der Dritte Stuhl) (Badawia 2002) centres on how migrants who have been successful in education deal with cultural differences. The study enters the debate about the effect of actual or professed 'cultural conflicts' that have been said to be disadvantageous for adolescent migrants' socialisation and education. Badawia opposes to the picture of life '*in between* two cultures' (Badawia 2002, p. 308) a life '*in* two cultures' (Badawia 2002, p. 308), that is, 'multiple culturality' as 'a new productive form of processing' (Badawia 2002, p. 308). In this light, culture is no longer seen as a hindrance to processes of education. The biographical point of origin of 'multiple culturality' is the notion of 'biculturality' (Badawia 2002, p. 308) as an empirical, verifiable, 'cognitive achievement for structuring one's environment' (Badawia 2002, p. 308), which illustrates parts of the social reality for the adolescents of migration backgrounds. It is a source and object of subjective processes of identity-creation leading to distinct identity aspirations.

Whereas Badawia examines the creation of identity of migrants who have been successful in education, Merle Hummerich deals in her study 'Success in Education and Migration' (Bildungserfolg und Migration) (Hummrich 2002) with the context of the 'internal' construction of the subject, and the 'external' socio-structural conditions of class, gender and ethnicity in the biographical transformation of young women (Hummrich 2002, p. 10). 'Internal' transformation implies here an active positioning to the 'structural categories that cause inequality' (Hummrich 2002, p. 304) and which are connected to changes in attitude. Here, the notion of generation becomes important, since the specific attributes of a generation lead to various ways of processing experiences. For migrants, an 'antimony of attachment and alienation' (Hummrich 2002, p. 305) can characterise the intergenerational relationship. This antimony, however, cannot be determined only on the grounds of the ambivalence of intergenerational relationships, which consists of both the institutional dimension (family structure) and the intersubjective dimension of family relationships. Hummrich adds a third dimension, the 'level of acting' (Hummrich 2002, p. 305f.), characterised by the poles of heteronomy and autonomy (Hummrich 2002, p. 305f.). Acting and biographical reconstructions by migrants regarding their parents might, according to Hummrich who follows Apitzsch (1999b), 'be interpreted as an attempt to create new traditions through migration and changing processes in view of the violations of traditions mediated by the parents' (Hummrich 2002, p. 309).[1]

Using the example of migrants who have been successful in education, it can be demonstrated that adolescent migrants succeed in realising forms of 'identity transformation' and self-positioning via the educational processes. They develop distinct structures in order to exploit and extend existing possibilities of action, and in the process, the pursuit of independence and autonomy is applied to the familiar context as well as to a society characterised by inequality. Identity establishment, education and coping with adolescence are crucial categories that determine the migrants' growing up in modern societies. The self-image of the adolescent migrant is shaped here by his or her ability to develop and realise specific goals.

The Creation of Tradition: Cultural Reorientation and Self-positioning The peculiarities of the situation of adolescents of migrant background are at the same time a question about the importance of cultural difference in life. Anne Juhasz and Eva Mey adopt a perspective in their study 'The Second Generation: Insiders and Outsiders'? (Die zweite Generation: Etablierte oder Außenseiter?) (2003), a biographical study on second-generation adolescents and young adults, that is directed towards social inequality and social mobility. They argue that a shift is taking place, 'away from "culture" and towards the "structure" of a society' (Juhasz and Mey 2003, p. 336).[2] They are, therefore, above all, interested in the 'interplay between a logic of inequality that is conditioned by capital and one that is conditioned by figuration' (Juhasz and Mey 2003, p. 297). This is supplemented by an analysis of the 'individual patterns of perception and acting that shape the social positioning of an individual decisively' (Juhasz and Mey 2003, p. 297). There are intentional

---

[1] On this occasion, a supplementary comment should be added that an intergenerational transmission is taking place as well. Alejandro Portes and Rubén G. Rumbaut have highlighted this fact in their study on two US generations. 'There is [...] strong evidence on the intergenerational transmission of both privilege and disadvantage' (Portes and Rumbaut 2001, p. 283).

[2] The critique of the cultural paradigm, as it forms the basis of, for instance, the so-called 'thesis of cultural conflicts' and the turning towards socio-structural explanation attempts in the research on migration, was brought forth, among others, by Dittrich and Radtke (1990) and Marvakis (1998).

forms of action that are situated in specific social and structural contexts; yet there is also a chance to broaden the individual range of possibilities and to reach biographical goals, for example, aspired social positions. Topics specific to migration, which are of importance for the intentional and active form of positioning, consist most of all of the parents' attitude towards return, and relationship to the country of origin and the relatives still living there (Juhasz and Mey 2003, p. 298). The return can, for instance, become an emotional burden on the family, or lead to the arrangement of a 'provisional life' in the country of migration. The relationships to the country of origin represent a burden most of all for the succeeding generations, since they are regarded as foreigners there. Juhasz and Mey specify limited access to cultural, economic and social capital (Juhasz and Mey 2003 ff.) as they appear in exclusion processes in schools, in parents' limited resources, in processes of stigmatisation based on lack of language skill, and in the search for training positions, for instance. According to Juhasz and Mey, belonging is refused if, because of a lack of group belonging, access to social capital and social recognition in the form of commitment cognitive respect and social appreciation is withheld (Juhasz and Mey 2003).

The idea that adolescents of migrant backgrounds grow up in a social space pervaded by plurality and unequal power relations is a common feature of new theoretical approaches developed in qualitative research. In this context, 'belonging work' and self-authorisation can be seen as strategies that refer to social belonging(s), centred on community and society, as well as to the question of the subjective ability to aim for self-realisation. The studies presented here distance themselves from the simplifying and homogenising assumptions often made in migration research. Conceptually and theoretically, however, the relevance of cultural distinctions is still prompting questions. Juhasz and Mey, for instance, attempt to analyse the biographies of second-generation adolescents of foreign origin on the grounds of social inequality, in order to develop a 'perspective away from "culture" and towards the "structure" of society' (Juhasz and Mey 2003, p. 336). With the concepts of 'national, ethnic, and cultural (multiple) belonging' (Mecheril), the 'struggle for belonging and recognition' (Riegel), and the 'third chair' (Badawia), concepts are created that refer directly to processes of cultural reorientation realised through social and cultural re-positionings. Biographical experiences are considered to be relevant as a whole and not just in relation to two cultural contexts that are different from one another or exist in a hierarchical relationship. But the various cultural reference points, too, that affect the lives of adolescent migrants are also considered relevant. Annette Treibel points out the relevance of (ethnic) cultural identity: 'For all generations, the ethnic identifications, which by all means are not homogenous, and the orientations towards their respective *community* play a crucial role. In this respect, it is important to assert that the existence of the *community* need not be identical with the neighbourhood someone is living in' (Treibel 2003, p. 194). Beyond that, ethnic identifications do not represent a 'relapse' into traditional patterns of action necessarily, so processes of 're-ethnicising' take on an independent character in fact individual *and* collective. Portes and Rumbaut refer to this as well: 'Even when the process involves embracing the parents' original identities, this is less a sign of continuing loyalty to the home country than a reaction to hostile conditions in the receiving society' (Portes and Rumbaut 2001, p. 284). Here, too, it is about processes of cultural repositioning in a social and cultural environment that limits the possibilities for action of migrants in general and adolescents in particular.

Apitzsch (1999a) has developed a theoretic-conceptual solution to the problem of the connection between 'culture *and* structure'. She describes the processes of cultural reorientation and self-positioning of adolescent migrants as 'creation of tradition' (Traditions*bildung)* (Apitzsch 1999a, p. 19). Juhasz/Mey and Hummrich also refer positively to this. Apitzsch prompts a rethink of the sociological concept of traditionality, whereby the ability of subjects to create their own biography in social conflicts is highlighted. 'Essentialising tendencies of "cultures of origin" are criticised strongly, the creation of traditions in the migration's destination societies and the share of biographical work in implementing these traditions are documented impressively' (Apitzsch 1999a, p. 19). However, biographical knowledge does not only provide a framework for everyday communication; the standards for a reciprocal acknowledgement of cultural traditions are also set through biographical representation in social conflicts (cf. Apitzsch 1999a, p. 19). The concept of 'modernity difference' is contrasted with the assumption of a 'post-conventional biographic development of tradition': 'A new individual autonomy of action is reconstructed, understanding it as an element of new emergent social practices' (Apitzsch 1999a, p. 19). In the context of adolescents of migrant background, the development of tradition, however, always presupposes the adoption of existing cultural significations as they are initially acquired in the context of the family and then in expanding, extra-familiar contexts. Only on this basis can the human proto-trust in community and society that takes place in the earliest years of life be developed. This then becomes a prerequisite for overcoming the ethnocentric limitations that have been acquired hitherto (cf. Jouhy 1996). It takes place because of individual and social learning processes (Mergner 1998, 1999). The limitation is based on the fact that in the early stages of their development, children only come into contact with a limited spectrum of cultural experiences and practices. Basically, this limitation applies to the children of migrants as well.

In adolescence, migrant youth are confronted with a developmental challenge, in the sense of having to master a double adolescence; they must detach themselves from their parents and turn to face society; in doing so, they move away from familiar cultural traditions and socio-cultural self-positioning in (at least) two different societies takes place—the one their parents came from and the one in which they currently living. This process of self-positioning has been observed and analysed for some time now in qualitative research on adolescents with migrant backgrounds, for instance, among those who have been successful in education (Badawia 2002; Hummrich 2002). It shows that adolescent migrants, because of their multicultural background, have available to them an extended range of possible (cultural) actions, which they can apply in the further productive shaping of their lives. At the same time, they can thereby succeed in overcoming existing forms of social inequality and discrimination.

Conclusion

My argument in this chapter is that developments in migration theory open new perspectives, especially regarding youth migrants and family migration; bringing youth and family migration into focus demands new theoretical approaches. Culture, too, becomes a more relevant issue; indeed, to understand better the contradictions and ambivalences of culture, diachronic and synchronic perspectives on it are important. As shown in the discussion of recent studies in migration youth research in Germany and Switzerland, the agency of young migrants in society is highlighted and the relevance and interplay of cultural, ethnic and social issues becomes clear. Following the discussion on 'belonging work', the 'struggle for belonging', and 'new social identifications', questions were posed about the characteristics of a young migrant's adolescence. Adolescence represents a space of possibilities in which processes of learning, education and development take place. The implication for the young migrants is that the belongings and patterns of action acquired thus far in their lives are altered and re-created in adolescence. In societies in which migration is still regarded as the exception, and forms and possibilities of social participation of migrants are often limited by segregation and racism. Under such conditions of social limits to learning respect for adolescent migrants is scarce. For the young migrants themselves, this implies that 'precarious identifications' are developing and society is turning out to be an unsafe place for them.

References

Anderson, B. (2006). *Doing the dirty work? Migrantinnen in der bezahlten Hausarbeit in Europa*. Berlin: Assoziation A.
Apitzsch, U. (1999a). Traditionsbildung im Zusammenhang gesellschaftlicher Migrations- und Umbruchprozesse. In U. Apitzsch (Ed.), *Migration und Traditionsbildung* (pp. 7–20). Wiesbaden: Westdeutscher Verlag.
Apitzsch, U. (Ed.). (1999b). *Migration und Traditionsbildung*. Wiesbaden: Westdeutscher Verlag.
Apitzsch, U., & Schmidbaur, M. (Eds.). (2010). *Care und Migration: Die Ent-Sorgung menschlicher Reproduktionsarbeit entlang von Geschlechter- und Armutsgrenzen*. Opladen/Farmington Hills: Barbara Budrich.
Badawia, T. (2002). *Der Dritte Stuhl*. Frankfurt am Main: IKO Verlag.
Bade, K. J. (2004). *Sozialhistorische Migrationsforschung*. Osnabrück: V&R Unipress.
Baumert, J., Stanat, P., & Watermann, R. (Eds.). (2006). *Herkunftsbedingte Disparitäten im Bildungswesen: Differenzielle Bildungsprozesse und Probleme der Verteilungsgerechtigkeit: Vertiefende Analysen im Rahmen von PISA 2000*. Wiesbaden: VS Verlag.
Bhabha, H. K. (Ed.). (1996). *Nation and narration*. London: Routledge.
Bhabha, H. K. (1997). Verortungen der Kultur. In E. Bronfen, B. Marius, & T. Steffen (Eds.), *Hybride Kulturen* (pp. 123–148). Tübingen: Stauffenburg
Borjas, G. J. (1989). Economic theory and international migration. *International Migration Review, XXIII*(3), 457–485.
Boyd, M. (1989). Family and personal networks in international migration. Recent developments and new agendas. *International Migration Review, 23*(3), 638–670.

Cox, P. (2007). Young people, migration and metanarratives. Arguments for a Critical Theoretical Approach. In T. Geisen & C. Riegel (Eds.), *Jugend, Partizipation und Migration* (pp. 51–66). Wiesbaden: VS Verlag.

Diefenbach, H. (2010). *Kinder und Jugendliche aus Migrantenfamilien im deutschen Bildungssystem: Erklärungen und empirische Befunde*. Wiesbaden: VS Verlag.

Dittrich, E. J., & Radtke, F.-O. (1990). *Ethnizität: Wissenschaft und Minderheiten*. Wiesbaden: Westdeutscher Verlag.

Eagleton, T. (2001). *Was ist Kultur?* München: C.H. Beck.

Erdheim, M. (1992). *Die gesellschaftliche Produktion von Unbewußtheit*. Frankfurt a. M.: Suhrkamp.

Faist, T. (2004). Grenzen überschreiten - zum Konzept Transnationaler Sozialer Räume. *Migration und Soziale Arbeit, 26*(2), 83–97.

Fawcett, J. T. (1989). Networks, linkages, and migration systems. *International Migration Review, XXIII*, 671–680.

Fürstenau, S., & Gomolla, M. (Eds.). (2009a). *Migration und schulischer Wandel: Elternbeteiligung*. Wiesbaden: VS Verlag.

Fürstenau, S., & Gomolla, M. (Eds.). (2009b). *Migration und schulischer Wandel: Unterricht*. Wiesbaden: VS Verlag.

Fürstenau, S., & Gomolla, M. (Eds.). (2011). *Migration und schulischer Wandel: Mehrsprachigkeit*. Wiesbaden: VS Verlag.

Geertz, C. (1987). *Dichte Beschreibung. Beiträge zum Verstehen kultureller Systeme*. Frankfurt am Main: Suhrkamp.

Geisen, T. (2005). Migration als Vergesellschaftungsprozess. In T. Geisen (Ed.), *Arbeitsmigration. WanderareiterInnen auf dem Weltmarkt für Arbeitskraft* (pp. 19–36). Frankfurt am Main: IKO Verlag.

Geisen, T. (2007). Der Blick der Forschung auf Jugendliche mit Migrationshintergrund. In C. Riegel & T. Geisen (Eds.), *Jugend, Zugehörigkeit und Migration* (pp. 27–60). Wiesbaden: VS Verlag.

Geisen, T. (2008). Kultur und Identität - Zum Problem der Thematisierung von Gleichheit und Differenz in modernen Gesellschaften. In L. Allolio-Näcke & B. Kalscheuer (Eds.), *Kulturelle Differenzen begreifen* (pp. 167–188). Frankfurt am Main: Campus.

Geisen, T. (2009). Vergesellschaftung statt Integration: Zur Kritik des Integrations-Paradigmas. In P. Mecheril, I. Dirim, M. Gomolla, S. Hornberg, & K. Stoyanov (Eds.), *Spannungsverhältnisse: Assimilationsdiskurse und interkulturell-pädagogische Forschung* (pp. 13–34). Münster: Waxmann.

Geisen, T., & Riegel, C. (Eds.). (2009). *Jugend, Partizipation und Migration: Orientierungen im Kontext von Integration und Ausgrenzung*. Wiesbaden: VS Verlag.

Glick-Schiller, N., Basch, L., & Szanton Blanc, C. (1997). From immigrant to transmigrant: Theorizing transnational migration In L. Pries (Ed.), *Transnationale migration* (pp. 121–140). Baden-Baden: Nomos Verlagsgesellschaft.

Hamburger, F., Badawia, T., & Hummrich, M. (Eds.). (2005). *Migration und Bildung*. Wiesbaden: VS Verlag.

Hobsbawm, E. J. (2003). Introduction: Inventing traditions. In E. J. Hobsbawm & T. Ranger (Eds.), *The invention of tradition* (pp. 1–14). Cambridge: Cambridge University Press.

Hoerder, D. (2002a). *Cultures in contact: World migrations in the second millennium*. Durham: Duke University Press.

Hoerder, D. (2002b). Migration als Ausgleichsprozess. In T. Geisen (Ed.), *Mobilität und Mentalitäten* (Vol. 1, pp. 258). Frankfurt a. M.: IKO-Verlag.

Hoerder, D., Hébert, Y., & Schmitt, I. (2005a). Transculturation and the accumulation of social capital: Understanding histories and decoding the present of young people. In D. Hoerder, Y. Hébert, & I. Schmitt (Eds.), *Negotiating transcultural lives: Belongings and social capital among youth in comparative perspective* (pp. 11–38). Göttingen: V & R Unipress.

Hoerder, D., Hébert, Y., & Schmitt, I. (Eds.). (2005b). *Negotiating transcultural lives: Belongings and social capital among youth in comparative perspective*. Osnabrück: V&R Unipress.

Hoerder, D., & Moch, L. P. (Eds.). (1996). *European migrants: Global and local perspectives*. Boston: Northeastern University Press.
Hummrich, M. (2002). *Bildungserfolg und Migration*. Opladen: Leske + Budrich.
Husa, K., Parnreiter, C., & Stacher, I. (Eds.). (2000). *Internationale Migration: Die globale Herausforderung des 21. Jahrhunderts?*. Frankfurt am Main: Brandes & Apsel.
Jouhy, E. (1996). *Bleiche Herrschaft - Dunkle Kulturen*. Frankfurt a. M.: IKO-Verlag.
Juhasz, A., & Mey, E. (2003). *Die zweite Generation: Etablierte oder Außenseiter?* Opladen: Leske + Budrich.
Lucassen, J., & Lucassen, L. (1997). Migration, migration history, history: Old paradigms and new perspectives. In J. Lucassen & L. Lucassen (Eds.), *Migration, migration history, history: Old paradigms and new perspectives* (pp. 9–40). Bern: Peter Lang.
Lutz, H. (2008). *Vom Weltmarkt in den Privathaushalt*. Opladen: Budrich.
Mannitz, S. (2006). *Die verkannte Integration*. Bielefeld: Transcript.
Marvakis, A. (1998). Wenn aus sozialen Ungleichheiten kulturelle Differenzen werden. *Forum Kritische Psychologie* (Heft 39), 42–58.
Massey, D. S. (2000). Einwanderungspolitik für ein neues Jahrhundert. In K. Husa, C. Parnreiter, & I. Stacher (Eds.), *Internationale Migration. Die globale Herausforderung des 21. Jahrhunderts?* Frankfurt am Main: Brandes & Apsel/Südwind.
Mecheril, P. (2003). *Prekäre Verhältnisse: Über natio-ethno-kulturelle (Mehrfach-)Zugehörigkeiten*. Münster: Waxmann.
Mergner, G. (1998). *Dominanz, Gewalt und Widerstand*. Hamburg: Argument Verlag.
Mergner, G. (1999). *Lernfähigkeit der Subjekte und gesellschaftliche Anpassungsgewalt*. Hamburg: Argument Verlag.
Metz-Göckel, S., Morokvasic, M., & Senganata, M. A. (Eds.). (2008). *Migration and mobility in an enlarged Europe*. Opladen: Barbara Budrich.
OECD. (2006). *Where immigrant students succeed - a comparative review of performance and engagement in PISA 2003*. http://www.pisa.oecd.org/dataoecd/2/38/36664934.pdf. Accessed 24 February 2007.
Piore, M. J. (1979). *Birds of passage: Migrant labor and industrial societies*. Cambridge: Cambridge University Press.
Portes, A., & Rumbaut, R. (2001). *Legacies: The story of the immigrant second generation*. Berkeley: University of California Press/Russel Sage Foundation.
Pries, L. (Ed.). (1997). *Transnational migration* (Vol. 12). Baden-Baden: Nomos Verlagsgesellschaft.
Pries, L. (2008). *Die Transnationalisierung der sozialen Welt*. Frankfurt a. M.: Suhrkamp.
Riegel, C. (2004). *Im Kampf um Zugehörigkeit und Anerkennung*. Frankfurt am Main: IKO Verlag.
Riegel, C., & Geisen, T. (Eds.). (2007). *Jugend, Zugehörigkeit und Migration: Subjektpositionierung im Kontext von Jugendkultur, Ethnizitäts- und Geschlechterkonstruktionen*. Wiesbaden: VS Verlag.
Schramkowski, B. (2007). *Integration unter Vorbehalt: Perspektiven junger Erwachsener mit Migrationshintergrund*. Frankfurt am Main: IKO Verlag.
Todaro, M. P. (1969). A model of labor migration and urban unemployment in less developed countries. *The American Economic Review, LIX* (1), 138–148.
Treibel, A. (2003). *Migration in modernen Gesellschaften*. Weinheim/München: Juventa.
Wimmer, A. (2005). *Kultur als Prozess: Zur Dynamik des Aushandelns von Bedeutungen*. Wiesbaden: VS Verlag.

Chapter 4
Beyond Limits and Limitations: Reflections on Learning Processes in Contexts of Migration and Young People

Pat Cox

Introduction

Migration is the social issue of this age (Harzig and Hoerder 2009); both migration *from* and migration *to* (Cortés 2007; Konseiga 2006). Interest in migration is widespread in political, legal and policy settings (Betts 2009; Loescher et al. 2008); among social scientists, educators, social workers; among health and medical workers (Castles and Miller 2009; Portes and DeWind 2008; Tunstall 2006).

In a migration context, speaking or writing about culture may refer to 'cultural differences' which challenge the normative societal and educational assumptions held by receiving nations: for example, Palmary (2007); Wright (1998); including challenges to assumptions about young migrant people's learning (Bilson and Cox 2007; Warwick et al. 2006). Young migrant people frequently encounter criticisms of their cultural heritage and practices (Bekerman and Kopelowitz 2008), or denial of their value and significance; such criticisms and denial can result in oppressive and limiting constructs of young migrant people. However, receiving nations' cultures are less fixed and more fluid than appearances suggest (Kushner 2006; Portes 2006), as are the cultures of young migrant people themselves (Gilroy 2010; Kasinitz et al. 2008).

Culture can be constituted, understood and analysed in many ways: for example, Elias (1978/1994); McGuigan (2009). For the purposes of this chapter, culture is more than cultural projects or forms of representation; culture is used in its broadest sense of shared practices which produce meaning; which permeate all aspects of social life (Calhoun and Sennett 2007) and which can be simultaneously affirmed, deconstructed and criticized (Gilroy 2010). In many western nations, culture often is ascribed the features of being essentialist, inherited and fixed; yet sociological analysis demonstrates cultures arising at particular moments in time and reflecting particular social or national developments (Hobsbawm and Ranger 1983;

P. Cox (✉)
School of Social Work, University of Central Lancashire, PR1 2HE, Lancashire, UK
e-mail: pcox2@uclan.ac.uk

McGuigan 2009), while the hegemony of influential social groups in structuring and maintaining cultures is frequently occluded (Gramsci 1971, 1985).

Despite widespread interest in migration, the significant roles that young migrant people play in both sending and receiving countries (GCIM 2005) are rarely acknowledged. They are members of a complex system of movements; as noted by Dobson (2009) and Harttgen and Klasen (2009), their actions and contributions are not captured fully by research studies. Migration can create choices for young people or expand existing ones; however, migration may not lead to improved opportunities if young people are refugees or asylum-seekers (Brownlees and Finch 2010).

The subjects of this chapter are young people who are migrants and the responsibilities of educators[1] in higher education (universities) in teaching and researching about migration. These two subjects rarely are linked; yet in researching and teaching about migration, particularly the migration of young people, educators are well placed to contribute to local, national and international debates on migration matters. In focussing upon young migrant people and in analysing the responsibilities of educators in teaching and researching about young people's migration and contributing to public learning and debate, the author draws upon Mergner's theorizing on 'learning' and 'social limits to learning'(2005a); the role of 'ambivalence' in human thought and action; 'identities' and 'universal equality' (1995, 2005c); 'morality of solidarity' (2005b) and education (2005c). Mergner emphasizes understanding of, learning about and conceptualizing the social world, social change and societal and inter-personal relationships and in his thinking new epistemological approaches are unfolded: their relevance to the linked subjects of young migrant people and higher education are discussed throughout this chapter. Arendts theorizing (1963, 1964, 1978) also contributes to analysis of these issues.

University education is regarded by many nations as essential to their expanding knowledge economies (Jessop et al. 2008) and as a source for the transmission of culture (Delanty 2001). However, criticism grows (Clegg 2008) that universities are retreating from what might be considered to be their original purposes (Benner 2003) and their role in, and contribution to, the public sphere (Calhoun 2008, 2009).

In this chapter it is argued firstly that educators should ensure that migration and the experiences and concerns of young migrant people are addressed within social, political and economic sciences; secondly, that educators must recognize how normative assumptions about learning, learning processes and culture may limit understanding and critical analysis of these issues; thirdly, that educators must encourage movement beyond debates about culture and beyond critiques of personal and social prejudice, commencing critical engagement with learning processes for students, for educators ourselves and for wider society. The aim is to engen-

---

[1] 'Educators' refers to university staff who both teach and undertake research. 'Young migrant people' include young people who arrive with families and carers in a planned way and those who may be 'forced migrants', including refugee and asylum-seeking young people.

der critically engaged thinking and praxes, when considering migration and when considering learning about young people's migration and culture within universities and in the public sphere.

In Part One, consideration of current issues in migration is followed by exploring the relevance of Mergner's thinking about learning, ambivalence, identity and education to migration and young migrant people. In Part Two, this same theorizing is applied to university education and to the responsibilities of educators in addressing issues for young migrant people; in developing understandings of cultural and social differences in learning processes and generating different debates around young people's migration, communities and societies, within universities and in the public sphere. The chapter begins with an overview of migration, including young people's migration.

Migration and Young People's Migration

In many western nations, migrant people of all ages frequently are characterized as existential threats (de Haas 2008; Huysmans 2005), rather than as people needing protection and support to integrate themselves into new surroundings (Cohen 2001; ICA 2008). Political, legal and policy responses to migration generally consist of increased bureaucracy and control through systems (Benhabib 2004); these are (apparently) pragmatic responses to 'overwhelming' 'numbers' of migrants (Goodman 2007). The impact of legal and policy structures on migrant people (Gibney 2004; Kushner 2006) is denied, as is the impact of exclusionary attitudes and praxes towards migrant people (Lewis 2005). Extreme nationalism—for example, Rydgren (2003); Wodak and Van Dijk (2000)—and other forms of prejudice, engender negative attitudes and hate crimes against migrant groups and individuals (Cooley and Rutter 2007; Lentin 2004).

Many young migrant people must engage with the concerns of adults in services in order to access support, adapting to policy requirements in receiving nations (Adams 2009; Hart 2008). However, policies and practices which lead to hostile treatment of adult migrants contribute to negative stereotyping and social exclusion of young migrant people also (Bilson and Cox 2007; Crawley 2010). Research and first-person accounts reveal varying understandings of migratory experiences among the generations, depending upon whether themselves or their parents are migrants (Burck 2007; Karpf 1996; Suárez-Orozco 2000).

This brief summary demonstrates that more complex theoretical approaches to migration are required (Geisen 2004; Kushner 2006; Portes and DeWind 2008). In the following two sections, 'social limits to learning' and 'ambivalence' (Mergner 2005a, c) in human thought and action, and their application to key issues in migration and young people's migration as summarized above, are explored and analysed.

Social Limits to Learning and Ambivalence

In Mergner's theory of learning, learning is conceptualized as a *social* (author's emphasis) process, which is influenced by numerous complex emotional responses to insights gained through learning. He asserts that humans oscillate between '…compulsion to learn' and a '…limit to learning' (Mergner and Pippert n.d., p. 248), arguing that each new learning activity begets new learning limits, which then are themselves transcended in an ongoing cycle. Within this non-linear and multi-dimensional theory of learning, everyone can be 'learning subjects' and 'acting subjects' (Mergner 2005a, p. 30). The dialectical model is rendered obsolete and historical determinism is challenged; the concept of social limits to learning acknowledges that the past influences, but does not necessarily decide the present or the future. And if learning processes are continuous, then opportunities for social change continually appear. Learning is potentially life-changing: '…a consciously transformative process of influencing one's own historical reality' (Mergner 2005a, p. 28).

The significance of the social limits to learning theory is that it includes *both* our human desire to learn *and* to apply learning limits (this author's emphasis), examining reasons why individuals, groups and communities comply temporarily or permanently with hegemonic structures and praxes which pervade social life; or resist, challenge, or overcome them; and the manner of compliance or challenge. This theorizing reveals possibilities for emancipatory politics and praxes:

'To overcome the social limits to learning pre-supposes a doubting mind, a sense of dissatisfaction with the existing states of affairs, the given social circumstances; it also pre-supposes vital needs of one's own' (Mergner 2005c, p. 150).

In emphasizing the significance of ambivalence in human thought and action, Mergner accounts for contradictions between personal and societal conformity or resistance: '…the concept of *ambivalence* is a tool for describing the relations between the open possibilities for decision and the diverse interests and motivations of human actors…' (Mergner 1995, p. 156).

He unites the concept of ambivalence with theorizing on social limits to learning, asserting that individuals, groups and communities must recognize the effects of ambivalence on learning: 'Learning is also impeded by the blindness for ambivalences within us…Learning needs trust in your own powers *and* the conceptual perception of your own ambivalences' (Mergner 2005c, p. 152).

Application of This Thinking for Young People's Migration

Both Mergner's conceptualization of the social limits to learning and of ambivalence in human action are relevant to key issues in migration. Mergner's theory of learning positions young migrant people as 'learning subjects' and 'acting subjects' (Mergner 2005a, p. 30). Young migrant people have agency (Adams 2009; Save the

Children 2001), and some choose short-term migration only (Bastia 2005; Hopkins and Hill 2008). Many have overcome their 'limits to learning' and 'ambivalences' (Mergner 2005a, c); their past will not necessarily decide their future (Warwick et al. 2006). However, young migrant people behaving as 'acting subjects' is not viewed positively everywhere, as research by Crawley (2010), among others, demonstrates.

Many nation states and their members choose to disregard the benefits of inward migration, casting migrant people only in negative terms. They set their own 'limits to learning', which are manifest in policies which deny or limit entry, and manifest in verbal and physical attacks on adult and young migrant people (Fekete 2001; Lentin 2004). 'Limits to learning' in receiving nations are also seen when the substantial contributions of migrant people are undervalued (Kushner and Knox 1999; Nguyen 2005) and the potential future contributions of young migrant people to revitalize social and political life (Carey and Kim 2006; Roudi-Fahimi and Kent 2007) are discounted.

Receiving nations' attitudes towards migrant peoples can be characterized as 'ambivalence': they vary across time and in relation to country of origin or current status, with some being welcomed more than others (Benhabib et al. 2007; Goodman 2007). Differences in attitudes are also experienced by young migrant people (Harttgen and Klasen 2009; Kushner 2006), influencing their sense of self-worth and how they view their futures (Crawley 2010; Warwick et al. 2006).

Mergner's (2005c) theorized about how 'identity' can be fashioned into both positive and negative constructs of individuals, groups and cultures and how concepts of equality and equalizing are not as beneficial as they appear. The applicability of this theorizing to migration and young migrant people is examined in the next two sections.

Identity and Abstract Equalizing: Morality of Solidarity

The enactment of the Freudian concepts of repression and projection (Freud 1979) at interpersonal levels in the subjugation of 'outsiders', and at social and political levels in the subjugation and destruction of 'other' cultures, interested Mergner, as did the construction of: 'instrumental-rational solutions, truths and norms' (Mergner 2005c, pp. 143–144) to justify such oppressions. He argues that human needs for identity and belonging can be manipulated into experiences of 'specious solidarity', where the interests of individuals: "… 'inside' are played off against everything categorized as foreign and 'external'. The ideological boundaries fossilize into rigid dogmatic truths; in this ossified form they are then defended, using any means necessary, as the protective sheath of one's own imagined identity" (Mergner 2005c, p. 145).

However, market requirements within receiving nations may supersede prejudice against 'others'; their entry may be justified according to the shifting need for labour (Mergner 2005c).

"Mergner insists on responding to non-indigenous people as individuals: …there can be no real compassion with and sensitivity for stereotyped anonymous groups… And no basis for building practical solidarity" (Mergner 2005c, p. 149). He notes that the term 'outsider' (Mayer 1975) is applied not only to non-indigenous people, but also to those within receiving societies who are perceived as 'other': '…the disabled, vagabonds, the elderly…even children' (Mergner 2005c, p. 145).

Forms of 'cultural patterning' which many of us assimilate when young, generate their own limits to learning; however, Mergner asserts that these limits can be transcended: "The aim of all learning is to recognize the objects, arrangements, and institutions handed down from the past in their human constructedness and to appropriate them anew in one's own interest" (Mergner 2005a, p. 28). He indicates possibilities of moving beyond limits and limitations, towards enriched understandings of self and others and towards social action:

> Cultural self-understanding and understanding of Otherness becomes possible where humans communicate with one another on a conceptual level, beyond the respective boundaries and limits into which they have been socialized and enculturated…cultural boundaries are at the disposition of acting subjects and their comprehended interests; they can be confronted and crossed. (Mergner 2005c, pp. 150–151)

Mergner doubted the value of 'abstract equalizing' (van der Linden 2005, p. 7), having been influenced by Mayer's (1975) critique of universal principles, including 'universal' equality. His consideration of 'identity', 'outsiders' and 'abstract equalizing', leads him to a close reading of Arendt's (1964) engagement with the relationships between rationality, human morality and solidarity (Mergner 2005b). Arendt declares: "…in general systems of ethical rules, individual conscience only functions in an 'automatic way' " (Arendt 1964, p. 205). Within such systems of ethical principles, individuals can justify action or inaction by reference to those principles, rather than by reference to their own conscience (Arendt 1978). Believing that morality needs to be grounded within individuals rather than within systems and rules, she contends that: '…doubters and sceptics…[who] do not cherish values and hold fast to moral norms and standards' (Arendt 1964, p. 205) think through issues and reach their own decisions grounded in that thinking. Arendt argues for independent human judgement of each situation as it arises, without reference to the past—'Denken ohne Geländer'—and thinking reflectively from other standpoints (Arendt 1978). And in this way, solidarity between individuals can flourish.

Application for Young People's Migration

Mergner (2005c) challenges members of receiving nations to review and break with cultural assumptions and ideologies from our upbringing which previously may never have been questioned. Implicit in Mergner's (2005c) insistence that non-indigenous people are individuals, is the possibility of creating different

4 Beyond Limits and Limitations: Reflections on Learning Processes 41

relationships between young migrant people and members of receiving nations and of co-creating alternative futures (Benhabib et al. 2007; Westwood and Phizacklea 2000), without dominance, without assimilation: '…genuine human relationships' (Mergner 2005c, p. 149). Mergner's conceptualization of 'instrumental-rational solutions' describes the migration controls developed in many western nations (de Haas 2008), with 'truths and norms' deployed to justify their actions (Huysmans 2005). National identities are constructed and maintained with 'specious solidarity', resulting in a conviction that 'other' cultures and young members of such cultures should be subjugated (Blok 1998; Hart 2008).

Allowing inward migration in order to meet the demands of capital may privilege adults above young migrant people, who may be viewed as economically inactive and therefore a burden upon services (Brownlees and Finch 2010; Harttgen and Klasen 2009). While young migrant people should not be forced into labour, misconceptions about 'burdens' overlook their future contribution to national life (Nguyen 2005) and ignore the needs of young migrant people for support in accessing housing, education (including higher education) and work (Adams 2009; Bilson and Cox 2007; HEFCW 2010).

Once young migrant people are stereotyped negatively, all forms of exclusion can be justified (Huysmans 2005). Arendt's thinking on individual conscience, foregrounding reflection, thinking and judgement, underpins Mergner's anticipation of a: '…morality of solidarity *between* individuals' (Mergner 2005b, p. 133; emphasis in the original); social relationships which are characterized by co-operation and communication. Such relationships are essential if young migrant people are to believe that their migratory endeavours are understood positively (Adams 2009; Crawley 2010); that they will be able to integrate into and contribute fully to social life (Carey and Kim 2006; Kushner and Knox 1999) in their selected receiving nation, without prejudice about their origin or status (Nguyen 2005); cross-cultural boundaries if they wish and in due time establish their own families (Portes et al. 2005).

Mergner's theorizing on education emphasizes learning processes for all involved in education. This is explored in the following two sections, with discussion of its relevance for young people's migration.

Mergner and Education

The theory of learning and social limits to learning links closely with Mergner's thinking about education. Marx and Engels (1881/1998) belief that: 'the educator must themselves be educated', influenced Mergner's (2005c, p. 150) ideas, which therefore apply to educators and learners alike. Education either 'bolsters bulwarks' or assists in 'overstepping boundaries and limits' (Mergner 2005c, p. 151). Mergner emphasizes the 'ambiguous' nature of education; education both reproduces cultural assumptions, norms and ideologies and: "…impart[s] knowledge and insight…Learning thus pre-supposes the communicative dissolution of one's own ossified past (and that of society) in the interest of the individual's own knowledge" (Mergner 2005a, pp. 27–28).

Mergner, Education and Young People's Migration

In analysing the ambiguities inherent in education, (Mergner 2005c) emphasizes its role in reproducing hegemonic cultural assumptions and norms (Gramsci 1971, 1985) and its role in challenging: '…traditional prejudice and inculcated superstition', presenting alternative analyses and critique (Mergner 2005a, c). In addressing the social issue of young people's migration, therefore, educators should be developing an: 'education that builds solidarity with the stranger' (Mergner 2005b, p. 137).

Young migrant people value education (Bilson and Cox 2007; Williams and Guémar 2008) and are keen to undertake university education in addition to schooling (Warwick et al. 2006). However, efforts by some universities to reach out directly to young migrant people and develop their capacities (HEFCW 2010) are at odds with legal and policy requirements concerning recruitment and monitoring (Jump 2010) and 'building solidarity' through education remains work in progress.

The relevance of Mergner's theorizing in analysing key matters for migration and young migrant people has been examined in Part One of this chapter; Part Two begins by outlining current issues in university education. In succeeding sections, aspects of Mergner's theorizing reviewed in Part One are applied to issues in university education, including the responsibilities of educators in addressing migration and the concerns of young migrant people; the development of understandings of cultural and social differences in learning processes for all 'learning subjects' in universities and in the public sphere.

University Education: Key Issues

In the twenty-first century, university (sometimes higher) education in the western world has become a means of accessing capital and resources (both material and symbolic) and a means for hegemonic groups to control others' access to capital and resources (Hooks 1994; Mohanty 2003). In addition to producing and reproducing knowledge and culture (Delanty 2001), university education frequently is complicit in the production and reproduction of social relations of power across disciplines and academic practices (Gillies and Lucey 2007; Mann 2008).

The current emphasis on 'vocationalization' and the widespread increase in student numbers arises from the influences of market requirements and managerialist approaches (Deem et al. 2008; Schimank 2005). The European Bologna Process, intended to standardize both teaching and academic awards in higher education, is not fully implemented and it is argued by educators across Europe: for example, Lorenz (2006), that this process results in commodification of higher education and of learning. Such critique links into national and international debates about whether educators are still intellectuals and intellectual leaders (Collini 2006; Eliaeson and Kalleberg 2008). Concerns are expressed about atelic conceptualizations of learning experiences within universities and the diminution of universities' social responsibilities and civic engagement (Greenwood and Levin 2003; McIlrath and MacLabhrainn 2007). And in an unequal world (Cox et al. 2008), many universities overlook opportunities to influence social change (Kraus 2008; Unterhalter and Carpentier 2010).

Despite, or because of, the foregoing, there is ongoing engagement with exploring universities' purposes and responsibilities: for example, Calhoun (2008); Habermas (1987); Lorenz (2006), including re-visiting von Humboldt's principle of unity in research and education (Benner 2003). Delanty (2001, 2003) emphasizes dialogue within universities and between universities and groups and communities in the public sphere. Clegg (2008) and Nixon (2008) acknowledge the potential for better dialogue between universities, groups and communities and educators' responsibilities to progress such dialogue. Calhoun (2009) and Greenwood and Levin (2003) argue for addressing the needs of minority stakeholders, rebuilding universities' relationships with communities and societies and reclaiming universities' social and civic responsibilities.

Individuals, groups and communities to whom universities previously were inaccessible undertake research in partnership with educators (Cox et al. 2008; Fine et al. 2003) and now lead their own research projects (Green 2008; Pitts and Smith 2007). For some, this poses epistemic threats to the established order and to the established research agenda; however, it is now agreed widely among researchers that once-marginalized individuals, groups and communities should be positioned as the 'source', rather than the 'object of' understanding (Geisen 2008; Green 2008).

University education generally occurs in public spaces of lectures and seminars; the transmission of knowledge is a public, regulated and controlled activity; learning may occur in public spaces or may be private activity in private spaces. Fromm (1978) emphasizes differences between 'having' and 'being' modes. In the former, students and educators 'have' and acquire knowledge; in the latter, students and educators pay attention to processes, seeking complex understandings of themselves and the social world. This latter ('being') experience is learning; including reflection on what is learned and how it is learned, revealing alternative possibilities for life in the social world (Bekerman 2008).

In the following sections the author explores the relevance of Mergner's theorizing to current key concerns in university education, leading to discussion of educators' responsibilities in addressing the two linked subjects of young migrant people and higher education.

Social Limits to Learning, Ambivalence and University Education

Mergner's theory of learning and learning limits acknowledges the influence of emotions and the complexity of human responses to insight and to knowledge, rather than assuming constant rationality on the part of social actors. Learning about and reflecting upon a range of research concerning young people's migratory and pre-migratory experiences and examining cultural understandings from different perspectives and experiences may lead to resistance (van der Linden 2005, p. 14), and both migrant and non-migrant students and educators in universities may construct our own 'limits to learning' in response (Mergner 2005a, c). However, while the past may influence students' and educators' learning, it does not determine the future: "The effort to consciously change one's own historical reality is what I understand 'learning' to be..." (Mergner 2005c, p. 150).

Open acknowledgement of the influence of ambivalence (Geisen 2008) in human thinking and action, would assist recognition of how it influences learning processes (Mergner 1995, p. 156). In deploying Mergner's theoretical work to facilitate students' exploration of issues for young migrant people, educators too may recognize the obstructive effects of our own 'limits to learning' and 'ambivalences' and can choose how and when to move beyond them (Mergner 2005c). Possibilities for more considered, less market-driven, approaches to teaching and research in universities (Fromm 1978) are revealed through Mergner's emphasis on reflection and self-reflection in relation to 'learning', 'learning limits' and being 'learning subjects' (Mergner 2005a, b).

Identity, Abstract Equalizing, Morality of Solidarity and University Education

Both research and first person narratives (Burck 2007; Williams and Guémar 2008) emphasize heterogeneity among migrant people; individuals not 'groups' (Mergner 2005c). His critique of 'abstract equalizing' (van der Linden 2005, p. 7) can be deployed by educators to examine how universalist approaches to policy and service delivery fail to apprehend the particular needs of young migrant people, and to challenge normative concepts such as 'equal treatment' with their concomitant assumption that such treatment will be of benefit to them (Mergner 2005b).

Knowledge is inextricably bound up with cultural values, assumptions and norms (Mohanty 2003), and Mergner's critique of false universalism reminds educators that knowledge in teaching and research developed in western settings may be appropriate to understanding emotions and experiences of individuals within these nations, but may not be applicable to everyone's emotions and experiences, particularly young migrant people; for example: Anderman (2002); Palmary (2007); Zack-Williams (2006). Sharing cultural stories and personal narratives facilitates multi-dimensional understandings of how world views and beliefs are constructed and held: '…the ability to engage in dialogue with alterity, with what is strange and unfamiliar' (Mergner 2005c, p. 150). Without such dialogue, we may not know what counts as beliefs within another person's or nation's worldview; see also Wittgenstein (1966).

Many educators are migrants ourselves, or the children, grandchildren and great-grandchildren of migrants (Cox 2007; Mohanty 2003). This facilitates questioning the concept of the 'fictive shared community' and the appeal of its 'specious solidarity' (Mergner 2005c, p. 145), through demonstrating that many western nations came into being through historical and recent migrations (Geisen 2004; Lucassen 2005). Therefore, claims that young migrant people should integrate into a prevailing indigenous culture are shown to be ill-founded (Mergner 2005c), as the culture itself is responding to numerous complex influences, including influences of earlier inward migration (Benhabib et al. 2007; Portes 2006). Young migrant people will understand: 'Everyone is from somewhere' (Kasinitz et al. 2008, p. 22) and this principle can become the basis for discussion with non-migrant and migrant students about issues of origin and culture: 'thinking in ambivalence on our own cultural ties and rootedness' (Mergner 2005c, p. 143); and exploration of changes within and between generations (Portes et al. 2005).

Arendt's (1978) insistence on personal responsibility for moral decisions, reflective thinking and the need for independent judgement in individual situations, encourages educators and students to move beyond concepts of individual and social prejudice, which are still culturally hegemonic positions, and surrendering our place as framers of narratives in order to begin: '…the task for an education that builds solidarity with the stranger. The methods and skills for *self-reflection* become here a necessary prerequisite for communication and co-operation' (Megner 2005b, p. 137, emphasis in the original).

Educators' Responsibilities

To acknowledge that university education is perfused with hegemonic social, cultural, political and economic discourses, should not lead to educators becoming complicit with this (Gillies and Lucey 2007). Educators must begin changing the terms of debates about migration, examining the attitudes and behaviour of the richer nations of the west (Arendt 1963; de Wet 2006), rather than blaming young migrant people; and responding to the learning requirements of migrant and non-migrant students from a range of cultural backgrounds (Bekerman and Kopelowitz 2008). It is well established that there is no 'view from nowhere' (Nagel 1986) that can be justified within teaching and research in an unequal world (Cox et al. 2008; Unterhalter and Carpentier 2010). To provide just two examples: normative concepts such as the nation state and its control of borders can be upturned to reveal their darker underside—oppressive treatment of displaced young people in need. Emphasis on state surveillance as a means of protecting citizens, positions some groups as a threat to citizens: young migrant people are one such group (Lewis 2005). And despite criticism (Newman 2008), educators must make our knowledge of young people's migration available to government and policy bodies, providing evidence and support which may help individuals or groups to be given leave to remain (Cohen 2001; ICA 2008).

Teaching which is informed by research can be a countervailing force to prejudice (Clegg 2008); research-informed teaching about and theoretically informed analyses of the social and emotional experiences of young people' migration ensure rigour in inquiry and debates (Geisen 2004; Portes and DeWind 2008). Learning develops as new groups, including young migrant people, enter universities, to study and to teach and research (Evans 2004) and revitalize learning. New thinking, some developed from young migrant people's own research (Warwick et al. 2006), challenges the status and production of existing knowledge and existing 'learning limits' (Mergner 2005a). To generate more complex understandings of young people's migration, educators must do more than 'add in' migration or adopt 'relativist' approaches (Mohanty 2003). Questioning the applicability of western knowledge in analysing migratory experiences and cultures and examining the structures and cultural assumptions of current curricula (Mergner 2005c) will become a significant component of learning. Working towards emancipatory learning praxes (Bauman 1999) there will be more research led by young migrant people and critical engagement with: '...knowledge that is meaningful' (Hooks 1994, p. 19); so that research and theory connect with students' and educators' lives and experiences (Mergner 2005a, b, c): '...a unity of life and thought' (van der Linden 2005, p. 7).

Migration, Learning, Ambivalence and Solidarity

Mergner's theory of the social process of learning, in which our desire to learn is in tension with learning limitations which we generate and transcend, positions everyone; students and educators, individuals, groups and communities, migrant and non-migrant as 'learning subjects' and 'acting subjects' (Mergner 2005a, p. 30). Learning limits in ourselves and others can be recognized and overcome; insight and recognition being pre-requisites when exploring issues of young people's migration and culture. Mergner's (1995, 2005c) conceptualization of the role of ambivalence in human thought and action explains personal and societal oscillation in the social world between inaction and action; conformity and resistance; predictable and unpredictable responses. Because learning processes are continuous (Mergner 2005a), possibilities for change in the social world remain always alive and open, irrespective of whether such possibilities for change are noticed or responded to. In endeavouring to accomplish change in the social world, strength gained from alliances with others similarly engaged is acknowledged: "Not until we... communicate with other like-minded interlocutors can we develop historical prospects for action..." (Mergner 2005c, p. 150).

As demonstrated throughout this chapter, Mergner's theorizing about 'learning' and 'social limits to learning' (2005a); 'ambivalence', 'identities' and 'universal equality' (1995, 2005c); 'morality of solidarity' (2005b) and education (2005c) is extremely relevant for creating more nuanced understandings of issues of migration and for young migrant people. His work assists in developing critical analyses of the short and longer-term psycho-social effects of migration on young migrant people, families and communities and the significance of culture and identity for young migrant people, generating possibilities for more informed debates about migration, identity and the interactions of different cultures, within universities and within the public sphere of receiving nations.

Conclusion: Young People's Migration and Learning; (re)-Connecting with Communities

Imagination is the capacity to think about the social world as if it could be otherwise and Friere (1994) notes the importance of: "Imagination and conjecture about a different world than the one of oppression …to the praxis of historical 'subjects' (agents in the process of transforming reality…)" (Freire 1994, p. 39). Retrieving universities' moral purposes and principles of social action, social responsibility and civic engagement (Greenwood and Levin 2003; Habermas 1987; Nixon 2008) and re-connecting with communities (Calhoun 2008, 2009) requires both imagination and determination.

Mergner (2005b, c) believes that 'practical solidarity' (Mergner 2005c, p. 149) is necessary to achieve social change; in similar vein Mohanty (2003) and Cox (2009) assert the need for coalition-building. Universities are part of the social world and can lead analysis and critique of major social issues such as young people's migration. As Delanty argues: "(the)…university is …a site of public discourses…universities…[could] become important agents of the public sphere, initiating social change rather than just responding to it" (Delanty 2003, p. 81). Adapting von Humboldt's principle of unity in research and teaching (Benner 2003), educators can bring the value of intellectual inquiry in learning, teaching and research undertaken by young migrant people to "…the service both of the disciplines and to communities outside academia" (Clegg 2008).

Undoubtedly, there is learning to be achieved and learning limits to overcome; for individuals, groups and communities, whether migrant or non-migrant, in coalitions and alliances and in endeavours to re-connect with the public sphere on issues of migration and culture; there will be ambivalence about how to achieve proposed changes and struggles to achieve solidarity; however, Mergner's work (1995, 2005a, b, c) shows that these issues can be recognized and engaged with. The social world is being transformed by migration and educators must engage fully and critically with young people's migration; within our disciplines, with our students and among ourselves and make the subjects of young people's migration and culture relevant to the communities and societies in which we are located.

References

Adams, M. (2009). Stories of fracture and claim for belonging: Young migrants' narratives of arrival in Britain. *Children's Geographies, 7*(2), 159–171.
Anderman, L. F. (2002, August). Cultural aspects of trauma. *CPA Bulletin*, 19–21.
Arendt, H. (1963). *On revolution*. Harmondsworth: Penguin Books.
Arendt, H. (6 August 1964). Personal responsibility under dictatorship. *The Listener*, 185–205.
Arendt, H. (1978). *The life of the mind*. New York: Harcourt Brace Jovanovitch.
Bastia, T. (2005). Child trafficking or teenage migration? Bolivian migrants in Argentina. *International Migration, 43*(4), 58–69.
Bauman, Z. (1999). *In search of politics*. Cambridge: Polity Press.
Bekerman, Z. (2008). Educational research need not be irrelevant. In P. Cox, T. Geisen, & R. Green (Eds.), *Qualitative research and social change: European contexts* (pp. 153–166). Basingstoke: Palgrave Macmillan.
Bekerman, Z., & Kopelwitz, E. (Eds.). (2008). *Cultural education - cultural sustainability: Minority, diaspora, indigenous and ethno-religious groups in multi-cultural societies*. New York: Routledge.
Benhabib, S. (2004). *The rights of others: Aliens, residents and citizens*. Cambridge: Cambridge University Press.
Benhabib, S., Shapiro, I., & Petranovich, D. (Eds.). (2007). *Identities, affiliations and allegiances*. New York: Cambridge University Press.
Benner, D. (2003). *Wilhelm von Humboldts Bildungstheorie*. Weinheim und München: Juventus.
Betts, A. (2009). *Forced migration and global politics*. West Sussex: Wiley Blackwell.
Bilson, A., & Cox, P. (2007). *Situational analysis of education in England: Report for save the children UK*. Preston: University of Central Lancashire.
Blok, A. (1998). The narcissism of minor differences. *European Journal of Social Theory, 1*(1), 33–56.
Brownlees, L., & Finch, N. (2010). *Levelling the playing field: A UNICEF UK Report into provision of services to unaccompanied or separated migrant children in three local authority areas in England*. London: www.unicef.org.uk.
Burck, C. (2007). *Multi-lingual living: explorations in language and subjectivity*. Basingstoke: Palgrave Macmillan.
Calhoun, C. (2008). Social science for public knowledge. In S. Eliaeson & R. Kalleberg (Eds.), *Academics as public intellectuals* (pp. 299–318). Newcastle upon Tyne: Cambridge Scholars Publishing.
Calhoun, C. (2009). Academic freedom, public knowledge and the structural transformation of the university. *Social Research: An International Quarterly of the Social Sciences, 76*(2), 561–598.
Calhoun, C., & Sennett, R. (Eds.). (2007). *Practicing culture*. Oxford: Routledge.
Carey, R., & Kim, J. (2006). *Tapping the potential of refugee youth*. New York: International Rescue Committee.
Castles, S., & Miller, M. J. (2009). *The age of migration: International population movements in the modern world* (4th ed.). Basingstoke: Palgrave Macmillan.
Clegg, S. (2008). Academic identities under threat? *British Educational Research Journal, 34*(3), 329–345.
Cohen, S. (2001). *States of denial: Knowing about atrocities and suffering*. Cambridge: Polity Press.
Collini, S. (2006). *Absent minds: Intellectuals in Britain*. Oxford: Oxford University Press.

Cooley, L., & Rutter, J. (2007). Turned away? Towards better protection for refugees fleeing violent conflict. *Public Policy Research, 14*(3), 176–180.
Cortés, R. (2007). *Remittances and children's rights: An overview of academic and policy literature.* New York: Division of Policy and Planning Working Papers UNICEF.
Cox, P. (2007). Young people, migration and metanarratives: Arguments for a critical theoretical approach. In T. Geisen & C. Riegel (Eds.), *Jugend, Partizipation und Migration: Orientierungen im Kontext von Integration und Ausgrenzung* (pp. 51–65). Wiesbaden: VS Verlag für Sozialwissenschaften.
Cox, P. (2009). 'Connectivity': Seeking conditions and connections for radical discourses and praxes in health, mental health and social work. *Social Theory and Health, 7*(2), 170–186.
Cox, P., Geisen, T., & Green, R. (2008). Introduction: The importance of qualitative research to social change - preliminary considerations. In P. Cox, T. Geisen, & R. Green (Eds.), *Qualitative research and social change: European perspectives* (pp. 1–11). Basingstoke: Palgrave Macmillan.
Crawley, H. (2010). 'No-one gives you a chance to say what you are thinking': Finding Space for Children's Agency in the UK Asylum System. *Area, 42*(2), 162–169.
de Haas, H. (2008). The myth of invasion: The inconvenient realities of African migration to Europe. *Third World Quarterly, 29*(7), 1305–1322.
de Wet, C. (Ed.). (2006). *Development-induced displacement: Problems, policies and people.* New York: Berghahn Books.
Deem, R., Hillyard, S., & Reed, M. (2008). *Knowledge, higher education and the new managerialism: The changing management of UK universities.* Oxford: Oxford University Press.
Delanty, G. (2001). *Challenging knowledge: The university in the knowledge society.* Buckingham: The Society for Research into Higher Education and Open University Press.
Delanty, G. (2003). Ideologies of the knowledge society and cultural contradictions of higher education. *Policy Futures in Education, 1*(1), 71–81.
Dobson, M. E. (2009) Unpacking children in migration research. *Children's Geographies, 7*(3), 355–360.
Eliaeson, S., & Kalleberg, R. (Eds.). (2008). *Academics as public intellectuals.* Newcastle upon Tyne: Cambridge Scholars Publishing.
Elias, N. (1978/1994). *The civilizing process: The history of manners and state formation and civilization* (trans: Jephcott, E.). Oxford: Blackwell.
Evans, M. (2004). *Killing thinking: The death of universities.* London: Continuum.
Fekete, L. (2001). The emergence of xeno-racism. *Race and Class, 43*(2), 23–40.
Fine, M., Weis, L., Weseen, S., & Wong, L. (2003). For whom? Qualitative research, representations and social responsibilities. In N. K. Denzin & Y. S. Lincoln (Eds.), *The landscape of qualitative research: Theories and issues* (pp. 167–207). Thousand Oaks: Sage.
Freire, P. (1994). *Pedagogy of hope.* New York: Continuum.
Freud, S. (1979). *On psychopathology: Inhibitions, symptoms and anxiety and other works.* Harmondsworth: Penguin Books.
Fromm, E. (1978). *To have or to be?* London: Abacus.
Geisen, T. (2004). People on the move: The inclusion of migrants in 'labor transfer systems' - The European case. In T. Geisen, A. A. Hickey, & A. Karcher (Eds.), *Migration, mobility and borders* (pp. 35–79). Frankfurt am Main: IKO Verlag.
Geisen, T. (2008). The notion of ambivalence: Human action and social change beyond analytical individualism. In P. Cox, T. Geisen, & R. Green (Eds.), *Qualitative research and social change: European contexts.* Basingstoke: Palgrave Macmillan.
Gibney, M. (2004). *The politics and ethics of asylum: Liberal democracy and the response to refugees.* Cambridge: Cambridge University Press.
Gillies, V., & Lucey, H. (Eds.). (2007). *Power, knowledge and the academy: The institutional is political.* Hampshire: Palgrave Macmillan.
Gilroy, P. (2010). *Darker than blue: On the moral economies of Black Atlantic culture.* Cambridge: Harvard University Press.

Global Commission on International Migration (GCIM). (2005). *Migration in an inter-connected world: New directions for action.* Switzerland: Global Commission on International Migration.
Goodman, S. (2007). Constructing asylum-seeking families. *Discourse Analysis Across Disciplines, 1*(1), 35–49.
Gramsci, A. (1971). *Selections from the prison notebooks.* London: Lawrence and Wishart.
Gramsci, A. (1985). *Selections from cultural writings.* Cambridge: Harvard University Press.
Green, R. (2008). Bringing about social change: The role of community research. In P. Cox, T. Geisen, & R. Green (Eds.), *Qualitative research and social change: European perspectives* (pp. 75–93). Basingstoke: Palgrave Macmillan.
Greenwood, D. J., & Levin, M. (2003). Reconstructing the relationship between universities and society through action research. In N. K. Denzin & Y. S. Lincoln (Eds.), *The landscape of qualitative research: Theories and issues* (2nd ed., pp. 131–166). Thousand Oaks: Sage.
Habermas, J. (1987). The idea of the university: Learning processes. *New German Critique, 41,* 3–22.
Hart, J. (2008). *Years of conflict: Adolescence, political violence and displacement.* Oxford: Berghahn Books.
Harttgen, K., & Klasen, S. (2009). *Well-being of migrant children and migrant youth in Europe: Discussion papers.* Georg-August Universität Göttingen: Ibero-America Institute for Economic Research.
Harzig, C., & Hoerder, D. (2009). *What is migration history?* Cambridge: Polity Press.
Higher Education Funding Council for Wales (HEFCW). (2010). *Widening access to refugees and asylum-seekers.* Cardiff Wales: Higher Education Funding Council for Wales.
Hobsbawm, E. J., & Ranger, T. (1983). *The invention of tradition.* Cambridge: Cambridge University Press.
Hooks, B. (1994). *Teaching to transgress: Education as the practice of freedom.* London: Routledge.
Hopkins, P., & Hill, M. (2008). Pre-flight experiences and migration stories: The accounts of unaccompanied asylum-seeking children. *Children's Geographies, 6*(3), 257–268.
Huysmans, J. (2005). *The politics of insecurity: Fear, migration and asylum in the EU.* London: Routledge.
Independent Asylum Commission (ICA). (2008). *Saving sanctuary: How we restore public support for sanctuary and improve the way we decide who needs sanctuary.* London: Independent Asylum Commission.
Jessop, B., Fairclough, N., & Wodak, R. (Eds.). (2008). *Education and the knowledge-based economy in Europe.* Rotterdam: Sense.
Jump, P. (2010, June). Border Agency 'unwavering' over research postgraduates. *Times Higher Education,* (10), 10–16.
Karpf, A. (1996). *The war after: Living with the holocaust.* London: William Heinemann.
Kasinitz, P., Mollenkopf, J. H., Waters, M. C., & Holdaway, J. (2008). *Inheriting the city: The children of immigrants coming of age.* New York: Russell Sage Foundation.
Konseiga, A. (2006). Household migration decisions as survival strategy: The case of Burkina Faso. *Journal of African Economics, 10,* 1–36.
Kraus, K. (2008). Policy analysis in education - multiplicity as a key orientation for research. In P. Cox, T. Geisen, & R. Green (Eds.), *Qualitative research and social change: European perspectives* (pp. 167–183). Hampshire: Palgrave Macmillan.
Kushner, T. (2006). *Remembering refugees: Then and now.* Manchester: Manchester University Press.
Kushner, T., & Knox, K. (1999). *Refugees in an age of genocide: Global, national and local perspectives.* London: Frank Cass.
Lentin, A. (2004). *Race and anti-racism in Europe.* London: Pluto Press.
Lewis, M. (2005). *Asylum: Understanding public attitudes.* London: Institute for Public Policy Research.

Loescher, G., Betts, A., & Milner, J. (2008). *United Nations High Commissioner for Refugees (UNHCR): The politics and practice of refugee protection into the 21st century*. Oxford: Routledge.

Lorenz, C. (2006). Higher education policies in the European Union, the 'knowledge economy' and neo-liberalism. *Social Europe*, 2006 (Autumn), 78–86.

Lucassen, L. (2005). *The immigrant threat: The integration of old and new migrants in Western Europe since 1850 (studies of world migrations)*. Champaign: University of Illinois Press.

Mann, S. (2008). *Study, power and the university: The institution and its effects on learning*. Buckingham: The Society for Research into Higher Education and Open University Press.

Marx, K., & Engels, F. (1998). *The German ideology: Including theses on Feuerbach and an introduction to the critique of political economy* [First Published 1881]. New York: Prometheus Books.

Mayer, H. (1975). *Aussenseiter*. Frankfurt am Main: Suhrkamp.

Mc Guigan, J. (2009). *Cultural analysis*. London: Sage.

McIlrath, L., & MacLabhrainn, I. (Eds.). (2007). *Higher education and civic engagement: International perspectives*. Hampshire: Ashgate.

Mergner, G. (1995). Zur Aktualität des Erziehungswissenschaftlers Ernest Jouhy. In G. Mergner & U. von Pape (Eds.), *Pädagogik zwischen den Kulturen: Ernest Jouhy. Zur Aktualität des Erziehungswissenschaftlers (Jahrbuch: Pädagogik: Dritte Welt)* (pp. 135–160). Frankfurt am Main: IKO-Verlag.

Mergner, G. (2005a). The theory of social limits to learning: On social history as a method. In M. dervan Linden (Ed.), *Gottfried Mergner: Social limits to learning: Essays on the archeology of domination, resistance, and experience* (pp. 20–31). New York: Berghahn Books.

Mergner, G. (2005b). Solidarity in a world of growing interconnectivity. In M. dervan Linden (Ed.), *Gottfried Mergner: Social limits to learning: Essays on the archeology of domination, resistance, and experience* (pp. 131–138). New York: Berghahn Books.

Mergner, G. (2005c). Compulsive and coerced identities: Once more on the theory of social limits to learning. In M. dervan Linden (Ed.), *Gottfried Mergner: Social limits to learning: Essays on the archeology of domination, resistance, and experience* (pp. 139–154). New York: Berghahn Books.

Mergner, G., & Pippert, R. (n.d.) Erziehungsstrategien und Lernperspektiven: Einführung in die Sozialgesichte der Erziehungen. (Unpublished, undated).

Mohanty, C. T. (2003). *Feminisms without borders: Decolonizing theory; practicing solidarity*. Durham: Duke University Press.

Nagel, T. (1986). *The view from nowhere*. New York: Oxford University Press.

Newman, M. (2008). Tribunal experts fear attacks on integrity. http://www.timeshighereducation.co.uk/story.asp?storycode=404239.

Nguyen, T. (2005). *We are all suspects now: Untold stories from immigrant communities after 9/11*. Boston: Beacon Press.

Nixon, J. (2008). *Towards the virtuous university: The moral bases of academic practice*. London: Routledge.

Palmary, I. (2007). Gender, race and culture: Unpacking discourses of tradition and culture in UNHCR Refugee Policy. *Annual Review of Critical Psychology, 6*, 125–133.

Pitts, M., & Smith, A. (Eds.). (2007). *Researching the margins: Strategies for ethical and rigorous research with marginalised communities*. Basingstoke: Palgrave Macmillan.

Portes, A. (2006, June). Institutions and development: A conceptual re-analysis. *Population and Development Review, 32*, 233–262.

Portes, A., & DeWind, J. (Eds.). (2008). *Rethinking migration: New theoretical and empirical perspectives*. New York: Berghahn Books.

Portes, A., Fernández-Kelly, P., & Haller, W. (2005). Segmented assimilation on the ground: The new second generation in early adulthood. *Ethnic and Racial Studies, 28*(6), 1000–1040.

Roudi-Fahimi, F., & Kent, M. M. (2007). Challenges and opportunities: The population of the Middle East and North Africa. *Population Bulletin, 62*(2), 3–19.

Rydgren, J. (2003). Mesolevel causes of racism and xenophobia. *European Journal of Social Theory, 6*(1), 45–68.

Save the Children UK. (2001). *Breaking through the clouds: A participatory action research (PAR) project with migrant children and youth along the borders of China, Myanmar and Thailand.* London: Save the Children UK.

Schimank, U. (2005). New public management and the academic profession: Reflections on the German situation. *Minerva, 43,* 361–376.

Suárez-Orozco, C. (2000). Identities under siege: Immigration stress and social mirroring among the children of immigrants. In A. C. G. M. Robben & M. M. Suárez-Orozco (Eds.), *Cultures under siege: Collective violence and trauma* (pp. 194–226). Cambridge: Cambridge University Press.

Tunstall, K. E. (Ed.). (2006). *Displacement, asylum, migration (Oxford Amnesty Lectures).* Oxford: Oxford University Press.

Unterhalter, E., & Carpentier, V. (2010). *Global inequalities and higher education: Whose interests are we serving?* Basingstoke: Palgrave Macmillan.

Van Der Linden, M. (Ed.). (2005). *Gottfried Mergner: Social limits to learning: Essays on the archeology of domination, resistance, and experience.* New York: Berghahn Books.

Warwick, I., Neville, R., & Smith, K. (2006). My life in Huddersfield: Supporting young asylum-seekers and refugees to record their experiences of living in Huddersfield. In P. Cox & S. Jackson (Eds.), *Themed issue of social work education:Promoting Children's Well-Being, 25*(2), 129–137.

Westwood, S., & Phizacklea, A. (2000). *Transnationalism and the politics of belonging.* London: Routledge.

Williams, J., & Guémar, L. (Eds.). (2008). *Fragments from the dark: Women writing home and self in Wales.* Swansea: Hafan Books.

Wittgenstein, L. (1966). *Lectures and conversations on aesthetics, psychology and religious belief.* Oxford: Basil Blackwell.

Wodak, R., & Van Dijk, T. (2000). *Racism at the top: Parliamentary discourses on ethnic issues in six European states.* Klagenfurt: Drava.

Wright, S. (1998). The politicisation of 'culture'. *Anthropology Today, 14*(1), 7–15.

Zack-Williams, T. B. (2006). Child soldiers in Sierra Leone and the problems of demobilisation, rehabilitation and reintegration into society: Some lessons for social workers in war-torn societies. In P. Cox & S. Jackson (Eds.), *Themed issue of social work education. Promoting Children's Well-Being, 25*(2), 119–128.

Chapter 5
The Concept of Ethnicity and its Relevance for Biographical Learning

Ursula Apitzsch

Introduction

Today, the social sciences consider it to be self-evident that ethnicity is *not* something natural, to such an extent that the idea that was common in the nineteenth and twentieth centuries, according to which ethnic groups are the natural units that later on may become states, has been completely reversed. We are now convinced that: "States produce nations and ethnic groups, and the way this happens is that the process by which states are formed is described as the work of (imagined) national communities" (Kneer 1997, p. 95). Everyone working in the social sciences today knows Benedict Anderson's famous definition of nations as "imagined communities" (see Anderson 1991, p. 14f.) and Eric Hobsbawm's statement about "'Traditions' which appear or claim to be old" but are in fact "quite often recent in origin and sometimes invented."[1]

Why is imagined shared ethnicity evidently such an important factor accompanying the coming into being of states and the integration of different groups within states? Contemporary social scientists are almost completely in agreement in the answers they give to this question. The core of these answers amounts to the argument that ethnicity is an important instrument in the struggle for scarce resources within a defined territorial and social space. It is one of a range of kinds of capital which provide an entitlement to enter social spaces (Bourdieu 1991, p. 32).

There is one problem, though, that all approaches to the question of ethnicity which look at it from the perspective of resource theory fail to address—whether these approaches be inspired by structuralism, structural functionalism, or systems theory. Ethnic movements create social dynamics that are *not* rational and not re-

---
[1] Hobsbawm 1996/1998, p. 1.

U. Apitzsch (✉)
FB 03 Gesellschaftswissenschaften, J.W. Goethe-Universität Frankfurt, Robert-Mayer-Straße 5, 60054 Frankfurt am Main, Germany
e-mail: apitzsch@soz.uni-frankfurt.de

stricted to the achievement of economic goals.[2] This observation identifies the crucial gap in the way resource theories treat ethnicity. These theories either ignore or underestimate the collective and gender dynamics involved in the coming into being of ethnicity.

This argument is not in any way intended to deny that ethnicity is a construct, or to represent it as a kind of force of nature. Nonetheless, even something that can be comprehended in social-constructivist terms can also lead to a catastrophic explosion, as if it were a natural event. To put this another way: even if we can analyze something as a social construct, that phenomenon can have the socially disastrous effects of a seemingly "natural" collective trajectory.

What I want to do here is to develop a way of looking at this issue that goes beyond the mere deconstruction of ethnicity. This is not just a matter of showing *that* ethnicity is constructed; it is also an attempt to show *how* the mysterious dynamics of ethnicity work and to identify, in particular, their consequences for the possibility of societal participation and the alternative of exclusion, which can go as far as physical destruction. The modern way of looking at ethnicity, deconstructing it from the perspective of how it is instrumentalized, is not altogether immune to the temptation to treat the scholar as the one who is able to grasp the functional social connections related to meaning and casualty, while implying that the acting subjects naturalize themselves in their ethnic justifications in order to gain societal benefits.[3] For education and learning this is of high relevance, since ethnicity can be seen and understood as a hindrance as well as a gain in the biographical processes of socialization.

---

[2] Max Weber put it differently in *Economy and Society*: "This artificial origin of the belief in common ethnicity follows the previously described pattern... of rational association turning into personal relationship. If rationally regulated action is not widespread, almost any association, even the most rational one, creates an overarching communal consciousness; this takes the form of a brotherhood on the basis of the belief in common ethnicity. At late as the Greek city state, even the most arbitrary division of the polis became for the member an association with at least a common cult and often a common fictitious ancestor." (Weber 1978, p. 389). We will come back to Weber's concept later on.

[3] After writing this essay in December 2007 for the introductory keynote paper of the ISA conference "Ethnicity and Biography" in Göttingen, I found a similar approach in Brubaker's book on *Ethnicity without groups* (2004). Brubaker criticizes "groupism" as the scientific reification of groups while thinking of them as existing entities, and simultaneously criticizes "social constructivism" as the pure intellectual habitus of showing that something has been constructed. Brubaker defines ethnicity as effectively working schemes, as "practical categories, situated actions, cultural idioms, cognitive schemas, discursive frames, organizational routines, institutional forms, political projects, and contingent events" (Brubaker 2004, p. 11). In this way, while paradoxically speaking of ethnicity without groups, in fact he focuses—following the relational definition of groups by Barth (1969)—on the ongoing negotiation of boundaries between groups which are conceived of as fluid formations and not as fixed cultural identities.

On the History of the Concept

Although "ethnicity" is derived from the Greek word *ethnos*, today it by no means signifies a people's consciousness that they form a collective. In his *Politics*, Aristotle distinguished between the *ethnos*, the native citizens of Athens, and the *demos*, the rest of the population. In the contemporary world, the meanings of these terms in everyday usage have been reversed: "ethnics" are always the others, and the autochthonous population does not think of itself as an ethnic group. As Lepsius (1988) emphasizes, "ethnos" has come to mean a traditional community, while modern, posttraditional society sees itself as a "demos," people acting collectively by democratic rules.

Max Weber was both the first scholar to grasp the modern, social-constructivist sense in which we speak of "ethnic groups" and the most sophisticated analyst of this question. In *Economy and Society*, originally published in 1922 but written before the First World War, Weber defined the characteristic self-consciousness of ethnic groups as their "group affinity, regardless of whether it has any objective foundation." He speaks here of the "*artificial* origin of the belief in common ethnicity" and defines it as follows "We shall call 'ethnic groups' those human groups that entertain a *subjective belief* in their common descent because of similarities of physical type or of customs or both, or because of memories of colonization and migration; this belief must be important for the propagation of group formation; conversely, it does not matter whether or not an objective blood relationship exists."[4] Weber argues that if ethnicity is asserted to be an original quality, God-given or provided by nature, it can be a useful way of pursuing interests in struggles over scarce resources.

Weber sees a fluid transition from ethnic to racist group definitions here:[5]

> The sense of ethnic honor is a specific honor of the masses *(Massenehre)*, for it is accessible to anybody who belongs to the subjectively believed community of descent. The 'poor white trash' i.e. the propertyless and, in the absence of job opportunities, very often destitute white inhabitants of the southern states of the United States of America in the period of slavery, were the actual bearers of racial antipathy, which was quite foreign to the planters. This was so because the social honor of the 'poor whites' was dependent upon the social déclassement of the Negroes.[6]

---

[4] Weber 1978, p. 389.

[5] There is an endless discussion in sociology about the appropriateness and the relation of the terms "race" and "ethnicity" to each other. Smelser et al. (2001) say : "Because race and ethnicity contain such a complex array of sustaining mechanisms and overlapping connotations, consistent definitions are hard to come by. Even the great sociology master, Max Weber, was frustrated in his efforts to deal with them." (ibid., p. 3) In my view, Weber takes ethnicity as the broader concept, because it means not only ascription (which in the case of the déclassement of black people by the 'poor white trash' Weber would call "racial"), but also self-positioning. My own use of "ethnicity" is still broader than Weber's, because (according to the concept of Stuart Hall) I also include meanings of ethnicity as different (imposed) positionings and their reflection by biographical work. For the history of discussion on the concepts of "race" and "ethnicity" see Bös 2005.

[6] Weber, ibid., p. 391.

Understood in this way, ethnicity is a complex social concept which sees that the ascription of certain qualities to oneself or others is a matter of construction, but at the same time suggests that the groups which do this instrumentalize these ascriptions by claiming that they are natural groups. In the tradition of Robert Park and the Chicago School, however, ethnic groups are not only seen as marginalized but also as culturally and politically productive groups. When Weber traveled through the USA in 1904, he was able to observe for the first time the political formation of the black population and the work of the black civil rights activists Booker T. Washington and William E.B. Du Bois, and became interested in this form of legitimate ethnic positioning. These encounters led Weber to the conviction that the explicit prohibition of marriage between blacks and whites in the southern states of the USA was a direct consequence of the emancipation of the slaves and struggles for civil rights. The notorious "one drop rule" stated that a single drop of black blood in a white person's ancestry, whatever their origins, meant they were automatically discriminated against and excluded from participation in civil affairs. In this way, white groups monopolized social power and honor by the racial construction of themselves and the others.[7]

Today new pan-ethnic categories such as "African-American," "Asian-American," etc. in the United States are also being interpreted as a result of the failure of social integration and the discrimination that follows from this. These pan-ethnic categories are seen as motivated by "the political requirements of competition for equal rights and material resources" (Neckel 1995, pp. 217–228, A7). "The demand that is now being put forward is no longer social integration regardless of all ethnic differences, but rather an officially guaranteed share of rights and resources that depends on the size and situation of the ethnic group" (Neckel 1995, p. 230).

We can see at this point that ethnicity can be conceived of in very different ways if it is connected to the concept of societal participation. On the one hand, when we think about Weber's example of the "ethnic honor" of the "poor white trash" in the southern states of the United States after the Civil War, it coincides exactly with what Talcott Parsons later called "ascription" and contrasted with "achievement."[8] In case of the devaluation of the other by ascription of certain "natural" qualities it means involuntary membership as distinct from the possibility of subjective positioning in society. Astonishingly, though, the very societal groups that have been the objects of ethnicizing identifications like the black civil movements in the United States consciously appropriated the term in a positive way, in order to pay tribute to the historical achievement of their group. Should they have rejected the ambigu-

---

[7] "Apart from the laws against biracial marriages in the Southern states, sexual relations between the two races are now abhorred by both sides, but this development began only with the Emancipation and resulted from the Negroes' demand for equal civil rights. Hence this abhorrence on the part of the Whites is socially determined by the … tendency toward the monopolization of social power and honor, a tendency which in this case happens to be linked to race." (Weber; ibid., p. 386).

[8] Parsons 1951, p. 172ff.

ous concept of ethnicity in favor of the "pure" concept of participation by equal citizenship?

As historical experience shows, all known concepts of citizenship construct belonging to a polity in such a way that it excludes certain groups of people in advance from certain possible achievements based on their civic performance.

I would like at this point to introduce a historical digression in order to demonstrate how historical enlightenment and objectionable ethnic ascription can occur simultaneously. My example is taken from Kant's lectures on the philosophy of nature and "On National Characteristics," from a period long before the concept of ethnicity was used. (I would like to thank Thomas McCarthy for bringing Kant's use of this argument to my attention.[9])

Participation Through Contract, Exclusion Through Belonging: The Example of Kant

In Kant's *Metaphysics of Morals* there is a sentence about the construct "the people" which anticipates Weber's later formulation about ethnic beliefs and their shared descent. At the beginning of §53, Kant says:

> "As natives of a country, those who constitute a nation (*Volk*) can be represented analogously to descendents of the same ancestors *even though they are not*."[10]

This very interesting quotation from a work published in 1797 clearly breathes the republican spirit of the French Revolution, which defines the people in terms of the belonging of persons within a territory under the rule of law, regardless of any natural differences that may exist between them. Participation is defined here as the fruit of the social contract, which the members of the republic have drawn up with one another and on the basis of which they place themselves under the authority of the state. As signatories to the contract, all persons are equal. No-one is more honored than others for reasons of birth or origin. The citizens, who are in the process of emancipating themselves from feudal society, invent an apparently rational construction derived from the ideas of contract and mutual recognition. At the same time, Kant understands that the citizens themselves transform the rational idea of participation on the basis of a contract into that of natural (family-like) belonging within a nation. Kant is aware that the idea of "natural" belonging is a construct, but he does not deny that it is an effective one.

However, in addition to the deconstructed collective idea of the nation, the Enlightenment thinker Kant allows a second idea to creep in—this time, a principle of individual "ethnic" ascription takes its place alongside the idea of the natural equality of all members of the polity. In his lectures on the "Observations on the Feeling of the Beautiful and Sublime" and "On National Characteristics," Kant explains the

---

[9] See also: McCarthy 2002, pp. 235–274.
[10] Kant 1966, p. 114. (My emphasis, U.A.)

reasons for the inferiority of certain groups of people who are unable to participate in the achievements of a polity. In a discussion of the suitability of Negro slaves as free workers, a much-debated issue at this time, Kant expresses his agreement with the argument that Indians and Negroes obviously had not inherited and would not transmit to their offspring the capacity to work hard and to become industrious persons, and that this inner natural disposition corresponded with the outer visible one:

> The Negroes of Africa have by nature no feeling that rises above the trifling. Mr. Hume challenges anyone to cite a single example in which a Negro has shown talents, and asserts that among the hundreds of thousands of blacks who are transported elsewhere from their countries, although many of them have even been set free, still not a single one was ever found who presented anything great in art or science or any other praise-worthy quality, even though among the whites some continually rise aloft from the lowest rabble, and through superior gifts earn respect in the world. So fundamental is the difference between these two races of man, *and it appears to be as great in regard to mental capacities as in color*.[11]

There are three aspects which seem to me of great significance in this text regarding the discourse about ethnicity (although the term itself would only come into use more than a hundred years later). Firstly, the fact that a supposed externally visible difference is assumed to be connected with an "internal disposition." Secondly, the fact that this projected "internal disposition" is conceived of as individually ascribed collective ethnicity.[12] Thirdly, this ascribed individual ethnicity is decisive for the question whether the moral agency of a person does or does not make this person a possible member of the collective contract that constitutes participation within a nation.

When I speak of the invention of individual ethnicity, I am using the term "individual ethnicity" to mean the identification of a person on the basis of external characteristics, and imagined "inner" qualities associated with these that are at-

---

[11] Kant, in Eze 1998, p. 55 (my emphasis). Eze selects this passage for his reader on *Race and the Enlightenment* from Kant's early publication "Observations on the Feeling of the Beautiful and Sublime" ("Beobachtungen über das Gefühl des Schönen und Erhabenen"), from 1764 (Werkausgabe Bd.II, 880). It seems that in this passage Kant connected the visible difference of black people with his imagination of their individual lack of moral agency. This connection, however, is not restricted to Kant's early writings. It can also be found in his lectures on the Philosophy of Nature, the lectures "Of the Different Races of Human Beings" (1775) and the "Anthropology from a Pragmatic Point of View" (1798). In "Über den Gebrauch teleologischer Prinzipien in der Philosophie" from 1786, Kant speaks of his vision of gypsies and their failure over generations to become industrious. He states that this "inner disposition" has to be seen as directly connected with their outer appearance: "*daß diese innere Anlage eben so wenig erlösche, als die äußerlich sichtbare.*" (Kant Werkausg. Bd.IX, S.157f.) For the debate on Kant's concept of reason and race, see Eze 2008. I am also referring to McCarthy (2004): He writes : "One thing that should be noted straightway regarding Kant's theorizing of 'race' is that he was not only at the forefront in Germany of the emerging discipline of anthropology, he was also fully abreast of, and in some crucial respect ahead of, contemporary discussions of the natural history of the human species. Thus his ongoing interchanges with Johann Friedrich Blumenbach, who is often deemed to have invented the modern, biologically based notion of race, were by no means unidirectional." (ibid., p 282).

[12] For "a critical account of Kant's unfortunate views on race", McCarthy refers to Eze 1997, pp. 103–140; McCarthy 2002, pp. 235–274.

tributed to that person. These characteristics and qualities are believed to connect the individual with an unspecified number of other people who are unknown to that individual, on the grounds that their imagined origins are the same. I am using the concept "individual ethnicity" in accordance with Paul Mecheril's distinction between "individual" and "subjective belonging," which I would like to recall briefly here.[13] The hallmark of individual ethnicity is that in each case it can only be seen by an external observer, not by the person identified. Individual ethnicity is essentially unhistorical, and therefore differs fundamentally from the political construct of participation. What I have attempted to show in my remarks on Kant is that it is quite possible for a deconstructive analysis of historical concepts such as "the nation" to go hand in hand with an obviously unthinking—if not racist—use of ascriptive categories, and that the scholar's attitude can even encourage thoughtless ascription insofar as internal causalities are more generally attributed on the basis of apparently objectively observed external differences, while the subjects observed are not involved in these attributions of causality.

This is generally also true for the concept of gender according to the modern understanding of the societal contract.

Ethnicity and Gender

In the modern nation state, the concept of ethnicity has a strong relationship with the category of gender. In traditional societies, the ethnic honor of men was usually connected with the patriarchal definition of proper behavior of women, particularly in relation to biological reproduction. In modern contract-based societies, the position of members of society is no longer defined by honor but by rights and duties. Carol Pateman, however, fears that the contract model of "fraternalism," or the nation as fraternity, which is replacing paternalism, does not in principle recognize that women have any public rights and duties. Rather, it banishes them from the public space of brothers and pushes them into the private space where paternalist power has survived (Pateman 1988, p. 4). This idea seems plausible to the extent that it is able to explain the constant private violence of men against women. Nira Yuval-Davis assumes that in classical contract theories, women are considered to be, so to speak, closer to nature, whatever this "nature" may be in terms of ethnicity.

In mixed marriages, patriarchal patrilinear law can be overridden by a stronger consideration, the creation of "natural" belonging and ethnic "honor" or "dishonor." In one section of her 1997 book *Gender and Nation*, Yuval-Davis relates an example from Britain:

> A man from Ghana tried in the 1970s to claim his British origin, stating the partiality clause in the British Immigration Act, and arguing that his African grandmother was legally mar-

---

[13] "Individual belonging means the belonging or non-belonging of an individual person seen from the perspective of an external observer; subjective belonging means the reality of belonging as experienced by individuals" (Mecheril 2003, p. 123, A.).

ried to his British grandfather. The judge rejected his claim, arguing that at that period no British man would have genuinely married an African woman. (Yuval-Davis 1997, p. 27)

It is noticeable that in this case there is a domination of patriarchal juridical concepts by racist arguments about belonging, and there is a further insinuation to the effect that a certain female person is entirely without honor. The legal position of patrilinear descent is not abandoned altogether, but in an individual case the attributed ethnicity is assigned a higher value as an indicator of belonging than legally grounded participation.

This observation is of some importance for the assessment of the mysterious way in which ethnic belonging functions as a construct. We recognize that ethnic belonging is a construct that can be handled in different ways in individual cases, but this does not make ethnic attribution any less socially dangerous—on the contrary, it makes it more dangerous and unpredictable. The example of the genocide in Rwanda illustrates this. Many Tutsi women who were married to Hutu men fled during the massacres to neighboring states, especially South Africa. There they told of their terrible experiences and fears. Their children should have been protected against persecution by the Hutus because Hutus observe the rule that family belonging is passed down via patrilinearity, but they were not able to trust this form of belonging as protection against genocide.[14] The reasons given as ways of defining ethnicity can change, and one must constantly check to see if they are connected with ensuring control over the resources of a group. It is important to note that such definitions of belonging can by no means be considered as self-evident and more original and fundamental than the construction of belonging by societal contract or personal choice. Rather, they are themselves constantly in need of reexamination. Groups defined as minorities by the dominant society and described as ethnic groups, or which have described themselves as such, have thus begun to reflect upon the history of ethnic ascriptions and to make themselves part of their particular national history by narrating their own victimization.

Ethnicity as Biographical Positioning

In view of the obvious dangers implicit in the ascription of individual ethnicity,[15] it is reasonable to ask anew why scholars like Stuart Hall, for example, have argued that the concept of ethnicity should be consciously appropriated in a positive way in order to pay tribute to the historical positioning and achievement of marginalized groups. The category is appropriate, Hall argues, precisely because the black subject and the black experience are not defined by nature. The concept of ethnicity

---

[14] Ingrid Palmary, a psychologist who coordinates the Gender, Violence and Displacement Initiative at the University of Witwatersrand, has reported on the topics that dominate the biographical narratives of the women affected. (Palmary, *Das Argument* 266, H.3/2006, pp. 402–410.)

[15] See also the examples given by Rosenthal (2004) from the former Yugoslavia.

5 The Concept of Ethnicity and its Relevance for Biographical Learning 61

can be used to construct that subject historically, culturally, and politically, and this can be done by the subject itself (Hall 1994, p. 21f.).

This way of looking at the issue is legitimate and productive as long as there are politically positioned groups and individuals who succeed in reversing ethnicizing processes of identification and stratification, giving them their own meaning, and so reinterpreting them biographically. This requires spaces for such groups' own experiences, the appropriation and reshaping of a wide range of traditions, and media and intellectual discourses that are at the disposal of these groups. In changing constellations, people recognize themselves as belonging to different collective identities, for example, through the mimetic rediscovery of shared resources and codes, but this does not make them into members of a collective subject. Bernhard Peters is surely right when he says that collective identities are a particular sort of social phenomenon, but they are not attributes of individuals (Peters 2003, p. 15).

The best proof of this is to be found in analyses of multiple ethnocultural belongings. In Germany, there are a large number of children of immigrants in the second or third generation who not only speak two standard languages perfectly but also speak one or more dialects to the same standard, i.e., as native languages. Without doubt, they belong to a cultural structure formed in a specific regional context, and can participate in this structure just as they participate in one or more national cultures. As social scientists and biography researchers, we have all experienced the intellectual pleasure to be derived from observing and admiring these forms of linguistic habitus and skilful switching between codes, but there is no way that in doing this we can identify a person unambiguously with one particular ethnic belonging. The factor that unifies these diverse affiliations is the biographical work of each individual, not an all-embracing ethnicity.

I would like to give another example of biographical work in the context of migration processes which not only produces ethnic memory without groups,[16] but may also produce a critical distance from existing groups while reflecting on ethnic memory.[17]

In her essay on "Bread, Book and Monument: Ethnic Memory and Beyond," Aleksandra Alund (1997) tells us about the 20-year-old student Hanna. Hanna's parents came from Turkey to Sweden as "Turkish" migrant workers when she was a very young girl. At that time, the only difference Hanna recognized between her own family and other Turkish families was the fact that her parents and other relatives spoke a different "dialect" at home. At the time of the interview, Hanna was studying international politics and the rights of minority peoples at a Swedish university. Only as a student had she discovered that her family were Assyrians, whose

---

[16] I refer to the title of Rogers Brubaker's book *Ethnicity without groups* (2007). I agree with his main hypothesis, that it is not so important to show *that* ethnicity is a construct but more important to show how this construction works and has been worked out in individual life and collective affiliations, and moreover that an individual may have very different ethnic belongings throughout a diachronic biographical follow-up of positioning. [?? Meaning of "follow-up of positioning" unclear, but perhaps a specialist reader would understand this]

[17] For this argument see also Apitzsch 1999a, 1999b, 2003.

ancestors are said to have lived in the region of the present south of Turkey for 2000 years with their own Christian church and their own Assyrian language. This language has been conserved by the study of the holy texts and everyday communication in Turkey as well as in the Diaspora. Hanna wants to feel "at home" in Swedish society, and therefore she has to do biographical work which concerns her family's tradition. It is the Swedish receiving society that made it possible for Hanna to learn the Assyrian language and to find out more about her Assyrian Christian religion. At the same time she recognizes the decline of tradition in her own community, and she sharply criticizes this:

> The decline of tradition means that good customs are getting weaker and bad ones stronger. Marrying the young people off seems more important than what one has taught them. They hold on hard, in the wrong way, and they haven't really understood that they're in Sweden. ...They keep their children away from Swedish friends. Their world is authoritarian and hierarchical. Children and parents can't talk with each other in a reciprocal fashion. Everything is decided from above and down. ... I don't mean that they should forget about food or about weddings. But you don't do your daughter a favor by marrying her off too early. ... Those who've married early and had kids are considered Assyrian—wholly and completely. Just because they've done that. In fact, however, they disappear. ...I want my younger siblings to grow up without feeling divided or being forced into paralyzing choices. That's why I'm needed at home. They must become both Assyrians and Swedes. If they don't learn Assyrian, they won't learn Swedish either. (Alund 1997, p. 150)

Why is she fighting so hard against what she calls the "decline of tradition"? Hanna explains her concept of an "ingrained tradition," which makes it possible for her to feel a full member of Swedish society. On the other hand, Hanna explains that Assyrian tradition outside Swedish society would never have had the same importance for her that it has today.

> In Turkey I wouldn't feel such responsibility and concern. Here in Sweden there are many opportunities, and I demand my right to become myself, with all that that means. In Turkey, others would take the responsibility, not me. (Alund 1997, p. 148)

Here Hanna makes it clear that the new importance of ethnic memory has to do with her own role in Sweden, with the "many possibilities" offered by this country. Her tradition has become something like a resource to help her find her place within Swedish society.

> Without Sweden I would never had been educated, or been able to know so much or to find myself. In Turkey I wouldn't have cared about Assyrian things. There I would have lived like everyone else. But here I have become myself. (Alund 1997, p. 148)

I think that what is being described here as the biographical positioning of a young Assyrian woman also applies to many female students in Germany with a Turkish migration background, though they have different resources for the biographical reconstruction of ethnic traditions. In German universities we often meet female Muslim students wearing impressive big scarves, the *türban*, which cover not only their hair but also part of their foreheads (Karakasoglu 2003). Most of these young women are daughters of Turkish immigrants from secular families who came to Germany 20 or 30 years ago. Their scarf is not their grandmothers' rural headgear but a symbol of belonging in the modern receiving society. In their new dress, these young women feel themselves respected by their own community as well as by the receiving society which—despite acts of discrimination—often regards them as experts in the culture attributed to them. They discover that they are coming to be recognized as "bargaining partners" between their own group and the receiving society. They finally feel that they have found their "style of life." They are creating their own traditional female style, while choosing consciously and individually which Imam and which religious school they want to follow. "Great tradition" for them has become a sort of "bricolage." Sigrid Nökel, in her study of the daughters of guest workers and Islam, gives empirical examples of this new "style of life" being regarded as a form of "nobilitation" of a person (Nökel 2002).

Some Conclusions

The idea of participation on the basis of citizenship rights established by a contract (as we have known it since the Enlightenment in the thought of Locke, Hume, Rousseau, and Kant) had to struggle from the start with the problem of the actual real conditions of an unequal and unjust society. The model does not explain who is permitted to conclude the contract, who is allowed to join, how relations between the autochthonous population and those joining later are to be regulated, and so on. It is true that our contemporary concepts of citizenship draw a fundamental distinction between a *ius sanguinis*, a "blood right" to participate that is guaranteed by heredity, and a *ius soli*, derived from the Latin *solum* meaning soil, i.e., the derivation of rights to citizenship from the territorial principle, as it has been formulated since the French Revolution. Historically, though, there never existed a pure *ius soli* (Brubaker 1992). The French revolutionary armies, and after them Napoleon's armies, spent long periods outside French territory, but it goes without saying that they did not want to lose their rights as French citizens and that they also wanted to pass these rights on to their children, who might be born outside France. Countries under greater pressure from immigration constantly had to deal with the opposite problem—how to define rules for participation that would protect the established citizens. Historically, therefore, the idea of participation on the basis of a territory shared by those inhabiting it has always been combined with various other principles for the definition of belonging. The most important of these is, without doubt, the principle that those who belong are those whose parents already belonged. The idea of the nation as children of the same parents arises from people's desire to be able to pass on their own position and resources in a privileged way to the next generation. The feudal state gave its subjects the feudal right to pass these privileges on, and the bourgeois state redefined them via the institution of property and—if necessary—via the various ways of defining ethnic belonging.

In conclusion, we can say that there is no way of accepting only the "good" concept of participation through contract and achievement while avoiding the "bad" concept of belonging by ethnic fate. On the contrary: we have to state that in all historical contexts "belonging" is always already an underlying condition of participation. Instead of ignoring it or only unmasking it as invention or pure illusion, we should study it very concretely not only as ascription but also as a possible achievement, in the ways it is being reconstructed in everyday practice by biographical work as well as collective positioning. A sociologist would be able to demonstrate that the image of the first "Black President" Barack Obama is a pure construct because Obama has two white and two black grandparents. Why isn't he called white and not black? At the same time, Obama's election as president has acquired its moving historical significance because millions of people identify with him as members of a group with a common history of being regarded and treated as unequal, and of having grandparents who were not allowed to eat in a restaurant. At the same time, we know that Obama belongs to lots of different groups. He is not only black, he also belongs to an elite, to the group of the most influential American intellectuals, and he is also a member of a Christian church and has a Christian identity as distinct from a Muslim one. In a word, he belongs to groups in multiple ways, and is not only defined by black ethnicity.

However, ethnic belongings are mostly not freely chosen. They are imposed on individuals by ethnic politics, and the individuals have to live through different ethnic regimes in order to reorganize their and their families' biographies through biographical work and through coping with different group identifications throughout their lives. This means that they have to exercise different ethnic positions in face of dominating or dominated social powers, but that as individuals they are never defined by just one ethnicity. So I would argue that, instead of speaking about ethnicity without groups (as Rogers Brubaker does), we should speak about ethnic groups without ethnic individuals. But, as I have shown in this chapter, ethnic groups are important reference points for individual action and biographical positioning. Therefore, they contribute substantially to questions of education and learning, since the belonging to one or more ethnicities or ethnic groups offers for the individual not only the chance to actively participate in social networks but also multiple options for identification(s). Being part of an established collective does put the individual into strong relations with others by referring to shared norms and values, shared cultural events and social practices. There is a need for individuals to produce identification(s), not only to bestow the own life with meaning and a sense of coherence but also to develop future aspirations and expectations. By picking up a concept from the Chicago School of Sociology (Park und Miller 1969) and applying to it a new biographically founded meaning, one could say that in this sense "ethnic self-identifications" are "bridges of transition," especially for migrants and minority members, marginalized in society, for successful processes of education and learning.

References

Alund, A. (1997). Book, bread and monument: Continuity and change through ethnic memory and beyond. *Innovation, 10*(2), 145–160.

Anderson, B. (1991). *Imagined communities: Reflections on the origin and spread of nationalism* (Rev. ed.). London: Verso.
Apitzsch, U. (Ed.). (1999a). *Migration und Traditionsbildung*. Opladen: Westdeutscher Verlag.
Apitzsch, U. (1999b). Politik mit der Ethnizität. In W. Glatzer (Ed.), Ansichten der Gesellschaft: Frankfurter Beiträge aus Soziologie und Politikwissenschaft (pp. 374–386). Opladen: Leske und Budrich.
Apitzsch, U. (2003). *Religious traditionality in multicultural Europe.* In R. Sackmann, B. Peters, & T. Faist (Eds.), *Identity and integration: Migrants in Western Europe* (pp. 91–107). Aldershot: Ashgate.
Barth, F. (1969). Ethnic groups and boundaries: The social organization of culture difference. Oslo: Universitetsforlaget.
Bös, M. (2005). Rasse und Ethnizität: Zur Problemgeschichte zweier Begriffe in der amerikanischen Soziologie. Wiesbaden: VS Verlag.
Bourdieu, P. (1991). *Physischer, sozialer und angeeigneter Raum.* In M. Wetz (Ed.), *Stadt-Räume* (pp. 25–34) Frankfurt a. M.: Campus.
Brubaker, R. (1992). *Citizenship and nationhood in France and Germany*. Cambridge: Harvard University Press.
Brubaker, R. (2004). *Ethnicity without groups*. Cambridge: Harvard University Press.
Eze, E. C. (1997). *The color of reason: The idea of 'race' in Kant's anthropology.* In *Postcolonial African philosophy* (pp. 103–140). Malden: Blackwell.
Eze, E. C. (1998). *Race and the enlightenment: A reader*. Malden: Blackwell.
Eze, E. C. (2008). *On reason: Rationality in a world of cultural conflict and racism*. Durham: Duke University Press.
Hall, S. (1992). *New ethnicities.* In J. Donald & A. Rattansi (Eds.), *Race, culture and difference*. Milton Keynes: Polity Press.
Hall, S. (1994). *Neue Ethnizitäten.* In *Rassismus und kulturelle Identität: Ausgewählte Schriften 2* (pp. 15–25). Hamburg: Argument. German Translation of:
Hobsbawm, E. (1996/1998). Inventing traditions. In E. Hobsbawm & T. Ranger (Eds.), *The invention of tradition* (1st ed., p. 1). Cambridge: Cambridge University Press.
Kant, I. (1966). *The metaphysics of morals* (ed. and trans: Gregor, M.). Cambridge University Press.
Kant, I. (1968a). *Beobachtungen über das Gefühl des Schönen und Erhabenen*, Werkausgabe in 12 Bänden, ed.by W.Weischedel, Bd.II (pp. 825–884). Frankfurt am Main: Suhrkamp.
Kant, I. (1968b). *Über den Gebrauch teleologischer Prinzipien in der Philosophie*, Werkausgabe in 12 Bänden, ed.by W.Weischedel, Bd.IX (pp. 139–170). Frankfurt am Main: Suhrkamp.
Kant, I. (1998). *On National characteristics, so far as they depend upon the distinct feeling of the beautiful and sublime.* In E. C. Eze (Ed.), *Race and the enlightenment: A reader* (pp. 49–57). Malden: Blackwell.
Karakasoglu (2003). *Custom tailored Islam? Second generation female students of Turko-Muslim origin in Germany and their concept of religiousness in the light of modernity and education.* In R. Sackmann, B. Peters, & T. Faist (Eds.), *Identity and integration: Migrants in Western Europe* (pp. 107–126). Aldershot: Ashgate.
Kneer, G. (1997). *Nationalstaat, Migration und Minderheiten: Ein Beitrag zur Soziogenese von ethnischen Minoritäten.* In A. Nassehi (Ed.), *Nation, Ethnie, Minderheit: Beiträge zur Aktualität ethnischer Konflikte* (pp. 85–102). Köln: Böhlau.
Lepsius, R. M. (1988). *'Ethnos' und 'Demos': Zur Anwendung zweier Kategorien von Emerich Francis auf das nationale Selbstverständnis der Bundesrepublik und auf die Europäische Einigung.* In *Interessen, Ideen und Institutionen* (pp. 247–255). Darmstadt: Westdeutscher Verlag.
McCarthy, T. (2002). *On reconciling national diversity and' cosmopolitan unity.* In C. Cronin & P. De Greiff (Eds.), *Global justice and transnational politics* (pp. 235–274). Cambridge: MIT Press.
McCarthy, T. (2004). *On the way to a world Republic? Kant on race and development.* In L. R. Waas (Ed.), *Politik, Moral und Religion – Gegensätze und Ergänzungen* (pp. 223–244). Berlin: Duncker & Humblot.

Mecheril, P. (2003). *Prekäre Verhältnisse: Über natio-ethno-kulturelle (Mehrfach-) Zugehörigkeit*. Münster et al.: Waxmann.
Neckel, S. (1995). *Politische Ethnizität: Das Beispiel der Vereinigten Staaten*. In B. Nedelmann (Ed.), *Politische Institutionen im Wandel* (pp. 217–236). Opladen: Westdeutscher Verlag.
Nökel, S. (2002). Die *Töchter der Gastarbeiter und der Islam*. Bielefeld: Transcript.
Palmary, I. (2005). *Family resistances: Women, war and the family in the African Great Lakes*. In *Annual Review of Critical Psychology, 4*, 54–65.
Palmary, I. (2006). *In der Konstruktion von „Rasse' steckt Gewalt gegen Frauen*. In: *Migrantinnen, Grenzen überschreitend. Das Argument 266, H.3/2006*, 402–410.
Park, R. E. und Miller, H. A. (1969, zuerst 1921). *Old-world traits transplanted*. New York: Arno Press.
Parsons, T. (1951). *The social system*. New York: Free Press.
Pateman, C. (1988). *The patriarchal welfare state*. In A. Gutmann (Ed.), *Democracy and the welfare state* (pp. 231–260). Princeton: Princeton University Press.
Peters, B. (2003). *Collective identity, cultural difference and the developmental trajectories of immigrant groups*. In R. Sackmann, B. Peters, & T. Faist (Eds.), *Identity and integration: Migrants in Western Europe* (pp. 13–36). Aldershot: Ashgate.
Rosenthal, G. (2004). "Ethnisierung der Biographie" und Traumatisierung. In M. Ottersbach und E. Yildiz (Eds.), Migration in der metropolitanen Gesellschaft: Zwischen Ethnisierung und globaler Neuorientierung (pp. 217–230). Münster: LIT.
Smelser, N. J., Wilson, W. J., & Mitchell, F. (Eds.). (2001). *America becoming: Racial trends and their consequences,* Vol. I. Washington, DC: National Research Council.
Weber, M. (1978). *Economy and society* (ed. G. Roth & C. Wittich). Berkeley: University of California Press.
Yuval-Davis, N. (1997). *Gender and nation*. London: Sage.

Chapter 6
"No Place. Nowhere" for Migrants' Subjectivity!?

Athanasios Marvakis

Critical Reflections on the Dominant Discourses About Integration[1]

> I move. From early on we are searching. All we do is crave, cry out. Do not have what we want. (*Ernst Bloch. The Principle of Hope. Oxford: Basil Blackwell, Vol. 1 (1986), pp. 21.*)
>
> What we need in terms of education, is not to learn that we are citizens of the world, but that we have distinctive/separate positions in an unequal world, and to be indifferent and global on the one side, and to support our individual interests on the other, do not constitute antitheses but theses which are combined in complex ways. Some combinations are desirable here, some no. Some are desirable here but not elsewhere, now but not then. Since we have learned this, we could start to confront successfully, from an intellectual point of view, the social reality (*Wallerstein* 1999, *p. 150*)

Much Too Much Talk About "Integration": Strong Medicine or a Strong Narcotic for Our Societies?

"Integration" is obviously a hot issue all around Europe with top priority on different agendas. Even a look in the media and/or a fast search in some of the language versions of Google combining, for example, terms like "migrants" and "integration" reveal many hundreds of thousands or even millions of entries. This very fact of media and electronic manifestation could convince us that "integration" for

---

[1] For the title I am borrowing from Christa Wolf, "Kein Ort. Nirgends" (1979, Berlin; Darmstadt). I want to thank my colleagues and friends Sofia Triliva and Kalliopi Miltsakaki for their help in making the text palatable English.

A. Marvakis (✉)
Department of Primary Education, University Campus - Building "Tower", Aristotle University of Thessalonica, 54124 Thessalonica, Greece
e-mail: marvakis@eled.auth.gr

thousands of different public agents is seemingly a suitable catch-word—if it is not taken as a political magic word, easy at hand to make societal phenomena understandable and social problems resolvable. And one could be astonished at how easily and how arbitrarily figures and allegations are literally thrown into the public space.[2] "Integration" is not only part of discourses "from above," since it seems to promise something also to all those who—from the perspective of the powerful—are "to be integrated."

Even a quick historical retrospection makes clear that "integration" is a political evergreen issue in Europe for the past several decades. Marios Nikolinakos in the beginning of the 1970s stressed the function of this concept in preserving the dominant power-relations: "All existing conceptualizations of integration (are) defensive; they articulate the attempts of a society to fight back the effects implied in the employment of guest-workers (Gastarbeiter)" (in: Gewerkschaftliche Monatshefte 1/1974, S. 22).[3]

My own engagement with discourses on "integration" is energized by a strong theoretical and political discontent, accumulated over the years, first, when I was conducting youth research in Germany in the 1990s (e.g., Held et al. 1996; Marvakis 1996). Second, the discontent continued to accumulate in a very different societal background when I moved to Greece in the mid 1990s and became involved in activism and research concerning migrants in this country.[4] During all these years it became clearer to me that "integration"—to say it diplomatically—is a much contaminated concept.[5] The facility with which it seemingly fits in every discourse (political, scientific, media, everyday) does not wipe off this contamination at all—on the contrary this augments the contamination!

As mentioned just before, grounded on the German tradition of Critical Psychology, I have been engaged for years in youth research/work and internationalist activism (Foitzik and Marvakis 1997). This particular background implies that all the theoretical and practical interventions I am participating in—conceived as "transformative/educative practices"—do not refer to some formalized social practices of education—e.g. to some more or less traditional schooling context. This is fitting with Mergner's (1999) notion of social learning processes, not as 'technicalities' in formalized schooling, but as integral part of an eventually self-organized process of political learning. In this context, "education"—as transformative interventions—refers more to what is dubbed in German as "politische Bildung" (civic learning/education). Furthermore, "Bildung"—as an ongoing social learning process—includes also practices of "self-education" (or self-transformation) by/in

---

[2] Just two actual examples from Germany: http://www.youtube.com/watch?v=sGE1-SsbKck&feature=youtube_gdata_player and http://www.youtube.com/watch?v=dGx7JcAfaJ0

[3] „Alle vorliegenden Konzepte zur Integration (sind) defensiv; sie stellen den Versuch einer Gesellschaft dar, sich gegen die aus der Gastarbeiterbeschäftigung ergebenden Wirkungen zu verteidigen."

[4] E.g., Marvakis et al. 2001; Marvakis 2004, 2005; Marvakis and Parsanoglou 2005; Marvakis et al. 2006; Dimitri et al. 2007.

[5] As are some more very popular concepts too, like for example "culture," "identity"…

activism. Practices, like for example writing, are in this context moments/kinds of critical self-reflection, which is itself part of the political self-education (or self-transformation) of the participating subjects. Guiding questions for such an "educative self-reflection" and "self-transformation" could be: How are we "talking" and "acting" politically? Which (political) aims are we claiming and which aims are we serving with our particular talking and acting? How far do our conceptual means/tools fit to our political "declarations"? How far are we subverting our own claims with our theoretical praxis and practice?

The argument here is that we are participating in (re)producing power-relations as they are, thus finally participating also in our domination, not by purpose or because of some individual "needs" to dominate or being dominated. Such a way of understanding/interpreting our own social practice or other social phenomena—by dubbing them with "psychological terminology"—make (some of) us potentially "feel good" (or feel better). However, it does not add a bit of clarification to our social practice, on the contrary it contributes to its disguise.

The (re)production of power-relations we are involved in has a lot to do with the social practices we are participating in (consciously or not, purposefully or not is a quite different issue/question). And the ways we are understanding and talking about our social world, as articulated in the discourses we are participating in are nor innocent, neither arbitrary, but very significant social practices for both: for understanding and changing our social world, but also for (re)producing power-relations dominating us. Our discursive practices are very efficient tools, for overcoming the "social learning barriers" ("soziale Lerngrenzen"—Mergner 1999), but also for keeping us confined within the existing social barriers. For this, it is very important for our social learning—as civic education/learning, politische Bildung, etc.—to reflect constantly on the particular perspectives and restrictions engulfed in and transported with the concepts we are using—as being theoretical/linguistic tools for understanding and changing our world.

This ongoing reflective practice is itself necessarily a social, a democratic and also an educative/transformative process. At the end of this chapter I will propose to catch this "self-transformative" process with the concept of "social self-understanding" (coined by Klaus Holzkamp—within the tradition of German Critical Psychology). In the context of a (political) self-education (as "politische Bildung") it is to have, to develop a "peer discourse" *with* others (peers) and less a report *about* others (e.g., as clients), offering reflections, clarifications, and hints for our common social self-understanding. The chapter aims to be useful exactly in such a context, in such a social practice and is less to be understood as some kind of reflection "about others" or some "instruction."

But let me first deploy my argument on "integration."

What constitutes my discontent? I want to try to give an answer deploying two interwoven arguments, hopefully, in this manner my discontent will become clearer and so will my approach. The first argument is about a certain and dominant "methodological functionalism"—in viewing people (here: migrating subjects) only as passive and as being driven—without subjectivity and without their own initiative in leading their life. The second argument points to a polarity in which the dominant view is capturing migrants. A polarity, which supplements the "abstraction" of migrants' subjectivity, having them allegedly only assimilating to the circumstances, being confined in choosing to whom or to whose demands they finally have to conform to.

One assertion seems to bear unchallengeable and self-understanding plausibility for a very broad political spectrum—from the Right to the Left. This self-understanding consists in the fact that the concept of "migration" is used as a code for very different assertions, all these having though in common that the actions of the migrant subjects have to be seen as mere "dependant variables" of a variety of conditions causing them—e.g., migration as caused by poverty, by persecution, etc. Thus, the concept of "migration" contributes more to obscuring the real interrelations and contradictions of our actions and far less to their exposure and clarification.

If we try to imagine why we human beings are (potentially) "migrating," then we will quickly come to an agreement that we are doing so because we have certain and concrete good reasons and not just because we are "driven" by something. And it will be even more difficult to find people migrating just to see "how migration is." My concern here is that approaching social phenomena abstracting from the subjectivity of the acting persons involved in those phenomena is not just a "theoretical" shortcoming or "mistake"—to be corrected—but much more it is a certain epistemological (thus "political") standpoint taken. And at this point it is irrelevant whether the standpoint is taken purposefully or "just" factually. Talking about migrants (and their "integration") without taking into account the various good reasons for human beings to make changes in their lives—sometimes with very high cost for their lives—is not just an example of "bad" or "good science." It is a very particular scientific perspective confining our view on migrants (and their integration) to the perception and "interests" of state bureaucracy and police. Such an epistemological (and political) standpoint constrains the "legitimate" aspects and questions in a social phenomenon like "migration" to those which are of interest only for certain social subjects in power.[6] An activist counterdiscourse to this politics in the social battlefield with the means of (a very particular) scientific approach has become known with the notion of "autonomy of migration" (e.g., Boutang 1998), aiming exactly at breaking with such a bureaucratic functionalism. "Autonomy of migration" focuses on the migrating subjects and the projects in their life, constituted and articulated in their trans-border mobility and in the social fights during this mobility.[7] This activist counter-discourse has consequently several linkages with a Critical Psychology (Marvakis 2010).

As we have already stated, "integration" constitutes a central and popular interpretative lens for looking at migrants. The main question here is not whether we are doing "right" or "wrong" working with this concept; the issue for us is that it guides

---

[6] By this it simultaneously casts away any opportunity to articulate a genuine social-scientific perspective on "migration."

[7] See: Karakayalı and Tsianos 2002; Bojadžijev 2005; Karakayalı 2006; Hess et al. (2009); Transit Migration Forschungsgruppe (2007).

our thinking and action only in a certain direction. According to this theoretical context the problems of migrants, especially those of migrant children, should be understood and explained as being reflected through the lens of a certain *lack*: it is the supposed lack which articulates itself because of the difference between their own way of "doing their life" and that of the way of the "host" population. Inherent in this "deficiency construct" is the notion that the individual migrant always encounters troubles and difficulties when she/he leaves her/his country or culture of origin and is confronted with new norms and new values. By this encounter she/he is (a) overwhelmed in coping with these new orientations, or (b) refuses to adjust, to subjugate to these new orientations. From this theoretical perspective, the starting point from which one should interpret the orientations of migrants and that of their children, as being articulated in problems and demands, is a double *polarity:* The polarity is constituted—on the one hand—of the "culture of the *homeland*" and on the other of the "*foreign* culture," i.e., the new *environment* or new *cultural milieu*, a milieu that is constituted by conflicting cultures of child-rearing, divergent societal demands, requirements and social orders, which are expected *from* and offer opportunities *to* the migrant subjects.

If we believe the mainstream literature then we have to accept as given that migrants (and particularly their children!) are living in a position that can be characterized as "in-between" (voluntarily or not), which is to be very burdening to them and encumbers them with a myriad of particular difficulties in acquiring useful or functional orientations and thus pushes them into a deficient or "lacking" position. From this perspective migrants should find themselves captured in a "conflict," that is in a position in-between divergent systems of orientations, i.e., cultures, which are moreover taken to be *homogenous* systems of social norms. The brains and hearts of the migrants are beating in the antagonistic rhythms of different social demands and presets. Especially the migrant children are forced to fight with two "inner" commitments, with two "determinations." The only remaining option for the migrant children is to choose amongst the different *external* determined demands and presets: Which social norms and demands should they adjust to or obey—those of their homeland or those of the host society?

In this theoretical context, focused on conflicting *external* demands and determinants with which the migrants are confronted, only a slight difference exist between the two main theoretical variants of this concept, that is the "ethnopluralistic" version and the version following "modernization theory": both variants differ only as to the particular "system of norms" they offer to migrants to choose, to obey and to align themselves with! Our (potential) objects-subjects under research, namely the migrants (and their children), seem to have no, or do not pursue any, independent interests, purposes, intentions; or there are no such interests recognized by the researchers and theoreticians. In the hallways of the concept of "integration" it is very difficult, if not impossible, to ascertain important differentiations concerning the good reasons of the migrants, like for example:

- Do their particular orientations serve "only" as an (un-critical) adjustment to and compliance with the specific societal demands and presets?

- Or is the subject putting up with the implied subjugation and reproduction of the societal demands on the ground of some personal strategic aims?
- Another qualitatively different foundation for someone's orientations consists in the conscious adoption of particular demands, because the subject views these orders as plausible and convincing.

And of course one could find some more good reasons!

As we can see, the concept of "integration" conceives and constructs orientation/action exclusively as adjustment, adaptation, finally as subjugation and conformism. Thus it has to offer to the migrants only adaptation to *pre*-defined and *pre*-delineated demands: whether these come from the "culture of the past" (i.e., country of origin, homeland, other "cultural burdens" to carry) or from the "culture of the present" (i.e., foreign/alien social environment, host society, current/actual problems). The concept of "integration" insinuates or even renders human beings as mere "vehicles" of cultural (or other) meanings and does not understand them as subjects. This gives us permission to question the potency of this concept and its usefulness for transcending our spontaneous and everyday consciousness. The aim of scientific thinking is not only to dress-up with scientific terminology all that, which is 'visible' or obvious to our every-day thinking, but—if we take our everyday thinking as a surface—to penetrate this surface and to approach the essence of all that is happening and experienced. On this background, we can say that the concept of "integration" not only does not penetrate the surface of what spontaneously seems as "apparent" to us (e.g., as "pushing us"), but it is putting an additional—let's say scientific—"foil" on our everyday consciousness and is thus cementing that surface by adding layers to it.

Following my argumentation so far one may agree with me in summarizing that for the concept of "integration" nothing new seems to be imaginable and possible concerning the orientations/actions of migrants beyond their "adjustment" and subjugation, and so it has nothing new to "offer" to our research objects, who are of course not "vehicles" or "media" of something, but living beings, subjects, in our case, migrants. As social scientists, trying to grasp migrants' realities with such a concept we are not "wrong" or "right" in doing so. We are just turning the deficiency of our theoretical comprehension—articulated in such concepts—into a deficiency of our subjects-objects to be researched. By this we are doing a good service—but certainly not to the objects of our scientific endeavor. As "servants of power" we are thus contributing to the social reproduction of ourselves and simultaneously are contributing to the social "pacification" of our "clients."

The Different Grammar of Integration

We are used to approach an issue starting with outlining its social semantic field. For our attempt to approach the social semantics of "integration" it is very useful to start with language differences. If we want to translate "integration" into Greek we have first to differentiate: On the one side we can translate it into "ολοκλήρωση" ("oloklirosi") stressing the facet of "completion." Or we can also translate it as "ενσωμάτωση" ("ensomatosi") highlighting the "incorporation," "embodiment." But the semantics of "integration" is multifaceted also in German, where we also have the same double-meaning.

This linguistic differentiation leads us directly to a practical and political question: who is the passive, and who is the active part in "integration"? Under which circumstances and for who exactly does "integration" mean improvement? When and for whom does it acquire assimilation? I want to try clarifying these questions using a few examples. With these, I am stressing less on "integration" as a social fact and I want to focus more on the contradictory expectations being tied to this concept. And, as we can imagine, these expectations are subject to permanent change, depending on the history and actual situation in the societies mentioned in the respective examples. These contradictory expectations are therefore implying different "grammar" of integration in play:

- *European Union*: Here "integration" implies primarily that different social groups or nation-states are voluntarily "assembling" into new social and cultural structures. The particular national identities are to be integrated into a greater whole, thus constituting a new all embracing unit(y), though without the different parts losing their idiosyncratic characters.
- In *Germany*—on the contrary—"integration" implies demands addressed to (foreign) individuals or groups to "incorporate" themselves, i.e., to adjust or assimilate to the behavioral patterns or notions of normality performed allegedly by the local majority. In concrete cases, this means that even family members of third-generation migrants have to fight for belonging to such a "local majority."
- The situation in *Ireland* (during the economic boom few years ago!) was different from Germany in so far as, based on the lack of hands and brains on the local labor-power market, "integration" was not questioned at all. The policies in Ireland were not pointing to migrants, but, on the contrary, were questioning and addressing the openness and ability of the local majority to integrate "others." And for educating this majority a significant set of courses and initiatives were financed by the government. As we can see clearly with this example, openness, tolerance and integrative capacity of the "locals" are considerable, lead to potential local advantages, and are key qualifications in the context of global capitalist competition.
- *Bolivia* is an example from those Latin-American states along the Andes where the indigenous population has not been eliminated by the European immigrants. "Integration" in this societal context is not related to figures in the same way as above, i.e. with majority and minorities in the population. Here the issue of integration is articulated in the imposed historical concrete power-relations. In these societies, integration means up to now nothing less than that the majority of the "local" population has finally to subordinate itself to the norms of the European migrant minorities.

All the examples above point out to the shortcomings of a perspective on "integration" seeing it only as an aspect of selection and/or exclusion. Such a perspective would inevitably reduce the discussion on some alleged deficits of certain groups and/or individuals to integrate themselves. But, as soon as we are looking at migration, and all the issues concerning integration, not only as a sheer social fact waiting out there for someone to "manage" it in different ways, as soon as we are positioning those issued (back) in their societal prerequisites and implications, from that moment on our concepts are starting to "dance." In this vein, if we start discussing "integration" as a social field of battles concerning the access to the societally produced wealth, from this point on we are able to see that the different policies/politics on "integration" are attempts to (re)organize exploitation, and are accompanied with certain "promises" towards different social groups. Such "integration promises" are attempts from the perspective of the powerful to achieve consensus and compromise on how exploitation is to be (re)organized; which normally means the (re)hierarchization of our opportunities in life (German: Lebenschancen). On the other side, the compromises contained in the different concepts and promises of integration are usually imposed by the various battles and resistances of migrants, but can also be founded on different calculi made by the powerful.

The above examples can show us that "integration" can be easily called for or even promoted by the capital, depending on the need for importing labor power and/or for disciplining its "local" labor power. If we switch sides and view "integration" from migrants' perspective, then we can observe that they are barely speaking about "integration" as such. Their actions are usually referring to concrete situations and problems, which migrants are trying to improve or to overcome. In the few cases they are using the concept of "integration" the provocative intention for this is more than obvious. As an illustration for this provocative manner I want to quote the German-Turkish weekly magazine "Persembe" (from February 2001):

> We are fed up with playing the victims for you. You are demanding 'integration', 'incorporation'. Nobody is asking us if we like the body in which we are to integrate ourselves. We want to change this body. (Quoted in German monthly magazine: IZ3 W 253/2001)[8]

From these observations we can conclude that the dominant discourses about integration are systematically ignoring the agency of migrants, as it is articulated in particular projects during their life or articulated in the broad range of ways they are encountering the challenges of their life—starting with singular demands and going to the all-embracing questioning of the existing social order. There is a supplementary benefit for the powerful in neglecting migrants' agency: once the field is divided, for example, into "locals" and "foreigners" the affinity of our problems and interests beyond ethnic boundaries is being obscured as are also the possibilities and necessities for common actions and demands.

---

[8] „Wir haben es satt, die Opferrolle für euch zu spielen. Ihr verlangt von uns 'Integration', ‚Eingliederung'. Niemand fragt, ob uns der Körper gefällt, in welchen wir uns integrieren sollen. Wir wollen den Körper verändern."

In summarizing the above argument we can say that the dominant variants of the discourses and promises of integration are one-sided articulations from the perspective of the powerful! In masking the real existing contradictions, "integration" cannot be discussed as a battlefield with its different actors and positions. The discourses and promises "from above" are *abstractions*, meaning desisting and looking away from the concrete demands and problems of the affected subjects. Such a one-sided concept about integration is a very practical and serviceable approach in/from the perspective of the administration or of the police. But it is in contradiction to any social-scientific perspective or to any notion of social sciences aiming at "picking up" and conceptualizing the problems and demands of affected subjects. And as long as social sciences are not relating themselves consciously to the contradictions inherent in the concept of "integration" they will continue to just serve the ruling politics of integration—independent of the personal intentions and aspirations of us individually.

The "Gastarbeiter" ("guest worker") as Example for a Fordist Integration Regime

As we have seen in the examples above, "integration" is not a single issue or fact. Depending on the historical and societal context, also the social grammar of the discourses is changing substantially. One method proposed in the context of the "autonomy of migration" approach is trying to (re)construct the particular battlefield, including the power-relations in it, where the participating actors are positioned in relation to each other and are making "their moves." In this vein and to give an example, I will try to outline in the following paragraphs very schematically the transformations of the battlefield of "integration" in Western Germany after the World War II. But in order to contextualize this outline, showing that "integration" is not a problem adhered solely to immigrants, a short historical flash-back to the nineteenth century is necessary.

The first huge "integration" in modern Western European countries was focused on the dangerous classes, the "mob," in German-speaking regions the "vaterlandslose Gesellen" (literally: buddies without homeland), meaning that the primary "subject" for the necessary "integration efforts" of that time was nobody else but the constituting proletariat. Capitalism had to deal with a self-produced and inevitable contradiction: The mobility of the workers—often initiated and/or forced by their previous expropriation—encompasses, on the one side, a substantial precondition for industrial development. Simultaneously, this mobility constitutes a potential danger for the ruling order and thus had to be regulated and controlled. As we can see, "integration" at that time was not at all a problem between "locals" and "foreigners." On the contrary, we could say that "integration" is the spot where labor and capital collide—though this is not the explicit topic of the discussion. And exactly this "being-not-the-issue" is very central for defending the dominant power-relations! From this point of view, the particular regulatory forms and characteristics expressed in different integration regimes (as mentioned in the examples above) appear as contradictory attempts to perpetuate—via making compromises—the control over a mobile and flexible labor power (e.g., migrants) and simultaneously keeping the expectations of that labor power as low as possible. If we overlook these contradictions and relations, then we are transferring the discourses about integration to a field where we are only talking (or even arguing) about the organization of exploitation, but without making exploitation an issue. And we could even say that with "integration" we are talking about exploitation without talking about exploitation.

The first phase in migration politics after World War II in Western Germany is characterized through its fordist integration regime, called also as "Gastarbeiter paradigm" (following the characterization of the immigrants as "guest-workers" in Germany). The compromise coming up in that historical battlefield as "agreement" between the different actors—trade unions, employers federations, state institutions, etc.—contained several components affecting the recruited foreigners: (a) priority of the locals concerning job allocation, (b) linking of rights to residence status, (c) incorporation in the social security system, and (d) dogma of temporary residence.

In realizing and regulating this integration regime the West German state held a central role. The recruitment of foreign labor power—along with the four components above—was a truly calculated strategy (concerning its flexibility, costs, etc.) of the political elites to deal with the lack of labor power in the West Germany during the 1950s, which worsened especially after the Berlin Wall was build. Some potential, but finally not preferred, alternatives to this chosen strategy included, for example: (a) increasing wages and competition between enterprises and industrial plants for labor power, (b) increasing the fraction of the population to work under wage labor conditions, e.g., by rising the percentage of wage-working women (but then who should take over the unpaid labor at home and the caring of the children?), and (c) improving the means of production, e.g., via replacing living labor power by improved machinery.

There is a differentiated bibliography about this "Gastarbeiter regime" from the perspective of the German majority society—in approving the regulation and control of migration and migrants or in criticizing these politics. The migrants themselves appear though in these debates mostly as objects of control, objects for care or even objects of "solidarity." Their subjectivity and autonomy is though covered by an eloquent silence.[9]

---

[9] As an exception to this silence see the reconstruction of the so-called "strike of the Turks" at a German plant of Ford Motors in August 1973 by Karakayalı (2001).

Neoliberal Transformation of Our Societies—Emerging of New Integration Regime(s)

The promise in the integration regime above (the "Gastarbeiter paradigm") addressed the migrants as a uniform group and is quite an easy one: "You can expect a regular wage and some social benefits, but you'll remain foreigners no matter how long you work and live here." On this background we have to ask about the respective promises in the post-fordist or neoliberal integration regime(s), as they are about to get shaped. Since the 1990s we can record massive changes in production in the capitalistic countries and can thus expect substantial changes also in the integration regimes along with these changes. The new emerging neoliberal "integration compromise"—oscillating between promises and (not only political) calculations—is constituted by mainly two components:

- Probably the first and most striking or obvious characteristic of this new emerging regime points to the successive individualization of different groups of immigrants, which also implies simultaneously the (re)hierarchization of these groups. A bunch of bureaucratic classificatory initiatives is segmenting the foreigners/migrants from anew and is being flanked with differentiated promises to these groups. Taking again Germany as an example we can list (incomplete), for example, the following hierarchically positioned classes of migrants:

  - "Late Repatriates" —ethnic Germans "resettled" from Eastern Europe
  - The—"inventoried"—former "Gastarbeiter," called now "Bestandsausländer"
  - Green Card holders
  - Refugees with exceptional leave to remain for humanitarian reasons
  - Migrants' family members
  - Illegalized immigrants—"without papers" called by the French expression "sans papiers"
  - Sexworkers and other immigrants working almost under slavery conditions

- The second component to emerge in the new regime is a consequence, or an extension of the first one: The promises are no longer addressed to groups, but more and more to individuals. These individuals have to perform certain characteristics and to put forth certain efforts *in advance*, quasi as entrance tickets for the "integration casino" of their particular society. For this neoliberal regime it is quite irrelevant how or from where the individuals obtained their "tickets"—as long as the regime does not have to pay for it. For this regime every diversity product of every single immigrant is welcome as a potential commodity—even the specific intercultural competences of the not perished (yet) immigrant children. "Integration" is therefore less and less a bonus, a *societal support*, a chance, a—literally—"promise" for something. It rather turns more and more to become a coercion, which although has to be gained first by the individual and by in advance provided exploitable features. By successfully attending certain "integration courses" or passing citizenship or naturalization tests an individual immigrant can attain the right to *apply* for residence. The social right for residence or existence has now to be authorized and certified in advance because of one's own "deficiency." Formulated differently we can say that immigrants are in advance suspected collectively of not being "able to integrate." And therefore each and everyone has to approve in advance their own "ability to integrate." The "dignity to enjoy hospitality" (as it is called in the respective German police act from 1938!) has been quasi translated into the "necessity to prove in advance one's individual ability to integrate." Using judicial terminology we could say that every single one should, as individual and in advance, provide evidence for their "innocence," i.e., their ability to integrate. It is not the prosecutor who has to provide evidence for ones "guilt," i.e., ones *in*ability to integrate; it is me who has to prove my *innocence*, my *ability*, in order not to be accused! This generalized suspicion—to harm (even willingly) the host society—with which migrants are faced could be interpreted as an inversion and suspension of the civil law principle of the "presumption of innocence." It is therefore legitimate for the Journalist Heribert Prantl to speak about integration as a monster (Newspaper "Süddeutsche Zeitung," April 12, 2004).

The shortcomings of the integration concept have inversed the understanding of who is responsible, ready and/or able to integrate. Demanding from the migrants just to subordinate to the dominant relations and beliefs is corresponding with common sense thinking, which in turn can be picked up easily by populist discourses and be disseminated by the powerful. As an example for this, we can quote from the policies concerning the foreigners in the German Federal State of Nordrhein-Westfalen. In its guidelines the government defines integration independently from one's origin as "attaining the ability by the individual to act autonomously in a free society."[10] The minister of the interior of the German Federal State of Schleswig-Holstein Ralf Stegner (SPD) has chosen integration to be a "duty," where any "counteracts" to this will be "punished with withdrawal of the residence permit or deprivation of social benefits" (weekly German newspaper "ak," Nr. 506, May 19, 2006, http://www.akweb.de). In our times of societal transformation, such official statements are examples not only of the way of dealing with immigrants in Europe, but are broadly applied to all socially weaker parts of the population. Each and every one of us is obliged to certify our ability to integrate!

The individualization of the integration policies tends to supersede the boundary between "locals" and "foreigners," which has been central for the previous fordist integration regime. The new development cancels the priority of the local majority over the immigrants, as self-understanding as it has been up to now. Thus, for example, the much discussed "elevator effect" in Germany (according to which parts of the local wage laborers can enjoy some social mobility because of the Gastarbeiter taking the lower positions in the social hierarchy) belongs mostly to the past. The

---

[10] „Erlangung der Fähigkeit des Einzelnen, in einer freien Gesellschaft selbstständig zu handeln," in: Lutz Hoffmann Presentation on a convention of the LAGA, 4./5. May 2002, in Herne, retrieved from http://www.laga-nrw.de/xd/public/content/index._cGlkPTg0_.html

belonging to the "locals" loses more and more its advantageous or even protective function.

We can generally observe processes which we may call provisionally as "fluidization of belonging." By this I mean the fading away of the—allegedly or not—protection enjoyed by all those who belong to a certain group or collective, who enjoyed some kind of guaranteed rights and benefits. This "fluidization of belonging" is actually a termination or cancellation of the (social) protection enacted by the powerful, which in concrete societal circumstances may include also the dominant majority of a population. For a current example for such a "fluidization" and a cancellation of social protection we can refer to the experiences of thousands of Greek Gastarbeiter in Germany since the spring of 2010. In the context of the discussions whether the other members of the Euro-Group should "help" the Greek state in getting (again) money loans,[11] wild (media and public) discourses boiled over in Germany stuffed with quick allegations about the laziness of the Greeks in Greece which then "swapped" and were easily attributed also to immigrants of Greek origin in Germany. The facility with which the protection of being a Gastarbeiter and belonging to Germany after decades of working and living there was cancelled, even by "locals" to which one had close relations, was widely and traumatically experienced by that "inhabitants of Germany with immigrant background" (as the Gastarbeiter are "officially" called). Furthermore, this example indicates that obviously there are no "social assets" any more, protecting people during a "crisis."

As we all know very well, capitalistic exploitation is very flexible concerning the used organizational forms and features. Sometimes it needs, supports, and uses racism. But not always and not necessarily everywhere! The process of reorganizing exploitation is well documented nowadays in our societies, where the populations are mixed from anew, with new social hierarchies being shaped. To provide proof of his or her own ability to become integrated individually means the provision of evidence for my own usability, which in a capitalist context means nothing else than providing evidence for my own exploitability. And this "duty" will less and less refer only to the part of the population with immigrant background.

Up to now we were talking about the multiple segmentations of the "foreigners" which were confronted with a wide range of differentiated and hierachized "promises of integration." It may sound odd, but up to now we have been talking about the (relatively) "privileged" segments of immigrants, where the subjects are forced by the new integration imperative to apply for integration by proving in advance and individually that they have enough credits to make such an application. However, the range of the new integration regime is much broader and also covers the segment of those illegalized immigrants who in fact do not "enjoy" any kind of "promise"—beyond a temporary and very precarious toleration. For the neoliberal conditions for production these illegalized subjects are the new cheap workers, agents of the flexible and mobile labor power—without any integration in the (social) system, which was an important component for the fordist regime. And,

---

[11] Which actually didn't mean anything else other than to loan (again) money to the Greek state with very high interest rate!

to talk about integration being confronted with the working and living conditions of these migrant groups demands a much more wide-ranging abstraction than we need in the discourses about the Gastarbeiter. However, the amount of abstraction from their living conditions needed here contains the danger to be cynical!

Social Self-understanding as Opposed to Integration!

Coming to the end of our discussion we can start thinking about the consequences on critical (social) science. In applying or using the concept of integration with its particular political grammar the very first danger we have to deal with is to lose our status as *political* subjects. Losing this status we would become unable to develop and articulate our own *political* discourse—through which we could make the shortcomings of the dominant views on integration visible and prospectively suspendable. From the perspective of a critical social science the question of "integration" or "nonintegration" is a pseudo-issue and trying to answer it one is getting involved inevitably in the dominant logic. Participating in this discourse, as it is being performed, we are aligned just to manage the (alleged or real) problems assigned by the powerful and to govern the subjects who are—according to the powerful—making problems. Consequently, we are becoming just technocrats in the power apparatus.

The argument I have tried to deploy up to now is quite straightforward: "Integration" is not just a "neutral" (probably good or bad) concept at hand, but it is a particular tool or even a weapon in the ongoing social struggles, because it is articulating or reflecting a certain social standpoint. And as an efficient tool it serves specific purposes. On the one side, as we have seen above, it helps withdrawing the attention from the dangerous societal contradictions by abstracting migrants' subjectivity and by redubbing the "issues."

And it is exactly this "redubbing" which also performs different potential subjective functions, particularly for the (respective) "locals": The "locals" can fantasize themselves as being powerful enough to allocate or to award something to others in need. Or at least they can imagine some participation in power, even if this participation is confined to answering into some microphone in front of me the question "How many immigrants 'my' country can take without sinking into social chaos." Such "micropolitics of participation in power" are very effective tools to co-construct some "fantastic" individual understanding about how our societies are "functioning." Furthermore, this "fantastic" logic helps us to push away our fear of the potential danger in finding ourselves in a similar position of "dependence" or "exclusion" as are the ethno-classes of immigrants at this historical moment. But we are probably well aware of the fact that this "help" for us is as "fantastic" as it is the social theory behind it. However, both "helpful" aspects of such a "fantastic" (or fake) logic hinder us finally to "universalize" the demand for solidarity. And such a confinement of solidarity to less than the whole population (e.g., only to "my" people) transports a *real* danger, which cannot be displaced, even not in my imagination. But, such subjective functionalities obtain more and more importance in our transitional era with our societies being transformed through new negotiations about the social hierarchization of the population. In this historical coincidence it has some short-term functionality for me to fantasize myself as being powerful, or to relocate the danger—even only in my imagination.

The substantial claim of every critical social science or social practice is constituted in trying to clarify the different subjective positions or perspectives being included in the dominant conceptualizations, even if/because these are substituted by placeholders. This substituting by placeholders deflects or mystifies the real "name," i.e., the naming of the different positions/perspectives of the subjects involved in the dominant conceptualizations. The claimed clarification is a basic prerequisite for making the subject positions accessible to reason/discourse and to (educative/transformative) practice. The dominant discourse is not only articulated by the dominant subjects in power. It is always worth reflecting about which perspectives/positions are articulated in/through our own discourses—beyond our declared and good intentions to resist the dominant discourses and practices. Resistance is—as it is solidarity—always practical, and it is not a matter of declaration.

So, summing up, we can state that instead of accepting our (sometimes well-paid) roles as *social engineers*, we have to develop ourselves into *political subjects*. This includes the necessity to encounter the many forms and circumstances where we think that we have to and we can determine the problems *of* and the actions *for* the others—without the others. But by this we are not only abstracting from, we are not only denying their subjectivity, but are simultaneously *subverting/undermining* our own subjectivity, i.e., our own possibilities to relate ourselves to the dominant coercions pushing *us* to "integrate." We cannot overcome these coercions by only taking abstractly the side of (the) others, or even by supporting their struggles practically. If we conceive these struggles as genuine solidary, then we have to initiate as well processes for "social self-understanding" (Osterkamp 2009, p. 171) about our common, though different, blockages and hindrances to act along our recognized necessities:

> Taking the other's perspective, however, does not simply mean imagining oneself in the other's place (only possible, in any case, in a rather limited way); instead, it is a process of social self-understanding aiming at gaining a meta-standpoint allowing us to grasp both the actual groundedness of each single perspective and their collusion in reproducing given power-relations. Such a process is tantamount to overcoming a merely descriptive access to the problems in favour of a constructive one by jointly concentrating on creating the possibilities for tackling the problems instead of merely reacting to them. (Osterkamp 2009, p. 171; see also: Holzkamp 2006)

It should be obvious to us that all the differentiated "offers" and "promises" to improve one's own situation by denying or discounting the above mentioned necessities are exactly part of the hindrances we have to deal with all together and in common.

References

Bojadžijev, M. (2005). *Die windige Internationale: Rassismus und Kämpfe der Migration*. Inauguraldissertation zur Erlangung des Grades eines Doktors der Philosophie im Fachbereich Gesellschaftswissenschaften der Johann-Wolfgang-Goethe-Universität zu Frankfurt am Main.

Boutang, Y. M. (1998). De l'esclavage au salariat: économie historique du salariat bridé. Paris: PUF.

Dimitri, A.,Marvakis, A., Parsanoglou, D., & Petrakou, I. (2007). Precarious trajectories: Migrant youth regimes in Greece. In G. Titley (Ed.), *The politics of diversity*. Strasbourg: Council of Europe Publishing.

Foitzik, A., & Marvakis, A. (Eds.). (1997). *Tarzan - Was nun? Internationale Solidarität im Dschungel der Widersprüche*. Hamburg: Verlag Libertäre Assoziation.

Held, J., Horn, H.-W., & Marvakis, A. (1996). *"Gespaltene Jugend" - Politische Orientierungen jugendlicher ArbeitnehmerInnen im Kontext gesellschaftlicher Veränderung* (unter Mitarbeit von Traudl Horn-Metzger, Wolfram Keppler und Christine Riegel). Opladen: Leske + Budrich.

Hess, S., Binder, J., & Moser, J. (Hrsg.). (2009). *No integration?! Kulturwissenschaftliche Beiträge zur Integrationsdebatte in Europa*. Bielefeld: transcript.

Holzkamp, K. (2006). Psychologie: Selbstverständigung über Handlungsbegründungen alltäglicher Lebensführung. *Forum Kritische Psychologie, 36*, 7–112.

Karakayalı, S. (2001). "Sechs bis acht Kommunisten, getarnt in Monteursmänteln." Die wahre Geschichte des Fordstreiks in Köln 1973. In *Stadtrevue, Nr. 10, Vol. 26.*, pp. 41–43; und in: http://www.kanak-attak.de/ka/text/fordstreik.html.

Karakayalı, S. (2006). *Zwei, drei, viele Wege ... Zur Genealogie illegaler Migration in der Bundesrepublik Deutschland*. Inauguraldissertation zur Erlangung des Grades eines Doktors der Philosophie im Fachbereich Gesellschaftswissenschaften der Johann-Wolfgang-Goethe-Universität zu Frankfurt am Main.

Karakayalı, S., & Tsianos, V. (2002). Migrationsregimes in der Bundesrepublik Deutschland: Zum Verhältnis von Staatlichkeit und Rassismus. In A. Demirović & M. Bojadžijev (Hrsg.). *Konjunkturen des Rassismus*. Münster: Verlag Westfälisches Dampfboot.

Marvakis, A. (1996). *Orientierung und Gesellschaft. Gesellschaftstheoretische und individualwissenschaftliche Grundlagen politischer Orientierungen Jugendlicher in Strukturen sozialer Ungleichheit*. Frankfurt/Main: Peter Lang.

Marvakis, A. (2004). Social integration or social apartheid? In M. Pavlu & D. Christopoulos (Eds.), *Greece as land of immigrants*. Athens: Kritiki. (in Greek).

Marvakis, A. (2005). Die Vernunft der Solidarität. In J. Held (Eds.), *Jugend in Europa – Integrationsprobleme, Partizipationschancen* (Beiträge der Internationalen Tagung vom 26. bis 29. 03. 2004 in Freudenstadt). Hamburg/Berlin: Argument.

Marvakis, A. (2010). Integration: Versprechen, Kampffeld und Chimäre. *Forum Kritische Psychologie, 54*, 81–94.

Marvakis, A., & Parsanoglou, D. (2005). Zur Kulturalisierung sozialer Ungleichheit. In R. Leiprecht et al. (Eds.), *International Lernen – Lokal Handeln*. London: IKO.

Marvakis, A., Parsanoglou, D. & Pavlu, M. (2001). Migrants in Greece: 'Problems', issues, subjects. In A. Marvakis, D. Parsanoglou, & M. Pavlu (Eds.), *Migrants in Greece* (pp. 13–28). Athens: Hellenika Grammata. (in Greek).

Marvakis, A., Parsanoglou, D., & Tsianos, V. (2006). "And though they move! ...". The revolution of hope and the autonomy of migrants. In *Synchronta Themata – special issue on "new conceptualizations on the phenomenon of immigration"*. (in Greek).

Mergner, G. (1999). *Lernfähigkeit der Subjekte und gesellschaftliche Anpassungsgewalt: Kritischer Dialog über Erziehung und Subjektivität*. (Ausgewählte Schriften Band 2). Hamburg/ Berlin: Argument.

Osterkamp, U. (2009). Knowledge and practice in critical psychology. *Theory & Psychology, 19*(2), 167–191.

Transit Migration Forschungsgruppe (Hrsg.). (2007). *Turbulente Ränder: Neue Perspektiven auf Migration an den Grenzen Europas*. Bielefeld: Transcript.
Wallerstein, I. (1999). Nor patriotism, neither cosmopolitism. In M. C. Nussbaum et al. (Eds.), *For my country: Patriotism or cosmopolitism?* Athens: Scripta (in Greek).

Chapter 7
Learning to Live Together—Towards a New Integration Society

Esteban Piñeiro and Jane Haller

Introduction

In the last two decades, Swiss policies on foreigners have been fundamentally restructured, as the guiding concept of integration has conquered the political arena in an exceptionally short time. Similarly in many European countries the idea became established, that in future, immigration will be necessary and therefore control and defensive measures in policies on migrants should be supplemented with a policy of "open doors" (Wicker 2004, p. 33). Only a close study of Swiss laws and government reports will enable us to recognize how integration policies reformulated the position of and the perspective on migrants by turning former foreigners into valuable members of Swiss society. Aiming for a peaceful coexistence of "natives" and migrants, the latter should participate in social and increasingly political life, ultimately gaining the same opportunities as the native Swiss. Reading the integration discourse, this can only be achieved through a variety of educational measures. Precisely this connection between integration and education will be the focus of our contribution.

We will start by giving a short outline of Swiss policies on foreigners and their reformulation according to integration policies in Chap. 1. This will be followed by an analysis of how integration is implemented and how education functions as a strategy of integration (Chap. 2). The first two parts of our contribution deal with the integration discourse in regard to what Laclau calls the social logic, that is the "truths" and rules according to which the integration discourse operates and renders social practices intelligible (Laclau 2007, p. 177). To make these social logics visible and understandable and as we see integration as a specific way of shaping the social, that is a form of regulating and governing people, we will use Foucault's theories on power, especially his studies on (neo-liberal) governmentality (2006a, b) and the concepts of sovereign, disciplinary, and bio-power (1979, 1983, 2001). The shifts that initiated and shaped the social logics of the current policies, thus developing and

E. Piñeiro (✉)
University of Applied Sciences Northwestern Switzerland, Thiersteinerallee 57, 4053 Basel, Switzerland
e-mail: esteban.pineiro@fhnw.ch

establishing specific aims and measures, are uncovered in a short historic outline in Chap. 3. In Chap. 4, we will deal with the question of how the ideal of integration is established, how varied interests are linked and how integration begins to spread to influence a large variety of areas of society. Perceiving and analyzing this with Laclau's and Mouffe's (1985) and Laclau's (2000, 2007) political theory of hegemony allows us to uncover the political logic, the dynamic force that shapes social order and is inherent in any process of social change (Laclau 2007, p. 117). This will enable us to determine the horizon of current integration policies, which model of society, i.e., which ideal of coexistence integration refers to. We will focus on the ideas and issues the integration discourse is connected to and which closures and demarcations are established through it. Finally, in Chap 5 returning to Foucault's perspective of governmentality, which looks at how political rationalities, forms of knowledge and governing are linked, we will analyze integration as a hegemonic project to govern a whole population. While to this point in the argumentation the emphasis lies on governing (that is educating) individuals, a broader perspective that takes in the population as well, will allow us to interpret integration as a form of risk management to establish the safety of the population. Furthermore, we will show how ultimately integration redraws the boundaries between the included and the excluded. Our contribution concludes with a critical perspective on the boundaries that are created and established through the integration policies.

New Swiss Policies on Foreigners

With over 1.6 million foreigners, Switzerland has one of the highest shares of foreigners in Europe (21% of the entire population). The Federal Office for Migration (BFM 2008) states that migration contributes more to the growth of the population in Switzerland than in classic immigration countries. By now second- and third-generation migrants are living in Switzerland. Piguet (2006) observes a high stability in the foreign population with more than 60% having a permanent residence permit, whereas in 1960 this was the case for less than 25%. In Switzerland, anyone who works during his/her stay or who remains for longer than 3 months requires a permit. A distinction is made between short-term residence permits (less than 1 year), annual residence permits (limited), and permanent residence permits (unlimited). In this context, it is important to note that Switzerland is not an EU/EFTA member state, which is why a number of bilateral agreements regulate relationships between Switzerland and the EU/EFTA member states, also in immigration matters (FZA 2002). This means European immigrants from the EU-17/EFTA states benefit from full freedom of movement, provided they work(ed) in Switzerland (Piguet 2006, p. 142). More than 60% of foreigners living in Switzerland come from EU-27/EFTA countries (BFM 2008). For citizens of all other countries (third states) there are quotas that only allow highly qualified managers and specialists to be admitted. It is this dual admission system, which characterizes Swiss admission policy today.

On the first of January 2008, the New Foreign Nationals Act (AuG) came into effect, replacing the former federal law on the residence and settlement of foreigners (ANAG) dating from 1934. Thereby the fundamental concerns of integration (Piguet 2006, p. 148) based on a broad political consensus and expressing the wishes of the Swiss sovereign were legally consolidated in article 4, Chap 8 of the AuG as well as in the ordinances VIntA 2000 and 2007. Integration policies are aimed at welcome migrants, addressed as integrated, integrateable or to be integrated. This distinguishing feature shapes the current admission policy to the Swiss territory. The new law on foreigners implements a bipolar regime with two tightly linked core areas (arts. 3 and 4 AuG): integrating migrants while simultaneously controlling immigration. The latter regulates entry into Switzerland, while integration organizes the "inside" of Swiss society. Both shape Swiss society by controlling who can enter Swiss territory and thereby who is allowed to become part of the Swiss community. Migration regulations expand as integration measures rely on immigration regulations, on a certain "insulation" to fruitfully structure the "inside" of society—the coexistence, collaboration, and compatibility of individuals on Swiss territory. At the same time, borders are drawn according to inclusion criteria formulated by the integration policies (art. 54 par. 1 AuG).

Today the matter of integration appears as the only way of dealing with foreigners. Not very long ago rotation models and quota policies aimed at the opposite, at preventing the integration of foreigners. Looking back just four decades to the 1960s, the debate on foreigners was fed by fears of "Überfremdung" (an "invasion" of Swiss society by foreign influences), of an infiltration of Swiss culture as an "intellectual contamination" (Studienkommission 1964, p. 133). Foreigners working in Switzerland were criticized as having different views on the state and community in general. They appeared unused to active participation in political life and as having a hostile attitude towards state authorities. Foreigners were thought to pose a not to be underestimated threat of "infecting" the Swiss population (Studienkommission 1964, p. 139). The policy on foreigners from the 1960s saw the foreign workers exclusively as a "raw" economic resource, managing them as anonymous, marginalized workers. The "supply of foreigners" was therefore regulated according to the demands of the labor market. These foreigners, who were seen as people in transition, have now become a recognized part of the population. As they are here to stay, migrants inevitably become socially and culturally visible. In the past decades migrants have shed themselves of the image of unwelcome foreigners and have become welcome fellow citizens, what we can call "indigenous migrants" (Wicker 2004, p. 34). Since the 1990s and even more clearly with the AuG a new conception of immigrants has established itself. The model of integration points to a valuable and useful human potential (Wicker 2004, p. 17; Leitbild Bern 1999). It is precisely this recognition and status improvement that is expressed in the term integration. Art. 4 par. 2 of the AuG states that integration should enable long-term and legally resident migrants to participate in economic, social, and cultural life. Integration is seen as a mutual process of give and take with the aim of enabling a peaceful "co-existence of Swiss and migrant residents based on the values of the federal constitution and reciprocal respect and tolerance" (art. 4 par. 1 AuG). The current understanding that migrants need to be integrated and have to be "integrateable" has led to a noticeable reformulation of policies on foreigners and ultimately to a new migrant subject.

Recognized as social agents, migrants should contribute in the long term and more broadly to the common good and may in turn participate in public life. While Switzerland appears to view itself as an immigration country, foreigners must in turn be willing to integrate themselves. They are encouraged to study the social and living conditions in Switzerland and especially to learn an official national language (art. 4 par. 4 AuG). The turn from policies focused on deficits to policies orientated towards resources is one of the characteristics of contemporary integration policies. Transnational mobility and migrants' potentials have become indispensable from an economic, demographic, and national-political point of view (Wicker 2004, p. 48; EKA 1996, p. 3; BIGA/BFA 1991, p. 2). Now nonintegrated foreigners are condemned as inferior and not worthy to stay. Formerly it was precisely the long-term and therefore visible residents that were seen as a threat, because they could potentially form, what is now called "parallel societies".

The current recognition of foreigners as part of the Swiss population goes hand in hand with the aim of giving them equal opportunities. The goal of integration is stated as "equal opportunities for the participation of foreigners in Swiss society" (art. 2 par. 1 VIntA). Crucially, integration no longer demands a unilateral effort from migrants, but is seen as a reciprocal approaching process between native Swiss and migrants. Art. 4 par. 3 of the AuG explicitly points out that integration depends on the willingness of migrants (to integrate themselves), but also on the openness of the Swiss population (Leitbild Basel 1999, p. 5), seen as a prerequisite for integration to become successful. Their contribution is part of a favorable framework that enables equal opportunities and the participation of the migrant population in public life, thereby helping to create a society envisaged in integration policies as made up of people with different origins living together and not next to each other (EKA 1996, p. 6).

Integration as Education

The new principles of learning and education appear clearly in the first Ordinance on the Integration of Foreign Nationals (VIntA). Herein integration encompasses all efforts that

(a) promote mutual understanding between the Swiss and foreign population;
(b) facilitate a coexistence based on shared fundamental values and behavior patterns;
(c) acquaint foreigners with the structure of the state, the societal and living conditions in Switzerland;
(d) create a favorable framework for equal opportunities and the participation of foreign population in societal life (art. 3 par. 2 VIntA 2000).

The policy on foreigners has become a pedagogy of foreigners, as the political interpretation of integration emphasizes a set of economic, social and cultural competences that foreigners must bring with them or need to acquire and develop through educational measures. The Ordinance on the Integration of Foreign Nationals of 2007 substantiated the required compatibility of knowledge, values, and norms moving from general principles to more concrete educational objectives. Art 4 VIntA 2007 notes that foreigners' contribution to their individual integration lies in:

(a) Respecting the constitutional order and the values of the federal constitution.
(b) Learning a national language spoken at the place of residence.
(c) Studying the living conditions in Switzerland.
(d) A willingness to participate in economic life and to acquire an education.

Studying, education, and qualifications form techniques of the integration policies and have become part of the policy on foreigners. Integration appears to rely on individual competences, as well as a specific education in living together and in realizing an economic potential. The degree of integration becomes measurable and achievable, as the expectations addressed at migrants are structured in a specific format, namely aimed at individual migrants, who need to learn a set of skills, ultimately to acquire a range of competences. These are economic, entrepreneurial (migrants take care of their own professional qualifications and education to gain access to the labor market and secure their livelihood), secondly social (migrants interact and communicate with the Swiss society, show social adaptability), thirdly normative (behavioral code according to the constitutional order and its values), and fourthly cultural (migrants learn a national language and acquire appropriate values and a compatible way of life). Overall integration policies appear to be realized through what we can summarize as a "cultural approach," as the question of a "fitting" culture touches on the most diverse societal systems. Migrants need to learn how to "fit" into society. This encompasses socio-cultural and socio-economic competences that are the criteria according to which integration is measured. Only thereby can a coexistence and the participation of migrants—the realization of their economic, social, and cultural potentials—be achieved.

According to the policies, integration as a form of education should work primarily through incentives, which is why *techniques of support* are favored. One of these incentives is that integrated migrants benefit from a better status in society (economically, socially, and legally), e.g., through the renewal of their residence permit. To help migrants integrate, the state also provides the framework that supports the acquisition of a national language, professional training and health care on a federal, cantonal, and communal level, as well as encouraging efforts to facilitate the mutual understanding between Swiss and foreigners (art. 53, par. 3 AuG). In addition a number of special measures are possible: language and integration courses, information services for a variety of social problems, integration programs for work and of the social welfare and social security authorities (art. 2 par. 3 VIntA).

Besides supporting techniques that offer a suitable framework, the *techniques of demands* emphasize the willingness and duty of migrants to integrate. The degree of integration and the diagnosed potential for integration—measured for instance as the readiness of migrants to study the living conditions and to learn a national language (art. 4 par. 3 and 4 AuG)—are factors in granting and extending residence permits and in questions of deportation or denied entry (art. 54 par. 2 AuG). Residence permits can be linked to the completion of an integration or language course. Compulsory (educational) measures can be written down in an integration agreement between the authorities and migrants, which after an evaluation of the individual case includes primarily educational aims and measures, as well as the consequences of violating the agreement (art. 5 par. 2 VIntA). Such "therapeutic" measures are aimed at migrants whose integration cannot be promoted solely through incentives.

So far our description leads us to the assumption that the integration policies create a type of migrant subject addressed as an active "entrepreneur" (Bröckling 2007, p. 46), who is meant to take care of his/her own integration. Individual potentials and efforts towards self-integration, proving oneself within a given framework of possibilities and measures are at the centre of the reformulated integration policies. A form of government can be observed here that is primarily understood as maintaining the conditions under which migrants are able to govern themselves, i.e., to integrate. Following Foucault (2006b, pp. 49, 300) educational techniques of self-governing can be read as operating according to a neo-liberal rationality. Neo-liberalism does not aim at direct domination or the repression of individuals, rather it gives subjects more freedom. It stresses the individual capacities for self-regulation (Lemke 1997, p. 256) and the autonomy of the individual that enable an indirect governing by providing a productive framework (equal opportunities, openness, and possibilities for participation). Individual freedom seen as self-determination and responsibility becomes one of the most important resources, as an entrepreneurial self-governing promises an efficient way of making migrants more productive, that is to aid them to handle their integration in an entrepreneurial way within a given neo-liberal (state) framework. The willingness of migrants to integrate is crucial, as integration is primarily a self-governed realization of opportunities in all areas of society.

In addition, the demands and requirements make a disciplinary approach visible that is characterized by techniques of control, evaluation, intervention, and ultimately of normalization (Foucault 1979). This power operates with permanent, consistent, and unobtrusive adaptation techniques. Essentially it consists of methods of enforcement that train and standardize human behavior (Foucault 1979, p. 181). The liberal forms of governing interlock with techniques of direct control, so support can be read as the demand to let yourself be supported and aided to fulfill your potential (Piñeiro and Haller 2009). Ultimately the demand consists of accepting the framework and playing by the rules of a neo-liberal society—resulting in being supported, making it possible for incentives to work and keep working.

After describing how the integration policies and educational techniques operate, in a next step our interest focuses on a historical approach to the integration discourse, as this further illuminates the social logic that is reflected in the concepts and different perspectives that have come together in and shaped the current integration policies and their implementation.

The Birth of Coexistence

Today's policies are anchored in the 1960s and present an at first glance paradox phenomenon: the opening of Switzerland and an acceptance of migrants in a time, when rising xenophobia manifested itself in public debates as "Überfremdungsangst" (fear of domination by foreign influences) which culminated in an attempted initiative against "Überfremdung" (Mahnig and Piguet 2004, p. 75). In 1964, a committee was formed to study the problem of foreign workers, dealing with the question of whether the state could afford (based on demographic and political considerations) to regulate immigration solely according to economic needs in view of the continually growing number of foreign residents (Studienkommission 1964, p. 7). As foreign workers had become an indispensable factor for the Swiss economy and due to the resulting growing number of long-term foreign residents, policies on foreigners could no longer solely be looked at as part of economic policies. However, the presence of a large number of (long-term) foreigners led to fears of their influence on Swiss culture and the dangerous effects of "geistige Überfremdung" (intellectual foreign infiltration) (Studienkommission 1964, p. 133). The solution to this dilemma of dependency and infiltration the committee suggested was to combat differing cultural characteristics. The idea of fending off cultural risks through integration (Eingliederung) was born. Integration in this first phase meant assimilation, yet the outlines of an idea of a reciprocal process, that integration can only succeed if foreigners are accepted by the Swiss, whereby the culture of the host country remains the decisive standard, are already visible. Difficulties in communicating, differing lifestyles, other views on cultural values, and the differences in customs were stated as reasons for the failure of assimilation (Studienkommission 1964 p. 142). The focus shifted to the whole person, no longer just a worker or a person fulfilling a specific economic role or function, but a social and cultural "worker" as well. According to this logic the threat of "Überfremdung" decreases with growing socio-cultural assimilation and the duration of residency (Niederberger 2004, p. 152). Therefore the policy on foreigners, which consisted of rotation and quota policies, was supplemented with an assimilation strategy. The selection of immigrants was influenced by the view that bridging a gap between two very different cultures was hardly ever successful (Studienkommission 1964, p. 145). The social logic, the discourse of simultaneous defense and integration that shaped the debate from the 1990s until now was prepared in the 1960s, the committee report appearing to give birth to current views on handling foreigners.

In the meantime the political landscape and the economic environment have changed. The rhetoric of "Überfremdung" and infiltration has vanished from the political vocabulary, but as we will see a similar spirit animates current integration policies. The idea of integration and of a socio-cultural fit between foreigners and the Swiss has been modulated and differentiated, not least after the opening towards citizens from EU/EFTA countries. In the 1990s the question of how to approach the EU while at the same time not heightening fears of "Überfremdung" became central (Mahnig and Piguet 2004, p. 96). Finally a Europe-friendly pragmatism led to Switzerland signing seven bilateral agreements including the Agreement on the Free Movement of Persons (FZA 2002), which came into force on the first of June 2002. With the bilateral agreements European migrants acquired nearly the same rights as Swiss citizens apart from political rights (Piguet 2006, p. 142; Kreis 2009). The Agreement on the Free Movement of Persons essentially brought about two marked changes: Firstly the AuG, the New Foreign Nationals Act, only applies for part of the foreign population, because the bilateral agreements regulate most aspects of immigration of EU citizens and the AuG regulates the immigration and integration conditions only for citizens from the rest of the world, from so-called third states (Piguet 2006, p. 145); therefore secondly the agreement results in an unprecedented opening of Switzerland to foreigners while integration measures and efforts to adapt and learn cannot be demanded of these migrants. To understand this development, we must take a closer look at a key document from the 1990s, the report on the conception and priorities of Swiss policy on foreigners that illuminates the social logic that has shaped Swiss policy on foreigners until today (Skenderovic and D'Amato 2008, p. 155). In this report the "three circles model" was introduced (BIGA/BFA 1991, p. 78), which was supposed to solve the dilemma of pursuing an economy-friendly immigration without strengthening fears of "Überfremdung." This model shifted the focus from the number of foreigners to an idea of cultural proximity, meaning that heterogeneity of immigrants living in Switzerland should be kept as low as possible. The three circles model allowed for a differentiation of foreigners into a hierarchy of three groups: culturally close people (EU/EFTA citizens) made up the first circle, citizens from states like the USA, Australia, Canada, and Eastern European states, with which Switzerland had close relations, belonged to the second circle, while everyone else was in the third group. The model of cultural proximity formed the basis for a differentiated form of "ethno diagnostics." According to this people from third states had slim chances of integrating due to a lack of sociocultural competencies and their immigration was therefore handled most restrictively (Hettlage and Tellenbach 1999, p. 278). This was meant to lead to a "culturally invisible immigration" (Piguet 2006, p. 73), which should ward off cultural risks, making them invisible to protect society and the population from "Überfremdung" and the fear thereof. A modified version of the model found its way into the AuG as a "two circles model" (Piguet 2006, p. 78), i.e., a dual admission system (EU/EFTA vs. non-EU citizens).

The three circles model, discredited as discriminating and even racist by the federal committee against racism (Mahnig and Piguet 2004, p. 100), inspired a counter model, which focused on the work experience and education potential of migrants, rather than their origins, favoring highly-skilled foreigners (Hettlage and Tellenbach 1999, p. 277). In this model the criteria of cultural compatibility appear to have been exchanged for qualification compatibility (Piguet 2006, p. 78). Current integration policies show that on the contrary the two criteria are interwoven in a new set of sociocultural and socioeconomic competences that include a whole range of economic, social, and cultural skills. Neither the three circles model nor the counter model were ever realized, but their social logics are inscribed in the new integration paradigm. Combining the two sets of criteria to classify people allows for more possibilities to govern them and thereby seems to enable the farthest-reaching integration possible. The opening of Switzerland appears to be a perfect strategy of risk management, as EU/EFTA citizens offer an optimal sociocultural and socioeconomic fit or at least have a great potential for integration. They pose a nearly neutralized risk, as they are culturally close and at the same time are considered an indispensable economic human resource (as long as they work in Switzerland).

The Will to Unity

So far we have attempted to clarify the social logic of the integration policies. To uncover the political logic that shapes the social order, in this chapter we will read integration as a hegemonic project following Laclau's and Mouffe's theory on hegemony. Thus we will change our focus from the microsocial practices and educational principles and technologies in the laws to a specific view of society we find implied in them.

Integration as a Hegemonic Project

The starting point for Laclau's and Mouffe's (1985; Laclau 2000, 2007) theory on hegemony is their conception of the social as the result of power struggles, as a politically created social order. The concept used to describe these constituting power struggles is called hegemony. This involves the attempt at creating and implementing a social order whereby the particular aims from a social sector are presented as realizing the universal aims of, e.g., a community as a whole (Laclau 2000, p. 50). One particular position assumes the representation of an imaginary totality (Laclau 2007, p. 70), created by differential positions in a given social order being made equivalent in what Laclau and Mouffe call a chain of equivalences. This imaginary totality also depends on all particularities excluding the same element (constitutive outside). What is more, only a so-called empty signifier can fulfill the function of representing diverse interests as a totality. The more elements a particular position represents, the more it loses its particular content and tends towards an empty signifier. Thus we propose, that integration functions as an empty signifier, linking different social demands and measures to represent a totality we will call "integration society." The starting point to an understanding of integration as an empty signifier is the indeterminacy, the often-criticized lack of a clear-cut definition (Bianchi 2003, p. 11). Precisely this vagueness and imprecision of the term will be understood in the next section as the "very condition of political action" (Laclau 2007, p. 18).

Integration is conceived of in a very broad sense, so it can affect all aspects of societal life from the coexistence of individuals, to education and health concerns, work integration, housing and settlement policies, as well as crime prevention (cf.

Leitbild Basel 1999; Leitbild Bern 1999; Integrationspolitik Zürich 1999). The contingent elements that are made equivalent to form a unity through integration policies are manifold: Today the concerns of integration influence all areas of migrants' lives, from their career planning to their hygiene. Migrants are not just meant to be integrated into the workforce, but rather should participate as equals in social, economic, cultural, and even political life, using their (acquired) socioeconomic and sociocultural skills to be part of society. While integration postulates equal opportunities for all members (of the same community) rather than the submission of a minority to a dominant culture and its social principles (assimilation), the recognition and equal treatment of migrants evidently only occurs within a society, where all individuals accept the same core traits. While the former model of assimilation is absorbed in the integration model, the "domesticated pluralism," i.e., the "harmonious cultural unity" is no longer achieved through a unilateral effort, but by a reciprocal, collective "rapprochement." For integration to work, all societal agents must work together. As a cross-sectional task, it depends on the efforts of federal, cantonal, and communal authorities, as well as nongovernmental agents like foreigners' organizations, employers and employees, private individuals, and companies. Consequently the Swiss are affected in that they are explicitly addressed in the AuG (Foreign Nationals Act), they must be open and help migrants to integrate. We can now even observe that not only migrants should be integrated, but also the disabled and able bodied, children and the elderly, men and women, people on welfare, etc. (Integration handicap; GIG 1995; Sozialhilfe Basel-Stadt). Everyone should have equal opportunities to become an active participant in social, cultural, and political life as a productive member of a "peaceful community" (Wyss 2009, p. 1362).

Community and Citizenship

It has become clear, that integration as an empty signifier unites particular interests, agents, and concepts, thereby creating a cohesive unity and bringing about a reformulation of the social. The harmonious unity is generated through shared core sociocultural and socioeconomic skills (language, values, norms, behavioral standards, education, and qualification standards). This specific form of coexistence implicit in the integration policies can best be expressed by referring to theoretical ideas on the community. A good example is Mason's (2000, p. 20) definition of a community understood as "a group of people who share a range of values, a way of life, identify with the group and its practices and recognize each other as members of that group" (cf. Taylor 2002, p. 15; Bauman 2009, pp. 7, 15). Based on this concept, it is our opinion that integration aims at a similar horizon and thereby shapes society according to an ideal of community. This new unity of Swiss nationals and migrants seems to be mirrored in a different, not nationally defined concept of membership, which can in turn be made visible by studying the citizenship discourse.

While membership used to be realized through national citizenship, integration policies have made the rules for inclusion more elastic (Mau 2007, p. 227; Piguet

2006, p. 168). National citizenship consisted of a double closure: concerning a territory and membership (Mau 2007, p. 216). However, integration policies subvert this logic of inclusion by flattening the hierarchy between national citizens and recognized migrants, giving them near equal social, civil, and even political rights (Mau 2007, p. 227). Through the integration dispositif, citizen's rights and legal statuses have become "socially" acquirable and depend on an individual's degree of integration. Migrants can therefore be educated and learn to become citizens. This reinterpretation of the former concept of membership (national citizenship) emphasizes the active membership and possibility of participation of new citizens in public life, nearly independent of their legal status as nationally defined citizens (passive membership) (Wimmer 2005, p. 128). This type of membership addresses migrants as "foreign citizens," as responsible, active, and culturally compatible subjects. Thus a unity of integrated citizens, that is national and "social" citizens, is created whereby openness to migrants produces a new closure. In this sense, being open and simultaneously making migrants new members must be understood as a political strategy of organizing pluralism (Balibar 2003, p. 196), only hereby making a community, i.e., a collective existence possible.

Based on our argumentation so far, it becomes clear how the empty signifier draws a boundary by reformulating the social. It represents the totality and at the same time defines what is excluded. The (unity of the) community can only be maintained through closure, through exclusion. This means, the diverse positions are linked by their rejection of a common excluded element. This antagonism, an irretrievable difference between inside and outside, is necessary to establish a community (Laclau 2007, p. 85; Balibar 2003, p. 123). In our case the new criteria for membership, having expanded from the distinction between national/foreigner to integrated/non-integrated, have at the same time shaped the excluded. They are therefore all those, who make no sense in this social order, who do not fit. This restructures the classification of foreigners: Most desired are highly qualified EU/EFTA citizens, promising an optimal cultural fit, followed by less qualified EU/EFTA citizens, as they are necessary for the labor market. Third state highly educated people are also needed, if they could not be recruited from EU/EFTA citizens. The last category is made up of undesirable third state citizens with a lower education and finally asylum seekers, sans-papiers and deportees (Wicker 2004, p. 33).

To uphold the border between a harmonious interior, a community of integrated citizens and the excluded, who do not have the potential for integration or who are not desirable, liberal forms of governing and disciplinary techniques are not enough. As can be seen in the explicit legal enforcement in integration agreements, if the incentives to submit to a disciplinary power (the techniques of support and demand on the "inside" of society) fail, a more radical type of power can come into play. A further type of power, which following Foucault we see as a sovereign power. This enforces and establishes a repressive demarcation between who is allowed to live in this society and who must be excluded, aiming at the abandonment, banishment or destruction of specific individuals. Sovereign power operates as an absorbing authority, an access right to things, time, bodies, and finally life (Foucault

1983, p. 132, 2001, p. 37; see also Lemke 1997, p. 98). In this case, integration works through oppression, i.e., deportation or through denial of entry at the border.

Education, Population, Security: Towards an "Integration Society"

To summarize, today's policies on foreigners and integration are influenced by the idea of defending society against risks, shaped in the 1960s as an "opening as closure." This came about as foreign potential has become existentially necessary for Switzerland; therefore its development depends on the recognition of migrants as equals. Thus we propose integration operates according to the social logic of membership and the ideals of citizenship. The heterogeneity (caused by the opening) must be weakened through community building and this is substantiated as we have seen in the new integration policies. According to our reading of the new policies, this unity of diverse members can only develop, if a regime is implemented that envisages a number of educational or rather culturalization and assimilation techniques of support and demand. This makes clear, why education appears to be the core of integration. "Social citizenship" can only be realized through education. Ultimately integration established a policy of community building that has led to a reformulation of the social as a unity based on a shared core. We can detect a shift here, as the unity of the community is no longer thought to be based on ethnic or nationalistic categories, nor a common history or blood and soil ideology, but on acquirable socio-economic and socio-cultural skills and traits that are the result of personal efforts. "Foreign" is re-coded to mean not integrated or not integrateable, therefore poorly educated and unqualified, culturally maladjusted, not speaking a national language, unproductive, etc. It is precisely the selection criteria integrated/nonintegrated that have led to an unprecedented openness especially towards EU/EFTA citizens, which can be read as a drastic weakening of the sovereignty of the Swiss state and national citizenship. However through the reconfiguration of society by creating a new imaginary community based on integration, a unity could be maintained, formed according to socio-cultural and socio-economic criteria rather than national citizenship. This reformulation of the social can be understood as a unity of national and "social" citizens.

With Foucault's analytics of governmentality and bio-politics this unity can be read as a population, which needs to be governed and protected in its entirety (Foucault 2001, p. 293; 2006a, p. 158). In this context governing is understood in the broadest sense as any form of guiding the conduct of individuals and groups. The core issue of governing is the risks to the population from inside and outside, such as nonintegrated or nonintegrateable migrants and "parallel societies." This power, securing and cultivating the population, Foucault calls bio-power. In the analytics of governmentality, disciplinary and liberal forms of governing individuals are linked with techniques for the regulation of the entire population. This includes among other things the registration, statistical measurement, and administration of the development of a population (2006a, p. 156). Individual health as an example and the "well-being" of a population are connected, aiming at a positive development of the population through the governing of individuals. Safety and the population are closely linked, whereby the former is an essential mechanism to govern the latter (Foucault 2006a, p. 162). Based on the elaborated social logics of a "risk management of closure through opening," that has developed in the last decades into "risk policies of citizenship", integration now appears as a governmental risk policy. Community building through education can thus be seen as part of a security technology, as a biopolitical mode of governing individuals and the population as a whole. Addressing the population as a community, the integration policies shape the population, re-drawing boundaries and conceptualizing the risks and safety of the population in a specific way; namely in line with socio-cultural and socio-economic categories, the integration criteria: All those suited to the population, the "integrateables" become part of the "body" of the "integration population". The uncovered mode of operation of integration policies brings the political logics of community building as a formation of a population to the fore. Community building is therefore a form of protection that at the same time produces a specific population of integrated people. The risk policies aim at creating a new, more harmonious, i.e., safer population made up of the Swiss and integrated migrants. Integration therefore, as the key to a peaceful coexistence in a harmonious community, aims at a strategic constitution of the population.

A governmental analysis enabled us to clarify how the idea of a community of national and "social" citizens ultimately constituting the population can be understood as a rationality that structures the governing of people. This way of thinking becomes interwoven with a neo-liberal rationality and together they structure the programs and technologies of integration. Through this entwinement, resulting in a form of government through neo-liberal community building, what we call the "integration society" develops.

Conclusion

Focusing on the risk managerial constitution of an "integration society" and its "outside," that is its boundaries, the effects of current risk and integration policies must be critically analyzed. There are far-reaching consequences connected to the shift of the distinction strategies from national/foreigner to integrated/nonintegrated. While we do not want to question the fundamental necessity of a demarcation between inside and outside, as discussed above following Laclau and Balibar (Laclau 2007, p. 85; Balibar 2003, p. 123), the mode of distinction has moved from the "border of the community" to its inside. From the formerly dominant differentiation national/foreigner realized for instance through the regulation of admissions, now the inside of society is shaped according to the principle of integrated/nonintegrated. Thereby integration appears to pervade all areas of society and affect all its members. The importance of education in integration becomes visible, as on the "inside" it creates a "harmonious diversity of integrated people", a "population of integrated people". In addition, at the border it also functions as a diagnostic instrument, determining who has the potential to join and fit in the "integration society". In the context of integration, education emerges as a technology of governing, as a political strategy to lead people according to the ideal of integration. Thereby it regulates the population to incorporate only integrated national and "social" citizens: Education serves the creation of an "integration society". Additionally integration, understood as a permanent education, redefines membership to become a constant task of regulation, as it is no longer legally settled once and for all at immigration. Instead integration opens a space for a permanent test of migrants in all areas of their lives; their integration can be continually monitored and evaluated. The status of social citizenship needs to be proved and is always at stake, as it is defined by actions and characteristics that might be found deficient, thereby questioning the right of membership. A new line is drawn between national and social citizens, as nationals appear to elude total exclusion and only social citizens can be affected by sovereign power. The discussed near equal status of Swiss and migrants is eroded precisely when migrants do not accept the integration chances they are given. Here the neo-liberal government based on individual entrepreneurship, motivation, and responsibility is replaced by a radical repressive mode of exclusion aimed at the nonintegrated (nonintegrateable) foreigners. In the hegemonic order of integration, a new form of exclusion emerges that focuses only on those who can or will not prove themselves in the neo-liberal "integration society". These need to be radically excluded as they pose a threat to the cohesion of the neo-liberal community based on consensus and the integration population as a whole. Ultimately the "integration society" seems to establish a tendency to eliminate heterogeneity in favor of "fitting" all eligible parts of society together through citizenship—creating an inside free of nonintegrated people. "Real members" are desired that although they have their own characteristics, must simultaneously display the common characteristics of the whole. This community centers on the dream of a world that with Balibar (1990) can be described as purified of all excessive identities, populated by people that are endowed with the characteristics that represent the community. It should have become clear, how education in this context works as a technology defining and enabling those, who can be counted as part of the "integration society" and are ultimately worth being integrated into the population. On the other hand the hidden inset of education is shown in all clarity when following Foucault (2001, p. 282) the right to "destroy life" in the name of population policy appears as a biopolitical necessity to secure the prosperity and survival of the population. This is precisely where the integration program appears to come into play: all viable, countable life and a productive coexistence are identified, created, and maintained through education as a strategy of integration. Following our analysis, education defines the threshold at which all alternatives appear to be eliminated, making a nonintegrated life and coexistence outside the integration society untenable. Any life or coexistence beyond integration is eradicated and what remains is the integration society without any parallel societies. In our opinion, the outside and rejects created by these processes of integration should become the focus of further critical thought.

References

ANAG. (1934). *Bundesgesetz über Aufenthalt und Niederlassung der Ausländer (ANAG)*. http://www.duebendorf.ch/dl.php/de/20050303185404/anag.de.pdf. Accessed 22 May 2009.
AuG. (2008). *Bundesgesetz über die Ausländerinnen und Ausländer vom 16. Dezember 2005*. http://www.admin.ch/ch/d/sr/1/142.20.de.pdf. Accessed 1 January 2008.
Balibar, É. (1990). Gibt es einen "Neo-Rassismus"? In É. Balibar & I. Wallerstein (Eds.), *Rasse Klasse Nation: Ambivalente Identitäten* (pp. 23–38). Hamburg: Argument.
Balibar, É. (2003). *Sind wir Bürger Europas? Politische Integration, soziale Ausgrenzung und die Zukunft des Nationalen*. Hamburg: Hamburger Edition.
Bauman, Z. (2009). *Gemeinschaften: Auf der Suche nach Sicherheit in einer bedrohlichen Welt*. Frankfurt a. M.: Suhrkamp.
BFM. (2008). *Bundesamt für Migration: Migrationsbericht 2008*. Bern. http://www.bfm.admin.ch/etc/medialib/data/migration/berichte/migration.Par.0004.File.tmp/bfm-migrationsbericht-2008-d.pdf. Accessed 8 August 2009.
Bianchi, D. (2003). *Die Integration der ausländischen Bevölkerung: Der Integrationsprozess im Lichte des schweizerischen Verfassungsrechts*. Zürich: Schulthess.
BIGA/BFA. (1991). *Bundesamt für Industrie Gewerbe und Arbeit, Bundesamt für Ausländerfragen: Bericht über Konzeption und Prioritäten der schweizerischen Ausländerpolitik der neunziger Jahre*. Bern.
Bröckling, U. (2007). *Das unternehmerische Selbst: Soziologie einer Subjektivierungsform*. Frankfurt a. M.: Suhrkamp.
EKA. (1996). *Umrisse zu einem Integrationskonzept: Eidgenössische Ausländerkommission (EKA)*. Bern.
Foucault, M. (1977). *Discipline and punish: The birth of the prison*. New York: Random House.
Foucault, M. (1979). *Überwachen und Strafen: Die Geburt des Gefängnisses*. Frankfurt a. M.: Suhrkamp.
Foucault, M. (1983). *Der Wille zum Wissen: Sexualität und Wahrheit 1*. Frankfurt a. M.: Suhrkamp.
Foucault, M. (1998). *The will to knowledge: The history of sexuality, Vol. 1*. London: Penguin.
Foucault, M. (2001). *In Verteidigung der Gesellschaft*. Frankfurt a. M.: Suhrkamp
Foucault, M. (2006a). *Sicherheit, Territorium, Bevölkerung: Geschichte der Gouvernementalität I*. Frankfurt a. M.: Suhrkamp.
Foucault, M. (2006b). *Die Geburt der Biopolitik: Geschichte der Gouvernementalität II*. Frankfurt a. M.: Suhrkamp.
FZA. (2002). *Abkommen zwischen der Schweizerischen Eidgenossenschaft einerseits und der Europäischen Gemeinschaft und ihren Mitgliedstaaten andererseits über die Freizügigkeit vom 21. Juni 1999*. http://www.admin.ch/ch/d/sr/i1/0.142.112.681.de.pdf. Accessed 8 July 2009.
GIG. (1995). *Bundesgesetz über die Gleichstellung von Frau und Mann*. http://www.admin.ch/ch/d/sr/151_1/index.html. Accessed 17 August 2009.
Hettlage, R., & Tellenbach, N. (1999). Migrations- und Integrationspolitik der 90er Jahre. In H. Nigg (Ed.), *Da und fort. Leben in zwei Welten. Interviews, Berichte und Dokumente zur Immigration und Binnenwanderung in der Schweiz* (pp. 277–285). Zürich: Limmat Verlag.
Integration handicap. *Schweizerische Arbeitsgemeinschaft zur Eingliederung Behinderter*. http://www.integrationhandicap.ch. Accessed 17 August 2009.
Integrationspolitik Zürich (1999, August). *Integrationspolitik der Stadt Zürich: Massnahmen für ein gutes Zusammenleben in unserer Stadt*. Stadtentwicklung der Stadt Zürich: Bereich Integrationsförderung.

Kreis, G. (Ed.). (2009). *Schweiz – Europa: wie weiter? Kontrollierte Personenfreizügigkeit*. Zürich: Verlag Neue Zürcher Zeitung.

Laclau, E. (2000). Identity and hegemony: The role of universality in the constitution of political logics. In J. Butler, E. Laclau, & S. Zizek (Eds.), *Contingency, hegemony, universality: Contemporary dialogues on the left* (pp. 44–90). London: Verso.

Laclau, E. (2007). *On populist reason*. London: Verso.

Laclau, E., & Mouffe, C. (1985). *Hegemony and socialist strategy: Towards a radical democratic politics*. London: Verso.

Leitbild, Basel. (1999). *Leitbild und Handlungskonzept des Regierungsrates zur Integrationspolitik des Kantons Basel-Stadt*. Ethnologisches Seminar der Universität Basel: Mai.

Leitbild, Bern. (1999). *Leitbild zur Integrationspolitik der Stadt Bern: Grundsätze. Organisation. Handlungsbedarf*. Gemeinderat der Stadt Bern.

Lemke, T. (1997). *Eine Kritik der politischen Vernunft: Foucaults Analyse der modernen Gouvernementalität*. Berlin: Argument.

Lemke, T. (2007). *Gouvernementalität und Biopolitik*. Wiesbaden: VS Verlag.

Mahnig, H., & Piguet, E. (2004). Die Immigrationspolitik der Schweiz von 1948 bis 1998: Entwicklungen und Auswirkungen. In H-R. Wicker, R. Fibbi, & W. Haut (Eds.), *Migration und die Schweiz* (pp. 65–108). Zürich: Seismo.

Mason, A. (2000). *Community, solidarity and belonging: Levels of community and their normative significance*. Cambridge: Cambridge University Press.

Mau, S. (2007). Mitgliedschaftsräume, wohlfahrtsstaatliche Solidarität und Migration. In J. Mackert & H-P. Müller (Eds.), *Moderne (Staats) Bürgerschaft: Nationale Staatsbürgerschaft und die Debatte der Citizenship Studies* (pp. 215–233). Wiesbaden: VS Verlag.

Niederberger, J. M. (2004). *Ausgrenzen, Assimilieren, Integrieren: Die Entwicklung einer schweizerischen Integrationspolitik*. Zürich: Seismo.

Piguet, E. (2006). *Einwanderungsland Schweiz: Fünf Jahrzehnte halb geöffnete Grenzen*. Bern: Haupt.

Piñeiro, E., & Haller, J. (2009). Neue Migranten für die Integrationsgesellschaft. Versuch einer gouvernementalen Gegenlektüre des Prinzips "Fördern und Fordern". In E. Piñeiro, I. Bopp, & G. Kreis (Eds.), *Fördern und Fordern im Fokus. Leerstellen des Schweizerischen Integrationsdiskurses* (pp. 141–170). Zürich: Seismo.

Skenderovic, D., & D'Amato, G. (2008). *Mit dem Fremden politisieren: Rechtspopulismus und Migrationspolitik in der Schweiz seit den 1960er Jahren*. Zürich: Chronos.

Sozialhilfe Basel-Stadt. *Integration in Arbeit, Soziale Integration*. http://www.sozialhilfe.bs.ch/informationen/schwerpunkte.htm. Accessed 10 November 2009.

Studienkommission. (1964). *Das Problem der ausländischen Arbeitskräfte: Bericht der Studienkommission für das Problem der ausländischen Arbeitskräfte*. Bern.

Taylor, C. (2002). *Wieviel Gemeinschaft braucht die Demokratie? Aufsätze zur politischen Philosophie*. Frankfurt a. M.: Suhrkamp.

VIntA. (2000). *Verordnung über die Integration von Ausländerinnen und Ausländern (VIntA) vom 13. September 2000 (Stand am 26. September 2000)*. http://www.bfm.admin.ch/etc/medialib/data/migration/buergerrecht/auslaendergesetz/anag_und_vollzugsverordnungen/deutsch.Par.0004.File.tmp/142.205.de.pdf. Accessed 22 May 2009.

VIntA. (2007). *Verordnung über die Integration von Ausländerinnen und Ausländern (VIntA) vom 24. Oktober 2007*. http://www.admin.ch/ch/d/sr/1/142.205.de.pdf. Accessed 22 May 2009.

Wicker, H-R. (2004). Einleitung: Migration, Migrationspolitik und Migrationsforschung. In H-R. Wicker, R. Fibbi, & W. Haug (Eds.), *Migration und die Schweiz. Ergebnisse des Nationalen Forschungsprogramms "Migration und interkulturelle Beziehungen"* (pp. 12–62). Zürich: Seismo.

Wimmer, A. (2005). *Kultur als Prozess: Zur Dynamik des Aushandelns von Bedeutungen*. Wiesbaden: VS Verlag.

Wyss, M. P. (2009). Ausländische Personen und Integration. In P. Übersax, B. Rudin, T. Hugi Yar, & T. Geiser (Eds.), *Ausländerrecht: Eine umfassende Darstellung der Rechtsstellung von Ausländerinnen und Ausländern in der Schweiz von A(syl) bis Z(ivilrecht)* (pp. 1345–1376). Basel: Helbing Lichtenhahn.

Chapter 8
Opportunities of Managing Diversity in Local Educational Programs

Andreas Thiesen

And the mixture is all of us—and we're still mixing.[1]

What's New With Diversity?

The topic of ethnographical research has switched from "faraway civilizations" to the complex character of "western" societies. The variety of Europe's postmodern society has been subject to several discourses in recent years. The concept of Diversity—some recently say "Super-Diversity" (Vertovec 2007)—is becoming a catchword when it comes to the description of multidimensional issues of social exclusion.

In the field of education, Diversity stands for a new kind of thinking about integration: When considering the needs of deprived persons, e.g. long-term unemployed or uneducated persons—frequently migrants and excluded minorities—suddenly everybody stresses individual and collective resources, potentials and skills. Compared to past concepts like *assimilation* (cf. Esser 1980) or *multiculturalism* (cf. Taylor 1994) this apparently completely different paradigm presents a strong incentive for a more precise study.

Among other things, the interest in the meanwhile interdisciplinary led Diversity-discourses is attributed to the changing social, political, economical, cultural and judicial parameters of the postmodern society—as a consequence of temporal and spatial shifting (cf. Rosa 2005). Of course one has to be clear that diversity is not so much a "product" of the postmodern era as it is the effect of it. Social change, value change, demographic change as well as a permanent differentiation and relocation of lifestyles require a serious consideration about the special status of pluralism and multiplicity. Moreover, cultural control systems and approved strategies of conflict

---

[1] This phrasing was coined by the American folk musician Woody Guthrie (Guthrie 1942).

A. Thiesen (✉)
Simrockstraße 26, Hannover 30171, Germany
e-mail: A_Thiesen@web.de

resolution have to be renegotiated; by the way: this is not a worstcase scenario, the conceptual expectation is: diversity contains potentials. The Diversity approach not only seems to enable the description of complex "variety" issues, but to *reflect* social categories and individual and collective attributions.

If diversity-sensitivity focuses on understanding "strange" perhaps sometimes paradoxical *Lebenswelten* and concepts of everyday culture, it might reveal different individual dispositions within the various milieus. Not least, the more we are witnessing a flexibility within cultural identities (cf. Hall 1999) we have to face the perspectives of intercultural competence and cultural "translation": most of all in the cities—like the sociologist Georg Simmel already noted at the beginning of the twentieth century (Simmel 2006)—and not so much in the rural areas. On that basis, I consider the following lines as an important contribution to a paradigm shift concerning the discussion about *Managing Diversity* in segregated urban areas.

I consider at first the theoretical outlines of the Diversity paradigm by consulting different disciplinary approaches. In doing so, I analyze which theoretical ideas, methods, not forgetting power-sensitive approaches, are up for renegotiation. Through this discussion process, we will be able to understand the ongoing "boom" of Diversity as well as its scientific "background". As educational program development is highly determined by its political parameters I therefore focus on the sociopolitical challenges of Europe's diverse societies in another step. Moreover, I examine the different spatial dimensions—EU policy and local politics—affecting the *chances* and *limits* of social and cultural learning. Concluding, I focus on the objectives and requirements of Diversity instituted in local educational programs as I try to design a specific conceptual framework for Diversity.

Theoretical Views on Diversity

Today Diversity is a topic of importance in several disciplines. While the economic sciences already have been dealing with *Diversity Management* since the eighties (cf. Vedder 2005), the social sciences, particularly the educational sciences, dealt with antidiscrimination, racism-critique or equal opportunities (cf. Melter and Mecheril 2009). However, the educational sciences have found a term for their discussions coining it *Diversity Education* (cf. Prengel 2006). In my further discussion I will use the definitions from social and cultural sciences to examine what is "behind" Diversity.

Diversity in the Field of Social Sciences

Although Diversity as a term has not been well developed theoretically and not yet standardized both within the social sciences nor transdisciplinary (Luig 2007, p. 87), it is an issue which affects diverse disciplines (cf. Krell et al. 2007a). Regarding the dimensions of Diversity from the view of social sciences, we notice that the socioeconomical dimension (like poverty, social disparity or exclusion) does not appear. Rather, the literature often offers a discussion about "gender", "ethnical background"/ "nationality", "age"/"generation", "disability"/"handicap", "religion"/"ideology" and "sexuality". As Diversity allows us to reflect on social attributed categories, it will not take the discussion further if we remain on certain, isolated dimensions. We see from the writings of Pierre Bourdieu that not so much the particulars about the characteristics—like gender, ethnicity or age—are crucial for the position of social actors and their specific *scope* when he talks about "social space". To a greater degree it is the *combination* of these characteristics and the *compatibility* with the specific requirements of the particular social spaces (cf. Geiling 2005, p. 1).

Three Perspectives on Diversity

In a video-interview Katherine Klein, Professor of Management in Wharton, claimed—obviously in reference to Gertrude Stein's famous quote "a Rose is a Rose is a Rose"— that "Diversity is not Diversity is not Diversity" (INSEAD 2009). It always depends on specific groups, settings and situations to determine the relevant dimensions of heterogeneity one has to handle with. The same is true if we consider the different discourses Diversity is subject to. Following the sociologist Albert Scherr we can identify at least three perspectives on Diversity (cf. Scherr 2008, p. 12):

(1) *Diversity as a functional understanding*:
The support of Diversity is subject to specific motives. For example firms, usually transnational operating concerns, expect economic advantages by practicing Diversity Management.
(2) *Diversity as an antidiscrimination discourse*:
Especially in Europe, Diversity is discussed on a political–judicial level, concerning the protection of individuals or groups.
(3) *Diversity as a critique of power and dominance*:
As Diversity is laid out in a horizontal and putatively individualistic way, there is a risk of obscuring connections of power and dominance.[2]

In the following, we may concentrate our attention especially on the second and third perspective on Diversity, but reflect its functional understanding as well.

Reflectivity as a Key Qualification for Educational Programs

Although there have always been related discourses within the social sciences—in conjunction with interculturality, social disparity or inclusion—they have mostly

---

[2] This is specially a domain of the Gender Studies.

been dealing with Diversity from the concerns about variety (e.g. variety of languages, theories or culture; Krell et al. 2007b, p. 8). In doing so, a second important connotation of Diversity—the concept of *difference*—is simply ignored. If Diversity is not read as *variety* and *difference* together, it will not be elaborated in a profound way (cf. exemplarily Fuchs 2007): We have to reflect that the diagnosis of "variety" alone is nothing more than a platitude in global times. Variety does not necessarily lead to certain social–political consequences. However, social and cultural difference may result in a need for politically administrated action. At the same moment the question of distribution of power becomes more important again: Who is defining Diversity? Who has got the prerogative of interpretation?

While we are dealing with Diversity we have to focus on the construction of subjective perception. In reference to Pierre Bourdieu, the sociologist Ingrid Breckner has pointed out that the level of perception of *social phenomena* highly depended on the subjective "incorporation of the objective structures of the social spaces" (Breckner 1999, p. 85). This phenomenological interpretation required communication as social actors had to disclose and explain their specific models of interpretation. According to that, the perception and experience, not least the categorization and judging of variety and difference, is vastly dependent on the subjects' ability to realize and reflect on their own constructed models.

The Significance of Cultural Capital for Managing Diversity

Using the example of education we can illustrate Pierre Bourdieu's way of thinking: Bourdieu invites us to combine the social goals Diversity is associated with—such as "participation" or "equal opportunities"—with its social structural reality. According to Bourdieu, the socializing institutions, before all the school, reproduce the social structure by "sanctioning" the unequal distribution of *cultural capital* which is founded on social transmission. Bourdieu makes a distinction between three forms of cultural capital: *incorporated cultural capital, objectified cultural capital* and *institutionalized cultural capital* (Bourdieu 2006, p. 112ff.):

(1) *Incorporated cultural capital*:
In this connection Bourdieu speaks of the embodied, *internalized* disposition of cultural capital—the level of education. It can only be acquired personally, by long-term investment. As "incarnated" personal property, incorporated cultural capital is part of the *habitus*. Certainly, this specific form of cultural capital is passed on through social transmission, but just "secretly" and not seamlessly. Only the bearer is able to "sell" his incorporated cultural capital in the form of products or services.

(2) *Objectified cultural capital*:
By adding this second variation of cultural capital Bourdieu refers to the material dimension. Objectified cultural capital consists of artifacts, such as paintings, monuments, designer furniture, literature etc. Objectified cultural capital can be passed on materially by its bearers. A material acquisition is also possible by investing economical capital or symbolically, by providing incorporated cultural capital.

(3) *Institutionalized cultural capital*:
Institutionalized cultural capital is nothing more than the product of the objectification of *incorporated cultural capital*. In the form of qualifications, degrees, titles etc., the bearers of institutionalized cultural capital come across the "deficit" of the embodied, only indirectly disposable characteristic of incorporated cultural capital. The institutionalization of cultural capital leads to acceptance and "comparability" of its bearers. However, the access to higher education depends on the social background and the disposition of *economical capital*. Nevertheless the transformation from economical to cultural capital may only be successful if degrees and titles are not traded, but rather stand for exclusiveness.

As we focus on the social importance of education, the three forms of cultural capital illustrate very clearly the relativity or the symbolism of social participation. With a closer look at the concept of Diversity, we realize that the cultural factor is obviously very important. That is why we necessarily have to define culture.

Diversity in the Field of Cultural Studies

While we consider the term of culture we are intentionally ignoring its naturalistic-material component: Not so much the physical cultivation and the technological progress is meant in this context, Diversity's terminological location is rather based on a metaphorical respectively symbolical comprehension of culture (cf. Hansen 2003, p. 11ff.; Eagleton 2000). Expressed in simplified terms we can understand "culture"—for the time being—as "the entirety of a collective's habits" (Hansen 2003, p. 17f.). Socially we might attribute the sum of all mental and artistic expressions of life to culture—be it in the form of education, art or social organization. Such a definition would refer to Raymond Williams and other representatives of the British cultural studies who particularly focused on the social determination of culture, everyday life behavior and the milieu-specific embodiment of culture e.g. different forms of communication (cf. Williams 1983).

If we enter the cultural studies, we are coming face to face with that central question of "power." The cultural studies are interested in the primacy of everyday "cultural power" (cf. Hörning 1999, p. 89). From such a perspective "culture" is not just connected to the level of its meaning and representation, but through this open-minded attitude to diverse lifestyles, the numerous, often implicit and nonsemantic forms of knowledge and life skills are brought to light (ib., p. 88).

The Social Contribution of Culture

By no later than the 1970s, it was Clifford Geertz who gave the term of culture a strong ethnological coloring (Geertz 1983, 1987). Geertz coined a semiotic comprehension of culture as he assumes that culture consists of a social coding that has to be decrypted. According to Geertz, culture is steadily produced and modified; as a result it is always subject to new interpretations by social actors: Culture cannot be objective. In so doing, Geertz expressly refers to Max Weber, who viewed man involved in a "homespun web of sense": While Geertz calls that "web" culture (cf. ib.: 9), he describes a nonstatic figure, waiting to get filled with life and being thickly described (cf. ib.: 21). That sort of cultural understanding allows us to realize that culture is always fragile and changing and helps us to understand the complex issue of Diversity again.

That creative location of culture I was drafting in my reference to Geertz is specifically organized on the state level of political representation. It is up to culture as some kind of "ethical pedagogy" (cf. Eagleton 2000, p. 7) to give a focus to the different ideas, visions and interests of individuals. Perhaps this is owed to the "humanitarian" role of culture. In this context the literary scholar Terry Eagleton stresses the social contribution of culture, claiming, "What culture does, then, is distil our common humanity from our sectarian political selves, redeeming the spirit from the senses, wresting the changeless from the temporal, and plucking unity from diversity" (ib.).

Such a reflexive perspective on culture allows us to deal with the cyclical "bubble" of Diversity in a critical way: On one side the complex mechanisms of power work against an entire overtaking of culture. On the other side we have to consider the *powerful control* of living conditions and lifestyles, despite their growing differentiation (Hörning 1999, p. 102). The impact of power on culture is most notably expressed in the imaginations, desires, artifacts and identities produced by the European, Japanese and North American culture industries—including hegemonic effects on international communication networks (cf. Hall 1999, p. 430). In this connection the sociologist Karl H. Hörning has shown the different functions of *social* and *cultural control*: While social control relates to individuals, groups or social relationships, cultural control describes authority over knowledge and skills. In historical terms, this differentiation goes back to the twentieth century when social control more and more contradicted the egalitarian principle of democratic societies. Making sure the balance of power required more subtle, allegedly non-ideological control mechanisms. By creating hegemonic cultural categories—like the selecting education system Bourdieu would call "institutionalized cultural capital"—the genesis of a political power vacuum was resisted early on (Hörning 1999, p. 103).

While we are able to distinguish between social and cultural control functions, it is not easy to decide which contemporary social conflict situations are of social or cultural origin. It seems natural that social and cultural tensions are rather mutually dependent. As people express themselves evermore through completely different lifestyles, we see that cultural commonalities are losing weight. As a result we are faced with problems of communication, translation and interpretation relating to every single dimension Diversity incorporates (gender, ethnicity, age etc.). In so doing, social actors reveal and question the accepted norms as they develop new distinctive identities (cf. ib.: 103f.).

The Concept of Shifting Identities

As the cultural studies emphasize the ambivalence and discrepancy of "culture" and "identity", we become sensitized to diverse lifestyles and mentalities. Yet we have to remember Bourdieu's idea of a relatively stable habitus, more than ever when we talk about "shifting identities" (Hall 1999, p. 430): All too often the cultural studies fueled an "extreme relativism" (Hörning 1999, p. 88) by disregarding social structural concepts like milieu-theories (cf. specially Vester et al. 2001).

The conceptual location of Diversity is neither definite nor consistent. The term itself pulls its weight. However, the cultural studies allow us to use Diversity as an integrated tool of analysis that concerns and combines relevant dimensions of heterogeneity, according to specific settings. The cultural studies oppose the conception of "totalized" cultural identities, considering individuals to be provided with definable and distinctly discriminable identities (Hörning 1999, p. 111). In this context identity is rather a multidimensional, often inconsistent and basically constructed issue. This assumption refers to Stuart Hall's concept of fragmented identities: Talking about variety, we have to focus the postmodern, subject-related variety of identities which is—to keep it short and simple—a result of globalization. Today we proceed on the assumption that identities are scattered and decentered. The "crisis of identity", powered by change of temporal and spatial determinations, is expressed in two respects: in relation to the location in the social and cultural world plus in terms of the person himself (Hall 1999, p. 393ff.). In this context, we notice a growth of choices between different identities in the centers of globalization—the cities and metropoles (ib.: 430).

Conflicting Scenarios on Cultural Difference

Diversity—compared with societal ideas like *multiculturalism* (cf. Taylor 1994)—increases sensitivity in dealing with differences *inside* a certain group, considering that all cultures are interwoven, highly complex and differentiated (cf. Eagleton 2000, p. 15). Generally we might consider the concept of multiculturalism—whose characteristics differ again between the single nation states—as an antipode of Diversity. Through the "discovery" of ethnic background "multiculti" usually narrows down to put minorities in a certain place (which most times is connected with gastronomic variety), instead of using flexible and modifiable conceptions of inclusion. So, when the discussion about permanent ethnic segregation in Europe begins we realize that *inter*cultural integration might be a satisfactory reaction to the complexity of cultural diversity.

All in all Diversity is not about "them" versus "us". We have to be aware of cultural stereotypes, remembering that all cultures are interwoven in some way. It will do to consult the anthropologist Arjun Appadurai to realize that the postmodern world has never been into a "Clash of Civilizations" (Huntington 1996), we rather witness a "clash of ideocides" or a "clash of civicides" (Appadurai 2006, p. 117).

This means that tensions can occur not just *across* but also *within* certain collectives—be it nations, cultures or small-scale milieus (cf. ib.: 118). In connection with the *postcolonial discourse,* we may finally focus on the concept of hybridity which has been coined by Homi K. Bhabha. Hybridity describes the "liquefication" of different cultural influences, set free not least by global migration movements. According to Bhabha, the diverse constellation of hybrid cultures changes normative cultural values on the national and subnational level. The challenge of cultural translation gets even more complex through this process while it requires a high level of sensitivity and empathy (Bhabha 2007).

Apart from that we may doubt the hegemonic force of a concept like hybridity—that has a close affiliation to the concept of ethnicity anyway: It is Appadurai again who points out the deeply rooted "Fear of Small Numbers" which is significant for *majoritarianism.* Accordingly, being in a majority is just not enough for aggressive—or like Appadurai says, "predatory"—identities: the smaller and weaker the minority, the bigger the ethnical rage of the majority (Appadurai 2006, p. 53). In a manner of speaking, such a perspective seems to contradict the concept of hybridity as well as the paradigm of shifting identities.

Concluding the theoretical framework so far, we realize that Diversity is dependent on its specific requirements of implementation. In the field of local educational program development we have to consider the effect of subjective perception as well as the importance of identity politics before we arrive at a decision, therefore leading us to know what is best for our addressees, as their needs would then be the basis for program development.

Political Background and Sociopolitical Challenges of Diverse Societies

While we are dealing with migration in a European context, we have to make clear what is behind this ambivalent issue: the European Commission has always been trying to promote inner-European labor-migration—without success so far (cf. Bach 2008, p. 147). At the same time we all have in mind a completely different form of migration as we recall the images of desperate refugees trying to reach Lampedusa.

Considering migration within the EU-27 we determine that Romanians are the most mobile EU citizens (1.7 million people or 5.4% of EU foreign population in 2008). Most of them usually resident in another EU member state live in Spain, Italy or Hungary while most of the Greeks crossing borders within the EU prefer to live in Germany (431.000 people or 1.4%). The biggest group among non-EU foreigners are Turkish citizens (2.4 million people or 7.9% of EU foreign population in 2008) while the second biggest group (1.7 million people or 5.6%) are Moroccans. Most of the Turks in the EU live in Germany while the majority of Moroccans in the EU resides in Spain, France or Italy (Eurostat 2009, p. 3f.; cf. Fig. 8.1):

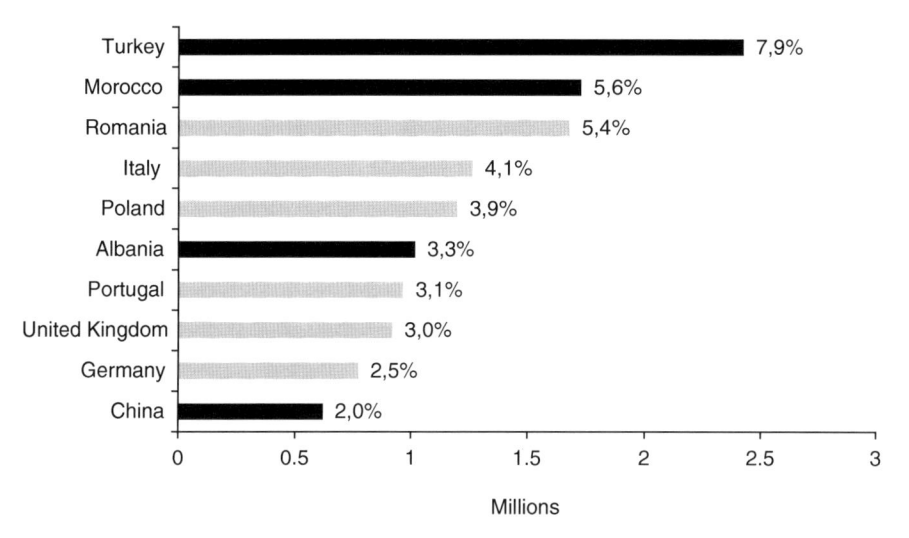

Country	Percentage
Turkey	7,9%
Morocco	5,6%
Romania	5,4%
Italy	4,1%
Poland	3,9%
Albania	3,3%
Portugal	3,1%
United Kingdom	3,0%
Germany	2,5%
China	2,0%

Fig. 8.1 Ten most numerous groups of foreign citizens usually resident in EU-27, as a percentage of EU total foreign population in 2008. Source: Eurostat (2009, p. 3) Citizenship of an EU-27 member state is marked with gray figure bars; citizenship of a non-EU country is in black

While on the international level the course is set for the advancement of Europe as an economic power, the responsibility for sociopolitical support rests mainly on individual nation states, regions and communities. In virtue of the European Employment Strategy, Diversity has always been related to European employment policy. By now, the providers of regional and urban development are required to encourage the cooperation between all relevant actors, for example within integrated development concepts. Above all the headline goals are full employment and social cohesion (cf. Ullrich 1999, p. 171ff.), as key qualifications seem to be the answer to "manage" one's own employability (cf. Wacker 2009).

"New Europe" and the Goals of Social Integration

The year 2010 is the *European Year for Combating Poverty and Social Exclusion* (European Commission 2009a) which is an example for Europe's strong publicity concerning the integration of Europe's multicultural population. Managing Diversity in Europe has become more important through the EU's latest enlargement. The fact alone that 25 different ethnic minorities live in Romania underlines this discovery (European Commission 2003, p. 98). As the year 2007 was the *European Year of Equal Opportunities for All* (European Commission 2009b) Europe's accentuation of diversity and inclusion—as well as the stress of national and regional heterogeneity—is somehow "amazing" and seems to cut across the hegemonic cultural understanding of the EU ("be mobile", "be flexible" and not least "be adaptable").

However, migration into prosperous regions has put cultural norms in motion. At the same time Europe's linguistic and cultural diversity causes barriers of communication (cf. Benz et al. 2000, p. 208; Bach 2008, p. 147).

On the one hand, there is a marked trend toward activating EU-employment policy. Economically—just like in the USA—the so called "high potentials" have to be expected on the minorities' side, due to the demographic transition (cf. Vedder 2006, p. 5f.). On the other hand, an increasing part of the population is not reached by the several relevant programs of the National Action Plans and is missing out on the promises of *Europeanization*. Experiencing immobility and exclusion in the middle of a dynamic environment may cause anti-European resentments as well.[3] In this connection it is full of irony that dealing with Europeanization and the slow downfall of the nation state forces us to think of the regionalism-discourse which dates back to the 1980s (cf. Elkar 1981).

As the European integration is taking place on the local, first of all the urban level, Diversity may be a mediating concept between the EU's symbolic policy and local politics for local educational program development. In this connection we have to consider the expectable tensions being expressed in the neighborhood.

Local Educational Programs—Tensions Between EU Policy and Local Politics

The challenges of Europeanization are particularly highlighted in the "detached" suburbs. The neighborhood serves as a place of learning (that implies the hegemonic conveyance of values and norms via the dominant groups of a district) and a place of stability (that implies the integrative efforts of the district's active social agents, e.g. key personalities or multipliers) (Urban and Weiser 2006). Different spatial-use-behavior or interests may lead to social conflicts, social disparity and exclusion (cf. Häußermann and Siebel 2004, p. 118). For example, segregation—especially social and ethnic forms (cf. Krummacher 2007, p. 111ff.)—illustrates the areal component of Diversity. At the same time it questions its physical existence on the basis of the spatial concentration of certain groups.

In the field of social urban development we necessarily come across the "phenomena" diversity: For example, in the deprived residential areas which are located on the outskirts of a city, there are often a high degree of social problems. Deficiencies of urban building, environmental problems, infrastructural deficits, social, economical and cultural issues, neighborly clashes and frequently negative images lead to *felt* and *physical* downward spirals (DIFU 2009). These deficiencies also can be seen as the key challenges to modern urban development. Urban development influences the change of urban structures as it is influenced by the interests of vari-

---

[3] These resentments renew questions about the legitimation of Euro-political decisions. For example, in Germany the ratification of the Treaty of Lisbon by means of plebiscite would certainly not be assured (cf. Wefing 2009, p. 9).

ous populations, particular social actors and subtle power structures as well. This always implies a certain degree of disparity between these social actors (cf. Häußermann and Siebel 2004, p. 118). The stepwise harmonization of that disparity leading to the establishment of social cohesion is the original content of social urban development.

When we talk about "resources" in highly deprived neighborhoods we likewise talk about a heterogenic mass of "outsiders" (Bude 2008). Considering the uneven *distribution* of resources like power, education or wealth we have to face the fact that particular resources—not least the autochthons' ones—are workable while others—which are generally the allochtones' ones—are not demanded or obviously obsolete. In short: Why can't migrants, irrespective of their (technical or professional) qualifications, apply their individual and collective resources profitably (cf. Thiesen 2009)? Consulting Bhabha again we are coming face to face with the *chances* of hybridity: There is much to be said for examining how far the autochthones can draw on the resources of the allochthones—resources they once were able to bring in, before they realized they are worth nothing by then.

Objectives for a Diversity-Based Local Educational Program

The challenge of a diversity-sensitive practice is to be able to deal with its own contradictions. We have to focus on the question of how the individual resources of a highly heterogenic urban population can be cultivated while coping at the same time with the mechanisms of workfare (cf. Esping-Andersen 2002, Wyss 2007).

As we begin to discuss Diversity—be it as a paradigm or be it as a concept—we immediately have to focus on the objectives for its implementation in an educational program; otherwise discussing Diversity would be pointless. As the objectives of local educational programs correspond structurally with the objectives of the EU, it is easy to name them: Employment development and social cohesion are at the heart of Europe's integration policy. Realizing that all European antidiscrimination efforts are linked to gainful employment, we have to deal with the effects of these efforts on the local community in a creative way while initiating local educational projects. These educational projects are being refinanced ever more through the European Social Funds. As communities effectuate more and more Europe's—or more precisely the EU's—political targets, local professional actors practicing Diversity Management have to walk a tightrope: They must combine manifold forms of activation to get a solid basis of support from their clientele.

Regarding new professions of the service sector, educational programming has to focus on key competences which are increasing importance to the workforce. Not just by chance the Organization for Economic Cooperation and Development (OECD) has mentioned "interacting in heterogeneous groups" in its selection of key competences (OECD 2005, p. 12). The variety of pluralistic societies has led to a boom of *soft skills* like empathy or the ability to work in a team. Above, the relevance of *social capital* is distinctly valued. This development actually carries a chance for eminently deprived groups like long-term unemployed or single parents. While educators detect and support their "hidden", not recognized potentials, they may run a chance to step into an "untrodden" field and create a new work order. This detection process may be done through the advancement of assessment tests or through more intensive biographical examination of their clientele. Local educators have to reflect what is "behind" the complex cultural settings they are dealing with. Remembering the concept of hybridity educators should examine the potentials of hybrid language. A vast number of young migrants create specific codes of communication by mixing vocabulary of different languages. This implies a high level of creativity and intelligence. Thinking of the concept of fragmented identities the example of hybrid language also exemplifies how specific milieus develop new ways of identification. Educators should not leave these skills unexploited. From another point of view they have to be aware not just to "use" their addressees' potentials for the sake of social cohesion—by educating intercultural multipliers, nannies, etc.— to express it vividly: The "needs" have to correlate with the "wants".

This leads me to the following questions I would like to link with the aforenamed theoretical framework: Regarding the level of management: Are local educational institutions sensitized to the issues of Diversity? Regarding the relevance of social transmission: In which way can allochthones "field" their skills in the domain of everyday culture? Regarding the relevance of cultural capital: Which opportunities does Diversity *hide* when trying to develop educational programming in deprived districts? Regarding the dependence on the specific situation: How do people in different social settings cope with diversity? And not least regarding the relevance of power: What kind of interests are behind the oppositions against the paradigm Diversity?

Without giving quick answers to those fundamentally important questions we can detect that Diversity in its political adoption is not so much about a new *way* of integration but all the more about its normative *objectives*: But, while every EU-financed project which focuses on employment and social cohesion must stress the importance of "resources," "potentials," or simply "talents" of their addressees, we have to consider that individuals use particular accesses to activate their specific resources—quantitatively and qualitatively.

To use an economic term: The "innovative" component of Diversity—in contrast to other concepts of integration—is on the one hand the appreciation of *individuality* and particular interests and needs. On the other hand it stresses *similarities* between different individuals or groups (cf. Vedder 2006, p. 10). Above all, the challenge is to determine the *missing link* between individualism and universalism. It seems natural to (re-)declare the human rights as a suitable link. In addition, we have to develop a universal framework for Diversity. Summarizing the mentioned influencing variables, Diversity needs a *contentual*, a *spatial*, an *institutional*, a *(everyday) cultural* and a *political–judicial framework* (see Fig. 8.2).

The concept of Diversity could definitely give new answers to the urgent questions of learning processes in heterogenic cultural settings. In doing so, diversity and pluralism are considered as chances while educational institutions:

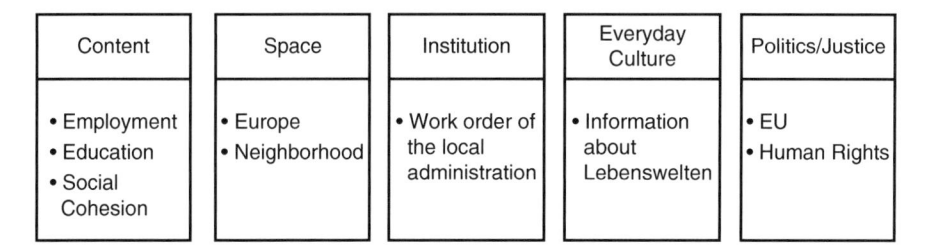

Content	Space	Institution	Everyday Culture	Politics/Justice
• Employment • Education • Social Cohesion	• Europe • Neighborhood	• Work order of the local administration	• Information about Lebenswelten	• EU • Human Rights

Fig. 8.2 Framework for Diversity in local educational programs

- encourage the multilingualism of migrants and minorities instead of constraining them to linguistic assimilation,
- take the visionary suggestions and—sometimes—creative strategies of avoidance of excluded persons seriously instead of stipulating terms they will not be able to discharge,
- appreciate the work experience of old people instead of infantilizing them,
- train their employees toward diversity-sensitive behaviors instead of pretending that there is no need.

Conclusion

Diversity *stresses* and likewise *overcomes* social and cultural differences. In doing so, the postulation of Diversity is full of contradictions. On one side every imaginable form of difference may be "examined" under the "microscope" of Diversity so that subjects are able to choose between different identities. On the other side Diversity accumulates all kinds of differences by relativizing them through its duplication. The politics of identity become irrelevant in this case (Mecheril 2009).

If Diversity, specifically in the context of the unequal access to education, really offers the chance to overcome culturally charged attributions, then a Diversity-based local educational program would finally appreciate that old paradigm called "equality of opportunity." Hannah Arendt once claimed that "having the right to have rights" is the basis for implementation of Human Rights. This applies to education as well. Diversity is a suitable concept for local educational programs as long as it considers the individual's need to have equal opportunities.

References

Appadurai, A. (2006). *Fear of small numbers: An essay on the geography of anger*. Durham: Duke University Press.

Bach, M. (2008). *Europa ohne Gesellschaft: Politische Soziologie der Europäischen Integration*. Wiesbaden: VS Verlag für Sozialwissenschaften.

Benz, B., Boeckh, J., & Huster, E.-U. (2000). *Sozialraum Europa: Ökonomische und politische Transformation in Ost und West*. Opladen: Leske & Budrich Verlag.

Bhabha, H. K. (2007). *Die Verortung der Kultur: Unveränderter Nachdruck der 1. Auflage 2000*. Tübingen: Stauffenburg Verlag.

Bourdieu, P. (2006). *Wie die Kultur zum Bauern kommt: Über Bildung, Schule und Politik*, hrsg. von Margareta Steinrücke, Hamburg: VSA-Verlag.

Breckner, I. (1999). Soziales in der Stadt des 21. Jahrhunderts: Beschaffenheit und Perspektiven. Vorgänge, 38 (1), S. 83–92.

Bude, H. (2008). *Die Ausgeschlossenen: Das Ende vom Traum der gerechten*. Gesellschaft, München: Hanser Verlag.

DIFU – Deutsches Institut für Urbanistik. (2009). Soziale Stadt – Programmhintergrund. http://www.sozialestadt.de/programm/hintergrund. Accessed 24 March 2009.

Eagleton, T. (2000). *The idea of culture*. Oxford: Blackwell.

Elkar, R. S. (Hrsg.). (1981). *Europas unruhige Regionen: Geschichtsbewußtsein und europäischer Regionalismus*. Stuttgart: Klett-Cotta Verlag.

Esping-Andersen, G. (2002). *Why we need a new welfare state*. Oxford: Oxford University Press.

Esser, H. (1980). *Aspekte der Wanderungssoziologie*. Darmstadt/Neuwied: Luchterhand Verlag.

European Commission. (2003). Equality, diversity and enlargement: Report on measures to combat discrimination in acceding and candidate countries, Luxemburg.

European Commission. (2009a). European Year for combating poverty and social exclusion. http://ec.europa.eu/social/main.jsp?langId=en&catId=637. Accessed 31 October 2009.

European Commission (2009b): European Year of equal opportunities for all. http://ec.europa.eu/employment_social/eyeq/index.cfm?&. Accessed 31 October 2009.

Eurostat. (2009). Statistics in Focus 94/2009, Citizens of European countries account for the majority of the foreign population in EU-27 in 2008. http://epp.eurostat.ec.europa.eu/cache/ITY_OFFPUB/KS-SF-09-094/EN/KS-SF-09-094-EN.PDF. Accessed 10 January 2010.

Fuchs, M. (2007). Diversity und Differenz – Konzeptionelle Überlegungen. In G. Krell, B. Riedmüller, B. Sieben, & D. Vinz (Hrsg.): Diversity Studies. Grundlagen und disziplinäre Ansätze, (S. 17–34). Frankfurt a. Main: Campus Verlag.

Geertz, C. (1983/1987). Dichte Beschreibung: Beiträge zum Verstehen kultureller Systeme. Frankfurt a. Main: Suhrkamp Verlag.

Geiling, H. (2005). Zur Theorie und Methode einer Stadtteilanalyse. http://212.12.126.151/cms/index.php?option=com_content&task=view&id=68&Itemid=262. Accessed 20 March 2009.

Guthrie, W. (1942). And the mixture is all of us and we're still mixing. Citation from "She came along to me". www.woodyguthrie.org/Lyrics/She_Came_Along_to_Me.htm. Accessed 11 November 2009; available on: Billy Bragg & Wilco (1998): Mermaid Avenue, Audio-CD, New York.

Hall, S. (1999). Kulturelle Identität und Globalisierung. In K. H. Hörning & R. Winter (Hrsg.): Widerspenstige Kulturen. Cultural Studies als Herausforderung, (S. 393–441). Frankfurt a. Main: Suhrkamp Verlag.

Hansen, K. P. (2003). *Kultur und Kulturwissenschaft*, 3 Aufl. Tübingen und Basel: A. Francke Verlag.

Häußermann, H., & Siebel, W. (2004). *Stadtsoziologie – Eine Einführung*. Frankfurt a. Main: Campus Verlag.

Hörning, K. H. (1999). Kulturelle Kollisionen. Die Soziologie vor neuen Aufgaben. In K. H. Hörning, & R. Winter (Hrsg.): Widerspenstige Kulturen. Cultural Studies als Herausforderung, (S. 84–115). Frankfurt a. Main: Suhrkamp Verlag.

Huntington, S. P. (1996). *The clash of civilizations*. New York: Simon & Schuster.

INSEAD – The Business School for the World. (2009). Diversity is not Diversity. Video-interview with Prof. Katherine Klein. http://tv.insead.edu/. Accessed 15 November 2009.

Krell, G., Riedmüller, B., Sieben, B., & Vinz, D. (Hrsg.). (2007a). Diversity Studies. Grundlagen und disziplinäre Ansätze. Frankfurt a. Main: Campus Verlag.

Krell, G., Riedmüller, B., Sieben, B., & Vinz, D. (2007b). Einleitung – Diversity Studies als integrierende Forschungsrichtung. In: Dies. (Hrsg.): Diversity Studies. Grundlagen und disziplinäre Ansätze, (S. 7–16.) Frankfurt a. Main: Campus Verlag.

Krummacher, M. (2007). Zum Umgang mit "Minderheitenghettos". In W.-D. Bukow, C. Nikodem, E. Schulze, & E. Yildiz (Hrsg.): Was heißt hier Parallelgesellschaft? Zum Umgang mit Differenzen, (S. 109–120). Wiesbaden: VS Verlag für Sozialwissenschaften.

Luig, U. (2007). Diversity als Lebenszusammenhang – Ethnizität, Religion und Gesundheit im transnationalen Kontext. In G. Krell, B. Riedmüller, B. Sieben, & D. Vinz (Hrsg.): Diversity Studies – Grundlagen und disziplinäre Ansätze, (S. 87–108). Frankfurt a. Main: Campus Verlag.

Mecheril, P. (2009). Diversity: Die Macht des Einbezugs. http://www.migration-boell.de/web/diversity/48_1012.asp. Accessed 17 September 2009.

Melter, C., & Mecheril, P. (Hrsg.). (2009). *Rassismuskritik. Band 1: Rassismustheorie und -forschung.* Schwalbach/Ts.: Wochenschau Verlag.

OECD - Organization for Economic Cooperation and Development. (2005). The definition and selection of key competences. Executive summary. http://www.oecd.org/dataoecd/47/61/35070367.pdf. Accessed 1 November 2009.

Prengel, A. (2006). *Pädagogik der Vielfalt: Verschiedenheit und Gleichberechtigung in Interkultureller, Feministischer und Integrativer Pädagogik,* 3 Aufl. Wiesbaden: VS Verlag für Sozialwissenschaften.

Rosa, H. (2005). *Beschleunigung: Die Veränderung der Zeitstrukturen in der Moderne.* Frankfurt a. Main: Suhrkamp Verlag.

Scherr, A. (2008). Alles so schön bunt hier? Eine Einleitung zum Themenschwerpunkt. In Sozial Extra Nov./Dez. 2008, 32. S. 11–12.

Simmel, G. (2006). *Die Großstädte und das Geistesleben.* Frankfurt a. Main: Suhrkamp Verlag.

Taylor, C. (1994). Multiculturalism: With commentary by K. Anthony Appiah, Jürgen Habermas, Steven C. Rockefeller, Michael Walzer, and Susan Wolf. Edited and introduced by Amy Gutmann. Princeton: Princeton University Press.

Thiesen, A. (2009). Vielfalt als Humanressource? Diversity als neues Paradigma in der Jugendberufshilfe. In L. Finkeldey & A. Thiesen (Hrsg.): Case management in der Jugendberufshilfe. Materialien für Theorie, Praxis und Studium der Sozialen Arbeit, (S. 143–156). Hildesheim: Olms Verlag.

Ullrich, O. (1999). Regionalisierung: Die räumliche Grundlage für eine zukunftsfähige Lebensweise. In L. Finkeldey (Hrsg.): Tausch statt Kaufrausch, (S. 171–184). Bochum: SWI Verlag.

Urban, M., & Weiser, U. (2006). Kleinräumige Sozialraumanalyse. Theoretische Grundlagen und praktische Anwendung – Identifikation und Beschreibung von Sozialräumen mit quantitativen Daten. Dresden: Saxonia Verlag.

Vedder, G. (2005). Denkanstöße zum Diversity Management. Arbeit, Heft 1/2005, S. 34–43.

Vedder, G. (2006). Die historische Entwicklung von Diversity Management in den USA und in Deutschland. In G. Krell & H. Wächter (Hrsg.): Diversity management: Impulse aus der Personalforschung, (S. 1–23) München und Mering: Rainer Hampp Verlag.

Vertovec, S. (2007, November). Super-diversity and its implications.*Ethnic and Racial Studies, 30* (6), 1024–1054.

Vester, M., von Oertzen, P., Geiling, H., Hermann, T., & Müller, D. (2001). Soziale Milieus im gesellschaftlichen Strukturwandel: Zwischen Integration und Ausgrenzung, Frankfurt a. Main: Suhrkamp Verlag.

Wacker, A. (2009). "Employability" – Anforderungen an Beschäftigte und Arbeitsplatzsuchende heute. In L. Finkeldey & A. Thiesen (Hrsg.): Case management in der Jugendberufshilfe. Materialien für Theorie, Praxis und Studium der Sozialen Arbeit, (S. 11–23) Hildesheim: Olms Verlag.

Wefing, H. (2009). Bis hierher, Europa. Die Zeit Nr. 7 v. 5. February 2009, S. 9.

Williams, R. (1983). *Culture and society 1780–1950,* 2nd Ed. New York: Columbia University Press.

Wyss, K. (2007). *Workfare: Sozialstaatliche Repression im Dienst des globalisierten Kapitalismus.* Zürich: Edition 8.

Chapter 9
Family Child-Raising and Educational Strategies Among European Mixed Couples

Sofia Gaspar

Introduction

This chapter reports original findings from a study of the socialization strategies among upper-middle-class European families of mixed nationality. Children from a bi-national EU milieu hold certain social, symbolic and economic resources that help protect them from marginal positions or discrimination in the host society, as this is quite a privileged social group in terms of social class and ethnic origin. European children from an affluent family and belonging to a homogeneous ethnic group in terms of race, culture, citizenship and religion normally become an 'invisible social group' within the host state. However, despite extensive research on immigrant children in recent decades, most publications by European scholars have been about underprivileged social groups belonging to migrant workers' communities (Thomson and Crul 2007; Crul and Vermeulen 2003). Hence, apart from some isolated attempts (Finnäs and O'Leary 2003; Wagner 1998), very little is known about child-raising strategies among privileged migrants.

The aim of this chapter is to examine the choices expressed by EU parents of mixed nationality residing in Lisbon for their offspring's socialization, specifically in relation to the transmission of linguistic capital, formal education (the school selected), and the nature of social networks.[1] Each of these parental options clarifies whether their socialization goals are developed in order to perpetuate their high status as a minority group (Finnäs and O'Leary 2003; Lieberson 1985) and the cosmopolitan capital normally associated to the family (Weenink 2008).

In light of the lack of information, the chapter is divided into five sections with the aim of expanding our knowledge in this field: taking EU social integration as a starting point, the next section argues that the rise of intra-European families is

---

[1] Some studies that contextualize social and family features of the Portuguese society can be found in detail in Torres (2008, 2004) and Torres and Silva (1998).

S. Gaspar (✉)
ISCTE-IUL, CIES-IUL, Av. das Forças Armadas, 1649-026 Lisbon, Portugal
e-mail: sofia.gaspar@iscte.pt

an emerging phenomenon that must be considered when studying privileged interethnic minorities. Some fundamental aspects of how parents raise transcultural children are then identified. The following section describes the methodology for the collection of the original data, before the analysis of the educational 'ideal types' that emerged from the empirical information. The final section summarizes the key points and examines the potential implications of 'privileged interethnic EU children' as a social group in the debates on upbringing processes among minorities.

European Mixed Families as an Emerging Social Type

The free movement of persons within the European Union has originated one of the most important mobility-promoting spaces in contemporary societies. The 1985 Schengen Agreement and the 1992 Maastricht Treaty set Europeans' geographical mobility beyond national borders and greatly facilitated access to other EU countries. This European measure, accompanied by a wave of migration in the globalized world and the rise of mass tourism, has contributed to the social and cultural blending of different national groups. Indeed, the most frequent reasons for moving cited by people within the EU—work education, tourism, personal self-fulfilment and emotional relationships—are motivating growing numbers of people and strengthening the European social integration process (Ackers 1998; Recchi and Favell 2009).

One point emerging in this context, which I have defended (Gaspar 2009, 2008) and others have also confirmed (Santacreu et al. 2009), is that *geographical mobility is fomenting the increase in European mixed marriages*. EU-free movers are emerging as a particular social group within the European matrimonial market and it thus becomes crucial to assess how these partnerships create specific transcultural family arrangements and socialization patterns for children. However, there is still a lack of research into intra-EU partnerships. Apart from certain exceptions (Ackers 1998; Braun and Recchi 2008; Gaspar 2009, 2008; Lauth Bacas 2002; Nowicka 2006; Santacreu et al. 2009; Santacreu and García 2008; Scott and Cartledge 2009), relatively little research has been dedicated to the theme when compared to mixed families with at least one non-European partner. To be precise, most studies on binational marriage in Europe have centred on unions between European natives and migrant workers from underprivileged European and non-European backgrounds (Cortina et al. 2008; González Ferrer 2006; Kalmijn and van Tubergen 2006; Klein 2001; Rodríguez García 2006; Rother 2008; van Tubergen and Maas 2007) with the aim of assessing the social integration of these minority communities within the host countries.

So why is an EU mixed marriage a sociologically relevant object of study? The marital union between citizens from different national contexts inside the EU (Gaspar 2008, 2009) is an excellent context to evaluate how particular values and social meanings are negotiated, constructed and developed on a daily basis within a

European political and institutional setting.[2] The legal status of EU partners provides them with secure basic conditions to live in a foreign country as part of a *privileged migrant group*, with their civil rights fully guaranteed by the host state. Marriage to another EU citizen does not involve the legal procedures applied to non-EU spouses and enables the couple to enjoy citizenship and free movement across intra-European borders. European nationality offers citizens more advantages than other groups of migrants regarding residence, geographical mobility, civil rights, legally guaranteed freedom from discrimination, and an easier access to employment. In short, EU citizenship is a powerful source of social inclusion and acceptance for ethnic minorities in the host society.[3] This legal system also guarantees the construction of *cross-border geographical mobility*, which can in time be experienced by both partners as a *private and internal in-between EU region* (Lauth Bacas 2002).

European citizens also tend to have more *symbolic prestige* associated with their nationality. 'Being European' or 'Western' might symbolize belonging to an ethnic group which enjoys positive advantages in an 'ethnic ranking system' and is therefore less likely to cause negative social discrimination in the host society. This idea is consistent with some of the studies that have furthered our knowledge of privileged migrants, revealing that nationality, profession or social class often confer these groups a positive social status (see O'Leary and Finnäs 2002; Stierna 2003; Wagner 1998). These findings highlighted the fact that *dominant minorities* can develop strategies to maintain and secure their class privileges and ethnic prestige even when part of a wider social community.

Accordingly, and as we are speaking of European ethnic minorities whose social status is symbolically valued, interethnic EU partnerships can be expected to encounter higher levels of social acceptance and integration than those between an EU citizen and non-EU partner (Gaspar 2009; Rother 2008; Scott and Cartledge 2009). This 'positive discrimination' may be transformed into symbolic capital that can act as a powerful tool in the adjustment practices developed into the host country. This is particularly relevant since belonging to a bi-national partnership produces specific conjugal dynamics inserted in a complex socio-cultural hybrid space, where both partners interact not only with natives of the host society but also with other foreign groups. Thus, both spouses and the whole family network (affinal and consanguineal) have to be reorganized around at least two different geographical and cultural places, which brings new forms of re-adaptation to all generations involved (Rodríguez García 2006). Even in the case of high assimilation levels, the internal structure these families tend to display creates and stimulates quite unique

---

[2] In the category 'EU countries' I include not only the EU-27 states but also neighboring countries (Iceland, Norway, Liechtenstein and Switzerland) that have privileged political and social relations with the EU.

[3] Although the social integration of a European citizen into another EU country tends to be easier than that of other types of migrant, this does not mean that this process is always unproblematic. Original research on intra-mobile migrants has shown that women, especially 'trailing spouses', still have social and legal difficulties in getting access to full citizenship inside the European Union (see Ackers 1998; Stalford 2005).

strategies, behaviours and patterns of cultural negotiation when compared to lifestyles of families from a single national background.

I shall now turn to issues related to upbringing patterns among interethnic minority families to shed light on whether EU relationships exhibit specific choices for children's socialization that warrant debate when considering wider rearing models for ethnic minority groups.

Upbringing and Education of Transnational Children

Due to their greater exposure to cosmopolitan influences and interactions, interethnic EU families tend to transmit these values to their children, whose lifestyles and behaviour are closer to transnational influences and mentalities than those of native children (Nowicka 2006; Wagner 1998; Weenink 2008). As the child-rearing plans of these couples are linked to different cultural and social codes of behaviour which interplay whenever a child is born, both parents have to negotiate and deal with cultural readjustment processes so as to achieve the best socialization outcomes for their offspring. In most cases, child-rearing strategies are merely defined as general sets of action and not as rigid predefined means or resources (social norms, values, beliefs and identities) which must be activated in the first years of a child's life. Only during the child's development do parents tend to re-adapt certain educational lines as the need arises (Rodríguez Marcos 2006). However, the necessity to negotiate and reconcile different national models of upbringing may not be free of tension and may force the family unit to come to some unforeseen agreements (see Rodríguez Garcia 2006).

According to previous studies, the main research areas into children's socialization in interethnic families involve language transmission, type of school selected and nature of the social family support networks (Deprez and Dreyfus 1998; Nowicka 2006; Rodríguez Marcos 2006; Wagner 1998). These choices are due both to the positive rewards and advantages they bring for the child's future, and also the importance attributed to affiliation within an ethnic group minority (Finnäs and O'Leary 2003). Choosing certain child-rearing strategies over others implies the capacity to select the most prestigious and powerful resources that can be converted into social capital and act as distinctive symbols to maintain an upper-middle-class position or guarantee the 'ethnic prestige' associated with particular national cultures (Lieberson 1985). The socialization options related to a child's future are thus good indicators of the social strategies of parents in dominant minorities to reproduce or attain social mobility in their class trajectories.[4]

Parents' decisions on *language transmission* usually involve retaining both native linguistic codes. However, the most educated groups were found to be more motivated and aware of the symbolic and positive benefits of the investment in

---

[4] A classical study on children's educational strategies across different social class positions is the one developed by Kellerhals and Montadon (1991).

bilingual skills than other less educated groups (Finnäs and O'Leary 2003; Rodríguez Marcos 2006; Wagner 1998; Weenink 2008). Nowadays the ability to express oneself in two or more languages is seen as a powerful resource that enriches the child's symbolic and social capital and augments his or her future competitive capabilities (Weenink 2007, 2008). On the other hand, bilingualism also acquires an affective meaning among transnational families as it enables the child to communicate with the extended family, especially grandparents and close relatives.

Research into bi-cultural education (Deprez and Dreyfus 1998; Nowicka 2006) has shown that the language of the destination society ultimately tends to dominate over other minority languages spoken within the family unit. Therefore, an interethnic child may not always have balanced bilingual skills or identify with both parents' original cultures equally as he/she will be governed by the leading culture of the host society. Another determinant aspect to the level of bilingual skills and cultural dominance in a child's identity is whether one of the parents is a national citizen. Research conducted by Deprez and Dreyfus (1998) in Paris and Dakar revealed that when one of the parents was a native citizen, the language transmission of the foreign partner was more likely to be disregarded within the family unit, whereas the two foreign languages tended to be preserved if both parents belonged to different national settings. Furthermore, the parent's gender is also thought to condition language transmission. Several studies have stressed the central role played by the mother in the child's linguistic development (Deprez and Dreyfus 1998; Finnäs and O'Leary 2003; Lomsky-Feder and Leibovitz 2010; Nowicka 2006), since she has been traditionally more involved in children's daily care in terms of household tasks and emotional support (Torres 2008; Torres and Silva 1998). This predominant role is therefore likely to make the mother more attentive to transmitting her native language and correcting the child's linguistic skills whether she is native-born or a foreigner.

A second area in which interethnic parents tend to invest is the type of *school system*. The selection of the formal education (private/public, national/international) is extremely important since it is one of the most powerful sources of ethnic transmission (Lieberson 1985; Finnäs and O'Leary 2003; Wagner 1998; Weenink 2008). Bi-national families put a lot of effort into choosing the most suitable school for their children although this choice is determined by their personal situation, the length of time they plan to stay in the destination country, future migration plans, the degree and nature of familial and community support networks and, most obviously, the quality attributed to different educational institutions.[5]

I believe the level of commitment to the country of residence is another very influential factor in parent's schooling decision. In fact, those registering their children in national schools tend to reveal a clear effort to assimilate. The use of formal national institutions symbolizes the wish for their children to socialize in a 'truly' homogeneous culture, thus boosting their level of social integration through personal relationships developed with local peers or the assimilation of the values,

---

[5] For a deep analysis of the formal and informal educational solutions adopted by Portuguese couples for their children in Lisbon, see the Torres and Silva (1998).

behaviours and practices of the host society they live in. However, as we are dealing with a social group from an upper-middle-class background, the reputation attributed to certain national school systems in terms of the quality of the curriculum and teachers may also be important when choosing a particular institution.

On the other hand, when an ethnic-minority school[6] is selected, this can be seen as a strategy for the reproduction or upward mobility of an upper-middle class (Weenink 2007, 2008). Studies conducted by Wagner (1998) and Weenink (2007, 2008) have shown that enrolment in international institutions not only follows a strategy of acquiring social prestige but also—and most importantly—the transmission of cosmopolitan capital to the children. In fact, international educational systems tend to be selective in their student recruitment, both because they are conceived as legitimate institutions for privileged ethnic-minority groups and they can only be afforded by upper-middle-class parents. The permanent movement of students enrolled in these schools justifies curricula contents that are easily transferable to other national environments and, therefore, suitable for the education of a 'transnational social elite'.

Apart from symbolizing a strategic choice for the reproduction of upper-middle social groups, minority-schools also represent one of the few resources available to interethnic parents for transmitting their languages and socializing children into an international atmosphere close to their cultural and national repertoires. These schools are often conceived as 'small societies' governed by their own social codes and formal educational principles which actually play an important role in the transmission of ethnic identification, not only by reinforcing linguistic skills but also by transmitting wider cultural references to specific foreign groups (Finnäs and O'Leary 2003; Lieberson 1985; Wagner 1998).

Hence, international schools also serve as a privileged meeting place where both children and parents can encounter people from different cultural origins who contribute to their affiliation with a transnational culture (Wagner 1998). Being part of a formal internationalized system may be an opportunity to participate in multicultural enclaves that tend to reinforce feelings of group cohesion and social identity. This illustrates the importance of *social networks* on mixed families' adaptation to a host society and the degree to which those networks are also related to certain parental educational choices.

National social ties that help people go about their daily lives and acquire a sense of belonging to a host society are extremely important to the success of both children and parents' social integration. Fluid and constant interaction between the migrant and his/her living environment can assist adjustment to migration since social contacts with the local citizens can lead to more rapid assimilation of the main culture. Besides, the social support system may be more directly linked to the locality when one member of the couple is a native of the host state than in situations where neither is a national citizen (Gaspar 2009; Rother 2008; Santacreu and García 2008;

---

[6] By 'ethnic-minority school' I mean the international institutions which can be found in any European city such as the British School, German School, and the French School.

Scott and Cartledge 2009).[7] Indeed, these couples may suffer more from the lack of informal and practical support (e.g. help with child care) and therefore intensify their transnational social contacts, which can sometimes mitigate the need for social assistance (e.g. profiting from grandparents' visits to invest more in professional or conjugal life) (Ackers 1998; Stalford 2005). In the face of integration difficulties in national support systems, a mixed (both national and foreign) or international network of friends therefore helps some families to overcome social isolation. Kinship ties with extended family members, friends, work colleagues, and neighbours can also shed light on families' choices about children's socialization. The experience and know-how of other transnational families about day-to-day matters such as schooling, medical care, child care services and affective support is a vital social capital in the migration adjustment process.

In short, although the upbringing of interethnic children is related to various macro- and microsocial processes that weave between the leading and minority cultures, some of the most important parental choices involve language transmission, the school system and the nature of social ties. After clarifying below the methodology adopted in my research, I shall reflect on the empirical evidence that has emerged in each mentioned dimensions.

Data and Methodology

A qualitative methodology was used in this study to provide insights into choices made by families regarding their children's upbringing. Although parents were contacted and asked to participate using a snowball technique, individuals from different social and cultural backgrounds were included as much as possible. After providing preliminary information by e-mail or telephone, semi-directed interviews of approximately 90 minutes were conducted with each parent. The interviews took place in the interviewee's home or office, the interviewer's home, or public places, and were conducted in English, Portuguese or Spanish, depending on each parent's language skills.

The information on child-rearing strategies was analysed using a set number of theoretical dimensions focusing on language transmission, type of school selected, and nature of the social family support networks.[8] Unlike previous investigations

---

[7] Research conducted by Torres and Silva (1998) on domestic and child arrangements in Lisbon has revealed that recurring to family networks (mainly to grandmothers) for child care assistance is less common than would have been expected among national Portuguese families (15–19% of the observed cases). However, the nature of this family help tends to increase to 20% if it is given on an informal and discontinuous basis, e.g. sometimes taking children to school or staying with them for a couple of hours when parents are unavailable.

[8] The interview was not limited to child-rearing issues but also included other dimensions such as duration of the couple's affective relationship, migration history, national and European identity, dynamics of conjugal life, division of household tasks, social integration, and future mobility plans.

focusing on just one partner (Scott and Cartledge 2009), both mother and father were asked the same questions separately to obtain each couple member's perspective on the child's upbringing. Hence, the data gathered were first scrutinized through content analysis of every participant's discourse, and subsequently coded into one of the pre-selected categories to create different *educational ideal types* for all family units. The MAXqda software package was used for the coding and retrieval of the data.

The original data reported here were collected from 24 individuals, representing 12 European interethnic families who had been living in the Greater Lisbon area for at least 1 year before the interview. On average, the couples had two children aged between 2 months and 10 years. The children of ten of the couples had dual nationality (both the father's and the mother's) with only two couples opting for single nationality for their offspring. The parents were recruited according to a particular group structure so as to control for gender and nationality:

- Portuguese men married to/cohabiting with European women (four couples);
- Portuguese women married to/cohabiting with European men (four couples);
- European men married to/cohabiting with European women of a third country (four couples).

An analysis of Table 9.1 reveals that the mean age was 37.1 years and men were slightly older (39.2 years) than the women (35 years). On average, the couple had been together for 9.5 years, including the dating period and the marriage or cohabitation. Ten couples were married and the remaining two were cohabiting. The socio-economic status of these parents was high and all interviewees were well educated—ten had a bachelor's degree, six a master's degree, and eight a PhD—and their professional lives were in keeping with these credentials. However, while in most cases both the mother and the father were working (nine dual-earner couples), three of the men were the sole breadwinners. A large proportion of the interviewees mentioned that they had lived in other foreign countries before Portugal (two, on average). This shows a fairly high mobility trajectory: among them, six out of eight Portuguese spouses had mobility experience of approximately 4 or 6 years in a foreign country, whereas their EU partners had a mean length of residence in Lisbon of about 6 years, ranging from 1.5 to 17 years. All participants were able to speak English competently, and had mastered at least four different languages.

Assessing Family Strategies on Children's Upbringing and Education

A content analysis of the data resulting from the interviews allowed the delineation of some ideal types of parental choice for language transmission (monolingual, bilingual, trilingual), formal education (public/private, national/international schools), and the nature of social family support networks (national, mixed, international).

9 Family Child-Raising and Educational Strategies Among European Mixed Couples 125

Table 9.1 Socio-demographic information of EU mixed families

Type of couple	Name	Sex	Age	Nationality	Length of relationship	Number of children	Age of the children	Nationality of the children	Languages of the children
PM-EW (Portuguese man-European woman)	Paulo	M	42	Portuguese	11 years	1	3 years	Portuguese and Greek	Portuguese and Greek
	Athina	F	38	Greek					
	Miguel	M	34	Portuguese	10 years	2	7 and 3 years	Portuguese and Maltese	Portuguese and English
	Gertrude	F	39	Maltese					
	Rodrigo	M	36	Portuguese	5 years	2	2 years and 3 months	Portuguese and Lituanian	Portuguese and Lituanian
	Ema	F	29	Lituanian					
	Bernardo	M	36	Portuguese	8 years	2	4 and 2 years	Portuguese and Polish	Portuguese, Polish some English
	Hanna	F	31	Polish					
EM-PW (European man-Portuguese woman)	Markus	M	39	German	10 years	2	3 years and 6 months	Portuguese and German	Portuguese and German
	Carlota	F	32	Portuguese					
	Albert	M	33	Belgian	9 years	1	2 months	Portuguese and Belgium	Portuguese and French
	Sara	F	33	Portuguese					
	Johann	M	42	German	10 years	2	9 and 6 years	Portuguese and German (oldest)	Portuguese
	Sónia	F	35	Portuguese					
	Jan	M	47	Belgian	2 years	1	3 months	Portuguese and Belgium	Portuguese
	Andreia	F	34	Portuguese					
EM-EW (European man-European woman)	Carlos	M	39	Spanish	6 years	2	2.5 years and 6 months	Belgium and Spanish	Spanish, French Portuguese
	Marie	F	30	Belgian					
	Sean	M	40	Irish	15 years	3	6 and 2 years, 3 months	French and Belgium	English and French
	Claire	F	40	F.-Belgian					
	Knut	M	47	Norwegian	15 years	2	13 and 10 years	French	French, Norweg. Portuguese
	Marguerite	F	43	French					
	Josep	M	36	Spanish	13 years	2	1 and 4	Spanish	Catalan, German Portuguese
	Angela	F	36	German					

As a result, three types of family child-raising strategies emerged—*family assimilation strategy*, *bi-national family strategy*, and *peripatetic family strategy*. The definition of these ideal types resulted from various combinations of criteria. The *family assimilation strategy* required at least two of the following: Portuguese as the dominant mother tongue, enrolment in a Portuguese state or private school and social networks that used native Portuguese citizens as the main source. The *bi-national family strategy* involved at least two processes: bilingual skills (mastering two languages equally), attendance at a national or international state/private school, and mixed or international social networks. Finally, inclusion in the *peripatetic family strategy* required at least two of the following patterns of socialization: trilingual skills without a clear dominance of one of the languages, the choice of a private or public international school, and international or mixed social networks as the main source of social capital.

Even though data analysis revealed no clear pattern in the relationship between the types of EU couple and the child-raising strategies, a scenario of social assimilation or bi-culturalism appears to be most likely when at least one of the parents is a native Portuguese citizen. Similarly, when both parents originate from two different countries (excluding Portugal), a peripatetic model is most common. If we now compare all the patterns observed, the *family assimilation model* is the most frequent (five cases), followed by the *bi-national family strategy* (four cases) and the *peripatetic family* pattern (three cases). Furthermore, and contrary to earlier investigations (Deprez and Dreyfus 1998), gender differences do not appear to determine child-raising choices in these families.

A detailed analysis of each ideal child-raising type is then elaborated in the next sections.

Family Assimilation Strategy

This strategy requires the couple to make a deliberate effort to assimilate into the host country. In this case, as mentioned before, certain issues involving language skills, type of school and social network links are very similar to those found within Portuguese society, whose social norms predominate over those of the European ethnic minority. Parental attitudes towards child-raising are therefore consciously in keeping with Portuguese culture on the development of a child's social and personal identity.

So how are these choices translated into specific family practices? According to the criteria set above, an *assimilation strategy* is developed when Portuguese becomes the dominant language, a local school is selected, and a predominantly Portuguese network is used. In short, Portuguese culture is taken as the benchmark. This is what happens in Johann (German) and Sónia (Portuguese) family: Portuguese is the only language spoken by the family, their children go to a state school and, though their circle of friends includes one or two foreigners, the core of their social network is Portuguese. Johann clearly explains why he does not speak German to his children:

> I made some attempts but I was never persistent! Apart from that, I used to feel I said things and no else understood! My wife didn't understand, and the kids didn't understand… Maybe it would have been easy if my wife understood German, it would have been easy to use German at home and Portuguese outside… But as she doesn't, I didn't do that. But I think I failed. If I had been persistent, my kids would have learnt. But that wasn't an important issue to me…(Johann, German, married to Sónia, Portuguese)

Johann's discourse reveals two central justifications for not teaching one's native language. Firstly, if one parent is unable to speak or understand the other's mother tongue, it interferes in communication between father/mother and child because one of the parents feels excluded by the other. In fact, when a parent communicates with a child, it often involves not only the two but it also is a subtle message to the other partner. Secondly, some individuals associate the decision to invest or not in language transmission with the symbolic significance or meanings attributed to their mother tongue. This attitude may well be related to weaker attachment to the original national identity or to permanent settlement and tend to increase a migrant's level of social and cultural assimilation. Moreover, the type of school the children attend is also consistent with an assimilation strategy. Economic and logistic factors can also contribute to the parents' decision when they opt for a particular school: as Sónia says, they chose a Portuguese state education not merely because they wanted their children '*to feel Portuguese and not feel different*' but also for economic reasons, as the German school was both extremely expensive and a long way from where they live.

Paulo (Portuguese) and Athina (Greek) can also be included among those adopting an assimilation strategy. Though both speak in their native languages to their son, he goes to a private Portuguese nursery and will later move into the national school system. Apart from one or two families, their social network is mainly Portuguese. Paulo recognizes that the preponderance of the national environment will be decisive in structuring his son's identity and upbringing and that Greek culture will represent a sort of 'imagined and exotic community' where they normally spend their summer holidays. The lack of educational structures (i.e. a Greek school) in Lisbon seems to determine the choice of school and influencing their son's national identity. As Athina notes,

> My son will never feel Greek the way I do… He's only going to feel Greek through me, through the relationship he has with me… And here in Portugal I don't think I can teach him much more than the language…(Athina, Greek, married to Paulo, Portuguese)

Although an assimilation strategy is more likely in a couple where one member belongs to the host society, this is not necessarily so. In fact, one of the couples interviewed—Josep (Spanish) and Annette (German)—came from two different foreign backgrounds but still considered the Portuguese pattern of child-raising preferable. For them, giving their children a cultural and geographical basis with which they could consistently identify was the most important aspect for their socialization. And although both speak to their sons in their mother tongue, Portuguese is spoken at home and they consider it the main source of communication between the couple and the children's best spoken language. Also, when mentioning the type of school selected, Annette explains:

> We are not going to put our children in international schools—either German or Spanish—because they already have these two cultures, these two languages, and they need to feel that they are based in one specific country. We think that they should feel Portuguese… Yes, they should feel that they are Portuguese! (Annette, German, cohabiting with Josep, Spanish)

In opting for the Portuguese state system, the couple clearly demonstrates their attempt to integrate into the receiving country and, ultimately, to avoid the feeling many interethnic parents experience of raising their children in a European 'no man's land'. They prefer to provide them with a sense of emotional and cultural belonging. Attendance at a state school will contribute to the development of a *'unique cultural input'* capable of guaranteeing good Portuguese as the first language and strengthening the social networks with Portuguese peers and their parents. Immersion in Portuguese society is then viewed as the 'ideal child-raising choice' for the acquisition of a solid and unambiguous cultural identity.

Bi-national Family Strategy

This second socialization pattern requires a 'living commitment' on the cultures of both parents, by making an equal investment in the transmission of the two national contexts of reference. This educational process creates a *bi-cultural upbringing* which not only implies acquiring different linguistic resources and national social codes, but may also means dividing families' lives between two places of residence. The discourse of these couples shows that the best solution for children is not simply *assimilation into one parent's country* but *simultaneous assimilation into those of both*. Markus explains this with particular clarity:

> I try to build an environment between Berlin and Lisbon… I think it will be good for our children if they feel two geographic anchors. And I feel we can build that, two places where they can relate to. I would like them to speak two languages perfectly (German and Portuguese), so that they can progress and identify with both countries. If we stay here in Portugal I would like them to go to a German school because I would be afraid that their German would not be perfect. I want them to speak in German, it is important to me… (Markus, German, married to Carlota, Portuguese)

Following a bi-national assimilation strategy also implies learning both parents' languages perfectly since bilingualism is assumed to be an enriching social capital and central to developing a 'truly dual identity'. In Markus's opinion, sending the children to the German school is an important way of ensuring that their formal education will take place within the culture of the ethnic minority parent. In fact, several of the couples included in this socialization strategy mentioned that sending their offspring to an international school was important to compensate for the cultural and symbolic dominance of Portugal. Besides, in Markus's view, raising children in a bi-cultural environment and thus giving them a solid sense of having a dual identity and two national attachments will not necessarily give them a sense of rootedness. As he explains,

We don't want to have 'Euro-children'. We want to have children raised with two European identities, but we don't want children that could feel everywhere and nowhere in Europe. (Markus, German, married to Carlota, Portuguese)

Like Markus and Carlota, Sean (Irish) and Claire (French-Belgian) try to raise their children by setting a bi-cultural identity. Although they represent a type of mixed couple that lives in a foreign state, this does not necessarily entail bringing the children up in a culture other than their own. As such, the leading role of Portuguese culture tends to be minimized as the family unit lives 'socially apart' from the host country. Language is one of the elements that most determines this socio-cultural isolation and their own social and working conditions in Lisbon: they have not mastered Portuguese, Sean's working environment is predominantly international, their children go to the French school, and almost all their friends are foreign. They are what are usually termed 'expatriates'. Moreover, they clearly show social reproduction practices by stressing the importance of raising their children in both an English-speaking and French-speaking cultural environment:

Our oldest daughter has been to French school. And she's going to do Secondary in an English school. For us it is very important to be completely equal, to keep both at the same level. So we know that her English is not that good but she understands it very well, she speaks it very well, but it is not as perfect as the French… So she'll do English Secondary School from the age of 12 or 11… (Claire, French-Belgian, married to Sean, Irish)

In Sean and Claire's child-rearing plans, there was quite evident competition in the search for a bi-cultural equilibrium in socialization. In fact, some partnerships reveal a subtle tension in the possible dominance of one culture over the other (Lomsky-Feder and Leibovitz 2010). In these situations, the child is brought up in an environment where the conjugal relationship frequently implies counterbalancing the dominant role of one parent's culture. But reaching perfect bi-cultural symmetry may prove impossible in the long run since it is also determined by the family's *length of stay* in a particular country (Deprez and Dreyfus 1998; Nowicka 2006).

Peripatetic Family Strategy

This last type of strategy involves the family-life routine being structured around at least three different cultures, i.e. the cultures of the mother and the father and that of a third country. The coexistence of multiple socio-cultural backgrounds in daily rituals, habits and behaviours frequently leads to the creation of a hybrid ethnic environment without the presence of a leading culture functioning as a matrix of reference. Moreover, parents who develop a peripatetic socialization pattern tend to perceive the host state as a *transitory place*, and hardly ever as a permanent settlement. This attitude contributes to a *detached life style* leading to instrumental choices in the receiving society that guarantee a minimum level of assimilation. The most usual scenario is that the children are raised speaking more than two languages, they normally attend an international school, and their social support system is characterized by non-native individuals who tend to reinforce this semi-social integration and perpetuate a permanently denationalized cultural life.

The family of Carlos (Spanish) and Marie (Belgian) illustrates this interethnic complexity. They both speak their native languages (Spanish and French) with their daughters, the older of whom attends a Portuguese state kindergarten and the younger spends the day at home with a Portuguese nanny. The children's upbringing is therefore structured around three linguistic codes, none of which is dominant. The parents realize that difficulties in language acquisition are a major consequence of this ethnic diversity:

> My oldest daughter speaks badly, she speaks very little... She speaks less than a child who only has one language... It is normal, but I thought it was going to be easier.... But I now realize she has difficulties because she has three languages... And I have to work a bit harder with her: to read her books to develop her languages a bit... (Marie, Belgium, married to Carlos, Spanish)

The family plans to send their daughters to the French school to ensure that at least one language is learnt correctly and also because they still do not know if they will settle permanently in Lisbon or will have to move to another European country for professional reasons. This scenario of future mobility frequently appears in the discourses of mixed couples, as having a partner of a different national origin always entails the possibility of moving to that country at some time. Sending children to international schools is not only a means of transmitting a formal education in one parent's native language but also a tactic for providing an education that can be easily transferred to another national context. As Carlos explains,

> We have decided that it is best for the girls to be educated in French. Why's that? It's very simple: as we still don't know how many years we are going to stay in Lisbon, and because there is the possibility that in three or four years time we have to move country, we don't want to compromise our daughters' future... So we think that there are likely to be French schools in any big city where we could go to, whereas you don't find Spanish schools everywhere... So this is a strategic option that enables us to consider all the scenarios that might appear in the future years... (Carlos, Spanish, married to Marie, Belgium)

When it comes to social networks and acquaintances, Carlos and Marie interact mainly with expatriates with children, or Portuguese people married to foreigners. These are therefore the most typical partnerships in their social support system and this helps reinforce the multicultural environment in which their children are raised and also to maintain a distance from Portuguese society.

Although a peripatetic strategy is generally found among mixed couples in which neither of the partners is a native citizen of the host society, this is not necessarily the case. Bernardo (Portuguese) and Hanna (Polish) take the same attitude to their daughters' upbringing. Regarding language transmission, Hanna says,

> I speak in Polish with my children... And my husband speaks with them in Portuguese, but we teach them English as well. We do that as a kind of a game, we also ask them things in English and they enjoy it. It's kind of a fun thing!' (Hanna, Polish, married to Bernardo, Portuguese)

The coexistence of three languages in a family environment where one of the parents is Portuguese is justified by the symbolic and functional usefulness of English in an international context. As Bernardo states at some point, '*English is the most useful language to use in any context*', and so the couple is strongly motivated to send their daughters to a private English-speaking school that can offer the best guarantee in terms of teaching quality (see also Wagner 1998; Weenink 2007). The plan to raise their children in an international setting is therefore a deliberate choice to transmit the appropriate cosmopolitan capital for a possible international lifestyle in the future. Furthermore, the family's social networks mainly involve foreigners or mixed couples:

> They are normally mixed couples… They are normally colleagues from the university, where at least one of the partners is a foreigner. And the kindergarten where our daughters go also has many children whose parents are not Portuguese. So they have immense contact with an international community. And that environment is similar to the one they also have. And that might help them not to feel so strange, so different from the other kids….
> (Bernardo, Portuguese, married to Hanna, Polish)

Bernardo and Hanna's child-rearing practices demonstrate an effort on social class reproduction trajectories, in that they favour both trilingual skills within the family unit and attendance of an international English-speaking school. They believe this will be an instrument for their daughters' acquisition of cosmopolitan capital and other prestigious resources that can position them in a privileged ethnic minority group (see Finnäs and O'Leary 2003; Wagner 1998; Weenink 2007, 2008). The couple is therefore implementing certain distinctive socialization strategies aimed at developing upper-middle-class practices and lifestyles where symbolic prestige is linked to an international environment.

Conclusion

Children belonging to ethnically dominant minority groups have hardly been taken into consideration in studies of migration and minority communities. However, this topic is particularly relevant in light of the EU intra-mobility space and the new socio-political conditions associated with migration in contemporary societies. When moving, EU migrants and their children have similar civic rights to those of nationals of the host states, making them a privileged social group when compared to other communities (Recchi and Favell 2009). In fact, mixed EU families represent both a challenge and an opportunity to observe how child-raising and social integration processes of ethnic minorities are created and possibly blend into a new culture.

This chapter fills the gap in the literature by focusing on the rearing strategies of upper-middle-class EU families of mixed nationality living in Lisbon. The results suggest that there are three ideal types of upbringing—*family assimilation strategy, bi-national family strategy*, and *peripatetic family strategy*—when deciding on priority educational areas like language transmission, the choice of school, and the nature of social networks (Deprez and Dreyfus 1998; Nowicka 2006; Rodríguez Marcos 2006; Wagner 1998). Furthermore, in accordance with previous studies, the findings showed that some variables intermeshed in this process—having a native parent (Deprez and Dreyfus 1998), the level of commitment to the country of residence (Gaspar 2009), and the culture of the destination society (Nowicka 2006)—seem to condition the adoption of certain socialization practices and the level of parental negotiation in cultural readjustment processes.

A major trend that came to light is that the couple is more likely to adopt an *assimilation educational strategy* when one of the parents is a Portuguese citizen. This follows Scott and Cartledge (2009) who showed that the likelihood of migrants '*going native*' was strictly dependent on whether they had a native spouse. Moreover, having a native parent also contributes to strengthening the family's level of commitment towards the residence country as language transmission, type of school selected and the nature of social peers are facilitated by the fact that one of the members of the household can function as a 'cultural bridge' to the family unit (Rodríguez García 2006). The development of this educational strategy ultimately leads to the dominance of Portuguese as the main language and as the prime social environment in structuring children's social identity and cultural affiliations, making their social integration much easier than other groups.

The adoption of a *bi-national educational strategy* motivates a cultural balance in the negotiation of which aspects from each parent's culture are retained or discarded in childrearing. It requires finding a balance in the transmission of both the mother and the father's native background, and it can trigger more tensions and family conflicts throughout the course of children's socialization. The bicultural atmosphere in which parents aim to raise their offspring implies that the child learns to switch cultural roles back and forth according to his/her context. However, this balance may not be sustained in the long term if the residence in the host country becomes permanent. In this case, stronger feelings of identification and attachment towards the residence society are likely to be developed, as it has been found in past investigations (Deprez and Drefys 1998; Nowicka 2006; Rodriguez Marcos 2006).

Finally, the research results also revealed that the absence of a native parent or weaker commitment to Portugal seem to influence the adoption of a *peripatetic educational strategy*. These parents are motivated by the desire to transmit *cosmopolitan capital* to their offspring (Wagner 1998; Weenink 2008, 2007), given that the transmission of bilingual skills, the transferability of the knowledge acquired in international schools, and the interaction with transnational communities are understood as strategies for reproducing educational models adjustable to a *moving culture*. Moreover, both *bi-cultural* and *peripatetic educational strategies* may reflect parents' wish to pass on ethnic affiliations linked to their native culture, and also to reproduce certain distinctive symbols of their upper-middle-class position as dominant minority citizens (Finnäs and O'Leary 2003; Lieberson 1985).

The socialization of privileged interethnic EU children is relevant both for the understanding of transnational migrant families and the social institutions interacting with them (schools, political representatives) and is therefore essential to furthering the debate on ethnic minority education. It is important that parents, teachers, educators and policy makers are aware of the diversity of the parenting process when dealing with interethnic EU children. In this interplay, various processes of ethnization may emerge within privileged migrant families: the fact of being a 'dominant minority' can entail important advantages when trying to negotiate recognition and legitimacy as an ethnic social group, and it also leads to processes of cultural reconstruction capable of promoting social cohesion and solidarity within multicultural settings both within and outside the EU.

Acknowledgements The author is particularly grateful to the editors of this volume, Zvi Bekerman and Thomas Geisen, for their ongoing encouragement to write this chapter and constructive observations on the content of the final version. She is also indebted to Anália Torres for insightful comments on an earlier draft of this text. Finally, she wants to express her gratitude to the 24 parents who generously agreed to share their family life stories for this research.

References

Ackers, L. (1998). *Shifting spaces – women, citizenship and migration within the European Union*. Bristol: Policy Press.
Brau, M., & Recchi, E. (2008). Interethnic partnership of Western Europeans: Between preferences and opportunities. *Revista OBETS, 1*, 73–87.
Cortina, A. C., Esteve, A., & Domingo, A. (2008). Marriage patterns of the foreign born population in a new country of immigration: The case of Spain. *International Migration Review, 42*(4), 877–902.
Crul, M., & Vermeulen, H. (2003). The second generation in Europe. *International Migration Review, 37*(4), 965–986.
Deprez, C., & Dreyfus, M. (1998). Transmission et usages des langues: Couples mixtes à Paris et à Dakar. In C. Philippe, G. Varro, & G. Neyrand (Eds.), *Liberté, Égalité, Mixité... Conjugales* (pp. 201–228). Paris: Anthropos.
Finnäs, F., & O'Leary, R. (2003). Choosing for the children: The affiliation for the children of minority-majority group intermarriages. *European Sociological Review, 19* (5), 483–499.
Gaspar, S. (2008). Towards a definition of European intra-marriage as a new social phenomenon. CIES e-working paper no. 48, CIES-ISCTE, Lisbon, 23 pp, online at http://www.cies.iscte/pt/destaques/documents/CIES-WP46.pdf. Accessed 10 Nov 2009.
Gaspar, S. (2009). Integración y satisfacción social en parejas mixtas intraeuropeas. *Discurso y Sociedad, 16*, 68–101 http://www.discurso.aau.dk/SociedadyDiscurso_16/Gaspar_SyD16.pdf. Accessed 29 Nov 2009.
Gonzaléz Ferrer, A. (2006). Who do immigrants marry? Partner's choice among single immigrants in Germany. *European Sociological Review, 22*(2), 171–185.
Kalmijn, M., & van Tubergen, F. (2006). Ethnic intermarriage in the Netherlands: Confirmations and refutations of accepted insights. *European Journal of Population, 22*, 371–397.
Kellerhals, J., & Montadon, C. (1991). *Les strategies éducatives des familles – milieu social, dynamique familiale et education des pré-adolescents*. Lausanne: Delachaux et Niestlé.
Klein, T. (2001). Intermarriage between Germans and Foreigners in Germany. *Journal of Comparative Family Studies, 32*(3), 325–346.
Lauth Bacas, J. (2002). *Cross-border marriages and the formation of transnational families: A case study of Greek-German couples in Athens.* Oxford: University of Oxford. Working paper online at www.transcomm.ox.ac.uk/working%20papers/WPTC-02–10%20Bacas.pdf. Accessed 26 June 2011.
Lieberson, S. (1985). Unhyphenated whites in the United States. *Ethnic and Racial Studies, 8*, 159–180.

Lomsky-Feder, E., & Leibovitz, T. (2010). Inter-ethnic encounters within the family: Competing cultural models and social exchange. *Journal of Ethnic and Migration Studies, 36*(1), 107–124.
Nowicka, E. (2006). Identity and socio-cultural capital: Duality of transnational people in Poland. *Ethnic and Racial Studies, 29*(6), 1072–1086.
O'Leary, R., & Finnäs, F. (2002). Education, social integration and minority-majority group intermarriage. *Sociology, 36*(2), 235–254.
Recchi, E., & Favell, A. (Eds.). (2009). *Pioneers of European integration – citizenship and mobility within the EU.* Cheltenham: Edward Elgar.
Rodríguez García, D. (2006). Mixed marriages and transnational families in the intercultural context: A case study of African-Spanish couples in Catalonia. *Journal of Ethnic and Migration Studies, 32*(3), 403–433.
Rodríguez Marcos, M. E. (2006). *Familias interculturales – La construcción de la interculturalidad de lo micro social a lo macro social.* Salamanca: Publicaciones Universidad Pontifica.
Rother, N. (2008). Better integrated due to a German partner? An analysis of differences in the integration of foreigners in intra- and inter-ethnic partnership in Germany. *Revista OBETS, 1,* 21–43.
Santacreu, O., Baldoni, E., & Albert, M. C. (2009). Deciding to move: Migration projects in an integrating Europe. In E. Recchi & A. Favell (Eds.), *Pioneers of European integration: Citizenship and mobility in the EU* (pp. 52–71). Cheltenham: Edward Elgar.
Santacreu F. O. A., & García, F. J. (2008). Parejas mixtas de europeos en España: integración, satisfacción y expectativas de futuro. *Revista OBETS, 1,* 7–20.
Scott, S., & Cartledge, K. (2009). Migrant assimilaton in Europe: A transnational family affair. *International Migration Review, 43*(1), 60–89.
Stalford, H. (2005). Parenting, care and mobility in the EU. *Innovation, 18*(3), 361–380.
Stierna, J. (2003). Etnicidad y reconocimiento social. Una perspectiva sobre integración social desde un análisis histórico del colectivo en Madrid. *Revista Española de Sociología, 3,* 99–118.
Thomson, M., & Crul, M. (2007). The second generation in Europe and the United States: How is the transatlantic debate relevant for further research on the European second generation? *Journal of Ethnic and Migration Studies, 33*(7), 1025–1041.
Torres, A. (2004). *Vida conjugal e trabalho.* Oeiras: Celta Editora.
Torres, A. (2008). Women, gender, and work: The Portuguese case in the context of the European Union. *International Journal of Sociology, 38*(4), 36–56.
Torres, A., & Silva, F. V. da (1998). Guarda das crianças e divisão do trabalho entre homens e mulheres. *Sociologia – Problemas e Práticas, 28,* 9–65.
Wagner, A.-C. (1998). *Les nouvelles élites de la mondialisation – une immigration dorée en France.* Paris: PUF.
Weenink, D. (2007). Cosmopolitan and established resources of power in the education arena. *International Sociology, 22*(4), 492–516.
Weenink, D. (2008). Cosmopolitanism as a form of capital: Parents preparing their children for a globalizing world. *Sociology, 42*(6), 1089–1106.
van Tubergen, F., & Maas, I. (2007). Ethnic intermarriage among immigrants in the Netherlands: An analysis of population data. *Social Science Research, 36*(3), 1065–1086.

Chapter 10
Opening a Gate to Citizenship: Media for Migrants

Esther Schely-Newman

Introduction

Migration involves shifting identities, a complex process that requires adjusting to different cultural norms, and accepting a new history and mythology. Becoming a participant member of the new community includes formal steps of citizenship as well as acquiring the language and becoming familiar with the group's ethos. Linguistic competence provides access to formal and informal socialization, to the history and ideologies, mythologies, and other banal aspects of nationalism and patriotism which are self-evident for 'natives' (Anderson 1983; Bhabha 1990; Billig 1995; Hall 1996; Krzyżanowski and Wodak 2007; Wodak et al. 1996). Subsequently, nation-states develop language policies which are part of the educational and political systems, aiming at socializing citizens in the formal and informal educational systems (Kramsch 2000). Media addressing migrants play a significant role in the process by framing events and telling the national stories on special occasions and national holidays.

This chapter treats texts in *Shaar Lamathil*, a weekly newsmagazine published by the Israeli Ministry of Education since 1956 as a pedagogical tool for teaching Hebrew to adult migrants. The analysis offers a diachronic perspective of how Israel presents itself to new citizens by analyzing texts used for teaching the language. Internal socio-cultural-political changes are reflected in texts addressed to different people in the process of learning the language of the host country. Focusing on a particular religious-national holiday, the feast of Hanukkah, allows for an analysis of modes for constructing national identity. The yearly repeated story of the holiday reflects basic myth and national ethos and reveals insights into the dynamic nature of myth, and the tension between tradition and change. The chapter suggests that socialization of migrants is achieved by concurrently fashioning a collective memory and standardizing rituals.

E. Schely-Newman (✉)
Noah Mozes Department of Communication and Journalism, The Hebrew University, Mount Scopus, Jerusalem, Israel
e-mail: msetti@mscc.huji.ac.il

A critical approach treating context, purpose of production, the medium, the intended audience, the language, genres, and other discursive strategies reveals the mechanisms that amplify the persuasive power of the texts and their implied ideologies (Fairclough 1995; van Dijk 2001, 2006; Wodak 2006). The Israeli case study thus provides insights into the role of media for migrants and the effects of simplifying the language to ease learning. These texts, I will argue, serve a double function—as a port of entry into the new society but also as a gatekeeper, requiring language competence to enter 'the promised land.'

Conceptual Framework

National languages allow citizens and residents to identify themselves with the collective and to fulfil other mundane functions for participation in everyday life. Nation-states based on migration need to create a sense of nationhood and a common cause, hence the significant role of national language as a unifying mechanism. Language plays a major role in the discourse of citizenship and serves as potential exclusionary mechanism that creates, regulates, and sustains the boundaries of the collective (Kramsch 2000; Kroskrity 2001; Milani 2008; Schmid 2001; Shohamy 2009; Tollefson 1991). Monoglot ideologies appear in citizenship discourse in multilingual societies such as Belgium and the United States, or states with lenient language requirements such as Sweden and Israel (Blommaert et al. 2006; Shohamy and Kanza 2009; Silverstein 1996; Spolsky and Shohamy 1999).

The ideological nature of language is expressed in the values attached to different languages, variations and modalities such as written or spoken, register, dialect or accent, including orthography. These ideologies explain the development of 'legitimate code' of a language and the hierarchy between different communication systems (Bourdieu 1991; Silverstein 1998). The level of language taught thus bears implications beyond its practical use; the right code is the key for entering different strata of society. Print literacy—the ability to read and write—is perceived as a marker of modernity, the basis for participation in civic life, economic and political activity; an index for "capacity of self representation and even as signs of fitness for democratic self rule" (Cody 2009, p. 352; Harris 2000; Purcell-Gates et al. 2004) More succinctly, literacy is "something that defines us as human beings, i.e., as normal members of our cultures" (Blommaert et al. 2006, p. 35).

Ideologies are created, represented, and reproduced in discourse; in the ways ideas are organized into texts, and coherent stories, as well as in decisions as to what variant of language will be taught and what texts will be used in educational settings. Texts that teach language to new citizens tell recent members of the group what they should know about the society they are joining; introducing immigrants to everyday life, geography, and history of the new country as well as nation building myth—information that is part of the formal and informal education systems for the 'natives.' These texts offer guidance into the way the collective ('we') behaves in comparison with the 'others'—minority groups, other religions or countries, including the previous identities (languages, customs) of the student. The prestige of textbooks (approved by state imprimatur) and the hierarchical settings of their use provide them with the authority for transmitting ideologies regardless of the subject matter presented (Heller and Martin-Jones 2001; Paxton 1999; van Dijk 2004).

National and religious holidays are an opportunity for the collective to celebrate its ubiquitous identity, strengthen the demarcations between members and outsiders. These yearly occasions shape and reinforce the collective memory, particularly for newcomers to the group who need to acquire the basic-official-hegemonic knowledge that establishes the foundations of the nation-state (Bird and Dardenne 1992; Zerubavel 1995). Pedagogical texts for adult migrants are an opportunity to partake this knowledge as part of the basic skills needed for life in the new society. The banal nationalism, instilled through formal and informal education, needs to be told, retold, and reinterpreted to migrants. The rhetorical power of such texts is greater, I will argue, because of the implicit connection between linguistic rules, pedagogical texts and the content they convey.

Israel: Language, Ideologies, Immigration

Hebrew has been used mainly for Jewish ritualistic purposes for two millennia, becoming a 'living' language for everyday purposes only in the last hundred years. The 'revival' of Hebrew was closely linked to the Jewish national movement, Zionism: the growing Jewish population in southern area of the Ottoman Empire (and later, British Mandatory Palestine), created a need for a common language, Hebrew. Concurrently, the emerging language became a symbol of the nascent Jewish community. Development of bureaucratic institutions and educational systems in Jewish Palestine, and the declaration of Hebrew as an official language of the British Mandate (along with Arabic and English) in 1922 supported the use and reinforced the ideological value of Hebrew. Israel's independence in 1948 sealed the linguistic transformation by declaring Hebrew (and Arabic) national languages of the new Jewish state (Harshav 1993; Spolsky and Shohamy 1999).

The official status of Hebrew as the language of the independent state of Israel encountered difficulties due to the nature of the new state. The July 1950 Law of Return declares all Jews potential citizens of the State of Israel: every Jew may activate this right upon arriving to the country without any further demands.[1] The new State of Israel absorbed large numbers of migrants who did not have a common language or culture, and the majority lacked competence in Modern Hebrew. More specifically: The Israeli Jewish population in 1948 was approximately 650,000; a number that was doubled in two years. The demographic increase included refugees

---

[1] The Palestinian–Arab population within the boundaries of Israel in 1948 and their descendants are also citizens, and maintain an independent educational system. Other individuals may obtain Israeli citizenship subject to different regulations that include knowledge of Hebrew (1970 amendment of the Law of Return).

and Holocaust survivors from post Second World War Europe, migrants from Arab countries at war with Israel since 1948, and Jews from other countries driven by the ideological fervor of living in a Jewish independent state. The role of the new state was therefore to transform all migrants into Hebrew-speaking Israelis; learning the language was a means for achieving a new cultural identity.

The need to create a common national ethos and identity was critical as was the need to accommodate the migrants with housing, occupation, education, and other needs. The melting pot paradigm of the first decades of Israeli statehood aimed at producing new citizens with little, if any, ethnic markers of identity including language, and to become a new Hebrew-Israeli-modern citizen (Olshtain and Kotik 2000). Language transformation was a major tool in this process. Migrants were expected to abandon old diasporic ways of life, including names, professions, and languages, in order to become Israelis; tolerance and retention for native languages were minimal and limited to languages with high prestige (Bar Yosef 1964; Ben-Rafael 1994).[2]

The pressures for assimilation and becoming 'one nation,' typical to the first decades of Israeli independence, began to ease with the passage of years. The struggle for letting Jews migrate from the Soviet Union in the late 1960s and early 1970s brought to Israel approximately 160,000 Russian-speaking migrants, and the breakdown of the Soviet Block in the 1990s increased the Russian-speaking Israeli population to nearly one million (of a population of 7.4 millions).[3] These migrants, arriving to Israel at a time of greater tolerance for multiculturalism, and their sheer numbers, increased their ability to retain Russian language and culture, expressed in a large number of Russian language newspapers, educational and cultural programs in Russian (Adoni et al. 2002; Anteby-Yemini 2004; Horenczyk 2000). The Russian-speaking Israelis became one of the groups that threaten the hegemonic center by suggesting alternative ways of being Israeli while retaining diasporic characteristics (Ben-Rafael 2001; Smooha 2008).

The population changes in Israel continue to pose linguistic challenges. Only 35% of the Jewish population upon independence (1948) were born in Israel, and thus may be considered native speakers of Hebrew. At the end of 2008 the percentage of Israeli-born citizen doubled to 70.7%. In absolute numbers, approximately 1.6 million Israeli citizens are migrants, 748,700 arriving since 1990.

The language challenge was exacerbated by the fact that migrants arrived from different cultures with varying degrees of linguistic skills from different language systems (L1), factors that necessitated developing special means for teaching Hebrew combined with socialization into the new and emerging national identity. Although knowledge of Hebrew is not a prerequisite for citizenship, Israel invests resources in teaching Hebrew to all citizens, young and adult, following language planning

---

[2] The history of ethnic relations in Israel and of the sociological study of this history was recently reviewed by Goldberg and Bram (2007). The impact of the melting pot pressures in the early years of statehood continues to be viable in the Israeli discourse and studies of Israeli identity. See for example, Goldberg et al. (2006), Schejter (2007).

[3] Statistical Abstracts of Israel, 2009; www.cbs.gov.il.

and policies that emphasize the superiority of Hebrew (Ben-Rafael 1994). These measures included developing (in the early 1950s) a unique system of intensive classes for teaching Hebrew in Hebrew (the *ulpan*), programs for teaching migrant children in schools, and literacy and basic adult education campaigns. *Ulpan* classes are perceived by the Ministry of Education more than language schools, but rather a place, "in which the immigrant acquires basic key terms from the national reservoir of associations and the collective national memory" (Aviad and Peretz 2003).[4]

Among the measures for teaching Hebrew to adult migrants, a simplified version of the target language (L2) was developed. Ivrit Kala, Simplified [easy] Hebrew, shares some characteristics of basic varieties of other languages: controlled lexicon, restricted grammatical forms and few syntactic constructions. Ease of learning and functionality are the main purposes for developing this language variety, for use at the initial stages of learning L2. In addition to primers in Simplified Hebrew, other texts were 'translated' in order to provide reading materials for adults learners, such as novels, popular science, and a weekly newsmagazine.

Simplified Hebrew was developed in order to provide a mode of basic communication for people arriving from different linguistic systems. Since Hebrew remained mainly in textual form for ritualistic purposes it lacked varied registers and styles. Teachers were impelled to create lists of common words and regenerate simple stylistic and grammatical forms. There are no fixed rules for simplification: lists of common words, ranging from 500 to 1500 continue to be compiled. Linguists and Hebrew teachers search for criteria defining basic lexemes, based not only on frequency but also on the range of texts in which they appear (Blum 1971).

While teachers of Hebrew as L2 and students find Simplified Hebrew easy to use, linguists warn against depleting language resources and 'watering down' literary texts. Papers published in the 1960s and 1970s debated the issues, and warned against the extensive use and reliance on simplified texts, urging educators to expand the variety of texts and let adult learners immerse in different registers and usage of Hebrew.[5] Survey of texts written for ulpan and other Hebrew classes at different times reveals a variety of texts according to the target population and the level of class. Primers for basic adult literacy include texts that speak of Israeli history, local flora and fauna, while texts for university students may include, in addition, issues such as gender relations. In recent years *Shaar Lamathil*, the weekly newsmagazine, has a more structured format with sections written in different registers for an easier transition from Simplified Hebrew printed in large fonts with diachritic signs to what is common in daily newspapers.

All texts for teaching Hebrew to adults were written, or at least approved, by the Division of Adult Education in the Ministry of Education. Despite their function as socializing agents, their context was not subject to critical evaluation for exposing their explicit and implicit ideologies (Fairclough 1995, 2005; van Dijk 2001, 2006;

---

[4] Hebrew quotes are translated by author.
[5] For example, linguists Shoshana Blum-Kulka, Raphael Nir, Uzi Ornan, and Hayim Rosen addressed the issue in *Orhot* a journal of adult education, in several issues, most notably, 1967 and 1976.

Wodak 2006). The main criterion for use of these materials was their efficiency in instilling grammatical rules and increasing register.

Media in Simplified Language

A unique kind of publication, a newsmagazine, was introduced into adult classes of Hebrew. On March 4, 1956, *ulpan* students received supplement reading material, a page entitled *Lamathil* [For the Beginner], recapping the news of the week. The publication soon became a regular weekly, including other features that provide learners with topics for class discussion and leisure literacy practices (e.g., crossword puzzles and stories).[6] A second version of the weekly magazine, addressing learners with low education levels was launched in 1961, but both weeklies merged in 1978 into *Shaar Lamathil* [A Gate for the Beginner]. The weekly now appears regularly in a 16-page tabloid format, with a variety of texts in different levels of difficulties for the student of Hebrew. The current circulation is approximately 20,000 copies sold to subscribers and in newsstands, and additional access through the internet. The actual number of readers is larger because many teachers use it in class.

The concept of using current events as basis for frequently updated reading material in L2 currently is being used in several private publications in the United States.[7] *Easy English Times*, Elizabeth Claire's *Easy English News*, and *News for You* (online) are written by teachers of English as second language, and address adult needs and interests. Similar to the Hebrew publication, they include national and world news, people in the news, sports, and special features such as history and geography. Simplification is achieved by brief texts, treating complex topics without using a high register vocabulary, providing background information, large fonts, and uncluttered design, as well as no advertising that may distract the reader. These publications address special interests of adults as explicitly declared in their Internet sites: "A world of information for the adult learner" (http://www.easyenglishtimes.com), "The purpose is to welcome immigrants to the United States and to help them learn about their new environment and society" (http://www.elizabethclaire.com).

Similarly, 'to know Hebrew is to know Israel,' declares the opening page of the English Website of *Shaar Lamathil*. The site spells out the benefits of the newsmagazine, "Israel's leading easy-Hebrew weekly.... Written in simple Hebrew with big, bold letters and vowels underneath. ...Distributed throughout Israel and around the world wherever Hebrew is read and taught" (http://slamathil.allbiz.co.il). Information about child rearing, military service, election campaigns and urging people to vote are some of the 'adult topics' included in the Hebrew newsmagazine.

---

[6] Interviews with current editors, Mr. Hayim Jacobson (May 4, 2003), Ms. Zippi Mazar (September 3, 2003), and Mr. Ygal Moldavsky (August 15, 2006).

[7] I was surprised to find after an extensive search and help from US colleagues only three such publication. I did not find similar ones in England. Thanks to Victoria Purcell-Gates and to Eric Jacobson for their help.

Although *Shaar Lamathil* reports news and is published on a regular basis, it differs from other media: it is primarily a pedagogical tool and the editorial policy is based on linguistic criteria rather than news worthiness. At present, due to the proliferation of media in different languages and channels, by migrants and for migrants, the newsmagazine is not the only source of information for recent immigrants (Adoni et al. 2002). Furthermore, because it is primarily a teaching tool, there is no attempt to foster a loyal readership; on the contrary, 'It is the only product that measures its success by how many people stop using it,' as stated by Mr. Jacobson.

The socializing agenda is explicitly declared:

> Then, like today […] we wanted you to be familiar with the institutions of the state, the industry, leaders and 'the small people' in towns and in the country. […] we wanted you to understand the problems and difficulties […] (Rachel Inbar, editor, supplement to *Lamathil* 1000 issue, 1976).

Twenty-two years later, the editor states similar purposes in a special issue marking the 1000 issue of the joint weekly publication, of *Shaar Lamathil*:

> *Shaar Lamathil* follows the state in historic moments and daily life, photographing Israeli reality, pointing at achievements as well as at difficulties. It continues to participate in the national endeavors of absorbing immigrants and of education (Zippi Mazar, editor, 1998).

Shaar-Lamathil fulfils basic media functions: to inform and entertain as well as socialize, coordinate, and categorize elements of social structure, pass on knowledge and inculcate values to the next generation. For new citizens *Shaar Lamathil* serves to complete their enculturation and improve their familiarity with basic information about the country and its people; a socializing agent that shapes the needs and perceptions of individuals and sets normative behavior patterns. The story of Hanukkah in Simplified Hebrew is analyzed to demonstrate these socializing functions.

Hanukkah: A Heroic Feast

Hanukkah means 'dedication' and refers to the purification and resumption of Jewish rituals in the Temple in Jerusalem that was defiled by Hellenistic pagan practices over two thousand years ago. A family of priests from Judea, known as the Maccabees, revolted against the religious persecutions by the powerful Greek Empire and succeeded in establishing an independent Jewish state in 166 BCE. Lighting candles for eight nights and performing the ritual blessing commemorates and gives praise to the divine intervention that led to the military and political victories.

The Jewish national revival movement (Zionism) found inspiration in Hanukkah as a historical model of successful fight for independence, and the holiday acquired an important place in the Zionist historiography. Hanukkah represents human heroism and a successful struggle against oppression that resulted in political independence. The Maccabee struggle is seen as a precursor to contemporary Israel, and as such it was an important event in Israeli Zionist ethos. In the educational system, Hanukkah continues to be celebrated with great drama and enthusiasm (Don-Yehiya

1992). For recent immigrants who are not yet familiar with the basic myths of the State of Israel, these stories need to be told and interpreted; like children, they too need to be introduced to the official history and rituals.

Research Methodology

Given the mandate of *Shaar Lamathil* as guide through language to recent members of Israeli society, I analyzed the presentation of Hanukkah, a national holiday, in this publication. Changes in the manner of socialization—from the pressures of transformation into one type of Israeli–Hebrew to multiculturalism and multilingualism—are assumed to have affected the presentation of Hanukkah. A content analysis of fifty consecutive years provides a panoramic picture of the holiday, its history, stories and the version(s) of rituals offered to recent members of the community.

For the purpose of the study, I have examined each issue of *Shaar Lamathil* published before, during, and after Hanukkah from 1956 to 2006, considering all texts, visual and verbal, that refer to the holiday. In most years there was one issue treating Hanukkah but occasionally there were two or three issues telling the story of the Maccabees in two consecutive weeks. In addition, for 18 years (1961–1978) there were two newsmagazines in Simplified Hebrew, thus the sample includes 68 years of texts. Issues of two major daily newspapers (*Haaretz* and *Yediot Aharonot* 1963, 1973, 1983, 1993, 2003) were included in the sample in order to add a comparative dimension.

Texts were categorized according to their content and genre: e.g., poems versus prose, or visual texts, news items, recipes, and stories, in order to analyze their functions. A primary question posed was the content: what historical events, contemporary stories, and ritual traditions are presented, what images accompany the texts. Other questions treat the voices heard: are all texts and traditions told from the same perspective, or are there different authors, and, as a result, what frames of interpretations are offered? Are there different group categories, who can be identified as 'other' and what discursive practices are used for such presentation? Grouping the different texts according to their type and function (see below), was complemented by a diachronic perspective to account for possible changes in the meaning of the holiday. The combined perspectives of content and discourse analyses, allow for a better understanding of the uniqueness of the medium as a major conduit for narrating Israeli national identity.

Hanukkah for Beginners: Findings

Throughout the last 50 years, texts in *Shaar Lamathil* appear in three distinct clusters of content: history (the events commemorated), ritual (how to celebrate), and stories from the recent past about individuals that link Hanukkah to everyday life.

The model was set in the first issue (*Lamathil* 31, November 28, 1956). Three texts about Hanukkah were published: A poem signed by the initials B.R. expresses the ongoing struggle of the Maccabee: alluding to the Sinai War (October–November 1956): 'The war for our independence is not over yet'; a photograph of a soldier lighting a menorah (Hanukkah candelabra), made of military helmets; and a story, set in Europe at the end of the nineteenth century, about a man who reconnects with his Jewish identity through fashioning a menorah and lighting candles while telling his family the story of Hanukkah for the eight consecutive nights (see below). These three texts frame Hanukkah as a national holiday having a continuous relevance to the Jewish people in Israel. The photograph creates a homology between the Maccabees and the Israeli Defense Forces (IDF), and the story reiterates the importance of cultural roots to the formation of national identity. The lack of historical narratives—what are the origins of the holiday—suggest that the editors assume a basic knowledge of the student-readers about the events, and thus offer only a national frame of interpretation.

In following years, other genres were introduced; for example, news about events taking place during the week of Hanukkah, particularly public events such as lighting candles in special sites, or the torch-carrying race from Jerusalem to the burial site of the Maccabees. This invented tradition bridges the two thousand years gap: twentieth-century Israeli youth reconnect with the heroic past by transporting a torch through historical sites. Other genres include recipes for traditional food, popular Hebrew songs, candelabras, and other traditional images decorate the pages of the newsmagazine with or without texts, as well as instructions about the ritual of candle lighting. The additional genres consistently remain within the triadic frame of history, ritual, and stories.

History—Crafting the Collective Memory

The first issue of *Lamathil* did not narrate historical events. B.R.'s poem declares, 'The heart lights up with the candles in memory of Maccabee heroism…' but does not elaborate. Over the years, the story is standardized in a double perspective of the past and the present. An illustration in the 1958 issue points to the current day miracle: A menorah with the same design as the official emblem of the State of Israel has a soldier standing guard. The beam of light from each candle attracts human figures arriving from different countries. The caption reads 'The greatest miracle of today—Ingathering of the Exiles' (Illustration 1). A simulation of a newspaper from the Maccabee historical time appeared in 1959 informing the readers about 'current events.' The homology to the present is explicit: 'Are we not witnessing miracles today? The first days of the state of Israel will also be remembered for thousands of years.'

This combined perspective constantly appears in different texts in the following years: 'The Maccabee wars—a modern fight for freedom,' or 'Hanukkah—Independence Day of Past Year.' Some texts are more elaborate than others, such as a

Illustration 1 "The Biggest Miracle of Today—Ingathering of the Exiles" *Lamathil* issue 132, December 10, 1958

special supplement to the 1965 issue of *Lamathil* concluding with: 'Our generation is able to see how history repeats itself and how a freedom movement of a few was able to restore independence to the people of Israel.' The nationalist perspective persists as attested by the text, 'The Hashmonean army—army of the people,' first published in 1984 and reprinted for the eighth time in 2006.[8]

Historical narratives of Hanukkah do not appear in daily Hebrew newspapers; for the general Israeli audience these stories are part of the national habitus, and the events are evoked by the rituals and the prayers. Mainstream media recognize the holiday in different ways, by essays about the meaning of Hanukkah as commentary to current events. For example, in 1973, following the war, *Yediot Aharonoth* published an essay about the meaning of sacrifices made by parents—the death of their children—for the common good, recalling a Hanukkah story.[9] Another example are essays framing the ideological struggle between Jewish and secular ideas in nineteenth-century Europe as a version of the fight against Hellenism (Brug 1993; Eden and Shavit 2003).

Ritual—That's How We Do It

The few religious requirements of Hanukkah have been supplemented with many customs developed over time in different communities. *Shaar Lamathil* focuses on lighting candles, reciting blessings, giving presents to children, singing, playing with a *dreydle* (a Hanukkah top), and eating the customary fried doughnuts (*sufganiyot*) or potato pancakes (*latkes*). These are edified verbally and visually: photographs of people performing, reports about special events for Hanukkah, recipes,

---

[8] Recycling texts is common, particularly during holidays. The fast turnover of readership probably accounts for this practice.

[9] The story of Hannah and her seven sons (Book of Maccabees II, Chap. 7, also appears the Babylonian Talmud and in Midrash) tells of a mother who encourages her children to refuse to perform pagan rituals knowing that they will be executed.

Illustration 2 "My Little Candles—So Many Stories" *Shaar Lamatchil*, issue 1271, December 23, 2003. (Photograph by Yariv Katz)

נֵרוֹתַי הַצְעִירִים - מָה רַבּוּ הַסִּיפּוּרִים

suggestions for presents, stories about the rituals, lists of 'what to do,' texts of blessings, lyrics of Hanukkah songs, and etymologies of lexemes common to the holiday complete the sanctification of these traditions.

Other rituals associated with Hanukkah are not ignored but are framed as belonging to specific groups, *minhagey edot* ('ethnic traditions'). Rituals are also presented by individuals: in 1961 Mr. Zakay from Mossul tells the readers of his ancestral Iraqi traditions, and in 1982 several women recount in first person how the holiday was celebrated in their home countries: Morocco, Yemen, Iran, and Iraq. These individual narratives about experiences prior to immigration stress what was not done in the countries of origin compared with the Israeli tradition. The emphasis on omissions adds a negative connotation to these ethnic rituals and prioritizes the all-Israeli version, represented in the authoritative and anonymous voice of *Shaar Lamathil*. Although the variety of rituals continues to appear yearly, the mode of presentation creates an exclusive Israeli 'we' that marks ethnic traditions as 'other' and even superfluous and irrelevant to the process of becoming Israeli. This difference in voice and presentation creates a rift between the present (and future) Israeli traditions and others that are passé, typical to exilic life.

Marginalization through representation is found in visual texts as well: photographs of specific groups: politicians, wounded soldiers or immigrants, as well as 'exotic' groups, families from Bukhara or Yemen dressed in traditional garb around the menorah. This practice of exotism—positively emphasizing what is different as strange and distant—is also a strategy of marking the 'other' (van Dijk 2004). No pictures of everyday Israeli adults performing the ritual, perhaps because the ritual is not newsworthy: 90% of secular Jewish Israelis light candles for Hanukkah, according to a poll taken in 2003 by *Yediot Aharonoth*. The ethnic variety of Israeli population appears in a positive framing only in the case of children. Almost every issue includes photographs of children—religious and secular, boys and girls, light and dark skinned—all performing the same ritual of lighting candles, or watching the lit menorah wearing the paper crown young children don in school celebrations, dressed in contemporary clothing (Illustration 2). This visual presentation reinforces the common future and the idea of 'ingathering of the exiles'—one culture reuniting different people with a common distant past (Hall 1996; Wodak et al. 1996).

General media mark the holiday by giving ample exposure to the same Israeli Hanukkah rituals, established as well as newly invented traditions. Recipes, recommendations for children's shows, advice about the nutritional value of fried doughnuts or which celebrities showed up at whose party, are common in the print and electronic media. The tradition of gift giving and the weeklong vacation of school children are opportunities for commercial entrepreneurship and marketing.

Stories—Rhetorics of Affect

Stories connecting the individual experience to national symbolism form the third predominant cluster of texts appearing in *Shaar Lamathil*. Instead of historical and philosophical arguments about the value of the holiday, which appear in regular newspapers, students of Hebrew read how people, just like themselves, struggled with difficulties and were able to overcome obstacles against all odds.

Adapted from folklore, personal narratives or literary sources, the stories concretize the abstract ideas of sacrifice, freedom and hope—motifs that occur in the historical narratives. The stories recall famous characters as well as simple people, e.g., a woodcutter who sees Hanukkah lights in the forest that guide him to safety, or a Jewish soldier who meets General George Washington while lighting Hanukkah candles at Valley Forge in 1777 (Schely-Newman 2008). For the new Israeli citizen reading his first stories in Hebrew, the stories provide a sense of being part of the struggling collective, and add to building his own share of collective memory and esprit de corps.

The function of narratives as a primordial form for socialization is evident in studies of children's linguistic development. We understand our own experiences and others' by transforming them into a narrative form, and recognize our universe through narratives. Stories are used to teach children about the right order of the world and interactional skills (Blum-Kulka 2005). A study of the responses to *Shaar* indicates that 84% of the readers found the stories as the most interesting part of the weekly magazine (Rahat 1977).

These stories, as all texts in Simplified Hebrew, are short and avoid digressions, texts are judged primarily on the basis of the language and the perceived ability of the students to cope with the linguistic level. Therefore simplification requires substitution of less common words; unfamiliar concepts are glossed or eliminated altogether for the benefit of brevity (Nir 1985).

Celebrating Homogeneity—Discussion

A diachronic view of Hanukkah texts for immigrants published over a 50-year period serves as an example of tensions between continuity and change from the point of view of the hegemonic center. *Shaar Lamathil* is published under the supervision of the Ministry of Education; thus texts can be expected to represent the "most institutionalize and conservative realm of collective memory" (Goldberg et al. 2006, p. 230). The social paradigm of a melting pot and the pressure to assimilate into a Zionist Israeli monolingual society has been weakened since the mid 1980s. Immigration to Israel evinces traits of transnational communities, and linguistic policies have become lenient towards multilingualism (Anteby-Yemini 2004; Ben-Rafael 2007; Spolsky and Shohamy 1999; Weingrod and Levy 2006). These changes are echoed in the stories of Hanukkah in *Shaar Lamathil*, though in a less pronounced manner than in the standard media.

The first issues of *Shaar Lamathil* presented one possible interpretation: Hanukkah is the precursor of Zionism, IDF soldiers are the incarnation of the Maccabees, and the return of the Jewish people to their long-lost homeland is a current-day miracle. The historic events follow the teleological depiction of Jewish history in the Zionist version, the public discourse of the first decades of Israeli independence, and the social paradigm of the melting pot. The consistency of this perspective is evident in recent issues: 'The heroic death of Elazar,' first appeared in 1967 and lastly in 2006, while 'The story of the Hashmonean—against all odds' (2005), presents the same idea in different words.

However, even *Shaar Lamathil* is not immune to social changes. As mentioned above, the first issue (1956) included a poem that stressed the importance of historical lessons, stating that as Israeli Jews,

> We must remember Maccabee heroism the same way we remember the Exodus from Egypt, each and every generation, because the battle for our independence is not over yet.

This and subsequent texts provided a monolithic, national interpretation of the historical events as the basis of the holiday. Forty-seven years later, in 2003, the editor, Ms. Zippi Mazar, muses over the meanings of Hanukkah:

> The holiday is a wonderful opportunity to talk to friends and family about the symbols of the holiday. [...] In my family we have a tradition, that each person will tell a story about a small victory in everyday life.

These reflections stress the importance of telling stories of heroism, disseminating the national narrative year after year in the Jewish way of remembering. However, Mazar's words offer a polysemic interpretation of heroism, widening the range of tellability: the personal is gaining legitimization. Not much else has changed: the current day miracle continues to be Jewish immigration, though from other sources.

Format changes introduced by Ms. Mazar since the late 1990s continue to retain the triadic focus. A new type of text has been introduced: etymologies and semantic fields of the holiday vocabulary that explain the common roots of words like *Hanukkiyah* (menorah) or *sufganiya* (fried doughnut); quotes and beliefs relating to light, fire, oil, add a different perspective to the presentation of Hanukkah. These columns remain within the boundaries of what has been established as the Israeli ritual, thus continuing to edify traditions connected to the lexical terms explored.

Hanukkah exemplifies the function of *Shaar Lamathil* for its audience, recent immigrants in Israel: ease their inclusion into Israeli society by cultural instruction via language socialization. The Maccabees provide a model for human heroism, personal sacrifice, and struggle for independence—a historical model that is transmitted to Israeli children from an early age (Handelman 1998). Recent immigrants need to emulate this 'correct' version which is spelled out for them in small doses in each issue of their newsmagazine. To celebrate Hanukkah as Israelis do, the new immigrants are told to forego their own traditions and stories and adopt what is provided in the new language and culture.

The need for developing an 'official/dominant' image of the past is different in migrant communities and deserves special attention (Shapira 2000). National and religious holidays are a fertile ground to produce and reproduce traditions and myth, and the educational system takes an active role in shaping a particular version of the memory. Supervised by the Ministry of Education, *Shaar Lamathil* replicates the official version of the national narrative and mythology expected to be part of the texts for new citizens; these texts give the immigrant an opportunity to inculcate the collective memory and be familiar with the local rituals. And yet, the ritualistic repetition of texts suggests an additional viewpoint of Jewish history and memory. Jewish historical experience transcends time; the meaning of the past lies within the present and the future. Jewish collective memory is ritualistic and cyclical—preserved in ritual, in the reading of Biblical texts during special times of the year, or in the texts recited during candle lighting of Hanukkah (Yerushalmi 1982). *Shaar Lamathil* offers the new citizen a simplified version of the holiday in a particular manner that links the past with the secular Zionist present (and future).

The innate authority of pedagogical texts is strengthened by other factors relating to the purpose of the texts and their intended audience: the use of narratives focuses the attention of readers to events and characters, to the surface plot; migrants learning the language of the new society may be more attentive to linguistic rules and new lexemes than to ideas embedded in them. The result is one 'correct' version of history and rituals that reinforce the unity of the Jews arriving to Israel from different traditions. Regardless of their backgrounds, readers are instructed to follow yearly the rituals prescribed by *Shaar Lamathil*: they light candles, observe the same foodways, sing the same songs, tell similar stories. The potentially manipulative power of the medium is used to establish homogeneity but also to suppress ethnic identity and variety. The combination of factors naturalizes implicit ideas and ideologies in the texts—they become immune to critical evaluation.

Migration, Media, Language—Concluding Remarks

Hanukkah in Simplified Hebrew demonstrates the power of pedagogical texts in transforming migrants' identities. Explicitly and implicitly, *Shaar Lamathil* instructs the readers about the rules of becoming Israeli through lessons in history-mythology and practical ways of celebrating. The texts—at all levels—are employed for the Israeli nation-building project: they introduce the migrants to the state of Israel, its institutions, population(s), and cultural lifestyle. Learning the language is presented as an important step in crossing the threshold of new Jewish–Israeli identity.

However, contemporary social trends challenge the idea of language as defining national identity. The proliferation of global languages, mainly English, work migration, transglobal diasporas, the World Wide Web—question the need for competence in the language of the host community as necessary for acculturation. People may reside in one country but lead social and professional lives in other spheres, virtual or actual. Israelis who migrated from the former Soviet Union maintain a rich cultural life in Russian and their Israeli identity is not defined solely by Hebrew (Anteby-Yemini 2004; Ben-Rafael 2001; Smooha 2008). Occasional remarks from students of Hebrew suggest rejection of the nationalistic-Jewish mission of pedagogical texts, wishing to learn the language rather than being culturally transformed.

The challenge for teaching language skills to migrants—and for pedagogical texts in the target language—is to find paradigms that provide knowledge and foster national identity without denying ethnicity. In sum: to open a gate rather than strengthen the barriers between 'us' and 'them' and between old and new identities.

References

Adoni, H., Cohen, A. A., Caspi, D. (2002). The consumer's choice: Language, media consumption and hybrid identities of minorities. *Communications*, *27*, 411–436.
Anderson, B. (1983). *Imagined communities.* London: Verso.
Anteby-Yemini, L. (2004). Being an Oleh in a global world: From local ethnic community to transnational community. In A. Kemp, U. Ram, & O. Yiftachel (Eds.), *Israelis in conflict: Hegemonies, identities and challenges* (pp. 144–161). Portland: Sussex Academic Press.
Aviad, R., & Peretz, M. (2003). The quiet revolution in language teaching: Assessment exams in the ulpan. In Y. Schlezinger & M. Muchnik (Eds.), *Studies celebrating thirty years of the Israeli association of applied linguistics* (pp. 9–25). Jerusalem: Zivonim. In Hebrew.
Bar Yosef, R. (1964). Desocialization and resocialization: The adjustment process of immigrants. *International Migration Review*, *2*(3), 546–558.
Ben-Rafael, E. (1994). *Language, identity and social division: The case of Israel*. Oxford: Clarendon Press.
Ben-Rafael, E. (2001). The transformation of diasporas: The linguistic dimension. In E. Ben Rafael & Y. Sternberg (Eds.), *Identity, culture and globalization* (pp. 337–351). Leiden: Brill.
Ben-Rafael, E. (2007). Mizrahi and Russian Challenges to Israel's dominant culture: Divergences and convergences. *Israel Studies*, *12*, 68–91.
Bhabha, H. K. (1990). DissemiNation: Time, narrative, and the margins of the modern nation. In H. K. Bhabah (Ed.), *Nation and narration* (pp. 291–323). London: Routledge.
Billig, M. (1995). *Banal nationalism.* London: Sage.
Bird, E. S., & Dardenne, R. W. (1992). Myth, chronicle and story: Exploring the narrative authority of news. In J. W. Carey (Ed.), *Media, myth and narratives: Television and the press* (pp. 67–86). Newbury Park: Sage.
Blommaert, J., Creve, L., & Willaert, E. (2006). On being declared illiterate: Language-ideological disqualification in Dutch classes for immigrants in Belgium. *Language and Communication*, *26*, 34–54.
Blum, S. (1971). How to be weaned from Simplified Hebrew? In S. Kodesh (Ed.), *Kamrat Book* (pp. 52–61). Jerusalem: Ministry of Education. In Hebrew.
Blum-Kulka, S. (2005). Modes of meaning making in children's conversation storytelling. In J. Thornborrow & J. Coates (Eds.), *The sociolinguistics of narrative* (pp. 149–170). Amsterdam: John Benjamins.
Bourdieu, P. (1991). *Language and symbolic power*. Cambridge: Polity Press.
Brug, M. (1993). There are enough Hashmoneans. *Haaretz*, December 10, 1993. In Hebrew.
Cody, F. (2009). Inscribing subjects to citizenship: Petitions, literacy activism, and the performativity of signature in rural Tamil India. *Cultural Anthropology, 24*, 347–380.

Don-Yehiya, E. (1992). Hanukkah and the myth of the Maccabees in Zionist ideology and in Israeli society. *Jewish Journal of Sociology, 34,* 5–24.
Eden, M., & Shavit, Y. (2003). All crazy buds of Jewish Antioch should be destroyed. *Haaretz,* December 25, 2003. In Hebrew.
Fairclough, N. (1995). *Critical discourse analysis: The critical study of language.* London: Longman.
Fairclough, N. (2005). Critical discourse analysis. *Linguistique, 9,* 76–94.
Goldberg, H. E., & Bram, C. (2007). Sephardic/Mizrahi/Arab-Jews: Reflections on critical sociology and the study of Middle Eastern Jewries within the context of Israeli society. In Medding P (Ed.), *Sephardic Jewry and Mizrahi Jews studies in contemporary Jewry* (pp. 227–256). Oxford: Oxford University Press.
Goldberg, T., Porat, D., & Schwarz, B. B. (2006). 'Here started the rift we see today': Student and textbook narratives between official and counter memory. *Narrative Inquiry, 16,* 319–347.
Hall, S. (1996). The question of cultural identity. In S. Hall (Ed.), *Modernity: An introduction to modern societies* (pp. 595–634). Cambridge: Blackwell.
Handelman, D. (1998). *Models and mirrors.* New York: Berghahn Books.
Harris, R. (2000). *Rethinking writing.* London: Athlone Press.
Harshav, B. (1993). *Language in time of revolution.* Berkeley: University of California Press.
Heller, M., & Martin-Jones, M. (Eds.). (2001). *Voices of authority: Education and linguistic differences.* Westport: Ablex.
Horenczyk, G. (2000). Conflicted identities: Acculturation attitudes and immigrants' construction of their social worlds. In G. Horenczyk & E. Olshtain (Eds.), *Language, identity and immigration* (pp. 13–30). Jerusalem: Magness Press.
Kramsch, C. (2000). *Literacy, equity, access for the immigrant learner. Language, identity and immigration.* In G. Horenczyk & E. Olshtain (Eds.), *Language, identity and immigration* (pp. 325–338). Jerusalem: Magness Press.
Kroskrity, P. V. (2001). *Regimenting languages: Language ideological perspectives.* Santa Fe: School of American Research Press.
Krzyżanowski, M., & Wodak, R. (2007). Multiple identities, migration, and belonging: Voices of migrants. In R. Cladas-Coulthard & R. Iedema (Eds.), *Identity troubles* (pp. 95–119). Basingstoke: Palgrave.
Milani, T. M. (2008). Language testing and citizenship: A language ideological debate in Sweden. *Language in Society, 37,* 27–59.
Nir, R. (1985). Simplification of Hebrew journalistic texts. In M. Zahari et al. (Eds.), *Nation and language: Festschrift for Ariyeh Tartakover* (pp. 277–288). Jerusalem: Magness Press. In Hebrew.
Olshtain, E., & Kotik, B. (2000). The development of bilingualism in an immigrant community. In G. Horenczyk & E. Olshtain (Eds.), *Language, identity and immigration* (pp. 201–217). Jerusalem: Magness Press.
Paxton, R. J. (1999). Deafening silence: History textbooks and the students who read them. *Review of Educational Research, 69,* 315–339.
Purcell-Gates, V., Jacobson, E., & Degener, S. (2004). *Print literacy development: Uniting cognitive and social practice theories.* Cambridge: Harvard University Press.
Rahat, R. (1977). A study of the paper Shaar Lakoreh Hahadash. *Iyunim, 8: The uneducated and the mass media.* Jerusalem: The Ministry of Education. In Hebrew.
Schejter, A. M. (2007). 'The pillar of fire by night, to shew them light': Israeli broadcasting, the Supreme Court and the Zionist narrative. *Media, Culture and Society, 29,* 916–933.
Schely-Newman, E. (2008). Local concerns, foreign heroes: George Washington in Israel. *Western Folklore, 67*(4), 351–378.
Schmid, C. L. (2001). *The politics of language: Conflict, identity and cultural pluralism in comparative perspective.* Oxford: Oxford University Press.
Shapira, A. (2000). Hirbet Hizah: Between remembrance and forgetting. *Jewish Social Studies, 7,* 1–62.

Shohamy, E. (2009). Language tests for immigrants: Why language? why tests? why citizenship? In G. Hogan-Brun, C. Mar-Molinero, & P. Stevenson (Eds.), *Discourses on language and integration* (pp. 45–59). Amsterdam: John Benjamins.

Shohamy, E., & Kanza, T. (2009). Language and citizenship in Israel. *Language Assessment Quarterly, 6*, 83–88.

Silverstein, M. (1996). Monoglot 'standard' in America: Standardization and metaphors of linguistic hegemony. In D. Brenneis & R. K. S. Macaulay (Eds.), *The matrix of language* (pp. 284–306). New York: Westview Press.

Silverstein, M. (1998). The uses and utilities of ideology: A commentary. In B. B. Schieffelin, K. A. Woolard, & P. V. Kroskrity (Eds.), *Language ideologies: Practice and theory* (pp. 12–145). New York: Oxford University Press.

Smooha, S. (2008). The mass immigration to Israel: A comparison of the failure of the Mizrahi immigrants of the 1950s with the success of the Russian immigrants of the 1990s. *Journal of Israeli History, 27*, 1–27.

Spolsky, B., & Shohamy, E. (1999). *The languages of Israel: Policy, ideology and practice.* Clevedon: Multilingual Matters.

Tollefson, J. W. (1991). *Planning language, planning inequality: Language policy in the community.* London: Longman.

van Dijk, T. A. (2001). Critical discourse analysis. In D. Schiffrin, D. Tannen, & H. E. Hamilton (Eds.), *Handbook of discourse analysis* (pp. 352–371). Malden: Blackwell.

van Dijk, T. A. (2004). Racism, discourse and textbooks: The coverage of immigration in Spanish textbooks. A Symposium on Human Rights in Textbooks. Istanbul.

van Dijk, T. A. (2006). Discourse and manipulation. *Discourse and Society, 17,* 359–383.

Weingrod, A., & Levy, A. (2006). Paradoxes of homecoming: The Jews and their diasporas. *Anthropological Quarterly, 79,* 691–716.

Wodak, R. (2006). Dilemmas of discourse (analysis). *Language in Society, 35,* 595–611.

Wodak, R., De Cillia, R., Riesigl, M., & Liebhart, K. (1996). *The discursive construction of national identity.* Edinburgh: Edinburgh University Press.

Yerushalmi, H. Y. (1982). *Zakhor: Jewish history and Jewish memory.* Washington, DC: University of Washington Press.

Zerubavel, Y. (1995). *Recovered roots: Collective memory and the making of Israeli national tradition.* Chicago: University of Chicago Press.

Chapter 11
Living in Different Worlds and Learning All About It: Migration Narratives in Perspective

Joanne Cassar

Introduction

Immigration to Malta[1] in the last few years has mainly been perceived as interrupting normality. The transitional process from a relatively homogenous society into a multiethnic one is actively resisted through political policies, which frame migrants as "inferior others" (Lee 2009, p. 155). Since 2002, the increasing number of boats carrying asylum seekers from sub-Saharan African countries to Malta has caused the proliferation of a public discourse, that is mainly made up of racist and xenophobic sentiments and which gave way to frequent discrimination, hostility, and negative stereotypes towards asylum seekers (Borg and Mayo 2006). The embodiment of this discourse in Maltese society permeates its social structures and constantly reminds Maltese citizens that the immigration situation has reached "crisis proportions." In general, African immigrants are located within discourses that define them as dependent, homeless, subordinate, nationless, undocumented, anonymous, clandestine, and a "burden." These discourses have been perceived as a means of protecting social security and acting as a form of a defense mechanism and "reflect the challenge posed by massive migration from the South to the North in the context of the intensification of globalization" (Mayo 2007, p. 2).

This chapter presents two case studies, which focus on the personal narratives of two Somali migrants who lived in Malta after the year 2002. One of them is Qassim Aways Saalim, who was interviewed by Maltese journalist Karl Stagno-Navarra (2009). The other asylum seeker is Warsame Ali Garare, whose story was told by Msnbc (2007a, b). These two men attempted to engage in the construction of knowledge as means of coping with the realities they faced as a result of their

---

[1] Malta is a small country in the Mediterranean Sea. It has a population of 400,000 people and is one of the countries in the European Union, which is mostly affected by African migration. It is one of the most densely populated countries in the world.

J. Cassar (✉)
Department of Youth and Community Studies, University of Malta, Msida, Malta
e-mail: joanne.cassar@um.edu.mt

migration experiences. Their perspectives demonstrate that migration offers possibilities of learning about life and learning from life. Their narratives are regarded as entailing a self-mediated process that reflects power structures operating in their host country. This process also entailed attempts by them to improve this society. This study employs a poststructuralist approach (Derrida 1976) and a critical paradigm to explore the nature of the migrants' experiential learning through an investigation of their problems and issues. The critical paradigm draws on Foucault's insights (1977a, b), who assumed that knowledge is not neutral but is a result of human interests. This paradigm attempts a deconstructive approach, which is adopted in putting forward a number of suggestions, with reference to educational strategies aimed at contributing towards a greater understanding of migration issues. This chapter takes up Stronach and MacLure's appeal, who argue that deconstruction "ought to be a central concern of educational research and theory" (1997, p. 32) and who refer to Derrida's definition of it as "a critical culture, a kind of education" (Stronach and MacLure 1997).

Methodology

Data were collected through internet websites. Repeated attempts to find internet narratives of women migrants who live/lived in Malta have yielded no results. This testifies to the invisibility of the articulations of migrant women, who come to Malta. The narratives of both case studies have been collected by journalists. The data were therefore not the result of responses to specific questions asked by myself. This is considered as a limitation of the study. In making use of secondary sources, I acknowledge that these data can be general and vague. The experiences of the two migrants, located in Malta are, however, very familiar to me, since I also share the same geographical territory and I am immersed in national debates surrounding migration issues. Since I am not a migrant, I consider myself as an "outsider," since I pertain to a different generation, social class, and culture from that of these two informants. Through the two case studies, I have questioned my familiarity with migrant issues and engaged myself in an understanding of the inherent uniqueness of the two migrants, as described by them.

Ali's narratives are supported by numerous photos and video clips, which reveal his voice and surroundings (Msnbc 2007a, b). While affirming that images are increasingly being considered as significant forms of data (Plummer 2001, pp. 59–66) and that they are a powerful means of doing research (Walker 1993), I acknowledge that photographic images are not created passively or objectively (Haraway 1991):

> …visual images are always constructed, and visualization is an accomplishment involving perspective and directional gaze, so none of these is directly and straightforwardly 'evidential' and 'representational'. (Mason 2005, p. 108)

The location of Qassim's and Ali's narratives in cyberspace, where the distinction of the virtual and the real world is blurred, could be considered problematic. These narratives have been mediated and filtered by the journalists who have presented their spoken narratives into written words. This creates an instability in language, which disrupts the meanings of texts (Derrida 1976). Although words carry their contexts with them, the fullness, completeness, and the presence ascribed to them is never fully realized (Derrida 1976). Consequently, it is difficult to arrive at conclusions.

I have not met these two migrants in person and have never contacted them. I am concerned that by limiting my encounter with them, I was perpetuating the existing barriers that exist between "us" (Maltese) and "them" (migrants). By concentrating on their existing narratives only, I acknowledge that I might have chosen to distance and alienate myself from them. Consequently, it is possible that I might have derived meanings from their narratives that were unintended by them. Woodward (2000) also shares these feelings, which resulted from not meeting her informants in person and from not talking to them. In order to reduce the risk of making my voice more central than that of the migrants (Wolf 1996), I have chosen to present their narratives at length.

Although I have "met" the two migrants in a digital environment populated by hundreds of thousands, or even millions of internet users, they have never met me. Amidst these preoccupations, my intention in writing about them is to affirm their voice and legitimate it through an exploration of their life experiences. By foregrounding their concerns, my intention is to do justice to their articulations by exploring how they used their migration experiences to learn. The framework which underpins this exploration is built on the assumption that people, who talk through their problems and embark on self-inquiry, increase their self-awareness (Babad et al. 1983).

Migrant issues are omnipresent and highly visible in the Maltese media, in electoral campaigns and electoral manifestos. Yet these same machineries hardly ever bring the migrant personal voices to the fore. Attempts at silencing, subduing, and hiding the migrants' voice is perhaps a coping strategy, which revolves around denial and which tries to suppress the Maltese people's own suffering related to a colonial past. Migrant people's attempts towards mobility is met with the realization that "the 'spectre' of the violent colonial process the 'old continent' initiated has come back with a vengeance to 'haunt' it" (Borg and Mayo 2006, p. 151). My methodological approach is concerned with "representing the actions of the relatively unknown, perhaps oppressed and ignored" (Goodley et al. 2004, p. 57). I have considered the migrants' narratives as attempts by them to open up, emerge from segregated underworlds, share knowledge and assert their migrant voice. Their narratives are considered "documents of life" (Plummer 2001), which inform others of their strengths and vulnerabilities. It is not the purpose of this chapter to speak for the migrants, especially because I myself am not a migrant. I acknowledge that the term "migrant" is problematic since migrants do not form a homogenous group. There are a number of complexities surrounding attempts to speak for the migrants, especially by academics (Galea 2008).

The migrants' stories only describe succinct snippets from their lives. Their text is a fragmented part of wider debates about migration, integration, learning, and their intersection. My interpretation of their narratives moves away from the idea of having fixed and grounded contexts. Meanings of words cannot be fixed in single texts since they refer to other texts and contexts; therefore creating a web of intertextuality in meaning. Words only have meaning in relation to other words and there is no absolute meaning of any word but rather meaning is always in flux and cannot be fixed in language (Derrida 1976). I have regarded the migrants' narratives as referring to events which are unfolding and in process. A number of events have led to the migrants' narratives. Their voices are mediated by the dynamics they experience daily, their culture and by the politics administered in Maltese society. Their personality, frame of mind, and attitude also played an important role in the construction of their texts. They might have suffered far beyond what they have said and they might have been hiding more pain than they could describe. On the other hand, they might have exaggerated and overinflated their anxiety. Some of their experiences might never emerge in the open but remain hidden inside their psyche.

These possibilities generate a proliferation of interpretations and multiple realities. Consequently, no single interpretation can be claimed to be the final one (Derrida 1976). From a poststructuralist standpoint, there are no facts or conclusions, but interpretations (Foucault 1972). I have adopted this approach, acknowledging that: "Single vision produces worse illusions than double vision or many-headed monsters" (Haraway 1991, p. 155).

Ali Garare

Ali Garare was brought up in Mogadishu (2010a, b). The civil war in Somalia was part of his daily living. Despite the tension and fear of being killed, he did his best to study, work, and teach. He is fluent in Arabic, English, French, and Somali as well as several African languages including Hausa, Swahili, and Zarma. But in 2002, in his late twenties, when the instability and fighting intensified, he had to leave everything behind him and flee. For two years he trekked through Kenya, Ethiopia, Sudan, Niger, and Libya. The daily conditions of his journeys were terrifying: "I always had problems.... It's so painful" (Msnbc 2007b). He travelled from country to country and through the desert without any official documents. Somali citizens were refused passports in their own country, so that they would not escape in order to form part of the military.

Ali then worked in Libya for six months to be able to pay for and organize his clandestine boat trip to Europe. When he had enough money, he was "smuggled" out of Tripoli in a crammed boat. After the third day at sea, the engine of Ali's boat broke down, leaving his group "floating," as they ran out of water. They sucked sugar cubes for survival. Their original destination was Italy but after six days at sea they managed to arrive in Malta unexpectedly. During the first three months in Malta, he stayed in "the most horrible place," (Msnbc 2007b) a prison-like, isolated detention center, while his asylum status was being decided on. After he was granted humanitarian protection, he was ordered to stay in a detention center run by the military.

Despite these horrific experiences, his leadership qualities and his enthusiasm to care for others stood out and shortly after he was released in 2005, he was asked to set up a center for migrants and work as a "social worker." This center was previously an abandoned school situated in a squalid, non residential area, located between a shipyard and red-light district. With very limited resources, Ali Garare tried to create a "home" for about six-seven hundred people, almost all of them young men, who came from numerous countries with different languages, cultures, religions, and cuisine. Creating a "home" was not easy as many felt disengaged. Most of them were destitute and withdrawn into themselves and felt isolated. They just stayed in their rooms. They suffered trauma caused by the horrors of war, attacks, and deaths which they had witnessed along their journeys. They were also disillusioned and felt a sense of shame at not being able to arrive in mainland Europe and support the families they had left behind. They were also immersed in the "burden discourse" and felt that they were to blame for the "immigration crisis." Having spent months and months in detention and then having to wait endlessly to be granted a passport, they felt that their long-held dreams of reaching Europe and starting a new life were fading.

Despite this lethargy and disabling depression, which engulfed the residents, Ali managed to involve them and together they took the initiative to create a small Africa inside the center by creating African "restaurants," tobacco stands, internet cafe', a "mosque," and barber shop. In this way, they created a small village, which gave "people a chance to start their own businesses" (Msnbc 2007b). The residents themselves "decided what to run and how to run it." They worked together to create it themselves, "as a community, as a group" (Msnbc 2007b).

The center has also raised awareness about their inhumane conditions and sought to protect their human and legal rights, especially in matters concerning the difficulties in determining their status as either migrants or refugees. Through his charismatic, humane, personal approach, Ali gave his fellow migrants emotional support: "They feel comfortable with me, and come to me to see if I can solve their problems" (Msnbc 2007b). Ali was described as very friendly; often stopping by to shake hands or embrace the migrants, who depended on his language skills to communicate their needs. Despite his busy schedule, Ali still found time to give a hug to a friend in need or help translate for a deaf Somali immigrant, since he also knows sign language and has taught himself the Maltese language. British expatriate Terry Gosden who heads the center said that: "The only reason we have the mental stability we have in the center is because of Warsame" (Msnbc 2007b). He also stressed that Ali is someone who "most countries would dream of having" (Msnbc 2007a).

The migrants at the center come from opposite political factions, which are at war. Ali was a peacekeeper amongst the migrants' disparate groups. Amongst the six hundred men living there, some "may have been on opposite sides of conflicts in Africa, (but) in the center they live together creating community in makeshift restaurants where people from Somalia, Eritrea, and Ethiopia can socialize with others from their own countries and eat familiar foods" (Msnbc 2007a).

While most of the residents at the center regarded him as their mentor and friend, Ali emphasized that his own life remains very insecure as he was uncertain of how he could leave Malta and settle permanently in a relatively safe and stable country. "The only dream I have is to live like anyone else, just to have normal stability in life" (Msnbc 2007a). He emphasized that he will never feel at home in a country that will not accept him. "I worry about the future," he said. "How long can we go on like this?" (Msnbc 2007a).

Qassim

Some migrants become reflexive as a result of traumas they endured and perhaps also because they have a lot of time at their disposal to think about their situation since in their confinement they have nothing to do all day. Qassim's story, reported both in the first and third person by Stagno Navarra (2009) demonstrates this attempt to become reflexive:

> Let no Maltese or any other European citizen witness the horrors of a lawless nation like mine, and never feel the urge of running away, not only from war, but also from certain death, where you are hunted down with guns and machetes because all you did was speak on a radio station and appeal for peace…
> He is also a journalist documenting his now one-year long stay in Malta, six months of which he spent in detention. Qassim—formerly of Radio Simba in the Somali capital Mogadishu—shows me two plain copybooks, where he is neatly documenting his ordeal as an asylum seeker.
> I am writing this because in the years to come, I want Europe to know what welcome my fellow people and myself have been given… I have lived in detention for months and lived in squalid conditions, until Allah heard my prayers and was released from my prison. After the cage, I was put in a tent… I worked as a radio speaker on Radio Simba broadcasting. Simba in Swahili means lion, and the radio was one of many that broadcasted appeals for peace. My radio director, my colleagues have all been killed. Others like me who managed to escape and kept up with their peace campaigns have been hunted down and been killed in Addis Ababa in Ethiopia, and in places as far as Nigeria.
> …he also describes his escape on foot and by truck through the dangerous route out of Somalia into Ethiopia, Sudan, Chad, and eventually into Libya where he hid in a farm for two whole months not to be caught by the Libyan police, until the day he set off on a boat towards Europe together with other Somali nationals. He was rescued by a Maltese patrol boat after spending three days stalled at sea, and he recounts his ordeal at the hands of the Maltese authorities in July of last year.
> …We were whisked into a bus when we arrived to shore, and taken for fingerprinting. After that we were just dumped into a big cage. I knew I reached a European member state, I was constantly asking myself is this really it? I started to doubt it, and forgot all about it as soon as I was just kept behind bars for months, living like an animal.
> Qassim has since been released into an open center after his request for humanitarian status was upheld by the Maltese government. He was transferred to the Hal Far tent village. But time and calendars don't even matter here. The worst is that people like Qassim and hundreds of others, have no idea of what is to happen with them. What future could they possibly have? He spends his days sitting on his bunk-bed, writing his diary and documenting

his life, and his homeland. "*I need books, paper, pens, internet,*" he says, while I promise to relay his requests to Reporters Sans Frontiers. Before I leave, Qassim asks me to take a picture of us together. He smiles and asks me not to forget him.

Qassim drew on his personal experiences of contradiction, subjugated knowledge and multiple positionings through his subversive voice. His narrative might have stemmed from his "obligation to confess" (Foucault 1978, p. 60), which:

> ...is now relayed through so many different points, is so deeply ingrained in us, that we no longer perceive it as the effect of a power that constrains us; on the contrary, it seems to us that truth, lodged in our most secret nature, "demands" only to surface.... (Foucault 1978)

My interpretation of Qassim's experiences and narratives of violence, as told by him during the interview, is viewed primarily from a lens of "deep admiration" towards him but it is also built on the assumption that he is considered an unheroic hero by numerous Maltese citizens. Qassim seemed to be very much aware of the power of narrative and regarded his stories as having political and historical importance, which can serve to alert others about the horrors of war. He seemed to believe that the act of writing in his diary granted him some form of agency to communicate the legitimization of his knowledge. His writings can be described as constructing sites of "conflicting forms of subjectivity, of political strategy waged mainly through language" (Humphries et al. 2000, p. 11). He considered his writings as having the potential power to break the cycles of violence. He also attempted to break his marginalization by drawing into himself and writing about new possibilities. The enclosed spaces within detention and the tent village are not limited to just being confined in a physical structure such as a detention center, but could also be regarded as a person's drawing within her/himself to gain self-knowledge.

Although Qassim strongly desired that nobody witnesses his horrors, at the same time he felt the need to perpetuate them by writing about them, so that they would not be forgotten. Through his journal writing he sought to find ownership of his voice. Power brings along resistance to counteract it (Foucault 1978). Within repressive discourses are the seeds of counter discourses that can subvert dominant views (Foucault 1977a). Qassim's writings might be considered a form of passive resistance against being fed the discourse that he is a "burden." Qassim described himself as a "dissident" (Stagno Navarra 2009). Alongside this resistance, however, he expressed accommodation to the power structures operating within his life. Although resistance might be a possible initial step towards empowerment, it is also "an essentially defensive relationship to cultural power" (Bennett 1998, p. 171). Qassim's use of the words "animal," "cage," and "prison" revolve around a discourse of victimization. The long-lasting effects of unsafe and inhumane asylum perpetuate feelings of shame and sadness. The asylum "is a juridical space where one is accused, judged, and condemned, and from which one is never released except by the version of this trial in psychological depth—that is, by remorse" (Foucault 1984, p. 158). Through his narratives he fought this "remorse" and strongly insisted that human beings should never be hounded and killed. His appeal not to be forgotten does not seem to be so much related to his own persona but rather to a collective consciousness about the horrific traumas of war.

Learning to Belong

These two migrants' biographies can be considered "evocative narratives" (Ellis and Bochner 2000, p. 744), which bring together an interplay of a multiplicity of power relations. Power and resistance practices are embedded in this interplay. The narratives demonstrate the difficulties involved in striking a compromise "between, on the one hand people's feelings, their moral choices, their relationship with themselves, and, on the other hand, the institutions that surround them" (Foucault 1988, pp. 161–162).

The migrants' entrapment in the detention center, tent village and in the migrants' center functions as a deterrent against new arrivals of migrants (European Commission against Racism and Intolerance (2007, p. 22). It is employed as a mechanism to stabilize the perceived fears of social insecurity caused by the migrants. Although the principle of social security in itself has its benefits, the ways that it is employed are not always coherent with the respect for the migrants' human rights. Foucault (1988) argues that social security can also be regarded as having "perverse effects," (p. 160), due to an "increasing rigidity of certain mechanisms and a growth in dependence" (Foucault 1988). To reconcile this "infernal couple" namely security-dependence Foucault proposes "a security that opens the way to richer, more numerous, more diverse, and more flexible relations with one self and one's environment, while guaranteeing to each individual real autonomy" (Foucault 1988, p. 161). This implies a certain degree of displacement from the state and assuming responsibility of one's well-being.

Ali and his fellow migrants were capable to an extent of working around the policies and institutions, which dictated their confinement in their center. Together they transformed the abandoned classrooms of the dilapidated old school into other type of "classrooms" where "peace education" and interfaith dialogue could be learnt. The "pedagogical" spaces they constructed, served to expose, challenge and expand their self-awareness. In their exploration and experimentation of their new world away from their native land, they sought and constructed a sense of familiarity and continuity.

Despite their search for pathways towards empowerment, both Ali and Qassim seemed to be aware of their voicelessness but they still attempted to tap into the potential transformative power of human beings. From this perspective, their narratives highlight their resilience and agency rather than their passivity. Operating within environments that disenfranchise migrants, Ali employed an ethic of care and assumed personal responsibility and accountability towards other migrants, without assuming superiority. Ali's involvement in the center helped to improve his personal situation and that of others. This attitude can be understood as leading to an expansion of knowledge.

Inside the center, the migrants' attempts at learning the process of enculturation to initiate new understandings of diverse social groups, signal the trajectories of both their individual personhood and of their nationhood. Both trajectories are in a process of transition. The migrants' encounters among heterogeneous groups necessitated them to adapt in a pluralistic and multicultural community through a process of homogenization. Migration offered them the ability to break down ethnic prejudices and go beyond conflicts present in their own homeland by giving way to mutual toleration and understanding. As they performed their migrant self, their inner feelings and thoughts were met with a plethora of cultural norms, which seemed to cause their private/public boundaries to collide.

Because the migrants faced common challenges, struggles and vulnerabilities they learned how to seek and appreciate commonalities, despite their differences. The migrants' connection with each other was not only based on the concept of shared identity as migrants but also on alliance. Their journey into their private, inner self took them towards taboo realms related to befriending the "other." In their desperation they were bound to reflexively ask why they were there, and what they needed to do to improve their situation, thus digging out their inner knowledge and resources. In their struggle to belong, they fought self-alienation. By inhabiting different cultural worlds, they learned how to adapt themselves in order to be accepted and survive. This means learning "how to move between worlds" (Mirza 2010, p. 135). This necessitates compromising and being a different person in different scenarios (Mirza 2010). Consequently, the migration experience demanded them to reframe their personal identity and learn to forge a new self in view of their intercultural encounters with diverse national identities. Their life as migrants taught them that freedom is "a constant attempt at self-disengagement and self-invention" (Rajchman, quoted in Sawicki 1991, p. 101). As they learned how to come to terms with emerging parts of themselves, they sought out means to establish material and emotional security and support. This exercise is also required of the host country, yet most Maltese citizens have been reluctant to take up this challenge but rather prefer to rely on hegemonic discourses (Mercieca 2007; Borg and Mayo 2006). Although migrants are often regarded as subordinate and marginalized, they provide invaluable insights about the host society.

Learning to Learn from Life: The Purpose of Education

The fear of the migrant has also migrated to Maltese schools and is also present among a number of Maltese students (Camilleri 2007). I regard schools as having the purpose of compensating for the lack of compassion towards migrants. I consider education as being able to provide alternative spaces, aimed at deconstructing dominant beliefs surrounding racist discourses and which contest the purpose of social spaces. Schools can provide illusionary spaces, which offer visions of a world, which does not yet exist fully and which is conducted by multicultural principles based on empathy, compassion and solidarity, through spaces that create "astonishment, surprise and enigmatic experience" (Mercieca 2007, p. 145). According to Foucault (1977b) however, schools adopt a "disciplinary machinery," which moves away from the idea of compassion. The gaze of surveillance present in detention centers is also present institutionally in schools:

> A relation of surveillance, defined and regulated, is inscribed at the heart of the practice of teaching, not as an additional or adjacent part, but as a mechanism that is inherent to it and which increases its efficiency. (Foucault 1977b, p. 176)

In teaching institutions, "The Normal is established as a principle of coercion in teaching with the introduction of a standardized education…" (Foucault 1977b; p. 184), which moulds attitudes and behaviors in particular ways to ensure that hegemonic power is safeguarded through the reproduction of ideas and values aimed at doing so. Yet within the embedded structures of domination surrounding human beings' lives, there could also be more open spaces of possibility. I suggest that schools, as centers of knowledge, provide spaces for the other to be deconstructed and also be able to create spaces that expose real possibilities for multiculturalism to dominate. Derrida (1992) holds that if such a thing as deconstruction exists, it is justice (pp. 14–15). Deconstruction entails uncovering the invisibility of dialogue in education curricula on migrant subjectivities. The asking of questions about the possible meanings and implications of migrant narratives is one way of facilitating this. Deconstruction allows educators to explore ways of dismantling racist and discriminatory viewpoints. In Derrida's view, deconstruction is neither a method, nor a set of rules or tools. It demands one to "perform something new," in one's own language, one's singular situation and signature "to invent the impossible and to break with the application …" (1996, pp. 217–218). Through deconstruction, education can function to make the real seem unreal, the familiar seem strange and to make knowledge both strange and familiar (Britzman 2000, p. 51) through representing, contesting and inverting notions about social spaces. Foucault (1994a) describes the utopia/real dichotomy by using the comparison of the mirror, which can be adopted to education:

> …The mirror is a utopia after all, since it is a placeless place. In the mirror I see myself where I am not, in an unreal space that opens up virtually behind the surface; I am over there where I am not, a kind of shadow that gives me my own visibility, that enables me to look at myself there where I am absent- a mirror utopia. (pp. 178–179)

In this sense, education "can see itself where it is not." This perspective regards education as a vehicle which is capable of crossing boundaries to depart from cultural, theoretical, and ideological borders (Giroux 1992) that are enveloped within the safety of "those places and spaces we inherit and occupy, which frame our lives in very specific and concrete ways" (Borsa 1990, p. 36).

Principles which foster respect for cultural diversity and multicultural dialogue through education have been advocated by a number of Maltese educators and researchers (Azzopardi 2008; Camilleri and Camilleri 2008; Galea 2008; Camilleri

2007; Mayo 2007; Borg and Mayo 2006). Together with these guidelines, I add the pedagogical principle of addressing the complexities of discourses in the curriculum (Cassar 2007, pp. 175–181) and examine the "regulatory effects" which are inherent to "all discourses" (Allen 2004, p. 159), as well as encourage students to critically examine the implications of multiculturalism and cosmopolitanism. A curriculum, which reflects on human tragedies, is promoted in order to challenge discursive spaces which frame immigration as necessarily dangerous and in need of resistance. I envisage schools as providing spaces of resistance to "hate speech" against migrants and to othering discourses, not simply by advocating tolerance but by deconstructing the justification of othering discourses and normative, racist dominance. Such liberating learning communities support students in progressing from passive recipients of knowledge, who perceive dominant discourses as sources of truth, to active thinkers engaged in the construction of knowledge through reason, intuition and collaboration. This implies the learning of a language to generate "alternative stories that incorporate vital and previously neglected aspects of lived experience" (White and Epston 1990, p. 31). This necessitates educational intervention, which aims towards social inclusion based on critical reflection on how negative stereotypes are formed in particular cultural formations and how they shape mentalities. These stereotypes are not limited to how images of the other are formed but also how "we" are constructed to accommodate and reproduce these stereotypes. The possibility of shedding the different layers of racism is built on the recognition that "…an anti-racist programme of education and social action can be successful only if rooted in political economy and an understanding of colonialism" (Mayo 2007, p. 9). When paraphrasing Derrida, Standish mentions the role of the professor (I extend this role to teachers), which suggests supporting students not only to open up to new concepts but also to "the impossible":

> The responsibility of the professor extends beyond the performatives of criticism to an openness to the event. It must extend beyond the 'masterable possible', which is the result of conventions and legitimate fictions, to the surprise of the impossible possible, which has the character of the arrivant. Openness to the impossible possible, something beyond the range of predetermined categories or a purely autonomous control (effective performance), is essential to the exercise and growth of the imagination that this professing requires. (Standish 2001, p. 18)

I relate the idea about "the openness of the event" (Standish 2001) to multicultural teaching, which should not be limited by a relativistic approach, but be open to possibilities and take students into unforeseen territories. In this sense, education itself becomes a migrant and migrates towards terrains of otherness and trespasses between dominant concepts related to different cultural and political boundaries that cultivate hegemony, in order to deconstruct these same concepts. De Lauretis (1987) asks: "How do changes in consciousness affect changes in dominant discourses?" (p. 16). She suggests enabling agency by moving between spaces contained by discourses and between "the space-off, the elsewhere, of those discourses" (De Lauretis 1987, p. 26). In this sense education is regarded as offering spaces for a journey into the personal feelings, experiences, reflections and narratives of students to explore issues revolving around the recognition that it is not the lack of space for humanity that causes racism but rather the lack of *safe* spaces (physical, political, pedagogical, mental, and emotional) available.

Conclusion

This chapter has discussed issues, which locate the migrant voice within mediated self-presentation. It has shown that learning from migrant narratives is not related to static constructs. Very often migration experiences are compelling and uproot one's life. They serve as defining moments in the migrants' lives. This does not happen automatically but requires continuous reflexivity and determination in seeking out new meanings: "Telling one's story may help in self-realization but may also be an exercise in self-delusion. Voice has to be treated with the same criticality as other biographical expressions…" (Griffiths 2003, pp. 81–82). This implies that with regards to migration learning experiences, what counts as knowledge includes the assessment and evaluation of narratives depicting everyday practices and actions.

What Qassim and Ali have learnt through their migrant experiences captures existential questions related to what it means to be human. Despite the hierarchical divisions of class, race, ethnicity, nationality and age, which interfere with their socioeconomic status, they have managed to gain access to particular spaces to voice their fears of exclusion and marginalization. The two case studies suggest that learning is not an automatic process. It requires stamina, courage and determination. While real-life experiences have the potential to lead to liberation from oppression (Freire 1970, 1994) migrants can easily adopt a fatalistic attitude and become unreflective victims of their situated experiences. Ali's and Qassim's narratives show that power goes to great lengths to survive; constructing new structures of power evidenced in spatialized, social, hegemonic cycles of knowledge and alterity. Their lived experiences and endeavors have brought them to seek answers to the question: "Is there anything other than a despairing location?" (Haraway, in Penley and Ross 1991, p. 6). The lived accounts presented by them are regarded as a channel through which they acquired new forms of learning. These are examined in the light of their emergent altered states as they struggle to integrate, belong, be accepted and "settle down." Their narrated life experiences demonstrate that resilience and coping strategies are a result of how they managed to work through personal and social networks with the local Maltese people and their politics. They embarked on a learning process in order to gain multicultural competence by striving to understand and appreciate the values, expectations and communication styles of Maltese and other traditions, which are remarkably diverse, without giving up their own, as much as possible. Their acquisition of learning emanates from their personal capabilities but also from cultural norms, which determine and mediate their understanding of what it means to live as a migrant and how to make sense of it. The learning from their experiences is understood as offering ways of functioning to cope with the uncertainties entailed in living in a new country and as a way to deal with new forms of citizenship and assimilation. This entails their skilful maneuvering of feelings of hostility and resentment towards migrants in Maltese society (Camilleri and Camilleri 2008) which have arisen out of the crisis discourse related to migrants (Busuttil 2008) and which are mainly the result of the fear of migrants and of the perceived threats and insecurity associated with them.

This chapter has proposed educational processes, which deconstruct hegemonic "whiteness" and power relations, which secure themselves through the stigmatization of the other. It suggests pedagogical practices, which address the consequences of discourses in relation to the complexities and multidimensionality of racism. This chapter suggests that the complexities surrounding discourses need to be addressed by school curricula and through pedagogy. This entails students to critically examine how discourses frame perceptions, interfere with human behavior and determine outcomes. This requires the learning of how to deconstruct the meanings and effects of discourses. The use of narratives and personal biographies as they emerge through the internet and other media, could be instrumental in establishing this task. Such practices also encompass the examination of the effects of colonialism on racism and are based on the recognition that the struggle for a multicultural society is placed amidst the struggle for the recognition of a Maltese national identity. The "us" (Maltese) and "them" (immigrants) discourse reiterates the same fragmentation of the "us" and "them" discourse in local politics. Foucault (1994b) outlines a reason for the division between human beings:

> We live in a legal, social, and institutional world where the only relations possible are, extremely simplified, and extremely poor…. Society and the institutions which frame it have limited the possibility of relationships because a rich relational world would be very complex to manage. (p. 158)

The purpose of education is to grapple with these complexities. In practical terms, this is achieved through the learning and promotion of communication skills related to interpersonal dialogue with migrants. This entails that students are engaged in discussions about the social elements surrounding multiethnicity, through teaching them how to clarify their thoughts, articulate themselves and develop agency in situations of ambiguity related to xenophobia and racism. The case studies presented suggest the promotion of critical understandings and the learning of negotiation skills in dealing with contradictory discourses about migration experiences emanating from lived realities, educational institutions, popular culture, friends and family. This approach is aimed at "resurrecting the subjugated knowledges" (Besley 2001, p. 77). It is against a schooled system based on transmitting knowledge to statically positioned learners but offers access to a language of empowerment, through an investigation of why xenophobia is prevalent and what it means for some adolescents to be part of ethnic minorities. Education policymakers have the task to examine structural problems that prevent these recommendations from reaching their potential by challenging institutional barriers and by interrogating the resounding silences that surround the promotion of multicultural principles in school curricula.

The migrants' narratives point out towards the importance of creating multiple possibilities within which a multicultural identity might flourish. They show that power can be renegotiated to challenge and eventually change socio-cultural structures and contexts. Ali's story suggests that experiential learning is facilitated through collective efforts, whereas Qassim struggles to break from isolation. In resisting and counteracting oppression, spaces of possibility are constructed to give way to less coercive ways of "governmentality" (Foucault 1991). Such ways emerge out of learning experiences. Learning problematizes, enriches, reshapes, and complicates the understanding of social phenomena, use of social space and the role of institutions. Yet, the migrant stories suggest that they do not always seek to eliminate the presence of regulations but rather they serve to facilitate an understanding of how these are formed and to whom they have to be accessible:

> There is no question that a society without restrictions is inconceivable, but I can only repeat myself in saying that these restrictions have to be within the reach of those affected by them so that they at least have the possibility of altering them. (Foucault 1994a, p. 148)

This vision gives agency and empowerment to migrants who live within discourses. Foucault (Foucault 1994a) was concerned with the sterile state of relations in modern culture and although very often he was reluctant to give pragmatic solutions to problems, he insists that "we should fight against the impoverishment of the relational fabric" and that we "should try to imagine and create a new relational right that permits all possible types of relations to exist" (p. 158).

References

Allen, L. (2004). Beyond the birds and the bees: Constituting a discourse of erotics in sexuality education. *Gender and Education, 16*(2), 152–167.

Azzopardi, A. (2008). A Raison d'Etre for multicultural education in Malta. *Malta Review of Educational Research, 6*(1), 118–128.

Babad, E. Y., Max, B., & Benne, K. D. (1983). *The social self: Group influences on personal identity.* Beverly Hills: Sage.

Bennett, T. (1998). *Culture: A reformer's science.* St. Leonards: Allen & Unwin.

Besley, T. (2001). Foucauldian influences in narrative therapy: An approach for schools. *Journal of Educational Enquiry, 2*(2), 72–93.

Borg, C., & Mayo, P. (2006). *Learning and social difference: Challenges for public education and critical pedagogy.* Boulder CO: Paradigm.

Borsa, J. (1990). Towards a politics of location: Rethinking marginality. *Canadian Women Studies, 11,* 36–39.

Britzman, D. P. (2000). Precocious education. In S. Talburt & S. Steinberg (Eds.), *Thinking queer: Sexuality, culture, and education* (pp. 33–60). New York: Peter Lang.

Busuttil, S. (2008). *Report on a Common Immigration Policy for Europe: Principles, actions and Tools.* European Parliament Session Document, Number 2331. http://simonbusuttil.eu/content/docs/Report_common_immigration_policy_for_europe.pdf. Accessed 28 June 2009.

Camilleri, J. (2007). *Do I belong?* Unpublished M.Psy dissertation, University of Malta, Malta.

Camilleri, J., & Camilleri, K. (2008). Do I belong? Psychological perspectives and educational considerations of young immigrants' school experiences. *Malta Review of Educational Research, 6*(1), 64–79.

Cassar, J. (2007). *Public and private spaces in adolescent girls' lives: School graffiti, sexualities and romantic relationship.* Unpublished Ed.D thesis, The University of Sheffield.

Derrida, J. (1976). *Of grammatology* (trans: Spivak, G. C.). Baltimore: Johns Hopkins University Press.

Derrida, J. (1992). Force of Law: The Mystical Foundation of Authority. In D. Rosenfeld and D. Carlson (Eds.), *Deconstruction and the Possibility of Justice* (pp. 3–67). New York: Routledge.

De Lauretis, T. (1987). *Technologies of gender; essays on theory, film, and fiction.* Bloomington: Indiana University Press.

Ellis, C., & Bochner, A. P. (2000). Autoethnography, personal narrative, reflexivity: Researcher as subject. In N. K. Denzin & Y. S. Lincoln (Eds.), *Handbook of qualitative research* (2nd ed., pp. 733–768). Thousand Oaks: Sage.

European Commission against Racism and Intolerance. (2007). *Third Report on Malta.* Council of Europe. http://www.mjha.gov.mt/downloads/documents/ecri_report.pdf. Accessed 24 May 2009.

Foucault, M. (1972). *The archaeology of knowledge and the discourse on language* (trans: Sheridan Smith, A. M.). New York: Pantheon.

Foucault, M. (1977a). *Language, counter-memory, practice: Selected essays and interview.* London: Blackwell.

Foucault, M. (1977b). *Discipline and punish: The birth of the prison.* London: Allen Lane.

Foucault, M. (1978). *The history of sexuality vol. 1: An introduction* (trans:Hurley, R.). New York: Pantheon.

Foucault, M. (1984). The birth of the asylum. In P. Rabinow (Ed.), *The Foucault Reader* (pp. 141–167). New York: Pantheon Books.

Foucault, M. (1988). Social security. In L. D. Kritzman (Ed.), *Michel Foucault, politics, philosophy, culture: Interviews and other writings 1977–1984* (pp. 159–177). London: Routledge.

Foucault, M. (1991). Governmentality. In G. Burchell, C. Gordon, & P. Miller (Eds.), *The Foucault effect: Studies in governmentality* (pp. 87–104). Hemel Hempstead: Harvester Wheatsheaf.

Foucault, M. (1994a). Different spaces. In D. Faubion (Ed.), *Essential works of Foucault 1954–1984, vol. 2,* (trans: Hurley, R.) (pp. 175–185). London: Penguin.

Foucault, M. (1994b). The social triumph of the sexual will. In P. Rabinow (Ed.), *Ethics, subjectivity, and truth: The essential works of Michel Foucault, 1954–1984 vol. 1.* (pp. 157–162). New York: New Press.

Freire, P. (1970). *Pedagogy of the oppressed.* New York: Seabury Press.

Freire, P. (1994). *Pedagogy of hope.* New York: Continuum.

Galea, S. (2008). Can the migrant speak? Voicing myself, voicing the other. *Malta Review of Educational Research, 6*(1), 15–28.

Giroux, H. A. (1992). *Border crossings: Cultural workers and the politics of education.* New York: Routledge.

Goodley, D., et al. (2004). *Researching life stories: Method, theory and analyses in a biographical age.* London: Routledge Falmer Press.

Griffiths, M. (2003). *Action for social justice in education.* Maidenhead: Open University Press.

Haraway, D. J. (1991). A Cyborg manifesto: Science, technology, and socialist-feminism in the late twentieth century. In D. Haraway (Ed.), *Simians, Cyborgs and women: The reinvention of nature* (pp. 149–181). New York: Routledge.

Humphries, B., Mertens, D. M., & Truman, C. (2000). Arguments for an 'emancipatory' research paradigm. In C. Truman, D. M. Mertens, & B. Humphries (Eds.), *Research and inequality* (pp. 3–23). London: UCL Press.

Lee, Y. (2009) Indigenous knowledge construction and experiential learning of Taiwanese Aborigines. *International Education Studies, 2*(2), 155–161.

Mason, J. (2005). *Qualitative researching* (2nd ed.). London: Sage.

Mayo, P. (2007). Gramsci, the Southern Question and the Mediterranean. *Mediterranean Journal of Educational Studies, 12*(2), 1–17.

Mercieca, D. (2007). On the borders: The arrival of irregular immigrants in Malta—some implications for education. *Ethics and Education, 2*(2), 145–157.

Mirza, H. S. (2010). Love in the cupboard: A conversation about success and sadness when class, race and gender collide in the making of an academic career. In B. A. Cole & H. Gunter (Eds.), *Changing lives: Women inclusion and the PhD* (pp. 119–136). Stroke on Trent: Trentham.

Msnbc. (2007a). *The changing face of Europe.* http://www.msnbc.msn.com/id/19227137/ns/world_news-frontier_europe/?story=village. Accessed 9 Oct 2009.

Msnbc. (2007b). Teacher creates a home for refugees like himself: Somali helps build an African 'village' on Malta, but yearns for 'stability'. http://www.msnbc.msn.com/id/18982950. Accessed 9 Oct 2009.

Penley, C., & Ross, A. (1991). Cyborgs at large: Interview with Donna Haraway. In C. Penley & A. Ross (Eds.), *Technoculture* (pp. 1–20). Minneapolis: University of Minnesota.

Plummer, K. (2001). *Documents of life 2: An invitation to a critical humanism.* London: Sage.

Sawicki, J. (1991). *Disciplining Foucault: Feminism, power and the body.* New York: Routledge.

Stagno Navarra, K. (2009, May 17). Let nobody witness my horrors. *The Malta Today*, p. 13. http://www.maltatoday.com.mt/2009/05/17/t13.html. Accessed 24 June 2009.

Standish, P. (2001). Disciplining the profession: Subjects subject to procedure. *Education, Philosophy and Theory, 34*(1), 5–23.

Stronach, I., & MacLure, M. (1997). *Educational research undone: The postmodern embrace.* Buckingham: Open University Press.

Walker, R. (1993). Finding a silent voice for the researcher: Using photographs in evaluation and research. In M. Schratz (Ed.), *Qualitative voices in educational research* (pp. 72–92). London: Falmer.

White, M., & Epston, D. (1990). *Narrative means to therapeutic ends.* New York: Norton.

Wolf, D. L. (1996). Situating feminist dilemmas in fieldwork. In D. L. Wolf (Ed.), *Feminist Dilemmas in fieldwork* (pp. 1–55). Colorado: Westview Press.

Woodward, C. L. (2000). Hearing voices? Research issues when telling respondents' stories of childhood sexual abuse from a feminist perspective. In C. Truman, D. M. Mertens, & B. Humphries (Eds.), *Research and inequality* (pp. 37–51). London: UCL Press.

Chapter 12
Early Childhood Education in Multilingual Settings

Drorit Lengyel

Introduction

In many parts of the world multilingualism has been the norm for a long time. Yet, especially in European countries with strong monolingual and monocultural traditions the complex forms of multilingualism that come with migration challenge education systems. As there are fixed pre- and misconceptions about growing up bilingual, which have a significant impact on education practices, there is the need to identify and clarify those conceptions and to find ways of adapting to linguistic heterogeneity.

Education research into bilingualism is concerned with questions about socialization in two or more languages, bilingual education in the family and institutional contexts, language promotion/support, language maintenance through education, and language loss (Baker 1988, 2001, 2002). Compared to the research that has been conducted on bilingualism and cultural diversity in the field of schooling, particularly in Europe, Canada, and the United States, there is far less *research* and *theorizing* in the field of early childhood education, though there is no lack of practical concepts and measures. One reason for this is the fragmentation of research traditions and theoretical approaches. Furthermore, in some countries, including Germany and Switzerland, early childhood education as a discipline with its own research agenda developed only in the 1970s (Fried and Roux 2006). As it is agreed that the early years of life are formative, one of the most important questions in early childhood education research is how best to support the development of children growing up with two or more languages, and how language education and promotion should be designed and organized in multilingual settings to meet the needs of children in early education.

In this chapter, I introduce an inclusive perspective for early childhood education in multilingual contexts that is based on the concept of the "plurilingual" individual

D. Lengyel (✉)
Modellkolleg Bildungswissenschaften – School of Education, Zentrum für Diagnostik und Förderung ZeDiF – Center for Assessment and Support, University of Cologne, Gronewaldstr. 2, 50931 Köln, Germany
e-mail: dlengyel@uni-koeln.de

child. As there is a tendency to ignore hybrid language experiences and uses, particularly in Europe, I first present some reflections on the traditional linguistic and cultural identity of education systems in Europe that contribute to the "persistent exclusion" (Gogolin 2002, p. 123) of children of migrant backgrounds from equal opportunities. A current example from Germany illustrates how education research discourse on multilingualism has shifted again toward discussing one language—the lingua franca. I then review some research findings on growing up bilingual, which reveal differentiations that affect education processes. As there are infinite settings and contexts in which multiple languages are spoken and acquired, we need to understand and recognize individual development paths and socialization conditions. This then leads into Sect. 4, in which I sketch the inclusive perspective that evolved from my ethnographic research in multilingual kindergarten settings. Within this perspective, I refer to the concept of plurilingualism, introduced in 2001 by the Council of Europe and its "Common European Framework of Reference for Languages," and integrate theoretical perspectives from the sociocultural approach, as well as from functional linguistics and second language acquisition research. In conclusion, I reflect on its potential for and possible impacts on (research on) early childhood education.

Monocultural and Monolingual Traditions in Education Systems, Practice, and Research

> Multilingualism and cultural diversity in Europe is not limited to the coexistence of different national cultures and languages, languages of certain groups of functional fields. It has to be described as a continuous process of border crossing. (Gogolin 2002, p. 126)

In Europe, discourse on multilingualism in educational contexts is confronted by a monolingual and monocultural ideological heritage. To give an example: one of the more common and typical phenomena of multilingualism is code-switching and code-mixing. The intertwining, overlapping, and mixing of languages in speech is commonplace in multilingual social practices all over the world. Still, it often is viewed as an unhealthy, impure use of language, revealing low linguistic competence (see Baker 2002; Tracy 2007). As Gogolin (1998, 2002) shows in her work on language and cultural policies in European education systems, it was the rise of the idea of the nation-state that led to what she calls a monolingual and monocultural habitus (*in sensu* Bourdieu). This idea is conceptually and ideologically based on the notion of cultural and linguistic homogeneity. "There is no doubt that differences on the surface level of concrete historical phenomena can be found, but independent of these, the self-conception of homogeneity is a common element of the European nation state" (2002, p. 127). Gogolin calls this a "fundamental myth of uniformity of language and culture among a people." This myth has lead to a defensive attitude about multilingualism and multiculturalism, which functions as a deep-seated belief that is neither explicitly nor consciously expressed. The notion of linguistic homogeneity also affects education systems, their structure, forms, and contents, and they implicitly reinforce the monolingual self-conception (cf. Vermes

1998, for France et al. 1994, for the Netherlands). Thus, there is a predominant conviction that monolingualism and cultural homogeneity in society and in education particularly, "is the only legitimate normality—is a characteristic of nation as such" (p. 127). The process of nation-building itself led to the assumption that linguistic diversity and the learning of languages are complicated matters; that bilingualism too early in childhood may confuse the child and negatively affect linguistic as well as cognitive development, and more.

It is clear that educational institutions come into conflict when serving bilingual children of migrant backgrounds. On the one hand, their orientation is toward the monolingual self-conception, defended by the public interests of the national majority. On the other hand, they must focus on the children and their families, and their multilingual childhood socialization. Education theory and practice therefore must reflect upon this contradiction. In European countries, the majority clearly prefers linguistic uniformity in education, a fact that recently has been rearticulated resolutely (Reich 2008).

The monolingual habitus is also expressed in early childhood education. Institutions and support programs focus on promoting the "national languages." In Germany, for example, a broad review of language support measures for children aged 3 to 6 years was conducted by Jampert et al. (2007), who show that the recent recognition of language and emergent literacy education led to measures that virtually promoted only German. The problem is most apparent when we look at language assessment activities in the early years. Here, language proficiency is measured with tests and instruments developed for monolingual children, with no questioning of their appropriateness and validity in the different context (see Lengyel Forthcoming; Lengyel et al. 2009). To summarize, giving multilingualism a chance in education systems cannot come without fundamental change to the national linguistic self-conception; there must be established a "multilingual habitus" among individuals and in education institutions.[1] This means that we must not only value linguistic diversity but also accept its potential and legitimacy, independently of the status of any particular language in a society. This is most important, since there is a strong tendency to organize languages hierarchically. The languages of migration (such as Romani across Europe; Turkish in Germany; Gujarati in the United Kingdom; Spanish in parts of the United States, and so on) are of especially low status, indicating the social and political status of the specific migrant community in the society.

This monolingual and monocultural habitus can also be observed in education research. Until the twenty-first century, it was assumed that linguistic and cultural diversity would no longer matter in national education systems. It was believed that the process of integration into the "host country" would lead to language and

---

[1] Professionals in the education systems across Europe are overwhelmingly monolingual. Thus, personal experience of and reflection upon multilingualism are missing. Gogolin (1994) argues that the monolingual orientation of educators is an intrinsic element of their professional habitus. The less conscious the individual teacher is of the existence of the monolingual habitus, the more effectively it operates.

cultural shifts: adoption of the language and culture of the host country, and the relinquishment of the native or first languages. Hence there was no need to research the consequences of raising children as bilingual, either for or in the educational field. As research has shown, however, minorities and migrants do not give up their languages and cultural practices. Instead, they form innovative transcultural-linguistic practices that reflect the circumstances in which they live (Cenoz and Hornberger 2008). Nonetheless, in mainstream education research, categories indicating linguistic diversity and different childhood experiences with languages when entering the education system are barely considered. Here, I argue that we need more precise and detailed categories to capture children's and students' multilingualism and its complexity. This is crucial to discovering the real significance of the effect of a child's or student's linguistic background on his or her education processes and achievements. As I show in part 3, there are different routes to becoming a bilingual individual; hence research questionnaires, especially in early childhood education, must include, at least, questions about first contact with the language of the education system—the lingua franca and instructional language; they should specify language use among family members, and they need to include information on literacy experiences in the first language.

Understanding the complex processes of educational practice (such as teaching, supporting, learning) within multilingual contexts is more difficult the greater the distance between the research question and the terrain of organizational or other external features of education processes. Education research that is interested in discovering the "inner sphere" such as interaction patterns, and implicit, underlying agendas, in order to understand what happens beneath the surface of easily observable phenomena, requires research designs that allow such a view. Incorporating ethnographic approaches seems most suitable here.

Recently, there has been a shift in education research back toward discussing bilingualism controversy (see Gogolin and Neumann 2009). Some researchers question the worth and benefit of bilingual education in general, using cost-benefit-analysis (cf. Esser 2006; Hopf 2005). Hopf from Germany, for example, argues for a "German only" early education for migrant children stating that "[m]ost families will, however, lack the motivation for engaging their children in intensive learning of the German language before school" (Hopf 2005, p. 245; my translation). His argument is prejudicial though, assuming that migrant families will not be motivated enough to send their children to educational institutions where they can acquire German as an additional language. But the attendance rate of 5-year-old children of migrant backgrounds in early childhood education institutions in Germany differs only marginally from that of the attendance rate of monolingual, national majority 5-year-old children. Over 90% of this cohort attends preschool or kindergarten (Autorengruppe Bildungsberichterstattung 2008); in other words, they participate very strongly. A cause for concern is, however, that approximately 30% of migrant children growing up bilingual (acquiring German as an additional language in early childhood) attend institutions that are attended by 50% or more bilingual children (Autorengruppe Bildungsberichterstattung 2008, p. 53). The acquisition of a second language in such a learning situation is a tenuous matter then, since native-speaker role models are missing, as are adequate strategies for promoting language learning (List 2007; Lengyel 2009; Tracy 2007). It is not lack of motivation on the part of migrant families that leads to this unsatisfactory situation, but rather social and spatial segregation processes in urban areas. This illustrates that there still is a need for education research, theory, and practice, in order to overcome assumptions and beliefs that are rooted in national thinking, and tend to reduce the complexity of forms of childhood bilingualism.

Research on Bilingualism and Its Implications for Language Education

> At best, bilingualism is a scale, moving from virtually no awareness that other languages exist to complete fluency in two languages. At what point on this scale do we declare children to be bilingual? How do we conduct research on the impact of a variable that we struggle to define? (Bialystok 2001, p. 8)

As the quotation from Ellen Bialystok suggests, one of the greatest problems in researching bilingualism is how to define the phenomena adequately. Furthermore, it has been noted since the 1980s that it was the monolingual who was traditionally the "standard" by which researchers measured the bilingual, and was thus implicitly the "uncrowned king of linguistics" (Mey 1981, p. 73). Walters (2005) indicates that (psycho-) linguistic research models, approaches, and methods designed to explore monolingualism still serve as the reference point for research in the field of multilingualism.

The study of bilingualism leads to general methodological problems in empirical research. Since there are myriad social conditions with which bilingualism is correlated, it must be separated from these variables, which seems, presently, to be almost impossible. Furthermore, the aim of controlled empirical designs is to identify factors for creating relevant groups in order to find reliable differences between them based on statistical evidence. Bialystok (2001) argues that there are two main complications here for researching childhood bilingualism. The first is that due to its complexity as a concept, bilingualism is not simply a variable that can be isolated. It is not possible to create groups of bi- and monolingual children that are comparable in every way except in the single, independent variable of being mono- or bilingual. The second complication is that bilingual children "are never exactly the same as an otherwise comparable group of monolingual children except for the number of languages they speak. In some inevitable sense, bilingual children live different lives than their friends and neighbors who may be socially, economically, and politically similar but speak only one language" (Bialystok 2001, p. 9). Therefore, whenever research is conducted in pedagogy—for example, when investigating the impact of a certain support method on bilingual children—it is essential to assure that the experiences of mono- and bilinguals in the study are as comparable as possible.

François Grosjean, a Canadian Psycholinguist, was one of the first to theoretically model the so-called bilingual (or holistic) view of the phenomena: "The bilingual is NOT the sum of two complete or incomplete monolinguals; rather, he or she has a unique and specific linguistic configuration. The coexistence and constant interaction of the two languages in the bilingual have produced a different but complete language system" (Grosjean 1985, p. 471). The bilingual uses his or her languages in daily life orally and/or in writing, and can have different language competencies in his or her languages; in some cases, the acquired languages have been mastered perfectly, and in others, one language is dominant. The first case seldom occurs—it is an ideal type that Oksaar (2003, p. 31) labeled "*Gleichsprachigkeit*" (languages in equal balance). The languages in the repertoire of an individual may be used for various purposes and in different domains, such as communicating within the family, socializing with neighbors, in discourses at work, and for expressing membership of a group. This is most relevant to early childhood education theory and practice since it takes account of the social and communicative circumstances of languages in use. As it suggests, bilingualism forms an integral and important part of the daily life experiences of children. I now discuss a German study that aimed to track these experiences. Its findings mirror linguistic reality in European societies, especially in urban areas, and probably also the realities in other countries with significant migration over the past 60 years.

How Do Children Experience Growing Up in Two or More Languages?

Large-scale studies of multilingual childhood experiences rarely incorporate children under 6 years of age. Some findings come from the study "Multicultural Childhood" (*Multikulturelles Kinderleben*) conducted in Germany in 2000 in which 1,208 children of migrant background, between 5 and 11 years old, were interviewed in Frankfurt, Munich, and Cologne; data on their social backgrounds were also included. These urban areas can be characterized as having a heterogeneous population; the findings can be summarized as follows: Almost all of the children involved in the study grew up with two or more languages. There are a myriad of factors impinging on their language acquisition, including age, social living conditions, and the linguistic atmosphere in their urban quarter, language preferences, and number of generations in the household.

The study also provides detailed information on the language patterns among the families: communicating with their mothers, almost 8% of the children report that they use German; 48% communicate with them in their first language and almost 45% mix languages. Concerning the fathers, again, 8% of the children communicate in German; 43% use the first language; and 49% mix the two. Communication among siblings is different: 21% use German as the main language; 22% use the first language; and 56% mainly mix the two languages.

The children of the study experienced their bilingualism outside of the institution as useful and enriching. When asked about their experiences entering the education system, they reported feeling constrained to speak only German, a language that most of them were just beginning to acquire. Nevertheless, German becomes the most important language for peer communication and interaction in the institution. The children do not conceive their bilingualism as "either this language or that language"; instead, their comprehension of growing up with different languages is holistic: their linguistic practices are flexible (code-switching, code-mixing, and translating), situational, and personal; multilingualism is the precondition for activity, it is what they experience (DJI 2000). We conclude from this that children in their early years do experience diversity but not as distinct isolated and/or contradictory systems, as adults often do. They create their own childhood linguistic culture using elements from their environment, and draw on their complete linguistic repertoire. The research also suggests that flexibility in language use and communicating in the first language outside of the family depends on the linguistic atmosphere in the region and the social environment. The effects of public space and language use have been found in other studies as well (cf. Keim 2007).

These findings imply that diversity of languages and cultural experiences is an important aspect of a child's daily life and a common element in his or her socialization. It also reveals that the way in which children use their languages is subject to infinite variation depending on extra- and intralinguistic factors. This variety often escapes the surveys on which much of the debate about the benefits and disadvantages of bilingualism in education is founded. For early childhood pedagogy though, it is important to take it into account in order to meet the needs of the children.

Paths to Growing Up Bilingual in Early Childhood

Romaine (1999, pp. 254–256) was one of the first to describe patterns of "home language bilingualism" after reviewing major studies of bilingual and second language acquisition. She systematized these patterns in their linguistic and social dimensions, focusing on the parents and their languages, the educational strategy in language use, and the social community in which the family lives. Each of these is relevant to the development of both the child and the family.

Type 1: One person—one language
The parents speak different native languages and both speak the language of the partner. One of the parental languages is the dominant language of the community. As a strategy for educating their child, the parents each communicate in their own language.

Type 2: Nondominant home language/one language—one environment
The parents have different native languages, one of which is nondominant, and the other of which is the dominant language of the community. As a strategy, both parents speak the nondominant language to the child at home. Outside the home (for example, in kindergarten), the child is exposed to the dominant language of the community.

Type 3: Nondominant home language without community support
The parents share the same native language, which is not the dominant community language. The parents speak their own language when addressing the child. Similar to type 2, the child acquires the second language only when outside the home, in particular in institutional settings.

Type 4: Double nondominant home language without community support
This type follows the rules from type 3. It is more complex though, since the parents have different native languages that they both speak to their child at home. Thus, the child becomes trilingual.

Type 5: Nonnative parents
In this case, the parents share the same native language, which is the same as the dominant language of the community. As an educational strategy, one parent addresses the child in a language that is not his or her native language.

Type 6: Mixed languages
The parents are both bilingual and sectors of the community may also be bilingual. The parents mix languages and code-switch when addressing the child. In this case, the input and exposure to the languages appears to be unsystematic, but research shows that code-switching it is a highly skilled form of language use and is a natural one in bilingual communities. From a research point of view, it is considered a rich and complex form of discourse. (cf. Auer 2009)

This classification[2] is useful because it allows differences and similarities to be identified: All children of types 1 through 6 become bilingual at home, but are acquiring their languages under different conditions that "undoubtedly lead to different levels of competence in each" (Bialystok 2001, p. 4). Considering multilingual settings across the world, especially in those western countries with much migration in the last 60 years, types 3 and 6 are the most common (cf. Reich 2005). Type 1 is best documented in research though it is the least common across the world, whereas type 6, the most common, is described seldom in research; type 3 has become of more interest in the last 15 years. Romaine (1999, p. 255) reasons that "a great many of the studies have been done by parents educated in linguistics, i.e., middle class professionals, investigating their own children's development." To sum up, second language acquisition research offers ways toward systematic classification that could be useful for education theory and research. Different language learners need different support—different paths to growing up bilingual imply different outcomes in competence in two or more languages, and, most importantly, these different types may be a helpful tool in surveys investigating the effects of different educational methods and measures.

---

[2] Another typification for childhood bilingualism, introduced by Genesee et al. (2004, p. 6), which may be useful for education theory as well. The authors differentiate between children from the majority ethnolinguistic community and those who are members of a minority ethnolinguistic community. With this distinction they focus on how widely the language is spoken and valued, and if it has high or low social status, socioeconomic power, and institutional support.

Research Findings from Second Language Acquisition Research

Language acquisition and development in monolingual cases has been documented relatively well for some languages. Yet, in bilingual cases, our knowledge is comparatively weak (see Oksaar 2003; Bathia and Ritchie 2004). Most notably there is a research gap in early childhood bilingualism within linguistic minority groups and those growing up in socially precarious circumstances. Also, there are few findings in the predominant cases where a second (or third) language variety is acquired in early childhood in immersive institutional settings without instruction, such as kindergarten or nursery school. It must be understood that acquiring a second language in early childhood is different from doing so at the age of eight or ten, or as an adolescent (these latter groups have been studied more intensively); early childhood is a phase when central cognitive processes develop, the first language is not yet fully acquired, and the first steps of detachment from the family, the first socialization instances, take place. When investigating second language acquisition in early childhood, it must be noted that children already "know" language: they have experienced the functions of language and goal-oriented communication in their first acquired language. List (2003) describes this as learning a second language through the filter of the first one.

Though there are gaps in research, there is no dispute that early second or third language acquisition beginning at the age of 2, 3, or 4 years has many similarities with first language development, for example, in grammatical development (Rothweiler 2006). The prosodic and phonetic developments in the second also benefit from early acquisition since the children are able to draw on perceptive and reproductive strategies (implicit, procedural learning), and slip into the new language through its sound and melody. Furthermore, it has been found that early childhood bilingualism involves the potential for early acquisition of metalinguistic competence and awareness, and that it provides advantages for learning languages in particular, and for learning in general (Bialystok 2009). To explain this, researchers draw on bilingual children's early language experience of finding out that a word does not "stick on objects of the real word" but instead refers to something. The early contact with the arbitrariness of two linguistic symbols helps them to understand that the forms and functions of words are based on conventions (List 2007, p. 39).

All in all, studies in second language acquisition underline the potential and advantages of growing up bilingual in early childhood, compared to foreign language learning in school, or second language learning in later years. Still, the inequality that often accompanies migration in many dimensions, as well as a monolingual habitus and the absence of institutional support, can twist this positive picture. Thus, for pedagogy it is important to take account of the individual child and his family, the linguistic atmosphere of the community in which the family lives, and other structural and social conditions. We can see the difference between a child who simply acquires a second language in kindergarten along with other children, who are second language learners as well, and the socialization that occurs in a situation where both languages are spoken at home (Lengyel 2009). Nevertheless, if education research, theory, and practice recognize the specific linguistic situation of bilingual children of migrant backgrounds and respond to it, then there are chances of supporting these children to develop their cognitive potential for language and other learning (Gogolin 2008, p. 85).

Early Childhood Education in Multilingual Settings as Language Education

In this section, I sketch my inclusive approach to early language education in multilingual settings (Lengyel 2009). It is based on research done in four different multilingual kindergarten settings in heterogeneous social milieus in urban areas of Germany.[3] The research focused on play situations with peers and professionals (including construction play, role play, and literacy settings) and the interactions therein. The aim was to develop an observation scheme with a set of criteria designed for *plurilingual* children and to design an inclusive perspective on language education in multilingual fields.

I use the term plurilingual here (Council of Europe 2001; Beacco 2007) because it grasps the dynamic and integrated practices of language socialization in multilingual settings; it does not suggest certain individual language proficiency but rather highlights the ability of each individual to communicate, to varying degrees, in two or more languages according to (day-to-day) needs and circumstances such as topic, interlocutors, and social context. Plurilingual competence is a dynamic concept, which is most useful for looking at phenomena of language mixing such as code-switching, borrowing, code-mixing, and so on. It underlines the fact that an individual's languages are in constant interaction and that individuals draw on their full language repertoire and resources to make meaning in context (Lengyel 2009, p. 27ff). It is inclusive because it also integrates "monolinguals," as they too can experience plurilingualism; for example, in peer-groups or early childhood education settings they are in touch with other languages, picking up words and meanings, and developing various skills to varying degrees.

---

[3] The research included 43 plurilingual children aged 3 to 6 years. The dominant minority language was Turkish, followed by Romani and Italian. Fourteen of these children spoke other languages, including Greek, Urdu, Berber, Croatian, and Portuguese. Only three of these children fitted the "type 1" scheme described earlier; the others either belonged to type 3 or type 6. Furthermore, three children were exposed to a language other than German (Sicilian, an Italian dialect, and Romani) as infants and toddlers, but later on were exposed to German by their mothers, still living in an environment where neighbors and friends spoke these other languages. This happened when the parents divorced and the other language was introduced by the father. These children are labeled in research "hidden bilinguals" (Nitsch 2007, p. 58f).

The Effects of Early Childhood Education—Some General Findings

There are studies on the effectiveness of early childhood education in general, especially in English-speaking countries and Scandinavia, documenting short-term effects (successful school enrollment). An important longitudinal study entitled "The Effective Provision of Pre-school Education" (Sylva et al. 2004), investigated the effectiveness of different forms of early childhood education such as nursery school, kindergarten, and preschool, between 1997 and 2003. Overall, children who are given the opportunity to gain experiences outside the family in their early years benefit in their cognitive and social development compared to those socialized solely in the family surroundings. The main factors here are the institutional quality, and intensity and duration of the education. Sylva et al. (2003) show that children from vulnerable groups benefit most, but only if they are in socially mixed groups. An OECD study (2001, 2006) gives further details: education designed with specific developmental and pedagogical orientations and objectives works better than that without a clear framework. However, there is also evidence that the family setting and home learning environment still have the greatest impact on children's development; in Germany, a recent study (Bertelsmann 2008) has reconfirmed that the parents' education background has the greatest influence on secondary school attendance. It also shows that among children from vulnerable groups who attend nursery school, the probability of secondary school attendance increases from 36% to 50%. In sum, there is clear evidence of the benefits of early childhood education, especially for children of migrant background in precarious social circumstances, which emphasizes the need for socially mixed groups, intensive and enduring strategies, a developmental orientation, and pedagogical goals.

These findings match general psychological research on cognitive processes and learning, where the three factors having the greatest effect are opportunities to learn, time spent actively learning, and the quality of pedagogical work in the education process (cf. Carroll 1989; Helmke and Weinert 1997). As noted above, in multilingual settings, all these dimensions affect the process and outcome of language development—in both the majority language and the first language. The inclusive approach sets out to track the opportunities to learn ("quantity"), the time spent actively in language learning in early childhood education settings ("quality"), especially in linguistic, cultural and socially diverse groups, and to combine this aspect with quality criteria for language education and support ("language education"), and thus may be helpful for developing early language education policies in linguistically diverse settings as well.

Toward Plurilingual Education—an Inclusive Approach

The inclusive approach is based on a constructivist view of the individual, which is based on the work of L.S. Vygotskij, a Russian psychologist who shaped what is called sociocultural psychology and theory at the beginning of the twentieth century.

He investigated the connection between speech and thinking, and the role of speech as a tool for cognitive development, individualization, and for higher cognitive processes, taking into account social contexts and cultural practices (Vygotskij 2002). Language is therefore seen as a cultural tool transmitting history and culture, as a symbolic system for communication, and as a cognitive tool (because thoughts are based on "inner speech"). The sociocultural approach influenced (second) language acquisition research (see Bruner 1987; Tomasello 2003; Lantolf and Appel 1994; Mitchell and Myles 2004), has a long tradition in education research focusing on schools, and is useful for analyzing classroom interaction and engagement in learning through communicating (Mercer 1995; Gibbons 2002, 2009).

Theorizing language education in multilingual settings is based on aspects of sociocultural theory: the social and cultural setting (heterogeneous groups in educational institutions), activity (play, interaction), languages in use, and cognitive engagement. Concerning the setting, the focus shifts from the individual child and his or her development to the group situation and the role of the child within it. The education group setting is seen as a "community of practice," similar to how it is defined by Eckhert and McConnell-Ginet (1992, p. 464). As a social construct, a community of practice is not only defined by membership but also by the practice in which participants engage. Individuals can be peripheral or core members, and engage to different extents in different ways. They may also have different access to the resources accumulated in the community, for example, linguistic and cultural repertoires.

Within an inclusive approach, a kindergarten group can be seen as a community of practice in which children from diverse backgrounds and with different communication skills in different languages come together and engage in play, interaction and learning, creating their own culture, combining repertoires and tools in a transcultural and translinguistic way. In the case of plurilingual children from migrant backgrounds, this concept offers the possibility to identify systematically their opportunities to access the resources and their opportunities for learning the lingua franca ("quantity"). It leads to a change in perspective: instead of looking for deficits in the individual, his or her social role within the community of practice and the learning opportunities are focused. For institutional education, this is important because it centers on what is most relevant: the pedagogical scope and how to frame the learning environment so that it fits the individual. As noted at the beginning of the chapter, this view is often expressed in general, but not when migrant children are discussed.

As was shown earlier, plurilingual children from migrant backgrounds in particular, attend education institutions where they have almost no peers acting as native-speaker role models of the lingua franca. Thus, the centrality of educators in this learning process becomes evident. It is not so much the proper arrangement of certain knowledge or linguistic features and language drills that is required, but rather the structuring of a framework in which children can engage in joint activity and thought, and access to the lingua franca as another cognitive and cultural tool with which to construct knowledge ("language education"). Pedagogical work in multilingual settings then is about coconstruction within sociocultural frameworks, giving children opportunities to construct cultural and linguistic knowledge that is also compatible with social education goals. Thus, active listening and observation are key competencies for educators. Observing children in play and peer interaction, we can discover how they engage in meaning-making in the specific context and the extent to which they begin to use language to understand and cope with social reality, and engage in problem-solving activities mediated by speech.[4] For example, the focus can be turned to the development from "here-and-now language" to the context-reduced speech (a higher degree of abstraction) that is required when talking about something that has yet to happen, or when negotiating characters and imaginative issues in role plays.[5] Focusing on language as a cognitive tool—instead of counting false conjugations or missing words—allows professionals to direct their attention to scaffolding social interaction, that is, to framing and creating stimulating surroundings and social interactions where children working in their zone of proximal development (Vygotskij 2002) engage in negotiating meaning toward self-regulation and higher forms of language use ("quality" of the learning process) (Lengyel 2009, pp. 144ff, 241ff).

From this perspective, taking up the children's languages is crucial to paving the way to participation in the community of practice for those who have little experience with the lingua franca of the institution, and also for building relationships. Embracing the languages acquired outside the institution can also occur on a metalinguistic level, which is cognitively more demanding (Bialystok 2009). Charged with curiosity, children aged 4 or 5 years are interested in comparing and contrasting languages, exploring word meanings and structural patterns; they like to play with language. This genuine interest can be employed in a pedagogical way. Such an approach also allows us to discover whether plurilingual children engage in code-switching, language mixing, and translating, which—as research suggests—are highly skilled forms of language use, revealing an ability to use language according to situational and interlocutors' needs. Translation demands metalinguistic awareness too, as meaning that was constructed in one language must be transferred to the other.

The inclusive approach suggests that supporting plurilingualism in early childhood education means—for all children—to promote activity and interaction in and through the languages that the children bring along; it means finding out about different varieties and registers, looking at differing language symbols, mixing them, and making them an object of thought. Plurilingualism then is established through *social practice* and *valuation* of different languages, varieties, and registers. The approach overcomes the usual division of the child's languages and allows plurilingual social practice to emerge. It enhances competence in linguistically and

---

[4] It is important to note that this development in whatever language the individual child acquires will differ from route to route. Children of type 1 may have good preconditions for managing these processes in both their languages, children of type 3 may rely more on the language in which cognitive concepts were first developed, whereas children of type 6 may rely on both languages in a more intertwined way (which might not be acceptable to the majority).

[5] Context-reduced speech is crucial in literacy development, typically for the languages of schooling, academic texts, and reading.

culturally diverse contexts, and captures a sociolinguistic reality in which the fusion of different languages characterizes today's communication processes.

There are some practical concepts and projects in early childhood education around the world based on some of these ideas, including family literacy, which aims to enhance the literacy skills of parents and children of migrant background (Desmond and Elfert 2008). For instance, parents create books in which they tell their children a story in all the languages relevant to the child. This is interesting because engaging children in reading, connecting them to books, reading stories aloud and discussing them, are powerful aids to children's later success in school (Cummins 2001; Guthrie 2004). Furthermore, so-called translanguaging approaches, developed in schools and increasingly the subject of research, especially in United Kingdom community schools (Chinese and Gujarati) (cf. Cresse Forthcoming; Cresse and Backledge 2010), might also be interesting for early childhood education. In these schools, monolingual instruction has been replaced by the use of two or more languages of instruction, intended to deepen understanding of the subject matter. In Germany, this approach was explored in an early childhood education setting attended mostly by children whose first language is Turkish.[6] These children receive language support in German and Turkish, in integrated rather than separate forms, working with both languages to make meaning and establish cognitive concepts. Such innovative measures in early childhood education need to be observed and analyzed in more detail.

Conclusion

In this chapter, I showed how monolingual and monocultural traditions in education research and practice are still at work when dealing with bilingual children from migrant backgrounds. Findings from research in early childhood bilingualism, language acquisition, and in the field of plurilingual childhood socialization suggest, however, that it is not bilingualism itself but rather the complex interplay of multiple factors and different paths of growing up bilingual which impact the linguistic outcomes of the children. The inclusive approach for language education, I sketched, looks in depth at these different paths as well as at the role of the individual child in the community of practice in the institutional setting. Thus, it may contribute to an understanding which neither attributes early childhood education problems to migrant children and their families themselves, nor traces them back to socialization in a language other than the mainstream one. Instead, it promotes

---

[6] This concept arose from support measures in a community kindergarten and has not yet been investigated further. The kindergarten was part of the German model program "Support for immigrant minority children and youth" (*FörMig*), in which, between 2004 and 2009, ten states created a network of "developmental partnerships" to provide an inclusive environment for all children and adolescents, and to establish continuous language education policies. For further information see www.uni-hamburg.blk-foermig.de.

recognition of the linguistically and culturally diverse settings in which children are socialized, and the integration of these experiences into education processes. For education practice the approach suggests that framing language learning situations in which joint construction can take place is a key to give children access to language as a tool for learning and to support them to find productive ways in which they can bring all their languages into the process.

References

Auer, P. (2009). Competence in performance: Code-switching und andere Formen des bilingualen Sprechens. In I. Gogolin & U. Neumann (Eds.), *Streitfall Zweisprachigkeit – The bilingualism controversy* (pp. 91–110). Wiesbaden: VS-Verlag.
Autorengruppe Bildungsberichterstattung. (Eds.). (2008). *Bildung in Deutschland 2008: Ein indikatorengestützter Bericht mit einer Analyse zu Übergängen im Anschluss an den Sekundarbereich I*. Bielefeld: Bertelsmann Verlag.
Baker, C. (1988). *Key issues in bilingualism and bilingual education*. Clevedon: Multilingual Matters.
Baker, C. (2001). *Foundations of bilingual education and bilingualism* (2nd ed.). Clevedon: Multilingual Matters.
Baker, C. (2002). *The care and education of young bilinguals*. Clevedon: Multilingual Matters.
Bathia, T. K., & Ritchie, W. C. (Eds.). (2004). *The handbook of bilingualism*. Oxford: Blackwell.
Beacco, J.-C. (2007). *From linguistic diversity to plurilingual education: Guide for the development of language education policies in Europe*. Strasbourg: Council of Europe.
Bialystok, E. (2001). *Bilingualism in development: Language, literacy, and cognition*. Cambridge: Cambridge University Press.
Bialystok, E. (2009). Effects of bilingualism on cognitive and linguistic performance across the lifespan. In I. Gogolin & U. Neumann (Eds.), *Streitfall Zweisprachigkeit – The bilingualism controversy* (pp. 53–68). Wiesbaden: VS-Verlag.
Bruner, J. (1987). *Wie das Kind sprechen lernt*. Bern: Hans Huber.
Carroll, J. B. (1989). The Carroll-Model: A 25-year retrospective and prospective view. *Educational Researcher, 18*(1), 26–31.
Cenoz, J., & Hornberger, N. (Eds.). (2008). *Encyclopaedia of language and education. 6: Knowledge about language* (2nd ed.). New York: Springer.
Council of Europe. (2001). *Common European framework of reference for languages: Learning, teaching and assessment*. Strasbourg: Council of Europe/Cambridge University Press.
Cummins, J. (2001). *Negotiating identities: Education for empowerment in a diverse society* (2nd ed.). Los Angeles: California Association for Bilingual Education.
Cresse, A. (Forthcoming). Translanguaging in multilingual classrooms. *Zeitschrift für Erziehungswissenschaft, 13*(4).
Cresse, A., & Blackledge, A. (2010). Translanguaging in the bilingual classroom: A pedagogy for learning and teaching? *The Modern Language Journal, 94*(1), 103–115.
Desmond, S., & Elfert, M. (Eds.). (2008). *Family literacy: Experiences from Africa and around the world: UNESCO Institute for Lifelong Learning/DVV international*. Hambug/Bonn.
DJI-Projekt "Multikulturelles Kinderleben" (Eds.). (2000). *Wie Kinder multikulturellen Alltag erleben: Ergebnisse einer Kinderbefragung*. www.dji.de/bibs/DJI_Multikulti_Heft4.pdf. Accessed 4 April 2010.
Eckhert, P., & McConnell-Ginet, S. (1992). Think practically and look locally: Language and gender as community based-practice. *Annual Review of Anthropology, 21*, 461–490.
Esser, H. (2006). *Sprache und Integration: Die sozialen Bedingungen und Folgen des Spracherwerbs von Migranten*. Frankfurt: Campus.

Fried, L., & Roux, S. (Eds.). (2006). *Pädagogik der frühen Kindheit*. Weinheim: Beltz.
Fritschi, T., & Oesch, T. (2008). *Volkswirtschaftlicher Nutzen von frühkindlicher Bildung in Deutschland: Eine ökonomische Bewertung langfristiger Bildungseffekte bei Krippenkindern. Studie im Auftrag der Bertelsmann Stiftung*. Bielefeld: Bertelsmann.
Genesee, F., Paradis, J., & Crago, M. (2004). *Dual language development and disorders*. Baltimore: Paul H. Brooks.
Gibbons, P. (2002). *Scaffolding language, scaffolding learning: Teaching second language learners in the mainstream classroom*. Westport: Heinemann.
Gibbons, P. (2009). *English learners, academic literacy, and thinking: Learning in the challenge zone*. Portsmouth: Heinemann.
Gogolin, I. (1994). *Der monolinguale Habitus der multilingualen Schule*. Münster: Waxmann.
Gogolin, I. (1998). Sprachen reinhalten – eine Obsession. In I. Gogolin, S. Graap, & G. List (Eds.), *Über Mehrsprachigkeit* (pp. 71–96). Tübingen: Stauffenburg.
Gogolin, I. (2002). Linguistic and cultural diversity in Europe: A challenge for educational research and practice. *European Educational Research Journal, 1*(1), 123–138.
Gogolin, I. (2008). Förderung von Kindern mit Migrationshintergrund im Elementarbereich. *Zeitschrift für Erziehungswissenschaft, 10*(Sonderheft 11), 79–90.
Gogolin, I., & Neumann, U. (Eds.). (2009). *Streitfall Zweisprachigkeit – The bilingualism controversy*. Wiesbaden: VS-Verlag.
Grosjean, F. (1985). The bilingual as a competent but specific speaker-hearer. *Journal of Multilingual and Multicultural Development, 6*, 467–477.
Guthrie, J. T. (2004). Teaching for literacy engagement. *Journal of Literacy Research, 36*(1), 1–30.
Helmke, A., & Weinert, F. E. (1997). Bedingungsfaktoren schulischer Leistung. In F. E. Weinert (Ed.), *Psychologie des Unterrichts und der Schule* (pp. 71–176). Göttingen: Hogrefe.
Hopf, D. (2005). Zweisprachigkeit und Schulleistung bei Migrantenkindern. *Zeitschrift für Pädagogik, 5*(2), 236–251.
Jampert, K., Best, P., Guadatiello, A., Holler, D., & Zehnbauer, A. (2007). *Schlüsselkompetenz Sprache. Sprachliche Bildung und Förderung im Kindergarten. Konzepte, Projekte und Maßnahmen. 2: Aktualisierte und überarbeitete Aufl*. Berlin: verlag das netz.
Keim, I. (2007). *Die "türkischen Powergirls": Lebenswelt und kommunikativer Stil einer Migrantinnengruppe in Mannheim*. Tübingen: Gunter Narr.
Kroon, S., & Vallen, T. (1994). Das nationale Selbstverständnis im Unterricht der Nationalsprache: Der Fall Niederlande. In I. Gogolin (Ed.), *Das nationale Selbstverständnis der Bildung* (pp. 151–182). Münster: Waxmann.
Lantolf, J. P., & Appel, G. (Eds.). (1994). *Vygotskian approaches to second language research*. Norwood: Ablex.
Lengyel, D. (Forthcoming). *Language diagnostics in multilingual settings with regards to individualized teaching and learning*. Strasbourg: Council of Europe.
Lengyel, D. (2009). *Zweitspracherwerb in der Kita: Eine integrative Sicht auf die sprachliche und kognitive Entwicklung mehrsprachiger Kinder*. Münster: Waxmann.
Lengyel, D., Reich, H. H., Roth, H.-J., & Döll, M. (Eds.). (2009). *Von der Sprachdiagnose und Sprachförderung: FörMig Edition Band 5*. Münster: Waxmann.
List, G. (2003). Sprachpsychologie. In K.-R. Bausch, H. Christ, & H.-J. Krumm, (Eds.), *Fremdsprachenunterricht* (pp. 25–31). Tübingen: Franke.
List, G. (2007). Förderung von Mehrsprachigkeit in der Kita. Expertise im Auftrag des Deutschen Jugendinstituts. www.dji.de/bibs/384_8288_Expertise_List_MSP.pdf. Accessed 17 April 2010.
Mercer, N. (1995). *The guided construction of knowledge: Talk amongst teachers and learners*. Clevedon: Multilingual Matters.
Mey, J. (1981). "Right or wrong, my native speaker": Estant les régestes du noble souverain de l'empirie linguistic avec un renvoy au mesme roy. In F. Coulmas (Ed.), *A festschrift for "native speaker"* (pp. 69–84). The Hague: Mouton.
Mitchell, R., & Myles, F. (2004). *Second language learning theories*. Oxford: Oxford University Press.

Nitsch, C. (2007). Mehrsprachigkeit – eine neurowissenschaftliche Perspektive. In T. Anstatt (Ed.), *Mehrsprachigkeit bei Kindern und Erwachsenen. Erwerb – Formen – Förderung* (pp. 47–68). Tübingen: Attempto Verlag.

Oksaar, E. (2003). *Zweitspracherwerb: Wege zur Mehrsprachigkeit und interkulturellen Verständigung*. Stuttgart: Kohlhammer.

Organisation for Economic Co-operation and Development OECD. (2001). *Starting strong: Early childhood education and care*. Paris: OECD.

Organisation for Economic Co-operation and Development OECD. (2006). *Starting strong II: Early childhood education and care*. Paris: OECD.

Reich, H. H. (2005). Forschungsstand und Desideratenaufweis zu Migrationslinguistik und Migrationspädagogik für die Zwecke des "Anforderungsrahmens". In K. Ehlich, H. denvan Bergh, U. Brel, B. Garme, A. Komor, H.-J. Krumm, T. McNamara, H. H. Reich, G. Schnieders, & J. D. tende Thije (Eds.), *Anforderungen an Verfahren der regelmäßigen Sprachstandsfeststellung als Grundlage für die frühe und individuelle Förderung von Kindern und Jugendlichen mit Migrationshintergrund* (pp. 121–169). Berlin: Bundesministerium für Forschung.

Reich, H. H. (2008). Kindertageseinrichtungen als Institutionen sprachlicher Bildung. *Diskurs Kindheits- und Jugendforschung, 3*(3), 249–258.

Romaine, S. (1999). Bilingual language development. In M. Barrett (Ed.), *The development of language* (pp. 251–275). Hove: Psychology Press.

Rothweiler, M. (2006). The acquisition of V2 and subordinate clauses in early successive acquisition of German. In C. Lleó (Ed.), *Interfaces in multilingualism: Acquisition and representation* (pp. 91–113). Amsterdam: John Benjamins.

Sylva, K., Melhuish, E., Sammons, P., Siraj-Blatchford, I., Taggart, B., & Elliot, K. (2003). The effective provision of preschool education (EPPE) Project: Findings from the pre-school period (DfES Research Brief RBX 15–03).

Sylva, K., Melhuish, E., Sammons, P., Siraj-Blatchford, I., & Taggart, B. (2004). The effective pre-school education (EPPE) project. A longitudinal study funded by the DfES 1997–2004. Final Report. University of London, Institute for Education. http://www.ioe.ac.uk/projects/eppe. Accessed 15 July 2010.

Tomasello, M. (2003). *Constructing language: A usage-based theory of language acquisition*. Cambridge: Harvard University Press.

Tracy, R. (2007). *Wie Kinder Sprachen lernen: Und wie wir sie dabei unterstützen können*. Tübingen: Francke.

Vermes, G. (1998). Schrifterwerb und Minorisierung als psychologisches Problem. In I. Gogolin, S. Graap, & G. List (Eds.), *Über Mehrsprachigkeit* (pp. 3–19). Tübingen: Stauffenburg.

Vygotskij, L. S. (2002). *Sprechen und Denken*. Weinheim: Beltz.

Walters, J. (2005). *Bilingualism: The sociopragmatic-psycholinguistic interface*. Mahwah: Lawrence Erlbaum.

Part II
Education in Multilingual Societies

Chapter 13
Migration, Minorities, and Learning: Understanding Cultural and Social Differences in Education

M. Lynn Aylward

The origins of the theoretical connections of human difference and culture have some of their foundations in the work of anthropologist Franz Boas. Within what can be described, in more progressive terms, as an antiracist framework, Boas promoted the consideration of cultures and cultural difference as a way to lessen the status of race in social science theory (Boas 1940). Boas proposed that culture rather than race was the category to explore and theorize in order to help explain and describe such human experiences as immigration. So what do we understand today about cultural and social difference in education, especially as it relates to the experiences of migration, minority groups and learning?

In September of 1998 I traveled to Nuuk, Greenland to attend the 11th Inuit Studies Conference. One session I attended was a presentation by two teacher educators from the Chukotka Region of Russia. Two experienced and competent women explained how they were promoting and preserving a local endangered Indigenous language through their professional practice at a small teacher education institute. Though my memory is fuzzy about most of the scholarly details (including the presenters' names), their passion was obvious and my admiration for their courage and commitment is as strong today as it was when I sat in that conference room in Nuuk. The barriers they faced seemed insurmountable. I remember turning at the end of the presentation to a Canadian colleague and saying something close to the idea that, "the survival of this language appears to be dependent upon these two women and a typewriter." These moments of clarity about the true significance of the contributions made by those who toil in academia are few and far between.

My story of the Inuit Studies Conference experience is not meant to oversimplify the complexities of the global struggles of minority communities, but rather is an attempt to foreground the activist intent that I believe to be at the foundation of the methodologies explored in all of the authors' studies contained in the book section that follows. Each of the seven chapters journey a struggle around language, culture, and identity with respect to various minoritized populations' interactions with formal education.

M. L. Aylward (✉)
School of Education, Acadia University, Wolfville, NS, Canada
e-mail: Lynn.aylward@acadiau.ca

The authors discuss cultural and social difference in education by examining the status and politics of indigenous and minority language education in Estonia, Croatia, and the Nunavut Territory of Canada; the experiences of diasporic immigrant student populations in the schools of Ireland, and Canada; and minority parents' views and expectations of schools in a Palestinian–Jewish school in Israel as well as the negotiations and conflict between Chinese immigrant parents and Canadian teachers. The agency of parents, teachers, administrators, students, and policy makers are included in these chapters as an in depth conversation about migration/diaspora, minoritization and learning contexts.

In Chap. 1, Kara Brown considers the state's role in the minority language instruction of Estonia, a country that gained independence from the Soviet Union in 1991. In particular Brown focuses on the two minority groups, Russian speakers and the Voro, an ethnic Estonian group. Brown argues that the Estonian government's provision of choice with respect to Estonian language policies is strongly connected with the wider communities' conceptions of "acceptable differences" for minorities (Urciuoli 1994).

Drawing on 15 years of minority-language policy research in Estonia, Brown gives precedence to the consideration of policy development by reflecting on data generated through long-term participant observations and semistructured interviews in Russian and Estonian-medium schools from 1995 to 2009. Brown's work is rooted in critical language theory and Urciuoli's "models of acceptable differences" anchors the discussion. The author explains how Estonian language proficiency and identification with Estonian language, culture, and history is the vehicle for integration in all public and private schools, with non-Estonian language instruction taking up a subordinate role. The Russian speaking (non-Estonian or Russophones) and the Voro are two distinct cultural groups that have different relationships to the state, however, Brown makes the point that they face some common issues in the creation of school-based Estonian language policy. The Russian speakers' status has changed significantly in the last 25 years from that of a privileged minority in a Soviet run Estonia to one of a minority group within the independent state of Estonia. The state's intentions for the Russophones are mainly around Estonian language acquisition. The Voro, a regional-language community, are considered to be fully integrated into Estonian life and therefore the state's interest is in ensuring a place for the Estonian language within the Voro community's language revitalization efforts. Layered on both of these minority groups is perhaps the more potent effect of Estonian-language education efforts through schooling—that of the fortification of Estonian ethnic identity. Brown suggests that current sociocultural and demographic changes will likely force the state to reconsider its "acceptable difference" model of language planning in Estonian medium schools in order to accommodate all residents of Estonia toward its goal of having Estonian language proficiency among non-Estonians.

In Chap. 2, Lynn Aylward continues to explore the articulations of cultural difference and schooling in her study of public schooling within the majority Inuit (Indigenous peoples) populated Nunavut territory of Canada. Aylward describes how there exists an ongoing and unique Conversation (Gee 2005) about the role of Inuit language and culture in the arctic territory that has as its main participants the policy makers, curriculum authors, teachers and government officials. Using data generated in interviews with experienced Inuit and non-Inuit teachers as well as interviews with expert Inuit curriculum authors, Aylward provides details of the *Inuit Qaujimajatuqangit* (Inuit ways of knowing and being) Conversation and how it shapes the structures of schooling in a learning context where Indigenous knowledges have been historically subjugated and/or erased. Aylward's discourse analysis of her participants' talk identifies specific cultural models and theorizations about how the world works with respect to Nunavut education and offers a comprehensive look at social and cultural difference in the Nunavut milieu. The *Inuit Qaujimajatuqangit* Conversation has three key discourses of *place* that characterize the dynamic of the everyday lives of students and teachers; place as context in schooling, place as power in schooling and place as the cultural negotiation of schooling. Aylward concludes by acknowledging the demanding social and political tensions of education in minoritized Indigenenous communities and points to how the *Inuit Qaujimajatuqangit* Conversation pushes back from the usual discourses of cultural difference as assimilationism, integration, and biculturalism toward a more complex interrogation that represents an anticolonial, intellectual, and social movement in Nunavut education.

In Chap. 3, Zvi Bekerman and Moshe Tatar offer the reader a glimpse into a unique learning context that speaks to our understandings of minority education in "an area engaged in one of the most intractable and intense conflicts of modern times" (p. #). As the authors explain, most of the Palestinian population in Israel attend monolingual Arabic schools, under the supervision of the national Jewish educational system while Jewish children attend monolingual secular schools. Substantive sociocultural differences exist between the two schools systems and an identified educational gap exists between the Jewish and Palestinian communities with the Palestinians possessing lower matriculation rates. The authors discuss the complex relations between families and schools, majority and minority, within two bilingual, binational integrated Palestinian– Jewish schools in Israel. Through an analysis of in depth interviews with Palestinian parents, Bekerman and Tatar discuss minority parents' views and expectations of their children's education with respect to their choice of an integrated school setting. The authors describe the challenges and opportunities expressed by the parent participants and uncover a "latent ambivalence" regarding the parental motives for choosing the bilingual, binational school system.

In Chap. 4, Jadranka Cacic-Kumpes moves the reader from the school level back to a broader analysis of the educational considerations of ethnic and cultural diversity in a pluralistic Croatian society. Cacic-Kumpes begins with the Council of Europe's intercultural stance that places education at the foundation of "managing cultural diversity, building European identity and developing cultural and ethnic pluralistic societies based on solidarity" (p. #). The author discusses whether or not it is possible to draw on several centuries of ethnic and cultural diversity affirmation in the Croatian education system and move on to conceptualizations of frameworks of contemporary integration processes. The importance of ethnic affiliations and "markers" have been a critical factor in Croatia's history with many former "Czech," "Hungarian," "Ruthenian," "Slovak," and "Serb" villages remaining ethnically homogeneous. Wars and the resulting new states have had a significant effect on ethnic structures and the status of ethnic groups, with some becoming "accidental diasporas" (Brubaker 2000). Cacic-Kumpes discussion of Croatian education takes up the relations of power among interest groups such as the ethnic elites as well as the mobilizing potential of ethnicity. The author puts a call out for the need to "regulate, organize and develop" a multicultural approach to education so that societal changes might follow (see p. 21). A dilemma is identified related to the need for segregated minority and majority schools or for integrated schools in an education system where ethnic and cultural diversity can be affirmed.

In Chap. 5, Laura Thompson examines the construction of a collective Francophone identity in the Canadian prairies in light of changing demographics; diversity created by recent immigration. Based on a qualitative analysis of three secondary school students' perceptions of their Francophone identity within the Anglophone province of Alberta, Thompson explores what it means to be Francophone, French-Canadian and Franco-Albertan in a postcolonial context. In consideration of the past, present and future categorizations of Francophone communities, the author reminds us that "French language may unify Francophones, but cultural identities separate them" (p. #). Thompson discusses how all educators need to grapple with ways to respond to an increasingly plural Francophone community while being specifically charged with teaching curriculum from multiple Francophone perspectives. Thompson's three participants' dialogues are positioned within a postcolonial framework in order to story the particulars of what she calls "here," "there," and "home." In the end, the author wants us to consider how French-speaking newcomers to Canada are welcomed. Are they recognized as "real" Francophones and "real" Canadians or does a crisis of representation remain?

In Chap. 6, Merike Darmody, Emer Smyth, Delma Byrne, and Frances McGinnity present the challenges of schooling the recent heterogenous immigrant population in Ireland who have arrived from new member States of the European Union. Considerations of the norms transmitted by the host country school environment are discussed within Bourdieu's cultural reproduction and transmission theories in order to highlight the experiences of immigrant students as they interact with Irish students and teachers. Through an initial questionnaire sent to 800 school principals and as well as interviews with students and staff in 12 case study schools (both elementary and secondary), research findings are discussed in terms of issues of language proficiency, institutional differences, peer social interactions, cultural distance, and cultural transmission. The authors relate how the ambiguous positioning of students who possess differing levels of cultural capital interacts with constructions of the "good" student by teachers and administrators. The research communicates that though Irish schools have become more culturally, linguistically, and religiously diverse, it remains to be seen how this diversity might disrupt the routine nature of the social reproduction of schooling.

In Chap. 7, Yan Gao gives some insights into the conflict and miscommunication that exists between English as a Second Language (ESL) parents and Canadian teachers in the province of British Columbia. Through a study of the particular communication patterns performed between ESL parents and secondary ESL teachers during a " Parents' Night" event, Gao provides both an intercultural and "dialogue across difference" informed analysis, based in part, on the work of Charles Taylor. Using a discourse analysis guided by systemic functional linguistics, the Parents' Night event dialogues are examined in two specific contexts of situation and culture. The majority of the participating parents were immigrants from Taiwan, Hong Kong, and mainland China. Data were generated in interviews, naturalistic observation and focus groups over a 3-year period during the Parents' night event and in activities related to planning for the event. Participants included ESL teachers as well as bilingual assistants. Gao presents the teachers' approach to Parents' Night and parents' reactions to parents' night in order to demonstrate the conflicting expectations and to make suggestions for how we need to reach beyond simplistic explanations of cultural difference to completely comprehend the challenges of ESL parent–teacher communications.

Giroux and Simon (1990) theorized that the language of curricula in schools teaches students how to "name the world" in particular ways and introduces them to certain social relations. Language is power and it ensures full access to and participation in education. Linguistic and cultural diversity in education contexts can be a "productive resource" (Cummins and Schecter 2003; Janks 2005; May and Janks 2004). Therefore, it is imperative for educators to continually question how institutions legitimate and organize knowledge. What knowledges count?

Canadian scholar Willinsky (1999) observed that museum curators' and anthropologists' questions of culture have a strong foothold within school curricula. He questioned how much has been accomplished by turning to culture as an alternative to race to construct social difference. There are evident and ongoing tensions between discursive constructions of culture and our understandings of cultural and social difference within education. Often we situate cultural and social difference in education as "deficit" or "otherness."

The studies contained in the following seven chapters point to the realities of the strategic political choices facing minoritized communities around the negotiations of cultural and social difference. Such vital negotiations, enabled within state or government policy (Brown, Cacic-Kumpes) by parents (Bekerman and Tatar, Gao), or among students and teachers (Aylward, Darmody et al., Thompson) may force existing institutions of schooling into moves toward potentially substantive structural change.

Chapter 14
The State, Official-Language Education, and Minorities: Estonian-Language Instruction for Estonia's Russian-Speakers and the Võro

Kara D. Brown

Historic changes in Estonia, from regaining independence from the Soviet Union in 1991 to joining the European Union in 2004, have dramatically transformed minority education in this Baltic state. This chapter focuses on the nonnegotiable starting point for developing school-based policies to accommodate and promote linguistic and ethnic difference—Estonian-language proficiency. In particular, I focus on the way the state's "acceptable difference" (Urciuoli 1994) approach to Estonian-language instruction for minorities creates differentiated opportunities for language maintenance and integration. To examine this theme, I take a comparative focus on language policies targeting two minority groups—the Russian-speakers, a largely immigrant-language community, and the Võro, an ethnic Estonian autochthonous group. The differences in these groups' size, history, and socio-cultural position have resulted in few comparative analyses of the impact of medium-of-instruction policies (for exceptions see Rannut 2004; Verschik 2005). Yet, these cultural and social divergences provide a rich spectrum to consider the state's common response to language difference in school through a focus on programmatic "choice." In response both to the state's tight conscription of "choice" and cultural–political urgency, both minority communities engage in policy resistance, which is reflected in their response to government-endorsed official-language education.

The data presented in this chapter are drawn from over 15 years of research on minority-language policy in Estonia. Given the limitations of space, this chapter considers policy, primarily, from a state perspective. My focus on the state recognizes, however, the multiple and diverse actors involved in policy appropriation including teachers, the international community, parents, and students. Qualitative methods used to gather data include long-term participant observation in Russian- and Estonian-medium schools in southeastern Estonia and in the capital (in 1995–1996 and 2001–2002 and 2004 academic years), semistructured interviews conducted in Russian, Estonian, and English with policy officials, teachers, and administrators (in the summers of 2008 and 2009), and an analysis of official

K. D. Brown (✉)
College of Education, University of South Carolina, Wardlaw Hall 136, Columbia, SC 29208, USA
e-mail: brownk25@mailbox.sc.edu

documents, correspondence, archival documents, and the public press concerning language planning. My research is guided by a critical language theory, which highlights issues of power and privilege in language policy. Along with other scholars of critical language policy (Pennycook 2006; Ricento 1998; Tollefson 2006), I recognize that language policies, ranging from those generated by the state to those perpetuated by nonstate actors "on the ground," tend to endanger the languages of the less powerful.

I open the chapter by introducing the concept of acceptable difference, which guides official-language education for minorities in Estonia. I then provide both a contextual and historical background to minorities in Estonia and the role of schools vis-à-vis Estonian-language learning in the twentieth and twenty-first centuries. In the third section, I examine ways the state has attempted to create new spaces via "choice" for language learning through curricular change in Russian- and Estonian-medium schools. I then consider how cultural–political urgency within both communities feeds resistance to state-based choice and differently positions the communities to take advantage of choice-based options. I conclude with a discussion of the resistance to state-based definitions of acceptable difference in the public and private education spheres.

Conceptual Framework

Urciuoli's (1994) "models of acceptable difference" suggests that when social and cultural "differences are safely contained" (p. 19) within a framework where the differences are understood to enhance contributions to the polity, then these differences are supported and allowed to flourish. Urciuoli's insight helps to frame the simultaneous containment and encouragement of minority languages in public education. In this Baltic country, the parameters for "acceptable difference" in the school sphere are informed by broad understandings of language identity and endangerment. The borders of "acceptability" are drawn with a concern for the development and protection of Estonian. As the sole official language and the mother-tongue of the ethnic Estonian population, Estonian constitutes the heart of civic and national identity. The central place of Estonian for ethnic Estonians is captured in the opening of the state's Estonian-language development plan "…without the Estonian language the Estonian people would not be what they are" (Ministry of Education and Research (2004, p. 3). Given the language's central role, notions of "acceptable difference" and state policy are guided, in part, by fear among ethnic Estonians about the endangerment of Estonian language. With only 1.1 million speakers worldwide, many consider Estonian to be an endangered language vulnerable to the homogenizing force of English, the regional dominance of Russian, and a decline in the population base of native speakers. Given this sense of endangerment, one purpose of schooling is to transform Estonia's minorities into communities that understand Estonian language, culture, and history.

The Estonian government also wants to use education as a tool to maintain elements of cultural and social distinctiveness for its linguistic and ethnic minorities. This commitment to maintaining and protecting diversity is reflected in the laws and global agreements signed by the state. In practice, "acceptable difference" means that, at minimum, as long as Estonian is taught in all public and private schools and in all grades, non-Estonian language instruction is permitted to varying degrees. Legal guarantees secure the position of the Estonian language in both Estonian- and Russian-medium public education: the State Constitution[1] and laws guarantee the right to education in Estonian language; 60% of the upper secondary school (10th–12th grade) curriculum in Russian-medium schools must be taught in Estonian by September 2011; the first foreign language taught in Russian-medium general schools (1st–9th grade) must be Estonian; and Russian-medium kindergartens (starting from age 3) must offer Estonian-language instruction.

The minority communities come to school with radically different skill bases in the official language. In practice, the state attempts to acknowledge these divergent linguistic profiles and promote distinct goals of school vis-à-vis Estonian-language instruction including maintenance and acquisition. The Võro largely speak Estonian as their first language (L1) while the Russian-speakers, to varying degrees, speak the official language as a second language (L2). As part of a previous majority, Estonia's Russian-speakers have benefited from systemic privileges that other minority groups lack including a well-established, fully functioning K-12 Russian-medium track public school system available in most parts of the country. In 2008/2009, 19% of all students (22,131) attend Russian-medium primary schools and 19.2% (6,015) were enrolled in Russian-medium upper secondary (10th–12th grade) schools.

If Russian-speakers had historic privileges in the educational sphere (e.g., Russian-medium schools), which facilitated Russian-language maintenance, schools have played a significantly different role for the Võro community; these institutions served as tools of ethnic homogenization. Historically, the state emphasized acquisition of *standard* Estonian during the first period of independence (1918–1940), an effort, which continued during the Soviet occupation. With Estonian-language acquisition for the Võro no longer a primary concern, the state has shifted its concern for setting standards to maintain a place for the state language in the context of Võro-language revitalization. For the Võro, the state shapes "acceptable difference" around the provision of opportunities to express difference within the ethnic Estonian community rather than by the promotion of Estonian-language learning (as with the Russian-speakers).

---

[1] Article 37, point 4 states, "All persons shall have the right to instruction in Estonian. Educational institutions established for minorities shall choose their own language of instruction."

Context

Minority Profiles

Estonia's Russian-speakers, also referred to as non-Estonians and Russophones, constitute a complex minority population. First, in the last 25 years (1985–2010), the Russian-speakers, who once enjoyed a privileged position due to their connection with a broader and powerful Russian majority in the Soviet Union, transformed into a minority population in an independent Estonia. Russian-speakers in Estonia are defined, in part, by their history of immigration to Estonia. The population of ethnic Russians, the largest group of Russian-speakers, grew substantially under the Soviet occupation of Estonia—from 3.9% in 1923–1934 (the interwar era of Estonian independence) to 25.6% in 2000–2001 (Hogan-Brun 2007, p. 556). Ozolins (1999) observes a major consequence of this significant in-migration during the Soviet period was the creation of a linguistic ecosystem marked by asymmetrical bilingualism with bilingual (Estonian-Russian) Estonians and monolingual Russian speakers. Moreover, a culture of expectations developed where the "monolingual (or russified) Russian speakers…expected to be able to work and receive any service in Russian" (Ozolins 1999, p. 10). The monolingualism of this Soviet socioeconomic order, what Rannut (2004, p. 4) identifies as "full scale Russian monolingualism for Russians," resulted in only 15% of the country's ethnic Russian population claiming to know Estonian in 1989 (Zabrodskaja 2009, p. 62).

The second aspect adding to the Russian-speakers' complexity is their ethnic diversity; they constitute a large (~380,000, Table 14.1), ethnically heterogeneous population loosely united by language. The term "Russian-speakers" refers not only to ethnic Russians, the largest minority group in Estonia, but also to some of the so-called "third nationalities" or ethnic minorities (e.g., Ukrainians and Belarussians) who use Russian as their language of communication, yet are not ethnic Estonian or Russian. Pavlenko (2008) highlights the complex linguistic aspect of their identity, noting that Russian speakers "challenge the common view of 'majorities' and 'minorities'" speaking "a regional lingua franca and a mother tongue of a multiethnic group of people" (p. 304). Irrespective of ethnicity and language, Russian-speakers represent a largely urban group with the population divided into four main areas: (1) Tallinn, Estonia's capital, where they are a little less than a half of the population; (2) Northeastern Estonia, where they constitute over 95% of the population; (3) other cities where Russians are less than 30% of the total population; and (4) the rural areas where the Russian population is dispersed (Rannut 2005). The geographic concentration of Russian-speakers serves both to maintain

Table 14.1 Population of Estonia by ethnicity, 2000 and 2008. (Source: Statistics Estonia 2009)

Year	Estonians	Russians	Ukrainians	Belorussians	Finns	Tatars	Others	Total
2000	935,884	354,660	29,259	17,460	11,974	2,610	20,224	1,372,071
2008	920,885	343,568	28,003	15,925	10,890	2,473	19,191	1,340,935

their language community and isolate them from an ethnic-Estonian and Estonian-language environment (Lapikova 1998, p. 7). Although culturally and linguistically different, Russian-speakers have overwhelmingly declared their political allegiance to Estonia. Since Estonia's independence, a majority of the country's Russian speakers have become Estonian citizens (84.1% of Estonia's population held Estonian citizenship), while 8.6% of the population represents citizens of other countries and 7.3% are of undetermined citizenship (May 2010, Ministry of Foreign Affairs 2010, p. 3).

The Võro have a strikingly different profile from the Russian-speaking community and represent a complex minority in their own right. The Võro, an autochthonous, regional-language community, akin to Catalan-speakers in Spain, identify themselves as ethnic Estonians and are fully integrated into Estonian cultural, political, and social life. This minority group speaks, to varying degrees of proficiency, Võro, an endangered local language. Although Võro[2] has its own history as a literary language and was used in the late nineteenth-century-schools, churches, and other public institutions, past policies promoting language homogenization among ethnic Estonians have contributed to the overwhelming majority of Võro-speaking Estonian as their L1. By the most recent estimates, about 50,000 people speak Võro (Koreinik 2007, p. 10) or approximately 5% of the ethnic Estonian population.[3] Few children speak Võro as their L1 (for exception see Saar 2002) or regularly use the language at home. According to one VI researcher's estimates, in 2009, approximately 20 children speak Võro as their L1. Given the decline in the number of L1 Võro speakers and a significant language shift across generations, a concerted effort to revitalize the language began over 20 years ago.

The Võro are also distinct from the Russian-speakers due to their legal status. While Estonia's Võro speakers constitute a numeric minority, the state does not consider them an official "ethnic minority," a category that carries certain privileges. The Law on Autonomy for Ethnic Minorities (1993) created by the state in the spirit of "acceptable difference," attempts to ensure that non-Estonian ethnic groups have the opportunity to maintain their language and culture in Estonia. According to the law, ethnic minorities are

> ...a group of Estonian citizens, who reside on Estonian territory, are in firm and lasting relations with Estonia, differ from Estonians by their ethnic origin, cultural identity, religion or language, who seek to maintain their cultural traditions, religion and language that are fundamental to their sense of national identity.

Verschik (2005, p. 293, citing Smith 2001, 2003) notes that these minority-defining criteria have generally divided the Russian and Võro communities by drawing "a clear distinction between autochthonous/indigenous 'national' minorities on the one

---

[2] Võro, considered a variety of the South Estonian language because it "differs significantly from standard and common Estonian in all linguistic aspects—phonology, morphology, syntax and vocabulary," has a literary history dating to the seventeenth century, when a New Testament edition first appeared in the language (Koreinik 2007, p. 5).

[3] These figures represent a rough approximation since the Estonian government does not count the Võro separately from other ethnic Estonians in the census.

hand, and 'new' or 'immigrant' ethnic minorities on the other criteria." For the Võro, who do not "differ from Estonians by their ethnic origin," they do not have the same legal grounds on which to organize school-based efforts to promote revitalization.

Triple Role of Schooling

The state's emphasis on Estonian language-learning has emerged as part, and in response to, the shifting purposes of schooling across the twentieth and twenty-first centuries. A longitudinal review of these purposes reveals three, at times overlapping, goals: Estonianization, civic integration, and Russification. "Acceptable difference" has taken different forms for the two minority groups depending on the era. In this section, I sketch the key features of these purposes and the ways that the state helped to shape Estonian-language learning opportunities for Russian-speakers and the Võro.

Estonianization

As a new state (1918–1940), one of the first purposes of Estonian-language education vis-à-vis the Estonian population was to fortify ethnic identity and to "create a modern and autonomous Estonian culture" (Raun 1985, p. 19) through Estonianization. Language planners along with school administrators and faculty promoted standard Estonian as the primary language of instruction in schools serving ethnic Estonians (Verschik 2005, p. 286). Regional "dialects" were officially and informally no longer an acceptable difference within public schools. Publishing in the regional-language, prominent during the nineteenth century faded with the rise of the Estonian nationalism near the turn of the century and through the time of Estonianization. In this period of, what Raun (2000, p. 136) identifies as, "the era of standardization of written Estonian," primers, grammar books, and dictionaries were used as tools to promote a single standard; the emphasis on the cultivation of a common national language and the promotion of ethnic solidarity, attempted to erase autochthonous languages, including Võro, from schools.

With the collapse of the Soviet Union and new era of independence in 1991, the Estonian state focused once again on the promotion and preservation of the Estonian. In particular, the state used specific strategies, like the "Estonian Language Development Strategy" (2004–2010) and "Estonian Language Development Plan" (2011–2017), to outline long-term commitments and priorities for language development; these language plans include support for the country's regional languages. The government's symbolic and financial support for the regional-language marks a significant shift in its position toward regional languages from restrictive Estonianization practices typical of the interwar (1918–1940) to an endorsement of "reinscription" or a reintroduction of the regional-language into schools (Brown 2010).

In the newly independent Estonia, the state has accommodated and endorsed, on the basis of voluntary choice, regional-language instruction in Southeastern Estonian schools. Since 1995, a new phase in state-supported Võro-language education has begun with a voluntary language program offered in about half the schools where Võro has historically been spoken. I discuss this support in greater detail in the next section.

Civic Integration

Civic integration has also guided state decision-making regarding Estonian-language learning in schools. Since independence, one of the primary goals in Estonia has been to create a school system that will aid in developing this civic identity and facilitating the integration of non-Estonians. Estonian-language instruction constitutes the cornerstone of these educational efforts. The Estonian government strives to use education, particularly Estonian-language schooling, to dismantle "ethnic cleavages" through

> a pronounced emphasis on inculcating social mores in a spirit of civic equality and fraternity. Part…of the contents of that education may be termed civic too. For it may be used to convey, through language (assuming there to be a lingua franca), history, the arts and literature, a political mythology and symbolism of the new nation….(Smith 1991, p. 119).

The government's prime concerns regarding the Russian-speaking minority—increasing Estonian citizenship acquisition and developing Estonian language skills—are distinct from the Estonianization goals targeting the regional-language speakers. The Estonian government promotes a shared civic Estonian identity, while not requiring a homogenous cultural identity. The state conception of "acceptable difference" is reflected in the multiple state-sponsored integration programs (e.g., State Programme: "Integration into Estonian Society 2000–2007" & State Programme: "Integration into Estonian Society 2008–2013") and initiatives (e.g., National Language Immersion Program), which depict integration as an additive rather than a subtractive process. The *Estonian Human Development Report* (1998) defines integration as

> a process, within which the non-Estonians residing in Estonia will join the local society's affairs as full-fledged participants. Integration means a gradual disappearance of these barriers, which are currently preventing many non-Estonians from becoming competitive in the Estonian labor market, benefiting from the educational opportunities, participating in the local culture and political affairs….Integration is not a change of ethnic identity; integration is not a loss of something, but the acquisition of new qualities necessary for survival in a modern Estonia. (Heidmets et al. 1998, p. 51)

The additive approach to integration reflected in the extract—civic Estonian plus ethnic identity—is a state-model of "acceptable difference" that garnered hard-earned praise and, in some cases, funding from international organizations, including the Organization for Security and Cooperation in Europe (OSCE), the European

Union (EU) and the Open Society Institute (OSI) (Laitin 2005, p. 53).[4] The state's integration efforts have also been an effective way to express and implement the Estonian government's commitment to minority rights as articulated through various laws, particularly the Law on Cultural Autonomy.

Russification

De jure and de facto Russification has also shaped the context for promoting Estonian-language education. De jure Russification during the Soviet occupation of Estonia (1940–1991) was driven by three models: (1) Russian monolingualism for Russians with minimal, if any Estonian-language instruction; (2) Estonian-Russian bilingualism for ethnic Estonians; and (3) assimilation of other non-Russian and non-Estonian ethnicities (Rannut 2004, p. 4) In practice, Russification meant an increase in Russian-language instruction in Estonian-medium schools, the rapid expansion of the Russian-medium school network, and the marginalization of Estonian-language education in Russian-medium schools. The de facto Russification of "third nationalities" or non-ethnic Russian groups, which began under the Soviets, continues in the post-Soviet era in Russian-medium schools where the majority of students are ethnic Russian. In post-communist Estonia, "third nationality" Russian-speakers are left with the choice to enroll in an Estonian-medium school, to continue attending Russian-medium schools or to organize their own national schools (Verschik 2005, p. 294). Since the foundation of a national school can be costly and challenging, and there is a long-standing tradition of attending, Russian-medium schools, many non-Russian students, except for Finns, remain in the Russian-medium schools, yet do not receive any instruction in their national language or culture.

Shaping "Acceptable Difference"

Since independence from the Soviet Union in 1991, the Estonian government has attempted to strike a balance between mandated change and embedded choice in its approach to Estonian-language policy in state schools. In the case of both the Russian-speaking and Võro communities, the state works to secure first the non-negotiable starting point for developing school-based policies to accommodate and promote linguistic and ethnic difference—Estonian-language proficiency. In practice, these policies strive to either secure the current position of Estonian-medium education or create new spaces for learning Estonian. To be sure, while the choice motif undergirds the policies directed toward both minority groups, the state differently crafts the options available for these communities.

---

[4] Estonia has also signed and ratified the *Framework Convention for the Protection of National Minorities*.

For the country's autochthonous Võro community, the state has developed a model of acceptable difference where instruction in the state language is preserved and regional-language education is offered as a supplemental and voluntary course. The roots of this state support—a response to the organized initiative of Estonian regional-language activists, the awareness of general "European" (i.e., the Council of Europe and the European Union) endorsement of regional and minority languages, and the government's continued appreciation of the regional languages as an enriching source of Estonian language and identity, has resulted in multiple initiatives to develop and protect voluntary regional-language education. The primary government programs that fund and develop instruction in regional languages include the "South Estonian Language and Culture Program State Program" (2005–2009), the "Old Võrumaa Cultural Program" (2010–2013), and the "Development Strategy of the Estonian Language" (2004–2010). The government also supports the regional-language through the Võro Institute (VI), a research and development organization funded primarily by the Ministry of Culture. The VI was established in 1995 as an independent institution to coalesce the work of a grassroots language-revitalization movement that emerged late in the Soviet period. The Institute compiles and publishes textbooks and teaching materials, organizes in-service teacher training seminars and academic conferences, recruits, organizes, and subsidizes teachers, and hosts extracurricular language competitions and camps for students.

In essence, acceptable difference for the autochthonous Võro community creates options or choices *within* the traditional framework of Estonian-medium schools. That is, since 1995 the government financially and ideologically supports a voluntary class offered in the regional language at the general school (grades 1–9) and/or upper secondary level (grades 10–12). In this framework, Võro is taught in addition to, rather than in place of, Estonian. The network of institutions teaching Võro has expanded over the last decade from 6 schools in 1997/1998 to 23 in 2009/2010, just under half the schools in the region. Approximately four hundred children, or about 5% of the total school population, receive some type of Võro instruction, which begins in third or fourth grade with basic primer instruction and can extend into the sixth and seventh grades with "home studies," a type of regional culture and history class.

In contrast to the maintenance base of the "choice" policy for Estonia's autochthonous minorities, the state's approach to Estonian-language learning for Russian-speakers rests on mandated change and choice from select state-endorsed models. As mentioned earlier in the chapter, the introduction and full development of a required Estonian-language curriculum functions as a cornerstone of the state's integration plan. The Ministry of Education and Research, the body with official responsibility for the definition and implementation of education policy, has required Russian-medium schools both to adopt state curricula in order to have subject-based uniformity in public schools and, for upper secondary schools (grades 10–12), to shift at least 60% of instruction to Estonian. Law has mandated both changes. The Ministry began to unify the curricula of the Russian- and Estonian-medium schools beginning in the late glasnost period (Estonian history in 1990/1991, Estonian literature and geography in 1991/1992, and civic education in 1992/1993) and completed the process in 1996 (Vöörman 1998, p. 1). The Basic Schools and Upper Secondary Schools Act (1997) required Russian-medium upper secondary level schools to transition to Estonian-language instruction by September 2007; this deadline was extended in 2007 to the 2011/2012 along with the Ministry-financed provision of 70,000 Estonian kroons (~ $ 5,860) per additional compulsory subject that is taught in Estonian beyond the required 60%.

The choice-based component embedded in the mandated curricular change lies in the school options for Estonian-language learning for Russian-speakers. In an effort to improve this community's language proficiency and fluency, two state-supported paths are possible for increased Estonian-language learning: (1) Estonian as a second language; and (2) Estonian immersion (see Table 14.2). Each option presents strengths and drawbacks with regard to Estonian-language instruction and home-language maintenance. First, the Russian-medium option with Estonian as a foreign or second language (ESL) provides for Russian-medium instruction with a set number of Estonian-language courses per grade. In post-Soviet practice, the number of hours allotted to Estonian study in Russian-medium schools has gradually increased. By 1998, the required number of hours of Estonian-language instruction ranges from 6 to 10 hours a week for first through third grade, 12 to 15 hours for fourth through ninth grades, and 9 hours for tenth through 12th grades. Embedded in this requirement is the mandate that a greater number of core classes be offered in Estonian. To this end, the 2011/2012 academic year marks a landmark point in the integration efforts targeting upper secondary students.

The second option for Estonian-language learning second is enrollment in an immersion program. Originally developed in cooperation with Canada and Finland, the immersion approach, begun in 2000, aims to develop fluency in Estonian while retaining the Russian L1. Within the immersion approach, schools can opt for (1) early language immersion (ELI), which begins with 100% immersion in kindergarten and first grade with a gradual, grade-by-grade introduction of Russian instruction, so by grades 6–9 Estonian and Russian instruction each constitute 44%

Table 14.2 State-approved Estonian and Võro language learning opportunities

Language	Format	Goal
Estonian		
Estonian-as-a-foreign language	Estonian is taught as a foreign language in a Russian-medium school	Estonian proficiency with a strong Russian base as student's L1
Immersion	Early immersion Partial early immersion Late immersion	Additive bilingualism
Estonian as medium of instruction	Enrollment into Estonian-medium school	Estonian fluency
Võro		
Elective class	Optional course offered during the school day	Proficiency
Hobby (after-school) class	Optional course offered after school	Introduction to the language

of the curriculum and 12% is dedicated to foreign-language instruction; or (2) late language immersion (LLI), which begins in the sixth grade with approximately 33% of the curriculum in Estonian and increasing to over 60% in the following three grades. In 2009/2010, 54 Russian-language schools and kindergartens participated in the language immersion program.

Shared Challenges

Despite the key differences in the choice-based Estonian-language learning policies, the two minority communities share a core challenge that both limits their ability to take full advantage of the "acceptable difference" model, and, equally as important, presents a basis for resisting "acceptable difference" as currently defined by the state. The common challenge is the urgency with which the respective language learning must take place (i.e., Võro and Estonian). Key aspects of this urgency, including demographic decline and uneven language program development, pose significant barriers to each minority communities' ability to capitalize on the choices embedded in state policy. A review of the aspects of urgency illustrates both the effective tapering of choices and the challenge to maintain linguistic diversity through the "acceptable difference" model.

Urgency in the Võro Context

Võro has survived into the twenty-first century, but not without significant language loss and shift. Researchers report a sharp decrease in the daily use of Võro across generations, a shift that adds particular urgency to developing effective school-based programs to promote language acquisition. According to recent studies, the following percentages claim to "not use Võro at all": 12% among 52–71-year-olds; 21% of 32–51-year-olds; and 62% of 14–16-year-olds (Ehala 2007, p. 47). Despite this steep decline, the statistics camouflage a potentially promising gap between language use and knowledge among the children's generation (i.e., 14–16-year-olds); in a recent survey 52% of children claimed their knowledge of Võro is "average" or "better" (Ehala 2007, p. 46). Given the endangered status of Võro, educators and language activists have struggled to determine the best ways to work with an Estonian-dominated public school system in order to revitalize their language.

In addition to language shift, the demographic decline has added to the sense of linguistic urgency, and, in part, contributed to school closure and the retirement of Võro L1 teachers. Schools throughout the county, especially those in the less populated, rural areas, face consolidation and closing due to the declining student population, tight budgets, and general concern about the quality of education in country schools. Since 2000, 11 schools in the region have closed including six schools hosting Võro programs. Language teachers acknowledged that they have little power to bring stability to rural schools, given the contemporary demographic and political trends signaling triple termination—the end of the school, the demise of the regional-language program and, in many cases, the close of their professional careers. Only 5 of the 26 schools offering Võro had more than one regional-language teacher in 2001/2002, and new, younger teachers are hard to recruit. In my research, I found teachers to be aware of the hole that their retirement will leave, but they express resignation at the effects of their decision. Annika, a veteran teacher, explained to me in an interview, "I might teach one more year, but then I will retire. I don't know if there will be another teacher willing to take on the Võro course once I'm gone" (Brown 2006, p. 136).

Urgency in the Russian Context

"Urgency" regarding the Russian speakers pertains in part to the connection between the collective level of Estonian-language skills and this community's persistent social and political isolation. The isolation of the Russian-speakers is linked directly with their lack of integration, as reflected in the Language Immersion Centre's webpage, "Approximately one third of the population of Estonia is of non-Estonian origin, the vast majority of whom do not speak Estonian and are not fully integrated into the mainstream of Estonian political, social and cultural life" (Language Immersion Centre n.d., p. 1). The burden on schools to address linguistic and civic isolation is particularly heavy given low Estonian-Russian-speaker intermarriage rates and the demographic concentration of Russian-speakers discussed earlier in this chapter. The importance of schools to help address this de facto segregation between the communities is reflected in a comment made by a Russian-speaking Latvian student in Sillamäe, "The only place where we can speak in Estonian is in Estonian-language class and as a conversation partner with our Estonian-language teacher" (Tiik 1999).

In addition to the urgency of addressing sociopolitical isolation through official-language education, the general demographic decline (i.e., low birth rates, high death rates, and high out migration) of Russians since independence has led to changes in language-learning structures and opportunities. Most significantly, the absolute number of Russian students and schools (see Table 14.3) has decreased, which creates a parallel tension between the maintenance of the tradition of Russian-medium education and introduction of greater opportunities for Estonian-language learning.

Table 14.3 Number of schools by language of instruction: 1990–2010. (Source: Ministry of Education and Research, Kõigi valdkondale statistilised Andmed, www.hm.ee-index.php_048055)

Academic year	Estonian	Russian	Mixed
1995–1996	600	116	26
2000–2001	566	100	19
2005–2006	492	79	22
2009–2010	465	61	28

Although more than a third of all students continue to be educated in Russian, the number of students learning in Russian and the number of Russian schools has dropped in the last 20 years. From 1990/1991 until 2006/2007, the percentage of children enrolled in Russian schools dropped from 36.8% to 20%. The decrease in the number of Russian-speaking students reflects, in large part, the overall drop in the total population of Russian-speakers in Estonia from 1991 to 1999, especially from 1990 to 1993, as a result of emigration from Estonia and falling birth rates.[5]

The population decline, as well as the low levels of post-Soviet immigration, threatens to end Russian-medium education in whole regions of the country due to the lack of Russian students; to this point, 3 out of 15 counties in Estonia have already closed their Russian-medium schools. The closure of Russian-medium schools has led to the enrollment of Russian-speaking primary and secondary students in Estonian schools; adding to this stream of Russian-speaking attendees of Estonian-medium schools are those students who enroll by choice (i.e., when a Russian-medium track is available but rejected) (Hogan-Brun 2007, p. 564). The most reliable data on this enrollment pattern emerge from 2006 to 2007 when over 4,500 Russian-speaking children attended Estonian-track primary or secondary schools constituting approximately 4% of all students in these schools (Estonian Integration Strategy 2008–2013, p. 7).

The uneven expansion of Estonian-language programs among the country's Russian-medium schools accompanies this demographic shift. While all Russian-medium schools are required to offer some level of instruction in Estonian, great disparity remains between the quality of the language programs offered in different regions of Estonia. For schools in the heavily Russian areas of Estonia, such as Narva, which are over 95% Russian-speaking, the transition to Estonian-medium instruction in at the upper secondary level has been challenging due, in part, to the late introduction (i.e., 1991) of Estonian-language courses in area schools. In contrast, in the more ethnic Estonian-dominant areas of the country, such as Tartu, or in the small cities and rural towns, such as Võru, the curricular transition to Estonian-medium instruction has proceeded more smoothly. Teacher training and readiness complicates the development and delivery of effective Estonian-language instruction. Part of the challenge is rooted in the stability of the teaching corps at the Russian schools. The turnover of Russian-medium teachers from the Soviet to the post-communist period has been small; and, the majority of the Russian-medium teachers, who received their training in Russia during the Soviet period, lack Estonian-language skills (Lapikova 1998, p. 9). The quality of the staff and its lack of Estonian-language training has significant ramifications for the implementation of Estonian-language programs in the post-communist period, which shapes the learning outcomes of students who opt for schooling in the Russian-medium track. The urgency and importance of developing an Estonian-skill base for Russian-medium

---

[5] The largest group of Russian-speakers, the ethnic Russians, has decreased in size from 474,834 people in 1989 to 343,568 in 2008. It is important to note that the rate of Russian-speaker emigration has significantly decreased since 1994 and most remaining Russian-speakers have decided to live in Estonia permanently.

teachers was highlighted in 2009, when legislation was passed that gave teachers 2 years to reach a degree of proficiency in Estonian or face losing their jobs.[6]

Discussion

The Estonian government has drawn clear parameters of "acceptable difference" for the official-language education of minority communities; as long as Estonian-language instruction is maintained or expanded, cultural difference, as illustrated in part by non-Estonian language learning, is tolerated and supported. At its core, the "acceptable difference" approach allows the state to further goals like civic integration and support for cultural diversity, while also providing space for the Russian-speakers and Võro to retain and develop distinct identity. Although the emphasis on Estonian-language education in these two minority communities serves different purposes (i.e., Estonian-language maintenance and Estonian-language skill development), the state adheres to the common approach of embedding choice in its Estonian language-learning policies. To be sure, for both populations, Estonian-language learning and instruction must be offered from preschool through 12th grade; yet, the groups have distinct options regarding the balance of Estonian and minority-language instruction. These options are constructed according to state-defined notions of "acceptable difference."

In pursuing a model of "acceptable difference" within separate Estonian- and Russian-medium schools, the state accomplishes two goals. First, the government communicates that it accepts and supports cultural and linguistic difference in public schools. Russian-medium schools provide the opportunity to maintain their schools as a symbol of security and as evidence of the concrete continuity of Russian language and culture in Estonia. Joshua Fishman argues that the preservation of some type of minority-language instruction provides a sense of belonging for that community.

> Disadvantaged populations are particularly dependent on this symbolism [of national language] since they lack the full array of other public symbols that advantaged populations display. The use of the disadvantaged language in the school is a symbolic statement in and of itself. It says, "We are here. We exist. We remain faithful to ourselves." The use of the disadvantaged language in the schools is a statement of public legitimacy on behalf of populations that possess few other symbolic entree into the public realm (1984, p. 54).

Although the Estonian state perceives Estonian rather than Russian to be a "disadvantaged" language, the government recognizes the practical and symbolic value of maintaining the Russian-medium schools. For the Võro community, the government's support for regional-language education communicates that linguistic diversity is accepted even for ethnic Estonians and merits a voluntary place in the public-school day. The "acceptable difference" model further helps to preserve distinct and

---

[6] The law also reforms the measurement scale of proficiency to bring it in line with EU norms as defined under the Common European Framework of Reference for Languages.

protective places for the fortification of the Estonian-language and for the cultivation of ethnic Estonian solidarity.

The state-defined borders of "acceptability"—that minority-language instruction is permitted only if Estonian-language instruction is guaranteed a primary role—applies equally to Estonian- and Russian-medium schools even if it comes at the cost of enhancing linguistic diversity and supporting language revitalization. The equal application of "acceptable difference" generates asymmetrical consequences for the Võro-speakers. For the Võro community, the government notions of "acceptability" means that exclusive instruction in the regional language (i.e., immersion pedagogy) is not permitted despite the community's fluency in Estonian and solidarity with other ethnic Estonians. One of the consequences of this model of acceptable difference is a limitation of pedagogical and programmatic development. First, immersion Võro-language programs remain outside the realm of what's permitted. Based on existing language laws, the state language (Estonian) must be offered in public schools from preschool through the secondary level. Given this restriction, grassroots' attempts to introduce the language nest approach to learning Võro, where teachers use only the heritage language with the young children, have been prohibited from the public education sphere. Although operating the language nest in the private sphere allows teachers the freedom to maintain the one-language immersion approach, it also excludes the community from key financial benefits and institutional support.

Second, the voluntary approach to funding Võro-language instruction has made vulnerable program development. In depending on willing teachers, the VI and other civil society organizations to develop and shape regional-language education,

> the government has abdicated its power to use state institutions for the maintenance and development of endangered languages. Without the charge of the state, civil society groups are left unable to compel a reluctant public to engage in the short- and long-term planning necessary for the preservation of the regional language. To help alter this balance, civil society groups will undoubtedly continue to pressure the government to sign the Council of Europe's "Charter on Regional or Minority Languages." (Brown 2009, p. 144)

As this passage reveals, the limitations of the Estonian government's programmatic approach to realizing "acceptable difference" for the Võro might result in language activists and educators turning to alternative, European-level notions of "acceptable difference" to broaden support and recognition.

The acceptable difference approach to official-language education also fails to acknowledge the socio-cultural limitations to realizing "choice" within this policy. For the Võro, continued school closure and language-teacher retirement "presents a challenge to the government's notion of the ability of the local level to take advantage of choices made by parents and students" (Brown 2010, p. 308). For the Russian-speakers, "choice" elements from Estonian-language learning policy are undermined, in part, by the historic uneven development of school-based Estonian programs and by the demographic decline resulting in the closure of Russian-medium schools. These developments result in limited rather than expanded options for Estonian-language learning including systematic involuntary submersion (i.e., the placement of all Russian-speakers into the closest Estonian-language school) and Estonian-medium school enrollment (in order to access higher-quality language instruction).

Both minority communities have challenged the government's current conception of "acceptable difference." Community-based resistance has resulted in new language-learning possibilities within both the public and private educational sphere. Evidence of this resistance can be found within the growing trend of enrolling Russian-speaking children into Estonian-medium schools—a response, in part, to the limited options for Russian schooling and preferred options for linguistic and cultural integration. With this choice, Russian-speakers opt to have their children study in Estonian-medium schools *without* additional support for maintaining their L1. Although data are limited, this trend appears to be concentrated at the early childhood level. For example, in 2009/2010, Russian-speakers constituted approximately 3% of the total population of Estonian-medium kindergartens. Verschik (2006) argues that this grassroots merger of ethnic communities into one school may be a prudent policy approach to promote future Estonian proficiency among non-Estonians. She suggests, however, that Estonian-medium schools will need to shift to accommodate all residents of Estonia.

> As the best results in Estonian as L2 are achieved in Estonian-medium schools, and as new immigrants continue to settle in Estonia, Estonian-medium schools have to change their character from the Soviet-time bastion of (defensive) Estonian identity into an institution that creates an integrative motivation and where students of various origins receive an education in the official language of the country. (Verschik 2006, p. 124)

Verschik's recommendation points to the need for a broadening of the "acceptable difference" ethos beyond Russian-medium to Estonian-medium schools to embrace partial responsibility for minority integration and enculturation into Estonian society.

The resistance within the Võro-speaking community to the state's foreclosure of immersion opportunities in public schools has been channeled into developments in the private sphere. A pilot Võro "language nest" opened in the 2009 for one day a week also to serve the youngest members of the community. The language nest, a result of NGO and public institute cooperation, promotes a one-language immersion approach to instruction through the exclusive use of Võro with a small group of children. While the immersion program does not benefit from the institutional and staff support that public kindergartens enjoy, the development of a differentiated early-childhood education to sustain Võro is evidence of local attempts to pass the language along to the next generation of Estonians and preserve it well into the twenty-first century.

In conclusion, the government's approach toward Estonian-language learning for the Võro and Russian-speaking minorities revolves around the central notion of providing options to maintain a community language alongside Estonian. The urgency in addressing the parallel linguistic situations—one involving regional language revitalization and the other a delicate balance between a well-established minority language and the underused state language—will undoubtedly challenge the current "acceptable difference" model in the upcoming decades. The local resistance to the government's notions of "acceptability" expressed in practices, like Estonian-medium enrollment and the development of private-sphere bases immersion early childhood programs, suggests a powerful dialectic between the government and minority communities about notions of difference in twenty-first-century Estonia and future directions for policy development.

References

Brown, K. D. (2006). Learning the language: International, national & local dimensions of regional-language education in Estonia (doctoral dissertation). Available from Dissertations and Theses database. (UMI No. 3229586).
Brown, K. D. (2009). Market models of language policy: A view from Estonia. *European Journal of Language Policy, 1.2,* 137–146.
Brown, K. D. (2010). Teachers as language policy actors. *Anthropology & Education Quarterly, 41*(3), 298–314.
Ehala, M. (2007). Sustainability of double ethnic identity in majority-minority settings: The case of Estonian and Võro. In R. Blokland & C. Hasselblatt (Eds.), *Language and identity in the Finno-Ugric world* (pp. 44–54). Maastricht: Shaker.
Estonian Integration Strategy. (2008–2013). http://www.kul.ee/webeditor/files/integratsioon/Loimumiskava_2008_2013_ENG.pdf. Accessed 1 May 2009.
Fishman, J. A. (1984). Minority mother tongues in education. *Prospects, 14,* 51–61.
Heidmets, M., Loogma, K., Raudma, T., Toomel, K., & Viik, L. (Eds.). (1998). *Estonian Human Development Report 1998.* Tallinn. http://www.tlu.ee/~teap/nhdr/1998/EIA98eng.pdf. Accessed 5 May 2010.
Hogan-Brun, G. (2007). Language-in-education across the Baltic: Policies, practices and challenges. *Comparative Education, 43,* 553–570.
Hogan-Brun, G., Ramoniene, M., & Rannut, M. (2007). Language policies and practices in the Baltic States. *Current Issues in Language Planning, 8,* 469–631.
Koreinik, K. (2007). *Võro: The Võro language in education.* Ljouwert: Mercator European Research Centre on Multilingualism and Language Learning.
Laitin, D. (2005). Culture shift in a postcommunist state. In Z. Barany & R. G. Moser (Eds.), *Ethnic politics after communism* (pp. 46–72). Ithaca: Cornell University Press.
Language Immersion Centre. (n.d.) History of the immersion program in Estonia. http://www.kke.ee/index.php?lang=eng&pages_ID=19&menus_ID=1&active_link_ID=50&mark. Accessed 15 April 2010.
Lapikova, N. (1998). Venekeelsest haridusest Eestis [Russian-language education in Estonia]. *Haridus, 2,* 7–12.
Ministry of Education and Research. (2004). *Development strategy of the Estonian Language: 2004–2010.* Tartu: Atlex.
Ministry of Foreign Affairs. (2010). Citizenship. http://estonia.eu/about-estonia/society/citizenship.html. Accessed 15 March 2010.
Ozolins, U. (1999). Between Russian and European hegemony: Current language policy in the Baltic States. Current Issues in Language and Society, 6, 6–47.
Pavlenko, A. (2008). Multilingualism in post-Soviet countries: Language revival, language removal, and sociolinguistic theory. *International Journal of Bilingual Education and Bilingualism, 11,* 275–240.
Pennycook, A. (2006). Postmodernism in language policy. In T. Ricento (Ed.), *An introduction to language policy: Theory and method* (pp. 60–76). Oxford: Blackwell.
Rannut, M. (2004). Language policy in Estonia. *Noves SL. Revista de Sociolinguistica,* Spring-Summer, 1–17. http://www6.gencat.net/llengcat/noves/hm04primavera-estiu/docs/rannut.pdf. Accessed 1 May 2010.

Rannut, Ü. (2005). *Keelekeskkonna mõju vene õpilaste eesti keele omandamisele ja integratsioonile Eestis* [Impact of the language environment on integration and Estonian language acquisition of Russian- speaking children in Estonia]. Tallinn: Tallinn University Press.
Raun, T. U. (1985). Language development and policy in Estonia. In I. T. Kreindler (Ed.), *Sociolinguistic perspectives on Soviet national languages: Their past, present and future* (pp. 13–35). Berlin: Mouton de Gruyter.
Raun, T. U. (2000). *Estonia and the Estonians* (2nd ed.). Stanford: Stanford University Press.
Ricento, T. (1998). National language policy in the United States. In T. Ricento & B. Burnaby (Eds.), *Language and policies in the United States and Canada: Myths and realities* (pp. 85–112). Mahwah: Erlbaum.
Saar, E. (2002). Haan'kasõh kynõldas latsiga maakiilt (People of Haanja speak the country language with children). Uma Leht, 5 March, 3.
Smith, A. (1991). *National identity*. Reno: University of Nevada Press.
Smith, D.J. (2001). Cultural autonomy in Estonia. A relevant paradigm for the Post-Soviet era? Working Paper 19/01 of the ESRC "One Europe or Several?" Programme. University of Sussex: ESRC.
Smith, D.J. (2003). Minority rights, multiculturalism and EU enlargement. The case of Estonia. Journal on Ethnopolitics and Minority Issues in Europe I. http://www.ecmi.de/j emie/ download/Focus 1-2003_Smith.pdf. Accessed 5 June 2005.
Tikk, Ü. (1999). Loobumine kartulikasvatusest keeleõppetalu kasuks. Õpetajate Leht 18 June. http://greta.cs.ioc.ee/~opleht/Arhiiv/99Jun18/elustenesest.html. Accessed 5 Dec 2001.
Tollefson, J. W. (2006). Critical theory in language policy. In T. Ricento (Ed.), *An introduction to language policy: Theory and method* (pp. 42–59). Oxford: Blackwell.
Urciuoli, B. (1994). Acceptable difference: The cultural evolution of the model ethnic American citizen. *POLAR: Political and Legal Anthropology Review, 17,* 19–36.
Verschik, A. (2005). The language situation in Estonia. *Journal of Baltic Studies, 36,* 283–316.
Verschik, A. (2006). Recent contributions to Estonian sociolinguistics. *SOLS Estudios de Sociolingüística, 7,* 121–126.
Vöörman, M. (1998). Õ nagu õpik [Õ as in textbook]. *Luup.* http://postimees.ee/luup/98/25. Accessed 14 Dec 1998. http://www.postimees.ee/luup/98/25/eesti2.htm. Accessed 1 Aug 2010.
Zabrodskaja, A. (2009). Language testing in the context of citizenship and asylum: The case of Estonia. *Language Assessment Quarterly, 6,* 61–70.

Chapter 15
The Inuit Qaujimajatuqangit Conversation: The Language and Culture of Schooling in the Nunavut Territory of Canada

M. Lynn Aylward

Introduction

Understanding cultural and social and difference within minoritized Indigenous education contexts necessitates the recognition that Indigenous knowledges worldwide have been framed by western epistemological and curricular constructs as subjugated knowledges (Barnhardt 2001; Castellano et al. 2000; Hampton 1993; Semali and Kincheloe 1999). In this instance, subjugation refers to the relations of power around efforts to include Indigenous knowledges in academic curriculum. Eurocentric public schooling in Canada has perpetuated damaging myths about Indigenous knowledges and heritages and has limited Indigenous students' potential through "cognitive imperialism" and "cognitive assimilation" (Battiste 1986; Battiste and Henderson 2000; Iseke-Barnes 2005). Marie Battiste, a Mi'kmaw scholar, describes these processes as the imposition of a Eurocentric worldview on Aboriginal people with the assumption of superiority. This cognitive manipulation has denied Indigenous groups their language and cultural integrity by consistently validating and legitimating one dominant language and culture (Royal Commission on Aboriginal Peoples 1996).

In response to school curricula that have been deemed irrelevant and/or inappropriate, Indigenous educators have provided many interpretations of what has been termed the "cultural divide" of education (Alaska Native Commission 1994). Many Aboriginal scholars and educators are making efforts to distinguish and discern how community cultural strengths can be utilized within school curricula and programs (Annahatak 1994; Arnaqaq et al. 1999; Battiste 2000; Knockwood 2004).

This chapter draws upon the main findings of my study of the construction of the role of Inuit languages and cultures within schooling in the Canadian arctic territory of Nunavut (Aylward 2006). The main aim of this research was to take into account the local community contexts in theorizations of social and cultural difference within schooling.

M. L. Aylward (✉)
School of Education, Acadia University, Wolfville, N.S., Canada
e-mail: Lynn.aylward@acadiau.ca

I propose that there exists a distinct *Inuit Qaujimajatuqangit Conversation* that permits a bringing together of the rich interconnections of the *how, what,* and *why* of the role of Indigenous languages and culture within current community-based schooling efforts in Nunavut. *Inuit Qaujimajatuqangit* is an Inuit epistemology that cannot genuinely make the translation in all its richness from the Inuit language of *Inuktitut* to English. *IQ* (as it has been nicknamed in *qallunaatitut*—English) is holistic and was first defined by Louis Tapardjuk of the Nunavut Social Development Council (NSDC) as "all aspects of traditional Inuit culture including its values, world-view, language, social organization, knowledge, life skills, perceptions, and expectations. *Inuit Qaujimajatuqangit* is as much a way of life as it is sets of information" (NSDC 1998). According to Gee (2005), a "Conversation" is an analytic tool or thinking device that provokes researchers to ask certain sorts of questions. This construct is especially useful as it permits a detailed discussion of the intertextualities and social languages present in the data and interwoven with the key themes related to the fields of Indigenous knowledges and minority education.

Construction of the Role of Inuit language and Culture in Nunavut Schooling

The Nunavut territory of Canada can be classified as a political compromise. In 1976, the Inuit Tapirisat of Canada, a national Aboriginal rights organization, proposed the creation of the territory of Nunavut as part of a comprehensive Inuit land rights settlement in the Northwest Territories. Slowly, methodically, and strategically, Inuit leaders negotiated with the federal government over the next two decades until the Nunavut Agreement was signed in Iqaluit on May 25, 1993. This agreement—covering one-fifth of Canada's land mass—represents the largest land rights settlement in Canada (Kusugak 2000). Inuit can certainly be considered a "minoritized" [1] group in reference to the power relations or marginalization experienced by Aboriginal groups in society today (McCarty 2002). However, the fact that Inuit maintain their majority status today, within a public government, is key to understanding the political and educational contexts of Nunavut, and indicates that constructing a role for Inuit language and culture within Nunavut schooling reaches far beyond the usual majority/minority binary.

Upon the creation of the Canadian territory of Nunavut in 1999, the newly formed territorial public government made a commitment to have Inuit traditional knowledge, language and culture as the foundation of "all we do" (Government of Nunavut 2000/2004). My study explored the significant concerns and troubles I observed while living and working as a non-Inuit educator in Nunavut. Why was there so much turmoil in school communities related to Inuit language and culture?

---

[1] Teresa McCarty, in writing about her work with the American Navajo Indian community, uses this term in order to more accurately convey the power relations or marginalization experienced by Aboriginal groups in society even though they may be living in a numerical "majority" situation; as is the case in Nunavut for the Inuit.

Why was it so challenging for Nunavut teachers to see a way forward for education that could be distinctly different from the colonial past? Over time these recurring concerns grew into a focused research question: *How has the role of Inuit language and culture been constructed within Nunavut schooling?*

My exploration of the role of Inuit language and culture in Nunavut curriculum and pedagogy demanded that I work within an anticolonial framework. Anticolonial discourse is linked to current decolonization movements and has its origins in the works of Frantz Fanon, Mohandas K. Gandhi, and Albert Memmi (Shahjahan 2005). The Nunavut context required an anticolonial discursive approach, meaning a "theorization of issues, concerns and social practices emerging from colonial relations and their aftermath" (Dei 2000, p. 117).

The particular discourse analytic approach of this study follows Gee's (1999) work in the area of applied linguistics and sociolinguistics. However, the method employed is not bound by a strict linguistic tradition. Gee's method of analysis and interpretation are taken up and practiced through the lenses of the anticolonial methodologies previously discussed. My research process attempted to remain firmly planted within the context of community schooling, curriculum, and the everyday of Nunavut educators.

I generated data about the construction of the role of Inuit language and culture within Nunavut schooling through an analysis of the interview transcripts from dialogue with 8 of the 12 *Inuuqatigiit* Curriculum authors about their journey of creating the *Inuuqatigiit* Curriculum. In addition, I analyzed the interview transcripts generated in discussions with five Inuit and five non-Inuit educators around the role of Inuit language and culture in their curricula and teaching practices. Specifically, my discourse analysis (Gee 1999, 2005) identified *situated meanings*, as well as naming and delineating *cultural models*.

According to Gee, *situated meanings* are the local meanings of text, grounded in actual practices and experiences. The situated meanings are connected to the cues and clues; key words and repeated phrases that enable a negotiation of understanding. These meanings are "assemblies" put together at the moment to suit a specific language context and purpose. Gee emphasizes that they are not definitions but flexible patterns that both come out of and construct our experiences. *Cultural models* are analytical thinking devices for pattern recognition in Gee's method of discourse analysis. They are the explanations for the patterns or assemblies of situated meanings and the theorizations about how the world works. Cultural models do not exist in any one person's head but are socially distributed and shared across a group. They are often invisible and become "what one sees with, but seldom what one sees" (Holland and Quinn 1987, p. 14).

Nunavut Curriculum Authors' Talk About Inuit Language and Culture

Inuuqatigiit: The Curriculum from the Inuit Perspective, was published in August of 1996 by the Northwest Territories Department of Education, Culture, and Employment. Dialogue with eight of the *Inuuqatigiit* authors in pairs, small groups and

Table 15.1 Summary of authors' situated meanings, motifs, and cultural models

Motif	Situated meanings	Cultural model
Coming Together	• Arguing against the original mandate • Minding the language and cultural gaps • Opposition to translations from English to Inuktitut • Reevaluating a professional stance	*Critique*
Working with elders	• Garnering strength and support • Sharing	*Inuuqatigiiniq*
Community response to *Inuuqatigiit*	• Resistance and conflict • Success and discovery	*Activism*
Dreams for the future of the *Inuuqatigiit* curriculum	• Foundation for teaching and learning • Equal status and legitimacy in relation to all curricula • Effecting school change	*Hope*

individually provided the text for the discourse analysis. This dialogue was guided by questions related to the following topics: the main purpose of the curriculum project; the process of creating *Inuuqatigiit* Curriculum; how the process affected their professional development, practice, or beliefs; and dreams about the future role of *Inuuqatigiit* in Nunavut schooling. The analysis is summarized in Table 15.1.

Coming Together

The motif of Coming Together encompasses the story of how the authors group came to be, how they made connections to the ways in which Inuit language and culture was addressed in the past and how they responded to stated reasoning by government officials about why certain curriculum development processes were undertaken. Working towards unity was emphasized by the *Inuuqatigiit* authors as they described their argument against the original mandate for the committee as set out by the Northwest Territories Department of Education. This mandate proposed the creation of two separate Inuit language documents: one for the eastern arctic and one for the western arctic. The authors discussed their refusal to create separate documents in terms of "making a stand"[2] by questioning the purposes and reasoning of the senior government officials' decision making.

In terms of minding the language and cultural gaps, the authors questioned why Inuit language was spoken about and planned for without the inclusion or recognition of Inuit cultural knowledges within curriculum. In their efforts to come together as a group the authors were forced to deeply examine and explore the purposes of having only Inuit language skills as the basis for the proposed curriculum. The

---

[2] Terms that were used repeatedly across the group and noted in webs of situated meanings during the analytic process are indicated in the text through the use of quotation marks. These phrases and related terms were often used by more than one participant and so are not individually referenced.

authors began to question the positioning of Inuktitut[3] as the "common language" for all Inuit and the assumption that Inuit culture was a uniform entity.

The authors' also voiced strong opposition to the historical practice of translation from English in the process of curriculum development. They wanted to "get away from the basal readers" technique and the focus on Inuit language in isolation; without context, without people.

The authors spoke of how the *Inuuqatigiit* committee work influenced other areas of their professional activity and caused them to re-evaluate their professional stance. They shared how they began to reflect more critically on all program activities related to Inuit language and culture with which they were involved. The power and dominance of the unquestioned content of the southern Canadian curriculum became much more obvious to the authors through their concurrent involvement with the *Inuuqatigiit* group, which also enabled them to clearly see and fundamentally question more of what was going on in their professional lives and overall in Nunavut education.

Evidenced by the authors' situated meanings within the motif of Coming Together is the emergence of what I call a cultural model of critique. They were beginning to see what previously they had taken for granted in terms of curriculum and instruction.

Working with Elders

The motif of Working with Elders had great prominence in the story of the creation of the *Inuuqatigiit* Curriculum. A sense of strength and support was constructed within the authors' talk as they recalled the more traditional ways in which learning occurred within family groups and how much that method had been disrupted by the colonial agents of early formal education efforts. They referred to the need to "go back," "remember," and recover their recollections of the teaching/learning process within their communities with elders and family members.

Once teaming with elders began, so did true sharing. Researching and working with the elders caused as much turmoil as it did harmony. The authors named how they began to practice their "Inuit ways" with each other, sharing laughter, food, tears, and painful moments. Many times the feeling of the group was referred to as that of family.

The process of the authors' reconnection with their Inuit cultural heritage is part of what I have named a cultural model of *Inuuqatigiiniq*. *Inuuqatigiiniq* is the concept of the quest for living in harmony with people or living and dealing with all relationships (Peesee Pitsiulak, *Inuuqatigiit* author, personal communication,

---

[3] Inuktitut is one of the Inuit languages used in Nunavut and the Northwest Territories. Inuinnaqtun and Inuvialuktun are classified by linguists as dialects of Inuktitut but many speakers claim they are Inuit languages. In addition, there are many regional dialectical differences within the language of Inuktitut.

April, 2005). The authors communicated the significance and importance of going backwards before they could go forward to meet their goal of establishing a strong and solid role for Inuit language and culture in Nunavut schools.

Community Response to *Inuuqatigiit*

In the fall of 1995, a draft of *Inuuqatigiit* was introduced and piloted in the arctic schools of the Northwest Territories and Nunavut. Regional committees of northern educators were created and the members were introduced to the curriculum. Along with the *Inuuqatigiit* authors, the regional committees were tasked with providing community-based in-services to school staff and District Education Authorities on the *Inuuqatigiit* Curriculum. Resistance and conflict were prominent features of the community response referred to by the authors' dialogue. The authors spoke of encouraging the sharing of stories during the community meetings even though some stories created a great deal of discomfort and pain among participants.

The authors described resistance and conflict in terms of Inuit teachers "neglecting" *Inuuqatigiit* and being "overwhelmed" by its goals. *Inuuqatigiit* was "hard to incorporate" and "it didn't apply at all" for some Inuit teachers; they were "never taught." Some non-Inuit teachers rejected the idea of teaching from *Inuuqatigiit* as it was not "part of their culture."

There was also a great deal of success and discovery in the community response to the *Inuuqatigiit* curriculum. The authors talked of *Inuuqatigiit* becoming a valuable "learning tool" and program support. It was extremely helpful in educating government departments and community organizations about Inuit language and culture.

A cultural model of activism was underpinning the authors' talk as they discussed the various elements of resistance, conflict, success, and discovery in reference to their interactions with Nunavut educators and community members during the implementation of the *Inuuqatigiit* Curriculum. The authors believed that the language and cultural activism of these in-services were invaluable to bringing forward more honest and genuine intercultural conversation within communities.

Dreams for the Future of *Inuuqatigiit*

The *Inuuqatigiit* Curriculum was viewed by the authors as a source of program leadership. They consistently presented it as a foundation for teaching and learning, a "core curriculum" and "an integration document." It was important to the authors that the *Inuuqatigiit* content be deemed legitimate and gain equal status within the world of curriculum development. They wanted a strong program presence for *Inuuqatigiit* in all community schools. They wanted it to be "required," "pushed," and "mandated" for use in schools by all levels of the Government of Nunavut. The

15 *The Inuit Qaujimajatuqangit* Conversation: The Language and Culture of Schooling   219

authors articulated their dreams for how the *Inuuqatigiit* Curriculum could effect change in Nunavut schooling philosophies and practices. They spoke about how the curriculum promoted educators' collaboration in terms of "team planning" and "team teaching." They viewed this as ways to support teachers, especially those who taught in Inuktitut.

The authors' dreams for the future of *Inuuqatigiit* were rooted within a cultural model of hope. The authors' dialogue indicated that they shared a vision of a more hopeful future with respect to the role of Inuit language and culture in Nunavut education and discussed some active ways of making the vision a reality. One of the authors' main hopes was that the *Inuuqatigiit* Curriculum would be assistive to change efforts focused on the development of a more culturally relevant and distinctive Nunavut High School graduation diploma.

Nunavut Teachers' Talk About Inuit Language and Culture

Ten experienced Nunavut teachers (five Inuit and five non-Inuit) shared stories of their teaching experience in Nunavut schools related to the role of Inuit language and culture within their practice. A discourse analysis of the interview transcripts is detailed in Table 15.2.

Bilingual Education

A prominent feature of the teachers' talk was the call to action for Nunavut residents around survival of the Inuit language. This call was voiced by many teachers, using terms such as "language loss" and "fighting" (for Inuit language programs). The

Table 15.2 Summary of teachers' situated meanings, motifs and cultural models

Motifs	Situated meanings	Cultural models
Bilingual education	• Survival of the Inuit language • Nature of bilingual programs in Nunavut • Necessary supports for bilingual education • Inuit language stream as a disadvantage	*Academic truths revitalization*
Use of *Inuuqatigiit* curriculum	• Incompatibility of Inuuqatigiit and Nunavut teachers' practice • Inuuqatigiit Curriculum as just a beginning • Inuuqatigiit Curriculum as a catalyst for change	*Disparity*
School and classroom practices of *Inuit Qaujimajatuqangit*	• Role of elders • School–community relationships • Establishing an Inuit culture-based school • Lack of resources or consistent support • Sources of conflict • Best of both worlds	*Struggle affirmation*

teachers' talk regarding survival of the Inuit language recognized the power of the language and minority rights legislation that were used in other jurisdictions for the protection and promotion of Indigenous languages. Teachers discussed the nature of bilingual programs and specific bilingual models being implemented in Nunavut schools. They used terms such as "transitional bilingual program," "mother tongue," "balanced" and "expert confidence" to describe the bilingual approaches and provided an analysis of currently used language-of-instruction models, as well as an academic, literature-informed review of their effectiveness. Teachers considered bilingual Education to be impossible without the necessary supports of bilingual educators or professional development in place to do the job. They referred to the need for schools to "get on board" and "get experts," and the fact that bilingual education success was not about the language but how it was taught.

Bilingual education in Nunavut was considered by the teachers as both a challenge and a problem with the Inuit language stream in school often constructed as an academic disadvantage. Specifically, the problems of bilingual education were often attributed to the language proficiency levels of individual students, families, and communities—also known as the "home/school language gap."

Arising from the teachers' situated meanings related to bilingual education is a cultural model I named as academic truths. The teachers expressed an unquestioned commitment to the "truths" founded within academic research related to bilingual education and language learning. They viewed successful bilingual education as substantially associated with languages-of-instruction models, language acquisition, and language proficiency. Comingling, resisting, and resonating with the academic truths cultural model was evidence in the teachers' dialogue of a cultural model of revitalization. The spirit of language and cultural revitalization present in the teachers' transcripts featured elements of language leadership, parent and elder involvement, minority rights, standards, and accountability.

Use of *Inuuqatigiit* Curriculum

An incompatibility between the *Inuuqatigiit* Curriculum and Nunavut teachers' practice was constructed on many levels in regard to both Inuit and non-Inuit teachers. They spoke about how the *Inuuqatigiit* Curriculum guide did not have enough for non-Inuit teachers to "go on," and the ideas were voiced that the Curriculum was "ridiculous," "useless," "difficult" and "challenging" for them. For Inuit staff, the teachers communicated how the residential schooling experience had disrupted the natural flow of traditional knowledge from parents to children. So in addition to reclaiming their language, many Inuit teachers were reported to be in the process of re-learning many Inuit cultural skills.

Inuuqatigiit was seen as only a beginning, with much more needed in order for it to realize its full potential in practice when compared to other subject specific curricula. However, teachers also spoke of how *Inuuqatigiit* was intended to be much more than "good as a start" or "barely a start" in terms of its spheres of influence.

Relating inequality to the *Inuuqatigiit* Curriculum, teachers referred to the advocacy required and spoke of using *Inuuqatigiit* as a "lonely place." They questioned the lack of resources provided to support the curriculum's implementation.

The *Inuuqatigiit* curriculum was considered a catalyst for change. Use of the *Inuuqatigiit* Curriculum was put forward as important groundwork that could help address some of the inequality around the role of Indigenous language and culture in schooling. *Inuuqatigiit* was described as "going backwards" to gather strength to go forward in terms of cultural programs as well as language renewal.

The situated meanings employed by the teachers activated what I see as a cultural model of disparity. Teachers believed there to be significant incongruity within the *Inuuqatigiit* Curriculum content and format as well as an incompatibility of the curriculum with teachers' background knowledge.

School and Classroom Practices of *Inuit Qaujimajatuqangit*

The storytelling around the role of elders in schooling was rich and engaging. Elders were considered the embodiment and lifeline of implementing the *Inuuqatigiit* Curriculum and establishing a presence for *Inuit Qaujimajatuqangit* in practice. Descriptions of elders gathering, speaking, teaming, and learning with students every day were prevalent. If these activities were not happening every day, teachers spoke of them needing to happen that often.

In relation to School/community relationships and the ways in which the community resources could benefit curriculum and programs, teachers communicated that they felt there was more openness overall to community/school partnerships in the past. They spoke about how the infusion of *Inuit Qaujimajatuqangit* into many school practices had become contrived and artificial. Inuit teachers voiced some of their dreams of an *Inuit Qaujimajatuqangit* school; an Inuit culture-based school. They envisioned a school "by and for Inuit" and a university based on Inuit language and culture. All teachers talked about efforts for cultural "integration" as being superior to curricular approaches that followed an additive model of cultural inclusion.

Concerns regarding the lack of resources, demands on teacher time, and the feasibility of offering culturally relevant programs infused with *Inuit Qaujimajatuqangit* arose often among the group. Teachers discussed "juggling responsibilities," "resourcing yourself," and not having enough people to do the work that needed to be done. There were many sources of conflict as teachers reported that communicating openly and honestly any concerns regarding specific curriculum, classroom discipline, or school structure was very challenging. Teachers spoke of "disconnections," "gaps," "divides," and "deep rivers" in terms of intercultural relationships and levels of understanding among and between some Inuit and non-Inuit teachers. They viewed working across difference as "uncomfortable," "intimidating," and "threatening."

The "best of both worlds" talk was intertwined with dialogue about providing possible solutions to the divisions that existed in the everyday of Nunavut education. Teachers spoke of making attempts to give equal status to English and Inuktitut and of further exploring Indigenous ways of knowing and doing so that students' experience would include addressing their cultural identity and some recognition of Inuit culture as a valuable fund of knowledge (Moll et al. 1992).

The cultural model of struggle emanates from the conflict and contradiction teachers described in their daily practice. Struggle was implicated at an interpersonal level, at an economic level and in relation to wider systemic issues and beliefs. Coexisting with struggle in the teacher data, there was a cultural model of affirmation that took up the ways in which *Inuit Qaujimajatuqangit* was articulated in teachers' school practices. *Inuit Qaujimajatuqangit* was believed to be both a culturally and linguistically affirming experience for Inuit students and staff in addition to being professionally satisfying for all school community members.

The *Inuit Qaujimajatuqangit* Conversation: Discourses of Place

Based upon the discourse analysis of the Nunavut teacher and curriculum author interview data, I propose that there exists a distinct Conversation within Nunavut schooling regarding the role of Inuit languages and culture. I would argue that the *Inuit Qaujimajatuqangit* Conversation is very much about *place* in several of the meanings currently recognized in curriculum and teaching. Drawing on Hutchinson (2004), Ellis (2004, 2005) Barnhardt (2008) and D.G. Smith (2000), I consider place as an ongoing dynamic that deeply connects to the everyday life of teachers and students. I am writing from a philosophy and a pedagogy that moves beyond geographical considerations with regard to Nunavut education and engages with the relationships and socially constructed realities of place (Casey 1997; Schubert 2004). This is different from, but none the less in keeping with, a broader understanding of place as the material and spiritual land of Nunavut (Takano 2005).

The *Inuit Qaujimajatuqangit* Conversation is the "ever present background" (Gee 2005, p. 49) for Nunavut schooling and its discourses provide an interpretation of the more global and culturally loaded terrain of Indigenous schooling. Drawing upon the analysis of educator and curriculum author interviews, I have identified the dominant discourses of the *Inuit Qaujimajatuqangit* Conversation and how they construct *place* as central to the debate around the role of Inuit language and culture in Nunavut schooling in three key ways:

- *Place as context in schooling:* Nunavut's distinct sociopolitical context
- *Place as power in schooling*: the status and identity of place in terms of Inuit languages and culture within Nunavut policy, curriculum, and practice
- *Place as a cultural negotiation in schooling*: the ways in which educators' make a place for Inuit language and culture in their curriculum, program, and practice

The discourses of place within the *Inuit Qaujimajatuqangit* Conversation are helpful tools in the deconstruction of the common storylines found in the fields of biculturalism and multiculturalism. The discourses of place as context, power and negotiation invite a further exploration of "place-based education"(G. A. Smith 2002). What follows is a discussion of the discourses and cultural models associated with each dynamic of place within the *Inuit Qaujimajatuqangit* Conversation.

Place as the Sociopolitical Context of Nunavut Schooling

The achievement of the political arrangement of Nunavut as an independent public government within the federation of Canada is unique to Aboriginal people's experiences in North America and represents a major institutional contribution to the decolonization discourse in the *Inuit Qaujimajatuqangit* Conversation. This decolonization discourse emanates, in part, from the establishment of a territory that reaps the rewards of a comprehensive Indigenous land claim; but the significance of this act is not the ownership of the land. It is about making space within the world for Indigenous voice and local decision-making about issues important to the sustainability of a way of life. Decisions around educating children are of vital importance in the reclaiming of voice.

The discourse analysis of the *Inuuqatigiit* authors' story demonstrated an experience of decolonization in the group process of creating the *Inuuqatigiit* Curriculum. The cultural models identified indicate how the authors purposefully engaged in critique, in activism, in becoming *Inuuqatigiiniq* (in harmony)and in the many practices of hope. A pivotal moment in the decolonization process of the authors happened when, as a group, they decided to take the curriculum in another direction from the originally mandated Inuktitut Language Arts project. Paired with resistance to promoting Inuit language through English translation, the authors established a beginning foundation for new ways for understanding how schooling could happen in Nunavut.

The Nunavut teachers' cultural model of affirmation activated dialogue about the goals of *Inuit Qaujimajatuqangit* in terms of changes to physical space with clear implications for the sociopolitical dynamics of place. Participants believe that education needs to be firmly anchored in Nunavut communities, on the land, outside classrooms, such that cultural and linguistic maintenance is possible. This is in contrast to present-day curriculum generally, which Gruenewald (2003) refers to as "placeless" in that it regulates, coordinates, and regiments experiences of learning. The teachers' desire to have schooling expand into the surrounding community follows the traditions of ecological place-based education and contributes to what Gruenewald refers to as a "critical pedagogy of place."

The *Inuuqatigiit* authors' motif of working with elders generates more local contributions to the *Inuit Qaujimajatuqangit* Conversation around curriculum integration and place. For example, the decision to partner closely with elders enabled the *Inuuqatigiit* authors to gather the strength and support necessary to define their own

Indigenous standpoint. It made sense to them to reestablish and connect with their heritage in order to meet the challenges that the newly created territory of Nunavut would bring. In establishing elders as experts, the authors positioned Indigenous knowledge as a foundation for teaching and learning rather than the knowledges of "other" historically isolated through essentialism and Aboriginality (McConaghy 2000).

Overall, in the consideration of place as the sociopolitical context of the Nunavut territory, the analysis of the data generated makes prominent the discursive formations of decolonization. Within the *Inuit Qaujimajatuqangit* Conversation, the concept of decolonization is characterized by the themes of deconstruction, discovery, and affirmation that are ongoing within the author and teacher talk. Indigenous scholar Taiaiake Alfred states that "true decolonization movement can emerge only when we shift our politics from articulating grievances to pursuing organized and political battle for the cause of our freedom" (2005, p. 11). There has been a tremendous amount of organized political battle happening in Nunavut since the creation of the *Inuuqatigiit* Curriculum, which I would argue is part of a genuine decolonization movement in education.

Place as Power, Status, and Identity in Nunavut Schooling

The places of Indigenous and Aboriginal education are immersed in interrogations of power relations (Bishop and Glynn 1999; Fitznor 2005; Johnston 1998). The *Inuuqatigiit* authors' cultural model of critique directly engages with discourses that construct place as power, status, and identity. The descriptions of their interactions with other committee members, Department of Education officials, and non-Inuit collaborators illustrated how the group was determined to deconstruct the usually hierarchical structure of working relationships. In addition, they confronted issues of domination and subordination from the beginning. Choosing to communicate in their own Inuit languages and refusing to follow the Eurocentric template of curriculum development, as well as establishing their own league of elder experts, stand as determined actions to changing the existing power structures.

Explicit references to power and status are evidenced within the cultural models of revitalization and academic truths. In the motif of bilingual education, teachers voiced how Inuit language revitalization efforts were in effect battles against language loss and the effects of "linguicism" (Skutnabb-Kangas 1988), whereby there had been obvious unequal divisions of power and resources. The involvement of parents, elders, and the whole community were implicated in successful models of bilingual education. Bilingual education was also considered an essential part of Inuit cultural survival and an academically sound response to English-only propositions. Teachers' engagement with the discourses of human rights, specifically minority-language rights of Francophone speakers within Canada, was about establishing Inuit language as powerful. Bilingual education in Nunavut has become a pathway for disrupting the social, ideological, and political order of schooling (Macedo and Bartolome 1999).

Structural and systemic difficulties that were identified within the bilingual education programs were attached to beliefs about how Inuit language and culture continuously struggles to survive in Nunavut. In response to these struggles, a discourse of anticolonialism emerges, emphasizing the role of affirmation and resistance for Inuit educators through the cultural models of critique revitalization and academic truths Many Indigenous groups have spawned anticolonial resistance education initiatives that are explicit in their intent to work against the residual colonial influences, whereby Aboriginal knowledge, histories, and experiences are excluded from curriculum (Bishop 2003; Pihama et al. 2002; G. H. Smith 1997; Smith 1999; G. H. Smith 2002). The discourse of anticolonialism at play within Nunavut education represents an explicit transformation of the existing power structures (Bishop and Glynn 1999; Fitzsimons and Smith 2000). The primary work of the *Inuuqatigiit* authors, along with the understandings of Indigenous knowledges expressed by the participating teachers point to the existence of the *Inuit Qaujimajatuqangit* intellectual and social movement.

Place as Cultural Negotiation in Nunavut Schooling

Within the *Inuit Qaujimajatuqangit* Conversation place was frequently constructed as a zone of consistent intercultural negotiation, with the discourse of biculturalism ever present. A "both worlds" orientation to Indigenous education operating in Nunavut is both highly resilient and highly problematic. As Battiste (2004) notes, the metaphor of bridging "two worlds" is part of how most non-Aboriginal people view the support necessary in order for Aboriginal students to "compete successfully" with non-Aboriginal students. Competition based on irrelevant standards is not at all the goal of Indigenous and community-based education in Nunavut, as evidenced in the statements made by the *Inuuqatigiit* authors in this study.

The teachers' negotiations of the importance of place relates to the concept of developing education Indigenous to place as set out by Aboriginal scholars Kawagley and Barnhardt (1997). Schooling oriented to community legitimates local Indigenous knowledges and world views and explores how they are juxtaposed with more dominant scientific perspectives. In this way Indigenous education moves towards "an emphasis on education in the culture, rather than education about the culture" (Kawagley and Barnhardt 1997, p. 15). The Nunavut teachers' cultural model of disparity underpins the ongoing intercultural negotiations and offers a critical view of the substantial daily efforts involved in making any place for Inuit language and culture in Nunavut community schooling.

Nunavut teachers' cultural model of struggle narrated stories of school and classroom practices of *Inuit Qaujimajatuqangit* that emphasized the many challenges of doing school. Teachers consistently voiced their concerns about their own professional effectiveness and relevance, as well as those of their colleagues and the school system as a whole.

The combined efforts of *Inuuqatigiit* authors and Nunavut teachers exemplify the intercultural challenges necessary in making education relevant to Indigenous peoples. Teresa McCarty's research over the past two decades with the Rough Rock Navajo community school in Arizona has examined similar situations and reinforces much of what was found in my study about the kind of cultural "border work" necessary within Indigenous education.

> It is undeniable that Indigenous schools and educators engage in such dialogue and interaction against a backdrop of oppression, and within school and community contexts that are contradictory and full of tension. For better or worse, schools are a prime arena in which these tensions are being confronted and negotiated. (McCarty 2002, p. 190)

Nunavut schooling and its schools are undeniably necessary as places of intercultural negotiation—places where power, identity, and status are contested and places connected to a distinct sociopolitical context.

Conclusion

Informed by an analysis of Nunavut educators' theorizations of how the world works, the findings of my study (Aylward 2006) partially map the contradictory Indigenous schooling milieu of the Nunavut Territory, confirming the view that education in minoritized Indigenous communities carries demanding social and political tensions (Barnhardt 2001; Bishop and Glynn 1999; Dinero 2004). The *Inuit Qaujimajatuqangit* Conversation detailed in this study represents a theoretical shift away from the dominant academic theories and discursive strategies of cultural difference and their connections to assimilationism, integration, and biculturalism towards a more complex interrogation of social and cultural difference.

Anthropological research on the educational experiences of minority students and the development of a cultural–ecological theories of minority student response to schooling have had a strong influence on North American educators' understandings of cultural difference (Ogbu 1992, 2003; Taylor 2002). Ogbu, for example, connected resistance and subordination within minority education communities to the diverse experiences of oppression. Ogbu promoted the idea that contemporary mistrust of schools by minority groups is based on historical patterns of discrimination, when his own data demonstrated that these attitudes stemmed from contemporary experiences of structural inequities within the education system (Foster 2005). Aboriginal scholars such as Nakata (2002) and Urion(1999) believe that the anthropological discourse of cultural difference has become dominant within many Indigenous education contexts promoting "difference as deficit" and "difference as otherness" in an attempt to explain cultural and social difference in education.

Urion warns that some constructions of cultural difference, as read within the confines of acculturation, can seriously restrict the legitimacy of Indigenous viewpoints and position academic success as the cultural property of the dominant culture. Even some efforts to take Aboriginal and Indigenous communities seriously within the field of education have created a species of cultural essentialism known as "Aboriginality" (McConaghy 2000). Academic assumptions of cultural difference within minority education contexts, especially Indigenous and Aboriginal settings, tend to focus on culture as ethnicity or race rather than taking up the more complex perspectives of the sociocultural dimensions of relationships within a community. There is not enough attention paid to the contributions that theorizations of community and place can make to the understanding of cultural and social difference in education. The *Inuit Qaujimajatuqangit* Conversation provides openings for such theoretical explorations.

The main message of the *Inuit Qaujimajatuqangit* Conversation for the field of minority education is the call for a comprehensive anticolonial agenda of systemic change.The *Inuit Qaujimajatuqangit* Conversation represents an anticolonial, intellectual, and social movement in Nunavut education that resists the polarities of biculturalism and engages with more culturally relevant discourses of decolonization and transformation. Cultural negotiation of Indigenous education is positioned by Nunavut educators as a way to engender strategies derived from a community that are contrary to deficit theories of cultural difference. By advocating for a culturally negotiated pedagogy that promotes the construction of schooling as a community-based institution, Nunavut educators promote a hopeful future.

References

Alaska Native Commission (ANCFR). (1994). *Final Report, Volume 2. Alaska Native Education: Report of the Education Task Force*. Alaska: Alaska Native Commission.
Alfred, T. (2005). Indigenous Pathways of Action and Freedom. Paper written coursework at Pacific Centre for Technology and Culture, University of Victoria. www.ctheory.net. Accessed March 2005.
Annahatak, B. (1994). Quality education for Inuit today? Cultural strengths, new things, and working out the unknowns: A story by an Inuk. *Peabody Journal of Education, 69*(2), 12–18.
Arnaqaq, N., Pitsiulak, P., & Tompkins, J. (1999). *Geese Flying in a Northern Sky*. Paper presented at the American Education Research Association (AERA), Montreal. April.
Ashcroft, B. (2001). *Postcolonial transformation*. New York: Routledge.
Aylward, M. L. (2006). *The role of Inuit Language and culture in Nunavut schooling: Discourses of the Inuit Qaujimajatuqangit Conversation*. Unpublished doctoral dissertation, University of South Australia, Adelaide.
Barnhardt, C. (2001). A history of schooling for Alaska native people. *Journal of American Indian Education, 40*(1), 1–30.
Barnhardt, R. (2008). Creating a place for indigenous knowledge in education. In D. Gruenwald & G. Smith (Eds.), *Place based education in the global age* (pp. 113–133). Mahwah: Lawrence Erlbaum.

Battiste, M. (1986). Mi'kmaq literacy and cognitive assimilation. In J. Barman, Y. Hebert, & D. McCaskill (Eds.), *Indian education in Canada: The legacy, Vol. 1* (pp. 23–44). Vancouver: University of British Columbia Press.

Battiste, M. (2000). Maintaining Aboriginal identity, language, and culture in modern society. In M. Battiste (Ed.), *Reclaiming indigenous voice and vision* (pp. 192–208). Vancouver: UBC Press.

Battiste, M. (2004). *Animating sites of postcolonial education: Indigenous knowledge and the humanities.* CSSE Plenary Address. Winnipeg Manitoba, May 29.

Battiste, M., & Henderson, J. S. Y. (2000). *Protecting Indigenous knowledge and heritage: A global challenge.* Saskatoon: Purich Press.

Bishop, R. (2003). Changing power relations in education: *Kaupapa Maori* messages for 'mainstream' education in Aotearoa/New Zealand. *Comparative Education, 30*(2), 221–238.

Bishop, R., & Glynn, T. (1999). *Culture counts: Changing power relations in education.* New York: Zed Books.

Casey, E. S. (1997). *The fate of place: A philosophical history.* Berkeley: University of California Press.

Castellano, M., Davis, L., & Lahache, L. (Eds). (2000). *Aboriginal education: Fulfilling the promise.* Vancouver: UBC Press.

Dei, G. J. S. (2000). Rethinking the role of indigenous knowledges in the academy. *International Journal of Inclusive Education, 4*(2), 111–132.

Dinero, S. C. (2004). The politics of education provision in rural Native Alaska: The case of Yukon Village. *Race, Ethnicity and Education, 7*(4), 401–419.

Ellis, J. (2004). The significance of place in the curriculum of children's everyday lives. *Taboo: The Journal of Culture and Education, 8*(1), (Spring-Summer), 23–42.

Ellis, J. (2005). Place and identity for children in classrooms and schools. *Journal of Canadian Association of Curriculum Studies, 3*(2), 55–73. http://www.csse.ca/CACS/JCACS/V3N2/PDFcontent/JCACS_3_2_g_Ellis.pdf. Accessed October 2009.

Fitznor, L. (2005). *Aboriginal educational teaching experiences: Foregrounding Aboriginal/Indigenous knowledges and processes.* Paper presented at First Nations, First Thoughts Conference, University of Edinburgh: May 5 & 6.

Fitzsimons, P., & Smith, G. (2000). Philosophy and indigenous cultural transformation. *Educational Philosophy and Theory, 32*(1), 25–41.

Foster, K. M. (2005). Narratives of the social scientist: Understanding the works of John Ogbu. *International Journal of Qualitative Studies in Education, 18*(5), 565–580.

Gee, J. P. (1999). *An introduction to discourse analysis theory and method* (1st ed.). New York: Routledge.

Gee, J. P. (2005). *An introduction to discourse analysis theory and method* (2nd ed.). New York: Routledge.

Government of Nunavut. (2000/2004). *Pinasuaqtavut: Our commitment to building Nunavut's future.* Iqaluit: Government of Nunavut.

Gruenewald, D. A. (2003). The best of both worlds: A critical pedagogy of place. *Educational Researcher, 32*(4), 3–12.

Hampton, E. (1993). Toward a redefinition of American Indian/Alaska Native Education. *Canadian Journal of Native Education, 20*(2), 261–310.

Holland, D., & Quinn, N. (Eds.). (1987). *Cultural models in language and thought.* Cambridge: Cambridge University Press.

Hutchinson, D. (2004). *A natural history of place in education.* New York: Teachers College Press.

Iseke-Barnes, J. (2005). Misrepresentations of Indigenous history and science: Public broadcasting, the internet, and education. *Discourse: Studies in the Cultural Politics of Education, 26*(2), 149–165.

Johnston, P. M. G. (1998). *He Ao Rereke: Education policy and Maori under-achievement: Mechanisms of power and difference.* Unpublished doctoral thesis. New Zealand: University of Auckland.

Kawagley, O., & Barnhardt, R. (1997). Education indigenous to place: Western science meets native reality. In G. Smith & D. Williams (Eds.), *Ecological education in action.* (pp. 117–142). Albany: State University of New York Press.

Knockwood, J. (2004). Creating a community-based school. In K. Anderson & B. Lawrence (Eds.), *Strong women stories: Native vision and community survival.* (pp. 191–201).Toronto: Sumach Press.

Kusugak, J. (2000). The tide has shifted: Nunavut works for us, and it offers a lesson to the *Broader Global Community.* (pp. 20–30).In J. Dahl, J. Hicks, & P. Jull (Eds.), Nunavut: Inuit regain control of their lands and their lives. Copenhagen: International Work Group for Indigenous Affairs.

Macedo, D., & Bartolome, L. I. (1999). *Dancing with bigotry: Beyond the politics of tolerance.* New York: St. Martin's Press.

McCarty, T. L. (2002). *A place to be Navajo: Rough rock and the struggle for self-determination in Indigenous schooling.* Mahwah: Lawrence Erlbaum.

McConaghy, C. (2000). *Rethinking indigenous education: Culturalism, colonialism, and the politics of knowing.* Flaxton: Post Pressed.

Moll, L. C., Neff, D., & Gonzalez, N. (1992). Funds of knowledge for teaching: Using a qualitative approach to connect homes and classrooms. *Theory into Practice, 31*(2), 132–141.

Nakata, M. (2002). *Indigenous knowledge and the cultural interface: Underlying issues at the intersection of knowledge and information systems.* Paper presented at the 68th IFLA Council and General Conference, August 18–24. Glasgow, Scotland.

Nunavut Social Development Council (NSDC). (1998, March 20–24). *Report of the Nunavut traditional knowledge conference.* Igloolik: Nunavut Social Development Council.

NWT, Government of. (1996). *Inuuqatigiit: The curriculum from the Inuit perspective.* Yellowknife: Department of Education, Culture and Employment.

Ogbu, J. (1992). Adaptation to minority status and impact on school success. *Theory into Practice, 31*(4), 287–295.

Ogbu, J. (2003). *Black students in an affluent suburb: A study of academic disengagement.* Mahwah: Lawrence Erlbaum.

Pihama, L., Cram, F., & Walker, S. (2002). Creating methodological space: A literature review of Kaupapa Maori research. *Canadian Journal of Native Education, 26*(1), 30–43.

Royal Commission on Aboriginal Peoples. (1996). *Royal Commission on Aboriginal Peoples Report.* Ottawa: Federal Government of Canada.

Schubert, W. H. (2004). Reflections on the place of curriculum. In. D. M. Callejo Perez, S. M. Fain, & J. J. Slater (Eds.), *Pedagogy of place: Seeing space as cultural education* (pp. ix–xxv) New York: Peter Lang.

Semali, L. M., & Kincheloe, J. L. (1999). What is Indigenous knowledge and why should we study it? In L. M. Semali, & J. L. Kincheloe (Eds.), *What is Indigenous knowledge?* (pp. 3–59). New York: Falmer Press.

Shahjahan, R. A. (2005). Mapping the field of anti-colonial discourse to understand issues of Indigenous knowledges: Decolonizing praxis. *McGill Journal of Education, 40*(2), 213–240.

Skutnabb-Kangas, T. (1988). Resource, power and autonomy through discourse in conflict: A Finnish migrant school strike in Sweden. In T. Skutnabb-Kangas & J. Cummins (Eds.), *Minority education: From shame to struggle* (pp. 251–277). Clevedon: Multilingual Matters.

Smith, G. H. (1997). *Kaupapa Maori as transformative praxis.* Unpublished Ph.D. thesis. University of Auckland.

Smith, L. T. (1999). *Decolonizing methodologies: Research and indigenous peoples.* New York: Zed Books.

Smith, D.G. (2000). The specific challenges of globalization for teaching and vice versa. *The Alberta Journal of Educational Research, XLVI*(1), 7–26.

Smith, G. A. (2002). Place-based education: Learning to be where we are. *Phi Delta Kappan, 83*(8), 584–595.

Smith, G.H. (2002). Protecting and respecting indigenous knowledge. In M. Battiste (Ed.), *Reclaiming indigenous voice and vision* (pp. 209–224). Vancouver: UBC Press.

Takano, T. (2005). Connections with the land: Land skills courses in Igloolik Nunavut. *Ethnography, 6*(4),463–486.
Taylor, D. M. (2002). *The quest for identity: From minority groups to generation Xers*. Westport: Praeger
Urion, C. (1999). Changing academic discourse about Native education: Using two pairs of eyes. *Canadian Journal of Native Education, 23*(1), 6–15.

Chapter 16
Ambivalence: Minority Parents Positioning When Facing School Choices

Zvi Bekerman and Moshe Tatar

Introduction

The importance of the field of education and schooling when dealing with minority students is well illustrated by a range of considerations: (1) The presence and treatment of minorities are highly politicized issues—in many countries this topic is one of the central issues of politics; (2) The treatment of minorities is a "litmus test" by which the openness of a society can be measured. Education is regarded as one of the most effective devices by which the acceptance of minority rights and tolerance towards minorities can be strengthened; and (3) Education is one of the most important vehicles by which the integration of minorities into mainstream society can be promoted.

Within this context minority parents' attitudes, perceptions, and behaviors vis-à-vis their children's education reflect the intricacies of the relations between minority and majority groups. Parental expectations of schools and of schooling are a pivotal factor within the complex relations between families and their children's schools (see, Seginer 1986, 1995; Tatar and Horenczyk 2000).

Many studies conceptualized parental expectations in terms of the views that parents hold regarding the highest level of education that their children will complete (see, e.g., Reynolds 1992). Over 20 years ago, Seginer (1986) proposed a more complex conceptualization of parental educational expectations and defined them as consisting of three dimensions: (1) realistic expectations—parental predictions of the level of academic performance of their children; (2) idealistic expectations—including the wishes and hopeful anticipations held by the parents related to their children in academic realms; and (3) standards of achievement—namely, the implicit measures by which the parents evaluate their children's academic attainments.

A more multifaceted situation is delineated when trying to understand the perceptions of parents that are members of minority groups regarding their children's

---

Z. Bekerman (✉)
School of Education, Melton Center, Hebrew University, Jerusalem, Israel
e-mail: mszviman@mscc.huji.ac.il

schools and specifically when analyzing their expectations vis-à-vis the educational institutions which their children attend (for a summary, see Seginer 2006).

In general, while some analyses have concluded that minority parents are less involved in their children's education than majority parents (e.g., Baker and Stevenson 1986) others do not support this conclusion (Catsambis 2002). It is well accepted that parental involvement varies with ethnicity and within ethnic minorities by level of education (e.g., Seginer and Vermulst 2002).

It has been suggested that there is an effect of parents' cultural belief systems vis-à-vis their involvement in their children's schools. For example Li (2001), using a qualitative approach to explore the expectations of Chinese parents who had recently immigrated to Canada, shows these parents to ground their expectations for their children in the Chinese tradition. These parents advise their children to pursue science-related careers as a means to overcome the perceived disadvantages experienced by the minorities within the Canadian society.

Different cultural beliefs about the benefits of schooling lead parents to adopt diverse involvement attitudes. Ogbu (1994) stresses two different types of parental attitudes. First, the one labeled, "effort optimism," an attitude that reflects parents trust in the schools to educate their children and that schooling ultimately facilitate their children's social advancement. Parents holding this attitude closely monitor their children's schoolwork, and encouraged them to excel at school. In contrast, the second type of parental attitude mentioned by Obgu, attributes the lesser involvement of minority parents in their children's schooling to their mistrust of the educational system. In this case, parents may develop a rather more instrumental approach to schooling (e.g., consider schooling as a means only for improving their children's academic achievement or helping them gain better jobs).

Hernandez Dimmler (2008) concluded that while a robust body of research with middle-class, European American families supports the relationship between parent expectations of their children's performances and student achievement; the scant research with low-income, ethnic minority families indicates that the expectations of these parents are less predictive of their children's attainments. Yet, parents' high mobility orientation (education of parents and their encouragement of the school career of their children) appeared to be a significant factor in the academic success of minority high school students attending western schools (e.g., see the case of Turkish and Moroccan high school students attending Dutch schools in van der Veen 2003). Moreover, parents' long-term goals and values for their children vary across ethnic groups. For example, researchers have found that some American ethnic minority groups tend to promote interdependence, and European Americans tend to promote independence, yet evidence of both orientations has also been found within each ethnic group (see for example, Suizzo 2007).

This chapter intends to add to present knowledge on minority parents' views and expectations of schools. Our analysis is based on qualitative data derived from Palestinian parents who send their children to a very atypical school setting in the Israeli educational system: the bilingual binational integrated Palestinian Jewish schools. Following, we will shortly describe the sociopolitical and sociocultural contexts of the Palestinian minority citizens of Israel and the educational initiative in which these parents and their children participate. After positioning ourselves as researchers we present our main findings followed by some preliminary conclusions.

The Sociopolitical Context of the Palestinian Minority in Israel

If stated succinctly it could be said that the Palestinian minority in Israel (18%) is treated by the Jewish majority (78%) as present absentees (Jamal 2007). Palestinians in Israel suffer from continuous structural inequalities. The discrimination against Palestinian citizens includes serious income gaps. Official figures point at a sustained gap in the income of the Palestinian and Jewish populations; the average Palestinian income stands at a 60% of the average Jewish income (Bendleck 2002). For the year 2002, 65% of the Palestinian labor force in Israel consisted of skilled and unskilled workers in the fields of construction, light industry, and services. Moreover while the Jewish professional/academic workforce occupies positions in a variety of governmental and private labor spheres Palestinians with an academic background are mostly employed in as teachers and headmasters within the educational Arab (Arab Israelis is the name given to Palestinian citizens of Israel by the Israeli Jewish hegemonic powers) system in Israel (Fares 2002). Of the 59,938 workers in the state's services in January 2000 only 2,835 (5%) were Arabs, most of whom worked in either the Ministry of Health or the Ministry of Education (Jamal 2007).

For the most part the Palestinian population in Israel attends monolingual Arabic schools. The Arab educational system in Israel though separate works under the supervision of the national Jewish educational system. The Palestinian educational system has been traditionally tightly supervised by the Israeli General Security Service and its high positions are held by Jews who dominate the contents taught in the curriculum and dictate the didactic and pedagogic concepts of instruction policy (Abu-Asbah 1997). Moreover, the system suffers a severe shortage in resources (Al-Haj 1995). Examinations of the contents of the Arab educational curriculum have found that they aim at creating a submissive Palestinian minority while trying to eliminate their national identity (Al-Haj 1995; Abu-Asbah 2004).

In spite of Israel's declared goals of offering equal opportunity to all its citizens through the educational system the gap between the Jewish and Palestinian sectors remains. For example in 1991, 45.4% Palestinian and 67.3% Jewish children earned a matriculation diploma, while in 2007, the percentage increased to 57.1% and 69.7%, respectively (Statistical Abstract of Israel 2008).

The Israeli case provides an outstanding example of the theoretical insight made by Brubaker (1996, 2004) that nationalizing states are active central players in generating social inequality and enforcing one cultural identity in the public sphere, while partially excluding subordinate social groups from the political game. Palestinians in Israel are victims to these nationalizing pressures.

The Sociocultural Context of the Palestinian Minority in Israel

For the most part the Palestinian culture in Israel is distinguished by its traditional, homogeneous, and collectivist orientation and well suits agrarian nonindustrial categories (Al-Haj 1995; Barakat 1993). Family structure is associated with stable, hierarchical roles (dependent on gender, family background, age) and children are expected to submit to adults and obey them (Haj-Yahia and Shor 1995). Daughters are educated in much stricter ways than sons and are encouraged to stay home and away from social interactions with males (Weller et al. 1995). Their autonomy is much more limited when compared to the relative openness with which males are exposed to outside modernizing trends (Antonovski et al. 1978). These norms, while minimizing self-criticism, promote adherence to norms and to group consensus (Barakat 1985).

The unique sociocultural background of the Palestinian population is reflected in its monolingual educational system (Abu-Nimer 1999). Within the classroom, there exists an authoritarian model of student–teacher relationships and a frontal teaching approach that is pedagogically very traditional. For teachers, there is a sense of conflict regarding their loyalty towards their employer, the Ministry of Education, and their loyalty towards their Palestinian community. Other major differences are apparent between the Palestinian and the secular Jewish educational sectors regarding the culture-bound behavioral norms of supervisors, principals, teachers, and students (Abu-Nimer 2004; Eilam 2002). Reflecting the cultural patterns of the wider Palestinian society, Palestinian teaching practices grant teachers ultimate authority, and Palestinian students' expressions of opinions, criticisms, liberal attitudes, or arguments tend to be discouraged. In the Palestinian sector, teachers are usually intolerant of students' independent behavior or criticism (Dwairy 2004) and base their educational strategies on memorization and rote learning (Al-Haj 1996). Similar accentuated behaviors are to be found in small communities and villages in rural areas (Dwairy 1998).

Jewish monolingual secular schools offer a strong contrast to the educational approaches just described. With different measures of success, they have regularly introduced new approaches to teaching and learning processes, such as cooperative and independent learning, inquiry, and alternative assessment. Also, at the managerial level, innovative approaches have been introduced in the Jewish sector; team management and democratic management styles are slowly being incorporated which promote and support students' active learning and independent thinking and encourage teachers to try new methods and develop creative ways of helping students to construct their own bodies of knowledge (Glaubman and Iram 1999). Thus, the atmospheres created in the two systems remain radically different. Jewish school rules invite students' free expression of opinions and critiques, cooperation with teachers, and participation in school life including parental involvement. Palestinian schools adopt much more conservative, exclusionary rules (Egan 1996). It is against these contrasting backgrounds that the population under study must be understood.

The Bilingual Binational Integrated Palestinian Jewish Schools

The schools whose parents' population we studied were first established in 1997 by the Center for Arab–Jewish Education in Israel, this initiative envisioned educational institutions that would be equally staffed by Palestinians and Jews and would equally use Arabic and Hebrew as languages of instruction. Their main goal was to raise youth who could both acknowledge and respect one another while at the same time cultivate loyalty to their own cultural heritage. In 1998, two schools were established, one in Jerusalem and the other in the Upper Galilee. In 2004, a third school was started in Kafer Karah, the first in a Palestinian city in the north of Israel. The most recent school opened in Beer-Sheva in 2006. The schools, today, serve a population of over 1,000 students.

The curriculum used in the schools is the standard curriculum of the state's non-religious Jewish school system, the difference being that both Hebrew and Arabic are used as languages of instruction. The schools employ what has been characterized as a strong additive bilingual approach, which emphasizes symmetry between both languages in all aspects of instruction (Garcia 1997). Two homeroom teachers, one a Palestinian, one a Jew, jointly lead all classes. These schools, still considered a curiosity in the Israeli educational scene, must pioneer solutions to multiple curricular problems raised by mixing Palestinian and Jewish populations. The problems have to do with cultural and identity borders and with historical discourses and interpretations including those that sustain the present violent conflict.

The schools could be considered as forming part of a relatively new trend which, although heterogeneous, consists of schools serving various social groups in Israeli society seeking educational services characterized by a particular educational, ideological, and/or pedagogical emphasis such as the Democratic schools. The relatively large number of trends may indicate a dialectical tension that exists between the egalitarian perspective which traditionally dominated Israeli education leading to the foundation of State schools, and the particularistic perspective, which is evident in the demand for religious (or other particularistic) education, privatization and parental choice (Nir and Inbar 2004). For a full description of the bilingual-integrated schools see (Bekerman 2004, 2005, 2008; Bekerman and Nir 2006)

Researchers Positioning

Before bringing this introductory section to an end, we would like to mention our Jewish background. Such a mention is made out of a sensibility towards theoretical perspectives which have pointed at the relevance of the researcher's sociocultural and historical trajectories in the performance of any research activity (Denzin and Lincoln 2000; Haraway 1991). This sensibility should be doubled in the case of this study, which is conducted in an area engaged in one of the most intractable and intense conflicts of modern times (Bar-Tal 2000). Indeed ethnic, national, and religious identities operate in the lives of people by connecting them with some individuals and dividing them from others (Appiah and Gates 1995). Still individuals negotiate their identities while constituting and being constituted by them (Harre and Gillett 1995; Sampson 1993). Though in present conditions our Jewishness might be a given, we want to believe that throughout our many years of life experiences and theoretical training in a variety of sociohistorical perspectives, we have come to at least be able to sustain a critical perspective on ourselves and the circumstances of our research. Thus, in addition to our own reflective and critical position, we have made sure throughout the research process to be assisted by figures fully identified with those groups which might not have an initial trust in our "ethnic/national/cultural presence." At all stages of the research we have worked with fully bilingual Jewish and Palestinian research assistants.

Methodology

In this chapter, we focus on Palestinian parents who were known to us as being actively involved in the school and to basically endorse the schools' declared aims. We justify this choice based on our desire not to include parents who might be carrying unfinished business, conflicts, or confrontations with school authorities which negatively "color" retrospectively their choice of the schools for their children. The sample includes 18 Palestinian parents from two of the schools presently active. Two hour, in-depth interviews were conducted in English and or Arabic with these parents. All interviews were audio taped and fully transcribed. They were then analyzed according to conventional qualitative methods (Mason 1996; Silverman 1993).

To ensure validity, the research team worked separately and collaboratively, using an interpretive method of coding (Erickson 1986) to ascertain confirming and disconfirming evidence of assertions arising from data sources. We monitored our first interpretative efforts through peer debriefing, paying special attention to the ways in which we as researchers allowed or did not allow for the preliminary coding to be influenced by our prior expectations or theoretical inclinations. We used negative case analysis to gain confidence in the hypotheses proposed. We carefully analyzed the data, looking for patterns and thematic issues of relevance, which were then coded as to allow for further analysis. The first codification, prepared independently by each of the two researchers involved, raised multiple categories (over 18). A second reading of all materials allowed us to reduce the categories by combining like terms and eliminating redundant ones. Throughout the process, intercoder reliability checks showed strong agreement between coders and high reliability for the coding scheme (Glassner and Loughlin 1987). Thus, we arrived at five main themes from which we created our final coding system. The five themes were named: on the parents' decision to send their children to the bilingual schools, parents' perspectives on identity and national commemorations, parents' future expectations from the children, parents' perceived prices paid by sending the children to the schools, and parents' perceived advantages of studying at the bilingual schools.

Population

Out of the 18 interviewees who participated in the study all but two where Moslem (one Armenian and another Christian). The parents' ages ranged from 35–45 years old. All interviewees held academic degrees in the social and natural sciences. Twelve of the parents interviewed had more than one child at the school at the time of the study. All the children in these families had joined the school in first grade and are today in grades 2 to 8. Parents sending their children to these schools could be characterized as belonging to an upper-middle socioeconomic class in Israeli society (Bekerman 2009).

Findings

General Background Information

Our first questions asked participants to offer some biographical personal insights. All seem to have had rather quiet and comfortable lives not tinted by any dramatic events related to the ongoing conflict which characterizes the Israeli society. When asked about perceived differences between Palestinians and Jews, two Palestinians who engaged in answering this question with some substantive observation mentioned the fact that the groups belong to different religious traditions but that there are many cultural similarities among the groups providing examples of life-cycle events and dietary restrictions.

Participants claimed that they have not encouraged or forced their children into practicing religion but they do celebrate the main feast in the Muslim calendar (*Ramadan, Eid Al Fitr & Eid Al Adha*). In addition, apart from two participants who were raised in a very religious home, all the Palestinian parents were raised in a traditional manner and were not forced or encouraged to practice religion,

> Religion-wise we barely had any influence, we weren't a religious house we were more traditional, we kept traditions like Ramadan and feasts but dressing-wise and practice-wise it was more secular, we didn't have any constrictions—like wearing a veil on your head or anything like that so there was great freedom in expressing yourself religiously—with no constrictions. We were secular in every manner. (Interview, 4)

When asked about the Palestinian–Israeli conflict the parents' responses were mild as they expressed a variety of political perspectives but none sounded extreme or threatening. One of the interviewees spoke about the conflict as a territorial one which cannot be easily justified and about the conflict creating religious extremism.

Others indicated their expectations that Israel (Jews) will soon correct the wrongs done to the Palestinian people offering them full rights as equal citizens.

For the Palestinians living in the context of the Israeli Jewish society, self-definition is not an easy task. The following excerpt shows the complexities expressed by the interviewees in their reports

> I am Arab, you know I speak the Arabic language. My// I'm from a Palestinian origin, because my grandparents were Palestinians before Israel came. I have the Israeli passport and I// so I live in this country and I have the passport. And I'm from Christian background, I'm not religious [...] no I don't feel very Israeli. I have Israeli friends, I live in this country, but I can't say I am Israeli. It's// because I don't get all the// it's true that, you know, I studied in this country, I work with everyone here, I have lots of Jewish friends, but to be to say (you are) Israeli you should also be able to hold the flag of the country and to be able to sing the national anthem and go to serve in the army. And this is// I can't-I can't feel any connection to these three things and I can't// though I can't go even to the army, because I have family in Lebanon, you know, my aunt lives there. She's Palestinian, who moved. I have lots of family, like in Jordan also. Like, it's a conflict here, you can't// one day will be peace and there will be know// when the country will be for everyone, also the political view of it will be like this, then I feel// I will say I'm Israeli, but now I can't say it. (Interview 15)
> The few who are ready to adopt Israeli as an identity category see it as imposed on them by the surrounding context "...because we are secondary citizens here, we forcefully had our land taken away from us and we were forcefully given these IDs and not by choice, I wouldn't choose to take this ID.... We're in a dilemma, we can't take back our land but we're living in a state that isn't ours. We have no feeling of belonging to this country, only to the land." (Interview, 8)

Palestinians clearly deny the possibility of considering Israel as both a democratic and a Jewish state; the states' Jewish character at present prevents their identification with it and adds to their sense of being discriminated against

> This is my problem here. I think it should be a state with no religion-no// religion is whatever. You know, for everyone, every religion. And for me it's not// like even the flag of Israel as an Arab it's hard for me to put this flag on my house. I don't feel any connection, because this flag is only for Jewish people and the sign is only for Jewish people. The flag should be for everyone, not only for Jewish people [...] so and also the countries national anthem. Also like if you look at the words it's only for Jewish people. (Interview, 15)

The parent's relationships to Jews in the country are tinted by the "conflict"; their possibility to connect to Jews and relate to them is dependent on holding to a strong differentiation between "individuals" and their national groups

> I'm working with them, I have friends, I go out with them. Listen, when you're talking about any, actually any person, either Jewish or Arab, when you're talking on the personal level you can make best friends. Not talk// but you shouldn't talk about politics. Ok? [...] Because if you talk about politics there's no way that you can get to an understanding with most of the Jews. And I'm saying most of them. (Interview, 14)

With their children, in the bilingual schools we researched, parents report on trying to avoid discussing political issues for they are worried about their reaction towards the Jewish children at the school. When doing so they seem to approach the issues with the same differentiation as the one mentioned above, they differentiate between individual and group affiliation

> It was very difficult for (name of child), he once asked us why we sent them to study with Jewish children if Jewish people kill Arabs. I explained to him that there are good Jews and there are bad Jews. He then told his sister that he wanted to tell their friends that not all Arabs are bad and that not all Jews are bad and that way they will all get along! (Interview, 5)

In general parents seem to have found ways to adapt to the present conflictual situation

> When you look from away on the conflict it's seems very big deal, but when you're living in it it's between people, you can be friend with everyone and// but I think it's hard to solve it with politics, but people in this school like it's a very good example that, you know, the people can live together. This is how I believe how this could be solved. (Interview, 2)

On the Decision to Send the Children to the Bilingual Schools

Almost all Palestinian parents mention that there decision to have their children join the school followed from the lack of "good" educational options in the Arab educational sector *"Doctor Lee (one of the founders of the school) was so correct as// In addition, we didn't find any frame, normal frame, for our children."* (Interview, 1)

Two interviewees explain that the *bagrut* (the Israeli matriculation certificate) was the main reason to join the bilingual school. *"[I]f I will be very honest with you I will tell you that I-I took this school only because of the, ah, final exams"* (Interview, 17). One other Palestinian parent mentions the lack of options in Jerusalem and that if she lived in the north, she would have not sent her children to this school. *"Maybe if I lived in another place, not in Jerusalem, like in Nazareth for example, I won't think about it, because there's lots of options also. For me there was no other options."* (Interview, 15)

The gaining of Hebrew language competence was high on the list of reasons for their choice *"I do not want my children to suffer as I did when entering the university, I want them to know Hebrew well, in Israel all universities teach in Hebrew"* (Interview, 5). Parents wanted their children to find it easier to meet the Jewish majority when joining them in higher education institutions

> …I also don't want my daughter's exposure to Jews be experienced as a traumatic one, I want them to feel strong, because that's just the way it is we're a minority as oppose to the Jews and so we feel less of a person than they are, that they are better than you.(Interview, 9)

Four parents mention the importance they saw in having their children participate in a multicultural environment in which they expected their children to encounter the "other" under hospitable conditions. One of the Palestinian parents put it emphatically *"the school allows me to leave my dream of co-existence."* (Interview, 3)

One other Palestinian interviewee says the "values" of the school were a main factor in his decision:

> But (.) I-I have to say something that (.) there is another (other than a good school) element that made me came to the school. This school is kind of school that gives (…) values that

no other school, public school, gives. For example: my children, my children have clear (.) opinion about (.) who they are, the Palestinians and (.) things that happen in the society. In a normal school, in a public school we are not talking about these things. We are afraid to talk like this. (Interview, 14)

Four other parents underlie the success of the schools in offering a multicultural environment in which each of the groups is recognized and respected while creating a sense of community and belonging:

We, in this school, (2) we are there to break prejudice, st-stereotypes. For example, it's very good a-a-a place to (..) to talk to the other in the same (..) level, you know. I'm looking at you at the same level as equals. Not (.) from above. (Interview, 15)

Palestinian parents were also looking for a school that will respect the students and that will not hurt or humiliate them (both emotionally and physically).

The Israeli society is a competitive one but to be successful in this society you have to have high self esteem...personality...assertiveness.... We looked for an education that teaches values because if a teacher beats students in year one, all her values are lost and there has no respect for the student as a person...he doesn't exist.... Teacher's love is stipulated by the grades that he receives. (Interview, 8)

In addition, Palestinian parents also speak highly about an educational environment which encourages and supports *"open-mindedness and curiosity"* for the children and that promotes *"inquiry."* (Interview, 8)

Parents also showed some ambivalence in their responses. They were, at times, critical of the Jewish cohort at the schools who had in the upper grades of primary school been dwindling based on the Jewish parents' appreciation that the bilingual schools offered limited socializing possibilities to their children. Yet, Palestinian parents expressed doubts regarding the possibility to organize all by themselves a school which would embody the educational approach which brought about their choosing of the bilingual school for their children. One of the parents put it succinctly

When we sent our kids to this school it was of very selfish reasons, there isn't one good school in the area here, I know each and every teacher here, where he studied and what, and who gets where and why. I know how teachers because teachers and who the principles are and why. We sent them to this Jewish Arab school because we want them to be respected, I don't care if they study Hebrew or not. I want them (the teachers) to respect them and not embarrass her and make her feel bad if she makes a mistake, I want them to be educated the way I educate them, with respect and love. This you won't find in the Arab schools here. Of course, I would never say that in the school because of selfish reasons. I'm afraid of the Arabs taking over the school, I'm afraid of there being only Arab teachers. (Interview, 10)

From the parents reports we also heard what we interpreted as an idealization of the Jewish society. Palestinian parents seemed to perceive Jews as more confident, kinder, having stronger personalities and being more patient and less violent. One of the interviewees stated,

It's just the way matters tend to be created from a small context into a larger one—sadly, it's (violence) found at home...it's not that I'm not proud of the Arab culture, I love our culture and I'm against the occupation and other things that the Jews have done but still, I like their way of education, I want my daughter to grow up and not be afraid to look the teacher in the eye...when I watch my daughters play with their Jewish classmates I don't see a difference between them but another Arab boy doesn't have the it in him, he gets shy and doesn't want to do anything or say anything, and he could get to the same level even though he wasn't in interaction with Jewish people, because that's where he comes from, the important thing is to know how to read, write and get good grades, that's all...but in the Jewish education they know to compliment the child, to give him to make him creative...get ready for life.

Another participant said,

> I used to get so upset seeing a Jewish boy on TV, he knows how to talk and express himself.... Why can't we do that? What do we lack? So when I heard about the Arab-Jewish school I told myself that I'm going to register her there no matter what anyone says.... There are many things that you can learn from the Jews.... I learned a lot from them in the past couple of years.... There are also negative things but a person can choose what to learn. For example, how they treat each other and myself, my daughter.... She can stay there (at school) a whole day and not want to go home. For us children have to start reading and writing from the minute they're at school but for Jews it's not like that, they build a personality, they teach you how to behave how to look at people and yourself. When Amal tells a story they listen to her until the end even if it's not interesting. (Interview, 3)

In addition, most Palestinian parents mention their decision to enroll their children in the bilingual school was supported by their immediate family. One of them believes that within the Palestinian community having children at the schools is highly regarded:

> No, no, in our area it's very excepted and it's even ah (..) it's like something that you are proud of....'I go the bilingual school!' You know. (...) Yes, yes, they all tell you...'Oh, you are so lucky, you go to this school'. (Interview, 9)

Identity and National Commemorations

One of the main challenges confronted by the bilingual schools is the educational curricular treatment of identity-related issues such as national commemorations and historical narratives. Contraintuitively, Palestinian parents are particularly satisfied with the way in which the bilingual schools deal with national days and holydays because they well know that regular monolingual (Arabic) schools are very much limited by the Israeli Ministry of Education in terms of how much (if at all) they can give expression to their own Palestinian narrative *"at the school our narrative is respected our children know and learn about the Nakba (day of the catastrophe)."* (Interview, 18)

Most interviewees spoke about the school's role in strengthening their childrens' identity. One of the parents talked about meeting people with other identities as a strengthening factor for his child's identity:

> I think yes. Yeah, better than separate schools, better than separate schools (...) Because as I told you, when you see the other you know yourself better. (...) When you see only yourself, when you look in the mirror you see only your face. And you can't compare your face with other faces. Okay?. (Interview, 16)

Future Expectations of/from the Children

All in all they expect their kids to grow to be independent, open-minded, and respectful towards others:

> I'm-I want to be that they be proud, that they are different, to analyze the differences in the society and find the ways (.) to live with the differences. To have their own, ah, (..) identity, way of thinking and (5) to be independent (..) not like in society, in our society because we depends all on each other, cousins, brothers, sisters, you know. And have:: their own future. And to decide, what to do. This is what my aim is. And they are looking for things (.) in (.) different perspectives (.) not like me or like their mother or like their cousins. (Interview, 14)

Prices Paid by Sending the Kids to the Schools

Though benefits are indeed mentioned by the parents (higher school quality, majority language competence) all identify some prices their children might pay for their participation in the bilingual initiative. When questioned about their fears what was mentioned as positive above regarding multiculturalism is now rephrased as a fear. The different behavioral codes among Palestinians and Jews are mentioned by parents. Palestinians are represented as being more traditional and the Jews as being more modernist. In this section of the interview assimilatory fears are expressed:

> We-we-we were afraid, because maybe we can lose our language. We:: (.) we were afraid because maybe aeh it's supposed to be:: aeh absorption or assimilation of our children by the Jewish people. (2) We were afraid aeh about our values. There are cultural boundaries, you know. I wanted (my child) to accept and to recognize my values, (.) my culture. Aeh (4) But I think, for example, oh, we were-were afraid about ah political situation. (Interview, 12)

Parents also expressed worries about their children's competence in Arabic

> "There is(are) <u>two</u> languages in the Arabic, spoken and written Arabic" he says "my son is paying a price. He is so slow in reading for example. He is like a Jewish student" (Interview, 4). Another parent said: "I wanted them to be happy. To speak Arab// good Arabic, and to speak good Hebrew. I was afraid that they will speak more Hebrew than Arabic, I didn't want that to happen. I want them to// and I didn't want them to mix languages together." (Interview, 15)

Advantages of Studying in the Bilingual School

In terms of advantages following from their childrens' participation in the bilingual initiative, parents mention both multicultural/bilingual and social issues.

Hasan as other Palestinian parents states that:

> …let's start with the simple things. That they learn two languages…that they have small classes, two teachers. It's all material things. But I think the most important things is beyond these things. This school (.)challenges (.) the kids. That from your first beginning, of your life (…) you have (.) to learn (.) the other. And I can say even (.) the enemy, okay? (..) You have to learn how to live with the enemy, how to make cooperation with this other. This challenge gives (.) my kids (.) things that (.) no other school can grant to them. (Interview, 10)

When asked about things the kids learn from their friends who come from different cultural background, Palestinian interviewees said:

> I think (..) self-confidence, a lot of self-confidence and to be proud of what you are. And this is one thing that many Palestinians don't learn to do. They are not proud of what they are. They are afraid (.) to show who they are and what they are. So, I think, I hope that my child would (.) learn this from the other side. (Interview, 11)

Conclusions

The rich data gathered suggest a complex picture which we will try to partially disentangle in our concluding remarks while being certain that much more efforts should be invested in the study of intricate minority–majority relations as these get organized around educational discourses.

The Israeli bilingual schools offer both opportunities and challenges for Palestinian parents. Palestinian participants in our study, while rhetorically agreeing with the aims of coexistence education and multiculturalism as these are expressed in the schools goals, see the schools, for the most part, as an opportunity for their children to gain access to a good/better education. Mobility more than recognition is what they are after, not necessarily because they reject the need for recognition but because they realize the present limitations of the Israeli sociopolitical context. They express appreciation for the more liberal approach offered by these schools' initiative. These upwardly mobile Palestinian parents measure the primary success of the educational effort not according to its liberatory power, but rather according to its role in developing their children's abilities to attain desirable positions in the "bureaucracies" of present dominant Western cultural traditions (Giroux 1994, 1995).

Still, parents show a latent ambivalence regarding their motives for registering their children in the bilingual binational integrated schools: On the one hand, Palestinian parents would like their children to conform to the majority-related behaviors and norms (being "assimilated") in terms of speaking Hebrew and adopting a more individualistic and assertive stance while encouraging open mindedness and curiosity qualities associated with the Jewish majority. Components that will facilitate their children's mobility within the Israeli strongly westernized society. On the other hand, this same assimilationist tendency raises in the Palestinian parents fears and threat-like feelings due to the implied risk of the loss of a sense of belonging to their cultural heritage—preserving the Arabic language and cultural norms.

We also read in the data gathered the presence of tensions in the parent's efforts to balance between the best interest of their children (high-quality education, a supportive educational environment for growth, etc.) and their own aspirations as parents (that their children will achieve a similar or higher status than the one they have attained in the majority society).

Finally, our research is aligned with Seginer's (1995) approach that stresses the importance of investigating parental expectations of schools. In her opinion this approach is especially relevant for potential interventions, because it suggests the kind of parental behaviors that help or hinder children's academic achievements. Seginer also puts forward a second approach based on students' perceptions of parental expectations—that focuses on the subjective reality as experienced by the children themselves and may allow us to understand the meanings that children give to their parents' expectations regarding their own school-based academic achievements. We suggest that further research should explore how the children understand parental expectations given that these might be considered powerful motives for their academic-related attitudes and behaviors.

The extent to which schools construct parental involvement and develop a "culturally sensitive" approach to the different groups of parents are pivotal keys for the understanding of school–family relations in culturally diverse contexts. Research has pointed the importance of identifying the culturally appropriate kind of parent participation for the different ethnic, religious, or national groups (Tatar 2008). School receptivity is one of the strongest predictors of parental school involvement within groups of parents across the different levels of education (see e.g., Overstreet et al. 2005). The ways by which schools construct parental involvement may invite and attract parents to schools or impede and keep them out of the educational settings. If educational systems are truly interested in developing culturally successful parental involvement programs, it is crucial that parallel and complementary processes should be developed and implemented both at the educational institution and at the community levels. Among the practical guidelines that should be taken into account we may mention the following (Tatar 2008; Whitaker and Fioe 2001): To assess the family's needs and interests in working with the schools. In parallel, evaluate the expectations and desires of school staff regarding the extent and nature of parental involvement; to develop multiple (and creative) outreach mechanisms to inform about involvement policies and programs and to involve key individuals in the educational setting and at the community level also at the planning level, so that programs will be endorsed by both parties; to recognize the community's historic, linguistic, or cultural resources in generating the appropriate parental involvement programs; and to evaluate the effectiveness of parental involvement programs and activities on a regular basis being open and flexible in adapting and accommodating parental involvement programs to the results of the evaluation.

Bibliography

Abu-Nimer, M. (1999). *Dialogue, conflict, resolution, and change: Arab-Jewish encounters in Israel*. Albany: SUNY.
Abu-Nimer, M. (2004). Education for coexistence and Arab-Jewish encounters in Israel: Potential and challenges. *Journal of Social Issues, 60*(2), 405–422.
Al-Haj, M. (1995). Kinship and modernization in developing societies: The emergence of instrumentalized kinship. *Journal of Comparative Family Studies, 26*(3), 311–328.
Al-Haj, M. (1996). *Education among the Arabs in Israel: Control and social change*. Jerusalem: Hebrew University Magnes Press.
Antonovski, H., Meari, M., & Blanc, J. I. E. (1978). Changing family life in an Arab village. In E. J. Anthony & C. Chiland (Eds.), *The child in his family: Children in a changing world* (Vol. 5, pp. 217–240). New York: Wiley.
Appiah, K. A., & Gates, H. L. (1995). *Identities*. Chicago: University of Chicago Press.
Baker, D. P., & Stevenson, D. L. (1986). Mothers' strategies for children's school achievement: Managing the transition to high schools. *Sociology of Education, 59,* 156–166.
Barakat, H. (1985). The Arab family and the challenge of social transformation. In E. W. Fernea (Ed.), *Women and the family in the Middle East: New voices of change*. Austin: University of Texas Press.
Barakat, H. (1993). *The Arab world: Society, culture and state*. Berkeley: University of California Press.
Bar-Tal, D. (2000). From intractable conflict through conflict resolution to reconciliation: Psychological analysis. *Political Psychology, 21*(2), 351–365.
Bekerman, Z. (2004). Multicultural approaches and options in conflict ridden areas: Bilingual Palestinian-Jewish education in Israel. *Teachers College Record, 106*(3), 574–610.
Bekerman, Z. (2005). Complex contexts and ideologies: Bilingual education in conflict-ridden areas. *Journal of Language Identity and Education, 4*(1), 1–20.
Bekerman, Z. (2008). The ethnography of peace education: Some lessons learned from Palestinian-Jewish integrated education in Israel. In S. Byrne, D. Sandole, J. Senehi & I. Staroste-Sandole (Eds.), *Handbook of conflict analysis and resolution* (pp. 144–156). New York: Routledge.
Bekerman, Z. (2009). Social justice, identity politics, and integration in conflict ridden societies: Challenges and opportunities in integrated Palestinian-Jewish education in Israel. In W. Ayers, T. Quinn & D. Stovall (Eds.), *Handbook of social justice in education* (pp. 138–151). New York: Routlledge.
Bekerman, Z., & Nir, A. (2006). Opportunities and challenges of integrated education in conflict ridden societies:The case of Palestinian-Jewish schools in Israel. *Childhood Education, 82*(6), 324–333.
Catsambis, S. (2002). Expanding knowledge of parental involvement in children's secondary education: Connections with high seniors' academic success. *Social Psychology of Education, 5,* 149–177.
Denzin, N. K., & Lincoln, Y. S. (Eds.). (2000). *Handbook of qualitative research* (2nd. ed.). London: Sage.
Dwairy, M. (1998). *Cross-cultural counseling: The Arab-Palestinian case*. New York: Haworth Press.
Dwairy, M. (2004). Culturally sensitive education: Adapting self-riented assertiveness training to collective minorities. *Journal of Social Issues, 60*(2), 423–436.
Egan, K. (1996). Narrative and learning: A voyage of implications. In H. McEwan & K. Egan (Eds.), *Narrative in teaching, learning, and research*. New York: Teachers College Press.
Eilam, B. (2002). "Passing through" a Western-Democratic teacher education: The case of Israeli Arab teachers. *Teachers College Record, 104*(8), 1656–1701.
Giroux, H. (1994). Doing cultural studies: Youth and the language of pedagogy. *Harvard Educational Review, 64*(3), 278–308.

Giroux, H. (1995). The politics of insurgent multiculturalism in the era of the Los Angeles uprising. In B. Kanpol & P. McLaren (Eds.), *Critical multiculturalism: Uncommon voices in a common struggle.* Westport: Bergin & Garvin.
Glassner, B., & Loughlin, J. (1987). *Drugs in adolescent worlds: Burnouts to straights.* New York: St. Martin's Press.
Glaubman, R., & Iram, Y. (1999). *Developments in teaching: The Israeli case.* Tel Aviv: Ramot.
Haj-Yahia, M. M., & Shor, R. (1995). Child maltreatment as perceived by Arab students of social science in the West Bank. *Child Abuse and Neglect, 19,* 1209–1219.
Haraway, D. J. (1991). *Simians, Cyborgs, and women: The revition of nature.* New York: Routledge.
Harre, R., & Gillett, G. (1995). *The discoursive mind.* London: Sage.
Hernandez Dimmler, M. (2008). Parent expectations, knowledge of student performance, and school involvement: Links to the achievement of African American and Latino children. Dissertation Abstracts International Section A: Humanities and Social Sciences. 68(8-A), pp. 3277.
Jamal, A. (2007). Nationalizing states and the constitution of â€˜Hollow Citizenshipâ€™: Israel and its Palestinian citizens. *Ethnopolitics, 6*(4), 471–493.
Li, J. (2001). Expectations of Chinese immigrant parents for their children's education: The interplay of Chinese tradition and the Canadian context. *Canadian Journal of Education, 26,* 477–494.
Mason, J. (1996). *Qualitative researching.* London: Sage publications.
Nir, A. E., & Inbar, D. (2004). From egalitarianism to competition: The case of the Israeli educational system. In I. Rotberg (Ed.), *Balancing change and tradition in global education reform* (pp. 207–228). Lanham: Scarecrow Education Pub.
Ogbu, J. U. (1994). From cultural differences to differences in cultural frame of reference. In P. M. Greenfield & R. R. Cocking (Eds.), *Cross-cultural roots of minority child development* (pp. 365–391). Hillsdale: Lawrence Erlbaum Associates.
Overstreet, S., Devine, J., Bevans, K. & Efreom, Y. (2005). Predicting parental involvement in children's schooling within an economically disadvantaged African American sample. *Psychology in the Schools, 42,* 101–111.
Reynolds, A. J. (1992). Comparing measures of parental involvement and their effects on academic achievement. *Early Childhood Research Quarterly, 7,* 441–462.
Sampson, E. E. (1993). *Celebrating the other: A dialogic account of human nature.* Hertfordshire: Harvester Wheatsheaf.
Seginer, R. (1986). Mother's behaviour and son's performance: An initial test of academic achievement path model. *Merrill-Palmer Quarterly, 32,* 153–166.
Seginer, R. (1995). Parents: The third partner in school processes. In H. Flum (Ed.), *Adolescents in Israel: Personal, familial and social aspects.* Even Yehuda: Reches (in Hebrew).
Seginer, R. (2006). Parents' educational involvement: A developmental ecology perspective. parenting. *Science and Practice, 6,* 1–48.
Seginer, R., & Vermulst, A. (2002). Family environment, educational aspirations, and academic achievement in two cultural settings. *Journal of Cross Cultural Psychology, 33,* 540–558.
Silverman, D. (1993). *Interpreting qualitative data.* London: Sage.
Suizzo, M. (2007). Parents' goals and values for children: Dimensions of independence and interdependence across four U.S. Ethnic groups. *Journal of Cross-Cultural Psychology, 38,* 506–530.
Tatar, M. (2008). Parents and schools: Chronicle of a conflict foretold? In A. Stavans & I. Kupferberg (Eds.), *Studies in language and language education* (pp. 411–427). Jerusalem: Hebrew University Magnes Press.
Tatar, M. & Horenczyk, G. (2000) Parental expectations of their adolescents' teachers. *Journal of Adolescence, 23,* 487–495.
Van Der Veen, I. (2003). Parents' education and their encouragement of successful secondary school students from ethnic minorities in the Netherlands. *Social Psychology of Education, 6,* 233–250.

Weller, A., Florian, V., & Mikulincer, M. (1995). Adolescents' reports of parental division of power in a multicultural society. *Journal of Research on Adolescence, 5*(4), 413–429.

Whitaker, T. & Fioe, D. J. (2001). *Dealing with difficult parents and with parents in difficult situations*. Larchmont: Eye on Education.

Chapter 17
Social Change and Minority Education: A Sociological and Social Historical View on Minority Education in Croatia

Jadranka Čačić-Kumpes

Introduction

Whenever people have the chance to formulate educational goals they usually desire to make use of the indubitable socializational power of the role of schooling. Consequently, the Council of Europe refers to the importance of education in its programmatic text on intercultural dialogues as a foundation for managing cultural diversity, building European identity, and developing cultural and ethnic pluralistic societies based on solidarity. "In a multicultural Europe, education is not only a means of preparing for the labor market, supporting personal development and providing a broad knowledge base; schools are also important for the preparation of young people for life as active citizens," which, inter alia, includes the respect of human rights "as the foundations for managing diversity and stimulating openness to other cultures" (*White paper…* 2008, p. 30). This concerns recognizing the right to diversity which, through the intercultural concept, was defined by the Council of Europe as early as during the 1970s. The intercultural concept, similarly to other concepts with which it is sometimes intertwined, sometimes equated, and sometimes differentiated (e.g., the concept of multiculturalism, integration, and social cohesion), appeared only when immigrants became sufficiently stable and visible groups so that host countries could no longer, by ignoring their cultural diversity, also ignore their basic human rights. Yet it should be said that societies were multicultural even before modern migration flows and globalization processes, and this multicultural aspect was regulated in various ways.

Specifically, a widespread interpretation exists that the modernizing pattern of compulsory, standardized, public, and mass education was conceived so as to politically socialize and nationally homogenize populations, and thus also to suppress existing cultural and ethnic differences with the goal of creating modern and efficient (nation) states. From this stems the simplified developmental scheme of education systems, which began with the national-homogenizing project in the nineteenth

---

J. Čačić-Kumpes (✉)
Department of Sociology, University of Zadar, Zadar, Croatia
e-mail: jcacic@unizd.hr

century and only in the second half of the twentieth century moved towards the affirmation of cultural and ethnic diversities. Despite the indisputable dominance of such a developmental scheme in the practice of education, it was not the only one. An example of another practice, of a certain type of (proto)multiculturalism dating from the very beginning of compulsory education, was represented by the Croatian school system in the multinational states in which Croatia[1] was included, until the late twentieth century.

This social historical sketch of the Croatian education system will put into context the reasons for which it diverged from the dominant modernizing pattern in the European framework, and the reasons for its continuous recognition of ethnic and cultural diversities, despite substantial sociopolitical changes. Chronologically, our review of regulations pertaining to ethnic and cultural diversities in Croatian schools will begin with the period after the Austro-Hungarian Compromise (*Ausgleich*) of 1867, which resulted in the creation of the Dual Monarchy. This was a period of modernization in the Monarchy and in its peripheral regions, including Croatia, which at the time was divided between various administrations[2] and in a *sui generis* position of internal colonialism relative to the centers of power in Vienna or Budapest. Next, this chapter will outline regulations involving ethnic and cultural diversities in schools in the Kingdom of Serbs, Croats, and Slovenes (in 1929 renamed the Kingdom of Yugoslavia),[3] and later in Socialist Croatia.[4]

A composite (multilayered) examination of this topic includes determining the sociohistorical contexts of the Croatian education system within social macroprocesses, as well as an examination of dominant ideologies in specific periods, of power relations, including power relations between the ethnic groups in individual states, of the interests of "ethnic" and political elites and of their reactions to regulating ethnic and cultural diversities within the education system.

Finally, a question arises: Is it possible to extract certain elements from this template of practically two centuries of affirming ethnic and cultural diversities in the

---

[1] The analytical unit in this chapter is Croatia (in its present borders), and this concept will be used for all periods and state framework(s) through which Croatia has passed. Croatia was a part of the Austro-Hungarian Monarchy until its break-up in 1918; later, until World War II, the country was part of the Kingdom of Yugoslavia, and finally it was included in the Socialist Federal Republic of Yugoslavia, until the latter's disintegration in 1991.

[2] The Monarchy was divided into an Austrian and a Hungarian part, and the Croatian lands found themselves under both administrations. Istria and Dalmatia were under Austrian administration, the Kingdoms of Croatia and Slavonia had a particular type of self-rule within the Hungarian part of the Monarchy, Međimurje and Baranja were under direct Hungarian rule, as was the city of Rijeka, which had a special status. The Military Frontier, until its demilitarization in 1881, when it was incorporated into the Kingdoms of Croatia and Slavonia, was under specific Austrian military administration.

[3] Here we will be dealing with the territory of present-day Croatia without Istria, Zadar, and several islands that were given to Italy in the peace treaty following World War I.

[4] Croatia, in its present borders, was one of the federal republics of Socialist Yugoslavia, and was defined in its last Constitution from that period (1974) as "the nation state of the Croat people, the state of the Serb people in Croatia and the state of the nationalities that live in it."

Croatian education system, which should be considered when conceptualizing education in the framework of contemporary integration processes?

Relating Ethnicity and Education: Theoretical Approaches

The very act of linking social changes, ethnicity, and education brings one to the problem of explanatory reductionism among the existing theoretic approaches. As Archer (1983) notes, this concerns, first of all, the fact that most theories treat education as something mysterious, adaptable to social demands, whereas sociologists of education have not considered the role of education in creating and maintaining the national collectivity (cf. Schnapper 1991). The role of education in forming the nation and national identity was more the concern of theorists of ethnicity, the nation, and nationalism. Despite an obvious overlapping of interests between the sociology of ethnicity and the sociology of education, overlapping knowledge between these two disciplines is lacking (cf. Hallinan 2000).

Theorists of ethnicity and nationalism talk of an intertwining of education and the concept of creating a nation state (e.g., Eriksen 2002; Gellner 1983; Hobsbawm 1975; Hroch 1985; Schnapper 1991, 1994; Smith 1983), which was foreseen as a program as early as the eighteenth century by Rousseau. In his instructions to the Polish government, Rousseau directed attention to the importance of national institutions in the formation of the nation: "I repeat: *national* institutions. That is what gives form to the genius, the character, the tastes and the customs of a people; what causes it to be itself rather than some other people; what arouses in it that ardent love of fatherland that is founded upon habits of mind impossible to uproot..." (Rousseau 1985, p. 11). In the nineteenth century, when modern nation states were formed, compulsory, standardized, public and mass education systems began to flourish, since "[a]ll who held ambitions to invent some nation made their vows to the cult of the school" (Schnapper 1994, p. 132).

Less important in this context are various theoretic disputes as to whether nationalist motives established mass education to shape the population into a "nation" (Smith 1983), or whether nationalism is the product of such education, which—as dictated by the economy—standardizes and unifies in order to establish a broad common basis for quick prequalification (Gellner 1983). Be it a precondition or a result of the formation of the nation, the system of standardized, compulsory, public and mass education has been assigned a role in homogenizing the nation, and is considered an indicator of modernity, an image of the Western World. Within the constructivist conception of the nation, it is seen as an "extremely powerful machine for the creation of abstract identifications" (Eriksen 2002, p. 90) that can impose national unity (Hobsbawm 1975).

The conclusions of theorists of ethnicity and the nation are followed through in Green's studies. Green believes that the system of general education can be understood primarily in connection with the process of state creation, in which politics and other social factors (economic ones, for example) have equal importance (cf. Green 1990). The pedagogical optimism of the ruling elite in nation states envisions in the schooling system the basis of modernity that ensures development and the desired functioning of society.

According to Robertson and Dale, the nation state, the universality of the state's structure and its functioning, and a focus on the importance of compulsory education for the development of modern states, seen as the basic traits of modernity, do not provide explanations for changes in the globalizing world. These authors list four forms of methodological reductionism: methodological nationalism, methodological statism, methodological educationalism, and spatial fetishism (Robertson and Dale 2008). Yet all considered it seems that the methodological reductionism of the mentioned *-isms* applies also to an earlier period. Namely, none of the noted approaches alone can explain how it was possible in the nineteenth century to establish and then to affirm continuously the right to cultural and ethnic diversity within the (Croatian) education system, during turbulent social changes and in spite of them. Therefore it seems advisable to analyze the school system on several levels, based on the morphogenetic perspective proposed by Archer (1979), in order that their synergy might provide an understanding of (proto)multicultural education systems outside of the usual Western-centric modernizing pattern.

However, before discussing minority schooling in Croatia it is important to gain at least a rough insight into changes in the ethnic structure and in relations between ethnic groups living in the country.

Ethnic Minorities in Croatia: A Sketch of Changes in the Ethnic Structure

Since the beginning of systematic and regular population censuses in Croatia, the population has also been recorded according to its ethnic affiliations, or else according to ethnic markers.[5] Because of this, it is possible to reconstruct Croatia's ethnic structure (see Table 17.1). The fact that the population was also recorded by its ethnic affiliations indicates the social and political importance given to ethnic diversity in the entire examined period.

The census data in Table 17.1 indicate a relatively high degree of national homogeneity in Croatia, in which Croats make up the absolute majority of the population (in a range between virtually 70% to virtually 90% of the total population). At the same time, the continuous presence of a large number of minority ethnic groups is noticeable. Although the number of their members has been falling, and national

---

[5] The question of ethnic affiliation was posed in censuses during the eighteenth century. The census of 1857 is considered the first modern census in the Habsburg Monarchy, but it only posed the question of religious confession. Later censuses asked respondents to declare their mother tongue and confession, and it is therefore possible, on the basis of these data, to estimate ethnic affiliation. From 1948 onwards, respondents could choose to declare or not to declare their ethnic affiliation.

Table 17.1 Ethnic structure of Croatia from 1880 to 2001 (%)

	1880	1910	1948	1961	1981	1991	2001*
Croats	69.83	68.53	78.72	80.29	75.07	78.10	89.63
Serbs	17.24	16.30	14.42	15.02	11.55	12.16	4.54
Czechs	0.92	0.91	0.77	0.56	0.33	0.27	0.24
Germans	3.85	3.45	0.27	0.10	0.05	0.06	0.07
Hungarians	2.80	3.51	1.36	1.02	0.55	0.47	0.37
Italians	3.11	4.50	2.01	0.51	0.25	0.45	0.44
Muslims/Bosniaks	–	–	0.03	0.07	0.52	0.91	0.47
Ruthenians and Ukrainians**	0.05	0.16	0.17	0.15	0.12	0.12	0.10
Slovaks	0.19	0.28	0.27	0.20	0.14	0.12	0.11
Slovenians	0.99	0.82	1.00	0.94	0.55	0.47	0.30
Yugoslavs	–	–	–	0.37	8.24	2.22	–
Other and unknown	1.02	1.54	0.98	0.77	2.63	4.65	3.73

Sources: *Narodnosni i vjerski sastav…* 1998; Census 2001
* Data for 2001 are not compatible with earlier data due to a different census methodology (as opposed to the previous censuses, in 2001 only the population present was surveyed). It is shown in this table only as an illustration of the general trend
** Ruthenians and Ukrainians were occasionally grouped into one category, and therefore in this comparative data for all census years they are shown as one group

homogeneity is increasing, one can also notice a growing trend in the overall number of different ethnic groups.[6]

The diversity of the ethnic structure was influenced by migrations, regardless of whether this involved immigration waves that began in the era of Ottoman conquests, or migrations within multiethnic/multinational states (Heršak 1993), in which the population participated often on the incentive of state politics (in colonization actions, for example). Conclusions on the systematic settlement of particular ethnic groups as a result of these migrations cannot be made from general illustrations of Croatia's ethnic structure, but rather the spatial concentration of minority groups in certain parts of Croatia needs to be considered (see Pan and Pfeil 2003, p. 68). In some territorial-administrative units (municipalities), especially in Eastern and Central Croatia, members of specific ethnic minorities make up a large percentage of the local population (sometimes a relative, or even absolute majority of the population), and many former "Czech," "Hungarian," "Ruthenian," "Slovak," and "Serb" villages have remained ethnically homogeneous (see *Narodnosni i vjerski sastav…* 1998).

Although wars brought about the greatest changes in the ethnic structure, important changes also occurred in more peaceful times. During such times, they were primarily associated with substantial transformations such as shifts in government that were followed by changes in the power relations among political elites, and in their interests, and in which ethnicity was often both an investment and a means of mobilization. Thus, for example, the number of Hungarians (Magyars) increased

---

[6] The *Constitutional Law on the Rights of National Minorities* of 2002 regulated the rights of 22 recognized national minorities in Croatia.

after the Croatian-Hungarian Compromise (1868), when Hungarian influence on Croatia's internal administration increased. It gradually surpassed the percentage of Germans, which had constantly risen in the period of absolutism, during which the state had pursued a policy of Germanization. On the other hand, there were no great oscillations in the trends among members of minority groups that had never been in a dominant position. For example, the percentages of Ruthenians, Czechs, and Slovaks always remained small, with a tendency towards stagnation and/or decrease, but without major shifts (cf. Table 17.1).

Apart from their effects on changes in the ethnic structure, wars, and the creation of new states on the ruins of supranational or multinational states had an impact on the status of ethnic groups, which became, as Brubaker (2000) labeled them, "accidental diasporas." This was true, for example, of the status of Hungarians, Germans, and Italians in Croatia after the break-up of Austria–Hungary. Until that point their position could not be considered, in the sociological sense, a minority status. Namely, despite their small share in the total population, by their other traits (political, economic, and generally social power) they were in a privileged position. The status of other ethnic groups that became diasporas after the break-up of Austria–Hungary did not change significantly. These changes in the power relations among ethnic groups appear to be, in all periods, a significant factor for understanding the realization of rights to a separate education, as well as the entire sociohistorical context in which the equality of rights to diversity is, at least formally, guaranteed to all recognized ethnic groups.

Minority Education in Croatia: Multiculturality in the School System

The regulation of ethnic diversity in education in Croatia, during the period when the country was a part of multinational/multiethnic states, can be discussed from at least two aspects. The first involves the construction of the Croatian national education system as an institutional basis for shaping national identity and achieving national homogenization, in conditions resulting from the long period of territorial disunification of the Croatian ethnic area under various administrations. The second aspect pertains to the institutionalization of the rights of minority (linguistic, religious, ethnic) communities to a separate education and, by this means, to forming and nurturing their separate identities. These two aspects interact with one another, and their interlinkage could be defined as a *sui generis* (proto)multicultural approach to diversity.

Although multiculturalism emerged on the scene only in the second part of the twentieth century, the notion that ethnic diversity could be given visibility in the public sphere gained force in Central Europe, and thus also in Croatia, as early as the "Springtime of Peoples." If we include among the postulates of multiculturalism legal recognition of minorities and protective legislation of their individual and group rights, as well as fostering the public expression of diversity and institutional

Table 17.2 Minority schools in Croatia from the nineteenth to the twentieth century (selective data) (Due to discrepancies in the data only one year has been selected for each examined period, simply to illustrate the continuity of minority schooling. The table presents data only on the number of separate schools, not on school departments with instruction conducted in the mother tongue. For more extensive information on the number of minority schools and class units in the examined period—see Čačić-Kumpes 2004)

	1890		1900	1932		1982	2007
	Croatia and Slavonia	Istria	Dalmatia	Banovina		Croatia	Croatia
				Sava	Littoral		
Czech	–	–	–	3	–	13	7
German	51	2	–	4	–	–	1
Hungarian	15	–	–	1	–	14	9
Italian	–	60	6	–	3	19	17
Ruthenian	2	–	–	–	–	1	–
Serb	10*	–	–	–	–	–	35
Slovak	2	–	–	–	–	–	–

Sources: Iz statistike o pučkoj školi 1909, p. 184; *Školstvo u Hrvatskoj i Slavoniji...* 1896, pp. 52–53; Franković et al. 1958, pp. 228–230; *Статистика школа...* 1933; *Statistički godišnjak Republike Hrvatske* 1991; *Statistički ljetopis* 2008
* This figure applies to 1885 and refers to the number of Serbian Orthodox schools

affirmation of cultural differences (cf. Abdallah-Pretceille 1999, pp. 26–28), then we could say that these elements were present already at the very beginning of compulsory public schooling in Croatia. In contrast to policies aimed at assimilation and national homogenization that dominated in the nineteenth and in the first half of the twentieth century, and contrary to the principles of liberal democracy, in which multiculturalism is often reduced to the requirement that people function in public life within the limits of a common cultural pattern and express their particularities in the private sphere, in Croatia—as early as the nineteenth century—the right to schools in one's mother tongue was already regulated and implemented (see Table 17.2).

An examination of the origin and the characteristics of ethnic minority education in Croatia in a time span of virtually two centuries reveals certain elements that influenced the need to conceptualize it, and to continue such a practice.

In the context of the Austro-Hungarian Monarchy, (proto)multicultural education in the Croatian area resulted from the fact that the Croatian school system was established on the periphery of a large empire, whose "military dynasticism" (Mann 1998) maintained its ruling power precisely by manipulating the rights of individual peoples. Language and religious confession were formally recognized ethnic markers, and their equality within the school system was legalized. Organization of education in the mother tongue was the result of balancing, on the part of the central authorities, between: (1) attempts to implement Germanization and Magyarization goals through education, (2) the protection of the group rights of ethnic minorities, and (3) attempts by local political elites to establish national education systems. Ethnic minority schools only partially reflected a certain numerical presence and territorial concentration of specific ethnic groups. This could be seen, for example, in the numerical overrepresentation of German and Hungarian schools relative to the share of Germans and Hungarians in the total population of individual areas (Čop 1988), and also in the influence of Serbs on enactment of the school law, etc. (Gross 1988). In the region of Istria and Dalmatia, although Croats made up the majority population, they had to struggle for their own school system against Italianization, in a situation of economic and political domination by ethnic Italians. In Baranja and Međimurje, which were under Hungarian administration, Croatian schooling receded before the pressure of Magyarization policies (Kokolj and Horvat 1977). In Rijeka, which was also under Hungarian administration, despite a Croatian relative majority in the population (48.16%), there were no Croatian schools in 1900 (Čop 1988). There were 14 Italian schools in Rijeka (Italians made up 34.23% of the city's population), and five Hungarian schools (Hungarians made up 5.7% of the population) (Čop 1988; *Narodnosni i vjerski sastav...* 1998). Yet it should be noted that attempts by interest groups to execute their plans through education—regardless of whether these plans involved assimilation or national emancipation projects, extending literacy, vocational training, or something else—were generally difficult to realize, since parents ignored their obligation, regulated by law, to send their children to school (Gross 1985). The authorities that had prescribed compulsory schooling did not exert much pressure on the predominantly rural populace to comply with its legal duty, and the latter itself did not perceive the purpose of education, nor imagine that its offspring could derive much use from it.[7] The school population started to increase more significantly, although not enough, only during the 1880s.[8]

After the collapse of the anational monarchy, Croatia became part of a monarchy (the Kingdom of Yugoslavia), which had national-integrating ambitions. The multiculturality of the new state was manifested through minority schools, guaranteed for in the peace agreements following World War I. As demanded by the League of Nations, newly formed states had to ensure new minorities the right of affirming their cultural and ethnic diversity (Macartney 1934). On such a basis, the continuation of minority education in Croatia was organized between the extremes of nonrecognition of majority rights (e.g., for the Roma population), or a type of revanchism (towards the Hungarians), and concessions made to certain minority groups due to their high "market price" on the diplomatic level (in the case of Germans and Italians) (cf. Димић 1997, Vol. 3). The curriculum, merely translated into minority languages, was identical for all groups, for members of the three constitutive people (Serbs, Croats, and Slovenes) and for ethnic minorities. The goal of education, although it crystallized only after several years of debate and numerous drafts of the school law (which was passed only 11 years after creation of the state), in the final

---

[7] If we recall Thomas's study of Polish peasants, education first has to become a general phenomenon before the peasants can recognize its usefulness in people's lives. Only then can it be accepted by the conservative village environment (see Thomas 1966).

[8] This increase in the school population is considered a result of the *First School Law* (1874), the first modern Croatian autonomous legal act, which applied to the territory of the Kingdoms of Croatia and Slavonia. Whereas, for example, during the absolutist period, in the 1850s, only about 30% of all persons obliged to attend school in the Kingdoms of Croatia and Slavonia actually did so (Gross 1985, p. 288), in the school year 1885/1886 this percentage rose to 63.6% (Statistički podatci o stanju pučkoga školstva... 1887, p. 36).

analysis boiled down to the idea of a particular Yugoslav melting pot, a potential amalgam that would receive its strength and main characteristics from values derived from the Serbian state tradition and Serbian Orthodox Christianity (Franković et al. 1958; Димић 1997, Vol. 2). Asymmetric power relations among ethnic elites and permanent opposition from the Western—economically more developed—part of the kingdom, towards the national-homogenizing project of the political center in the East, directly led to the collapse of the state at the beginning of World War II.

On the ruins of the previous state, which had been called the "dungeon of peoples," the authorities of new Socialist Yugoslavia, if they wished to preserve the old state framework, had to unite the constitutive peoples around the notion of their equality—and regardless of the fact that giving importance to the national question was not in line with the new ruling ideology. Namely, this ideology was based on class internationalism, not on ethnic or national bonds. Yet normative equality did not exclude actual selectivity in implementing the right to diversity. Thus, for example, members of constitutive Yugoslav peoples residing outside of their home republics[9] could not realize their right to schooling in their mother tongues (see Čačić-Kumpes 2004), and minority groups such as Germans and Austrians were in effect marginalized. Other ethnic minority groups continued to have their own schools and/or class units (depending on the size of the group), as well as an adjusted school curriculum and, finally, in the 1970s, regulations were formulated that called to mind the interculturalist concept that began to surface at that time in Europe. Interlinking majority and minority cultures was anticipated in legal provisions regarding the mandatory teaching of the language of the environment. This meant that Croats were obliged to learn minority languages in areas of Croatia in which minority groups made up the majority of the population. As for members of constitutive peoples living outside of their home republics, it should be noted that educational contents pertaining to their own cultures was incorporated into the curriculum of Croatian schools.[10] On the other hand, one might conclude that disregarding the rights of constitutive peoples to education in their mother tongues in a certain sense reveals the ruling elite's interest in nurturing affiliation to the Yugoslav community, instead of to separate national communities, that is, the ruling elite's interest in suppressing separate national feelings and developing a specific type of supranational identity (Yugoslavism as a metanationality). However, such an educational goal was never explicitly defined.

Changes in Croatian education systems illustrate that education systems are closely linked to the formation of the state, to the type of state, and to its organization and dominant ideology (see Table 17.3).

---

[9] The constitutive Yugoslav peoples were Croats, Macedonians, Montenegrins, Muslims (after the break-up of Yugoslavia—Bosniaks), Serbs, and Slovenes.

[10] Material concerning the history, geography, literature, art, and music of all constitutive Yugoslav peoples was added to the curriculum, although it was not equally represented. In the 1980s the political elite assessed that it was necessary to increase the level of unity, and thus prescribed an obligatory "common core" of material that was to be introduced into the curricula in all Yugoslav republics (*Socijalistički samoupravni preobražaj odgoja i obrazovanja* ... 1985).

Table 17.3 Regulating ethnic and cultural differences in Croatian schools

Period		1868–1918	1918–1941	1945–1991
State framework		Anational dual monarchy	Unitary monarchy	Federation of (mostly) national Republics
Position of Croatia		Several politically and territorially divided entities on the periphery of a multiethnic empire	An undifferentiated part of the whole (until the establishment of the Banovina of Croatia in 1939)	A national republic in a multinational federation (of socialist republics)
Origin of regulations for diversity		The ruling elite	The League of Nations	The ruling elite
Ideal of togetherness		Loyalty to the dynasty	Integral Yugoslavism	"Brotherhood and unity," internationalism
Relations between ethnic groups (or peoples) and ethnic processes	Legislated	Equality	Equality	Equality
	Targeted	Plural coexistence	Melting pot	Cultural permeation
	Actual (dominant)	Hierarchized coexistence	Assimilation	Plural coexistence

17 Social Change and Minority Education

Fig. 17.1 Representation of the "national" group of subjects in the weekly schedule of school subjects in Croatia in three multinational/multiethnic states (Sources: *Naredba*... 1875; *Nastavni plan i program*... 1933; *Osnovna škola* 1960)

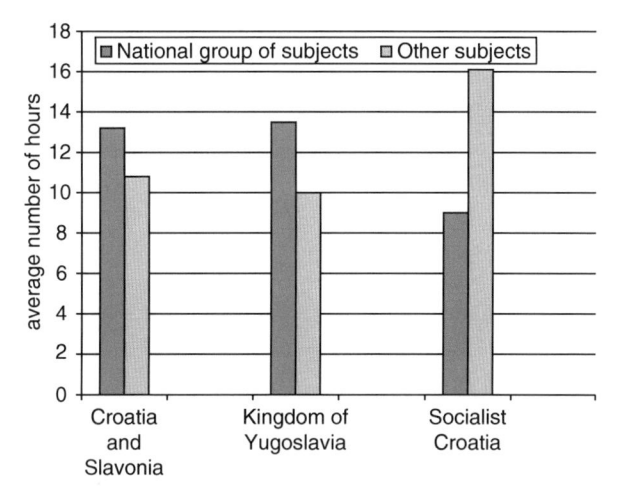

Croatia found itself in the framework of states that were constituted as multiethnic/multinational entities, and in each of them recognition of ethnic diversity was in various ways both a basis and a guarantee for their formation and survival. This had a crucial effect on multiculturality in the education system. However, the influence of the broader sociohistorical context, which was dominated by the concept of the nation state with a culture-unifying education system, manifested itself through the aspirations of representatives of political elites, especially of elites among the more powerful ethnic groups. One of the indicators of this tendency was also the incorporation of the so-called national group of subjects in school programs. Thus, for example, at the time of the Kingdom of Yugoslavia the percentage of hours in the school curriculum scheduled for the national group of subjects was slightly greater than the percentage of hours planned for other subjects, in comparison to the same ratio in the nineteenth century, and much greater than was the case in Socialist Croatia (see Fig. 17.1). Yet it would not be fully accurate to interpret greater representation of national content in individual curricula only as a means of implementing the state's national-homogenizing concept. It must in addition be linked to broader sociohistorical conditions and to changes in the very conception of schooling. The social role of schools, as demonstrated by the French example, shifted from schools being nurturers of the nation to becoming training places for work and finally institutions to prepare pupils for further education (cf. Schnapper 1991; Queiroz 1995).

The Croatian school system, as it developed on the European periphery, was not isolated from outside influences, yet it only partially followed the mentioned pattern. It adapted itself primarily to Croatian sociohistorical conditions. Although the social role of schools in Croatia also moved towards increasingly pronounced goals of preparing pupils for work and further education, the nurturing function of schools was always imposed as their primary task. The contents of this task changed as the dominant ideology changed. However, in contrast to the continuous function of nurturing the nation, which was characteristic of most European school systems, the nurturing function of Croatian schools changed depending on the state framework. At the beginning, schools had the function of raising pupils in a spirit of loyalty to the dynasty, later they had instilled in them an artificial identity of integral Yugoslavism, and finally they had to shape individuals with a feeling for the "unity and brotherhood" of all Yugoslav "peoples and nationalities" and for class-based internationalism (cf. Čačić-Kumpes 2004).

When discussing cultural and ethnic diversity, it should be noted that compulsory public schooling was, from its beginning, an institution that made cultural differences visible in the public sphere. In over ten school acts, from the first autonomous Croatian school law of 1874, through the Yugoslav law of 1929 to the Croatian laws during Socialist Yugoslavia, the "tribes [= peoples] of other language," "national minorities," or "Yugoslav peoples and nationalities," respectively, were given the right to separate education. This right included establishing separate schools and/or class units, special or adjusted curricula, qualified teachers who were speakers of the pupils' mother tongue, and textbooks with adapted contents. Such a pattern of organizing minority schools, once established, paradoxically did not change, despite substantial social changes: namely, changes in the state framework, the sociopolitical system, and the dominant ideology.

Since these social changes also involved elimination of the influence of previous dominant groups, changes in the education system were effectuated in a restrictive form.[11] In this way room was made for profound changes in the identification patterns that had been established for the needs of education in previous periods. Therefore, the persistence of a virtually ideal type of institutionalization of multicultural approach in the school system is even more amazing. Yet the answer, it seems, lies probably in the fact that the way in which minority schooling was organized came from "above," that is, it derived primarily from the interests and needs of state authorities and political elites, and only to a lesser degree, and more rarely, from attempts to affirm respect for cultural differences in a multiethnic/multinational state through education. So one could say that education was structurally removed from reality, distanced from the interests and the needs of those for whom it was, at least declaratively, organized. Namely, by encouraging affirmation of ethnic differences through group affiliations, prescribing the right to separate education to members of ethnic groups brings up certain questions. First of all, it is questionable how much and to what degree such a scheme contributes to preserving and fostering minority ethnic identities. The realization of this right in Croatia during a period of two centuries certainly had an impact on the continuity of minority ethnic identities. This is also apparent in the fact that members of minority groups, who from the very establishment of the school system had minority schools and departments, continuously declared their ethnic affiliation (and mother tongue), and were always a part of Croatia's ethnic structure, despite also always having a relatively small share

---

[11] Archer distinguishes two strategies for reducing the monopoly of dominant groups in education: the substitutive and the restrictive strategy. By changing regulations in a restrictive manner, the monopoly of the dominant group is reduced through force, not through competition (Archer 1979). The main factor that enables a group to apply restrictive policies is that it has access, to a certain degree, to the state's legislative mechanisms.

in the country's total population (cf. Tables 17.1 and 17.2). On the other hand, the "disappearance" and reappearance of minority schools is also evident, especially after turbulent social changes (cf. Table 17.2). This was not only the result of an actual dispersal or influx of members of ethnic minorities, but furthermore derived from their status in society, which also implies the question of the possible negative effects of separate schooling. Separate education based on group rights, namely, can likewise segregate members of ethnic minorities, and a certain type of pressure to ascribe identity may have such an influence that not only frameworks of identity, but also life styles, are imposed on individuals, especially in small environments.[12] Finally, the separate education of members of individual ethnic minorities, regardless of whether it has either positive or possibly negative effects for them, in actual fact isolates ethnic cultures. In ethnically mixed areas, however, an interweaving of cultures does occur (which includes all possible forms of cultural contact), at least as unintended consequences of everyday life.

Finally, it seems that a social historical review of (proto)multiculturalism in the Croatian school system in multiethnic/multinational states to a certain degree provides ideas for possible conceptualization of education projects in countries, which—although they are ethnically or nationally relatively homogeneous—do not deny their multicultural nature, and which are in the process of integrating themselves into a supranational community.

Concluding Remarks

It is an undoubted fact that education systems are reflections of the states that organize them, and also of various influences from the broader sociohistorical context. Yet this fact does not help us fully to explain the continuity of the multicultural approach to ethnic and cultural diversity in education in Croatia. Therefore, it is necessary to understand, on the one hand—relations of power among interest groups, that is, ethnic elites on the level of the state and on the local level, and on the other—the mobilizing potential of ethnicity.

Starting from such an understanding, and a particular combination of primarily meso- and macroapproaches, this chapter has presented a rough sketch of the multicultural approach to diversity in Croatian education systems during the period when Croatia was a part of multiethnic/multinational states. This sketch points to a specific linkage of elements, which may have had an effect on the institutionalization of minority education, and it also indicates the advantages and shortcomings of such a particular form of (proto)multiculturality in education.

It has been shown that legal regulation of the right to ethnic and cultural diversity is the basic requirement for realizing both this right as well as educational goals

---

[12] Examples of such consequences can also be found in the Croatian school system, although available analyses primarily deal with the present period (see NDC… 2005), which is not treated in this chapter.

aimed at reproducing such diversity. Besides this basic requirement, it is important that the state secures the conditions in which such education can function, that is, an appropriate infrastructure. Furthermore, since the area under examination is one in which it is difficult to separate the emotional and cognitive sides of learning, it is important that values gained through learning conform to the values of society. Namely, limiting the right to ethnic and cultural diversity mainly to schooling, by its pedagogical optimism in fact isolates schools from other parts of society and reduces their presupposed effectiveness. Such noneffectiveness is less evident on the identificational level,[13] and more obvious when dealing with socialization values directed towards the equality of ethnic groups and to tolerance, and against xenophobia, racism, and ethnocentrism. It has been shown that relations of power and relations between ethnic groups in society were not only manifested in the organization of minority schools (from underrepresentation right through to the disappearance of schools for certain minority groups). These relations were also reproduced, despite the fact that schools, through educational goals that were defined by legal regulations and curricula, were supposed to encourage the equality of various ethnic cultures. Finally, schools cannot successfully develop values that are difficult to define outside of the classroom in everyday life, that is, which are not practiced in broader society.

Furthermore, it has been shown that a need exists permanently to regulate, organize, and develop contents within the multicultural approach to education, because reliance only on the mere continuity of this approach is not sufficiently correlated to changes in society. Yet, breaking this continuity has a negative effect on relations between members of ethnic groups and on the groups themselves, who are thus denied already existing rights. Once a certain level of rights has been attained it cannot be reduced, since this would be experienced as unjust by members of individual ethnic groups. Perpetuated discontent has always surfaced when the power ratio has been changed, or when social conditions that favor an expression of discontent have appeared.

Therefore, in the end, it seems we need to remember that the goals of education must be set on the basis of existing conditions in society (Dewey 1916). These goals are not created simply by the fact that a certain group possesses enough power to impose them. They must be sufficiently general so that all can accept them, and sufficiently flexible so that no one is excluded. On the organizational level, a dilemma exists as to the need either for separate minority and majority schools and/or class units, or for integrated schools. Justification for separate minority schools in Croatia was confirmed through the continuity of separate identities in periods when, either on the local (Croatian) or on the global level, there was a tendency to neglect the

---

[13] The effect of schools on shaping identity is weaker than the effect that factors of primary socialization have on the individual (Berger and Luckmann 1966). In connection with this, the relative success of separate minority schools in nurturing and preserving ethnic identities in the Croatian school system can be explained precisely by the connection between factors of primary socialization, the schools and the state, which through legislative means regulated and institutionalized the visibility of ethnic minorities, and in so doing designated separate identity as a social value.

right to diversity. On the other hand, the idea of "unity in diversity" implies the simultaneous intertwining of cultures, and not their separation based on the principles of cultural relativism. In an age of celebrating diversities and of networking that surpasses temporal and spatial borders, it seems, therefore, that new organizational forms of education should be developed, through which ethnic and cultural diversity could be affirmed.

References

Abdallah-Pretceille, M. (1999). *L'éducation interculturelle*. Paris: Presses Universitaires de France.
Archer, M. S. (1979). *Social origins of educational systems*. London: Sage.
Archer, M. S. (1983). Process without system. *Archives européennes de sociologie, 24*(1), 196–221.
Berger, P. L., & Luckmann, T. (1966). *The social construction of reality*. Garden City: Doubleday.
Brubaker, R. (2000). Accidental diasporas and external 'homelands' in Central and Eastern Europe: Past and present. Vienna: Institute for Advanced Studies (Political Science Series 71). http://www.sscnet.ucla.edu/soc/faculty/brubaker/Publications/19_Accidental_Diasporas.pdf.
Čačić-Kumpes, J. (2004). Multiculturality in Croatian education. In M. Mesić (Ed.), *Perspectives of multiculturalism – Western and transitional countries* (pp. 315–329). Zagreb: Faculty of Philosophy Press & Croatian Commission for UNESCO.
Čop, M. (1988). *Riječko školstvo (1848–1918)*. Rijeka: Izdavački centar Rijeka.
Статистика школа под Министарством просвете на дан 15 маја 1932 год. (Израдио Н. С. Тујковић). (1933). Београд: Министарство просвете Краљевине Југославије.
Dewey, J. (1916). *Democracy and education: An introduction to the philosophy of education*. New York: Macmillan.
Димић, Љ. (1997). *Културна политика у Краљевини Југославији 1918–1941* (Vols. 2–3). Београд: Стубови културе.
Eriksen, T. H. (2002). *Ethnicity and nationalism* (2nd ed.). London: Pluto Press.
Franković, D. et al. (1958). *Povijest školstva i pedagogije u Hrvatskoj*. Zagreb: Pedagoško-književni zbor.
Gellner, E. (1983). *Nations and nationalism*. Ithaca: Cornell University Press.
Green, A. (1990). *Education and state formation: The rise of education systems in England, France and the USA*. London: Macmillan Press.
Gross, M. (1985). *Počeci moderne Hrvatske: Neoapsolutizam u civilnoj Hrvatskoj i Slavoniji 1850–1860*. Zagreb: Globus.
Gross, M. (1988). Zakon o osnovnim školama 1874. i srpsko pravoslavno školstvo. In *Zbornik radova o povijesti i kulturi srpskog naroda u Socijalističkoj Republici Hrvatskoj*, Vol. 1 (pp. 75–117). Zagreb: JAZU.
Hallinan, M. T. (2000). On the linkages between sociology of race and ethnicity and sociology of education. In M. T. Hallinan (Ed.), *Handbook of the sociology of education* (pp. 65–84). New York: Kluwer Academic/Plenum.
Heršak, E. (1993). Panoptikum migracija. *Migracijske teme, 9*(3–4), 227–302.
Hobsbawm, E. J. (1975). *The age of capital: 1848–1875*. London: Weidenfeld and Nicolson.
Hroch, M. (1985). *Social preconditions of national revival in Europe: A comparative analysis of the social composition of patriotic groups among the smaller European nations*. Cambridge: Cambridge University Press.
Iz statistike o pučkoj školi. (1909). *Narodna prosvjeta, 4*.
Klodič-Sabladoski, A. (1910). Povijest školstva u austrijskom Primorju [Istra]. *Narodna prosvjeta, 5*.

Kokolj, M., & Horvat, B. (1977). *Prekmursko šolstvo: Od začetka reformacije do zloma nacizma*. Murska Sobota: Pomurska založba.
Macartney, C. A. (1934). *National states and national minorities*. London: Oxford University Press.
Mann, M. (1998). *The sources of social power: Vol. 2. The rise of classes and nation-states, 1760–1914*. Cambridge: Cambridge University Press.
Naredba od 24. kolovoza 1875. broj 2949., kojom se izdaju naukovne osnove za obće pučke i gradjanske škole u kraljevinah Hrvatskoj i Slavoniji. (1875). Zagreb: Tiskara "Narodnih novinah".
Narodnosni i vjerski sastav stanovništva Hrvatske 1880–1991. po naseljima, Vols. 1–5. J. Gelo et al. (Eds.) (1998). Zagreb: Državni zavod za statistiku Republike Hrvatske.
Nastavni plan i program za osnovne škole Kraljevine Jugoslavije. (1933). Zagreb: St. Kugli.
NDC—Nansen dijalog centar. (2005). Ispitivanje odnosa roditelja prema kvaliteti osnovnog školovanja njihove djece u Vukovaru: Izvješće o kvalitativnom istraživanju. Osijek. http://www.ndcosijek.hr/pdf/istrazivanje.pdf
Osnovna škola. Odgojno-obrazovna struktura [1959]. (1960). Zagreb: Školska knjiga.
Pan, Ch., & Pfeil, B. S. (2003). *National minorities in Europe: Handbook*. Wien: W. Braumüller.
Queiroz, J.-M. de. (1995). *L'école et ses sociologies*. Paris: Nathan.
Robertson, S., & Dale, R. (2008). Researching education in a globalising era: Beyond methodological nationalism, methodological statism, methodological educationism and spatial fetishism. In J. Resnik (Ed.), *The production of educational knowledge in the global era* (pp. 19–32). Rotterdam: Sense.
Rousseau, J.-J. (1985). *The Government of Poland*. (trans. W. Kendall). Indianapolis: Hackett (Original work published 1782 [1771]).
Schnapper, D. (1991). *La France de l'intégration: Sociologie de la nation en 1990*. Paris: Gallimard.
Schnapper, D. (1994). *La communauté des citoyens: Sur l'idée moderne de nation*. Paris: Gallimard.
Smith, A. D. (1983). *Theories of nationalism* (2nd ed.). New York: Holmes & Meier.
Socijalistički samoupravni preobražaj odgoja i obrazovanja u SR Hrvatskoj 1974–1984. (1985). Zagreb: Školska knjiga.
Školstvo u Hrvatskoj i Slavoniji od njegova početka do konca god. 1895. uz pregled humanitarnih i kulturnih zavoda. (1896). Zagreb: Kr. IIrv.-Slav.-Dalm. Zem. vlada.
Statistički godišnjak Republike Hrvatske. (1991). Zagreb: Republički zavod za statistiku Republike Hrvatske.
Statistički ljetopis. (2008). http://www.dzs.hr/Hrv_Eng/ljetopis/2008/PDF/26-bind.pdf.
Statistički podatci o stanju pučkoga školstva u Hrvatskoj i Slavoniji svršetkom školske godine 1885/6. (1887). *Službeni glasnik kr. hrv. slav. dalm. zemaljske vlade, odjela za bogoštovje i nastavu*, komad III, 31. ožujka 1887, pp. 23–53.
Thomas, W. I. (1966). *On social organization and social personality. Selected papers*. M. Janowits (Ed.). Chicago: University of Chicago Press.
White paper on intercultural dialogue "Living together as equals in dignity." (2008). Strasbourg: Council of Europe.

Chapter 18
Reimagining Home in Alberta's Francophone Communities

Laura A. Thompson

Introduction

In the prairie province of Alberta, Canada, the recent phenomenon of French-speaking newcomers, who are multicultural, multiracial, multilingual, multiethnic, and multifaith, is putting into question the concept of a collective Francophone identity. On the one hand, Canadians would be challenged to identify Alberta as having a historical or emergent Francophone identity. On the other hand, changing demographics due to immigration are challenging the already elusive concept of Francophone identity across Canada, thus making the notion increasingly difficult to define. The question therefore is twofold: what is the meaning of Francophone heterogeneity in Alberta's Francophone communities, and what is the relevance of identity formation on Francophone education in an era of increasing Francophone pluralism on the Canadian prairies?

In this chapter, I would like to explore how three secondary school students perceive and construct their Francophone identity as lived in the predominantly Anglophone province of Alberta (about 4,000 km west of Québec, the predominantly Francophone province of Canada). Specifically, I would like to consider how stories of history, memory, language, and geography explore the lived experiences of Francophone youth in Alberta, especially during a time of rapid change. I draw this chapter's analysis from postcolonial authors such as Rushdie (1991), Hall (1994), and Bhabha (1994/2006) who contend that identities are not static but lived and are complicated by multiple and shifting subject positions, a fluid conception of identity which recognizes hybridity and difference. By looking at interrelated notions of living in-between and imagining home through a postcolonial lens, I see the borders of a singular Francophone identity within a heterogeneous school community as blurred and the chances for conceptualizing multilayered "Francophone" cultures and belongings as possible. To better understand the complexity of Francophone identity within Alberta, I situate the discourses of identity within a context of a

L. A. Thompson (✉)
School of Education, Acadia University, Box 57, Wolfville, Nova Scotia, Canada B4P 2R6
e-mail: laura.thompson@acadiau.ca

changing Canada in a globalized world as well as social and educational policy and curriculum documents for Francophone (school) communities. In conclusion, I suggest possible ways that educators can encounter these new challenges of complicating matters of Francophone identity, community, and belonging in an era of multiplicity.

Representing Francophone Identity

In order to understand (Franco-)Alberta's changing circumstances, it is important to reflect on how blurred borders of and shifting spaces of "Francophoneness" recast static definitions of "the Franco-Albertan" in a postcolonial context. Three terms will be used in this chapter: "Francophones," "French-Canadians," and "Franco-Albertans." While all three refer to French-speaking peoples, they are not used interchangeably. Canada has two official languages, English and French, and "Francophones" is the most general term to refer to those whose mother tongue is French[1] (Statistics Canada 2007). "French-Canadians" refers to the descendants of French settlers who came to North America in the seventeenth and eighteenth centuries, and the term was widely used until the 1960s. In Alberta, French-Canadians became known as Franco-Albertans, short for Francophone-Albertans. But with six out of ten "Franco-Albertans" born elsewhere in Canada and the world (based on 2001 Census data; see Fédération des communautés francophones et acadienne [FCFA] 2004, p. 4), it is becoming difficult to define who counts as "Franco-Albertan" because Francophones from other places and of various origins are contributing to the development of diasporic cultural identities within the Alberta francophonie.

In thinking about how Francophone identity is (and has been) represented in Alberta (or not), it is important to reflect critically on the emergence of new Francophone communities in Alberta and how the interplay of past and present (and future) problematizes fixed formulations of identity and belonging as White, Catholic, and French-Canadian (and if bilingual, then French-English bilingualism). Hall (1994) defines identity "as a 'production' which is never complete, always in process, and always constituted within, not outside, representation" (p. 392). How we come to name ourselves and our experiences and how we name those of others implicate not only subjectivities, but rather subject positions, which are complicated by varying and incomplete positions in a given time and place. While contextualizing is important, paying attention to the deep layers of difference is critical to reconsider the histories and cultures of "Francophones" in this time and place because, as Hall argues, "the difference *matters*" (p. 396, author's emphasis). Case in point: the French language may unify Francophones, but cultural identities separate them. For example,

---

[1] Statistics Canada (2007) defines mother tongue as the "first language learned at home during childhood and still understood by the individual at the time of the census." Based on Canada's most recent census in 2006, 1 out of 5 Canadians is Francophone.

the discourse of la Francophonie[2] places French speakers, wherever they may be (from), as "sharing a common language" and underpins all Organisation internationale de la Francophonie (OIF) activities "by the desire to promote and reinforce the use of French" throughout the world (OIF 2009). However, the discourse of the historical Alberta francophonie does not readily recognize the cultural implications of world-wide French colonial diasporas, that is, the dispersion and settlement of other French speakers of multiple races, religions, and cultures now in Alberta.[3] In other words, as member countries and governments of la Francophonie are dissimilar, so too are the peoples who make up the francophonie, including those who have settled and continue to settle in Alberta, because diasporic "Francophones" have different narratives of the past. This profound historical difference in cultural identity means that Alberta Francophone identity "belongs to the future as much as to the past" because cultural identity "is a matter of 'becoming' as well as of 'being'" which is subject to "the continuous 'play' of history, culture and power" (Hall 1994, p. 394). And in the current context of globalization, economic migration, cultural vitality and community renewal, this means that Francophone identity in Alberta is contingent on narratives of *both* the past and the future.

The future of minority Francophone communities lies in the colonial past through present-day public policy that is shaping Francophone diasporas. The Government of Canada has been promoting Francophone immigration in English-speaking Canada, including Alberta (Canadian Heritage 2004, 2008; Immigration and Citizenship Canada 2006). The federal government has been encouraging the integration of Francophone newcomers in all parts of Canada because community vitality and renewal is increasingly dependent on French-speaking newcomers from elsewhere across Canada and around the world (e.g., Canadian Heritage 2008; Jedwab 2002; Statistics Canada 2007). Francophone immigration policy, then, is influencing how the discourse of a static and seemingly continuous French-Canadian collective identity, memory, and home continues to be repositioned and even disrupted in an era of globalization. "Diaspora does not simply refer to dispersal," as Ashcroft et al. (2002a) explain, "but also to the vexed questions of identity, memory and home which such displacement produces" (pp. 217–218).

In his essay *Imaginary Homelands*, Rushdie (1991) invites us to consider profound uncertainties and new possibilities of identity and belonging in an era of change. He introduces his essay by questioning the peculiarity of an old photograph of a house, the interplay of past and present and one's sense of home. The

---

[2] *L'organisation internationale de la Francophonie* (OIF), with a capital F, refers to the international organization of 70 member states and governments on five continents, for whom French is an official or working language (OIF 2009).

[3] While the federal government's solution to enhance the vitality of Francophone communities (and the French language) is Francophone immigration, demographic shifts can also be met with resistance in Francophone minority communities who have long struggled for recognition. In their policy paper on fostering Francophone immigration, Immigration and Citizenship Canada (2006) states that the fight for Francophone schools and school governance as well as the recognition of fundamental rights "has sapped the communities' energy and has caused them to be somewhat closed off from others for several decades" (p. 2).

photograph reminds Rushdie, while revisiting Bombay, "that it's my present that is foreign, and that the past is home, albeit a lost home in a lost city in the mists of lost time" (p. 9). As Rushdie attempts to come to terms with another place/representation of home (especially as a migrant), and in thinking about the changing Alberta Francophone context with increased migration and immigration to the bountiful province, I picture a similar image. The past of the historical Franco-Albertan community (i.e., homogeneous White, Catholic, and French-Canadian) is home. However, like Rushdie's family home in his lost city of Bombay, the landscape of Francophone identity has changed and, therefore, should not be seen the same way, that is, "monochromatically" (p. 9). Rather, the history of Francophones in Alberta should not "restore the past" to a static sense of self, but become "whole," as a place with multiple histories and memories. And if Alberta were represented as a place with a history to reclaim, then one would have to ask what history and for whom.

Yet, the historical Franco-Albertan community is looking back to a homogeneous White, Catholic, and French-speaking community, while the emergent heterogeneous Francophone community is also looking back to different homelands from which the Canadian and world francophonies derive. Francophone spaces include Québec, Acadie, Lebanon, and numerous African countries, all of which were colonized by French-speaking European powers. In other words, there is a simultaneous looking back, or sense of loss. As Rushdie (1991) argues, those who are "out-of-country and even out-of language may experience this loss in an intensified form" (p. 12). And while Alberta Francophones share a common humanity of loss, the simultaneous looking back by both the historical and emergent communities creates a more profound sense of loss and sense of place. It also contributes to a haunting sense of uncertainty in a place where many "Francophones" inhabit, and have inhabited, many different "Francophone" homes and where they currently share the Francophone space in Alberta. This haunting tension ultimately creates "fictions, not actual cities or villages, but invisible ones, imaginary homelands, [francophonies] of the mind" (Rushdie 1991, p. 10). This can be seen as problematic for two reasons: because competing visions of homeland, real or imaginary, can conflict and because reflecting multiple visions of homeland and belonging in Francophone schools, communities, and curricula continues to be resisted in a place where ascribed notions of being Francophone have been constructed as being faithful to the traditional French-Canadian past of language, culture, and identity.

Francophones and non-Francophones educators alike need to come to terms with the increasingly plural Francophone presence in Alberta because shifts in Francophone demographics are influencing the social, cultural, political, religious, linguistic, economic, and educational landscape of the province. Between 2001 and 2006, the share of the Francophone population in Canada decreased due to the rapid growth of the overall immigrant population, displacing French and the official language group. In Alberta, however, the proportion of Francophones is increasing (only one of two provinces in Canada) due to immigration and interprovincial migration (Statistics Canada 2007, p. 16). Moreover, from 1999 to 2008, total Francophone school enrolment in Alberta's Francophone jurisdictions grew by 147.6%.[4] Considering the demographic need for French-speaking newcomers to counter low Francophone birth rates and to boost Canada's linguistic duality (Immigration and Citizenship Canada 2006; Quell 2002; Statistics Canada 2007) and considering Alberta's growing prosperity, it is accurate to say that the sharp increases in enrolment in Alberta's Francophone schools are primarily due to the arrival of newcomers to the province.

Furthermore, Alberta educational policy and social studies curricula clearly identify understanding Francophone peoples, perspectives and experiences as central to its educational goals. In 2001, the Alberta government introduced a framework for French first language education, and while the overall goals include "an openness to the world" generally, they also specify the importance of Francophone education in focusing on community belonging and pride. One expected outcome is that Francophone education will "introduce and instil an appreciation for the multiethnic, multilingual and intercultural nature of the Francophone community" (p. 12). Moreover, all social studies educators (including Anglophones) are mandated to teach, from Kindergarten to Grade 12, multiple Francophone perspectives. Alberta Education's (2005) social studies curriculum provides learning opportunities for students to "understand the multiethnic and intercultural makeup of Francophones in Canada," including "the historical and contemporary realities of Francophones in Canada" (p. 2).

While Francophone education in Alberta faces many challenges (e.g., funding levels, infrastructure issues, and anglicized families), profound demographic shifts in Alberta's francophonie are putting into question the very nature of the Franco-Albertan (school) community. The challenge, therefore, means rethinking who belongs to this community and reconsidering curriculum. Given the increasing pluralism in Francophone communities in Alberta and given the provincial curriculum mandates, it is critical for the Francophone educational milieu to reflect and value the diverse nature of lived Francophone experiences (Alberta Education 2005; Couture and Bergeron 2002; FCFA 2001, 2004; Gérin-Lajoie 2006; Moke Ngala 2005).

Theoretical Framework

The purpose of my inquiry was to seek a deeper understanding of the plurality and complexity of (youth) narratives within the "Franco-Albertan" lived experience. The interpretive process was multifold: contextual, dialogic, and poststructural (de Certeau 1988; Fine 1994; Foucault 1988; Saukko 2005) as well as postcolonial (Bhabha 1994; Burton 2003; Gikandi 1996, 2004). Rereading my participants' responses from postcolonial perspectives meant better understanding how they perceive their world(s) because my ten participants, an ethnoculturally diverse group of

---

[4] Based on 2009 statistics provided by the Information Services Branch of the Government of Alberta's Ministry of Education (2009), there are 5 Francophone school jurisdictions and 32 Francophone schools in Alberta. In 1999, there were 3 Francophone school authorities and 18 Francophone schools in Alberta.

Francophones attending the same high school, described their experiences of living in-between languages, cultures, and homes, thus positioning themselves and the category "Francophone" in different ways.

In a world of increased migration and globalization, of shifting borders and spaces, and of increased hybridity and difference, categories of identity and nation can become unstable (Burton 2003; Gikandi 1996, 2004). In the context of my research, revisioning constructions of Francophone identity in Canadian and Albertan contexts were informed by postcolonialism because "the Francophone" is constructed through differing worldviews in general and discourses of language, culture, and identity in particular. The interplay between and among discursive spaces of language, power, and resistance becomes all the more interesting because it complicates how one goes about describing who is Francophone in Alberta (and Canada) and what the Francophone world entails. Moreover, postcolonialism problematizes sociocultural and political realities of the French language across Canada and within the Francophonie, and of competing British and French legacies in the discursive space of belonging and living in-between.

The Research Project

What insights do student stories of lived Francophone experiences in Alberta offer about the francophonie in an era of accelerating pluralism? Drawing from the initial study, a small-scale research project that sought to understand this question, I am discussing the lived experiences of three out of the ten 12- and 13-year-old participants because these three represent the traditional and emerging communities of Francophones in Alberta. I am reporting on six one-on-one interviews and one focus group interview, to explore and discuss how they were making sense of their mixed social, cultural, and linguistic identities, and to build on their life histories.[5] I pursued my research in a Francophone school setting, not only because it is in this place that I can currently best study the lived experiences of Francophone students, but also because the notions of culture, language, and identity are deeply entrenched in educational policy and curriculum documents (e.g., Alberta Education 2005; Alberta Learning 2001). Furthermore, I selected an urban Francophone Catholic high school in Alberta as the research site because it reflects an increasingly diverse school community. Now the heterogeneous student population includes a significant proportion of students from African and Middle Eastern backgrounds, namely immigrants, refugees, and first-generation Canadians. These students tend to be either Catholic or Muslim. The majority of students are Caucasian and Catholic from various regions of Canada, namely Alberta, Québec, and Acadie. Students generally

---

[5] In the initial study, the ten student participants were invited to take part in interviews, which involved two one-on-one interviews as well as one focus group involving all participants. Participants were also invited to review the verbatim transcriptions of their two individual interviews. The series of three interviews lead to the writing of ten life history narratives.

speak two languages and increasingly three or four (e.g., French, English, Lingala, Kinyarwanda, Swahili, Spanish, and Arabic).

The student participants in this research project are connected by place, in the sense that they live in the prosperous province of Alberta, where all attended the same Francophone Catholic secondary school in an urban center during the 2005–2006 school year. For the initial study, participants were intentionally selected based on criteria such as gender, race, ethnicity, language background, birthplace (theirs and their parents'), and family milieu (e.g., two Francophone parents, Francophone/Anglophone, and Francophone/other). For Creswell (1998), establishing criteria for purposefully selecting participants within a large cultural group is useful to show different layers of experience. By presenting multiple perspectives of Francophone youth of different origins, I am in a better position to describe the complexity inherent in Francophone (school) communities in Alberta.

For the purpose of this chapter, I have chosen the responses of Léonie, Rania, and Karen, who chose their own pseudonyms. Léonie, born and raised in Alberta, is proud that her Franco-Albertan heritage goes back over 100 years.[6] Rania, of mixed Lebanese and Canadian heritage, and born and raised in Alberta, is proud to be trilingual. Karen, born in Rwanda and newcomer to Alberta but not to Canada, prefers to call herself "*Franco-Canadienne*" and "*Franco-Rwandaise*" and is adapting to life in Alberta. Together, their stories become part of a collective of Canada's and/or Alberta's Francophone story or, as Greene (1996) remarks, stories of community and difference "become part of the flow of the culture's story" (p. 42). And becoming part of a collective or flow involves interweaving stories, experiences, and meanings that draw attention to other narratives. Put another way, in telling their own story, they are also narrating it to wider stories of diversity, difference, history, and community (Goodson 2005). The words of the interviewed participants can help us better understand the multifaceted experiences and meanings of historical, contemporary, and emergent Francophone communities, including interrelated notions of living in-between and imagining home.

Relocating Alberta and Francophone Identity

In this chapter, I use the term diaspora as generally referring to the dispersion of peoples from their original homeland (often countries with a history of European colonialism), involving large and small patterns of migration due to varying political and economic conditions. Diaspora can be described as geographical, historical, and cultural, but as some postcolonial critics argue, diaspora is not merely geographical; it is "a central historical fact of colonization" (Ashcroft et al. 2002a, p. 217 and 2002b, p. 68). Alberta Francophones are diasporic because they make up

---

[6] Canada is a young country (created in 1867) and the province of Alberta younger still (created in 1905). Léonie's Franco-Albertan family would be considered a founding family of Alberta's Francophone community.

an ambiguous collective of French speakers (first language and increasingly second and third language) from various ethnocultural, racial, and religious backgrounds and having ties—primarily because of the French language—to a political, cultural, and linguistic geography that is the *francophonie internationale*. The Albertan francophonie, then, is a composite portrait produced by combining French-speaking peoples from different Francophone colonial hearths (there), creating distinct diaspora communities in Alberta (here). It is important to remember that these are not unitary, homogeneous, common, and noncontested spaces.

Rather, as McLeod (2000) explains, they are "composite communities" that are constructed: "Differences of gender, 'race', class, religion and language (as well as generational differences) make diaspora spaces dynamic and shifting, open to repeated construction and reconstruction" (p. 207). For example, within Alberta alone, there are multiple and varied diasporas (e.g., Acadian, African, and Arab) overlapping to create composite Francophone communities and it is important to understand how such diasporas play out in the context of Alberta. Ultimately, this difference can be recognized in the eyes of my young participants, including Léonie who is from a founding Franco-Albertan family. While none of my participants expressed their Franco-Albertan identity in purist terms, Léonie—who is proud of her French-Canadian and Catholic roots—alludes to the authenticity of one's Franco-Albertan origins.

> [Ê]tre Franco-Albertain, je pense qu'il faut que tu viennes de l'Alberta, parce que c'est comme ça que c'est.[7]

For Léonie, being Franco-Albertan means being from here because that's the way it is.

Léonie's use of the verb *venir de* speaks to one's particular origins, coupled with her insistence on the particular of Alberta (*il faut que*), makes her truly Franco-Albertan. It must be noted that Léonie did not come to this statement easily. My probing question on the possibility of Francophones new to Alberta calling themselves Franco-Albertan incites this long yet nuanced response by Léonie:

> Je sais pas. Bien, ça dépend pour moi parce que…comme plutôt non…mais aussi il y en a [*des francophones*] qui ont leur culture, mais ils sont nés en Alberta. Alors, je pense que oui, ils peuvent dire ça [*qu'ils sont Franco-Albertains*] parce qu'ils sont nés en Alberta puis ils sont juste comme ça. Ensuite il y en a qui viennent du Liban ici, puis je ne pense pas qu'ils peuvent dire ça [*qu'ils sont Franco-Albertains*]. Je pense qu'ils peuvent dire que «je suis Franco-Libanais» ou Franco-whatever d'où ils viennent. Mais d'être Franco-Albertain, je pense qu'il faut que tu viennes de l'Alberta, parce que c'est comme ça que c'est. Juste que tu sois né ici. Je sais pas trop, it's weird.[8]

---

[7] To be Franco-Albertan, I think that you need to come from Alberta, because that's the way it is.

[8] I don't know. Well, it depends for me because…well maybe no…but also they are some [*Francophones*] who have their own culture, but they are born in Alberta. Therefore, I think that, yes, they can say they are [*Franco-Albertan*] because they were born in Alberta and they are just like that. Then there are those who are from Lebanon and come here, but I don't think they can say that [*they are Franco-Albertan*]. I think that they can say that "I am Franco-Lebanese" or Franco-whatever where they're from. But to be Franco-Albertan, I think you have to be from Alberta because that's the way it is. Just that you are born here. I don't know, it's weird.

Léonie does not believe that Francophone ancestry and culture must be from Alberta alone. She recognizes the plurality of Francophone origins worldwide and here, in her home province. However, as Léonie becomes protective of Alberta as the traditional home of Franco-Albertans, she defines being Franco-Albertan in opposition to other Francophones. For example, Léonie does not think that all French-speaking newcomers to Alberta can call themselves Franco-Albertan, whether they be from other parts of Canada or the world. At first, she has difficulty making up her mind about who counts as Franco-Albertan. But as she considers Alberta's diverse Francophone population, she realizes that some of the others were born here as well, confusing her thinking. Beginning her answer with *ça dépend*, she moves to say *oui*, but then decides that being from here makes one Franco-Albertan, that being born here suffices. Ultimately, she concludes by saying "it's weird."

Living In-Between: Complicating Categories of Identity

In the National Film Board of Canada documentary film, *Between: Living in the Hyphen* (Nakagawa 2005), Canadian interviewees of mixed cultural and racial identity share their feelings of confusion that come from living in-between. One interviewee specifically refers to the "weird collision" when you find yourself between cultural identities and having to understand that difference. It is not because my 12- and 13-year-old participants are either young or inarticulate that they have difficulty making sense of identity and difference. History and memory, coupled with living in-between languages and cultures, make it difficult for anyone to articulate what identity formation is all about. And the collision between here and there, living in-between homes and hyphens, only complicates these matters. For Léonie, then, *une Franco-Albertaine de souche*[9] who is witnessing the change to the historicity of her traditional community, it must be confusing to distinguish between here and there. On the one hand, here is the *Alberta français* her family and ancestry have preserved and protected for over 100 years. And Léonie, a well-liked and respected student who has close friends from various social locations, knows that other Francophones in Alberta are born here as well. On the other hand, she does not recognize their origins as being authentically Franco-Albertan. Thus, the here is now complicated because there is here: there was born here.

To borrow from Rushdie (1991), it is Léonie's present Alberta that is "foreign" to her, with its heterogeneous French-speaking population being born in her home province and claiming to be Francophone Albertans. But Léonie's past Alberta is "home, albeit a lost home in a lost [province] in the mists of lost time" (p. 9) because Francophone others, who hail from different Francophone colonial places and cultures, are taking root in her home. This sense of loss coupled with a profound

---

[9] The expression *de souche* usually refers to old stock, as in White and Catholic Franco-Albertans who were born and bred in Alberta and who can trace their ancestry back to the original settlers of New France.

sense of place creates a tension in Léonie as she attempts to make sense of her Franco-Albertan community, past and present, and who rightly belongs. But, as Léonie has learned, that's not the way it is supposed to be *"parce que c'est comme ça que c'est."*

Léonie's nuanced and complicated response is interesting because she is living in-between (tensions of) a historical Franco-Albertan community and an emergent diasporic Francophone one. And living in a diaspora means living in-between and imagining "home" in different ways. For Léonie, this means constructing a sense of Franco-Albertan home that is pure, unchanged, and unchanging. *"Juste que tu sois né ici,"* or just that you are born here, alludes to an imagined *Alberta français*. Léonie's sense of Franco-Albertan identity is well-grounded in this place (*ici*) and well-founded in time and her sense of belonging is closely tied to a historical *Alberta français* comprised primarily of *Franco-Albertains de souche*.

If Franco-Albertan lineage or parentage is at issue for Léonie, and given the increasing numbers of ethnically diverse Francophone newcomers to Alberta, then perhaps the definition/perception of one's "home" also is. This is the case for Rania and Karen whose dreams of "home" have been influenced by different experiences of migration and involving the places of Lebanon, Rwanda, and Ontario. Rania is a Lebanese-Canadian born and raised in Alberta, and she imagines Lebanon—her parents' homeland—as her own. During both individual interviews, Rania speaks of Lebanon often, more so than of Alberta, and dreams of her family's extended stays in this warm and beautiful place.

> Oui, j'adore aller au Liban parce que toute ma famille est là. Puis la température, puis les beach, puis les océans, puis tous les… ya. Puis le manger, c'est tellement bon. Le poisson là, c'est vraiment bon.[10]

Rania's emotional attachment to Lebanon is strong and as her responses illustrate, experiences of migrancy affect both the migrant parents and their Canadian-born children because the families have constructed how they think about their "home" and Alberta, where they live. Although Rania and her family return to their "homeland" for extended visits, the result of living in Alberta means that Lebanon becomes constructed and, accordingly, Rania's Francophone/Canadian/Lebanese subject positions are discontinuous.

By discontinuity, I mean the split that exists between the idea of "home" and the experience of returning "home." Drawing from Avtar Brah's *Cartographies of Diaspora*, McLeod (2000) concludes that "home" is a mythic place of desire in the diasporic imagination. In this sense it is a place of no-return, even if it is possible to visit the geographical territory that is seen as the place of "origin" (p. 209). To "return home" is impossible because, as Rushdie (1991) argues, "the past is a country from which we have all emigrated, that its loss is part of our common humanity" (p. 12). [And being alienated from one's homeland] "almost inevitably means that we will not be capable of reclaiming precisely the thing that was lost; that we will,

---

[10] Yes, I love going to Lebanon because all of my family is there. And the temperature, and the beaches and the oceans, well all of the… And the food, it's so good. The fish there, it is very good.

18 Reimagining Home in Alberta's Francophone Communities

in short, create fictions, not actual cities or villages, but invisible ones, imaginary homelands" (p. 10).

How Rania, along with the other young Francophones, see "home" impacts the local Francophone community because their way of being in the world can be problematic for a community which imagines itself as here (in Alberta)—and as unified. When I ask Rania how she identifies herself, she gives this response:

> Je suis moitié-moitié. Moitié Canadienne, moitié Libanaise. Je ne dis pas francophone en général. Parce que ça, c'est juste comme juste comment je le dis. Franco, ça ne va pas vraiment dans ma tête. Parce que je parle seulement français quand je suis à l'école ou avec quelqu'un qui parle français.[11]

For Rania, then, who longs to be in Lebanon, speaking French and attending a Francophone school do not seem to help her develop a sense of belonging here— to *l'Alberta français*. And this discontinuity not only contradicts the role of the Francophone school, but also illustrates how the construct of "home" represents a "disjunction between here and there" and "a fractured, discontinuous relationship with the present" (McLeod 2000, p. 211). Rania's response displaces the Francophone (school) community of Alberta because Rania herself occupies a displaced position within two constructed and fractured spaces: home and school. Her "home" is lodged in memory, like Léonie's and Karen's, but her imaginary homeland not only houses individual ideas of belonging, her sense of self as not being Francophone disrupts the very notion of Franco-Albertan community and collectivity as one. Alberta's francophonie is disrupted by personal memories and by the diasporic present, whether it be French Canadian, Arab, or African, or overlapping fragments of these diasporas.

Helping to create, or at the very least direct our individual and collective attention to, hybrid and incomplete Francophone identities in *Alberta français* is the increasing number of Black African and French-speaking immigrant and refugee families in the predominantly English province of Alberta. Karen, who moved from the province of Ontario in 2005, does not yet feel at home in Alberta. Thus, she prefers to call herself Franco-Canadian rather than Franco-Albertan because she is not "used to here."

> J'aime mieux Franco-Canadienne parce que je ne suis pas vraiment Albertaine maintenant. Je ne suis pas vraiment habituée à ici. Oui [*on peut devenir Franco-Albertain*], si on vit plus d'années ici et on est used to here.[12]

Over time, Karen may be willing to associate more with Alberta but, in the meantime, she perceives herself as Franco-Canadian. For Karen, it is a question of belonging, and as she still does not identify with belonging here, she cannot imagine herself as Franco-Albertan. Karen agrees that one can become Franco-Albertan

---

[11] I am half and half. Half Canadian, half Lebanese. I don't usually say that I am Francophone. Because it is just, like, just how I say it. Franco, it doesn't really jive with me. Because I speak French only when I am at school or with someone else who speaks French.

[12] I prefer Franco-Canadian because I am not really Albertan right now. I am not really used to here. Yes [we can become Franco-Albertan], if we have lived here longer and we are used to here.

with time, once one has grown "used to here." But Karen has experienced multiple geographical locations, both real and imagined. While Karen also calls herself Franco-Ontarian, because *Ontario français* was her "second home" for 8 years of her life, she prefers to say that she is Franco-Rwandese. Karen was born in Rwanda, where she learned to speak French.

> Oui, [*je me dis Franco-Ontarienne*] un peu, parce que maintenant, Franco-Ontarienne, c'est ma deuxième…it's like my second home. J'étais là [*en Ontario*] presque toute ma vie. Je me dis Franco-Rwandaise un peu parce que c'est où je parlais français. C'est d'où je viens. Je suis née là. Je suis Franco-Rwandaise comme vraiment, puis un peu Franco-Canadienne.[13]

Karen's response to my question is particularly interesting to me because she speaks to a multilayered Francophone identity: home, birthplace, mother tongue, another tongue, and another home. She also quantifies her response by adding "un peu" to each statement: once again Karen speaks to a sense of becoming and belonging. *Peu à peu*, she became Franco-Rwandaise, then Franco-Ontarienne; little by little, Karen belongs. At the same time, she also leaves the door open to become Franco-Albertan, a subject position contingent on residence. Therefore, identifying with one particular group or another involves a dynamic process of being and belonging, an ambivalent space that juxtaposes perspectives, places, and times against each other.

Drawing from Bhabha (1994/2006), Karen's subjectivity, her Francophone senses of self, like her homes, cannot be fixed in time and space. Rather, they situate "home" as evershifting (Fine 1994), as imagined (McLeod 2000) and as incomplete (Huddart 2006), confusing the categories of Franco-Albertan identity and allowing for multiple Francophone subject positions in the same place all at once. Thinking of Alberta's Francophone communities as diasporic, in its fluidity, in its hybridity, "in its crossing of borders, opens up the horizon of place" (Ashcroft et al. 2002a, p. 218). And it is in this place of in-between that Karen can be both "Franco-Rwandaise comme vraiment, puis un peu Franco-Canadienne" and perhaps never be "used to here." While Karen dreams about returning to Africa some day, especially to visit with her aunts and cousins, she would like to see how it is to live in Rwanda.

> Oui, je veux voir mes tantes et mes cousins et tout ça. Pour voir comment c'est, comment c'est y vivre. Comme nous, on est plus chanceux qu'eux, parce qu'ils n'ont pas beaucoup de choses. Puis pour nous, don't take advantage of what you have. To learn qu'on a beaucoup et on doit être content de ça.[14]

Karen and her refugee family's experience of migration is dramatically different from Rania's, but both participants continue to imagine their homelands, which ori-

---

[13] Yes, [*I say that I am Franco-Ontarian*] a little, because now Franco-Ontarian, it's my second… it's like my second home. I was there [*in Ontario*] almost my whole life. I self-identify as Franco-Rwandese a little because that is where I spoke French [*learned to speak French*]. It is where I am from. I was born there [*in Rwanda*]. I am Franco-Rwandese really, and a little Franco-Canadian.

[14] Yes, I want to see my aunts and cousins and all that. To see how it is, how it is to live there. For us, we are luckier than they are because they do not have a lot of things. And for us, do not take advantage of what you have. To learn that we have a lot and we should be content knowing that.

ents them in Alberta. Although Karen dreams about visiting her Rwandese relatives, living in Rwanda where she and her family are originally from, being in Canada has helped her develop a sense of being in a privileged place, although where she belongs is still being negotiated—between Africa and Canada, between Ontario and Alberta, between there and here.

For Rania and Karen, like Léonie, these three young people are creating Lebanons, Rwandas, and Albertas of the mind because they are living in-between memories of history and geography, between imaginaries of past and present in two distinct geographical locations. Bhabha's notion of hybridization is useful when discussing Francophones' sense of selves because, like Rushdie, Bhabha (1994/2006) pushes the limits of purist claims of authentic cultural identities. In fact, he diverts our attention away from the idea of pure cultures to shed light on the "impurity" of cultures and, as Huddart (2006) explains this diversion, "cultures are the consequence of attempts to still the flux of cultural hybridities" (pp. 6–7). For Huddart, Bhabha insists on paying attention to the ongoing process that is cultural hybridity because it is what happens in-between cultures and identities, between self and other, and this is what is crucial to understand. To be Francophone, then, is to be in process, to be culturally mixed, to be and live in-between.

In general, my three participants speak to the postcolonial condition of imagining homelands and living in-between borders. While they all live in-between places (places with particular histories, languages, and cultures), their narratives tell us that searching for "here" and "there" and, ultimately, "home" is not an easy feat. Léonie, Rania, and Karen, who are confronted with mixed and mediated messages of here in relation to there and vice versa, remind us that borders are blurred and spaces shift, even in the same geographical location. The somewhere in-between, then, becomes more crucial when discussing a world of Francophone imaginings and reimaginings. Making sense of a world of in-betweens helps us to accept that, when we say we are "Franco-whatever" (or not), we are allowing for (dis)comfort, (dis)continuity, and uncertainty as well as possibilities of difference. Living in a diasporic Francophone community in Alberta means thinking about the disruptive effects of migration, but also the new, creative possibilities of being in a truly Francophone world. That is, bringing "there" home to Alberta "here" can help an increasingly diverse group of Francophones reconceptualize Francophone communities, Francophone homelands, and the Francophone world. As McLeod (2000) writes, the notion of home is "a valuable means of orientation" because it gives us a sense of our place in the world, not only telling us from where we originated but also where we belong. He also points to the concept of being "at home," of "occupy[ing] a location where we are welcome, where we can be with people very much like ourselves" (p. 210). But what happens to the idea of "home" and being "at home" in the "Franco-Albertan" community when Francophones from various places, throughout Canada and the world, come here? How does reimagining "home" and "community" in a pluralistic Francophone-Alberta help to orient ourselves towards a reimagination of grand narratives of Francophone identity?

Conclusion: Being in Relation with Francophone Others in an Era of Multiplicity

Jean Vanier (2003), in his book *Finding Peace*, suggests that real peace is about relationship, being in relation with other, and that a quest for peace means moving from a place of mourning to a place of gentle or personal encounter. As he writes, "We begin to move towards peace as we move away from our own labels and the labels we have put on others, and meet heart to heart, person to person" (p. 42). Working towards peace and, in turn, love and justice requires "hard work," emphasizing that "it can bring pain because it implies loss—loss of certitudes, comforts, and hurts that shelter and define us" (p. 44). Imagining a different Francophone home in Alberta can be painful not only because a rapidly shifting Franco-Albertan community is witnessing an intensified coming together of Francophone peoples in "their" home, but also because young people who make up this community are shifting towards a fluid, hybrid, and diasporic Francophone identity.

With respect to developing further possible ways on how to encounter these new challenges of complicating identity and reimagining home in complex Francophone spaces, it is important to consider the implications for classrooms, curriculum, and educational policy. In Canada, where teachers must draw on government-mandated curricula and where teachers in the Francophone school system must also rely on policy documents to support the Francophone educational project, it is important to reflect critically on what educators and school communities are being told about being "Francophone" and how they, in turn, understand and teach "Francophoneness" in an era of multiplicity. Essential for being with Francophone others is a deeper, more nuanced understanding of what "Francophone" means in culturally mixed spaces. How do students and teachers conceptualize "Francophone" identities and perspectives? If the mandate of the Francophone school is "to provide a schooling experience built around Francophone language, culture and community" (Alberta Learning 2001, p. 10), then it seems imperative to me that we first understand how young people and teachers understand "Francophoneness" in general and how they construct "Francophone language, culture, and community" in particular.

This personal and pedagogical process of understanding, recognition, and acceptance will require that school boards support teachers' efforts in reaching out to the increasing number of students and families who bring with them very different stories of being "Francophone." Simply acknowledging Francophone diversity at the local level and the importance of Francophone immigration to the vitality of Francophone communities at the provincial level does not suffice. For if Francophone newcomers are not welcomed or recognized as "real" Francophones and as "real" Canadians, then the crisis of representation will persist because French-speaking and English-speaking Canadians continue to accept static definitions of who counts as Francophone in Canada. Canadian teachers and curriculum developers should not be satisfied with "Francophone diversity," rather, they should challenge it by naming the narrow constructions and moving beyond celebratory approaches of a multicultural Francophone Canada.

As McCarthy et al. (2005) argue, it is important to contest "culture" in curriculum because it is an all-too-often "undertheorized" concept "still commonly treated in education as a pre-existent, unchanging deposit, consisting of a rigidly bounded set of elite or folkloric knowledges, values, experiences and linguistic practices specific to particular groups" (p. xix). By acknowledging that the word "Francophone" itself can neutralize the politics of home, representation and identity, educators can conceptualize "Francophone culture" critically by paying greater attention to the continued insistence on Eurocentric curriculum and identity in Canada. How well prepared and equipped are teachers and school board leaders to meet educational policy and curriculum objectives of countering assimilation and integrating students into the "Francophone culture community locally, nationally, and globally" which "is achieved through cultural and community experiences and commitments that nurture the Francophone identity and sense of belonging" (Alberta Learning 2001, p. 11)? This means professional development opportunities need to be provided to prospective and practicing teachers so that they can engage critically with their own understanding of cultural identities and their own histories as well as current thinking drawing on notions of white privilege, race, culture, and identity. This also means that teachers will need to supplement government-approved teaching materials to support planning and student learning in a culturally complex and evershifting Francophone world. Ultimately, this requires further research to map the "kinds of curricula–broadly defined–young people [and teachers] draw on to understand, explain, and live through the world around them" (McCarthy et al. 2005, p. xxviii).

By framing a discussion of Francophone curriculum perspectives within postcolonialism, a diasporic, hybrid postcolonial (Albertan) francophonie will be better explained, if not explained differently. The challenge of overlapping multiple and different "Francophone" languages, cultures, and identities becomes reconceptualizing Francophone curriculum perspectives to represent the complex layers to the Francophone world in Alberta in pluralistic and problematic ways. Such a reconceptualization is necessary if Francophone education is to contribute to the vitality and renewal of Francophone communities across Canada.

References

Alberta Education. Curriculum Branch. (2005). *Social studies kindergarten to grade 12.* Edmonton: Author.
Alberta Education. Information Services Branch. (2009). Statistics, student population, student population by grade, school and authority, Alberta (tables). http://education.alberta.ca/department/stats/students.aspx. Accessed 4 April 2009.
Alberta Learning. French Language Services Branch. (2001). *Affirming Francophone education—foundations and directions: A framework for French first language education in Alberta.* Edmonton: Author.
Ashcroft, B., Griffiths, G., & Tiffin, H. (2002a). *The empire writes back: Theory and practice in post-colonial literatures* (2nd ed.). London: Routledge.
Ashcroft, B., Griffiths, G., & Tiffin, H. (2002b). *Post-colonial studies: The key concepts.* London: Routledge.

Bhabha, H. K. (2006 [1994]). *The location of culture*. London: Routledge.

Burton, A. (Ed.) (2003). *After the imperial turn: Thinking with and through the nation*. Durham: Duke University Press.

Canada. Canadian Heritage. (2004). Official languages—community development and linguistic duality. *Bulletin, 9*(2), 41–42. http://www.patrimoinecanadien.gc.ca/progs/lo-ol/bulletin/vol9_no2/plan3_e.cfm#3h. Accessed 30 March 2005 from Canadian Heritage.

Canadian Heritage. (2008). *Roadmap for Canada's linguistic duality 2008–2013: Acting for the future*. Ottawa: Author.

Canada. Immigration and Citizenship. (2006). *Strategic plan to foster immigration to Francophone minority communities*. Ottawa: Author.

Couture, C., & Bergeron, J. (2002). Le multiculturalisme francophone et la question de la différence. In C. Couture & J. Bergeron (Eds.), *L'Alberta et le multiculturalisme francophone: témoignages et problématiques* (pp. 15–18). Edmonton: Centre d'études canadiennes de la Faculté Saint-Jean et l'Association Multiculturelle Francophone de l'Alberta.

Creswell, J. W. (1998). *Qualitative inquiry and research design: Choosing among five traditions*. Thousand Oaks: Sage.

de Certeau, M. (1988). *The practice of everyday life* (trans: Rendall, S.). Berkeley: University of California Press.

Fédération des communautés francophones et acadienne (FCFA) du Canada. (2001). *Parlons-nous! Dialogue*. Ottawa: Author.

Fédération des communautés francophones et acadienne (FCFA) du Canada. (2004). *Francophone community profile of Alberta*. Ottawa: Author.

Fine, M. (1994). Working the hyphens: Reinventing self and other in qualitative research. In N. K. Denzin & Y. S. Lincoln (Eds.), *Handbook of qualitative research* (pp. 70–82). Thousand Oaks: Sage.

Foucault, M. (1988). Technologies of the self. In L. H. Martin, H. Gutman, & P. H. Hutton (Eds.), *Technologies of the self: A seminar with Michel Foucault* (pp. 16–49). Amherst: University of Massachusetts Press.

Gérin-Lajoie, D. (2006). La contribution de l'école au processus de construction identitaire des élèves dans une société pluraliste. *Éducation et francophonie, 34*(1), 1–7.

Gikandi, S. (1996). *Maps of Englishness: Writing identity in the culture of colonialism*. New York: Columbia University Press.

Gikandi, S. (2004). Poststructuralism and postcolonial discourse. In N. Lazarus (Ed.), *The Cambridge companion to postcolonial literary studies* (pp. 97–119). Cambridge: Cambridge University Press.

Goodson, I. F. (2005). *Learning, curriculum and life politics: The selected works of Ivor F. Goodson*. London: Routledge.

Greene, M. (1996). Plurality, diversity, and the public space. In A. Oldenquist (Ed.), *Can democracy be taught?* (pp. 27–44). Bloomington: Phi Delta Kappa Educational Foundation.

Hall, S. (1994). Cultural identity and diaspora. In P. Williams & L. Chrisman (Eds.), *Colonial discourse and post-colonial theory: A reader* (pp. 392–403). New York: Columbia University Press.

Huddart, D. (2006). *Homi K. Bhabha*. London: Routledge.

Jedwab, J. (2002). *Immigration and the vitality of Canada's official language communities: Policy, demography and identity*. Ottawa: Office of the Commissioner of Official Languages.

McCarthy, C., Crichlow, W., Dimitriadis, G., & Dolby, N. (2005). Transforming contexts, transforming identities: Race and education in the new millennium. In C. McCarthy, W. Crichlow, G. Dimitriadis, & N. Dolby (Eds.), *Race, identity and representation in education,* (2nd ed., pp. xv–xxix). New York & London: Routledge.

McLeod, J. (2000). *Beginning postcolonialism*. Manchester: Manchester University Press.

Moke Ngala, V. (2005). *L'intégration des jeunes des familles immigrantes francophones d'origine africaine à la vie scolaire dans les écoles secondaires francophones dans un milieu urbain en Alberta: conditions et incidences.* Unpublished master's thesis, University of Alberta, Edmonton, Alberta, Canada.

Nakagawa, A. M. (Director). (2005). *Between: Living in the hyphen* [video recording]. Montréal, Québec: National Film Board of Canada.

Organisation internationale de la Francophonie (OIF). (2009). *Organisation internationale de la Francophonie: Qui sommes-nous?* http://www.francophonie.org/Qui-sommes-nous.html. Accessed 6 December 2009.

Quell, C. (2002). *Official languages and immigration: Obstacles and opportunities for immigrants and communities*. http://www.ocol-clo.gc.ca/archives/sst_es/2002/obstacle/obstacle_e.htm. Accessed 3 October 2006.

Rushdie, S. (1991). *Imaginary homelands: Essays and criticism 1981–1991*. London: Granta & Viking Penguin.

Saukko, P. (2005). Methodologies in cultural studies: An integrative approach. In N. Denzin & Y. Lincoln (Eds.), *The Sage handbook of qualitative research* (3rd ed., pp. 343–356). Thousand Oaks: Sage.

Statistics Canada. (2007). The evolving linguistic portrait, 2006 census, Catalogue 97–555-XWE2006001, Released 4 December 2007. http://www12.statcan.ca/census-recensement/2006/as-sa/97-555/index-eng.cfm?CFID=2774042&CFTOKEN=22898055. Accessed 18 May 2009.

Vanier, J. (2003). *Finding peace*. Toronto: House of Anansi Press.

Chapter 19
New School, New System: The Experiences of Immigrant Students in Irish Schools

Merike Darmody, Emer Smyth, Delma Byrne and Frances McGinnity

Introduction

Exceptional economic growth from the mid-1990s onwards transformed Ireland from a country of emigration to one of large-scale immigration. In general, immigrants to Ireland have been a highly heterogeneous group in terms of nationality, language skills, ethnicity, religion and legal status. However, the largest group of recent immigrants has come from the new member states of the European Union. Within the last decade, there has also been a marked increase in the number of immigrant families coming to Ireland accompanied by school-age children (Central Statistics Office [CSO] 2008). This has presented challenges to schools who previously catered to a relatively ethnically homogenous student intake, mainly Catholic, White and mono-cultural (see Devine 2005). Ireland is therefore a particularly interesting case study because of the extent, pace and heterogeneity of recent immigration. Furthermore, a striking feature of the Irish situation is the high level of educational qualifications among the immigrant population (CSO 2008). All of these features mean that the experience of immigrant students in Ireland may differ from the experiences of young immigrants in 'classical immigration countries'.

International research has highlighted the crucial role of schools in the integration of children and young people into the new society (Gitlin et al. 2003). Immigrant children spend a large part of their day at the school of the 'host' country, where they encounter students and teachers from the majority culture and learn to adjust to a new institutional environment. In these environments, dominant cultural norms are transmitted by teachers and students explicitly—via the formal (curriculum of a subject area), or implicitly—via hidden (attitudes, values, beliefs and behaviour) curriculum (Ross 2003; Apple 1971). Social interaction with peers and teachers is therefore a crucial influence on the settling-in process of new students (Cummins 2001; Dimakos and Tasiopoulou 2003) and has important implications for access to and acquisition of culturally relevant knowledge and norms. These processes

M. Darmody (✉)
The Economic and Social Research Institute, Whitaker Square, Dublin 2, Ireland
e-mail: merike.darmody@esri.ie

are also important at macro level, as cultural transmission aids the integration of immigrant children. School is also the first setting where being an 'insider' or an 'outsider' is actively negotiated between pupils and teachers.

This chapter critically employs the cultural reproduction framework to explore the experiences of immigrant students in Ireland. In doing so, it draws on data from a pioneering, large-scale, mixed methods study on school provision for immigrant students,[1] comprising both primary and secondary school sectors. This chapter draws on focus group interviews with Irish and immigrant students, placing their accounts in the context of the perceptions of school principals and teachers.

Recent Migration to Ireland: Children and Youth

The economic boom in Ireland from the 1990s onwards resulted in a marked expansion in employment and the emergence of labour shortages. Such shortages resulted in an unprecedented increase in immigration to Ireland: net migration increased from 8,000 per annum in 1996 to almost 70,000 per annum in 2006. According to census figures from 2006, just over 10% of the population (almost 420,000 people) were foreign nationals. The immigrant flow was disproportionately made up of working-age adults. However, the number of immigrant children and young people also increased: In 2006 almost 7% of the 5–19-year-old group were foreign nationals. A significant minority of these are of UK origin, and, combined with children of US origin and a number of other nationalities, about 40% of immigrant children are from English-speaking countries. Approximately 40% of all foreign nationals are from the EU15 or EU10 countries. There are also more African children than Asian children in the 5–19 age group, though fewer Africans than Asians in the whole population.

In their recent study, Smyth et al. (2009) estimate that immigrant students made up approximately 10% of the primary school-going population and 6% of the secondary population in 2007. The distribution of immigrant students across schools in the two sectors is quite different: The vast majority of secondary schools have at least one immigrant student but immigrants make up a relatively modest proportion of students (2–9%) within each school. The primary school sector is more polarized: Four in ten schools have no immigrant students while in some schools immigrant students make up more than a fifth of the total cohort. It is important to note that the body of immigrant students in Ireland is very heterogeneous with students coming from a number of different countries and speaking over a hundred different languages. A response to the needs of these students which puts in place appropriate policy initiatives requires better understanding of the experiences of these young people and the cultural processes that shape those experiences. The critical use of cultural reproduction theory facilitates such an understanding.

---

[1] For the purposes of this study, an 'immigrant student' is defined as a student whose parents were born outside Ireland.

Theoretical Framework

This chapter uses the cultural reproduction or transmission framework to trace the experiences of immigrant students in the school setting in Ireland. Cultural reproduction theory, put forward by Bourdieu, originated as a framework for understanding social class differences in the transmission of advantage from one generation to the next. Bourdieu emphasized the role of economic, cultural and social resources in this process and suggested that individuals develop a class-specific habitus, that is, a set of dispositions, orientations and values, which guide their behaviour (see Bourdieu 1977). From this perspective, middle-class children develop within the home the kinds of cultural and social skills which facilitate their progress in the school system, and have exchange value in the wider society. This cultural capital consists of familiarity with the dominant (largely middle class) culture in a society (Bourdieu 1977). The dominant culture is also transmitted through educational system, as schools are not socially neutral institutions (Wong 1998). However acquired, at home or in school or both, cultural capital of the dominant group can be converted into social and economic advantage in later life. In contrast, the mismatch between home and school cultures, where home culture lacks recognized 'currency', contributes to the underperformance of working-class children and, hence, more limited life chances.

While initially formulated in terms of social class, Bourdieu's theory of cultural capital has been expanded by subsequent theorists (see, for example, Lareau and Horvat 1999; Goldstein 2003; Monkman et al. 2005) to take account of cultural diversity in terms of nationality and/or ethnicity. These authors suggest that the policies and practices of the school are familiar to students from the dominant group, that is, the 'insiders' who possess this information as a part of their cultural capital, whereas members of minority immigrant groups, possessing different cultural capital, norms and values, are often in the position of 'outsiders' (Bourdieu 1984). Later, in his *Practical Reason: On the Theory of Action*, Bourdieu (1998) argues that the 'outsider' status of immigrants may differ across groups since some immigrant families are more likely than others to be in a position to access information on the education system of the receiving country and internalize its cultural preferences (Weine et al. 2004). The ease with which immigrant families adapt to the culture of the 'host' country also depends on their social class background (Lareau and Horvat 1999).

For immigrant children, the school is their primary source of contact with the majority culture, and thus an important site for acquiring knowledge of the lingua franca of the receiving country, culturally relevant knowledge, skills and attitudes of the receiving country (Park-Taylor et al. 2007; Trickett and Birman 2005). However, immigrant children and their parents are less likely than the native-born population to possess the insider know-how to successfully navigate their way through the school system—to have 'the feel for the game' (Bourdieu 1977). These families often rely on 'grapevine knowledge' (see Ball and Vincent 1998). Immigrant students therefore depend on positive social interaction with peers and teachers in order to plot a course through the new educational system and to translate newly acquired social and academic knowledge into success both in and beyond school (Boyer 2000; Saez-Marti and Sjögren 2007). Teachers play a key role in helping students develop more open and inclusive attitudes (Cummins 2001), essential for creating a supportive environment for immigrant students and transmitting culturally relevant knowledge. However, schools and teachers may also act (consciously or subconsciously) to legitimate the dominant culture (Bernstein 1975) and thus contribution to the undervaluation of minority cultural and social capital (Gibson and Ogbu 1991). For many immigrant students, interaction with other immigrants also provides a useful social network: peers from the same country of origin can provide information that helps the new arrivals to become familiar with the new organizational structure as well as social spaces in the school (Goldstein 2003). Social knowledge can also be transmitted by indigenous peers by social activities, i.e. play and sports. The more included the immigrant students are in these activities, the more cultural knowledge they acquire (Davis 2005).

The 'mismatch', or cultural distance, between home and school cultures may vary across nationalities or linguistic groups as well as social class depending on various types of capitals at their disposal. In addition, immigrant children come to the 'host' country with their own attitudes to learning and learning styles—influenced by practices in the home country—that may be dissimilar to the ones practiced in the receiving country (Baluja 2001).

In this chapter, at micro level, we conceptualize immigrant children and their parents as possessing different quantities of economic, social and cultural capitals that are necessary for successful education in the 'host' country. Thus, highly educated immigrant parents may be 'outsiders' in terms of not knowing how the new school system operates but in other respects may be 'insiders' since they know the kinds of behaviours which are likely to contribute to school success. A further refinement of the cultural transmission perspective is also necessary. Bourdieu's work on social and cultural reproduction has frequently been criticized for being overly deterministic[2] (see Jenkins 2002) and therefore at odds with emerging educational research which emphasizes the importance of children's voice and agency (see Clark et al. 2003). Later refinements of Bourdieu's framework have allowed for the fluid nature of social reproduction, arguing that 'an individual's class and racial position affect social reproduction, but they do not determine it' (Lareau and Horvat 1999, p. 50). We therefore focus on the perspectives of young people on their school experiences and regard them as active agents, who can shape their relations with teachers and peers.

A good deal of research on immigrant children and young people has focused on the factors shaping academic achievement (see, for example, Organisation for Economic Co-operation and Development [OECD] 2006). Here we focus not on academic outcomes but the experiences of social interaction with peers and teachers. International research has indicated that the successful integration of new ar-

---

[2] Other commentators have, however, denied this position arguing that Bourdieu allows for individual agency (see, for example, King 2005; Grenfell and James 1998).

rivals is essential for ensuring social cohesion in the 'host' countries and for the well-being of immigrants themselves (OECD 2006; Eurydice 2004). Furthermore, Irish research has indicated that for all students positive interaction with teachers contributes to school completion, higher academic performance and more positive social/personal development outcomes (Smyth 1999). Since peers play an important part in children's school experiences and socialization (Smyth et al. 2009), the chapter also considers the experiences of both Irish and immigrant students.

Methodology and Data

This chapter draws on a large-scale study of school provision for immigrant children at the primary and secondary levels.[3] The study used a mixed methods approach combining quantitative and qualitative research methods in order to provide a better understanding of the phenomenon, gaining a fuller picture. Firstly, data from the postal questionnaires provided an overall picture of provision for immigrant children in Irish schools. Secondly, interviews provided voices for the key personnel and students in the case study schools and enabled the authors to tap into rich and invaluable information.

The survey stage provided nationally representative data on ethnic diversity in primary and secondary schools. It involved a postal survey of a sample of 800 primary school principals and all secondary school principals, selected to be representative of the population of schools in terms of school size, school type, location and disadvantaged status. The survey provided a unique insight into the issues facing schools in catering for the educational needs of different groups of pupils.

The national survey of school principals was used to determine the criteria for selecting six primary and six secondary schools for case study analysis. These schools were selected to capture key dimensions of the experiences of different schools in managing diversity. Within each of the schools, interviews were carried out with principals and a selection of teachers with various functions. Within primary schools, group interviews were carried out with older (fifth or sixth class) students in order to explore their perspective. Within secondary schools, interviews were carried out with small groups of second- and fifth-year students. Interviews explored the issues raised in the postal survey in much greater detail, allowing us to explore potentially different perspectives within the school. Group interviews were carried out separately with Irish and immigrant students in each of the schools. A total of 43 group interviews were conducted with students while 82 in-depth interviews were carried out with school personnel. Interviews were recorded, transcribed and coded. These case studies yielded more detailed insights into issues relating to diversity 'on the ground' in schools.

---

[3] The original research was funded by the Department of Education and Skills, Ireland. However, the views expressed in this chapter are those of the authors.

In this chapter, we mainly draw on both student interviews and teacher accounts to provide a holistic view of the integration process. The following section presents the main issues identified by both teachers and students with regard to the experiences of immigrant students in Irish schools. The perspectives of teachers and students are presented *in tandem*, in order to provide more comprehensive understanding of cultural transmission and social learning in the school context.

Research Findings

Language Proficiency

Proficiency in the language of the 'host' country is a vital component in the cultural transmission process. Bernstein (1971) has described language 'as the major process through which culture is transmitted' (p. 119). Not surprisingly, the Green Paper on Migration and Mobility (European Commission 2008) identifies proficiency in the language of instruction as a key factor for success of immigrant students at schools of 'host' countries. According to both teacher and student accounts, proficiency in English was one of the major challenges for most immigrant students participating in our study, impacting on both academic progress and social integration:

> The language barrier is the biggest one, definitely. … It can be quite isolating I think for the students themselves when they don't have the language and their peers all around them are having conversations and laughing and messing at lunch time and they don't know what's going on, I think that's the biggest issue really. (Secondary school teacher)

Similar sentiments were expressed by immigrant students themselves who reported feeling isolated and uncomfortable, at least when first arriving at the new school:

> Because when people like ask you to play with them like, they could be asking you forever because you don't know what they're on about or anything. (Primary school pupils)

Even where students already had some English language skills, accent and the informality of day-to-day speech made the situation difficult:

> My English is not perfect, I learn English in Poland but here I cannot understand sometimes because I learn pure English, not here, it's different.

Integration into the new school setting and academic success requires not only conversational fluency in English but the specialized terminology required for academic subjects, an issue which was particularly pertinent for older (secondary school) students.

> Well I knew English before I came, not much but I knew a lot so it helped me out. But I did find it hard like…you know the terminology in Maths and everything I was just like 'oh my god what is he talking about?'.

It could be argued that language difficulties may disadvantage immigrant children in terms of options available for them in future either in tertiary education or high position jobs in the labour market.

According to the European Commission (2008) immigrant children require a full command of the language of the receiving country for full integration (p. 8). For many new arrivals mother tongue as part of the cultural capital 'looses currency' through the immigration process and lingua franca of the receiving country becomes vital in accessing information about and functioning in the new environment, learning about 'rules of the game' (Bourdieu 1984). Proficiency in the 'new' language has implications not only for immigrant children themselves but also their parents who may also lack language proficiency (see Smyth et al. 2009). In our study, English language proficiency therefore emerged as a necessary condition for the cultural transmission process in Irish schools. However, it was not a sufficient condition since, as will be seen in the analysis that follows, even proficient English speakers could assume 'outsider' status in the new school system.

Institutional Differences

For many immigrant children and young people, moving to Ireland involves a major cultural shift that also includes making the transition from one educational system to another. Research evidence shows that the problem for many immigrant pupils is that the schools in a receiving country—vehicles of dominant culture—have certain expectations of the 'new arrivals', in line with the school ethos and expectations (European Commission 2008). In our study, teachers generally acknowledged that moving to a new country constitutes a major change and upheaval in the lives of immigrant students in terms of adjusting to a new language, culture and educational system:

> It's a new country, a new language, new culture, new system; it must be very difficult for some of them. ... I wouldn't even go to estimate how difficult it is for them, very difficult I'd say. (Secondary school teacher)

Reflecting the relatively recent nature of immigration into Ireland, almost all of the immigrant students in the study had begun their schooling career in their native country, although some of the younger immigrant students in primary schools had begun their education in Ireland. In general, school organization and process in Ireland were seen as very different from those in their home countries—reflecting cultural distance of the national education systems. Firstly, Irish schooling, especially at secondary school level, was generally seen as less strict, with less formal relations between teachers and students than many immigrant students had previously experienced.

> In Ireland I think a lot of people use bad words. I think in Poland when you use bad words... Yeah, you are suspended.

A number of immigrant students from Africa remarked on the absence of corporal punishment in Ireland:

> It would be less strict than in Nigeria, yeah. They are really, really strict, they are like...if you don't do your homework you are hit with a cane, if you are late you get hit with a cane, anything you do they hit you.

Secondly, several immigrant students in secondary school referred to a difference in academic demands, mainly finding the schoolwork easier than in their home country.

> Yeah, they are different to Poland schools because in Poland it's very difficult, it's a lot of subjects, lots of study but here it's not bad.

Moving to a new educational system means that immigrant students are 'outsiders' in terms of knowing how the new system operates. However, the fact that many of the students had previously experienced strict schools with a strong emphasis on academic standards meant that they often demonstrated the kinds of behaviour and attitudes to schoolwork that are valued by the school system (right dispositions). Considering the high levels of academic achievement among most adult immigrants in Ireland (discussed earlier in the chapter) it could be argued that despite lower levels of economic and different cultural and social capital, they have positive dispositions towards academic success that could in future be exchanged to success in education and beyond.

There is some research evidence which indicates that social relations between teachers and minority ethnic students are somewhat less positive than those for native-born students (see Irvine 1990; Fine 1991; Nieto 1992), and immigrant students are seen to have issues with discipline (Monroe 2005), in certain countries. Several of these studies reflect teacher expectations that are informed by acceptable behaviour and attitudes. However, in Ireland, Devine (2005) found that teachers generally hold positive views of immigrant students, especially those who come from Eastern Europe. Immigrant students in Ireland are generally considered to be motivated learners who display positive attitudes towards school and teachers (Vekic 2003; Devine et al. 2004; Darmody 2007).

In general, the primary and secondary school teachers participating in this study held positive views on immigrant students, in line with earlier research by Devine and Kelly (2006): '*[T]hey would be very intelligent most of them*' (Secondary teacher), '*they're very motivated, and sometimes they're more motivated than normal students...They're not problematic people, they're lovely to deal with, they're gorgeous in fact...diligent workers*' (Secondary teacher). Immigrant students themselves reported getting on well with Irish teachers. However, some teachers tended to construct immigrant students as 'other' while legitimizing native-born students as 'normal', as seen from the quote above.

In those case study schools serving a working-class intake, teachers at times clearly contrasted the harder working, better-behaved immigrant students with the 'local' students who were seen as more disengaged from school. This difference was seen as rooted in the higher educational aspirations of immigrant parents for their children.

> A lot of them are very, very able children and this is a...school which would have a high number of educationally disadvantaged children. ...I would have said the advent of the newcomer children would have lifted the base because as I'm sure the teachers told you

some of their parents are very, very ambitious for them and they would be the children of the up and at it, you know. (Primary school teacher)

In sum, immigrant children and their parents are faced with negotiating their way through a school system with which they are unfamiliar and which may differ from the one in their home country—rendering them 'outsiders'. This can result in a mismatch between culture and expectations at home and school. At the same time, the highly educated profile of immigrant parents in Ireland, coupled by the prior experience among a significant number of immigrant students of an academically orientated, strict school context, can mean that immigrant children engage in their schoolwork and behave in the classroom in ways that are valued by the school system. Arguably, this can facilitate their experience of cultural transmission process at school.

Social Interaction with Peers

As well as encountering a new school system, immigrant students are faced with a new peer group. According to the European Commission (2008), peers have a substantial influence on the achievement of immigrant children (p. 7). In only a few Irish schools (see above) do immigrant children join schools with substantial numbers of other immigrants; even fewer attend schools with significant numbers of peers from their own national or cultural group. This means that many immigrant children do not have social networks from their own country from where to gain 'insider knowledge' of the system. Most immigrant students in the study reported that they did not know anyone in the school before they came, which was seen as making the first day at school particularly daunting:

> I think it's still hard because you're used to the people that were in your other school or where you are from and then if you move to a new school you kind of like feel scared because there's not much people you know.

In contrast, knowing someone in the school beforehand was seen as easing the transition process, providing a 'familiar face' but also a degree of insider information on how the school operates.

A number of teachers in the case study schools remarked on the tendency of immigrant students to 'group together', particularly if they were recent arrivals. This pattern was seen to vary across national and cultural groups with Eastern European students seen to mix better compared to other immigrant groups:

> The Eastern Europeans mix very well. The Africans tend to stay among themselves. (Secondary teacher)
> The Chinese in particular are a very close knit group that won't mingle with other students. (Secondary school teacher)

Social integration was also seen to vary by student age and stage, since it is harder for older students to integrate into already established friendship groups, whereas younger students coming into first year may find making friends with Irish students easier as everybody is 'new' and they can gradually build up friendships. A number of Irish students similarly reported that immigrants tended to socialize with each other at break times; leading to a degree of segregation in friendship patterns running along nationality and language lines:

> They all kind of make their own little groups and they're all from different countries.

Arguably, this may make general integration process of the new arrivals longer and more difficult.[4] This degree of segregation appeared to coexist, for the most part, with relatively friendly relations between immigrant and Irish students. However, national data indicate that immigrant children are more likely to experience bullying than their native-born peers (Molcho et al. 2008). In the same vein, immigrant students in a number of the case study schools in our study reported being bullied or seeing their classmates bullied on the basis of nationality.

> The only way they think is to slag and throw stuff, do whatever, just anti-social behaviour. Well they think that, well only one or two of them 'ah foreigners' you know, because they are in our country.

In secondary schools, such bullying was seen as more common among younger students, but was also evident at primary level:

> (An Irish student) turned around and told me 'what are you doing here, get back to Africa'.
> …
> Say oh go home you stupid Lithuanian and stuff like that.

In general, a degree of segregation in friendship patterns is likely to limit the extent to which immigrant children can absorb cultural and social capital from their Irish-born peers. Where bullying occurs, this is likely to further impede the cultural transmission process. Segregation is reinforced by 'withdrawing' immigrant students from some subject classes for additional English language support.

Cultural Distance

Immigrant students in Ireland come from a range of European and non-European countries. Thus, the cultural distance, or gap between cultures, may vary depending on nationality, ethnicity, language and other factors. The extent of cultural distance is likely to influence cultural transmission processes in the school. As a result, European immigrants were seen by teachers as having more similar styles of interaction to Irish students than non-European, especially African, families:

> For me here, they would say that the Africans would keep things among themselves, they will not come forward, in relating to personal problems or difficulties. And we have difficulties here with some parents who will come up, and who will, in front of us, will hit their children, the Africans in particular. (Secondary school teacher)

---

[4] However, socializing with students from the same linguistic background provides immigrant students with an opportunity to help to maintain fluency in their mother tongue.

19 New School, New System: The Experiences of Immigrant Students in Irish Schools

In two of the secondary schools, there were perceived problems with social interaction between female teachers and some male immigrant students reflecting different cultural norms in Ireland and Iraq:

> But that case now there's a young fellow there in third year from Iraq and he's a very aggressive young fellow and he doesn't like women. And he gets very aggressive and sometimes really aggressive towards female teachers and other students ... (Secondary school teacher)

In addition, some immigrant female students at second level found it difficult to address a male teacher when experiencing social difficulties:

> Yeah, any boy teacher, because like two years in a row we had to fix our fights ourselves because we were too shy to say something to men so we had to wait and say it to our duty teachers.

It can be argued that students coming from very different national and family backgrounds may find it harder to adjust to the social norms in Ireland. The likelihood of students being bullied appeared to be greater for more culturally distant groups, with African children more likely to experience bullying than their Eastern European counterparts (see also Devine et al. 2004):

> When [she] first came to this school the boys used to call her like Smarty and.
> M&M's.
> Chocolate.
> Chocolate with chocolate fudge on top and stuff.
> ...
> It was horrible.
> (Irish primary students)

Perhaps the most striking example of the cultural 'gap' between home and school related to the situation of asylum-seeking and refugee children, especially those who were unaccompanied minors. Unaccompanied minors and asylum-seeking children face specific challenges when entering a new country. Generally, they lack informal social support networks that would facilitate the adjustment process. Some teachers participating in this study commented on the personal difficulties and trauma experienced by unaccompanied minors, factors that are likely to affect their settling-in process:

> We're all very conscious, all the teachers are conscious that...they live in hostels...and [Student T] now at the moment, is between houses...and it's very difficult. [Student W], in first year, who moved...and they have two buses to get. So that's now that must be very difficult. ...We had one girl, a number of years ago, who had experienced savage [events], I mean this girl had seen slaughter and you name it. (Secondary school teacher)

In one school, teachers acknowledged additional difficulties posed by the processes involved in applying for asylum:

> I mean we had [a large number of] unaccompanied minors in the ages between fifteen and seventeen and eighteen, and they were going through the asylum process, on their own, and this was impacting on them significantly because in most cases, in the initial stages, I mean it is quite a complicated process, it's a very legalistic process, and for a young lad to be going through that on his own! (Secondary school teacher)

Historically, Irish primary schools are denominational in nature, with four-fifths of the schools under Roman Catholic management. Immigrants to Ireland are not only linguistically and culturally diverse, but differ from the majority of Irish population in their religious profile. At present, there are Educate Together multidenominational schools at primary school level and two Muslim schools which means that many Catholic schools have immigrant students with different religious background. In one school, major difficulties around the issue of religion were reported by a teacher with a Muslim child in a Catholic school:

> They had a huge difficulty around religion, because it is a Catholic school and they were Muslim themselves, but they had a fear, somewhere along the line they had a fear that we would try to change their children to Catholics and we didn't have Kurdish and they didn't have English to explain, every child is welcome,…if we say a prayer they don't say their prayer, they get quiet time and things like that, you know. (Primary school teacher)

A degree of cultural distance could impact not only on social interaction but also on learning, since some school subjects require knowledge of Irish, or at least European, subject areas. Typical comments from immigrant students included:

> We didn't do good in like history or something because it was all about Ireland and stuff.

Cultural Transmission: A One-Way Street?

In theory, cultural transmission can be a two-way process, with each group of children as active agents learning from the other. In terms of cultural awareness, some schools in this study had celebrated specific festivals or events associated with other national groups while some classes had done projects on different countries. However, these approaches have, by and large, remained 'tokenistic' and are more likely constructing immigrant children as 'other'.

> We have an international day for international kids.
> …
> Like they dress up in their national costumes and…
> They bring in their food.

In other cases Irish students asked informally about the immigrant's country in the course of everyday conversation.

> We sometimes ask [him] about how to say things and stuff in Lithuanian.
> …
> Well if you get into a conversation with them… sometimes you end up talking about like where they are from. And that can be like really interesting.

Considering that intercultural education in Irish schools is still in early stages, many Irish students reported knowing little about other cultures, especially those of non-European countries. One group of immigrant students at primary level described a lack of awareness among Irish students of religious differences:

> I don't think people from Ireland know much about our culture because they have a different one like I'm Orthodox and they're Christian so I don't think they'd know much about Orthodox since they haven't really been there or they're not Orthodox.

Furthermore, another group of immigrant students felt that Irish young people had very stereotyped notions of their countries:

> I'll tell you what happened like. They don't care, just because they show in the Trocaire [Irish NGO] right, they are going to show children in Trocaire in Sudan with no water and all messy shoes, no shoes on, all carrying big pillows on their heads. Everybody thinks ah jungle boy! And they call me (laughing) jungle boy.

These findings would suggest that the 'transmission' process is one-way, with immigrant students expected to learn the appropriate behaviour and cultural mores from their Irish peers. However, the majority of the Irish students interviewed also expressed positive views about recent immigration, feeling it made Ireland a more diverse society and allowed exposure to different cultures:

> Ireland would be a very boring place if there was only Irish people.

While this learning about different cultures is often only infrequently enshrined in formal school learning, it has the potential to transform the habitus of Irish schools, in keeping with Olneck's (2000) discussion of the implications of multiculturalism for the nature of cultural capital.

Discussion and Conclusions

This chapter explored the experiences of immigrant students in Irish primary and secondary schools. Ireland represents an interesting case study because immigration has been rapid and heterogeneous, and immigrants are a largely highly educated group. The scale and speed of immigration has potentially significant consequences for socio-cultural reproduction within the school context. Irish schools had little prior experience of catering for a diverse student intake, and, at least in some respects, were required to rapidly adjust their provision and practice to reflect their new students. In addition, teacher training has not adequately prepared teachers for the newly multicultural student body (see Smyth et al. 2009). Possessing different cultural, social and linguistic capital, children and young people entered the new school setting as 'outsiders' with little knowledge of how to navigate the new school system, what rules are to be followed and what practices are rewarded; often with limited proficiency of the lingua franca to access this knowledge. Furthermore, the dispersion of immigrant students across schools, coupled with the variety of nationality and linguistic groups in the immigrant population, meant that immigrant students could not generally rely on social networks of students from their own community. In other countries, such peer social capital has served as an important resource for children in acquiring cultural capital (see, for example Goldstein 2003; Stanton-Salazar and Dornbusch 1995). On the other hand, however, the educational profile of immigrant families means that many immigrant students already have the kinds of engagement with schoolwork and behaviour that is valued by the school system, and that makes successful cultural transmission (both direct and indirect) possible. However, we acknowledge that, because of their specific circumstances, a small proportion of immigrant students (especially unaccompanied minors) may have greater difficulties in settling in and engaging with schoolwork.

The interaction of these processes means that immigrant students in Ireland occupy an ambiguous position, possessing different levels of social and cultural capitals. For the recognition of cultural capital during migration, the form of cultural capital is significant (Nohl et al. 2006)—in other words, only the type of cultural capital is recognized that is valued by the 'host' country or institution. Their 'outsider' position is reinforced by a number of factors, including lack of English language proficiency, differences between their previous school experience and the Irish school system and a degree of segregation in friendship patterns between immigrant and Irish students. However, especially in working-class school contexts, immigrant students are constructed as 'good students' by teachers, regarded as generally hardworking, engaged and well-behaved. Thus, they possess some forms of cultural and social capital which are likely to facilitate their school success and social integration as they have adopted 'insider' norms (reflecting middle-class values); forms of cultural capital that has currency in the educational system of a receiving country.

Recent large-scale immigration to Ireland has had significant consequences for school practice, with most schools now providing English language support as well as social supports for immigrant students (see Smyth et al. 2009). In terms of formal learning, however, cultural transmission continues to be one-way, with immigrant students required to learn about Irish culture, and to date little adaptation of the curriculum has been made to reflect cultural diversity. With 'intercultural education' approach still in its infancy, the children of a dominant culture have often very limited and stereotypical views of the 'other' as discussed earlier in the chapter. Possessing very different types of cultural, social and economic capital; the 'new arrivals' often experience that their background is under-valued and are expected to adapt to the 'local' norms and rules. In the same vein, Arshad et al. (2005) in Scotland and Daoud (2003) in the USA note that immigrant children are being seen as essentially different by their native-born peers and teachers and are expected to adopt values and norms transmitted to them by school policies and practices. In addition, many immigrant children tend to adopt the social norms, speech and belief systems similar to their majority ethnic peers. Through these processes one can clearly see that, the school system reinforces existing social inequalities, by favouring children of the dominant social/cultural status groups, especially the middle-class families that owe their status position to levels of educational attainment. While considering the relatively high levels of educational attainment of Irish immigrants who may possess the 'right type' of cultural capital and favourable dispositions towards education, it remains to be seen if this compensates for other spheres, necessary for successful integration. As yet, little use has been made of the cultural capital and experiences that immigrant children bring into Irish classrooms. At the same time, though, Irish schools are now more diverse, culturally, linguistically and religiously, and this diversity has the potential to challenge and transform the nature of social reproduction within schools and thus on society more broadly. Failure to do so may have serious consequences on general integration of immigrant population and on social cohesion.

References

Apple, M. W. (1971). The hidden curriculum and the nature of conflict. *Interchange, 2*(4), 27–40.
Arshad, R., Diniz, F. A., O'Hara, P., Sharp, S., & Syed, R. (2005). *Minority ethnic pupils' experiences of school in Scotland (MEPESS)*. Scottish Executive: Education Department.
Ball, S. J., & Vincent, C. (1998). I heard it on the grapevine: 'Hot' knowledge and school choice. *British Journal of Sociology of Education, 19*(3), 377–400.
Baluja, K. (2001). *Teachers' perceptions of catering to the mathematical needs of immigrant students*, ACE Papers, Issue 11.
Bernstein, B. (1971). *Class, codes and control. Vol. 1: Theoretical studies towards sociology of language*. London: Routledge and Kegan Paul.
Bernstein, B. (1975). *Class, codes and control. Vol. 3: Towards a theory of educational transmissions*. London: Routledge and Kegan Paul.
Bourdieu, P. (1977). Cultural reproduction and social reproduction. In J. Karabel & A. H. Halsey (Eds.), Power and ideology in education. Oxford: Oxford University Press.
Bourdieu, P. (1984). *Distinction: A social critique of the judgment of taste*. Cambridge: Harvard University Press.
Bourdieu P. (1998). *Practical reason: On the theory of action*. Stanford: Stanford University Press.
Boyer, P. (2000). Evolutionary psychology and cultural transmission. *American Behavioral Scientist, 43*(6), 987–1000.
Central Statistics Office [CSO]. (2008). Census 2006. *Non-Irish nationals living in Ireland*. Dublin: Stationery Office.
Clark, A., McQuail, S., & Moss, P. (2003). *Exploring the field of listening to and consulting with young children*. Sheffield: DfES.
Cummins, J. (2001). Babel babble, cultural and linguistic diversity in education, a mainstream issue. In C. F. Baker and N. H. Hornberger (Eds.), *An introductory reader to the writings of Jim Cummins: Bilingual education and bilingualism*. New York: Multilingual Matters.
Daoud, A. M. (2003). The ESL kids are over there: Opportunities for social interactions between immigrant Latino and White high school students. *Journal of Hispanic Higher Education, 2*, 292–314.
Darmody, M. (2007). Strengthening the school social climate. In P. Downes, & A. L. Gilligan (Eds.), *Beyond educational disadvantage*. Dublin: Institute of Public Administration.
Davis, H. M. (2005). *Cultural transmission of social knowledge in preschool: A Costa Rican perspective*. New York: Longman.
Devine, D. (2005). Welcome to the Celtic Tiger? -- Teacher responses to immigration and increasing ethnic diversity in Irish schools. *International Studies in Sociology of Education, 15*, 49–71.
Devine, D., & Kelly, M. (2006), I just don't want to get picked on by anybody: Dynamics of inclusion and exclusion in a newly multi-ethnic Irish primary school. *Children & Society, 20*, 128–139.
Devine, D., Kenny, M., & MacNeela, E. (2004). Experiencing racism in the primary school – Children's perspectives. In J. Deegan, D. Devine, & A. Lodge (Eds.), *Primary voicesequality, diversity and childhood in Irish primary schools*. Dublin: Institute of Public Administration.
Dimakos, I. C., & Tasiopoulou, K. (2003). Attitudes towards migrants: What do Greek students think about their immigrant classmates? *Intercultural Education, 14* (3), 307–316.

European Commission (2008). *Green paper: Migration and mobility: Challenges and opportunities for EU education systems.* Brussels: European Commission.

Eurydice (2004). *Integrating immigrant children into schools in Europe.* http://www.eurydice.org/ressources/eurydice/pdf/catalogue_2003/catalogue_2003_EN.pdf. Accessed 12 October 2007.

Fine, M. (1991). *Framing dropouts: Notes on the politics of an urban public high school.* Albany: SUNY Press.

Gibson, M. A., & Ogbu, J. U. (1991). *Minority status and schooling: A comparative study of immigrant and involuntary minorities.* New York: Garland.

Gitlin, A., Buendia, E., Crosland, K., & Doumbia, F. (2003). The production of margin and center: Welcoming-unwelcoming of immigrant students. *American Educational Research Journal, 40*(1), 91–122.

Goldstein, T. (2003). Contemporary bilingual life at a Canadian high school: Choices, risks, tensions, and dilemmas. *Sociology of Education, 76,* 247–264.

Grenfell, M., & James, D. (1998). *Bourdieu and education: Acts of practical theory.* London: Falmer Press.

Irvine, J. J. (1990). *Black students and school failure: Policies, practices, and prescriptions*, Westport: Greenwood.

Jenkins, R. (2002). *Pierre Bourdieu.* London: Routledge.

King, A. (2005). Structure and agency. In A. Harrington (Ed.), *Modern social theory: An introduction* (pp. 215–232). Oxford: Oxford University Press.

Lareau, A., & Horvat, E. M. (1999). Moments of social inclusion and exclusion: Race, class and cultural capital in familyschool relationships. *Sociology of Education, 72*(1), 37–53.

Molcho, M., Kelly, C., Gavin A., & Nic Gabhainn, S. (2008). *Inequalities in health among school-aged children in Ireland.* Galway: HBSC Ireland.

Monkman, K., Ronald, M., & Theremene, F. D. (2005). Social and cultural capital in an urban Latino school community. *Urban Education, 40*(4), 4–33.

Monroe, C. R. (2005). Understanding the discipline gap through a cultural lens: Implications for the education of African American students. *Intercultural Education, 16*(4), 317–330.

Nieto, S. (1992). *Affirming diversity: The socio-political context of multicultural education.* White Plains: Longman.

Nohl, A.-M., Schittenhelm, K., Schmidtke, O., & Weiss, A. (2006). Cultural capital during migration—A multi-level approach to the empirical analysis of labor market integration amongst highly skilled migrants, *FQS, 7*(3), Art. 14.

Organisation for Economic Co-operation and Development [OECD] (2006). *Where immigrant students succeed—A comparative review of performance and engagement in PISA 2003.* Paris: OECD.

Olneck, M. (2000). Can multicultural education change what counts as cultural capital? *American Educational Research Journal, 37,* 317–348.

Park-Taylor, J., Walsh, M. E., & Ventura, A. B. (2007). Creating healthy acculturation pathways: Integrating theory and research to inform counselors' work with immigrant children. *Professional School Counseling, 11*(1), 25–34.

Ross, A. (2003). Teachers as symbols of societal power: What cultural icon are we?. In A. Ross (Ed.), *A Europe of many cultures* (pp. 217–223), London: CiCE.

Saez-Marti, M., & Sjögren, A. (2007). *Peers and culture.* Working Paper No. 349. University of Zurich Institute for Empirical Research in Economics.

Smyth, E. (1999). *Do schools differ? Academic and personal development among pupils in the second-level sector.* Dublin: Oak Tree Press/ESRI.

Smyth, E., Darmody, M., McGinnity, F., & Byrne, D. (2009). *Adapting to diversity: Irish schools and newcomer students*, Dublin: ESRI.

Stanton-Salazar, R. D., & Dornbusch S. M. (1995). Social capital and the reproduction of inequality: Information networks among Mexican-origin high school students. *Sociology of Education, 68*(2), 99–115.

Trickett, E. J., & Birman, D. (2005), Acculturation, school context, and school outcomes: Adaptation of refugee adolescents from the former Soviet Union. *Psychology in the Schools, 42,* 27–38.

Vekic, K. (2003). *Unsettled hope: Unaccompanied minors in Ireland, from understanding to response*. Dublin: Marino Institute of Education.

Weine, S. M., Ware, N., & Klebic, A. (2004). Converting cultural capital among teen refugees and their families from Bosnia-Herzegovina. *Psychiatric Services, 55,* 923–927.

Wong, R. S-K. (1998). Multidimensional influences of family environment in education: The case of socialist Czechoslovakia. *Sociology of Education, 71*(1), 1–22.

Chapter 20
Beyond Cultural Differences: Understanding and Negotiating the Conflict Between Chinese Immigrant Parents and Canadian Teachers

Yan Guo and Bernard Mohan

Introduction

The results of the 2006 Census of Canada showed that almost 6,293,000 people, or about one out of every five in the country, spoke languages other than English or French as their mother tongue (Statistics Canada 2008). The Canadian K-12 English as a second language (ESL) population included considerable numbers of students who were at risk of educational failure (Gunderson 2004; Watt and Roessingh 2001). Research shows that the school achievement and social growth of ESL students are significantly increased when schools actively encourage parental participation (Henderson and Mapp 2002; Hiatt-Michael 2007). However, some research suggests that whereas white parents were increasingly participating in their children's education, ESL parents' contacts with their children's schools were actually decreasing (Moles 1993).

ESL parent voices are not always heard or solicited, yet parents may be very concerned about the appropriateness of ESL instruction. For example, the Calderdale decision was formulated in England in the 1980s after a group of ESL parents successfully sued a school authority because they felt their children were ghettoized in an ESL program (Leung and Franson 2001). Consequently, the Ministry of Education prohibited ESL programs throughout England, and ESL teachers now work as support teachers within content classes. In North America, California Proposition 227, known as the Unz Initiative, passed with a 63% approval in 1998 and eliminated all forms of ESL instruction and bilingual programs except immersion (Crawford 1997), with large numbers of Hispanic parents voting against ESL and bilingual education. Parents believed that their children were not learning English quickly enough. Thus, the message is clear: Even where many parents are satisfied with ESL programs, it is important to reach groups who are not satisfied and may not fully understand the program. It is important for educators to listen to ESL parents. The above two examples reveal another mechanism as well: Politicians can take ESL parents' dissatisfaction as an excuse to reduce ESL funding. As a result, ESL students may not get the support that they need.

Y. Guo (✉)
Faculty of Education, University of Calgary, 2500 University Drive NW, Calgary, AB, Canada
e-mail: yanguo@ucalgary.ca

Over the years, research has also repeatedly revealed that limited communication between ESL parents and teachers has been a serious problem confronting educators (Gougeon 1993; Guo 2006, 2007; Ran 2001; Salzberg 1998); in fact, the Alberta Beginning Teachers' Survey (Malatest et al. 2003) indicates that the difficulties beginning teachers have in communicating with ESL parents also plague many experienced teachers (Faltis 1997). The issue of communication between schools and ESL parents has moved to the foreground recently. In British Columbia, Canada, the Vancouver and Richmond school boards have both been approached with proposals for the establishment of more traditional schools. Most of the parents supporting these proposals were recent Chinese immigrant parents who were unhappy with the work their children were doing in Vancouver and Richmond public schools (*The Globe and Mail*, 1 February 1999); these parents asked for "teacher-led instruction, a homework policy, dress code or uniforms, regular study and conduct reports, frequent meetings between parents and teachers, and additional extra-curricular activities" (Sullivan 1998, p. 15). It is worth noting that this debate has been presented as being between two familiar sides, the traditional and the progressive, a contrast that does not always fit local conditions. There is a danger that the ready-made rhetoric of the public debate may turn attention away from classroom realities and that calls for simplistic solutions may distract attention from valuable educational approaches to real needs. In the Richmond school district, difficulties of communication with Chinese immigrant parents have become a major political question (Gaskell 2001). Yet communication between schools and ESL parents is a relatively neglected research area despite the fact that miscommunication has the potential to derail the provision of multicultural and minority education.

Theoretical Framework

This study examines communication between ESL parents and high school ESL teachers in a "Parents' Night" (PN) event organized to increase understanding of the ESL program. We will discuss three "views" which we will apply to the data. First we will consider the widely known intercultural communication or intercultural differences view. Then we consider Taylor's "dialogue across differences" view which aims to overcome differences. Finally, we discuss the more comprehensive systemic functional linguistics view which enables us systematically and holistically to describe the discourse of the event, and locate it in its contexts. In the data analysis, we will examine the three views as explanations for a conflict that occurred.

Intercultural Communication

Intercultural miscommunication centers on differences between groups which result in differences in interpretation in communication. It "occurs when large and important cultural differences create dissimilar interpretations and expectations about how to communicate competently" (Lustig and Koester 2003, p. 50). R. Scollon and S. Scollon (2001) explain that the discourses of our cultural groups "make it more difficult for us to interpret those who are members of different groups. We call these enveloping discourses 'discourse systems' … The major sources of miscommunication in intercultural contexts lie in differences in patterns of discourse" (pp. xii–xiii). Discourse systems include the following aspects of culture: ideology, socialization, forms of discourse, and face systems.

Li (2006) provides an example of an interview study of ESL parents and teachers that discusses intercultural differences (but not communication). She explored culturally contested pedagogy by examining the views of language education (traditional, teacher-centered, code emphasis vs. progressive, student-centered, meaning emphasis) of Chinese middle-class parents and mainstream teachers in a publicly funded elementary school in Richmond B.C., Canada. She proposed a "pedagogy of cultural reciprocity" so that teachers and parents might work together more successfully. In a critical review Wamba (2006), drawing on Freirian work, points out that Li's single focus on Chinese educational culture has value, but is hardly an adequate explanation of all educational disagreements between teachers and Chinese parents. Nor does it address the *educational* question: What is best for the learner? Wamba underlines the need to study actual parent–teacher interactions where teachers knowledgeable about second language and culture learning aim at reconciling differences about the education of their children.

The core of this approach centers on differences between groups which result in differences in interpretation in communication, which in our study we will call "mismatches", and examine them particularly through reflection data.

"Dialogue Across Differences"/Practical Reasoning

Where the intercultural approach concentrates on differences, the "dialogue across differences" view aims to overcome differences and resolve conflicts to bring us together. This view comes from the philosopher Charles Taylor who accepts that the modern age is plural in two respects; there is an irreducible plurality of values and cultures, and there is also a plurality of forms of reflection, with any form of reflection being conditioned by the author's culture and other factors. For Taylor, unlike many postmodern writers, it does not follow that one must simply accept the irreducible plurality (Tully 1994, p. xiv). Taylor believes what he calls "practical reason" offers the possibility of a rational arbitration of differences between conflicting views in culture, ethics and other areas by reasoned argument aiming at validity. Since it deals with difference and dialogue (Taylor 1994, 1997), this arbitration could be called a "dialogue across differences". Going beyond the aim of a more perspicacious appreciation of differences between interlocutors, the goal of practical reason is to reach agreement between disputing positions. As such, practical reason provides an alternative to lapsing into subjectivism and relativism. Practical reason "starts from something that is common to the two (or more) positions in the dispute...it is directed at the participants in the conversation and at the things they posit or value." Practical reason "strives, through the comparison, questioning and rearticulation of views, either towards some reconciliation of differences or to persuading the interlocutors that they should come to agree that one position is better" (Abbey 2000, p. 166).

We undertook an exploratory analysis which looked for what were, in our view, some relevant features of "practical reasoning" that might apply to the presentations at PN. We looked for discourse evidence of: (1) awareness of commonalities and differences between the views of parents and teachers; (2) awareness of values in those views, both positive values (e.g., aims and goals) and negative values (which we call "concerns"); (3) reasoned arguments which aim at reconciling differences.

Systemic Functional Linguistics: Text in Context

We need to connect the dialogue across differences approach to discourse analysis, and apply it along with the intercultural communication approach to parent–teacher communication data. It would be desirable not to limit ourselves to these two approaches but to use a holistic description of discourse which could reveal other issues. Since Parents' Night is a school event, it would be wise not to ignore the educational context of this discourse. Finally, it would be advantageous if our discourse analysis was systematically related to linguistic analysis so that relevant issues could be brought into sharp focus.

To meet these requirements, we will use the more comprehensive systemic functional linguistics (SFL) perspective of "text in context" which enables us systematically and holistically to describe the discourse of the event and locate it in its contexts. SFL studies text in context, following "the principle that language is understood in relation to its environment" (Halliday 1999, p. 1). One type of context is the "context of situation" (Halliday and Hasan 1985, p. 52 ff.), the immediate environment of the text. Its three components are: (1) the field of discourse, typically subdivided into the social activity and its goal(s) versus the topic of discourse (e.g., the social activity or speech-event of Parents' Night versus the topics it deals with), (2) the tenor of discourse (e.g., the social roles and relations between teachers, parents, and students) and (3) the mode of discourse (e.g., the medium and role of language, such as presentations to the whole audience, smaller group discussions). Our analysis of discourse will illustrate all three but will particularly focus on field. The second type of context is the "context of culture," the broader background against which the text has to be interpreted. Halliday illustrates how the field, mode and tenor of any text in school "are instances of, and derive their meaning from, the school as an institution in the culture" (Halliday and Hasan 1985 p. 46). Our analysis of the context of culture of Parents' Night is selective and our discourse analysis (e.g., of practical reasoning) is informal, but indicate how a more thorough analysis might develop. Detailed linguistic analysis is beyond the scope of this chapter.

The SFL description of our data provides unique insights into ESL parent–teacher communication. We will examine all three views as possible explanations for a conflict that occurred at Parents' Night.

In the context of ESL education in Canada, our study investigated the communication processes between ESL teachers and parents through ESL Parents' Night. Two initial research questions guided our study:

1. How do teachers approach Parents' Night? Why?
2. How do parents react to Parents' Night? Why?

Methodology

Research Site

The study was conducted at Milton Secondary School (a pseudonym) located on the west side of Vancouver, British Columbia. Milton was chosen for three reasons: (1) diversity in student population, (2) its ESL program, and (3) its ESL Parents' Night. A secondary school with about 1,700 students from grades 8 to 12, is situated in a quiet, middle-to upper-middle-class neighborhood. Sixty-two percent of the students spoke a language other than English at home. The approximate number of students studying in the ESL program in the first year of the study was 200, in the second year, 160 students, and in the final year, 120 students. Many of the students were recent immigrants from Taiwan, Hong Kong, and mainland China. The ESL— program consisted of a number of noncredit content-based courses such as ESL science which integrated the instruction of the English language and subject matter simultaneously. The exceptions were physical education and math which were mainstream classes. The students at Milton generally stayed in the ESL program for 2 years. The program had organized an ESL Parents' Night for more than 10 years. These nights allowed teachers to inform parents about the philosophy of the ESL program and students and to explain the differences in educational systems between Canada and their home societies.

The investigator was introduced to the teachers and parents as a researcher from a Canadian university who studied the processes of home–school communication. She played the role of participant observer (Spradley 1980), seeking to "maintain a balance between being an insider and an outsider, between participation and observation" (p. 60). As requested by teachers, she explained Parents' Night to the parents on the phone, presented information gathered from the parents at the teachers' planning meetings, interpreted for Chinese parents at Parents' Night, and reported parents' feedback to the teachers after Parents' Night.

Participants

Nine ESL teachers and six bilingual assistants participated in the study. All of the teachers participated in the planning, delivery, and feedback sessions of the Parents' Night. They also involved their students in the entire process. The bilingual assistants were trained graduate research assistants who were also experienced ESL teachers. Before the Parents' Night, teachers sent home invitations in English to parents, explaining that the purpose of the event was to inform parents about the ESL program. The assistants followed up the invitations to parents in Mandarin, Cantonese, or English. Many Chinese parents were postsecondary educated entrepreneurs, investors, or professionals from Taiwan, Hong Kong, and mainland China.[1] In the parent questionnaires, parents stated that the major reason they immigrated to Canada was for their children's education. The parents had been in Canada from a few months to 4 years. The bilingual assistants served as interpreters at Parents' Night.

Data Collection

Three research methods—interviews, naturalistic observations, and focus groups—were used for data collection over a 3-year period. The researcher observed 12 ESL department planning meetings for Parents' Night, four for each event. At these meetings, teachers discussed their purposes and educational philosophies for Parents' Night. Three annual ESL Parents' Nights were observed. Observations focused on how teachers and students made their presentations, how parents asked their questions, and how teachers responded. With the consent of the teachers and parents, the 12 planning meetings and three Parents' Nights were audio recorded and subsequently transcribed.

The researcher interviewed six bilingual assistants individually. Each interview ranged from 30 to 50 minutes. Before Parents' Night, bilingual assistants telephoned 257 parents/guardians to explain the purpose of the event in Mandarin or Cantonese. On referral from the assistants, the researcher made a further 105 follow-up calls with parents/guardians to clarify the nature of the parents' concerns. After Parents' Night, the assistants also talked to the parents informally to get their feedback on the event, particularly about their reactions to teachers' and students' presentations and whether their concerns were addressed. Parents' feedback was recorded in bilingual assistants' and the researcher's field notes. The parents did not provide consent for formal face-to-face interviews, but allowed the bilingual assistants and the researcher to take notes during telephone conversations. The bilingual assistants listened to and recorded parents' questions and

---

[1] This is not to say that the Chinese are a homogeneous cultural group. In fact, there are significant differences in the political, economic, social, and educational systems between China, Hong Kong, and Taiwan, thus caution in generalizations about Chinese parents is needed.

comments. The interviews with the assistants focused on parents' interpretations of the ESL program, parents' major concerns, and their strategies for working on these concerns.

After Parents' Night, the researcher also interviewed nine ESL teachers individually. Each interview ranged from 30 to 80 minutes. Three teachers were interviewed twice because of their active involvement in Parents' Night. These interviews allowed teachers to reflect on their experience with the event and to articulate their beliefs about ESL education.

A focus group with eight ESL teachers and four bilingual assistants was also conducted after individual interviews were completed. The summary of the interviews was duly reported and the group also reviewed data about the parents' feedback conveyed by six bilingual assistants. The focus group generated more information about teachers' and parents' perspectives of ESL learning and parents' concerns, valuable data used for purposes of triangulation.

Data Analysis

The process of qualitative data collection and analysis is recursive and dynamic, as suggested by McMillan and Schumacher (2001). Data analysis in this study was ongoing throughout the data collection period. The ongoing analysis helped to identify emerging themes. The inductive analysis strategy was applied to the interview data in order to understand how participants approached Parents' Night. Observation data of the teachers' planning meetings were also analyzed inductively to identify teachers' goals for Parents' Night. This was accomplished by searching for patterns that emerged from the data rather than being imposed on data prior to collection (McMillan and Schumacher 2001). More systematic analysis was conducted after the data collection was completed and the interviews were transcribed.

Findings and Discussion

Parent's Night was a complex event, and its first opening typically began in the school auditorium, where the school principal welcomed ESL parents and students. Next a school area superintendent outlined provincial and school–district ESL policy. Other staff then reviewed services such as ESL counseling and multicultural liaison. In the second part of the evening, teachers and others spoke about the ESL program. In the third part, teachers, parents, and students moved to seven individual homerooms, where the ESL teacher explained the program and answered questions from students, and where students showed portfolios of their work to their parents.

Context of Culture: Description

A central aspect of the context of culture of Parent's Night was an underlying concern of teachers and parents about the educational progress of ESL students. Above we have reviewed research studies that show that in Canada in high school ESL learners are highly likely to fail to graduate, that ESL learners need to develop grade-level academic language proficiency, that an ESL student who arrives in grade 8 with minimal English will find it hard to graduate from grade 12, and that such students face an insoluble conflict between taking content courses and taking ESL courses. Students in the study school district had to complete a noncredit ESL program before they could enter a full range of content courses. Adequate ongoing support is not available when they leave the ESL program. This information is essential background for understanding the texts of Parents' Night when reference is made to such key lexical phrases as: (1) the ESL program, (2) student language learning, (3) conversational and academic language proficiency, (4) the length of time taken to exit from ESL program to mainstream, (5) student learning in the mainstream, and (6) graduation. ESL teachers and parents share a common interest in the educational progress of ESL students, but experience it differently through their different roles. They may therefore concentrate on different aspects of the intractable problem of ESL student progress in high school systems. ESL teachers may aim for the best use of student time in the ESL program, while parents may worry about their child's progress to graduation.

Context of Situation

Field 1 (Social activity/speech event): Speech-event of Parent's Night in Canada.
 Main goal: Inform all parents about ESL education (as opposed to arbitrate serious differences with individuals).
 Field 2 (Topic): Institutional: The ESL program and the Canadian education system generally.
 Tenor: Formal: School officials and teachers speaking to ESL parents and students.
 Mode: Pre-planned spoken monologue with a large audience in the auditorium; pre-planned presentations and dialogue with a smaller audience in the homerooms.

Teachers' Approach to Parents' Night

This section considers teachers' goals for PN and then examines how they realized these goals in the speech-event, noting evidence of Taylor's "practical reasoning". Accordingly, we will look for discourse evidence of reflection on both parents' and teachers' views and values, and of reasoned arguments aimed at reconciliation of differences.

Teachers identified three goals for Parents' Night: (1) to inform parents and students about the ESL program and Canadian education system, (2) to promote understanding for parents of students' language acquisition and learning and the progression from ESL to mainstream, and (3) to demonstrate student strengths in reading, writing, listening, and speaking through presentations/activity.

Here we illustrate goal one, discussing other goals as needed.

> Our students are primarily Chinese from either Hong Kong or Taiwan, where the predominant mode of instruction is rote learning. Students are motivated by demanding and strict teachers who give tests regularly and expect students to memorize what is said in the classroom. Our more lenient approach, based on developing thinking skills and creativity is already a huge shift for parents to grasp. When we throw in non-graded ESL classes where grade 8's are mixed with grade 12's and where beginners are grouped with advanced English speakers, parents are sometimes bewildered ... As professional educators, teachers in the ESL department recognize the need to educate our parents, as well as our students, to the goals and philosophy behind our system.... As they (parents) continually "push" their children to "work hard" and get out of ESL, we feel it essential to organize a Parents' Night every year to introduce our parents to these new ideas. (Teacher 5, interview)

Here the teacher compares educational approaches in Hong Kong/Taiwan and Canada, reflecting on a contrast between views and values of ESL parents and of teachers (e.g., rote learning vs. thinking skills) and a sense of parents' concerns about leniency and multilevel classes. Seeing an urgent professional responsibility to inform all parents about how Canadian programs were different from those of the families' emigrating societies, the teacher describes Parents' Night mainly as a mass educational information event, which limits the scope for Taylor's "practical reasoning" through arbitration dialogues between individuals.

Parents were vitally concerned with exit from the program and the length of time students stay in the program. The table on the next page shows speakers addressing this concern and giving reasoned arguments to justify the philosophy of the program and reconcile parents to it but not to arbitrate differences:

The table illustrates how an ESL specialist from the local School Board drew her knowledge of other schools to endorse the program and student time spent in it. A teacher from the ESL program justified the average stay in the program on the basis of research, drawing on Cummins (1991) to explain to parents the difference between conversational proficiency and academic language proficiency. An ESL science teacher and a mainstream science teacher jointly described how they cooperatively taught the academic science discourse required for the mainstream. Thus they "practiced what they preached"; their cooperative presentation onstage paralleled their topic of cooperation in teaching science register. Current ESL students presented their comparison of education in Canada and Taiwan, highlighting differences in student-centered instruction, different kinds of homework, cooperative learning, and learning language in context. They also "practiced what they preached"; their responsible participation in a student group presentation paralleled their description of Canadian education.

Speakers	Justification of the ESL Program
An ESL specialist from the local School Board	You are very fortunate that your children are at this school. The ESL program is one of the finest in the city. I'd also let you know it takes a long time for students to learn English. I work with all elementary and secondary schools in this area, and the average time students spend in the ESL program or with the ESL support in this area of the city is two to 3 years.
An ESL teacher	It is more difficult to understand the textbook than just to talk to your friends on the phone about what you want to do on Saturday night. Conversation skills take about 1 to 2 years to master while academic language proficiency takes 5 to 7 years. So really 2 years in ESL is a minimum. Academic language proficiency refers to things like thinking processes, reading for information from textbooks, writing an essay, making a presentation whereas in conversation you get context.
A mainstream science teacher and an ESL science teacher	Even though some may think that science involves less English, actually there are many new vocabulary terms and students must be able to read and understand textbooks and the teacher's notes. Also assignments must be written using an acceptable level of English. What we would like to do now is show you how ESL science prepares the students for mainstream classes. In ESL science I teach students how to write definitions and note-taking skills step by step. In mainstream science it is expected that students already know how. In ESL science I teach students how to write lab reports step by step, and in mainstream classes it is taught in grade 8, but by the time students are getting into other grades it is assumed that they know. Unless students come in at grade 8 level, they learn it in ESL science, or they don't learn it.
Current ESL students	S1: The teachers here like students to be responsible, like students to ask questions, and also let students participate. S2: The homework is also different. In Taiwan, all homework is copying everything from the textbook, but here teachers give students homework by presentation, or read newspaper, or to prepare for a presentation. You have to go to the library and do all the work by yourself. S3: The teachers here have students do group work. They often divide students into different groups and discuss a topic. In my home country, Taiwan, we all sit in our own seats, and listen to the teacher. S4: We also have TV and video in our classroom, sometimes we watch movies to learn things.

With respect to Taylor's model, there is therefore discourse evidence that the teachers and their supporters worked to reconcile differences with parents by recognizing common goals (success in the mainstream), identifying differences (different approaches to education and to language learning), and offering reasons based on needs of the students, research about academic discourse, evidence of "science register cooperation" between the ESL teacher and the mainstream science teacher and experience of participants in the ESL program. SFL provides tools to examine this discourse evidence in much sharper detail, as we have indicated by noting the parallel between what speakers "practice" and what they "preach," which is a parallel between speech-event (field 1) and topic (field 2). A similar parallel is looked for when, as qualitative researchers, we compare the transcript of the PN with the teacher's description of the goals for the PN, or with parents' reactions to the PN.

Parents' Reactions to Parents' Night

The parents showed a range of reactions to Parents' Night.

New Parents. The most positive reactions were from "new" parents. These parents were relatively new to Canada. Their children were relatively new to the ESL program. They usually did not know much about the Canadian educational system and were anxious about their children's progress in school. This group of parents seemed to be happy with the general information about school policies and the ESL program provided at Parents' Night. This is evident from the fact that many of these parents expressed their appreciation. They asserted that the energy and effort put into it was very worthwhile. For example, parents commented:

- The Parents' Night was very helpful to me because I learned so much about the ESL program.
- Now I know how many courses that my son takes in the ESL program.

It appeared that these parents accepted the teachers' goals for Parents' Night as an educational speech event. The "new" parents were a difficult group for the teachers to communicate with, for obvious reasons. Parents' Night was successful for them, and this success underlines the importance of making parents aware of the underlying assumptions of the ESL Program.

Even so, there were some communication difficulties that appeared to be due to intercultural mismatches. For example, "new" parents were unfamiliar with Parents' Night as a school event. As one of the parents stated:

> In Taiwan we were used to learning about our own children by means of marks on report cards. When we were invited to go to the Parents' Night we did not know why we need to go.

When invited, many parents were initially unwilling to come to Parents' Night, not understanding what the evening was about. Since the parents knew little about the ESL program, it was difficult for them to recognize that the educational assumptions of the ESL program were different from those in Taiwan. Hence it was difficult for them to recognize the need to understand these differences. Parents' Night seemed to be a new concept for them. They came to Parents' Night to learn about their own children, not to learn general information about the program. Simply put, their initial question was "Can you give me information about my child?"

"Experienced" Parents. The "experienced" parents were people whose children had typically been in the program for at least 1 year or more, and who were therefore fairly familiar with the ESL program, more familiar with Parents' Night as a school event and more aware of the teachers' view of its purposes. They knew more

about the Canadian educational system and had a high level of anxiety about their children's progress in school. Parents were concerned that ESL classes took time away from mainstream classes, and viewed 2 years in the ESL program as too long for their children. Some considered the ESL program as useless because students did not gain academic credits for it, a clear case of undervaluing ESL programs because school systems undervalued them. Consequently, a main question was: "When will my child exit the ESL program?"

Many of the "experienced" parents were therefore strongly dissatisfied with the topics covered at Parents' Night. Some of these parents said that Parents' Night was "a waste of time," and they would not come again.

For example, parents said:

- I would not come to Parents' Night because I have been to Parents' Night before, but my concerns were not addressed. It was useless to come because what I really wanted from the teachers was to ask them to give ESL students an exit test so that I would know when my children were ready to move to the mainstream classes.
- I would like to meet the teacher individually to discuss how well my child is doing in ESL. I don't feel I should go to Parents' Night unless I can talk to the teacher.

In sum, new parents were interested in the topics of PN, learning about the ESL program so that they could support their children's progress through school. Initially, though, they had a problem with PN as an unfamiliar speech event. In striking contrast, many experienced parents, familiar with PN as a speech event, rejected its topics, wanting discussion of different topics ("my concerns," "how well my child is doing").Thus the distinction between speech event (field 1) and topic (field 2) is vital for understanding the difference between parents' reactions.

We have seen above how teachers tried to address this concern about time in the ESL program in a variety of ways. Why were parents and teachers seeing things differently?

In small group discussions with the bilingual assistants, parents expressed strong concerns about their children not being able to graduate. They worried that the ESL program would slow down their children's progress to graduation and university:

- What happens if my kid has two courses left before he graduates? He has to leave high school at 19. What happens then if you cannot graduate with the system?
- Did you go to school here? How long did you stay in ESL? What do you think of the ESL program? Do you think the ESL program slowed you down in the process of going to university?

Similar concerns were shown in parents' responses to the Parents' Night questionnaire. Many of the parents wanted their children to go to university but considered that they would not graduate at the correct age if the ESL program slowed down their progress. Consequently, they wanted their children to exit the program quickly for the mainstream.

How can we explain this conflict between the ESL teachers and many of the experienced ESL parents? With respect to intercultural differences, we do not believe that this conflict is fundamentally intercultural, though intercultural differences certainly aggravate it. It is true that there were a number of cultural mismatches between parents and teachers, and that mismatches always contribute to a "fog of interpretation." For example, the new parents were unfamiliar with the speech event or social activity of PN. But the concerns of the experienced ESL parents with the ESL program cannot be adequately explained as a matter of cultural mismatch. The urgent concern of the experienced parents was the *length of time* their children were in the ESL program, not its educational philosophy. There was no evidence that *this* concern would be resolved by altering the ESL program towards a better cultural match, e.g., towards traditional Chinese language education practices.

With respect to diversity dialogues and practical reasoning, can one explain the situation with the experienced parents as a failure by the ESL teachers to create a dialogue across differences, despite all of their very real efforts? Would more effort have resulted in a consensual dialogue? While dialogue is very important, it does not seem to be an adequate explanation of the situation, because it was not the newer parents who were at odds but the more experienced parents, who had more understanding of the ESL teachers' arguments. In fact, it was our strong impression that many of the experienced parents were no longer open to a dialogue about the ESL program. They were concerned about progress in the mainstream. Turning to the wider "context of culture" surrounding Parent's Night, a more adequate explanation appears to be the underlying problem of ESL student progress, which cannot be solved by parent–teacher communication and negotiation. We have noted how these parents have high aspirations for their children, that large numbers of their children will fail to graduate, and that these learners face an almost insoluble dilemma of balancing language development with subject-matter development in the mainstream. Any parent in this situation would try to make sure their child had the very best conditions for success as they saw them and would be anxious for exit. This is not a concern special to a particular cultural group. While the ESL teachers were focused on necessary language development via the ESL program, these experienced parents were focused on the very different issue of progress in the mainstream, with a view to graduation within the normal time limit. The tragedy of an inequitable education system for high school ESL students with minimal English is that it places these two goals at odds with each other, and it therefore places ESL teachers and parents at odds with each other. Worse still, negative feedback by parents about the ESL program can be, and has been, misused by educational policy makers to reduce rather than increase educational support for these ESL students.

To address these frustrations, and create an ongoing dialogue between parents and teachers, the school established an ESL parent committee. Note that this strategy exchanges the mainly monological, formal and institutional PN for improved conditions for parent–teacher negotiation in a different context of situation: a small-group, immediate-response situation of dialogical conversation (MODE), a more informal situation with more equal power and more frequent contact (TENOR), where more potentially divisive topics can emerge through a more accommodating speech-event (FIELD).

Conclusion and Implications

What are some of the implications of this study for theory and research? The intercultural model was very helpful in identifying cultural differences which were sources of misunderstanding, as it was designed to do. The lack of ESL parents' visible involvement in schools is often attributed to cultural differences (Dyson 2001; Ogbu 1995; Wan 1994; Yao 1988). The results of this study suggest that we need to go beyond cultural differences to understand the difficulty of ESL parent–teacher communication. The findings of the study reveal that there were conflicting expectations of Parents' Night between teachers and parents. The teachers perceived the Parents' Night as an educational event to provide general information about the ESL program, whereas the parents viewed it as a venue to voice their concerns. Such a mismatch of expectations could make their communication difficult even before meeting at Parents' Night.

More importantly, simply attributing communication problems to cultural differences or to ESL parents being reluctant to participate in their children's education (Wan 1994; Yao 1988) is to sweep over the importance to examine actual processes of ESL parent–teacher interactions. Taylor's dialogue/practical reasoning model is therefore an essential addition to any study of intercultural groups which is interested in studying the possibilities of consensus across differences. It was helpful in recognizing teacher strategies at Parents' Night that were aimed towards consensus with parents, while noting that the conditions for full dialogue were neither aimed at nor present at the mass meeting of Parents' Night. Mass meetings for parents may run the danger that teachers maintain knowledge and authority through their use of specialist vocabularies and professional registers, while placing the immigrant parents in a position of receivers of educational information (MacLure and Walker 2000). Mass meetings may find parent participation strongly limited by the structure of power marginalized parents face within the school space (Cline and Necochea 2001; Lareau 2003). Thus schools need to consider whether events are structured in ways that foster cross-communication instead of one-way transmission and to open up opportunities to listen to ESL parents' voice, as this school did by developing an ESL parent committee.

Compared to the intercultural model, Taylor's model picked out very different aspects of the data, data that would otherwise have been ignored, and applied different criteria to them. To relate these two models systematically and holistically to discourse data, this study found it crucial to use a SFL perspective, which guided us to look at the context of culture, context of situation, and field of PN as speech event and topic. These aspects are entry points for detailed linguistic analysis of relevant issues. They are possible factors of misunderstanding in any situation of intercultural communication, and possible factors of importance in any dialogue across differences. Context of culture helped account for the conflict between the experienced parents and teachers, difference of context of situation for the dialogical strategy of mitigating conflict with an ESL parent committee, and field as speech event and topic for justification strategies for PN presentations, differences in reactions between new and experienced parents and more generally the link between interview data and observations of PN. Thus there are great advantages if future studies use a SFL discourse analysis and perspective to analyze a range of models within a series of contexts.

What are some of the practical implications? What can be done to mitigate the conflict between teachers and experienced parents? Parent's Night is a highly appropriate forum to discuss the aims of an ESL program with new parents but not to negotiate conflict with experienced parents who want their child to exit the program. In their case Parent's Night as an ESL parent–teacher communication process was problematic and was not able to resolve their differences, placing the resolution of this conflict in doubt. Some experienced parents said that they wanted an individual parent–teacher conference about their child's progress. These were regularly available at the school during the school year. If the parent was not satisfied with the result of these, the parent could appeal to the school administration to exit their child. But this is to treat a symptom rather than address its underlying causes. We have noted that the school had created a school-level ESL parent committee. This can play a role in mediating between parents and ESL teachers, communicating information, examining conflicts, developing ways that parents and teachers can cooperate more, and exploring possible educationally responsible changes in the ESL program that are within the ESL teachers' control. Finally, the committee can open a dialogue about progress in the mainstream. In the relatively affluent school in this study, ESL students often had a large number of private tutors, who tutored them for several mainstream courses, and the ESL teachers at the school had held meetings with groups of private tutors to seek ways of coordinating their joint efforts. Where circumstances permit, then, this committee can also form a link between parents, teachers and private tutors to support students' progress in the mainstream towards graduation.

However, none of the above forms of ESL parent–teacher communication can solve the problem that underlies the conflict over exit: That the high school ESL graduation rate is unacceptably low and that the educational system fails to support ESL students adequately. This will require changes in high school policy and operation (such as a whole school support policy, bilingual education where possible, and credit for ESL courses) and changes in teacher education. In urban school districts where the percentage of ESL students is more than 40 or 50%, such changes are long overdue.

These changes are beyond the power of ESL parents and ESL teachers at the school level, and it is unlikely that such changes in school policy and teacher education will come about without strong lobbying by ESL parents and ESL teachers in combination. ESL parents and teachers share a common concern that ESL students graduate from high school at a rate that reflects their abilities and achievements. It would be appropriate for a partnership of ESL parent organizations and ESL teacher organizations at the school–district level and above to focus on this common concern and to work for changes in the education system which will bring it nearer to reality.

Acknowledgment An earlier version of this revised chapter appeared in Language and Education, 22(1), 17–33. It is reprinted here with the kind permission of the journal editor.

References

Abbey, R. (2000). *Charles Taylor*. Princeton: Princeton University Press.
Cline, Z., & Necochea, J. (2001). ¡*Basta Ya!* Latino parents fighting entrenched racism. *Bilingual Research Journal, 25*, 1–26.
Crawford, J. (1997). The campaign against proposition 227: A post mortem. *Bilingual Research Journal, 21*(1), 1–29.
Cummins, J. (1991). Conversational and academic language proficiency in bilingual contexts. In J. H. Hulstijin & J. F. Matter (Eds.), Reading in two languages. *AILA Review, 8*, 75–89.
Dyson, L. (2001). Home-school communication and expectations of recent Chinese immigrants. *Canadian Journal of Education, 26*, 455–476.
Faltis, C. (1997). Joinfostering: Adapting teaching for the multicultural classroom (2nd ed.). Upper Saddle River: Prentice-Hall.
Gaskell, J. (2001). The "public" in public schools: A school board debate. *Canadian Journal of Education, 26*, 19–36.
Gougeon, T. (1993). Urban schools and immigrant families: Teacher perspectives. *The Urban Review, 25*, 251–287.
Gunderson, L. (2004). The language, literacy, achievement, and social consequences of English-only programs for immigrant students. In J. Hoffman & D. Schallert (Eds.), *The NRC yearbook* (pp. 1–27). Milwaukee: National Reading Conference.
Guo, Y. (2006). "Why didn't they show up?": Rethinking ESL parent involvement in K-12 education. *TESL Canada Journal, 24*(1), 80–95.
Guo, Y. (2007). Multiple perspectives of Chinese immigrant parents and Canadian teachers on ESL learning in schools. *Diaspora, Indigenous, and Minority Education: An International Journal, 1*(1), 43–64.
Halliday, M. A. K. (1999). The notion of 'context' in language education. In M. Ghadessy (Ed.), *Text and context in functional linguistics* (pp. 1–24). Philadelphia: Benjamins.
Halliday, M. A. K., & Hasan, R. (1985). *Language, context, and text: Aspects of language in a social-semiotic perspective*. Victoria: Deakin University Press.
Henderson, A. T., & Mapp, K. L. (2002). *A new wave of evidence: The impact of school, family, and community connections on student achievement*. Austin: Southwest Educational Development Laboratory.
Hiatt-Michael, D. B. (Ed.). (2007). *Promising practices for teachers to engage families of English language learners*. Charlotte: Information Age.
Lareau, A. (2003). *Unequal childhoods: Class, race, and family life*. Berkeley: University of California Press.
Leung, C., & Franson, C. (2001). England: ESL in the early days. In B. Mohan, C. Leung, & C. Davison (Eds.), *English as a second language in the mainstream* (pp. 153–164). Harlow: Pearson Education.
Li, G. (2006). *Culturally contested pedagogy: Battles of literacy and schooling between mainstream teachers and Asian immigrant parents*. Albany: SUNY.
Lustig, M. W., & Koester, J. (2003). *Intercultural competence: Interpersonal communication across cultures* (4th ed.). New York: Allyn & Bacon/Longman.

MacLure, M., & Walker, B. (2000). Disenchanted evenings: The social organization of talk in parent-teacher consultations in UK secondary schools. *British Journal of Sociology of Education, 21*(1), 5–25.

Malatest, R. A., et al. (2003). *Efficacy of Alberta teacher preparation programs and beginning teachers' professional development opportunities, 2002 survey report*. Unpublished manuscript. Edmonton: Alberta Learning.

McMillan, J., & Schumacher, S. (2001). *Research in education: A conceptual introduction* (5th ed.). New York: Longman.

Moles, O. C. (1993). Collaboration between schools and disadvantaged parents: Obstacles and openings. In N. F. Chavkin (Ed.), *Families and schools in a pluralist society* (pp. 21–49). Albany: SUNY.

Ogbu, J. (1995). Cultural problems in minority education: Their interpretations and consequences-part two: Case studies. *Urban Review, 27*, 271–297.

Ran, A. (2001). Travelling on parallel tracks: Chinese parents and English teachers. *Educational Research, 43*(3), 311–328.

Salzberg, J. (1998). *Taiwanese immigrant parents' perceptions of their adolescent children's ESL learning and academic achievement*. Master's thesis, University of British Columbia.

Scollon, R., & Scollon, S. (2001). *Intercultural communication: A discourse approach* (2nd ed.). Malden: Blackwell.

Spradley, J. (1980). *Participant observation*. New York: Holt, Rinehart & Winston.

Statistics Canada. (2008). *The evolving linguistic portrait, 2006 Census*. Ottawa: Statistics Canada. http://www12.statcan.ca/english/census06/analysis/language/pdf/97-555-XIE2006001.pdf. Accessed 28 June 2010.

Sullivan, A. (1998, March 11). Chinese lead traditional school drive. *The Vancouver Courier*, p. 15A.

Taylor, C. (1994). The politics of recognition. In A. Gutmann (Ed.), *Multiculturalism: Examining the politics of recognition* (pp. 25–73). Princeton: Princeton University Press.

Taylor, C. (1997, September 21). *Negotiating the differences*. Interview conducted by CBC Radio. Toronto, Ontario, Canada.

Tully, J. (Ed.). (1994). *Philosophy in an age of pluralism: The philosophy of Charles Taylor in question*. Cambridge: Cambridge University Press.

Wamba, N. (2006). A review of: "Culturally contested pedagogy: Battles of literacy and schooling between mainstream teachers and Asian immigrant parents by Guofang Li." *Reading & Writing Quarterly, 22*(3), 299–304.

Wan, Y. (1994). *Immigrant Chinese mothers' involvement in K-6 United States schools: A participatory study*. Unpublished doctoral dissertation. University of San Francisco.

Watt, D., & Roessingh, H. (2001). The dynamics of ESL dropout: Plus ca change… *Canadian Modern Language Review, 58*, 203–222.

Yao, E. (1988). Working effectively with Asian immigrant parents. *Phi Delta Kappan, 70*, 223–225.

Part III
Heterogeneity and Learning in Schools

Chapter 21
Introduction: Heterogeneity, Belonging and Learning in Schools

Irina Schmitt

In this part of the book we address the role of education for ethnicized and otherwise minoritized children and young people, and these children's and young people's influence on discourses and practices of education. From these debates, the position of institutionalized education as a major factor in nation re-building is more than obvious. That nations interpellate specifically gendered subjects is not new; schools are spaces for the re-production of very specific subjectivities in very specific national contexts.

The texts in this part offer crucial perspectives on the currency of this issue, addressing the historically embedded contemporary struggles over representations of ethnicized and otherwise minoritized children and young people, and over conceptionalizations of education as central issues in new and old immigration societies. Interestingly, it seems that most societies choose to figure out how to address the challenges they face internally, with little reference to earlier experiences in other societies. Beyond the respective insights into specific national contexts, these texts give us an understanding of both the transnational interconnectedness of politics and ideologies and the limitations of national policy making and practice. (Needless to say, transnational policy making, having a tendency towards conservation rather than transformation, cannot be considered the quick-fix solution, either.)

Children and young people, in this debate, inhabit quite contradictory roles: "Our children" are vulnerable to "stranger danger", a discourse that co-constitutes notions of belonging and strangeness and also constructs public spaces through definitions of who is understood to be a stranger or someone who belongs (Ahmed 2000). At the same time, "the innocence of the child is what is most at risk from the proximity of strangers" in discourses of stranger danger (Ahmed 2000). But what, then, about the child who is positioned as stranger? The texts in this part discuss vividly the implications of both too much and too little reflection on notions of difference. "Different" children—by virtue of their immigration status, ethnification, racialization, or gendering—come to embody both stranger danger and the need of protection of the innocent child. They are positioned as "endangering" the well-

I. Schmitt (✉)
Centre for Gender Studies, Lund University, PO Box 117, Lund 22100, Sweden
e-mail: irina.schmitt@genus.lu.se

oiled machinery of education, the well-known strategies of nation-building that are in place, or even "our" children's learning. They come to be seen as disruptions of the educational order, and in most educational contexts disruption is equaled with "problem." Yet, as the authors in this part show, these "disruptions" are a chance to contextualize education systems historically, showing patterns of earlier migrations, for example, in order to understand more recent immigration; and conceptually, by analyzing nationally specific—again historically embedded—notions of education.

Theoretical and Methodological Polyphony

Geographically, the authors in this part analyze education policy and practice in Switzerland, Britain, Germany, Canada, Sweden, the USA, Greece, Portugal, Argentina and Spain. The texts in this part shed light on re-production of inequalities and discrimination and the impact of education policies, on specific policy strategies that are aimed at migrant and minoritized children and young people, as well as on didactic strategies to address classroom heterogeneity. This part can also be read as a conversation about research methodology and theoretical frameworks in the intersectional fields of migration, youth and education studies. While we agree on the need to critically reflect on nation-states' strategies towards young people, we have different ideas on how to frame our critique.

Both politically and methodologically, children and young people remain relatively invisible; and many education and youth researchers can attest to the lack of interest in research with groups that have so little direct political influence. Yet, the analysis of children's and young people's situation and experiences can offer necessary reflections to address issues of inclusion and exclusion in the societies discussed here. The need for containment inherent to nation-states is offset by children's and young people's negotiations of belonging:

> [Y]oung people's cultural and geographical mobility seriously challenges the state, as youth seek out opportunity regardless of state. The understanding of socialization as mono-cultural and mono-national will have to be revised in light of acquisition of transcultural competencies as well as of many-cultured pasts. (Hoerder et al. 2005a, p. 31)

In these texts, we share a critical perspective on nation-states implicatedness in education, as well as an interest in "problem solving", to borrow the often-used concept in national educational tests. The texts also show that many immigration societies have been timid in their approaches towards an education system and education practice that more than professes to embed heterogeneity structurally and pedagogically.

The analysis of educational regimes as reflective of as well as productive of national regimes of belonging is not in itself a new idea, but one that apparently needs to be brought to both researchers' and policy makers' attention with painstaking regularity. Debates about family language use in schools or the role of parents in the education process are the stuff media hypes are made off. Nations, it seems, are rather fragile entities, and their existence is easily threatened by young people who are transculturally and multilinguistically competent. (While I write this, German politicians suggest, again, to inscribe the hegemony of German as the only language of the nation into the basic law.) And class-based societies cannot tolerate the disconnection of young people's educational achievements from their parents' and guardians' socio-economic position; rather, many societies invest in the reproduction of class positions through education, making families responsible if their children's do not succeed in —read, can make the system work for them—the education system. That these national strategies need to be read in their interrelation, and as gendered, is obvious in the following texts.

Decentering Education—The Texts

With the first text, "Dealing With Diversity and Social Heterogeneity—Ambivalences, Challenges and Pitfalls for Pedagogical Activity", Christine Riegel sets the stage for our conversations about the role of schools in learning about differences in societies. Importantly, Riegel reminds her readers that intersectional analyses allow us to take into account "multifaceted and diverse individual circumstances in a shared space characterized by inequitable social structures". Based on data from a joined study "Preventing Right wing Extremism and Ethnical Violence in Swiss Schools", Riegel analyzes if and how societal inequalities are reflected in schools. Multilingual societies such as Switzerland offer additional insights in terms of the structures of difference that define a society.

Riegel points to an ambivalence inherent to schools, by reading schools simultaneously as spaces of heterogeneity where students and teachers with diverse experiences meet, and spaces of homogenization, as schools, by their structure, tend to oversee these heterogeneous experiences and at the same time segment students based on, among other aspects, age and standardized achievements. In these negotiations of heterogeneity and homogenization, teachers can be seen as the link between institutional and individual discrimination, and Riegel focuses the analysis in her text on teachers' strategies towards the heterogeneity in their schools. Riegel's notion of "doing normality" and her analysis of the use and critique of discourses of equality that cover up demands of assimilation, while reflecting the specific experiences of the Swiss study, can be usefully adapted in other contexts. Riegel convincingly points out that change cannot merely be situated on the interpersonal level and in a demand for individual recognition, but needs structural change and a reflection of the societal contexts of education.

The following text offers readers a comparative perspective and a reflection of long-term implications of policy choices and adaptations. In "A learning curve: The Education of Immigrants in Newcastle-upon-Tyne and Bremen from the 1960s to the 1990s", Sarah Elizabeth Hackett decenters the more common perspective on education in migration societies that focuses on metropolitan centers. Instead of adding to the discussion of education for immigrant children in national capitals and large cities, she turns the gaze to less-analyzed places, Newcastle-upon-Tyne in northeast England and Bremen in northwest Germany. By analyzing educational policies and strategies, Hackett shows that local solutions could subvert national trends, such as in Newcastle-upon-Tyne, where in the late 1960s the choice not to disperse immigrant students all over town (admittedly at least partly grounded in fewer numbers) lead to relatively better outcomes for immigrant students. Hackett also points out the need to understand the discrepancy between societies that perceived immigration as long-term and societies that saw students' participation in education as short-term and focused on their "return", as was common in western Germany in the 1970s and 1980s. Hackett reminds readers that immigration policy has long-term outcomes, and that, for example, the (western) German refusal to accept the reality of immigration needs to be read as one reason for ongoing problematic outcomes in international tests.

The third text—my own—attempts a comparative analysis of education policies in Sweden, Canada and Germany. With "School Policies, Gender-Sex-Sexuality and Ethno-Cultural Re-production in Sweden, Canada and Germany", my interest is to analyze the role of gender-sex-sexuality in school policies in relation to the construction of ethnicized belonging in immigration societies. I argue that school policies are part of national discourses regarding values and norms of gender and relationships that inform and in turn are informed by concepts of ethnicized belonging. Furthermore, the analysis of school policy texts allows insights into conceptualizations of young people and their societal role in the context of ongoing neo-liberal re-configurations of schools and societies.

With this text, I am also discussing the limits of anti-discrimination legislation, and notions of "minorities," as I understand the limitations experienced by minoritized young people as also working on nonminoritized young people. An intersectional analysis is needed to understand the implications of education legislation and practice that makes invisible or excludes specific students, in order to be able to reflect on the strengths of norms and their meaning for all children and young people in schools, and to see the skills and abilities of minoritized youth and consider them as experts rather than victims.

Claudia Koehler discusses in her text the "Effects of the Head Start Program in the USA as Indicators of Ethnic Inequalities". Basing her analysis on 13 evaluation studies, Koehler offers explanations for why participating in the US early education program Head Start does not, despite decades of work, ameliorate inequalities in education for children from minoritized communities. In fact, research underlines that the most disadvantaged children have the least to gain from the program. It seems striking that such a long-term effort such as Head Start continues to be in place without a serious reflection of the effects—or the lack of effects—discussed by Koehler. Her suggestions for program adaptation also point to the larger frameworks researchers and policymakers need to take into account; the discriminational praxes that disadvantage, for example, many African-American adults can translate into educational disadvantages for children. Again, an intersectional analysis shows that racialization/ethnification and economic position need to be understood in their relation.

In their text "Project-Based Learning to Enhance Recognition and Acceptance of Cultural Diversity in the Primary School", Christos Govaris and Stavroula Kaldi take the discussion from policy analysis to empirical reflection. In their study at a Greek elementary school that included both interviews and teacher-led activities, the authors try out an educational program that aims to allow mainstream-Greek and minoritized students to understand both the historicity and the contemporary meanings of migration to their town as well as the implications for their classroom. Govaris' and Kaldi's focus on teaching methodology is informative, as it reveals the need not only for policy and curriculum change, but also for change in the strategies that structure everyday interactions in schools. In reflecting on the uses of problem-based learning and the frameworks of intercultural education, Govaris and Kaldi also open, I would argue, possibilities for teachers who wish to effect change in their own classrooms, and to create a "community of learning" both for children from mainstream families and for minoritized children.

Teresa de Jesus Seabra de Almeida takes into account socio-economic inequalities in her analysis of migrant students' achievements in school. In her study on "Ethnicity, Social Inequalities and School Performance", Seabra questions and expands the Bourdieuian framework that explains cultural discontinuities for working-class children in the middle-class context of school, by intersecting this framework with data about migrant children and young people. The research for this study was conducted in the context of the Plan for Immigrant Integration of the Portuguese government, as no statistical information about families' social conditions and national backgrounds had been available previously. Seabra disentangles notions of cultural difference and difference in social conditions, and analyzes these also in relation to gender, by analyzing school success of students from Indian and Cap Verdean families in Portugal. This study is striking as it questions the still-common assumption that immigrating students should use the language of their new home-country only. As Seabra shows in her text, Indian students who use both their family language and Portuguese, are more successful in school than students from Cap Verdean families, although the cultural difference for students from Indian families is considered more pronounced. Seabra also underlines that students adapt their social and educational strategies, based on the understanding that students' agency is often overlooked. Finally, she points out the role of family involvement in students' education as a decisive factor.

The part closes with another comparative study. The text by Ana Bravo-Moreno and Jason Beech on "Migration, Educational Policies and Practices: Constructing Difference in Buenos Aires and in Madrid" offers reflections on the "powerful triangle" of structure, culture and agency that work to empower or disempower young people in the context of migration. By discussing conceptual traditions and their translation into current approaches—the idea of assimilation in Buenos Aires and the idea of compensation in Madrid—Bravo-Moreno and Beech highlight the limitations of education settings that do not account for the specific experiences of migrant students. Both Argentina, as a traditional immigration country, and Spain, where immigration is seen as a more recent phenomenon, could, the authors argue, profit from intercultural models of education. The underlying notion that migrant students should adapt to the given situation leads to "institutional misrecognition" of migrant students in both settings; it also positions the responsibility of adaptation on the students. Interestingly, the research participants in Buenos Aires reflected on the daily use of nationalistic symbolism in school as something they felt familiar with, and did not liken it to the discrimination they experienced outside of school. While the practice of nationalism might be considered excluding to immigrant children, the similarity in educational culture to their previous education experiences seemed to be more important for the participating students. The authors are also able to show the relationship between political decisions and school experiences, when they show that public funding and political support for private schools is rising, and that immigrant students have only limited access to these schools.

Pedagogies of Shame and Anger

In these texts, schools are reflected upon as spaces where national historically embedded trajectories find expression in specific policy decisions, as much as in the seemingly individual strategies employed by teachers. Reading schools in such an embedded way allows us to analyze students' successes—or the lack thereof—beyond their or their families' abilities and resources. The analyses offered in this part engage history, policy and education praxes and thus allow us to read the discourses and praxes of education in schools as praxes of national belonging and exclusion, and to keep working on locally specific yet globally embedded strategies of change.

Implicitly or explicitly, the texts in this part address pedagogical opportunities. Depending on our frames of reference and theoretical vocabulary, this can be discussed using terminology of citizenship (Invernizzi and Williams 2008) or of a range of critical pedagogical interventions (Giroux 1991), such as intercultural, multicultural, or transcultural pedagogies (Göhlich et al. 2006), anti-racist pedagogy (Dei et al. 2000), feminist (Larson 2005; Sykes 2004) or norm-critical and anti-oppressive pedagogy (Bromseth and Darj 2010; Kumashiro 2000, 2002). Kevin Kumashiro categorizes the field of critical pedagogies, finding "education for the other", "education about the other", "education that is critical of privileging and othering" and "education that changes students and society" (Kumashiro 2000). Kumashiro suggests that

> [broadening] the ways we conceptualize the dynamics of oppression, the processes of teaching and learning, and even the purposes of schooling is necessary when working against the many forms of social oppression that play out in the lives of students. Doing so requires not only using an amalgam of these four approaches (which many educators already do), but also "looking beyond" the field to explore the possibilities of theories that remain marginalized in educational research. (Kumashiro 2000, p. 25)

In the European context, the concept of interculturality has been entrenched into education frameworks. The authors of the report "Sharing Diversity. National

Approaches to Intercultural Dialogue in Europe", written for the European Commission in 2008, suggest the following working definition of interculturality:

> Intercultural dialogue is a process that comprises an open and respectful exchange or interaction between individuals, groups and organisations with different cultural backgrounds or world views. Among its aims are: to develop a deeper understanding of diverse perspectives and practices; to increase participation and the freedom and ability to make choices; to foster equality; and to enhance creative processes. (European Institute for Comparative Cultural Research 2008, p. xiii)

This reflects an understanding common in Europe that is based on cultural difference, focusing on the appreciation of cultural belongings and expressions "other than my own". It also entails the strengthening of minority cultures, both indigenous and immigrated. In my reading, this understanding does, however, inscribe a conceptualization of distinct cultures, and even a hierarchization between "majority" and "minority" cultures. How does this work for children and young people who learn to negotiate their own belongings and positions in many-cultural contexts?

My interest in terminology might be petty. Yet, I persist, with your permission, to explore this further. How can we—researchers, activists, teachers—capture and discuss experiences and strategies dealing with diverse diversities? Some years ago, I participated in a research network under the heading of transculturalism, initiated by a Canadian research organization, at a time when the notion of multiculturalism seemed to lose its appeal for many in Canada. The concept of transculturalism promised to integrate the lessons learned from multiculturalism; we focused on transculturation as ongoing negotiations of belonging and highlighted young people's competences rather than re-producing migrant young people's status as problematic (Hoerder et al. 2005b).

Yet, how do we subvert the tendencies to—sometimes inadvertently—re-hierarcize belongings? One suggestion might be Michalinos Zembylas' pedagogy that challenges traditional notions of (national) pride and shame. "This kind of pedagogy also suggests developing a mode of critique that comprehends the affective economies of schooling as well as their effects on students and teachers' lives", Zembylas argues (Zembylas 2008, p. 275).

And still, I am not satisfied. In writing this introduction, I learned from Sara Ahmed's discussion of the possible racist implications that can be traced in and all too uncritical excitement about "diversity":

> What does it mean to embody diversity? This is a question I have learnt to ask myself over time. It is an unsettling question. The turn to diversity is often predicated on the numbers game, on getting more of us, more people of colour, to add colour to the white faces of organisations. So if we are the colour, then we are what gets added on. Whiteness: the world as is it coheres around certain bodies. We symbolise the hope or promise that whiteness is being undone. (Ahmed 2009, p. 41)

Ahmed discusses "doing diversity" and the personal and political frustrations of "being diversity" (Ahmed 2009, pp. 43, 45). Indeed, she offers and demands a change in perspective: This cannot be about the graceful proposition of inclusion of the "other" from the lofty and comfortable chairs of majority researchers and policy makers. Ahmed's experience of being positioned as the good example for institutional integration can probably be recognized by many teachers who unwittingly serve to represent "diversity" in their schools. Writing as a White middle-class European lesbian academic, I am not entitled to appropriate Ahmed's anger, but I need to learn from it if I want to be able to make any useful propositions in these debates. Yet it is, incidentally, akin to the anger I experience in doing research on queer/ed young people. Education is serious business, and sometimes painfully personal.

Of course, the R-word is not comme-il-faut in many university departments nor in political institutions. Ahmed discusses how institutions can attach negativity to those who make obvious how deeply engrained exclusionary structures are, disavowing those who are thus objectified their subjectivity, expressed, for example, in anger and seething criticism, as these become personal expressions rather than justified critique. Yet, racism, in its many forms and impersonations, lies at the bottom of many of the struggles encountered and reflected by the authors in this part of the book. At this moment, I believe that we need to learn from this anger, rather than aim to resolve it.

> Racism is not something you can get over. We won't get over it. It is not over. To get over it before it is over would be to keep things in place. We must be the trouble they claim us to be: we must persist in being the cause of their trouble. It is time for us to reclaim our place as angry Black feminists even as we inhabit different places. The angry Black feminist, who insists on speaks about racism, who is not happy with diversity, can do things. We don't even know yet just what she can do. We need to be bad at embodying diversity. We need to fail to be happy for them. We need to stay as sore as our points. (Ahmed 2009, p. 51)

References

Ahmed, S. (2000). *Strange encounters: Embodied others in post-coloniality*. London: Routledge.
Ahmed, S. (2009). Embodying diversity: Problems and paradoxes for Black feminists. *Race Ethnicity and Education, 12*(1), 41–52.
Bromseth, J., & Darj, F. (Eds.). (2010). *Normkritisk pedagogic: Makt, lärande och strategier för förändring*. Uppsala: Centrum för genusvetenskap, Uppsala universitet i samarbete med RFSL ungdom.
Dei, G. J. S., Calliste, A., & with the assistance of Margarida Aguiar (Eds.). (2000). *Power, knowledge and anti-racism in education*. Halifax: Fernwood.
European Institute for Comparative Cultural Research. (2008). *Sharing diversity: National approaches to intercultural dialogue in Europe: Study for the European Commission*. http://www.interculturaldialogue.eu/web/files/14/en/Sharing_Diversity_Final_Report.pdf. Accessed 13 Dec 2010.
Giroux, H. A. (1991). Border pedagogy and the politics of modernism/postmodernism. *Journal of Architectural Education, 44*(2), 69–79.
Göhlich, M., Leonhard, H.-W., Liebau, E., & Zirfas, J. (Eds.). (2006). *Transkulturalität und Pädagogik: Interdisziplinäre Annäherungen an ein kulturwissenschaftliches Konzept und seine pädagogische Relevanz*. Weinheim: Juventa.
Hoerder, D., Hébert, Y., & Schmitt, I. (2005a). Introduction: Transculturation and the accumulation of social capital: Understanding histories and decoding the present of young people. In D. Hoerder, Y. Hébert, & I. Schmitt (Eds.), *Negotiating transcultural lives: Belonging and social capital among youth in comparative perspective* (pp. 11–36). Göttingen: V+R Unipress (2nd ed. 2006 University of Toronto Press).

Hoerder, D., Hébert, Y. M., & Schmitt, I. (Eds.). (2005b). *Negotiating transcultural lives: Belongings and social capital among youth in comparative perspective*. Göttingen: V+R Unipress (2nd ed., 2006 University of Toronto Press).

Invernizzi, A., & Williams, J. M. (2008). *Children and citizenship*. Los Angeles: Sage.

Kumashiro, K. (2000). Toward a theory of anti-oppressive education. *Review of Educational Research, 70*(1), 25–53.

Kumashiro, K. (2002). *Troubling education: Queer activism and antioppressive pedagogy*. New York: Routledge Falmer.

Larson, L. M. (2005). The necessity of feminist pedagogy in a climate of political backlash. *Equity & Excellence in Education, 38*(2), 135–144.

Sykes, H. (2004). Pedagogies of censorship, injury and masochism: Teacher responses to homophobic speech in physical education. *Journal of Curriculum Studies, 36*(1), 75–99.

Zembylas, M. (2008). The politics of shame in intercultural education. *Education, Citizenship and Social Justice 2008 3: 263, 3*(3), 263–280.

Chapter 22
Dealing with Diversity and Social Heterogeneity: Ambivalences, Challenges and Pitfalls for Pedagogical Activity

Christine Riegel

Introduction

Education and learning rarely happen in socially and culturally homogeneous contexts, but rather are characterized by social differences and social inequality. Formal learning locations like schools mirror the social and cultural heterogeneity of the society, but this heterogeneity is rarely adequately considered by educational and institutional frameworks. Therein lie challenges and difficulties for pedagogical action. In general, but especially in the context of school, dealing with social differences in societies marked by social heterogeneity is fraught with ambivalences. Ambivalence is inherent in the task of recognizing both equality and difference under conditions of social inequality and hierarchical relations of power. In this chapter the controversial field of "equality" and "difference" will be examined. The main questions are on social processes and on everyday practices of "doing differences" in the context of school education, and on the questions, how teachers deal with social differences, social heterogeneity, and social inequality in pedagogical work, and how they act in situations where the conflicting demands of "equality" and "difference" manifest themselves.

First, I describe the structural contexts for dealing with heterogeneity in society and especially in the contradictory institutional context of school. Then, based on classroom observations and interviews with teachers who participated in an intervention study on "Preventing Right Wing Extremism and Ethnicized Violence in Swiss Schools" (see Oser et al. 2007, 2009), I will reconstruct ambivalences and pitfalls in dealing with differences and discuss dangers like Othering and negative attribution in contexts of asymmetrical power relations in society and in hierarchical context of school. In conclusion I accentuate the powerful intersection of social differences and their consequences for social structures, representations, and practices and finally I will point out implications for educational practice.

C. Riegel (✉)
Institute of Education, Social Pedagogy, Freiburg University of Education,
Kunzenweg 21, 79117 Freiburg, Germany
e-mail: christine.riegel@ph-freiburg.de

Therefore I focus on the social and institutional contexts of schooling in central Europe, with particular reference to Switzerland, where study was carried out. This also means, that the chapter is written from a central European position and point of view.

Diversity in the Context of Social Inequality

Diversity and social heterogeneity not only refer to a variety of ways of life and social backgrounds, but also to (socially constructed, but significant) differences—distinctions that have social implications, mark symbolic boundaries, and structure the entire society. Social heterogeneity is directly connected to social inequality including the asymmetrical distribution of power and dominance. Thus social differences like gender, class and ethnicity are always related to hierarchical and bipolar distinctions (like white–black, male–female, rich–poor, healthy–ill, north–south, west–east…) and unequal evaluations and unequal access to social resources and power. In social relations of power and inequality diverse social-structure categories and differences like, for example, gender, class, ethnicity, body, age, sexuality, religion, geographical location etc. empirically overlay and affect each other. The concept of intersectionality is useful in considering and analyzing how these complex levels and positions work together, as they focus and examine the interdependence of various lines of social difference (Crenshaw 1989; Davis 2008; Lutz et al. 2010; McCall 2005; Riegel 2010; Winker and Degele 2009). These intersecting lines of social structure categories and their associated inequalities and relations of dominance and oppression (Hall 1994) mutually affect each other and—as a conglomerate—effectively construct social meaning. But social differences are no fixed structures; the social construction of hierarchical organized categories like race, class, gender and their intersection are generated, produced, and reproduced by social processes and practices of "doing difference" (Fenstermaker and West 2001; West and Fenstermaker 1995). Therein lies the potential to change these hierarchical power relations. But also, there is a danger of participating in, recreating and reproducing in everyday practices and discourses the dominant and hegemonic categorizations—through using dominant representation and practices of differentiation. Social differences are effects of praxes of social differentiation and also function—as inequality structuring social categories—in social representations (narratives, discourses, images, norms) and social practices with effects of inclusion and exclusion, like in differentiations in "We" and "The Other". The term "Othering" describes social practices und processes, which constitute humans, social groups, and societies as "Others"—by categorization and evaluation as different—combined with hierarchical thinking and evaluation. Thereby the subjectivity of "the Other" is ignored and missed, and "the Other" is consequently excluded from the hegemonic discourses of power (Broden and Mecheril 2007; Eggers 2005; Spivak 1985). This is a selective and meaningful differentiation and discrimination between "We" and "The Others", linking to diverse social categories like gender, class, ethnicity, body, age, and so on.

Further, social heterogeneity refers to the existence of multifaceted and diverse individual circumstances in a shared space characterized by inequitable social structures, which further shape the respective scope of possibilities ("Möglichkeitsraum", see Holzkamp 1983) for individual students. Considering social heterogeneity at school means more than paying attention to students in all their individuality and variability, and it also means attending to the differences that are associated with social inequality in their life circumstances, social positioning, possibilities, and limitations.

The question that arises is: to what extent is the connection between heterogeneity and inequality in society reflected in the educational system and in the schools? In order to address this question, the framework and organizational structure of schools is examined.

Heterogeneity in School: Institutional Minefields in Dealing with Equality and Difference

In the context of school education we can observe areas of conflict and ambivalence in structures for dealing with difference and social heterogeneity (Kutscher 2008; Wenning 2004). Here I refer especially to the education system of Switzerland,[1] but the problems which will be shown in the following are similar in other middle European countries like Germany. Even if social differences, diverse backgrounds and living circumstances of the students are a daily fact of life in society and in schools, the school system, the organization of the institution, of instruction and of teacher education carry on as if social heterogeneity were not a fact of life (Leiprecht and Kerber 2005). School—as a crucial educational institution—finds itself pulled in two opposing directions: homogenizing and segmenting.

On the one hand school aims toward homogenization. Schools seek to standardize study groups and educational goals, in which case social heterogeneity is seen as a disturbance and is minimized by the organization as far as possible. This is apparent in multi-element educational systems when students are divided and assigned to classes, stages and school levels within school classifications—not to mention establishing standardized achievement norms and age homogeneity. Beyond that, the educational system is conceptualized as monocultural (Allemann-Ghionda 1999)

---

[1] The Swiss school system can be divided into primary level (first to sixth year), lower secondary level (to ninth year), and upper secondary level, which constitutes the first phase of noncompulsory education. In the upper secondary level students can choose among the following types of education: Matura schools (as precondition for later access to university), middle schools and basic vocational education and training schools. Primary level and lower secondary level are obligatory for every child and are free, universal public schools. (see: http://www.sbf.admin.ch/htm/themen/bildung_en.html, 14 May 2010).

and is shaped by the monolingual habitus (Gogolin 2008). Also in Switzerland, with four national languages, each school usually has only one main language which has to be used in classes. Students' knowledge and use of other languages are often ignored or viewed as problematic. At the same time there is an unexpressed orientation toward "the normal pupil"(which is conceptualized as white, Christian, middle-class, male, heterosexual, healthy)—whose actual existence is in question today, more than ever. In addition, the content of the curriculum and of didactical material like textbooks (Höhne et al. 2006) themselves too often ignores the history of globalization and colonization as well as the daily reality of diversity within society and within schools; in the end, the appropriate structural and organizational conditions for learning in the heterogeneous context are not created (Gomolla and Radtke 2009; Leiprecht and Kerber 2005). Usually social differences are ignored or seen as a perturbation. Intercultural education is at best a fringe area in school, which is only brought into play when problems arise (like prejudices and conflicts between youngsters or school problems of immigrant students). Intercultural learning is more often seen as a problem to be dealt with, rather than as a transversal or mainstreaming task or demand.

In failing to adequately acknowledge and address differences there is a great risk that education will neglect the diversity of different preconditions and living circumstances of divers student bodies. This is why the tendency toward homogenization can lead to social segmentation and discrimination of those who don't precisely fit the (hidden, unspoken) norm. On the background of these strategies of homogenization the formal "postulate of equality", the requirement to treat students with equality, becomes paradoxical. For Bourdieu and Passeron (1971), this is "the illusion of equal opportunities". There is a great risk that education will reproduce, rather than ameliorate, conditions of inequality (Wenning 2004) and disguise relations of power (Bourdieu and Passeron 1973). There arise considerable inequalities of opportunity in educational systems and there is a systematic bias in the education system. International studies like PISA and national-level reports on educational achievement show that minority group students, immigrants and students from poor families have a disproportionate risk of failure in school and in vocational training (Haeberlin et al. 2004; OECD 2007). Migration background, ethnicity, class and gender are all important factors (i.e., social categories) of differentiation that influence students' prospects and possibilities. Unequal educational opportunities for students from migrant and socially disadvantaged families arise not only because of inequality in social circumstances and/or inequalities in access to social, economic, and cultural capital, but also can be directly attributed to school practices including discrimination (conscious or unconscious) on the part of the teachers and the schooling system. Studies, like those of Gomolla and Radtke (2009) in Germany, Haeberlin et al. (2004) and Kronig et al. (2007) in Switzerland and of Gomolla (2005) in an international comparative perspective (England, Germany, Switzerland) show institutionalized discriminatory practices and organizational factors in schools, which are conducive to a systematic disadvantage and unfair treatment and judgment of the activity and achievement of students—with a ethnicized, class or gender bias (Weber 2005). These are structurally unfair preconditions as well as daily classroom practices and discourses that discriminate and prejudge children and young people from immigrant and socially disadvantaged families. This is particularly obvious when decisions are made about levels and types of schooling, in the transition, for example, from one school level to the next one as well as, and particularly, in the transition from schooling per se to vocational or professional training. Here we speak of institutional discrimination (Feagin and Feagin 1986; Gilborn 2002) because racism, gender-bias, class-based praxis and thinking is in the organization of school, educational objectives and in everyday routines of the school.

The gap between social heterogeneity and the urge toward homogenization on the one hand, as well as the gap between the requirement for equality and the practice of discrimination on the other thus represent structural and institutional areas of conflict in how schools deal with difference. With these background thoughts in mind, in the following section we address the question of how teachers deal with social differences, social heterogeneity and inequality in their orientation as well as their everyday behavior.

Dealing with Social Differences in School

The empirical basis for the data used here comes from interviews with teachers and classroom observations at schools in Switzerland which were done in connection with a research project "Prevention of Right Wing Extremism and Ethnicized Violence in Schools. An Intervention Study on the Impact of Teacher Training Programs in Switzerland" (Oser et al., from 2004 to 2006), funded by the Swiss National Fund. In this intervention study we developed a prevention program for secondary schools, involving both students and teachers. The entire process—the implementation of the program in classes by teachers as well as the workshops for teachers—was evaluated by quantitative and qualitative methods (Oser et al. 2007, 2009). Unlike the intervention study that focused on how students responded to a racism-prevention program, this current paper analyzes how teachers deal with diversity and social differences in their pedagogical work. Classroom observations were done during the period of time when the teachers implemented the intervention in their classes; the qualitative interviews were done after the end of the project, asking the teachers for their experiences during the project and with dealing with heterogeneity in general. The qualitative analysis refers to the methodology of Grounded Theory (Strauss 1987).

Teachers' Perceptions of Heterogeneity

Teachers quite consciously perceive and judge the heterogeneous composition of their student body. In interviews they refer to differences along social structure lines like social origin, national, ethnic or cultural affiliation, residence location, religion, language and gender. Beyond that, they attend to differences in physical and cognitive level of development as well as students' educational abilities, which is itself a central area of school evaluation and decision-making. Social and individual differences and the tendency toward increasing heterogeneity are thus clearly noticed by teachers, even though those differences may be variously evaluated. Although when teachers speak freely about heterogeneity in everyday conversation or in interviews, it is also clear that they have different appraisals and assessments. Social heterogeneity is regarded

- as common and/or matter of course in today's society, in which the school reflects the image of the society, and/or
- as a positive challenge for instruction and educational work (in the sense, for example, of statements like "otherwise would be boring it"), and/or
- as problem and difficulty.

The teachers' evaluations can be quite intertwined, exist side by, and/or vary depending on the context. Here we want to emphasize the discursive connection between problematizing heterogeneity and the simultaneously narrow view of cultural differences. If heterogeneity is evaluated as problematic, then the teachers focus mainly on immigrant students and their cultural background, which are made salient so that problems are seen as one-sided in an ethnic or cultural context (Diehm and Radtke 1999). Furthermore, teachers consider heterogeneity as a burden in connection with structurally unfavorable conditions, e.g., large classes, no additional support or educational personnel, etc., so that heterogeneity is viewed negatively. Note the problem shift, when attention and discourse concentrate on problematizing migrants, the Other, as themselves problematic instead of responding to the unfavorable structural conditions. Interestingly, teachers broach the issue of social heterogeneity in school out of respect to their students but do not tackle intragroup differences of the teaching body and their respective social status and privileges.

The main point here is that when the faculty (predominantly part of the autochtonous dominant majority) discuss the heterogeneity of the students they focus mostly on students from immigrant families and they see them as Other (while ignoring other differences and building a homogeneous image of them), assessing their presence positively, in that "they" enrich the educational environment, or negatively as a burden—but in any case conceptualized as other, different.

Ambivalences in Dealing with Social Differences

Dealing with the delicate areas of equality and difference is on the background of the inadequate institutional consideration of social heterogeneity largely left to the teachers. The ambivalences and paradoxes in dealing with social differences that were addressed in the introduction intensify against this background. Teachers are confronted with ambivalent requirements in handling differences and diversity in their pedagogical tasks and in their work with students. Given all of this, heterogeneity can become—depending upon context, personal orientation, and tolerance for ambiguity—a positive, potentially developmental challenge or a burden. In this connection the question of how to deal with social differences arises for teachers (again and again), whether they employ the principle of equality or the principle of distinction and differentiation; and/or whether they rely on yet other alternative principles. Initially, we can identify two poles in how teachers deal with diversity: One pole favors equal treatment of students, and seeks to move away from differences and focus on the common requirements and conditions for all students. The other pole represents the acknowledgment of differences and the attempt to treat each case fairly in consideration of those differences. The first variant is connected with playing down, minimizing and perhaps silencing discussion of difference. The second variant is connected with raising the subject of differences for discussion (either explicitly or implicitly). Each in and of itself poses risks, and the implementation of either is paradoxical, as shall be explicated in the following.

Minimizing the Discussion of Differences: The Danger of Ignoring Different Circumstances

Comments from teachers of this orientation are symptomatic when they refer explicitly to the postulate of equal treatment: "We treat all students equally here, we make no differences between the students, nor do we label them", or "the same rights and obligations apply for all pupils". Such discourse patterns that argue from principles of equal treatment and justice, predominate in the argumentation against making special arrangements for Muslim students in swimming classes, during Ramadan and about the practice of wearing a head scarf—discourses, that dominate and are relevant representatives of such discourse, among others, in different countries in Central Europe (Karakasoglu 2003). References to equal rights and obligations are the basis for the approach to integration of minorities and immigrants that demand being as inconspicuous as possible, and accommodating to the local way of life (also constructed as homogeneous). Differences are to be ameliorated unidirectionally, by the voluntary adaptation of the minority to the majority. The question of dealing with differences is directly related to predominating discourses of assimilation or nonassimilation. In the cases and contexts raised here (discourses around fasting, head scarves, etc.) the postulate of equality implicates ethnocentrism and racism. Here the danger is that referring to equal treatment implies that the dominant paradigm and predominating conceptions of norms, rules, and standards are conformed to, and perhaps strengthened.

Further, with reference to the requirement of equal treatment, i.e., similar demands, there is always a risk that with such a perspective students' diverse life-situations—which are always connected with unequal preconditions for learning and scopes of possibilities—are also ignored. Thus, despite the expectation of equal treatment and equal demands, unequal conditions are reproduced. This structural limitation on possible educational (and hence societal) opportunities for students from immigrant and/or poor families is often not seen by members of the majority society. Rather, the prevailing ideology is promoted, namely, that through readiness to perform, will, effort and sufficient support by the family both scholastically and vocationally much or everything can be achieved. This is a personalized perspective on success and failure and a snapshot of unequal assumptions and possibilities under the conditions that social inequalities are neglected. The risk and consequences of such a perspective of ostensibly equal treatment are to reproduce social inequality and also to strengthen the culture hegemony (Gramsci).

Other teachers, involved in the intervention study, have another perspective and valuations of dealing with social heterogeneity in school. A secondary school teacher, for example, sees the postulate of equal treatment quite critically and under today's conditions of social heterogeneity, deems it unworkable.

Int.: Is equal treatment of all pupils even possible, given heterogeneity?

Teacher: No, (smiles) no, absolutely not. So, uh, I think that it's also a little, uh, an outdated saying: all students are treated equally. That is (…) no, no, it doesn't work at all. […], they are completely different (…) things that the students bring along with them in terms of resources, educational preparation, (…) problems which they drag along that permit or prevent learning. Just let me give you a small example. In one family they read to the children, in another family they watch television, or the child has his or her own television in the room, and in a third family the child has nothing at all, neither someone reading aloud to them, nor television. Clearly one cannot achieve the same goals with these three children within the same timeframe, since they have completely different preconditions.

This teacher considers students' widely varied social circumstances to be important starting points for doing adequate and appropriate schooling. He sees adequately dealing with diversity as basic to finding a suitable way to support each individual student. Such a subject-oriented attitude, with the focus on the student's scope of possibility (Möglichkeitsraum), in terms of both their resources and limitations, is an option to account for the diversity among students and offering each student the same opportunities to learn, given the broad range of background circumstances.

In contrast, to take the equality postulate literally (see above), without considering context differences, can only be part of an ideology, or a construction of "normality" which poses normal as over and against deviations from the norm, and with such polarization comes the tendency toward exclusion.

Addressing Difference: The Risk of Inflexible Attribution and of Othering

However, ambivalences and risks occur within the recognition and consideration of differences as well. Another teacher names the danger of attribution in her reflections about dealing with differences in school. She not only considered the postulate of equal treatment, but also the differentiated perception and evaluation of students as thoroughly ambivalent:

> I find it difficult. I can't say what's correct or not. Accordingly, I must also say here, if one wanted to deal with each particular and be correct, then one probably bumps rather rapidly into the limits; that is, one quickly runs into the danger of being just and fair or not. So then things still happen in such a way that one acts rather racist. Although one did not want that actually at all. The prejudice still gets the upper hand. [...] If I think now of how students behave in class, out of the ordinary, rather in-your-face behavior, then perhaps I (...) allow the hot-tempered boy who comes from a southern European country, more leeway than I might with a hot tempered girl, but from Switzerland (laughs). I don't know for sure, but I could imagine that. So I (,), I've never thought it through to end.

In this teacher's statement the ambivalence of dealing with difference and equality becomes clear, including with regard to justice: She reflects on the one hand the difficulty in being fair under all different conditions with respect to the complexity of a class; on the other hand the potential risk of constructing or strengthening ethnicized, racialized *and* gendered attributions and norms—as she herself recognized when she reflected critically on her own behavior with respect to the consideration of differences.

The danger exists in addressing and focusing on differences, that these are emphasized and made salient, and thus their effectiveness as social affiliation markers are strengthened. Above all, this is problematic regarding the dominant view of Others, as has been mentioned, because it presents a one-sided focus on minorities or marginalized people, so that, for example, cultural differences of students from immigrant families are highlighted as aberrant or deviant, and differences in general are attributed to cultural or ethnic characteristics. Here, then, there is a risk of inflexible, rigid attribution and of reducing individuals to a set of collectively attributed characteristics. This can lead again to a one-sided perception of students, e.g., with an ethnicized perspective. Rather such fixed attributions pose the risk of making them "special" or excluding them. Such practices and discourses of Othering are often part of everyday routines and of interactions between teachers and students.

Such a process appears in a classroom situation, in which a teacher is discussing the positive consequences of immigration. The teacher gives some examples of what she means by this, for instance, the influence of international culinary styles and foods. Then she suddenly turns to a student and asks:

> *Where does your mother do her grocery shopping?*
> The student hesitates for a moment and then says:
> *She buys groceries everywhere, in Migro, Coop... (5 sec. delay) My mother doesn't actually cook Brasilian very often at all, more often Asian.*

In this situation it becomes clear, that by addressing the girl and the grocery-practices of her mother, cultural differences (assumed by the teacher) are emphasized and the daily practices of the girl or her mother are ethnicized. Here it comes to a situation of Othering and ethnicization, not to mention gender-related attribution, naming the mother as the person responsible for grocery shopping and cooking. This happens presumably despite the quite well-intended animus of the teacher (attempting to give a good example of multicultural life in Switzerland). But the girl apparently cannot identify herself with this role and so when she answers, she tries to locate herself explicitly in the majority society—by saying that her mother shops in established Swiss supermarkets. After a short pause she even goes beyond that, by stressing that her mother does not cook (ethnic) food from her country of origin, but rather, she cooks internationally, which in Europe and elsewhere means Asian cuisine. She demonstrates that her mother not only does not cook based on her ethnic roots, but rather, she orients the mother as a global Trendsetter and thereby also counters the unexpressed assumptions of the teacher. Even if the girl responds to the culturalized image by using the strategy of building a counter image, this situation illustrates well the powerful impact of the teacher's gendered-ethnic attribution, from which the pupil can free herself only with difficulty.

This example clearly shows, that by raising and focusing on the national-ethnic-cultural belonging (Mecheril 2003) or the background of students from immigrant families, there is a corresponding danger of ascribing fixed-attributions and Othering. The subtle but powerful mode of Othering and inclusion–exclusion is attributed when social differences are marked.

Othering and Negative-Attribution as a Component of Educational Action

The school as a centralized, hierarchically structured educational facility represents in this connection a quite ambivalent and risky platform for action. The establishment of attributional as well as Othering processes has a particularly powerful impact as a consequence of the predominating imbalance of power and the tendency to fuse educational content with discriminatory discourses and practices. Here the reproduction of attributional and Othering processes can also come into play in intercultural work. This is exemplified in the following instructional situation. On the topic of integration and living together, a class with very few immigrant students led by an autochthonous teacher, negative pictures and stereotypes of ethnic Others are addressed and reproduced. This is reconstructed in the following:

Student 1:	To me, foreigners who live in Switzerland should adapt.
Student 2:	But and still one should leave their own customs to them.
Student 3:	One ought to allow them their own particular characteristics, like religion, as well.
Teacher:	But the religion should not have restrictive effects, for example, when religion limits girls, for example, by requiring them to wear a head scarf or preventing them from participating in physical education classes, and such like. We've already talked about that. In what other areas are Muslim girls limited?
Student 1:	They can't join clubs.
Student 4:	They can't have a boyfriend.

Teacher:	Yes, and sometimes they are also forced, against their will, to marry someone they hardly know and are brought back to Turkey.
Student 3:	Yes, but this isn't alike in all families, there are also very open parents, who have nothing at all against it.
Student 5:	That always depends on parents.
Medley of voices:	There are also very open foreigners.

From the first contributions of the students, differences are made. They speak—from the majority perspective—about the Others, "the foreigners, who live in Switzerland". They proceed from the assumption of a specific Swiss majority culture, from which Others deviate. Religion seems to be a noteworthy difference. The teacher's comments are of particular interest as she fashions and emphasizes difference in the above educational discourse. She constructs and outlines a picture of Muslim girls in a typical question and answer format—in which discussion, by the way, there is no Muslim girl. Also, in this case, talking about the Other becomes a means to shape and devalue people, as deviant and incompatible with the majority society. The teacher moves the general discussion of differences in a particular direction by opening a chain of association, which leads from religion, to Muslims and then to religious restrictions and prohibitions for girls. Various lines of difference are touched and taken up: religion, culture, gender, sexuality, generation relationships; thereby a deficient and also negative picture of Muslim girls is drawn. In addition, normality conceptions are brought into play, such as, e.g., that it is standard that girls of these students' age have a boyfriend and, further unexpressed, it is assumed that they are heterosexual. In this way the (societally agreed-upon) attributions toward Muslim girls across a range of social categories and difference lines are overlaid and become a conglomerate (of gender, ethnicity, religion, age, sexuality) from which the picture is fashioned. The overlay and intersection of diverse social differences joins itself to a picture, which places "one's own" as superior over and against "the Other".

The practices of "doing difference" (West and Fenstermaker 1995) and "doing normality" generate and strengthen societal markers for inclusion and exclusion. In addition, "talking about Others" (as seen in this school communication) is also a common hegemonic practice of Othering (Broden and Mecheril 2007; Riegel 2011 forthcoming).

The teacher powerfully steers this discussion. Moreover, through her position as teacher, her substantive message, her power to define within the learning content and teaching discourse, is reinforced. The dominant discourse and well-known, popular (stereotyped) picture of Muslim girls is repeatedly made salient and strengthened through the teachers' comments and questions. Hence the students' "knowledge" is consolidated.

It is important to note here that the construction of Other in the context of schooling, not only perpetuates ethnic and ethnically derogatory images of Other, but also intertwines those images directly with the educational message and the subject matter. Teachers' gendered racialized statements serve as school-specific knowledge.

The students access this image accordingly, initially by responding in the typical classroom question–answer game, thus participating in the reproduction of the dominant paradigm. Later, however, the students also actively resist the teacher in their attempts to qualify, to relativize and limit the teacher's generalizations.

Questioning the statements of a teacher or even resistance in the hierarchical context of school is, however, fraught with difficulties for students. The result of the experience is much too dependent on the good graces of the teacher. This is reflected, for example, in the so-called "school diary" in which a student (of another class) makes reference to a lesson, and, in the following, notes his disagreement with the statements of his teacher.

> I had understood it that way. I wanted to ask if he was trying to say that in our culture it's normal to beat up on others, or what? That is wrong. Of course there are such people, but they're not only Turks, and certainly the majority of Turks are not like this. I don't know exactly what he [Note: the teacher] meant, but it seemed to me that he wanted to tell the class: Watch out for the Turks. People have to be careful with any human being, if one doesn't know that person. I simply felt insulted, but I did not say anything because I did not want to attack my teacher.

This note shows that students are sensitive to teachers' statements and attributions, especially if they feel themselves in any way connected to or a part of the group about whom the teacher is talking. Freedom of expression is possible for students within the context of unequal power between teachers and pupils, but only with difficulty. With a view to the possible or feared consequences (sanctions, bad impressions that have an impact on grades, etc.) it may make sense for students to withhold their responses, retorts or challenges to the attributions and pictures presented by the teacher. Here we see how difficult it is in the hierarchical context of school, in the face of the sovereignty of the teachers, as well as the hegemonic discourse and dominance structures, to resist the attributions of teachers and prevailing norms and dismissive discourses.

Racialized attributions and ethnicization of life, motivation and reasons for action by migrants and the (unstated) distinction between "We and the Others" serves to standardize social groups monolithically, and thereby establish boundaries between them. Thereby the view is one-sided and addressed to those who are conceptualized as Other and often connected with depreciation. The (privileged) situation of majority group members remains unaddressed or is taken as a yardstick. Social representations and discourses are also evident and in effect in the educational context, with exclusionary and discriminatory consequences for students construed as Others.

These consequences are not necessarily intended by the actor. Rather, these actions are framed and rendered obvious by the conflicting institutional parameters for dealing with difference and equality (see above) as well as by societal predominant structures, practices, and discourses of racism (Essed 2002; Osterkamp 1997), which provide the social context for exclusion and discrimination against those who are made Other. Thus, in line with Weiß (2001) we speak of "racism against intention" ("Rassimus wider Willen"). But even if the impact and the outcome of their practices are not intended, they contribute to racism and discrimination and the reproduction, passing on their structures in everyday life and society. Here, we highlight that Othering as well as exclusionary and culturalizing discourses contribute to unequal opportunities for students that institutionalize and establish discrimination in schools. The last example, particularly, makes clear the way in which educators' thinking and action with regard to immigrants and minorities influence and effect professional action. In the educational setting of the school, where knowledge is transmitted, the reproduction of such images and discourses has an even greater power of enforcement, so that the contents of images (as for example of Muslim girls) become social facts as a result of the school institutions power to frame. Thus "talk about the Others", which can lead to Othering, takes place from a doubly powerful position—first from the perspective of the majority society, and then from the position of teacher. Lastly, reproducing established symbolic boundaries, belongings and relations of power while focusing on cultural differences is as well a risk of intercultural education (Diehm and Radtke 1999; Riegel 2011 forthcoming).

Conclusion and Pedagogical Implications

In conclusion, we maintain that dealing with social difference and diversity is ambivalent—particularly under conditions of social inequality where social differences are used to order and to segregate society and to exclude or discriminate people or social groups, which are not in accordance with the cultural hegemony. With reference to social differences (especially ethnicity and gender) we encounter two opposing dangers: On the one hand, there is the problem and the danger of producing and reproducing dominant and established categorizations and attributions and thus of maintaining and perpetuating dominant social demarcations, which result in exclusion, subordination or forcible normalization. But on the other hand, not to consider social differences—as social structure categories—carries the inherent danger of ignoring different starting points and social opportunities and thereby continuing to reproduce social inequality. In any case there is a high risk to strengthen and reproduce the dominant power relations and hegemonic system—in the intersection of heteronormative gender relations, racial ethnic relations, hierarchical class relations, and normative body relations (see Winker and Degele 2009). What is becoming obvious in the empirical examples is, that constructed images and narratives about the Others indeed focus mainly on named "cultural" differences. But these images are constructed by linking other social differences and hierarchical difference relations, like gender/heteronormativity, age/generation, body, religion and ignoring other differences like class. The intersection of different categories can have reinforcing, or in some cases neutralizing or alleviativing effects. By this intersection and interdependency of diverse differences, the image of the Other is formed as not compatible with "our own". The link, the combination and merging to other social images and gender, body, sexual norms has the (reinforcing) social function of protecting the superior position and quality of "one's own" and the symbolic and factual exclusion of social affiliation and power. Here, the analytical perspective of intersectionality is useful for reconstructing processes of Othering as well as for processes of inclusion and exclusion (Riegel 2010). Regarding the intersection of diverse social differences and of relations of power can be a fruitful perspective as well for developing and reflecting educational practices in contexts of socially heterogeneous contexts.

What can we learn from this for educational practice and for organization of schools? How can we find an adequate way to deal with the identified risks and ambivalences? How are we to escape the dilemma between fixed attribution and ignorance of social differences without reproducing exclusion and discrimination?

In the context of relations of social inequality, cultural hegemony and hierarchical power relations, which are also operative in the school context, this is a difficult task—without a clear and unambiguous "solution" of these contradictions. Dealing with difference is a balancing act between equality and recognizing differentiation. A balancing act, that Pat Parker, a Black, lesbian left-wing activist and poet expressed in the poem "For the White Person Who Wants to Know How to Be My Friend": "The first thing you do is to forget that I'm Black. Second, you must never forget that I'm Black" (Parker 2000).

The balance is due to the recognition, on the one hand, of diversity, multiple affiliations and belonging as well of differences without ascribing attributions to individuals and thus (consciously or unconsciously) discriminating and excluding. On the other hand it also requires the consideration of different social conditions and the subject-oriented perception and support of students in their scope of possibilities, without ignoring personal, cultural, or structural conditions, and to bring to consciousness the meaning of privileged or nonprivileged positions. (cf: Blakeney 2000; Siddle Walker and Snarey 2004; West 2001).

So the difference between dealing with a constant swing back and forth between raising and ignoring the issue of difference, a fragile tightrope that, under the circumstances of social inequality and segmentation, can't be escaped, and yet whose respective dangers and pitfalls can be brought to consciousness.

This requires (not only) for teaching persons constant and critical reflection of prevailing images that categorize and order patterns and of the processes of "doing difference", and their consequences for students and for social (power) relations, but also a critique of social and institutional discriminating mechanism and processes of social dominance and repression and its own involvement in it. This includes not least, awareness of and reflection on one's own social position, privilege and power, both in the position of teacher (or researcher) as well as in social space. This kind of reflection needs self-criticism and criticism of the hegemonic system. And, it needs theoretical background or instruments as well as space and time for it—which is usually absent in everyday life at school. With this background one consequence for schools and for the education of teachers is, to give time and room space for reflection, mentoring, and to develop perspectives for changing and for alternatives for action. This has to be considered in teacher training and education, but also in everyday communication in school. In the described research project, where teachers were involved in teacher trainings and mentoring over the whole period of intervention, they used this space for reflecting on their own thinking and behavior, especially on problematic situations of Othering like those described here. They evaluated this as an important learning process for dealing with social differences and social heterogeneity.

However, consequences for education cannot be limited to the level of consciousness raising and self-reflection, but also need structural changes and consequences in the organization of schools and teaching. It needs an institutional and didactic framing, that acknowledges differences between students, without fixing and limiting them to these differences and their linked stereotypes, but rather, representing diversity in the whole range of life environments of the students in didactical material, in curricula, in designing class rooms and buildings and in formation and mixture of teaching staff, which also includes executive positions. This also means recognizing and allocating space for multilingualism and a diversity of living styles of students and parents as well as an explicit positioning against all kinds of discrimination, of racism, sexism, heteronormativism, classism, bodyism and agism. This includes for social hegemonic groups to share their privileges with others.

Ultimately it is not about the question of recognition of difference, but rather of the production of circumstances for social justice and equal opportunity. This is a necessary change of perspective away from a difference-oriented look at Others or the discussion of difficulties in dealing with heterogeneity, to a focus on structural, social, and societal conditions and limitations necessary to achieve equal opportunities.

Acknowledgment I would like to express my sincere gratitude to Ronnie Blakeney for the inspiring discussions, linguistic editing and translation.

References

Allemann-Ghionda, C. (1999). *Schule, Bildung und Pluralität: Sechs Fallstudien im europäischen Vergleich*. Bern: Lang.
Blakeney, R. (2000, July 7–11). *Invitation to the dance: Migration, multi-culturalism and moral development*. Paper presented at the conference 'On the Making of Moral Citizens?' Association of Moral Education, Glasgow, Scottland.
Bourdieu, P., & Passeron, J.-C. (1971). *Die Illusion der Chancengleichheit*. Stuttgart: Klett.
Bourdieu, P., & Passeron, J.-C. (1973). *Grundlagen einer Theorie der symbolischen Gewalt: Kulturelle Reproduktion und soziale Reproduktion*. Frankfurt/Main: Suhrkamp.
Broden, A., & Mecheril, P. (2007). Migrationsgesellschaftliche Re-Präsentationen: Eine Einführung. In A. Broden & P. Mecheril (Eds.), *Re-Präsentationen: Dynamiken der Migrationsgesellschaft* (pp. 7–28). Düsseldorf: IDA NRW.
Crenshaw, K. (1989). Demarginalizing the intersection of race and sex: A Black feminist critique of antidiscrimination doctrine. *The University of Chicago Legal Forum (Feminism in the Law: Theory, Practice and Criticism)*, Vol. 1989, 139–167.
Davis, K. (2008). Intersectionality as a buzzword: A sociology of science perspective on what makes a feminist theory successful. *Feminist Theory, 9*(1), 67–85.
Diehm, I., & Radtke, F.-O. (1999). *Erziehung und Migration: Eine Einführung*. Stuttgart: Kohlhammer.

Eggers, M. M. (2005). Rassifizierte Machtdifferenz als Deutungsperspektive in der Kritischen Weißseinsforschung in Deutschland. In M. M. Eggers, G. Kilomba, P. Piesche, & S. Arndt (Eds.), *Mythen, Masken, Subjekte. Kritische Weißseinsforschung in Deutschland* (pp. 56–72). Münster: Unrast.

Feagin, J. R., & Feagin, C. B. (1986). *Discrimination American style – institutional racism and sexism*. Malabar: Krieger.

Fenstermaker, S. B., & West, C. (2001). "Doing difference" revisited: Probleme, Aussichten und der Dialog in der Geschlechterforschung. In B. Heintz (Ed.), *Geschlechtersoziologie* (pp. 236–249). Opladen: Westdeutscher Verlag.

Gilborn, D. (2002). *Education and institutional racism*. London: University of London, Institute of Education.

Gogolin, I. (2008). *Der monolinguale Habitus der multilingualen Schule* (2nd ed.). Münster, New York: Waxmann.

Gomolla, M. (2005). Institutionelle Diskriminierung im Bildungs- und Erziehungssystem. In R. Leiprecht & A. Kerber (Eds.), *Schule in der Einwanderungsgesellschaft: Ein Handbuch* (pp. 97–109). Schwalbach: Wochenschau Verlag.

Gomolla, M., & Radtke, F.-O. (2009). *Institutionelle Diskriminierung: Die Herstellung ethnischer Differenz in der Schule*. (3rd ed.). Wiesbaden: VS Verlag.

Haeberlin, U., Imdorf, C., & Kronig, W. (2004). *Von der Schule in die Berufslehre: Untersuchungen zur Benachteiligung von ausländischen und von weiblichen Jugendlichen bei der Lehrstellensuche*. Bern: Haupt Verlag.

Hall, S. (1994). 'Rasse', Artikulation und Gesellschaften mit struktureller Dominante. In S. Hall (Ed.), *Rassismus und kulturelle Identität: Ausgewählte Schriften 2* (pp. 89–136). Hamburg: Argument Verlag.

Höhne, T., Kunz, T., & Radtke, F.-O. (2006). *Bilder von Fremden – Was unsere Kinder aus Schulbüchern über Migranten lernen sollen*. Frankfurt a.M.: Wolfgang-Goethe-Universität.

Holzkamp, K. (1983). *Grundlegung der Psychologie*. Frankfurt a.M.: Argument.

Karakasoglu, Y. (2003). Die "Kopftuch-Frage" an deutschen Schulen - Kontroverse Positionen im Spiegel rechtlicher und öffentlicher Diskurse. In U. Kloeters, J. Lüddecke, & T. Quehl (Eds.), *Schulwege in die Vielfalt: Handreichung zur Interkulturellen und Antirassistischen Pädagogik in der Schule* (pp. 61–84). Frankfurt a. M.: IKO Verlag.

Kronig, W., Eckard, M., & Haeberlin, U. (2007). *Immigrantenkinder und schulische Selektion: Pädagogische Visionen, theoretische Erklärungen und empirische Untersuchungen zur Wirkung integrierender und separierender Schulformen in den Grundschuljahren* (Vol. 2). Bern: Haupt Verlag.

Kutscher, N. (2008). Heterogenität. In H.-U. Otto & T. Coelen (Eds.), *Grundbegriffe Ganztagsbildung: Das Handbuch* (2nd ed., pp. 61–70). Wiesbaden: VS Verlag.

Leiprecht, R., & Kerber, A. (Eds.). (2005). *Schule in der Einwanderungsgesellschaft: Ein Handbuch*. Schwalbach: Wochenschau Verlag.

Lutz, H., Herrera Vivar, M. T., & Supik, L. (Eds.). (2010). *Fokus Intersektionalität - Bewegungen und Verortungen eines vielschichtigen Konzepts*. Wiesbaden: VS Verlag für Sozialwissenschaften.

Lutz, H., & Wenning, N. (Eds.). (2001). *Unterschiedlich verschieden: Differenz in der Erziehungswissenschaft*. Opladen: Leske&Budrich.

McCall, L. (2005). The complexity of intersectionality: Signs. *Journal of Woman in Culture and Society, 30*, 1771–1800.

Mecheril, P. (2003). *Prekäre Verhältnisse: Über natio-ethno-kulturelle (Mehrfach-)Zugehörigkeit*. Münster: Waxmann Verlag.

OECD (2007). *PISA 2006. Science Competencies for Tomorrow's World*: Vol. 1: Analysis, PISA, OECD Publishing.

Oser, F., Riegel, C., & Tanner, S. (2007). *Prävention von Rechtsextremismus und ethnisierter Gewalt an Schulen: Eine Interventions- und Evaluationsstudie mit Lehrerweiterbildungsmassnahmen in der Schweiz. Schlussbericht*. Fribourg: Departement Erziehungswissenschaft, Universität Fribourg.

Oser, F., Riegel, C., & Tanner, S. (2009). Changing devils into angels? Prevention of racism and right-wing extremism at school as a sensitising activity. In M. A. Niggli (Ed.), *Right-wing extremism in Switzerland: National and international perspectives* (pp. 231–251). Baden Baden: Nomos.

Parker, P. (2000). For the White person who wants to know how to be my friend. *Callaloo, 23*(1), 73–77.

Riegel, C. (2010). Intersektionalität als transdisziplinäres Projekt: Methodologische Perspektiven für die Jugendforschung. In C. Riegel, A. Scherr, & B. Stauber (Eds.), *Transdisziplinäre Jugendforschung* (pp. 65–89). Wiesbaden: VS Verlag.

Riegel, C. (2011, forthcoming). Folgenreiche Unterscheidungen: Repräsentationen des ‚Eigenen und Fremden' im interkulturellen Bildungskontext. In S. Bartmann & O. Immel (Eds.), *Das Vertraute und das Fremde: Differenzerfahrung und Fremdverstehen im Interkulturalitätsdiskurs*. Bielefeld: Transcript.

Walker, V., & Snarey, J. R. (2004). *Race-ing moral formation: African-American perspectives on care and justice*. New York: Teachers College Press.

Spivak, G. C. (1985). The rani of Simur: An essay in reading the archives. In F. Barker, P. Hulme, M. Iversen, & D. Loxley (Eds.) F. B et al. (Ed.), *Europe and its others* (Vol. 1, pp. 128–151). Colchester: University of Essex.

Strauss, A. L. (1987). *Qualitative analysis for social scientists*. Cambridge: Cambridge University Press.

Weber, M. (2005). "Ali Gymnasium" – Soziale Differenzen von SchülerInnen aus der Perspektive von Lehrkräften. In T. Badawia, F. Hamburger, & M. Hummrich (Eds.), *Migration und Bildung* (pp. 69–81). Wiesbaden: VS Verlag.

Weiß, A. (2001). *Rassismus wider Willen: Ein anderer Blick auf eine Struktur sozialer Ungleichheit*. Wiesbaden: Westdeutscher Verlag.

Wenning, N. (2004). Heterogenität als nette Leitidee der Erziehungswissenschaft? Zur Berücksichtigung von Gleichheit und Verschiedenheit. *Zeitschrift für Pädagogik, 50*(2), 565–582.

West, C. (2001). *Race matters*. New York: Vintage Press.

West, C., & Fenstermaker, S. (1995). Doing difference. *Gender and Society, 9*(1), 8–37.

Winker, G., & Degele, N. (2009). *Intersektionalität: Zur Analyse sozialer Ungleichheiten*. Bielefeld: Transcript.

Chapter 23
A Learning Curve: The Education of Immigrants in Newcastle-upon-Tyne and Bremen from the 1960s to the 1980s

Sarah E. Hackett

The importance of educational experiences amongst immigrant youths in Britain and West Germany remains undisputed in the literature.[1] Since the 1960s, both countries have witnessed a vast increase in the number of immigrant pupils enrolled in schools, causing the emergence of such terms as 'educationally disadvantaged', 'equal educational opportunity' and 'multi-racial education' (Willke 1975; Rist 1979b; Tomlinson 1986). Regarding Britain, scholars have especially highlighted the problems endured by Afro-Caribbean pupils, and the educational hindrance caused by language needs and belated government responses (Taylor 1974; Kirp 1979a; Parekh 1986). The literature addressing Germany concludes that immigrant schoolchildren have become concentrated in the least prestigious schools, suffered inequality within the apprenticeship and training system, and that many have left without a diploma (Wilpert 1977; Faist 1993; Alba et al. 1994). This chapter will complement these works by presenting a historical assessment of the education of immigrants in Newcastle-upon-Tyne and Bremen, providing a voice to those beyond the foci of Birmingham and Berlin who, despite belonging to well-established communities, have remained relatively silent in the literature. It will do so by means of an analysis of government documents from the 1960s through to the 1980s, a period for which material is readily available and one which charts vital changes in approach in both cities' education sectors. It will start by offering an extended look at the general immigration and education policies of both countries.

Although there is no doubt that immigrant youths in Britain and Germany have traditionally endured hardships and disadvantages within the education sector, there is a fundamental difference in ideology that has shaped both countries' immigration policies post-1945. Britain's role as the imperial hub for a quarter of the world's surface has led to the creation of the socioeconomic and cultural entity of the Commonwealth. Depending on pre-existing links and bonds, immigrants arrived to

---

[1] This chapter will simply refer to "Germany" from this point onwards.

S. E. Hackett (✉)
University of Sunderland, SR1 3PZ Sunderland, UK
e-mail: sarah.hackett-1@sunderland.ac.uk

Britain as ex-subjects of the imperial project, largely with the intention of settling indefinitely. They had the right to enter Britain and to obtainritish citizenship, and were entitled to vote as well as work in the civil service. Furthermore, the literature has emphasised the extent to which these colonial ties played a role in initial reasons for migrating (Layton-Henry 1992; Joppke 1996, p. 477; J. Herbert 2008). It has been Britain's colonial history that gave way to an immigration pattern in which migrants arrived independently with social and economic aspirations. Alternatively, in West Germany, immigrants arrived as nothing short of economic pawns in the country's prospering economy. Due to its economic miracle of the 1950s, recruitment contracts were signed with eight countries (Panayi 2000). The result was a guest-worker rotation system that generated privately negotiated economic immigration. Guest-workers in West Germany were seen as nothing more than a temporary phenomenon, a group of immigrant workers whom Herbert termed 'a reserve labour army' (U. Herbert 1990, p. 211).

Comparisons between British and German cities with regards to immigrant experiences have rarely been pursued. One example is Boyes and Huneke's study on Turks in Berlin and Pakistanis in Bradford which, although a valuable contribution to the field, was nevertheless a comparison between two cities that had little more in common than their large immigrant communities (2004). Newcastle and Bremen, however, are home to well-established South Asian and Turkish communities respectively,[2] and are two cities that allow for an effective comparison due to shared historical, economic and social characteristics. Both acted as major European ports, suffered economic downturns during the 1970s and 1980s, and have since become post-industrial landscapes struggling with commercial readjustment. Most importantly, it has been argued that both cities have a strong sense of regional identity, a trait that has feasibly helped shape the experiences of their respective immigrant communities. Regarding Newcastle, scholars have established that this city sits at the centre of a region that prides itself on being a welcoming host (Todd 1987; Renton 2006). To the contrary, Bremen has arguably historically been home to a 'special urban identity' that has acted as a catalyst for jingoism and xenophobia (Buse 1993).

Despite these claims, these cities have been largely overlooked in the literature. Bremen's history of immigration has very much been overshadowed by its role as a centre of emigration in a similar way to the manner in which Newcastle's has been

---

[2] According to the censuses, Newcastle's Indian, Pakistani and Bangladeshi population stood at 1,202 in 1961, 2,697 in 1981, 3,457 in 1991 and 5,704 in 2001. However, these figures include only those people born in India, Pakistan and Bangladesh, and not any descendants born in Newcastle. The real figure of this immigrant community, therefore, was undoubtedly much higher. This information has been provided by the Office for National Statistics. The microfilm containing the data for the 1971 census has been misplaced and this information can, therefore, not be accessed. Bremen's immigrant community has traditionally been much larger. In 1979, the state of Bremen had an immigrant population of 41,700, the vast majority of which were from some of the former recruitment countries (Turkey, Yugoslavia, Portugal, Italy, Spain and Greece). By 2001, the state's immigrant population had risen to 79,000. Furthermore, as was the case throughout Germany, it was Turks who constituted a large proportion of this figure as a result of family reunification. These statistics have been obtained from the Bremische Bürgerschaft Bibliothek (City Parliament Library of Bremen) and the Statistisches Landesamt Bremen (Statistical Land Office of Bremen).

marred by the experiences and reputation of South Shields, a North-Eastern city that has been home to a substantial immigrant population since the late 1800s (Hoerder 1993; Lawless 1995). However, there are certainly reasons for which this neglect should be reversed. Bremen, and indeed the whole of Germany's poor performance in the PISA (Programme for International Student Assessment) study in 2000 has brought the German education system to the forefront of the political and scholarly agenda (OECD 2001). Regarding Newcastle, a recent study concluded that the integration of the city's refugee pupils largely depended on individual schools, calling into question the impact of overarching local policies and measures (Whiteman 2005). This chapter therefore has both historical poignancy and current relevance. It is through these two case studies that the extent to which Britain and Germany's differing immigration histories lay at the foundation of succeeding education policies will be assessed, and their holistic impact on learning and social contexts revealed.

The policies adopted by both governments during the 1960s were marked by the very absence of a strategy. In Britain, there was no clear-sighted policy at a national level during this decade. As Male pointed out, the 1963 Robbins Report on higher education did not even mention immigrants, the 1963 Newsom Report dedicated less than two pages to the educational obstacles faced by Black youths and the 1967 Plowden Report devoted only six pages to immigrant children (1980, p. 292).[3] In West Germany, during the 1960s, the federal government did little more than call for compulsory education to be extended to immigrant youths (Rist 1979b, p. 357.). Furthermore, it was deemed unnecessary for education legislation to be directed at immigrant children. This was because their long-term integration was considered futile as their stay in Germany was only to be temporary. It is perhaps then not surprising that it was not initially recognised that the educational needs of immigrant children required catering for (Wilpert 1977, p. 475).

In Britain, the 1965 dispersal policy signalled a departure from previous inactivity (Ministry of Education and Science 1965). This policy advised that ethnic minority children should be divided amongst different schools rather than becoming concentrated in only a selected few. It stated that no school or classroom should be more than circa one-third immigrant, believing that high concentrations of immigrant pupils would prevent integration (Gillborn 1990, pp. 145–146; Grosvenor 1997, pp. 53–55). This policy clearly paved the way for what was to become the British government's assimilationist approach towards the education of immigrant children during the late 1960s and 1970s. This was based on the belief that immigrants should be absorbed into British society, and that the preservation of minority languages and cultures should have a much lower priority (Mullard 1982, p. 121). It was believed that the dispersing of immigrant pupils would enable a faster acquisition of the English language as well as ensuring that schools were not transformed due to an influx of a large number of immigrants (Kirp 1979b, pp. 272–273). It soon became apparent, however, that not all immigrant pupils were benefiting from

---

[3] The Robbins Report considered the future of higher education in the UK, the Newsom Report assessed the education of less able pupils and the Plowden Report examined primary school education.

this policy (Figueroa 1991, p. 76). Consequently, the 1970s and 1980s witnessed a shift in Britain from an assimilationist approach to a multicultural one. This new approach was documented in the 1985 Swann Report, which advocated a multi-ethnic school curriculum, and promoted ways in which school pupils would learn about and appreciate a variety of cultures, ethnicities and languages (Rex 1987, pp. 13–15). Although it has been difficult to assess the exact impact of the report's recommendations, some initiatives were taken, such as an interest in increasing the number of teachers from an ethnic minority background (Arora 2005, pp. 86–87).

Whilst Britain exchanged an assimilationist education policy for a multicultural one, federal states across Germany adopted a plethora of policies of both types. In other words, schools in some states focused more on long-term integration than those in others. Differences quickly emerged in the quality and length of German language classes, the importance placed on mother-tongue languages and culture, and access to education and training (Wilpert 1977, pp. 476–477). Although one might assume that there are benefits to implementing local measures for local immigrant communities, many scholars have repeatedly highlighted the shortcomings of these education policies, with Rist asserting that immigrant children received a 'double message' from the German education system (1979b, p. 362). Whilst Germany's education policies towards guest-worker children undoubtedly portrayed a widespread uncertainty concerning its position as a nation of immigrants, those of Britain increasingly represented a country that arguably attempted to define itself as multicultural.[4]

Despite the fact that their approaches have differed as a result of immigration history, there is little doubt that each nation's respective debate concerning the education of immigrant children is still ongoing. The same contention that was witnessed during the 1970s with the emergence of Coard's groundbreaking work (1971) on West Indian children in the British school system, and during the 1980s with the Honeyford Affair and the Burnage High School incident,[5] is today seen in the debate over the wearing of Muslim veils in British schools. Similarly, the ever-present discrimination and lack of opportunities suffered by Turks in Germany's education system, as reported by scholars during the 1970s and 1980s, has more recently been reinforced by the OECD's PISA study in 2000, which concluded that Germany trails significantly behind in the education of immigrants compared to other European countries (Baumert et al. 2001; Ammermueller 2007). It is through this chapter's historical microcosmic assessments that two cities' attempts to address the cultural and social differences in the process of learning are revealed, and the impact that national immigration legislation has on local education policy exposed.

---

[4] For an introduction to the claim that Germany is not a country of immigration, see Joppke, (1999, pp. 62–99). For an introduction to multiculturalism in Britain, see Modood (2007).

[5] The 1985 Honeyford Affair took place in Bradford and consisted of a headmaster publishing various articles that challenged the concept of multicultural education. In the 1986 Burnage High School incident, an Asian boy was murdered as a result of a racist attack.

Newcastle-upon-Tyne[6]

Newcastle's local authority's education policies towards immigrant pupils have historically reflected Britain's role as the receiver of both organic and permanent immigration. One of the major concerns expressed during the 1960s was the acquisition of the English language. It was believed that schools with a larger number of pupils from an ethnic minority background were becoming characterised with a lower standard of English (TWAS 5 December 1967, p. 1). As a result of this apprehension concerning the increasing number of immigrant children in the city's schools,[7] Newcastle's local authority seems to have considered implementing the Ministry of Education and Science's 1965 dispersal policy. Although Newcastle did not have any schools that were one-third immigrant, there were two primary schools, Westgate Hill Junior and Westgate Hill Infant, that had 70 and 51 immigrant pupils, and which were 19.8% and 20% immigrant, respectively (TWAS 5 December 1967, p. 1). Despite this concentration, however, it was decided that the difficulties posed by high numbers of ethnic minority children would be addressed within the individual schools concerned (TWAS 5 December 1967, p. 2). Part-time teachers were appointed to assist with language skills and the immigrant pupils' overall integration.

Although not in Newcastle, the dispersal policy was considered and introduced by local authorities across Britain. Under the measure adopted by Ealing's education authority, Asian pupils were expected to apply to a central office and be dispersed to different schools in the area (Male 1980, p. 293). During the mid1960s, Bradford and Southall's local authorities transported immigrant pupils to schools in neighbouring areas so as to avoid their concentration in others (Miller 1966, p. 253). Some cities, such as Bristol, did not have to resort to the dispersal policy as racial mixing was achieved by the fact that most schools were built on the outskirts of the city, away from the centre of the ethnic population (Kirp 1979b, p. 276). It is perhaps not surprising that Newcastle City Council did not introduce the dispersal policy during the 1960s. Firstly, compared to cities like London and Bradford, Newcastle had a very small immigrant community that was undoubtedly deemed more manageable. Secondly, although there were indeed some immigrant pupils who had little knowledge of the English language, the Education Committee was potentially assured by the fact that they were still of primary school age and therefore still young enough to acquire the language quickly. The link between age and language acquisition is stressed in the literature and the situation in Newcastle was undoubtedly less severe than that of other cities, such as Birmingham (Dustman and Fabbri 2003).

It is not surprising then that the situation in one particular secondary school caused much concern. In November 1967, Slatyford Comprehensive School was

---

[6] See also Hackett (2009).

[7] According to the Education Committee document of 5 December 1967, in November 1967, there were 585 immigrant pupils in Newcastle's schools. This was an increase from 348 in January 1964.

10% immigrant, a figure that was significantly higher than that of any other of Newcastle's secondary schools, and was deemed as having a language problem. Out of 124 immigrant pupils, 34 spoke English to an acceptable standard, 21 had some knowledge of English and 18 had no knowledge of the English language whatsoever (TWAS 5 December 1967, p. 3). Unlike those immigrant children at primary school age, those arriving to Slatyford Comprehensive School were doing so with relatively few years of school life remaining. During the 1960s and 1970s, works increasingly focused on the attainment of the English language by immigrant children and the consequences of poor language acquisition are still continuously highlighted with regards to both Britain and Germany (Derrick 1977; Dustman and Fabbri 2003; Von Below 2007). Regarding Newcastle, the Education Committee initially suggested that those immigrant pupils with language problems be sent to a reception centre where they would undergo intensive English language tuition until they were deemed ready to rejoin their respective classes.

This was a scheme that was implemented by local authorities throughout Britain during the 1960s, including those of Inner London, Huddersfield and Birmingham (Miller 1966, p. 256; Loewenberg and Wass 1997). Newcastle's Commonwealth Working Group, however, disregarded the idea, stating that it was preferable for problems to be addressed within the standard classroom. This may have been because it was believed that the school had sufficient resources to address the problem or due to the fact that reception centres were often perceived as hindering integration, rather than promoting it. According to Miller (1966, p. 255), 'some immigrant groups…have regarded the reception class as a form of segregation. Schools have found it difficult to classify immigrant children and have occasionally placed them initially in a class for retarded children'. Despite the fact that the Newcastle City Council did not introduce the dispersal policy for either the city's primary or secondary school immigrant students, there was nevertheless a keen focus on the acquisition of the English language and an overall assimilation into British society. Although there has traditionally been much debate surrounding the reasoning behind the 1965 dispersal policy, there is no doubt that a provision for long-term immigration and integration lay at its foundations. In other words, whether this assimilationist position should be seen as merely the forcing of immigrant pupils to abandon their own languages and cultures for 'superior' ones pertaining to the host society, or a consequence of a fear that schools would soon become overrun with ethnic minority children, this approach was based on the idea of permanent settlement (McKay and Freedman 1990, p. 388; Grosvenor 1997, pp. 50–51).

This notion of long-term immigration and integration was further reinforced by the approach that the Newcastle City Council adopted during the 1980s. During the second half of this decade especially, education policies across Britain were partially shaped by the 1985 Swann Report, also known as *Education for All*. It asserted that pupils should be educated in a multicultural environment and should be 'mainstreamed' rather than being isolated from their indigenous counterparts (Committee of Inquiry into the Education of Children from Ethnic Minority Groups 1985; Chivers 1987; Verma 2007). Furthermore, this multiculturalist approach arguably influenced local government measures before 1985 with the 1981 Rampton Report, also issued by the Swann Committee.

This transition from an assimilationist education system towards a multicultural one was adopted fairly quickly in Newcastle. Schools were asked 'to review their curricular, organisational and administrative policies to ensure they are free of any institutional racism' (TWAS 18 September 1985b, p. 1). Newcastle's council focused on promoting ethnic minority language and participation, and the combating of racist incidents (TWAS 15 March 1985; TWAS 6 February 1984, p. 2). Twenty mother-tongue teachers, for example, were to be divided between the city's primary and secondary schools (TWAS 18 September 1985a, p. 3). It is, however, essential to realize that by promoting mother-tongue languages within the city's schools, the council was in fact breaching the Swann Report, which suggested that whilst ethnic minority languages should be encouraged, they should not be incorporated within mainstream schools. (Broeder and Extra 1999, p. 88). This was done because there was concern that not all ethnic minority children would have the external support needed to maintain their mother tongues (TWAS 18 September 1985a, p. 2). Overall, however, there is no doubt that it resulted in a more multicultural approach. Other measures included staff training in ethnic minority languages, courses in language teaching methodology and the promoting of language awareness in schools (TWAS 18 September 1985a, p. 3).

A further consequence that the Swann Report had on Newcastle's local authority consisted of suggestions designed to combat racism. Anti-racism training was to be offered to Education Officers, Advisors and Head Teachers, a centralised system for the reporting of racial incidents was to be established, the curriculum was to include anti-racist teaching, and kitchen staff was to be trained for the provision of ethnic minority diets (TWAS 18 March 1987, p. 43; TWAS 9 July 1985, pp. 1–3). Again, these measures were not particular to Newcastle. Similar steps were also taken in Birmingham, for example, in an attempt to respect Muslim religious and cultural traditions (Joly 1989; Ansari 2004, pp. 318–320). It is on the reporting of racial incidents that Newcastle's local government appears to have largely focused during the following years, and the mid- to late-1980s witnessed the emergence of reports that recorded racial incidents that took place within the city's schools (TWAS 9 July 1985, pp. 3–5; TWAS 18 March 1987; TWAS 22 March 1988).

Bremen

As with Newcastle, Bremen's education policies regarding immigrants have also historically adhered to national mandate, but one reflecting confusion and uncertainty. Education in Germany is state-controlled and differs from one *Bundesland* to another, lacking centralised accountability and a clear integration policy (Hill 1987; Hanf 2001). This has resulted in each German state implementing the type of policy it prefers. In Bavaria, for example, a large emphasis was put on mother-tongue languages as it was believed that immigrants' integration into German schools would prove difficult. To the contrary, Berlin's policy prepared immigrant children primarily for a future in Germany and strove for integration, believing that it was unrealistic by the mid 1970s to still assume that guest-workers would be returning 'home' (Rist 1979a). Still other states implemented the combined model, which promoted both German and mother-tongue languages. Bremen's position towards the education of immigrant pupils was close to that of Berlin in that its main aim was to promote integration into German society. During the mid 1970s, Bremen's government introduced a variety of measures addressing the education of immigrants. Like in Newcastle, this was undoubtedly linked to the increase in the number of immigrant schoolchildren, which between 1970 and 1977 had risen from just over 1,000 to an estimated 5,300. This was primarily due to family reunification, which was largely heightened by the change in allowances for children (*Kindergeld*) and the 1973 recruitment halt (Statistisches Landesamt Bremen, April 1978, p. 100). Starting in January 1975, these allowances were only available for those children living in Germany, causing many immigrants to call for their children to join them (Rudolph 2006, p. 105).

Bremen's approach was detailed in a state government document dating from April 1977 (Bremische Bürgerschaft Bibliothek, 25 April 1977). There were a variety of measures through which integration was hoped to be achieved, such as the promotion of day care centres amongst immigrant families and additional German language classes. On the whole, it was deemed that preparation classes were only meeting the needs of a small proportion of immigrant pupils and that more needed to be done to assist with the acquisition of the German language. Secondly, there was also an emphasis placed on the fact that not all immigrant children remained in Germany, but that some would eventually return to the homeland. Thus, it was thought necessary that measures should extend to the maintaining of mother-tongue languages and native cultures. This was to be done at day care and youth centres. It was the policy in Bremen that mother-tongue language instruction was the responsibility of the countries of origin. However, the local government assisted with the organisation of language classes and expressed a desire to incorporate mother-tongue lessons into the city's schools if and when possible.

Bremen was by no means particular in providing for the learning and maintaining of mother-tongue languages. Krefeld and the state of North Rhine-Westphalia separated German and non-German children for some school subjects and brought them together for others, thus promoting teaching in both German and mother tongues. Other areas, such as Lower Saxony and Baden-Württemberg, permitted immigrant children to choose their mother-tongue language as their first foreign language in schools. The aim was for children to learn these languages whilst also receiving the same education as their German counterparts (McLaughlin and Graf 1985, pp. 247–248; Beck 1999, p. 8). The fact that these disparities existed between different German states was not only evidence of a lack of a national policy, but also of the uncertainty surrounding the future of the country's guest-workers. Differences also existed between the approaches taken in Bremen and Newcastle. Firstly, whilst Newcastle seemed keen to tackle problems within the respective schools, Bremen involved day care and youth centres. This might have been because Bremen's schools alone simply could not implement all necessary measures. After all, many of the measures suggested in the April 1977 report, such as the involvement of parents and the hiring of extra workers of a Turkish background, would have been much more difficult to implement within mainstream classrooms. Secondly and most importantly, there is a fundamental difference between the two cities' types and chronology of approach. Whilst Newcastle's local authority was pursuing only long-term integration already by the late 1960s, Bremen, despite having opted for the integration model, was nevertheless considering immigrant youths' return to the homeland still during the late 1970s. Again, this reflects the grassroots legacy of Britain's and Germany's immigration histories.

A government document of 1980 detailing recommendations regarding the situation of immigrant youths in Bremen's schools records what appears to be a more enhanced focus on integration into German society and stresses the desire for German and immigrant children to sit side by side in the same classroom (Bremische Bürgerschaft Bibliothek, 1 September 1980). The acquisition of the German language was to be further promoted so that immigrant youths would be able to attain a good quality school-leaving qualification, something that has always been perceived as problematic amongst ethnic minorities in Germany (Alba et al. 1994; Worbs 2003). In the document of September 1980, Bremen's Secretary of Education suggested a dispersal policy similar to that proposed in 1965 by the Ministry of Education and Science in Britain. In Britain, the policy stated that the number of immigrant pupils in either one school or classroom should not exceed one-third of the total number of students. In Bremen, however, as in Berlin, the figure suggested was 20% (Rist 1979a, pp. 251–254). Whilst Newcastle did not have any schools that approached the one-third limit, Bremen had a number of schools that exceeded 20%. In the school year of 1979–1980, there were a total of 344 classes that were 20% or more immigrant, constituting 17.9% of the city's classrooms (Bremische Bürgerschaft Bibliothek, 1 September 1980, p. 8).

The dangers and shortcomings of dispersal policies have been well documented and there were additional measures that Bremen's local authority suggested implementing at this time (Jancke 1976). These included an increase in the number of teaching posts in the city's schools in order to support the learning needs of immigrant children and the tackling of compulsory school attendance. For the school year 1979–1980, notification regarding compulsory school education was provided in mother-tongue languages for immigrant parents. In addition, it was decided that immigrant parents applying for *Kindergeld* had to provide confirmation of compulsory school attendance. The results of these measures were seen almost immediately. With regards to vocational schools, for example, the percentage of registered students increased from 65% in 1978–1979 to 80% in 1979–1980. These measures mark a clear contrast with the situation in Newcastle and Britain as a whole where, although the literature has often depicted language problems and poor government responses, there has never been widespread poor attendance at compulsory school age. There is little doubt that, overall, ethnic educational inequality has historically been more evident in Germany (Baumert and Schümer 2001; Kristen 2006).

Changes were also proposed within schools. Additional help was to be provided for pupils whose German was not advanced enough to allow them to participate in regular classes. Preparation classes were to be available for those youths whose German was very basic. It was decided, however, that pupils should not stay in preparation classes for more than two years as the aim was for them to become integrated alongside their German counterparts as quickly as possible. In schools with smaller numbers of immigrant pupils in which preparation classes were not available, support groups were to be formed and, although they would still take part in mainstream classes, special assistance was provided (Bremische Bürgerschaft Bibliothek, 1 September 1980, pp. 14–15). Some immigrant pupils were to be able to choose their mother-tongue language as a school subject instead of a foreign language, a measure that was not particular to Bremen, but was offered in other German states (Broeder and Extra 1999, p. 82). Concern was expressed over the type of schools that the city's immigrants were attending. Scholars have repeatedly highlighted the three different tracks of German secondary education, consisting of *Hauptschule* (minimum or elementary education), *Realschule* (intermediate education), both of which often preceded apprenticeships, and *Gymnasium* (grammar school), which lead to university, and argue that immigrant youths, especially Turks, became concentrated in the lower school classifications (Frick and Wagner 2001; Kristen and Granato 2007). These concerns and policies all reflect the long-term legacy of Germany's guest-worker rotation system.

Conclusion

There are several conclusions that can be drawn from this bureau-political study of immigrant education in Newcastle and Bremen. From the 1960s to 1980s, both cities implemented a variety of policies. Whether these took the form of after-school centres, an intensified focus on the English and German languages, or ways in which to guarantee employment, it rapidly became clear that they were only satisfying a segment of the immigrant pupils' ethno-cultural needs. Both cities have been home to immigrant youths who have found themselves torn between two educational cultures. This has resulted in learning not being confined to the classroom, but rather being pebble-dashed across both cities in the shape of mosques and temples, religious youth centres and family-run businesses, which acted as conduits of indigenous cultural education. In other words, Newcastle and Bremen's immigrant youths have found themselves adhering to assimilationist or integrationist policies whilst still pursuing cultural self-determination. This illustrates not only the breach between host government policies and immigrant needs, but also the extent to which it can influence the learning process.

Nevertheless, Newcastle appears to have encountered fewer obstacles with regards to immigrants and education than much of the literature suggests. The 1965 dispersal policy that played such a role in Inner London and Bradford was never introduced in Newcastle, and the consistent educational underachievement so widespread across Britain never witnessed (Tomlinson 1991; Modood et al. 1997). This might possibly have been the result of Newcastle's comparably smaller immigrant community. Whilst some cities were confronted with classrooms that were overwhelmingly comprised of immigrant pupils during the 1960s and 1970s and thus adhered to national mandate, Newcastle was able to address any issues arising within schools and did not need to implement all elements of the assimilationist model in an attempt to promote the English language and culture.

It initially appears as though the same conclusion might be drawn regarding Bremen. This is a city that has never been at the centre of the abundant literature addressing immigrant educational underachievement in Germany (Gang and Zimmermann 2000; Schierup et al. 2006, pp. 159–160). Furthermore, the September 1980 government report highlighted how Bremen surpassed other German cities regarding the number of immigrant youths attaining a school-leaving qualification (Bremische Bürgerschaft Bibliothek, 1 September 1980, p 16). Yet by the 2000s, the PISA results certainly told a different story. The 2000 study concluded that immigrant pupils in Bremen trailed significantly behind their German counterparts regarding reading literacy scores. The 2003 study reached similar conclusions for the city-state of Bremen in mathematics, reading literacy and the usage of the German language (Prenzel et al. 2005, pp. 267–298). In fact, Germany as a whole performed well below the OECD average in all three test subjects with regards to both German and immigrant pupils. Many reasons have been offered for this poor performance, especially in reference to immigrant pupils, such as the strong link between socioeconomic status and educational performance, or the fact that the German school system requires pupils to be streamed at an early age, often before immigrant youths have reached an adequate level in the German language (Kristen 2000; Worbs 2003).

It has also been suggested that immigration law has had an impact on PISA results with traditional immigration countries, such as Australia and Canada, performing better than their European counterparts because they have tended to choose immigrants with a good educational background and those who are able to contribute to the country's economy (Entorf and Minoiu 2004; Ammermueller 2007). The UK, however, appears to be an exception to this paradigm, which Entorf and Minoiu (2004) suggested is down to a high influx of Western migrants. However, maybe this result should not be as surprising as Entorf and Minoiu (2004) claimed it to be, and perhaps Western migrants are not the sole reason for it. In the same way that immigration law has impacted upon the PISA results of Australia and Canada, there is no doubt that it has also done so for those of Britain and Germany. The legacy of Britain and Germany's immigration histories and policies are seen in both Newcastle and Bremen. Many immigrants who arrived in Britain during the 1940s and 1950s for the long-term had experienced the British education system, were familiar with British culture and many regarded Britain as a natural second home (Favell 2001; J. Herbert 2008). This was often coupled with the entrepreneurial and educationally proactive culture of the subcontinent. In Germany, to the contrary, guest-workers arrived as temporary relief to the country's full employment economy and took part in an immigration scheme that involved few social provisions or costs on behalf of the German government (Panayi 2000; Green 2004). This has doubtlessly enforced social limits on the holistic process of learning.

These case studies have demonstrated the long-term ramifications of two very different immigration histories, but have also exposed factors that could inform modern immigration and integration policy. Newcastle has disclosed the benefits of a smaller and more manageable immigrant community, whilst Bremen has revealed the struggles surrounding the integration and education of immigrant youths in a Germany that claimed it was not a nation of immigrants. Whilst it is apparent that Germany's official denial hindered the integration of immigrant youth, it must be recognised that this renunciation is slowly being reversed. The Immigration Act of 2005, for example, included the promotion of integration amongst immigrant communities, whilst the German Islam Conference of 2006 paved the way for increased dialogue between the German government and the country's immigrant population. These developments combined with the PISA results will undoubtedly secure the education of immigrant youth a place on the German political agenda. In Britain, the Muslim Council of Britain, for example, has been pursuing similar goals for more than a decade. It is certainly the conclusion of the research here that this should continue and increase.

Newcastle and other British cities' local authorities prepared for the permanent integration of immigrant youths from the outset, whilst Bremen's government's ability to implement local policies for local immigrant communities as a result of Germany's federal administration was overshadowed by the ambiguity surrounding the country's guest-workers and Germany's continuous claim that it was not a country of immigrants. It appears as though, in both cases, the legacy of national immigration histories prevailed, rendering the differences between Britain's centralised and Germany's federal administrations practically redundant. Education policy in some areas like Bavaria did not even consider the integration of immigrant youths and even those cities that did, such as Berlin, have been criticised for pursuing assimilation rather than multiculturalism, and for not accommodating the needs of immigrant pupils. In other words, whilst Britain's history and policies created a paradigm for educational stability, Germany's led to a sense of uncertainty and obscurity. It appears that the shadow of the suitcase not only fell on Southampton dockside and Munich central station, but across 50 years and into the classrooms of contemporary immigrant schoolchildren.

References

Alba, R. D., Handl, J., & Müller, W. (1994). Ethnische Ungleichheit im deutschen Bildungssystem. *Kölner Zeitschrift für Soziologie und Sozialpsychologie, 46,* 209–237.
Ammermueller, A. (2007). Poor background or low returns? Why immigrants in Germany perform so poorly in the Programme for International Student Assessment. *Education Economics, 15*(2), 215–230.
Ansari, H. (2004). *'The infidel within': Muslims in Britain since 1800.* London: C. Hurst.
Arora, R. (2005). *Race and ethnicity in education.* Aldershot: Ashgate.

Baumert, J., & Schümer, G. (2001). Familiäre Lebensverhältnisse, Bildungsbeteiligung und Kompetenzerwerb. In J. Baumert, E.Klieme, M. Neubrand, M. Prenzel, U. Schiefele, W. Schneider, et al. (Eds.), *PISA 2000: Basiskompetenzen von Schülerinnen und Schülern im internationalen Vergleich* (pp. 323–407). Opladen: Leske + Budrich.

Baumert, J., Klieme, E., Neubrand, M., Prenzel, M., Schiefele, U., Schneider, W., et al. (2001). *PISA 2000: Basiskompetenzen von Schülerinnen und Schülern im internationalen Vergleich.* Opladen: Leske + Budrich.

Beck, E. (1999). Language rights and Turkish children in Germany. *Patterns of Prejudice, 33*(2), 3–12.

Boyes, R., & Huneke, D. (2004). *Is it easier to be a Turk in Berlin or a Pakistani in Bradford?* London: Anglo-German Foundation for the Study of Industrial Society.

Bremische Bürgerschaft Bibliothek. (25 April 1977). *Antwort des Senats zur kleinen Anfrage der Fraktion der FDP vom 1. März 1977 (Drs. 9/445) Kinder ausländischer Arbeitnehmer* (Drucksachen Band 3 9/451–9/620 March 1977-October 1977, Bremische Bürgerschaft Landtag 9. Wahlperiode, Drucksache 9/484).

Bremische Bürgerschaft Bibliothek. (1 September 1980). *Bericht über die Lage der schulpflichtigen Kinder von Ausländern* (Drucksachen Band 2 10/251–10/450 June 1980-March 1981, Bremische Bürgerschaft Landtag 10. Wahlperiode, Drucksache 10/300).

Broeder, P., & Extra, G. (1999). *Language, ethnicity & education: Case studies on immigrant minority groups and immigrant minority languages.* Clevedon: Multilingual Matters.

Buse, D. (1993). Urban and national identity: Bremen, 1860–1920. *Journal of Social History, 26*(3), 521–537.

Chivers, T. S. (Ed.). (1987). *Race and culture in education. Issues arising from the Swann Committee report.* Windsor: NFER-Nelson.

Coard, B. (1971). *How the West Indian child is made educationally sub-normal in the British school system: The scandal of the black child in schools in Britain.* London: New Beacon for the Caribbean Education and Community Workers' Association.

Committee of Inquiry into the Education of Children from Ethnic Minority Groups. (1985). *Education for all: The report of the committee of inquiry into the education of children from ethnic minority groups.* London: HMSO.

Derrick, J. (1977). *Language needs of minority group children: Learners of English as a second language.* Windsor: NFER.

Dustman, C., & Fabbri, F. (2003). Language proficiency and labour market performance of immigrants in the UK. *The Economic Journal, 113*(489), 695–717.

Entorf, H., & Minoiu, N. (2004). PISA results: What a difference immigration law makes. *IZA Discussion Paper, 1021.*

Faist, T. (1993). From school to work: Public policy and underclass formation among young Turks in Germany during the 1980s. *International Migration Review, 27*(2), 306–331.

Favell, A. (2001). *Philosophies of integration: Immigration and the idea of citizenship in France and Britain* (2nd ed.). Basingstoke: Palgrave.

Figueroa, P. (1991). *Education and the social construction of 'race'.* London: Routledge.

Frick, J., & Wagner, G. (2001). Economic and social perspectives of immigrant children in Germany. In E. Currie & T. Wunderlich (Eds.), *Deutschland, ein Einwanderungsland?: Rückblick, Bilanz und neue Fragen* (pp. 299–326). Stuttgart: Lucius & Lucius.

Gang, I., & Zimmermann, K. (2000). Is child like parent? Educational attainment and ethnic origin. *The Journal of Human Resources, 35*(3), 550–569.

Gillborn, D. (1990). *'Race', ethnicity & education: Teaching and learning in multi-ethnic schools.* London: Unwin Hyman.

Green, S. (2004). *The politics of exclusion. Institutions and immigration policy in contemporary Germany.* Manchester: Manchester University Press.

Grosvenor, I. (1997). *Assimilating identities: Racism and educational policy in post 1945 Britain.* London: Lawrence & Wishart.

Hackett, S. (2009). The Asian of the North: Immigrant experiences and the importance of regional identity in Newcastle-upon-Tyne during the 1980s. *Northern History, 46*(2), 293–311.

Hanf, T. (2001). Education in a cultural lag: The case of Germany. *International Journal of Educational Research, 35*(3), 255–268.
Herbert, U. (1990). *A history of foreign labor in Germany, 1880–1980: Seasonal workers, forced laborers, guest workers.* (trans: Templer, W.). Ann Arbor: University of Michigan Press. (Original work published 1986).
Herbert, J. (2008). *Negotiating boundaries in the city: Migration, ethnicity, and gender in Britain.* Aldershot: Ashgate.
Hill, A. (1987). Democratic education in West Germany: The effects of the new minorities. *Comparative Education Review, 31*(2), 273–287.
Hoerder, D. (1993). The traffic of emigration via Bremen/Bremerhaven: Merchants' interests, protective legislation, and migrants' experiences. *Journal of American Ethnic History, 13*(1), 68–101.
Jancke, E. (1976). Zur schulischen Situation der Kinder ausländischer Arbeitnehmer in Berlin. *Forum, 4*, 94–99.
Joly, D. (1989). Ethnic minorities and education in Britain: Interaction between the Muslim community and Birmingham schools. *Muslims in Europe, 41.*
Joppke, C. (1996). Multiculturalism and immigration. A comparison of the United States, Germany, and Great Britain. *Theory and Society, 25*(4), 449–500.
Joppke, C. (1999). *Immigration and the nation-state: The United States, Germany, and Great Britain.* Oxford: Oxford University Press.
Kirp, D. (1979a). *Doing good by doing little: Race and schooling in Britain.* London: University of California Press.
Kirp, D. (1979b). The vagaries of discrimination: Busing, policy, and law in Britain. *The School Review, 87*(3), 269–294.
Kristen, C. (2000). Ethnic differences in educational placement: The transition from primary to secondary schooling. *MZES Working Paper, 32.*
Kristen, C. (2006). Ethnische Diskriminierung in der Grundschule? Die Vergabe von Noten und Bildungsempfehlungen. *Kölner Zeitschrift für Soziologie und Sozialpsychologie, 58*(1), 79–97.
Kristen, C., & Granato, N. (2007). The educational attainment of the second generation in Germany: Social origins and ethnic inequality. *Ethnicities, 7*(3), 343–366.
Lawless, R. (1995). *From Ta'izz to Tyneside: An Arab community in the North-East of England during the early twentieth century.* Exeter: University of Exeter Press.
Layton-Henry, Z. (1992). *The politics of immigration: Immigration, 'race' and 'race' relations in post-war Britain.* Oxford: Blackwell.
Loewenberg, M., & Wass, B. (1997). Provision for the development of the linguistic proficiency of young immigrants in England and Wales and France: A comparative study. *Comparative Education, 33*(3), 395–409.
Male, G. (1980). Multicultural education and education policy: The British experience. *Comparative Education Review, 24*(3), 291–301.
McKay, S., & Freedman, S. (1990). Language minority education in Great Britain: A challenge to current U.S. policy. *TESOL Quarterly, 24*(3), 385–405.
McLaughlin, B., & Graf, P. (1985). Bilingual education in West Germany: Recent developments. *Comparative Education, 21*(3), 241–255.
Miller, H. (1966). Race relations and schools in Great Britain. *Phylon, 27*(3), 247–267.
Ministry of Education and Science. (June 1965). *The education of immigrants.* (Circular 7/65). London: HMSO.
Modood, T. (2007). *Multiculturalism: A civic idea.* Cambridge: Polity.
Modood, T., & May, S. (2001). Multiculturalism and education in Britain: An internally contested debate. *International Journal of Educational Research, 35*(3), 305–317.
Modood, T., Berthoud, R., Lakey, J., Nazroo, J., Smith, P., Virdee, S., et al. (1997). *Ethnic minorities in Britain: Diversity and disadvantage.* London: Policy Studies Institute.
Mullard, C. (1982). Multiracial education in Britain: From assimilation to cultural pluralism. In J. Tierney (Ed.), *Race, migration and schooling* (pp. 120–133). Norfolk: Thetford Press.
OECD. (2001). *Knowledge and skills for life: First results from PISA 2000.* Paris: OECD.

Panayi, P. (2000). *Ethnic minorities in nineteenth and twentieth century Germany: Jews, gypsies, Poles, Turks and others*. Harlow: Longman.
Parekh, B. (1986). The concept of multicultural education. In S. Modgil, G. Verma, K. Mallick, & C. Modgil (Eds.), *Multicultural education: The interminable debate* (pp. 19–31). London: Falmer.
Prenzel, M., Baumert, J., Blum, W., Lehmann, R., Leutner, D., Neubrand, M., et al. (2005). *PISA 2003: Der zweite Vergleich der Länder in Deutschland – Was wissen und können Jugendliche?* Münster: Waxmann Verlag GmbH.
Renton, D. (2006). Hostility or welcome? Migration to the North East of England since 1945. *Paper in North Eastern History, 15*.
Rex, J. (1987), Multiculturalism, anti-racism and equality of opportunity in the Swann Report. In T. S. Chivers (Ed.), *Race and culture in education. Issues arising from the Swann Committee report* (pp. 1–16). Windsor: NFER-Nelson.
Rist, R. (1979a). On the education of guest-worker children in Germany: A comparative study of policies and programs in Bavaria and Berlin. *The School Review, 87*(3), 242–268.
Rist, R. (1979b). On the education of guest-worker children in Germany: Public policies and equal educational opportunity. *Comparative Education Review, 23*(3), 355–369.
Rudolph, C. (2006). *National security and immigration: Policy development in the United States and Western Europe since 1945*. Stanford: Stanford University Press.
Schierup, C., Hansen, P., & Castles, S. (2006). *Migration, citizenship, and the European welfare state: A European dilemma*. Oxford: Oxford University Press.
Statistisches Landesamt Bremen. (April 1978). *Schulbesuch und Schulerfolg ausländischer Schüler* (Statistische Monatsberichte der Freien Hansestadt Bremen, 30. Jahrgang).
Taylor, F. (1974). *Race, school and community*. Windsor: N.F.E.R.
Todd, N. (1987). Black on Tyne: The black presence on Tyneside in the 1860s. *North East Labour History Society, 21*, 17–27.
Tomlinson, S. (1986). Political dilemmas in multi-racial education. In Z. Layton-Henry & P. Rich (Eds.), *Race, government & politics in Britain* (pp. 187–203). Basingstoke: Macmillan.
Tomlinson, S. (1991). Ethnicity and educational attainment in England: An overview. *Anthropology and Education Quarterly, 22*(2), 121–139.
Tyne & Wear Archives Service (TWAS). (5 December 1967). *Immigrant pupils in schools* (Commonwealth Immigrants Working Group of Planning Committee 19 Sep. 1966–6 May 1968 MD.NC/149).
Tyne & Wear Archives Service (TWAS). (6 February 1984). *Co-opted members* (Local Government and Racial Equality Sub-Committee of Corporate Joint Sub-Committee 18 March 1983–17 July 1985, Local Government and Racial Equality Sub-Committee MD.NC/162/1).
Tyne & Wear Archives Service (TWAS). (15 March 1985). *The Swann Report: Digest of the report of the Swann Committee on 'Education for All'* (Local Government and Racial Equality Sub-Committee of Corporate Joint Sub-Committee 18 September 1985–15 July 1987 MD.NC/162/2).
Tyne & Wear Archives Service (TWAS). (9 July 1985). *Report of racial incidents* (Local Government and Racial Equality Sub-Committee of Corporate Joint Sub-Committee 18 March 1983–17 July 1985 MD.NC/162/1).
Tyne & Wear Archives Service (TWAS). (18 September 1985a). *Mother-tongue teaching report on the schools language survey conducted in Newcastle-upon-Tyne schools* (Local Government and Racial Equality Sub-Committee of corporate Joint Sub-Committee 18 September 1985–15 July 1987 MD.NC/162/2).
Tyne & Wear Archives Service (TWAS). (18 September 1985b). *The Swann Report* (Local Government and Racial Equality Sub-Committee of Corporate Joint Sub-Committee 18 September 1985–15 July 1987, City of Newcastle-upon-Tyne Education Committee, Schools Sub-Committee and Racial Equality Sub-Committee MD.NC/162/2).
Tyne & Wear Archives Service (TWAS). (18 March 1987). *Monitoring of racial incidents in schools* (Local Government and Racial Equality Sub-Committee of Corporate Joint Sub-Committee 18 September 1985–15 July 1987 MD.NC/162/2).

Tyne & Wear Archives Service (TWAS). (18 March 1987). *Strategies for combating racism – head teachers' courses* (Local Government and Racial Equality Sub-Committee of Corporate Joint Sub-Committee 18 September 1985–15 July 1987 MD.NC/162/2).

Tyne & Wear Archives Service (TWAS). (22 March 1988). *Monitoring of racial incidents in schools* (Local Government and Racial Equality Sub-Committee of Corporate Joint Sub-Committee 6 August 1987–16 March 1988 MD.NC/162/3).

Verma, G. (2007). Diversity and multicultural education: Cross-cutting issues and concepts. In G. Verma, C. Bagley, & M. Jha (Eds.), *International perspectives on educational diversity and inclusion: Studies from America, Europe and India* (pp. 21–30). Abingdon: Routledge.

Von Below, S. (2007). What are the chances of young Turks and Italians for equal education and employment in Germany? The role of objective and subjective indicators. *Social Indicators Research, 82*(2), 209–231.

Whiteman, R. (2005). Welcoming the stranger: A qualitative analysis of teachers' views regarding the integration of refugee pupils into schools in Newcastle upon Tyne. *Educational Studies, 31*(4), 375–391.

Willke, I. (1975). Schooling of immigrant children in West Germany, Sweden, England: The educationally disadvantaged. *International Review of Education, 21*(3), 357–382.

Wilpert, C. (1977). Children of foreign workers in the Federal Republic of Germany. *International Migration Review, 11*(4), 473–485.

Worbs, S. (2003). The second generation in Germany: Between schools and labor market. *International Migration Review, 37*(4), 1011–1038.

Chapter 24
School Policies, Gender-Sex-Sexuality and Ethnocultural Re-production in Sweden, Canada, and Germany

Irina Schmitt

Setting Out—Looking for Stories of the Nation and the Role of Gender-Sex-Sexuality in School Policies

Schools are places of learning—of the acquisition of academic knowledge and skills, as well as the adoption and incorporation of social knowledge. At school, knowledge about societal norms is effectively transmitted and re-produced in daily interaction. School policies provide part of the framework that structures this knowledge transfer. Policies, in turn, are informed by—gendered—discourses of social participation in the context of nation-state reasoning. I am interested in the national investments in specific notions of gender-sex-sexuality, in the entanglements of neonationalist projects in Europe and North America with complex strategies leading at the same time to the exclusion of queer and queered subjectivities, and to their use as symbols of liberal democracies, effectively racializing/ethnifying insider and outsider gender-sex-sexualities (Puar 2007).[1]

This chapter aims to analyze this complexity by discussing school politics from three Western immigration societies, Germany, Sweden, and Canada.[2] The transnational comparison and the intersectional approach will address current limitations in education policies and public discourses (Nash 2008). The interest in policy is also motivated in the United Nations Convention on the Rights of the Child that stipulates the need to act in children's "best interest" when making laws and policies (UN 1989, Article 3).

---

[1] I use the term queered to describe the processes of othering that have little to do with identity and more with discriminatory structures and practises, while queer, in my understanding, implies self-positioning.

[2] This choice reflects my shifting points of departure: Originally situated in Germany, I was interested Canada, and then Sweden, as two of the often cited "good practice" examples. As I shifted my geographical location, so did my focus: I now look at the "good example" as a critical insider-outsider.

I. Schmitt (✉)
Centre for Gender Studies, Lund University, Box 117, 221 00 Lund, Sweden
e-mail: irina.schmitt@genus.lu.se

Education, Henry Giroux reminds us,

> is always political because it is connected to the acquisition of agency. As a political project, education should illuminate the relationships among knowledge, authority, and power. It should also draw attention to questions concerning who has control over the production of knowledge, values, and skills, and it should illuminate how knowledge, identities, and authority are constructed within particular sets of social relations. In my view, education is a deliberate attempt on the part of educators to influence how and what knowledge and subjectivities are produced within particular sets of social relations. (Giroux and Polychroniou 2008)

While education is certainly not restricted to schools, schools are spaces where issues of values and the authority over their representation are most obvious, and therefore merit constant reflection.

There are important differences in the national debates about values regarding gendered, sexualized, and ethnicized belonging in the three societies I refer to in this chapter. While Canadian society has about 40 years experience of conceptualizing ethnocultural diversity as an integral part of Canadian-ness, Germany waited till 1998 to officially acknowledge immigration as a societal factor that merits political attention. Sweden's cultural consensus on "equality" as well as the positive appearance in the PISA study, despite current political and structural changes towards more conservative approaches in education, makes that comparison insightful (OECD 2000, p. 45). The perceptions of migrant young people differ significantly in the societies discussed here. While especially in Germany, but also in Sweden, a discursive juxtaposition of cultural and sexual belongings is used in the ongoing construction of a "national identity", this is less the case in Canada (though gender vs. religious rights are also discussed, see Schmitt and Winter 2009).

By analyzing how policy texts create implicit knowledge about and explicit presentations of—ethnicized—norms of gender-sex-sexuality in the context of schools, I hope to clarify the discursive and structural frameworks that make schools "safe" or "unsafe" spaces for (groups of) young people. I follow the tradition of researchers and activists who point out the high risks faced by queer and queered children and youth (Kosofsky Sedgwick 1991) while at the same time being aware of the limitations of the notion of "queer kids as victims" (Rasmussen et al. 2004).

Neither gender, nor sexuality nor indeed sex, come to us naturally (Butler 1993). Young people both learn to "be" a certain gender-sex-sexuality and performatively construct gender-sex-sexuality in interrelation with other aspects of identification and stratification. For young people who are considered to be "different in more ways than one" issues of social justice and belonging can be even more crucial than for their peers (Belling et al. 2004).

To make my ideas tangible, I will focus on one example of school policies per country, choosing the countries' capitals Berlin, Stockholm, and Ottawa. The subject of civics/social studies will offer a distinct insight in the understandings of citizenship and belonging in these societies. A brief presentation of studies on homophobia and other forms of discrimination experienced by young people, done by NGOs, public bodies, and academics, shall serve to contextualize these normative statements.

Notions of "Youth"—Agency in Dangerous Times?

Young people and their representations are limited by an understanding and the legal fixation of young people as innocent and impressionable, in need of protection and basically subjected to adults (Mellor and Epstein 2006, p. 381; Rofes 2005, p. 66). At the same time, young people—especially in some of their othered impersonations—are considered dangerous, to themselves and "society at large". Thus, the analysis of school policies needs to be embedded in a refiguration of our understandings of "youth".

Children and young people are a focal point of national negotiations of sexuality (Pellegrini 2009). The invocation of normalized notions of children and youth also informs students' understanding of self and others. Queer theorist Judith Jack Halberstam suggests an "'epistemology of youth' that disrupts conventional accounts of subculture, youth culture, adulthood, race, class and maturity" (Halberstam 2008, p. 27). The issue at stake is much broader than voicing (justified) concern about minoritized youth, or even young people's well-being in general. Rather, young people might be read as reflection and indication of changes in societal understandings of belonging, as David McInnes and Cristyn Davies suggest:

> What might happen if the melancholic presence of the sissy boy in schools is considered as a lively point of reflection rather than as a call to tolerance of homosexuality? (McInnes and Davies 2008, p. 115)

This is a challenge to read the normative text of policies in a way that allows for the nonnormative. It is central to not consider gender nonconformative, queer/ed and ethnicized young people as either a "tool" that initiates and propels otherwise unnecessary changes, nor as carrying the main responsibility for such changes. It is important to acknowledge young people as coproducers of belongings and hierarchizations, without understating adults' responsibilities (Kumashiro 2000, p. 38).

Analyzing School Policies—Framing "Who I Should Be"

Schools, as spaces where apparently private experiences need to be negotiated with public rules and norms, are exemplary for the ongoing re-production of what is considered "normal" and which presentations of selfhood are readable and recognized (Marshall and Gerstl-Pepin 2005, pp. 124–125).[3] In the mostly heteronormative setting of schools, lesbian, gay, bisexual, transgendered, and intersex youth (and teachers) are confronted with additional "social work" and sometimes additional

---

[3] The discourse about underachieving boys is just one example of the role of gender in schools (Connell 1996), with successful girls and the supposedly overpowering presence of female teachers as main culprits. Little is written about the overpowering presence of White teachers on children of color, or the possibly damaging effects of a mainly heteronormative staff on queer/ed students.

risks (Martinsson et al. 2007; Meyer 2009). Discourses that regulate gender-sex-sexuality use and in turn inform conceptualizations of ethnicized national belonging (Frosh et al. 2002; Luibhéid 2002; Nordberg 2008; Puar 2007; Schmitt 2010b; Spindler 2006).

Three theoretical tools are useful for this analysis. Intersectionality is, if used critically, an approach to analyze interdependent power relations, most prominently gender, class, and ethnicity (de los Reyes and Mulinari 2005; McCall 2005; Nash 2008). More recently, categorizations such as sexuality, gender identity and ability are addressed. The concept of heteronormativity is used to critically refer to the ongoing discursive re-production of heterosexuality as exclusively normal. Working with the concept of heteronormativity means to analyze if and how subjects, both those written into the policies and those analyzing the policies, are implied as generally heterosexual and as conforming to norms regarding gender-sex-sexuality (thus, this is not mainly about intimate interactions, but about social praxes) (McGregor 2008).[4] Lastly, I use comparative analysis to reflect the movement towards educational globalization that is, for example, manifest in international comparative tests (Marshall and Gerstl-Pepin 2005, pp. 212–226). This movement is not unproblematic, but also holds a moment of learning from societies with differing understandings of education and social justice. Thus, I engage Clare Hemming's call for a particularity that is globally situated (Hemmings 2007, pp. 26–27).

Analysis of social regulations cannot be limited to policy analysis (Butler 2004, p. 40; Paechter 2001, p. 45). Policy analysis does, however, offer an understanding of the normative societal consensus through which inclusion and exclusion are formulated (Marshall and Gerstl-Pepin 2005, pp. 118–119). Reading texts as a reality in themselves, rather than as a referent to a reality outside of the text, has become a sound tradition in feminist (education) studies (Bacchi 2005; Foucault 2003, p. 34; Smith 1993 [1990]). School laws and curricula can be seen as "powerful policy artefacts" (Marshall and Young 2006, p. 67). That discourses are produced by and in turn produce (human) subjectivities and interrelations, is important to remember in reading policy texts (Bacchi 2005).

Sharon Todd reminds us of the ontological demands inherent in curricula: The regulative moment of policies is not just a structure, it works to alter students (Todd 2001). Following Todd (following Derrida), this "ontological violence," that is, the internalization of rules, regulations, and discourses actually changes "who I am" and has strong normative implications (Todd 2001, p. 435). Legal and structural frameworks not only reflect, but also constitute the "gendered subject of the law" (Ahmed 2000, p. 53).

Discussing policies implies some confidence that change within or with the tools of "the system" can create profound social change and refers to the understanding that young people's "safety" can be achieved by using government structures. Yet, writing policy is much easier than implementing effective long-term strategies to

---

[4] I have written about the need to dislodge the researcher as implicitly heterosexual elsewhere (Schmitt 2008b, 2010a).

counteract discrimination (McGregor 2008). The notion of "safety" in itself invites critical examination, as Mary Lou Rasmussen shows:

> [Tropes] of "safe space", like notions of inclusion, are difficult to critique. However, on closer scrutiny it is apparent this operates as a dividing practice producing material and symbolic exclusions...it is also necessary to take into account the power relations that underlie the invocation of "safe space" in educational contexts... (Rasmussen 2004, p. 138)

Analyzing policies dissects how gendered, sexualized, and ethnicized norms are perceived and created through the documents that govern schools and their everyday affairs. It is clear that policies need to be seen as situated in and representations of their specific social and political contexts (McGregor 2008, pp. 3–4). On the following pages, I will present central aspects of school policy texts for Berlin, Stockholm, and Ottawa. The different structures in the three societies in question—federal in Germany and Canada, and more centralist with a focus on regions in Sweden—obviously produce different formats of school policies. Generally, all three contexts have antidiscrimination legislation, to differing degrees embedded in the school policies.

Discourses of Citizenship and Difference—Berlin

The German legal and societal framework has long positioned diversity as problematic. Recently, some important policy changes have been accomplished, as, for example, the Civil Partnership Act of 2001 and the General Equal Treatment Act of 2006, that affords an antidiscrimination framework. The debate about the "integration" of ethicized groups is very present in German public discourse. The German education system maintains the reproduction of exclusion, one symptom being that "second generation" students generally are less successful in school than "first generation" students (OECD 2006, p. 2). At the same time, the lack of positive examples reproduces the image of migrant students' educational "failure". This debate is markedly gendered, invoking a traditionally patriarchal "other".

While no national studies on homophobia and transphobia in schools exist, a study with German young people found that 61% express homophobic sentiments (iconkids & youth 2002). Two studies are interested in the role of migrant young men as perpetrators of homophobic violence (MANEO 2007; Simon 2008). This perceived causality between migration and homophobia refers to the German understanding of national belonging: The "migrant young men" in these studies might have been born in Germany, but are considered "foreigners" by state institutions as well as in these studies. The "othering" of homophobia is one aspect of the continuous "othering" of patriarchal traditions that inhibits serious discussion of patterns of exclusion and violence in Germany.

As Germany is a federal republic, educational responsibility lies mainly with the states (*Länder*), partly coordinated by the Standing Conference of the Ministers of Education and Cultural Affairs of the Länder. Berlin is a city-state, with its own education policy. I base my analysis on the Berlin school law of 2004 (Senatsverwaltung für Bildung, Wissenschaft und Forschung Berlin 2008), and the curriculum for civics of 2006 for grades 7–10 (Senatsverwaltung für Bildung, Jugend und Sport Berlin 2006).[5]

The School law stipulates:

> Every young person has the right to a sustainable school education and upbringing regardless of their sex, their descent, their language, their origin, a disability, their religious or political beliefs, their sexual identity and the economic or social standing of the guardians. (Senatsverwaltung für Bildung, Wissenschaft und Forschung Berlin 2008, pp. § 2, 1; this and all following translations by the author)[6]

Aiming to follow these regulations, all Berlin curricula are opened by a four-page introduction marking a common normative ground, both regarding gender and ethnicity. There is a strong focus on learning in a many-cultural society and the importance of intercultural competences. This introductory text also includes a paragraph that highlights that "girls and boys should be strengthened in their difference and individuality" (Senatsverwaltung für Bildung, Jugend und Sport Berlin 2006, p. 7).

The curriculum for civics (*Sozialkunde*) refers to two main discourses: a discourse of rights (and obligations), and another, interlinked discourse of difference. The authors of the curriculum focus on the role of learners within the democratic state as active citizens. Democracy is considered a good in need of constant protection. In terms of classroom methods, this means that students should be able to "adopt different perspectives" (Senatsverwaltung für Bildung Jugend und Sport Berlin 2006, p. 14).

The field of civics is structured in topics. Under the topic of "young people and politics," grades 7–8, the text states among others "ways of life and life situations of different social groups and cultures such as children, youth, women, men, lesbians, gay men, migrants, old people, and disabled people" as learning context (Senatsverwaltung für Bildung Jugend und Sport Berlin 2006, p. 27). The authors of the curriculum suggest possible cross-references with the learning on sexuality and sexual orientation in biology class. Under the topic of "human rights", the authors of the curriculum position human rights as "an expression and means of measurement of the process of civilisation" (Senatsverwaltung für Bildung Jugend und Sport Berlin 2006, pp. 16, 29). While knowledge about human rights is an important basis for discussions of national and global social injustices, the way human rights are positioned here creates a strong hierarchization of societies.

In this framework, to "translate basic principles of constitutional and social democracy" is a central personality trait (Senatsverwaltung für Bildung, Jugend und Sport Berlin 2006, p. 14). It is embedded into a societal norm of a pluralistic society that is manifest through "peaceful solutions for conflicts of interests" (Senatsverwaltung für Bildung, Jugend und Sport Berlin 2006, p. 26). This is an interesting notion, especially in Berlin, where heterogeneity is an integral part of young people's everyday lives. It indicates the assumption that young peoples' experiences

---

[5] See Boeser and Späte for an overview on research on "gender issues and civic education" (Boeser 2005; Späte 2005).

[6] The German term *Geschlecht* invokes both sex and gender.

of "differences" tend to be fraught with problems and that a rights-based learning experience will allow them to overcome such differences. There is no reference to the young peoples' transcultural experiences and skills as being something learning can build on (Schmitt 2008c).

The authors of the curriculum point out that being able "to work cooperatively and product-oriented in groups" are considered essential for survival and success in the job market (Senatsverwaltung für Bildung, Jugend und Sport Berlin 2006, p. 19). Thus, intercultural competences are not presented as a value in themselves, as the recurring reference to the normative frameworks such as human rights might imply; they serve another goal in the context of neoliberal market interests.

The focus on human rights and the "principles of freedom and equality" (Senatsverwaltung für Bildung, Jugend und Sport Berlin 2006, p. 19) is similarly intriguing within a context that still affords strongly differentiated access to the labor market and, incidentally, to political office, with a marked bias against young people with migration background (Burkert and Seibert 2007; Granato 2001; OECD 2006).

Responsible Freedom in the Market of Schools—Stockholm

Sweden is a constitutional monarchy; government is unitary, with elected regional and communal administrative bodies. Sweden is internationally renowned as a gender-equal society with gender-aware education (Seemann 2009), though critics point to the still significant gender pay gap (Lundberg 2007) and everyday racism (Schmauch 2006).

In a study on abuse in schools, 82% of the research participants never or rarely heard about homosexuality in sex-education (Osbeck et al. 2003, pp. 134–138). A survey by the national organization for sexual equality found troubling examples of discrimination in textbooks (Ryng et al. 2003). This is supported by a more recent annual report on police-registered hate crime that states a rise in sexuality-related hate crime in 2008 by 46% in comparison to 2007; transphobia was registered specifically for the first time (Klingspor and Molarin 2009, pp. 57–63, 64–65).

Swedish school education is generally free and comprehensive, and in preschool and the compulsory *grundskolan* (grades 1–9) based on a national curriculum; the responsibility for education lies with each municipality.[7] The documents I am using for my analysis are parts of the current national curriculum and the new version that has recently passed parliament (Skolverket 2006, 2010a, 2011), the Stockholm *Skolplan* (Stockholms Stad 2008) and the national syllabus for civics (Skolverket 2000a). After revision of both the school law and the national curriculum for *grundskolan* in summer 2010, the subject-specific syllabi have been rewritten and scheduled to be implemented in fall 2011 (Skolverket 2010b). While under the new law local school plans are no longer compulsory, it will be the responsibility of lo-

---

[7] The national plan also covers higher secondary education and adult education, *Sameskolan* (grades 1–6) for children of Sami families, and special schools.

cal authorities and principals to plan and document education (Skolverket 2010b, Chap. 4, § 2–6; 2011). I present the analysis of the existing school plan as indication of how documents might be framed. Also, following the implementation of the new antidiscrimination legislation in 2009, schools have to write an annual antidiscrimination plan (Skolinspektionen 2008). However, the *Skolinspektion* found that 9 out of 10 schools fail to adequately address this task.

As the current version, the new national curriculum opens with statements on "Fundamental values" and "Understanding and compassion for others" (Skolverket 2006, p. 3, pages refer to the English-language version; 2010a, 2011 my translation).[8] In addition to "gender, ethnic belonging, religion or other belief, sexual orientation or disability, or subjected to other degrading treatment" (Skolverket 2006, p. 3), and in accordance with antidiscrimination legislation from 2009, the new text also includes transgender identity, age, ability as grounds for nondiscrimination (Skolverket 2010a, 2011).[9] In both versions, this first page refers to "the ethics borne by Christian tradition and Western humanism" that should be "achieved by fostering in the individual a sense of justice, generosity of spirit, tolerance and responsibility" (Skolverket 2006, p. 3, 2010a, 2011, p.7).[10] This is supported later on in the document; one of the "Goals to attain in the compulsory school" is that students should be "familiar with central parts of our Swedish, Nordic and Western heritages" (Skolverket 2006, p. 10, 2010a, p. 4, 2011, p.13). This clearly demarcates the ethnocultural ground on which education should be based.

At the same time, students should learn an "understanding of other cultures" and "appreciate the values that are to be found in cultural diversity" (Skolverket 2006, pp. 3, 4). According to the new text, they should both be knowledgeable about national minorities in Sweden (Jews, Roma, Sami, Finns, and people from Tornedalen) and be able to cooperate with people based on knowledge about similarities and differences in living conditions, culture, language, religion, and history in the new text (Skolverket 2010a, p. 11, 2011, p.14).

The Stockholm school plan is titled "A world-class school!" (Stockholms Stad 2008; my translation). In the opening paragraph, the authors underline that "Education gives people the power to form their own live" (Stockholms Stad 2008, p. 5). Students shall learn in an environment free from fear and anxiety. High priority is given to teachers as the students' main resource for learning. The introduction ends with an interesting point: schools are to be free from political intervention. The text clearly points to the notion of schools as service providers in a market of other educational service providers. With the growth of the private education sector, public

---

[8] To discuss all the changes and continuities in the new text would be beyond the scope of this chapter. The official statements highlight more clarity with regards to responsibilities and rights (which also implies more control for the private sector), more centralized content in all subjects, assembled syllabi for different school forms; national tests in year 3, 6, and 9, and a more detailed grade scale (Skolverket 2010c; for a more detailed discussion see Schmitt (in press)).

[9] From 2006 to 2009, school-specific antidiscrimination legislation existed.

[10] Similar references can be found in some German school laws, for example, in North Rhine-Westphalia, Baden-Wuerttemberg, Bavaria, and the Saarland.

schools are now competing for students (Lund 2008).[11] Thus diversity (*mångfald*) has a double meaning, denoting both the changes due to immigration and a growing awareness of indigenous minorities as well as the changes in school policy that lead to growing competition in the "market of schools." Read together with the investment in the individual that is tangible throughout the school plan, this creates a tension with the national curriculum that refers to the need to "contribute to the pupil's sense of togetherness and solidarity and also to developing their sense of responsibility for people outside of the immediate group" (Skolverket 2006, p. 8, 2010a, p. 9, 2011, p.12).

The Stockholm school plan highlights the role of education in a multicultural society. Gender is discussed in a chapter on norms and values, where it is written that boys and girls should have the same chances for development (Stockholms Stad 2008, p. 12), but it does not refer to sexuality and gender nonconformative gender identities (i.e., transgender and intersex).[12] In contrast, ethnicity and disability merit their own paragraphs in the school plan, and indeed serve to highlight the focus on diversity. The text also states that schools should not go over the parental home's responsibilities, which invites ambivalent interpretations: While, especially in multicultural societies, parental rights can have an important function in counteracting universalist learning contexts, children's and young people's position looses importance. All students are to feel safe in their school; therefore the school plan outlines a zero tolerance approach against mobbing, offending treatment, and violence. It is stressed that sexual assault is unacceptable (Stockholms Stad 2008, p. 12).[13]

The old national curriculum for civics (*samhällskunskap*) is embedded in the curriculum for social studies, which includes also geography, history, and religion (Skolverket 2000b). The civics curriculum specifies:

> The subject contributes to pupils' ability to understand their own and others' conditions and values, and thus also be able to distance themselves from and actively counteract different forms of repression and racism. The education should be open to different ideas and encourage their expression, as well as promote respect for each person's intrinsic value, irrespective of gender, class and ethnic background. The equal rights and opportunities of boys and girls, women and men should be actively and consciously clarified. (Skolverket 2000a)

While gender is repeatedly mentioned, sexual identifications are only implicit in both the civics curriculum and the school plan.[14]

The new course plan for civics for grades 7–9 mentions "young people's identities and lifestyles and how they are informed by, for example, socioeconomic back-

---

[11] The new law limits some of the priviledges for private schools.

[12] A study on the Swedish school plans specifies that 1 out of 269 school plans mention sexual identity, 14 take up sexuality/sexual orientation/homophobia (Oscarsson 2005).

[13] The Ombudsperson for Children and Students (*Barn och elev ombudet*), set within the structures of the school inspection, is in charge of controlling all contexts that affect children und students (http://www.skolinspektionen.se/BEO/).

[14] To clarify: the Swedish texts mentions *kön*, a term that conflates "sex" and "gender"; the English translation mentions "gender".

ground, gender and sexual orientation" as part of the central content (Skolverket 2011, p. 202 my translation).

Rights, Responsibilities, and Consequences—Ottawa

Canada is a federal state consisting of 13 provinces and territories that are also responsible for education. Schools aim to present specific profiles to attract their "clientele", and fees are paid to cover costs for material. While education policies are decided on by the provinces, the local school boards are in charge of translating policy into praxis. Next to the public school boards, there are Catholic school boards and French school boards. Independent schools also offer other faith-based education. Canada offers extensive legal antidiscrimination provisions; especially the Policy of Multiculturalism of 1971 has had an enormous impact on Canadian politics and national identity. Similarly, the struggles for sexual rights since the 1980s have created important political changes (Warner 2002); the Canadian government introduced same-sex marriage in 2005 (Schmitt 2008a). Yet, a national study on young peoples' experiences of homophobia and transphobia in schools indicates that many queer/ed young people feel unsafe in their schools and regularly experience verbal or physical abuse (Égale Canada et al. 2009).

The texts discussed here are the document "Violence-Free Schools Policy" (Ontario Ministry of Education 1994), "Bill 157 Keeping our kids safe at school" (Ontario Ministry of Education 2009), the curriculum for social science and humanities for grades 9–10 (Ontario Ministry of Education 1999b) and the curriculum for health and physical education for grades 9–10 (Ontario Ministry of Education 1999a).[15]

The Ontario ministry of education, responsible for Ottawa, presents a focus on normative values and the consequences of transgressions. The document "Violence-Free Schools", in place since 1994, stipulates grounds for nondiscrimination and is in itself noteworthy for the early inclusion of sexual orientation as a reason for nondiscrimination. The text states that every school must have a code of conduct that is regularly revised, that states

> unequivocally that physical, verbal (oral or written), sexual, or psychological abuse; bullying; or discrimination on the basis of race, culture, religion, gender, language, disability, sexual orientation, or any other attribute is unacceptable (Ontario Ministry of Education 1994).

Further, the text states, with reference to the document "Antiracism and Ethnocultural Equity in School Boards. Guidelines for Policy Development and Implementation 1993" (Ontario Ministry of Education 1993), that

> Curriculum must be free of bias and must reflect the diverse groups that compose our society. It must enable "all students to see themselves reflected in [it]" and "provide each student with the knowledge, skills, attitudes, and behaviours needed to live in a complex

---

[15] In the field of social sciences, Ontario students study Social Studies grades 1–6, History and Geography grades 7–8, and Social Sciences and the Humanities grades 9–10.

and diverse world" (Antiracism and Ethnocultural Equity in School Boards). (Ontario Ministry of Education 1994)

This statement points to the role of policy makers and teachers and is also noteworthy as it very clearly states the necessity of punishment: Homophobia, as well as racism, is considered a "serious violent incident" that is to be reported to the police (Ontario Ministry of Education 1994). Thus antidiscrimination is not only perceived as a matter of democratic values, but is embedded in a strong regulatory framework. This is even supported by the new Bill 157 Keeping Our Kids Safe at School that focuses on "reporting and responding to incidents" (Ontario Ministry of Education 2009). The Bill outlines student behavior that can lead to suspension or expulsion, such as bullying (Ontario Ministry of Education 2009, p. 2), and, like "Violence-Free Schools," underscores teachers' responsibility to respond to "inappropriate and disrespectful behavior" in a student, such as

> racist, sexual, sexist or homophobic comments, slurs and jokes or graffiti, as well as those activities and behaviours outlined on page 2 that can lead to suspension or expulsion (Ontario Ministry of Education 2009, p. 5)

The Ontario curriculum for social sciences and humanities is comprised of general social science, family studies, philosophy, and world religions. Grades 9 and 10 are focused on family studies (Ontario Ministry of Education 1999b, p. 4). The definition of "family" is relatively broad in this document, including "nuclear, blended, single-parent families; foster care; adoption; sibling relationships" (Ontario Ministry of Education 1999b, p. 20). In a chapter on Diversity, Interdependence, and Global Connections, students are expected to

> describe variations in the roles of adolescents and in expectations of females and of males among families within Canada and in other countries. (Ontario Ministry of Education 1999b, p. 20)

The curriculum for health and physical education, grades 9–10, while not within the social sciences, offers an interesting additional perspective on the discussion of family, by highlighting the importance of "responsible sexuality" (Ontario Ministry of Education 1999a, p. 15). Thus, students must be enabled to "explain the consequences of sexual decisions on the individual, family, and community" (Ontario Ministry of Education 1999a, p. 10).[16] Homosexuality is not mentioned throughout the curriculum, though a new interim curriculum for grades 1–8 defines sexual orientation in a glossary as a

> person's sense of sexual attraction to people of the same sex, the opposite sex, or both sexes. (Refer to the Ontario Human Rights Commission's Policy on Discrimination and Harassment because of Sexual Orientation, at www.ohrc.on.ca.) (Ontario Ministry of Education 2010, p. 217)

Also, parents can decide to withdraw their child from "any component" of the course "where such a component is in conflict with a religious belief held by the parent or student" (Ontario Ministry of Education 1999a, p. 5). In the negotiation of "cultural" versus sexual rights, this is enlightening.

---

[16] Interestingly, the curriculum for grades 1–8 also refers also to "respect for life."

At the same time, extensive Canadian antidiscrimination legislation and the debates about and implementation of "gay marriage" have considerably changed the meaning of family and indeed sexuality, and the Ontario curriculum is bound to these legal and normative frameworks. Read together, these text leave an ambivalence: The strong focus on the family (and the concept of "responsible sexuality" expressed in the health and physical education curriculum) transmits a sense of conservative values embedded in a neoliberal discourse of individual choice, while the documents "Antiracism and Ethnocultural Equity in School Boards" and "Bill 157" focus on diversity, respect, and consequences of discriminatory behavior.

Results—Sexual Individuals, Ethnic Communities?

Finding the nation in notions of gender-sex-sexuality in school policy texts is an evasive task, not least as these texts are under regular revision. I argue that national inscription in these texts occurs on two levels: school policies interpellate the national context; and they reference ideals of subjectivity.

The selected texts offered some similarities. Most basically, they all refer to existing antidiscrimination legislation; thus, ethnicity, gender, and sexuality (and gender identity) are inscribed as grounds for nondiscrimination in rights-based discussions. They also showed the tendency to present ethnicity as a group marker, whereas sexuality is an aspect of individualization (within the notion of responsibility in the Canadian example). Following this indication, nonheteronormative sexualities might be—problematically—read as an example of neoliberal notions of the individual.

While it is encouraging to find references to sexuality as ground for nondiscrimination in all three contexts, this also refers to my basic concern: as is evident from the studies mentioned in all three contexts, homophobia and transphobia remain serious challenges. Clearly, the reference to (hetero)normative frameworks such as human rights is not sufficient to decenter normative understandings of young people's sexualities. Sexual diversity needs to be more clearly embedded in social and content-based learning, as well as in (national) discourses of belonging, if we are to address the problematic othering of queer/ed youth.

To different degrees, the discourse of neoliberal management of learning is prominent in all three settings. The increasing focus on market applicability of education and the increase in discourses of neoliberal economy ties in with current nationalisms we encounter in many Western nation-states (Davies and Bansel 2007, p. 251). This includes the rehierarchization of young people in schools, and a redefinition of gendered discourses on school achievement (Francis and Skelton 2009, p. 15).

The focus in the three contexts differs: The German policy and curriculum invoked a problematizing notion of (ethnocultural) difference. The Swedish texts invest more in the individual, while marking a clear ethnocultural context of belonging. The Canadian texts most directly write about consequences, both for young people engaging in sexual interaction, as well as for perpetrators of violence on grounds of gender and sexuality, and racialization/ethnification. Most importantly, all three contexts lack a more explicit engagement in the reflection of the interdependences of racialization/ethnification, and gender and sexualities.

Conclusion

Why am I—along with other education researchers—engaging in such an analysis? Is it not limited to small groups of people, "minorities"? Who are, as I write myself, covered by antidiscrimination legislation? The relevance is twofold: First, studies indicate that minoritized young people are often, if not generally, limited in their choices and experience threats to their well-being. Second, the workings of normative frameworks affect all members of learning communities. To present subjectivities that are "successfully normal" is hard work, and belonging, to school communities and nations, is done through gendered and sexualized ethnicities. The lack of intersectional analysis within the policy documents implicitly creates mutually exclusive groups of "others".

Madeleine Arnot suggests "the integration of sexuality education into citizenship programmes" (Arnot 2004, p. 19). In order to understand the intricate entanglements of citizenship, sexuality, and belonging, young people need to have access to information that addresses the complexity of these issues. At the same time, it is necessary to revise the images of and discourses about young people. Positioning minoritized young people as in need of tolerance limits the ways we can call for and indeed think change, because we focus on queer/ed and ethnicized youth as victims in need of support or as dangerous aggressors. We need to reflect on the meaning of norms for all children and young people in schools; we also need to focus on skills and abilities of minoritized young people and consider them as experts rather than victims.

While "homosexual youth" have been discovered by school authorities to some extent, transgender youth, and even more so intersex youth, are still very much at the periphery of educational as well as academic and political vision. Individualized or identity-based approaches are limited if stigmatizing school cultures remain intact (Meyer 2009). The inclusion of antidiscrimination legislation in school policies is essential; yet, it is not sufficient. Further translation into curriculum and into everyday experiences in schools is needed. In these efforts, it is central to remember the interdependences of power relationships young people experience. As the late Eric Rofes pointed out:

> It is not enough to say that antigay, sexist, or racist bigotry makes the lives of children and youth into hell on earth. The frequently quoted statistics on the disproportionate toll suicide takes on gay and lesbian youth […] are as much an indictment of 'adultism' as of homophobia. Testimonies of queer youth can be heard as narratives of heterosexism and homophobia, as well as ageism and the technologies that police childhood. (Rofes 2005, p. 69)

Rofes' reference to the interdependences of gender-sex-sexuality and ethnicity is an important reminder for researchers and policy makers as such complexity is missing in the curricula texts discussed in this chapter. More comparative qualitative research is needed to understand these powerful interdependences and more political interaction is needed to translate them into everyday reality for young people.

References

Ahmed, S. (2000). *Strange encounters: Embodied others in post-coloniality*. London: Routledge.
Arnot, M. (2004). *Gender equality and opportunities in the classroom: Thinking about citizenship, pedagogy and the rights of children*. Paper presented at the Beyond Access: Pedagogic Strategies for Gender Equality and Quality Basic Education in Schools, 2–3 February, 2004. Accessed 15 Feb 2010.
Bacchi, C. (2005). Discourse, discourse everywhere: Subject 'agency' in feminist discourse methodology. *NORA. Nordic Journal of Feminist and Gender Research, 13*(3), 198–209.
Belling, P., Bolter, F., Dankmeijer, P., Enders, M., Graglia, M., Kraan, K., et al. (2004). *Different in more ways than one: Providing guidance for teenagers on their way to identity, sexuality and respect*. Düsseldorf: Ministerium für Gesundheit, Soziales, Frauen und Familie des Landes Nordrhein-Westfalen.
Boeser, C. (2005). Gender issues and civic education—the discussion in Germany. http://www.sowi-online.de/journal/2005–2/pdf/gender_boeser.pdf. Accessed 11 Feb 2010.
Burkert, C., & Seibert, H. (2007). Labour market outcomes after vocational training in Germany: Equal opportunities for migrants and natives? IAB Discussion Paper. http://doku.iab.de/discussionpapers/2007/dp3107.pdf. Accessed 11 Feb 2011.
Butler, J. (1993). *Bodies that matter: On the discursive limits of "sex"*. New York: Routledge.
Butler, J. (2004). *Undoing gender*. New York: Routledge.
Connell, R. W. (1996). Teaching the boys: New research on masculinity, and gender strategies for schools. *Teachers College Record, 98*(2), 206–235.
Davies, B., & Bansel, P. (2007). Neoliberalism and education. *International Journal of Qualitative Studies in Education, 20*(3), 247–259.
de los Reyes, P., & Mulinari, D. (2005). *Intersektionalitet: Kritiska reflektioner over (o)jämlikhetens landskap*. Malmö: Liber.
Égale Canada, Taylor, C., Peter, T., Schachter, W. K., Beldom, S., Gross, Z., et al. (2009). Youth speak up about homophobia and transphobia. The first national climate survey on homophobia in Canadian schools. Phase one Report.http://egale.ca/extra/CG_Taylor__Climate_Survey__Phase_One_Report.pdf. Accessed 28 Mar 2011.
Foucault, M. (2003). *Die Ordnung des Diskurses: Mit einem Essay von Ralf Konsermann*. Frankfurt a. M.: Fischer.
Francis, B., & Skelton, C. (2009). 'The self-made self': Analysing the potential contribution to the field of gender and education of theories that disembed selfhood. In J.-A. Dillabough, J. McLeod, & M. Mills (Eds.), *Troubling gender in education* (pp. 10–23). London: Routledge.
Frosh, S., Phoenix, A., & Pattman, R. (2002). *Young masculinities: Understanding boys in contemporary society*. Basingstoke: Palgrave.
Giroux, H., & Polychroniou, C. (2008). Rethinking democratic education in the new millennium. An interview with Henry Giroux. *Teachers College Record*. Accessed 27 Oct 2009.
Granato, M. (2001). Qualifizierungspotenziale in Deutschland nutzen: Jugendliche mit Migrationshintergrund und berufliche Ausbildung. http://www.sowi-online.de/reader/berufsorientierung/granato.htm. Accessed 11 Feb 2010.
Halberstam, J. (2008). The anti-social turn in queer studies. *Graduate Journal of Social Science, 5*(2), 140–156.
Hemmings, C. (2007). What's in a name? Bisexuality, transnational sexuality studies and Western colonial legacies. *The International Journal of Human Rights, 11*(1), 13–32.
iconkids & youth. (2002). Pressemitteilung. 61 Prozent der deutschen Jugendlichen lehnen Homosexuelle ab. Noch größer sind die Vorbehalte gegen "Ökos", "Punks", und "Skinheads". http://www.iconkids.com/deutsch/download/presse/2002/2002_2.pdf. Accessed 11 Feb 2010.
Klingspor, K., & Molarin, A. (2009). *Hatbrott 2008. Polisanmälningar där det i motivbilden ingår etnisk bakgrund, religiös tro, sexuell läggning eller könsöverskridande identitet eller uttryck*. Stockholm: Brottsförebyggande rådet.
Kosofsky Sedgwick, E. (1991). How to bring your kids up gay. *Social Text, 29*, 18–27.

Kumashiro, K. (2000). Toward a theory of anti-oppressive education. *Review of Educational Research, 70*(1), 25–53.
Luibhéid, E. (2002). *Entry denied: Controlling sexuality at the border*. Minneapolis: University of Minnesota Press.
Lund, S. (2008). Choice paths in the Swedish upper secondary education—a critical discourse analysis of recent reforms. *Journal of Education Policy, 23*(6), 633–648.
Lundberg, J. (2007). Gender pay gap decreasing but wide variations between sectors. http://www.eurofound.europa.eu/ewco/2007/06/SE0706019I.htm. Accessed 11 Feb 2010.
MANEO. (2007). *Gewalterfahrungen von schwulen und bisexuellen Jugendlichen und Männern in Deutschland. Ergebnisse der MANEO-Umfrage 2006/2007*. Berlin: MANEO – Das schwule Anti-Gewalt-Projekt in Berlin. Accessed 11 Feb 2010.
Marshall, C., & Gerstl-Pepin, C. I. (2005). *Re-framing educational politics for social justice*. Boston: Pearson/Allyn and Bacon.
Marshall, C., & Young, M. D. (2006). Gender and methodology. In C. Skelton, B. Francis, & L. Smulyan (Eds.), *The Sage handbook of gender and education* (pp. 63–77). Thousand Oaks: Sage.
Martinsson, L., Reimers, E., Reingarde, J., & Lundgren, A. S. (2007). Norms at work: Challenging homophobia and heteronormativity: RFSL. http://app.rfsl.se/apa/37/public_files/TRACE_Norms_at_Work.pdf. Accessed 14 May 2010.
McCall, L. (2005). The complexity of intersectionality. *Signs: Journal of Women in Culture and Society, 30*(3), 1771–1800.
McGregor, C. (2008). Norming and forming: Challenging heteronormativity in educational policy discourses. http://www.umanitoba.ca/publications/cjeap/articles/mcgregor.html. Accessed 6 May 2010.
McInnes, D., & Davies, C. (2008). Articulating sissy boy queerness within and against discourses of tolerance and pride. In S. Driver (Ed.), *Queer youth cultures* (pp. 105–121). New York: State University of New York Press.
Mellor, D. J., & Epstein, D. (2006). Appropriate behaviour? Sexualities, schooling and heterogender. In C. Skelton, B. Francis, & L. Smulyan (Eds.), *The Sage handbook of gender and education* (pp. 378–391). Thousand Oaks: Sage.
Meyer, E. J. (2009). *Gender, bullying, and harassment. Strategies to end sexism and homophobia in schools. Foreword by Lyn Mikel Brown*. New York: Teachers College Press.
Nash, J. C. (2008). Re-thinking intersectionality. *Feminist Review, 89*, 1–15.
Nordberg, M. (2008). *Maskulinitet på schemat – pojkar, flickor och könsskapande i förskola och skola*. Stockholm: Liber.
OECD. (2000). *Knowledge and skills for life. First results from the OECD Programme for International Student Assessment (PISA) 2000*. Organisation for Economic Co-operation and Development. http://www.pisa.oecd.org/dataoecd/44/53/33691596.pdf. Accessed 12 May 2010.
OECD. (2006). *Wo haben Schüler mit Migrationshintergrund die größten Erfolgschancen: Eine vergleichende Analyse von Leistung und Engagement in PISA 2003 – Kurzzusammenfassung, 2006*. Organisation for Economic Co-operation and Development. http://www.oecd.org/dataoecd/2/57/36665235.pdf. Accessed 12 May 2010.
Ontario Ministry of Education. (1993). Antiracism and ethnocultural equity in school boards. Guidelines for Policy Development and Implementation 1993. http://www.edu.gov.on.ca/eng/document/curricul/antiraci/antire.pdf. Accessed 11 Feb 2010.
Ontario Ministry of Education. (1994). Violence free school policy. Second Printing 1994. http://www.edu.gov.on.ca/eng/document/policy/vfreeng.html. Accessed 11 Feb 2010.
Ontario Ministry of Education (1999a). The Ontario Curriculum, Grades 9 and 10: Health and physical education. http://www.edu.gov.on.ca/eng/curriculum/secondary/health910curr.pdf. Accessed 11 Feb 2010.
Ontario Ministry of Education (1999b). The Ontario Curriculum, Grades 9 and 10: Social sciences and humanities. http://www.edu.gov.on.ca/eng/curriculum/secondary/sstudies910curr.pdf. Accessed 11 Feb 2010.

Ontario Ministry of Education (2009). Bill 157 keeping our kids safe at school. http://www.edu.gov.on.ca/eng/safeschools/KeepKidSafeSchool.pdf. Accessed 26 Nov 2010.

Ontario Ministry of Education (2010). Health and physical education. Interim Edition. http://www.edu.gov.on.ca/eng/curriculum/elementary/healthcurr18.pdf. Accessed 26 Nov 2010.

Osbeck, C., Holm, A.-S., & Wernersson, I. (2003). *Kränkningar i skolan. Förekomst, former och sammanhang.* Göteborg: Göteborgs Universitet.

Oscarsson, K. (2005). *RFSL Rapport om Skolplansundersökningen.* Stockholm: Riksförbundet för sexuellt likaberättigande.

Paechter, C. (2001). Using poststructuralist ideas in gender theory and research. In B. Francis & C. Skelton (Eds.), *Investigating gender: Contemporary perspectives in education* (pp. 41–51). Buckingham: Open University Press.

Pellegrini, A. (2009). *Pedagogies of fear: Contemporary U.S. debates over sex, religion, and childhood.* Paper presented at the Critical Feminist Dialogues on Sex Education, Violence and Sexology: Between Agency, Pleasure, Shame and Pain: A Conference for GEXcel Themes 4 & 5 "Sexual Health, Embodiment and Empowerment: Bridging Epistemological Gaps", Department of Gender Studies, Linköping University.

Puar, J. K. (2007). *Terrorist assemblages. Homonationalism in queer times.* Durham: Duke University Press.

Rasmussen, M. L. (2004). Safety and subversion: The production of sexualities and genders in school spaces. In M. L. Rasmussen, E. Rofes, & S. Talburt (Eds.), *Youth and sexualities: Pleasure, subversion, and insubordination in and out of schools* (pp. 131–152). New York: Palgrave Macmillan.

Rasmussen, M. L., Rofes, E., & Talburt, S. (Eds.). (2004). *Youth and sexualities: Pleasure, subversion, and insubordination in and out of schools.* New York: Palgrave Macmillan.

Rofes, E. E. (2005). *A radical rethinking of sexuality and schooling: Status quo or status queer?* Lanham: Rowman & Littlefield.

Ryng, A., Sysimetsä, T., & Blomqvist, M. B. (2003). *"Homosexualitet är inte olagligt om man är över 15 år". Inkludering och exkludering av homosexuella, bisexuella och transpersoner i biologiböcker.* RFSL Ungdom. http://www.rfslungdom.se/sites/default/files/biobokgranskning.pdf. Accessed 15 Feb 2010.

Schmauch, U. (2006). *Den osynliga vardagsrasismens realitet.* Umeå: Sociologiska institutionen, Umeå universitet.

Schmitt, I. (2008a). From 'security risk' to charter rights—gender, sexuality and the Canadian politics of integration. *Zeitschrift für Kanada-Studien, 28*(1), 46–69.

Schmitt, I. (2008b). 'Ich besorg' dir Viagra für deinen Freund' – Heteronormativität als methodologische Herausforderung in der Forschung mit Jugendlichen. In U. Freikamp, M. Leanza, J. Mende, S. Müller, P. Ullrich, & H.-J. Voß (Eds.), *Kritik mit Methode? Forschungsmethoden und Gesellschaftskritik* (42 ed., pp. 253–268). Berlin: Karl Dietz Verlag.

Schmitt, I. (2008c). *Wir sind halt alle anders: eine gesellschaftspolitische Analyse deutscher und kanadischer Jugendlicher zu Zugehörigkeit, Gender und Vielkulturalität.* Göttingen: V&R Unipress.

Schmitt, I. (2010a). Do you have a boyfriend? Feeling queer in youth and education research. *Lambda Nordica. Tidskrift för homo/lesbisk/bi/transforskning, 15*(3–4), 15–39.

Schmitt, I. (2010b). 'Normally I should belong to the others'—young people's gendered transcultural competence in creating belonging in Germany and Canada. *Childhood (spec. ed. Children and Migration: Identities, Home and Belonging, eds. Caitríona Ní Laoire, Naomi Bushin, Fina Carpena-Mendez, Allen White), 17*(2), 163–180.

Schmitt, I. (in press). Sexuality, secularism and the nation—reading Swedish school policies. Sexualities in Education: A Reader. T. Quinn and E. R. Meiners. New York: Lang.

Schmitt, I., & Winter, E. (2009). Current debates on citizenship and belonging: Multiculturalism, gender and sexuality. In K.-D. Ertler & H. Lutz (Eds.), *Canada in Grainau/ Le Canada à Grainau. Canadian Studies/Études canadiennes: The State of the Art* (pp. 129–153). Frankfurt a. M.: Peter Lang.

Seemann, M. (2009). *Geschlechtergerechtigkeit in der Schule. Eine Studie zum Gender Mainstreaming in Schweden.* Bielefeld: Transcript.

Senatsverwaltung für Bildung Jugend und Sport Berlin. (2006). Rahmenlehrplan für die Sekundarstufe I Jahrgangsstufe 7–10, Sozialkunde, Hauptschule, Realschule, Gesamtschule, Gymnasium. http://www.berlin.de/imperia/md/content/sen-bildung/schulorganisation/lehrplaene/sek1_sozialkunde.pdf. Accessed 11 Feb 2010.

Senatsverwaltung für Bildung Wissenschaft und Forschung Berlin. (2008). Schulgesetz für das Land Berlin (Schulgesetz – SchulG), vom 26. Januar 2004 (GVBl. S. 26), zuletzt geändert durch Zweites Gesetz zur Änderung des Schulgesetzes vom 17. April 2008 (GVBl. S. 95). http://www.berlin.de/imperia/md/content/sen-bildung/rechtsvorschriften/schulgesetz.pdf. Accessed 11 Feb 2010.

Simon, B. (2008). Einstellungen zur Homosexualität: Ausprägungen und psychologische Korrelate bei Jugendlichen mit und ohne Migrationshintergrund (ehemalige UdSSR und Türkei). *Zeitschrift für Entwicklungspsychologie und Pädagogische Psychologie, 40,* 87–99.

Skolinspektionen. (2008). Starkare ställning för barn i ny lagstiftning. http://www.skolinspektionen.se/Documents/BEO/barn-och-elevskyddslagen.pdf. Accessed 11 Feb 2010.

Skolverket. (2000a). Compulsory school. Syllabus. Civics. http://www3.skolverket.se/ki03/front.aspx?sprak=EN&ar=0809&infotyp=24&skolform=11&id=3887&extraId=2087. Accessed 11 Feb 2010.

Skolverket. (2000b). Compulsory school. Syllabus. Social studies. http://www3.skolverket.se/ki03/front.aspx?sprak=EN&ar=0809&infotyp=23&skolform=11&id=3882&extraId=2087. Accessed 11 Feb 2010.

Skolverket. (2006). Curriculum for the compulsory school system, the pre-school class and the leisure-time centre Lpo 94 (Läroplan för det obligatoriska skolväsendet, förskoleklassen och fritidshemmet Lpo 94). http://www.skolverket.se/publikationer?id=1070/ (http://www.skolverket.se/publikationer?id=1069). Accessed 11 Feb 2010.

Skolverket. (2010a). Del ur Lgr 11: Läroplan för grundskolan, förskoleklassen och fritidshemmet: kapitel 1 och 2. http://www.skolverket.se/content/1/c6/02/21/84/Lgr11_kap1_2.pdf. Accessed 20 July 2010.

Skolverket. (2010b). Sammanfattning av skollagens 29 kapitel (2 July 2010). http://www.skolverket.se/sb/d/3885/a/20552. Accessed 20 July 2010.

Skolverket. (2010c). Skola i förändring. Om reformerna i den obligatoriska skolan. http://www.skolverket.se/publikationer?id=2427. Accessed 26 Nov 2010.

Skolverket. (2011). Läroplan för grundskolan, förskoleklassen och fritidshemmet 2011. http://www.skolverket.se/publikationer?id=2575. Accessed 6 May 2011.

Smith, D. E. (1993[1990]). *Texts, facts, and femininity: Exploring the relations of ruling*. London: Routledge.

Späte, K. (2005). Forgotten documents—gender and curricula work in civic education: The case of Germany. *Journal of Social Science Education,* (2).

Spindler, S. (2006). *Corpus delicti. Männlichkeit, Rassismus und Kriminalisierung im Alltag jugendlicher Migranten*. Münster: Edition Diss, Unrast-Verlag.

Stockholms Stad. (2008). En Skola i Värlsklass! Skolplan för Skolplan för Stockholms Stad. http://www.stockholm.se/Global/Stads%c3%b6vergripande%20%c3%a4mnen/Skola%20%26%20Arbete/Styr-%20och%20st%c3%b6ddokument/Skolplan%202008.pdf. Accessed 11 Feb 2010.

Todd, S. (2001). 'Bringing more than I contain': Ethics, curriculum and the pedagogical demand for altered egos. *Journal of Curriculum Studies, 33*(4), 431–450.

UN. (1989). Convention on the Rights of the Child. Entry into force 2 September 1990, in accordance with article 49. http://www2.ohchr.org/english/law/crc.htm: United Nations High Commissioner for Human Rights. Accessed 14 May 2010.

Warner, T. (2002). *Never going back: the history of queer activism in Canada*. Toronto: Toronto University Press.

Chapter 25
Effects of the Head Start Program in the USA as Indicators of Ethnic Inequalities

Claudia Koehler

Introduction

The history of the USA is based on immigration and the coexistence of different ethnic groups (the term "ethnic group" hereinafter refers to ethnic as well as racialized group). However, this coexistence has not completely come along with equality: Ethnic minorities, specifically African-Americans and Hispanic-Americans, have been more disadvantaged than White-Americans among others in reference to educational performance, labor market participation, and income.

For the functioning of a societal system it is vital that all ethnic groups are integrated. This implies the equal occupation of positions within the functional spheres of the society,[1] mainly the labor market. A facilitator for this, if not a precondition, is the successful completion of the educational system. Hence education has a key function for the social integration of minorities (Esser 2000).

Education in a broader sense is considered as a means of overcoming handicaps, achieving greater equality and acquiring wealth and social status. It is perceived as one of the best means of achieving greater social equality (Sargent 1994). The accomplishment of this goal depends among others on the quality and effectiveness of the respective educational system and the existence of equal rights among all members of society. Thus, under certain circumstances the educational system may not only not accomplish this goal, but cause the social and ethnic reproduction of inequality.

In the USA, it was not until the Civil Rights Movement of the 1960s that equal rights were granted to all ethnic groups. The program Head Start was launched in 1965 in order to enhance equal chances for all children by providing a large-

---

[1] Esser's theory was developed in the context of migrants in Europe. Therefore he uses the term "host society". For analytical purposes his theory is here with slight adaptations applied to ethnic minorities in general, regardless of migrant status.

C. Koehler (✉)
European Forum for Migration Studies (EFMS), Schuetzenstrasse 51, 96047 Bamberg, Germany
e-mail: claudia.koehler@uni-bamberg.de

scale early education program for disadvantaged children, and has been running with some adaptations since. A large proportion of participating children have been African-American and increasingly Hispanic children. A major goal of the program is the successful educational and social development of the participants. If this goal was reached, an important contribution to the integration of the participating ethnic minorities would be accomplished. The analysis of evaluations conducted on the impact of Head Start on African- and Hispanic-Americans, however, shows that Head Start has not been successful in reaching this goal.

After outlining the development and structure of Head Start and summarizing major results of evaluations, this chapter seeks to identify the reasons for ethnic differences in the effects of the program. Concepts of social limits of learning and of the achievement gap are applied to analyze the validity of test results and factors within and beyond Head Start which contribute to the fading of effects for ethnic minorities. Subsequently, the impact on dimensions of integration is analyzed by a set of indicators and suggestions for the improvement of the effectiveness are provided.

Formation and Theoretical Background of Head Start

The launch of the Head Start program in 1965 was the consequence of the then social and political situation as well as the theoretical understanding, that **minority groups**, mainly African-Americans, were decisively **disadvantaged** in reference to educational achievements, income level, labor market participation, and living standards. The Civil Rights movement of the 1960s had activated the awareness of the need of action against ethnic inequalities (Vinovskis 2005, pp. 35–40).

In the context of the launch of the space shuttle Sputnik by the Soviet Union in 1957, the US government considered investments in better-quality education as the clue for getting ahead of the **scientific race** (Vinovskis 2005, p. 14).

In approaching these issues, politicians and scientists drew on developmental psychology as well as on medical theory and the experiences of pilot projects:

At the end of the 1950s the **environmental approach** evolved: Unlike the earlier belief that human intelligence was determined by inheritance, the intellect was now primarily considered as a result of experiences within the first 5 years. Environmentalists such as Skeels, Hunt and Bloom concluded that this time frame was the best period for intervention (Stoyle 1973; Zigler and Valentine 1979, pp. 6/7). This approach was supplemented by the **"culture of poverty"—approach** by Lewis: With the continuing social and economic depression the culture of poverty is passed on from generation to generation (Alexanian 1967, In Zigler and Valentine 1979, p. 8). Thus, it was considered vital to include the family into intervention measures in order to change the ecological circumstances as a precondition for the success of interventions (Bronfenbrenner 1974).

Medical theories argued that children of poor families more frequently suffered from physical and psychical illnesses, tended to be malnourished and receive less medical care than more advantaged children. Health deficiencies would hinder children's adequate development (Zigler and Valentine 1979, p. xxiv).

Previously conducted **model projects** of early childhood education (such as the Early Learning Project by Susan Gray in Nashville and the Children's Center in Syracuse) proved an increase of the IQ and verbal competences of participants (Zigler and Valentine 1979, p. 11).

Structure of Head Start

The program aims at compensating for educational disadvantages that are caused by social disadvantages through measures of early education by the beginning of school. Besides the cognitive support, the program includes medical care and healthy nutrition as well as parental support and community networking (U.S. Department of Health & Human Services 2007).

In 1965 Head Start started off as a summer program with 560,000 children participating in 3,300 programs all across the USA (Butler 1968, p. 6). After 1969, Head Start was turned into a full-year program. Participation numbers rose up to around 900,000 per year (Child Trends Data Bank 2007).

Target Groups, Financing, and Coordination

The **main target group** of the program—explicitly—were **disadvantaged children** in general. As the majority of this group were **African-American children** (and to a smaller extent Native-American children) at that time, they were the implicit target group (Kuntz 1998, pp. 2–6).

Over the years the **ethnic composition** of Head Start participants changed: Until 2002 participants were predominantly of African-American origin, afterwards the proportions of Hispanics, Whites as well as "others" have increased (cf. Fig. 1).

Due to the specific focus of Head Start on disadvantaged children, the participation likelihood of 3–4-year-olds is the largest for African-American and the smallest for White-American children (Child Trends Data Bank 2007). **African-American children** represent the group strongest affected by poverty. The majority of them grow up with single mothers in segregated and insecure neighborhoods, and lack adequate access to medical care. They have worse school-related preconditions than White children, specifically in reference to cognitive, social, and problem-solving competences (U.S. Census 2001, 2007; Westat 2005).

The majority of **Hispanic Head Start children** are first- and second-generation immigrants. The disadvantages described for African-American Head Start children predominantly apply to Hispanic Head Start children as well. In addition, this group is subject to disadvantages which come along with their immigrant status (U.S. Census 2007; Westat 2005).

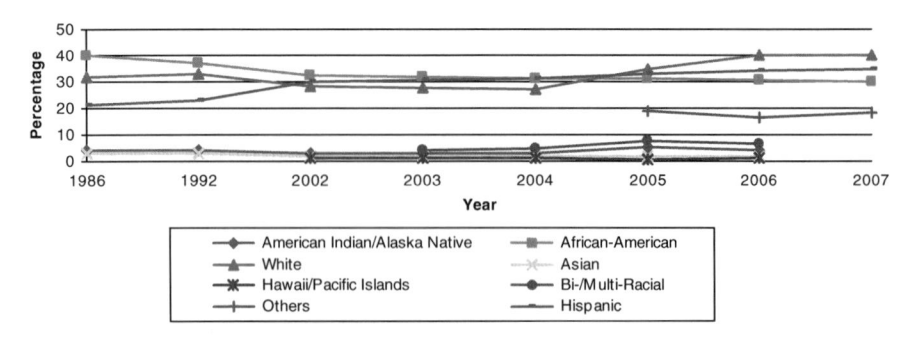

Fig. 1 Ethnic composition of head start participants 1986–2007. (Source: Administration for Children and Families 2007, own design; data on American Indian/Alaska Native, White, Hawaii/Pacific Island and Bi-/Multi-Racial not available for 2007)

With respect to social structural, familiar and cognitive aspects, **White Head Start children** enjoy the best preconditions among the analyzed groups (U.S. Census 2001; Westat 2003).

For the **second target group—parents**—two aspects of their inclusion within Head Start in reference to the respective theoretical understanding can be differentiated:

1. Components of the program which aim at improving parental abilities (e.g., parenting, educational, or job-related measures) are based on the understanding that the cause of poverty originates from the individual (the parents) (Kuntz 1998, pp. 7–8).
2. Aspects of the active inclusion of parents in the program (e.g., in decision-making processes, as volunteers, and as employees) rest on the understanding that the cause of poverty is rooted in the system, and not in the individual (Kuntz 1998, pp. 7–8).

Originally the program incorporated both aspects; the first aspect, however, has gained prevalence (Sissel 1999). This is in accordance with the general opinion that deficits are not rooted in the system of society but in the individual himself.

Financing and coordination of Head Start are conducted by the Federal Government; the responsible department is the Department of Health and Human Services (DHHS) (The White House 2007). Head Start programs are carried out by over 1,400 local organizations; among them are schools, universities, health centers, regional municipalities, religious organizations, and tribal authorities (U.S. Department of Health & Human Services 2007). The supporting institutions have to apply for finances with the DHHS which provides 80% of the expenses; the remaining 20% have to be covered by the municipality (The White House 2007). The allocation of the federal funds among the states is in accordance with the number of eligible children (preschool children whose family income is below a certain level). Mostly, the number of approved places is lower than the number of all eligible children within the catchment area. The institutions then have to make a decision on who to accept: Neidell and Waldfogel (2006) show that primarily the neediest children are chosen. Head Start participants are therefore subject to a double negative selection: First, referring to the eligibility to the program and second, referring to the selection into the program (Neidell and Waldfogel 2006).

Functional Theory of Head Start

In the following a model of the functional theory of Head Start is suggested which demonstrates the implied logic of the program. It incorporates the relevant elements (the basic problem, the intervention to tackle this problem, the target groups and the respective measures, the preconditions for an impact, the intended impact, and the major goal as a product of the impact) and their interdependence. The model implies that the goal can only be reached, if all the previous elements are successfully integrated into the program.

The elements printed in standard letters indicate the original version of the program; the bold letters indicate adoptions which the later analysis suggests in order to reach the goal for all participating ethnic groups.

Functional theory of Head Start

Problem: The educational performance of disadvantaged US American children (especially African-American children) lacks far behind more advantaged children.
Intervention: Head Start is launched as a summer, and later all year early education program.
Target groups and measures

Disadvantaged children / **all children**			Parents	
Early education	Medical attendance	Healthy nutrition	Involvement in decisions and activities of center	Counselling and seminars

Preconditions for impact

Increased participation and acceptance of the program	**Higher and persistent** quality of personal and program design	Purpose oriented financial input
Similar expectations and attitudes of teachers towards all children	**Broad social and ethnic composition of Head Start classes**	

Impact

Children's cognitive and social competences increase	Children's physical health and abilities increase	Parental abilities and involvement in children's development increase	Parental labor marked integration improves	Networks of support evolve and are available for families in need

Goal: Children from disadvantaged families enter school with the same chances as more advantaged children and develop their potentials into long-term social and educational success.

Effects of Head Start in the Context of Minority Integration

During its four decades of conduction, Head Start has been the subject of numerous evaluations of its effects. Within this chapter a total of 13 relevant studies were reviewed. Five of them were selected for a detailed analysis of the impact of Head Start on ethnic minorities (see the Appendix for the list of reviewed studies). These studies were chosen for reasons of actuality (conduction within the last 15 years), representativeness, measurement of dimensions relevant for integration, and differentiation of results by ethnic and racial background.

For the analysis the **theory of integration** developed by Esser (2000)—in continuation of the theory by Lockwood (1964)—is applied. Esser differentiates between system and social integration. **System integration** means the cohesion of a social system (e.g., a society) as a whole. It occurs through interdependences of actors on markets, institutions, and orientations of actors. Ethnic stratification—as expressed by social distances between ethnic groups, cultural and local segmentation, and the institutionalization of ethnic communities—represents a danger to system integration. **Social integration** is considered as a precondition for structural integration. It consists of four dimensions:

1. The structural dimension is the attainment of equal access to and positions in the major institutions of society.
2. Within the cultural dimension cognitive, cultural, and behavioral patterns of minorities adapt to the society.
3. The social dimension refers to private and group relations.
4. Minorities' feelings of belonging represent the emotional dimension (Esser 2000).

Moreover, it appears necessary to include characteristics of the majority population, such as the openness of institutions and attitudes towards minorities. For the purpose of measurement a set of indicators can be allocated to each of the dimensions. A successful impact on minority integration would show in an adjustment of the variations of the dimensions of social integration between majority and minority population (Esser 2000).

After summarizing major results and analyzing ethnic differences in results, this paragraph illustrates the impact of Head Start on minority integration by dimensions of integration and indicators allocated to them by Entzinger and Biezeveld (2003).

Major Results of Evaluations on the Impact of Head Start

In the following, results of the analyzed evaluations are summarized differentiated by ethnicity.

African-American Head Start participants: Short-term effects were proven for the reduction of unwanted behavior (Westat 2005) and for cognitive improvements. The latter disappear in the comparison with siblings (Currie and Thomas 1993, 1995). This is an indication for spill-over effects resulting in a gain of cognitive abilities for siblings (Garces et al. 2000).

Positive cognitive effects on children under 4 years (Westat 2005; Mathematica Policy Research, Inc. & Columbia University Center for Children and Families 2006) indicate that very early intervention is particularly effective for African-Americans.

In the long run, a reduction of the likelihood of delinquency directly (Currie and Thomas 1995), and as a spill-over effect on siblings was proven (Garces et al. 2000).

Due to the existence of spill-over effects for African-American children an underestimation of effects has to be assumed for this group as most evaluations are based on the comparison between siblings.

Hispanic Head Start participants: Positive effects were demonstrated for health and behavior-related aspects and for English language competences (Currie and Thomas 1993, 1996; Westat 2003, 2005). These effects partly disappear after the age of 8 years (Currie and Thomas 1993).

As a long-term effect a reduction of the likelihood of class repetition was proven (Currie and Thomas 1993; Neidell and Waldfogel 2006). As the majority of evaluations do not analyze long-term effects for Hispanic children separately, no definite conclusion can be drawn on the existence of these effects.

White Head Start participants: Short-term effects exist for cognitive (Currie and Thomas 1993, 1995) and health-related aspects (Westat 2005). Long-term effects were demonstrated for educational performance in general (Currie and Thomas 1993), the reduction of grade-repetition (Currie and Thomas 1993, 1995), the probability of high school completion and college attendance, the income level (Currie and Thomas 1995; Garces et al. 2000), health and the reduction of the likelihood of teenage parenthood (Currie and Thomas 1993).

A cost-benefit analysis came to the result that the benefits of Head Start exceed the costs only in the case of White participants (Currie and Thomas 1995).

The results demonstrate that effects of Head Start vary largely between the herein differentiated groups: Only for White participants, nearly all intended short- and long-term effects were measured. This achievement can be considered as an illustration of what Head Start is capable of effectuating. However, the basic goal of the program—to enable all children to start school on equal preconditions and competences and to perpetuate these competences into educational and social achievements—has not been reached.

The following section seeks to identify the forces which lead to the disappearance of positive effects of Head Start over time for African-Americans. As the ethnic category of Hispanic-Americans only recently was included in evaluations, the results are not sufficient enough to lead to reliable assertions about coherences of long-term effects for this group.

Why Do Effects of Head Start Disappear over Time for African-Americans?

In the context of disparities in educational achievements among different ethnic groups, the concepts of social learning, social limits of learning, and of the achievement gap have been discussed. The basic assumption of the **social learning theory** is that learning behavior is subject to the influence of the individual itself (i.e., his or her life history of learning and experiences) as well as the environment (i.e., those stimuli that the person is aware of and responding to) (Bandura 1977, Rotter 1982). According to Rotter (1982) behavior can be predicted by four main components: behavior potential, expectancy, reinforcement value, and the psychological situation. **Behavior potential** is the likelihood of engaging in a particular behavior in a specific situation. **Expectancy** is the subjective probability that a given behavior will lead to a particular outcome or reinforcer. Expectancies are formed based on past experience. **Reinforcement value** refers to the desirability of the outcomes of behavior: a person will exhibit the behavior with the greatest reinforcement value. The **psychological situation** refers to the fact that people interpret situations and their environment subjectively, therefore the way they behave is not based on an objective array of stimuli but on their subjective interpretation (Rotter 1982).

The **theory of social limits of learning** ties in with this concept, specifically with its assumptions on subjectivity: It assumes that social limits of learning stem from the fact that people base their perceptions of the environment and of situations on present experiences as well as on cultural and historical learning experiences (Mergner 2005). These experiences differ between ethnic groups and result in differences in behavior in the learning environment.

Elements of the theory of social limits of learning are utilized to explain the **achievement gap** which has been observed in several educational contexts between ethnic majority and minority groups (primarily referring to higher achievements of White-Americans vs. African- and Hispanic-Americans). In explaining the achievement gap cultural and environmental as well as structural and institutional factors are considered:

1. **Cultural and environmental factors**
   For long-term school success the dynamic between parents, children and school is of high importance (Woodhead 1993; Consortium on Longitudinal Studies 1983). This dynamic incorporates negative aspects for ethnic minorities (Wolff and Stein 1967, In Butler 1968, pp. 14–15; Ferguson 1998b):

   a. **Parental support and expectations:** African-American parents tend to have lower academic expectations in their children than White parents (Ferguson 1998b; Sadowski 2001). Students do better in school when they have assistance from a parent with homework. This is a problem for many minority students due to large numbers of single-parent households and the increase in non-English-speaking parents (Suarez-Orozco and Suarez-Orozco 1995).

b. **Teachers' expectations:** Teachers have lower academic expectations in African-American pupils than they have in White pupils. Teacher's low expectations reflect on their teaching methods and content, and on their attitudes towards students; they accumulate over time (Ferguson 1998b; Sadowski 2001). Such ethnicity-specific expectations within the school systems are a form of institutional racism (Hochschild 2003). Teacher's attitudes influence African-American pupils more than White pupils (Ferguson 1998b; Sadowski 2001).
c. **Students' expectations:** African-American children tend to have low self-expectations and feel the pressure to come up to the expectation of low performance. This "stereotype-effect" hinders them from tapping their whole potentials and may lead to the rejection of academic achievement per se. As a "peer-effect," African-American students who perform well in school might be blamed to "act white" by their peers (Ferguson 1998b; Fordham and Ogbu 1986). In accordance with the "expectancy" component of the social learning theory (Rotter 1982) minority students may not be motivated to do well in school and consciously reject the achievement ideology—the idea that studying hard will pay off in the form of upward social mobility—because they feel that this ideology does not apply to them (Fordham and Ogbu 1986; Jencks and Phillips 1998).
d. **Cultural capital in tests:** Schools often inadvertently test students on their knowledge and familiarity with white, middle-class cultural capital—which minority students are often unfamiliar with—instead of their abilities and knowledge of the subject matter. This results in disadvantages in test scores for minority students (Takanishi 2004; Allen et al. 1970, In Zigler and Valentine 1979, p. 9; Zigler et al. 1973, In Currie and Thomas 1993).

2. **Structural and institutional factors**

    a. **Segregation due to residential segregation:** Minority students tend to come from low-income households and are more likely to attend poorly funded schools based on the districting patterns within the school system. Schools in lower-income districts tend to employ less-qualified teachers, have larger classes, and fewer educational resources (Roscigno et al. 2006; Currie and Thomas 1998).
    Social learning theory emphasizes the importance of the environment on students' performance. Accordingly, the quality of a school has a decisive impact on the school performance of a child. According to Ferguson (1998a), African-American elementary school pupils particularly profit from small classes and well-qualified teachers.
    b. **Segregation due to tracking:** Schools tend to place students in tracking education groups as a means of tailoring lesson plans for different types of learners, primarily related to socioeconomic status and cultural capital. As a result, minority students are over-represented in lower educational tracks (Vander-Hart 2006). Hispanic- and African-American students are often wrongly placed into lower tracks based on teachers' and administrators' expectations.

Students in lower tracks tend to have less-qualified teachers, a less challenging curriculum, and fewer opportunities to advance into higher tracks (Hochschild 2003). Research suggests that students in lower tracks suffer from social psychological consequences of being labeled as slower learners, which often leads children to stop trying in school (Hallinan 1994).

c. **Wealth:** Within the concept of wealth, supported among others by Conley (2003), Oliver (2003), and Ditomaso (2003), differences in performance of African- and White-American children are ascribed to family wealth—the entity of all family belongings. The wealth of a family saves it over economic hardships, helps family members to acquire belongings, and finances education. The knowledge about the family's wealth imparts trust in the abilities of their ancestries in children. According to the theory of social limits of learning, these history-based experiences have a meaningful impact on present learning behavior (Mergner 2005).

The distribution of wealth varies decisively among ethnic groups. The discrepancies can be ascribed to the historic as well as persisting discrimination of African-Americans and Hispanic-Americans. Wealth explains most of the difference between educational and social attainments of African- and White-Americans: When controlling for wealth, African-Americans and Whites have the same rates of college degrees, labor market participation, and welfare dependency (Conley 2003; Oliver 2003; Ditomaso 2003).

In the following, the discussed concepts are applied to the specific case of analyzing the question why effects of Head Start correlate with ethnicity. The discussion is based on the assumption that the long-term success of Head Start (or any other early childhood intervention program) is based on the program itself *and* on the conditions (e.g., at home, in the neighborhood, and at school) that the child is exposed to during and after the intervention. After notions on the reliability of the results, which evaluations are based on, causes within and beyond Head Start are discussed.

Reliability of the results

Following the argument of the concept of the achievement gap on **culturally biased tests**, it can be assumed that the test design within Head Start is more favorable for White children. Hence effects of Head Start on ethnic minority children would be underestimated.

An alternative hypothesis is based on the **selection into the program**: A larger proportion of eligible African-American children participate in Head Start than eligible White children (O'Connor 1998). White participants represent the most disadvantaged White children; the same does not apply to African-Americans. If aspects of selection were linked to program outcomes, the effects on White children were overestimated (Currie and Thomas 1995).

Causes within and beyond Head Start

Due to the structure of Head Start there is a high **qualitative diversity of programs**. It is assumed that low-quality programs are primarily attended by minorities. The reason for this could be of structural and institutional nature: Minorities are overrepresented in disadvantaged neighborhoods, which goes along with Head Start centers of low quality. An additional reason could be of cultural and environmental nature: Due to low expectations of parents and teachers centers where minorities are overrepresented place less focus on cognitive and academic aspects than others (Entwisle 1995).

The quality of early childhood programs has an important impact on the effects, especially for African-American and Hispanic-American participants: Increased quality within Head Start and the use of a high-quality curriculum such as "High/Scope" leads to more positive effects on African-American participants (Westat 2003). The same is proven for programs similar to Head Start but of higher quality (Barnett 1995, pp. 26–29, 42–46). The following early intervention programs are characterized by a similar design as Head Start, similar target groups, and similar goals. In contrast, they apply a higher quality of teaching and of curriculum, operate with smaller classes and better qualified teachers, and have more restricted thematic focuses, as opposed to the rather broad focus of Head Start:

The **Perry Preschool project** (1962–1967) was an all-week, half-day, center-based program with the use of the "High/Scope" curriculum and with the inclusion of home visits. The funding was private and classes were small. The focus was on the intellectual, social, and emotional domains. All participants were 3–4-year-old disadvantaged African-American children. Long-term effects in comparison with a control group prove higher educational attainments, smaller drop-out rates, higher college enrolment, lower crime rates and lower welfare dependency (Bogard 2004).

The **Abecedarian project** (1972–1977) was an all-week, full-day, center-based program for infants up to kindergarten age lasting 1 year. The curriculum focused on cognitive and literacy dimensions and included healthcare and family support. The teacher–child ratio was low. All participants were disadvantaged African-American children. The funding was private. Long-term effects prove higher educational attainments, higher scores on cognitive measures and lower rates of teen pregnancy than comparison groups (Bogard 2004).

Child–Parent Centers were established in the 1970s in Chicago and are still being operated. The centers provide full-day service to 3–8-year-olds with federal, state, and local funding. The areas of focus include social, cognitive, academic, mathematic, and language skills with parental involvement. In small classes individual attention is provided. Long-term effects on African-American participants prove lower grade retention, lower drop-out rates, lower arrest rates, and higher math and reading skills than comparison groups. Moreover, "…entry into good elementary schools accounted for the largest effect of the sustainability of the impact of high quality pre-k." (Bogard 2004, pp. 1/2).

Other early intervention programs which proved successful for African-American participants include the Syracuse University Family Research Program and the Yale Child Welfare Project.

As demonstrated in the above discussion on **structural and institutional factors** of the achievement gap, minority children are **disadvantaged in schools** because of housing and tracking segregation and the specific negative impact of low-quality teaching which comes along with it. This correlation is not only a function of the social disadvantage of ethnic minorities: Even though all Head Start participants are socially disadvantaged, African-American former Head Start children predominantly attend schools of lower quality whereas White former Head Start children mainly attend schools of medium quality (Currie and Thomas 1998). In accordance with the discussion of the achievement gap, the negative impact of school segregation and low-quality teaching was demonstrated for former Head Start participants by O'Connor (1998): African-American former Head Start children who live in wealthy states with low proportions of minorities perform decisively better in school than in other states.

Hence it must be assumed that the effects of Head Start for African-American children are diminished through the impact of their structural and institutional disadvantage in reference to schools as well as by the impact of **cultural and environmental factors** (Ludwig and Phillips 2007).

The above analyzed evaluations use the family income as controlling variable for the social background. However, several authors, among them Conley (2003), Oliver (2003), and Ditomaso (2003), argue that **wealth** has a higher significance and therefore is a more suitable variable for the measurement of social capital. Assuming the validity of the high explanatory potential of wealth, it seems as if interventions like Head Start have only little potential of balancing out inequalities which have grown and established over a long period of time.

Contributions to the Integration of Ethnic Minorities Through Head Start

Given the above analysis, this section seeks to identify which contributions to the integration of ethnic minorities—specifically of African-Americans and Hispanics—have been accomplished by Head Start. This analysis is conducted by an allocation of the evaluation results and structural components of Head Start to the interpretable indicators of social integration which have been developed by Entzinger and Biezeveld (2003) for each of four dimensions of integration. These four dimensions (socioeconomic, cultural, legal/political integration, and attitudes of majority population) are largely in correspondence with the above-described dimensions by Esser (2000) (see Chap. 4). A remarkable difference is notable for the last dimension: Instead of analyzing the identification of minorities with the majority population, Entzinger and Biezeveld (2003) analyze the attitudes of the majority population towards minorities. Not all developed indicators can be interpreted in the context of Head Start, for the legal/political dimension none of the indicators is interpretable. Subsequently notions on the impact of Head Start on system integration are made.

In the following table indicators of the three interpretable dimensions are analyzed. The subject is not an analysis of minority integration per se, but of the contributions of Head Start to their integration (Table 1).

In addition to the analyzed indicators Head Start has other effects, such as on health-related aspects, which were not analyzed by the indicators above.

Which conclusion on the contributions of Head Start to the social integration of minorities can be drawn from the analysis?

The socioeconomic dimension of integration is in accordance with the structural dimension within Esser's (2000) model. Structural integration is considered as a precondition for all other dimensions of social integration, the latter being the precondition for system integration. As no long-term effects of Head Start on the placement of ethnic minorities could be proven, the conclusion has to be drawn that Head Start does not sustainably contribute to the social integration of minorities. Accordingly, a precondition for **system integration** is not provided. The notions on residential and school segregation as well as school tracking indicate the existence of ethnic stratification. If components of structural and institutional and/or cultural and environmental disadvantage of minorities were transmitted through Head Start, the program would contribute to ethnic stratification.

An aspect which has not been analyzed so far is the impact of **minorities' orientations**. An intervention program like Head Start could evoke feelings of loyalty among minorities towards the society as the program is experienced as an effort of the majority society to improve the situation and chances of minorities. If this proved true, it would represent a contribution to system integration.

Adoptions of the program which aim at its potential for the enhancement of integration should focus on the components which are suitable for contributing to structural integration. Aspects which might contribute to structural and institutional and/or cultural and environmental disadvantages should be critically analyzed and, if applicable, corrected.

Conclusion and Approaches of Improving Head Start's Potential for Contributing to Minority Integration

The analysis observes an achievement gap between the effects of Head Start for minority participants versus White participants. Furthermore, the findings suggest that Head Start has not sustainably contributed to the social integration of minorities and to the system integration.

The analysis concludes that—given the following adoptions—Head Start could more effectively contribute to minority integration:

Table 1 Effects of Head Start on dimensions of social integration of minorities (indicators drawn from Entzinger et al. 2003)

Indicator	Effect on indicator by Head Start participation
Socioeconomic dimension of integration	
Labor market participation	Head Start has no effect on labor market participation (Garces et al. 2000). Considering the cases of family members of Head Start participants finding employment within the program, a small contribution to labor market integration can be ascribed to Head Start.
Income level	Head Start has no effect on the income (Currie and Thomas 1995; Garces et al. 2000).
Social benefits dependency	Head Start does not affect social benefit dependency (Currie and Thomas 1993).
Educational achievements	Short-term effects of Head Start are proven for all ethnic groups (on participants as well as on siblings), long-term effects on minorities are only demonstrated for the reduction of the likelihood of grade repetition of Hispanic participants (Currie and Thomas 1993, 1995, 1996).
	Considering spill-over effects, long-term effects on minority participants might exist. However, the available data suggest that long-term effects on educational performance only exist for White children. In this case, Head Start would not have managed to contribute to minority integration within its major focus area of education.
Housing conditions and segregation	The data do not explicitly inform on that indicator. However, housing conditions are strongly related to the income level. Head Start does not affect minority income (Currie and Thomas 1995; Garces et al. 2000). Data on schools attended by former Head Start participants suggest a severe segregation, especially in the case of African-Americans. Hence it can be assumed that Head Start does not contribute to housing-related integration.
Cultural dimension of integration	
Attitudes and behavior in reference to basic rules and norms of the society	Head Start affects the social behavior of all participants positively; the affected fields of behavior vary between the ethnic groups (Westat 2005, 2006). Consequently, Head Start contributes to integration in the field of social behavior.
Language competences	Head Start affects language competences of African-American participants and their siblings as well as of Hispanic participants positively (Westat 2005, 2006), hence it contributes to integration in the field of language competences.
Delinquency	For African-American children the likelihood of delinquency is reduced by Head Start participation (Currie and Thomas 1995).
Attitudes of majority population towards minorities	
Discrimination	There is no direct data on discrimination within or as a result of Head Start. If the above-described observances on prejudice-based behavioral patterns of teachers of schools (Ferguson 1998 [2]; Sadowski 2001) applied to Head Start teachers as well, the program would negatively influence integration in this field. However, this is a vague assumption which is not based on reliable analysis.

Table 1 (continued)

Indicator	Effect on indicator by Head Start participation
Perception of minorities by majority population	With the major goal of Head Start being the advancement of disadvantaged children, sympathy for children enhanced the public support of the program from the beginning (Kuntz 1998, pp. 5–6). The general acceptance of the program facilitates the conduction of other social measures which are incorporated into the program and benefit not only children but also adult members of minorities.
Measures enhancing cultural diversity	Head Start pursuits a multicultural approach which is practiced in the form of multicultural classroom materials and festivities. In this sense Head Start contributes to cultural diversity.

Program quality should be increased, e.g., through better qualified teachers, the use of higher-quality curriculum such as High/Scope and smaller classes, as a means of improving the educational impact on minority participants. Equal quality standards should be implemented in all Head Start centers and segregation within centers should be avoided. Teachers should be encouraged to have equal expectations towards all children, regardless of ethnic and social origin.

Especially African-American children could profit from an expansion of very early interventions. Long-term effects could be increased by follow-up intervention in school-age, the allocation of former Head Start children to schools of medium or higher quality and the avoiding of ethnic segregation and tracking in schools.

A long-term goal should be the adoption of the wealth level of ethnic minorities to the level of Whites by the elimination of discriminating practices which lead to the reproduction of wealth inequalities.

Increasingly, a preschool system has been suggested which is available for all children, not only for disadvantaged children. This system should be based on income-dependent fees and strict qualitative standards (Morgan 2004). This would have the advantages of an increase of program quality and participation rates, and a broader social composition of participants. The ethnic composition of the social disadvantaged population would not be reproduced through the ethnic composition of Head Start participants. At the same time, children whose families are slightly above the income line for Head Start but cannot afford a private program could participate.

These advantages again could lead to a relevant impact on minority integration because cultural and environmental factors of disadvantage for minorities could be diminished within Head Start, and due to spill-over effects especially African-Americans could profit from higher participation rates. Moreover, it would be less likely that the quality and the focus of programs as well as attitudes and expectations of teachers vary with the ethnic composition of the class.

The access to the program regardless of ethnic and social origin is in accordance with the principle of equal chances which is not only a basic part of the US constitution but also the constitutive idea of Head Start.

References

Administration for Children and Families. (2007). Head Start Fact Sheet. http://www.head-start.lane.or.us/general/statistics.html. Accessed 11 Dec 2007.

Alexanian, S. (1967/1979). Language project: The effects of a teacher-developed pre-school Language Training Program on First Grade Reading Achievement. Report D-1. Boston: Boston University, Head Start Evaluation and Research Center. (ED022563). In E. Zigler & J. Valentine (Eds.), *Project Head Start: A legacy of the war on poverty*. New York: Free Press.

Allen, K. E., Turner, K. D., & Everett, P. M. (1970/1979). A behavior modification classroom for Head Start children with problem behaviours: Exceptional Children 37. In E. Zigler & J. Valentine (Eds.), *Project Head Start: A legacy of the war on poverty* (pp. 119–128). New York: Free Press.

Bandura, A. (1977). *Social learning theory*. New York: General Learning Press.

Barnett, S. (1995). Long-term effects of early childhood programs on cognitive and school outcomes. *The Future of Children, 5*(3). http://www.futureofchildren.org/usr_doc/vol5no3ART2.pdf. Accessed 31 Jan 2008.

Bogard, K. (2004). Summary of selected longitudinal studies that inform PK-3. National Association of State Boards of Education (NASBE). www.fcd-us.org/usr_doc/bogardlongstudycomparisonnew.pdf. Accessed 20 Jan 2008.

Bronfenbrenner, U. (1974). *Is eary intervention effective?* Department of Health, Education, and Welfare, Office of Child Development., Washington, DC.

Butler, A. L. (1968, July). From Head Start to follow through. *Bulletin of the School of Education Indiana University, 44*(4).

Child Trends Data Bank. (2007). http://www.childtrendsdatabank.org/indicators/97HeadStart.cfm. Accessed 8 Nov 2007.

Child Trends Data Bank. (2008). http://www.childtrendsdatabank.org/basic.cfm. Accessed 9 Feb 2008.

Conley, D. (2003). Interview with Dalton Conley (edited transcript). California Newsreel. http://www.pbs.org/race/000_About/002_04-background-03–03.htm. Accessed 4 Feb 2008.

Currie, J., & Fallick, B. (1990/1993). From school to work: Minimum wages and educational attainment. In J. Currie & D. Thomas (Eds.), *Does Head Start make a difference?* NBER working paper series (Working paper no. 4406). National Bureau of Economic Research. Mimeo: UCLA.

Currie, J., & Thomas, D. (1993). *Does Head Start make a difference?* NBER working paper series (Working paper no. 4406). National Bureau of Economic Research.

Currie, J., & Thomas, D. (1995). *Does Head Start make a difference?* (JEL 138, H43). http://www.econ.ucla.edu/people/papers/currie/hdstaer.pdf. Accessed 25 Jan 2008.

Currie, J., & Thomas, D. (1996). *Does Head Start help Hispanic children?* NBER working paper series (Working paper no. 5805). National Bureau of Economic Research.

Currie, J., & Thomas, D. (1998). *School quality and the longer-term effects of Head Start*. NBER working paper series (Working paper no. 6362). National Bureau of Economic Research.

Ditomaso, N. (2003). Interview with Nancy Ditomaso (edited transcript). California Newsreel. http://www.pbs.org/race/000_About/002_04-background-03–07.htm. Accessed 4 Feb 2008.

Entwisle, D. R. (1995). The role of schools in sustaining early childhood program benefits. *The Future of Children, 5*(3), 133–142. http://www.futureofchildren.org/usr_doc/vol5no3ART2.pdf. Accessed 5 Nov 2008.

Entzinger, H., & Biezeveld, R. (2003). *Benchmarking in immigrant integration*. European Research Center on Migration and Ethnic Relations (ERCOMER), Faculty of Social Sciences, Erasmus University Rotterdam. http://www.ec.europa.eu/justice_home/funding/2004_2007/doc/study_indicators_integration.pdf. Accessed 12 Nov 2007.

Esser, H. (2000). *Soziologie. Spezielle Grundlagen Band 2: Die Konstruktion der Gesellschaft*. Frankfurt a. M.: Campus.

Ferguson, R. F. (1998a). Can schools narrow the black-white test score gap? In C. Jencks & M. Phillips (Eds.), *The black-white test score gap.* Washington: Brookings Institution. http://www.learningpt.org.gaplibrary/text/howcan.php. Accessed 4 Feb 2008.

Ferguson, R. F. (1998b). Teachers' perceptions and expectations and the black-white test score gap. In C. Jencks & M. Phillips (Eds.), *The black-white test score gap.* Washington: Brookings Institution. http://www.learnigpt.org/gaplibrary/text/teacherperceptions2.php. Accessed 4 Feb 2008.

Fordham, S., & Ogbu, J. U. (1986, September). Black students' school success: Coping with the "burden of 'acting white'". *The Urban Review, 18*(3).

Garces, E., Currie, J., & Thomas, D. (2000). *Longer term effects of Head Start.* NBER working paper series (Working paper no. 8054). National Bureau of Economic Research.

Hallinan, M. (1994). Tracking: From theory to practice. *Sociology of Education, 67*(2), 79–84.

Hanushek, E. A., Kain, J. F., & Rivkin, S. G. (2002). *New evidence about Brown v. Board of Ecucation: The complex effects of school racial composition on achievement.* Working paper 8741. National Bureau of Economic Research. http://www.learningpt.org/gaplibrary/text/researcherslink.php. Accessed 4 Feb 2008.

Hochschild, J. L. (2003, December). Social class in public schools. *Journal of Social Issues, 59*(4), 821–840.

Jencks, C., & Phillips, M. (1998, September–October). America's next achievement test: Closing the Black-White Test Score Gap. *The American Prospect, 9*(40), 44–53. http://www.prospect.org/print/V9/40/jencks-c.html. Accessed 5 Nov 2008.

Kuntz, K. R. (1998). A lost legacy: Head Start's origins in community action. In J. Ellsworth & L. J. Ames (Eds.), *Critical perspectives on Project Head Start: Revisioning the hope and challenge.* (pp. 1–38) New York: New York State University Press.

Lockwood, D. (1964). Social integration and system integration. In Z. Zollschan & W. Hirsch (Eds.), *Explorations in social change.* (pp. 244–256). London: Routledge & Kegan Paul.

Ludwig, J., & Phillips, D. A. (2007). *The benefits and costs of Head Start* (Working paper series no. 07–09, February). National Poverty Center. http://npc.umich.edu/publications/u/working_paper07–09.pdf. Accessed 4 Feb 2008.

Mathematica Policy Research, Inc. & Columbia University Center for Children and Families. (2006). *Early Head Start benefits children and families: Early Head Start research and evaluation project.* Administration for Children and Families, U.S. Department for Health and Human Services. http://www.earlychildhoodrc.org/events/presentations/raikes.pdf. Accessed 28 Jan 2008.

Mathematica Policy Research, Inc. (2007, March). *FACES 2006 study design.* Administration for Children and Families. http://www.acf.hhs.gov/programs/opre/hs/faces/reports/faces-studydesign.pdf. Accessed 20 Nov 2007.

Matthews, H., & Ewen, D. (2006). *Reaching all children? Understanding early care and education participation among immigrant families.* Center for Law and Social Policy., Washington, DC. http://www.clasp.org/publications/child_care_immigrant.pdf. Accessed 31 Jan 2008.

Mergner, G. (2005). Social limits to learning: Essays on the archeology of domination, resistance, and experience. Bergham Books. New York: Oxford University Press.

Morgan, G. (2004). A Head Start for all children. In E. Zigler & S. Styfco (Eds.), *The Head Start debates.* (pp. 407–502) Baltimore: Paul H. Brookes.

Neidell, M., & Waldfogel, J. (2006). *Spillover effects of early education: Evidence from Head Start.* New York: Oxford University Press. Columbia University. https://weblamp.princeton.edu/chw/papers/neidell_spillover_effects_headstart.pdf. Accessed 12 Nov 2007.

O'Connor, R. E. (1998). Race and Head Start participation: Political and social determinants of enrolment success in the States. *Social Science Quarterly, 79*(3), 547–556. Blackwell, Malden. http://cat.inist.fr/?aModele=afficheN&cpsidt=2012002. Accessed 4 Feb 2008.

Oliver, M. (2003). Interview with Melvin Oliver (edited transcript). California Newsreel. http://www.pbs.org/race/000_About/002_04-background-03–05.htm. Accessed 4 Feb 2008.

Portes, A., & Hao, L. (2004, August 17). The schooling of children of immigrants: Contextual effects on the educational attainment of the second generation. *PNAS, 101*(33), 11920–11927. http://www.pnas.org/cgi/reprint/101/33/11920. Accessed 11 Feb 2008.

Roscigno, V. J., Tomaskovic-Devey, D., & Crowley, M. (2006, June). Education and the inequalities of place. *Social Forces, 84*(4), 2121–2145.

Rotter, J. B. (1982). *The development and applications of social learning theory. Selected Papers.* New York: Praeger.

Sadowski, M. (2001). Closing the gap one school at a time. *Harvard Education Letter.* http://www.edletter.org/past/issues/2001-mj/gap.shtml in: http:///www.learningpt.org/gaplibrary/text/whatis.php. Accessed 4 Feb 2008.

Sargent, M. (1994). *The new sociology for Australians* (3rd ed.). Melbourne: Longman Chesire.

Sissel, P. A. (1999). *Staff, parents, and politics in Head Start: A case study in unequal power, knowledge, and material resources.* New York: Farmer Press.

Stoyle, J. (1973/1979). Culture, cognition, and social change: The effect of the Head Start experience on cognitive patterns. Philadelphia: Temple University, Child Development Research and Evaluation Center for Head Start (ED086315). In E. Zigler & J. Valentine (Eds.), *Project Head Start: A legacy of the war on poverty.* New York: Free Press.

Suarez-Orozco, C., & Suarez-Orozco, M. (1995). *Immigration, family life, and achievement motivation among Latino adolescents.* Stanford: Stanford University Press.

Takanishi, R. (2004). Levelling the playing field: Supporting immigrant children from birth to eight, children of immigrant families. The future of children, *14*(2), 61–79. Summer. http://www.futureofchildren.org/usr_doc/takanishi.pdf. Accessed 14 Feb 2008.

The White House. (2007). http://www.whitehouse.gov/infocus/earlychildhood/hspolicybook/html. Accessed 29 Nov 2007.

US Census. (2001). [Data file]. http://www.census.gov/prod/2001pubs/c2kbr01-1.pdf. Accessed 9 Nov 2007.

US Census. (2007). [Data file] http://www.census.gov/compendia/statab/tables/08s0049.xls. Accessed 8 Feb 2008.

US Department of Health & Human Services (DHHS). (2007). http://www.headstartinfo.org/recruitment/cdp.htm. Accessed 27 Oct 2007.

VanderHart, P. G. (2006). Why do some schools group by ability? Some evidence from the NAEP. *American Journal of Economics and Sociology, 65*(2), 435–462.

Vinovskis, M. A. (Ed.). (2005). *The birth of Head Start: Preschool education policies in the Kennedy and Johnson administrations.* Chicago: The University of Chicago Press.

Wolff, M., & Stein, A. (1967/1968, July). Head Start six months later. *Phi Delta Kappa, 48,* 349–350. In A. L. Butler (Ed.), From Head Start to follow through. *Bulletin of the School of Education Indiana University, 44*(4).

Woodhead, M. (1993). When psychology informs public policy. In E. Zigler & S. Styfco (Eds.), *Head Start and beyond: A national plan for extended childhood intervention.* New Haven: Yale University Press.

Zigler, E., & Valentine, J. (1979). *Project Head Start: A legacy of the war on poverty.* New York: Free Press.

Zigler, E., Abelson, W., & Seitz, V. (1973/1993). Motivational factors in the performance of economically disadvantaged children on the PPVT. *Child Development, 44,* 294–303. In J. Currie & D. Thomas (Eds.), *Does Head Start make a difference?* NBER working paper series (Working paper no. 4406). National Bureau of Economic Research.

Studies Reviewed Within the Analysis of Evaluation Results

Currie, J., & Thomas, D. (1993). *Does Head Start make a difference?* NBER working paper series (Working paper no. 4406). National Bureau of Economic Research.

Currie, J., & Thomas, D. (1995). *Does Head Start make a difference?* (JEL 138, H43). http://www.econ.ucla.edu/people/papers/currie/hdstaer.pdf. Accessed 25 Jan 2008.

Currie, J., & Thomas, D. (1996). *Does Head Start help Hispanic children?* NBER working paper series (Working paper no. 5805). National Bureau of Economic Research.

Garces, E., Currie, J., & Thomas, D. (2000). *Longer term effects of Head Start.* NBER working paper series (Working paper no. 8054). National Bureau of Economic Research.

Mathematica Policy Research, Inc. (2007). *FACES 2006 study design.* Administration for Children and Families, March. http://www.acf.hhs.gov/programs/opre/hs/faces/reports/faces-studydesign.pdf. Accessed 20 Nov 2007.

Neidell, M., & Waldfogel, J. (2006). *Spillover effects of early education: Evidence from Head Start.* Columbia University. https://weblamp.princeton.edu/chw/papers/neidell_spillover_effects_headstart.pdf. Accessed 12 Nov 2007.

Westat. (2003). Head Start FACES 2000: A whole-child perspective on program performance. Administration for Children and Families, U.S. Department of Health and Human Services (DHHS). http://www.acf.hhs.gov/programs/opre/hs/faces/reports/faces00_4thprogress/faces00_4thprogress.pdf. Accessed 21 Jan 2008.

Westat. (2005). Head Start impact study: First year findings. Administration for children and families, U.S. Department of Health and Human Services (DHHS). http://www.acf.hhs.gov/programs/opre/hs/impact_study/reports/first_yr_finds/first_yr_finds.pdf. Accessed 23 Jan 2008.

Westat. (2006). FACES 2003 Research brief: Children's outcomes and program quality in Head Start. Administration for Children and Families, U.S. Department of Health and Human Services (DHHS). http://www.acf.hhs.gov/programs/opre/hs/faces/reports/research_2003/research_2003.pdf. Accessed 23 Jan 2008.

Chapter 26
Project-Based Learning to Enhance Recognition and Acceptance of Cultural Diversity in the Elementary School

Christos Govaris and Stavroula Kaldi

Introduction

During the decade of 1990s, Greece was transformed to an immigrant receiving country, which has led to a scientific discourse about dealing with cultural diversity in action. Since then there is an increasing need to learn to accept and live together with people with immigrant background. For this, the present chapter focuses on promoting recognition and acceptance of cultural diversity in the Greek elementary school via project-based learning.

Currently, more than 1,000,000 people from foreign countries live in Greece, mainly from the Eastern European and South Eastern European countries. About 10% of pupil population consists of children with immigrant background which in numbers is translated into 130,000 pupils. An attempt is made to correspond to the challenges of the current reality imposed by the cultural and linguistic diversity via curriculum changes and adaptations to the new conditions and teachers' in-service training in the Greek school system. Based on the results of PISA research, pupils with immigrant background are left behind compared to the native pupils concerning the academic performance in the three main subject areas (reading, mathematics and science) (see OECD 2003, 2006, 2007a, b). School appears to be facing a series of difficulties and dilemmas regarding the educational management of diversity in the classrooms. Factors that influence and, furthermore, hinder dealing with the cultural and linguistic diversity positively should be searched in relation to people with immigrant background social status and to how natives act towards and interact with them outside and within the school system.

Published research on social relationships in European multicultural societies indicates the existence of discrimination attitudes and stigmatizing immigrants from large parts of the native population. These attitudes appear to have a special breadth in the Greek multicultural society (European Monitoring Centre on Racism and Xe-

---

C. Govaris (✉)
Department of Primary Education, School of Humanities, University of Thessaly,
Argonafton & Filellinon, 38221 Volos, Greece
e-mail: govaris@uth.gr

nophobia 2005; Sarafidou et al. 2010). Prejudices and resistance against immigrants as well as the multicultural nature of the modern Greek society are not simply traced amongst the adults, but also amongst children and adolescents. Evidence from recent research in Greece about pupils' attitudes and perceptions of multiculturalism (see Govaris et al. 2006) shows that the majority of the participants face immigrants with prejudices. The majority of Greek pupils do not wish for cultural contacts with the immigrant pupils[1] and they prefer a model of social relations between native and immigrant people which aims to culturally assimilate immigrant people in the Greek society. Taking into consideration this social reality and the declared aim of the European Union about respecting and promoting cultural and linguistic diversity, we must ask a fundamental question about the role and importance of schooling in preparing future generation to live together creatively in a social space characterized by cultural pluralism and constant cultural changes. In this chapter we present some findings of a pilot study in which a project with an intercultural content was implemented in an elementary school classroom, aiming to decrease ethnic stereotypes and prejudices and, at the same time, to structure intercultural competencies.

In this study the terms 'multicultural' and 'intercultural' are used to describe different meanings in the Greek scientific discourse. 'Multicultural' refers to the description of a society in which different ethnocultural groups of people coexist whereas 'intercultural' refers to educational practices in a multicultural society. The term 'intercultural education' is not understood and used commonly by different groups of educational scientists in Greece and in the international context. There are two main contradictory directions to refer to the intercultural education (Hohmann 1987; Hormel and Scherr 2004; Auernheimer 2006). The first direction is based on the position that the different cultural groups have distinct limits and differences and education should aim to experience and 'meet' the other culture through pointing the cultural differences in a context of harmonious social coexistence amongst the different ethnocultural groups. The second direction is based on the principle that the concepts of culture and cultural differences can be dynamic concepts and is opposed to the approach of the first direction which views cultural differences as distinct limits between cultural groups, promoting, in this way, existing types of ethnic stereotypes and prejudices. In the present study the approach of the second direction is accepted as a frame of reference. Therefore, education must aim to reduce the social processes of immigrants' segregation and decategorize dominant images of 'foreign and other'. In addition, education should aim to recognize cultural differences and decategorize institutional processes which hinder pupils with immigrant background to equally participate in the educational process.

---

[1] Immigrant pupils' refer to pupils who come from families with an immigrant background and this does not imply a stigmatized term.

Contextual Information About Multiculturalism and Intercultural Education in Greece

During the decade of the 1990s, Greece from being an emigrant country was transformed into an immigrant one. The Greek state reacted to the new social reality by passing a new law about 'Intercultural Education and Education of Repatriated Greeks' in 1996. This law describes a version of intercultural education which is focused on a static definition of the concepts of 'culture' and 'cultural differences'. Such a version, though, cannot contribute to the quest for critical learning in contrast to procedures of ethnic discrimination and immigrants' separation. On the contrary, it could contribute, as Damanakis points out (1997) to consolidating the existing ethnic prejudices and restricting pupils with immigrant background into nonexisting cultural differences (see also Skourtou et al. 2004). At the level of school education, reception classes and additional teaching provided to pupils with immigrant background were established as necessary for these pupils to learn quickly the Greek language. Learning the Greek language is an essential condition in order to achieve school integration for pupils with immigrant background, but it cannot be considered to be the only one. We could admit that, regardless of the progress in the national scientific discourse on interculturalism in Greece (see Damanakis 1997; Markou 1997; Govaris 2001; Gotovos 2002; Georgogiannis 2006), all the efforts carried out from schools in the next decade were focused on disseminating the principles of teaching Greek as a second language and producing teaching materials for this (see Skourtou 2008).

When the national curriculum was reconstructed and new syllabuses were produced in 2003, we could observe an extended endeavour to integrate interculturalism in the school learning procedures. An important difference to the old curriculum is detected as the new curriculum establishes a social frame of reference on which central aims of education are chosen and rationalized. More specifically, a change in the orientation from the national to the international social frame of reference is met. Within a scene of contemporary international advancements, issues about the role and aims of the education systems in a globalized environment are adopted. The reasons for this change in the orientation of the national curriculum can be explained by the fact that the internationalization of culture, the globalized economy and multiculturalism are not simply recognized as basic characteristics of the school's social environment, but they are also evaluated as educational challenges, which can be translated into fundamental aims of education: resistance to the dominance of a mono-cultural model of society and to phenomena of xenophobia and racism.

It is therefore, observed that the new curriculum in Greece employs a new quest in the orientation of education in terms of principles and aims of intercultural education. In other words, it can be claimed that there is a shift from the position of 'neglecting differentiation'—which characterized the old curriculum—to the position of 'respecting cultural and linguistic diversity'. Nevertheless, a closer look at the new curriculum reveals a dense web of restrictions which enclose the initial intention of recognizing multiculturalism into a deadlock. More specifically, multiculturalism is defined as an ethno-cultural pluralism, as a situation where different ethnic cultures with distinct limits in the interaction relations between them co-exist. It is therefore evident that the opening of the new curriculum towards multiculturalism is characterized by ambivalence: meeting the 'other' is projected as an opportunity to enrich 'oneself's identity', but also as a danger of losing/undermining 'oneself's identity'. This ambivalence permeates all intercultural references in the new curriculum and intercultural learning takes place in a tensed atmosphere which derives from this approach of the 'other' mentioned above. This approach includes limitations regarding daily classroom teaching. Teaching practices which start with a static conceptualization of culture and specific cultural differences are limited to meeting and understanding an abstract and without history 'other'; in other words, they are entrapped in a version of understanding the 'different other' with an egocentric and ethnocentric character. Thus we consider that curriculum promotes a version of intercultural approach which contributes to the consolidation of an ethnocentric way of thinking and finally, to strengthening the limits and discrimination between social groups rather that weakening them.

Theoretical Background

In social psychology prejudices are defined as attitudes with value weight and content which are neither based on the empirical reality nor examined considering their objective validity. Prejudices' basic elements are negative feelings and acts of stigmatizing. Ethnic prejudices are these negative attitudes and perceptions of people or groups of people towards members of another group/ethnicity. At this point we should clarify that prejudices are not present in some people's attitudes but they are also present in a general social level (social discussion) or in institution level (i.e. in law texts, in school syllabuses, in literature texts). Prejudices exist in processes of categorizing social groups and act as rational knowledge in order to separate and reject specific social groups. According to Bruner (in Vanderbroeck 1999, p. 80) the picture we frame for people is related to the social power they may have. Differences in power, in the social position and in wealth play a significant role in shaping people's perceptions about other people. Therefore, prejudices are not just invented by people casually, but are directly relevant to the social structures and conditions and are socially intervened via the social discussion or the institution level (i.e. mass media, school knowledge) (see Govaris 2001). As Hatcher and Troyna (2000) mention, societies offer children a series of social orientations and interpretative patterns with racist charge. These patterns are used by children in understanding and interpreting specific situations around them.

It is evident from previous research about prejudices in childhood that young children at the age of 4 have ethnic awareness under the meaning of evaluative opinion for in-groups and out-groups (Doyle and Aboud 1995; Milner 1996; Rutland 1999; Vandenbroeck 1999; Jones and Foley 2003; Govaris et al. 2006). Children can acknowledge characteristics and the social value of an ethnic group before they have contact with that group. Children like adults use categorization to simplify the cognitive process when evaluating self and other (see Allport 1954; Jones and Foley 2003; Govaris et al. 2006). Many studies support decategorizing or recategorizing as the most effective way to stop the many biases that follow categorization (e.g. stereotypes, hate, conflict) and that are the definition of prejudice. Decategorization instead promotes a co-operative interdependence (Gaertner et al. 1989; Devine 1995; Brown 1996).

Project-Based Learning, Co-operative Learning and Intercultural Education

Within the context of child-centred learning, project-based teaching method has become increasingly prominent as a response of schooling to the challenges of the twenty-first century. The project-based learning (P-BL) involves the study/research of a topic in depth where students' interests, ideas, questions and predictions form the experiences lived and the works/activities undertaken; it is a collaborative activity between the teacher and pupils, the latter being often in groups. The main characteristics of P-BL are described in the literature as follows (Frey 1994; Harris 2002; McGrath 2002; Solomon 2003): students can become communicative, creative and develop practical thinking as they are engaged in active inquiry/discovery, exploration and decision making; knowledge is based on experience and experimentation in real/authentic life. In relevant literature about the effects of P-BL on multi-ethnic classrooms, it is shown that pupils can develop positive attitudes towards peers from different ethnic backgrounds (Kaldi et al. forthcoming).

A significant part of P-BL is the collaborative activity amongst pupils in order to carry out the task assigned. Co-operative learning is based on constructivism including talking and listening, questions, argument and sharing (Jarvis et al. 1998). In literature on educational studies, co-operative learning is generally understood to be learning that takes place in an environment where pupils in small groups share ideas and work collaboratively to complete academic tasks (see Slavin 1985; Webb 1985; Johnson and Johnson 1989; Sharan 1990; Davidson and Kroll 1991; Hertz-Lazarowitz 1992; Veenman et al. 2000). There exist though different models for co-operative learning which vary considerably in their assumptions about the nature of learning and about the roles of teachers and pupils in the classroom (Sharan 1990).

Published research on the process of learning during co-operative group work has showed that academic performance should be examined within the social context and that academic and social processes interrelate in various ways. Webb (1985) and Hertz-Lazarowitz (1992) have demonstrated that behaviour changed within groups in the course of time and group members' experiences during group work were different between them. In particular, Webb (1985) illustrated that there were differences in the group perceptions related to gender, academic skills and status of each group member. Hertz-Lazarowitz (1992) claimed that group members acquired group skills and moved beyond their individuality managing thus, to interact in a high academic level.

The effects of co-operative learning in culturally and racially heterogeneous groups have been researched thoroughly. Aronson et al. (1975) researched co-teaching amongst pupils in heterogeneous groups of black, white and Chicano children and found that pupils liked and helped each other significantly more after the 6-week intervention program. Lucker et al. (1976) designed the 'Jigsaw Method' in which white, black and Chicano fifth and sixth graders studied together in four to six person groups and measured the academic benefits of this method. Rooney-Rebeck and Jason in the USA (1986) investigated the effects of cooperative group peer tutoring on the inter-ethnic relations of elementary school age children. Direct observations of social interactions on the playground and sociometric indices were used to measure interethnic associations before and after an 8-week program. The findings suggest that a cooperative peer tutoring classroom structure can have a positive measurable effect on the inter-ethnic behaviour and academic learning of school children. Eitan et al. research in Israel (1992) about immigrant pupils' low self-esteem in multicultural classrooms included co-operative learning in an educational program which had positive effect on pupils' academic and social self-image and suggested that teachers should link academic and social elements when they plan teaching in multicultural classrooms. Overall, co-operative learning has been found to influence positively the social relations with pupils of different ethnic backgrounds and mainstreamed special education pupils and their class peers.

Therefore, co-operatively structured settings combine several of the optimal conditions that might be effective in preventing or reducing prejudice (Rooney-Rebeck and Jason 1986), in decategorizing or recategorizing self and others.

Summing up, we could claim that native and immigrant pupils who have their own experiences and information/knowledge about the social value/hierarchy of their group, are met in the multicultural school. Taking this for granted we should ask how we could refer to immigrant pupils' cultural differences during teaching without strengthening the existed social evaluations/discriminations and without attributing to them cultural traits which can cause feelings of insecurity in a social environment with intense pressures for cultural assimilation. The question we should ask is directly linked to how we understand the fundamental principles and aims of *Intercultural Education*. Therefore, we briefly outline how we understand intercultural education as follows: We accept intercultural education which is based on:

- **A dynamic concept of culture and cultural differences.** Within the frame of such a conceptualization the prime interest of teaching is associated with the pupils' subjective meaning about their cultural differences (i.e. the meaning of languages, origin, religion, etc.).
- **A dynamic concept of identity.** Immigrant pupils' identity should not be exclusively defined according to their ethnic origin. Therefore, schooling must provide those pupils with opportunities to experiment and negotiate with their identity.

- **The principles of 'recognition and indirect reference' to cultural differences** (see Diehm 1995 and Govaris 2001). This principle could be defined as "attitude of awareness towards the individual peculiarities and diversity of experiences" (Diehm 1995, p. 143) which characterize children's personalities. This principle can be implemented via teaching when pupils are regarded as individuals who have the right to be recognized in the line of their entire social affiliations, subjective meanings and knowledge derived from them. The principle of indirect reference underlines the necessity for teaching in which differentiation is not an exclusive characteristic of immigrant pupils, but a basic one of all pupils. Furthermore, implementing the principle above in teaching could prevent the corroboration of perceptions such as "all native pupils are one and the same, all immigrant pupils are different from us" and contribute to an understanding of differentiation provided by the corpus of all pupils. Finally, looking at children as people who experience life through their special and important relationships facilitates us to overcome an established and mistaken attitude towards immigrant pupils as anonymous representatives of a closely united ethnic group. According to the principle above in teaching we do not come across to the 'young Albanian', but to 'Miri'—the name of a child with Albanian passport—as a person with specific needs, desires and experiences. Children must become familiar and understand the meaning of these different individual experiences, desires and practices rather than any characteristics of a general and abstract, for example, 'Albanian' culture.

Within the framework above teaching should aim to (a) develop communication competencies in a multicultural society, (b) produce content of multiple types of differentiation and (c) critically juxtapose with the social structures which 'determine' the quality of social relations. As Markou points out (1997, p. 31) foreign and native pupils must learn to understand themselves within the process of life conditions. Self-consciousness shaped in this way can transcend self and is sensitive in exclusion, prejudices, discrimination and racism.

Fundamental Ideas About the Educational Program

Taking into consideration the current multicultural character of the Greek society, published research on the significance of co-operative learning in the multicultural school environment and the fundamental principles of intercultural education, we suggest that the process of constructing knowledge and attitudes which can reduce ethnic stereotypes and prejudices and can promote relations between native and immigrant pupils should take place in the Greek elementary school under the principles of recognition and indirect reference to cultural differences. Searching the multiculturalism of certain Greek towns such as Volos historically and at the present time can offer opportunities for implementing the above.

The historic dimension of multiculturalism of the town of Volos is mainly related to the refugees from Asia Minor in the region of N. Ionia as well as the time long presence of Greek Roma. Searching for the historic dimension of multiculturalism we aim to make pupils (a) become aware of the cultural contacts through time and the development of cultural pluralism in this town, (b) ask questions about issues of excluding groups of people who live in Greece for many decades (such as Roma) and of the relativist perception about entire cultural homogeneity of the native population. We anticipate, in other words, that pupils can apparently understand that there are certain, different and through time causes of human mobility, that 'different people' either defined as 'foreigners' or 'natives' were always present and what we describe as cultural development is closely related to the cultural agitations resulting from the cultural contacts between different groups of people. Searching for the present time dimension of the town of Volos we aim to make pupils understand the causes of human mobility at present times and get to know personal histories and routes of people who have immigrated to Greece, in order to understand, accept and appreciate them.

Thus, by creating such as frame of reference we provide pupils with the opportunities to narrate a special story of mobility/immigration, directly or indirectly relevant to their families. Immigrant pupils' stories can then become important links in this chain of life histories presented in the classroom environment by all pupils.

It is significant to note that these individual stories have many elements in common. One of these is the town of Volos in which they all live at present. Therefore, we reach the second fundamental aim of this educational program: processing and integrating materials and information such as pictures, narratives, photos from all stories of human mobility in producing one narrative story about the development of the multiculturalism of Volos. This story can be written in all languages spoken by pupils (mother tongue and any other second languages) and will be presented in a website on the internet. Pupils' participation in searching and constructing the human history of the town and its publication (by creating the website) can offer identification experiences with the town and can support immigrant pupils to give meaning to their own linguistic capital via the town they live as a point of reference. **Native pupils will get to listen and see their peers' mother tongue and will experience multilingualism as cultural wealth.**

Methodology

The methodology applied in this pilot study is qualitative and used the case study research design (Yin 1994; Bassey 1999) and the research methods of interview, informal discussion and classroom observation (Cohen et al. 2000). A grade 6 class of an elementary school in the town of Volos was the actual case study of the present pilot research and the selection process was based on the volunteer character of the class teacher. The participants of the research process included 21 pupils, five of whom were immigrants' children and the class teacher. Interviews were conducted with the pupils and the class teacher whereas informal discussions only with the class teacher. Observation was participant and nonparticipant. The class teacher kept a journal of the activities and events in the classroom during the educational program.

The educational program lasted for 5 weeks and planned activities were implemented between 2 and 3 teaching hours a week. Issues raised during the activities were also discussed in teaching hours of other subjects.

Limitations

The present study is limited in the use of certain methodological tools. We did not use a sociometric index about pupils' relationships and immigrant pupils' position in these relationships because we did not want to create any further problematic situations. This was also the reason why we avoided conducting a quantitative study about the existence of ethnic prejudices. The educational program we developed consists of a pilot implementation aiming to act as the beginning of a series of activities which would not be limited in the classroom environment and would have a positive effect on school culture as well as develop a school culture of recognizing, participating and integrating immigrant pupils and their families.

Another limitation of the present study is pupils' limited experiences of innovative teaching and learning methods such as project-based and co-operative learning. We have not managed to evaluate the effects of these limitations in the course of the educational program, however, we have collected data about the program's improvement which are not discussed in this chapter.

Implementation of the Educational Program in a Grade 6 Classroom

The implementation of the educational program depended on the class teacher's will to differentiate her teaching according to her pupils' needs and extend her learning about multiculturalism and intercultural education. Before the start of the program she mentioned that she had raised issues of immigration and multiculturalism during lesson in the Greek language. At this point we should emphasize that the new national curriculum and syllabus implemented for a second school year in Greek schools have an intercultural orientation, the implementation and breadth of which is not simply possible via occasional references to 'foreigners'.

The class teacher said she had noticed that immigrant pupils were not fully accepted from some native peers in the classroom as well as during breaks. From the overall informal discussions with the class teacher we concluded that immigrant pupils were experiencing a classroom peer climate between acceptance and discrimination and that the class teacher could not spend much of her teaching time to some immigrant pupils' learning difficulties due to the new syllabus pressures to be effectively implemented. We can admit that even though the new syllabus offers some opportunities for differentiated learning, class teachers are not adequately equipped to differentiated teaching and do not feel competent to do so.

The main axes of activities implemented during the program were the following:

- Refugees from Asia Minor
- Internal mobility within Greece
- Immigration
- Maps of mobility/immigration

From these activities the outcomes in terms of pupil work were materials and texts produced in Greek and there were negotiations during group work in order to decide the languages of translating these texts and materials.

Regarding teaching methods the teacher applied group work and class discussions. The main themes of the activities were first discussed in the whole class, explanations were given about the group work to be undertaken and then pupils worked in groups investigating each axis of the program. All groups were assigned the same activity at a time. Then a whole class discussion was taking place presenting materials, texts and information which raised the issues we present in the findings.

Procedure of the Research Process

The educational program was planned by the class teacher around the basic issues discussed with the research team. The plan was open to pupils' ideas and suggestions therefore, it included important elements of project-based learning (pupils' active involvement by providing ideas and suggestions in planning activities as well as their own experiences). The process of learning was beyond simply collecting information and events and became active when pupils were given opportunities to contribute with and provide their own meanings openly.

During the research process we met pupils three times: at the beginning, in the middle and at the end of the program. At the beginning we carried out a group interview to explore what they knew about the history of their town, if and how they linked this history with immigration, how they understood concepts of 'differentiation' and 'foreign', whom foreigners they knew and whom they wished to meet. In the second and final visit we collected information about issues which were important for pupils.

Meetings were also organized with the class teacher after a planned visit to observe the lessons carried out. She provided the researcher with her views about the progress of the activities, their impact on pupils and pupils' expressed ideas and suggestions.

Findings and Discussion

Examining the findings from this education program we point out issues which indicate that there were certain learning outcomes as developed earlier.

Key Points of the Findings

"How Did We Reach the Same Town?"—Different Routes with the Same Destination

At the point of the program where pupils were working on describing their families' or ancestors' or friends' routes of immigration/mobility with coloured lines on a Mediterranean map a female pupil commented "different routes, but they all lived or live here in Volos….we live here, we are different but in what do we differ? I don't understand…". The teacher utilized pupil's phrase and asked all pupils to think what makes their family unique and different. Thus pupils searched the individual elements of their culture and identity experiencing the differentiation in presenting themselves. They also discovered that many of these differences had a common cultural baseline and universal human needs of self-expression, such as music and its importance in family cultures.

From this point onwards an attempt to gradually move away from stereotypical images of an ethnic group to present the uniqueness of self was made. This is depicted in native pupils' phrases about their immigrant peers: "all Albanians are not the same, they differ amongst them, as we differ with those people who live in other towns to villages. My father told me that on the islands people listen to different music and have different dances to ours here" (Yiannis). Therefore the group work and the presentation of self individuality led to a critical reflection about cultural differentiations within native pupils' ethnic group. Differentiation was experienced during co-operative work as normality and not as an exception. Therefore, co-operative classroom structure led to improving inter-ethnic behaviour which is similar to what Rooney-Rebeck and Jason (1986) claimed in their work. We cannot claim though that some ethnic stereotypes were decategorized as there were a few comments during the class discussions as follows: "From appearance you make out who is Albanian".

In total, pupils revealed their understanding of differentiation through their expression of individuality as an important element of each life history and not simply of the 'other' pupils. It was important for them to research and present their individuality in the group work. In this work—unlike previous research [i.e Hertz-Lazarowitz (1992) who argued that, after group work, group member moved beyond their individuality], we argue that the individual contribution to studying family life histories was important and assisted in developing an empathetic attitude towards immigrant peers and their families.

What a 'Weird Language' Do You Have?—Hierarchical Categorization Patterns of Languages (Evaluating Languages)

During the activity in which pupils drew on the map of people's routes a language issue emerged: in what language should we write/refer the places of origin? Native pupils argued that it should be written in Greek because everyone in the class could read it. Orlando (Albanian boy) claimed that his mother tongue has almost the same fonts with the English which they all learn at school. A native pupil answered that "the Albanian language is not highly valued as English" (Yiorgos) depicting the complexities emerging from evaluating the prestige of certain languages (i.e. English).

At this point of co-operative learning a 'simmering' issue which was mainly immigrant pupils' concern came forward: "How will our native peers react when hearing our mother tongue?". During traditional teaching immigrant pupils are not given opportunities to negotiate issues of identity and pupils participating in this program were used to deal with such questions. Therefore, the issue mentioned above was not raised from the beginning of the program having a twofold consequence: immigrant pupils do not negotiate issues of identity and native pupils do not speculate on what values in individuality and more specifically, in our case, the value of immigrant pupils' mother tongue.

The negotiations about selecting another language, except Greek, to present the routes of mobility/immigration during the group work illustrated the taken for granted view of native pupils that immigrant peers must culturally assimilate to the dominant culture of the society and their difficulty to move beyond the dominant evaluation of some languages' prestige.

To Whom Does This Town Belong?

Acceptance of the Albanian language during this program occurred when pupils had to decide in what languages the website would be published/presented. As all pupils agreed that the website could be read by a variety of web viewers they came to a conclusion that Albanian language should be included. At this point one can wonder whether this kind of acceptance indicates a more positive and permanent attitude towards people with immigrant background. Nevertheless, during this educational program, many native pupils expressed a genuine curiosity about the way of writing and reading Albanian and their satisfaction when managed to spell a few Albanian words. The contribution of one Albanian boy (Orlando) was valuable when he had brought with him a Greek-Albanian dictionary in order to check the translation of the texts having been already produced in Greek. The above can illustrate the beginnings of identification with a heterogeneous group and a new environment of living based on linking mother tongue with the history of the new place of residence.

During pupils' discussions in group work about creating the website some pupils expressed their concerns about whether this town belonged to all people living in it, even to foreigners who might leave some day. In expressing their concerns and views we came up with hidden recoils between accepting and not accepting immigrant pupils.

What was positive during these discussions was that group work provided ground for externalizing fears and arguments in order to negotiate with the issue of 'who has got the right to be identified with this town'. This issue however, can be argued for the rest of the educational program.

Conclusion

In concluding the educational program proposed and implemented by an elementary school class provided ground for presenting three main themes:

a. Elementary school pupils of the researched case study expressed their prejudices with no hesitation and more specifically, native pupil population showed clearly their prejudices about immigrants. Therefore, from this case study we can claim that we have a picture of expressing prejudices in a school environment. Thus we must take this issue into consideration when planning and implementing intervention educational programs in the future.
b. Through co-operative learning the aims of the educational program were almost met: via communication processes, such as discussion in the group work and exchanging ideas and issues about family histories of route mobility/immigration, native pupils got to know peers from immigrant families; they speculated on difficulties of daily life which immigrants face and empathized with them when they had to search for their own family histories of route mobility and/or immigration.
c. Through this educational program a process of searching what native and immigrant population in the town of Volos have in common and can unite them was launched which must be continued in order to meet a working target for elementary school classes, that is, developing a *community of learning*. A whole school teaching approach must be developed in which collaborative action in learning should be promoted. The more pupil collaboration in school and community issues, the better understanding, accepting and appreciative they can become.

Therefore, we should direct ourselves in searching what we need to change in the teaching methodology in classes and schools in order to provide pupils with more opportunities to understand, accept and appreciate each other.

References

Allport, G. W. (1954). *The nature of prejudice*. Cambridge: Addison-Wesley.
Aronson, E., Blaney, N., Sikes, J., Stephen, G., & Snapp, H. (1975). The Jigsaw route to learning and liking. *Psychology Today, 8,* 43–50.
Auernheimer, G. (2006). Gleichheit und Anerkennung als Leitmotive Interkultureller Pädagogik. In A. Tanner, H. Badertscher, R. Holzer, A. Schindler, & U. Streckeisen (Hrsg.), *Heterogenität und Integration* (pp. 29–45). Zürich: Seismo Verlag.
Bassey, M. (1999). *Case study research in educational settings*. Buckingham: Open University Press.
Brown, R. (1996). Intergroup relations. In M. Hewstone, W. Stroebe, & G. M. Stephenson (Eds.), *Introduction to social psychology* (pp. 530–561). Oxford: Blackwell.
Cohen, L., Manion, L., & Morrison, K. (2000). *Research methods in education* (5th ed.). London: Routledge & Falmer.
Damanakis, M. E. (1997). (in Greek). *Repatriated and foreign pupils' education in Greece: An intercultural approach (Η εκπαίδευση των παλιννοστούντων και αλλοδαπών μαθητών στην Ελλάδα: διαπολιτισμική προσέγγιση)*. Athens: Gutenberg.
Davidson, N., & Kroll, D. L. (1991). An overview of research on cooperative learning related to mathematics. *Journal for Research in Mathematics Education, 22*(5), 362–365.
Devine, P. G. (1995). Prejudice and out-group perception. In A. Tesser (Eds.), *Advanced social psychology* (pp. 466–524). New York: McGraw-Hill.
Diehm, I. (1995). *Erziehung in der Einwanderungsgesellschaft. KonzeptionelleÜberlegungen für die Elementerpädagogik*. Frankfurt a. M.: IKo Verlag.
Doyle, A., & Aboud, F. E. (1995). A longitudinal study of White children's racial prejudice as a social-cognitive development. *Merrill-Palmer Quarterly, 41,* 209–228
Dunne, E., & Bennett, N. (1994). *Talking and learning in groups*. London: Routledge.
Eitan, T., Amir, Y., & Rich, Y. (1992). Social and academic treatments in mixed ethnic classes and change in student self concept. *British Journal of Educational Psychology, 62*(3), 364–374.
European Monitoring Centre on Racism and Xenophobia. (2005). *Majorities' attitudes towards minorities: Key finding from the Eurobarometer and the European Social Survey*. fra.europa.eu/fraWebsite/attachments/EB2005-summary.pdf.
Frey, K. (1994). *Die Projektmethode* (5th ed.). Weinheim: Beltz.
Gaertner, S. L., Mann, J., Murrell, A., & Dovidio, J. F. (1989). Reducing intergroup bias: The benefits of recategorization. *Journal of Personality and Social Psychology, 57,* 239–249.
Georgogiannis, P. (2006). *Teachers' intercultural competence and readiness*. Patras: Own Publication.
Gotovos, A. (2002). (in Greek). *Education and diversity (Εκπαίδευση και Ετερότητα)*. Athens: Metaichmio.
Govaris, C. (2001). (in Greek). *Introduction to intercultural education (Εισαγωγή στη Διαπολιτισμική Εκπαίδευση)*. Athens: Atrapos.
Govaris, C., Athanasiadis, I., Xanthakou, Y., & Kaila, M. (2006). Griechenland als Einwanderungsland. Akkulturationseinstellungen, Diskriminierungsbereitschaft und Stereotype von einheimischen SchülerInnen. In J. Held (Hrsg.), *Perspektiven der myltikulturellen Gesellschaft Universität Tübingen* (pp. 52–67). Tübingen: Universität Tübingen.
Harris, J. (2002). Activity design assessments: An uncharacteristic consensus. *Learning and Leading with Technology, 27*(7), 42–50.
Hatcher, R., & Troyna, B. (2000). Ethnisierungsprozesse und Kinder. In Th. Quehl, (Hrsg.), *Schule ist keine Insel. Britische Perspektiven antirassistischer Pädagogik* (pp. 88–102). Münster: Waxmann.
Hertz-Lazarowitz, R. (1992). Understanding students' interactive behavior: Looking at six mirrors of the classroom. In R. Hertz-Lazarowitz & N. Miller (Eds.), *Interaction in cooperative groups: The anatomy of group learning* (pp. 71–102). New York: Cambridge Press.

Hohmann, M. (1987). Interkulturelle Erziehung – Versuch einer Bestandsaufnahme. *Ausländer Kinder in Schule und Kindergarten, 4,* 4–8.

Hormel, U., & Scherr, A. (2004). *Bildung für die Einwanderungsgesellschaft. Perspektiven der Auseinandersetzung mit struktureller, institutioneller und interaktionaler Diskriminierung.* Wiesbaden: VS Verlag.

Jarvis, P., Holford J., & Griffin, C. (1998). *The theory and practice of learning.* London: Kogan Page.

Johnson, D. W., & Johnson, R. T. (1989). *Cooperation and competition: Theory and research.* Edina: Interaction Book.

Jones, L. M., & Foley, L. A. (2003). Educating children to decategorize racial groups. *Journal of Applied Social Psychology, 33*(3), 554–564.

Kaldi, S., Filippatou, D., & Govaris, C. (forthcoming). Project-based learning in primary schools: Effects on pupils' learning and attitudes. *3–13 Education,* 1–11.

Lucker, G. W., Rosenfield, D., Sikes, J., & Aronson, E. (1976). Performance in the interdependent classroom: A field study. *American Educational Research Journal, 13,* 115–123.

Markou, G. (1997). (in Greek) *Introduction to intercultural education. Greek and international experience (Εισαγωγή στη Διαπολιτισμική Εκπαίδευση. Ελληνική και Διεθνής εμπειρία).* Athens: Center for Intercultural Education, University of Athens.

McGrath, D. (2002). Getting started with project-based learning. *Learning and Leading with Technology, 30*(3), 42–50.

Milner, D. (1996). Children and racism: Beyond the value of the dolls. In W. P. Robinson (Eds.), *Social groups and identities: Developing the legacy of Henri Tajfel* (pp. 249–268). Oxford: Butterworth-Heinemann.

OECD. (2003). *Literacy skills for the world of tomorrow - further results from PISA 2000,* OECD/UNESCO-UIS, Paris.http://www.uis.unesco.org/TEMPLATE/pdf/pisa/PISAplus_Eng.pdf.

OECD. (2006). *Where immigrant students succeed: A comparative review of performance and engagement in PISA 2003,* OECD, Paris. http://www.oecd.org/dataoecd/2/38/36664934.pdf.

OECD. (2007a). *PISA 2006: Science competencies for tomorrow's world,* OECD, Paris. http://www.oecd.org/dataoecd/16/28/39722597.pdf.

OECD FACTBOOK. (2007b). *Educational outcomes for children of immigrants,* OECD, Paris. http://www.thepresidency.gov.za/learning/reference/factbook/pdf/12–03-01.pdf.

Rooney-Rebeck, P., & Jason, L. (1986). Prevention of prejudice in Elementary School Students. *Journal of Primary Prevention, 7*(2), 63–73.

Rutland, A. (1999). The development of national prejudice, in-group favouritism and self-stereotypes in British children. *British Journal of Social Psychology, 38,* 55–70.

Sarafidou, J., Govaris, C., & Loumakou, M. (2010, August 25–27). Identifying blatant and subtle ethnic prejudice among primary school children. Paper presented at the European Conference in Educational Research (ECER10), Helsinki, Finland.

Sharan, S. (1990). *Cooperative learning: Theory and research.* London: Praeger.

Skourtou, E. (2008). Linguistic diversity and language learning and teaching: An example from Greece. *Scientia Paedagogica Experimentalis, XLV*(1), 175–194.

Skourtou, E., Vratsalis, K., & Govaris, C. (2004). (in Greek) *Immigration in Greece and education. A review of the existing situation -- challenges and perspectives of improvement (Μετανάστευση στην Ελλάδα και Εκπαίδευση. Αποτίμηση της υπάρχουσας κατάστασης -- Προκλήσεις και προοπτικές βελτίωσης).* Athens: IMEPO.

Slavin, R. E. (1985). An introduction to cooperative learning research. In R. E. Slavin, S. Sharan, S. Kagan, R. Hertz-Lazarowitz, C. Webb, & R. Schmuck (Eds.), *Learning to co-operate, co-operating to learn* (pp. 5–16). London: Plenum Press.

Solomon, G. (2003). Project-based learning: A primer. *Technology and Learning, 23*(6), 20–30.

Troyna, B., & Hatcher, R. (1992). *Racism in children's lives: A study of mainly- White primary schools.* New York: Routledge, Chapman, and Hall.

Vandenbroeck, M. (1999). *The view of the Yeti: Bringing up children in the spirit of self-awareness and kindredship.* Hague: Bernard Van Leer Foundation.

Veenman, S., Kenter, B., & Post, K. (2000). Cooperative learning in Dutch primary classrooms. *Educational Studies, 26*(3), 281–302.

Webb, C. (1985). Cooperative learning in mathematics and science. In R. E. Slavin, S. Sharan, S. Kagan, R. Hertz-Lazarowitz, C. Webb, & R. Schmuck (Eds.), *Learning to co-operate, co-operating to learn* (pp. 173–176). London: Plenum Press.

Yin, R. K. (1994). *Case study research: Design and methods* (2nd ed.). London: Sage.

Chapter 27
School Performance of Children of Indian and Cape Verdean Immigrants in Basic Schooling in Portugal

Teresa Seabra

Introduction

The relationship between pupils' social environment and the results they obtain at school is clearly documented, as is underachievement among certain groups of immigrant pupils and those who belong to different ethnic minorities. Research conducted, especially in countries with a stronger immigration tradition than Portugal, such as the United States and the United Kingdom, has revealed that among various groups of immigrant pupils, those originating from Asian countries tend to have the best results and black immigrants have the worst (Demack et al. 2000; Vernez and Abrahamse 1996).

Much less attention has been given to study of school achievement that conjugates the differentiation of various national origins and "ethnic" conditions with the family's class condition and/or educational qualifications. However, available research has demonstrated that this is important as it leads to significant changes in the conclusions that can be drawn about the school performance of immigrant children. While immigrant pupils from socially disadvantaged families tend to obtain better results than their native counterparts, this is not the case for pupils from socially advantaged families (OECD 2006; Kao and Tienda 1995; Vallet and Caille 2000). Could these results be generalized to all immigrant groups or are they only found in groups of certain national origins? If the social conditions of the family of origin were taken into consideration, would the gaps in the school performance between different groups be reduced to such an extent that speaking of differences in performance due to immigrant origin would cease to make sense?

We know that the differences between family culture and school culture go a long way toward explaining the problems that children and young people from the working classes experience in obtaining good results at school: while middle-class children and young people experience a cultural continuity at school, there is a rupture in relation to those from working classes (Bourdieu and Passeron 1970). From

---

T. Seabra (✉)
Department of Sociology, ISCTE–Instituto Universitário de Lisboa, 1649-026 Lisbon, Portugal
e-mail: teresa.seabra@iscte.pt

this stance, how can we explain the fact that the immigrant groups that are culturally most distinct from the host society (the case of Asians in Western society) obtain the best results? What explains the school achievement of these groups where family culture is radically different from that of the school?

The importance of school contexts is also documented in international research. Inequalities in the characteristics of the educational system, in school organization (allocation of pupils at schools and of teachers to classes and shifts) and the different treatment given by teachers to different types of pupil also affect school performance. The classic research conducted on the effects of the class or teacher reveal that: (a) the social heterogeneity of the class (and the school) benefits pupils originating from working classes (Ball 1986); (b) the success of pupils from the middle and upper classes is boosted by positive expectations that teachers transmit to them (Becker 1952; Rosenthal and Jacobson 1968); and (c) low expectations (of teachers, pupils and parents) intensify the growing difficulties that pupils from working classes face in adapting to the school system. Could it be that pupils of immigrant origin are treated differently in their school life? What kind of school experience do children and young people of immigrant origin have?

Following an analysis of the effects of the homogenization of families' social condition (social class and educational level) on the school results of pupils of different national origins, I will examine the relationship of a wide range of practices in the family/school context with the school performance of each group of students. In this way, we aim not only to provide more in-depth knowledge about the situation of immigrant children in Portuguese society, but also to shed light on the meaning of these variables in this relationship.

I start by explaining the methodology used and then we summarize the situation of immigrants' children in Portuguese schools and compare pupils of Cape Verdean and Indian origin in Portugal, as these two groups have striking differences in school performance: while Indian pupils have a very good performance that of the Cape Verdeans is poor.[1]

Methodology

The methodology articulates quantitative and qualitative research which compliments each other. More specifically, the former aims to reveal the family conditions and dynamics and the pupil's school experience, while the latter strives to obtain an in-depth understanding of the migratory experience of families of Cape Verdean and Indian origin with both their country(s) of origin and their host country.

The quantitative research involved a questionnaire given to pupils attending basic schooling (aged 10–12 years) at eight schools in the Loures and Lisbon municipalities, which we will call IALL, complemented by data collection at each of these

---

[1] The statistics available demonstrated this contrast (Entreculturas database/ME—1994/1995–1997/1998—and Giase/ME—2000/2001–2003/2004).

schools and interviews with the school directors. The empirical data were collected from pupils attending basic schooling in the Lisbon Metropolitan Area between March and April 2003. The intentional sample was formed using the pupils' diverse social conditions and national origins as criteria. The survey covered 837 pupils, 369 of whom were of immigrant origin (40%)[2]—110 from Cape Verde and 109 from India. The questionnaire provided data about the pupil (school trajectory, language(s) used, relationship with the school, fellow pupils and teachers, school rules, learning strategies, and school and vocational aspirations and expectations) and his/her family context (social profile, practices related to schooling and aspirations).

The qualitative study was made by means of semidirective interviews with parents of children of Cape Verdean and Indian origin. The aim of the interviews was to glean information about their migratory trajectory, strategies for integration in Portuguese society, the relationship with their culture of origin, social habits and educational strategies. The interviews conducted with six families of Indian origin and five of Cape Verdean origin followed an interview script. We interviewed whichever parent was available for interview; this was the mother in all cases with the exception of one Indian family when both parents were present. The recorded interviews were transcribed and then subjected to content analysis.[3]

Portuguese Data on School Performance of Children of Immigrants

Since 1986, Portugal's school system has been organized into two levels over 12 school years: 9 years of basic education and 3 years of upper secondary schooling.[4] Most Portuguese schools are part of the public education system. In 2006/2007, only 11% of schools belonged to the private sector. The system is selective as pupils' transition to the next school year is not guaranteed and pupils who have failed the year a number of times are channeled to a form of "second opportunity" training (vocational training).

Over the last three decades, children from socially disadvantaged families have been remaining at school longer. Moreover, the school population has become increasingly diversified due to the inclusion of growing numbers of pupils of immigrant origin (Giase/ME 2006).

In 2008, an estimated 4.1% of the resident population of Portugal consisted of legal immigrants. Whereas in previous decades immigrants came largely from the

---

[2] A pupil is considered of immigrant origin when at least one parent or grandparent was born in a foreign country.

[3] Full results of the research can be seen in Seabra (2010).

[4] The Portuguese school system comprises nine school years of Basic schooling (EB) divided into three cycles: 4 years in the first (1st CEB), 2 years in the second (2nd CEB) and 3 years in the third (3rd CEB)—followed by 3 years of Secondary/High School.

Table 27.1 School performance by nationality (Portugal, 2008/2009)[a]. (Source: Data provided by GEPE/Ministry of Education)

Nationality	Pupils (number)	Transition rate (pass rate)					
		1st cycle	2nd cycle	3rd cycle Regular	CEF	Upper secondary Regular	Vocational
Portugal	*1,285,361*	*96.6*	*93.0*	*86.8*	*82.7*	*79.7*	*87.2*
Immigrants	*70,508*	*92.2*	*84.5*	*75.9*	*81.1*	*61.5*	*81.2*
Brazil	17,699	92.8	82.3	71.7	77.9	50.4	82.1
Cape Verde	10,195	84.6	74.5	61.9	80.5	45.9	81.3
Angola	6,040	91.0	82.9	71.7	84.1	58.6	81.0
Ukraine	4,197	94.4	92.4	84.9	90.5	65.4	84.5
Guinea Bissau	4,096	88.6	78.9	66.8	79.8	43.9	78.9
France	3,110	95.5	93.1	87.9	–	73.9	81.4
S.Tomé Príncipe	3,062	89.9	78.4	70.4	83.0	53.0	74.3
Romania	2,466	91.3	85.2	77.0	–	72.3	–
Moldavia	2,457	98.1	93.8	87.2	–	69.3	81.7
Switzerland	1,993	97.4	95.6	89.8	–	81.6	90.6
Germany	1,949	96.4	94.7	88.7	–	80.4	–
United kingdom	1,774	91.4	90.6	79.8	–	74.8	–
Spain	1,376	95.4	84.1	89.7	–	86.3	–
China	1,219	95.3	86.2	71.9	–	73.3	–
Russia	690	96.8	95.3	82.1	–	64.6	–
United States America	619	97.4	–	92.0	–	73.2	–
Mozambique	493	88.0	–	78.3	–	–	–
Holland	482	90.4	–	87.9	–	–	–
Venezuela	471	99.0	–	85.5	–	71.2	–
Bulgaria	465	90.7	85.1	80.6	–	–	–
Guinea-Conakry	405	–	–	–	–	–	–

[a] No percentage is given when the number of pupils is fewer than 100

PALOP,[5] more recent migratory flows have changed and in 2010 27% are from the PALOP, 24% from Brazil, 19% from the European Union, and 17% from Ukraine or Moldavia.[6]

In the school system, the most recent available data (Table 27.1) indicate that 70,508 children and young people with a foreign nationality attend basic and secondary schooling, i.e., 5.2% of pupils. They originate mainly from the PALOP (34%)—especially Cape Verde and Angola—and Brazil (25%).

Generally speaking, immigrants' results are not as good as those of Portuguese pupils. A comparison with the average immigrant performance reveals that pupils from Cape Verde, Guinea-Bissau, S. Tomé, Brazil and Angola obtain the worst results (in decreasing order).

---

[5] Portuguese-speaking African Countries (former-colonies): Angola, Cape Verde, Guinea-Bissau, Mozambique and S. Tomé and Principe.

[6] http://www.sef.pt/portal/v10/PT/aspx/estatisticas/index

The diversity of national origins is reflected especially in the multiplicity of pupils' mother tongues. A survey conducted by the Ministry of Education in the 2001–2002 school year (DEB 2003) detected roughly 17,535 pupils in the first 9 years of schooling with a mother tongue other than Portuguese and there were 230 different languages of 140 minorities. The mother tongue of around half of these pupils was Creole, followed by Romany and French.

Once the qualifications of these pupils have been formally recognized, they are admitted to the Portuguese education system using the so-called "immersion model" where pupils are directly exposed to the language of the host country. In 2001, Decree Law 6/2001(18 January), recognized that this was insufficient and Portuguese is now also taught as a second language. The law stated that "schools should provide specific curricular activities for the teaching of Portuguese as a second language to pupils whose mother tongue is not Portuguese" (article 18°).

The intercultural approach to curricula is comprehensive in basic schooling by fostering tolerance and respect for difference, especially by means of intercultural extracurricular activities such as themed events and festivals and student exchanges (Eurydice 2004). Some higher education teacher training institutions have begun to include intercultural education as part of their curriculum but there are no explicit policy guidelines for this (Casa-Nova et al. 2006).

In 2007, the Portuguese Government approved a Plan for Immigrant Integration.[7] The 17 measures in the field of education include the need to make the teaching of Portuguese as a second language a priority area in teacher training, the "ethnic composition" of balanced classes, and the equipping of schools with "teaching materials to support intercultural and anti-racist education." Support for research into this field of knowledge, i.e., the schooling of immigrant children, is also provided for in this plan.

No statistical information is available in Portugal on both the social condition and national origin of the pupils' families in the analysis of unequal school results. To this end, I conducted research in state schools in the Lisbon Metropolitan Area that encompassed both native pupils and children of immigrants.

The Differences Between the Performance of Pupils of Indian and Cape Verdean Descent

As mentioned above, the aim of the research was to examine how family and school are linked to the difference in performance between pupils of Indian and Cape Verdean origin.

Which is the predominant factor: cultural differences or very distinct social conditions? Whereas Cape Verdeans' *social* conditions contrast with those of the host society, Indians are faced with a *cultural* contrast. Does Indian pupils' school and

---

[7] Council of Ministers Resolution nr 63-A/2007 in *Diário da República*, 1st series, nr 85, 3 May 2007.

social integration therefore mean that the cultural dimension of ethnicity is less important than the social dimension, as argued by Machado (2002)? Or could it be precisely the Indians' cultural specificities that favor this integration? How do these two factors work together?

I first examine whether the different results detected in the national statistics remain when pupils belonging to families in the same social condition are considered. I then analyze the relationship of school performance with family and school contexts.

School trajectories when families' social conditions and national origin are controlled

These pupils have a very distinct school performance: 38% of native pupils had to repeat at least 1 year during their school pathway, compared to 27% of Indian pupils and 56% of pupils of Cape Verdean origin. The findings corroborate international research, as females in all groups perform better. The smallest difference is found among pupils of Indian origin (girls: 25% and boys: 28%) and the greatest among pupils of Cape Verdean origin (girls: 47% and boys: 65%). The group of pupils that finds it most difficult to succeed at school is therefore clearly identified as boys of Cape Verdean origin.

When we controlled the families' social condition, the results of immigrant pupils converged with those obtained in other countries (Fig. 27.1): (a) there is a significant reduction (50%) in the difference between native pupils and those of Cape Verdean origin when the families' social circumstances are homogenized; when the father has a low level of schooling (4 years at most), they obtain better results than natives; (b) in contrast to this, including family variables accentuates the advance of pupils of Indian origin except in the case of those from middle/upper-class families. In other words, the superior results of immigrant origin pupils in socially disadvantaged situations become more evident.

In short, the differences in school performance are found to be consistent and the relative ranking of the results remains even though the uniformity of families' social conditions changes the distance between the groups.

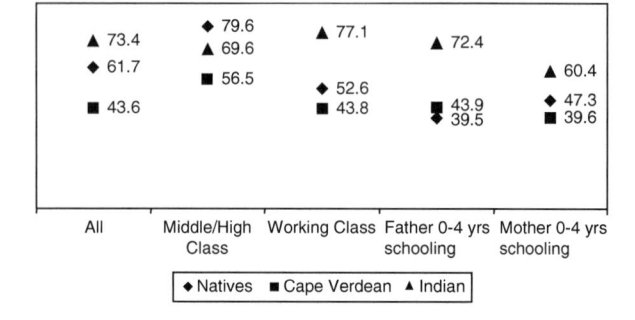

Fig. 27.1 School success in accordance with families' national origins and social conditions. (Source: IALL 2003)

Due to the difference found in the school results achieved by the pupils of the different national origins under analysis, a broad set of variables was then studied in order to shed light on the relationship with the unequal performance identified, such as variables linked to family trajectories and the relationship with the culture of origin, the level of contact with mainstream society, family practices in relation to schooling, and the school experience of these two groups of pupils.

Indian and Cape Verdean Families in Portugal

The families of these different groups have very different migratory trajectories, which express their respective traditional paths:

1. The large majority (76%) of families of Indian origin had lived in Mozambique before settling in Portugal, 5% came from other African countries of the Indian Diaspora such as Kenya and Tanzania and 19% came from India.
2. The large majority (68%) of families of Cape Verdean origin migrated directly from Cape Verde and of those where there had been mixed marriages with other nationalities (32%), all were with people from African countries and the majority (18%) from PALOP.

The discourse of the families interviewed (ten mothers and one father) revealed that they used different strategies to adapt to the society in which they live. Families of Cape Verdean origin focus on assimilating into Portuguese culture and the specificities of their ancestors' culture play an important but secondary role. Families of Indian origin live permanently in two cultures and their culture of origin never takes second place.

These families' relations with their cultures of origin are largely dictated by the specificities of the religion to which the families of origin belong, i.e., Hinduism. In various situations and phases of life, being Hindu involves going to and staying in India, even if temporarily, and belonging to a *community* even though they experience many class or caste distinctions. As the following citations demonstrate, they constantly feel and recreate their *origins* as if they were totally transposed to another city anywhere in the world.

> -We wear normal clothes for our day to day lives. It's only when we go to parties that we all wear Indian clothes.
> *And do they like it?*
> They love it.
> - *So perhaps they'd like to go to school like that, would they?*
> - No. They've never asked me if they can go to school in Indian dress, only to parties.
> (Shetal, born in Diu, India, 6 years of schooling, shop owner)

> I wear normal clothes, I wear the other clothes and things at parties and just now and then when the weather is really good too.
> (...)For example, I like Christmas things, my children like participating in Christmas and we have our Christmas.

> For example, we have our birthdays in Indian too; and today it was my husband's birthday and so I did all those things that we do on his birthday… it's on the same day but it's just that our calendar changes the date, our calendar works differently. Today was one day, and now on the 19th it'll be his birthday…
> (Carima, born in Diu, 6 school years, housewife)

Carima's and Shetal's offspring separate the two worlds well: they do not want to *be different* at school, just as they do not want to *be different* in the community. The case that best illustrates this situation is that of Julia's son. Julia was also born in Diu and owns a clothes shop. She said, "my son speaks Gujarati and Portuguese correctly but when he is at school he refuses to speak Gujariti with other Indians who have not mastered Portuguese (he said "It is as if they were in India!"). When he is in the community, he only speaks Gujariti and he really enjoys it and teaches the other boys who still cannot speak it correctly."

Families develop this "multiple identity" in their offspring from an early age and these children become carriers of a "cultural plasticity", of an "identity made up of multiple belongings" that favors their integration in the host society and, in particular, in school contexts.

It is a different situation in the case of the families of Cape Verdean origin, as they work hard not to forget their *origins* in the awareness that there is a risk they will be erased from memory. The cultural contrasts between their origin and the country in which they live are less marked (Machado 2002, p. 47). They understand that as they are Portuguese they should not act differently but this does not stop them from having a "symbolic ethnicity" in practice (Gans 1982/1962) by evoking, recreating, and maintaining practices from the past, even a distant past: language, traditional foods, and music.

> Yes, it's good they know because it has to do with our culture. It's a language that …we came to Portugal, we speak Portuguese but…I don't think we should forget that Creole is our parents' language of origin. For me Creole is like a treasure that has been put away and it has to be kept there always so it isn't forgotten. It's like our heritage.
> *And what other aspects of the culture do you worry about besides language? Or other than Creole.*
> I worry about Creole, but I often cook Cape Verdean food…I make *cachupa*…I make fish soup but they don't like that much….we do it because it's something that stays, it's part of the family heritage. We don't talk much about what it was like over there, about the music. At the weekend we put on some African music and get on with our work…
> (Maria, born in Cape Verde, 9th school year, day-nursery assistant)

In short, we see here two ways of being an immigrant in the host country: one among families of Indian origin that can be defined as "knowing how to live on two platforms" (an expression used by one of the interviewees) and the other commonly found among the families of Cape Verdean origin interviewed that consists of "being Portuguese without forgetting their roots."

The language spoken at home and with friends is an indicator of the relationship with the culture of origin. Table 27.2 compares the two groups of children and shows that pupils of Cape Verdean origin use Portuguese more than those of Indian descent who speak their language of origin more often (Hindi, Urdu, and mainly Guajarati). While nearly half the pupils of Cape Verdean origin (42%) spoke only

Table 27.2 Pupils' everyday language by national origin. (Source: IALL 2003)

		Cape Verdean origin	Indian origin
At home	Only speak Portuguese	44.4	20.2
	Speak Portuguese and another language	37.0	57.8
	Don't speak Portuguese	18.6	22.0
	Total (no)	*108*	*109*
With friends	Only speak Portuguese with both friends	75.0	62.5
	Speak Portuguese only with one friend	14.1	15.6
	Don't speak Portuguese	10.9	21.9
	Total (no)	*92*	*96*
At home and with friends	Only speak Portuguese	42.4	17.7
	Bilingualism in both situations	7.6	12.5
	Bilingualism in one of the situations	45.7	60.4
	Don't speak Portuguese	4.3	9.4
	Total (no)	*91*	*96*

Portuguese in their everyday life (at home and with their two best friends), this was only true for 18% of the Indian pupils. While Cape Verdean families often only spoke Portuguese, Indian families were more frequently bilingual.

This raises doubts about the common assumption that directly links better school performance to a greater use of the Portuguese language at home. If this was the case, the children of Indian immigrants would be expected to speak more Portuguese at home in light of their success at school; however, precisely the opposite is true and bilingualism does not undermine their school performance. It is important to highlight language-related differences: School results are always better when pupils only speak Portuguese at home. However, whereas the Indian pupils' results are not as good when they do not speak any Portuguese, the Cape Verdeans obtain the worst results when they are bilingual. In short, bilingualism at home has the opposite effect on school success in these two groups of pupil.

The intensity of the pupils' contact with Portuguese society was assessed and an indicator formed that included responses to each of the following variables: their own and their parents' and grandparents' place of birth, national origin of their closest friends and language used in everyday life (at home and with their best friends). When the two groups are compared, the children of Indian origin have greater contact with Portuguese society: While 33% of the pupils of Indian origin had "great contact"[8] with Portuguese society, this was true of only 11% of the children of Cape Verdean origin.

On analyzing a set of family practices related to schooling, differences can be seen between these two groups of pupils (Table 27.3): it is more usual for pupils of Indian

---

[8] Each variable has the value 0 or 1 as a response depending on the absence or presence of the attribute. Different levels of contact with Portuguese society were defined from the sum resulting from this indictor: *Great* when the value was more then 27; *Average* when it was between 22 and 27; *Little* if lower than 22.

Table 27.3 Summary of family practices related to schooling. (Source: IALL 2003)

	Cape Verdean origin	Indian origin
Speak only Portuguese at home	44.4	20.2
Pupils accompanied outside of school hours	56.4	59.6
... by adults	56.4	76.6
Control over homework	88.1	91.7
Support with school difficulties (only working class)	77.5	91.7
... by parents	42.5	31.3
... by friends, neighbors or others	15.0	27.1
Dialogue about school	80.0	74.1
(main subject)	(none)	(results)
Family's school aspirations		
Go to the university	62.7	32.1
Don't know	24.5	36.7

origin to be around adults outside school hours, homework is better controlled, people outside the family are called on more frequently to help with difficulties at school and the dialogue about school focuses more on school results (grades, tests, etc.).

Might the school achievement of pupils of Indian origin be linked to these differences? In fact, these data suggest that exerting stricter, more direct control over compliance with school obligations, as well as organizing a broader support structure to deal with difficulties by calling on people from the surrounding community (neighbors, friends, etc.) might have positive effects on school results. However, the Cape Verdean families have higher school aspirations for their children and talk more about their school life and the Portuguese language is more usually spoken at home, which could favor their school performance.

It is well known that school achievement is related to more than just the family profile, as the school experience also influences results and school success requires support in the two domains.

School Experience of Cape Verdean and Indian Pupils

According to the indicators at our disposal, if we compare the overall school experience of the two groups, the Cape Verdean pupils have a less positive experience than Indian pupils (Table 27.4). They suffer from more ghettoization in class formation,[9] are less satisfied with the school attended, feel less empathy with core subjects (Portuguese and math), feel less support from teachers and do not have such a good relationship with fellow pupils. Their practices do not foster school achievement, as they do not abide by school rules, are less proactive when in doubt and request less help from teachers.

---

[9] A recent study comparing national systems (OECD 2007, p. 277) identifies the negative impact on student performance (in science) of ability steaming for all subjects within schools.

Table 27.4 Summary of school experience of pupils of Cape Verdean and Indian origin. (Source: IALL 2003)

	Cape Verdean origin	Indian origin
Attended "classes for repeat pupils"[a]	35.6	15.1
High satisfaction with school attended[b]	22.7	31.2
"Empathy" with core subjects[c]	19.1	24.8
"Teachers help me when I answer wrong"	41.0	53.4
Positive relationship with schoolmates[d]	41.8	51.9
"My schoolmates make fun of me"	30.9	23.9
"When I have difficulties I…		
Do nothing	7.3	2.8
Ask for help from teachers"	59.1	68.8
"I have been given warnings for bad conduct"	56.0	13.3
"I have been through disciplinary procedures"	15.0	3.7

[a] We consider "classes for repeat pupils" when more than 50% of pupils had repeated at least one school year

[b] Indicator resulting from the relationship between the number of aspects referred as positive and the number of aspects referred to as negative: where the number of positive aspects is greater than the negative = "high"; if the number of positive and negative aspects is equal = "moderate" and if negative aspects are greater than positive = "low"

[c] We considered it to be an "empathetic" relation if the pupil referred to enjoying Portuguese or Math and did not refer to either when they identified subjects they disliked

[d] Variable resulting from the indictor created from the sum of the answers for four indicators: number of friends at schools (0–1–2); being made fun of (or not) by schoolmates (0–1); schoolmates are (or not) one of negative aspects of school (0–1); schoolmates are (or not) one of aspects mentioned on what needs to be changed at school (0–1). The most favorable answers always corresponded to 1 (or 2 in the case of having two friends at school) and unfavorable answers always corresponded to 0. Scale: 0–2 = negative; 3 = neutral; 4–5 = positive

The study of how school variables affect the results of pupils of different national origins is still in its early stages and as yet there are no well-founded conclusions. While the first studies indicated that black pupils who attended heterogeneous classes in predominantly white schools had an unequivocal advantage (Coleman et al. 1966; Oakes 2005 [1985]; Rist 2003 [1973]), more recent research has found that this effect is not uniform and varies according to the minority group in question—heterogeneity appears beneficial in cases where this is associated with other advantages (e.g., pupils of Asian origin) but prejudicial when the groups are in extremely unfavorable social conditions (Portes and Hao 2005; Portes and MacLeod 1996, 1999; Portes and Rumbaut 2001).

Another important finding that research has persistently demonstrated is that pupils from disadvantaged social backgrounds are particularly sensitive to the school context. This is corroborated by the comparison of results in international exams: "It is found that the difference between countries is what most marks the performance achieved by pupils from disadvantaged backgrounds. In contrast, the youths from privileged backgrounds are successful in a much more homogeneous fashion from one country (and therefore one education system) to another, thus confirming their greater sensitivity to the context." (Duru-Bellat 2002, p. 165).

School (under)achievement is undoubtedly a multidimensional and relational social phenomenon. It includes and implies family and school socialization, the relationship between the two and the school's relationship with the society to which it belongs, especially with the wide-ranging social inequalities found in that society and with the interaction between the school and the labor market. It is also known that "the combination of the factors is more important than each factor alone" (Bressoux 1994). A recent study by Millet and Thin on "ruptures at school" yet again highlights the importance of the confluence of factors in the production of a given situation: "The processes of ruptures at school are combined and result from an articulation of different dimensions of the pupils' school life, each dimension interwoven with the others, making it viable and strengthening it and without which it would have neither the same meaning or effect" (2005, p. 295). In addition to the instability, uncertainty, and threats experienced by the family, there is a process of the reciprocal rejection of school (of pupils and teachers and the institution). The PISA 2006 results (OECD 2007) underline this interdependence between different factors: When a set of school variables that have effects on performance is considered, the authors note that "most of this effect is not attributable to the school factors acting wholly independently of demographic and socioeconomic factors, but rather a combined effect of the two" (p. 277).

We know that, in the case of immigrant children and young people, the process is even more complex because other variables are involved: on one hand, the "modes of incorporation" (Portes 1999), and on the other "community forces" (Ogbu 2003). In relation to the "modes of incorporation", the groups that encounter the greatest school difficulties are: (ai) those with a historic relationship of subordination and/or involuntary minorities (Blacks and Mexicans from New Mexico in US America); (b) groups holding subservient roles in the socioeconomic structure; and (c) the pupils who have immigrated most recently. In the case of the Indian and Cape Verdean communities living in Portugal, it is true that the historic relationship of subordination of the latter is much more recent and present (until 1974), while the former belonged to former African colonies (Mozambique) but not as a colonized group. We also found significant differences related to "community forces": a stronger feeling of belonging to a community due to common religious practices among the Indian families. In her analysis of the school success of the Sikh community in California, Gibson (1988) identified "accommodation without assimilation" as one of the "community forces" of this group that supports their performance.

Conclusions

The findings of this research reveal that pupils of Indian origin attending state schools in Portugal have a very good school performance and are superior even when we consider the families' social condition. The data suggest that their families are stricter and control compliance with school obligations more directly, and that they organize a broader support structure to deal with difficulties by calling on people from the surrounding community (neighbors, friends, etc.), adults are more present outside school hours, dialogue about school focuses more on school results (grades, tests, etc.) and this is associated with a more positive school experience than their Cape Verdean school fellows—better relations with classmates, greater support from teachers, more active learning habits, and attend classes with fewer re-sit pupils.

There appears to be no foundation for the common assumption that the higher nonachievement rate of Cape Verdean pupils is linked to greater use of Creole (which in this case does not occur), the lack of dialogue in the family about their education or the family's low expectations of schooling.

Without directly questioning the validity of the theory of cultural continuities (the advantage of cultural continuity from the family to the school universe is not in question), the data reveal the limitations of this theory insofar as continuity is not a necessary condition for school achievement. It is weakened by the fact that pupils are able to strategically adapt their behavior to different contexts. Might cultural versatility be just as important as cultural continuity?

We found that the transmission of cultural heritage to children from Indian families did not impede their adaptation to school in the host society. By enriching their identities, which were always hybrid and changeable, the children went through an exercise of plasticity and adaptability—they managed the particularities depending on the contexts—and this seemed to favor their success at school. Indian children live in different worlds. They know each world; they act and interact according to the rules of each. They intentionally activate two or more different cultures depending on the dominant culture of the milieu of which they are part at each moment, and therefore develop greater flexibility and adaptation. We can speak of the construction of multiple identities by means of a "plural assimilation" process. A recent study of second-generation immigrants living in New York (Kasinitz et al. 2008) reveals the advantage of being between two different social systems: "[The second generation] allows for creative and selective combinations of the two that can be highly conducive to success. In developing a strategy for navigating challenges, second generation youngsters do not have to choose whether being foreign or being American is 'better'. They can draw on both cultures" (pp. 354–355).

In short, on one hand the improvement of school results which is necessary for some groups of immigrant pupils involves: (a) disseminating among families the principles and reasoning for the school model as it is only when families understand them sufficiently that they can contribute to their children's adaptation to this model; (b) strengthening families ties with their culture of origin, which as we have seen is not an obstacle to school achievement; (c) educational policies that ensure effective learning of the Portuguese language, which is particularly important for pupils of African origin whose language is similar to Portuguese and thus gives rise to greater confusion; and (d) public policies that ensure pupils are monitored by adults outside the school timetable. On a more indirect though no less important level, there is a need to develop a more cosmopolitan culture that values cultural exchanges, hybridism, and change resulting particularly in the reduction of urban segregation that affects many immigrant populations.

References

Ball, S. (1986). The sociology of the school: Streaming and mixed ability and social class. In R. Rogers (Ed.), *Education and social class*. London: Falmer Press.

Becker, H. S. (1952). Social-class variations in the teacher-pupil relationship. *Journal of Educational Sociology, 25*(8), 451–465.

Bourdieu, P., & Passeron, J.-C. (1970). *La Reproduction: Éléments pour une théorie du système d'enseignement*. Paris: Minuit.

Bressoux, P. (1994). Les recherches sur les effets-écoles et les effets-maître. *Revue Française de Pédagogie, 108*(juillet-août-septembre), 91–137.

Casa-Nova, M. J., Seabra, T., Mateus, S., & Caldeira, R. (2006). Migration and ethnicity in curricula of Portuguese Public Universities: Sociology and anthropology degrees. In S. Jacobs (Ed.), *Pedagogies of teaching 'race' and ethnicity in higher education: British and European experiences*. Birmingham: C-SAP: University of Birmingham.

Coleman, J. S., Campbell, E. Q., Hobson, C. J., McPartland, J., Mood, A., Weinfeld, F. D., et al. (1966). *Equality of educational opportunity*. Washington: Government Printed Office.

DEB. (2003). *Caracterização Nacional dos Alunos com Língua Portuguesa como Língua Não Materna*, Departamento de Educação Básica.

Demack, S., Drew, D., & Grimsley, M. (2000). Minding the gap: Ethnic, gender and social differences in attainment at 16, 1988–95. *Race Ethnicity and Education, 3*(2), 117–143.

Duru-Bellat, M. (2002). *Les inégalités sociales à l'école. Genèse et Mythes*. Paris: PUF.

Eurydice. (2004). Integrating immigrant children into schools in Europe. European Commission, Directorate—General for Education and Culture.

Gans, H. (1982/1962). *The urban villagers*. Free Press.

Giase, ME. (2006). Alunos matriculados por grupo cultural/nacionalidade 2000/2001–2003/2004, GIASE/ME.

Gibson, M. A. (1988). *Accommodation without assimilation—Sikh immigrants in an American high school*. Ithaca: Cornell University Press.

Kao, G., & Tienda, M. (1995). Optimism and achievement: The educational performance of immigrant youth. *Social Science Quarterly, 76*(1), 1–19.

Kasinitz, P., Mollenkopf, J., Waters, M., & Holdaway, J. (2008). *Inheriting the city: The children of immigrants come of age*. New York: Russell Sage Foundation/Harvard University Press.

Machado, F. L. (2002). *Contrastes e Continuidades: Migração, Etnicidade e Integração dos Guineenses em Portugal*. Oeiras: Celta.

Millet, M., & Thin, D. (2005). *Ruptures scolaires – L'école à l'épreuve de la question sociale*. Paris: PUF.

Oakes, J. (2005[1985]). *Keeping track—how schools structure inequality*. New Haven: Yale University.

OECD. (2006). Where immigrant students succeed—a comparative review of performance and engagement in PISA 2003: OCDE. Document Number.

OECD. (2007). *PISA 2006: Science competencies for tomorrow's world*. Document Number.

Ogbu, J. (2003). *Black American students in an affluent suburb—a study of academic disengagement*. Mahwah: Lawrence Erlbaum.

Portes, A. (1999). *Migrações internacionais: Origens, tipos e modos de incorporação*. Oeiras: Celta.

Portes, A., & Hao, L. (2005). La educación de los hijos de inmigrantes: efectos contextuales. *Migraciones, 17*, 7–44.

Portes, A., & MacLeod, D. (1996). Educational progress of children of immigrants: The roles of class, ethnicity and school context. *Sociology of Education, 69*(October), 255–275.

Portes, A., & MacLeod, D. (1999). Educating the second generation: Determinants of academic achievement among children of immigrants in the United States. *Journal of Ethnic and Migration Studies, 25*(3), 373–396.

Portes, A., & Rumbaut, R. (2001). *Legacies: The story of immigrant second generation*. Berkeley: California University/Russell Sage Foundation.
Rist, R. (2003[1973]). *The Urban School—a factory for failure*. New Jersey: Transaction.
Rosenthal, R. A., & Jacobson, L. (1968). *Pygmalion in the classroom: Teacher expectations and pupil's intellectual development*. New York: Hold, Rinehart and Winston.
Seabra, T. (2010). *Adaptação e Adversidade: o desempenho escolar de alunos de origem indiana e cabo-verdiana no ensino básico*. Lisboa: ICS/UL.
Vallet, L.-A., & Caille, J.-P. (2000). La scolarité des enfants d'immigrés. In A. Van Zanten (Ed.), *L'école: l'état des savoirs*. Paris: La Découverte.
Vernez, G., & Abrahamse. (1996). *How immigrants fare in U.S. education*. Santa Mónica: RAND.

Chapter 28
Migration, Educational Policies, and Practices: Constructing Difference in Buenos Aires and in Madrid

Ana Bravo-Moreno and Jason Beech

Introduction

The aim of this chapter is to analyze the formal education of Latin American immigrants in the cities of Buenos Aires and Madrid. The text compares the overall situation of Latin American immigrants in Madrid and Buenos Aires, their general educational trajectories in these cities, and examines the legislation on immigration in each country, and the education policies that relate to immigrant students.

In addition, the chapter captures the perspective of students and how they perceive and evaluate their school experiences in their city of residence. Dewey (1997) argued that experiences involve a transaction between objective conditions (or the environment) and the active interpretations of individuals. Thus, we understand that students constitute their own school experiences through a permanent interaction with the "school environment" that is itself shaped by its context. The data was generated by in-depth interviews with 31 school students and 18 teachers, head-teachers, directors of studies and counselors in seven state high schools (four in Madrid and three in Buenos Aires).

Migration and Education in Spain and in Madrid

Spain has 46 million inhabitants, of which 5.2 millions (11%) are foreign-born (INE 2008). During the past 10 years, the number of immigrants has increased nine-fold. Few countries have seen such a dramatic change in their population in such a short period of time particularly since Spain used to be a country of emigration until the 1970s.

Official statistics on education and immigration in Spain make comparisons difficult and less informative than might be expected. Nevertheless, and overall

---

A. Bravo-Moreno (✉)
Facultad de Ciencias de la Educación, Universidad de Granada, Campus de Cartuja,
18071 Granada, Spain
e-mail: abravo@ugr.es

profile of migrant students in Madrid can be offered. Most likely, the student is Latino,[1] Moroccan, Sub-Saharan African, Eastern European, or Chinese. Many of these students struggle academically and many never make it beyond Compulsory Secondary Education (ESO). If we take a look at their schools, most likely there are between 20 and 30 students per class and classroom instruction is largely focused on the state's standardized exams. In the students' home environments the parents most likely work two or more jobs or they are unemployed. There are more than 1,057,000 unemployed foreigners in Spain (INE 2009). They live at or below the poverty line or are members of the working poor. In many cases these children find themselves being raised by their mother. The parents most likely work in jobs that are unstable or in the informal economy.

According to the Ministry of Education (2009) the total number of foreign students was 743,696 (9.7%) in the academic year 2008–2009 compared with the case of Madrid where the percentage was 13.8. Thirty percent of immigrant students fail and do not finish compulsory secondary education. Only one in 50 continues into postcompulsory secondary education (2 years) or into intermediate vocational training. Thus, only 33% of immigrant youth aged between 16 and 18 years is enrolled in school compared to 83.6% of Spaniards. These students are also marked by a high level of absenteeism (PISA 2005). They experience family circumstances and economic inequality that hinder their education. Consequently both the education and the labor market situation of these young people remain a concern. In general, one-fifth of the population aged 15 to 19 is not in education, the eighth highest percentage among OECD and partner countries (Ombudsman's Report 2003).

Politics, Educational Policies, and Social Justice

There are 17 regional autonomous governments in Spain that have full responsibility for education and health care as well as other social programs. Autonomous communities are ruled by a government elected by a unicameral legislature. In Madrid, the conservative party (PP) took office in 2003. The ideology of the Madrid government contrasts with the Spanish national government that belongs to the Spanish Socialist Workers' Party (PSOE). There have been problems as to how the regional government of Madrid invests public money on Education: The Superior Court of Justice has received nine sentences against the regional government of Madrid for its educational policies in less than a year.[2] One of them originated when public funds were used to finance single sex schools linked with the Opus Dei.[3]

---

[1] The areas of origin of migrant students for the academic year 2008–2009 were as follows: 40.7% from South America, 3.7% from Central America, 28.8% from Europe, 20.6% from Africa, and 5.3% from Asia and Oceania (Ministerio de Educación 2009, pp. 6–9).

[2] Público. 2010. "La educación de Esperanza Aguirre choca con la justicia" 6th of February.

[3] Ultraconservative movement within the Roman Catholic Church.

The Minister of Education criticized the conservative government of Madrid stating that education is a public service: "They (the conservative party) speak about parents' freedom of choice regarding schools, the majority of immigrant students attend state schools and they do not receive extra funding. That is not social justice. Privately run schools funded by the State must have rights and obligations the same as state schools" (Público 2010 p. 30). The most complete and reliable survey on the situation of immigrant students in Spain was released in April 2003 by the Spanish Ombudsman in cooperation with UNICEF (2003). The main concern expressed in this report referred to the high level of concentration of immigrant students in state schools.

Assimilation and Compensatory Education vs. Intercultural Education

Spain's education system has undergone significant changes in the last 30 years. A number of major educational reform laws were promulgated; some of them affected primary and secondary education. The Organic Law on the Right to Education (LODE) in 1985 established free compulsory education and required schools to respect the different languages and cultures of Spain. In 1990, the Organic Law on the General Organization of the Educational System (LOGSE) extended compulsory education from 8 to 10 years.

Nevertheless, the challenge of immigrant education was not specifically addressed. There was no reference to it in one of the most recent education reforms: the Constitutional Law of Quality of Education (LOCE 2002). The aim of this law was to reduce drop out rates and improve the quality of education. Yet, this reform only vaguely touched upon the issue of immigrant education, simply stressing that the law would also benefit immigrant students (BOE 2002). Scant attention was paid to their needs and to the training teachers of immigrant students may undergo. More importantly, the law presented itself as being based "on the humanistic values of our European cultural tradition." None of the "values" on the basis of which the new law was formulated makes any reference to multiculturalism or diversity as a crucial component of education. For Cros et al. (2004) public authorities and, in particular, the University should train educators in "intercultural pedagogy", incorporating this course in the study programs for initial teacher training. Currently, there are few courses on "intercultural education" or "socio-cultural diversity" included in these programs in Spain. Instead, individual effort, quality of education, rigorous methods of assessment, social consideration for teachers, and autonomy of the institutions are the main points addressed in the Law. It simply offers vague guidelines as to how the regional administrations should deal with immigrant education, but provides no specific indication of any financial support from the central administration or, for example, of significant changes in the curriculum.

This means that autonomous communities have been left to their own devices to resolve the issue of diversity. As a result of the lack of central guidelines, the Spanish education system is reacting in a number of ways, which differ from one autonomous community to another (Cachón Rodríguez 2003).

In the case of Madrid the institutional response to migrant students has been the creation of the Compensatory Education Regional Plan, which started in 1999 and includes the following measures:

1. Transitional classrooms which cater to immigrant students whose mother tongue is not Spanish. They also attend several lessons each day in an ordinary classroom.
2. Educational compensatory classrooms which are aimed at students between the ages of 14 and 16 who are at risk of leaving school due to family or social problems and who might not otherwise obtain a secondary school diploma. These students must be 2 years behind the norm for their age or they must have serious difficulties adjusting to formal educational settings.
3. Mother tongue and culture programs (for Arabic and Portuguese only) in line with agreements between the Spanish government and the governments of Morocco and Portugal.
4. External compensation services, outside the school timetable: the aim is to develop socioeducational spaces for cooperation with the local community in schools and to improve the educational process of the students in disadvantaged situations.

Nevertheless, these measures of "inclusion" fall within the framework of compensatory education which is aimed at compensating for a perceived deficit in the student. Therefore this approach does not locate the responsibility for the challenges that migrants' education may pose within the educational system, which is unable to provide a suitable answer to diversity. The model of compensatory education is not compatible with intercultural education as it does not demand any change to mainstream educational institutions or society. Bernstein claimed that "education cannot compensate for society" (Bernstein 1970). He argued that it makes no sense to talk about offering compensatory education to children "who in the first place, have as yet not been offered an adequate educational environment" (Bernstein 1971, p. 191). Bernstein also drew attention to the internal organization of the school which "creates delicate overt and covert streaming arrangements which neatly lower the expectations and motivations of teachers and taught." Madrid educational policies are built on the same kind of pathological views of disadvantaged students and families that Bernstein emphasized:

> The concept 'compensatory education' implies that something is lacking in the family, and so in the child. As a result the children are unable to benefit from schools. It follows then that the school has to 'compensate' for the something which is missing in the family and the children become little deficit systems. (1971, p. 192)

Changes affecting the whole educational system are not being proposed. Only specific measures within the framework of assimilation to mainstream are offered to provide with answers to specific problems. However, this is not sufficient to build social cohesion. A profound debate within the political and educational community is both urgent and necessary about the educational model and the kind of society that would foster parity in social participation for its members. The compensatory approach adopted by the regional government of Madrid clashes with intercultural education which is a holistic and transforming approach that involves and affects all members of society. Although when interculturalism or multiculturalism is represented as the accommodation of or negotiation with cultural groups, this encourages us to view the world through the prism of separate and distinct cultures: Hispanic culture, Chinese culture, as if each culture has some core characteristics that once mastered brings the magic of successfully teaching in multicultural schools (Wang and Olson 2009. We see ways of life struggling to survive; we see clashes of cultures. As Phillips (2007) argues, the aim is to practice an intercultural education that dispenses with reified notions of culture or homogenized conceptions of the cultural group and yet retains enough robustness to address cultural inequalities.

Freire (1970) stated that "a curriculum for the disadvantaged must begin as closely as possible to the pupils' direct experience" because "without such an approach, the abstract cannot be attained" (1970, p. 83). However, difficult as it may be, articulating the connections and disconnections between home and school must be worth exploring more consistently. This approach also invites a shift in the teacher–student relationship from an authoritarian approach to a dialogic approach (Freire 1970). Imposing our own notion of what multicultural education should be, despite self-perceived good intentions, replicates the transmission mode of teaching an oppressive education.

Wang (2004) argues that what has made these strategies effective is instructors' increasing understanding of students and their efforts to make teaching relevant to students' lived experiences including their lack of experiences in diversity issues for autochthonous students. These educators actively attempt to understand the reasons for students' resistance and to build bridges to work productively through it rather than simply denouncing it. Such efforts we would prefer to phrase as teaching in "a third space" promote intercultural dynamics for transformative education.

Segregation Within Segregation

Segregation in this context refers to the clustering of migrant students in state schools. Many migrant children are in schools in which they form the majority of the school population. In Madrid, state schools enrolled 75.8%, and fully subsidized private schools and purely private schools enrolled 17.8% of migrant students (Ministerio de Educación 2009). The conservative government of Madrid has preferred to increase public funds to subsidize private Catholic schools, while state schools are decreasing in demand, partly due to the presence of immigrant children. Only one in five immigrant students is registered in fully subsidized private Catholic schools (Ombudsman 2003). Since many private Catholic schools are funded by the State it would be expected that they would share the responsibility for educating immigrant students.

When migrant students arrive in Madrid during the school academic year there are School Committees which are in charge of supervising the admission of migrant children to state and fully subsidized private schools. According to the head-teachers interviewed for this study, these Committees tend to allocate migrant children in state schools, which may constitute another reason for explaining the concentration of migrant students in state schools. This asymmetrical allocation of immigrant students and access to state-funded schools needs to be audited and revised to assure that equal opportunity is respected and immigrants are equally treated. This controversial situation is in opposition with some of the basic principles for schools in Spanish legislation. The LODE Act of 1985 (the Organic Act on the Right to Education) established that both state education and private education financed by the State were to be free of cost and that both types of schools would have the same criteria regarding the admission of pupils.

What can segregation explain in relation to underachievement and social cohesion of migrant children? According to a report published by the European Commission, concentration of migrant children in schools hinders their academic performance. Discrimination is often a major factor affecting the achievement of migrant students. Strengthening the support function of schools with large numbers of migrant students requires extra financial resources (European Commission 2008). Since peers play an important part in school achievement and socialization, school segregation hinders school achievement and social cohesion.

There is solid research evidence showing that peers have a substantial influence on student achievement. The more "advanced" their fellow students the better the minority students did. Minority children exposed to classmates with higher educational aspirations increase their own (Wells and Crain 1997); expectations are higher in integrated schools compared to segregated schools (Cohen 1995, 1993). Minority students in integrated schools are more likely to attend college and get better jobs after graduation (Wells and Crain 1997; Ortfield and Eaton 1996). Farley (2006, p. 58) concludes in his review "that the great majority of studies show that the achievement of majority group and/or middle-class students does not decrease" in integrated schools.

Head-teachers interviewed for this study stated that Spanish parents did not want their children to attend schools where there is an important presence of immigrant students because they believed their children will learn less in such schools. Some teachers also told the interviewer that they did not want their own children or grandchildren to attend state schools because they shared the same view. Manuel a counselor with 37 years of experience in state schools said:

> I've got two granddaughters. I cannot even think to send them to a state school. I've always believed in public education, but now there is too much imbalance. Most immigrant students are in state schools, some of them with 70% immigrant students. Integration cannot succeed with that proportion. I want a more equilibrated educational environment for my granddaughters.

Many middle class parents remove their children from state schools because it is perceived as a symbol of social status (Jacott and Maldonado 2004), but also because they prefer their children not to mix with immigrants. Jon, a 16-year-old boy from Quito (Ecuador) who arrived with his family in Madrid when he was 8, talks about the perception people have on his school:

> People call my school a school of immigrants, of Latinos, of underachievers. In my class the majority of students are foreigners from Latino America, some from Rumania, some from Senegal. I've heard people say they don't want their children coming to this school because of that.

Jon epitomizes what many students and teachers interviewed for this study stated. According to Crain and Stuart (1999) segregation may perpetuate itself; children who attend segregated schools may live segregated lives as adults. They lack a network of friends in the larger labor market to point them toward job openings, have a harder time in their language, presenting themselves to employers; they are not relaxed with autochthonous supervisors, and are angrier and less able to deal with the demands of integrated settings.

Within this segregated system there is further segregation perpetrated by some teachers' prejudices toward immigration. Personal beliefs held by teachers regarding immigration will affect how immigrant children are treated and therefore their school performance (Schneider et al. 2006). Classroom behavior, as well as the quality and the frequency of teacher–student interaction will be determined by expectations, stereotypes, attitudes, and motivations that the teacher holds with respect to his or her students (Rumbaut 2005).

Mariela, one of the students interviewed for this study aged 17, from Santiago de Chile arrived in Madrid when she was 9 years old. Now she is studying her last year of compulsory secondary school. She attends a compensatory class because she is 1 year behind. That class is composed of seven pupils, four from South America and three from Spain. Mariela comments on her teacher's attitudes toward South Americans: "My teacher says things like 'I hate South American accents, there are South Americans whose physical features resemble those of monkeys.'" Her sister, Lucía, 1 year older, who attends the same compensatory class, remarked that the same teacher "calls us 'sudacas'[4] and our Spanish classmates say that we are inferior to Spaniards, that we are nothing. This happens regularly, and I feel very angry and sad when I am treated like that".

Even though these students told their parents who went to speak with their tutor and the head-teacher, the racist comments continued and aggravated because their teacher learned they had told their parents and the school. When we spoke with the counselor of the school she acknowledged that the head-teacher had received formal complaints about that particular teacher before, but could not do anything because that teacher was on a permanent contract and racism "is very difficult to prove".

Research shows that denied support is the most significant form of discrimination in the education of migrant children (European Commission 2008). To the extent that racist discourses deny rights that victims consider fundamental, for example, the right to share the same space, to relate with classmates in a positive way, to live in the country in which they are residing, these discourses may be experienced as forms

---

[4] A derogatory term for South Americans.

of violence. Therefore, by leaving the cause of violence intact, teachers' responses may not have an impact on the broader student body or eliminate the hegemony of racist discourses and the rejection and isolation of immigrant students. Intervention strategies ought to be devised in order to help all students and teachers to interrogate racist attitudes and discourses; this could enable them to transform these discourses and the violence they perpetuate. Such strategies transcend the discussion of cultural diversity to address the political dimensions of racism and racist violence as a means of understanding and improving intercultural relations (Hooks 1994).

Thus, the compensatory approach of the educational system in Madrid has serious weakness and fails in providing immigrant students an education that contributes to parity in social participation. Immigration in Spain is a relatively new phenomenon that implied dramatic changes in population. However, no centralized strategies have been devised to attend to the educational needs of immigrant students. The government of Madrid has reacted by creating a Compensatory Educational Regional Plan, based on the notion of assimilation and compensatory education that takes a starting point a perceived "deficit" in immigrant students. At the same time, as has been shown, formal and informal rules result in the segregation of immigrant students in state schools, and in certain schools in particular that tend to be avoided by autochthonous students. These processes are in sharp contrast with an intercultural education that could, in theory, contribute to social cohesion through a more holistic and transformative approach involving all the community in the educational system. In addition, accounts of student experiences show that some teachers systematically deny support to immigrant students and they even have racist attitudes toward them. Therefore, we suggest that a profound debate is needed to reflect upon the ways in which the educational system may not be contributing to social cohesion.

In the next section, the case of Buenos Aires will be compared with the above analysis of Madrid, showing how different historical migration trajectories and overall approaches to the education of immigrants can fall short of attending to the specific needs of migrant students, albeit in a very different way.

Migration and Education in Argentina and Buenos Aires

Immigration has been a fundamental trait in the construction of the Argentine nation since its independence from Spain in 1816. During the nineteenth century, the promotion of European immigration was used as one of the main strategies to "civilize" and "modernize" the newborn nation, and in this way immigrants became coprotagonist of national progress. Argentina has been described as a country *of* immigrants (not a country *with* immigrants) (Novick and Oteiza 2000).

Between 1880 and 1930 a great number of immigrants settled in Argentina, most of them of European origin. Massive immigration deeply restructured the profile of Argentine society. The 1.8 million inhabitants existent in 1869 became 7.8 million in 1914, and, during that same period, the population of the city of Buenos Aires went from 180,000 to 1.5 million. In 1895, two out of three inhabitants of the city were immigrants and by 1914, when many of these immigrants had children born in Argentina, 30% of the total population was foreign-born, 28% from Europe, and only 2% from other American countries (INDEC 2009; Romero 2001). The newly arrived introduced different cultural traditions, languages and values, contributing to existing cultural diversity; which at the time was seen as an obstacle in the state-led project of constructing a modern nation.

The educational system was designed with the aim of homogenizing the population under the new "Argentine culture" that would guarantee political stability and legitimize the power of the central state. Primary schools expanded rapidly through most of the Argentine territory. Under the firm control of the state, each and every school in Argentina had to function in exactly the same way, offering the same content, at the same time, with the same methods, and using the same didactic materials (Gvirtz et al. 2008). At the time, the French Republican ethos of equality of opportunity had a strong influence on the educational system, reinforcing the notion that all students had to receive exactly the same education.

Another salient historical characteristic of the Argentine educational system was (and still is) the use of nationalistic rituals to promote national identity. The Argentine flag is raised at the beginning of the school day and lowered at the end, the national anthem and other national songs are sung, national holidays are celebrated with formal ceremonies, and schools are decorated with images of national heroes. Although the pomp and formality of these rituals has faded away, it is still compulsory for schools to follow them (Amuchástegui 2000; Eleazer 2005).

Argentina, and especially Buenos Aires, was constructed discursively as an European enclave in South America. The historical narratives that were promoted in schools and other institutions in order to construct and develop national identity were based on the idea that Argentina was a *crisol de razas* [an ethnic melting pot]. However, this imagined melting pot included only people with different European origins. Indigenous people have been almost invisible in these narratives,[5] and when they were considered, they were portrayed as backwards people that were an obstacle for progress and civilization (Grimson 2006).

In the last three decades the profile of immigration in Argentina has changed substantially. A marked decrease of European immigration implied a growth in relative terms of migrants from neighboring countries and Peru. Political discourses did not include these contemporary immigrants—mostly South Americans—as coprotagonist of a national project. On the contrary the "invasion" of South American immigrants was blamed for the problems that Argentina was going through (Grimson 1999).

However, immigration from neighboring countries to Argentina is not a new phenomenon. The first national census in 1869 showed that migrants from neighboring countries represented 20% of foreign-born population. Due to the reduction of immigration flows from other countries, the proportion of immigrants from

---

[5] However, the invisibility of indigenous ethnicities in Argentina is a discursive construction that is not based on demographic data, since Argentina has a higher proportion of indigenous people than Brazil (Grimson 2006).

neighboring countries grew to 61% of all foreign immigrants in 2001. However, the overall proportion of immigrants from neighboring countries and Peru has been quite stable since 1869, ranging from 2–2.9% of the total population (INDEC 2009).

In the 1990s South American immigrants started to be more visible in the city of Buenos Aires. Economic growth in Argentina, and a favorable exchange rate attracted regional migrants, especially from Peru, Bolivia, and Paraguay. In addition, migrants from these countries that had traditionally settled in areas close to the borders, started to move into Buenos Aires and other the big cities (Ceva 2006). As social networks expanded in the metropolitan area, the costs of migrating to Buenos Aires were reduced, and a process of territorial segregation started in which migrants tended to settle in certain areas that became Bolivian, Paraguayan, or Peruvian enclaves (Sassone and Mera 2007). This process of segregation also included a cultural dimension: the neighborhood is given a specific name (such as the Bolivian "Barrio Charrua"), religious, national, and ethnic celebrations are organized, and newspapers, radios, and restaurants that cater to that specific community are opened (Sassone and Mera 2007).

As a result of the growth of ethnic plurality in a city that defined itself as "European", immigration started receiving much attention in the media and in public debates. Overall, there were two types of reactions and positions in the debate. One position was reflected in the passing of Law 25,871 in 2004 that defined a new political approach to immigration, based on the ideal of an "inclusive, multicultural society, integrated to the region, that respects the rights of foreigners and values their cultural and social contribution" (Novick 2005, p. 11). It grants immigrants and their families equal access to social services such as education, health, justice, work, and social security. In education, all foreigners, regardless of their legal status, are granted the right to enroll in public and private institutions at all levels in the same conditions as nationals do.

On the other hand, racist and xenophobic discourses blamed immigrants from other South American countries for the high unemployment rates (especially after the economy stagnated in the mid 1990s), for the "overload" of public services (health and education), and for the growth in criminality (Aruj et al. 2002, Albarracín 2005).

This type of views, combined with the political and economic collapse of 2001, and a huge increase in poverty rates and in the gap between the income of rich and poor (Gasparini and Cruces 2008), was translated into a typical phrase in public opinion: "We are now really Latin Americans". There was a strong feeling that the distinctive characteristics of Argentina in relation to other Latin American countries (a strong middle-class, low poverty rates and "European flavor") were gone.

Migration, Education, and Segregation in Buenos Aires

As in Spain, official statistics on education and migration in Argentina are scarce and not very informative. Nevertheless, an overall profile of immigrant students in the city of Buenos Aires can be offered. According to official data of 2006, there are 30,816 foreign students enrolled in preschool, primary, and secondary education in Buenos Aires. Eighty-seven percent of these students come from neighboring countries and Peru. The distribution by nationality within this group shows that 42% come from Bolivia, 26% from Paraguay, 24% from Peru, 4% from Uruguay, 3% from Brazil, and 1% from Chile. It is important to note that these numbers do not consider the sons and daughters of immigrant parents that were born in Argentina, but are socially considered to be Bolivian, Paraguayan, and so on (Grimson 2006).

In Argentina, state schools mainly cater for the most economically disadvantaged sectors of the population. Private enrollments are concentrated within the families with the highest incomes (Narodowski and Nores 2002). This situation particularly affects the big urban centers, where the increase in private schools has had the most significant impact (Narodowski and Nores 2002). In the City of Buenos Aires, 53.5% of students attend state schools and 46.5% are enrolled in private schools.

Overall, immigrant students tend to concentrate in state schools (80%). By looking at the state–private distribution of immigrant students by nationality it is possible to see how socioeconomic status relates with the national origin of migrants and the type of education they receive. There is an overall direct relation between the nationality of Latin American immigrants and socioeconomic status as reflected in the job market. Paraguay, Bolivia, and Peru have provided mostly unqualified labor, while Uruguayan and Brazilian immigrants tend to work in more qualified jobs (Ceva 2006).[6] This difference is reflected in public–private enrollments (although it is not so clear for the case of Uruguay). The percentage of enrollments in public schools is of 95% for Bolivia, 86% for Paraguay, 85% for Peru, 71% for Uruguay, and 51% for Brazil.

The Argentine educational system has suffered a progressive de facto school segregation based on social class, generating implicit subsystems of education (Veleda 2009; Neufeld and Thisted 1999). This segmentation by social class happens even within the public sector (and obviously within the private sector where fees determine directly who can access which school). In this way, some schools have been labeled as "stigmatized schools", they are discredited, associated with a low-quality education, and thus, avoided by those who have more resources and possibilities to choose a school for their children—mainly the middle classes (Neufeld and Thisted 1999).

The spatial distribution of immigrant students in the city of Buenos Aires shows that foreign-born students, and especially Paraguayans, Peruvians, and Bolivians, tend to concentrate in the southern part of the city, where the highest levels of poverty can be found. These districts also have the highest dropout rates, and the worst overall academic performance. Even within these districts, immigrant students tend to concentrate in certain schools. One of the head-teachers interviewed for this study explains how this happened:

> In our case, since the population, mostly Bolivians and Peruvians and a few Paraguayans, started to come to this school—since they chose this school for their education - the number of Argentine students fell.

---

[6] There is not much research on Chilean immigration in Argentina.

Thus, a similar process to the one described for Madrid can be observed. Argentine parents do not want their children to go to a school were there is a significant presence of immigrant students and this perpetuates and reinforces the concentration of migrant children in certain schools. In this way, many migrant children (and the Argentine children of immigrants) attend schools in which they form the majority of the school population.

There is no specific data on the educational trajectories and/or academic performance of immigrant students in Argentina, nor in Buenos Aires—an indicator that the challenge of immigrant education has not been considered as an issue that requires special attention and specific political and pedagogical strategies. Overall, in Argentina the most relevant variable related with academic performance and educational trajectories is socioeconomic class (Cerrutti and Binstock 2005; Llach 2006). Thus, it is quite possible that immigrant groups follow similar patterns, since no special adaptations have been designed to attend to their specific educational needs. However, other issues such as family support and language difficulties might play a role in differentiating the academic performance of immigrant students from their autochthonous peers of similar socioeconomic backgrounds.

The segregation of immigrant students in certain schools has a negative effect, perpetuating the spatial and social segregation of immigrant groups in the city. Many of the immigrant students who were interviewed mentioned that they spend most of their free time with other migrant children. They tend to stay in their neighborhood, and only a few of them had visited other parts of the city. Furthermore, in some cases they said that their parents do not allow them to go out, and they spend most of their time in their own house, since they live in "dangerous areas" and parents wanted them to avoid problems such as crime and drug use. Thus, it is difficult for them to develop wider social networks since they are isolated and do not participate much in integrated social settings outside of school. In theory, the educational system should create opportunities for students of different backgrounds, and primarily for minority students, to meet and interact, contributing to overall social cohesion. However, in the case of Buenos Aires and Madrid, the systems seem to be reinforcing social fragmentation and the segregation of immigrant groups.

Assimilation, Invisibility, and the Republican Ethos

In Argentina (and in Buenos Aires) no special pedagogic or institutional devices have been designed to attend to the specific needs of immigrant students. The institutional response to the challenges posed by immigrant students at the macrolevel has been limited to granting immigrants access to institutions, regardless of their legal status, and giving foreign-born students the possibility of applying for scholarships that help economically disadvantaged students pay the costs of books, travel, and other expenses.

This weak adaptation can be explained at least by three factors. In the first place, the challenge of immigrant education is very visible in certain districts and in certain schools where immigrant students tend to cluster, but it has not been significantly considered as a general challenge that needs to be addressed by the central authorities. Secondly, the huge increase in poverty in the last four decades in Argentina has placed the problem of redistribution at the center of educational debates, while issues linked with cultural recognition have received very little attention. Finally, the Republican ethos of equality of opportunity is still very strong in the views of legislators, educational authorities, and teachers. From this point of view, the fairest way to deal with differences is to treat everybody in the same way, disregarding the need for group identity politics. This view was very strong among principals and teachers in the schools that participated of this study.

In the schools we visited there where almost no specific pedagogical or institutional strategies aimed at attending to the special needs of immigrant students. Furthermore, in conversations we had with teachers and principals it was evident that they did not believe that foreign-born students required any special attention. When teachers did mention adaptations they referred to the need to give students "care and affection", but this is something they said they did for most of their students, not because they were immigrants, but because they were poor, and in their views they did not receive much emotional support from their families.

Minority groups can suffer from institutional misrecognition when their differences are overrecognized, and they are systematically segregated and treated in a different way than other groups. This is what seems to be happening in schools in Madrid. However, misrecognition can also happen when the differences and specific needs of minority groups are not recognized (Fraser and Honneth 2003). This is what happens in Buenos Aires, where no attention is given to the specific needs of immigrant students and consequently no specific devices to help them have been created.

In the overall assimilationist view that dominates education policies and practices in Buenos Aires it is the responsibility of students to "assimilate to Argentine culture". Students who were interviewed said that they had to participate in nationalistic rituals. Most of them mentioned that they had suffered from discrimination in the streets (not so much in schools). In some cases they noted that this happened in the first few years after their arrival, and that then it had stopped. When asked about whether she had been discriminated against, a Peruvian girl said:

> Yes, when I was little, the other kids called my sister and me "*negra peruana* (Peruvian negro)"... but know, since we've changed it has stopped, because now we dress and makeup differently.

A Bolivian student in another school gave a similar answer:

> At the beginning it was difficult here, especially because I was discriminated against. It happens with everybody who has arrived recently, because it is easy to tell that you come from another country. But I was wrong in the way I thought... I was little and I didn't understand.

Theses comments are illustrative of how the students that were interviewed tended to blame themselves for the initial discrimination and thought that it was something that they changed about them that made it stop.

Interestingly, students seemed to be quite at ease and comfortable with the approach of schools and teachers in Buenos Aires. All of them marked a very clear distinction between the discrimination they suffered (and saw their family or friends suffer) in the streets and what happened in schools. They did not express any bad feelings about participating in nationalistic rituals—this type of ritual is also practiced in schools in their countries of origin, and thus they saw it as a natural event. Most of them said they had good relationships with teachers and peers, and pointed out to some teachers or tutors that have given them some kind of emotional or academic support. Therefore, some informal support networks between adults and students existed, but these were dependant of the good will of certain people, and were mostly based on providing emotional support to address specific problems of the students, not necessarily aimed at facilitating overall social democratization, equality, and parity of participation in social life. Nevertheless, the school experiences of the students that were interviewed were quite positive from their point of view.

However, we also grasped in the discourse of adults in schools some stereotypes, and nostalgic views about European immigration that reflect how migration from neighboring countries in Buenos Aires revitalizes ethnic tensions that date back to colonial times. The head of a school mentioned with pride that the school used to be referred to as the *"Belgrano Shule"*[7], because of the great number of students from the Jewish community they had. When we suggested that those were also immigrant families, she immediately reacted: "No, no, that was something else", and explained how their "old" graduates had become "important people", doctors, lawyers, and so on. Implicit was the notion that their current students had no chance of becoming "important people", that they had some kind of deficit. "We have become Latin Americans", said another teacher disdainfully. The alleged deficit was associated with stereotypes such as the slowness and quietness of Bolivians and Peruvians, with their socioeconomic origins (that included deficits in their families, their homes, and their previous education among other things) and with ethnicity. One teacher, for example, emphasized how the color of the skin was more important than the nationality in terms of defining which students had academic difficulties: "There are kids here that come from the [Argentine] provinces of the north that look very similar to Bolivians, they have the same physiognomy…in general you can see that those with [academic] problems are the ones with dark skin". Therefore, nationality, social class, and ethnicity were muddled up in the discourse of adults in schools, that overall were not happy with the type of students they had.

In Buenos Aires, students and adults who participated of this study reported no cases of discrimination by teachers. However, the overall approach of obscuring differences by ignoring the specific needs of immigrant children also falls short of providing an adequate education to foreign-born pupils. Thus, it is clear that in Buenos Aires more visibility should be given to the educational needs of migrant students and some institutionalized policies dealing with their specific needs should be devised in order to introduce the concept of intercultural education that was absent from political discourses, policies, and practices.

---

[7] Names of schools are fictitious in order to protect their anonymity and confidentiality.

Conclusion

Both Madrid and Buenos Aires have experienced substantial changes in the profile of migration trajectories. The growth and visibility of ethnic and cultural plurality in two cities that saw themselves as having certain cultural and ethnic homogeneity, has altered imagined homogenized identities, socioeconomic affiliations, and placed political and educational systems under tremendous strain. New political, economic, educational, and ethnic tensions between groups often build upon previous social constructions and historical relations between these groups. Thus, Spain's colonial past, and the image of Argentina as a European enclave in South America have a significant influence in the ways in which Latin American migrants are othered, and national identities and senses of belonging are negotiated.

In both cities the overall approach is based on the notion of assimilation to an imagined mainstream culture. Within this general approach, misrecognition of the specific needs of immigrant students takes place in schools in both cities, although in very different forms in each location. In the case of Madrid, differences are emphasized through specific compensatory practices aimed at immigrant groups. In Buenos Aires differences are obscured and, to a certain extent, ignored. Nevertheless, both educational systems need to rethink the way in which they deal with immigrant students and with injustices rooted in sociocultural patterns of representation of specific groups. These two cases emphasize the need to reflect upon "the extent to which race, religion, or ethnicity [and nationality] should be highlighted or obscured in educational settings and what form such saliency (or dimness) should take" (Bekerman et al. 2009, p. 226).

We suggest that the concept of "integration", which is (at least implicitly) based on the idea of assimilation to the dominant culture, needs to be questioned. Educational systems should move beyond the imagery of territories as spatially fixed geographical containers for social processes. Moreover, intercultural education should be based on the inclusion of the interests of all groups, especially those that have faced and are facing discrimination. Thus it calls for revolutionary practices and guidelines from policy makers, educators, and educational communities informed by an ethics of social justice and a language of critique against exploitation on all fronts. Thus education needs to be treated within a broader ideological and political framework and as a catalyst for thinking about social democratization, equality, and citizenship.

Acknowledgment We would like to thank AECID (Agencia Española de Cooperación Internacional y Desarrollo) for their financial support which has enabled us to conduct this study.

References

Amuchástegui, M. (2000). El orden escolar y sus rituales. In S. Gvirtz (Ed.), *Textos para repensar el día a día escolar, escolar,* Buenos Aires: Santillana, pp. 59–77.
Aruj, R., Novick, S., & Oteiza, E. (2000). *Inmigración y Discriminación Políticas y Discursos. Inmigración y Discriminación Políticas y Discursos*. Buenos Aires: Grupo Editor Universitario.

Bekerman, Z., Zembylas, M., & Mcglynn, C. (2009). Working toward the de-essentialization of identity categories in conflict and postconflict societies: Israel, Cyprus, and Northern Ireland. *Comparative Education Review, 53*(2), pp. 213–234.
Bernstein, B. (1970) *Education cannot compensate for society,* New Society, 26 February 1970, pp. 344–347.
Bernstein, B. (1971). *Class, Codes and Control,* Vol. 1, London: Routledge and Kegan Paul.
Cachón Rodríguez, L. (2003). *Inmigrantes jóvenes en España: Sistema educativo y mercado de trabajo.* Edición Injuve: Castilla la Mancha.
Cerrutti, M., & Bistock, G. (2005). *Carreras truncadas: El abandono escolar en el nivel medio en la Argentina.* Buenos Aires: UNICEF.
Ceva, M. (2006). *La migración limítrofe hacia la Argentina.* Buenos Aires: Prometeo libros.
Crain, R. L., & Stuart, W. A. (1999). *Stepping over the color line: African-American students in White suburban schools.* New Haven: Yale University Press.
Cros, F., Yael, D., & Kantasalami, K. (2004). *Attracting, developing and retaining effective teachers. Country note: Spain.* Paris: OECD.
Dewey, J. (1997). *Experience and education.* New York: Touchstone.
Eleazer, M. (2005). *La Nación de la Escuela Un análisis de los actos escolares en contextos de crisis.* Master's thesis, Escuela de Educación, Universidad de San Andrés, Buenos Aires, Argentina.
European Commission. (2008). *Education and migration: Strategies for integrating migrant children in European schools and societies: A synthesis of research findings for policy-makers.* Ness.
Farley, J. (2006). School integration and its consequences for social integration and educational opportunity. In F. Heckmann & R. Wolf (Eds.), *Immigrant integration and education: The role of state and civil society in Germany and the US.* Bamberg: European Forum for Migration Studies.
Fraser, N., & Honneth, A. (2003). *Redistribution or recognition? A political-philosophical exchange.* London: Verso.
Freire, P. (1970). *Pedagogía del oprimido.* Montevideo: Tierra Nueva.
Gasparini, L., & Cruces, G. (2008). *A distribution in motion: The case of Argentina. A review of the empirical evidence.* Working paper, CEDLAS, Universidad de La Plata.
Gobierno de la Ciudad de Buenos Aires. (2006). Relevamiento anual 2006.
Grimson, A. (1999). *Relatos de la diferencia y la igualdad: Los bolivianos en Buenos Aires.* Buenos Aires: Editorial Universitaria de Buenos Aires.
Grimson, A. (2006). Nuevas xenofobias, nuevas políticas étnicas en Argentina. In A. Grimson & E. Jelin (Eds.), *Migraciones regionales hacia la Argentina: Diferencias, desigualdades y derechos.* Buenos Aires: Prometeo.
Gvirtz, S., Beech, J., & Oria, A. (2008). Schooling in Argentina. In S. Gvirtz & J. Beech (Eds.), *Going to school in Latin America.* Westport: Greenwood Press.
Hooks, B. (1994). *Teaching to transgress. Education as the practice of freedom.* New York: Routledge.
Instituto Nacional de Estadísticas y Censos [INDEC] (n.d.). http://www.indec.gov.ar/. Accessed November 2009.
Instituto Nacional de Estadística [INE] (2008). Survey of the Active Population.
Instituto Nacional de Estadística [INE] (2009). Survey of the Active Population.
Llach, J. (2006). *El desafío de la equidad educativa.* Buenos Aires: Granica.
Ministerio de Educación. (2009). *Datos y cifras. Curso 2009–2010.* Madrid: Ministerio de Educación.
Narodowski, M., & Nores, M. (2002). Socio-economic segregation with (without) competitive education policies: A comparative analysis of Argentina and Chile. *Comparative Education, 38*(4), pp. 429–450.
Neufeld, M. R., & Thisted, J. A. (Eds.) (1999). *"De eso no se habla...": Los usos de la diversidad sociocultural en la escuela.* Buenos Aires: Eudeba.

Novick, S. (2005). La reciente política migratoria argentina en el contexto del MERCOSUR. In S. Novick, A. Hener, P. Dalle (Eds.), *El proceso de integración Mercosur: de las políticas migratorias y de seguridad a las trayectorias de los inmigrantes*. Buenos Aires: Instituto de Investigaciones Gino Germani, Facultad de Ciencias Sociales, UBA.

Ombudsman's Report. (2005). On schooling the immigrant child 2003. http://www.defensordelpueblo.es

Ortfield, G., & Eaton, S. E. (1996). *Dismantling desegregation: The quiet reversal of Brown v. Board of Education*. New York: New Press.

Oteiza, E., & Novick, S. (2000). *Inmigración y derechos humanos. Política y discursos en el tramo final del menemismo*. Documento de Trabajo 14, Buenos Aires: Instituto de Investigaciones Gino Germani, Facultad de Ciencias Sociales, Universidad de Buenos Aires.

Phillips, A. (2007). *Multiculturalism without culture*. Princeton: Princeton University Press.

PISA. (2005). *Education at a glance*. Paris: OCDE.

Romero, L. A. (2001.) *Breve historia contemporánea de la Argentina*. Buenos Aires: Fondo de Cultura Económica de Argentina S.A.

Rumbaut, R. G. (2005). Children of immigrants and their achievement: The role of family, acculturation, class, gender, ethnicity, and school contexts. In R. D. Taylor (Ed.), *Addressing the achievement gap: Theory informing practice*. Greenwich: Information Age Publishing, pp. 23–59.

Sassone, S., & Mera, C. (2007). *Barrios de migrantes en Buenos Aires: Identidad, cultura y cohesión socioterritorial*. Presented in the European Congress of Latin American Studies.

Veleda, C. (2009). Regulación estatal y segregación educativa en la provincia de Buenos Aires. *Revista de Política Educativa*. 1(1).

Wang, H., & Olson, N. (2009). *A journey to unlearn and learn in multicultural education*. New York: Peter Lang.

Wells, A. S., & Crain, R. L. (1997). *Stepping over the color line: African American students in white suburban schools*. New Haven: Yale University Press.

Part IV
Higher Education

Chapter 29
Introduction: Higher Education

Marisol Clark-Ibáñez

Introduction

The three chapters in this part represent the diverse experiences of minorities in higher education. Each chapter highlights the challenges of the everyday work and school life of teachers who educate international students in Australia, African immigrant students in the United States, and undocumented Latino college students in the United States. The chapters focus on the methodological, theoretical, and practical implications of the research and population. Together, they create a broad and detailed understanding of how culture, class, community, and dominant discourses shape the experiences of minority students.

Summaries

In the first chapter of this part, Ruth Arber describes the intersection of pedagogy and culture of international students attending Australian secondary schools. Her research draws on interview data from two science teachers and how they speak about their teaching of international students. She explains that as public schools lose government funding, fee-paying international students present an important income generator for Australian schools; most of the students come from Asian countries. While science teachers may try to provide an inclusive and dynamic curriculum for all of their students, in practice international students are often viewed through a deficit perspective.

Arber takes the reader through a comprehensive and theoretical discussion of culture as it relates to multicultural education and hegemonic notions of race and ethnicity. The context of science education is pertinent to this issue because, as she

---

M. Clark-Ibáñez (✉)
Department of Sociology, California State University San Marcos,
333 S. Twin Oaks Valley Road, San Marcos, CA 92096, USA
e-mail: mibanez@csusm.edu

argues, science curriculum is so often thought of as culture free but it is "part of a historical process of cultural construction." Indeed, Arber finds that the two science teachers imbue their own cultural bias on their international students, at times drawing on "us versus them" distinctions and to describe how they are different from local students. Using rich interview data, Arber also finds that teachers conceptualize the international students as "the other" and seek to "break barriers" and "confront them" in order to socialize them to the Western pedagogical standards. Yet, the teachers describe innovative and successful teaching methods that seem to mostly benefit local students. The language and cultural challenges of the international students seem to be insurmountable for them to bridge the gap between the two learning populations.

Arber concludes the chapter with an extensive and thoughtful reflection on how to create meaningful curriculum for all students. Specifically, she argues that we need to first explore and understand the normative expectations that underlie our curriculum. We must be able to "clarify the value, ideas, behaviors, and practices" that are integral to science curriculum in order to make it culturally inclusive. To develop a more reflexive curriculum, Arber presents a framework that would incorporate the interactions between individuals, institutional structures, and normative contexts. This, she hopes, could begin to decrease the teachers' estrangement from their international students.

In the second chapter of this part, Joash Matua Wambua and Cecil Robinson present how African immigrant students experience college and the role of "the self" in their academic success. In the United States, for statistical purposes African students (immigrants) are combined with African-American students. Yet, the authors point out several differences between the groups; in particular, the East African students in this study have parents with higher educational levels, come from families with higher income, and possess higher educational aspirations. One of the main issues that make this group vulnerable is the assimilation process and keeping their cultural heritage—a strength that if lost, could jeopardize or slow down their academic and economic progress. Therein lies the focus of the chapter: identity and pressures to adapt to mainstream American culture and African-American subcultures.

The researchers rely on the social-psychological notion of "possible selves" to understand how African students (when compared to African-American students) perceive their current identity, future success, and fear of failure. Possible selves, the authors describe, "represent what we might become, what we hope to become, and what we fear becoming." They operationalized this abstract notion by introducing the concept of achievement goals, which is how students work toward general goals. They argue, convincingly, that racial identity is linked to academic achievement. Using innovative questionnaires, they sought to understand how African students perceive themselves.

Their findings paint a fascinating picture of the lives of African students. They perceive themselves as different from African-American students at their university; this leads to lower awareness of racism, higher cultural connectedness to the African immigrant community, and higher achievement scores. African students are experiencing their racial-ethnic status in a different way than African-American students, despite various institutional and social means to lump the two groups together.

Another component to the research was to look at within group differences among the African immigrant students; they found that attending a 4-year university (as opposed to a 4-year college or 2-year community college) led to stronger, more successful possible selves.

However, in general, doing well academically was an important part of the African immigrant identity when compared to African-American students. Because universities may not recognize the differences between these groups, the opportunity to strengthen this self-identity or even build cultural coalitions between the two groups are lost. Academic counselors and other university agents can capitalize on the goal setting ability that is part of the African students' identity. Finally, avenues still left to explore in this area of research were the issues of tribal groups, status, and gender.

In the third chapter, Marisol Clark-Ibáñez, Fredi Garcia, and Gricelda Alva describe the experiences of undocumented Latino immigrant college students who live in a Southern California community that is openly hostile to immigrants. Undocumented students, by California law, may attend the university (or other place of higher education) but are not eligible for any public financial aid. These students are also not able to work legally or apply for a driver's license. Undocumented students are in a liminal state—they possess the right for education but cannot legally work or live in the United States.

The research study discovered that the university provides a safe haven. The students' status is not openly questioned because the university uses student identification numbers instead of Social Security numbers. (This is an important distinction because in the United States, it is the basis of almost every transaction with social institutions and for which undocumented students are not eligible.) Students are able to pursue their academic aspirations in relative safety. The authors found that students gained "educational citizenship," meaning they claimed their rights for a meaningful schooling experience. Yet, within this safety zone, they must maintain private their immigration status or, at minimum, be quite careful with whom they share this information.

Through in-depth qualitative interviews with 19 participants, the researchers were able to capture the ways in which the students' status of invisibility or ability to "pass" (as a citizen) also had a shadow side. This includes holding back their own thoughts during class discussions and the stress of constantly maintaining their secret status, even when such information is pertinent to the completion of assignments, field trips, or internships. The undocumented college students in this study also poignantly discussed the emotional toll that it takes to not being able to fully participate in the normative college activities such as driving a car, going out to eat or drink where nonschool identification cards are required, studying abroad, and working in jobs that would further their professional aspirations.

Evidence of resiliency was found in this study. Despite numerous odds and an uncertain future after graduation, all the students interviewed doggedly pursued their educational dreams for themselves and their families. Many aspire to attend graduate school. Yet, the role of the university and its institutional agents in supporting the students was mixed. Numerous recommendations for universities were outlined, including protecting the university from antiimmigration groups; creating awareness of faculty about the challenges facing undocumented students so that pedagogy, assignments, and field trips reflect this sensitivity; and, supporting current legislation that would provide a path to citizenship for undocumented students.

All three chapters reflect the need for a better understanding of these minority populations—international students, African immigrants, and undocumented Latinos. This improved understanding, the authors collectively claim, could improve the educational outcomes for these students.

Discussion

Invisibility in the Literature and in the Social World

Little has been written about African immigrants, undocumented students, and the pedagogy of teaching international students. And, there is a striking parallel in that all three chapters touched on the issue of invisibility either implicitly or explicitly. The African and Latino students are not necessarily viewed in their own separate categories by the university and yet they possess unique characteristics that greatly shape their educational experiences. The international students were "seen" negatively by their teachers but as actors in the classroom they were considered passive; as learners, the international students' talents and personal ambitions were invisible to their teachers.

Universal Design as Good Learning for All

Upon reflecting on the three chapters, the idea of "universal design" came to mind. I borrow this term from the field of disability studies and the pedagogy of online learning. Universal design implies that the design of class, when catered correctly to a disabled student, could improve the learning for all students. For example, the international students in Arber's study struggle with the English and the science content. However, for most students—regardless of native language—chemistry is like learning another language. This is also the case, traditionally, for issues of gender and science learning. Research finds that girls, compared to boys, learn science differently and have a more passive participation style. All students benefit if the science teachers approached all students with patience, understanding, and the realization that gender and culture should be taken into consideration.

In the case of East African students, the authors argue that advisors should tailor their services with the assumption that these students already have in their value system the need to succeed, set goals, and possess self-motivation; yet, one can imagine the amazing benefits of an academic advisor who adopted this proactive attitude of high expectations for all students.

The undocumented students explained how some assignments, field trips, and class discussions led to their inability to fully participate. Yet, other students who are marginalized (low-income) or who may protect a secret identity (gay or lesbian) may also benefit from their professors' careful consideration as to the cost of assignments, the time needed outside of class, the issue of transportation and gas, and creating safe spaces for class discussions.

Home Cultures and Student Strengths

Finally, what became clear to me upon reflecting on the three chapters is the loss of human capital and potential when we do not tap into students' strengths and home cultures. In the case of the international students in Australia, because the teachers perceived them as "the other," they missed the opportunity to know their strengths, ambitions, and motivations in terms of learning and their education. Clearly, these are students who may be independent and could possess extraordinary skills by mere fact that they chose (or where chosen) to study abroad. Teachers fail to build upon and capitalize on these (and potentially other) characteristics that could lead to deeper learning and a more cohesive classroom community.

Similarly, East African students are typically not seen by others as different from their African-American peers. Therefore, advisors, professors, fellow classmates, and other university actors miss the opportunity to learn from these students and also further build their potential. Fortunately, it seems that at least in the 4-year university context, the African immigrant students experience support and self-motivation by seeing themselves as different from their African-American counterparts and the negative labels that apply to these students. Yet, in the other educational contexts mentioned in the study, the African students do not seem as fortified by their own culture.

For the undocumented Latino students, the community and political climate make them afraid to reveal their immigration status, even when pertinent for relationship building or classroom assignments. Blocking a part of who they are often leads to their sadness and stress—emotional states not conducive to learning.

Conclusion

In summary, the three chapters represent minorities in higher education in diverse contexts. Taken together, they demonstrate universalities related to inequality in schooling. Students' identity and cultural validation are not fully realized. Pedagogy and student services are compromised for the students because of their unique social location. It becomes clear, when combining the findings of the chapters, that institutes of higher education and its members must be proactive in ameliorating these inequalities.

Chapter 30
Encountering An-Other: The Culture of Curriculum and Inclusive Pedagogies

Ruth Arber

Introduction

> Claims that Melbourne is a racist city have angered a population proud of their cultural diversity...The perception is damaging to Melbourne's reputation—which has suffered economically from declining Indian student enrolments and tourist numbers. (The Herald Sun, *January 11, 2010, p. 6*)

The different configurations that underpin the ways that identity and difference are played out within a globalized world, their impact on the ways that cultural flows are constructed and interpolated, and their consequences frame recent media discussion about international student programs in Australia. I am interested in the ways that the notions that underpin these debates are understood and practiced in demographically diverse and internationally networked classrooms, in the analysis of these notions as the subject and object of cultural knowledge and behavior, in the relationship between these practices and the categorization of identities, and in the implications of these understandings for the development of inclusive pedagogies. In an interdependent and ostensibly Anglophone world, the indispensability of the English language and a Western education as a resource places pressure on families to pay to educate their children *trans*nationally. In a fiercely competitive market, Australia is now third after Britain and the United States as a provider of secondary education to international students, and education provision is its third largest service export (Australian Government 2009). Local government schools are now able to augment limited government funding by providing education to fee-paying international students.

The debate in the article described above emerged from a series of incidents, including the stabbing to death of an Indian student. The discussion challenges perceptions that Australia is a multicultural country whose long experience in immigrant and refugee education makes it well placed as a provider of education for fee-

---

R. Arber (✉)
Faculty of Arts and Education, School of Education, 221 Burwood Highway,
Burwood 3121, VIC, Australia
e-mail: ruth.arber@deakin.edu.au

paying international students. It begs questions about the ways that we need to think about education for international students and whether and how it follows from the work of providing education for immigrant and refugee students and for students generally as they work within a world markedly changed by global flows and digital interchange. My focus in this chapter is on the manifestation and consequences of cultural understanding and practice for the ways in which two science teachers in Melbourne, Australia, attempt to provide an inclusive pedagogy for fee-paying international students. At stake are the ways in which schools are able to provide comprehensive and far-thinking education for all of their students—including international students.

Changed demographic, technical, and fiscal imperatives over the last decade call for pedagogies that provide all students with access to thinking, interrogative, and life skills for a globalized world (Deng and Luke 2007). Science curriculum statements particularly express the need for education to be "dynamic and progressive" in a society that "is being continually confronted, challenged and redirected by ideas borne from people's curiosity, imagination and dreams about what might be possible" (VELS 2009). Yet too often, pedagogies for international students support a deficit view of teaching practice, with an emphasis on parochial and technical expertise and the simplification of language and culture to their discrete and systemic characteristics rather than their embodied and ontological aspects (Carroll and Ryan 2005). The manifestation of culture and its relation to identification are at the core of the lacuna between the ideal of a science curriculum for all students and what is provided.

Multidimensional and multifaceted, culture integrates the skills and knowledge that make up educational pathways even as it prescribes the terms and conditions under which these skills and knowledge are constructed. Culture, seen through modernist lenses, is described as the behaviors, habits, norms, customs, and values held in common and circumscribed by group identification (see Goldberg 1994, p. 70). When understood through these same lenses, multicultural education is about the preservation of the exotic and strange cultures of another. Such celebrations of alternative cultures are in stark contrast to demands to ameliorate inadequacies exposed within other and deficit cultures (Arber 2008b). On the other hand, the literature and debates about globalization often describe culture as fluid and malleable, separable from social and historical framing, and "colorblind" in its ascription of identities and contexts (e.g., McKay 2002). The skills and knowledge integral to a curriculum for an internationalized economy are reduced to the simple technical and linguistic skills that are required to work within a depoliticized and homogeneous global culture (see Rizvi's 2009 important analysis). These notions of culture are entangled with discourses of race and identity to mediate the ways that groups (ethnic, refugee, indigenous, international student) belong within school communities. In the case of international school education, these discourses interact with other discourses concerned with postcolonialism, neoliberalism, and naïve cosmopolitanism to mediate the ways international students and their cultures are defined against that which is normal and included (or excluded) within schools and curriculum (Arber 2008b, 2009).

To develop a more comprehensive view of inclusive education for all students, we need to understand the practiced, systemic, and normative circumstances that surround the definition and implementation of school curriculum; to describe their relation to the conception and normalization of culture; and to interrogate their implications for identification practices. I make my argument in four moves. The first move looks at the multidimensional notion of culture, its relation to practice and identification of individuals and its implications for inclusive pedagogy for international, refugee, and immigrant students in Australian secondary schools. The second move examines the different ways that two science teachers at one school in Melbourne, Australia, describe good pedagogy for international students. It is argued that teachers often fail to understand the variability of, and relationships between, culture and the technical and meaningful aspects of their teaching content—even as they describe the culture of their international students as homogeneous, unchanging, and foreign. In the third move, I set out the principles of a two-dimensional frame to explore the reflexive and multifaceted dimensions of culture which frame a comprehensive and inclusive curriculum for diverse student cohorts entering changed worlds. The final move interrogates the slippage that occurs between understandings about culture and the identification of individuals on the one hand and the articulation of inclusive pedagogy on the other. The notion of culture as reified and unchanging underpins modern and multicultural discourse and intersects with more recent notions of language and identity as endlessly fluid and inconsequential. If contemporary curricula are to be more inclusive, the practices, systemic conditions, and normative mores that define and mediate classroom interactions and curricula need to be understood reflexively, and the practices, systemic conditions, and normative mores that define and mediate them interrogated and implemented in other ways.

Culture and the Curriculum

Culture describes both the practices and ideas that are made routine in everyday lives and the nexus between everyday objects and events, their embodiment within everyday behaviors and practices, and their manifestation within historically defined social worlds (Bauman 1999). Intricately bound together with language, the notion of culture contains within it our confidence in the materiality of a familiar and everyday world and our imagination of it (Anderson 1991). Gee and Green (1998) define the imaginative aspects of culture as pertaining to a "meaning model", or Discourse (with a capital D). These ways of being and understanding the world frame the socially accepted principles that define identities and actions within and across contexts. They are differentiated from the discourses (with a small d) or the practices "of thinking, feeling, believing, valuing, and of acting that can be used to identify oneself as a member of a socially meaningful group or 'social network'" (Gee 1996, p. 131). In this respect, language ("concerned with the production and exchange of meaning") and culture ("concerned with the giving and taking of meaning between members of a group") are intertwined (1996, p. 131). Language describes the ways that we understand and speak about the social world in which "we" act and in which "meaning is produced and exchanged", even as it is the principle means through which we conduct our everyday lives (Hall 1997, p. 2). The culture of day-to-day practices is negotiated through the commonalities that accrue from shared history and traditions. The world and its history (and the ways that people are positioned, belong, and share in that history) and the implications of a shared past for the present and future are the foundations for and construct the product, culture (Kramsch 1998, p. 7).

Culture, like language, is therefore reflexive. It simultaneously takes its meaning from its context even as it constructs the very context of what it is to "mean and be in the first place" (Gee and Green 1998, p. 127). In Bourdieu's terms, the everyday ideas and practices which make up the habitus[1] of the everyday practice are mediated by the rules and structure of institutions and negotiated within the larger fields of social, economic, and cultural relations. Bourdieu's notion of "symbolic domination" refers to the ability of certain social groups to maintain control over others by establishing their view of reality and their cultural practices as the most valued and, perhaps more importantly, as "the norm" (Bourdieu 2007). The articulation of cultural objects and their use within systemic structures and ontological context is crucially concerned with the definition of the normative condition of the "ordinary person" and of "everyday ideas and behaviours" (Luke 2003, p. ix).

In a social world mapped out within the quagmire of unequally empowered and competing discourses, language and culture become the site and subject of the different ways people can behave, are understood, and are included within a society. The character of voice and the bodily performance of language—like physical characteristics such as skin color—mark who we are and what we can become (Arber 2008a, b; Rizvi 2005). The social construction of that-which-we-are-called-to-be is far from merely superficial. Subjectivity is in a sense a "performance" in which a self-conscious performer chooses an act, which is "performed". Power operates through the creation of different subject identities in ways that strengthen and legitimize them through countless acts of reiteration and performance that seek "to introduce a reality rather than report on an existing one" (Butler 1997, p. 33). The identification of individuals and their categorization as belonging to a group needs to be understood as an "achievement" that takes place as a matter of "human activity...shaped and reinterpreted as a kind of cultural activity conducted together with one's partners and neighbours and negotiated within the variousness of historical and social contexts" (Bekerman 2003, p. 7).

Language and culture provide the mechanism and the framing context for the formulation of school curricula—including science curricula. So often thought of as culture free, scientific method and thought are nevertheless part of a historical process of cultural construction (Bishop 1995). The internationalization of scien-

---

[1] Habitus refers to the commonsense and shared ways of understanding and behaving developed within the everyday conditions of institutional life (Bourdieu 2007).

tific thought through the mechanisms of postcolonial conquest and administration; the interconnectivity of popular culture, technology, and communication; and the linkages between education institutions and communities—all add weight to the perception that science is universal and natural. The culture of science describes activities, values, thoughts, and behaviors framed by particular ways of being within, and working within, that world (Lemke 2002). In the formal context of the school, the curriculum categorizes and integrates the practices, norms, values, and beliefs of educational culture. These understandings and behaviors—as they are formalized within government and school policy and everyday practice, and shaped within the Discourse structures—inform the "hidden curriculum", which shapes ways of thinking and behaving within the school defined as "normal" (Giroux 2001). Such essential notions of "normal thinking" mediate the objects, processes, and meaning making contained within curriculum subject matter. The material and notional aspects of science curriculum—as it formalizes the encoded, embodied, and ontological aspects of what it means to do science—define its cultural terms and conditions and the manifestation of its policy and practice.

Research Project and Methodology

The case studies explored in this chapter are taken from a larger study that explores the impact of fee-paying international students on secondary education provision in Victoria, Australia. Since 2004, this study has included a statewide survey of nearly 200 schools (Arber and Blackmore 2007), and case studies of 16 government schools (Arber 2008b; Arber and Blackmore 2007). Case studies include open-ended interviews with school representatives, purposefully sampled to include English-language teachers and class teachers. Using grounded and naturalistic research methods, focus questions concerned with the implementation and impact of international student programs were organized into patterns to identify conceptual issues, establish links, and explore specific instances illustrative of wider shifts (Denzin and Lincoln 1998).[2]

In this chapter, case study methodology is used to describe the day-to-day practices of two teachers at a Melbourne state secondary school as they speak about

---

[2] Open-ended questions asked of teachers in case studies focus on the following:

1. Tell me about yourself and the work you do.
2. Describe the school and your classroom. Describe the students in your class.
3. Describe the ways you teach your subject matter to your students. What do you see as being good curriculum and practice for your students? What do you see as being changed? Why?
4. What obstacles or enabling factors within and outside of the school impact on the ways that you can implement your curriculum and practice?

their work with international students. The essential feature of a "naturalistic method" of human inquiry (Lincoln and Guba 1985) is that people understand the world around them through the meaning they give to their day-to-day actions. The ad hoc and changing everyday experiences of practitioners are valued and examined, and the thoughtful comments of good teachers about their practice are considered carefully as a first step towards building a compendium of good teaching practice in schools (Smith 1987, p. 8).

The interweaving and competing discourses that link the sociohistorical trajectories that map out the day-to-day experience of the social world formulate the relation between day-to-day practice and the taken-for-granted "historical forever". This "terrain of imagination", which frames everyday practice and social conditions (Anderson 1991; O'Callaghan 1995, p. 22), describes a multilayered complexity of discoursal space that is profoundly material as different notional forms are played across patterned fields of power that constitute and transform social relations and identities. It explores the relation between culture as it refers to the ways of understanding and being in the world and culture as it constructs that understanding. Both a participant in the researched context and an observer of it, the researcher can view these spaces of "imagination" from three different, but integrated vantage points: that of (a) *narrational practices* (the seemingly ad hoc individual experiences and stories that describe the ways experiencing individuals understand and participate in their day-to-day worlds); (b) *narrational fields* (the debates and arguments that make up contingent and often disjunctive ways in which meaning and practice are related to a particular conceptual or practical domain); and (c) *narrational maps* (the logic, or terms and conditions of the debate as they appear as essential ways of knowing and being in the world).[3]

In the next section, I examine examples of the ways two teachers speak about science teaching as a way of interrogating the ambiguous notions that articulate the nexus between the complex ways that teacher's perceptions about culture and its practice are played out in their pedagogy.[4]

The Culture of Pedagogical Practice

The tree-lined streets, two-story houses, and landscaped gardens that surround the green ovals of Inglebank Secondary College provide a vision of gentrified suburban Melbourne that is deceptive. Few parents in the immediate vicinity send their children here. The majority of domestic students come from outside this upper middle-class and traditionally Anglo-Australian area, including some who travel kilometers to come to the school from Melbourne's outer suburbs. They come from a diversity

---

[3] See Arber (2008b) for a more detailed explication of this framework for analytical abstraction.

[4] The names of all individuals and schools have been changed to maintain anonymity. Data from this case study taken from much larger research projects have been discussed elsewhere (Arber 2008a, p. 9).

of ethnic and non-English-speaking backgrounds and are mostly of low socioeconomic background, of mixed academic aspiration and ability. The school, one of the first government schools to do so, implemented an international students program to maintain student numbers and funding. There are now nearly 80 international students at the school: 60% are from China; the rest are from Hong Kong, Thailand, Taiwan, Korea, Japan, and East Timor.

The chemistry teacher at Inglebank, Dale Collins, describes how good pedagogies for international students might be understood:

> ...you've got to create pictures in their minds and hope that you're skilled enough to put the right picture in their minds. It is a skill that takes a long time to develop. And it's OK in your own language, but we will then deal with second language speakers, it's another ball game again... So images that I build up in chemistry are sometimes very difficult for non-English-speaking-background kids to deal with.
> Ruth: Can you kind of...
> Collins: ...well if I was trying to introduce the concept of bonding in chemistry, how it works, that it's electrostatic in origin. Positive and negative charges, I use imagery or diagrams. Sometimes they're a little...
> Ruth: ...you have to explain it in more detail cause I'm not much of a chemist. So [if] you were going to...bonding, what kind of imagery would you mean?
> Collins: All matter is made up of atoms etc. And they're all bonded together electrostatically, that is positive and negative attractions.

The pedagogies Collins has developed to explain his material to his students has (at least) three principles. First, the essential vocabularies and principles of chemistry thinking can be modeled. Chemistry is described as an overarching notional and behavioral medium containing symbols and structures that are systematic and rule based. It has a substantive condition in which "All matter is made up of atoms etc.", which are "all bonded together electrostatically" and have "positive and negative charges". A first principle of learning chemistry is to define and categorize these terms and conditions, which make up the language of chemistry.

Secondly, the systemic and unitary elements of chemistry, which make up the embodied nature of chemistry, are located and described in relation to each other. Chemistry is envisioned as embodied within a multidimensional everyday world. The concept of "bonding" in chemistry refers to the ways in which atoms are drawn together "electrostatically" through their "positive and negative charges". Over time, Collins has developed "skills" and knowledge that make the concrete nature of the chemical world visible to his students. Chemistry pedagogy describes the skills and knowledge the teacher employs in order to convey that reality, including the use of molecular model kits, diagrams, and software.

Thirdly, understanding these rules involves the development of an overarching picture or image which needs to be understood if students are to be able to understand chemistry itself. It is a matter of telling a "story", providing an "image" that will help students develop the "right picture in their minds". These ways of thinking are described within normative frameworks that are held to represent chemistry generally. They assume that we are part of an everyday world made up of miniscule particles that function in relation to one another and which can be interacted with through human agency. Understanding the subject matter of chemistry assumes that students not only understand chemical concepts, but that they understand and can work within the meaningful framework on which the discussion of chemistry is predicated.

Collins prides his ability, acquired over the years, to integrate his students (both local and international) into the particularities of the ontological context that provides the terms and conditions for understanding chemistry. Collins' concern that students get the story right can be read in two ways. The first describes a dedicated teacher's concern that his students understand correctly the notions he describes. The second suggests that that science and chemistry might be understood differently through the lens of different languages and cultures and at different times. The meaning frameworks that Collins defines are themselves framed through the taken-for-granted mass of discourse that describes his subject matter and the ways it should be understood and practiced in his classroom. To induct his students meaningfully into the classroom, the institutional and normative frames that provide this shaping context must be explored.

Collins finds his push to implement his preferred teaching pedagogies mediated by institutional demands and mores. The "pressure" of getting through the curriculum on time forces him to work through the course rapidly and to prepare students to cover specific exam content. He finds that his teaching effort is focused on more technical aspects of curriculum and that he has little time to work with the ontological understandings he argues are crucial to the study of chemistry as:

> There's also the added pressure on a teacher that they've got to get through a curriculum. But you can't slow down too much or diverge too much. You've got to stay fairly well on track 'cause you've got an obligation to get through a certain body of information or content...and you just don't have the time to get up to all of them.

Moreover, Collins has developed his pedagogic skills in response to what he perceives as the pedagogical needs of his students. He describes these needs as a binary between the ways international and local students work within the classroom, which is constructed in relation to the cultural background of his students and places them against what are to him "normal" ways of behaving in classrooms:

> For me initially, I found...I didn't have any skills in knowing how to engage them, because by and large they don't question you. They don't ask questions. They don't put their hands up. They don't respond. They don't tell you if they've got difficulties. Because I think that's the way their education systems were set up. They don't ask questions of the teacher.

The skills Collins describe here pertain to the pedagogies he has developed to include his students within his teaching. These are defined as a negative relation to the ways in which a good student would be expected to behave. He is frustrated by the ways in which international students "don't question", "don't ask questions", "don't put their hand up", "don't respond", "don't tell you if they have difficulties". His repetition of "they don't" emphasizes his frustration with the cultural attributes of students who do not seem to behave in the way he expects of them. The "they" he describes appears as a cohesive and homogeneous mass of students who share some cultural attributes: reluctance to ask and answer questions and competence to understand but not to speak about chemistry. More than a matter of inappropriate individual behaviors, Collins suggests that his students' behaviors reflect cultural characteristics drawn from a foreign and unhelpful home culture. The difficulties that his students have in asking questions are attributes, Collins argues, of "their" culture and "the way their education systems were set up". An East/West binary is set up between international students whose teachers in their own country are not only "reserved", but "aloof" and "not to be questioned", and students who are used to "our system", where students are expected "to question". Collins assumes

> that in their own countries the teacher is more reserved, aloof, is not to be questioned. Whereas our system of education expects students to question, not to just absorb. And by questioning, that makes your lesson much more enjoyable.

Intertwined within Collins' discussion about the knowledge and skills he has developed to introduce the normative context of science discussion is a second way of thinking that describes a binary relation between a cohesive and homogenous cultural alterity (otherness) shared in common by international students and the everyday world of our culture. Crossing between their culture and "ours" is not a fluid condition, but rather a matter of breaking "the ice", or "the barriers":

> I've found to break the ice I have to always confront them one on one during class…And confront them about questions and make them talk to me. And break down those sorts of barriers, and then it starts to work.

Throughout his discussion, Collins' focus has been on the complex pedagogies required to teach abstract chemical notions to students who might not have the linguistic and cultural tools to understand them easily. He argues that within the science subjects chemistry makes the biggest linguistic and conceptual demands on students in their classroom work, and this argument underpins his concern about the difficulties international students have learning about chemistry in a second language. The skills and knowledge he has developed to "engage" his students and induct them into the chemistry culture, work towards providing students with the vocabularies and meaning frameworks they require to work with their subject matter. Collins' argument that language is a "big barrier" to his ability to work with his students takes on different connotations as he switches his conversation focus from his students' linguistic abilities to what he understands as the cultural differences they exhibit. His efforts to "engage" his students—which initially sounds like a perennial appeal made by a teacher frustrated in his efforts to interest his students because of their poor language ability—are described in terms of needing to "break the ice" and "break down…barriers" between groups of students who carry particular cultural attributes. These attributes are essentially differentiated from those held by "ourselves"—a community of "selves", which Collins assumes he is part of and which he understands as differentiated, and which he differentiates, from the cultural attributes of international students.

Even as Collins demonstrates his awareness of the meaning frameworks he weaves for his students to induct them into the chemistry story, he remains unaware of his own positioning within ontological frameworks that identify and position international students as foreign and deficient. A more ambivalent reading of the quote above describes a teacher's engagement with a student who is shy and reticent and separated by a cold, brittle, opaque barrier that needs be shattered and/or melted if communication is to take place. To communicate with his students, Collins tells me, twice, he needs to "confront" them, to "make them" talk to him. His students, no longer to be engaged with, or even to be warmed to, are understood as reluctant others who need to be forced to speak.

Collins' complex understanding of the linguistic and cultural multidimensionality of his subject matter provides him with the skills and knowledge to induct his students into the culture of chemistry. His ability to do this is nevertheless constrained by barriers that are cold and hard and beyond which recalcitrant students need to be forced to transcend if they are to answer his questions. What "it" is that "starts to work" in order to "break down those sorts of barriers" suggests an ambivalence that underpins Collins' engagement with his students.

Encountering the Other

The relationship between teacher definitions of curriculum and practice, notions of culture and the identification and positioning of international students is made apparent in a second teacher interview. Jane Arthur, a physics teacher at Inglebank, explains how attention to the conceptual and mechanical aspects of her teaching content is central to her teaching approach:

> Well a lot of the concepts I visually do with apples and things like this. I use my data show…So I do a lot of visual stuff. Because sometimes you get lots of…pracs…And I have a lot of dictionary sort of stuff…I also go through lots and lots of questions. This means this. This means this. The examiners want this. They ask this or this.
> I model. Do a lot of [modeling] of one question, but all the questions are different… Always go, how to problem solve… Then they have to explain each line and things like this—what rules have been used. And so I have to do a lot of that.

Like Collins, Arthur understands that her subject content and related language notions need to be discussed at several levels. She encourages the use of dictionaries to teach essential vocabulary; she models the appropriate communication genre; she provides time for problem-solving practice; and she uses data displays to focus the subject information and to demonstrate the different section of the data analysis. Integral to her teaching approach are concrete examples of abstract concepts contained in the course:

> Arthur: I also try and make it real life things…I always ask them first what their interests and where their interests are going to lie…So I can draw in those and use as examples when I'm trying to teach the concepts.
> Ruth: Can you give me an example of that?
> Arthur: One girl wants to be an astronaut this year. So when I'm doing certain things like forces and things, we have to do weightlessness, but I'm applying those, that sort of thing.

Arthur understands her teaching content as pertaining to embodied notions that can be explained to students in encoded and systematized ways. Students find the language they need in dictionaries and learn the grammar they require to discuss their subject matter. She is concerned that her students should describe the ways that such physical understandings are manifested in the material world. Her classroom practices ground the physical notions she describes within the students' everyday world. Examples emerge from her students' aspirations and interests: excursions to Lunar Park, games with "hacky sacks" and "slinkies", and jumping from chairs with bent and straight legs.

Arthur teaches things "like forces and things" and "weightlessness", exemplifies them, models them, and applies them. She is frustrated by the lack of preparation students have had to work with the linguistic forms they require to be able to work with the notions that she introduces to them. Students come to the school ill prepared to work within the language system: Arthus contends that:

> in language schools, the language stuff before they come is very basic. Some of them can barely understand what's going on.

Teaching practices implemented by Arthur are concerned with the vocabularies and grammar of physics and the ways that they can be modeled, exemplified, and discussed in the material world. Classroom practices, including the use of dictionaries and student translators, are insufficient to induct her students into their subject matter. Despite Arthur's attempt to demonstrate her subject matter in the real world, students find it difficult to work with the meaning of her subject matter. Unlike Collins, Arthur does not consider ways to make the meaning base of her subject matter transparent. Students struggle to find words to make material the scientific notions and practices Arthur describes within a vague and undefined physical context.

The growing ambivalence that Arthur exhibits towards her students is developed further in the following quote. Predicating her comments with the premise that "Last year" she was "the only Anglo Saxon", Arthur responds to my questions:

> Ruth: How do they get on? I mean what's it like having so many ESL and international students?
> Arthur: Interesting when you're the only Anglo Saxon.
> Ruth: In what respect?
> Arthur: Well I only speak English and even…I haven't got the American twang either. I always say data [dahtuh[5]] instead of data [daytuh]…
> Arthur: I say data [dahtuh] as in English. And then I say dance [dahns] and prance [prahns], and castle [kahsul] and things…
> Arthur: Yes. Because everybody speaks in a different inflection and things like this so I understand the first part of the year certain things are asked, to write things down, but even then…A lot of them don't want to write anything down. They don't really want to write anything down so I give them a certain amount of board notes…
> Ruth: But you were talking too…it sounds almost a lonely situation?

Underlying the conversation with Arthur is a second conversation neither of us broach directly. Arguing that she is the only Anglo Saxon in the classroom, Arthur changes the subject to talk about ways that everyone is different. My reference to her point that she is the only Anglo Saxon, by asking whether she feels lonely, is immediately understood as referring to her initial comment. Despite her assertion

---

[5] Pronunciation convention used by Macquarie Online Dictionary (Accessed 16/12/2009).

that difference did not matter, the theme remains the silent underpinning of our conversation—remained of utmost importance to us. Arthur's discussion of her relationship with her students is made in several moves. In the first part of the quote above she suggests that all people are different and that she shares in that difference: Arthur's argument is that as she has an Australian accent rather than an American accent she, like her students, is different. Her assertion of equivalence between her having a different accent and the linguistic and cultural behaviors and vocabularies her students bring to their study suggests that the differences she describes seem momentarily not to matter, even as they delineate clearly Arthur's sense that she is different from the students in her classroom:

As the conversation continues, the "colorblindness" that underpins her assertion of raced difference slips away.[6] Arthur's students behave contrary to the ways that are expected. They exhibit cultural mannerisms that seem insurmountably different from those exhibited by ourselves. As the conversation continues Arthur's frustration shifts from her annoyance with her particular students to the nebulous and ambivalent quality of the stereotype. Increasingly international, refugee and migrant students—whether from China, Malaysia or Cambodia—behave in similar ways and lose their individuality to become a homogenous mass of others who are "used to just regurgitating" and "just rote learn".

> Arthur: Because they don't want to do anything and if they're used to Chinese teachers as 'god' and they say everything is right. Now I ask questions even if they say the right answer: 'Why do you say that?', and they have to justify it. That's really putting them on the spot because they have to justify it, and they say hold on, justify why you said that. And they have to say out in front of everybody why they were saying that. That's a big thing for Chinese students and Malaysian students that are used to just regurgitating it...Now China—it's sort of the teacher instinct. India is very similar. And they rote learn. Whereas in Cambodia they do more older style things.

The differences shared by her students are now seen as primordially and essentially differentiated—a far cry from her light-hearted analysis of her Australian-accented English. It is not just the students' identities but their culture and societies that are characterized as homogenously other and problematic. In the quote above, teachers who work within the very different cultures represented by international and immigrant students are described as working by "teacher instinct". It is a move that defines teachers from countries as differentiated as China, India, and Cambodia as primitive and faulty and as lacking rationality in the development of their teaching principles.

Interwoven with the conversations that I have had with Collins and Arthur about their pedagogy are other discourses that mediate the ways that they understand their students and their subject matter. Arthur's embodiment of her subject matter within the everyday of her student's lives reflects her understanding of the corporal aspects

---

[6] The multicultural literature describes "colorblindness" as the discourse direction which describes all people as different within a community (see Frankenberg 1993). Those who understand themselves as representative of "normality" simultaneously claim for themselves exotic difference even as they identity certain communities—in this case international and migrant students—as different, and as outside of the mainstream community.

of science. Collins' well-honed teaching skills provide a narrative context for his subject matter, allowing him to speak to the meaningful as well as the symbolic and technical aspects of chemistry. The notional depth and breadth that underpins the ways these two teachers understand their pedagogic culture is interlaced with other understandings that shape the ways their students are identified and included within the classroom.

The Culture of Curriculum and Inclusive Pedagogies

The reflexive and multifaceted dimensions of culture provide a two-dimensional frame to set out a comprehensive and inclusive curriculum for a diverse student cohort entering a changed world marked by global flows and digital interchange.[7] The horizontal axis of my proposed framework delineates the different points from which culture can be defined—as object, as its use in practice, and as the symbolic conception of their practice (Kramsch 1998, p. 1). To be meaningful, curriculum must clarify the symbolic codings through which the world is presented, engage with the visceral and material world that is that social world, and explore the normative notions (values, beliefs, ideas) that provide and draw from the meaning, or narrative, of the thinking and practice that frames the curriculum context. Failure to develop the narrative or storied aspect of culture is to reduce subject matter to its technological and instrumental aspects and it mediates the ways in which students can participate meaningfully within the curriculum. The analysis of discussions by two science teachers of their pedagogy broadens and deepens our understanding of what is at stake here. Collins' view of his subject matter, broader and deeper than that of Arthur, is concerned with the normative, or storied, understanding of subject matter. The systems and elements of chemistry are located within a normative context with its own vocabulary and systemic rules. The overall story or meaning framework that provides the narrative for his chemistry thinking provide the "pictures", the "images", that he strives to build in his students' minds.

Science enjoys a preeminent place within the contemporary curriculum because it can explain the world as we know it and provide the analytic and interpretive skills needed to develop and to participate within that knowing. It provides "one view of the world which is influencing and influenced by social values and which changes as our knowledge and understanding…evolves" (VELS 2009). To be meaningful, the science curriculum needs to explore and to clarify the values, ideas, behaviors, and practices that are integral to its development. It must make clear the symbolic codings through which the science world is presented and engage the visceral and material world that is that science world. The relationship between the material and the symbolic worlds is realized through the meaning or narrative that provides the

---

[7] I would like to thank Professor Paul James, Professor of Globalization, and Cultural Diversity in the Globalism Research Centre and Director of the Global Cities Institute, RMIT, for conversations that provided the groundwork for the thinking behind this framework.

frame and the object of science thinking and practice. To fail to develop the narrative or storied aspect of science culture is to reduce science to its technological and instrumental aspects and mediates the ways in which students can participate meaningfully within its curriculum. In Arthur's terms, it is to be given the "language stuff" without providing the contextual terms and conditions that provide its cultural and linguistic meaning.

Followers of science culture, so often concerned with interrogating notions that have failed to change in the past, habitually fail to interrogate the terms and conditions of science thinking and behaving. The acknowledgment of science curriculum as cultured and as having technical and symbolic aspects that are meaningful insists that we make transparent and interrogate the normative culture that underpins science thinking as it is encoded, embodied, and meaningful—and as it is articulated within the historical trajectories of Eastern and Western interchange, European colonial retreat, and technological interconnectivity. Such a move provides space for science to be taught in more holistic and culturally inclusive ways. Moreover, it provides space for the provision of far-thinking creative and innovative thinking that can explore the changed conditions of time, space, and identity that frame the ways we live and work within a technologically complex and interconnected contemporary world. It forcefully interrogates notions that they-do-not-do-that-there, and insists that the shadow curriculum we espouse be made transparent and accountable.

It is not just that curriculum is cultured, but that it is negotiated reflexively within a context defined by and defining of language and culture. The vertical axis of my framework insists that the multidimensional interactions that take place between individuals, institutional structures, and normative context be questioned. The seemingly ad hoc individual experiences and stories that describe the ways experiencing individuals understand and participate in their day-to-day worlds are negotiated within and negotiate the everyday systemic and conceptual and practical domain of school life. They are practiced within the changing and unequally empowered essential ways of knowing and being in the world that provide their subject and object. In interconnected worlds and marked by histories of Eurocentric colonization and the ascendancy of English as an international language, parents seek out Western and Anglophone education for their children. Discourses about good pedagogy, science thinking, and culture mediate the realization of access provided to school curriculum. These understandings intersect with discourses of normalcy against otherness to define international student as other identities and mediate their access to the curriculum, just as they do for migrant, refugee, and ethnic students.

Conclusion

The question of inclusive education provision for international students in Australian schools cannot be explored separately from the commonsense notions about identity and difference that provide the cultural framing of the discussion. The constructed identity of who-we-are negotiated through the logic of that which we-are-not (ambivalent, grounded in fantasy, and decentered from itself) defines the characteristics of students of another culture, differentiated and far removed from our own. The ambiguous terms of the stereotype describe the characteristics of who-they-are and the essential, primordial, and unchanging elements of an-other and esoteric culture. The international (now immigrant/refugee/ethnic) student comes to represent that which is abnormal, uncomfortable, out of control. The move to control and make comfortable the culture of another—forever disrupted, slipping, and incomplete—underpins the teachers' continuing estrangement from their students, even as it supports their confidence in their reflexive practice. Collins' concern for students who do not act as they should, their different cultures separated from his own by membranes as brittle as ice, and Arthur's "loneliness", or awareness of being "the only Anglo Saxon" in the classroom, surrounded by others who behave in ways that are completely foreign, hint at cultures of race and identity understanding that mediate the implementation of inclusive and internationalized science curriculum within local schools.

The concentration of the encoded and embodied aspects of culture and language and the neglect of its normative and ontological aspects not only leads to the assumption of the right story without ever saying what it is; it fails to provide students with the normative understandings they require to properly explore the curriculum. Too often this means that the culture of pedagogy becomes renegotiated in ways that redefine international students, and therefore the curriculum provided to them, as deficient and simple: devoid of anything more than its encoded and technical aspects; parochial in its application and separated from the very meaning aspects that nevertheless continue to provide their framing power.

The study of international student programs in Australia provides insight into the changed demographic of classroom populations in a time of global interchange and participation and into the impact of these changes on education. These changes, along with the changes in technological and digital interchange and ever-faster modes of transportation, impact on the ways that notions of identity and difference are played out and cultural flows are understood, interpreted, and practiced. Calls for comprehensive and far-thinking curriculum and pedagogies lay out the requirements for pedagogical changes that provide access to lifelong and analytic skills and intercultural competencies. A more comprehensive and inclusive curriculum demands that the cultural overlay that frames classroom practice be understood reflexively to interrogate and to implement in other ways the practices, systemic conditions, and normative mores that define and mediate classroom interactions and curricula.

References

Anderson, B. (1991). *Imagined communities: Reflections on the origin and spread of nationalism.* London: Verso.

Arber, R. (2008a). Interrogating 'imagined' communities: Exploring the impact of international students in local schools. *Race and Ethnicity and Education, 11*(4), 387–405.

Arber, R. (2008b). *Race, ethnicity and education in globalised times*. Dordrecht: Springer.

Arber, R. (2009). Discourses of antagonism and desire: Marketing for international students in neighbourhood schools. *Globalisation, Societies Education, 7*(2), 109–112.

Arber, R., & Blackmore, J. (2007). *Impact of internationalisation on secondary schooling and teachers*. Unpublished study. Melbourne: Deakin University.

Australian Government, Australian Education International (2009). International student data. http://www.aei.gov.au/AEI/MIP/Statistics/StudentEnrolmentAndVisaStatistics/Default.htm. Accessed 18 September 2009.

Bauman, Z. (1999). *Culture as praxis*. London: Sage.

Bekerman, Z. (2003). Hidden dangers in multicultural discourse. *Race Equality and Teaching, 21*(3), 36–42.

Bhabha, H. (1994). *The location of culture*. Abingdon: Routledge.

Bishop, A. J. (1995). Western mathematics: The secret weapon of cultural imperialism. In B. Ashcroft, G. Griffin, & H. Tiffin (Eds.), *The post-colonial studies reader*. London: Routledge.

Bourdieu, P. (2007). *Bachelors ball: The crisis of peasant society in Béarn*. London: Polity Press.

Brah, A. (1996). *Cartographies of diaspora: Contesting identities*. London: Routledge.

Butler, J. (1997). *Excitable speech: A politics of the performative*. New York: Routledge.

Carroll, J., & Ryan, J. (Eds.). (2005). *Teaching international students: Improving learning for all*. London: Routledge.

Deng, Z., & Luke, A. (2007). Subject matter: Defining and theorizing school subjects. In F. M. Connelly, M. F. He, & J. Phillion (Eds.), *The Sage handbook of curriculum and instruction*. Thousand Oaks: Sage.

Denzin, N., & Lincoln, Y. (1998). *The landscape of qualitative research: Theories and issues*. Thousand Oaks: Sage.

Dwyer, R. (1997). *White*. London: Routledge.

Frankenberg, R. (1993). *White women, race matters: The social construction of whiteness*. London: Routledge.

Gee, J. (1996). *Social linguistics and literacies: Ideology in discourses*. Bristol: Taylor & Francis.

Gee, J., & Green, J. (1998). Discourse analysis, learning, and social practice: A methodological study. *Review of Research in Education, 23*, 119–169.

Giroux, H. (2001). *Theory and resistance in education: Towards a pedagogy for the opposition*. Westport: Bergin & Garvey.

Goldberg, D. T. (1994). *Racist culture: Philosophy and the politics of meaning*. Oxford: Blackwell.

Hall, S. (1997). *Representation: Cultural representations and signifying practices (Culture, media and identities series)*. Milton Keynes: Open University.

Kramsch, C. (1993). *Context and culture in language teaching*. Oxford: Oxford University Press.

Kramsch, C. (1998). *Language and culture*. Oxford: Oxford University Press.

Lemke, J. (2002). Ideology, intertextuality, and the communication of science. In P. H. Fries, M. Cummings, D. Lockwood & W. Spruiell (Eds.), *Relations and functions within and around language* (pp. 32–55). New York: Continuum.

Lincoln, Y. S., & Guba, E. G. (1985). *Naturalistic inquiry*. Thousand Oaks: Sage.

Luke, A. (2003). Introduction. In J. Miller (Ed.), *Audible difference: ESL and social difference in schools*. Sydney: Multilingual Matters.

McKay, S. (2002). *Teaching English as an international language: Rethinking goals and approaches*. New York: Oxford University Press.

O'Callaghan, M. (1995). Continuities in imagination. In J. N. Pieterse & B. Parekh (Eds.), *The decolonisation of imagination*. London: Zed Books.

Rizvi, F. (2005). International education and the production of cosmopolitan identities, Globalization and higher education, RIHE International publication series 9. https://www.ideals.illinois.edu/bitstream/handle/2142/3516/TSRizvi.pdf?sequence=2. Accessed 5 December 2009.

Rizvi, F. (2009). Teaching global interconnectivity. http://www.curriculum.edu.au/verve/_resources/Rizvi_Teaching_Global_Interconnectivity_v.1.pdf. Accessed September 2009.

Smith, D. (1987). *The everyday world as problematic: A feminist sociology.* Toronto: University of Toronto Press.
State Government of Victoria, Victorian Curriculum and Assessment Authority (2009). Victorian essential learning standards, P1–10 curriculum learning standards, introduction to science. http://vels.vcaa.vic.edu.au/science/intro.html. Accessed 16 September 2009.
Youdell, D. (2006). *Impossible bodies, impossible selves: Exclusion and student subjectivities.* Dordrecht: Springer.
VELS. (2009). see State Government of Victoria, Victorian Curriculum and Assessment Authority.

Chapter 31
Possible Selves and Goal Orientations of East-African Undergraduate Students in the United States

Joash M. Wambua and Cecil Robinson

Introduction

The United States is a leading destination for many immigrants. In 1998, 20% of all the children in the United States were immigrants (Hernandez 1999), and one of every five children under the age of 18 in the United States has at least one foreign-born parent (National Center for Educational Surveys 2000). Increasing among this immigrant population is Africans.

English-speaking Africans began to favor the United States after the passage of the 1965 Hart-Cellar Immigration Act, which allowed for the admission of immigrants based on their skills, professions, or relationship to families in the United States (Okome 2002). This trend increased in 1990 with the passing of the Diversity Visa Lottery Law, which offered immigrant visas to high school graduates from underrepresented countries. As a result of the immigration laws, of the nearly 38 million people classified by the US Census Bureau as Black, African-American, approximately one million are African born (Eissa 2005). Next to Caribbean immigrants, Africans constitute the largest flow of blacks to America (Reid 1986).

Although there are a significant number of African immigrants in the United States, there is little research literature about African immigration to the United States especially when compared to the research literature about European, Asian, and Hispanic immigration. Of the available research, most is comprised of case studies on the causes for migrating, demographics, and social conditions of African immigrants in America (Bangura 2005). For example, Takyi (2002) documented the experiences of African immigrants. He identified four reasons for African immigration to the United States: political instability in their countries, the historical structural paradigm of dependence relations, changing immigration policies in the United States and the search for educational opportunities. Though education is a reason for immigration, he does not describe their educational experiences. Indeed, little has been written about the education of African immigrants in the United

---

J. M. Wambua (✉)
Miles College, 1652 Heritage Place, Birmingham, Al. 35210, USA
e-mail: wambua@juno.com

States (Traore and Elcock 2003). One reason for this lack of research may be the categorical methods of the US Census Bureau—African Immigrants are not separated from African-Americans.

The conflation of Africans and African-Americans poses a problem because there are substantial historical and sociocultural differences. Africans have a collectivist culture, while African-Americans have an individualistic culture (Triandis 1995). Another difference is the distinction between voluntary and involuntary minority statuses (Ogbu 1983, 1991). Ogbu posited that African-Americans are involuntary immigrants whose minority status is a result of historical subjection after forced migration (i.e., descendants of slaves), and tend to have an oppositional approach to society. In contrast, African immigrants are voluntary immigrants whose minority status is a result of their choice to migrate to the United States. Voluntary immigrants generally have an instrumental approach to their host society and institutions, holding them as valuable and useful.

Such differences are important because academic achievement is associated with employment opportunities (Muslow and Murry 1996). African-born residents in the United States are highly educated, urbanized, and have one of the highest per capita incomes of any immigrant group (Katende 1994; Butcher 1995). Three quarters have some college experience and one in four has an advanced degree (Speer 1994). These figures surpass those of African-Americans. Another reason why these differences and lack of research on African immigrants is important is that a lack of research denies the American public, and policy makers, opportunities to explore the many urgent and intriguing issues concerning black immigrants and contributes to the neglect of their special needs (Rong and Brown 2001).

Rong and Brown specifically suggested the need for research focusing on the development of beliefs and attitudes affecting African immigrants' self-perceptions, ethnicity and identity, and on strategies to manage the pressure to adapt. Their suggestion in combination with the growing African immigrant population in the United States and the limited educational research on African immigrants was the impetus for this study, which examined motivational characteristics, racial–ethnic identities, and sociocultural measures of African immigrants.

Possible Selves and Achievement Goal Orientation

Goals represent a cornerstone within achievement motivation, providing anchors around which students gather energy and determine viable pathways to achieve them. Two types of goals that function within academic settings are general goals and achievement goals (Pintrich 2000). General goals are broad goals that represent a future orientation, or a sense of becoming that an individual is striving for. As such, future general goals provide direction for students to direct energy and attention. Those without general goals lack direction and motivation, and are at-risk for low academic success. Achievement goals describe how students work toward general goals. That is, achievement goals orient student motivation as they strive to achieve their general goals. In this study, we examine general goals through the concept of possible selves, and achievement goals through academic goal orientation (Pintrich 2000).

Possible selves is a motivational construct that examines the extent to which individuals think about and conceptualize what their future may hold and the extent to which they create strategies to act on their future goals (Markus and Nurius 1986). Possible selves represent what we might become, what we hope to become and what we fear becoming. These future goals motivate behavior when individuals link their present condition to these potential goals through a set of self-representations that lead to the goal (Markus et al. 1990). We chose to use possible selves because it is a strong predictor of academic success (Oyserman et al. 1995; Oyserman and Markus 1990) and persistence (Leondari et al. 1998); has been used successfully cross-culturally (Oyserman et al. 2001); and is relevant to young people who spend a lot of time contemplating what the future might hold for them (Lobenstine et al. 2001).

Achievement goal theory identifies two types of goals: mastery and performance goals (Ames 1992). Students with mastery goal orientation engage in academic work in order to improve their competency. They work toward future goals as a means to learn and better themselves, attribute failure to lack of effort, choose moderately challenging tasks, and use more self-regulating strategies (Ames 1988). Students with performance goal orientation engage in academic work in order to demonstrate their abilities to outside observers. Their focus is not on learning the material, but on competent performance. As such, they prefer less challenging tasks and use surface processing (Ames 1992; Dweck and Leggett 1988). Although the terms used for achievement goal orientation varies (Anderman and Midgley 1997; Elliott and Dweck 1988; Nicholls 1984), research consistently describes the types of goals similarly, and finds benefits of mastery over performance goals.

Racial–Ethnic Identities and Gender Differences

African students face more adjustment problems in relation to universities in host countries than do their native counterparts (Adelegan and Parks 1985; Pruit 1978). Like other immigrants to the United States, African students earn a living through traditional entry-level employment. When these kinds of jobs are compounded with the demands of attending school, it makes for a difficult life. One of the tasks immigrants face in acculturating to the United States is learning how to ethnically classify themselves within America (Walters 2000). Racial–ethnic identities develop throughout the lifespan and impact reference groups by the determining traits and competencies of a social identity; establishing and communicating the status of social identities; and forming the basis of social feedback regarding one's traits, competencies, and values (Leonard 1995).

Racial–ethnic identity improves academic competence when one embeds achievement as integral to one's racial–ethnic group and uses it as a defining in-group value to focus attention and motivation on ways to learn and succeed (Oyserman et al. 2001). This bolsters academic efficacy by making achievement a function of ingroup membership. Previous research highlights differences in the racial identity of African and African-American graduate students (Bagley and Copeland 1994), but more research is needed on the racial identities of African undergraduate students to examine how identities may affect their academic goals and motivation.

Research also needs to differentiate between men and women. A comparative overview of Africans in the United States identified socialization factors that disadvantage women (Maundeni 1999). This leads to increased stress to female students, lower self-esteem and feelings of shame and guilt. Possible selves may be particularly useful for the assessment of female self-esteem because it includes feared selves and past research demonstrates its relationship to female self-esteem (Knox et al. 2000).

Purpose

This study explores possible selves, academic goal orientations and racial–ethnic identities of male and female East-African undergraduate students in the United States. Based on this objective, the research question for this investigation was: What is the relationship among possible selves and academic goal orientations and how does the relationship vary by racial–ethnic identity and gender among East-African undergraduate students in the United States?

Method

Participants

Black-African undergraduate students from four postsecondary schools in the Southeast United States participated in this study. The schools were located across two states and consisted of one public research university, two 4-year historically black colleges, and one community college. Most participants (91%) were from the East-African countries of Kenya, Tanzania, and Uganda ($N=175$). Because the sample was skewed, a decision was made to use the East-African sample and drop the other participants. This decision limited the number of participants but had the benefit of approximating greater cultural similarity. Although this study does not account for the diverse tribes within East Africa, it represents greater homogeneity than considering all African countries.

There were 47% females and 53% males, with ages ranging from 19 to 30 years. Students either attended a 4-year university (46%), a 4-year college (17%), or a 2-year community college (37%). There was even distribution among academic standing (freshman, sophomore, etc.), and the majority had health (46%) or business (28%) related majors. The length of time in the United States ranged from less than 6 months to more than 7 years. About half of the students (49%) received financial support from their families.

Materials

Demographic Information

A self-report questionnaire asked students to provide background information about gender, age, length of time in the United States, academic standing, academic major, and familial financial support to attend school as family resources predict school outcomes (Coleman Report 1966).

Possible Selves Questionnaire

The possible selves questionnaire (PSQ; Oyserman 2004) measures what people believe they might become (expected or hoped for selves), what people are afraid of becoming (feared or avoided selves), the strategies people use to become or avoid becoming, and the relationship between expected and feared selves. To assess expected selves, participants generated a list of goals. "Think about next year—imagine what you'll be like, and what you'll be doing next year. In the lines below, write what you expect you will be like and what you expect to be doing next year." Next, participants indicated whether they are currently working on the goal or expectation. If participants indicated they were working on the goal, then they wrote strategies they were using to attain the goal.

To assess feared selves, participants generated a list of their avoided selves. "Think a minute about ways you would not like to be next year—*things you are concerned about or want to avoid being like.* Write those concerns or selves to-be-avoided in the lines below." Next, participants indicated whether they were currently working on avoiding that concern. If so, then participants wrote strategies they were using to reduce the chances their concern would describe them next year.

Coding participants' responses was completed using the method specified by Oyserman (2004). Counts were created based on the list of student generated expected and feared selves. The counts included only expected and feared items that students were actively pursuing or avoiding, respectively, through a listed strategy. These lists were compared to identify the number of balanced possible selves, which has maximal motivational effectiveness (Oyserman and Markus 1990). A balanced possible self resulted when an item in the expected possible selves list corresponded to an item in the feared possible selves list. As such, balanced possible selves were the number of pairs of expected and feared possible selves that contain opposite sides of the same issue in the same domain. Using balanced possible selves is a reliable method that produces scores ranging from 0.42 to 3.23 (Oyserman 2004; Oyserman et al. 2006; Oyserman and Markus 1990). Two independent raters identified the number of balanced possible selves with an interrater reliability of .87.

Personal Achievement Goal Orientation Scale

The personal achievement goal orientation scale (PAGOS) is a subscale from the Patterns of Adaptive Learning Scale (PALS; Midgley et al. 2000). The PAGOS has 14 items that are rated on a five-point Likert scale ranging from 1 (strongly disagree) to 5 (strongly agree), measures three types of goal orientations with adequate reliability ($.74 \leq \alpha \leq .89$) and mean scores ranging from 2.56 to 4.57. *Mastery goals* orient students to develop or improve competence (e.g., "One of my goals in class is to learn as much as I can."). *Performance approach goals* orient students to demonstrate their competence (e.g., "One of my goals is to show others that I'm good at my class work."). *Performance avoidance goals* orient students to avoid the demonstration of incompetence (e.g., "One of my goals in class is to avoid looking like I have trouble doing the work.") (Midgley et al. 2000).

The Racial–Ethnic Identity Assessment

The Racial–Ethnic Identity Assessment (REIA; Oyserman et al. 1995) measures three components of racial-ethnicity. *Connectedness* is positive ingroup identification and pride in one's ethnic group. *Awareness of racism* is negative outgroup perceptions. *Embedded achievement* is the extent to which academic achievement is viewed as an integral part of one's ethnic group (Oyserman et al. 2001). The REIA contains 14 items that are rated on a five-point Likert scale ranging from 1 (strongly disagree) to 5 (strongly agree), and has adequate reliability ($.58 \leq \alpha \leq .79$) (Altschul et al. 2006; Oyserman et al. 2006). The items used in this study were modified to reflect African instead of African-Americans students. The connectedness subscale contains four items (e.g., "I feel that I am a part of the African community."). The awareness of racism subscale contains four items (e.g., "Some people will treat me differently because I am black."). Embedded achievement has four items (e.g., "If I work hard and get good grades, other Africans will respect me").

Procedure

Students were recruited through announcements on bulletin boards, community meetings, and at International and African student Association meetings. Additional students were recruited by word of mouth using a snowball technique. Participants were informed about the study, signed informed consent forms, and received, completed and returned a packet of information that contained a cover letter, a questionnaire consisting of the demographic questions and surveys (PSQ, PALS, and REIA) and a pencil to record their responses.

Results

Descriptive Statistics

The possible selves and goal orientation scores were consistent with previous research, and goal orientation and racial–ethnic identity measures demonstrated adequate scale reliability (Table 31.1). These results lend evidence about the reliability and validity of students' responses to the survey items. The racial–ethnic identity scores, however, deviated from the previous research.

Racial–Ethnic Identity of East-African Students

Connectedness scores were slightly higher for East-African students ($M=4.53$) compared to African-American students ($M=4.29$; Altschul et al. 2006). Higher connectedness regarding one's ethnic group is likely related to the collectivist nature of African culture, which has greater focus on relationships and group membership. This is in contrast to the individualistic US culture with greater focus on independence and distinction from others (Markus and Kitayama 1991; Triandis 1995).

Embedded achievement scores were higher for East-African students ($M=4.55$) compared to African-American students ($M=3.83$; Altschul et al. 2006). The importance of academic achievement on ethnic identity is evident in their actions to pursue higher education degrees in the United States. Although part of a collectivist culture, the importance of education led these students to leave families, tribes, and countries to make their pursuit a reality. Further, the importance of academic

Table 31.1 Means, standard deviations, and reliability coefficients for possible selves, goal orientation and racial–ethnic identity ($N=175$)

	M	SD	α
Balanced Possible Selves	1.55	.98	–
Expected Possible Selves	2.54	1.09	–
Feared Possible Selves	2.24	1.16	–
Mastery Goal Orientation	4.72	.45	.80
Performance Approach Goal Orientation	2.57	1.05	.82
Performance Avoidance Goal Orientation	2.72	1.24	.83
Racial–Ethnic Identity: Connectedness	4.53	.62	.74
Racial–Ethnic Identity: Embedded Achievement	4.55	.54	.53
Racial–Ethnic Identity: Awareness of Racism	2.96	.87	.57

achievement as a component of racial–ethnic identity increased the longer students lived in the United States to pursue their education ($r=.20$, $p=.01$). Embedded achievement as a component of East-African's ethnic identity is also consistent with the previous research. As mentioned in the introduction, African residents in the United States are highly educated (Butcher 1995; Katende 1994; Speer 1994), whereas many African-American students develop an oppositional identity to educational achievement (Ogbu 1991).

East-African students also reported a lower awareness of racism ($M=2.96$) than African-American students ($M=3.56$; Altschul et al. 2006). East-African students have spent most of their lives in countries that are overwhelmingly black. As the dominant race in their countries, they are much less likely to have encountered or be aware of racism. More likely, students would have greater awareness of tribalism if the students belonged to a minority tribe.

Although students were raised in a predominantly black country, they assumed a minority status once they entered the United States. Research suggests contexts that make membership to one's racial–ethnic group salient are likely to result in individuals defining the self in racial–ethnic terms, that is to redefine their racial–ethnic identity (Cross and Markus 1991; Oyserman et al. 2003). To test whether their awareness of racism increased once they entered the United States and assumed a minority status, we examined the relationship between awareness of racism and length of stay in the United States. We found that awareness of racism remained unchanged regardless of length of stay ($r=-.08$, $p>.10$). These findings do not support claims about the contextual development of racial–ethnic identity. Instead, the findings are consistent with developmental research that suggests awareness of racism is incorporated into one's racial–ethnic identity by early to mid adolescence (Bigler et al. 2003; Quintana and Segura-Herrera 2003). Alternatively, we think that context may matter, but that our finding may highlight differences in the ways that East-African students experience minority status than African-Americans in the United States. Whereas East Africans may view American Whites as different, they also may see them as instrumental in attaining their educational goals (Ogbu 1991). Further, they may not view American Whites as former slave owners and the legacy that endures for African-Americans. Using this same line of argument, it is conceivable that students who grow up in South Africa, with a significant white population and legacy of apartheid, would have greater awareness of racism because the context makes their racial–ethnic identity more salient. Similarly, living and studying in England may also provide a context that changes the way East-African students experience minority racial–ethnic status because of the brutal legacy of British colonization of East-African countries, resulting in increased awareness of racism into their racial–ethnic identities.

Taken together, the results highlight differences between East-African and African-American students on each component of racial–ethnic identity. The different racial–ethnic identities of these students provide additional evidence supporting the need to disambiguate African immigrants from African-Americans in census data and educational research in the United States.

Personal and Environmental Factors Influencing Possible Selves

Identifying significant personal and environmental factors provided insight into the possible selves of East-African students, and allowed us to control for these factors when examining the relationships between possible selves, academic goal orientation and racial–ethnic identity. Multiple regression analyses were used to test which factors were related to possible selves. The personal factors tested were: age, academic standing (freshman, sophomore, junior, or senior), and self-support (the degree to which the student was financially independent or dependent on financial aid from others). The environmental factors tested were: school (university, 4-year college, 2-year community college); length of stay (amount of time students have lived in the United States; and academic major. Results suggest two environmental factors—*length of stay* and *school* (whether the student attended a 4-year university) and one personal factor—*self-support*, were significantly related to possible selves.

Balanced possible selves was related to length of stay ($\beta=.375, p<.01$) and attending a 4-year university ($\beta=.219, p=.04$). Students who attended a 4-year university and lived in the United States for a longer period of time had a greater number of balanced possible selves than students who attended a 4-year college or 2-year community college and only recently moved to the United States. Expected and feared possible selves, components that constitute balanced possible selves, were each related to length of stay and self-support ($\beta s \geq .219, ps \leq .01$). The longer students lived in the United States and greater financial independence led to an increased number of expected and feared possible selves.

These findings highlight the importance of personal and environment factors on the development of East-African students' possible selves as students acculturate from a collectivist culture into an individualistic culture. Possible selves are measures of the number of future goals that students are actively trying to pursue or avoid. Using goals to drive current action is goal-directedness, the central principle of action-regulation for individualistic cultures (Kitayama et al. 2007). This acculturation appears to be occurring at the person level, as financial independence (which requires planning for the future) leads to a greater number of future goals or possible selves. Academic and societal environments also seem to influence acculturation as well. Studying at a 4-year university has greater academic options, and may be more demanding and less intimate (faculty-to-student ratio) than a 4-year college or 2-year community college. This type of academic environment requires greater planning and self-regulation to be successful—all aspects of goal-directedness—and leads to increased possible selves. Finally, the United States in general is highly individualistic and goal-directed. The longer students live within this social milieu, the more they take on its characteristics.

Relationship Between Possible Selves and Academic Goal Orientation

The main purpose of this study was to explore the relationship between possible selves and academic goal orientation of East-African students. Results suggest a significant relationship. A regression model that controlled for personal (self-support) and environmental factors (length of stay and school) indicated that academic goal orientation (mastery, performance-approach, and performance-avoidance) was significantly related to possible selves [$R^2=.198$, $F(6168)=6.906$, $p<.001$]. However, mastery goals was the only goal orientation that predicted possible selves ($\beta=.18$, $p=.013$). This finding is inconsistent with previous research that suggests performance-approach goals influence possible selves (Anderman et al. 1999), and highlights another potential difference between African-American and East-African students.

Possible Selves, Academic Goal Orientation, and Gender

To examine whether the relationship between possible selves and goal orientation varied by gender, we first tested for gender differences between the reported possible selves and academic goal orientation scores. Analysis of variance revealed no gender differences across any measure ($ps>.10$). Next, we elaborated on the regression model described above and found that gender was not related to possible selves ($p>.10$). Finally, we tested whether gender interacted with goal orientation to predict possible selves, and found no significant relationships ($ps>.10$), indicating that students' possible selves and goal orientations do not vary by gender. These findings are consistent with previous research (Leondari et al. 1998; Oyserman et al. 1995). However, the results do not support research that argues possible selves differ across gender within diverse populations in the United States (Knox et al. 2000; Oyserman and Fryberg 2006).

Possible Selves, Academic Goal Orientation, and Racial–Ethnic Identity

To examine whether the relationship between possible selves and goal orientation varied by racial–ethnic identity, we elaborated on the regression model described in the previous two sections. We found that none of the measures of racial–ethnic identity (connectedness, embedded achievement, and awareness of racism) was directly related to possible selves ($ps>.10$), and also found that East-African students' possible selves and goal orientations do not vary by racial–ethnic identity ($ps>.10$). Our findings contrast with previous research that demonstrated a significant relationship between racial–ethnic identity and possible selves for African-American, Asian American, Latina/o and White students (Kao 2000; Oyserman et al. 2006; Oyserman et al. 1995; Oyserman et al. 2003). This finding lends additional evidence to differences between African and African-American students studying in the United States.

Discussion

Although the United States is experiencing a wave of African immigration, little research exists compared to other immigrant groups. This research gap is problematic because it prevents the American public and its policy makers to address issues concerning African immigrants. This chapter attempted to address a small slice of the needed research. Specifically, the need for research regarding beliefs and attitudes affecting African immigrants' self-perceptions and identity, and strategies to manage the pressure to adapt as racial–ethnic minorities in the United States (Rong and Brown 2002). In the sections below, we discuss differences identified between East-African and African-American students, the policy implications of these differences, and future directions for this work.

Differences Between East-African and African-American Students

One reason for the limited research on African immigrants in the United States is conflation with African-Americans even though there are documented cultural and academic differences between these groups. As mentioned in the introduction, Africans have a more collectivist culture and take on a voluntary minority status within the United States. African-Americans have a more individualistic culture and take on an involuntary minority status (Markus and Kitayama 1991; Ogbu 1983, 1991; Triandis 1995). There are also differences in educational achievement (US Census Bureau 2000).

An important finding of this chapter is the differences between East-African and African-American students' racial–ethnic identity, academic goals, and motivation. These differences are important because each is related to the cultural and academic differences described above.

Culture affects the development of racial–ethnic identity. Collectivist cultures orients the self toward group-centeredness, whereas individualistic cultures orients the self toward self-centeredness. Our results suggest that East-African students' appropriated group-centeredness not only as a cultural practice or meaning system, but also as a component of their racial–ethnic identity as evidenced through a greater sense of connectedness with their African community compared to African-Americans.

Racial–ethnic identity, academic goals and motivation also appear to affect positive academic outcomes. Academic achievement was highly embedded within the East-African community; that is, doing well academically was a greater source of respect and more important part of one's identity compared to African-Americans. This result in conjunction with a high sense of connectedness creates a greater likelihood of academic success because it is no longer an externalized achievement, but an integral part of themselves and as a member of their African ethnic group.

The high sense of connectedness and embedded achievement may also explain the low awareness of racism. As we argued earlier, low awareness may have resulted from growing up in countries that are mostly black. However, after entering the United States they assumed a minority status making their ethnicity more salient. This should have led to increased awareness of racism the longer they lived in the United States, but this was not the case. The length of time had no affect. This is not to say that racism is any less present for African or African-American students. Rather, African students did not perceive it and was therefore a less salient component of their racial–ethnic identity. One possible explanation is that the connectedness and embedded achievement components of their racial–ethnic identity were the most salient and well developed. Therefore, the East-African students may view American whites as different, but more importantly, view them as instrumental in attaining their educational goals as a means to remain true to their connected, embedded achievement selves.

East-African students also had goal orientations that were more supportive of academic achievement than African-Americans. African-American students' achievement of future goals is often driven by an externalized motivation to demonstrate competence to teachers and classmates by outperforming classmates on assignments and exams (Anderman et al. 1999). Our findings demonstrate that East-African students' possible selves are influenced by mastery goals, a drive to achieve future goals through an internalized motivation to learn by mastering the material covered in academic course work and putting forth the necessary effort to develop and continue to improve upon that mastery. This type of orientation leads to challenging goals, greater persistence in goal pursuit, and increased attainment of goals (Schunk and Zimmerman 2006).

Policy Implications

Although collectivist East-African culture influences the racial–ethnic identity of its students, our study also demonstrates that these students are acculturating into an individualistic US culture. The longer East-African students live in the United States, they increase the number of expected, feared, and balanced possible selves—each of which represent goal-directed action and regulation characteristic the individualistic cultures (Kitayama et al. 2007). However, as East-African students acculturate in the United States, they may take on characteristics of US students that may place them at risk academically and move away from characteristics of an

African identity that supports academic achievement. Each has policy implications for higher education counselors, faculty, and administrators.

In this current culture of accountability in the United States, an unyielding emphasis has been placed on demonstrating performance related to an increasing number of academic standards. The longer East-African students live and study in the United States, the less they may rely on their current orientation of mastery to drive future goals. Consistent with current US educational practice, they may instead rely on a demonstration of performance to drive future goals. To combat this possibility, sustain East-African students current goal motivation, and to change current US students' goal motivations, we think that higher education faculty and administrators need to promote a culture of mastery goals in the classroom. School and classrooms that support mastery goal structures are effective in promoting and sustaining students' mastery goal orientations (Murayama and Elliott 2009; Patrick and Ryan 2008; Retelsdorf et al. 2009).

To support mastery goal structures and East-African students' continued academic success, we also think it is important that schools provide a physical and psychological space to support a sense of connectedness to their African culture by connecting students to other East-African and African students, and supporting cultural activities—traditional dinners, dances, among other activities. As students acculturate into US culture, their sense of connectedness and by extension, embedded achievement, may be threatened. In this study, we found that connectedness and embedded achievement form a sense of self for East-African students, which ties their identity to academic success. If this identity shifts, due to acculturation into an individualistic culture, then their academic success may also be placed at risk as well. Supporting a space for culturally relevant practices on campus may create more opportunities for East-African students to successfully figure themselves into the college campuses in the United States, while allowing them to maintain their sense of African identity.

In addition to our recommendations listed above, we also think academic advisors at 2-year community colleges and 4-year colleges need to place increased emphasis on goal setting for East-African students. Collectivist cultures direct persons' attention to the harmony of the group, not personal achievement. The primary purpose of this chapter was to explore how East-African students form future goals, or possible selves, as such goal setting is highly predictive of academic success. We make this recommendation because our findings indicate that attending a 4-year university leads to increased number of possible selves for East-African students and that there are no effects for the other institutions we studied. There are two likely reasons for this finding. First, students live in the United States longer when attending a 4-year university compared to a 2-year community college, which creates greater opportunity to acculturate into a goal-oriented individualistic culture. Second, students attending a 4-year university compared to a 4-year college may face more demanding academic course offerings with less individual support due to the size of the institution. This kind of environment requires more goal setting, self-regulation, and planning. To combat these potential negative institutional affects for any international student from a collectivist culture, academic advisors at

2-year community colleges and 4-year colleges need to spend a greater amount of time planning and setting future master-oriented goals with students.

Finally, as we have highlighted throughout this chapter, our findings provide additional evidence about the significant differences between East-African and African-American students. As such, we argue that schools and other social and political institutions need to discontinue practices of grouping the two groups as one. From an educational standpoint this policy may have adversely affect East-African's academic achievement, as grouping East-African immigrants as African-Americans may elicit identities vulnerable to stereotype threat and academic underachievement (Gibson and Ogbu 1991; Steele and Aronson 1995).

Future Studies

This chapter represents an initial exploration into the academic attitudes, beliefs and motivations of East-African college students studying in the United States. This study has provided baseline data about their beliefs and provides outcomes that highlight differences between, and support calls for separating African immigrants from African-Americans in educational policy, practice, and research. However, as an initial exploration, it also raises as many questions as it answers. In this section, we discuss future studies needed to extend our findings.

Future studies need to include a wider range of outcome variables to develop path models of African immigrant students' academic success including, grade point average, school retention and graduation rates, and additional measures that assess subjective, physical and psychological well-being. In addition, longitudinal studies are needed to create developmental models of African immigrant students' academic success and assimilation into an individualistic US culture.

Additional studies also need to include a more diverse African student population. Studies need to examine if our findings hold true for other African regions (e.g., North, West, and South Africa) and countries. Also, we need to recognize that country boundary lines were the result of colonization, and that future studies should also take into account potential tribal differences, which are more natural and historical cultural markers.

Future studies also need to examine a wider range of educational settings. This study focused on college students who grew up and developed their identities in East Africa. The results might differ for first- and second-generation African immigrant students who attend primary, middle, and high school in the United States and have to negotiate between the individualistic, performance-based culture of schooling in the United States and collectivist culture of their parent's heritage.

This study also focused on African immigrants who grew up in a predominantly black country, attending school in a predominantly white country that historically is not an African colonizer. Future studies need to tease apart each of these ethnic-racial and historical-political components. For example, the racial–ethnic identities, specifically the awareness of racism, may be quite different for African students from South Africa or Zimbabwe. These identities may affect motivation variables, attitudes about and relationship to schooling in a predominantly white higher educational schooling system such as the United States. Furthermore, the racial–ethnic identities and relationship to schooling might also differ for African immigrants who attend schools in countries that are historically seen as colonizers (e.g., Kenyans attending school in England, or Rwandans attending school in France).

Future studies need to explore whether African immigrants are able to develop a bicultural identity as they live and go to school in the United States and other countries of destination. That is, studies need to explore whether African immigrants are able to maintain their African racial–ethnic identity while developing an identity as an immigrant in another country. Finally, studies need to explore if educational policy and practice can be developed to promote African immigrants continued academic success.

Conclusions

The conflation of African immigrants with African-Americans has contributed to the low volume of research on the African immigrants, even though there are documented differences between the two groups. This chapter discussed findings that demonstrate that differences extend to motivation and racial–ethnic identities, and that these differences have policy and practice implications for the future academic success of students who immigrate from East Africa. Although more research is needed, this chapter represents a first step in ensuring that the academic needs of African students are met after they immigrate into the United States.

This chapter also highlights the need to consider differences of other immigrant groups in the United States and other countries. As the global community becomes more intricately woven with each other, it is not sufficient to create educational institutions and classrooms that fail to differentiate students because they have similar skin pigmentation. Rather, we need to consider a range of potential differences beyond skin color that affect current and future educational aspirations and achievements, such as cultural history that forms their identity, academic motivation, and shapes their vision of what they can be in the future. Although this chapter only tackles a small slice of potential differences, we hope it becomes an impetus for future studies that continue to tease out such differences and explore how each finding can be used to better meet the needs of our global citizens as they migrate from one country to another.

References

Adelegan, F. O., & Parks, D. J. (1985). Problems of transition for African students in an American university. *Journal of College Student Personnel, 26,* 504–508.

Aloyse-Young, P. A., Henningham, K. M., & Leong, C. W. (2001). *Journal of Early Adolescence, 21*(2), 158–181.

Altschul, I., Oyserman, D., & Bybee, D. (2006). Racial-ethnic identity in mid-adolescence: Content and change as predictors of academic achievement. *Child Development, 77*(5).
Ames, C. (1988, April). *Achievement goals and student learning strategies*. Paper presented at the annual meeting of the American Educational Research Association, New Orleans, 1155–1169.
Ames, C. (1992). Classrooms: Goals, structures, and student motivation. *Journal of Educational Psychology, 84*(3), 261–271.
Anderman, E. M., & Midgley, C. (1997). Changes in achievement goal orientations, perceived academic competence and grades across the transition to middle-level schools. *Contemporary Educational Psychology, 22*, 269–298.
Anderman, E. M., Anderman, L. H., & Griesinger, T. (1999). The relationship of present and academic selves during early adolescence to grade point average and achievement goals. *The Elementary School Journal, 100*(1), 3–17.
Bagley, C. A., & Copeland, E. J. (1994). African and African American graduate students' racial identity and personal problem-solving strategies. *Journal of Counseling & Development, 73*, 167–171.
Bangura, A. K. (2005). African immigration and naturalization in the United States from 1966 to 2002: A quantitative of the Morris or the Takougang. Hypothesis. http://file///D/purehost/articles/bangura.html. Accessed 3 January 2005.
Bigler, R., Averhart, C., & Liben, L. (2003). Race and the workforce: Occupational status, aspirations, and stereotyping among African American children. *Developmental Psychology, 39*, 572–580.
Butcher, K. (1995). Black immigrants in the United States: A comparison with native blacks and other immigrants. *Industrial and Labor Relations Review, 47*, 265–284.
Cross, S. E., & Markus, H. R. (1991). Possible selves across the lifespan. *Human Development, 34*, 230–255.
Dweck, C. S., & Leggett, E. L. (1988). A social-cognitive approach to motivation and personality. *Psychological Review, 95*, 256–273.
Eissa, S. O. (2005). Diversity and transformation: African and African immigration to the United States. Immigration policy brief. The American Immigration Law Foundation. www.ailf.org/ipc/diversityandtransformationprint.asp. Accessed 15 May 2007.
Elliot, E. S., & Dweck, C. S. (1988). Goals: An approach to motivation and achievement. *Journal of Personality and Social Psychology, 54*, 5–12.
Frazier, L., Hooker, K. Johnson, P. M., & Kaus, C. R. (2000). Continuity and change in possible selves in the later years: A 5-year longitudinal study. *Basic and Applied Social Psychology, 22*, 237–244.
Gibson, M. A., & Ogbu, U. (Eds.). (1991). *Minority status in schooling: A comparative study of immigrant and involuntary minorities*. New York: Garland.
Hernandez, D. J. (1999). Children of immigrants, one fifth of America's children and growing: Their circumstances, prospects and welfare reform. Master lecture presented at the biannual meeting of the Society for Research in Child Development held April 15–18 in Albuquerque, NM.
Holland, D., Lachicotte, W. Jr., Skinner, D., & Cain, C. (1998). *Identity and agency in cultural worlds*. Cambridge: Harvard University Press.
Kao, G. (2000). Group images and possible selves among adolescents: Linking stereotypes to expectations by race and ethnicity. *Sociological Forum, 15*, 407–430.
Katende, C. (1994). *Population dynamics in Africa*. Doctoral Dissertation, University of Pennsylvania.
Kitayama, S., Duffy, S., & Uchida, Y. (2007). Self as a cultural mode of being. In S. Kitayama & D. Cohen (Eds.), *Handbook of cultural psychology* (pp. 136–174). New York: Guilford Press.
Knox, M., Funk, J., Elliott, R., & Bush, E. G. (2000). Gender differences in adolescents' possible selves. *Youth & Society, 31*(3), 287–309.
Leonard, T. (1995). Narrative structure in a cognitive framework. In G. Brudy, J. Duchan, & L. Hewitt (Eds.), *Deixis in narrative: A cognitive science perspective* (pp. 421–460). Lawrence Erlbaum.

Leondari, A., Syngollitou, E., & Kiosseloglou, G. (1998). Academic achievement, motivation and future selves. *Educational Studies, 24*(2), 153–163.

Lobenstine, L., Pereira, Y., Whitley, J., Robles, J., Soto, Y., & Sergeant, J. (2001). Possible selves and pastels: A truly socially contextualized model of girlhood. Paper presented at *A New Girl Order: Young Women and Feminist Inquiry Conference*. London.

Markus, H., & Kitayama, S. (1991). Culture and the self: Implications for cognition, emotion, and motivation. *Psychological Review, 98,* 224–253.

Markus, H. R., & Nurius, P. (1986). Possible selves. *American Psychologist, 9,* 954–969.

Markus, H., Cross, S., & Wurf. E. (1990). The role of the self-system in competence. In R. J. Sternberg & J. Kolligian, Jr (Eds.), Competence considered (pp. 205–225). New Haven: Yale University Press.

Maundeni, T. (1999). African females and adjustment to studying abroad. *Gender and Education, 11*(1), 27–42.

Midgley, C., Maehr, M. L., Hundra, L. Z., Anderman, E., Anderman, L., Freeman, K. E. et al. (2000). *Patterns of Adaptive Learning Scales (PALS)*. Ann Arbor: University of Michigan.

Murayama, K., & Elliott, A. (2009). The joint influence of personal achievement goals and classroom goal structures on achievement-related outcomes. *Journal of Educational Psychology, 101*(2), 432–447.

Muslow, M. H., & Murry, V. M. (1996). Parenting on edge. *Journal of Family Issues, 17,* 704–721.

National Center for Educational Surveys (NCES) (2000). http://nces.ed.gov./ccd

Nicholls, J. G. (1984). Achievement motivation: Conceptions of ability, subjective experience, task choice, and performance. *Psychological Bulletin, 91,* 328–346.

Ogbu, J. U. (1983). Minority status and schooling in plural societies. *Comparative Education Review, 27,* 169–172.

Ogbu, J. U. (1991). *Minority status and schooling*. New York: Garland.

Ogilvie, D. M. (1987). The undesired self: A neglected variable in personality research. *Journal of Personality and Social Psychology, 52,* 379–385.

Okome, M. O. (2002). *The antimonies of globalization: Causes of contemporary African immigration to the United States of America*. www.africamigration.com/archives_01/m_okome_globalization_01.htm

Oyserman, D. (2004). Possible selves questionnaire. *Possible selves citations, measure and coding instructions*. Institute of Social Research, University of Michigan.

Oyserman, D., & Fryberg, S. (2006). Possible selves of diverse adolescents. In C. Dunkel & J. Kerpelman (Eds.), *Possible selves: Theory, research and application*. Huntington: Nova.

Oyserman, D., & Markus, H. R. (1990). Possible selves and delinquency. *Journal of Personality and Social Psychology, 59,* 112–125.

Oyserman, D., Gant, L., & Ager, J. (1995). A socially contextualized model of African-American identity: Possible selves and school persistence. *Journal of Personality and Social Psychology, 69,* 1216–1232.

Oyserman, D., Harrison, K., & Bybee, D. (2001). Can racial identity be promotive of academic efficacy? *International Journal of Behavioral Development, 25,* 379–385.

Oyserman, D., Kemmelmeier, M., Fryberg, S., Brosh, H., & Hart-Johnson, T. (2003). Racial- ethnic self-schemas. *Social Psychology Quarterly, 66*(4), 333–347.

Oyserman, D. Terry, K., Bybee, D., Terry, K., & Hart-Johnson, T. (2003). Possible selves as roadmaps. *Journal of Research in Personality, 38,* 130–149.

Oyserman, D., Bybee, D., & Terry, K. (2006). Possible selves and academic outcomes: How and when possible selves impel action. *Journal of Personality and Social Psychology, 91,* 188–244.

Patrick, H., & Ryan, A. M. (2008). What do students think about when evaluating their classroom's mastery goal structure? An examination of young adolescents' explanations. *Journal of Experimental Education, 77*(2), 99–123.

Pintrich, P. R. (1989). The dynamic interplay of student motivation and cognition in the college classroom. In M. L. Maehr & P. R. Pintrich (Eds.).

Pintrich, P. R. (2000). The role of self-regulation in self-regulated learning. In P. P. Boekaerts & M. Zeidner (Eds.), *The handbook of self-regulation* (pp. 451–502). New York: Academic Press.

Pruit, F. J. (1978). The adaptation of African students to American society. *International Journal of Intercultural Relations, 2,* 90–118.

Quintana, S., & Segura-Herrera, T. (2003). Developmental transformations of self and identity in the context of oppression. *Self and Identity, 2,* 269–285.

Reid, J. (1986). Immigration and the future of the U.S. Black population. *Population Today, 14,* 6–8.

Retelsdorf, J., Butler, R., Streblow, L., & Schiefele, U. (2009). Teachers' goal orientations for teaching: Associations with instructional practices, interest in teaching, and burnout. *Learning and Instruction, 20,* 1–17.

Rong, X. L., & Brown, F. (2001). The effects of immigrant generation and ethnicity on educational attainment among young African and Caribbean Blacks in the United States. *Harvard Educational Review, 71*(3), 536–565.

Rong, X. L., & Brown, F. (2002). Socialization, culture, and identities of black immigrant children: What educators need to know and do. *Education and Urban Society, 34*(2), 247–273.

Schunk, D., & Zimmerman, B. (2006). Competence and control beliefs: Distinguishing the means and ends. In P. Alexander & P. Winne (Eds.), *Handbook of educational psychology* (pp. 349–367). Mahwah: Lawrence Erlbaum.

Speer, T. (1994). The newest African Americans aren't black. *American Demographics, 16*(1), 9–10.

Steele, C., & Aronson, J. (1995). Stereotype threat and the intellectual test performance of African-Americans. *Journal of Personality and Social Psychology, 69,* 797–811.

Takyi, B. K. (2002). The making of the second diaspora: On the recent African immigrant community in the United States of America. *The Western Journal of Black Studies, 26* (1), 32–43.

Traore, T., & Elcock, S. (2003, July 27–30). Serving undocumented and illiterate immigrants: A creative process. National HIV Prevention Conference, Atlanta, Georgia.

Triandis, H. C. (1995). *Individualism and collectivism.* Boulder: Westview.

US Census Bureau. (2000). U.S. Census Bureau: 10 years on the web. http://www.census.gov.

Walters, J. R. (2000). Dispersal behavior: An ornithological frontier. *Contier, 102,* 479–481.

Chapter 32
A Passport to Education: Undocumented Latino University Students Navigating Their Invisible Status

Marisol Clark-Ibáñez, Fredi Garcia-Alverdín and Gricelda Alva

Introduction

This chapter focuses on the educational and social lives of undocumented Latino university students who live near the United States–México border in a politically conservative community. Being undocumented, in our study, means that these students do not have US citizenship or legal residency, although some students have some type of legal status (e.g., work permit but no residency). The students in our study traverse sites from home to school that are characterized by border checkpoints and immigration raids. Just getting to campus can be perilous.

The undocumented college students in our study are part of a unique group. While they have a legal right for higher education, they possess few formal financial resources and precarious citizenship status. Yet, they have made it through the educational pipeline. The PEW Hispanic Center reports that about 50% of Latinos do not finish high school, and of those who graduate, only about a third go on to some type of college. A third of this group goes on to a 4-year college, and only 2% of all Latinos who go onto college are undocumented because most undocumented youth do not realize they can attend college (Abrego 2006). This study focuses on undocumented Latino students who made it through the primary and secondary school pipeline and are working toward graduation at a 4-year college.

In this chapter, we describe the students' college experiences and show how their status as undocumented people affects their learning. We found factors that positively impact their educational experiences such as supportive institutional personnel and the relative invisibility of their legal status on campus. Interestingly, their invisibility shaped their inability to interact fully in the classroom and engage in classroom debates. In addition, our participants described an overwhelming feeling of fear, anxiety, and hopelessness due to the hyper hate community that surrounds the university and other societal factors.

M. Clark-Ibáñez (✉)
Department of Sociology, California State University San Marcos, 333 S. Twin Oaks Valley Road, San Marcos 92096, CA, USA
e-mail: mibanez@csusm.edu

By contrasting the climate of the community that surrounds the college campus to the university itself, we will show how students fight against, negotiate, and at times succumbed to structures of domination as seen through actions of agents of the local, national, and state law enforcement agencies and the local actors who advocate against the students' rights to an education. We will also show the important ways in which undocumented college students are savvy—how they use the tools and resources of the university to build social capital and manage their identity and status. Thus, we aim to present a complex situation of resistance through negotiation.

Ultimately, our study addresses the following questions pertaining to undocumented students: How is learning shaped by the surrounding community? What is the role of the university, as an institution, to support undocumented students' learning? How might we improve the educational outcomes of undocumented students through the communities in which they live and learn?

Undocumented Latino Students

Undocumented Latino students[1] in the United States live under contradictory legal statutes. They are considered illegal and are subjected to laws that would lead to their immediate deportation. (Unfortunately, most undocumented students have no memory of or even family in their birth country.) However, other laws give undocumented students the right to attend school and .institutions of higher education. A tension between living illegally and being educated legally exists for the participants in this study.

The UCLA Center for Labor, Research, and Education (2007) reports that there are approximately 2.5 million undocumented youth under the age of 18 were living in the United States. Approximately 65,000 undocumented students graduate from US high schools each year. Of this number, about 26,000, undocumented youth reside in the state of California.

Only 2% of Latinos who go on to college are undocumented, and of this group just a small number attend a 4-year university while a significant number attend a 2-year community college. Participants in our study reflect a typical undocumented college student profile: they were brought to the United States at an early age, have mixed status within their family (some family members are citizens or legal residents while others are not), and most excelled in high school so as to be granted admission to the university without special circumstances or consideration. They represent a unique group because few undocumented high school students know that they can enroll in college or university.

California state law (Assembly Bill 540) allows undocumented students who have attended state high schools for three or more years to attend a college or uni-

---

[1] Our study focuses on Latino undocumented students, the most populous in the United States.

versity. They are eligible to pay in-state tuition, but they are excluded from receiving state or federal financial aid. Therein lies one of the main problems facing undocumented students—most are ineligible to work legally, they come from low-income families, and are not able to receive financial aid (National Immigration Law Center 2006). Moreover, many private scholarships require a social security number, which undocumented students do not possess. The reality of attending university, despite being academically prepared, becomes an enormous challenge because of the financial barriers. In addition, undocumented students also confront sociolegal challenges in the greater community.

Community Context[2]

Our study takes place in San Martin, California, a medium-sized city about 50 miles from the US–México border. Over one-third of the residents in San Martin are Latino, and in surrounding cities one-third to one half the residents are Latinos. Research and local media describe the region as hostile to Latino immigrants in general and undocumented immigrants in particular. For example, there are numerous reports of border patrol check points, local police traffic stops, city policies and laws against undocumented immigrants, and antiimmigrant protests (Sifuentes 2008). Cities in this region have routinely passed ordinances against immigrant labor, overnight parking, and rental policies discriminating against undocumented people. This has created a climate of fear and distrust between immigrants and local authorities. The students in our study feel unsafe trying to physically navigate their way through city and county streets to the college campus (see the Findings section for further detail).

Federal ICE agents (Immigration and Customs Enforcement) conduct routine raids at work places and homes. While they are formally charged with seeking fugitives who are non-US nationals, they have been cited for casting a wide net in immigrant communities. In addition, the creation of ICE Detention Centers has increased causing further fear among immigrants. ICE agents have also begun collaborating with local police agencies across the United States. Thus, the local police's mission to "protect and serve" is tainted by fear that only those who are US citizens are afforded the protection of the police.

The police checkpoints, in particular, add another dimension of fear and hostility. A person who is undocumented cannot obtain a driver's license, yet the region has a weak public transportation system. Many must drive to get to work or to perform simple chores (e.g., grocery shopping, going to the bank). Many cities are targeting undocumented immigrants by impounding their cars. Recently, the American Civil Liberty Union, a national civil rights organization, decried the excessive use of po-

---

[2] All people, locations, organizations, and groups have been given pseudonyms.

lice/border patrol checkpoints in this region that usually take place near immigrant communities and communities of color (Rodriguez 2006).

Also, this region's proximity to the border and military bases make it a conservative area where patriotism, mixed with antiimmigrant sentiment, create a hostile environment for immigrants and a safe-haven for groups such as the Minutemen, an antiimmigrant vigilante group. The Minutemen have caused panic and disrupted everyday life. For example, they aggressively protested at a church event that would have aided immigrants in obtaining acceptable identification documents granted by the Mexican consulate.

Other antiimmigrant groups such as "Friends of the Border Patrol" and various cities' "Citizens Brigades" have formed to protest day laborers and migrant workers. The hate-groups are quite active and seem to target those who are perceived as helping immigrants. These examples of fear and hostility are what undocumented students have to deal with on an everyday basis.

College Context

Situated in the midst of this region characterized by antiimmigrant activity is a medium-sized, public university, San Martin State College (SMSC), where the students in our study are enrolled. Diversity, multiculturalism, and academic excellence are some of the cornerstone values and principles of its founding. About one-fourth of the students are Latinos along with smaller populations of Black, Asian, Pacific Islanders, and Native American students. The majority of the students on campus are white.

The campus has been affected by the hate groups in the region—faculty of color reported tires slashed and threats against their lives. In addition, students of color report that the campus police have racially profiled them. In short, SMSC is like most institutions in the United States—reflecting (and at times actively promoting) the societal norms, ills, and inequities of its surrounding community. What makes SMSC different is that it has a clear foundation and mission that counters racism, ignorance, and xenophobia.

Literature Review on Undocumented Students

Because our study is exploratory and inductive, it is useful to understand the state of the current research in order to put our findings and analysis into context. Currently, the literature on the lives of undocumented college students is small, interdisciplinary, and growing. We have identified four main themes related to the experiences of undocumented students.

Social Capital and Social Networks

Social capital involves "personal connections that facilitate access to jobs, market tips, or loans" (Portes 2000, p. 3). Social capital can serve as a resource and enhance resilience especially at times of adversity. In the form of social support, it is found to be extremely important to the success of this population, as confirmed by studies about college students in general (Gloria et al. 2005). However, negative or unsupportive networks may be more detrimental to undocumented students than the student body at large (Gloria et al. 2005). We plan to ask students about the people who help them (and those who are less helpful) in the educational setting. We anticipate that relationship with peers will be an important asset to our participants (Tierney and Venegas 2006).

Educational Resilience

Educational resilience refers to students who succeed academically regardless of adversity. It is defined as "the heightened likelihood of success in school and other life accomplishments despite environmental adversities brought about by early traits, conditions, and experiences" (Wang and Gordon 1994, p. 46). Resilience indicates competence despite of adversity (Luthar et al. 2000). Such adversity may include health, poverty, and other social conditions. The concept of educational resilience does not refer to an attribute, but rather on "alterable factors" that promote educational success. Such factors include: social competence, problem-solving skills, autonomy, and having a sense of purpose. Other factors include: personal attributes like motivation and being goal oriented, positive use of time, family support, school and classroom learning environment (Waxman et al. 2003).

Perez et al. (2009) uses the concept of educational resilience to demonstrate that undocumented students who make it to college are academically prepared—they have been able to overcome many obstacles in their lives. Some examples of risk factors for college going undocumented students include working more than 20 hours per week during high school, feeling a sense of rejection due to undocumented status, low parental educational attainment, and coming from a large family. Despite these obstacles, students persevered.

Perez and colleagues claim that having a collection of environmental (e.g., value volunteering, extracurricular activities, parents valuing schooling) and personal protective resources (e.g., value schooling) helps students from being at risk of failing academically despite having psychosocial conditions (e.g., undocumented status, socioeconomic difficulties, and low parental education), which could affect their academics negatively.

We build upon Perez and colleagues: while the literature has mainly focused on the challenges to this student population, our stance on undocumented college students is that they are a resilient student population. We expand upon these findings in our interviews so as to identify the strategies employed by undocumented students such as how they cope with challenges in the classroom and community and identify their educational successes.

Institutional Dynamics

The university setting itself (mentoring, campus climate, and perpetuation of stereotypes in the curriculum) is another factor that affects the experiences of undocumented students (Herrera 2007; Rincón 2008). An important school of thought in the field of Sociology of Education is the idea that our educational institutions perpetuate the broader inequalities in society. Schools create the curriculum and academic expectations that valued some students' home and cultural experiences and devalues others. Much of this research has been conducted in grade school. In our study, the undocumented students have made it to the university, despite various legal and school-related obstacles. Thus, we will be examining the role of the university.

Emotions and Educational Success

Loneliness is also related to undocumented status (Abrego 2008; Martinez-Calderón 2009). Dozier (1993) found that some undocumented students felt that their status prevented them from creating "close emotional relationships" because they feared what others would do once they knew about their status.

In particular, the stress of financial struggles negatively impacts undocumented students' success (Herrera 2007; Hudson et al. 2008). The stress of finances is also related to students reporting hopelessness. Some may feel forced to remain in less desirable working conditions due to fear of not being able to find another job. This is because of their inability to work legally. Face-to-face interviews, rather than surveys, will be essential to be able to not only be able to see the emotions as students tell us about their experiences. Also, knowing this might be a critical issue, we provided an information packet that contained information regarding counseling, financial, and legal resources to every participant.

Finally, this study has another important contribution: we highlight and forefront the students' voices. Most research is focused on quantitative educational attainment outcomes and graduation rates. Another segment of the research is based on the usage of financial aid. A third segment of the literature on undocumented students is based on policy and law, not necessarily how the undocumented students experience the laws that govern them (Abrego 2008 is an exception). We fill in the gap on this topic by providing qualitative accounts of undocumented students' lived experiences. As you will read in our Findings section, qualitative data have led us to more sophisticated theory building and analysis of the undocumented students' lives.

Methods and Data Analysis

Our study used a qualitative methodology to capture the lived learning experiences of Latino undocumented students. Through the use of in-depth interviews, we captured the educational experiences of undocumented Latino students within an environment/region that reflects an antiimmigrant sentiment manifested by law and public opinion, to name a few.

Recruitment took place at SMSC using snowball and targeted sampling techniques. We contacted those who work with organizations focused on undocumented students and asked them to pass along our contact information to others who might be interested in participating. We distributed flyers throughout student support services and contacted Latino student organizations. E-mail was primarily used as a way to set up appointments and for further communication between research participants and researchers. We also fielded inquiries from potential participants through phone calls and personal meetings.

Our sample consisted of 19 SMSC undocumented Latino college students: 16 females and 3 males. (The limited number of males in our study reflects the lack of Latino males in higher education.) Our participants' ages ranged from 18 to 24 years old. Three were pursuing a postbachelors degree. Also, our sample included a variety of majors within Social Sciences, Business, Biological Sciences, and Math. Most participants' age of arrival to the United States ranged from 2 to 13. All but one participant are first-generation college students.

Following the recruitment phase, the prospective participants contacted us to set up a place and time for interviews. We conducted the interviews as guided conversations, which was ideally matched with our study's goal: to allow the participants to communicate their experiences from their unique perspectives (Denzin 1997). Our interview questions focused on an array of issues ranging from participant's identity to educational learning experiences. Interviews were conducted in public locations; steps were taken to ensure confidentiality and protection of participants. Each interview averaged 45 minutes to an hour and was audio recorded. Interviews were transcribed and participants assigned pseudonyms. We took extraordinary care to protect the identity of our interviewees. The interviews were conducted between August 2008 and December 2008.

As a research team and individually, we analyzed the data using the grounded theory approach (Strauss and Corbin 1990). Grounded theories require researchers to make comparisons and ask questions of the data. We began individually conducting open coding by reading the 19 transcripts on our own. Our next step was to conduct axial coding: we met to discuss themes and reveal how we coded the data. We discussed the merits of our coding and came up with several concepts in common. We returned to selectively code the data on our own again. Then, we returned to the interviews to code them more specifically. Finally, we wrote the analysis together. This process allowed the data to "speak" rather than the researchers fitting the data into a specific box. Also, the three researchers coding individually and together allowed for a higher level of reliability.

Findings and Discussion

Several themes became apparent as we coded the data. Most importantly, we discovered new analytical frameworks for understanding the students' experiences. Many are borrowed from research in related fields but never applied to undocumented college students. First, we found that students are navigating their way to school through a hyper hate community climate. Second, when students arrive at the university, they operate with a "passport" for learning that can be freeing and also silencing. Third, the overall stress and fear that students experience can adversely affect their schooling. We found, however, that undocumented students are a resilient group and successfully (albeit painfully) steer their way through the educational system.

Navigating a Hyper Hate Community Climate

We argue that the undocumented students in our study traverse through a hyper hate community climate. We created this concept to capture the intersections of federal, state, regional, and city laws and policies, along with the action of civic hate groups; taken together, they form a web that oppresses, scares, and diminishes undocumented immigrants. (See Community Context, Sect. 2.)

The idea of a hyper hate community climate is similar to those describing "white space" (Lewis 2003). The concept of "white space" emerged out of racialized space literature (e.g., residential segregation) in the social sciences and refers to the norms, policies, and procedures that result in reproducing white privilege. Our concept differs in that it conceptualizes multiple levels of hostility toward immigrants and draws together the community and university.

All of the participants in this study discussed the difficulty of getting to campus and maneuvering in the community. This finding is reflected in recent qualitative studies on undocumented students' experiences (Martinez-Calderón 2009). For example, Laura expressed, "I do get very depressed. You think que no afecta mucho pero sí afecta. [You think that it does not affect you but it does affect.] School would have been much easier. Or driving. I can't [drive] here because there is a checkpoint. I wish that I could travel pero no puedo [but I can't]. Simple things like that." Andrea worried about shopping for groceries: "They can come into stores, como El Tigre [like supermarket The Tiger], and they can actually ask you for your papers and that make me feel, 'Wow.' You realize how bad things [could] get."

Elisa described, "I live in a city that is very conservative, where checkpoints are almost routine." Fear of living as an undocumented person in this community is a very real emotion for these students. Monica shared, "What if my parents get deported? They do drive without a license. ICE has raided work. I fear that my family might be deported. I fear losing everything we have worked for."

Most participants explained that they were alerted about roadblocks and checkpoints by text messaging, through the internet, news, and informal networks on and off campus. Thus, the key to navigating the hyper hate community climate is social capital, which recall involves "personal connections that facilitate access to jobs, market tips, or loans" (Portes 2000, p. 3). It is based on trust, reciprocity, norms, and networks, which may translate into material goods (Adger 2003). Interestingly, many researchers have used this concept to understand educational outcomes. However, we found that social capital is crucial to surviving the act of physically coming to and from to the university, where it is presumed undocumented students will have a better educational outcome.

Educational Citizenship

We found evidence that students perceive their ability to attend the university as a passport to educational citizenship. We borrow this concept from Benmayor (2002), who has written extensively about cultural citizenship and the university. Specifically, she writes that cultural citizenship affirms "the right for Mexican origin students to receive quality education, to be on college campuses in significant numbers, and to be appropriately supported in their academic and career development" (p. 97). The way that most undocumented students claim their education is by remaining undetected as undocumented immigrants. They must register with the university as being "AB540" but federal law protects their privacy, as it does all university students in the United States.

Invisibility has its benefits: navigating around the university does not create a fear of being deported compared to their feeling in the outside community. However, their invisibility can be silencing and negatively affect their learning. In the following subsection, we discuss this dilemma in detail.

Our findings indicate that the college campus in general is a relative "safe haven" because the citizenship status of students is invisible. Monica explained, "I feel welcome on campus. Since not everyone talks about [their legal status], I don't feel any hostility toward AB540 students. I feel that I am treated as any other student." Recently the campus decided to use student identification numbers, rather than Social Security numbers in order to prevent identity theft. For undocumented students, this change has deep significance. Gisela described, "I feel comfortable [at SMSC] because in here they don't ask you like for your social security number. All you use is your [student] ID. So, you get all over school with your ID, so that is like your passport for school." Leticia bluntly said, "We blend in with everyone."

Thus, most participants "pass"—they manage their undocumented immigrant identities. Goffman's (1963) concept of "passing" is crucial to understanding how students see themselves. Being undocumented is a stigma in this society that requires them to manage their identity in a variety of ways. Most do so successfully by not making their stigma (being an undocumented immigrant) visible to others.

Yet, this invisibility or passing has several shadow sides. The social isolation participants felt forced them to be less reliant on peers, thereby losing out on potential gains from social capital and putting them at greater risk for depression and dropping out. The invisibility also caused them to be less likely to speak out in debates or discussion about immigration in the classroom.

All the participants in our study felt socially and academically isolated at various points in their schooling. As mentioned previously, having social capital is one way that students succeed in school. However, because of their hidden identity, some students cannot capitalize on their social ties because they keep their status a secret. Also, this type of isolation can lead to depression and leaving school (Tinto 1993).

As Mercedes stated, "Most students are not aware that we are here. There is not enough awareness. I don't feel comfortable talking about my legal status because I don't know others'." In fact, the undocumented students themselves are not sure who else is undocumented. Laura expressed, "I don't know who doesn't have papers here, so everyone I see is born here."

Most participants kept their status to themselves and rarely shared it with their friends. Jose explained, "[My friends] ask me, 'Why don't you have an ID. Why don't you have a driver's license? Why don't you do this and that?' I would be like, 'Man, I am busy!' I did not tell them because I did not want them to consider me a charity case or anything. I guess I don't really trust them. I would feel more secure if they did not know because…they could tell someone and…I could be deported."

Maritza said that she did not know anyone with her status, adding, "I don't feel comfortable to tell anyone." She regretted the few times she has revealed her status and explained that friends "were just like, 'Wow, can't you just fix it?'" She went on to explain, "They were trying to tell me I was dumb and that I didn't know [how to get out of the situation] but it's really hard [for others] to understand." Elisa shared that it took her 2 years to reveal her status to her best friend because "you need to know who you can tell and who you can't." We noted in many of the interviews that the issue of trust and who to trust was crucial to the participants.

There are two reactions to this shadow side: taking a risk to reveal one's identity and political action. A few participants in our study informally found social support in others who were in similar situations. Gisela remembered, "When I was doing my credential, I had…two friends who did not have a green card as well. We just kind of, you know, [said to each other] 'Let's just go for it, just go for it. We can't give up now because we are almost done.'" Isabel cherished the opportunities to help others in her situation. She explained, "People that I know, who are in the same situation as me, are younger than me. They use me as a role model. When they tell me their difficulties about what's going on, I tell them my difficulties and what helped me out to keep on going." Clearly, peer support can be crucial to a student's success but if very few know each other, this becomes problematic.

Also, students formed a club at SMSC called "United In Education," devoted to supporting and advocating for undocumented students. Its rallies, outreach efforts, and fundraising activities may contribute to wider understanding of undocumented students' experiences, challenges, and contributions. Interestingly, this club creates visibility for undocumented students and their plights, but also inadvertently increases the risk of exposure, which is described by participants below.

Another shadow side of gaining access to higher education is that being "invisible" (in terms of their immigration status) may have a chilling effect on classroom learning for undocumented students. Participants noted that hostility and lack of safety arose in classroom discussions on immigration.

In terms of learning, most feel that they cannot speak up in debates as much as they would like to because they fear retaliation. Gisela explained, "I kind of keep everything to myself…Like if we are having a class argument, I might say stuff about it. I feel like 'Oh, you have no idea what its like to be illegal.' I just think that to myself because I don't express it." Mercedes described a recent incident: "In my History class, the topic of immigration was brought up. I tend to hold back and do not want to let them know my point of view. Afterwards, I would feel bad." Students participate but do so cautiously and at their own peril. They know they are expected to participate and they want to. However, they "hold back" as seen in Mercedes' comments.

Research on the chilly classroom has traditionally focused on gender and these studies can give us additional insight into its effects (Hall and Sandler1982). Professors may give preferential treatment or allowing "disparaging remarks" toward women. The chilly classroom climate is also created by *students themselves (*Fassinger 1995). In terms of being undocumented and not revealing one's identity, there is more risk involved.

Most of our participants were similar to Cecilia, who expressed, "You know when you are in the classroom, you can't really say your point of view. Like you know someone who is in the classroom might disagree with your opinion, but what if someone disagrees *badly*?" She echoes the fear of a peer going to an extreme (e.g., reporting the student to immigration). Women who are documented or nonimmigrants do not feel this sort of pressure and fear. Martinez-Calderón (2009) also found that students are "pushed into the shadows" because of fear of visibility and discovery as undocumented. Disagreements occur in most classrooms but, for these students, the stakes are too high if a student who is conservative or is against "illegal" immigration decides to report them to ICE. De Genova (2002) reports that this is a common and real fear for most undocumented people.

Decades of research show that participation in the classroom is crucial to students learning (Hollander 2002; Karp and William 1976). Because students are hesitant to fully reveal their ideas for fear of being discovered, they remain less actively involved in discussions about social policy regarding immigration.

The third shadow side of gaining educational citizenship is that the students in this study must manage their identity, which causes stress in their lives. It should be noted that Latina/os, regardless of status, experience more stress and depression than non-Latina/os due to racism and unequal treatment (Araújo-Dawson 2009).

In our sample, the status of the participants negatively shapes how they experience their classes and the opportunity to learn. Mercedes summarized her feelings, "I have felt overwhelmed and stressed out. Being in this situation, it is so easy to give up." Elisa revealed, "I have cried a lot. I know my situation and I know I can go away easily. It just sucks because I work so hard and I think I deserve to be here."

Isabel, like many of our participants was visibly upset in the interview when she explained her feelings regarding her status: "I just feel hopeless right now. A couple of days ago, I broke down [she begins to cry] in the car with my brother because I felt hopeless. I told my brother, 'You are seventeen, you are working and giving me money to pay for gas.' I felt dumb. I am the older one and I am supposed to help you out and not al revez....Me siento tan inutil [not in reverse...I feel so futile]" Isabel was managing role conflict: as an older sister, she is the one supposed to be supporting her little brother but, as an undocumented young person, she is the one who needs his support. (Families with mix status are not uncommon.) These students felt acute anguish about their status and the related economic and social limitations.

Students seemed to bolster themselves by strongly believing that their predicament is not fair or their fault. They identified the adverse conditions faced due to their status—the types of jobs they must have and the lack of mobility in the community—and expressed their bitterness. Recall, these are exceptional and academically talented students who have made it through the leaky educational pipeline for Latinos in the United States, as discussed previously.

While all the participants spoke about managing their negative emotions due to their status, Maritza was one of the most descriptive. For example, she mourned not having a "regular job" and admitted, "I hate my job 'cause I had to go clean houses with my mom like Friday, Saturday, and Sunday to pay for my tuition and...babysit at night." She also reflected on the relative privilege that she noticed when she babysat: "I babysit Caucasian kids and they have everything. I keep asking myself: I have been here. I've been getting an education. They have rights that I don't and I have been here all my life. I don't understand that." Maritza became very emotional in an interview when she recalled that she was awarded a scholarship but then it was taken away because she did not have a social security card.

All the participants explained how they give themselves positive talks to keep on going with their education as a way of combating depression and hopelessness. For example, Martha shared how she tells herself, "I have to be strong, I have to be strong." Others spoke of an inner-strength, such as Aurora described: "I just have this thing within me that I'm not going to give up, you know... I know that in the future everything will change and I will be ok but I just cannot give up because, I mean, I have been here all my life and I don't know why they won't give me an opportunity." What is key here is that the students do not internalize their lack of future opportunities. The students' opportunities do not match their aspirations; this is a reverse phenomenon compared to studies about other students of color and working class students, where the lack of opportunities dampen students' aspirations (MacLeod 1995).

In fact, most students decided on additional schooling as a way to cope with not being able to join the workforce in their chosen professions. Paula described the next steps in her life: "Ph.D. is next. I see myself working in the field of biomedical research to find a cure for cancer or diabetes." Maritza, Elisa, and Mercedes also want to pursue a doctorate. Maritza explained her reasoning for going on to a doctorate program, "I think that education—they can't take that away from you." Andrea and Cecilia aspired for professional Master's degrees. The students' goals of additional schooling reflect the values of the Latino family for education and working hard (Glick and White 2004; Martinez-Calderón 2009).

Political involvement was again mentioned as a way to stay motivated. Most cited their participation in the college club, "United In Education." José described what is helpful to him: "We just talk about…you know…even though con nuestro status how it is so we can keep going maybe…Right now, we are encouraging [each other] to finish our education so when the [DREAM Act] passes, we'll be ready to go. I guess that's a way to keep motivated."

Finally, most of the students were first-generation college students, meaning they are the first in their family to attend a 4-year university. The main motivation to keep on their journey comes from their family. Laura excitedly explained, "I want to do this so I can help my entire family. Not just me, my dad, my mom, and my sister but mis tios, mis tias, todos [my uncles, my aunts, everyone]! It's what keeps me going." Students draw upon their social support and economic hope for a better future. Their collective attitude, as opposed to an individualist one, becomes a strength from which they derive their determination (Benmayor 2002).

The Role of Campus Actors

Thus far, we have discussed how the students themselves feel about and manage their immigration status. However, the university campus has an important role in setting the tone and offering resources that could directly affect the trust building and educational successes of these students.

Certain institutional actors were perceived as being advocates and mentors. Participants revealed that they are savvy in figuring out with whom they are "safe" to discuss their status. Elisa explained, "I know who I can go to, which professors will be open and supportive of me." Most named specific counselors and staff people who worked in various programs related to student support services and who have specific social justice agendas. Stanton-Salazar (2001) has found that these actors, institutional agents, are crucial for the success of marginalized students. In contrast, other units of student services were reported as rarely utilized by the participants. In particular, participants repeatedly mentioned academic advising, financial aid, and the career center as services they did not feel supported them or were helpful. The key seemed to be being explicit about welcoming undocumented students and clearly communicating an understanding of their situation.

Faculty awareness (or lack thereof) seemed to have a major impact on students' educational trajectory. Two participants in the teacher credential program encountered the most trouble. Routine requirements for working or interning in schools such as fingerprints and background checks put undocumented students in a tricky situation. Students can reveal their status to their professors, find ways to negotiate around the requirements (volunteering), or drop out of the class. Martiza chose to reveal her status to her professor but was still deeply emotional about having to do so. She described learning about needing to be fingerprinted: "I was devastated inside of me because I was like 'Oh my God! Will I be able to continue?' Right after class I went to the professor and told the truth. I was like, 'I am in this situation. What can I do?' I worked with the professor but every time I would cry after class. I had to just deal with it."

Another participant Laura recalled when she needed to be hired as a student teacher to obtain her credential but could not because of her undocumented status. Her professor told her to drop the class if she could not be a student teacher. Laura went through a stage of fearing that she would drop out of the program and felt great grief, however, she found a way to be a "guest teacher" to complete the obligations of the credential program. These are additional steps that other students, who are citizens, do not need to undertake or manage.

Does the campus explicitly work toward empowering and supporting undocumented students? Not exactly. Units and individuals seem to do a good job of positively affecting the experiences of our participants. However, the very invisibility that allows students to maneuver on campus with relative ease also means that other important units and individuals, such as academic advising, financial aid, program coordinators, internship programs, and professors are uninformed and potentially harming the academic well being of the students in our study.

Recommendations and Conclusions

Based on our research findings, we believe there are various recommendations for universities and learning. First, the university must adopt a "zero tolerance" policy for antiimmigration hate activities. Currently, the undocumented students in our study conceptualize the university as a safe haven. However, if the "hyper hate community climate" creeps into the university setting, this sense of safety will erode and threaten their legal right to attend college.

Second, adopting informed and aware pedagogy seems to be important for supporting undocumented students' learning. Faculty members need to be aware of the presence of undocumented students, their rights, and the barriers they face. For example, when professors assign projects (e.g., service learning) or fieldtrips off campus, they should create alternatives for those who have limitations in transportation and physical movement in the region. Introducing additional assignments, such as journaling, could lessen some of the stress undocumented students felt in classroom discussions.

Third, student support services that are currently underutilized by undocumented students should begin a campaign and efforts to become more informed and sensitive to the needs of our participants. In addition, the counseling department should work with student clubs that feature Latinos (and other students of color) to begin culturally sensitive outreach efforts and create peer-counseling programs.

Finally, the state and national levels, the passage of the Development, Relief, and Education for Alien Minors Act (DREAM Act), would pave the way to citizenship for undocumented students, thereby dramatically lessen the stress and uncertainty felt by the participants in the study. This legislation would also make eligible grants, scholarships, and loan programs.

Our study shows the ways in which undocumented students experience learning in a hostile region that is characterized by a "hyper hate climate." The participants conceptualize the university as a safe-haven because their legal status is not the focus of their identity and role as a student. However, students' "invisible status" negatively affected their learning experience and how they seek social and academic support. Social support is essential for our participants when dealing with their status. Undocumented students seemed to experience an array of mental distresses due to their current status. As a consequence, students are not able to legally work and are economically constrained when financing their education. However, undocumented students are resilient and go above and beyond to persevere with their academic studies, their respective roles within their own families, and as members of a society that does not welcome them.

References

Abrego, L. J. (2006). I can't go to college because I don't have papers: Incorporating patterns of Latino undocumented youth. *Latino Studies, 4*(3), 212–231.

Abrego, L. J. (2008). Legitimacy, social identity, and the mobilization of law: The effects of Assembly Bill 540 on undocumented students of California. *Law and Social Inquiry, 33*(3), 709–734.

Adger, N. W. (2003). Social capital, collective action, and adaptation to climate change. *Economic Geography, 79*(4), 387–404. JSTOR database. Accessed 11 August 2009.

Araújo-Dawson, B. (2009). Discrimination, stress, and acculturation among Dominican women. *Hispanic Journal of Behavioral Sciences, 31*(1), 96–111.

Benmayor, R. (2002). Narrating cultural citizenship: Oral histories of first-generation college students of Mexican origin. *Social Justice, 29*(4), 96–121.

Bourdieu, P., & Passeron, J. (1977). *Reproduction in education, society, and culture*. London: Sage.

De Genova, N. P. (2002). Migrant "illegality" and deportability in everyday life. *Annual Review of Anthropology, 31*, 419–447.

Denzin, N. (1997). *Interpretive ethnography*. Thousand Oaks: Sage.

Dozier, S. B. (1993). Emotional concerns of undocumented and out-of-status foreign students. *Community Review, 13*, 6–39. Academic Search Premier database. Accessed 10 February 2009.

Fassinger, P. A. (1995). Understanding classroom interaction: Students' and professors' contributions to students' silence. *The Journal of Higher Education, 66*(1), 82–96. JSTOR database. Accessed 9 September 2009.

Glick, J. E., & White, M. J. (2004). Post-secondary school participation of immigrant and native youth: The role of familial resources and educational expectations. *Social Science Research, 33*, 272–299.

Gloria, A. M., Castellanos, J., & Orozco, V. (2005). Perceived educational barriers, cultural fit, coping responses, and psychological well-being of Latina undergraduates. *Hispanic Journal of Behavioral Sciences, 27*(2), 161–183. Sage Journals Online. Accessed 9 June 2008. doi: 10.1177/0739986305275097161.

Goffman, E. (1963). *Stigma: Notes on the management of spoiled identity.* Englewood Cliffs: Prentice-Hall.

Hall, R. M., & Sandler, B. R. (1982). The classroom climate: A chilly one for women? *Project on the Status and Education of Women, Association of American Colleges.* ERIC database. Accessed 9 September 2009.

Herrera, A. R. (2007). Continuing the dream: Assisting undocumented students in higher education. www.universityofcalifornia.edu/.../ETS07_AB540_workshop_5-2-07.ppt. Accessed 1 June 2008.

Hollander, J. (2002). Learning to discuss: Strategies for improving the quality of class discussion. *Teaching Sociology, 30*(3), 317–327.

Hudson, R., Towey, J., & Shinar, O. (2008). Depression and racial/ethnic variations within a diverse nontraditional college sample. *College Student Journal, 42*(1), 103–114. PsycINFO Database. Accessed 2 June 2008.

Karp, D., & William, Y. (1976). The college classroom: Some observations on the meanings of student participation. *Sociology and Social Research, 60,* 421–439.

Lewis, A. (2003). *Race in the schoolyard: Negotiating the color line in classrooms and communities.* New Brunswick: Rutgers University Press.

Lopez, G., & Chism, N. (1993). Classroom concerns of gay and lesbian students: the invisible Minority. *College Teaching, 41*(3), 197–204. JSTOR database. Accessed 9 September 2009.

Luthar, S. S, Cichetti, D., & Becker, Bronwyn. (2000). The construct of resilience: A critical evaluation and guidelines for future work. *Child Development, 71*(3), 543. Academic Search Premier. Accessed 10 August 2009.

MacLeod, J. (1995). *Ain't no makin' it: Aspirations and attainment in a low income neighborhood.* Boulder: Westview Press.

Martinez-Calderón, C. (2009) Out of the shadows: Undocumented Latino college students. Institute for the Study of Social Change, ISSC Fellows working papers, University of California, Berkeley. Paper ISSC-WP-34. http://repositories.cdlib.org/issc/fwp/ISSC_WP_34. Accessed 12 January 2009.

National Immigration Law Center. (2006). Court upholds California in-state tuition law (AB540). http://www.nilc.org/immlawpolicy/DREAM/Dream006.htm. Accessed 15 June 2008.

Perez, W., Espinoza, R., Ramos, K., Coronado, H. M., & Cortes, R. (2009). Academic resilience among undocumented Latino students. *Hispanic Journal of Behavioral Sciences, 20*(10). http://hjbs.sagepub.com. Accessed 13 February 2009.

Portes, A. (2000). The two meanings of social capital. *Sociological Forum, 15*(1), 1–12. JSTOR database. Accessed 10 August 2009.

Rincón, A. (2008). *Undocumented immigrants and higher education: Sí se puede!* El Paso: LFB Scholarly Publishing.

Rodriguez, M. (2006, June 28). Vista approves day-laborer law. *The San Diego Union Tribune.* http://www.signonsandiego.com. Accessed 11 July 2009.

Sifuentes, E. (2008, August 10). REGION: Escondido's checkpoints big business. *North County Times, 1.* http://www.nctimes.com. Accessed 11 July 2009.

Stanton-Salazar, R. (2001). *Manufacturing hope and despair: The school and kin support networks of U.S.-Mexican youth.* New York: Teachers College Press.

Steele, C., & Aronson, J. (1995). Stereotype threat and the intellectual performance of African American students. *Journal of Personality and Social Psychology, 69*(5), 797–811.

Strauss, A., & Corbin, J. (1990). *Basics of qualitative research.* Newbury Park: Sage.

Tierney, W., & Venegas, K. (2006). Fictive kin and social capital: The role of peer groups in applying and paying for college. *The American Behavioral Scientist, 49*(12), 1687–1703.

Tinto, V. (1993). *Leaving college: Rethinking the causes and cures of student attrition.* Chicago: University of Chicago Press.

UCLA Center for Labor, Research and Education. (2007). Undocumented students: Unfulfilled dreams. http://www.labor.ucla.edu/publications/reports/Undocumented-Students.pdf. Accessed 14 June 2009.

Wang, M. C., & Gordon, E. W. (Eds.). (1994). *Educational resilience in inner-city America: Challenges and prospects*. Hillsdale: Erlbaum.

Waxman, H., Gray, J. P., & Padron, Y. N. (2003). Review of research on educational resilience. *Center for Research on Education, Diversity & Excellence*. Research Reports. Paper rr_11. http://repositories.cdlib.org/crede/rsrchrpts/rr_11. Accessed 11 July 2009.

Part V
Religion and Learning

Chapter 33
Introduction Part 5: Religion and Learning

Eoin Daly

Introduction

Religious diversity in the education context provokes myriad dilemmas on policy, pragmatic and normative levels. The integration of minority religions within public education systems poses challenges for learning and policy; but this relates at a broader level to normative and political debates surrounding national identity, multiculturalism and assimilation. While educationalists are preoccupied with the influence of religion over learning processes, and social scientists with the dynamics of integration in the context of religion and learning, political and legal theorists are concerned with religion and learning as a site of conflicting normative and social claims on the values of religious freedom, equality, multiculturalism, and individual autonomy, which refracts and exemplifies states' public philosophies. The salience of culture and religion in the learning process is set within a broader normative and policy question of how a reconciliation between individual autonomy and respect for religious diversity may be achieved. The challenge of ensuring that individuals' religious preferences are neither undermined by a dominant culture, nor used to essentialize them within a particular group or community, appears particularly intense in this context. What are religious minorities' responses to the social and political processes assigning particular statuses and identities to them, and to the use of educational systems in the formation and reproduction of both identity and belief? The concepts of recognition and identity will create a strong tendency towards differentiated structures for the accommodation of learning processes amongst children of minority religious backgrounds, but again, the politics of recognition invites critical appraisal as much on the plane of its terms of implementation—*whose claim* is recognized?—as on the abstract, normative level. Religious diversity may give rise to claims to recognition and the differentiation of learning structures along these lines—but how are these claims resisted with reference to liberal conceptions of the individual rights of child-citizens within minority communities? In turn, how are

E. Daly (✉)
School of Law and Government, Dublin City University, Glasnevin, Dublin 9, Ireland
e-mail: eoin.daly@dcu.ie

these liberal discourses related to conceptions of national identity and belonging that require migrants to adopt to the culture of the dominant majority—particularly in the context of western responses to Islam? What, in other terms, is the relationship between the claim to cultural self-determination of minority religious groups, and countervailing conceptions of liberal-individual rights in this specific context of religion and learning? This peculiar context invites analysis of the politics of identity not only through the prism of religious minorities' claim to recognition, but also, from the standpoint of the alternative politics of identity—the communitarian and nationalist values of "social cohesion"—that are deployed against this, and which resist multiculturalist attempts to recognize, facilitate and even promote the influence of religion on learning.

Thus, evaluation and description is needed of the dynamics of the interaction between religious minorities and educational structures attuned to dominant majorities, but also, of the prevailing discourses surrounding the terms of integration imposed on religious minorities in Europe in particular, in the context of ongoing polemic surrounding the position of Islam, in particular, in "the West." In this vein, it is important to consider the dynamics of integration of religious minorities in the education context in the light of evolving discursive concepts of national belonging and identity, in a context where the processes of belief formation and reproduction are also peculiarly sensitive to the exercise of state power. Of particular importance is the relationship between social inequality and religious discrimination, given the disparities in social and political capital—the relative dearth of power and resources—that may hinder religious minorities in negotiating and instrumentalizing public educational structures. Thus, of particular interest is the relationship between social exclusion and religious diversity in educational contexts. An understanding of the nature and structure of the social inequality that affects religious minorities in this context may inform policy and normative debates. In light of the intersection between sociological and normative questions in the context of religion and learning, the four chapters included in Part 4 approach these questions both at the policy and empirical as well as normative levels.

In "Negotiating the School Curriculum for the Malay Muslims in Singapore," Charlene Tan and Hairon Salleh examine the negotiation of Singapore's school curriculum by the Malay Muslim community. Beginning with an exploration of the historical context of the Muslim Malay experience in the British colonial period, the authors consider how this community "negotiated their objective situation and their subjective everyday practices in the school curriculum." Moreover, they analyse this community in view of the role of religion as a marker of cultural identity "in an age of globalisation marked by change and uncertainty." Tan and Salleh touch upon the broader question of the "tightrope," as they term it, between the imperatives of cultural and religious self-determination on one hand, and that of social mobility and integration on the other.

Tracing a not unfamiliar account of resistance to British (secular) education in the colonial era, as a tool of cultural and religious assimilation, the authors describe Muslims' assertion of religious and cultural identity through a longstanding preference for Islamic schools. In the post-colonial era, this assertion of identity was mirrored in Malays' resistance to the imposition of the English language. This culminated in the successful negotiation of educational structures by the Malays in order to assert their control over the religious, linguistic and cultural parameters of learning. The transition to minority status following Singapore's independence in 1965, however, was accompanied by a greater preparedness to embrace the English language instruction, in order to promote educational achievement and social mobility—which was mirrored in turn by declining enthusiasm for Muslim Madrasahs. However, the international religious revival, from the 1980s onwards, coupled with dissatisfaction towards secular schooling, led Malay parents to place renewed emphasis on Islamic as an anchor of identity, and reassert cultural self-determination. On foot of this, the secular Singapore state has taken steps to intervene in the hitherto private madrasah system, in order to assert a minimal control over secular educational standards.

Using a qualitative case study research design, the authors analysed recent developments within the madrasah system, including the reactions of its stakeholders to recent reforms—including positive perceptions of the impact of these reforms on student achievement, as well as doubts surrounding their administration and practical implementation. The authors conclude that their study demonstrates the impact of "changing political, economic, and social conditions" on the Muslim Malay community, with the promise of opportunity and social mobility bearing heavily on educational preferences. They argue that the madrasahs have adapted to broader economic and social trends, meeting national, as well as Islamic aspirations. They conclude that given increased state intervention "the prospects of the madrasahs depend largely on how the madrasahs see their mission and their relationship with the state"—notwithstanding a certain resistance on the part of some madrasahs to the modernizing and secularizing influence of state reforms. In negotiating educational structures as a religious minority, the Malay Muslims have "rejected ascribed cultural attributes by the state and taken ownership of their religious, cultural and social processes and outcomes."

In "Educational processes and ethnicity amongst Hindu migrants," Helena Sant'ana considers the case of Hindu migrant women in Portugal, arguing that "the contingencies that have surrounded the Hindu migratory process towards Portuguese territory were historically and sociologically decisive in determining how that population socialized its members, particularly with regard to instigating female education." She argues that the educational practices of Hindu women have had an impact both upon the construction of ethnicity and the integration of this minority. She considers, furthermore, whether immigration has changed the traditionally gendered ways in which the utility of education has been perceived amongst Hindus, as well as women migrants' perception of their own role.

By employing a qualitative methodology entailing the establishment of a network of Hindu contacts in the Lisbon area, and using a combination of interview and ethnographic work, the author used a "snowball method," exploiting social networks, to ascertain Hindu women's experiences. This is set within the context of an historical conception according to which Hindu women "received a form of socialization completely in keeping with the values of Hinduism," and received little formal schooling; the dominant conception of virtue was set within matrimony. Hindu migration from Mozambique to Portugal saw the emergence of stronger associational means for the preservation of identity, promoting ethnic social capital—in a context with a greater risk of "identity loss," partly by virtue of state educational intervention. However, the construct of ethnicity may be seen as facilitating a form of social control over the individual. Sant'ana also documents the link between socioeconomic status and gender inequality, in educational opportunity, within this community—with low socioeconomic status apparently being correlated with a higher degree of control by the group over the individual. The author's field work enabled the observation of "survival techniques" used by women with little access to formal education, involving the "manipulation" of tradition in order to readjust traditional gender roles. The construction of ethnicity may hold Hindu women "hostage in a highly gender stratified society."

Considering tendencies towards both "defensive" and adaptive behaviours within minority religious groups, the author considers how, notwithstanding a certain pull towards the "communitarization" of Hindu migrants to Portugal, ethnic conscience remains an "ambivalent" phenomenon. The distinctiveness of Hindu customs is qualified "by the need to adapt locally," as exemplified by linguistic practices. The author observes how "older women recreate socializing models of Hinduism by manipulating religious, social and cultural levels." Hindu women are argued to "actively create integration networks by manipulating the rules that govern relationships of both belonging and meaning." However, the "female socializing model" also weakens the capacity for integration. Thus, "ethnic closure" emasculates the potential agency of Hindu women. The author concludes that the choice between the informal education cementing tradition, and the formal education offering mobility and integration, "is not an easy choice in some cases, and in others it is not even a choice at all."

In "Integration by Other Means: Hindu schooling in the Netherlands," Michael S. Merry and Geert Driessen address the growing salience of religion, as distinct fromo culture and ethnicity, in the "politics of integration." This is considered specifically in terms of schools conceived as tools for promoting and facilitating integration. The authors discuss how Hindu schools in the Netherlands facilitate integration "by other means," assessing how well integration is facilitated by schools predicated on "voluntary separation". This is considered alongside the role of Hindu-specific schools in promoting faith-identity and emancipation.

In an historical context of discrimination against Hindu immigrants to the Netherlands, primarily of Surinamese origin, the authors consider first the relatively rapid integration of Dutch Hindus. Detailing the establishment of Hindu schools on foot of greater educational freedoms granted in the Netherlands in the 1970s, the authors note the role of Hindu schools in catering for children from socioeconomically disadvantaged backgrounds, and the relative absence of polemic and controversy pertaining to them, in comparison to Islamic schools. They consider the role of Hindu schools in light of their recognition and funding by the state on foot of constitutional principles of educational pluralism.

In addition, the authors note the relative academic success of Hindu schools in relation to other minority religious schools, and the faster rate of integration by those attending such schools, in light of their emphasis on encouraging integration and tolerance as well as fostering Hindu identity. Noting that advocates of Hindu education claim that taking account of pupils' shared religious background enhances the learning process, the authors argue that Hindu schools "represent a form of emancipation," in the context of the broader politics of integration. They provide "a means by which ethnic identities are nourished and grow."

Nonetheless, the authors argue that "a majority of children and staff in Hindu schools share more in common by virtue of a shared Surinamese cultural background, and with this shared background the Dutch language provides additional cohesive support," with Hinduism a "convenient artifice for binding these items together." This is an interesting paradox given the focus of the Dutch framework on facilitating schools that accommodate a religious, rather than a cultural specificity. This is set within a broader tension between the autonomy of religious groups in this education context, and the claims of the nation-state vis-à-vis the integration of religious minorities. The authors question the "integration"-oriented argument against faith schooling by postulating that the tendency to segregation amongst minorities is one shared by the majority group, in the form of "social class affinity," they also question whether mixed schools will necessarily lead to better outcomes for pupils. Moreover, the capacity of schools to protect "fragile identities" may have a positive effect on individual students: "integration by other means" also refers to "being integrated with oneself and one's 'own' community." Therefore, the authors conclude: "Hindu schools contribute to emancipation by attending to the religious and cultural identities of children of Surinamese background so that, (seemingly) paradoxically, they can more effectively integrate into the mainstream society."

In "Precarious religious liberties in education: the salience of social and demographic contingencies under a formally pluralist public philosophy," Eoin Daly considers the difficulties faced by minority religious groups in a jurisdiction—the Republic of Ireland—where educational pluralism is constitutionally guaranteed, yet its exercise depends on certain social and demographic contingencies, such as whether a particular community enjoys the numerical "critical mass" enabling it to establish state-funded schools under a formally pluralist legal framework. Thus, despite the constitutional neutrality of the state towards religion, the right of religious freedom is distributed unequally in this context, as a function of the power relations within and between various religious and other groups in society. The absence of secular public schools in the Republic of Ireland—a legacy of resistance to British state education in the colonial era—means that in the absence of the resources and capital necessary to the processes of school establishment and recognition, non-Catholics may have little choice other than to avail of schools committed to imparting Catholic doctrines and ethos. Thus, the exercise of the right to religious freedom is made contingent on the establishment and recognition of schools specifically attuned to particular beliefs; this represents a disparity between the formal state neutrality between religions in the process of school funding and recognition, and the goal of equal religious liberty for individuals, irrespective of the relative bargaining power of their communities.

The rationale for the denominational education model in Ireland has evolved, historically, from an idea of religion and religious education as a privileged public good, to a quasiutilitarian justification centring on the secular goods of diversity and choice. It no longer centres on the idea of religion as one of the "anchoring points of national identity." Yet under the contemporary model of formal pluralism, the religious freedoms of religious minorities remain vulnerable to disparities of bargaining power and human capital that bear heavily upon them in the process of school recognition. Certain minorities, by virtue of their weaker social position, are ill-positioned to instrumentalize the secular good of "choice." The author concludes: "the denial of religious liberty rights for minorities no longer arises from any essentialized conception of citizenship, from any established doctrine or identity, but instead lies in the failure of public institutions to safeguard these rights independently of social and political power relations."

The chapters in this Part 4 touch upon certain common themes, normative, policy-based and empirical, in the field of religion and learning—in particular, of schools as sites of conflict between political agendas of integration, and the attempts of minority groups to retain their capacity for self-determination, and to maintain cultural and religious distinctiveness. How do minorities negotiate between the opportunities represented by integration, and the exercise of cultural and religious self-determination, as much on the individual as the collective level? This is considered by Tan and Salleh, as well as Merry and Driessen. Similarly, as Sant'ana considers, how do migrants negotiate traditional power structures within their communities in asserting their agency and self-determination? Furthermore, how do the nationalist and liberal-democratic politics of integration impact upon the agency and educational freedoms of minority communities? In some of the chapters, there is a common theme of post-colonial resistance to shared or secular schooling as a tool of assimilation. Finally, certain of these chapters consider: in what ways are minority religious communities disadvantaged in seeking to instrumentalize the supports and benefits offered within the public educational systems of secular European states? The contributions by both Daly and Merry & Driessen touch upon the disparity between freedom of educational principles and the diminished opportunities for relatively peripheral minorities, poorly endowed in various forms of power and social capital, to exercise this freedom.

Chapter 34
Integration by Other Means: Hindu Schooling in the Netherlands

Michael S. Merry and Geert Driessen

Introduction

With migratory patterns globally on the rise, the language of integration now reverberates prominently within the industrialized nation–states. For decades cultural and ethnic differences were the primary markers of immigrants but increasingly there is now a shift onto *religion*. The politics of integration entails that ethnic minorities—be they immigrants, asylum seekers, or even indigenous—accept the dominant political and cultural norms of the host society (cf. Vasta 2007). Yet 'integration' is an ideologically loaded concept with many implicit features whose meanings are not entirely evident either to the immigrant or to the native population. Consequently, there is much debate concerning its conditions, indicators and requirements (cf. Berry 2003).

Schools are arguably the most effective means of enacting the aims of integration. In many societies, schools are at least partly designed to be places, where children of different backgrounds converge to learn together, and also to learn about, and from, one another.[1] Therefore, schools that to the dominant group seem segregated present a serious challenge to the aims of integration. But not all schools with separate pupil populations are alike; some are the legacy of *de jure* segregation and white flight, but others host relatively homogeneous minority pupil populations by choice. That is, theirs is a form of *voluntary separation*. This chapter is an exploration into one type of school about which very little has been said, viz., the Hindu school in the

---

[1] Dutch educational policy now departs from the idea that persons live in a multicultural society and that it should be the explicit task of schools to prepare children to function adequately in them (NMEC 2007). Indeed, the current government now claims that the multicultural society has not worked (echoing comments from Angela Merkel in Germany and David Cameron in the United Kingdom). Further, the Minister of Education Van Bijsterveldt recently announced that national efforts to desegregate schools are no longer a national priority.

M. S. Merry (✉)
Faculty of Social and Behavioural Sciences, University of Amsterdam, Nieuwe Prinsengracht 130, 1018 VZ Amsterdam, Netherlands
e-mail: m.s.merry@uva.nl

Netherlands. These schools consciously promote cultural and religious distinctiveness with the aim of facilitating emancipation and integration by other means.

The primary aim of this chapter is to assess how well, and by what means, Hindu schools try to accomplish the aims of integration in a vernacular that is predicated on voluntary separation. Though Hindu schools are open to non-Hindu children, their primary aim is to educate children of like cultural and religious background. And, like other schools whose instructional design is religiously specific, Hindu schools have faith-building, identity formation and emancipation among their central aims. We will explore the specific cultural and religious components that are used to form the identities of children, and how these are operationalized as emancipatory practices. In particular, we will examine how these features are conceptualized, developed and connected to learning, and how Hindu schools concretely prepare pupils to negotiate their place in a society in which they are visible minorities. Further, to the extent possible, we will investigate whether the academic outcomes Hindu schools strive for are bearing fruit.

Our study will be based on a review of the available literature, Hindu school websites[2], analyses of general demographic data from Statistics Netherlands and school composition data from the Dutch Ministry of Education, analysis of the yearly school-specific evaluation and monitoring reports from the Dutch Inspectorate of Education, and semi-structured interviews with the administrator of the Hindu School Foundation and the deputy principal of a Hindu school. When compared to research on Muslims in Western societies, or, for that matter, Islamic schools, research carried out on Western Hindus, and certainly Hindu schools, is virtually non-existent. Only a handful of media reports are available, all of them merely announcing the opening of Hindu schools. Indeed, the very first qualitative dissertation ever carried out on Dutch Hindu schools was completed in late 2008 at the University of Tilburg.[3] Consequently, gathering and analysing peer-reviewed data on Hindu schools in the Netherlands, where they fall within the ambit of state-provided education, is for the time being only possible by referring to official reports and by making school visits. Thus given the virtual absence of any studies on Hindu schools, both theoretical and empirical, this chapter aims to fill an important gap.

We proceed as follows. First, we describe the central features of Hinduism. While the theological and/or philosophical tenets of Hinduism are central to the pedagogy of Dutch Hindu schools, we will explain why religion per se is not the most important contribution to the children who attend them. Next, we examine the colonial history of Dutch Hindus and elucidate why Dutch Hindus have managed to integrate into Dutch society at a far quicker pace than some other immigrant groups. We then look into the reasons for the establishment of Hindu schools in the

---

[2] See http://www.shrivishnu.nl/; http://www.shriganesha.nl/; http://www.shrilaksmi.nl/; http://www.shrikrishna.nl/; http://www.shrisaraswatie.nl/; http://www.vahon.nl/; also see http://www.youtube.com/watch?v=x8709uYIwfE and http://www.youtube.com/watch?v=Pxnr5ZRKgSo&feature=related. Each of the school's websites includes a prospectus with, among other things, information on the school's founding history, religious-philosophical orientation, educational goals and contents, didactical approach, staff, provisions for special needs pupils, parental participation, and pupil achievement.

[3] The thesis defense was attended by the first author.

Netherlands, showing how the Dutch system of education facilitates schools of this sort. Next, we explore the process of identity formation and how this complements the emancipatory aims of Hindu schools. Finally, we will consider a number of challenges that Hindu schools may face in the coming years.

Hindu Belief

Hindu oral tradition dates back at least to the eighth millennium BCE. It is believed that sacred knowledge was 'heard' by *rishis* (seers) and orally transmitted. These *sruti* texts, 'heard' by sages during meditation, were eventually canonized and are known today as the Vedas. Hinduism is best described as a *henotheistic* religion, meaning that it is a plural form of monotheism: a polytheism within a monotheism. Similar to the way Muslims describe the 99 attributes of God, Hinduism's purported 330 million gods are more properly interpreted as manifestations or expressions of the one divine Being, Brahmā. Sometimes Brahmā is described in terms of a Hindu trinity, or *trimurti,* with Brahmā or Ishvara as Creator Lord, Vishnu as preserver, and Siva as destroyer. Taken together they symbolize the circle or *samsara* of life. Whatever the case, *bhakti* or personal devotion to an individual god (e.g. Kali, Sarasvati, Ganesh) is an integral part of ordinary Hindu practice.

The basic human condition in Hinduism is suffering, and the root of all suffering is ignorance. Suffering is governed by the laws of karma. What one reaps, one also sows; deeds shape not only the character but also the soul. The wheel of life or sequence of change (*samsara*) is one that each Hindu hopes to escape. Moving up through a series of reincarnations enables one to gradually attain a level (*Brahmin*) where one can be released (*moksha*) from this life. No matter how many reincarnations one has, the self (*atman*) remains the same; it only assumes different bodies. Detachment from impermanent things, and union (*samadhi*) with the Absolute is the ultimate spiritual aim.

Metaphysically, Hindus accept the impermanence (*annica*) of things. Attachment to impermanent things is seen as a key obstacle to enlightenment in Hinduism. What persons perceive is ultimately *maya* or illusion owing to the sentiments, memories and personal projections we cast onto impermanent things. Because we rely upon our sense perceptions, there is something real about what we encounter, but in their essence, there is only *maya*. Attachment is due to ignorance (*avidya*), which misperceives what is Real.

The foregoing represent rather high-minded ideals which do not occupy the thoughts of ordinary Hindus. However, most Hindus do endeavour to model their lives upon the principles of *Hindū dharma,* which refers to the ethical way of life and thought. A broad term, *dharma* encompasses customs, duties, social welfare, ethics and health. All devout Hindus espouse *ahimsa* or non-violence, and they apply this concept to both humans and non-humans alike.[4] The vast majority of Hin-

---

[4] That said, every 5 years there is a major Hindu festival in Bariyapur, Nepal, during which more than 200,000 animals are slaughtered *en masse* to honour the goddess Gadhimai. The 2009 festival

dus also believe that tolerance of religious difference is essential. Wisdom distilled from the Upanishads suggests that every person carries a spark of the divine, that the human race is an extended family, and that the truth is one, though the wise call it by many names. Unlike Judaism, Christianity and Islam, in Hinduism generally there is far less emphasis on doctrinal purity or scriptural authority. Hinduism easily incorporates features from other religions (notably from those which have formally split from Hinduism such as Jainism, Buddhism and Sikhism) and thus except for fairly recent politicized movements in India, very few if any exclusivist theological claims are made.

Dutch Hindus

By far most Dutch Hindus originate from Surinam, which was a Dutch plantation colony from 1667 until 1953. In 1975, it became an independent republic. In the intermediary period, it was granted a system of limited self-government. Between 1873 and 1916, approximately 35,000 indentured labourers were brought to Surinam from the British Indian states of Bihar and Uttar Pradesh by Dutch colonial interests in order to replace recently freed African slaves. Paid labour was scarcely better than slavery itself.

Most Indian migrants had backgrounds in farming and migrated to Surinam due to severe drought and famine in India. Eighty per cent of the Indian arrivals were Hindu. Upon their arrival, they found themselves vulnerable both to prejudice from other groups, whether indigenous or those with African or mixed European-African ancestry (Creole), whose social position was often worse. Unlike in neighbouring Guyana, a British colony, Dutch efforts to convert Hindus was not the norm. Instead, similar to the way they organized their own society in the Netherlands, the colonizers separated the various groups in Surinam, a pattern which still holds. Different religious and ethnic groups generally occupy different areas and villages in a pattern of relatively peaceful co-existence (Vertovec 1995).

During the indentured labour period, Hinduism in Surinam underwent major changes in orientation, redefining itself in its new environment. Eventually the caste system, a central feature of *vaishnavite* Hinduism in northeastern India, was abolished, a process brought to completion with the arrival of the anti-Brahmin and more strictly monotheistic *arya sarnaj* movement. Moreover, unlike neighbouring British colonies, where efforts to Anglicize the Indian population were part of a protracted assimilationist campaign, the use of Hindi—the official language of India—continues to be used in formal situations and for religious purposes (Koefoed and Jadoenandansing 1993). It was estimated that in 2009 Surinam had 482,000

---

was predictably met with protests from animal rights activists, as well as many prominent Buddhists, Jains and Hindus. See Bhanot 2009.

inhabitants, of whom 37% are of Indian descent, and approximately 27% of whom adhere to Hinduism (CIA 2009).[5]

In the immigration process to the Netherlands, various waves can be discerned. First, came the Surinamese elite for higher education. In the 1960s, other groups followed their example. It was not until the 1970s, and especially upon receiving independence from the Netherlands in 1975 that large numbers of poorer Surinamese, particularly from the ethnic minority Chinese, Javanese and Indian groups, re-settled in the Netherlands for political reasons and to seek out better economic opportunities. After 1980, immigration continued for reasons of family reunification and formation. The arrival of non-white immigrants, concentrated mainly in the larger western urban centres, resulted in discrimination, particularly for black Surinamese, both in the housing and labour markets (Bovenkerk 1978; Van Amersfoort and Van Niekerk 2006).

Of the approximately 225,000–300,000 persons of Indian descent living in the Netherlands today, 85% have immigrated from Surinam. In 2004 there were 99,000 Hindus in the Netherlands, of which 83,000 originated from Surinam, and 11,000 from India (CBS 2009). Whereas a significant percentage of Surinamese Hindus once retained dual citizenship, owing to changes in Dutch immigration policy in the mid 1990s, many have opted exclusively for Dutch citizenship, though they retain the right to return to Surinam if they wish. Today, the largest concentrations of Surinamese can be found in Amsterdam, Rotterdam, The Hague and Almere.

Notwithstanding the earlier setbacks, Surinamese immigrants have managed to integrate in the Netherlands in spite of their visible minority status. While the socio-economic position of Afro-Surinamese and Indo-Surinamese relative to Dutch society was nearly the same in the first 15 to 20 years, different patterns of social mobility emerged with the latter eventually making faster progress (Van Niekerk 2004). Command of the Dutch language, high rates of intermarriage with native Dutch, and an historical relationship with the Netherlands have eased their transition relative to other groups. Other evidence suggests that the hierarchally organized and community-oriented Indian community, together with a strong social cohesion and control, an entrepreneurial work ethic and high social aspirations, all combine to explain the rapid integrative advancement of Dutch Hindus.[6] In addition to support for the Surinamese community, Hindus also enjoy government sponsored weekly television and radio programming, organized and run by Hindus, which focuses on issues affecting the Hindu community in the Netherlands and abroad. Today, Dutch Hindus are cast as model minorities, certainly when compared to the largest immigrant groups in the Netherlands, the Moroccans and Turks (cf. Dagevos and-Gijsberts 2007).

---

[5] About 1% of Surinamese of Indian descent are Christians and 20% are Muslims (Koefoed and Jadoenandansing 1991).

[6] Scholars have used a situational analysis to better understand the dynamics between the reception in the receiving society, the design of government policies which aim to assist immigrant groups, the labour market conditions, and the social composition of the ethnic community (cf. Vermeulen and Penninx 2000).

Dutch Hindu Schools

Freedom of Education

Since the revision of its constitution in 1917, the Netherlands has guaranteed educational freedoms, together with full support for funding, to establish special (*bijzondere*) schools with religious or didactic aims and methods. Article 23 of the Dutch constitution was the result of a hard-fought-over school struggle (*schoolstrijd*) for public recognition and funding between Protestants and Catholics on the one hand, and secular Liberals on the other. This struggle can be seen as part of an emancipation process of the indigenous Dutch religious social groups.

Many 'special' schools (e.g. Jenaplan, Steiner, Montessori) are very popular, especially among well-educated, white parents; others, which represent religious denominational differences, also remain popular, and in fact continue to educate a majority of Dutch children. This remains something of a paradox in the Netherlands: while secularization has steadily progressed in all societal sectors since the 1960s, the number of religious schools has remained constant with a market share of 67% (Driessen and Merry 2006). At this moment, 33% of all primary schools are public schools, 30% are Catholic, 26% are Protestant, and the rest are schools of smaller denominations including branches of orthodox Protestant, Islamic, Jewish and Hindu schools.

Notwithstanding their specific denomination, all schools promote, to one degree or another, shared beliefs, values, habits and interactions among school and community members.

The Founding of Hindu Schools

While the Dutch state has played a facilitative role in fostering educational pluralism, not all religious schools have been welcomed with open arms. For example, in their 20-year history, Islamic schools have struggled under an image problem; during periods of political crisis (e.g. following 9/11 or the murder of Dutch film provocateur Theo van Gogh by a Muslim extremist in 2004) public sentiment briefly turned against the Muslim minority and a number of Islamic schools were vandalized (Buijs 2009). In addition, it has become clear that in terms of their pupils' achievements the 43 Islamic schools that are in existence now have not succeeded in living up to their expectations. Recent scandals involving fiscal mismanagement by the schools' boards have only worsened their reputation (Driessen 2008; Merry and Driessen 2009).

Like Islamic schools, Hindu schools cater mostly to a cultural and religious minority, but more importantly to a higher then average percentage of socio-economically disadvantaged children.[7] Furthermore, like Islamic schools, Hindu schools represent a form of voluntary separation, one that appears to conflict with the rhetoric of integration. Yet in contrast to Islamic schools, Hindu schools are fewer in number, manage to produce better than average academic results, have not been subject to scandal, have received very little media attention, and recent school openings have been welcomed by the Ministry of Education.

Presently there are six Hindu primary schools in the Netherlands. They are located in Den Haag (2), Amsterdam, Rotterdam, Utrecht and Almere. The first Hindu primary school was founded in 1988 (at the same time as the first Islamic school), the sixth and most recent opened its doors in 2008. (There are now plans to establish a Hindu secondary school.) That it took so long before the first school was established is a bit surprising considering that the Dutch pillarized school system, based on the principle of freedom of education, offers any denomination the same opportunity to establish its own schools. The reasons for the long delay may have been simply a shortage of pioneers and educational expertise among Surinamese immigrants; further, for a long time there has been a trust in the quality of Dutch education; finally there are important differences in orientation between first- and second-generation immigrants (Van Amersfoort and Van Niekerk 2006; Van Niekerk 2000).

Motives for establishing Hindu schools vary, but they include concern for the academic reputation, a desire that one's children become acquainted with the cultural background of the parents, and the hope that they will play a positive role in the integration process of Hindu youngsters (Bloemberg and Nijhuis 1993; Roels-ma-Somer 2008; Teunissen 1990). Because Hindu schools follow the constitutional guarantees which permit schools to be founded on the basis of a worldview or philosophy, each of these is fully funded by the Dutch state. While they are free to favour Hindu teachers and principals, all schools are expected to follow the attainment targets in terms of teaching matter set by the Ministry of Education. Most of the pupils in Hindu schools of course have a Hindu background, but in at least one Hindu school, owing to its diverse neighbourhood characteristics and strong academic reputation, more than 25% of the children are either Muslim or Christian. Perhaps also surprising is that this school has a number of Muslim teachers.

To understand the position of Hindu schools in a broader perspective, i.e. the Dutch denominational school landscape, a comparison was made between a number of demographic background characteristics of Hindu schools, Islamic schools, Catholic schools, Protestant schools, public schools and the average Dutch primary school. This analysis was based on national population data concerning the 2008–2009 school year. In that year there were 6,891 primary schools of which 32.9% was public, 30.1% Catholic, and 26.2% Protestant Christian; the rest represented a number of small denominations. There were 6 Hindu schools (or 0.1%) and 41 Islamic schools (or 0.6%). All of the Hindu schools are situated in the large cities in the western part of the Netherlands, while most Islamic schools are located in the large cities in the western and southern part.

---

[7] The percentage of children from low-educated families varies from one school to another. In Amsterdam the figure is 53%, in Rotterdam 50%, Utrecht 53%, Den Haag 47%, and Almere 38%.

Table 34.1 Demographic characteristics of various categories of denominational schools and the average Dutch primary school (school year 2008–2009; means per school)

	Public	Catholic	Protestant	Hindu	Islamic	Average
Number of pupils	210	255	211	276	228	225
% Ethnic minorities	14.5	9.8	8.2	77.0	89.2	11.1
% Disadvantaged	19.6	15.5	14.0	44.5	63.4	16.1
% Turkish	7.0	5.3	5.6	1.4	31.4	6.3
% Moroccan	7.2	6.0	5.9	0.0	43.0	6.8
% Surinamese	3.8	2.6	3.5	71.9	3.1	3.6
% Antillean	2.0	1.5	1.9	1.0	1.1	1.8
Total number of schools	*2,264*	*2,075*	*1,806*	*6*	*41*	*6,891*
Total number of pupils	*474,643*	*529,329*	*380,278*	*1,654*	*9,331*	*1,552,894*

Table 34.1 summarizes the demographic characteristics of the different school denominations: the number of pupils (i.e. school size); the percentage of ethnic minorities (at least one of the pupil's parents was born in a Mediterranean country or a non-English speaking country outside of Europe or is a refugee); the percentage of disadvantaged pupils (i.e. their parents are low-educated and/or perform manual labour or are without a job and/or are from ethnic minorities[8]); and the percentages of Turkish, Moroccan, Surinamese, and Antillean pupils, respectively.

There are a number of striking differences between the various denominational types of schools. For starters, Hindu schools are the largest schools. Although both Hindu schools and Islamic schools are known as so-called black schools, Hindu schools cater to far fewer ethnic minority and disadvantaged pupils (77 v. 89% and 45 v. 63%, respectively). The latter probably has to do with the fact that Surinamese Hindus in general are better educated and in paid jobs than Turks and Moroccans. In addition, in the case of Hindu schools the main country of origin by far is Surinam, while for the Islamic schools this is (either) Morocco or Turkey. This also explains the differences in mean disadvantaged status of the schools: the Moroccan and Turks immigrated to the Netherlands as (unskilled) guest workers, while many of the Surinamese already had received an education in Surinam and immigrated in order to pursue higher education in the Netherlands. The bottom line of the table shows that the total number of pupils attending a Hindu (or Islamic) school is very small indeed.

---

[8] These indicators stem from the Educational Priority Policy, where they were used to award schools with (many) disadvantaged pupils extra facilities (cf. Driessen and Dekkers 2008). Recently this classification system has been changed in such a way that only the parents' education level has remained a relevant indicator.

Characteristics of Hindu Schools

As we have already mentioned, the vast majority of children who attend Dutch Hindu schools have a Surinamese background, and many also have parents with lower SES. Nevertheless, Dutch Hindus appear not only to perform, on average, better than other minority groups in schools (Van Niekerk 2004), they also appear to integrate at a faster rate than other non-Western immigrant groups. Partly this is because of shared characteristics with Dutch society, but also social aspirations among Dutch Hindus are consistently high, and in general their orientation is towards the mainstream culture. Dutch Hindus hold that one has to adapt to the country where one lives, actively participate in its social and political life, and abide by the laws of the country. Hindu schools prepare their pupils to live in a multicultural society by instilling discipline, tolerance and mutual respect, especially towards adults. These are reinforced by explicit staff expectations and parental support of the school mission. Role-modelling proper attitudes and dispositions reinforce a school ethos of peace and respect.

The ethos of a Dutch Hindu school is further structured in the following ways: time for meditation is a part of daily school life; images of Hindu gods adorn classrooms and hallways; texts from scriptures such as the *Bhagavad Gita* and *Upanishads,* or epic poetic texts from the *Mahabharata* and the *Ramayana,* can be publicly seen; Indian dance and music may also fill up as much as two hours of school time per week; finally, though major Christian holidays are also celebrated, Hindu festivals such as Diwali and Phagwa (Holi) are community-wide festivities which attract a lot of public attention and participation.

Hindus believe they have a duty both to themselves and to the community in which they find themselves. Both obligations comprise their educational and spiritual vision. The child is part of the class community and learns to function as part of this community. Therefore, whole-class instruction is an important feature of Hindu schools. At the same time, Hindu schools try to cultivate each child's development by attending to individual needs. School is thus preparation for membership and participation in society and the Hindu school endeavours to supply each child with the requisite dispositions, knowledge and skills. Though Hindu schools have a holistic orientation, they are generally more subject matter-oriented than process-oriented and there is a strong emphasis on discipline and cognitive achievement.

Unlike most Islamic schools, girls and boys take class instruction, but also physical exercise and swim classes, together. Active parental participation and involvement in the school life and at home is encouraged. However, this is not always accomplished. Reasons for this are that Surinamese children disproportionally live in single-parent families (up to 60%) and if this is not the case both parents work. Pupils at Hindu schools follow the same basic curriculum as pupils at other Dutch schools. This also includes the obligatory subjects, 'intercultural education' and 'religious and ideological movements' (such as Christianity, Islam and Judaism). While Hindu schools use the same textbooks as other schools, there is considerable flexibility in how the school meets its learning goals and attainment targets.

Teachers aim to develop a Hindu worldview and identity by integrating cultural and religious beliefs into ordinary instruction. This is known as *dharma* education. Though the regular subjects are taught, the Hindu school also offers Hindi instruction for one to two hours per week, but in all subjects instruction is given in Dutch. Hindu schools strive to foster unity among the staff and pupils through shared mantras, prayer (at the start and end of the school day), and a vegetarian diet (though not all families are vegetarian). Yet far more than Hinduism, what children in a Dutch Hindu school mainly share in common is their Surinamese cultural background. Because most teachers have a Surinamese-Hindu background, staff and pupils share a similar ancestral history and experience, which strenghthens both the relationship between teachers and pupils and overall internal school cohesion. This can also be seen in the school didactics, i.e. the fact that more individual attention is given to the cultural needs of pupils (Bloemberg and Nijhuis 1993; Roelsma-Somer 2008).

Quality and Achievement

The Dutch Inspectorate of Education visits schools on a regular basis and checks to see whether they are meeting the required instruction standards on a number of quality criteria.[9] These criteria are elaborated in a framework that focuses on the structure of the learning process with the following elements: educational content; learning/teaching time; educational climate; school climate; teachings methods; response to individual needs; active and independent learning; results and development of pupils.

The findings of the Inspectorate's most recent reports for the years 2005 and 2006 are summarized in Table 34.2 (see Inspectie van het Onderwijs 2009).

This table shows that on most aspects Hindu schools score 'sufficiently' or 'strongly'. Importantly, with regard to the schools' output as measured by standardized achievement tests, all schools score at least equal to, but often above, the level of other schools with a comparable socio-ethnic pupil population. For the first four schools in Table 34.2 information is available concerning the situation in 2008. The Inspectorate's conclusion is that since 2005 or 2006 the situation at these four schools has improved to such a degree that there are no worries regarding the schools' quality and there thus is no need for further inquiry.

---

[9] As of 2007 the Inspectorate only visits schools when there are (indications of) problems.

Table 34.2 Results quality evaluation reports Inspectorate of Education for 2005 and 2006

School	Contribution to educational quality 2005 and 2006						Achievement test results
	Not/ hardly	Insufficiently	Sufficiently	Strongly	N/A	Aspects	
Shri Saraswatie	0	3	25	4	1	33	at or above level comparable schools
Shri Krishna[a]	0	5	2	0	4	11	N/A
Shri Laksmi	0	6	20	3	2	31	at or above level comparable schools
Shri Vishnu	0	10	22	4	1	37	at or above level comparable schools
Algemene Hindoe-school[b]							at or above level comparable schools

[a] At the time of the Inspectorate's visit this school was operational for just one year.
[b] This report only focused on the schools' achievements.

A Closer Look at Hindu Schools

Introduction

Hindu schools are founded and predicated upon many of the same principles invoked by other religious minority groups in the Netherlands, including Muslims, Jews and Evangelicals. That is, its defenders argue that a Hindu education, one that takes account of the relevant shared cultural and religious values and backgrounds of the pupils, including child rearing practices in the family, enhances the learning process. In addition, Dutch Hindu schools recognize that instructional design, strong leadership and school organization that builds upon these shared features is the key difference between a school with a high concentration of minorities and one that has turned cultural homogeneity to its advantage.

Hindu schools represent a form of emancipation. They are emancipatory for reasons both external and internal to the educative process. Some of the external reasons have to do with colonial and post-colonial practices and identities; cultural and religious minority stigmatization in a secularized society; experiences with prejudice and racism; the rhetoric of integration that permeates government speak; and finally, the tremendous pressures attending the model-minority stereotype, viz., internal and external expectations to out-perform other, less favourably evaluated, minorities and to show oneself more 'integrated'.

Yet reasons internal to the educative process may also be cited, including higher rates of personal well-being and improved academic performance that derive from culturally integrated learning strategies. Indeed, Hindu schools are sites where faith but perhaps especially cultural background, can easily be incorporated into the instructional design owing to the core mission of the school. Like other community-based schools, Hindu schools provide a caring ethos, high expectations, a culturally relevant curriculum, and a core set of shared values. More than the curriculum itself, a Hindu school's daily rituals, routines and practices, role-modelling and leadership, relational bonds and trust, and strong community support, all contribute to a unique learning experience in which the Hindu child is placed at the centre of instruction.

In what follows we examine a number of teachings and practices found in Dutch Hindu schools and assess them both for their ability to forge a distinctive identity, one conducive to emancipation and thus their ability to prepare children for integration by other means. We then consider whether there may be challenges awaiting Dutch Hindu schools in the coming years.

Hindu Schooling and Identity

Like any major world religion, Hinduism is vastly complex, includes numerous subdivisions and incongruous teachings, and cannot easily be reduced to a simple core of beliefs or practices. Though it contains important canonical texts, none of them is accepted as authoritative by all Hindus. Further, while Hinduism comprises many doctrines, unlike other religions for which right belief (*orthodoxy*) is paramount, Hinduism is chiefly a religion of customs, habits and practices largely informed by one's cultural roots in India. As Indians continue to migrate throughout the world, reflecting many of the social class differences in Indian society, those cultural and religious roots evolve and are transformed by the new environments in which persons of Indian ancestry find themselves. In many cases, religious identity is renewed, re-discovered, or re-invented in a land of immigration.

The renewal of a religious identity in a new land is nothing new. For immigrants, religious organizations become the primary means by which ethnic identities are nourished and grow. Minority groups are also confronted with the experience of being a minority, and a visible minority at that, which causes many to search for their roots As Kurien (2001, p. 265) writes,

> ...religion and religious organizations increase in salience for immigrants because of the disruption and disorientation caused by the immigration experience and because religious organizations become the means to form ethnic communities and identities in the immigrant context.

It is of course true that determining what a *Hindu* identity entails in the Dutch environment is not entirely clear. On a straightforward reading of Hindu school literature, and in speaking with school personnel, Hindu identity is defined and described as one who recognizes *as one's own* the loosely assembled beliefs and practices to which Hindu schools subscribe.

Yet as we have argued, a majority of children and staff in Hindu schools share more in common by virtue of a shared Surinamese cultural background, and with this shared background the Dutch language provides additional cohesive support. Within the existing constitutional framework in the Netherlands, Hinduism—as a religious worldview—becomes the convenient artifice for binding these items together. Even in the absence of constitutional provisions, religion frequently mediates cultural bonding among expatriates. Kurien explains, "[in] immigrant contexts, religion becomes the means of creating ethnic communities and identities and so the attachment to religion and religious institutions is intensified" (Kurien 2001, p. 289).

As we have seen, Hindu schools also map onto the Dutch model which facilitates *religion-based* schools but not, strictly speaking, *culturally based* ones. To illustrate the centrality of cultural cohesion in Hindu schools, there is an awareness in the Dutch Hindu community that those of Surinamese descent and Hindus who immigrate directly from India share very little in common; despite a shared religion, interactions between the two groups are in fact quite limited. Further, besides the probable differences in shared culture and language, Hindus who immigrate directly from India are more likely to be influenced by caste thinking[10] than their Surinamese counterparts, and India continues to be a far more patriarchal society than either Surinam or the Netherlands.

So while there is no doubt that Hindu schools aim to foster a shared Hindu ethos, through the propagation and repetition of basic beliefs and practices, celebrations of religious festivals, participation in silent meditation, and a vegetarian diet, the emphasis is largely *culturally* based, and thus the actual Hindu-ness of what Hindu schools do may not run very deep. All children and school staff participate in the shared activities, tolerance towards other beliefs and traditions is strongly encouraged, and mutual respect towards one another in school is certainly expected. Yet except perhaps for the singular interpretation these things are given, tolerance and mutual respect are hardly the exclusive domain of Hindu schools. Indeed, these virtues are promoted and found in most schools, and in the Netherlands they are incorporated within the aims of compulsory citizenship instruction. What Hindu school staff say in response to this is that while other schools claim to promote them, they fail to deliver. Yet as an empirical matter, this hypothesis is difficult to assess.

---

[10] The majority of Dutch Hindus follow the *Sanatan Dharm*, a spiritual form of Hinduism influenced by the Bhagavad Gita and the Upanishads and which emphasizes equality, while a minority follow the more recently formed *Karma Veda*, whose founder, Swami Dayanand, aimed to ground Hinduism in its so-called original sources, the Vedas, and among its beliefs there is the requirement that only those from the Brahman caste are able to become priests.

Hindu Schools and Emancipation

As we have shown, the Dutch constitutional freedom of education resulted from a struggle over equal treatment, specifically for equal financial support for both denominational and non-denominational or public schools. This struggle was not restricted to education, but was rather part of a general emancipatory process of social and religious groups in the Netherlands that penetrated all aspects of Dutch society. An important consequence of this has been the maintenance of a delicate balance between the autonomy of the different social and religious groups on the one hand, and the integration of these groups within the encompassing framework of the nation-state on the other (cf. Spiecker and Steutel 2001). Today, despite steady secularization, religious schools continue to be defended as an important avenue of emancipation. Proponents of Hindu schools appeal to the role separate schools have played in the historical emancipation of, for example, Dutch Catholics (Teunissen 1990).

Yet opponents of separate schools, and perhaps especially of Islamic and Hindu schools, argue that voluntary separation will only aggravate segregation within the education system and lead to permanent societal isolation. Further, separate Hindu schools will not succeed in providing quality education, in part because of the concentration of low SES pupils, and therefore they will be associated with school failure and cultural separatism. The ethnic separation within the education system will coincide with ethnic separation within other societal institutions which will result in ethnic enclaves or even ghettos (Teunissen 1990). One hears in these concerns a worry that segregated schools of any sort are simply bad policy, bad for the Dutch majority but especially so for ethnic minorities. Correspondingly, integrated schools, or schools with a racial/ethnic 'balance'(though usually with a native Dutch majority) promise better educational and experiential outcomes for children, but also better outcomes for society because integrated schools are believed to strengthen social cohesion in the public sphere (cf. Merry and New 2008).

Though commonly voiced, this criticism contains a number of question-begging assumptions. First, it is assumed that segregation is a situation created by minorities themselves. While minority groups certainly exhibit preferences for living close to one another, the same of course can be said of majority groups for reasons having to do with social class affinity, access to specific resources, or shared cultural and religious background. Separation is of course also determined by forces outside the control of individuals themselves, including affordable rents or white flight, which in the Netherlands has resulted in rather obvious segregation in both neighbourhoods and schools in several cities (cf. Karsten et al. 2006; Musterd and Ostendorf 2009).[11]

---

[11] It should be noted that the integrated v. segregated school discussion presently underway in the Netherlands for the most part is a hypothetical discussion. The situation is such that most Hindu parents wishing their child to attend another school in their district would likely have as their only choice a school with a high concentration of poor minorities, where the chances of meeting middle-class white pupils are very small indeed.

But the criticism also assumes, without evidence, that an integrated school is better—both in terms of quality as well as in terms of preparing children to live together—than one that is (voluntarily) separate. Here the logic of integration, hinted at above, assumes that mixed schools per se yield better outcomes in academic performance and individual well-being than more homogeneous schools, and also that mixed schools provide the blueprint for how society ought to be organized. In most Western societies, including the Netherlands, it continues to be assumed by liberal elites that simply mixing schools will yield positive outcomes. Thus educational policy, whose aim it is to maintain racial/ethnic balance—for example recent restrictions on parental choice in the Dutch city of Nijmegen[12]—is often predicated on the belief that by mixing pupils of different backgrounds the performance of the disadvantaged pupils will go up and the performance of the advantaged pupils will mostly be unaffected.

Yet while a concentration of socio-economically disadvantaged pupils in one school building certainly increases the challenges both to teachers and pupils, too frequently the remedies offered are rather simplistic. As for the academic outcomes, a recent review into this so-called school-mix effect does not support this hypothesis (Driessen 2007), while on the level of societal outcomes, the 'benefits' continue to be postulated rather than demonstrated (see Blokland and Van Eijk 2010). This is *not* to say that integrated schools are a bad idea, or that real benefits will not accrue to—particularly disadvantaged—pupils from different backgrounds who interact with one another. Even so, more thinking needs to be done beyond simply mixing schools. While a mixed pupil body is doubtless one variable worth taking into consideration,[13] other important features are surely equally important: (1) teacher quality and retention, (2) committed school leadership, (3) parental educational level and involvement, (4) shared community values, (5) role-modelling of school staff, and (6) the cultural relevance of learning material.

For proponents of Hindu schools, like proponents of *any* form of voluntary separation, what they do is not 'segregationist'. For starters, the reasons for separation are to reinforce the potentially fragile identities of children from immigrant families who are more likely to experience bullying or harassment, discrimination or exclusion, but also ambivalence towards a culture with which they may not identify (Merry and New 2008; Villalpando 2003). There is much evidence to suggest that this is often the case for 'visible minorities' in the Netherlands, including children of Surinamese background (Van Niekerk 2004, 2007). Hindu schools, then, assist children in being proud of their cultural background and also to become 'good'

---

[12] The new measures were implemented in April 2009; similar initiatives are currently underway in other Dutch cities.

[13] Unsurprisingly, all-White schools (and neighbourhoods) are generally seen as "normal", while predominately non-White schools and neighbourhoods are perceived as "segregated" (cf. Bonilla-Silva 2003). As for mixed schools, there continue to be problems with homogeneous classrooms. There also is plenty of evidence that children normally self-select who they will interact with based on shared interests and preferences (cf. Moody 2001; Tatum 1997).

Hindus. Securing a stronger identity can enable pupils to defend themselves against ignorance and prejudice, both as individuals and as a group.

Defining what it means to be a member of the Dutch Hindu community on one's own terms improves the chances of escaping imposed stereotypes offered up by the media and a school system that otherwise does not address cultural difference except in the most superficial way. Proponents of Hindu schools see that one of the best ways to do this is to explicitly address the minority position of Hindu children relative to the broader Dutch context. Separate schooling as a provisional measure can thus contribute to a child's self-esteem and autonomy, but also to an inward sense of belonging to one's cultural group and also outward towards Dutch society (cf. Merry 2005). Thus, as the title to our chapter suggests, *integration by other means* engages in double entendre, for it signals different and possibly conflicting ways of being 'integrated': (a) being integrated with oneself and one's 'own' community, and (b) integration into the broader society. Both forms of integration, however, involve expectations internal to their specific processes that may serve to alienate rather than emancipate. These include essentialisms of Hinduism but also expressions of tokenism by the majority population.

Conclusions

In this chapter, we have demonstrated how Hindu schools, within the Dutch context, operate as an important form of cultural and religious mediation for children who otherwise may face higher risks of school failure. Like other community-based forms of education, Hindu schools contribute to emancipation by attending to the religious and cultural identities of children of Surinamese background so that, (seemingly) paradoxically, they can more effectively integrate into the mainstream society. Hindu schools therefore purport themselves to be an avenue of integration by other means.

Even so, we have also shown that despite the challenges Dutch Hindus have faced, they continue to be a rather successful minority relative to other minority groups. This can be explained in terms of a tight community structure, fluency in the Dutch language, high social aspirations, and a generally favourable position relative to other immigrant groups, some of whom struggle under more intense pressures to integrate.

Yet despite the many positive features of Hindu schools that we have elaborated, there are a few challenges that may arise in the coming years. The first is whether Hindu schools, and the Hindu community at large, will be influenced by—and exploit—the prevailing anti-Islamic ethos, casting themselves as the 'model minority', the tolerant, peaceful alternative to Islam. This will prove a very difficult temptation to resist, particularly when Dutch Islamic schools continue to be viewed as undesirable, and prominent voices in Dutch politics openly rail against the prevalence of Muslim minorities in Dutch cities.

Related to this, and already beginning to manifest, is the creeping influence of Hindu nationalist politics from India onto those in the diaspora. Contrary to the manner in which Dutch Hindus portray themselves as peace-loving and tolerant, the *Hindutva* movement in India is a highly intolerant strain of religious fascism that for decades has grown in size and political power. Indeed, it has already shown itself capable of extending its influence abroad (see Kundu 1994; Zavos 2009).[14] The comparative juxtaposition of Hinduism and Islam, with Hinduism being seen as the preferable of the two, has the potential to aggravate tensions by making unfair evaluations between two decidedly different minority groups with completely different pre-immigration and post-immigration histories. With this expanding influence there are reasons to wonder whether the 'supremacy' of Hinduism—as the only legitimate religion of India—will influence the ideas and attitudes of Hindus abroad, especially when political currents in Hinduism cannot be restricted to the Indian subcontinent (cf. Kurien 2007; Vertovec 2000).[15]

Related to these challenges is the need for Hindu schools to take its claims of mutual respect and emancipation seriously not only by *tolerating* what others believe and do, but by critically examining Hinduism's historical role in establishing fixed castes of people, with some persons destined to permanently lower positions, and others relegated outside the caste system altogether, viz., the Dalits. Other topics that could come up for critical discussion might be various patriarchal customs (e.g. control of temples), or the limited freedom to exit one's Hindu culture (cf. Spinner-Halev 2005). Whatever the case, Hindu schools have the ability to use religion as a critical resource, one directed against cultural practices that fail to exhibit either emancipation or mutual respect.

Finally, one very real challenge for Hindu schools is whether they can remain 'authentically' Hindu. Fostering strong Hindu identity in a society where Hinduism is a strange, exotic (and sometimes fashionable) religion poses special challenges, but so do the expectations from parents that Hindu schools first deliver on academic excellence, second on cultural support, and only third on the Hindu faith itself. Unlike Dutch Islamic schools, which struggle to foster an Islamic ethos owing to a severe shortage of Muslim teachers, Hindu schools for the moment have strong community support and its staff are overwhelmingly of Hindu background. Yet like mainstream Christian schools, Hindu schools may before long have the exact same religious identity crisis if the Hindu faith is only an ancillary concern for most of its members. Correlated to this, given the high social aspirations of the Dutch Hindu community, and the manner in which Hindus are generally seen as model minorities in the Netherlands, the arguments for emancipation of a vulnerable minority may cease to resonate.

---

[14] One could mention escalating tensions between British Sikhs and Hindus during the late 1980s and early 1990s due to struggles in Punjab, or violent outbursts in Britain following the destruction of the Babri Masjid in Ayodhya in 1992.

[15] This influence does not move in one direction. Indians in diaspora can wield great influence on Indian politics. Wealthy and well-educated Hindus in southern California, for instance, have been major benefactors of *Hindutva* in India. (See Kurien 2007).

References

Berry, J. (2003). Conceptual approaches to acculturation. In K. Chun, P. Balls Organista, & G. Marín (Eds.), *Acculturation: Advances in theory, measurement, and applied research* (pp. 17–37). Washington, DC: American Pyschological Association.

Bhanot, A. (2009). The Gadhimai Sacrifice is Grotesque. *The Guardian.* http://www.guardian.co.uk/commentisfree/belief/2009/nov/25/gadhimai-animal-sacrifice-nepal. Accessed 26 November 2009.

Bloemberg, L., & Nijhuis, D. (1993). Hindoescholen in Nederland. *Migrantenstudies, 9*(3), 35–52.

Blokland, T., & Van Eijk, G. (2010). Do people who like diversity practice diversity in neighborhood life? Neighborhood use and the social networks of 'diversity seekers' in a mixed neighbourhood in the Netherlands. *Journal of Ethnic and Migration Studies, 36*(2), 313–332.

Bonilla-Silva, E. (2003). *Racism without racists: Color-blind racism and the persistance of racial inequality in the United States.* Lanham: Rowman & Littlefield.

Bovenkerk, F. (Ed.). (1978). Omdat zij anders zijn: Patronen van rasdiscriminatie in Nederland. Amsterdam & Meppel: Boom.

Buijs, F. (2009). Muslims in the Netherlands: Social and political developments after 9/11. *Journal of Ethnic and Migration Studies, 35*(3), 421–438.

CBS. (2009). Bevolking. http://statline.cbs.nl. Accessed 3 July 2009.

CIA. (2009). The world factbook: Suriname. https://www.cia.gov/library/publications/the-world-factbook/geos/NS.html. Accessed 7 July 2009.

Dagevos, J., & Gijsberts, M. (2007). Integration report 2007. Summary. In J. Dagevos & M. Gijsberts (Eds.), *Jaarraport integratie* (pp. 311–326). Den Haag: SCP.

Driessen, G. (2007). *"Peer group" effecten op onderwijsprestaties: Een internationaal review van effecten, verklaringen en theoretische en methodologische aspecten.* Nijmegen: ITS.

Driessen, G. (2008). De verwachtingen waargemaakt? Twee decennia islamitische basisscholen. *Mens & Maatschappij, 83*(2), 168–189.

Driessen, G., & Dekkers, H. (2008). Dutch policies on socio-economic and ethnic inequality in education. *International Social Science Journal, 59* (193/194), 449–464.

Driessen, G., & Merry, M. (2006). Islamic schools in the Netherlands: Expansion or marginalization? *Interchange, 37*(3), 201–223.

Inspectie van het Onderwijs. (2009). *Schoolwijzer.* http://www.onderwijsinspectie.nl. Accessed 3 July 2009.

Karsten, S., Felix, C., Ledoux, G., Meijnen, W., Roeleveld, J., & Van Schooten, E. (2006). Choosing segregation or integration? The extent and effects of ethnic segregation in Dutch cities. *Education and Urban Society, 38*(2), 228–247.

Koefoed, G., & Jadoenandansing, S. (1991). De Surinamers. In J. J. de Ruijter (Ed.), *Talen in Nederland* (pp. 157–205). Groningen: Wolters-Noordhoff.

Koefoed, G., & Jadoenandansing, S. (1993). Surinamese languages. In G. Extra & L. Verhoeven (Eds.), *Community languages in the Netherlands* (pp. 51–67). Amsterdam: Swets & Zeitlinger.

Kundu, A. (1994). The Ayodhya aftermath: Hindu versus Muslim violence in Britain. *Immigrants and Minorities, 13*(1), 26–47.

Kurien, P. (2001). Religion, ethnicity and politics: Hindu and Muslim Indian immigrants in the United States. *Ethnic and Racial Studies, 24*(2), 263–293.

Kurien, P. (2007). *A place at the multicultural table: The development of an American Hinduism.* Piscataway: Rutgers University Press.

Merry, M. (2005). Cultural coherence and the schooling for identity maintenance. *Journal of Philosophy of Education, 39*(3), 477–497.

Merry, M., & Driessen, G. (2009). Islamic schools in North America and the Netherlands: Inhibiting or enhancing democratic dispositions? In P. Woods & G. Woods (Eds.), *Alternative education for the 21st century: Philosophies, approaches, visions* (pp. 101–122). New York: Palgrave Macmillan.

Merry, M., & New, W. (2008). Constructing an authentic self: The challenges and promise of African-centered pedagogy. *American Journal of Education, 115*(1), 35–64.
Moody, J. (2001). Race, school integration and friendship segregation in America. *American Journal of Sociology, 107*(3), 679–716.
Musterd, S., & Ostendorf, W. (2009). Residential segregation and integration in the Netherlands. *Journal of Ethnic and Migration Studies, 35*(9), 1515–1532.
NMECS. (2007). *The education system in the Netherlands 2007.* http://www.minocw.nl/documenten/eurydice_2007_en.pdf. Accessed 24 June 2009.
Roelsma-Somer, S. (2008). *De kwaliteit van hindoescholen.* (Unpublished doctoral Dissertation, University of Tilburg)
Spiecker, B., & Steutel, J. (2001). Multiculturalism, pillarization and liberal civic education in the Netherlands. *International Journal of Educational Research, 35*(3), 293–304.
Spinner-Halev, J. (2005). Hinduism, Christianity, and liberal religious toleration. *Poltical Theory, 33*(1), 28–57.
Tatum, B. (1997). *Why are all of the black kids sitting together in the cafeteria? And other conversations about race.* New York: Basic Books.
Teunissen, J. (1990). Basisscholen op islamitische en hindoeïstische grondslag. *Migrantenstudies, 6*(2), 45–57.
Van Amersfoort, H., & Van Niekerk, M. (2006). Immigration as a colonial inheritance: Post-colonial immigrants in the Netherlands, 1945–2002. *Journal of Ethnic and Migration Studies, 32*(3), 323–346.
Van Niekerk, M. (2000). Paradoxes in paradise: Integration and social mobility of the Surinamese in the Netherlands. In H. Vermeulen & R. Penninx (Eds.), *Immigrant integration: The Dutch case* (pp. 64–92). Amsterdam: Het Spinhuis.
Van Niekerk, M. (2004). Afro-Caribbeans and Indo-Caribbeans in the Netherlands: Premigration legacies and social mobility. *International Migration Review, 38*(1), 158–183.
Van Niekerk, M. (2007). Second-generation Caribbeans in the Netherlands: Different migration histories, diverging trajectories. *Journal of Ethnic and Migration Studies, 33*(7), 1063–1081.
Vasta, E. (2007). From ethnic minorities to ethnic majority policy: Multiculturalism and the shift to assimilationism in the Netherlands. *Ethnic and Racial Studies, 30*(5), 713–740.
Vermeulen, H., & Penninx, R. (Eds.). (2000). *Immigrant integration: The Dutch case.* Amsterdam: Het Spinhuis.
Vertovec, S. (1995). Indian indentured migration to the Caribbean. In R. Cohen (Ed.), *The Cambridge Survey of world migration* (pp. 57–62). Cambridge: Cambridge University Press.
Vertovec, S. (2000). *The Hindu diaspora: Comparative patterns.* London: Routledge.
Villalpando, O. (2003). Self-Segregation or Self-Preservation? A critical race theory and Latina/o critical theory analysis of a study of Chicana/o college students. *International Journal of Qualitative Studies in Education, 16*(5), 619–646.
Zavos, J. (2009). Negotiating multiculturalism: Religion and the organisation of Hindu identity in contemporary Britain. *Journal of Ethnic and Migration Studies, 35*(6), 881–900.

Chapter 35
Negotiating the School Curriculum for the Malay Muslims in Singapore

Charlene Tan and Salleh Hairon

An important aspect of understanding cultural and social differences in the learning processes is the role played by religion for minorities. As a powerful cultural and identity marker, religion is increasingly regarded as a spiritual anchor in an age of globalisation marked by change and uncertainty. This is true especially for Islam where an international religious resurgence is noticeable in the Muslims' dressing, lifestyles, religious practices and social interactions (Kadir 2004; Millard 2004; Tan 2007a). Like Muslims in other parts of the world, the Muslim minority community in Singapore walk on a tightrope to balance their self-determination with social mobility and integration in schools and other social spheres. This chapter examines how the Malay Muslim community in Singapore negotiated their objective situation and their subjective everyday practices in the school curriculum.[1] We use the term "curriculum" to refer to "the totality of learning experiences provided to students so that they can attain general skills and knowledge at a variety of learning sites" (Marsh 2004, p. 5).

This chapter is divided into four sections. We begin with a brief historical survey of the Malay Muslims in Singapore and their schooling experiences during the colonial period under the British. This is followed by an analysis of how they negotiated their curriculum since Singapore's self-government from the British in the late 1950s. The next section focuses on current efforts to "modernise" the madrasah curriculum, with a case study of the recent changes that have taken place in one madrasah in Singapore. The chapter ends with some observations about the negotiation processes and outcomes for the Malay Muslims as well as the prospects for madrasahs in Singapore.

---

[1] It is not an aim of the chapter to provide a detailed discussion of the historical evolution of the religious and secular schools for the Malay Muslims in Singapore; readers are invited to peruse an established body of literature on that topic (e.g., Roff 1967; Doraisamy 1969; Siddique 1986; Ahmad 1971; Haikal and Yahaya 1997; Sahib 2000; Aljunied and Hussin 2005; Chee 2006).

C. Tan (✉)
Policy and Leadership Studies, National Institute of Education, NIE2-03-64, 1, Nanyang Walk 637616, Singapore
e-mail: charlene.tan@nie.edu.sg

Background on the Malay Muslims in Singapore

Singapore is a multi-ethnic and multi-religious country in Southeast Asia with more than 4.9 million residents, comprising Chinese (74.2%), Malays (13.4%), Indians (9.2%) and other ethnic groups (3.2%). A majority of the population are Buddhists (42.5%), followed by Muslims (14.9%), Christians (14.6%), Taoists (8.5%), Hindus (4.0%) and those who professed to have no religion (14.8%). Among the ethnic groups, the Malays are the most homogenous with 99.6% of them being Muslims,[2] with the rest of the Muslims (about 15%) comprising Indians, Chinese, Arabs and Eurasians. As almost all Muslims are Malays in Singapore, this chapter shall focus on Muslims who are Malays or "Malay Muslims", and use the two terms, "Malays" and "Muslims" synonymously throughout the discussion.

Islam was spread to Southeast Asia around the fourteenth century by Arab and Indian traders, culminating in the formation of a Muslim community in Singapore at the beginning of the nineteenth century. When Sir Stamford Raffles arrived in Singapore in 1819, there were already about a hundred Malay fishermen and a small number of about 30 Chinese (Haikal and Yahaya 1997). Although the Malays formed the majority in Singapore in the beginning, they were subsequently outnumbered by the Chinese who migrated from China; the Chinese formed 53% of the population by 1830 and 65% of the population by 1867 (Haikal and Yahaya 1997). The Malays were to remain as a minority population until the 1960s where they enjoyed a majority status for a brief period (1963–1965) when Singapore merged with Malaya, Brunei, Sabah and Sarawak to form the sovereign country of Malaysia. When Singapore became independent on 9 August 1965, the Singapore Malays found themselves as a minority community once again—a situation that has remained till today. But it is important to point out that although the Singapore's Muslim population is small in absolute terms, it is the largest Muslim minority in Southeast Asia in percentage terms (Funston 2006).

The educational goal of the British colonial government in the early nineteenth century was to provide a basic secular education to the masses and groom a small group of educated elite from the Malay aristocratic class in English schools (also known as English-medium schools). But the British educational policy was met with apathy, caution and resistance by the Muslim community. An English education was rejected by most Muslims as it was perceived as anglicising, deculturalising and christianising the Muslims (Zoohri 1990). As the British also initiated the setting up of the Malay schools (also known as Malay vernacular schools or Malay-medium schools) which were schools that taught the Malay language and used Malay as a medium of instruction, these schools were also viewed suspiciously by the Malay Muslims. The unfavourable perception was aggravated by the discovery of

---

[2] It should be noted that the "Malays" are not homogenous and include various ethnic sub-groups such as Malay, Javanese and Baweanese. Djamour (1953, as cited in Aljunied 2009, p. 8) classified the Malays in Singapore into two types: immigrants from the peninsula who had lived in the colony for several generations; and Indonesian immigrants who were mainly Javanese, Baweanese, Bugis and Banjarese.

the Bible being used as a schoolbook in the Malay schools where Qur'anic lessons were held; that led to protests from Muslim parents and reinforced their refusal to send their children to the Malay schools (Aljunied and Hussin 2005).

Rather than passively accepting the British agenda, the Muslims took control of their objective situation by establishing and consolidating their own religious schools as learning sites to educate their own children in the Islamic faith and nurture religious elites for their own community. So resistant were the Muslims towards secular education that many of them would rather send their children to faraway Islamic schools than to enrol them in the English or the Malay schools nearby. The rejection of the latter continued even after World War II where few Muslims were enrolled in the English schools and no Malay secondary schools existed during that period due to a lack of demand.

Negotiating Curriculum

During Singapore's Self-Government and Merger

In contrast to the early colonial period when the Malays were uninterested in and negative towards the Malay schools, the 1950s and 1960s witnessed a change in their attitude where they became keen to promote the Malay language and culture. That change of heart was motivated largely by the political events of Singapore's partial internal self-government from the British in the 1950s, full self-government in 1959 and subsequent merger with the Malaya in 1963.[3] Unlike the predominantly Chinese population in Singapore, the majority population in Malaya comprised Malays who shared close ethnic, religious and familial ties with the Malays in Singapore. Merger with the Malaya was therefore enthusiastically embraced and anticipated by the Malays in Singapore who relished the thought of relinquishing their minority status in Singapore; at the same time they welcomed the likelihood of the Malay language being elevated to a majority language and Islam privileged as the state religion.

The above political developments contributed towards the Malays strengthening their resistance towards the learning of the English language in favour of the Malay language and culture. A notable event was the proposal of a Re-orientation Plan by the Education Department of the colonial administration in 1951. The plan was to equip the Malay graduates for the job market and to compete more effectively with other ethnic groups (Zoohri 1990). It recommended that the Malay language should be taught in the Malay schools only in the first 3 years and English should be the

---

[3] The Malay states known collectively as Malaya then were ruled by the Malay Sultans in the fifteenth century and were colonised by the British since 1786. Malaya attained its independence from the British in 1957 and became known as the Federation of Malaya. In 1963, the Federation of Malaya merged with Singapore, Brunei, Sabah and Sarawak to form the sovereign country of Malaysia.

medium of instruction from the fourth to the seventh year for all subjects exceptthe Malay Language and Literature. Top pupils would be given the opportunity to be transferred to the English schools to complete the Senior Cambridge Examination in the English medium. However, the plan fell through as it was strongly opposed by the Malay community led by the Kesatuan Guru-Guru Melayu Singapura (KGMS; Singapore Malay Teachers' Union). Many Malays objected to the Plan due to the oft-repeated concern that their children might adopt foreign values contrary to their religious beliefs and practices and abandon their traditional beliefs and practices (Haikal and Yahaya 1997). The objection to learning English was so strong that the colonial government failed the second time in 1956 when it put forward a modified proposal for Muslim children. The revised proposal recommended that Mathematics and Science be taught in English but only from Primary six upwards (Zoohri 1990). Expectedly, that proposal was rebuffed again by the Muslim community, this time led by the Majlis Pelajaran Melayu (MPM; Malay Education Council) which was formed in 1955. Comprising KGMS and other Malay organisations, MPM successfully campaigned for the restoration of the Malay schools and establishment of secondary and tertiary Malay education from the late 1950s (Zoohri 1990). The governing party, People's Action Party (PAP) acceded to the Muslims' request by choosing Malay as the national language and building more the Malay schools. Malay-medium secondary classes were introduced in 1960 and the first Malay secondary school, Sang Nila Utama was established in 1961 (Zoohri 1990).

The merger from 1963 to 1965 witnessed a greater opposition to the English schools and a concomitant assertiveness of the Malay language and culture by the Malays in Singapore who were the majority population in Malaysia. The turn of events in the 1950s and 1960s illustrate the successful negotiation process and outcome of the Malays in schooling their children based on their own terms. A consequence is that the Chinese and Indian children had the opportunity to learn both English and their indigenous languages from Standard I in their vernacular schools, while the Malay children chose to learn only Malay in their schools (Doraisamy 1969). This contrasting approach towards the schooling of the children of different ethnic groups had long-term repercussions for the Malay community, as we shall see later.

During Singapore's Independence

Singapore was separated from Malaysia after a short-lived merger due to political differences to become an independent sovereign state in 1965. That left a huge psychological impact on the Malays as they had once again become a minority community in Singapore. However, the special position of the Malays was formally recognised in the Singapore's constitution where the Singapore government states that it shall protect and promote the Malay language and the Malays' political, educational, religious, economic, social and cultural interests.[4] However, the Singapore government was careful not to appear to favour any particular ethnic group and preferred instead to promote ethnic and religious harmony, social cohesion, national identity and national economic development. The government implemented a number of educational reforms such as bringing all state schools (known as national schools) under a common national educational system, introducing a uniform curriculum and locally produced textbooks, and making moral and citizenship education compulsory. Underlying these educational reforms is the government's belief that small states are vulnerable to global events and not masters of their destiny. Therefore, they need to be developmentalist by optimising their limited manpower through education to produce a competent, adaptive and productive workforce (Tan 2009).

This time the Muslims responded differently towards the Malay schools and the English schools. Centuries of spurning the English schools and the English language had unfortunately contributed towards an educational under-achievement of the Malay community. Other historical factors such as the apathy of the Malay Sultans towards educating the masses and the British colonial policy to restrict an English education to a small group of Malay elite also aggravated the educational marginality of the Malays. All the above led to a gap in educational performance and socio-economic status between the Malay community and other ethnic groups in Singapore—a disparity that persists till today (Zoohri 1990; Tan 2007b; Mutalib 2008). Graduates of Malay schools and madrasahs in the mid 1960s and 1970s found themselves disadvantaged in their career prospects compared to those educated in the English schools. Aware of the remote possibility of Singapore's re-unification with Malaysia and the economic advantage of mastering English, most Muslim parents concluded that schooling in a secular national school was the most pragmatic choice for their children. Consequently, a majority of the Malay parents opted to send their children to study full-time in national schools where the medium of instruction was English, rather than to the Malay schools or madrasahs. Hence, the enrolment in the Malay schools fell from 7% to 2.3% in 1975 (Ali 1996); the same applies to the madrasahs which will be discussed in the next section. It was clear to many Muslims that the acquisition of English and "secular" knowledge was the path to survival and success in employment, career advancement, material comfort and status in society.

---

[4] Article 152 on Minorities and special position of Malays states as follows (Attorney-General's Chambers (2009):

(1) It shall be the responsibility of the Government constantly to care for the interests of the racial and religious minorities in Singapore.
(2) The Government shall exercise its functions in such manner as to recognise the special position of the Malays, who are the indigenous people of Singapore, and accordingly it shall be the responsibility of the Government to protect, safeguard, support, foster and promote their political, educational, religious, economic, social and cultural interests and the Malay language.

Responses from the Madrasahs

The madrasahs, which placed a much greater stress on Islamic education than the Malay schools faced dwindling enrolment. The madrasahs were also affected by the Singapore state agenda of emphasising economic development and the pragmatic desire of Muslim parents to enhance their children's job prospects, especially for their sons. Graduates of madrasahs had great difficulty finding jobs as they lacked both the qualifications and skills needed in a newly industrialised city. Even if the madrasahs had tried to prepare their graduates for the new economy, they were unable to do so due to insurmountable challenges in the 1960s and 1970s. As private schools that lacked the government's support, madrasahs were generally poorly managed and funded with no proper administration, benchmark and standardisation in the administration, finance, curriculum, examination, recruitment of teachers and teachers' training (Othman 2007). Other prevailing social and economic factors beyond the madrasahs' control also contributed to the reduced enrolment in the madrasahs. One such factor was the resettlement of the Malays from their villages to housing estates in different parts of the country as part of urban development of Singapore, leading to a loss of a critical mass to attend the madrasahs in the neighbourhood (Sahib 2000; Othman 2007). The lowest point for the madrasahs was in the 1970s where they were regarded as a place of last resort for school drop-outs from national schools (Bakar 2006). By the early 1980s, the number of full-time madrasahs was reduced to six which is the current number in Singapore.

However, the trend of declining enrolment in the madrasahs was reversed in the 1980s. That was due to several external and internal factors. Externally, the Muslims in Singapore were influenced by the international Islamic resurgence in the Middle East and North Africa from the late 1970s (Bakar 2006). As a community that places great importance on religious nurture, a number of Muslim parents increasingly felt dissatisfied with the lack of religious education in secular national schools and the corresponding perception that these schools bred social ills (Sahib 2000).[5] Unlike Malaysia which is a Muslim majority country that officially adopts Islam as the state religion and includes Islamic studies as a school subject in national schools, Singapore is a secular state with no official religion and upholds a strictly secular curriculum in national schools. Although Islamic studies was introduced in the Malay schools as an examination subject from 1958, that option was removed with the closure of the Malay schools in the early 1980s (Othman 2007).[6] Another internal factor was that the madrasahs took steps to position themselves as not just religious schools but institutions that could meet the changing needs of

---

[5] That the Malay Muslim community places a great importance on religion is seen in a survey where 88% of Malays indicated that "It is very important that people know that I am a member of a religion" (Ooi 2005; Tan in press). In contrast, only 38% of Chinese answered "yes" to the same question.

[6] It is uncertain when the Malay schools were formally closed. While Othman (2007) claims that it was in the 1970s, Bakar (2006) maintains that it was in 1983. What is certain is that the Malay schools started to be phased out by late 1970s due to dwindling enrolment.

the Muslims. In other words, the madrasahs, cognisant of the changing socio-economic conditions in the late 1960s, negotiated their practices by offering academic subjects to their students, on top of the usual religious subjects. For example, one madrasah incorporated academic subjects in 1966 while another madrasah took one step further to prepare their students to sit for the General Certificate of Education "O" (Ordinary) and "A" (Advanced) level examinations in 1971 (Chee 2006).

The desire of the Muslim community to achieve their dual goals of retaining their cultural self-determination and ensuring social mobility through the learning of academic subjects (i.e., English, Mathematics and Sciences) led to a renewed support for their own religious schools. The enrolment for all the six madrasahs increased progressively from the 1980s to the 2000s, with the madrasahs having to turn away applicants due to lack of places (Bakar 2006). For example, there were 135 Primary 1 students enrolled in the madrasahs in 1986 but the number rose to 464 students in 2000; the total student population also rose from over 2000 in 1991 to about 4,500 in 2001 (Tan 2009). The number of applicants to the madrasahs has constantly outstripped the number of places offered in the six madrasahs due to logistical limitations of the madrasahs to take in all the applicants. For example, there were about 800 students who applied to study in the six madrasahs but only over 400 were accepted in 2001 due to physical constraints of the madrasahs (Bakar 2006). Currently, only about 4,000 students or 4% of all Muslim children are enrolled in the six full-time madrasahs in Singapore.

Current Efforts to "Modernise" the Madrasah Curriculum

Efforts Made by the Government

In keeping with the colonial practice, the Singapore government mandated that national schools remain secular while Islamic education falls within the purview and responsibility of the Muslim community. But state concerns with the increased popularity of madrasahs in the last few decades, coupled with low academic standards in the madrasahs and international Islamist terrorism, have led to the government taking more interventionist steps to "modernise" the madrasah education. Two significant strategies adopted by the government are worth highlighting here (for more details see Tan 2008, 2009; Tan and Hairon 2008).

First is the Compulsory Act implemented in 2003 which requires all children to complete the mandatory 6 years of primary education in national secular schools that are under the Ministry of Education (MOE). All children will sit for the Primary School Leaving Examination (PSLE) at the end of 6 years; this means they will be assessed on four compulsory subjects (English, Mother Tongue Language, Mathematics and Science) just like their counterparts in the national schools. The government allows Muslim children attending madrasahs on a full-time basis to remain in their madrasah only if they meet the minimum performance benchmarks set by MOE. Madrasahs that meet the PSLE benchmark twice in a 3-year period from 2008 can continue to take in Primary 1 pupils. Those who fail to do so will face the prospect of their students being posted to another madrasah where the students meet the PSLE benchmark, or be transferred to a national school. In tandem with the academic benchmark for the madrasah is the government's decision to cap the total enrolment of primary 1 pupils of the madrasahs at 400 each year beginning from 2003.

Secondly, the government succeeded, through the Majlis Ugama Islam (MUIS) (Islamic Religious Council of Singapore)[7] in persuading three of the six full-time madrasahs in Singapore to be part of the "Joint Madrasah System" to be implemented in 2009 (Tan 2009). This serves to raise the academic standards of the madrasahs through a specialisation in either primary or secondary education. While one of the three madrasahs will focus on primary education, the other two will have only secondary classes. Of the two madrasahs providing secondary education, one will offer a purely academic track with school subjects largely similar to those in the national schools. The goal is for the graduates to proceed to secular institutions—junior college, polytechnic and/or secular universities. The other madrasah offering secondary education will provide two tracks: the "religious track" for students keen on Islamic tertiary education where they will apply for pre-university Islamic studies and then enrol in Islamic universities; and the "hybrid track" for students to study both religious and academic studies to qualify them for both Islamic and secular institutions. It appears from the madrasah revamp that the government is actively pushing for two streams or tracks of madrasah education with a priority to channel more madrasah students to the academic track (Tan 2009).

A Case Study of the Curricular Changes in a Madrasah in Singapore

Endeavours to "modernise" the madrasah curriculum to help these institutions cope with both academic and religious learning are on-going in the madrasahs in Singapore. It is therefore instructive to examine one such madrasah in Singapore based on a research project the authors are currently involved in.

The madrasah has introduced a few main curricular changes since 2002. First, the medium of instruction for all religious subjects except Arabic from Primary 1 to 6 students is English. This marks a significant departure from past practices where the medium of instruction, except for English and Malay lessons, was Arabic. The rationale is to give the primary students a firm foundation in English since it

---

[7] MUIS, the highest bureaucracy in charge of Muslim matters in Singapore, is a statutory body to advise the President of Singapore on all matters relating to Islam in the country. It is responsible for setting the Islamic agenda, shaping religious life and forging the Singaporean Muslim identity. Its main functions include the construction and administration of mosques development and management, and the administration of Islamic religious schools and Islamic education.

is one of the core academic subjects that all primary six students have to sit for at the PSLE. Secondly, the madrasah adopts the MOE syllabi for the key academic subjects, namely English, Mathematics and Science. It also increases the curriculum time for academic subjects from about 50% to about 60%. There were also preparations made to focus on improving the students' academic performance, such as banding students based on their academic abilities, remedial lessons, and workshops on Mathematics and Science for students and interested parents. Teachers are given opportunities for professional development through courses and workshops to better equip them to teach the academic subjects. Student-centred pedagogies are also infused into the curriculum across the subjects where activities such as playing games, singing and solving puzzles are common. Information and Communication Technology (ICT) is embraced to encourage students to exercise their initiative and shape their own learning.

The research project adopted a qualitative case study research design. Data were collected from content analysis of policy documents, reports and newspaper articles pertaining to the madrasah and madrasah education in Singapore, and interviews, including one-to-one and focused group interviews. For the latter, interviews were conducted with the key community members of the madrasah, which included the chairman, an external curriculum consultant, an internal curriculum development officer, 6 teachers of graduating classes, 10 parents of the graduating student and 20 graduating students. Preliminary findings were made with regard to the impact of the recent education reforms in madrasah education. While the content analysis provided the contextual information for the case study, the interviews surfaced the perceptions of the key stakeholders of the madrasah that pertain to the changes that had taken place at the madrasah. The preliminary findings were derived from an analytic induction process in data analysis where open and selective coding strategies were used.

This section highlights some preliminary research findings on the curricular changes at the madrasah. On the whole, the key community members of the madrasah had both positive and negative perceptions of the recent education reforms in madrasah education. With regard to the positive aspect, the chairman expressed satisfaction at being able to change the mindset or cultural values of people in the organisation. He also expressed the satisfaction of being able to fulfil the divine calling of "being the best nation" (Kuntum khaira *Ummah*). He believed that the changes that are taking place at the madrasah could be a model to other madrasahs in Singapore, the region, and the rest of the world. On the part of teachers, they supported the review and accountability processes in place to ensure academic achievement. For example, when teachers were required to analyse their respective students' formative and summative academic results, they were indirectly constrained to review the effectiveness of their teaching strategies so as to provide justifications for students' academic performance. They were also satisfied that the philosophical support for the changes in the madrasah was clearly articulated to them. The emphasis on student achievement had impacted not only the effectiveness of teachers teaching and the review and accountability processes, but also the professional development of teachers. Teachers were provided with greater resources and opportunities for professional development. Resources were also provided to support the programmes necessary to both achieve academic and Islamic education expectations. The programmes essentially sought to bring about excellent outcomes in both academic and Islamic education.

With regard to the negative aspect of the perception of the recent education reforms, teachers generally viewed the changes as being too fast, too much and lacking stability, which had the potential to lead to teacher burnout. Besides being involved in pedagogical changes, they were also involved in a range of administrative work needed to support these changes. The over demand of workload placed on teachers had negatively impacted on teachers' time for reflection, which was perceived to be important in helping teachers make continual improvements in classroom teaching and learning. The heavy workload also had undermined the practice of *Usrah* (family) where teachers come together to discuss about work and the underlying philosophies of their work. The demanding workload also posed the danger of making the change programmes unsustainable, especially when demands consistently exceed the resources for change. On the whole, the negative aspects of change did have the potential to frustrate or undermine the positive aspects of change. There were also evidences to suggest that bureaucracy outside of the madrasah may add on to the teachers' workload and stress. With regard to the professional development of the staff members, the messages were mixed. Although greater resources and opportunities were provided to teachers, some professional development platforms were viewed as having little relevance to their work. For example, the teachers might have enrolled in a course or workshop that they believed added little value to their teaching effectiveness.

The interviews with key community members of the madrasah also revealed the extensive and intensive curricular changes for the Primary 6 students at the madrasah. This was due to the fact that 2008 was the first time in which madrasah students' academic performance in PSLE was monitored by the education ministry. As mentioned earlier, madrasahs that fail to meet the PSLE benchmark stipulated by MOE will have to be closed. In general, more time had been allocated for the preparation of PSLE 2008. The focus was on increasing instructional time on the key subjects of English, Mathematics and Science, which includes conducting lessons on Saturdays, and increasing the students' familiarity with the PSLE exam papers such as going through mock exams and tests. Prior to the PSLE for about a period of 1 month, students were required to stay back after school from 3 to 5 pm everyday for extra classes. The teaching of non-academic subjects was also stopped in order to give more time for the teaching of these key academic subjects.

Outside vendors were also called in to improve the quality of teaching and learning in these key academic subjects such as Mathematics. Besides outside vendors, the madrasah had also received help from non-profit organisations and partners to support the teachers to better prepare the students for the PSLE. Parents whose children had been identified to be not preparing well for the PSLE were counselled by relevant school staff members. The madrasah had also put in place a system of assessing the students' academic strengths and weaknesses along with monitoring them prior to the PSLE. The overall objective is to improve students' learning and academic outcomes of these key subjects for students regardless of ability level. Besides changes that had been made to the preparation of students for the PSLE, the school management also saw the importance of providing conducive organisational structures to support this preparation. The following are examples: off-loading Primary 6 teachers' work; the termination of ineffective practices; getting the support of parents; and teacher professional development that are aimed primarily at securing academic results.

From the perspective of the Primary 6 students, the preparation for the PSLE had been very intensive and pressurising. The students were given a whole range of activities such as worksheets, extra classes, homework, lessons during holidays, workshops for science and maths, motivational talks, camps and outings, lectures on changing attitudes, additional help for selected students from teachers from national schools, and de-stressing activities (such as visits to the Dairy Farm) to help students cope with the pressure of PLSE preparation. The students also perceived that the teachers had high expectations on them. The teachers were seen as becoming stricter and placing great emphasis on academic achievements, pushing them to achieve their best in academic performance. The learning demands in the classroom had also increased. The rationale for doing well in the PSLE is multi-faceted. Based on the interview data from Primary 6 students, the following were their rationale for wanting to do well in the PSLE: determining life success, determining the future survival and existence of the madrasah, scrutiny by the government, wanting to compare themselves with students from the national schools, and maintaining the honour of the madrasah, Islamic education and the Malay Muslim community as a whole.

In general, the staff, parents and students of the madrasah had developed a great sense of urgency in securing good academic achievements in the PSLE. However, this was not without problems. First, some teachers felt that the priority over PSLE has made the non-academic subjects such as the *Tarbiyah*, which comprises religious subjects such as the history and teachings of Islam, become less important. Second, some teachers perceived that students were confused by the different teaching styles used by teachers and different service providers. Third, it was perceived that the lower-ability students in the madrasah did not believe that they were able to do well or pass the PSLE. Fourth, some teachers considered teaching mixed abilities as a great challenge. Fifth, the threat to sustainability was real in view of securing continuous additional funding to match the increased change demands.

Finally, the interviews with key community members of the madrasah revealed their key aspirations for madrasah education. These aspirations were articulated more clearly and explicitly by the madrasah management especially the chairman although the teachers, parents and students also shared these aspirations. Their practices essentially were the embodiment of these aspirations. First, they aspired to integrate religious and secular knowledge—the pursuit of the ideal man (*insan al-kamil*) who is well-versed in both religious and normal sciences. Secondly, they aspired to be able to apply both religious and secular knowledge in context, and hence making a contribution to society. One community member expressed this value in the following quote:

> That is what we want to see, that they [students] are good practising Muslims—a *muttaqi* [God fearing person]. So, they can specialise in their fields, but they will be knowledgeable, practising Muslims. And if they become a scientist, and whatever success that they achieve, they would say *Alhamdulillah* [praise be to Allah] and it is for the benefit of humanity.

The findings of the study illustrate how the madrasah, although compelled to make changes in response to the national agenda, had managed to negotiate its objective situation by reforming its school curriculum in ways consistent with their Islamic identity and aspirations. Our findings also show that the negotiation processes, far from easy and smooth-sailing, are filled with challenges and tensions from and among the various stakeholders of the madrasah community.

Conclusions

The Negotiation Processes and Outcomes for the Malay Muslims in Singapore

There are three concluding observations from our examination of the schooling experiences of the Malay Muslims in Singapore. The first two observations concern the negotiation processes and outcomes for the Malay Muslims in Singapore, while the third observation focussed on the prospects for madrasahs in Singapore.

First, the Singapore example shows how the Muslim minority community in the country is not immune to changing political, economic and social conditions. These conditions crucially influenced the rewards of education opportunities, materials, political power, and/or social status for the schools, whether they are English schools, Malay schools or madrasahs. One could trace the Muslims' shifting educational preferences, demands and actions—from rejecting English and Malay schools during the British colonial period, to advocating Malay schools in the self-government and merger period, and preferring the English schools and madrasahs after independence. One could also see the changing role of the madrasahs, from concentrating on producing religious elites in the beginning to the added mission of nurturing Muslim professionals with the requisite skills and knowledge for the modern world. As religious institutions, the madrasahs have demonstrated great responsiveness to changing needs and demands of the Muslim community. In doing so they showed that they are not above pragmatic concerns and not immune to the vicissitudes of larger social, economic and political forces.

Secondly, it is evident that many Muslims themselves would like to receive a balanced education which combines their religious pursuit with the learning of academic subjects for the modern age. As pointed out earlier, there has been a discernible shift since the late 1960s in the madrasahs' mission from solely training religious teachers and scholars in the beginning to the added goal of preparing their graduates for a knowledge economy. Bakar (2006) points out that the madrasahs today aim at "meeting parental expectation for an alternative education for their children that pivots around Islam, and fulfilling the national expectation to maintain its relevance in the face of an economy that values skilled and knowledge workers" (p. 43). Such a sentiment to integrate the sacred with the secular is also reflected in the madrasah students and graduates. A survey of 52 former and current madrasah students in Singapore indicates that the most cited motivation for them to choose to study in a madrasah is "to have a balance of religious and secular education" (84.6%) and "to learn Islamic values and culture" (84.6%) (Rukhaidah 2001). The same survey shows that 92.3% regarded English as absolutely essential for living in Singapore, linking it to "making money" (98.1%), "building a stable career" (96.2%) and "networking for contacts" (100%).

It is important to note that such a dual emphasis is not a foreign idea to the Islamic tradition. For instance, Muslim theologian Al-Ghazali points out that both religious sciences (or sacred knowledge) such as the articles of faith, and non-religious (or profane knowledge) such as arithmetic and natural sciences are important in Islamic thought and should be integrated into the curriculum (Buang 2008). But the juggling of both religious and academic subjects remains a daunting task for the madrasahs. Faced with limited financial support, inadequate modern facilities, many untrained teachers and low pay, the madrasahs are struggling with poor academic performance when compared with the national schools. This explains why a majority of Muslims today (about 96%) prefer to send their children to national schools and provide part-time Islamic instruction to their children after school hours.[8] Kong's (2005) research study involving interviews with Muslim parents informs us that there are Muslim parents who viewed madrasahs as largely religious institutions with a low level of English proficiency and inadequate emphasis on academic subjects.

Prospects for the Madrasahs in Singapore

In view of the changes and challenges faced by the madrasahs, what are the prospects of the madrasahs in Singapore? Given the religious significance of the madrasahs for the Muslim community, it is expected that the madrasahs in Singapore will continue to exist and be strongly supported by the parents, religious leaders and the Muslim community. However, against a backdrop of the Compulsory Education Act, the state requirement for all madrasahs to meet the minimum PSLE performance benchmark, and the call from MUIS for the madrasahs to reform their curricula, all the madrasahs are facing the pressure to cope with these external demands, albeit in different ways and with varying degrees of success. The prospects

---

[8] Muslim children may attend Islamic classes in one of the twenty-seven part-time "mosque madrasah" which are mosques that provide part-time basic Islamic education to students who attend nation schools. Besides the mosque madrasah, Muslims may also receive part-time religious instructions from private Islamic kindergartens, and programmes and activities organised by Muslim organisations (Tan 2007a).

of the madrasahs depend largely on how the madrasahs see their mission and their relationship with the state.

For "modern" madrasahs such as the one in our case study, they are likely to cope with the changes better due to their readiness to accept the state's recommendations and assistance, such as adhering closely to the syllabi used in national schools, utilising the state-endorsed textbooks and underscoring academic achievements. The receptivity of these madrasahs can be explained by their belief that the madrasahs have a duty not only to nurture religious teachers and leaders but also Muslim professionals who are successful and respected in a knowledge economy. For these madrasahs, their religion serves as a powerful motivating factor, not a hindrance, for their students to excel academically. As illustrated in an earlier quote from a Muslim community member, madrasah graduates who become successful professionals are regarded as exemplary Muslims who excel for the praise of Allah (*Alhamdulillah*). Such a mission for the madrasah is in alignment with the government's goal for graduates of these institutions to rise to the challenges of a globalised and modern world. It also helps that these madrasahs have traditionally maintained a positive relationship with the state. For example, the madrasah in our case study has been working closely with MUIS for years, and its current premise—a brand new campus with modern facilities—shares the same building as MUIS. In short, a mission that is compatible with the state agenda, together with the openness to curricular changes and a willingness to collaborate with the government, suggests that the curricula changes to "modernise" the madrasahs, such as those adopted by the madrasah in our case study, are likely to be sustainable. While these changes are not sufficient to enable the madrasahs to compete with the national schools (due to factors such as relatively low funding, limited facilities and resources, and lower academic qualifications of the madrasah teachers), the changes nevertheless are salutary for the madrasahs to meet the PSLE performance benchmark and balance both academic and religious subjects.

On the other hand, there are other madrasahs in Singapore that are not as receptive as the "modern" madrasahs towards the state's call for them to channel more time and resources to academic subjects and produce Muslim professionals in a knowledge economy. These madrasahs believe that their primary focus is religious inculcation rather than "secular sciences" which are academic subjects such as English, Mathematics and Sciences. An example is a madrasah in Singapore with this mission: "Mastering of the Arabic language is a pre-requisite for the understanding of the Al-Quran and Hadiths (Prophetic Traditions), the two fundamental sources of Islamic Jurisprudence, less in importance, is the acquisition of knowledge in the secular sciences" (cited in Tan 2009). For these madrasahs, religion, in contrast to the "modern" madrasahs, serves as a justification and a unifying force for them and their supporters to resist the "modernising" attempts by the state. Besides, these madrasahs may perceive the state initiatives and overtures as attempts to control or even close down the madrasahs. Consequently, their reluctance to carry out state-endorsed curricular changes and their uneasy relationship with the state is likely to lead to continual negotiations with the state and other stakeholders (including

MUIS, the "modern" madrasahs and segments of the Muslim community) on the future of these madrasahs.

This chapter illustrates the Malay Muslims' changing responses to their schooling realities under a secular state in a globalised and modern world. In managing their objective situation and adjusting their subjective practices especially for madrasah education, the Malay Muslims in Singapore reject ascribed cultural attributes by the state and take ownership of their religious, cultural and social processes and outcomes. Their experiences exemplify the fluidity and complexity of the discursive duality of the Muslim minority in negotiating their educational circumstances and practices to combine social and economic progress and cultural authenticity in a multicultural and predominantly Chinese society under a secular state.

Acknowlegement The authors thank the Nanyang Technological University for funding their research project; the chairman, staff, parents, students and other stakeholders of the madrasah for the research materials and their interviews; and Ms Diwi Binte Abbas for rendering valuable research assistance.

References

Ahmad, S. (1971). Singapore Malays, education and national development. *Suara Universiti, 2*, 41–45.
Ali, H. (1996). Culture, cognition and academic achievement of Malay students in Singapore. Unpublished PhD dissertation, National Institute of Education, Nanyang Technological University.
Aljunied, S. M. K. (2009). British discourses and Malay identity in colonial Singapore. *Indonesia and the Malay World, 37*(107), 1–21.
Aljunied, S. M. K., & Hussin, D. I. (2005). Estranged from the ideal past: Historical evolution of madrasahs in Singapore. *Journal of Muslim Minority Affairs, 25*(2), 249–260.
Attorney-General's Chambers. (2009). Singapore statutes online. http://statutes.agc.gov.sg/. Accessed 21 Aug 2009.
Bakar, M. A. (2006). Between state interests and citizen rights: Whither the madrasah? In N. A. A. Rahman & A. E. Lai (Eds.), *Secularism and spirituality: Seeking integrated knowledge and success in madrasah education in Singapore* (pp. 29–57). Singapore: Marshall Cavendish.
Buang, S. (2008). Religious education as locus of curriculum: A brief inquiry into *madrasah* curriculum in Singapore. In A. E. Lai (Ed.), *Religious diversity in Singapore* (pp. 342–361). Singapore: Institute of Southeast Asian Studies and Institute of Policy Studies.
Chee, M. F. (2006). The historical evolution of madrasah education in Singapore. In N. A. A. Rahman & A. E. Lai (Eds.), *Secularism and spirituality: Seeking integrated knowledge and success in madrasah education in Singapore* (pp. 6–28). Singapore: Marshall Cavendish.
Djamour, J. (1953). *Family structure of the Singapore Malays: Report to the Colonial Social Science Research Council (Scheme R. 281).* London: Colonial Office.
Doraisamy, T. R. (Ed.). (1969). *150 years of education in Singapore.* Singapore: Teachers' Training College.
Funston, J. (2006). Singapore. In G. Fealy & V. Hooker (Eds.), *Voices of Islam in Southeast Asia: A contemporary sourcebook* (pp. 71–75). Singapore: Institute of Southeast Asian Studies.
Haikal, H., & Yahaya, A. G. (1997). Muslims in Singapore: The colonial legacy and the making of a minority. *Journal of Muslim Minority Affairs, 17*(1), 83–88.
Kadir, S. (2004). Islam, state and society in Singapore. *Inter-Asia Cultural Studies, 5*(3), 357–371.

Kong, L. (2005). Religious schools: For spirit, (f)or nation. *Environment and Planning D: Society and Space, 23,* 615–631.
Marsh, C. (2004). *Key concepts for understanding curriculum* (3rd edn.). London: Routledge-Falmer.
Millard, M. (2004). *Jihad in paradise: Islam and politics in Southeast Asia.* Armonk: ME Sharpe.
Mutalib, H. (2008). *Islam in Southeast Asia.* Singapore: Institute of Southeast Asian Studies.
Ooi, G.L. (2005). The Role of the Developmental State and Interethnic Relations in Singapore. *Asian Ethnicity, 6*(2), 109–120.
Othman, A. B. (2007). The role of madrasah education in Singapore: A study on the philosophy and practice of madrasah education in a secular state and plural society. Unpublished Master's thesis, International Islamic University Malaysia, International Institute of Islamic Thought and Civilisation.
Roff, W. R. (1967). *The origins of Malay nationalism.* New Haven: Yale University Press.
Rukhaidah, S. (2001). Language and identity among Singapore madrasah students. Unpublished honours thesis, National University of Singapore.
Sahib, H. B. (2000). Islamic education in Singapore: Past achievements, present dilemmas and future directions. In I. Alee & H. Madman (Eds.), *Islamic studies in ASEAN: Presentations of an International Seminar* (pp. 69–85). Pattani: College of Islamic Studies, Prince of Songkla University.
Siddique, S. (1986). The administration of Islam in Singapore. In T. Abdullah & S. Siddique (Eds.), Islam in Southeast Asian studies (pp. 315–331). Singapore: Institute of Southeast Asian Studies.
Tan, C. (2007a). Islam and citizenship education in Singapore: Challenges and implications. *Education, Citizenship and Social Justice, 2*(1), 23–39.
Tan, C. (2007b). Narrowing the gap: The educational achievements of the Malay community in Singapore. *Intercultural Education, 18*(1), 71–82.
Tan, C. (2008). (Re)imagining the Muslim identity in Singapore. *Studies in Ethnicity and Nationalism, 8*(1), 31–43.
Tan, C. (2009). Globalisation and the reform agenda for madrasah education in Singapore. *Diaspora, Indigenous, and Minority Education, 3*(2), 67–80.
Tan, C. & Hairon, S. (2008). Continuing madrasah education in Singapore: towards teachers as reflective practitioners. *Educational Awakening: Journal of the Educational Sciences, 5*(1), 81–101.
Zoohri, W. H. (1990). *The Singapore Malays: The dilemma of development.* Singapore: Kesatuan Guru-Guru Melayu Singapura [Singapore Malay Teachers' Union].

Chapter 36
Precarious Religious Liberties in Education: The Salience of Demographic and Social Contingencies Under a Formally Pluralist Public Philosophy

Eoin Daly

Introduction

The relationship between pluralism and religious liberty is fraught with ambiguity in the public education context. Religious liberty principles preclude that children of minority beliefs should be assimilated in the dominant religious tradition, giving rise to demands for state support for schools catering specifically for minority beliefs. Conversely, resistance to differentiated provision for minorities hinges upon the claimed "neutrality" of public education (and public philosophy) towards religion and identity. This contribution addresses the religious liberties of minorities in the public education system of the Republic of Ireland, which has, historically, devolved the public education function to schools owned and operated by religious denominations, on the basis of formal equality or neutrality towards these. This model seeks to secure religious liberty in education by attuning the public education function to the religious identities prevailing in Irish society on the basis of formal pluralism. Yet increasingly, the devolution of public education to denominational intermediaries is justified in religiously neutral terms, with reference to the secular goods of diversity and choice. However, migration has dramatically illustrated the limitations of this model. It has preserved a preponderant position for the dominant religious community, and resulted in a precarious and unequal guarantee of religious liberty for religious minorities.

This contribution describes the treatment of religious minorities in a public education system underpinned by a political legal framework which is formally neutral towards religions at the level of public philosophy, but which provides public education almost exclusively through schools operated under the "patronage"[1] (man-

---

[1] Education Act 1998, s. 8(1); the Minister for Education may recognise private persons as "patrons", to whom the Board of Management is accountable in upholding the "characteristic spirit", or "ethos", of the school.

E. Daly (✉)
School of Law and Government, Dublin City University, Glasnevin, Dublin 9, Ireland
e-mail: eoin.daly@dcu.ie

agement and ownership) of a de jure plurality, but a de facto hegemony, of religious denominations. It charts the transition in justifications for denominational education from those privileging religious identity as a recognised public good, in the vein of communitarian or romantic nationalism, to a secularised discourse which instead justifies the broadly clerical "patronage" of schools on the basis of ostensibly neutral imperatives of diversity and choice. I discuss how religious liberty rights remain vulnerable in this context despite this secularisation of public philosophy.

A Formally Pluralist "Patronage" Model

Ireland's legal framework for public education has been determined in part by a colonial history, and consequently, the post-colonial function of public education in cementing romantic-nationalist identity in the independent state. Difficulties in securing the religious liberty rights in the public education context are attributable, primarily, to the fact that approximately 92% of pulicly funded schools in Ireland are owned by, and under the "patronage" of, the Roman Catholic Church, while 98% are operated by a religious denomination (Mawhinney 2009, p. 50). Therefore, only 6% of recognised schools are operated by non-Catholic denominations, and 2% non-sectarian. Due to the "fundamentally different" development of primary education in Ireland under British rule, the state never provided a system of public education owned and administered by local authorities, largely due to nationalist resistance to what was perceived as the imposition of British state education (Hyland 1989; Glendenning 2008). The task of education was left primarily to voluntary effort on the part of the churches. The preponderance of voluntary confessional schools constitutes "an unusual historical feature" of Irish education, which represented the aim of "providing Catholic children with a Catholic education" (Glendenning 2008, p. 290). Notwithstanding the British authorities' attempts to introduce "mixed" non-sectarian education, "the mixed education principle was gradually abandoned as the [19th] century progressed...as the church–state relationship became closer" (Glendenning 2008, pp. 303–304). Hyland writes:

> The Irish system of national education was fundamentally different... In England and Scotland 'parallel' systems had evolved, that is, denominational schools existed side by side with local authority controlled schools... In Ireland provision was never made for a separate system of primary schools controlled by the local authority, largely because... voluntary effort had adequately met the demand for elementary education. (1989, p. 95)

Despite early attempts both to impose non-sectarian national education and to separate religious and secular instruction in recognised schools, primary education remained deeply sectarian past independence, notwithstanding the non-sectarian tenor of independent Ireland's first constitution (1922).[2] Just as the rejection of British

---

[2] Article 8 provided: "Freedom of conscience and the free profession and practice of religion are, subject to public order and morality, guaranteed to every citizen, and no law may be made...to

state education represented resistance to assimilation into a British identity[3], the state's commitment to the de facto Roman Catholic character of public education reflected the importance of religion as a cement of nationalist identity in the nascent state (see generally Hogan 1987; Lee 1989). As late as the 1980s, Whyte observed that the Catholic Church had "carved out for itself a more extensive control over education...than in any other country" (1980, p. 21).

The prevailing justification for the denominational character of public education centred on the Catholic, ethos of the independent Irish state, despite its liberal orientation at the constitutional level. The partition of Ireland left an overwhelming Catholic majority in the independent state, which strongly influenced legislation and policy over subsequent decades. The ruling party in the 1930s "availed itself of every opportunity to show that it supported orthodox Catholic teaching" (Hogan 1987, p. 52). Catholic nationalism was tempered by constitutionally required toleration of the Protestant and Jewish minorities, whose schools were recognised and funded on a formally equal basis. This may be viewed as part of the post-independence accommodation with the Protestant minority, expressing vestiges of the republican origins of the nationalist movement (Pettit 2005).

The 1937 Constitution synthesised this liberal-republican heritage with the romantic nationalist, or what might today be termed the "communitarian" recognition of a Christian, sometimes specifically Catholic national identity. The preamble links the struggle for national independence to religion, invoking "the Most Holy Trinity", acknowledging "our obligations to our Divine Lord, Jesus Christ". It thus "defines its ultimate notion of the good in explicitly religious terms" (McCrea 2009, p. 6). Religion was recognised as a public good which the state pledged to "honour and respect".[4] The initial text recognised "the special position of the Holy Catholic Apostolic and Roman Church".[5] However, also recognised were the Protestant and Jewish congregations existing at the time. Given the pressures placed on the framers to formally establish the Catholic Church (Keogh 1988), the constitutional provisions on religion, which include guarantees against discrimination and disabilities on religious grounds, have been seen as a "skilful endorsement of religious pluralism" (Hogan and Whyte 2003).

---

affect prejudicially the right of any child to attend a school receiving public money without attending the religious instruction at the school, or make any discrimination...between schools under the management of different religious denominations".

[3] In *Crowley v. Ireland* [1980] IR 201, 216, Justice O'Higgins stated: "[Article 42] was intended to avoid imposing a mandatory obligation on the state directly to provide free primary education. This might have led to the provision of free primary education in exclusively state schools. Rather was it intended that the state should ensure by arrangements it made that free primary education would be provided. When one remembers the long and turbulent...struggle for the right to maintain [Church] schools...one can well understand the care with which the words used must have been selected".

[4] Article 44.1.

[5] Article 44.1.2 was removed through the Fifth Amendment (1972).

The Salience of Empirical and Social Contingencies Under a Formally Pluralist Framework

The 1937 Constitution recognises, albeit without explicitly stipulating, the confessional character of the public education system. A system reliant on predominantly clerical patrons interposed between state and citizen is juridically grounded by constitutional references to the rights of parents; the state is obliged to "provide for" free primary education, with "due regard" for the rights of parents, "in the matter of religious and moral formation".[6] The only explicit reference to the denominational character of state-funded schools appears in the prohibition of discrimination in their funding.

Legislation providing State aid for schools shall not discriminate between schools under the management of different religious denominations, nor be such as to affect prejudicially the right of any child to attend a school receiving public money without attending religious instruction at that school.[7]

Thus, the preponderant position for religious "patrons" has been preserved within a constitutional framework of formal neutrality emphasising liberal norms of individual choice, but also, the respect due to religion within the public sphere.[8] This is underpinned, at least, in part, by the romantic-nationalist idea of a shared religious identity as one of the anchoring points of citizenship. This framework juxtaposes a high degree of formal priority for the rights of individuals in the choice of their beliefs, with a permissiveness towards the devolution of the public education function to clerical patrons committed to imparting particular religious beliefs. While ostensibly valorising individual freedom of religious choice, it does not assume the necessity, for religious liberty, of a universal system of secular public education relegating religious education to the private sphere. Yet while shunning the secularist ideal, this framework underpins the predominantly confessional alternative with reference to parental rights, representing a formally pluralist legal framework for a public education system in which religion occupies a hegemonic position—with citizens in many geographical areas consequently having access only to Catholic-ethos schools.

What are the implications for minority groups? Specifically, what value lies in the formal guarantee of the equality of minority religions, where social and demographic inequalities mean that many may have little choice but to avail of schools committed to imparting beliefs other than their own? First, the formal neutrality of this framework is configured at the level of the group rather than the individual. It does not require that individuals, of whatever beliefs, have access to education through institutions in which their beliefs are accommodated, but that religious groups enjoy formal equality (non-discrimination) in accessing state funding and

---

[6] Article 42.4.

[7] Article 44.2.4.

[8] Article 44.1 provides: "the homage of public worship is due to Almighty God", and "the State... shall respect and honour religion". Article 44.2 states: "freedom of conscience and the free profession and practice of religion are, subject to public order and morality, guaranteed to every citizen", and "the State shall not impose any disabilities or make any discrimination on the grounds of religious belief, profession or status".

recognition of schools. This inevitably entails inequalities in the guarantee of religious liberty in this context, as a function of the power relations prevailing both between and within religious and other groups (Daly 2009). It represents formal equality for religious groups, rather than equal religious liberty for individuals. While this model is formally pluralist, the scope of the mere plurality of school patronage to protect basic rights is conditioned by arbitrary conjunctural factors, demographic and social. It does not guarantee the "internal" conditions of respect for pluralism in state-funded schools, which might guarantee the religious liberty of minority pupils who must attend these. As outlined below, these inequalities bear particularly heavily on those migrant minorities that lack the power and resources necessary to exercise the right to religious liberty within this system. While demographics represent a significant determinant of such inequalities, I aim to outline the broader multidimensional character of the power disparities that render persons' enjoyment of religious liberty subject to a variety of "social and natural contingencies" (Rawls 1997).

First, I describe how this framework leads to inequalities in the guarantee of religious liberty between those differently situated in demographic and social terms. The constitutional guarantee of formally equal support for minority religious schools fails to translate into equal religious liberty for individuals because its exercise is contingent on certain conjunctural factors. Insofar as the possibility of attending a school of one's own religion represents a guarantee of religious liberty, it is confined to those persons positioned within a "critical mass" of co-religionists which may warrant the establishment and recognition of an appropriate school in a particular area (Daly 2009). The right to attend a school other than one imparting a Catholic ethos hinges on the existence of a sufficiently numerous and mobilised group of co-religionists who may make the demands on public authority necessary to secure public education in accordance with their beliefs. The High Court ruling in *O'Shiel v Minister for Education*[9] illustrates this limited scope of formal constitutional pluralism. It involved a claim by parents to receive state recognition for a primary school operating under the Steiner pedagogy. The Court rejected the state's defence that it had sufficiently discharged its constitutional obligations by funding 15 primary schools, all Catholic, in proximity to the school seeking recognition. Justice Laffoy described this stance as "render[ing] worthless the guarantee of freedom of parental choice, which is the fundamental precept of the Constitution", and as "incompatible with the lawful preference of *an appreciable number of parents in the locality*".[10] She concluded: "it would pervert the clear intent of the Constitution to interpret that obligation as merely obliging the State to fund a single system of primary education which is an offer to parents on a 'take it or leave it' basis".[11] This is neatly transferable to cases involving religious claims: the state cannot refuse to support a denominational school where required by an "appreciable number" of parents in a locality.

---

[9] [1999] 2 IR 321.

[10] [1999] 2 IR 321, 347, 344.

[11] *Ibid.*

The Primacy of "Critical Mass"

The exercise of formal religious liberty rights in this context is thus made vulnerable to the contingency of the "critical mass", or "appreciable number" of co-religionists. Therefore, this formal constitutional pluralism operates, in reality, as function of the power relations between different religious groups, distributing religious liberty rights unequally on the basis of the relative social prevalence of the groups to which individuals belong. Its benefits are limited to those well positioned to muster the various resources necessary to seek state accommodation of their claim; as outlined below, demographic "critical mass" is not the sole determinant of inequality in the guarantee of religious liberty rights in this context, with disparities in political and social capital bearing particular salience for minorities. It is self-evidently impossible for any state to provide parents, in all areas, with schools specifically attuned to their religious or other beliefs, given the scarcity of resources and the diversity of beliefs. Those whose peripheral or minority beliefs are not accommodated in this framework must therefore accept a lesser degree of religious liberty. They must choose between foregoing the benefit of public education altogether[12], and availing of schools committed to inculcating beliefs incompatible with their own.

The consequent impact upon the religious liberty of those minorities who must avail of Catholic schools must be viewed in light of the role of denominational schools, as recognised in law, in inculcating a religious ethos and worldview throughout the broad school environment. The desire of church authorities to maintain a majority of co-religionists in schools under their patronage and ownership has resulted in legislation protecting their right to discriminate on religious grounds in enrolment[13], leading to controversial incidents in which non-Catholic migrant children in particular have experienced great difficulty in securing enrolment in *any* primary school place.[14] Such policies have been justified on the basis of the "right" to uphold the religious ethos of denominational schools.[15] Moreover, such schools are permitted to integrate their religious ethos into secular aspects of school life, a policy termed the "integrated curriculum" (Mawhinney 2007). As empirical research has shown, this compromises the efficacy of the constitutional guarantee of a child's right to withdraw from religious instruction. The right to withdraw solely from timetabled classes is ineffective where the religious ethos of a school, and the associated doctrines, pervade the whole school day (Mawhinney 2006). Although it might be argued that this policy violates the constitutional religious freedom guarantees, it is inconceivable that, since it mandates the provision of public education through institutions committed to imparting religious doctrines, the Constitution

---

[12] Under Article 42.3, parents cannot be required to avail of schools "established by the State".

[13] Equal Status Act 2000, s. 7.

[14] In 2007, the state established an "emergency" primary school in Dublin catering almost exclusively for migrant children. They had been unable to gain access to any primary school: priority was accorded to those possessing Catholic baptismal certificates, as permitted in legislation. "Ireland forced to open immigrant school", *The Guardian*, September 25, 2007.

[15] *Campaign to Separate Church and State v. Minister for Education* [1998] 3 IR 321.

could fully guarantee the integrity of non-coreligionists' beliefs against the confessional character of state-funded schools. It is unrealistic to expect that the rights of sceptics, non-conformists and religious minorities could be adequately accommodated in institutions whose very purpose may lie partially in the defeat of these competing forms of belief (Daly 2008).

Minority Children, Religious Learning and the "Integrated Curriculum"

Mawhinney (2006) and Alvey (1991) have documented the effect of this policy upon minority children. The aim of imparting a religious ethos which, according to administrative guidelines, must "inform and vivify the whole work of the school"[16], may result in such children becoming subject, whether inadvertently or otherwise, to inculcation in religious doctrines contrary to those, if any, in which they are instructed by their parents. Mawhinney's recent empirical research on the operation of the "integrated curriculum" reveals two important trends. First, the "opt-out" mechanism has proven difficult to implement, and ill-respected in practice. According to 50% of respondents, no opt-out provision whatsoever was provided even for timetabled religious instruction classes. Of those opt-out provisions from religious classes actually offered, among the most common option was "to be collected from school by parents" (2007, p. 390). Second, minority children have tended to become subject to the casual or inadvertent imparting of schools' religious doctrines, with many respondents describing these influences as both "subtle" and "pervasive" (2007, p. 391). While instruction in different and conflicting religious or other doctrines may well have certain developmental effects on children, the rights-based critique of the denominational model need not rely on any such knowledge. It applies insofar as the instruction of children in comprehensive doctrines, whether inadvertent or otherwise, has not been subject to the consent of their parents. This deontological approach does not rely on any evidence of empirical "harm" arising from involuntary instruction in religious doctrines. Since religious liberty constitutes "a right of individuals to non-interference...in the choice of religious belief or affiliation" (Clarke 1984, p. 15), it does not apply solely where discernible forms of harm result. Clarke argues that "there is no need to show that particular religious indoctrination causes some determinate...harm...rather *any* indoctrination causes the harm of a denial of fundamental rights" (1984, p. 220).

Thus, in the absence of a "critical mass" of coreligionists in a particular area, the residual guarantee of withdrawal from religious instruction classes within Catholic-ethos schools is itself balanced against the interests of the Church inculcating its ethos throughout the school environment. It represents an unequal guarantee of this right in relation to those who may either attend non-denominational schools where

---

[16] *Rules for National Schools* (Dublin: Stationery Office, 1965), rules 54(1) and 59(5).

these are established, or those reflecting their own religious beliefs. In the *Campaign* case[17], the Supreme Court held: "the Constitution cannot protect [the non-coreligionist child] from being influenced, to some degree, by the religious 'ethos' of the school".[18] As outlined below, prevailing justifications for such compromises to minorities' religious liberties have evolved, over decades, towards a quasi-utilitarian paradigm of "choice".

Power Relations in Public Education Beyond "Critical Mass"

The most obvious determinant of inequalities in the guarantee of religious liberty in this context is that of demographic "critical mass". If the "right" to receive state support for a school operating under a particular religious ethos constitutes a guarantee of religious freedom, it is inadequate for those not situated within a "critical mass" that warrants such recognition. The Education Act 1998, broadly neutral in religious terms, empowers the Minister for Education to recognise schools according to criteria including "the need to reflect the diversity of educational services", but also, that *"the number of students who are attending or are likely to attend the school is such or is likely to be such as to make the school viable"*.[19] The prior administrative rules provided that schools could be recognised only "where the number of pupils of a particular denomination in that area is sufficient to warrant the establishment and continuance of such a school".[20]

However, this demographic criterion is not the only form of contingency or chance determining the extent of individuals' religious liberty rights in this context. "Critical mass" is a necessary, but not a sufficient condition: where it exists in a particular area, seeking appropriate provision, it is not incumbent on the state to take the initiative. It is left to the initiative of that community itself, which as well as attaining "critical mass", must arrange for the initial establishment of a school. In the aforementioned case, the parents attained a "critical mass", but their school failed to make adequate provision for the teaching of the Irish language, as Steiner-trained teachers were not competent in this respect.[21] The state was entitled to impose "rational" criteria for recognition, "proper criteria for eligibility".[22] The Court observed that the state, in order "to accommodate the expression of parental conscientious choice", must not necessarily "accede to an application for financial aid

---

[17] [1998] 3 IR 321.

[18] *Ibid*, 357.

[19] Section 10(2)(a). The Minister must also have regard to "the effective and efficient use of resources".

[20] *Rules for National Schools*, Chap. 1, rule 3.

[21] [1999] 2 IR 321, 356.

[22] [1999] 2 IR 321, 348.

from any group of parents who are united in their choice of primary education".[23] Moreover, "it is...incumbent on the State... ...to ensure that need and viability are properly assessed".[24] This means that "critical mass" groups seeking school recognition must also possess certain resources, or capital. It may be extremely difficult for certain groups to meet the neutral or "rational" criteria required. It is not the state's obligation to provide the full extent of resources necessary to give effect to parents' choices, but merely to give support where certain criteria are met in advance.

Evidently, criteria requiring such forms of human capital may bear disproportionately on peripheral religious communities, whose faith is not historically implanted in Ireland, whose schools are not already established, and which suffer a relative deficit in the resources necessary to establish and seek recognition for new schools. Various forms of knowledge and social networks are necessary to the negotiation of this framework for such groups. Without these collective resources, parents may have no option but to avail of public education through institutions committed to imparting beliefs and doctrines they oppose.

Furthermore, the process of school recognition is somewhat vulnerable to the discretion or grace of the state authorities. One of the "objects" of the Education Act 1998 is "to promote the right of parents to send their children to a school of the parents' choice", but this is qualified with reference to "the effective and efficient use of resources".[25] The state's discretionary power potentially creates a danger of minority communities having to ingratiate themselves to certain political agendas, whether capricious, or bearing a "rational" veneer, or otherwise. The adequate accommodation of minorities may also be subject to the goodwill of the churches operating existing recognised schools, both in accommodating minorities in these schools, and in transferring these to non-sectarian patronage following demographic changes. An example is provided in the negotiations surrounding the proposed "handover", to state control, of a number of Catholic-ethos schools in Dublin, following greater demand for non-denominational education in Ireland in recent years. Archbishop Martin described the "almost monopoly" of the Catholic Church as "a historical hangover that doesn't reflect [modern] realities and is in many ways detrimental to the possibility of maintaining a true Catholic identity in Catholic schools" (Carbery 2009). He signalled an intention to facilitate "diversity" in educational provision in response to social change, by transferring control of some schools to secular control, while also recognising tensions between maintaining the confessional ethos of schools and safeguarding the rights of non-coreligionists. Thus, while secularisation has led to pressures for change, this depends on the cooperation of those in a historical position of dominance, and perhaps, who identify such changes as serving their own interests in better maintaining the confessional integrity of their remaining schools. The legal framework of formal pluralism better serves the interests, and upholds the rights of those who, through accidents of

---

[23] [1999] 2 IR 321, 347.
[24] [1999] 2 IR 321, 348.
[25] Section 6(1)(e).

historical chance, have already acquired a network of recognised schools, with this constituting a form of power or capital necessary to secure the basic rights as well as the broader interests of that group.

The Example of Special Arrangements for the Protestant Minority

An example of the salience of disparities in political and social capital is provided by the special provisions historically made for the Protestant minority. In contrast to recently implanted religions, this community has been present in the state over centuries, despite its precarious position following the partition of Ireland in the 1920s. Protestant primary schools were historically funded on an equal basis to Catholic schools, where Protestant populations existed. However, when free secondary education was introduced in the 1960s, it became clear that while 75% of Catholic students would benefit from the scheme, only 7.5% of Protestant students would similarly benefit, because:

> the majority of the [Protestant] group, *because of their size and geographical distribution*, would have to attend Protestant boarding [residential] schools if they were to receive an education in accordance with their parents' convictions (Glendenning 2009, p. 336).

Successive governments therefore administered an annual "block grant" for Protestant fee-paying secondary schools, to offset fees payable by residential students, on the basis of a means test. It was not paid to Catholic fee-paying schools. Its purpose was to permit Protestants to avail of a secondary school reflecting their religious beliefs. The state also administered an "ancillary grant", to cover non-teachings costs not normally provided to fee-paying schools, in order to put the Protestant fee-paying sector in a position of parity with the "free" Catholic schools. This reflected the fact that Protestant schools served a dispersed community, and therefore had to accept residential students, and therefore could not avail of the free secondary system while meaningfully serving this community. The "ancillary" grant was abolished amidst recent education cutbacks, with the government citing the constitutional requirement of non-discrimination[26], even though the criterion for the grant, of serving a dispersed community, might be seen as a secular or neutral one.[27] The decision provoked widespread polemic, invoking the religious liberty of the Protestant minority.[28]

---

[26] P. McGarry, 2009. The Minister stated: "to continue the grant that was available would be unconstitutional because it was being given to the Protestant denomination and being refused to the Catholic denomination".

[27] Mary Hanafin, then Minister for Education, stated: "the block grant has its origins in the desire of the State to enable students of the Protestant and Jewish persuasions to attend schools which reflect their denominational ethos". Dáil Éireann, Volume 638, October 2, 2007. Furthermore, the Supreme Court held in *Quinn's Supermarket v Att. Gen.* [1972] IR that the State could observe distinctions on religious grounds where necessary to guarantee religious freedom.

[28] E. Waugh, 2009.

First, the very necessity of such special provision neatly illustrates the shortcomings of the ostensibly pluralist patronage model. Despite the formal neutrality of the free secondary education scheme, the demographic weakness of the Protestant minority rendered the idea of a "right" to attend a school reflecting one's religious beliefs essentially meaningless. It illustrates the reliance of the patronage model on groups being sufficiently well positioned to establish schools in all areas. The exercise of this right is made subject to the type of arbitrary contingencies represented by Protestants' "scattered" demographic profile. Special arrangements for particular communities could not be considered an adequate safeguard of religious liberty for all non-Catholics. Such ad hoc arrangements are incapable of guaranteeing the religious liberty of all those who might seek public education in accordance with whatever religious or other doctrine, of enabling persons of all beliefs to attend schools specifically attuned to these.

While the Protestant community did not attain "critical mass" in most areas, it possessed the political capital necessary to convince successive governments to make special provision for its needs. This illustrates the importance, within the patronage model, of minority communities' capacity to advance political claims to accommodation, to have the state exercise its discretionary power in their favour. Other communities do not enjoy the same capital, political-moral claim, or even the recognition of "minority" status, which the Protestant community could draw upon in advancing its claim. A prerequisite to its claim was the existence of recognised schools which, for other communities, do not exist at all. Despite the government's stance, the special measures are arguably a constitutionally permissible form of religious accommodation[29], yet it could not be claimed that they are constitutionally required, for all beliefs that might exist. The discretion of public authority therefore represents a further determinant of inequality in the guarantee of minorities' religious liberties. This undermines the idea of basic liberties being put beyond the "calculus of social interests", and "taken off…the political agenda" (Rawls 2001, p. 115). Protestants' religious liberty has been vulnerable not only to their demographic decline, but to the subsiding of the goodwill historically extended by the state. For more peripheral communities, deficits in social and political capital translate as a yet more precarious religious liberty in this context.

Constructing Religious Liberty at the Level of the Group: The Rawlsian Critique

I have previously argued that the inequalities in the guarantee of liberty of conscience inherent in the patronage model are best critiqued through the prism of Rawls's justice as fairness (Daly 2009). Rawls's theory represents a social contract approach to constructing principles of justice appropriate to a society of citizens conceived as free and equal (Rawls 1996, 1999, 2001). The principles of justice appropriate to the

---

[29] Note 27 above.

"basic structure" of social institutions are those which would be accepted in a hypothetical deliberative position of fairness, the "original position", in which the parties are represented symmetrically, as free and equal, ignorant both of the power disparities prevailing in ordinary society, and the content and social prevalence of their own "comprehensive" doctrines (1997, p. 17). Rawls insists that the principles of justice regulating public institutions must transcend the "calculus of social interests" and "accidents of natural endowment" (2001, p. 105). Rawlsian justice precludes any particular "comprehensive" doctrine as a basis for public justification; principles of justice are derived independently of any such conception, "metaphysical" or otherwise, of final human ends (1999, p. 11). The principles of justice, and the basic liberties, are instead specified as primary goods, the "all-purpose means" necessary to enable persons to exercise the two "moral powers", including the capacity to pursue a conception of the good "over a complete life" (2001, p. 57).

Thus, Rawls's theory insists on the independence of justice from those contingent features of society regarded as "arbitrary from a moral point of view" (1999, p. 17). It imposes two distinct dualisms or abstractions, reflecting the peculiar role of principles applicable to political institutions, rather than voluntary associations, and the distinct role of political philosophy in relation to the "comprehensive" knowledge represented by theology or philosophy. It posits that under utilitarianism, the aim of maximum aggregate utility across society may result in the liberties of some being sacrificed for the sake of a "greater good shared by others", justice must instead protect rights independently of any such bargaining game. Furthermore, religious liberty rights are abstracted from any comprehensive doctrine, secular or religious, which might specify the final ends which these rights serve; citizenship cannot be based on any set of final ends or identities that citizens are presumed to share ("abstraction from doctrine"). However, where citizenship is defined in "neutral" terms, open to diverse final ends, identities and way of life, basic rights must be guaranteed independently of the power disparities prevailing in any given society, of the arbitrary advantages distributed unequally as a function of the hazards of natural chance ("abstraction from contingency").

The legal framework for guaranteeing religious liberty in public education in Ireland cannot be regarded as independent from the various "social and natural contingencies", particularly demographic "critical mass", as well as the various resources and capital necessary to achieve school recognition. While the "residual" guarantee of withdrawal from religious instruction is, in the ways outlined, an inadequate guarantee of this right, the guarantee represented by school recognition is vulnerable to contingencies that are "arbitrary from a moral point of view". Individuals' guarantee against interference in their choice of beliefs is made subject, in the first place, to their positioning within a "critical mass" necessary to school recognition, and then, to whether persons' conscientious choices remain wholly consonant with the ethos promoted by that group. The premise of "equality in the assignment of basic rights and duties" (Rawls 1999, p. 13) is undermined by a legal framework which leaves the protection of religious liberty subject to power and bargaining disparities. It is not an adequate scheme of religious liberty because it leaves its protection vulnerable to the relative prevalence and bargaining powers of the groups to which individuals may belong, undermining the idea that "the rights secured by justice are not subject to political bargaining" (Rawls 1999, p. 4).

This inequality of rights is itself the product of a trade-off between the basic liberty of conscience and the interests of certain groups in having public education provision devolved to institutions reflecting their beliefs. However, this inequality is not based on any formal distinction or civil disability directly related to religious affiliation. As outlined, minority religions possessing sufficient forms of capital are also capable of attaining state support for their schools, and therefore, of guaranteeing religious liberty for their adherents. The inequality in the distribution of this right may therefore be seen as operating within as well as between religious groups. While religious liberty is subject to adherence to a "critical mass", it also depends on the conscientious acceptance by individuals of the full range of beliefs held within the group; the categories between which religious liberty is unequally distributed are fluid and transient. It cuts across "majority" and "minority" categories: the mere fact that, say, a liberal Catholics may avail of schools matching their nominal religious affiliation, does not necessarily guarantee their freedom from arbitrary interference in their choice of beliefs. To argue otherwise would be to assume an implausible, consistent degree of unity between clerical patrons and those they serve. It would be a mistake to view these inequalities as operating simply between the different religious and other groups; instead, it must be seen as reflecting the multidimensional power relations operating within, as well as between groups. Individuals' religious liberties are vulnerable to a variety of conjunctural factors other than that of nominal religious affiliation, not just to the potential caprice, grace, and discretion of the state, but that of the "patron" as privileged interlocutor.

The parties represented in the Rawlsian original position reserve for themselves the choice and determination of their beliefs. They cannot "take chances" with their liberty of conscience by accepting that the range of recognised schools may, as a matter of mere probability or chance, accommodate their beliefs (1999, p. 181). Rather than guaranteeing religious liberty equally for *individuals* irrespective of the arbitrary outcomes of demographic and social chance, Irish law recognises formal equality between *groups* in accessing state support for their schools. This cannot translate as equal religious liberty for individuals, because it does not mean that all forms of beliefs and preferences may be equally accommodated, or that such group-oriented provision will accommodate the choices even of those nominally situated within such groups. The imperative of "diversity" in educational provision is bounded by various demographic, political and resource-based limitations; the "rights" into which it is translated are not fully adequate for persons differently situated in social terms.

The Transition to "Choice"-Oriented Justifications

The discourses surrounding denominational education have demonstrated a shift in legitimation strategy, from one emphasising religion as a public good or basis of national identity, to ideas of "choice" and diversity, defined in neutral and secular terms. In both legal rulings discussed, the state's responsibility to support denominational schools, and to recognise the largely unfettered inculcation of doctrines within such schools, was rationalised from the standpoint of parental "choice", rather than any conception of religion as a privileged locus of the public good. This transition has taken place notwithstanding the bellicose theistic references remaining in the Constitution.[30] Individuals are accordingly recognised, albeit in a flawed and partial sense, as "self-authenticating sources of valid claims" (Rawls 2001, p. 23). In *O'Shiel*, the parents seeking recognition for a Steiner school did not have to constitute any recognisable "community" to lay claim to state support for this model; their right was constructed exclusively in terms of "choice" rather than any comprehensive identity. Their claim was constructed as self-authenticating in the sense that the Court appeared to view it as equivalent to religious preferences which might otherwise be claimed to encumber adherents in a deeper sense. Similarly, the *Campaign* ruling justified the denominational character of recognised schools not in terms of the rights of school patrons or religious communities, but only the rights of individual parents, of whatever persuasion. The neutrality towards religion per se, or shift towards ends neutral values of choice, contrasts sharply with older jurisprudence. Justice Gavan Duffy stated in *Re Tilson* that "religion holds in the Constitution the place of honour which the community has always accorded to it",[31] while Justice Walsh proclaimed in *Quinn's Supermarket v. Att. Gen.* that "we are a religious people".[32]

When the patronage model is justified with reference to individual preferences, rather than religion as a public good, it is remarkably susceptible to the Rawlsian critique of utilitarianism. He suggests: "there is no reason…why [under utilitarianism]…the violation of the liberty of a few might not be made right by the greater good" (1999, p. 23). However, the shift from a communitarian to an individualist, "choice"-oriented justification for the denominational model creates certain tensions, since any legitimation predicated merely on choice, rather than on any intrinsic value in community *per se*, cannot coherently rely on the privileging of communitarian intermediaries. An explanation for this ideological confusion may lie in the very recent pedigree of the "choice"-oriented justification. In a secularised society, the appeal to individual "choice", rather than to any freestanding importance of religious identity may, despite its flaws, provide a more palatable justification for the denominational model, and may be capable of commanding broader support and legitimacy.

Whatever its flaws, the quasi-utilitarian paradigm of "choice" appears democratic in a limited sense, as it does not assume any communal end, belief or affiliation as prior to individual agency. It may have resonance in neoliberalism, in its emphasis on private involvement maximising "choice" in public services, and in its conflation of liberty with the minimisation or restraint of public authority. Meeting the preferences of education-consumers may override the "higher-order interests"

---

[30] Note 9 above.
[31] [1951] IR 1, at 14.
[32] [1972] IR 1, at 21.

of others consequently made subject to the inculcation of these preferences. To this vaguely neo-liberal doctrine of "choice", the egalitarian liberalism of Rawls' justice as fairness, affirming citizens' capacities to determine their conceptions of the good, offers a potent riposte to ideologies which leaves the guarantee of rights, if no longer subject to the hazards of established doctrines or idealised collective identities, then vulnerable to the arbitrary hazards of market-like forces.

Neutralised Citizenship, Precarious Rights

Despite the (partial) abstraction of citizenship from comprehensive doctrine in Ireland—in the shift to a secular, "choice"-oriented legitimation which replaces the idea of religion as a public good—religious liberty remains vulnerable, under a secularised public philosophy, to political and social power relations. The confessional character of schools is no longer justified in terms of "ghostly entities like collective will or national spirits" (Dworkin 1978, p. xi), or idealised systems of shared final ends, in the vein of romantic nationalism, that Rawls critiques as inappropriate as a basis for public justification in a society characterised by "reasonable pluralism" (1996, p. 4). Instead, it is justified in terms of secular goods of diversity and choice, but the "choice" it offers is vulnerable, for individuals, not only to their communities' relative powers, but also, to the enduring symmetry of their conscientious preferences with those of the group to whom the state has entrusted their representation.

The rights-based critique of clerical patronage in public education must account for its potential to underpin not only the domination of minority communities by state authorities, but also, the power relations between the privileged intermediaries recognised as patrons, and marginal voices within communities. While public philosophy and justifications for the patronage model have been broadly secularised, the function of identity-orientation is then merely devolved to the intra-communitarian level, with individuals' religious liberty claims bound up with the group to which the state arbitrarily delegates their representation. The failure to dissociate religious liberty rights from contingent affiliations stymies and jeopardises the secularisation of public philosophy, since individuals' rights are subsumed within the broader interests of groups with whom their conscientious choices may not durably and fully coincide. The idea of shared final ends or pre-political commonalities may dissipate at the level of the formally "neutral" secular state, but it persists at the level of the community. In Ireland, while citizenship might no longer be tethered to any conception of shared ends and values, the patronage model sees a secular "neutral" state specify the contours and requirements of citizens' rights with reference to their religious affiliations. This contrasts with Rawls's conception of citizens as "claim[ing] the right to view their persons as independent from and not identified with any particular conception of the good, or scheme of final ends" (2001, p. 21).

Thus, absent from the 'choice'-oriented justification is evidence of the concrete relationship between the ethos of schools, determined by school patrons, and the actual preferences of the members of the community. There is, at best, a casual relationship between school ethos and citizens' choices. While the Minister must have regard, in exercising his powers, to "the need to reflect the diversity of educational services", the legislation specifies no mechanism whereby the actual preferences of parents may be reflected in recognised schools. The Minister is not required to graft the ethos of recognised schools to the actual "choices" of parents, in whatever prevalence they exist. This might mean that while provision for public education through exclusively Catholic schools in a particular area might be justified with reference to the overwhelmingly Catholic demographics of that area, that itself is not a sufficient basis on which to legitimate the doctrines taught in the schools, even within the flawed, quasi-utilitarian paradigm of "choice". A demographic assessment of prevailing religious affiliations prevailing in a particular area would not in itself suffice to ascertain the more complex choices and preferences of individual citizens. This may overlook the potentially complex relationship between religious affiliation and other commitments. Liberal Catholics, for example, may wish for their children to attend a non-denominational or other school, for whatever reasons(Alvey 1991); where Catholic parents do wish for their children to attend Catholic schools, this itself is insufficient to establish that the doctrines imparted by the school accord with their choice. This issue is likely to be even more salient for minority groups given the relatively narrower range of school choices available. In either case, access to a school reflecting one's religious affiliation in the broad sense cannot be regarded as a reliable guarantee of undominated "choice". Yet the discourses surrounding denominational education are constructed as though the ethos of schools were determined by parents themselves, through their corporate will. The conflation of the "ethos" prescribed by various educational patrons, and the conscientious choices of parents, sits uneasily with the idea of citizens as "valid sources of self-authenticating claims". The simulacrum of representation characterising the patronage model parodies the putative dissociation of citizenship from religious identity.

Conclusion

This contribution has charted the adaptation of the peculiar model of educational patronage, formally non-sectarian but overwhelmingly confessional in real terms, from a legitimation rooted in romantic nationalism, to one appealing to secular values, more palatable to the liberal mind, of choice and diversity. It has illustrated the enduringly precarious status of the religious liberties rights of minority communities under a secularised legal framework, which remains reliant on private initiative and various forms of political bargaining, resulting, in turn, in persisting inequalities in the guarantee of this right, weighing disproportionately on these groups ill-positioned to instrumentalise the secular good of "choice". The denial of religious liberty rights for minorities no longer arises from any essentialised conception of citizenship, from any established doctrine or identity, but instead lies in the failure of public institutions to safeguard these rights independently of social and political power relations. The formally pluralist system of educational patronage described maintains a subordinate position for minority groups, under a veneer of secular neutrality.

References

Alvey, D. (1991). *Irish education: The case for secular reform*. Belfast: Athol Books.
Carbery, G. (2009). Catholic control of schooling not tenable, says archbishop. *The Irish Times*, June 17.
Clarke, D. (1984). *Church and state: Essays in political philosophy*. Cork: Cork University Press.
Clarke, D. (1998). Education, the state and sectarian schools. In T. Murphy & P. Twomey (Eds.), *Ireland's evolving constitution: 1937–1997* (pp. 41–51). Oxford: Hart Publishing.
Daly, E. (2008). Religious freedom and the denominational education model in the Republic of Ireland: The shortcomings of 'accommodationist' reform. *Education Law Journal, 9*, 242–258.
Daly, E. (2009). Religious freedom as a function of power relations: Dubious claims on pluralism in the denominational schools debate. *Irish Educational Studies, 28*(3), 235–251.
Dworkin, R. (1978). *Taking rights seriously*. London: Duckworth.
Glendenning, D. (2008). *Religion, education and the law*. Dublin: Tottel.
Hickey, T. (2009). Freedom as non-domination and the Islamic *Hijab* in Irish schools. *Dublin University Law Journal, 39*, 127–153.
Hogan, G. (1987). Church-state relations in Ireland from independence to the present day 1987. *American Journal of Comparative Law, 35*, 47–73.
Hogan, G., & Whyte, G. (2003). *JM Kelly: The Irish Constitution*. Dublin: Butterworth.
Hyland, Á. (1989). The multi-denominational experience in the National School System in Ireland. *Irish Educational Studies, 8*, 91–99.
Keogh, D. (1988). The Irish constitutional revolution: An analysis of the making of the constitution. In F. Litton (Ed.), *The constitution of Ireland: 1937–1987* (pp. 65–89). Dublin: Institute of Public Administration.
Lee, J. (1989). *Ireland 1912–1985: Politics and society*. Cambridge: Cambridge University Press.
Mawhinney, A. (2006). The opt-out clause: Imperfect protection for the right to freedom of religion in schools. *Education Law Journal, 2*, 27–43.
Mawhinney, A. (2007). Freedom of religion in the Irish primary school system: A failure to protect human rights? *Legal Studies, 27*(3), 379–403.
Mawhinney, A. (2009). *Freedom of religion and schools: The case of Ireland*. Saarbrücken: VDM.
McCrea, R. (2009). The recognition of religion within the constitutional and political order of the European Union. *LSE 'Europe in Question' Discussion Paper Series*.
McGarry, P. (2009). O'Keeffe to discuss cuts' impacts on Protestants. *The Irish Times*, October 22.
O'Connell, R. (1999). Theories of religious education in Ireland. *Journal of Law and Religion, 14*(2), 433–523.
Pettit, P. (2005). The tree of liberty: Republicanism, American, French and Irish. *Field Day Review, 1*, 28–41.
Rawls, J. (1996). *Political liberalism*. Cambridge: Harvard University Press.
Rawls, J. (1999). *A theory of justice*. Cambridge: Harvard University Press.
Rawls, J. (2001). *Justice as fairness: A restatement*. Cambridge: Harvard University Press.
Waugh, E. (2009). Why protestant schools pose a test of the Republic's democracy. *The Belfast Telegraph*, October 13.
Whyte, J. (1980). *Church and state in Modern Ireland*. Dublin: Gill and Macmillan.

Chapter 37
Educational Processes and Ethnicity Among Hindu Migrants

Helena Sant'ana

Introduction

This chapter focuses primarily on Hindu migrant women residing in the metropolitan area of Lisbon.

The Hindu population are mostly settled in the municipal areas of Lisbon and Loures (Santo Antonio dos Cavaleiros, Chelas, Portela de Sacavém and Quinta da Vitória), and a small number in the Porto region.

Almost all of this population migrated to Portugal from Mozambique in the late 1970s, due to the uncertainty surrounding the process of decolonization. Later during the 1990s as a result of the process of family reunification another type of migration emerged directly from India, in particular from the Diu and Gujarat States, as well as from the Central African Republic (Malheiros 2001).

This chapter aims to prove that the contingencies that have surrounded the Hindu migratory process towards Portuguese territory were historically and sociologically decisive in determining how that population socialized its members, particularly with regard to instigating female education. There is an overall agreement that culture, as well as the socialization process and education, are directly related to the construction of ethnicity. In this case the educational practices of the female Hindu population have had a strong influence both upon the structure of ethnicity and upon the way in which the ethnic minority has integrated. The educative pattern (both formal and informal) in Hindu society differs for both genders, because what is of importance is the utility of education. This implies that school attendance is only necessary when serving some practical purpose. In the case of men what is required is to achieve a socially and economically prestigious profession; whereas women need only learn enough to be a good mother and housewife[1] (Malheiros

---

[1] See "*The Anuários Estatísticos da Província de Cabo Verde* (1932–1970)".

H. Sant'ana (✉)
Universidade Técnica de Lisboa–ISCSP Rua Almerindo Lessa–Polo Universitário do Alto da Ajuda, 1349-055, Lisboa, Portugal
e-mail: hsantana@iscsp.utl.pt

1996; Menon-Sem and Shiva Kumar 2001, Hirst and Lynn 2004). How do the immigrants deal with educational differences within a new social context? Is it necessary to ask if the migration process brings about any change in the concept of utility regarding the procedure of female education? How do they react in contact with other educational systems? Does this have any impact upon their role as a woman? How does this population bridge the gap between formal and informal female education? Are the Hindu migrant women manipulated by the patriarchal system as the gatekeepers of tradition within a new cultural context or are they given more licence and self-control?

Methodology

This article is part of the research that took place between 2005 and 2008. This work focuses primarily on Hindu women residing in the metropolitan area of Lisbon. This Hindu population, mostly from Mozambique, has set itself in Lisbon Metropolitan area, specifically in the municipality of Lisbon and Loures: in St. António dos Cavaleiros, Chelas, Portela de Sacavém, Quinta da Vitória; and a small number in the region of greater Porto.

This is a population comprised of individuals who lived in Mozambique, and migrated to Portugal from the late 1970s, due to the uncertainty associated with the process of decolonization. From the 1990s, the process of reunification of the families will emerge new migrations derived directly from India in particular of Diu and the State of Gujarat.

The decision to undertake the study of Hindu women residing in Portugal encountered certain obstacles in obtaining examples. Where were these women? Since this is a heterogeneous group, which is neither confined to specific quarters nor confined to specific neighbourhoods and mostly of Portuguese nationality, because Hindu women are found living in large practically anonymous condominiums, made up of an invisible web of tight neighbourhood relationships of the ethnic community (a community that both oversees and supports the life of all) and also because it is a population dispersed across an urban mosaic (and which in most cases is naturalized) it became neither feasible nor practical to carry out quantitative research.

The appeal was therefore to establish a network of female contacts which ranged across the greater Lisbon area. Intimacy has been negotiated slowly.

Encounters were far from easy and contacts were compromised, conducted out of sight amid the small invisibilities of daily life. Hindu women are distant beings. That distance is the result of being confined in large town apartments.

The decision to undertake the study was based upon qualitative research, where the combination of interview and ethnographic work being deemed the best choice.

The research design was conducted through ethnographic research with filed work and life story interviews. The life story is a semi-structured interview which focuses upon social, educational, career and development factors. This also allows for the exploration of the migratory, residential and relational universe, observing such characteristics as: household composition and the maintenance of network alliances as well as self-help and friendship (Denzin and Yvonna 2000).

Twenty-seven women and ten men participated in the interviews ranging in age from 18 to 75. Three of the women were born in Portugal, one coming directly from India to get married, and the rest lived or were born in Mozambique. All of the men had lived in Mozambique before migrating to Portugal. The sample was obtained through a snowball method using their social networks. In some cases this meant, given the proximity of kinship between women, the interviews were conducted in the presence of other women. This engendered an interaction characterized by rich exchanges of experiences, memories and confessions.

Some of the respondents are of the same family. In some cases were interviewed mothers and daughters, mothers in law and daughters in law, or husbands and wives. In other cases, since it was used the snowball method, the interviews were conducted with neighbours from the community, and Hindu people who attend the Hindu temples in Lisbon (*see annex in the end*).

Indian Women in Mozambique—Type of Education

It was not until the 1930s that Indian women began to migrate to Africa, generating among the local population multiple family businesses, in which the woman would act as an active worker in the shop while simultaneously interacting with the local African population.

The female role slowly began to gain importance in the diaspora, not only in view of its influence upon the adaptation of the families of the *cantineiro*[2] and country merchants, but also when it came to the interaction between Indians and Africans (Ribeiro 1930; Reis 1973).

The progressive coming of women from India to the colony and the formation of extensive families took on an unexpected function. Since the stigmatization process had been started a few decades earlier, the formation and fixation of Hindu families as well as the need to preserve the caste system generated close endogamous relationships among the Hindu group (regardless of caste) resulting in seclusion from the Europeans (Castro 1932; Rita-Ferreira 1988).

---

[2] *Cantineiro* was an expression used to popularly define those merchants who opened their shops in the woods, near the villages of African populations. The largest number of *cantineiros* was found among Hindu and Muslim Indians. Despite the negative opinion of Portuguese rulers about the effect that Indians had on commercial traffic, totally contradictory to the economical interests of the state, their influence was extremely important. The presence of such populations was instrumental in diffusing monetary economy among southern populations and influenced spontaneous migratory flows to the new mining centres in South Africa.

The *cantineiros* sought to establish themselves strategically close to the borders with South Africa, profiting from the huge traffic of African miners returning to their villages.

Unlike the Europeans, Indian women learned the local language, habits, and medical practices, which they combined with knowledge of popular Hindu (Ayurvedic) medicine occasionally acting as midwives or healers and their knowledge commanded respect and status among the ethnic groups.

Female interaction between Hindus and Africans altered feeding habits, adding new tastes and adapting cooking procedures, thereby increasing the capacity of adaptability between the two groups.

Mitha tells an example of such an important interaction:

> In India I knew how to cook nothing but *rotli*, *rotlá*, fish and vegetarian food. Later I learned to cook African food, Portuguese food, Indian food, and even *mithá* (a traditional Indian sweet that is especially eaten during festivities). I learned from my mother-in-law who was already living in Africa and knew how to mix the two cuisines very well. She made the best *achar* in the whole region. [Mitha 1960]

The feminine presence in the colony stimulated associated and selective education among young Hindus, and it also stressed the socialization of children within the cultural models of Hinduism.[3]

During the 1940s and 1950s, two private schools belonging to Hindu associations appeared: the *Escola da Associação Hindu*, located in Beira, which was mainly concerned with elementary education for the Indo-British, and the *Escola Bharat Samaj*, in Lourenço Marques, which is still open today (despite a short interlude during the civil war) (A.E.P.M., 1957–1970).

The Gujarati Hindus preferred to maintain private schools, ruled and subsidized by the Hindu religious associations, on a par with Portuguese schools, so that their children not only kept in touch with their mother tongue but could also benefit from a set of identity–forming principles, in order that "the culture would not be lost".

Nevertheless, school attendance varied greatly between the two sexes. Girls studied very little, both in the Portuguese schools and in those belonging to the Hindu associations; their levels of study only rising during the 1960s and 1970s. Such girls usually ceased their education at elementary level.

Gujarati families with higher economic potentials sent their daughters to India after elementary education, placing them in private boarding schools, where they received a form of socialization completely in keeping with the values of Hinduism. They were brought up to be the guardians and transmitters of Hindu traditions, tak-

---

[3] The word Hinduism only entered the English vocabulary during the seventeenth century, becoming synonymous with those who professed the Hindu religion and had not converted to Islamism. Hinduism is not the translation of a word and in India it still cannot represent a religious union, being rather a form of identity in view of the other ethnic and religious groups that inhabit the same territory. To be Hindu "(…) is not a primordial identity that can be changed nor made infinitely flexible. It is not dependent on will. It is an identity acquired through social practice and constantly negotiated in changing contexts" (Vertovec 2000, p. 7). In that sense, Hinduism is a phenomenon of multiple definitions. To be a Hindu does not merely mean belonging affectively to a common religious collective, it constitutes a *habitus* with implications in all areas of individual and community life.

ing into consideration the migratory context within which the needs of adaptability frequently distorted the transmission of the purest sense of *dharma*.[4]

Women are socially prepared from infancy to fulfil their main goal: to become wives and then mothers. Becoming a wife demands a long apprenticeship, which the bridegroom's family takes into consideration during the proceedings of matrimonial alliance, including such requisites as the familiarity with religious rites and the ability to pass them on.

According to the Hindu conception, no woman will find her place in society without fully adopting her role as a sexual partner, since women are considered as being complementary to their companions (Ghosh 1989; Dhruvarajan 1989).

Hindu tradition states that the main goal of marriage involves religious duty (*dharma*), progeny (*praja*), and finally conjugal love (*rati*). In that sense, marriage is an instrument for attaining the highest expectations in the life of a Hindu. It is a sacrament (*samskara*) of the greatest importance because only the married man can perform the religious rites correctly, since most of them must be performed by the couple before the sacred fire (*agni*). But whereas men perform several sacraments during their lives, women are consecrated at one single time—marriage: the event that truly bestows social status upon them. As an organic and mystical form of complementariness, the union resulting from marriage is considered indissoluble and irrevocable (Ghosh 1989; Mukherjee 1978)

The importance of the matrimonial alliance in caste endogamy was so great that some young girls born in Mozambique were sent to India to honour and perpetuate the matrimonial alliances thereby maintaining the identity of cohesion between emigrant and autochthon Hindus. Such young women hardly attended school at all:

> I completed the fourth grade in Mozambique and then I married and went to India, to the house of my in-laws, when I was 16 years old. [Radha 1962]

---

[4] The concept of *dharma* is associated with the idea of ritual purity. The purity/pollution duality has become a principle that organizes space and social relationships in Indian society, "a principle recognized in the *dharmasastras* which sees social ethnicity as the maintenance of order and of limits between groups and genders, governed by degrees of purity and impurity" (Flood 1996, p. 57).

The hierarchical vision of Indian society recommended a different *dharma* for each human group and for each sex. Female socialization categorically imposes obedience to the *dharma*, this being an absolute imperative that cannot be mistaken for divine will or for individual conscience.

Dharma is above all a form of social control which leads towards the cohesion of social groups, in order to maintain a certain (ideal) social order for the whole of man's most important needs.

The female *dharma* expressed in the sacred books also implies a dedication to the *artha* (made up of material interests, wealth and success in undertakings) and the *kama* (which includes sensation and the pleasure of the senses).

Kama appears (in the ancient texts) as the feminine *svadharma*. No woman will find her place in society without fully assuming her role as a sexual companion. Within that domain they are considered as being complementary to their companions. One's *dharma* affects the other's *dharma*. If every Hindu man's moral and religious obligation is to fulfil his *dharma*, then the woman's consists of expressing her service to her husband, as to a god, to whom she must respond in amorous terms.

> I married at 14. I had been asked to marry since I was 12 and then my mother said that I could marry when I was 14, and so it was. We had no say at all, because that's the way it is in our religion, mother would command and we had to get married. I only attended the first grade. [kirti 1958]

The young women who studied in India usually stayed there from nine or ten years of age until about 18 or 20. They would return to Mozambique at the beginning of adulthood, when they had finished their studies and got engaged by parental agreement, or even after marriage.

Generally speaking, parents were not interested in their daughters studying for many years, simply enough to learn how to read and write and to be able to carry out domestic chores, in order to please their future husbands' families.

While in India they would stay with close relatives or, in the case of wealthier families, in boarding schools, and the prime objective was to prepare the girls to be the vehicles of cultural transmission within a migratory context. As guardians of Hinduism, women would be able to reproduce their maternal culture in Africa, just as they were to do in the second migratory cycle to Portugal.

> It was important to stay in India for a few years. There was not much study, but we learned our whole culture, in the place where our parents and forefathers had been born. Afterwards, when we got married, we could hand down that culture to our children. [Kasturi 1946]

The Hindu woman's ideal is to be virtuous and dedicated to her husband, not only as a dogma or ideal set by men, but as a life rule internalized by women (Dhruvarajan 1989; Biardeau 1972, 1981; Mukherjee 1978; Fuller 2004). Although in the present context the *patrivata*[5] is not the ideal model for the future, it still contributes to the self-esteem of women and to increase their prestige and power. Formal education was not a part of the life of Hindu women (in the recent past), this, coupled with them not having the capacity to achieve financial gain, as they did not work, kept them chained to domestic life. Gauri exemplifies the mentality of the Hindu woman through her mother, an immigrant in Mozambique:

> My mother did not study and she didn't want to, because she used to say: Why should I study? I have to work at home, so why study? But it is no longer like that now. Who would work away from home 35 years ago? Now many women do, my nieces do because they studied. Even after getting married they can go on working. Nowadays with television everybody knows what goes on in the world, so women no longer have that *pativratya* ideology. Men are not like that any more either. Before women had to obey their orders but now each one has autonomy. For instance, when we have a marriage we bring the whole household together and we decide. If someone wants to travel, we decide everything together. [Gauri 1947]

Moreover, while girls studied only up until the first grades of high school, the education of boys, especially those from Diu, was not overly long either. Hindu boys were socialized in the sense of being secluded from the Europeans; they were educated mainly to become merchants within their half-closed universe, as Devraj states:

---

[5] The *Prativratya* ideology considers that female spiritual salvation is rooted in total devotion and subordination to the husband.

I nearly had to take a stand in 1950. But Hindus placed their sons to study near them, so they could control them and ensure that they would not go around with other people. Then there was the monetary issue. People often would not have the monetary capacity to support a son studying away from home, because at home if there is enough food for three, there is also enough for four or five. For that reason boys did not study much. [Devraj 1950]

Educational Gaps

After the process of decolonizing Mozambique in 1975 and particularly during the 1980s, thousands of Hindus migrated to Portugal and scattered *communities* of Hindus who had previously resided in Mozambique met and interacted, forming cores of interests, depending upon unstable balances and on the reshaping of social classes that took place in Portugal after the revolution.

The Hindus who migrated to Portugal would seek to reconstruct their identity while still reflecting upon the regionalisms, based on the differences in uses, feeding habits and rituals that separate sub castes.

Migration to Portugal brought important changes in the organization of the Hindu association movements and in the role of women in those movements. The territorial spread of the Hindu population in Mozambique changed in Portugal to the forming of mutual knowledge and help networks. Migration to Portugal also led to an increase in the preserving of identity in a more visible form, through the re-foundation of associations, clubs and organizations. These groups were set up within a network promoting ethnic social capital (Putnam 2000) and their goal was to further socialization as well as to promote social and identity cohesion among their members.

During this second migratory period and because of the changes experienced by large families, Indian women began to initiate, in a more visible and sustained way, a transnational movement which, in turn, led to a migratory ebb and flow, with the exchanging of wives, visits and even more extended contacts, in order to keep cultural ties ever present. The social environment in modern Portugal contains a greater risk of identity loss. Hindu girls and boys are now forced to attend Portuguese schools and to complete compulsory scholarships. Contacts with those from other cultures turned cosmopolitan Lisbon into a greater danger than that seen in Mozambique. Hindu families protect themselves from the cultural contamination from "others" by focusing themselves as a group in the neighbourhood or at the temple.

In addition, a Hindu youth may have some Portuguese friends at school, but the network bond is not a strong one. In this particular case the concept of social control is close to Durkheim's concept of social integration. Durkheim (1897/1976) basically said that the greater integration of an individual into a group, the greater control the group has over the individual. Accordingly, ethnicity is a source of social control that remains current through family education. Hindu children speak their native language—Gujarati, and their parents send them to school at the temple to learn and write Gujarati, conceptualize mathematics in Gujarati and also to attend classes of Indian culture and religion.

The children usually attend Portuguese classes in the neighbourhood before commencing secondary education. Although they may be enrolled at the beginning, for the early years of schooling, they do not always remain in school. Babita recounts an episode which reflects the reality in many families of lower socio-economic status:

> I raised three children alone. My husband never helped me either at school or at hospitals, or with enquiries. He didn't even know how old the children were. One day when Joshi was in the 9th grade and Lalli was in the 8th, my husband called me and told me: enough studies! Which grades are they in? Then you don't know? And I told him which grades they were in, but my husband decided that it was time to leave school and go to work. The eldest still finished the 12th grade at night and then gave up. [Babita 1947]

However, if it were a girl who could drop out between second grade and third grade, she would be the first to abandon the classes, as Sima states:

> When I was 14 I was in the 2nd grade and my mother said to me "You are going to leave school next year, I would prefer you to help me at home rather than do nothing outside". [Sima 1992]

After one year Sima became engaged to a young Hindu from the same caste, and never studied again.

The fact is that Hindu boys are encouraged to finish high school, although a lesser number go on to university. But the reduced access to higher education among the Hindu population does not necessarily mean there is an adaptative process with extreme monetary difficulties. The cause lies in the rules laid down in the family *habitus*, as the stock strategy for a professional path undertaken by male members of the family.

Nakul is the owner of a small grocery business in Santo Antonio. He has three children, two boys and a girl. In his view:

> I would like it if one of my sons were to inherit the business. I've being working so hard to achieve it ...but I don't believe it any more. One of them wants to work at the airport, and the other, well he's still little but has a great talent for informatics.
> And what about your daughter, he was asked?
> - My daughter is very good looking like me. She rules everything in our home, but as you know when she gets married she will live with her in-laws. [Nakul 1948]

Poor families are also more likely to keep girls at home to look after younger siblings or to work in the family business. If a family has to choose between educating a son or a daughter because of financial limitations, typically the son will be chosen.

Education among Hindus is distinguished by caste/class together with gender. Hindus who live in slums have poorer levels of literacy and a difficult path through schooling. Girls in the same circumstances have a propensity to reach lower levels of literacy, marry very young and depend entirely upon their husbands and in-laws.

Bernstein (1975) considers that socially underprivileged families are carriers of a restricted code, i.e. with strong ties to the context and predominance of the collective over the individual. In this case the parents are the genuine holders of authority, and tend to educate their children in order to obey and accept the established order.

On the contrary, parents from higher classes are more flexible and more socially integrated. Following the same line of thought, Kellerhals and Montandon (1991) argue that parents from higher classes value autonomy and curiosity, and prefer children of a voluntary nature, while working class parents have a preference for order, discipline and...cleanliness.

Although there is no sufficient research on this issue that simultaneously takes into account ethnic diversity, social class and education, certain similarities between the behaviour of the caste and the different classes in the Hindu population may be inferred (Seabra 1994).

Currently, there is a tendency to overlap class and caste; this tends to dilute the statutory differences associated with the castes, especially in migratory contexts. The Hindus of higher castes also belong to higher social classes, or even the middle class, and this group reinforces the importance of maintaining studies in both sexes. Nevertheless, the usefulness of a higher education for girls is simply to find an educated and rich husband. The fact is that even when girls have a higher education and they get married they usually stop working to devote their lives to motherhood.

On the other hand, during field work a Luso-Indian female university graduate spoke autonomously about choosing a profession:

> I graduated this year and I'm applying for all the jobs that, but I still haven't found any work. But anyway I've decided not to go to work in my parents' shop [Reema 1985]

And Hansa, her friend says :
> I've decided to open my own business. I've got a degree in management, I've been thinking why not have my own career? My parents do not quite agree, but we live in other times. [Hansa 1985]

More traditional families fear that a young educated girl with professional ambitions may take some risks by opting for problematic solutions such as escaping from the cultural mainstream. So a young woman with superior academic training can be eyed with suspicion. Since she's more free-thinking, this denotes a propensity for questioning the rule governing behaviour and socializing which are imposed upon women. In the short term she will represent a threat to the familiar stability, insofar as she can deny her stridharma (Fuller 2004; Biardeau 1981).

Mitter (1991) asserts that a more educated woman will strive for changes in values: promoting the organization of women's right's movements; creating unions; editing magazines and newspapers and taking part in TV and radio programmes as well as denouncing the conditions in which women are victims and are the influences of a patriarchal regime against women's rights.

The author also detects that the representation of women in the mass media is almost always negative and stereotyped, where women have a low self-esteem. As Mitter says:

(...) Even if an increasing minority of working women in big cities are becoming more liberated, the majority still have no economic independence, no conviction of their worth and no acceptable social alternatives. They accept the way things are and learn some survival techniques (...) (1991, pp. 135–136)

During the field work it was possible to observe what kinds of survival techniques were developed by those women, particularly those who had little access to formal education.

Without education, without a profession and without the possibility of independence, the only alternative is the manipulation of one's own prison—tradition. Women from the lowest social strata will peacefully recreate their own socialized models, reinventing tradition in order to readjust the gender roles in a patriarchal family.

Women of higher social classes/castes try to mitigate the influence of tradition by prioritizing roles. The roles of freedom daughters and daughters in-law, allow them an alternative way of life where family relationships have become more egalitarian, but there are too few them. If we take into account that even those women who find themselves in positions where they are not able to exercise any power (not only political power, but also the power to act for their own ends but also the power to have an education and be free agents) still have alternatives at their disposal, then it can be seen that Hindu women have found a way of becoming free agents, released from their limited range of actions which is their influence on the domestic and semi-domestic front.

Once immigrated appears an opportunity to stress that agency throughout their role as domestic educators and main agents of socialization. In that sense, one might ask whether such women, acting accordingly to a generational hierarchical logic, where the eldest, mothers, mothers- in-law and grandmothers, might be responsible for the ethnicity of the members of the ethnic minority? On he other hand, the maintenance of an ethicized behaviour, grounded in informal female education close the Hindu girls hostage in a highly gender stratified society.

Education and Ethnicity: Why the Woman?

During the colonial period the main aim of Portuguese policy was an assimilation model. However, the Hindu community in Mozambique withstood acculturation and created a strategy of social encapsulation, keeping strict social rules and religious norms.

Hindus as an ethnic group tend to carry on with their endogamic characteristics, to generate patrilineal networks of parenthood that are restricted within the space of the group, coupled with avoiding consanguine relations with outsiders. Even so, immigrant populations, including those whose integration is defensive or ethnically self-centring, have the capacity to adjust to new realities, attempting to adapt their habits and customs, recreating other habits and customs or reinventing traditions. To use Cohen's expression, "the ethnic group uses traditional rules and ideologies to reinforce their distinguishing features in the context of a contemporary dynamic situation" (Cohen 1978, p. 118). Hindus who have immigrated to Portugal show contrasts that are manifest at the levels of religion, language, self-centred sociability, matrimonial patterns characterized by strong endogamy, and residential concentration. Self-centred sociability favours residential concentration, and the networks of relationships of an inter-ethnic nature favour communitarization. Nevertheless, it is important to underline that ethnic conscience is an ambivalent phenomenon, as stressed by Quintino:

37 Educational Processes and Ethnicity Among Hindu Migrants

> Ethnical actors are neither enforced to assimilate the dominant culture nor to develop a double identity, they can have a more expressive primary identity that is fed into the private sphere and a secondary identity that can be used to permanently negotiate with the outside world and that conciliates primordial fragments and circumstantial fragments. (Quintino 2004a, p. 65)

Ethnicity combines interests and affective ties. There is, in ethnicity, a visible set of means of identification, such as language, eating habits, music and names. The ethnical identity of a Hindu in Portugal is also marked by differences in class and caste, which mark the social context of those individuals. Their religious background works both as a means of integration and group cohesion (although different groups belonging to as many religious modalities may exist within one common ethnic group), allowing the individuals to understand that they belong to a common religious and ideological collective: *to be a Hindu*.

Hindus in Portugal, as well as in other countries where they have established themselves, maintain clearly defined customs and eating habits, despite the slight changes experienced by the need to adapt locally. And such distinct eating habits, ways of dressing, hairstyles, ways of decorating their homes, as well as physical gestures, tastes and cultural interests, constitute the cultural elements of an ethnic belonging, acquired during the process of primary socialization, continue for a lifetime and are mainly kept present by women (Romanucci-Ross and De Vos 1995).

The products that serve the dietary needs of Hindus are so inherently different that the need to acquire them led to the setting up of specialized firms that import those very goods, as well as a whole set of small ethnic shops that serve the material needs of the group's culture.

With religion, language constitutes one of the major factors of separation and boundary that constitute ethnic identity. In Portugal, the language of the diaspora is Gujarati, which is spoken among the members of each household; it is taught by mothers as the first language and is taught in the existing Hindu associations. This is so that youngsters born in Portugal will not loose the roots of their identity. In the words of one of the teachers:

> It is important to teach our children our language so that our culture is not lost.

The strong feeling of identity that comes from linguistic manipulation also produces effects of separating between the group and the outside population. A kind of linguistic isolation is achieved, a relative closing in of the group, whose members speak among themselves under the protection of a kind of barrier when it comes to being understood by "others", especially the Portuguese.

The national language is spoken outside, where boundaries merge. Inside the house the mother tongue predominates, a language from a distant, in some cases never visited, but eternally present, motherland. It is thus assumed, like in Parekh (1996, 1998), that the Asian communities are by nature ethnical, that is to say, that they are visibly differentiable, linked together by social ties stemming from shared practices, languages and inter matrimonial habits; they have their own histories, collective memories, geographical origins, world views and ways of social organization. Such ethnic traces separate the groups and make their distinguishing features emblematic (Romanucci-Ross and Lola De Vos 1995).

To implant the Hindu identity in the complicated post-colonial process it was necessary to emphasize tradition. In that case a reinvention of the past was developed to serve the interests of the caste and the gender, that it so say, partial interests. It is the older women who manipulate invented tradition, by means that are believed to be strategic, because according to Bond and Gillian (1994) one of the ways for the manifestation of power in history is "the construction of individual and collective identities (for instance, racial, ethnical and national). Such social construction is part of the process of the invention of traditions" (Bond and Gillian 1994, p. 13).

Throughout interviews and field work it was possible to notice a number of indicators that hierarchically summarize the way older women recreate socializing models of Hinduism by manipulating religious, social and cultural levels. These, as a whole, represent the cultural dimension of ethnicity. The data, which were diverse in range depending upon the importance of the action, reflect a rather uniform position among all of the women who were interviewed, without any noticeable distinctions regarding generation, caste or social class.

From a macro point of view, some theories regarding gender discuss the poor capacity of agency and feminine power among Indian women (Shiva e Mies 1983; Anthias 2000; Connel 1987; Hirst and Lynn 2004), but from a meso or micro point of view a new female role emerges within this sound migratory context, albeit limited by the patriarchal socializing structure (Bhachu 1996; Rodrigues 2007).

Hindu women actively create integration networks by manipulating the rules that govern relationships of both belonging and meaning but their power rests mainly in generational factors and also in life cycle and instrumental roles.

With the exception of a very limited group, the female socializing model weakens or even nullifies their capacity for cultural integration. Most of these women, even the youngest, are relatively confined to exercising the means for adaptation and cultural transmission, which in ever more globalizing societies are emptied of their original meaning. To quote Machado (1992, 2002) the ethnic closure of the Hindu group in one sense exercises a levelling pressure, while also serving to castrate the potentials of feminine agency within the domain of emancipation, whereas in another sense that same strategy also serves to (re)create the imaginary Hindu identity portrayed by older women.

Generally, older women (who came from Mozambique) settle upon the fabric of a social structure they neither dare understand nor question and where the exercise of power mostly occurs, that is among their own gender. In this sense, Hindu society demonstrates similarities to the patria-lineal system of Islamic societies[1], noticed by Lacoste-Dujardin (1993) among Algerian women. Since women are seen by men as being potentially subversive,[2] the way to exercise an effective control over what they do has been by "privileging and celebrating the maternal function", because "once they are immobilized and dedicated to the task of procreating the paternal lineage, and are dedicated to raising their children, the mothers are converted to the interests of lineage along a male path, and therefore should no longer be seen as a threat" (Lacoste-Dujardin 1993, p. 166).

The Hindu women under study still reproduce the primordial idea of a "feminine nature", a notion that was quite fashionable during the time when studies on gender relative to the traditional female role began. They live in the urban area of the Lisbon Metropolitan Area, establishing wide relationship networks that cover the city like a net. However, it is a semi-closed net whose contacts are established almost exclusively among their peers. The way of life characterizing the Hindu group is the closest example of the model of encapsulation conceptualized by Hannerz (1980). Although the male group may be seen as having a wider social integration network, since its quotidian life demands frequent contacts with the rest of the population, either by being self-employed on a commercial level, or by working for someone else, the female group, however, demonstrates a tendency for self-centring, as it is not allowed the fortune of upward professional and individual mobility.

Conclusion

When trying to answer the questions posed at the beginning of this article it can be said that the study has revealed that Hindu women in Portugal are faced with a gap between two types of education.

On the one hand women face an informal education based on socialization subject to the rules imposed upon them as women, which determines what kind of life they must follow, inhibited through the choices of fulfilling the demands of dharma. On the other hand, society offers them the alternative of formal education, professionalism and independence.

It is not an easy choice in some cases, and in others it is not even a choice at all. Still, there are very few young women who complete higher education or even reach intermediate level. The majority work in the family business not receiving any salary or they become housewives after getting married. Although with little formal education some of the women who were studied have opened businesses and have become entrepreneurs, on their husband's behalf, but still maintain a high capacity of agency and for decision-making within the family business.

They run small shops on their own, while husbands engage in other businesses sometimes extensions of family business, or they are employed in small companies. The Hindu tradition imposed upon women as "captives" into domesticity has tended to decrease, but has not yet finished. There is a fashioning of the ideal woman married, at home, maintaining the secular traditions.

Nevertheless, the economic pressure, the desire to pursue a profession, and an increase in schooling has slowly led to a change in the position and visibility of women. The Hindu woman (mainly the youngest) wants to get a better education, wants to live outside of the neighbourhood and wants to accomplish different sociocultural professional goals than those of the "imagined" female. Slowly the control of the ethnic and family network is reduced, and the more educated woman increasingly integrate the labour market.

Annex

Characterization of the sample

Interviewed woman	Year of birth	Place of birth	Profession	Literary qualifications	Marital status	Number of children	Year of migration to Portugal
E1	1931	India-Diu	housewife	1° year of 1° cycle	married	3	1982
E2	1935	India-Gujarat	housewife	4° year of 1° cycle	widow	2	1990
E3	1946	India-Diu	Teacher	Secondary education	widow	3	1998
E4	1947	India-Gujarat	housewife	4° year of 1° cycle	married	2	1989
E5	1947	India-Diu	House-maid	1° year of 1° cycle	married	3	1987
E6	1949	India-Diu	housewife	4° year of 1° cycle	married	1	1980
E7	1952	Mozambique	Family business	4° year of 1° cycle	married	4	1983
E8	1952	Mozambique	Public servant	Graduate	married	1	1974
E9	1957	Mozambique	housewife	4° year of 1° cycle	married	3	1983
E10	1958	Mozambique	housewife	1° year of 1° cycle	married	6	1982
E11	1960	India-Diu	Family business	2° year of 2° cycle	married	2	1985
E12	1960	India-Diu	Family business	Complete 3° cycle	married	3	1995
E13	1962	Mozambique	housewife	4° year of 1° cycle	married	3	1980
E14	1962	Mozambique	housewife	2° year of 2° cycle	married	2	1987
E15	1964	India-Gujarat	housewife	4° year of 1° cycle	married	2	1985
E16	1965	India-Gujarat	Family business	2° year of 1° cycle	married	1	1994
E17	1967	Mozambique	Family business	Secondary education 12th year	divorced	1	1985
E18	1968	India-Gujarat	Family business	Secondary education 10th year	married	2	1992
E19	1970	Mozambique	Hospitality industry	4° year of 1° cycle	widow	1	1983
E20	1972	Mozambique	housewife	Secondary education 11th year	married	3	1993

37 Educational Processes and Ethnicity Among Hindu Migrants

Annex (continued)

Interviewed woman	Year of birth	Place of birth	Profession	Literary qualifications	Marital status	Number of children	Year of migration to Portugal
E21	1974	India-Gujarat	Cosmetic industry	Secondary education 12th year	married	1	2000
E22	1977	India-Gujarat	housewife	University student	married	1	1998
E23	1978	India-Bombay	housemaid	1° year of 1° cycle	married	3	1982
E24	1981	Mozambique	Family business	Secondary education 12th year	married	1	1995
E25	1985	Portugal	Unemployed	graduated	single		
E26	1985	Portugal	Unemployed	graduated	single		
E27	1992	Portugal	Unemployed	2° year of 2° cycle	single		

Interviewed man	Year of birth	Place of birth	Profession	Literary qualifications	Marital status	Number of children	Year of migration to Portugal
E1	1935	Mozambique	Retired	4° year of 1° cycle	married	1	1980
E2	1937	India-Diu	Family business	2° year of 1° cycle	married	3	1985
E3	1939	India-Gujarat	Retired	4° year of 1° cycle	married	5	1980
E4	1943	Mozambique	Taxi driver	2° year of 2° cycle	married	4	1983
E5	1944	India-Diu	Retired	Graduated	married	3	1978
E6	1945	Mozambique	Family business	2° year of 2° cycle	married	2	1980
E7	1948	Mozambique	Family business	2° year of 2° cycle	married	3	1979
E8	1950	India-Goa	Public servant	2° year of 2° cycle	married	3	1983
E9	1959	Mozambique	Family business	Complete 3rd cycle	married	2	1979
E10	1969	India-Gujarat	Family business	Complete 3rd cycle	married	3	1983

References

Anthias, F. (2000). Metaphors of home: Gendering new migrations to Southern Europe. In F. Anthias & L. Gabriella (Eds.), *Gender and migration in Southern Europe* (pp. 15–48). Oxford: Berg.
Bernstein, B. (1975). *Towards a theory of educational transmission*. London: Routledge.
Bhachu, P. (1996). The multiple landscapes of transnational Asian woman in the diaspora. In V. Amit-Talai & C. Knowles (Eds.), *Re-situating identities: The politics of race, ethnicity and culture* (pp. 283–304). Ontário: Broadview.
Biardeau, M. (1972). *Clefs pour la Pensée Hindoue*. Paris: Seghers.
Biardeau, M. (1981). *L'Hinduism: Anthropologie d'une Civilization*. Paris: Flammarion.
Bond, G. C., & Gillian, A. (1994). *Social construction of the past: Representation as power*. London: Routledge.
Castro, L. d. (1932). A nefasta influência da imigração asiática na colónia de Moçambique. *Boletim da Sociedade de Estudos da Colónia de Moçambique, 5*(1), 30–45.
Cohen, R. (1978). Ethnicity: Problem and focus in anthropology. *Annual Review of Anthropology, 7,* 379–403.
Connel, R. W. (1987). *Gender and power: Society, the person and sexual politics*. Cambridge: Polity Press.
Denzin, N., & Yvonna, L. (2000). *Handbook of qualitative research*. Thousands Oaks: Sage.
Dhruvarajan, V. (1989). *Hindu woman and the power of ideology*. Nova Deli: Vistaar.
Durkheim, É. (1976 [1897]). *Le Suicide*. Paris: PUF.
Fuller, C. (2004). *The camphor flame: Popular Hinduism and society in India*. Princeton: Princeton University Press.
Ghosh, S. K. (1989). *Indian woman through the ages*. Nova Deli: Ashish Publishing House.
Hannerz, U. (1980). *Exploring the City*. New York: Columbia University Press.
Hirst, J. S., & Lynn T. (2004). *Playing for real: Hindu roles model, religion and gender*. New Delhi: Oxford University Press.
Kellerhals, J., & Montandon, C. (1991). *Les Stratégies éducatives des families – milieu social, dynamique familial et education des pré-adolescents*. Nuechâtel: Delachaux et Niestlé.
Lacoste-Dujardin, C. (1993). *Las Madres contra las Mujeres: Patriarcado e Maternidad en el Mundo Árabe*. Madrid: Cátedra.
Machado, F. L. (1992). Etnicidade em Portugal: Contrastes e politização. *Sociologia, Problemas e Práticas, 12,* 123–136.
Machado, F. L. (2002). *Contrastes e Continuidades: Migração, Etnicidade e Integração dos Guineenses em Portugal*. Oeiras: Celta.
Malheiros, J. (1996). *Comunidades Indianas na Área de Lisboa: Geografia de um Reencontro*. Lisboa: FLL.
Malheiros, J. S. M. (2001). Arquipélagos migratórios: transnacionalismo e integração, Universidade de Lisboa, *cyclostyled*
Menon-Sem, K., & Shiva Kumar, A. K. (2001). *Women in India: How free, how equal?* Report commissioned by the office of resident coordinator in India.
Mitter, S. S. (1991). *Dharma's daughters: Contemporary Indian woman and Hindu culture*. New Brunswick: Rutgers University.
Mukherjee, P. (1978). *Hindu woman: Narrative models*. Calcutá: Sagan.
Parekh, B. (1996). Minority practices and principles of toleration. *International Migration Review, 30*(1), 251–284.
Parekh, B. (1998). Integrating minorities. In T. Blackstone, B. Parekh, & P. Sander (Eds.), *Race relations in Britain: A developing agenda* (pp. 1–22). London: Routledge.
Putnam, R. (2000). *Bowling alone: The collapse and revival of American community*. Nova Iorque: Simon and Schuster.
Quintino, M. C. R. (2004a). *Migrações e Etnicidade em Terrenos Portugueses*. Lisbon: ISCSP, UTL.

Reis, C. S. (1973). *A População de Lourenço Marques em 1894*. Lisbon: Centro de Estudos Demográficos.
Ribeiro, C. M. (1930). *Os Indo-Portugueses perante a História da Colonização de Moçambique*. Lourenço Marques: J. L. Cezário de Nazareth.
Rita-Ferreira, A. (1988). Moçambique Post-25 de Abril: Causas do Êxodo da População de Origem Europeia e Asiática, em *Moçambique, Cultura e História de um País,* Coimbra, Instituto de Antropologia.
Rodrigues, I. de A. R. (2007). *No Feminino Singular. Identidades de Género de Mulheres Chinesas Migrantes em Lisboa*, Dissertação de Mestrado, Cyclocited, UTL, ISCSP.
Romanucci-Ross, L., & De Vos, e G. (orgs.) (1995), *Ethnic identity: Creation, conflict and accommodation.* Walnut Creek: Altamira Press. *Reconsidered*, Nova Iorque, Annals of the New York Academy of Sciences.
Seabra, T. (1994). Estratégias familiares de socialização das crianças, ISCTE. Lisboa: Cyclostyled.
Shiva & Mies. (1983). Ecofeminismo, Lisboa, Piaget.

Part VI
Community, Work and Learning

Chapter 38
Community, Work and Learning

Georgina Tsolidis

Bourdieu (1993) reminds us that there are many types of racism. In particular, he highlights the forms of racism that entrench the power of the dominant class in subtle ways by providing a rationale for the existing unequal relations. The racism of intelligence is a particularly virulent form of such racisms because it is linked to a seemingly natural or innate talent. This performs the task of masking power more convincingly because unlike the inheritance of property for example, intelligence is a form of embodied capital. In this sense, intellectual racism is like other forms of racism—it relies on essentialism and is expressed through euphemisms, in this case mechanisms such as IQ tests. Such mechanisms render what are class or social differences into differences of talent and therefore nature. Instead of accepting a naturalised account of difference, Bourdieu urges us to question why groups that experience discrimination, such as immigrants, come to be considered through frameworks that stress their lack of intelligence or lack of psychological resilience in relation to formal educational structures. As part of this exploration, he cautions us to remain vigilant about our own position as educationists and be mindful of how our work can reinstate forms of intellectual racism.

The papers in this section of the collection provide excellent illustrations of Bourdieu's argument that educationists should consider power and their role in bringing its unequal distribution into the public gaze. These authors focus on cultural difference and in so doing bring into the realm of vision the complex relations that operate globally but embed educational inequality locally. Through their scholarship, we are exposed to the schooling experiences of minority students in Greece, the USA, Cyprus and Australia. Yet one of the most interesting aspects of this collection is the broad understanding of education that is adopted. Learning is not just what happens in the classroom, it happens in the community and in the home. Examples of this broad understanding of education come from Brazil, Dubai and the families and youth subcultures of Europe.

It is particularly salient to acknowledge various forms and contexts for learning in relation to ethnic minority communities because their experiences of formal

---

G. Tsolidis (✉)
University of Ballarat, PO Box 663, Ballarat, Victoria, 3353, Australia
e-mail: g.tsolidis@ballarat.edu.au

education can often be negative and thus their learning enters other domains. Rather than restrict education to formal structures such as schooling, these authors take into account how learning is enacted through dynamic social relations, including those concerned with work and cultural practices. These authors engage with an eclectic range of practices in an eclectic range of national and social contexts. Taken together they illustrate how learning for transformation can occur across a wide spectrum. At one extreme seemingly benign spaces are explored through everyday practices, such as dance, to the other extreme, where curriculum policy discourses that are intended to evoke national identity in conflict situations are examined.

Zembylas examines multicultural education in the context of deep-seated conflict. National curriculum for Cypriot primary school students is explored as a means of considering how schooling engages with divided societies and in this case divided nations. By using discourse analysis, Zembylas is able to illustrate how this curriculum elides 'Cypriot' with 'Greek', and 'Turkish' with 'Other'. In this sense Cyprus is connected to Greece and the nation is narrated as an extension of various episodes of Greek history. The author argues that given the division of the island which occurred so long ago and resulted in a thorough and protracted division of the conflicting communities, the curriculum rather than an attempt at collective memory is a re-collection of knowledge acquisition. This occurs through the teaching of language, history and importantly a form of national emotion whereby students are asked to stay connected through feeling the pain of invasion and the loss of how things were in the past. As an alternative to this, Zembylas puts forward an argument for critical forms of multiculturalism, particularly given that the population of Cyprus is becoming increasingly diverse. Critical multiculturalism allows students to engage in dynamic views of culture and identity premised on dialogical pedagogical approaches. Such approaches allow students to understand the politics of knowledge and challenge essentialist views of ethnic identity that link it to past events. This has the potential to develop critical hope and a sense that reconciliation is possible.

New and Merry offer insights into Romani identity and schooling. They present an exploration of Greece as a nation within which are captured various approaches to the education of young people from the Romani community. They elaborate the issues using the concept of stigmatisation and argue that the Greek approach to the Rom is emblematic of what happens throughout Europe. Through a discussion of four Greek locations, we are introduced to a spectrum of approaches that rely on segregation and sustained indifference to the educational needs of Romani young people, through the programmes that are considered successful because they provide inroads into Greek society without the loss of identity. Stigmatisation is understood as crucial to the success or otherwise of these approaches. This is a psychosocial process whereby Romani can come to accept themselves as incapable rather than attribute this to the isolation and rejection they experience in mainstream society. The authors argue that stigma reduces the potential for learning and suggest that conscientisation assists the Rom resist it.

Tsolidis considers the public pedagogies of national belonging through space set aside to commemorate the fallen. The Melbourne Shrine of Remembrance was built during the Great Depression to honour those who fell during World War I. It now serves as a memorial for the fallen in a range of wars. The Melbourne Shrine is also a space where students are inducted into national narratives. On occasions such as Remembrance Day, many hundreds of students visit the Shrine and take part in commemorative services that are understood to mark critical episodes in nationhood. The Shrine is also the focus for minority commemorative services. In the case of the diasporic Greek community, students from community schools where Greek language and culture are taught visit the Shrine of Remembrance to mark the end of Ottoman occupancy on Greek National Day. This sharing of sacred spaces offers a broader lesson to young people on how to negotiate the memories of past generations whilst taking their place in contemporary Australia. In this context, Tsolidis argues that the Shrine of Remembrance illustrates Foucault's notion of heterotopia because it brings together contested representations of the constitution of 'Australian'.

In their paper, Lee and Madyun offer insights into the educational experiences of Somali students in the USA. They argue that while such students experience discrimination because of their refugee status, being working-class and racialised, there are discrepancies between them with regard to how they utilise social networks available to them. The authors are interested to find out the reasons behind differential use of social capital structures within family, community and schools and argue that this may explain high and low educational achievement rates. They suggest that a student's capacity to map resources and be strategic in how they utilise these is a critical marker of academic success and that this should be incorporated into academic programmes for such students.

Social networks are also the focus of the paper by Christ who is concerned with Filipina migrants in Dubai (United Arab Emirates). She considers everyday knowledge and how this is utilised by these women in order to negotiate life as migrant workers in a multiethnic environment. These women need to consider the local Arabic culture but also engage with people from a range of ethnic minorities who also work in Dubai. Christ argues that local knowledge is critical to their success in Dubai. This knowledge is taken to include factual information and skills; however, it is understood as responsive to situational dynamics and based on the 'laboratory of life'. Once acquired Filipina migrants exchange this knowledge with others from their community, newly arrived in Dubai. Christ argues that ethnicity is a critical marker in Dubai and this is reinforced by these migrant women workers who induct compatriots into the skills necessary to work and live in Dubai as a Filipina. Transfer of knowledge is restricted to members of the community and there exist expectations of reciprocity.

Ferreira and Pohl draw on a large EC-funded research project with a focus on youth to explore young people's agency in the context of social change. The study combined reports from Denmark, Spain, Germany, Finland, Romania and Portugal. These were supplemented with workshops that involved key policy makers and practitioners. The aim was to examine transitions to adulthood including from school to work. Ethnic subcultures appeared significant for young people, including those who were born in their parents' country of settlement. These subcultures provided support given such young people often felt isolated within mainstream society as well as within their own families. The authors argue that despite the risk of being stigmatised as members of gangs or tribes, young people who participate in such subcultures use them as informal learning environments. Most particularly, this informal learning assists them to make meaning of their lives and self-position rather than respond to how they are positioned by mainstream society.

In her paper Saucer examines the Afro-Brazillian art of Capoeira. This is a dance form that incorporates martial arts movements. It was invented by slaves as a means of camouflaging a self-defence strategy through dance. Capoeira is complex and involves a group of people who form and circle while two enter it to perform the sequences of movement, which combine dance, acrobatics and combative movements such as kicks. Those in the circle clap to maintain rhythm. It assisted the enslaved to develop resilience against oppression. Given this legacy, it remains associated with the marginalised groups including youth who experience social exclusion. It is referred to as a social movement and associated with liberatory politics. Saucer is primarily interested in the psychological dimensions of Capoeira, including those related to social learning. She argues that Capoeira is important for socially excluded youth as they use it to transfer between informal and formal learning. Individuals can gain access to economic capital as teachers or paid professionals but importantly they can access 'symbolic capital' through respect, trust and power.

The family home becomes the locus for informal learning in a paper by Cairns and Growiec who explore young people's mobility predispositions. They argue that young people can learn to be geographically insular through living in the family home with parents. In globalised times this may have a negative impact on their later lives. The authors utilise the social capital concepts of 'bonding' and 'bridging' to understand the impact on living in the family home for long periods of time. 'Bonding' reinforces exclusive identities and homogenous groups while 'bridging' creates outward looking identities and enables individuals to form relationships across distinct social groups more successfully. Cairns and Growiec argue that living with parents can have financial benefits. However, the informal learning that occurs through the family home can make young people reluctant to imagine mobility in their lives. In turn this restricts their capacity to take advantage of international opportunities.

These authors make obvious, in Bourdieu's terms, how the table needs to be turned so that the focus remains on education systems and their propensity to fail particular groups of students. Students can be failed even when they succeed academically. In systems that reward the hegemonic there is an imperative to assimilate in order to succeed academically. In relation to working class students' academic success can constitute a form of 'classing up' (Ball et al. 2002) whereby students risk leaving behind elements of their families, their communities and themselves. This argument has a particular poignancy when our major interest is the education of minorities (Tsolidis 2006). Minority students risk leaving behind elements of their identity as fundamental as language and the ability to communicate with their parents. Rather than remain complicit by focusing on students and whether or not they can achieve within a system that privileges dominant forms of knowledge, these authors shift our attention to education systems and how these attempt to confirm limited ways of knowing.

Through various case studies we are presented with how systems and schools can enact culturally inclusive pedagogies. We are provided with stark contrasts of this with reference to Romani students and the schools that support them relative to those that do what ever is possible to exclude them. In the Cypriot context, an argument is put forward for critical multiculturalism. This provides students with the ability to understand limited representations of nationhood and to develop hope in a divided society. At another level, we come to understand that being a refugee in the USA provides opportunities through community and family networks. The argument is made that schools need to acknowledge these and their potential and teach students how to make strategic use of them.

Importantly also, through these papers, we are provided with insights into spaces where informal learning takes place, for example, families and public spaces inhabited by youth subcultures. The authors produce powerful examples of resilience and optimism because they illustrate how education is not limited to formal systems of learning—there is life after school and there is the opportunity to learn and succeed without going down traditional pathways. This 'real life' learning provides important ways of understanding how the world works and how power relations can be redirected. Taken together this collection of chapters creates opportunities for us to understand how those from minorities engage with learning and how this learning navigates around systems, schools, families, communities and work.

Zembylas provides insights into how systems can work to inhibit as well as grow new ways of understanding difference. In Cyprus the curriculum framework discussed assumes an 'us' and 'them' and in so doing reinforces a binary rather than a potential unity of difference. A Cyprus that is home to an increasingly diversified community needs to develop education frameworks premised on critical multiculturalism to better serve its youth. In a similar vein, New and Merry argue that schools need to shift their practices in order to accommodate the experiences, needs and identities of Romani youth. Active exclusion of students marked as 'different' has implications for a whole society, not just those on its outskirts. The corollary of this are inclusive forms of schooling which have the potential to enrich the broader Greek community as well as Romani students specifically.

Lee and Madyun and Tsolidis consider adolescents but do so through their experiences outside the classroom. In the case of Somali youth in the USA, Lee and Madyun argue that networks prove pivotal to academic success. The capacity to draw on resources outside the classroom is what differentiates the 'good' student. Large social and familial networks exist for all these Somali students but until drawn upon strategically, these can remain incidental to learning. In the case of Greek students in Australia, Tsolidis describes how the Melbourne Shrine of Remembrance is a space through which young people are inducted into national narratives. This site for honouring the fallen is used by mainstream and community schools to induct young people into particular forms of belonging. Sometimes these ways of belonging need to be negotiated and it is left to young people to sift through the memories of their parents and grandparents and reconcile them with their own sense of self.

Ferreira and Phol, Saucer, Cairns and Growiec, and Christ all consider informal learning that has little to do with schooling. Ferreira and Phol examine how the family home has the potential to limit global citizenship by teaching young people reluctance to move. In globalised times mobility is valued and the comforts of home may work towards reducing its appeal. On the other hand, young people who experience alienation, including in their homes, look to youth subcultures as a means of forming identities. Cairns and Growiec illustrate how this assumes a set of social skills that while developed and rehearsed at a micro level, nonetheless prepare young people for work. In a similar vein, Saucer describes how Capoeira provides an opportunity to develop skills that are 'sell-able' in the immediate sense, that is, providing classes for novices at a price, but this form of dance also works to build confidence and resilience, which enables more successful social engagement without the compromise of self. Christ's paper considers those who are in full-time formal employment. Her paper on Filipina workers in Dubai illustrates how skills commonly ignored through formal education are the most important when negotiating multiethnic societies through transnational networks. Being a Filipina is the requirement and this provides immediate access to knowledge and its transferral through reciprocal arrangements, vital for survival in a city far away from home.

While each paper offers something specific, it is also important to take a bird's eye view. Spivak (1993) argues that as researchers we can only offer insights related to one part of a whole. It is incumbent on us to fit the pieces together so that they may speak to each other also. These papers bring together perspectives responsive to vastly different national contexts and in so doing delineate a view of a globalised world. A powerful message is that while there is movement of labour, capital and culture across increasingly irrelevant borders, there is also an imperative for people to remain distinct by holding on at some level, to what it is they bring with them to new situations. This is not a form of ossification but instead a means of capturing and drawing upon a form of cultural capital bequeathed to us by our forebears. As Hall (1996) argues, it is a backward move that takes us forward by combining the past with the present to create the 'new' ethnicities of the future. In fundamental ways these authors speak to identification and how this process is influenced by various forms of learning. It is this tension between the social and the individual, coupled with the tension between the local and the global that resonates most notably across this collection of papers.

References

Ball, S. J., Davies, J., David, M., & Reay, D. (2002). 'Classification' and 'judgement': Social class and the 'cognitive structures' of choice in higher education. *British Journal of Sociology of Education, 23*(1), 51–72.

Bourdieu, P. (1993). *The racism of 'intelligence', sociology in question* (trans: R. Nice). London: Sage.

Hall, S. (1996). The meaning of new times. In K. Morely & K. Chen (Eds.), *Critical dialogues in cultural studies*. New York: Routledge.
Spivak, G. (1993). *Outside in the teaching machine*. New York: Routledge.
Tsolidis, G. (2006). *Youthful imagination: Schooling, subcultures and social justice*. New York: Peter Lang.

Chapter 39
Multiculturalism in a Deeply Divided Society: The Case of Cyprus

Michalinos Zembylas

Introduction

With increased migration, contemporary societies are becoming more and more diverse. Consequently, diversity and multiculturalism create new challenges and opportunities for school curricula in nation-states. Curriculum reform efforts, as a response to multiculturalism, have become the center of fierce debates and criticisms in the last two decades. On one hand, well-known critics of multicultural education (e.g., Ravitch 1990; Schlesinger 1991) claim that the implementation of multicultural educational reform intensifies divisions and threatens national and social cohesion; on the other hand, proponents of multicultural educational reform (e.g., Banks 2007; Duarte and Smith 2000; Gutmann 2004; Nieto 1999) suggest that common values may be the result of repression of diversity and thus assimilation and monocultural ideological perspectives should be resisted.

Balancing unity and diversity is a continuing challenge in contemporary multicultural societies. Unity without diversity results in hegemony and oppression; diversity without unity leads to separatism and fragmentation (Banks 2007). The challenge to all multicultural societies is to recognize diversity and yet at the same time promote social cohesion. But what happens in a society in which issues on immigration, multiculturalism, and multicultural education are further complicated with matters of conflict and national collective memory? What are the implications of curricular goals to strengthen the national ethos in a conflict-ridden society that increasingly becomes more multicultural, yet minorities are viewed as rival groups aiming to diminish the rights and privileges of the majority ethnic group?

In light of the absence of work that analyzes the issue of multicultural curriculum reform in deeply divided societies (Al-Haj 2003, 2004, 2005) as well as the notion that there are no universal multicultural education approaches independent of sociopolitical contexts (Bekerman 2004; Sleeter 1992), this chapter explores the

M. Zembylas (✉)
Open University of Cyprus, P. O. Box 24801, Nicosia 1304, Cyprus
e-mail: m.zembylas@ouc.ac.cy, zembylas@msu.edu

current ideological ethos of the Greek-Cypriot national curriculum and its implications for multicultural education understandings. Cyprus has been and still remains a deeply divided (and segregated) society due to the protracted nature of conflict between Greek Cypriots (who live in the south) and Turkish Cypriots (who live in the north). At the same time, immigration to Cyprus has grown over the last few years, consisting of immigrants and labor workers from East Asia, Eastern Europe, the former Soviet Union, and the Middle East; there has also been some internal movement of Turkish Cypriots from the north (occupied by Turkey) to the south of Cyprus, especially after the partial lift of restrictions of movement in 2003. The goal of this chapter is to map the curriculum dynamics, mainly in subjects that are important to issues of identity and culture (specifically, Modern Greek Language, History, and a special subject called "*I Know, I Don't Forget and I Struggle*"), of the national curriculum for primary education (Ministry of Education and Culture 1996) and discuss the potential consequences for multicultural education in light of the increasing presence of various minorities in Cyprus. This analysis is important at this point and time because there are efforts for comprehensive curriculum reform and thus it is valuable to clarify the theoretical assumptions and implications of existing curriculum dynamics.

Theoretical Framework

There are two major approaches toward multiculturalism: mainstream and critical multiculturalism (Al-Haj 2003). Mainstream multiculturalism emphasizes difference and the importance of recognizing diversity; however, it fails to consider the role of power relationships in society and the majority's control of minorities (Giroux 1993). By contrast, critical multiculturalism adopts a comprehensive view of diversity, challenges inequalities, and acknowledges the role of power relations in shaping dominant discourses and practices. Attention is not focused on superficial differences but on those differences that are linked to social injustices. Central to this approach is the recognition of the ideological mission of schooling and the role of teachers as cultural gatekeepers who transmit values of the dominant culture (Kincheloe and Steinberg 1997). The common denominator of both the mainstream and the critical approaches, as Al-Haj (2004) states, is an emphasis on the rights of all groups (including minorities) to preserve their cultural uniqueness.

The struggle over religious, ethnic, and other rights has particularly become a major source of debates and tensions in regions of interethnic conflict. The question often asked in this regard is whether the struggle for recognition of difference and preservation of the national ethos of a specific group "goes hand in hand with multicultural ideology" (Al-Haj 2005, p. 49). On one hand, cultivating a national ethos is considered important for maintaining recognition of collective rights in societies in which those rights are perceived to be threatened by interethnic conflict and increasing immigration; on the other hand, focusing only on recognition and national ethos promotes further segregation and marginalization, because each social group cares about its own culture and puts aside concerns about social injustices (Al-Haj 2004; Steiner-Khamsi 2003). Writing in the context of the Middle East conflict, Al-Haj concludes that "the introduction of a multicultural ideology seems to be an impossible task when a specific national ethos stands at the center of the school curriculum. This is especially true in states that are experiencing an 'intractable conflict' in which the past is used to justify the present" (2005, p. 47). Along similar lines of thought, Bekerman (2004) emphasizes that

> Multiculturalism as understood today [i.e. mainstream], might not be a good formula for countries that are still unstable. These might be in need of a much more careful and critical approach. […] [I]interethnic tensions are aggravated by educational reforms that highlight each ethnic group both sequentially and in isolation. (p. 603)

In other words, it is suggested that multicultural initiatives that aim at assimilating minorities or immigrants or alleviating existing conflicts may actually have the opposite effect, that is, sharpening tensions. Mainstream multicultural approaches in conflict-ridden areas are "lacking in that the reality of the nation-state is not sufficiently accounted for" (Bekerman 2004, p. 604) in curriculum reform efforts. This oversight, points out Bekerman, is detrimental to multicultural education reform initiatives in conflict-ridden areas.

It is now well-documented that education is an important vehicle through which conflicting sites legitimate their positions through the formation of school curricula that perpetuate *us-and-them* categorizations (Davies 2004; Zembylas 2008). School curricula are utilized as instruments for promoting a national ethos that strengthens the nation to cope with the conflict and thus, in this manner, the conflict is perpetuated (Bar-Tal 2004). The question is whether school curricula can, at the same time, be used *both* for promoting a national ethos in response to conflict *and* for strengthening multicultural ideas and values. Two approaches have been proposed as a response to this question (Al-Haj 2005).

The first approach—the *compatibility approach*—essentially states that national ethos and multicultural ideals are compatible and, in fact, national attachment reinforces democratic, civic, and multicultural values (Miller 1993). The reinforcement of national identity, in other words, does not necessarily imply that multicultural diversity is undermined. However, the perception about the compatibility of national ethos and multicultural ideas should be viewed with caution in conflict-ridden societies. As Yiftachel (1999, 2000) argues, it is possible that more emphasis may be placed on safeguarding the rights and privileges of the dominant ethnic group rather than on including rival minority groups. Such an approach has been termed *ethnocratic multiculturalism* (Al-Haj 2004), a type of multiculturalism which differs from other types in that "it draws the borders of legitimacy according to an exclusive ethno-national basis, rather than on the basis of inclusive values" (p. 681). Contrary to perceptions about compatibility, this approach makes choices at the end of the day because a regime that is immersed in conflict will want to retain the ethnonational character of the state—thus perpetuating tensions between ethnocratic and multicultural principles—if it wishes to remain in power.

Unlike the compatibility approach, the *incompatibility approach* emphasizes that nation-building should not be an educational aim because it is incompatible with multicultural ideas: "[I]t [nation-building] creates loyalties that tend to be factional rather than encompassing society as a whole" (Al-Haj 2005, p. 50). This is especially the case in deeply divided societies, as Enslin (1994) points out, because "members of the society have different sets of memories and myths, in which other members are often depicted as enemies rather than compatriots. It is difficult to locate a common nationhood here" (p. 28). Consequently, a view of history that reinforces us-and-them categorizations can hardly prevent the perpetuation of animosity between rival groups living in the same country. In addition, school curricula that nurture national ethos further the alienation of minority groups whose narratives are not represented in the school system (Al-Haj 2003, 2005).

Balancing national ethos and multiculturalism, therefore, may sound like a promising idea in theory; however, in practice it proves to be much more difficult to achieve (Bekerman 2004). For this reason, it is suggested that multicultural efforts could benefit from *small openings* (Zembylas 2008) that deemphasize bipolar differences and problematize the hegemonic power of national ideology (Bekerman 2007; Bekerman and Maoz 2005; Steiner-Khamsi 2003; Zembylas and Bekerman 2008). In particular, Steiner-Khamsi (2003) argues that "we should move away from educational approaches that tend to see each student or each youth as a representative of a specific nation, race, ethnicity or religion" (p. 26). Similarly, Bekerman and Maoz (2005) state that goals such as peace and coexistence education may be better achieved if the emphasis on separate identity and culture is somewhat relaxed. According to them, strengthening coexistence might not be achieved if alternative options to the ones dictated in the past are not pursued.

Critical multicultural approaches can make important contributions to curriculum reform initiatives in conflict-ridden societies. The advantage of these approaches is that they help educators expose the hidden hegemonic discourses of the nation-state ideologies (Bekerman 2007); doing so does not imply that such discourses are necessarily subverted, however, critical approaches show how the authority of these discourses is constituted and constituting and thus the mechanisms with which this is accomplished can be resisted (Zembylas and Bekerman 2008). Critical multiculturalism has a transformative political agenda that is not limited in the coexistence of different ethnic cultural groups (some of which may be in conflict) but is committed to approaches that help educators create new imaginings of hope for overcoming segregation.

Education in Cyprus: Conflict and Multiculturalism

Conflict

Cyprus has been a divided society since violent intercommunal clashes in 1963–1967; in 1974, Turkey invaded after a failed military coup attempt to unify Cyprus and Greece. The island is since divided in the northern part (in which Turkish Cypriots live) and the southern part (in which Greek Cypriots live). Before the Turkish invasion, Greek Cypriots constituted approximately the 80% and Turkish Cypriots the 18% of the island's population. The division of Cyprus as a result of the Turkish invasion came with population displacements of around one third of a total of 600,000 Greek Cypriots to the south and 45,000 Turkish Cypriots to the north. As a result of the lack of contact for many years, the division of the island has been almost complete: geographically, culturally, and politically. Since 2003, there has been a partial lift of restrictions in movement; many Greek Cypriots and Turkish Cypriots have crossed to the other side to visit their homes but there is still a considerable number of Greek Cypriots (around 50%) who refuse to go to the north because they consider it unacceptable to show passports to the Turkish-Cypriot checkpoints in order to "visit" their own country.

In conflict-ridden societies, such as Cyprus, education is segregated along ethnopolitical lines and so educational systems are blamed for perpetuating divisions and conflict (Bush and Saltarelli 2000). In this sense, a deeply divided society produces a deeply divided curriculum (Al-Haj 2005). Existing literature addressing education in divided Cyprus (e.g., see Bryant 2004; Hadjipavlou-Trigeorgis 2007; Kizilyürek 1999; Spyrou 2006; Zembylas 2008, 2010b) shows indeed that the educational practices of both Greek Cypriots and Turkish Cypriots (who are educated separately) have been systematically used to create negative stereotypes about the Other. For example, it is shown that primary and secondary school curricula and pedagogies implore students to remember each side's glories, honor the heroes who fought the enemy/other, and despise the other side.

Recently, in the south there has been an increasing number of "multicultural" schools, that is, schools attended by minority children from various cultures, including those children whose parents are migrant workers or married to someone from another culture. Occasionally, there are a few Turkish-speaking children whose parents stayed in the south after the war of 1974 or moved there recently; thus the challenge in these schools becomes even more complex in light of the unresolved political problem and the intractable conflict between Greek Cypriots and Turkish Cypriots.

Multicultural Education in Cyprus

Of the current inhabitants of Cyprus, 13.7% are non-Cypriots (Statistical Service of the Republic of Cyprus 2006). The changing profile of the population in Cyprus has affected the schools and the educational system. While in the school year 1995–1996, the percentage of nonindigenous students in Greek-Cypriot schools was 4.41%, in 2010–2011 this percentage has risen almost to 12%. There are now some Greek-Cypriot schools where nonindigenous children constitute the large majority (80–90%) of the school population.

Multicultural education is relatively new to Greek-Cypriot schools and society. Although policy documents and official curricula include strong statements about humanistic ideas and respect for human rights, justice, and peace, in practice non-Greek Cypriot children are seen as deficient and needing to be assimilated (Panayiotopoulos and Nicolaidou 2007). The current model of intercultural education being implemented in the Republic of Cyprus (with respect to primary education) is a mainstreaming program in which language learners attend classrooms with indigenous Greek-speaking children. Schools which have an increasing number of nonindigenous children become part of a Zone of Educational Priority and receive additional help—such as extra hours for assisting nonindigenous students to learn the language. The primary goal is to provide intensive Greek lessons and specialized assistance to nonindigenous students; to this end, specialized materials (activity and work books) developed in Greece are sent to schools. Finally, the Pedagogical Institute of Cyprus organizes in-service training seminars for teachers in multicultural education (on a voluntary basis) and a three-hour meeting at the beginning of school year for new principals.

Curriculum Analysis

In what follows, I will concentrate on the national curriculum for primary schools in the Greek Cypriot educational system (Ministry of Education and Culture 1996) and particularly on three subjects that are supposed to affect identity and culture (cf. Al-Haj 2003) as well as issues of unity and diversity: Modern Greek Language, History, and "Gnorizo, Den Xechno kai Agonizomai" [I Know, I Don't Forget and I Struggle], the latter being a special school subject focused on teaching children about the occupied territories in north Cyprus and the need to keep memory alive. The central question that guides this analysis is the following: Which concepts related to multiculturalism and reconciliation are found in the primary school curriculum? The concept of reconciliation is chosen because it constitutes a major process by which deeply divided societies recover the ability to function effectively after violence (Bar-Tal 2004); in addition, recent research also highlights the significance of reconciliation in curriculum reform efforts in conflict-ridden societies (Cole 2007). This investigation is important because it is the first of its kind in Cyprus to conduct curriculum analysis in light of the increasing demands for multicultural education; therefore, it has important implications not only for present curriculum reform efforts in the Greek-Cypriot educational system but also for possible convergences and divergences with respect to tensions around national ethos and multiculturalism in other conflict-ridden societies.

The method used to conduct the curriculum analysis is critical discourse analysis (Fairclough 1995, 2003). I analyze the language of curriculum documents in relation to power and ideology; that is, I examine how the basic constructs and acts of categorizations that are relevant to national ethos constitute acts of power which create particular inclusions and exclusions (of social groups and identities) and depend on assumptions about naturalized realities. Denaturalizing these taken-for-granted assumptions and the underlying hegemonic ideologies is a key task of critical discourse analysis and this is precisely the reason that this approach is appropriate for the purpose of this chapter.

Modern Greek Language

The curriculum for Modern Greek Language begins with an outline of the primary education philosophy about language. In the general introduction, the philosophical statement begins by describing language as the manifestation of *"the deeper physiognomy of every people"* and continues: *"It [language] constitutes a point of recapitulation and synaeresis of all moments of the people's diachronic course, it is an extract of memories and origins that are tied to its being and help people realize their historical continuity and sameness"* (Ministry of Education and Culture 1996, p. 79). This introductory paragraph focuses on the fact that language expresses history, culture, and identity of a national group; at the same time, this description fails to consider that language also defines *how* the notions of history, culture and identity are conceived and vice versa (Bekerman 2007). This rather monological and static view of language, culture, and identity implies the existence of a common and unchanged nature for all people belonging to a national group and speaking the same language.

In the rest of the Modern Greek Language curriculum, the document focuses on each of the six language skills that students need to develop: listening and oral expression, reading, written expression, basic conceptual and orthographic vocabulary, grammar, handwriting, and studying and source utilization skills. The description of the curriculum goals focuses primarily on the technical skills needed for language expression and communication. One curriculum goal that deserves special attention, however, is the one referring to the acquisition of *"basic conceptual and orthographic vocabulary that is determined by the Greek curriculum program,"* and the fact that *"Because of Cyprus's distinctiveness [i.e. compared to mainland Greece], the basic conceptual and orthographic vocabulary is enriched with words that are directly relevant to the Cypriot reality"* (ibid., p. 86). Following this goal for grades 3–6 is a list of 51 terms relevant to the Turkish invasion, occupation, refugeedom, the struggle for liberation against the British in the 1950s and so on. Interestingly, one of the terms suggested, *Cypriot*, is employed as equivalent to the term *Greek* (see also Papadakis 2008), while the terms *Turkish Cypriot* or *Greek Cypriot* are nowhere to be found in the curriculum document. The primary students are taught, then, that the only native Cypriots are Greek in origin.

In general, the analysis of Modern Greek Language curriculum indicates that this curriculum does not include goals oriented toward multicultural and/or reconciliation education. An important element of this curriculum is the *monological* understanding of language, identity, and culture, despite contemporary theorizations in many social sciences that conceptualize identity and culture as dialogic processes depending largely on language (Bekerman 2005, 2007). According to Bekerman (2005), "languages are exuberant tools of meaning making; they produce and express identity, [and] create connectedness in political and social communities" (p. 15). Therefore, language both carries and constructs interpretations of this world; to speak a given language means to embrace a specific vision of reality. The Modern Greek Language curriculum seems to ignore this perception about language and thus remains lodged in monological perspectives that do not nurture dialogic possibilities found in multicultural and reconciliation ideas. Bekerman (2007) and Zembylas and Bekerman (2008) discuss the consequences of monological perspectives and argue that schools grounded in a single language and a single narrative essentially prevent efforts toward coexistence and multicultural education. If current reform efforts in Cyprus aim to overcome these monological perspectives then the monolithic national ethos need to be seriously reconsidered.

History

The general aim of the subject of history in primary education is *"...to help students learn and appreciate the historical life and the cultural heritage of Cyprus and Greece and construct a national consciousness as members of the Greek nation and as inhabitants of semi-occupied Cyprus"* (Ministry of Education and Culture 1996, p. 133). The twofold "agenda" of the subject of history is clearly revealed in this aim: firstly, history has to teach students information about the heritage of Cyprus and Greece; secondly, it has to construct and enhance Greek national identity, particularly in light of the fact that half of the country is under Turkish occupation. A problematic aspect of this aim is the failure to distinguish between *heritage* and *history* (Lowenthal 1998). Essentially, this aim understands school history as heritage and transmits exclusive myths of origin and continuity for the Greek nation (and its manifestation in Cyprus). For example, objectives such as, *"The students should realize the historical continuity of the Greek nation and appreciate the contribution of Hellenism in the development of European civilization"* (Ministry of Education and Culture 1996, p. 133), and *"The students should understand the tragedy of our homeland as a result of the coup d'etat and the Turkish invasion and occupation and to strengthen their fighting morale for national righteousness"* (ibid., p. 134)—bluntly confirm the utilization of the subject of history to enhance a monolithic national ethos grounded in heritage rather than in critical history. Understanding the subject of school history as heritage rather than as history restricts opportunities for critical reflection and cultivates *blind patriotism* (Schatz et al. 1999).

This national ethos is grounded in the fundamental perception that Cyprus is basically an extension of the history of Greece (Papadakis 2008). For example, the terms "Greece" or "Greek" is used in the titles or in the short descriptive paragraphs of 20 out of the 25 themes of the history curriculum in grades 3–6. The following are some examples: *"Religion in Cyprus and Greece in ancient times"*; *"The Greek civilization in Cyprus"*; *"Basic characteristics which united the Greeks in ancient Greece and Cyprus"*; *"Life in ancient Greece and Cyprus"*; *"The struggles of Greeks for freedom in Greece and Cyprus"*; *"The modern history of Cyprus and the struggles of Greeks for freedom on the island*" (Ministry of Education and Culture 1996, pp. 134–136). It should also be noted that the content development of the subject of history follows the three key periods of the history in Greece: ancient Greece, medieval Greece and the Byzantine period, and modern Greece. Therefore, the goal of "*the historical continuity of the Greek nation*" is promoted through emphasizing ancient Greece as the beginning of history, succeeded by the glorious Byzantine period, and followed by the modern traumatic events of the Turkish invasion and occupation.

Interestingly, no references are made to the other communities that constitute the population of Cyprus, that is, the Turkish Cypriots, Maronites, Armenians, and Latinos. The constant reference to Greece reveals a disregard for all the other communities except from the Greek Cypriots. Both the general aim and the objectives of the history curriculum are orientated toward the shaping of the students' Greek national identity in a static manner. As previously mentioned, these objectives fail to promote a dynamic and dialogic notion of culture and identity; the history curriculum for primary education constitutes a classic example of how history is used to construct and maintain a sense of national community and identity (VanSledright 2008). A fundamental element of this national ethos is that one of the objectives provokes students to "*struggle*" for their country and sacrifice their "*personal interest*" for "*the national interest*" (Ministry of Education and Culture 1996, p. 134). This objective is in line with one of the general goals of the primary education curriculum, that is, "*the inflection of a spirit of struggle for liberating the occupied land*" and "*the realization of the [students'] obligation toward the Turkish occupied country*" (ibid., p. 19). The 2004 Report of the Commission for Education Reform as well as recent research on history textbooks by Papadakis (2008) confirm the analysis presented here, emphasizing the nationalistic character of textbooks and the Helleno-ethnocentric and culturally monolithic curriculum.

On the other hand, however, it is interesting to note that the history curriculum also includes *humanist* elements, such as references to peace, democracy, and respect for other cultures. Examples of these curriculum objectives are: "*The students need to appreciate the accomplishments of other countries and people [...] [and] to develop positive attitudes towards them*"; "*to appreciate [...] the importance of peaceful procedures in solving differences between states*"; "*to understand the human relations that are necessary for the harmonious coexistence of people*"; "*to realize the importance that the ideals of democracy, freedom and peace have for humanity in global history*" (Ministry of Education and Culture 1996, p. 133). It should be noted that all the above objectives seem to refer to the relations between people of different countries and there is no clear effort made to clarify whether the term "*other people*" may refer to other indigenous communities of Cyprus (e.g., the Turkish Cypriots).

Based on the above analysis, there seem to be two different and seemingly contradictory ideological frames in the history curriculum. On one hand, there is an emphasis on enhancing a monolithic national ethos; this frame aims to educate students to become devoted patriots through the Greek nation's language, culture, religion, and values; on the other hand, there are also references to humanity, peace, and coexistence; this frame is grounded in humanist ideals and objectives that promote skills such as *"critical examination"* and *"the distinction of facts from opinions"* (ibid., p. 134). In a sense, then, these two different ideological frames constitute what Derrida (1992) calls *national humanism*. In his essay "Onto-Theology of National Humanism," Derrida warns us against the combination of both a nationalism grounded in a national idiom *and* the absorption of this idiom (its differences from other idioms) by universalism. Humanism as a theme needs to be reconsidered, argues Charalambous (2007), because it conceals the nation's self-interestedness (under the cover of humanist values) and yet at the same time the humanist promise for peace, freedom, and democracy is nationalized because the history curriculum emphasizes only the injustices against the Greek nation. Therefore, the history curriculum serves the nation's needs and interests (see also, Boehmer 2005).

"I Know, I Don't Forget and I Struggle"

In the introductory paragraph of the curriculum "I Know, I Don't Forget and I Struggle", it is stated that people's identity is dependent on their history and culture. It is particularly emphasized that in the difficult times that Greek Cypriots go through

> the danger of our extinction is apparent, [so] we have an obligation not only to keep the memory of everything that violence, injustice [...] took from us, but also to become attached to our heritage dynamically, because heritage [...] constitutes all the beliefs and manifestations of social and spiritual life of our people [...] and the simplest deviation from our heritage will possibly overturn the consciousness of the new generation, and the long term danger will be this generation's natural and national extinction. (Ministry of Education and Culture 1996, p. 93)

In the rest of the introductory paragraph there are ideas about the historical continuity of Hellenism and the need to strengthen students' national identity; these statements are made on the background of descriptions about the fear of *"national extinction."* In the rest of the "I Know, I Don't Forget and I Struggle" curriculum, there are three general aims that are broken down in several objectives: the first aim focuses on knowledge about the occupied territories of Cyprus and the enhancement of memory and fighting spirit for returning to these territories; the second aim deals with human rights and their relevance to the situation in Cyprus; and the third aim focuses on the diachronic traditions, attitudes, and values that contributed to the national and natural survival of *"Cypriot Hellenism."* As it will become obvious in the following brief analysis of these aims, the main idea is the need for strengthening the students' Greek national identity as well as their commitment to struggle for the liberation of their occupied homeland.

The first aim is: *"To help students gain knowledge about our enslaved land, to keep the memory of our occupied land alive and to cultivate and enhance optimism, faith and the fighting spirit for return"* (Ministry of Education and Culture 1996, p. 93). An interesting point can be raised about the use of the term *"memory."* If one takes into consideration that most of the students to which this curriculum is addressed have never been to the occupied territories (or at best, they have visited them, after the partial lift of restrictions in 2003) a paradox arises: how can students "*remember*" something that they have never known or seen? This curriculum, then, invokes memory through the sacralization of the past (Bell 2003); in a sense, students are asked to remember not what they have experienced but what they are taught. Although the intentions of this curriculum may focus on the nationalization of memory (Zembylas 2008, 2009), what the students are essentially asked to accomplish is not (collective) memory but recollection of knowledge acquisition.

The more specific objectives related to the first aim focus on knowledge acquisition about the occupied territories and seek to confirm these territories' Christian and Hellenic character. The objectives are in line with similar ones in the curricula of Modern Greek Language and History, concentrating on an essentialist and static view of the Greek nation, the national identity, and the Hellenic origin of Cyprus. For example, this essentialist view of identity and the nation is apparent in the following objective: "*[The students need] to realize the importance of what we have lost—a part of our self—and to realize the need to regain the occupied land, reunite Cyprus and preserve its liberty*" (Ministry of Education and Culture 1996, p. 94). Other objectives focus on enhancing students' commitment to struggle for returning to the occupied territories: "*[The students need] to realize and understand that without efforts and struggles regaining our occupied land is not possible*"; "*to learn and implement activities with which students can help in the struggle for return*" (ibid., p. 94). The omission, here, is similar to that in the previous two curricula; that is, there is no reference to the two conflicting communities in Cyprus.

The second aim is: "*To help students learn and understand human rights, as they appear in international declarations and to work consciously, responsibly and dynamically for their dominance in our land*" (ibid., p. 95). At first glance, this aim and the objectives that follow have the humanist tone that is also met in some other parts of the primary education curriculum. For example, the following objectives are included: "*[The students need] to understand, implement and promote the democratic ideals and the democratic procedures as individuals and as groups and to cultivate a spirit of love, unity, acceptance and mutual understanding*"; "*to realize that all people have rights, which have to be respected*"; "*to develop a positive attitude towards cooperation, acceptance and coexistence with other people*"; "*to respect others' national and religious identity* (ibid., p. 95). Again, all of these objectives fail to specify the "*other*" (e.g., Turkish Cypriots) and refer instead to a general other. There is only one objective referring to the diverse cultural character of the island: "*[The students need] to learn the diversity of the synthesis in Cypriot society (Greeks, Turkish, Maronites, Armenians) and to work for the harmonic coexistence of all inhabitants*" (ibid.). Although this is an important element for multicultural and reconciliation education, as it is the first time that it is recognized that Cyprus is not a homogeneous Greek community but there are other groups as well (the Latinos are not mentioned though; also no references are made to immigrants because this document has been written years before the influx of immigrants in Cyprus), there are two problematic issues.

Firstly, the four groups (Greeks, Turkish, Maronites, Armenians) are not presented as part of a coherent state but as members of the "*society*" at large and, therefore, it is implied that they do not necessarily have common bonds within the state or continuous historical copresence. Although it is not implied whether continuity and commonality are the *correct* criteria with which a community is judged to be indigenous or not, these criteria are used with respect to the Greek-Cypriot community. Therefore, in the context of the document's primary focus on Greek national identity, it is implied that these criteria do not apply to the other communities and consequently, these groups may not be considered *indigenous*. Secondly, the two communities in conflict are not named as such, that is, *Greek Cypriots* and *Turkish Cypriots*, but as Greeks and Turks. These two terms maximize the distance between the two ethnic groups and place them at two opposing poles: Greece and Turkey. The physical, historical, cultural, and religious bonds between the Greeks of Cyprus and those living in the *motherland* are legitimized through the repeated use of the terms "*Cypriot Hellenism*" or "*Greeks of Cyprus*," at the same time that the presence of Turkish Cypriots is utterly ignored. The Turks (no distinction is made between the Turks and the Turkish Cypriots) are repeatedly named as the invaders and the cause for all the troubles that (Greek) Cypriots experience. The phrase "*I don't forget*" is essentially a symbol that allows no space for recognition of the traumas of the Turkish-Cypriot community; these have been completely forgotten (Papadakis 2005).

Finally, the last aim is: "*To help students learn, understand, appreciate and respect all those elements (traditions, attitudes, values, customs) that contributed to the national and natural survival of the Cypriot Hellenism during its long history and to contribute to facing the dangers experienced by our land*" (Ministry of Education and Culture 1996, p. 96). In addition to the repeated essentialist views on the historical continuity of Cypriot Hellenism and Greek national identity, this aim and its related objectives utilize emotions to highlight the trauma of living in a semioccupied country. The nationalization of emotions (Zembylas 2008, 2009, 2010b) is shown in the following examples: "*[The students need] to mention and justify the elements that keep refugees and generally the [Greek-Cypriot] people emotionally tied to their land*"; "*to become emotionally moved through experiencing customs and traditions of our occupied land*"; "*to learn about the living of the inhabitants of occupied Cyprus before and after the invasion, and to collect information that show nostalgia for return from those who were uprooted*" (Ministry of Education and Culture 1996, p. 96). The nationalization of emotions aims at making students and teachers become invested in national norms that reify particular perceptions (e.g., the Greekness of the land; the need to be emotionally invested and committed to the struggle for liberating Cyprus and so on).

Conclusion and Implications

This chapter has explored the current ideological ethos of the Greek-Cypriot national curriculum for primary education. In particular, the analysis has mapped the curriculum dynamics, mainly in subjects that are important to issues of identity and culture—that is, Modern Greek Language, History, and a special subject called "I Know, I Don't Forget and I Struggle." This exploration has led to the conclusion that the curriculum for the aforementioned three subjects reflects an essentialist and monological conception of the Greek ethnonational culture and identity and thus is very far from multicultural and reconciliation education. In fact, it reflects perceptions closer to ethnocratic and mainstream multiculturalism; it functions as a powerful tool of maintaining the status quo and acting as *memory agent* (Podeh 2000) that crystallizes the Greek-Cypriot collective memory rather than legitimating the presence of minority groups.

It has also been suggested that the use of humanist ideas—such as "*human rights*," "*justice*," "*democracy*" and the like, or phrases such as "*critical examination*" and "*cultivation of attitudes and values towards others*"—are purely in contrast to the dominant ethnonational ethos of the curriculum. Humanism, therefore, is appropriated by the dominant nationalized discourse and thus becomes national humanism (Derrida 1992). In this sense, the construction and strengthening of Greek national identity as a curriculum aim is shown to be incompatible with multicultural ideas (Al-Haj 2005). Turkish Cypriots, as the largest minority group, are absent from the curriculum and stand outside Cyprus's legitimate political and cultural boundaries, which only include the Greek population. The emphasis on legitimating the "*Greekness*" of the educational system as well as Cyprus in general, leads almost inevitably to the disregard of the notion of reconciliation with Turkish Cypriots. This curriculum fails to raise the status of the Turkish Cypriots as a minority and the contradiction between humanist discourse and Greek ethnonational aspirations. Similar to Al-Haj's study of textbooks in Israel, this exploration indicates that "The entire question of a civil culture is missing […] [and] the spirit of the discussion merely reinforces the ethno-national culture" (2005, p. 66) of the Greek Cypriots.

Under these circumstances, the curriculum under investigation hardly leaves any space for critical multicultural education that might help promote a civic culture on the basis of humanist ideas such as peace and reconciliation. My conclusion here agrees with Al-Haj's (2005) finding (concerning the conflict in the Middle East):

> A curriculum that places defense of a hegemonic narrative at its core cannot lead to multicultural education, even according to the mainstream model of multiculturalism. This is especially true in a society that is still living in the shadow of conflict and in which a large group of citizens maintains a counternarrative to the hegemonic one. […] As a result, the use of education to promote the national ethos inevitably turns education into a means for deepening the…rift instead of a system that helps pave a shared civility. (pp. 67–68)

What is needed, therefore, in curriculum reform efforts in the Greek-Cypriot community is to develop curricula that emphasize critical multiculturalism and leave room for competing narratives and different identities (Bekerman 2004; Zembylas and Bekerman 2008). Critical approaches that aim at school and social transformation offer possibilities to extend the conversation in ways that allow the production of new imaginings of civic responsibility rather than the confirmation of conflicts based on ethnicity, religion, race, nationality, and other social divisions. Insisting on perpetuating these divisions, writes Bekerman (2004), "might make us vulnerable to the trap of serving the nation-state ideology which bears much responsibility for present interethnic conflict[s]" (p. 605).

Hodgkin (2006) suggests that curricula, especially in conflict-ridden areas, should offer students opportunities to engage in the discussion of multiple historical understandings and narratives. She suggests that students have to be encouraged to analyze and critique biased and partisan perspectives and learn to develop their own understanding of the past instead of sanitizing curricula and textbooks. Roudometof (2002) also argues that monolithic representations of the past contribute to the perpetuation of everlasting saga between conflicting communities. Monolithic narratives leave no room for dealing with the legitimacy of other narratives and fail to make a transition toward a multicultural education that might help promote a civil society. Curricula should be used instead as tools to promote critical perspectives both about humanist ideas and national ideologies.

Consequently, it is valuable that current educational reform initiatives in Cyprus consider the importance of dynamic views about identity, nation, and culture and how those views promote critical multiculturalism in more effective ways. Curricula need to incorporate more human rights perspectives without diminishing the importance of past traumas and memories, yet abandoning essentialist positions (Davies 2004). Also, curriculum revisions in the Greek-Cypriot community should create opportunities for critical dialogues so that empathy, multiperspectivity, solidarity, and social justice are nurtured (Zembylas 2008, 2010a). Finally, the educational and curricular needs of minorities and migrant populations need to be taken into consideration (Al-Haj 2004).

Educators and their students in Cyprus need to look beyond present curricula and the reproduction of existing knowledge and problematize the politics of identity and culture. Curricula that wish to disrupt the normalizing politics of identity and culture must engage students in critical multicultural and reconciliation education. This is a challenge to many educational systems and practices that are built on monological approaches; however, curricula are neither neutral nor separate from political circumstances. Unraveling the political aspects of curricula—both as analytic tools and as points of departure for cultivating individual and collective civic consciousness and critical multiculturalism—creates possibilities for enriching our critical perspectives about the implications of particular curriculum dynamics. Education in conflict-ridden societies needs curricula that account for the intersections of competing narratives, power relations, and critical hope (Zembylas 2007) for peace and reconciliation.

Acknowledgments I want to thank my research assistant, Yolanda Panteli, for her contribution in the curriculum analysis.

References

Al-Haj, M. (2003). Jewish-Arab relations and the education system in Israel. In Y. Iram (Ed.), *Education of minorities and peace education in pluralistic societies* (pp. 213–227). Israel: Bar Ilan University.

Al-Haj, M. (2004). The political culture of the 1990s immigrants from the former Soviet Union in Israel and their views toward the indigenous Arab minority: A case of ethnocratic multiculturalism. *Journal of Ethnic and Migration Studies, 30*(4), 681–696.

Al-Haj, M. (2005). National ethos, multicultural education, and the new history textbooks in Israel. *Curriculum Inquiry, 35*(1), 47–71.

Banks, J. A. (2007). *Educating citizens in a multicultural society* (2nd ed.). New York: Teachers College Press.

Bar-Tal, D. (2004). Nature, rationale, and effectiveness of education for coexistence. *Journal of Social Issues, 60*(2), 253–271.

Bekerman, Z. (2004). Potential and limitations of multicultural education in conflict-ridden areas: Bilingual Palestinian-Jewish schools in Israel. *Teachers College Record, 106*(3), 574–610.

Bekerman, Z. (2005). Complex contents and ideologies: Bilingual education in conflict- ridden areas. *Journal of Language, Identity, and Education, 4*(1), 1–20.

Bekerman, Z. (2007). Rethinking intergroup encounters: Rescuing praxis from theory, activity from education, and peace/co-existence from identity and culture. *Journal of Peace Education, 4*(1), 21–37.

Bekerman, Z., & Maoz, I. (2005). Troubles with identity: Obstacles to coexistence education in conflict ridden societies. *Identity: An International Journal of Theory and Research, 5*(4), 341–357.

Bell, D. (2003). Mythscapes: Memory, mythology, and national identity. *British Journal of Sociology, 54*(1), 63–81.

Boehmer, E. (2005). *Empire, the national, and the postcolonial, 1890–1920: Resistance in interaction.* Oxford: Oxford University Press.

Bryant, R. (2004). *Imagining the modern: The cultures of nationalism in Cyprus.* London: Tauris.

Bush, K. D., & Saltarelli, D. (2000). *The two faces of education in ethnic conflict: Towards a peacebuilding education for children.* Florence: UNICEF.

Charalambous, Y. (2007). Intercultural education or "national humanism": Reading anti-racist literature in Greek-Cypriot secondary education. Paper presented at the World Congress of Comparative Education, Sarajevo, Bosnia & Herzegovina.

Cole, E. (Ed.). (2007). *Teaching the violent past History education and reconciliation.* Lanham: Rowman & Littlefield.

Davies, L. (2004). *Education and conflict: Complexity and chaos.* London: Routledge.

Derrida, J. (1992). Onto-theology of national humanism (Prolegomena to a hypothesis). *Oxford Literary Review, 14*(1), 3–23.

Duarte, E. M., & Smith, S. (2000). *Foundational perspectives in multicultural education.* New York: Longman.

Enslin, P. (1994). Should nation-building be an aim of education? *Journal of Education, 19*(1), 23–36.

Fairclough, N. (1995). *Critical discourse analysis: The critical study of language.* London: Longman.

Fairclough, N. (2003). *Analyzing discourse: Textual analysis for social research.* London: Routledge.

Giroux, H. (1993). *Living dangerously: Multiculturalism and the politics of difference.* New York: Lang.

Gutmann, A. (2004). Unity and diversity in democratic multicultural education: Creative and destructive tensions. In J. A. Banks (Ed.), *Diversity and citizenship education: Global perspectives* (pp. 71–96). San Francisco: Jossey-Bass.

Hadjipavlou-Trigeorgis, M. (2007). Multiple realities and the role of peace education in deep-rooted conflicts: The case of Cyprus. In Z. Bekerman & C. McGlynn (Eds.), *Addressing ethnic conflict through peace education: International perspectives* (pp. 35–48). New York: Macmillan.
Hodgkin, M. (2006). Reconciliation in Rwanda: Education, history and the state. *Journal of International Affairs, 60*(1), 199–210.
Kincheloe, J. L., & Steinberg, S. R. (1997). *Changing multiculturalism*. Buckingham: Open University Press.
Kizilyürek, N. (1999). National memory and Turkish-Cypriot textbooks. *Internationale Schulbuchforschung, 21*(4), 387–396.
Lowenthal, D. (1998). *The heritage crusade and the spoils of history*. Cambridge: Cambridge University Pres.
Miller, D. (1993). In defense of nationality. *Journal of Applied Philosophy, 10*(1), 3–16.
Ministry of Education and Culture. (1996). *Curriculum for the primary education in the frame of the nine-year education*. Nicosia Department of Primary Education, Curriculum Development Unit (in Greek).
Nieto, S. (1999). *The light in their eyes: Creating multicultural learning communities*. New York: Teachers College Press.
Panayiotopoulos, C., & Nicolaidou, M. (2007). At a crossroads of civilizations: Multicultural educational provision in Cyprus through the lens of a case study. *Intercultural Education, 18*(1), 65–79.
Papadakis, Y. (2005). *Echoes from the dead zone: Across the Cyprus divide*. London and New York: Tauris.
Papadakis, Y. (2008). Narrative, memory and history education in divided Cyprus: A comparison of schoolbooks on the "History of Cyprus." *History & Memory, 20*(2), 128–148.
Podeh, E. (2000). History and memory in the Israeli education system. *History & Memory, 12*(1), 65–100.
Ravitch, D. (1990). Multiculturalism: E pluribus plures. The American Scholar, (Summer), 337–354.
Roudometof, V. (2002). *Collective memory, national identity and ethnic conflict: Greece, Bulgaria and the Macedonian question*. Westport, Connecticut and London: Praeger.
Schatz, R., Staub, E., & Lavine, H. (1999). On the varieties of national attachment: Blind versus constructive patriotism. *Political Psychology, 20*(2), 151–174.
Schlesinger, A. M. Jr. (1991). *The disuniting of America: Reflection on multicultural society*. New York: Norton.
Sleeter, C. (1992). *Keepers of the American dream*. London: Falmer.
Spyrou, S. (2006). Constructing "the Turk" as an enemy: The complexity of stereotypes in children's everyday worlds. *South European Society and Politics, 11*(1), 95–110.
Statistical Services of the Republic of Cyprus. (2006). *Demographic report*. Nicosia: Cyprus Statistical Services.
Steiner-Khamsi, G. (2003). Cultural recognition or social redistribution: Predicaments of minority education. In Y. Iram (Ed.), *Education of minorities and peace education in pluralistic societies* (pp. 15–28). Israel: Bar Ilan University.
VanSledright, B. (2008). Narratives of nation-state, historical knowledge, and school history education. *Review of Research in Education, 32*(1), 109–146.
Yiftachel, O. (1999). Ethnocracy: The politics of Judaizing Israel/Palestine. *Constellations, 6*(3), 364–390.
Yiftachel, O. (2000). Ethnocracy and discontents: Minorities, protest and the Israel polity. *Critical Inquiry, 26*(4), 725–756.
Zembylas, M. (2007). *Five pedagogies, a thousand possibilities: Struggling for hope and transformation in education*. Rotterdam: Sense.
Zembylas, M. (2008). *The politics of trauma in education*. New York: Macmillan.
Zembylas, M. (2009). Making sense of traumatic events: Towards a politics of aporetic mourning in educational theory and pedagogy. *Educational Theory, 59*(1), 85–104.

Zembylas, M. (2010a). Critical discourse analysis of multiculturalism and intercultural education policies in the Republic of Cyprus. *The Cyprus Review, 22*(1), 39–59.

Zembylas, M. (2010b). Racialization/ethnicization of school emotional spaces: The politics of resentment. *Race Ethnicity & Education, 13*(2), 253–270.

Zembylas, M., & Bekerman, Z. (2008). Dilemmas of justice in peace/coexistence education: Affect and the politics of identity. *The Review of Education, Pedagogy & Cultural Studies, 30*, 399–419.

Chapter 40
Learning Who They "Really" Are: From Stigmatization to Opportunities to Learn in Greek Romani Education

William New and Michael S. Merry

With the accession of Romania and Bulgaria to the EU in 2007, the total population of Roma living in the EU rose to above 7 million, making the Rom in many respects the 28th member nation, albeit a dispersed, territoryless nation with glaring deficits of self-governance and sovereignty. The EU and other transnational government and nongovernment entities committed considerable economic and political resources to correcting the dire human rights situation for Rom during the accession process for postcommunist nations, but the lack of sustained progress or political will to effect fundamental change in many member nations has put the issue back on the first page across the EU. Accompanying efforts to improve Romani education has produced a plethora of research conducted by and for national and transnational governmental agencies involved in education, human services, and minority rights. A matching set of research has been conducted by local, national, and transnational NGOs, most notably perhaps the European Roma Rights Center (ERRC) and various organizations affiliated with the Open Society Institute.

While most NGO and government-sponsored research is of professional quality, its core purpose is advocacy or policy analysis, and topics are selected with an eye for furthering these goals. For instance, the ERRC volume, Stigmata (2004), which documents discrimination against Romani students in several European countries, has the intent of supporting its legal actions against local and national governments, and providing rationale for increased enforcement of antidiscrimination laws already in place. Recently, NGO research documenting successful educational programs for Romani students has become more common, much of it funded through the Decade of Roma Inclusion (see EU MONITORING AND ADVOCACY PROGRAM, 2007 for example). Compared to research produced by government and nongovernment agencies, peer-reviewed research on Romani education is scant, tending to focus on analyses of local and national reform efforts that, in the view of the researchers, fail to address the needs of Romani students. Notable among publications in English are Claveria and Alonso (2003) on Spain, Igarashi (2005) on the Czech Republic,

W. New (✉)
Beloit College, Beloit, 53511 WI, US
e-mail: newb@beloit.edu

Kende (2000) on Hungary, Levinson (2007) on England, and Chronaki (2005) and Zachos (2009) on Greece. All these researchers choose a qualitative methodology, and nearly all evince an explicit commitment to human rights and sympathy for their Romani subjects. But despite the existence of many excellent ethnographies and histories of the Rom, and the widespread popular and governmental interest in Romani issues, most prominent European journals of education are yet to publish an article on Romani education, there are no book-length treatments of Romani education, and publication in the languages of nations with large Romani populations is rare. The contrast between this lacunae and the wealth of research literature on the education of migrant and other minorities in Europe, not to speak of the enormous body of North American research literature on minority education, is striking.

The purpose of this chapter will be to explore the opportunities for learning available to Romani youth in a specific national context. We have chosen Greece as our case, because recent developments there with respect to Romani education are peculiar to the idiosyncratic history and sociopolitical structure of Greece and emblematic of struggles for improved educational opportunities for Romani students across Europe. Choosing to focus on a single national case is motivated by three related notions: (a) opportunities to learn and opportunities for social integration are always inextricably linked to the histories of specific nations; (b) minority education always depends on the specific structures of governance, that is, policy reform, that prevail in these nations; and (c) efforts toward educational reform are part of the social and economic structure of the nations of which the Rom are a part. There are, of course, some general truths to keep in mind: the Rom everywhere are the object of pernicious process of stigmatization; they are the poorest of the poor, usually marginally employed or unemployed; they experience problems with housing; their access to education and health care is very limited, even in countries where education and health care are supposedly universal; and they are most often believed by majority populations (and media and politicians) to cause their own misery.

We address the question of learning for Greek Romani youth through the psychosocial construct of stigmatization. According to advocates for Romani rights and scholars, the most damaging kind of school segregation is that which results in a stigma on Romani students that cannot be eradicated, contributing greatly to the social isolation and dreadful living conditions experienced by most Rom. Recent research provides a conceptual basis for understanding the dynamics of rejection and its many modalities of response, and for understanding the political and cultural underpinnings of the iterative process of stigmatization. This will allow us to address one of the central issues of Romani education reform, and minority educational reform generally: why does integration or inclusion, *per se*, not necessarily produce the kind of improved prospects for individual students or for the minority community as a whole that we were led to expect? In our Greek case, we can approach this question by contrasting the learning opportunities for Romani youth in situations of exclusion or "separate and very much not equal," and the learning opportunities for Romani youth in integrated, albeit assimilatory, school settings. Data for these cases come from several sources, including ethnographic studies of Romani education in Greece, research generated by NGOs, governmental agencies and the courts, historical studies of the Rom, and media reports.

The Rom in Greece: An Historical Tradition of Stigma

The first mention of the Rom in Europe is from an eleventh century hagiography composed on Mt. Athos (in Greece): the Emperor in Constantinople calls upon the help of a group of religious heretics known as the *Atsigani,* who are "notorious for soothsaying and sorcery" (Fraser 1992, p. 46). From the word Greek *atsigani,* the other common European terms for designating the Rom—*cigan, cikán, zigeuner, tsigani, zingari, cigányuk*—are derived. In the thirteenth century, a permanent settlement of Rom who called themselves "Egyptians" was documented in Western Greece: from this misnaming comes the common English term *gypsy,* the Spanish term *gitano,* the Bulgarian *gjupci,* and the *agjiptani* of Kosovo, also referred to as *ashkali,* derived from Palestine. In current and historical usage, all these terms are derogatory, but the extent and quality of the meaning depends critically on the context of usage: on who is speaking to whom in what place and it what circumstance. While terms like *cikán* (Czech) and *zigeneur* (German) are implicated in long histories of violence and marginalization, politically correct terms like Roma may be implicated in a different history of subjugation: in different contexts, each can contribute to the reproduction of the structures of stigma.

A great deal of evidence about the Rom exists from the Ottoman period, which extended roughly from the mid fourteenth to the beginning of the twentieth century. The north Indian origins of the Rom have been known from linguistic evidence since the eighteenth century, but this was never part of the common knowledge about the Rom in the Balkans (including what is now Greece) under Byzantine, and then Ottoman rule. They were perceived as foreigners who spoke an incomprehensible and private language of unknown origins, engaged in various exotic cultural practices, were "black as Indians" (Marushiakova et al. 2001, p. 68) and had as low a regard for their multiethnic Balkan neighbors as their neighbors had for them. Notwithstanding their social isolation, the Rom were an intimate part of that multiethnic society, with complex social and religious relations with other groups and with the governing authorities. The northern provinces of Macedonia and Thrace—which did not come under direct Greek rule until the twentieth century and are the most ethnically diverse regions of Greece—have historically been home to the largest population of "Greek" Rom, though many were more closely associated with either Bulgarian or Turkish (Muslim) communities.

During Ottoman rule, the Rom had a special status and the same measure of autonomy accorded to other groups, related in part to whether they claimed to be Christian or Muslim, or neither. Most Rom appear to have followed a seminomadic lifestyle, usually settling in or near a town during the winter months: the efforts of the Ottomans to curtail nomadism related to the difficulty of collecting taxes from nonsedentary populations. But the wandering of the Rom was a very important part of their identity, for themselves and for others. The Rom provided needed services to the towns and cities they visited during the warm months: they had special skills in music and dance, metalworking, fortune telling, and sale and training of animals, to name a few occupations. They also took on "dirty work" that others did not want. Despite their ongoing and important social relations with non-Rom (*gadje*), they were—in the words of a nineteenth-century Bulgarian historian—"despised by the Turks and hated by the Christians... [T]he surrounding population views the Gypsies as everywhere else—an in impure, intellectually and morally inferior race" (quoted in Marushiakova et al. 2001, p. 75). What the Rom thought about the *gadjo* is not known, but one might infer some degree of reciprocity of feeling, along with a keen awareness of their vulnerability to hostility from the majority population.

Stigmatization and Identity Threat

Multiple definitions of stigmatization are in circulation, but for our purposes we employ the following definition provided by Pryor et al. (2004, p. 436): "A person who is stigmatized is a person whose social identity, or membership in some social category, calls into question his or her full humanity—the person is devalued, spoiled or flawed in the eyes of others." As a social psychological process, stigmatization depends on the ambivalence of the dominant group—ferocious prejudicial feelings coexist with nearly insurmountable defenses to any self-understanding of prejudice—and on the double-bind in which relentless discrimination is internalized by individual members of the targeted group. Stigmatization tends to be viewed either as a psychological process, originating in false generalizations about the nature of a person or a group and remediable through education, or as a sociopolitical process originating in exploitation and subordination, remediable through revolution or political reform (Gaines and Reed 1995). In the first explanation, derived from Allport's (1954) landmark work on prejudice, one supposes that eradicating the prejudice of the "stigmatizers" might undo the process of stigmatization, and that prejudice, insofar as it is grounded in false beliefs and cognition, ought to be responsive to the right kind of teaching.

The sociopolitical argument, on the other hand, depends more on systemic, unintentional discrimination, which is certainly a feature of the stigmatization of the Rom and other vulnerable minority groups. In Greece, for instance, the near complete unavailability of adequate housing for many Rom results in their continued residence around garbage dumps and polluted industrial sites, reinforcing the stereotype that the Rom do not wish to be like or live near civilized people (Guy 2009). But the argument for systemic discrimination, without an accompanying explanation for interpersonal dimensions of discrimination, is not adequate to account for the persistence of discrimination and its effects even after sociopolitical reforms have been achieved.

The history of the Rom in Greece and the Balkans suggests that stigmatization is social, psychological, and political at the same time, and highly adaptive to changing circumstances. That is to say, prejudice against the Rom has survived, undiminished, radical regime changes, alternations in ethnic identity and organization, efforts at eradication, ups and downs in economic fortune, language change, relocations and dislocations…the history that is lost to forgetfulness (and re-education) appears to have been remembered in the structures of stigmatization. Link and Phelan (2001) identity five necessary components for the experience of stigmatization: (1) distinguishing and labeling differences; (2) associating differences with negative attributes (or stereotypes); (3) separating us from them; (4) status loss and discrimination; and (5) the dependence of stigma on power. Applied to Romani students, the process begins with the labeling of educational differences; associating these differences in academic ability with the established Gypsy stereotype (which these differences both confirm and extend); physically and symbolically separating the affected children from "our children" (upon whom they might have negative effects); and resulting in, or confirming, the low status of the Roma child (and community), which serves to justify discrimination. The predicament for the stigmatized individual and group is constant because the mechanisms for discrimination, and for legitimating discrimination, are flexible and extensive. "There are many ways to achieve structural discrimination, many ways to directly discriminate, and many ways in which the stigmatized person can be encouraged to believe that they should not enjoy full and equal participation in social and economic life. Moreover, if the mechanisms that are currently in place are blocked or become embarrassing, new ones can always be created" (Link and Phelan 2001, p. 380).

The operation of stigmatization is associated with scores of negative affective and cognitive consequences, all impacting academic learning. Padilla (2008, p. 25) summarizes prior research in saying that

> the [stigmatized] person may experience a wide range of emotions such as feelings of depersonalization, lack of belonging, anger, frustration and depression…If the person experiences negative evaluations because of the stigma associated with their ethnic group from multiple sources—peers, teachers, mass media—the person may also experience an increased arousal level in similar social contexts in which they have felt threatened on other occasions. Thus, highly stigmatized individuals may experience generalized threat in many social contexts.

Other researchers report depersonalization, a sense of meaninglessness, lethargy, reduced affect, and self-awareness: that is, stigmatization produces emotional numbness (Twenge et al. 2003). The operation of stigma, as a system of aversive discrimination, may also produce traumatic stress with long-term physical and psychological consequences (Carter 2007; Butts 2002; Hicks 2004). For those individuals least able to adapt, stress responses can be severe, including intrusion of memories and thoughts of the initial injury, hypervigilance, difficulty sleeping, depression, and anxiety. Even when symptoms are less severe, the experience of persistent stress has negative psychological and behavioral effects, which may serve in practice to reproduce the stereotypes upon which the stressing acts of discrimination are based. One might think of behavioral stereotypes as the accumulated response to being placed in aversive situations, turned back on the victim as a reinscription of the original injury. According to Derks et al. (2009), social identity threat impairs cognitive performance generally by lowering motivation and investment in performance in high-status domains (like school), and increases the likelihood of individuals removing themselves from the threatening situation.

Rejections of all kinds are a threat to what appears to be a universal human goal of being valued, accepted, and belonging (Smart Richman and Leary 2009). The generalized outcome of rejection are "hurt feelings," often resulting in heightened desire for relationship, urges to defend oneself against the source of hurt feelings, or avoidance of further rejection by withdrawal. Individuals adopt different strategies or behaviors dependent on their own particular character or circumstances, and on the basis of specific social conditions. For instance, stigmatized individuals who believe that they are somehow in the wrong, that they caused their own hurt feelings, and who have some hope or faith in the possibilities of repairing the relationship, or a belief that repair of the relationship is essential to their well-being, are likely to put most of their energy in reparation. This may take the form of compliance, dissimulation, accommodation, behavioral change, change in appearance and presentation. In a racial context, authors such as Fanon (1967) are likely to see this strategy as a sign of self-loathing, or, in Allport's terminology, as "intrapunitive" (Gaines and Reed 1995). When individuals perceive rejection and the threat to well-being as chronic, pervasive, and unfair, and hold little expectation that valuable relationships with the aggressive parties could be successfully maintained, they tend to adopt either a confrontational or avoidant mode of "antisocial" response (Smart Richman and Leary 2009). For most Rom in Greece, the experience of rejection by members of the dominant culture is an everyday occurrence. And the realities of systemic discrimination in housing, education, health care, and civil rights are unremitting.

Clearly, stigma operates generally to decrease the potential for learning of those who bear the stigma, particularly in high-status domains. But there are significant differences in how stigma is experienced, and how its consequences are distributed, for Romani students in different kinds of settings and at different developmental levels. We are interested here to make distinctions with respect to learning between highly segregated settings and integrated settings. These distinctions will also bear on the destiny of the Rom as a culture and people: it is a somewhat paradoxical result of their long history of ostracism and avoidance that the Rom have escaped the total assimilation into majority populations that has been the fate of many other small ethnic groups, with the concomitant "extinction" of their "small languages" and life-ways (Marushiakova et al. 2001; Hancock 2002; Petrova 2003).

An integral counterpart to international imperatives to improve educational quality for Romani youth is the imperative to "preserve" the Romani culture in doing so. Linking phenomena of social identity threat to notions of self- and group-affirmation provides some insight into how differently positioned Romani students might respond to their educational milieu. Successful affirmation of either individual or group identity can serve as an antidote of sorts to the demoralizing effects of stigmatization, and sustain motivation to achieve, even in difficult circumstances (Crocker et al. 1998; Derks et al. 2007).

Of course, the extent to which individuals are identified by themselves or others with a social group varies as a matter of personality, history, and context. Individuals with low-identification with a low-status group—for example, the Romani student in a regular Greek classroom studying Greek—may choose to stress strategies of self-affirmation—for example, learning to read and write Greek as well as his or her Greek peers—and downplay his or her Romani identity. Recalling the psychological ambivalence of dominant group prejudice, in league with Greek cultural pressures toward democracy and tolerance, we can predict considerable sympathy from teachers and fellow students for this strategy. But, Derks et al. (2009, p. 199) suggest that

> [a]lthough individual upward mobility is often seen as providing the royal road toward achieving large-scale equal opportunity and social change...there is ample reason to believe individual mobility is not sufficient. That is not to say that it is not important for individual group members to strive for high performance in status-defining domains. However, to achieve more widespread social change it is crucial that successful upwardly mobile members of stigmatized groups remain concerned with the welfare of their groups.

But do the ingrained structures and processes of stigmatization allow for any large measure of continued identification with their group by upwardly mobile individuals? What remains unclear is whether there are other routes to more widespread social change that do not require of Romani students that they relinquish their membership in Romani community life and their claims to a Romani identity.

Exclusion and Inclusion of Romani Students in Greek Education

Romani education in Greece is of generally deplorable quality, but there are significant differences between the worst cases—outright school exclusion—and the best cases—integrated, albeit assimilatory, schooling with some degree of extra support for Romani students. Looking closely at these two poles helps us to understand the differential workings of stigmatization in a complex society, and how the opportunities to learn are structured, and for what purpose, in different locations in this society.

Examples of Exclusion—Nea Kios and Aspropyrgos

In 2000 in Nea Kios, an agricultural village of slightly more than 2,000 inhabitants located in the Peloponnese, local authorities evicted the Roma from their town, including the schools. In 2005 in Aspropyrgos, an industrial town just northwest of

Athens, with a population of around 27,000, local authorities and parents refused entry to Roma students to a public elementary school, and instead built a small facility for the exclusive attendance of Romani students. These cases are emblematic of the strategies of local authorities, rural and urban, across Greece with respect to Romani education, and of the tenuous relationship between local municipalities and populations and the Greek central government. In both Nea Kios and Aspropyrgos, the Romani population is especially impoverished. Local people in these towns tend to think of "their" Rom as outsiders, not belonging by right to their communities, and not deserving of a share of the inadequate public services available.

Nea Kios

After the Greek assault on Turkey ended in catastrophe, the 1922 Treaty of Lausanne required a massive population exchange between Greece and Turkey. Nea Kios was founded by Greek refugees from Kios, an ancient city on the Black Sea in what is now Turkey. The integrity of the local community is grounded in proud memories of these refugee origins, and the attempted expulsion of Rom from Nea Kios is rationalized in terms of restoring/protecting this core identity from pollution. Not coincidentally, the legal rationale for the eviction of the Rom was an administrative sanitary regulation by which they found the Rom living in Nea Kios to be a "health hazard" (Petrokou and Dimitrakopoulas 2002). Within a month, the Greek Ombudsman, prefect-level prosecutors and politicians in Athens were involved in the case, all with the purpose of persuading authorities in Nea Kios to desist in their openly "racist" policies. Formal complaints were issued, but they languished in the Courts before being dismissed (without notice to the complainants) in 2005 (Greek Helsinki Monitor 2009), signaling that the continuing, though now somewhat relaxed, segregation of the Rom in Nea Kios is, if not legitimate, beyond the reach or concern of nonlocal Greek authorities.

Upwards of 100 Romani families live in the Argolis prefecture in and about Nea Kios. About 30 families live on land they own, though most of them have not built permanent houses. Others live in olive orchards, and about 30 families live on polluted public land next to an olive oil processing refinery, which also serves as an illegal dump. Families live in shacks made of various materials, with little in the way of running water or sewage facilities. The children of this settlement sporadically attend a school operated by Greek teacher and Romani rights activist. Children from other settlements attend nearby Greek schools, but very few continue past elementary grades (Petrokou and Dimitrakopoulas 2002). Representatives from the local police and the Director of Primary Education described the possibilities for Romani education as dim, due to the shortcomings of the Romani students and their families:

> Roma families don't really want their children to attend school. They only enroll to get the benefit and they never come again.... Roma students are dirty and they smell. Other children don't want to be friends with them...[They] are free to attend any school they want, but the Roma are reluctant to integrate into society, the local people do not have any

problem with them. There is no racism in the schools of Argolis. (Petrokou and Dimitrakopoulas 2002)

All the requisite conditions of stigmatization are clearly present in Nea Kios. Romani children are identified as different from Greek children; their perceived differences are associated with and reinforce the Gypsy stereotype (families don't want to send their children to school or to integrate, children smell and are dirty); the distinction between "our" children and Gypsy children is articulated; the Gypsy children lose status by virtue of overt discrimination and their failure at high-status activities like schooling; the process is legitimated and enforced through channels of official power, including housing regulations, policing, and the labor market.

Aspropyrgos

Barring enrollment of Romani students in the elementary schools of Aspropyrgos has been ongoing for more than a decade, accompanied by persistent protest from Greek and international NGOs and typically ineffectual responses from the Greek Ombudsman and the Ministry of Education. In July 2005, two school headmasters provided a rationale for not allowing Romani children in their schools (International Helsinki Federation 2006, p. 2):

> These children live in a place they have occupied illegally, a place for depositing garbage, without electricity and without water. As a consequence of these wretched living conditions, the children have skin conditions…and many other illnesses, such as hepatitis and also diseases passed on to them by rat bites…. We would also report the vigorous reactions of the Parents' and Guardians' Associations and remind you that between the Pontics and Gypsies there is a vendetta, which…led…to the loss of one Romani life…[A] commonly acceptable solution needs to be found by competent authorities.

When the "competent authorities" did not provide a solution by the opening of school, non-Romani parents protested vehemently the inclusion of any Romani students in "their" schools, boycotted the school, and forcibly prevented the entry of any Romani students, resulting in a police presence to protect these children, though there were reports that the police stood by when non-Romani parents pushed and taunted Romani children. Late in October, Romani parents were pressured to agree to send their children to an annex some distance from the regular elementary schools and the Romani settlement (International Helsinki Foundation 2006), which they began attending. At this time, the regular school reopened without its former Romani students.

The eventual solution to the dilemma in Aspropyrgos was the construction of three new buildings exclusively for the elementary education of Romani children. A visitor (DeviousDiva January 2007) reported that the Romani children

> are sent to this "special" school where the teaching hours are…short, 8am until 12.30pm. The teachers…are there for a year at best and are then moved somewhere else. As there are only three rooms, children of different ages are taught in the same classroom…. There are 50 children enrolled there but most of the time attendance hovers at around 50%. As one of the teachers there pointed out, it is not their job to find out why a child is absent for three

days or more.... This is impossible to do when most of the families here have no telephone. They...do not have the means to check up on them and there are no social workers to cover the school. So the children just don't turn up or appear sporadically and that's the end of it.

This resulting class-action suit eventually found its way to the European Court of Human Rights (2008), which ruled in *Sampanis et al. v. Greece* that the policy of forced segregation in Aspropyrgos violated Article 14 of the European Convention on Human Rights, which prohibits discrimination in general, in connection with Article 2 of Protocol 1, which guarantees the right to education. In addition, the Greek government was found to have failed to provide an effective remedy, in violation of Article 13. Immediately following the *Sampanis* decision, the municipality renamed the annex 12th primary school, but only Romani students were enrolled. The facilities were repaired following vandalism over the summer, and chemical toilets and water were provided (for a short time) when representatives visited from the European Commission on Racial Intolerance (ECRI). While the school remains completely segregated and unequal in terms of the resources—in continued violation of the ruling by the European Court of Human Rights—the arrangement has been approved by the Greek ministry of education and Ombudsman (Greek Helsinki Monitor 2009).

What do Romani children, who are excluded in these ways from regular schooling, learn, and how can we characterize their experience of learning? On one hand, most of the elementary-age children in Nea Kios, Aspropyrgos, and many other similar municipalities across Greece have limited direct contact with non-Roma people and their cultural byways. They grow up speaking some combination of Romanes and Greek, they are exposed to the cultural practices of self- and group-affirmation common to their communities, they are cherished by their own parents and relatives, and often even by their teachers in Romani schools, and they have little basis for comparison by which they would judge their life conditions to be intolerable. This may protect them from some aspects of stigmatization—overt rejection, hurt feelings, depersonalization, self-loathing—but they are of course still subject to separation from the majority, to status and opportunity loss, and to general and pervasive disempowerment. What they do not learn, among other things, is how to read or write, how to do math, Greek history, and perhaps most importantly with respect to future prospects, they do not learn how to comport themselves as Greeks, essential tools for access to the language and social capital of power (Delpit 2006). And eventually, the protection against the most personal injuries of stigmatization provided by the insulation of their community must prove insufficient. The lives of even insulated Romani children are marked by incidents of overt discrimination and violence, like the actions of non-Romani parents toward Romani children attempting to enroll in school, and by the inescapable correlates of poverty: hunger, excessive cold and heat, illness, and mortality. By early adolescence there is also inevitably increased personal contact between Romani youth, very few of whom stay in school, and non-Romani persons, and this contact tends in places like Nea Kios and Aspropyrgos to feature the worst expressions of prejudice and derogation. From these experiences, Romani youth learn who they "really" are in the world and how to defend themselves psychologically and physically from stigma.

Examples of Inclusion—Flampouro and Agia Varvara

In the remote village of Flampouro northeast of Thessaloniki in Macedonia, a predominantly Roma community has flourished since at least the nineteenth century. Nearly all the students in the elementary school are Romani, but most graduates go on to an integrated secondary school a few miles away in the provincial capital. Academic performance and graduation rates of Flampouro's Romani students compare favorably to Greek averages (Zachos 2006). Similarly, Agia Varvara, at the northwestern edge of Athens, features a long-standing and economically stable Romani population. Local elementary schools include sizable Romani—as well as immigrant—minorities, there are some special programs to support the academic progress of Romani students, curricular materials focusing on Romani culture, and a general concern among faculty and administration to maintain an atmosphere of tolerance and mutual respect (New 2004).

Flampouro

Flampouro is a farming community of slightly more than 1,000 residents, the site of yearly music and cultural festivals that draw many performers, local non-Romani visitors, and tourists. Though Flampouro's Rom are sedentary, not corresponding to the storybook Gypsy wanderer, the village has an international reputation as a Romani heritage town (McDowell 1970). As a center for Romani cultural activities, Flampouro also has importance for the regional Romani population. Zachos (2006) has documented the political and educational history of the Rom of Macedonian Flampouro, focusing on (a) the atypical success of Romani students, (b) the established, sedentary status of the region's Rom (contrasting to the stereotype of the Rom as a nomadic people), and (c) the political awareness and activism of the local Rom, founded on experience during World War II in the resistance, and related association with the left-oriented National Liberation Front and the communist party. According to Zachos (2006, p. 24), the egalitarian, antidiscriminatory ethos promoted by the communist party in its earlier days served to lift the Rom

> out of passiveness, since it seems that the new worldview and the new supplies with which these people confronted life and society after their contact with the people and the ideas of the Left, altered their criteria and forced them to reconsider their values, attitudes and behaviors. These people were armed with an optimistic view of life that increased their combative spirit as well as their resolution to work in order to improve their living standards.

The "conscientization" that Zachos describes has been associated with successful resistance to stigma and discrimination (Freire 1970). It seems to be an important organizing principal, combines with of a particular set of historical and geographic characteristics, that has produced a state of affairs in which most young Rom from Flampouro are literate, and many have gained positions of authority and respect in the region.

Multiethnic Macedonia has been the locus of national identity conflict since Greece assumed control from Bulgaria in 1913 at the end of the Second Balkan War. The Greek government employed education as a primary means of assimilating the diverse populations of Macedonia into the Greek nation: language and history were paramount concerns. An elementary school was established in Flampouro in 1914, where its monolingual Romani children were educated to become Greeks. Notably, given Zachos's thesis of political conscientization, data are indicating that until 1948, the educational outcomes for Romani students in Flampouro were typically of those of other Greek Roma, but since that time enrollment and graduation have steadily risen. Flampouro itself has a reputation for offering "a secure environment free from intense ethnic conflicts and annoying, offensive behavior" (Zachos 2006), but Romani high school students are exposed to the typical run of derogatory treatment, though this is undoubtedly tempered by the longstanding residence and political participation of Romani people in the area.

Agia Varvara

Like Flampouro, the Romani community of Agia Varvara has a long continuous history in one location, and has achieved modest levels of social prosperity and educational success. The municipality is an active member in a network of Greek municipalities working on issues of Romani social integration, has received considerable funding for its Romani projects, the schools are integrated, most Romani students graduate from secondary school, and some onto university and professional studies. The Pan Hellenic Gypsy Cultural Association, still very active today, was founded in Agia Varvara in 1939 and continues to be headquartered there. The population of the elementary school in Agia Varvara is approximately 30% Romani, with also a significant population of immigrant children from Albania and Russia. Most of the Romani students spend one period a day working with a specialist on language arts, since this is the area of instruction in which the Romani students have, or are perceived to have, the most difficulty. It is also the most important subject in any Greek school. While the teachers responsible for Romani students sometimes complain about the lack of resources and their lack of training in Romani culture and language, they are highly attentive and sympathetic to their students, both in their own classes, and advocating for them in other classes. The faculty is aware of the school's status as a model for Romani education in Greece: many express dismay at those aspects of the mandated curricula which are less than ideally multicultural, which is to say, the entire state-mandated curriculum, in which an unproblematic and uncontested Greek identity is presupposed and strongly promoted. Some faculty members were, however, much less charitable in their assessments of Romani parents, fearing and resenting their complaints, especially the threat of being called a "racist," and showing considerable disdain for the "family life" that led to homework not being done, and to occasional extended absences (New 2004).

One Romani graduate of the school, Christos Vassileiou, has gone on to become a well-known physician in Athens. "For the standards of my race, it is revolutionary to be working in the medical field," he says, modestly recounting his life history of overcoming insuperable obstacles and achieving the impossible (Gerasimos 2009). "If you are a Gypsy, you cannot expect help from any quarter. You come across only walls and locked doors. Throughout your journey you need to keep your ears closed and remain committed to your goal." He attributes a great deal of success to being brought up in Agia Varvara, where there was the possibility of integrated, nondiscriminatory schooling, where the everyday psychological violence of racial stigmatization was mitigated by the presence of nonstereotypical Romani adults, and other youth, and where exposure to mainstream Greek life was available to a Romani child. Where other successful Romani students have fully assimilated into the Greek mainstream, and renounced their subordinate Gypsy identities and associates. Vasilleiou devotes some time and professional energy to the respiratory health of Romani youth.

The Romani students of Flampouro and Agia Varvara do learn, as well as other Greek students, the lessons of school: most importantly, they learn how to read and write Greek, and how to "be" Greek. Some of the factors that at least partially protect the minority students in these locales from the debilitating effects of general stigmatization are economic stability; an established presence in a single place; some degree of political awareness and organization; an appreciation for their ethnic/cultural identity; relatively civil relations with their *gadje* neighbors; and the availability of mature models of successful navigation of educational and social systems that do not favor Romani success. In the five-part scheme of the stigmatization, perhaps the most important levers for change are agency—as in not being completely subject to the exercise of the power of a hostile other—and the resources to avoid the full measure of individual or small group identification with the worst elements of the Gypsy stereotype.

But success poses a challenge to those minority individuals positioned to achieve it, and to the Romani minority as a whole. In a classroom in Agia Varvara, for instance, a teacher asked the students, more than a third of whom were Rom, if any could speak a language other than Greek. Several raised their hands, but all of them answered that they could also speak English—an overstatement at the least—and none volunteered that they could speak Romanes, or Albanian, or Russian (New 2004). Dr. Vasilleiou attests to the assimilatory success of his education, in which his volunteerism and concern for the oppressed can be easily understood as expressions of Greek virtues: "At school I was taught Ancient Greek History. Greece is my homeland, my home. And if the need arises, I will defend her" (Gerasimos 2009). While an educated Rom in Athens might have opportunities to disappear into the mainstream society, an educated Rom in Flampouro might well—as most educated rural Greek youth do—emigrate to either Thessaloniki or Athens (Zachos 2006). For members of low-status groups, performance in status-defining domains like school presents in the best case a challenge to self-affirmation, and in the worst case, the "categorization threat" that one's affiliation with the stigma attached to the group will make the challenge insuperable. Individuals are prone, in this situation, to downplay the extent to which their individual performance affirms the group's identity, and to play up the extent to which it confirms their own identity, as meritorious, as potentially free from stigma (Derks et al. 2007; 2009; Merry and New 2008). There may be reason to question the common wisdom that the upward mobility of individuals from vulnerable groups contributes to large-scale equal opportunity or lessening of the ingrained processes of stigmatization. Whether the situation of the children of Nea Kios and Aspopyrgos can be improved without the active concern of the successful students of Agia Varvara and Flampouro is also an open question.

Conclusion

In this chapter, we have explored the learning and life experiences of a vulnerable minority group—the Rom of Greece—in the context of an historical, multidimensional theory of stigmatization. For around a thousand years, various Romani groups have lived alongside—though usually at some distance—from their multiethnic neighbors in the Balkans, and the complex heritage of these historical relationships can still be observed in Greek society today. Contemporary social psychological theories of stigmatization describe a multipart, self-reinforcing system of prejudice and power that serves to keep those considered somewhat "less than human" (Goffman 1986) in their place. The psychological consequences of stigmatization for youth are many, but all converge in decreasing material opportunities to learn, and further, disincline stigmatized Romani students to engage in school learning even when it is available. Stigmatization can have differential effects on individual and group fortunes, depending on local circumstances. We examined four cases of Romani education in Greece—two in which extreme prejudice led to school segregation and exclusion for impoverished Romani communities, and two in which more successful Romani communities achieved great levels of social integration and academic success.

Where physical, psychological, and structural violence is rife, and educational opportunities very poor, Romani youth usually grow up without mastering even basic academic skills; there is also a tendency to avoid contact with non-Romani persons as much as possible, and to reproduce the socioeconomic conditions of scarcity that characterize their parents' lives. While ethnic identity might be preserved under such conditions, it is a beleaguered and degraded identity, fodder for the continuing cycle of stigmatization. The consequences of life in extreme poverty themselves—illness, lack of access to clean water, malnutrition, for example—have the effect of validating for the legitimacy of the stigma for those prejudiced against the Rom. The inclusion of children with lice and other infectious diseases in public schools, for instance, can be represented as a "nonracial" concern, and justification for exclusion, in contexts—like Greece generally—where systemic racism is generally not recognized and often vehemently denied at local levels and in official circles.

In Flampouro and Agia Varvara, the educational outcomes for Romani students are more positive, and insofar as individual success signals acceptance of conventional Greek identity, with Romani identity being downplayed, these individuals may escape many of the consequences of stigma and stereotype. But while it appears that these particular communities are relatively self-sustaining as enclaves of "model" Romani life, there are few signs that the existence of these communities is much benefit to the poorest—indeed the majority—of Romani people in Greece. The example of Rom who have "pulled themselves up" and live (more or less) like other Greeks may do as much to strengthen the stereotype of the "bad" Gypsy which serves as a rationale for the subjugation of those who are not able to rise above appallingly adverse circumstances. In fact, the complete absence of any possibility of self-improvement for those who live in places like Nea Kios or Aspropyrgos can then be reinterpreted—at personal and institutional levels—as symptoms of Gypsy irresponsibility, indolence, and as evidence of moral and intellectual deficiency. The presence of a "good Gypsy" may thus reinforce the stereotype of the "bad Gypsy." This may account, to some extent, for the intractability of segregated, egregiously unequal Romani schooling in Aspropyrgos and many others places in Greece, even in a political climate where intolerance and racial/ethnic inequality are popularly recognized as illegitimate. This reflects, in one way, on the historic nature of governance in Greece, a highly centralized system where decisions are most often contingent on political interests—in the worst possible sense of political—and where the edicts of the central government are not respected or enforced at local levels. In another way, it reflects on the paradoxical flexibility and obduracy of stigmatization, which seems able to alter its form in response to new conditions without diminishing its effects.

References

Allport, G. W. (1954). *The nature of prejudice*. New York: Basic Books.
Baumeister, R. F., Bratslavsky, E., Finkenauer, C., & Vohs, K. D. (2001). Bad is stronger than good. *Review of General Psychology, 5*(5), 323–370.
Butts, H. F. (2002). The black mask of humanity: Racial/ethnic discrimination and traumatic stress disorder. *The Journal of the American Academy of Psychiatry and Law, 30*(2), 336–339.
Carter, R. T. (2007). Racism and psychological and emotional injury: Recognizing and assessing race-based traumatic stress. *The Counseling Psychologist, 35*(1), 13–105.
Chronaki (2005). Learning about 'learning identities' in the school arithmetic practice: The experience of two young minority gypsy girls in the Greek context of education. *European Journal of Psychology of Education, 20*(1), 61–74.
Claveria, J. V., & Alonso, J. G. (2003). Why Roma do not like mainstream schools: Voices of a people without territory. *Harvard Educational Review, 573*(4), 559–590.
Crocker, J., Major, B., & Steele, C. (1998). Social stigma. In D. T. Gilbert, S. T. Fiske, & G. Lindzey (Eds.), *The handbook of social psychology* (4th ed., Vol. 2, pp. 504–553). Boston: McGraw-Hill.
Delpit, L. (2006). *Other people's children: Cultural conflict in the classroom, Updated edition*. New York: Basic Books.
Derks, B., van Laar, C., & Ellemers, N. (2007). The beneficial effects of social identity protection on the performance motivation of members of devalued groups. *Social Issues and Policy Review, 1*(1), 217–256.

Derks, B., van Laar, C., & Ellemers, N. (2009). Working for the self or working for the group: How personal and social self-affirmation promote self-improvement among members of devalued groups. *Journal of Personality and Social Psychology, 96*(1), 183–202.
DeviousDiva. (2007, January) *The Roma series.* http://deviousdiva.com/the-roma-series/. Accessed 9 July 2009.
European Court of Human Rights. (2008). *Sampanis v. Greece, application no. 32526/05.* Strasbourg: European Court of Human Rights.
European Union Monitoring and Advocacy Program (2007). *Equal Access to Quality Education for Roma, Volume1.* Budapest:open society Institute.
Fanon, F. (1967). *Black skin, white masks.* New York: Grove Press.
Fraser, A. (1992). *The gypsies.* Oxford: Blackwell.
Freire, P. (1970). *Pedagogy of the oppressed.* New York: Seabury Press.
Gaertner, S. L., & Dovidio, J. F. (2008). Addressing contemporary racism: The common ingroup identity model. *Nebraska Symposium on Motivation. Nebraska Symposium on Motivation, 53,* 111–133.
Gaines Jr., S. O., & Reed, E. S. (1995). Prejudice: From Allport to Dubois. *American Psychologist, 50*(2), 96–103.
Gerasimos, K. (2009, February 2). Greece: Doctor-role model for Roma says "the Third World is next door, in Aspropyrgos." *Eleftheros Typos,* http://www.e-tipos.com/newsitem?id=75693.
Goffman, E. (1986). *Stigma: Notes on the management of spoiled identity.* New York: Touchstone.
Greek Helsinki Monitor. (2009, April). Parallel summary report on Greece's compliance with the international convention on the elimination of all forms of racial discrimination. http://www2.ohchr.org/english/bodies/cerd/docs/ngos/GHM_Greece75.doc. Accessed 13 July 2009.
Guy, W. (2009). *Peer review—integrated program for the social inclusion of Roma, Greece. Discussion paper.* Vienna: OSB Consulting.
Hancock, I. F. (2002). *We are the Romani people.* Hertfordshire: University of Hertfordshire Press.
Hicks, J. W. (2004). Ethnicity, race and forensic psychiatry: Are we color-blind? *Journal of the American Academy of Psychiatry and Law, 32*(1), 22–33.
Igarashi, K. (2005). Support programmes for Roma children: Do they help promote exclusion? *Intercultural Education, 16*(5), 443–452.
International Helsinki Foundation. (2006, February 6). *Letter to Marietta Yannakou, minister of education on Roma placements in Aspropyrgos.* Athens: Greek Helsinki Watch.
Keil, C., Blau, D., Keil, A., & Feld, S. (2003). *Bright Balkan morning: Romani lives and the power of music in Greek Macedonia.* Somewhere: Wesleyan University Press.
Kende, A. (2000). The Hungary of otherness: The Roma (gypsies) of Hungary. *Journal of European Area Studies, 8*(2), 187–201.
Levinson, M. P. (2007). Literacy in English gypsy communities: Cultural capital manifested as negative assets. *American Educational Research Journal, 44*(1), 5–39.
Link, B. G., & Phelan, J. C. (2001). Conceptualizing stigma. *Annual Review of Sociology, 27,* 363–285.
Marushiakova, E., Popov, V., & Kenrick, D. (2001). *Gypsies in the Ottoman Empire: A contribution to the history of the Balkans.* Hertfordshire: University of Hertfordshire Press.
McDowell, B. (1970). *Gypsies: Wanderers of the world.* Washington: National Geographic Press.
Merry, M. S., & New, W. (2008). Constructing an authentic self: The challenges and promise of African-centered pedagogy. *American Journal of Education, 115,* 35–64.
New, W. S. (2004). Are you George Bush's brother? Fieldwork in a Greek school during the American war on Iraq. Paper presented at meeting of Canadian Anthropology Association/ Société Canadienne d'Anthropologie (CASCA).
Padilla, A. M. (2008). Social cognition, ethnic identity, and ethnic specific strategies for coping with threat due to prejudice and discrimination. *Nebraska Symposium on Motivation. Nebraska Symposium on Motivation, 53,* 7–42.
Petrokou, E., & Dimitrakopoulas, I. N. (2002). Racism and local authorities: The case of Roma in Nea Kios. *ANTIGONE.* Athens: RAXEN National Focal Point.
Petrova, D. (2003). The Roma: Between a myth and the future. *Social Research, 70*(1), 111–160.

Pryor, J. B., Reeder, G. D., Yeadon, C., & Hesson-McInnis, M. (2004). A dual process model of reactions to perceived stigma. *Journal of Personality and Social Psychology, 87*(4), 436–452.

Smart Richman, L., & Leary, M. R. (2009). Reactions to discrimination, stigmatization, ostracism, and other forms of interpersonal rejection: A multimotive model. *Psychological Review, 116*(2), 365–383.

Twenge, J. M., Catanese, K. R., & Baumeister, R. F. (2003). Social exclusion and the deconstructed state: Time perception, meaninglessness, lethargy, lack of emotion, and self-awareness. *Journal of Personality and Social Psychology, 85*(3), 409–423.

Zachos, D. (2006). Roma, egalitarianism and school integration: The case of Flampouro. *Journal for Critical Education Policy Studies, 4*(4), 1–28. www.jceps.com/?pageID=article&articleID=76.

Zachos, D. (2009). Citizenship, ethnicity and education in Modern Greece. *Journal of Modern Greek Studies, 27*(1), 131–155.

Chapter 41
Learning Difference in the Diaspora—Sharing Sacred Spaces

Georgina Tsolidis

Introduction

Hall reminds us that identification utilises "…resources from the past resources of history, language and culture in the process of becoming rather than being: not 'who we are' or 'where we came from', so much as what we might become, how we have been represented and how that bears on how we might represent ourselves" (Hall 1996, p. 4). The experiences of the grandchildren and great grandchildren of Greek immigrants to Australia are a means of exploring such becoming. Identification is relevant to the individual and who she/he may become but also intersects with the collective vision or social imaginary—the way national belonging is represented. Young Australians who muster personal resources that speak of other places and other times, illustrate the role of cultural difference within the social imaginary of Australianness.

Australianness is responsive to context, to perspective and to discourses that shape individuals. Through time and space we come to understand our communities and ourselves in particular ways. As policies related to immigration have shifted over time, the social imaginary of how Australianness is constituted has evolved also. Spatiality offers a useful frame for exploring diasporic Greekness and its potential to unpack the place of cultural difference in the Australian social imaginary. The Melbourne Shrine of Remembrance is examined as a space that at various times comes to represent divergent ways of being Australian. Thus young people through their schools, become the focus of pedagogies of belonging that are also public.

The Shrine is a focus because it is a significant marker of Australianness. It was built during the Great Depression to honour the ANZAC (Australian and New Zea-

---

This research was supported under Australian Research Council's Discovery Projects funding scheme (project DPO557512). The views expressed herein are those of the author and are not necessarily those of the Australian Research Council.

G. Tsolidis (✉)
School of Education, University of Ballarat, PO Box 663, Ballarat, VIC, 3353, Australia
e-mail: g.tsolidis@ballarat.edu.au

land Army Corps) soldiers who fell during the First World War. The ANZAC tradition began at Gallipoli and is linked to a national coming of age. April 25, 1915 was the first time Australian troops had participated in military action during the First World War with the aim of opening up the Dardanelles for the allied navies against fierce Ottoman opposition. Over 8,000 Australian soldiers fell in what became an 8-month campaign. Processions to the Shrine commemorate such events and include large numbers of students. The Shrine is also the destination for the Melbourne Greek community when it marks Greek National Day, which is linked to the struggle for independence against Ottoman rule. This occasion also involves large numbers of students through community-based schools established to teach Greek language and culture. Through such events young Australians are inducted into various and sometimes conflicting narratives of nation. Because of this, the Shrine is understood as a site where the social imaginary of Australianness can be explored in relation to absences and presences.

Spatiality

Foucault nominates space as the anxiety of our time. He argues that in the Middle Ages space was a critical social force. Spaces were established as a hierarchy with those places marked as close to the celestial considered sacred and those close to the ground considered profane. According to Foucault it was Galileo's discovery of infinitely open space that dramatically shifted Middle Age understandings. "…a thing's place was no longer anything but a point in its movement…" (Foucault 1986, p. 23). Nonetheless, our lived experience still reflects the sanctification of space through dichotomies such as private and public space, family and social space and leisure and work space. "All these are still nurtured by the hidden presence of the sacred" (Foucault 1986). Space is not understood as a vessel, empty and homogenous, waiting to be filled. Instead external space is constituted through heterogeneous sets of social relations that demark sites with various levels of significance.

Foucault delineates utopias and heterotopias. Utopias are sites with no real place in society; instead these are imagined or unreal spaces, often used to represent a perfected set of social relations. Heterotopias, on the other hand, are real sites fundamental to the way a culture represents itself and because of this include contested images simultaneously. Foucault likens heterotopias to mirrors because they reflect an image that is simultaneously real and illusory but are themselves material. Through the mirror we discover our absence from the place where we think we are. Heterotopias are capable of juxtaposing several, often incompatible spaces in the same real place.

"From the standpoint of the mirror I discover my absence from the place where I am since I see myself over there" (Foucault 1986, p. 24).

Foucault offers us a powerful way of understanding the role of the Melbourne Shrine of Remembrance. It is a sacred space that represents a set of social relations that link Australianness, through the ANZAC tradition to sacrifice for freedom, being loyal to allies, mateship and courage. It is also a heterotopia where diverse elements within society come to commemorate events that occurred in other places and other times. Thus the Shrine becomes a mirror that reflects the place of minorities in Australian society and by doing so also helps us to discover absences. For Australian minorities there is an absence from the place of origin and a metaphorical absence from their place of settlement.

Australianness—A Shifting Terrain

While attracting and accepting large numbers of non-British immigrants after the Second World War the immigration policy was underpinned by a clear understanding that 'Australian' had British underpinnings. When British immigrants failed to come in the desired numbers, despite incentives such as assisted passage schemes, the government diversified source countries. Nonetheless, a 'British type' was established using physical features and cultural compatibility against which other groups were measured. In this schema, immigrants from Italy, Greece and the former Yugoslavia, relative to those from Northern Europe, were simultaneously least desirable and imperative for the rapid industrialisation planned. (de Lepervanche and Bottomley 1988; Castles et al. 1988).

Initially, it was envisaged that all immigrant communities would assimilate into Australian society. The massive immigration programme was coupled with policies of assimilation and integration. Both policies, in more or less dramatic ways, emphasised the benefits of sameness. By the 1970s it became evident that some immigrant communities were becoming earmarked by their low incomes, poor housing, lack of English language skills and limited career opportunities. Inadequate and inappropriate services, including education, were recreating similar circumstances for the children of such immigrants. There was increasing concern about 'ethnic ghettos' forming particularly in Melbourne and Sydney. In the 1980s multiculturalism was developed as a response. This policy sought to provide support for minorities and some acknowledgement of the benefits of cultural difference. Multiculturalism has been critiqued for paying lip service to cultural difference, rather than challenging the British constitution of Australia (Jakubowicz 2002). Rather than precipitate real structural shifts, multiculturalism brought aspects of cultural difference to the fore that made minorities appear less threatening to xenophobic 'locals'.

Education was critical to multiculturalism. The children of immigrants were targeted as a means of creating social cohesion. Multicultural education policy was a highly contested discourse. Ethnic minority lobby groups sought the possibility of upward social mobility for the children of immigrants, including through programmes that rewarded skills such as mother tongue literacy. For conservative forces, it was anticipated that the children of immigrants could be better settled through programmes that aimed at assimilation while providing some acknowledgement of cultural difference (Tsolidis 2001, 2008a).

The notion of culture clash had framed the education of these migrant children. They faced the burden of having to reconcile their family values with those of mainstream society and education became pivotal in a framework that sought to compensate minorities for their 'un-Australianness'. The students, who are the focus of this paper, are the children of the generation who grew up being compensated for their parents' Greekness. Thus, these young people's experiences reflect the success or otherwise of policies related to national belonging and cultural difference. The Melbourne Greek community offers an interesting case-study of this post-war experience, having been earmarked as resistant to assimilation and more recently lauded as an example of successful integration. As a prominent diasporic community, their engagement with the Shrine of Remembrance as a sacred space will be considered as a means of considering cultural difference and Australianness more generally.

Background

The Melbourne Greek community was the focus of a study, the aim of which was to examine the ways in which young people come to represent themselves culturally (Tsolidis and Kostogriz 2005). Schooling and its engagement with processes of self-fashioning was a focus. The analysis presumed that space and time evoke a dynamism that mediates the social relations that nuance collective memories, lifestyle and aesthetic preferences, etc. This community was situated in a number of spaces intended to illustrate micro, messo and macro levels of spatiality, interrelationships between these and how they are mediated by power. Schools, families and individuals were considered in relation to each other as well as national and transnational contexts.

The study was conducted over a 3-year period through community-based schools or 'after hours schools' (Tsolidis and Kostogriz 2008). These operate outside normal school hours. Students engage with Greek language and culture in various ways and at different levels. In some cases, a relatively recently arrived community may involve volunteers with no teaching background to maintain Greek as a mother tongue. Other schools aim to keep young people connected to Greekness in relatively minor ways. In other instances, the school may be part of a large commercial venture, which employs trained teachers, including some from Greece to teach the great grandchildren of immigrants Greek as a second language. Many of these schools enable students to sit formal state-run examinations in their final years of schooling (Arvanitis 2000, 2004; Tsounis 1974). The schools selected for the study, operated in a variety of Melbourne suburbs and were attended by communities with various migration histories and socio-economic backgrounds.

I have argued elsewhere (Tsolidis 2008b) that the transient nature of 'after hours schools' does not allow research to be conducted in ways that are immediately recognisable. Such schools are constituted in borrowed spaces and as such are illusive. There are no filing cabinets. There is no staff room where teachers converge and discuss the day's events and there are no stockpiles of curriculum that mark shifts in pedagogy over time. Instead teachers see a shifting array of students for 2 or 3 hours each week. These students' knowledge of and interest in Greek language and culture is extremely varied. In this short period of time, teachers juggle the twin aims of teaching as much as possible, in ways recognised by parents as rigorous, and keeping the students relatively happy and entertained, a priority given they are doing extra school rather than sport or other recreational activities. In these environments, researchers are left to work in the crevices of a system already under duress.

The study was founded on the principle of reciprocity whereby a bilingual teacher of Greek was employed as part of the research team to conduct classes. Data were gathered by eliciting work from students. The teaching allowed us to collect data in a way that 'gave back' to the community and provided an authentic way of engaging with students on relevant issues. Issues of identity are explored commonly within the language curriculum and we were able to gain rich research data from how students described their identification. Teaching methods varied in response to the opportunities made available by schools, the type of curriculum already on offer and students' engagement with the issues being explored.

Students read texts, watched films, listened to music or read poetry and on this basis described their identification. They wrote essays reflecting on significant cultural markers in their lives. They put together portfolios that contained artefacts, which together represented how they saw themselves. Students included photographs, clothing labels, pictures from magazines of sporting and music heroes, words from songs or poems, etc. Students also held classroom discussions, which were audio-taped and transcribed. While the teaching and its outcomes varied in response to the type of school and existing curriculum imperatives, students' work nonetheless, relayed markers significant to their cultural identity. These student texts were analysed thematically and differences between schools and students were considered. The themes were constituted through understandings shared across the various groups of students—ways of representing their cultural experiences. Students, for example, used 'home' with reference to Greekness. 'Home' was not only where they were domiciled but also those forms of eating, speaking, smelling and listening they associated with being Greek, which also occurred in other people's homes and in Greece, where they did not live (Tsolidis and Pollard 2010). In addition, photographs were taken of spaces that were significant within Melbourne for their Greekness—streetscapes in specific suburbs, houses that looked from the outside like those described by students in their written work, particular shopping malls and community schools. These photographs were used to capture Greekness through spatiality. Photographs were taken of the annual procession to the Melbourne Shrine of Remembrance on Greece's National Day. These became a form of recording and representing the occasion by the researchers.

The research aimed to explore the relationship between spatiality and subjectivity and was framed by poststructuralist epistemologies that assume multiple truths and the significance of situationality —the idea that we capture a moment in time when we conduct an interview or observe a class. In addition, it was framed assuming the potential of research, including that which is non-traditional, to reinscribe privilege. This also includes the privilege implicit in the researcher's perspective and authorial power. Thus spatial–temporal possibilities foreshadow privilege not only through the repertoire of methods available to the researcher but also through interpretation and analysis. In this sense research that considers lived experience in the context of wider social processes and structures becomes a balancing act "…of being true to the lived and being aware of the commitments and limits of its 'truth'"(Saukko 2003, p. 56).

Educating Spaces

Spaces are not containers but instead a dynamic between social and material relations, characterised by power. This view of space takes into account the material and the social with enormous explanatory potential for education. Schools or classrooms are not seen as places within which teaching and learning is contained, but instead as part of the pedagogic dynamic whereby the material conditions influence the social relations and vice versa. McGregor (2004) comments that, rather than pre-given and timeless, we need to understand space as emergent, arising out of relations between individuals, including those who may not be present at a given time. Spatiality allows us to safeguard against reinstating a binary between space and time and simply reversing their order of significance (Usher 2002).

The Melbourne Shrine of Remembrance on Greek National Day is such an emergent space marked by dynamic relations between the material and the social, underpinned by complex power relations that mediate generations, ethnicities and mainstream and minority institutions including language, nation, schooling and collective memories of war. Those who have fallen in other countries fighting wars related to other times are not there but nonetheless, remain highly visible in a space earmarked as significant because it is dedicated to their memory. It is also a space that on this and other occasions constitutes a very public pedagogy of belonging. In this instance it is used by 'after hours schools' to show case how they connect young people to their Greekness.

The Shrine is a beginning point for exploring learning that occurs in spaces where cultural homogeneity remains contested. Melbourne is one of the most heterogeneous cities in Australia and has been at the heart of what is presented as successful multiculturalism. The Melbourne Greek community is one of the largest and most visible minorities with a strong identity, promulgated through various institutions including schools, media outlets, cultural and political associations and the Greek Orthodox Church. The march to the Shrine brings into focus how a space taken to be sacred because of its symbolic worth, also mediates a public pedagogy of belonging. In this instance, a public pedagogy related to difference and the possibility of democratic citizenship. The power relations that underpin this pedagogy are pronounced because they speak to contested views of nation. These relations are pronounced also, because they are played out through young people brought into this space by schools concerned to induct them into cultural ways of being that are reminiscent of other times and places. So while the sacred space speaks uniformly to nation, war and the 'unknown soldier', it is also a space wherein the discursive construction of these concepts remains contested.

The Shrine of Remembrance—A Sacred Space

Sacred spaces are spaces set aside for their spiritual power, commemorative features or representative significance. The Melbourne Shrine of Remembrance has immense significance. It is physically imposing and, dominates the skyline. Recently, the Victorian Planning Minister refused a building permit for a development because its height threatened to overshadow the Shrine (Premier of Victoria 2009). It is surrounded by gardens with a long and wide path leading to a series of steps that focus attention on the entrance. The eternal flame burns in a cauldron in the forecourt. The building is fashioned after the tomb built for King Mausolus of Caria, one of the seven wonders of the world. It combines the Doric columns of a Greek temple with a stepped pyramid roof. Built to commemorate those who fell during the First World War, it was opened in 1934. It was financed primarily through public donation; particularly noteworthy given this occurred during the 1920s, a period of high unemployment (Shrine of Remembrance n.d.).

It is one of the most symbolically enriched buildings in the city and serves to focus attention on the ANZAC legacy and its importance within the Australian national imaginary. It becomes the site for commemorations, notably Remembrance Day. There is growing participation by young people, who mark the contribution of Australian service men and women including those within their families. Many come wearing school uniform and medals awarded to deceased relatives. This is part of the ANZAC revival, a renewed interest in the ANZAC tradition as a way of marking Australianness.

ANZAC and the National Imaginary

The ANZAC legend is represented as the coming of age of Australian national character when, distilled with reference to mateship, sacrifice and honour, through the dramatic loss of life during the First World War (Brett 2004; McKenna 2006). Rather than fade with the passing of veterans, this tradition has been revived. Each year, larger numbers of young people commemorate the fallen, including school students at the Dawn Service at the Shrine.

This ANZAC revival has been debated, because of its possible manipulation by politicians in their efforts to nuance the national imaginary (Ball 2004; Manne 2007; Cranitch 2008). The respective roles of former Prime Ministers Keating and Howard are noteworthy. For Keating, the priority was establishing a sense of Australia as independent from Britain and with a clear sense of its place in the Asia Pacific region. For Howard, the priority was maintaining Australia's traditional attachment to Britain—a harking back to the Menzies's era when national identity remained uninterrupted by apologies to the indigenous peoples and multiculturalism. Keating and Howard promulgated divergent views of Australian national identity and while both honoured the sacrifices of Australian service men and women, the image of Keating bending to kiss the soil at the Kakoda Track is a significant gesture that points to war efforts that by comparison to Gallipoli, are removed from the service of King and Empire.

The ANZAC revival has associations with a conservative government and its attempts to rekindle a sense of Australia reminiscent of the 1950s when being White and British remained relatively uncomplicated by cosmopolitanism. At the time, this sense of Australianness was coupled with a deferential coupling to the United States in its war on terror; an increasingly exclusive immigration policy which included placing refugee families behind razor wire in detention centres; a steadfast refusal to apologise for the treatment of indigenous peoples, including the forced removal of children from their families; and a preference for narrow forms of citizenship (including through testing), over multiculturalism. This was an unselfconscious advocacy for a national narrative that many saw as regressive and divisive.

While the ANZAC revival on its own, may not be seen as a harbinger of narrow and xenophobic interpretations of national identity, in the context of such policy shifts it is less benign. This period was marked by the 'culture wars', the 'war on terror' and the infamous Cronulla riots (Poynting 2006). These riots involved youth identified as Muslim or Arabic and those represented as Australian in violent confrontation over the Australian way of life. Many of those opposed to immigration draped themselves in the Australian flag. Senior members of Government went into the public arena with comments about 'mushy multiculturalism' and argued that those who did not respect Australian values were not welcome in the country.

Unsurprisingly, the values identified as Australian became a matter of debate. There were strong statements from the Government that marked Australian values in relation to mateship, which in turn was linked to the ANZAC tradition. So strong was the ANZAC story line within this hegemonic representation of Australianness that when the then Government of Australia issued a national statement on the teaching of values to all Australian schools, the document cover featured a representation of Simpson and the donkey. This is a story of heroism that has become emblematic of the battle at Gallipoli. Simpson remained unarmed but confronted enemy fire in order to carry the injured back on his donkey. He died after only weeks of service and has become a metaphor for values heralded as particularly Australian and worthy of emulation (Tsolidis 2010).

The election of the Rudd Labour Government in 2007 became an opportunity for a review of how Australianness was projected. The Rudd Government was quick to act with reference to the long-awaited apology for the forced removal of Aboriginal children from their families. However, it has been less enthusiastic about overturning the Howard Government's removal of 'multiculturalism' from the national policy lexicon and returning to a more Keating-esque view of the significance of the ANZAC legacy. In 2008 Keating revived this debate by describing the view that

Australian nationhood was born or redeemed at Gallipoli as; "An utter and complete nonsense". Instead, he argued that Gallipoli was shocking for Australia and its representation remains marked by the ambivalence that surrounds Australia's view of itself. (Keating 2008) Rudd chose to publically distance himself from Keating's comments. Instead he stated; "That [Gallipoli] is part of our national consciousness. It's part of our national psyche, it is part of national identity" (Rudd 2008). Further to this, the Prime Minister claimed that this was in keeping with how 'ordinary Australians' understood the significance of ANZAC.

The Place of the Ordinary

The place of the 'ordinary' in the manufacturing of a national imaginary cannot be taken for granted, particularly in Australia where egalitarianism is presented as core business to its nature. Politicians lay personal claim to being ordinary regardless of political affiliations. As a conservative, Howard argued his lower middle class roots as 'ordinary'. Ironically the Labour Prime Minister Keating, who grew up in ordinary circumstances has been satirised because of his collection of French antique clocks, his passion for designer suits and his obscure musical tastes (Company B and Casey Bennetto 2007). Gregg (2007) makes the point that 'ordinary' is commonly used as a corrective to 'elite', which in political discourses remains connected to the intellectual—those who inhabit cafes and wine bars and are generally out of touch with the common person. Gregg considers that 'ordinary' is also readily juxtaposed to other categories such as the politically correct, those concerned with environmentalism and the Muslim, who becomes a euphemism for those who resist assimilation.

Greek National Day as Less Ordinary

Greece marks its National Day by commemorating the rise against Ottoman Rule on 25 March 1821. In Melbourne, this is marked with a procession to the Shrine of Remembrance. The procession captures elements critical to the Melbourne Greek community and is welcomed by dignitaries, including key political, community and church leaders. The welcoming party includes the Premier of Victoria, other Ministers and members of the Victorian and national Government with relevant portfolios or those who have a link to Greece through birthright, leaders of the Victorian Greek community and representatives of the Greek Government. The procession includes folkloric, philanthropic, sporting and cultural groups and fraternities formed to support those who emigrated from Greece. It also includes the Cypriot community, which marches under its national flag. Members of the army and police force with Greek heritage are part of the procession.

However, schools feature most obviously. Five-year-olds through to 18-year-olds march behind banners stating the name of the school they attend. Teachers accompany them and in most cases these students wear uniforms or costumes that denote Greekness in some way—allusions to classicism and national or regional costume. There is both a sense of celebration and solemnity as the students file past the dignitaries and lay wreaths at the eternal flame. Police officers from the 24-hour guard for the Shrine, carry a bayonet and wear the uniform of the Australian Light Horsemen who have a strong association with the ANZAC legend (The Shrine of Remembrance n.d.). The visual pastiche that is created by young people wearing colourful costumes alongside khaki-clad guards is evocative. The students are surrounded by excited parents who photograph them as they move through the sacred space to the sound of marching drums and chatter. In contrast the men who guard the Shrine are similar to each other in age and height, monochromatic, standing solemnly and silently in a manner that makes them almost blend into the stone of the Shrine's structure. These students and soldiers share the same sacred space yet their presence marks different collective memories, reminiscent of other times and places. And it is the sharing of this space that bespeaks a new narrative of contested belonging.

This contested belonging was played out most dramatically, with an incident that developed between the custodians of the Shrine and the Greek community in 2005. The Custodians suggested that the annual National Day March was being conducted inappropriately and that the Greek community needed to meet established guidelines. The Australian national flag had to be incorporated, speeches needed to be translated into English and all flags needed to be dipped as these were moved past the Cenotaph. These requirements were represented as universal to all those who entered the sacred space by the Custodians and peculiar to the Greek community by some of its members. These views became emblematic of a sense of Australianness that made the sacred space exclusive of those whose affiliations did not coincide with the hegemonic. The Greek flag was unwelcome, minority memories were unwelcome and the expression of these in languages other than English was unwelcome. The Greek community was given the choice of entering this space on these conditions or not entering the space. They chose to march to the site behind the Greek national flag and not contest the right to enter the space marked as sacred. Instead hundreds of people milled around on the footpaths at the bottom of the hill rather than progress up the path to the Shrine, which by design was intended to be reminiscent of Greek democracy—all in all, a somewhat ironic conflation of events in the eyes of some. Attendant to this view was the argument that Greeks had lost lives defending Australian soldiers in Greece and vice versa and the Shrine Trustees needed to be mindful of such strong wartime partnerships (Kalimniou 2005). According to one Shrine official (personal telephone conversation, 13 July 2009) 'trouble with the Greeks' was recurring and the events of 2005 were noteworthy only because these had been sensationalised in the press. This Official noted that all ceremonies held at the Shrine needed to meet the same requirements and the Greek community regularly flaunted these, particularly the need to dip flags and translate speeches. He noted that it was common for a speech that took up to 15 minutes in Greek to be accompanied by a 3-minute English translation.

The annual National Day March most often proceeds without incident. However, the 2005 controversy illustrated that the taken-for-granted assumptions about this sacred space demark it as Australian in particular ways. There is no questioning of the assumption that English language and the Australian flag are requisite. Why does it remain unthinkable that a Shrine honouring the unknown soldier cannot accommodate those soldiers commemorated by communities with affiliations to other times, places and languages? Why are such memories marked as alien? Instead a link is developed between those with affiliations to other countries and un-Australianness. This incident while quite benign, brings into view starkly, the complexities that surround nationhood and belonging. Given the Australian flag itself incorporates the flag of another country (United Kingdom), this is not so much a battle over affiliations with somewhere else, but more about the power relations that underpin a vision of which affiliations matter. It is also about the transience of such matters—what matters to whom, when and why. And importantly, it illustrates how sharing sites marked as sacred, can become a dynamic public pedagogy of belonging for young people is spaces marked by cultural heterogeneity.

Being the Same and from Somewhere Else

Interest in spatiality has increased in the context of globalisation. The significance of place, particularly with regard to nation, has been diminished by arguments that the movement of capital, people and culture (Robertson 1996; Soja 1989; Usher 2002) have created an unprecedented blurring of boundaries and destabilised the link between ethnicity and nation. Regardless of whether the basis for ethnic identification is language, religion, skin colour or kinship, instead of being contained within defined parameters, ethnicity has "...become a global force forever slipping through the cracks between states and borders" (Appadurai 1996, p. 41). Ethnicity becomes a basis on which a group of people identify, regardless of locality. There is also the sense that while not delineated by place, ethnicity draws on time as a means of denoting difference. In the case of the soldiers and students who share the Shrine as sacred space, identification captures events that occurred in a distant past, that nonetheless remain cultural resources that can be reworked to conjure a sense of community. So it is that young Australians travel to Gallipoli in order to define their sense of Australianness and other young people march to the Melbourne Shrine of Remembrance in order to embrace that element of their personal history that is Greek. And in both cases, this identification is anchored to the gravitas of distant wars and shameful loss of life. The links between spaces, collective memories and identification can be somewhat counter-intuitive. In the case of the ANZAC revival, ambivalence of belonging is played out with regard to relations with Britain and Australia's sense of place within the Asia Pacific region. In the case of Greek National Day commemorations, there is an ambivalence of belonging played out vis-a-vis Greece and Australia—broadening the definition of 'Australian' through a link with a place long left behind. Both cases are marked by unequal power relations and linked to ethnic identifications initiated by 'retrospective affiliations'. An aim here, is to explore how such 'retrospective affiliations' grind up against each other and in so doing tell another story about Australian society. In Australia, the national imaginary remains ambivalent regarding the significance of cultural difference—on the one hand, Australia is represented as a nation of immigrants and is characterised by its success as a multicultural experiment; on the other hand, there has been an entrenched resistance against understanding Australia as other than a British bastion in south east Asia (Hage 1998). Because of this, minority identification has been forged through nostalgic yearnings for places left behind, as well as strident resistance to xenophobia.

Appadurai nominates the tension between homogeneity and heterogeneity as the primary characteristic of cultural globalisation and argues that while culture may be global it is not necessarily homogenised. Instead he states:

> Thus the central feature of global culture today is the politics of the mutual effort of sameness and difference to cannibalize one another and thereby proclaim their successful hijacking of the twin Enlightenment ideas of the triumphantly universal and the resiliently particular. (Appadurai 1996, p. 43)

Appadurai's depiction of sameness and difference cannibalising one another arguably applies to diasporic identifications such as those of interest here. The Melbourne Greek community is one of the largest in the world and over many generations has established a visibility through schools, churches, media, sporting clubs and specific spaces earmarked as Greek. In Australia these institutions are marked as different by virtue of their apparent Greekness and their form of Greekness is different to that experienced in Greece. Yet such institutions share a sameness with other spaces marked as somehow Greek in other parts of the world where large numbers of emigrants from Greece have settled (Tsolidis 2009). This cannibalism between sameness and difference can be illustrated also through contestatory views on how national identity is represented in countries such as Australia, where there is a strong historic link to migration. The procession to the Melbourne Shrine of Remembrance illustrates how particularism and universalism lock horns through nationhood and belonging. On one level, the Shrine of Remembrance remains a monument to sameness—a space that marks Australia as white, masculine and linked to Britain. This view of belonging is fractured through the entry of foreign flags, foreign histories and 'foreigners' who insist that their legacies are somehow Australian also.

Public Pedagogies of Diasporic Becoming

The central role of students in commemorations at the Shrine of Remembrance illustrates how such spaces are critical to public pedagogies of belonging. Students are brought to this space by schools to remember wars and their forebears' contribution. They march to remember the ANZAC tradition and the Greek struggle for independence. No doubt some students would be involved in both marches, including as survivors of soldiers who fought in places such as Crete, earmarked as significant in bringing Greeks and Australians together during the Second World War (Kape 2009; Kyritsis 2009). For young people with connections to the Melbourne Greek community, such marches illustrate diasporic becoming and the power relations that mark such identifications under conditions of cultural heterogeneity. This is an experience of social learning from the margins.

Giroux reminds us that an element of politics "…focuses on where politics happens, how proliferating sites of pedagogy bring into being new forms of resistance, raise new questions, and necessitate alternative visions regarding autonomy and the possibility of democracy itself" (Giroux 2004, p. 74). He argues that pedagogical sites have proliferated with the advent of neo-liberalism and many of these sites are constituted in the public domain, relevant to, but often ignored by cultural studies (Giroux 2003). Sports and entertainment and the associated media, technology and advertising are public pedagogies that need to be politicised. I have argued elsewhere how this argument applies to events such as the Olympics or the Commonwealth Games and how these become public pedagogies of belonging. Similarly, it is possible to conceive of the Shrine as a pedagogical site. This is a space with symbolic worth 'where politics happens'. For Giroux, culture is the medium through which people come to understand power and begin to mediate its exercise through the dialogical relations between the private or individual and the public or collective, framed by larger social conditions. Such processes of socially ameliorated agency facilitate identification because the pedagogical function of culture is central to democracy as it shapes our assimilation and our resistance to dominant ways of understanding.

Giroux draws on Castoriadis (1997) who argues that the normative role of pedagogy is a contradictory one. One aim is to develop the learner's capacity for independent learning and reflexivity. The goal is to teach the capacity to learn and anything else that may be taught along the way should be incidental to this aim. Paradoxically, the other pedagogical aim is to induct the individual into existing institutional practices such as language, family and values. This is instruction in conformity. However, Castoriadis argues that institutions are fabrications of a collective imaginary and as such are how the collectivity represents itself. Nonetheless, once conjured, these institutions take on the sense of being pre-given, fixed and self-perpetuating. Rather than maintain their power through coercion they are powerful because individuals participate in their fabrication and pedagogy is instrumental to this process. Pedagogy has the paradoxical task of producing autonomous subjects, who nonetheless internalise existing institutions. Castoriadis argues that the capacity for independent thinking and reflection is the way of addressing this paradox and the similar paradox of politics, which he names the impossibility of politics, that is, democracy's dependence on democratic individuals and vice versa. It is the task of pedagogy to protect democracy by creating independent and reflective thinkers who can function internal to institutions.

The cultural politics of education are manifest in debates about the formal curriculum and its relationship, particularly to state-administered assessment and entry into higher education. Pedagogies linked to culture that is performed in public spaces is less scrutinised. Yet the public pedagogies performed in spaces such as the Shrine of Remembrance, have enormous cultural and therefore pedagogic worth. This is illustrated by the convention of bringing groups of young people to such spaces and drawing lessons for them formally, through the development of specific tutorials and curriculum materials (The Shrine of Remembrance). Importantly also is the significance given to their participation at events in such spaces. Each year, the media celebrates the involvement of young people at commemorative services at the Shrine of Remembrance. Mainstream media will interview young uniformed students about the ANZAC tradition and what it means to them as they participate in related wreath-laying services. Similarly, the Australian Greek media will feature the young people who march to the Shrine to mark Greece's National Day. Such occasions are developed into complex sets of social relations that mark the space as networked between generations, ethnicities, nations, collective memories of wars as these are played out through young people's induction into a social imaginary linked to Australianness.

Drawing on the arguments made by Giroux and Castoriadis, the Shrine of Remembrance is understood here as a pedagogic space that engages with democracy and provides powerful lessons to young people about the nation as an institution, its character as heterogeneous or otherwise and the possibilities available to them to cultivate a sense of belonging as minority youth and the basis on which this can be done. The marches to the Shrine perform significant cultural labour. This sacred space carries the burden of a national imaginary linked to the competing goals of valuing and de-valuing difference. Through the relatively benign example of whether the Greek National Day March can occupy this space, students learn that an aspect of their identity is seemingly under erasure and at risk of being denied legitimacy by authorities who are taken to speak for those who have paid the ultimate sacrifice for their nation. Yet through this relatively minor skirmish, ostensibly over flags and translations, lurks a fundamental rupture between those who understand nation as a space wherein social relations build heterogeneity and those who seek to construct nation as homogeneous, bounded by perimeters that require policing and where entry is conditional on leaving aspects of self, deemed incompatible, outside. Importantly, also young people learn a lesson in 'double speak' as Australia, and the Greek community specifically, are paraded as evidence of successful multiculturalism, yet the imperative to perform a narrow rendition of 'Australian' is simultaneously promulgated.

Conclusion

In neo-liberal times, Giroux nominates as the most important task of progressive education that of creating the "…conditions for students to address how knowledge is related to the power of both self-definition and social agency" (Giroux 2003,

p. 11). With regard to young people whose self-definition mediates other places and other times through the lived experience of a now that is laced with racism and xenophobia, there is a temptation to draw on essentialism in a politics of identity. For the young people who are the focus in this paper, consolidating an identity as either Greek or Australian can appear an easier option, particularly when various forms of schooling and public pedagogies of belonging work to compound rather than complicate ethnic boundaries and therefore binaries. As educators we need to assist students to "...refuse the 'comfortable' discourses of essentialism and separatism" (Giroux 2003, p. 77). Instead young people's capacity for active citizenship on the basis of belonging needs to be acknowledged and developed. In Australia belonging is inextricably linked to migration and policies of settlement including multiculturalism. Giroux argues that living a radical form of multicultural citizenship assumes young peoples' capacity to understand their everyday experience through the range of social injustices that are expressed through institutional practices. He argues that as part of this process educators must acknowledge the learning that takes place in public spaces outside school. Here the Melbourne Shrine of Remembrance is understood as a sacred space within which ethnic minority youth reconcile subjectivity through contested discourses of belonging. It becomes the mirror through which we discover our absence from the place where we think we are.

Its physical structure, location, the means by which it was built and its designated task of remembering the fallen in what is understood as the defence of democracy, gives the Shrine enormous symbolic significance. It is strongly aligned to the ANZAC tradition, which in turn is linked to Australian nationhood in socially dramatic, albeit contested, ways. The narrative of nationhood linked to the ANZAC tradition continues to resonate, enjoying what has been described as a revival. It holds a specific place in debates about Australianness as is illustrated by recent statements made by Prime Ministers and former Prime Ministers. These leach into the education arena, including through policy such as the National Statement of Values where the ANZAC spirit is taken to symbolise the Australian ethos of 'mateship' represented as a core value that should be learnt by students (DEST 2005).

That the Shrine has become the preferred space for a diasporic community to represent a collective memory of other times, other places and other wars reinforces the site's significance as a cultural marker. Yet the social relations that mark the space as significant also lay bare the contradictory discourses that constitute Australianness. This is evident in the controversy between the Trustees of the Shrine and the Greek community over protocols for processions. The requirement that all speeches be translated in full and the need for the Australian flag to be included on all occasions can be interpreted as a prescribed homogeneity. The response of disciplining minorities seeking to use the space in non-hegemonic ways illustrates the role of cultural difference in the shifting and often contradictory representations of nationhood, including with reference to the status of minority communities. The Greek community, which can be troublesome, is also held up as exemplar of successful multiculturalism by a Prime Minister concerned with the capacity of minorities to integrate.

Social relations constitute spaces in dynamic and responsive ways. These are relations that include those who may not be there. These relations are mediated by power. In the sacred space constituted around the Melbourne Shrine of Remembrance, the fallen are drawn upon to provide meaning to the institution of nation. In the case of the Greek community they remember those who fought against Ottoman Rule. In the case of the ANZAC tradition, Australian troops rallied in what was understood as a defence of democracy, spearheaded by Britain which was owed a strong allegiance. In both cases, young people are inducted through their schooling, into the cultural significance of these events. These constitute public pedagogies of belonging and for diasporic youth they also instruct on belonging and the terms on which this is made possible.

References

Appadurai, A. (1996). *Modernity at large: Cultural dimensions of globalization*, Minneapolis: University of Minnesota Press.
Arvanitis, E. (2000). *Greek ethnic schools in transition: Policy and practice in Australia in the late 1990s.* Unpublished PhD thesis, RMIT University, Victoria.
Arvanitis, E. (2004). *Greek ethnic schools In Australia in the late 1990s: Selected case studies, on-line monograph.* Melbourne: RMIT.
Australian Government Department of Education, Science and Training. (2005). *National framework for values education in Australian schools*, Canberra: Department of Communications, Information Technology and the Arts.
Australian War Memorial. http://www.awm.gov.au/commemoration/anzac/anzac_tradition.asp. Accessed 11 Nov 2009.
Ball, M. (2004). What the Anzac Revival means? *The Age Newspaper*, April 24, http://www.theage.com.au/articles/2004/23/108261632741. Accessed 15 July 2004.
Brett, J. (2004). The Howard Era—In retrospect border control? *Australian University Review 46*(2), 3–8.
Castles, S., et al. (1988). Mistaken Identity : Multiculturalism and the demise of nationalism in Australia. Sydney: Pluto Press.
Castoriadis, C. (1997). *World in fragments: Writings on politics, society, psychoanalysis, and the imagination*, Stanford: Stanford University Press.
Company B Original Casting Recording and Cassey Benenetto. (2007). *Keating!*
Cranitch, T. (2008). ANZAC a 'politically pliable' legend, *Eureka Street*, http://www.eurekastreet.com.au/article.aspx?aeid=68.36. Accessed 25 July 2009.
de Lepervanche, M. and G. Bottomley. (Eds.) (1988). *The cultural construction of race*, Annandale: Sydney Association for Studies in Society and Culture, No. 4.
DEST. (2005). *National Framework for Values Education in Australian Schools*, Commonwealth of Australia, Canberra.
Foucault, M. (1986). Of other spaces. *Diacritics, 16*(10), 22–27.
Giroux, H. (1996). *Living dangerously—Multiculturalism and the politics of difference.* New York: Lang.
Giroux, H. (2003). Public pedagogy and the politics of resistance: Notes on a critical theory of educational struggle. *Educational Philosophy and Theory, 35*(1), 5–16.
Giroux, H. (2004). Cultural studies and the politics of public pedagogy: Making the political more pedagogical. *Parallax, 10*(2), 73–89.
Gregg, M. (2007). The importance of being ordinary. *International Journal of Cultural Studies, 10*, 95–104.
Hage, G. (1998). *White nation: Fantasies of white supremacy in a multicultural society.* Sydney: Pluto/Comerford and Miller.

Hall, S. (1996). Who needs identity? In S. Hall & P. Du Gay, P. (Eds.), *Questions of cultural identity* (pp. 1–17). London: Sage.

Jakubowicz, A. (2002). *White noise: Australia's struggle with multiculturalism, working through whiteness: International perspectives* (pp. 107–125). New York: State University of New York.

Kalimniou, D. (2005, April 11). Hugh Gilchrist: Australians and Greeks. *Neos Kosmos*, p. 14.

Kape, F. (2009, April 27). Greeks and ANZACS: Allies and brothers. *Neos Kosmos*. http://neoskosmos.com/news/en/node/874. Accessed 31 July 2009.

Keating, P. (2008, October 31). Paul Keating's speech. *The Age Newspaper.* http://www.theage.com.au/national/paul-keatings-speech-20081031-5f1h.html. Accessed 19 March 2009.

Kyritsis, S. (2009, April 20). Greek RSL on ANZAC Day. *Neos Kosmos*. http://neoskosmos.com/news/en/node/833. Accessed 30 July 2009.

Manne, R. (2007, April 25). The myth that made us. *The Age Newspaper.* http://www.theage.com.au/news/robert-manne/the-war-myth-that-made-us/2007/04/24/1177180648069.html?page=2. Accessed 19 March 2009.

McGregor, J. (2004). Spatiality and the place of the material in schools. *Pedagogy, Culture and Society, 1*(3), 347–372.

McKenna, M. (2006, June 6). The patriot act. *The Australian Newspaper.* http://www.theaustralian.news.com.au/story/02086721813244-25132,00.html. Accessed 23 March 2009.

Poynting, S. (2006). What caused the Cronulla riot? *Race and Class, 48*(1), 85–92.

Robertson, R. (1996). *Globalization: Social Theory and Global Culture*, London:Sage Publications.

Rudd, K. (2008, October 31). Keating wrong on Anzac pride—Rudd, *Daily Telegraph*. http://www.dailytelegraph.com.au/news/national/keating-wrong-on-anzac-pride-rudd/story-e6freuzr-1111117909410. Accessed 29 July 2009.

Saukko, P. (2003). Doing research in cultural studies. London and Thousand Oaks: Sage.

Shrine of Remembrance (n.d.). Education program background information. http://www.shrine.org.au/content.asp?Document_ID=1415. Accessed 30 July 2009.

Soja, E. (1989). *Postmodern geographies: The reassertion of space in critical social theory*, London: Verso.

The Premier of Victoria Media Releases, From the Minister for Planning, Brumby Labour Government Acts to Protect the Shrine. (2009, June 23). http://www.premier.vic.gov.au/minister-for-planning/brumby-labor-government-acts-to-protect-shrine.html. Accessed 30 July 2009.

Tsolidis, G. (2001). *Schooling, diaspora and gender, being feminist and being different*. Buckingham: Open University Press.

Tsolidis, G. (2008a). Australian multicultural education: Revisiting and resuscitating. In G. Wan, (Ed.), *The education of diverse populations: A global* perspective (pp. 209–225). Netherlands: Springer.

Tsolidis, G. (2008b). The (im)possibility of post-modern ethnography: Researching diasporic identities in spaces not included. *Ethnography and Education, 3*(3), 271–282.

Tsolidis, G. (2009). Living diaspora 'back home': Daughters of Greek emigrants living in Greece. In E. Tsatsoglu (Ed.), *En/gendering Greek diaspora communities: Work, community and identity in the Greek diaspora*. New York: Mellen.

Tsolidis, G. (2010). Simpson, his donkey and the rest of us: Public pedagogies of the value of belonging. *Educational Philosophy and Theory, 42*(4), 448–461.

Tsolidis, G., & Kostogriz, A. (2005). ARC discovery grant: Transcultural literacies—diaspora, identity and schooling (DPO557512).

Tsolidis, G., & Kostogriz A. (2008). 'After hours' schools as core to the spatial politics of in-betweeness. *Race Ethnicity and Education, 11*(3), 319–326.

Tsolidis, G., & Pollard, V. (2010). Home space:Youthful identification in the diaspora. *Diaspora, Indigenous, and Minority Education: An International Journal, 4*(3), 147–161.

Tsounis, M. (1974). *Greek ethnic schools in Australia*. Canberra: Australian National University.

Usher, R. (2002). Putting space back on the map: Globalisation, place and identity. *Educational Philosophy and Theory, 34*(1), 41–55.

Chapter 42
Deciphering Somali Immigrant Adolescents' Navigation and Interpretation of Resources Embedded in Social Relationships

Moosung Lee and Na'im Madyun

Introduction

Does the presence of social resources embedded in social networks always lead immigrant youth to succeed academically? Recent research equipped with a social capital perspective has revealed the positive mechanism of social relationships promoting academic success for some of the least advantaged immigrant students in the United States. (see Gandara 1995; Portes and Fernandez-Kelly 2006; Stanton-Salazar 1997). Such research has revealed how social capital (i.e., resources embedded in social networks that convey sets of values such as norms, trust, and reciprocity) is generated and why social capital plays a key role in academic success. With these recent research findings of social capital effects, there have been numerous policy interventions and school–community efforts initiated to provide supportive social networks (e.g., smaller learning communities, mentoring programs, and school–family partnerships).

However, it has been found that some minority students engage in the networks and others do not. Current social capital research explains this behavior by arguing that students differentially appropriate social capital due to the conditioning of their racial and class categories, i.e., White middle-class students tend to possess more social capital and utilize social capital better than students of color from poor working-class backgrounds. This social capital explanation seems valid, but how do we explain the behavior of students within the same racial and class categories (e.g., African immigrant working-class) that possess similarly good networks yet utilize the resources embedded in those networks dissimilarly from their peers for their

M. Lee (✉)
Educational Policy and Leadership, Hong Kong Institute of Education, 42-1F-D4,
10 Lo Ping Rd. Tai Po, Hong Kong
e-mail: mslee@ied.edu.hk

N. Madyun
Postsecondary Teaching and Learning, University of Minnesota-Twin Cities, 206 Burton Hall,
Minneapolis, MN, USA
e-mail: madyu002@umn.edu

academic success? This suggests that neither the magnitude nor the consistency of social capital effects on the least advantaged students in education is clear despite several systematic studies on poor immigrant students' academic success.

Again, the critical question is 'why' do some disadvantaged ethnic minority immigrant students utilize social capital as latent opportunity structures embedded in their family, school, and community where their academic paths are conditioned, while other peers situated in similar social conditions do not? In fact, this 'why' question is based on an unexpected, emerging finding from our ongoing social network analysis of Somali immigrant adolescents in the United States. We found that even though some low-achieving Somali students were embedded in similarly large networks from which high-achieving Somali students actively drew resources, they did not fully utilize their large networks and therefore possessed less social capital.

To further investigate this unexpected finding in this study we placed stress on revealing (1) how differently Somali immigrant students navigate resources embedded in their similarly large networks and (2) how dissimilarly Somali immigrant students interpret meanings from their social networks. By exploring the Somali immigrant youth's navigations and interpretations of their social relationships, we aimed to provide more nuanced findings and implications for existing social capital research of immigrant youth that might explain divergent academic paths from similar beginnings.

Literature Review

Social Capital and Educational Experiences and Outcomes of Poor Immigrant Adolescents

Social capital refers to resources embedded in our social relationships, which are utilized for desirable, democratic intentions. Consistent with the positive feature of social capital,[1] Dika and Singh (2002) crystallized three consistent findings of social capital in association with educational outcomes. First, social capital has a positive association with educational attainment such as reducing dropout rates and increasing college enrollment. Second, social capital has a positive effect on academic achievement, increasing standardized test scores. Third, social capital is positively linked to psychological factors which have been predictive of educational outcomes such as educational aspirations.

Considering social capital has certain positive social functions derived from our social structures, the consistent research findings are not surprising (Lee 2010). Therefore, at this point, a more critical question is: Is social capital similarly helpful for the educational experiences and outcomes of poor immigrant adolescents who by definition might have dissimilar social structures? Researchers have argued that

---

[1] It is fair to say that there is a dark side to social capital. For example, Sampson et al. (1999) argue, "social capital can be drawn upon for negative as well as positive goals" (p. 636). Those interests can be democratic or perverse.

there exists a different mechanism for generating social capital by class. Diamond and Gomez (2004, p. 421) have reported that "parents' involvement orientations are informed by their backgrounds (e.g., their social class, race, and prior educational experience)." They identified that middle-class parents tend to be more actively involved with school matters than are working-class parents. Lareau (1989) has shown that middle-class parents, in comparison to working-class parents, better understand the value of school, and thus are more likely to intervene in school matters in order to secure for their children the benefits of school (cited in Dumais 2002). Class becomes important because it plays a key role in shaping the type and degree of parental involvement, and parental involvement is a major form of social capital generation in schooling (Horvat et al. 2003). The degree of parental involvement has also been tied to the achievement motivation of students in general (Goodenow and Grady 1993) and for certain immigrant populations of color (Ibanez et. al. 2003). Not only does parental involvement influence achievement motivation, but in a slightly broader context, the quality of the social relationships and the perception of social support surrounding the student also influences academic motivation (Ahmed et al. in press). In middle-class neighborhoods, social support, positive role models, and higher parental involvement are more likely to be present than in poorer neighborhoods thus producing more social capital to increase the achievement motivation and eventual academic outcomes of the youth. According to Harrington and Boardman (1997), the middle class is even more likely to possess a redundancy of social capital that can compensate for a lack of family social capital by connecting individuals to other resourceful people or institutions (cited in Dumais 2002).

However, do all these findings enable us to posit that the middle-class family always has more social capital than the working-class family? Devine's (2004) recent work provides a more comprehensive picture of the existing research. Her research shows that the working class as well as the middle class possesses substantial social capital, connoting that social capital is not a "zero-sum game" between the two classes (cited in Apple 2006, p. 458). This adds to the importance of exploring social capital with disadvantaged groups. Ethnic minorities residing in poor urban areas have limited socioeconomic resources in their communities, yet they sometimes form social capital (bonding) through ethnic enclaves by uniting limited resources when faced with serious neighborhood disadvantages (e.g., high poverty and crime). Recent research supports this. Bankston (2004) explained how ethnicity comes to play as social capital among some Southeast Asian immigrants. Social disadvantage facing many immigrants sometimes ironically encourages them to mobilize possible socio-economic resources within their ethnicity networks (Madyun and Lee 2010a). Rankin and Quane (2000) also found a positive link between neighborhood poverty and community involvement. Similarly, Schieman (2005) documented the positive association between neighborhood disadvantage and donated/received social support. In short, social capital can be intentionally mobilized for immigrant adolescents from poor surroundings through promoting deliberate social actions (e.g., policy interventions, civil movements, or volunteering). In this regard, social capital could be a resource which is achievable and redistributable beyond class and race.

On Somali Immigrant Adolescents and Their Educational Experiences

Amongst Black immigrant groups in the United States, we focus particularly on poor Somali immigrants. They are one of the most disadvantaged populations among ethnic minority groups, due in part to being refugees when they immigrated to the United States.[2] Within this context, there are several common socioeconomic conditions shaping the educational experiences of the Somali immigrant adolescents in the United States: their educational experiences are often racialized, classed, and linguistically isolated.

Racialization is one crucial feature that conditions Somali immigrants in the United States, which is a specific social mechanism reshaping Somali students' racial identity. Simply by being labeled as 'Black' (based on their skin color), Somali students are often confronted with racialization—"a socially constructed process where race becomes the predominant way of defining oneself or being defined by others" (Bigelow 2008, p. 28). Unfortunately, being labeled as Black in American society often means being placed in a racial power-relation mechanism where Blacks can be perceived and treated as 'second class citizens' (Torres 2006). This status, which has existed persistently in American society, can lead to a climate ripe for 'stereotype threat' (Steele 1995), by often weakening Blacks through indirectly or directly activating stereotypes of lazy and unintelligent (cited in Torres 2006).

Another related challenge facing Somali adolescents stems from the issue of their Blackness. By being labeled as Black, they are assigned stereotypes consistent with Blacks in America; at the same time, Somali immigrant youth often bring definitions of selves that are ill-fitted for American conceptualizations of Blackness. This means that Somali immigrant youth are pushed to negotiate their racial identity mostly within frameworks established by US Black communities (Kusow and Bjork 2007). However, Somali adolescents tend more to conceptualize their Blackness based on their own cultural and homeland identity. They try to deny the way that Blackness is defined in American society as prescribing their racial identity (see Kusow 2006). While some Somali youths adopt Black American vernacular English or hip-hop clothing, a majority of Somali youths still hold national and ethnic identities (Bigelow 2008). Nonetheless, mainstream society categorizes them as Black, which can lead them to face inequality stemming from a tacit racial hierarchy and further support an interest for some to define their identity outside of traditional African-American culture. Unfortunately, this may also lead to marginalization from Black communities who resist broader perceptions of Blackness (Kusow 2006).

Furthermore, the impact of race on Somali immigrants is inextricably linked to class stratification. In fact, Somali Americans immigrating into the United States

---

[2] The terms "Black" and "African American" are used interchangeably in this study. However, we used the term "US-born African American students" or "US-born black students" in order to distinguish nonimmigrant African-American students from recent African immigrant students.

were given probationary refugee status which implied a categorization of poor working-class or even underclass. This introduced class as another social structure determining opportunities and constraints. To cope with limited socioeconomic resources stemming from their class status, there has been a tendency for collective settlement in particular US communities. These collective settlements appear separate from other racial–ethnic groups, including US-born Black Americans. This residential segregation, in turn, adds to Somali immigrants' lives in the United States as being classed.

Finally, there is a polarization among Somali students in terms of linguistic isolation. Limited English proficiency (LEP) is another issue facing recent Somali immigrants. Although education is highly valued in Somali communities, the LEP issue has a significant influence on the development of content knowledge (e.g., science and math) and academic skills (Hersi 2005). More importantly, Somali youths' linguistic isolation which is in part a consequence of collectively settling aggravates the language development issue.

Research Design

The Overall Research Framework: A Case Study

Our research began with the case study based on a qualitative follow-up design in data collection to elaborate and expand quantitative results (Creswell 2002). Students' social network data gathered from a social network survey served as the foundation for a series of statistical analyses in order to examine the association of social capital with the academic achievement of Somali immigrant adolescents. After our preliminary analysis of the network data, an important but unexpected finding emerged from the network analysis, which later became our research question for the present study, i.e., even though some low-achieving Somali students were embedded in similarly large networks from which high-achieving Somali students actively drew resources, why did some low-achieving Somalis students poorly utilize their large networks for academics and therein possess less social capital? In other words, because there were some students who did not fit the "large network-high achievement" pattern in our analysis, further investigation was undertaken to understand this. To this end, we used a subtype of sequential explanatory design—residual and contrasting analysis (Onwuegbuzie and Teddlie 2003), which will be discussed later in this section.

Site Selection

In order to obtain substantial target populations, we chose a public school located in a large urban/inner-city area where comparably large immigrant populations reside in contrast to other suburban or rural areas where such populations are less prevalent. The public school is located in a typical, large urban/inner-city in the upper Midwest; hereafter let us refer to the school as "Baro Prep." The major characteristic of Baro Prep is that it is a predominantly Somali American K-12 school (71.5% as of 2006). The rest of the students enrolled in the school are US-born African Americans. Besides the relatively large number of Somali students enrolled in the school, there are other important reasons why we chose Baro Prep.

Importantly, in 2006 a majority of students (90.2%, i.e., 395 out of 438) in the school were Title 1 students who received free or reduced price lunch services. Despite having large numbers of low-SES students, compared to other public schools in the same school district, the school showed relatively high school performance in statewide assessments. For example, the school was one of the few charter schools in the school district that made Adequate Yearly Progress (AYP) in recent years. This was quite impressive for a school with a large concentration of limited English proficient (37.4%) and Title 1 (90.2%) students.

Social Network Data Collection

For this study, two fundamental approaches to network data collection were used: complete network and egocentric network. That is, while we employed complete network data for students' relations within the sample school, at the same time we used egocentric networks of each student to identify students' relations beyond the school. Because the school is the key social venue where students can access resources, we gathered complete network data from the school in order to capture substantial ties in that place. Complementarily, we tried to minimize the social boundary issue by gathering egocentric networks from each student.

There were 130 students enrolled from 9th to 12th grade in the school. Due to time and cost, we limited our complete network data collection to a subgroup that shared an extracurricular activity. As a result, 47 students were asked to list the closest peers within the group through a self-administered network paper survey. Coupled with the complete network, encompassing all social relationships among the 47 students, we collected egocentric network data from each student. The same self-administered paper survey was used. In the survey, the students were asked to name close and important persons in their networks. The students, then, were asked to indicate the category of relationship (e.g., teachers, friends, or acquaintances).

Reflecting the school characteristics described above, a majority of students sampled were from poor working-class backgrounds. Of the 47 students, 43 received either free or reduced lunch services, and their parental occupations were in the category of working-class jobs. In addition, six US-born African-American students were included in the 47 students because they were also affiliated with the subgroup. Although our target population is Somali immigrant students, the six nonimmigrant African-American students were also included because they were originally the members of the subgroup, i.e., if they were removed from the sample, the social network map of the subgroup will be distorted.

Qualitative Data Collection

For the qualitative data collection in this study, by purposive sampling based on the students' achievement levels (i.e., high or low G.P.A.) and network type (i.e., large or small), we selected eight students out of the 47 in order to elaborate and expand findings from network analyses. Specifically, we selected four students who had a 'high achievement with large network' pattern. Conversely, we selected two students who had a 'low achievement with small network' pattern. These six students belonged to the major tendency (i.e., high achievement with large network, or conversely, low achievement with small network). The other two students are residual cases whose results deviated from the major tendency. That is, S5 (i.e., Student ID #5) and S47 showed low achievement even with their large networks. The purpose of selecting these two students was to explore the phenomenon of our primary interest, which is deviation from the primary pattern (high achievement with large network). Each student was interviewed individually for about one hour in a conference room at Baro Prep. All interviews were audio recorded to examine the primary theme. In addition, after conducting each interview, the first author wrote certain analytic memos based on impressions and reflections from each student in order to capture more nuanced information.

Network Data Analysis

The collected network data were analyzed by the UCINET 6 and Netminer 3, social network analysis programs. Readers can find more detailed explanations about network concepts used in this study in the following section. By placing detailed explanations of the network concepts in the following section where those concepts are examined, we intend to provide a better understanding of the network concepts for readers.

Qualitative Analysis of Interview Data

Our analysis focused on two emerging residual cases (i.e., S5 and S47) that deviated from the main network pattern (i.e., high achievement with large networks). We, then, focused on two other cases (i.e., S8 and S41) who were exemplary students that followed the main network pattern. By contrasting these two groups, we attempted to seek answers to our research question. The co-interviewer transcribed all the interviews verbatim.[3] After conducting the first interview with the students, we began looking for codes and themes related to the research question. In this process, we also utilized memos, including the analytic reflections, after conducting each interview. After conducting multiple readings of each transcript and memo, we began seeking and developing a coding scheme related to the research question. After building the coding scheme to categorize (coding and thematic analysis) the interview data, we contextualized the data by integrating each individual profile into the data.

Findings and Discussions

Social Network and Academic Achievement: A Brief Introduction of Findings

The network data generated from the 47 students encompassed 373 actors and 1,434 social ties, showing the complex web of social relationships that condition the 47 students. Figure 42.1, for example, illustrates how one of the residual cases (i.e., S47, low achiever with good network) is placed in the entire work. In the sociogram below, the actors represent the individuals (e.g., family members, peers, teachers, or neighbors) connected to other individuals. The 1,434 social ties are based on a dyadic relationship, a social tie between two actors. There are also directions between all dyadic relationships. This means that the entire network is a directional network, showing the flow of some kinds of network content from one actor to the other actor. In this network each tie expresses general social support. In particular, the bold ties surrounding S47 indicate her own network.

Table 42.1 further illustrates several characteristics of the four students. In the table, "degree" refers to the number of social ties incident to an actor (or node). Because the network is a directional network, we need to specify the direction of each degree: in-degree ties refer to chosen ties by others (i.e., incoming ties) and outdegree ties means chosen ties by self (i.e., outgoing ties).

Notably, all of the four students have good social networks in terms of network size. For a comparison, we divided the 47 students into two groups: high-achieving versus low/mid-achieving groups based on their GPA.[4] Notably, the four stu-

---

[3] Notably, a few parts of the verbatim transcripts were edited for clarifying the contexts of interviews.

[4] Because of a lack of standardized achievement information such as state-mandated test scores, grouping students by G.P.A. needed to be done carefully. Therefore, labeling of the achievement groups is based on information from the school principal. According to his data and experience with the school over the last few years, students whose G.P.A. is higher than 3.2 have a higher chance of going to 4-year universities, including major state universities. Conversely, students

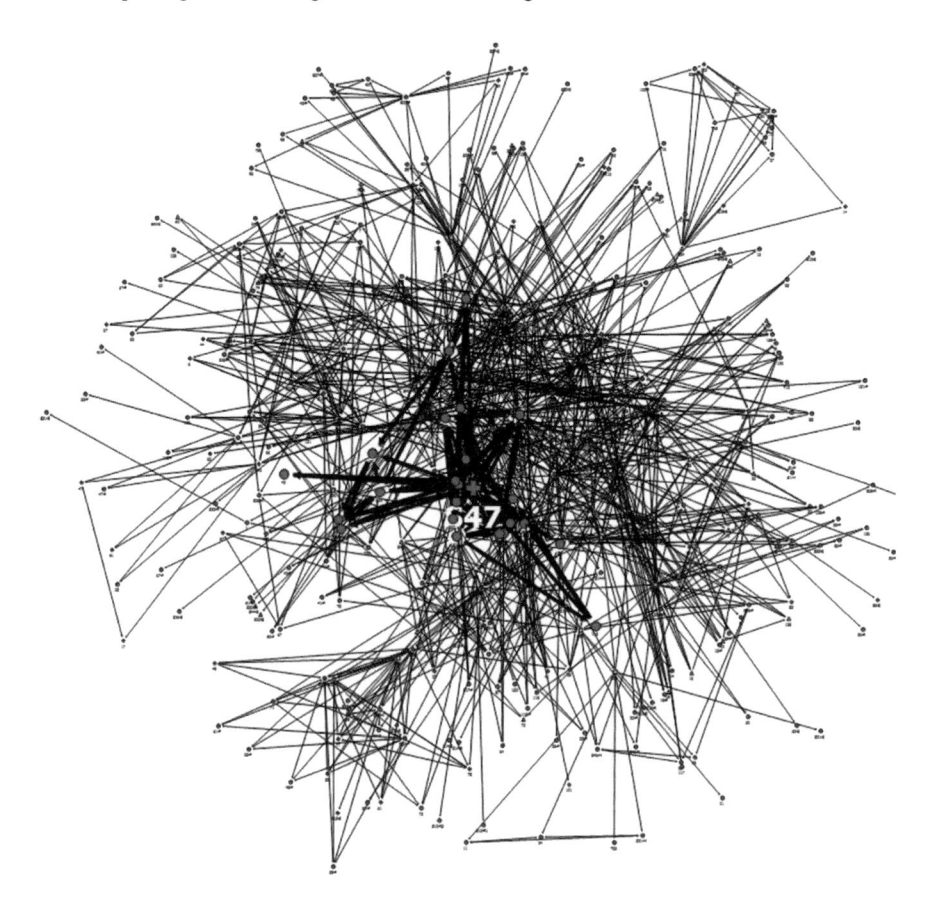

Fig. 42.1 S47's network in the entire network

dents were well connected with supportive individuals (e.g., institutional agents, neighbors, family members, and peers). The number of individuals connected with the four students was at least similar or higher than the average of both the high-achieving and low/mid-achieving students. Specifically, the average number of supportive individuals that the high-achieving students had was 18.4 and for the low/mid-achieving students it was 14.8. However, the number of supportive individuals that the four students possessed in their networks ranged from 18 to 32. The four students had three institutional agents (e.g., teachers, social workers, counselors, administrators, etc.) who were connected with them. This was slightly higher than the average number of institutional agents that the two achieving groups had. In short, the four students showed similar or higher numbers than the average of the

---

whose G.P.A. is lower than 2.3 have quite a low chance of attending college. As a result of this grouping, we identified 34 low or mid achievers and 13 high achievers. For a simple comparison, we combined the low and mid achievers into one group.

Table 42.1 Key network characteristics of the four students

Student group	Nodes (total)	Nodes (institutional agents)	Ties (total)	In-degree	Out-degree
S5 (low achiever)	18	3	63	5	16
S47 (low achiever)	23	3	244	6	22
S8 (high achiever)	32	3	138	11	28
S41 (high achiever)	19	3	87	6	19
Average of low/mid-achieving group	14.8	2.28	49.2	2.6	13.9
Average of high-achieving group	18.4	2.72	66.4	3.7	17.3

high-achieving group in all the measured areas. This suggests that the four students had better networks than their peers in terms of network size. The remaining question is despite their large networks, why were the levels of their academic achievement contradictory? One explanation would be weaker academic abilities of the two low achievers. However, based on our interview data, it appears more plausible that the main reason for their contradictory achievement was due to different abilities in navigating social resources and having dissimilar interpretations in drawing from their relatively large networks.

Two Emerging Themes

Based on the contrasting and residual analysis, two themes related to the research question emerged. They were:

Theme 1: The high achievers tend to have an ability to map out resources in a specific and strategic way, compared to the low-achieving students who chart their resources in a vague and less logical way.

Theme 2: The academic expectation of the Somali students is based on their previous observations of the academic pathway of their ethnically identical reference group. In particular, the positive observations or optimistic social contexts are significant in developing motivation and creating positive assessments (or negotiating the higher threshold of academic expectation) of opportunity structures in general and academic expectations in particular.

Theme 1: Vague Versus Specific and Strategic Mapping of Supportive Networks

Cognitively, one distinctive feature of the two groups (i.e., S5 and S47 vs. S8 and S41) was that they have different abilities in mapping out their social networks in general and supportive people in particular. When they were describing people supportive of their school work, Abid (S5) and Farah (S47) tended to list supportive individuals in a vague or less logical way. They could not come up with proper names immediately, which contrasted the fact that their networks include a substantial number of individuals.

Interviewer: When you have some personal problems who might help you?
Abdi (S5): Around my neighborhood.

Even though his network showed 22 ties with peers, he did not list any of his friends as helping individuals. Rather, he mentioned his neighbors. Thus, we asked him to list the names of some of those neighbors. Abdi could not come up with any specific names of caregivers in his neighborhood. He seemed to in general characterize his neighbors as potentially supportive people.

Furthermore, even though he mentioned participating in *Admission Possible* (i.e., nonprofit organization helping disadvantaged students go to college) as the most positive experience at Baro Prep, he did not list any names of institutional agents in *Admission Possible* as supportive individuals.

Interviewer: What is the most positive experience [in this school]?
Abdi (S5): *Admission possible*…. It's [*Admission Possible*] a program that helps low income people, it helps them prepare for the ACT and SAT, they help you find scholarships…you visit colleges and sometimes you stay overnight…. We [he and other participants in *Admission Possible*] sometimes stay after school and right now we are in this program called *Admission Possible*, working on resumes and stuff like that and teacher recommendations and we go to the teachers and give them our resumes and they give us teacher recommendations.

In the case of Farah (S47), her mapping out of supportive individuals was somewhat disconnected. We asked her to choose close friends from among as many of those ties as possible. Farah simply mentioned, she has "a lot, too many [friends]." She eventually named two: "(S26) and (S16)… [Of the two] (S16), she helps me when I moved here, she helped me pick class…I didn't know how to volunteer in hospital…she helped me." In contrast to her choice of (S16) as the closest friend, (S16) did not choose Farah as a close friend on her own survey. Neither did the other friend named as a close friend by Farah (S47). Farah (S47) did not seem to falsely exaggerate her relationships given that she received six ties from other peers that she did not choose (i.e., she does not view the six peers as close friends). All this implies is that she seemed to perceive her network in a way different than conventional logic—not mutually chosen ties. Farah may view some ties as close even though they are not aware of this closeness. However, by experience, we know that resources or information can be drawn from individuals more effectively when they are willing to share or give them. Thus, people like Farah may not be as successful in drawing resources from such people if the closeness of those relationships is not openly mutual.

In contrast, Aishafa (S8) was very specific in pointing out supportive individuals for her school work (mainly homework). Despite the nonpresence of her father (i.e., divorce), Aishafa (S8) had many supportive people surrounding her for schoolwork, including family-based members such as her elder brother, mother, and uncle. In the interview, she very specifically came up with names of other significant people who help with homework.

Aishafa (S8): (S20) is a cousin and (S41) is a friend I know from ninth grade. (S20), we've known each other since kindergarten and her mom and my mom are very close.... When I am at home, they [S20 and S41] call me and tell me to do this page and they give me examples of what the teacher was doing on the board...(S20)'s mother, she tells me to be good, she is like a mother to me.... I have a friend, she's 40 something, she used to be a [volunteer] tutor for us [Aishafa's family] when we lived in Skyline.... I have a really good teacher, he is Mr. T and he's my role model and that's the class I take Monday, Wednesday and Friday.... Mrs. U, she is a really good teacher [as well]...

The interview above reveals that Aishafa not only has supportive others but also some of the supportive others are closely connected. Her mother and her best friend's (S20) mother "are very close." (S20)'s mother "is like a mother" to her and tells her "to be good." This interlocking relationship for Aishafa is viewed as intergenerational closure—social capital produced by social relationships among parents who know and interact with their children's friends' parents (Coleman 1988), which is a major form of social capital mediated by family members. In social disorganization theory, the presence of too many female-headed households is viewed as a critical factor in undermining social control (Sampson 1997), because it suggests less intergenerational closure and thereby less supervision of others (Madyun and Lee 2010b). However, this is not true in Aishafa's case. In addition, her mentioning of the tutor helping her family indicates the presence of supportive others in her neighborhood.

In addition, Aishafa (S8) not just specifically maps out her supporters, but also more strategically utilizes her supportive people.

Interviewer: Which do you think is more important between recognition from teachers and from peers?

Aishafa (S8): recognition from teachers...because they know you, if you're a good person and you don't talk [too much in class]...and are very attentive and you understand what the teacher is saying, maybe the teacher can write a recommendation, but if your friends say you're a cool person, they [the teachers] are not going to listen to them [friends].... If you do good here they're going to give a good recommendation for colleges next year.... Most of the time they like…they think girls are like…if you hang around with the wrong crew, they are going to say "oh she is one of them"…I think Mr. T would say I am a successful person and Dr. I might say I am a successful person…. Mrs. U, she told me at the conference, "she [Aishafa] is a good girl…"

The interview above reflects a feature of Aishafa's strategic scaffolding of institutionalized resources by paying more attention to teachers' recognition. She values key Baro Prep staff members' evaluations of her. Note that Dr. I is the principal of the school; Mr. T is the most influential and popular teacher (given that he has the highest eigenvector centrality score and receives the most number of ties from the 47 students among the 23 institutional agents in our network data); and Mrs. U is the teacher with the third largest ties with students. Aishafa also knows that being labeled a "successful person" by those institutional agents is important for maintaining good relationships with them and obtaining a strong letter of recommendation for going to college. Thus, she tries not to be labeled as 'one of them' [i.e., the wrong crew from the point of view of key staff]. Once Boissevain (1974) defined this type of strategic relational approach as network orientation, referring to "[network orientation being] interpersonal relations [which] are structured and influenced by people's entrepreneurial impulses, where people seek to manipulate their ties to attain goals and solve their problems" (as cited in Stanton-Salazar and Spina 2000, p. 8).

Similarly, Sala (S41, a high achiever) also mentioned the importance of not being labeled as among the wrong crew by influential institutional agents such as the principal of the school.

Interviewer: What are the expected ways of behaving and interacting in this school?
Sala (S41): You have to behave good and don't 'mess' with Dr. I.

In summary, one distinguishable feature of the two high-achieving students is that they have an ability to map out resources (in particular, institutional resources) in a specific and strategic way, compared to the other two low-achieving students who chart their resources in a vague and disconnected way.

Theme 2: Negotiating Threshold of Academic Expectations—"They Used To Be Like Me."

Notably, all of the four students viewed going to college as the most important pathway for their social mobility. For example, when we asked Farah (S47), a low-achieving student, to describe herself in ten different ways in order of importance, she said "I am from Somali, I am a girl, I am a student, I need go to college, I need success..." In fact, the view of attending college as the most effective instrument of their life success is commonly identified throughout the interviewed students. This is partly because the school climate of Baro Prep is based on a college-oriented culture. Somali culture values education and the presence of high educational aspirations is a somewhat commonly identified phenomenon amongst ethnic minority students (Conchas 2005).

However, while all of the four students showed high academic aspirations, it is particularly interesting to look at certain negotiations of the academic levels given their similar networks and contexts. Before going further, it should be noted that academic aspirations and expectations are subtly different although those two concepts share similar psychological orientations to academic value. Academic aspirations indicate some level of hopefulness of future academic performance beyond one's realistic expectation, whereas expectations refer to beliefs regarding future academic performance based on more realistic self-assessments (Portes and Rumbaut 2001).

When we asked about her plan to go to college, Farah (S47) responded that she wants to go to City-State University because "they [City-State] have many programs." Then, we further asked why she does not consider other major state universities such as the University of Big-Ten, which provides more various programs. At first, her answer was that "my cousin, she goes to City-State University." After finishing the interview with her, when we asked her the same question, she said "at least I can expect I may be able to attend City-State University." This shows that while Farah plans to go to college, her preference to City-State University is not based on certain objective criteria such as reputation or programs of the university, but based on the "possibility" that she can get into the university. That is, she feels like she may follow the same educational pathway as her cousin whose socioeconomic conditions are similar to hers. In other words, Farah's realistic assessment of her attending college depended upon on the surroundings where she negotiated her possibility of having higher education in the future and may not be consistent with her aspirations.

A similar psychological pattern was found in Aishafa's case. That is, as Aishafa noticed some Somalis who were in similar life situations like her and went to college similar to Aishafa, she also negotiated the level of her academic expectations based on other observations. The following interview with Aishafa (S8), the high achiever, reflects this interpretation.

Interviewer: Are you in Upward-Bound or AP?
Aishafa (S8): I am going to be in one of them next year, I can't do it this year because I am a 10th grader, there is a test to go to AP [Advanced Placement], and then most of the people I know passed, I am very sure I am going to pass...they used to be like me. So, I feel like I will go to AP and attend some "good" [with an emphasis] college.

Aishafa (S8) believes that she will get through the test for Advanced Placement classes because 'most of the people' she knows passed the test. Notably, she pointed out that the most of the people 'used to be like me.' That is, those academically successful Somalis surrounding Aishafa were not a different group of people. They were people who were placed in the same disadvantaged situations as Aishafa. This makes her confident in her admission to AP and also a 'good' college.

In a similar vein, Sala (S41, high achiever) showed confidence in her future college enrollment because her elder sister is enrolled in a college. Notably, Aishafa's 'used-to-be-like-me' statement is similarly identified from Sala's interview.

Interviewer:	What school does she [Sala's elder sister] go to?
Sala (S41):	University of Big-Ten.
Interviewer:	What does she study?
Sala (S41):	She studies medicine.
Interviewer:	What do you want to do in the future?
Sala (S41):	I want to be an OBGYN.
Interviewer:	So you have an elder sibling who studies medicine at the U of Big-Ten, does that make you more confident?
Sala (S41):	Yeah, it makes me confident because she is doing it, so I can do it as well. I want to go to Harvard.
Interviewer:	Do you see many [academic] successes from Somali students who go to good colleges?
Sala (S41):	Yeah,…if they don't do drugs and stuff, which they are getting into.
Interviewer:	When you see Somali students who graduate from this school [Baro Prep] and go to Ivy League schools or other major universities, does that make you study harder?
Sala (S41):	It makes me happy and confident that I could do anything.
Interviewer:	What if you could identify only one [Somali] who would go to college, and many other [Somali] students could not go to college, do you think you could try to go to college?
Sala (S41):	Yeah, I still can try to go to college.
Interviewer:	Even though there was one?
Sala (S41):	Yeah. It could still be changed, it could be me or the other person.

Sala showed confidence of her going to good colleges like her elder sister. That is, her assessment of opportunity through education was very positive based on her experience and observation of other Somali students' academic success, including her sister.

In brief, the academic expectation of Farah (S47), Aishafa (S8), and Sala (S41) are based on their previous observations of the academic pathway of their ethnically identical peers. In the cases of Aishafa (S8) and Sala (S41), the positive observations or optimistic social contexts are significant in developing motivation and creating a positive assessment of opportunity structures in general and academic expectations in particular. Conversely, Farah's (S47) assessment of her attending college is less informed by potential resources of her network and is more dependent on the quality of her cousin as critical academic social tie. This suggests that even though those three students have similarly large networks, the type of people they had in close social relationships was more important than the number of people i.e., having academically oriented (or academically successful) Somali people in their networks was the major difference.

Concluding Remarks

A finding that emerged from this study was that students equipped with a large social network of relationships do not always succeed academically. To understand this finding, we tried to unravel how the students navigated the resources embedded in their networks and thereby reveal their interpretations of those social relationships. Findings show that the two groups differed based on (1) a cognitive difference in mapping out resources and (2) different levels of negotiations for academic expectations based on cumulative, previous experiences.

These findings suggest that we need to pay attention to agency-structure interplay of human behaviors amid the structure-dependency feature of human actions in order to fully understand the meaning of adolescents' social relationships. In other words, on the one hand, the significant influence of sociocultural contexts (e.g., racialized and classed social structures imposed on Somali immigrants) plays a key role in shaping poor Somali adolescents' social relationships and thereby social capital. On the other hand, Somali adolescents' ability in navigating resources embedded in their social relationships and their interpretations of self, other, and society are not merely imposed by such social structures but socially negotiated (Blumer 1969). We know by experience that individuals' social behavior or conduct is not entirely determined by social structures (Giddens 1984), because individuals' behaviors do not merely mirror structural conditions (Blumer 1969).

In conclusion, the phenomenon of Somali students having similarly large networks but different academic achievement seems to be associated with their ability in charting social resources and their interpretations of themselves and others, all of which are, in turn, conditioned by sociocultural contexts facing Somali adolescents. Therefore, we need to link 'negotiated order' (agency interpretation) and 'social exchange' (structure dependency) frameworks (Stolte et al. 2001) to examine how comprehensively social capital affects academic pathways. We believe that such an exclusive concept (i.e., either predominantly agent-oriented perspective or predominantly structural-functional focus) cannot fully uncover the varied possession and utilization of resources embedded in the social relationships of ethnic minority adolescents and the factors that lead to differing interpretations of those resources. In this regard, the findings as a consequence of such an approach (combining agency interpretation with structure dependency) provide some possible explanations about why some ethnic minority adolescents utilize social capital for their academic success as latent opportunity structures embedded in the family, school, and community where their academic paths are conditioned, while other peers situated in similar social relationships do not. In terms of practice, the finding suggests that the quality of educational programming will be critical in the designing of opportunities and the delivery of resources for students. Instructors and educators will not be able to assume that students can adequately recognize their opportunities and understand how to apply their potential resources. In addition, mentoring programs and individual advocates should be trained in demonstrating to students more than just that a goal is possible, but why the goal is possible.

References

Ahmed, W., Minnaert, A., Van Der Werf., G., & Kuyper, H. (in press). Perceived social support and early adolescents' achievement: The mediational roles of motivational beliefs and emotions. *Journal of Youth and Adolescence*, http://www.springerlink.com/content/n2g0721549017q05/fulltext.html. Accessed 12 Oct 2009.

Apple, M. (2006). How class works in education: Review of class practices—how parents help their children get good jobs. *Educational Policy, 20*(2), 455–462.

Bankston, C. (2004). Social capital, cultural values, immigration, and academic achievement: The host country context and contradictory consequences. *Sociology of Education, 77*(2), 176–179.

Blumer, H. (1969). *Symbolic interactionism: Perspective and method*. Englewood Cliffs: Prentice-Hall.

Boissevain, J. (1974). *Friends of friends: Networks, manipulators, and coalitions*. Oxford: Basil Blackwell.

Coleman, J. (1988). Social capital in the creation of human capital. In A. H. Halsely, H. Lauder, P. Brown, & A. S. Wells (Eds.), (2002). *Education: Culture, economy, society* (pp. 80–95). Oxford: Oxford University Press.

Conchas, G. Q. (2006). *The color of success: Race and high-achieving urban youth*. New York: Teachers College Press.

Creswell, J. W. (2002). *Educational research: Planning, conducting, and evaluating quantitative and qualitative research*. Upper Saddle River: Merrill Prentice Hall.

Devine, F. (2004). *Class practices: How parents help their children get good jobs*. Cambridge: Cambridge University Press.

Diamond, J. B., & Gomez, K. (2004). African American parents' educational orientations: The importance of social class and parents' perceptions of schools. *Education and Urban Society, 36*(4), 383–427.

Dika, S. L., & Singh, K. (2002). Applications of social capital in educational literature: A critical synthesis. *Review of Educational Research, 72*(1), 31–60.

Dumais, S. A. (2002). *The educational pathways of white working-class students*. Unpublished doctoral dissertation, Cambridge: Harvard University.

Fordham, S., & Ogbu, J. (1986). Black students' school success: Coping with the "burden of acting White." *The Urban Review, 18*(3), 176–206.

Fredericks, K., & Durland, M. (2005). The historical evolution and basic concepts of social network analysis. *New Directions for Evaluation, 107*, 15–23.

Gandara, P. C. (1995). *Over the Ivy walls: The educational mobility of low-income Chicanos*. Albany: State University of New York Press.

Giddens, A. (1984). *The constitution of society: Outline of the theory of structuration*. Berkeley: University of California Press.

Goodenow, C., & Grady, K. E. (1993). The relationship of school belonging and friends' values to academic motivation among urban adolescent students. *Journal of Experimental Education, 62*, 60–71.

Harrington, C. C., & Boardman, S. K. (1997). *Paths to success: Beating the odds in American society*. Cambridge: Harvard University Press.

Hersi, A. A. (2005). Educational challenges and sociocultural experiences of Somali students in an urban high school. In V. Gonzalez & J. Tinajero (Eds.), *NABE review of research and practice*, (*Vol. 3*, pp. 125–144). Mahwah: Lawrence Erlbaum.

Horton, H. D., Allen, B. L, Herring, C., & Thomas, M. E. (2000). Lost in the storm: The sociology of the black working-class, 1850 to 1990. *American Sociological Review, 65*, 128–137.

Horvat, E. M., Weininger, E. B., & Lareau, A. (2003). From social ties to social capital: Class differences in the relations between schools and parent networks. *American Educational Research Journal, 40*(2), 319–351.

Ibanez, G. E., Gabriel, P., Kuperminc, G. P., Jurkovic, G., & Perilla, J. (2004). Cultural attributes and adaptations linked to achievement motivation among Latino adolescents. *Journal of Youth and Adolescence, 33*(6), 559–568.

Kusow, A. M. (2006). Migration and racial formations among Somali immigrants in north America. *Journal of Ethnic and Migration Studies, 32*, 533–551.

Kusow, A. M., & Bjork, S. R. (2007). *From Mogadishu to Dixon: The Somali diaspora in a global context*. Trenton: Red Sea Press.

Lareau, A. (1989). *Home advantage: Social class and parental intervention in elementary education*. Lanham: Rowman & Littlefield.

Lee, M. (2010). Researching social capital in education: Some conceptual considerations relating to the contribution of network analysis. *British Journal of Sociology of Education, 31*(6), 779–792.

Madyun, N., & Lee, M. (2010a). Neighborhood ethnic density as an explanation for the academic achievement of ethnic minority youth placed in neighborhood disadvantage. *Berkeley Review of Education, 1*(1), 87–112.

Madyun, N., & Lee, M. (2010b). The influence of female-headed households on Black achievement. *Urban Education, 45*(4), 424–447.

Onwuegbuzie, A.J., & Teddlie, C. (2003). A framework for analyzing data in mixed methods research. In A. Tashakkori & C. Teddlie (Eds.), *Handbook of mixed methods in social and behavioral research* (pp. 351–384). Thousand Oaks: Sage.

Portes, A., & Fernandez-Kelly, P. (2006). *No margin for error: Educational and occupational achievement among disadvantaged children of immigrants.* Princeton: The Center for Migration and Development. http://cmd.princeton.edu/papers/wp0703.pdf. Accessed 14 Dec 2007.

Portes, A., & Rumbaut, R. G. (2001). *Legacies: The story of the immigration second generation*. Berkeley: University of California Press.

Rankin, B. H., & Quane, J. M. (2000). Neighborhood poverty and the social isolation of inner-city African American families. *Social Forces, 79*, 139–164.

Sampson, R. J. (1997). Collective regulation of adolescent misbehavior: Validation results from eighty Chicago neighborhoods. *Journal of Adolescent Research, 12*(2), 227–244.

Sampson, R. J., Morenoff, J. D., & Earls, F. (1999). Beyond social capital: Spatial dynamics of collective efficacy for children. *American Sociological Review, 64*, 633–660.

Schieman, S. (2005). Residential stability and the social impact of neighborhood disadvantage: A study of gender-and race-contingent effects. *Social Forces, 83*, 1031–1064.

Stanton-Salazar, R. D. (1997). A social capital framework for understanding the socialization of racial minority children and youth. *Harvard Educational Review, 67*(1), 1–40.

Stanton-Salazar, R. D., & Spina S. (2000). The network orientations of highly resilient urban minority youth: A network-analytic account of minority socialization and its educational implications. *The Urban Review, 32*, 227–261.

Steele, C. (1995). Stereotype threat and the intellectual test performance of African-Americans. *Journal of Personality and Social Psychology, 69*, 797–811.

Stolte, J. F., Fine, G. A., & Cook, K. S. (2001). Sociological miniaturism: Seeing big through the small in social psychology. *Annual Review of Sociology, 27*, 387–413.

Torres, K. (2006). *Manufacturing blackness: 'Skin color necessary but not sufficient.'* Unpublished Ph.D. dissertation. Pennsylvania: University of Pennsylvania.

Chapter 43
Agency and Everyday Knowledge of Filipina Migrants in Dubai, United Arab Emirates

Simone Christ

Introduction

Dubai—the name of this city entails a certain degree of connotation, namely that of a city characterized by superlatives. The world's first ever seven-star hotel, the *Burj Al Arab*, the world's largest tower, artificial islands shaping palms, and even the world are located in Dubai. Dubai will soon possess the world's largest airport, the world's largest hotel, the world's largest shopping mall as well as the world's largest leisure park (Arnu 2007, p. 11).[1] The media enthusiastically refer to these immense construction projects; however, it rarely presents the hidden side of this development.

Indians form the numerical majority of this desert city whose development makes large numbers of foreign workers indispensable, leading to a less-known superlative: nearly 90% of the labor force are migrants (Marchal 2005, p. 100). In this multiethnic environment, Filipinos form the fifth largest group of foreigners. The United Arab Emirates (UAE) is only one, but albeit important destination country for labor migration from the Philippines, where about 10% of the population live abroad (Philippine Overseas Employment Administration 2004).

Large migration movements nowadays are not permanent, but have a temporal character. Migration of workers is in general restrained to the duration of the labor contract; therefore, workers are considered as *Overseas Contract Workers* (OCW) (Hugo 2004, p. 44). In the Philippine context, the Philippine government coined the term *Overseas Filipino Worker* (OFW).

Contract labor migration can be considered as temporally and circular—after the end of the contract, the worker has to return to his country of origin. The character-

---

[1] Research in Dubai was done in 2007. In the meantime, the effects of the global financial crisis led to new developments, which are not yet subject in this chapter.

S. Christ (✉)
Institute of Oriental and Asian Studies, Department of Southeast Asian Studies,
University of Bonn, Germany
e-mail: simone.christ@uni-bonn.de

istics of the temporal labor migration do not allow any space for formal education processes. Workers are not allowed to pursue further education in the destination country. Although the structures of temporal labor migration are adverse to formal learning processes and these outer conditions limit education, workers arriving in the destination country are subject to various informal learning processes. This chapter aims to answer the two following questions: First, what kind of knowledge and skills do Filipina migrant workers have to cope with everyday life in Dubai? Second, how is this knowledge transmitted? It will be argued that social networks serve as the most important means of knowledge transfer for Filipina migrant workers in Dubai. Most aspects of everyday knowledge are only shared and transferred within the Filipino community. Although a wide range of anthropological studies cover the topic of Filipina labor migrants (e.g., Constable 1997; Parreñas 2003; Shinozaki 2005; Weekly 2005; Weyland 1997), this cognitive aspect of migration is barely taken in consideration.

Data for this chapter were collected in a three-month anthropological fieldwork in Dubai (October to December 2007). In this context, methods like participant observation, in-depth interviews, mental mapping, free listing, and ranking were used. The samples of the study are female labor migrants from the Philippines, mostly working in the hotel industry.

Theoretically, the research questions relate to discussions about local knowledge, which are discussed in the next section. Special characteristics of the sending country as well as the receiving country in relation to migration are given. Afterward, some dimensions of local knowledge of Filipina migrants in Dubai are exemplarily presented where it is demonstrated that social network ties are the most crucial means for knowledge transfer.

Local Knowledge—a Universal and Situational Approach

To assess learning processes and knowledge outside formal education, various concepts can be used. The concept informal learning refers to learning that takes place outside formal education (institutional schooling with degrees) and nonformal education (short-time voluntary educational programs outside the formal school curriculum). Referring to Schugurensky, informal learning consists of three forms: self-directed learning, incidental learning, and socialization (Schugurensky 2000). However, for the purpose of this chapter, the concept of local knowledge is preferred over the concept of informal learning. Compared to informal learning, local knowledge refers to certain localities, local situations, and problem-oriented solutions. Local knowledge encompasses skills and knowledge, which are in general shared by a group, e.g., a certain ethnic group, and is less oriented on individuals. The concept of local knowledge seems more appropriate to study Filipina migrants since their learning processes are shared within the ethnic groups of Filipinas in the UAE and differ from individual learning experiences as well as from knowledge of other ethnic groups in the UAE.

According to Antweiler, the core of local knowledge is "a form of knowledge and performance found in all societies, comprising skills and acquired intelligence, which are culturally *situated* and responding to *constantly changing* social and natural environments" (Antweiler 2004, p. 27, original emphasis). Consequently, local knowledge "is a universal form of knowledge common to all human beings" (Antweiler 1998, p. 477). Local knowledge differs in different situations, cultural, or natural environments; a paddy farmer in Southeast Asia necessarily exhibits different skills than a banker in Luxembourg in order to cope with the environment. This situational character of local knowledge indicates that knowledge is a social product (Antweiler 1998, p. 476). As a social product, it is by no means static, but subject to dynamic processes and social change. It is socially constructed.

Antweiler developed a general model of local knowledge, combining both its universal as much as its situational character (Antweiler 2004, pp. 16–17). This model stresses ten crucial aspects:

1. Local knowledge combines factual knowledge and action-oriented skills.
2. It adapts to situational dynamics.
3. It is based on an empirical local basis, the "laboratory of life" (Antweiler 2004, p. 16).
4. Its orientation is holistic.
5. Due to its tacit nature, it is often implicit and unconscious.
6. Means of transfer is informal learning.
7. It is not opposed to scientific knowledge, but even exhibits a scientific character because of its methodical approach.
8. It is directed by the principle of optimal ignorance.
9. Criterion of evaluation is practical efficacy.
10. It results in actions and solutions of problems broadly accepted by local communities (Antweiler 2004, pp. 16–17).

Culture of Migration in the Philippines

Recent statistics show that one out of six Filipino families and at least one family member is working abroad (Mangahas 2008). This is an impressive indication how labor migration has become an integral part in the daily lives of many Filipinos. The Philippines can be called a culture of migration (Lauser 2004) since labor migration penetrates all levels of society: state, households, and families as well as individuals.

The significance of migration becomes obvious on the state level. Due to its state-regulated migration institutions, the Philippines is characterized as the "prototype of a labor exporting country" (Semyonov and Gorodzeisky 2005, p. 47). Even though the history of migration in the Philippines can be traced back to precolonial times, it was only in the 1970s that the state actively engaged in the regulation of migration. At that time, the Philippine economy suffered from the recession of the global world economy and of martial law which was imposed by President Marcos.

By initiating a state-sponsored migration policy, Marcos expected economic gain resulting from the remittances of labor migrants (Reiterer 1997, p. 290). He glorified them as "new heroes"—a term that is until now frequently used by the government and media (Parreñas 2003, p. 53; Mangahas 2008). In 1982, the institutions built by Marcos were restructured and the *Philippine Overseas Employment Administration* (POEA) was formed. This government agency controls the recruitment of Filipino workers. It campaigns for the employment of Filipino workers in foreign countries and recruits prospective migrants in the Philippines. In 1995, the "Migrant Workers and Overseas Filipino Act" indicated a shift from the former focus solely on the economic benefits of migration toward the welfare and protection of migrants.

Today's labor migration is on contractual basis and is circular. In general, labor migrants do not immigrate permanently in the host country, but stay there only for the time of the contract. The kind of work is mostly indicated as the "3Ds": dirty, degrading, and dangerous/difficult (Chin 2003, p. 317). During the first years of state-sponsored labor migration, apart from destinations like the United States and Europe, the migration flow was directed to the Middle East where the economy was booming and workers for the large infrastructure projects were needed. Since the 1990s, the Asian *Newly Emerging Economies* (Malaysia, Hong Kong, Singapore, and Taiwan) were known as a new destination region for contract workers. However, not only the destinations but also the employment sector diversified within the last years. The demand for service workers increased especially for domestic helpers, an employment traditionally regarded to be female work. This paved the way for the *feminization of migration* (Han 2003, p. 61; Lutz 2007, p. 30). Whereas in 1975, 70% of all OFWs were men and only 30% women, nearly 30 years later, the ratio is exactly the opposite (Weekly 2002, p. 281). Statistically speaking, most women migrants are between 20 and 29 years old, unmarried, and originate from the island of Luzon. Half of them even hold some kind of college education (Asis 2001, p. 31).

On the familial level, large numbers of families are affected by migration. The family is the central institution in Philippine social organization to which each individual gives his loyalty, commitment, and sacrifices. On the other hand, individuals rely on their families for social status and prestige in society. Families consider migration as a means to diversify household risks (Han 2003, p. 129). Migrants working abroad are considered to be part of their households in the Philippines and are expected to contribute to the family income. Moreover, families reduce the costs of migration. By activating their social network, they provide prospective migrants with the financial means necessary for recruiting costs, travel expenses, and social contacts. Migrants often choose destinations where they already have social network ties.

On the level of individuals, labor migration serves as a culturally accepted strategy of everyday life. For one of the informants, Sheila, migration to Dubai was motivated by the desire to forget her love problems.

Summarizing, geographical mobility is intrinsically tied to being Pinoy/Pinay (Lauser 2004, p. 12) and is a significant component of society. Today, the Filipino diaspora is dispersed worldwide (Llorente 2007); however, the majority is concentrated in North America, Europe, Middle East, and East Asia. The UAE—despite having only two million inhabitants—constitutes the second most important destination in 2006. By considering the number of new hires and rehires, 99,000 (12.6%) Filipinos entered a contract in the UAE. The largest destination is Saudi Arabia with 223,000 (28.4%) new hires and rehires, and the third largest is Hong Kong with 97,000 (12.3%).

The Multiethnic Receiving Society of the UAE

The UAE is a member of the Gulf Cooperation Council (GCC)[2] and shares similar characteristics in terms of the social, economic, and political system with the other member states Bahrain, Qatar, Kuwait, Oman, and Saudi Arabia (Kapiszewski 2001, p. 4). Therefore, the UAE serves as a good example for labor migration to the oil-rich states of the Middle East.

The UAE's economic development is based on oil and natural gas. In 1962, commercial production of oil commenced in Abu Dhabi; 4 years later, oil was discovered in Dubai (Dean 2005, p. 1181). Financed by oil revenues, large infrastructure projects were initiated and foreign labor was recruited to build streets, ports, and sewage systems. Initially, the foreign labor force originated from other Arab countries like Egypt or Jordan. The oil crisis in 1973 brought higher oil revenues for the GCC states and labor recruitment was thereupon expanded to South and Southeast Asian countries. Payment for Asian workers was (and still is) lower than for Arab workers.[3] In the 1980s, further differentiation of employment structure—especially the creation of new jobs in the service sector—was followed by a larger demand for women migrants. Despite the feminization of migration, the inequality of the gender ratio is enormous: more than two-third of the population is male (Dean 2005, p. 1186).

Employment of workers is contractual and after the expiration of the contract, new migrant workers substitute the former. The implementation of the rotation principle aims to avoid the consolidation of migrant communities (Gesemann 2003, p. 361). The immense recruitment of foreigners is the reason for the large demographic inequalities between Emirati nationals and foreigners. In 1975, already 70% of the total population were foreigners; this rate even increased to 82% in 2004 (Janardhan 2007). The Filipino community is the fifth largest migrant group in the UAE after India, Pakistan, Sri Lanka, and Egypt (Kapiszewski 2001, p. 62). Concerning these figures, the UAE has a high degree of cultural heterogeneity.

---

[2] The member states of the GCC cooperate in terms of foreign policy, security policy, and economy; migration policies are also discussed in this forum.

[3] Literature differentiates Asian workers (mostly from India, Pakistan, Bangladesh, Sri Lanka, and the Philippines) from Arab workers (mostly from Jordan, Egypt, or Yemen) although Jordan and Yemen geographically belong to Asia.

In the authoritarian political system of the UAE, political rule is not authorized by elections, but lies in the hand of hereditary monarchs. Constitution and law prohibit the formation of political parties and nongovernmental organizations; the latter are engaged in the protection of migrants' rights in less restrictive states. Moreover, unions are not allowed so that there is no representation of workers' interests (Ghaemi 2006, p. 57). Protesting against inhuman working conditions is sanctioned, e.g., strike leaders have to face deportation. Above all, other liberal rights such as freedom of assembly are restricted. One reason is the perception of migrants as a possible threat to the internal security of the state. Since nationals form the minority, potential political uprisings of the foreign majority are considered a permanent threat (Janardhan 2007). Poor working conditions and insufficient guaranty of liberal human rights are topics frequently addressed by human right organizations like Human Rights Watch (Ghaemi 2006).

Legal conditions further affect the everyday life of migrant workers. In the Gulf States, a distinct legal feature symbolizes the dichotomy in the relationship between nationals and foreigners: the sponsorship system (Kafala system). Every foreign employee depends on a sponsor, who, in general, is a national. A sponsor is needed to issue a visa and without agreement of the sponsor, employees are not allowed to change jobs. The sponsorship system is a very powerful system,[4] which also serves as an additional income for the sponsors. It reproduces the existing social structure (Gesemann 2003, p. 360). Moreover, the dichotomy between nationals and foreigners is perpetuated by the fact that apart from a few exceptions, foreigners cannot obtain Emirati citizenship and that the residence permit is tied to employment or an employed immediate family member.

In conclusion, migration is considered by the UAE government as contrary to social solidarity and as a threat to political power. Essentializing processes of ethnization perpetuate social inequalities and the social exclusion of labor migrants. The conditions of the receiving society restrain formal learning processes and social mobility.

The Role of Formal Education for Filipino Migrants in the UAE

At a first glance, the Gulf societies seem to conform to the typical features of a plural society where "social orders […] live side by side, yet without mingling, in one political unit" (Furnivall 1980, p. 60). Further introspection and a closer ethnographic look on the daily interactions, however, suggest that there are manifold relationships between the different ethnic groups, which transcend the economic sphere. Nevertheless, there is one point in Furnivall's theory that is especially true for these countries: nationality and ethnicity—not qualification

---

[4] Longva (1997, pp. 77–109) gives a sociological account on the power relations of the sponsorship system.

or the educational background—determine job opportunities and class membership. In general, nationals occupy leading positions in the public sector. Executive positions in the private sector are mostly filled with either nationals or Westerners. Arabs or highly skilled Indians work in middle-income occupations; Egyptians, Palestinians, or Lebanese, for example, are employed as teachers and Indians or Iranians as physicians. Indian and Pakistani construction laborers as well as women from the Philippines, Sri Lanka, Indonesia, and recently also from Ethiopia working as domestic helpers constitute the low-income sector (Kapiszewski 2001, p. 60; Niethammer 2008, p. 16). Workers from Asia are, in general, ascribed with certain characteristics: They are efficient, obedient, and easier to control (Kapiszewski 2001, p. 60). Essentializing processes of ethnization and culturalization lead to stereotyping of migrants. In these essentialized definitions, culture and ethnicity are the most crucial factors for social status in the society.

In the case of Filipinos, these essentialized perceptions of culture and ethnicity determine job opportunities of Filipino migrants. A large number of OFWs are college graduates, but only a minority of them find work according to their qualifications, due to the ethnical hierarchy. Within the low-wage sector, Filipinos get a higher salary than other nationalities like Sri Lankans since Filipinos are associated with certain characteristics, for example, modernity and fluency in English. On the other hand, Filipinos receive a lower salary than their Arab colleagues for the same work and even if this colleague has lesser formal education. Although Filipinos benefit from the ethnic hierarchy within the low-wage sector, college education and formal education are of no avail for them and therefore often a source of frustration. The 48-year-old Filipina Maria, a college graduate of management, works as a waitress in a hotel, a work which is only done by young women in the Philippines. She complains:

> In the Philippines, I was the assistant store manager in a multinational company. I'm a management graduate. […] The proud comparing to your previous job, you really went to zero. […] It's been a hard time for me to accept the situation—crying. You cannot apply for what you have in the Philippines. It's different here, as I experienced, they're looking for Western graduates and mine was not included. But in terms of capacities, I know, I can. (Interview with Maria, October 26, 2007)

Women without a college degree in general appreciated the opportunity of working in Dubai, because they were not able to find an appropriate job in the Philippines. On the other hand, women from the Philippines with a college degree were frustrated because of being overqualified in their work. Table 43.1 will give an outline about the socioeconomic background of the women in the study.

As shown, formal education does not matter much in the ethnicized social hierarchy in the UAE. Being labor migrants, there is no way for them to pursue further education in the receiving society. Often Filipino migrants assess their stay abroad as deskilling. However, processes of learning take place in the everyday life of Filipino migrant. The next chapter will give some examples of local knowledge Filipina migrant workers possess in order to cope with their everyday lives in Dubai.

Table 43.1 Biographical background of the interviewees. (Source by the author)

Name	Age	Highest educational achievement	Marital Status	Number of children	Previous migration experiences	In Dubai since	Number of jobs in Dubai
Maria	48	Bachelor in Management	ma	2	–	1 y	1
Valerie	34	2 years in College, no degree	s	2	–	2 y	1
Alaine	34	2 years in College, no degree	ma	3	2 y in a garment factory in Taiwan	1 y, 5 m.	3
Cristina	23	Bachelor in Computer Science	s	–	–	1 y, 8 m.	6
Sheila	33	Bachelor in Customs Administration	s	–	5 y in an electronic company in Taiwan 2 m as a domestic worker in Hong Kong Tried to enter Germany without a valid visa, deportation	1 y, 4 m.	2
Mai	37	Bachelor in Agriculture	s	–	5 y, 2 m in an electronic company in Taiwan	1 y, 5 m.	2
Ligaya	27	Bachelor in Marine Biology	s	1	–	1.5 y	4
Cathrine	32	Bachelor in Nursing	s	–	–	4 y	1
Letti	26	Bachelor in Accountancy	s	–	–	1 y	1
Eden	29	High School	s	–	–	1 y	1
Shella	24	High School	s	–	6 m as entertainer in Japan	1 y, 6 m.	1

ma = married, s = single, y = year, m = month.

Dimensions of Local Knowledge in the Context of Migration: Some Examples

Even though labor migrants in the Middle East are largely perceived by their economic activity, an ethnographic look shows that in the emic view of Filipina migrants other areas are equally important, for example, their engagement in manifold social relationships.

Knowledge concerning economical aspects—relating to the fact that mostly migration of OFWs is economically motivated—is an important dimension of local knowledge. It includes:

- Knowledge about the search for employment, using formal ways (newspaper or Internet) and informal ways (social network, asking *kabayan* (fellow country man) on the street, and walk in);
- Knowledge about legal aspects, e.g., aspects concerning immigration and labor laws (visa, sponsor, and labor act);
- Educational background,[5] e.g., foreign language skills (English), specific knowledge gained in college, and official recognition of this knowledge through college degree;
- Knowledge about remittances, which are supposed to be cheap and reliable (financial institutions are preferred over informal ways);
- Knowledge about everyday living without spending too much, e.g., self-restriction to consuming, knowledge about close and cheap supermarkets, and knowledge how to budget wisely;
- Knowledge about distraction and relaxation from everyday life without spending a huge amount of money, e.g., cooking, sleeping, and going to disco.

Despite the relevance of economically related local knowledge, everyday life in migration is not entirely constrained to economic activities. Negotiating social relationships is an important part of everyday life. Knowledge about social relationships comprises:

- Knowledge about successful support of the family, which includes all economic aspects of local knowledge mentioned above;
- Knowledge about interpersonal relationships to Filipinos, e.g., general informal rules of interpersonal interaction (patience, amicability, and respect), specific informal rules of interpersonal interactions with Filipinos (not to interfere in personal matters of *kabayan*, to be humble). The norm of reciprocity is prevalent. In the accommodation, informal rules of living together acceptably in a tiny space (e.g., informal rules to regulate usage of the bathroom in the mornings) are followed.
- Knowledge about interpersonal relationships to non-Filipinos, e.g., general informal rules of interpersonal interaction (patience, amicability, and respect) and knowledge about intercultural communication;
- Knowledge about how to solve different problems like emotional problems, problems with the employer, visa problems, and harassment.

In the next section, some of these dimensions will be described in detail. According to the model of local knowledge, it becomes obvious that all these facets are socially situated and mirror the specific conditions of the receiving and sending society. The actual conditions of the receiving society determine the kind of local knowledge Filipina migrants need to cope with their social situation as labor migrants. For

---

[5] In the narrow sense of the word, knowledge gained through education as well as knowledge about legal aspects are not parts of local knowledge. However, both are in the emic view significant aspects and therefore cannot be ignored.

example, the legal setting of an easy entry to the UAE with a visit visa requires Filipina migrants to gain knowledge about the search for employment.

Search for Employment

As mentioned above, employment is the prerequisite for a residence permit; migrant workers who lose their employment contract have to return to the Philippines and often suffer the stigma of failure. Though recruitment to the UAE is channeled through agencies, the vast majority of Filipinos enter the country with a visit visa in their passports. The tourist visa is valid only for 60 days and before it expires, they need to find employment. Therefore, knowledge about the search for employment is, on the one hand, a precondition for migration to Dubai, on the other hand, also a requisite while abroad, considering that a large part of the informants was currently looking for a new job and has had other employments in Dubai before.

What ways are applicable for finding jobs? Formal and informal ways can be employed and frequently, the women use a combination of both. A formal way of finding employment is searching the classified advertisements in the newspapers or the Internet. However, by applying through job advertisements, Filipina migrant workers face ethnic discrimination already institutionalized in the UAE. Ethnic discrimination highly constrains the pool of potential applicants by determining their nationalities. For example, browsing the classified advertisements in the local newspaper, it becomes evident that employers oblige a certain nationality of their preferred employee: one employer requires an Indian housemaid, another asks for a Filipino nanny and beauticians, and a third requests an attractive Russian or Filipina waitress with good pleasing personality. Sometimes, employers even require a certain visa type in order to prevent spending for the visa of their prospective employee.

Informal methods are also widespread. Three different kinds are frequently used. First, Filipinas approach potential employers by asking the predominantly Filipino staff in malls or at hotel receptions for vacancies. The curriculum vitae (CV) of the applicant is given to the staff in order to be submitted to the Human Resource Department. The common social and cultural background of the Filipino applicant and the staff makes it easier for the application to be passed and submitted to the right persons. Social expectations regulate that *kabayans* assist their co-Filipinos. Second, job seekers approach other Filipinos whom they accidentally meet at the street. They ask for their cell phone numbers and potential job vacancies. Filipinos who recently entered the UAE use this tactic; Eden shares her experience:

> If they saw me, they're asking me about this. 'Excuse me, can I ask you?' [...] If I know, of course, I help. They're asking me first: 'Are you working?' 'Yes.' 'Where you're working?' 'Here, only near here.' Then they're asking: 'I'm searching for a job. If ever your company is hiring, can you please give my CV?' 'Ok, no problem. [...] This is the fax number, this is

the telephone number, you can ask and call if you need'. (Interview with Eden, November 29, 2007)

Third, the social network is involved in the search for employment. Frequently, friends, relatives, or acquaintances based in Dubai know where current job openings are, e.g., one woman was informed by her Sri Lankan boyfriend about the opening of a new hotel and the need for a large number of staff. Together with five of her roommates, she submitted her CV and all were hired immediately.

The example of search for employment stresses that local knowledge responds to changing social environments. The social experience of being a migrant abroad obliged to send money back to the family as well as the conditions of the receiving society make knowledge about search for employment indispensable. This example also shows that local knowledge also entails action-oriented skills.

Intercultural Relationships

By considering the enormous cultural diversity in Dubai followed by the recruitment of foreign workers, knowledge about intercultural relationships comprises an essential part of local knowledge typical for Dubai. Filipino migrants working in the hotel industry are exposed to people with different cultural backgrounds. Colleagues originate from India and Sri Lanka and the hotel owners of the above-mentioned hotel are Sri Lankans. Guests residing in the hotel come from Iran, Europe, Russia, Kazakhstan, China, and many other countries. On the contrary, contact with locals is negligible. Daily interactions with colleagues often cause personal affection and friendships, some even resulting in intercultural love attachments. In the sample, some Filipinas have Sri Lankan boyfriends. Love attachments are a popular and never-ending topic, which the women discuss passionately. Love attachments are a hint that everyday life is not only dominated by employment, but that there is some space to live a self-responsible private life. Roaming around with the boyfriend or going to restaurants are ways to forget about work and just feel like an "ordinary" young woman enjoying life. Talking to the boyfriend relieves homesickness and other emotional problems. Despite the emotional character of these relationships, the priority for these women is doubtless the responsibility to their families. Expecting that their families will not tolerate a Muslim boyfriend from Sri Lanka, some of the women keep silent about their boyfriends to avoid confrontation. Cristina's relationship to her Egyptian boyfriend was challenged by their different cultural backgrounds and practices. She could not accept that while walking with her boyfriend, he walks in front of her and not beside her:

> While we were walking, he wants to go first. Hello, I'm also human! He wants to go first while I'm in the back. […] If the lady passes in front of the guy [in his country] it means that this lady is making dishonor with this guy. […] I told him: If you don't want I go ahead, I'm going to make my own way. […] At least, somehow he changed. (Interview with Cristina, November 4, 2007)

Intercultural misunderstandings are especially striking when it comes to social contacts with men. Nearly all of the younger women experienced some misunderstandings, especially in the area of the typical joking relationship between young men and women common in the Philippines, when they try to apply them to other nationalities.

> In the Philippines you can joke about the guys. You can call them: 'Hey honey!', 'Hey sweetheart', they tell you back like that. Here, if you flirt with them, they think you're together! I had experiences like that. I smile on people, I don't think anything about it. And then they said: 'If you smile at them they think you like them! [...] It's very rude if you don't smile at people so now I try to put my hand down. In the Philippines, that's how we joke, it's very playful. With flirting it's different also. But here, you have to be really, really careful. Because they think you're easy and they can have you if you're like that. (Interview with Ligaya, October 21, 2007)

Ligaya and her Filipina friends had to experience that their behavior, which they learnt in the socialization process in the Philippines, has a different meaning outside the Filipino cultural reference frame. In Dubai, they feared to be mistaken for loose women, so they learnt to appropriately change their behavior.

As shown, the social reality of everyday life is framed by intercultural relationships. However, the depth of the bonds of these contacts is individually different and ranges from intercultural contacts in the workplace to love attachments. To successfully act in the intercultural setting, knowledge about aspects of intercultural communication is unavoidable as demonstrated by the example of the Filipino joking relationships. The example shows that local knowledge is based on an empirical local basis; it is gained in the experiences of everyday life.

Transnational Families

The family is often characterized as the core of Filipino social organization. Following Jocano,

> the notion of kinship lies deep in the heart of Filipino community social organization. It is its nucleus. It affects, if not dominates, the shaping of local institutions, values, emotions and actions. (Jocano 2001, p. 66)

Ties to the family left behind will not be cut off in migration, but rather the family is the guiding principle in migration. In the case of Sheila, her migration to Dubai was motivated by the desire to find a Filipino husband, but despite this fact, the most significant for her is her family:

> Supposed to be I have my boyfriend or husband soon. Maybe, he is my third priority: God, family and he. I cannot prioritize first my husband. (Interview with Sheila, November 7, 2007)

Due to the strong social relationships to the families in the Philippines, migrants consider themselves to be part of their transnational families (Parreñas 2003, p. 80). Theories of transnationalism consider the social, political, religious, and economic relationships between individuals and organizations which transcend the boundaries of nation-states (Pries 2008). Migration is not considered to be a one-time movement, but rather a circular process. Resulting from this, identities and activities can be tied to more than one place.

Transnational social family ties of Filipina migrants become present in many examples. Although physically absent, the family is socially very present and mothers try to correspond to their role as mothers even while being abroad: For example, modern communication technologies like Internet, telephone, or text messages make participation in family life possible. Mothers calling home unexpectedly at any time of the day are one example of mothers checking on their children to see where and how they are. Another striking example is sending of remittances, which stresses that migrants form a part of the transnational household. The motivation for sending remittances is a recurrent theme observable in the statements and social actions of the women. Whatever the rationale for migration was, support of the family is common to all Filipino migrants. A statistical survey conducted by Semyonov and Gorodzeisky confirms that more than 97% of all OFWs send remittances to their Philippine household (Semyonov and Gorodzeisky 2005, p. 54). According to Maria,

> Your intention is to help your family in terms of monetary aspects. For us Filipinos coming here, by hook and by crook, you have to send money to the Philippines. (Interview with Maria, October 26, 2007)

Therefore, knowledge how to successfully support the family in the Philippines is another facet of local knowledge omnipresent in the everyday life of Filipina migrants. Knowledge how to successfully support the family embraces many different aspects, for example, knowledge how to find work abroad, knowledge how to remit money efficiently, or knowledge how not to spend money in Dubai despite of high-living expenses. In conclusion, knowledge about the successful support of the family is not an aspect ranking at the same level as the before-mentioned dimensions but rather a guiding theme or leitmotif or migration.

Social Networks and Knowledge Transfer

The social network is not the only way to transmit local knowledge, but by far the most significant one. Compared to the more informal character of social networks, formal ways of knowledge transfer also exist. The diverse offers provided by the Philippine government are one example: The state institution POEA provides possible migrants with technical support concerning the formalities of recruitment procedures or visa requirements. For instance, NGOs based in the Philippines (e.g., Kanlungan Centre Foundation, c.f. Alunan 1997), individual OFWs sustaining their own website (e.g., OFW Connect 2007), or special journals for OFWs (e.g., The Filipino Expats 2005) assist migrants by giving country profiles or even job advertisements for the UAE (e.g., Pinoy UAE 2008). Despite these large possibilities of gaining knowledge relevant for migration, only one of the informants stated having used it.

More vital is obtaining knowledge through own experience, i.e., predominantly observing or trial-and-error. Although the newcomers are, for example, briefed by experienced migrants how to properly behave in intercultural relationships with men in order to avoid misinterpretations, some only become aware of this matter when their jokes with guys are mistakenly understood as sexual "pick-up lines."

However, the significance of experience and formal ways of knowledge transfer are negligible compared to the importance of the social network. Social network theories describe the social structure in form of social relations between different actors whose actions largely depend on the structure of their social network. The actors are connected to each other by different levels of interdependency. In migration studies, social network analysis is commonly done in order to study support and help migrants get from their social network.[6]

Prior to the decision to migrate, ties in social network play a crucial part for Filipina migrants since they provide the potential OFW with information about different countries. The women in the sample owe a large part of their previous knowledge—how life is like for OFWs in Dubai—to people from their personal network.

Arriving in the UAE, the visa sponsors are the first contact persons, and they are mostly friends or relatives who already work in the UAE. The visa sponsor usually picks up the newcomer at the airport and shares food and accommodation. In the UAE, low-wage earners reside either in crowded staff accommodations provided by the company or in bed spaces—shared rooms with about 10–15 persons. Bed spaces are strictly segregated by the social category ethnicity: Filipinos, Indians from Kerala, or Nepali do not mingle, but occupy rooms only with other countrymen. These bed spaces are commonly the entry point to the migrants' stay in Dubai and the place where "old hands" instruct newcomers and transfer local knowledge. Newcomers are informed about the formal procedures of applications, potential employers, and best wages. "Old hands" comfort or give deflection when feelings of emotional distress occur. Some of them brief the recently arrived about socially "correct" behavior in Dubai, motivated by a sense of responsibility they feel for their *kabayan*, as stated by Cathrine:

> The newcomers, I have to tell them that: "This in this country, you must avoid this. […] If not necessarily, don't speak with them [other nationalities, S. C.]. Avoid strangers. If you think that they can harm you, avoid them. As much as possible you must be very careful because we don't know what is in their mind." […] You have to protect yourself and you have to protect each other. You have to protect your countrymen also from others. You must [be] responsible for them also (Interview with Cathrine. December 5, 2007)

In the accommodation provided by the employer and also the bed spaces rented by Filipinas, all dimensions of local knowledge are shared. To intentionally expand their personal networks, some migrants even manage to integrate strangers. As mentioned before, newcomers approach other Filipinos who they accidentally cross paths with in order to ask for job opportunities, possible accommodations, or telephone numbers. In some cases, cell phone numbers are exchanged; by adding the number in the directory, the former strangers now belong to the personal network.

---

[6] For social network analysis, see Wasserman and Faust 1994. For studies on migration and social networks in cultural anthropology, see Brettell (2000, pp. 107–108).

It is obvious that this is merely used to contact other *kabayan,* not other nationalities. Within the Filipino community, the expectation to get valuable information by approaching strangers seems to be taken for granted. Sheila explains her incentive:

> I didn't ask: "Why should I help you? Do I know you?" No need because I'm also a Filipino. I know the situation. The first time we are here is hard. At least, if he can find a job, he will remember: "Oh, there is a Filipino who helped me." (Interview with Sheila, November 7, 2007)

Since support was given to Sheila when she was new in Dubai, she feels obliged to share her own positive experience. Mutual help and transfer of knowledge do not seem to be solely altruistic acts of individual persons, but rather a socially anticipated behavior. The norm of generalized reciprocity is the shared ideal in the OFW community, to which all Filipinos should correspond regardless whether they know each other or are strangers. Generalized reciprocity means that it is not the recipient of support who is expected to return support to the giver; although a return of help is expected, the return can be delivered to any member of the Filipino community at any time. Even though generalized reciprocity is the action-guiding norm, not everybody complies with it and some even take advantage of inexperienced newcomers. But, in general, Filipinos disfavor persons not conforming to this norm. Eden, for example, was outraged by a Filipina nurse who refused to give her medicines because of formalities, although Eden suffered heavy pains in her kidneys. "She is a Filipino lady, but *she didn't act like a Filipino*" (Interview with Eden, November 29, 2007, author's emphasis). On the whole, transfer of knowledge is restricted to the Filipino community, which emphasizes the role of ethnicity with regard to local knowledge and knowledge transfer. Only a few facets are also shared outside the community, most notably work-related issues, such as how to find employment or legal aspects concerning work or residence. Sri Lankan or Indian (boy) friends serve as intermediaries between different networks and are therefore valuable sources of information.

Conclusion

For the purpose of this chapter, the concept of local knowledge was preferred over informal learning. Whereas informal learning refers more to individual learning experiences, the approach of local knowledge clearly focuses on shared patterns of behavior in certain localities. This also refers to the social category ethnicity since migrants originating from the locality of the Philippines form an inclusive ethnic group in the UAE by keeping boundaries to other ethnic groups. Ethnicity is a guiding principle in the multiethnic environment of Dubai. It was shown that in the UAE, ethnicity and not formal education is the prevalent feature to determine job opportunities, wages, and even the social structure. As labor migrants, Filipina migrants are excluded from the engagement in further formal education in the UAE and even face deskilling experiences. On the other hand, the migrants themselves perpetuate the importance of ethnicity which becomes evident in different examples: Bed spaces, where newcomers are instructed and local knowledge is shared, are ethnically segregated. Moreover, except for knowledge concerning legal aspects or search for employment, all other dimensions of local knowledge are shared only within the Filipino social network and facilitated by the social norm of generalized reciprocity.

However, the "local" of the local knowledge has also to be understood geographically. It refers to certain localities and local situations and responds to changing environments. In the case of Filipina migrants, the conditions of the receiving and the sending country influence the kind of knowledge Filipinas have. Referring to the receiving society, the demographic imbalance between Emirati citizens and foreigners, for instance, is one reason why Filipinas experience cultural difference not in terms of social contacts with Emiratis, but with other foreigners. Competence in intercultural communication becomes indispensable. Conditions of the sending society like the importance of the family lead to transnational households and stress the significance of knowledge about the successful support of the transnational family as the guiding principle of migration.

References

Alunan, G. (1997). *Destination Middle East: A handbook for Filipino women domestic workers.* Quezon City: Kanlungan Centre Foundation.
Antweiler, C. (1998). Local knowledge and local knowing: An anthropological analysis of contested "cultural products" in the context of development. *Anthropos, 93*(4–6), 469–494.
Antweiler, C. (2004). Local knowledge theory and methods: An urban model from Indonesia. In A. Bicker, P. Sillitoe, & J. Pottier (Eds.), *Investigating local knowledge. New directions, new approaches* (pp. 1–34). Aldershot: Ashgate.
Arnu, T. (2007, May 16/17). Im Übermorgenland. *Süddeutsche Zeitung, 112,* 11.
Asis, M. (2001). Country study 1: Philippines: The return migration of Filipino women migrants: Home, but not for good? In C. Wille & B. Passl (Eds.), *Female labour migration in South-East Asia: Change and continuity* (pp. 23–93). Bangkok: Asian Research Centre for Migration.
Brettell, C. (2000). Theorizing migration in anthropology: The social construction of networks, identities, communities and globalscapes. In C. Brettell & J. Hollifield (Eds.), *Migration theory: Talking across disciplines* (pp. 97–137). New York: Routledge.
Chin, C. (2003). Organisierte Randständigkeit als staatliches Modell: Frauen und Migration in Südostasien. In U. Hunger & D. Thränhardt (Eds.), *Migration im Spannungsfeld von Globalisierung und Nationalstaat.* Leviathan Sonderheft 22 (pp. 313–333). Wiesbaden: Westdeutscher Verlag.
Constable, N. (1997). *Maid to order in Hong Kong: Stories of Filipina workers.* Ithaca/London: Cornell University Press.
Dean, L. (2005). *The Middle East and North Africa 2006.* Europe regional surveys of the world. (52nd ed.). London: Routledge.
Furnivall, J. S. (1980). Plural societies. In H.-D. Evers (Ed.), *Sociology of South-East Asia* (pp. 85–96). Oxford: Oxford University Press.
Gesemann, F. (2003). Arbeitskräfte ohne Rechte: Migration im Nahen Osten. In U. Hunger & D. Thränhardt (Eds.), *Migration im Spannungsfeld von Globalisierung und Nationalstaat.* Leviathan Sonderheft 22 (pp. 346–366). Wiesbaden: Westdeutscher Verlag.

Ghaemi, H. (2006). Building towers, cheating workers: Exploitation of migrant construction workers in the United Arab Emirates. *Human Rights Watch November 2006. 18*(8E). http://hrw.org/reports/2006/uae1106/. Accessed 27 December 2007.

Gulf News. (December 7, 2007). *Classifieds.*

Han, P. (2003). *Frauen und Migration: Strukturelle Bedingungen, Fakten und soziale Folgen der Frauenmigration.* Stuttgart: Lucius & Lucius.

Hugo, G. (2004). International migration in Southeast Asia since World War II. In A. Aris und E. N. Arifin (Eds.), *International migration in Southeast Asia* (pp. 28–70). Singapore: Institute of Southeast Asian Studies.

Janardhan, N. (2007). Redefining labor market rules. In A. Sager (Ed.), *Gulf yearbook 2006–2007* (pp. 199–214). Dubai: Gulf Research Center.

Jocano, F. (2001). *Filipino worldview: Ethnography of local knowledge: Anthropology of the Filipino people V.* Quezon City: Punlad.

Kapiszewski, A. (2001). *Nationals and expatriates: Population and labour dilemmas of the Gulf cooperation council states.* Ithaca: Reading.

Lauser, A. (2004). *Ein guter Mann ist harte Arbeit: Eine ethnographische Studie zu philippinischen Heiratsmigrantinnen.* Bielefeld: Transcript.

Llorente, S. (2007). A futuristic look into the Filipino diaspora: Trends, issues, and implications. *Journal of Filipino Studies.* http://journaloffilipinostudies.csueastbay.edu/html/cfsj-csueb-2007.html. Accessed 6 June 2008.

Lutz, H. (2007). *Vom Weltmarkt in den Privathaushalt: Die neuen Dienstmädchen im Zeitalter der Globalisierung.* Opladen: Barbara Budrich.

Mangahas, M. (May 5, 2008). Measuring the OFW advantage. *Philippine Daily Inquirer.* http://opinion.inquirer.net/inquireropinion/columns/view/20080524-138480/Measuring-the-OFW-advantage. Accessed 21 July 2008.

Marchal, R. (2005). Dubai: Global city and transnational hub. In M. Al-Rasheed (Ed.), *Transnational connections and the Arab Gulf* (pp. 93–110). London: Routledge.

OFW Connect. (2007). *VB's OFW-conncet for Filipino migrant workers around the globe.* http://www.ofw-connect.com. Accessed 19 February 2008.

Parreñas, R. (2003). *Servants of globalization: Women, migration and domestic work.* Manila: Ateneo de Manila University Press.

Philippine Overseas Employment Administration (POEA). (2004). *Stock estimates of overseas Filipinos as of December 2004.* http://www.poea.gov.ph/html/statistics.html. Accessed 9 February 2007.

Philippine Overseas Employment Administration (POEA). (2006). *OFW global presence: A compendium of overseas employment statistics.* http://www.poea.gov.ph/stats/2006Stats.pdf. Accessed 3 February 2008.

Pinoy UAE. (2008). *Pinoy UAE.* http://www.pinoyuae.com. Accessed 2 February 2008.

Pries, L. (2008). *Die Transnationalisierung der sozialen Welt: Sozialräume jenseits von Nationalgesellschaften.* Frankfurt am Main: Suhrkamp.

Reiterer, G. (1997). *Die Philippinen: Kontinuität und Wandel.* Wien: Sonderzahl.

Schugurensky, D. (2000). *The forms of informal learning: Towards a conceptualization of the field.* NALL working paper no. 19. http://www.oise.utoronto.ca/depts/sese/csew/nall/res/19formsofinformal.htm. Accessed 16 November 2009.

Semyonov, M., & Gorodzeisky, A. (2005). Labor migration, remittances and household income: A comparison between Filipino and Filipina overseas workers. *International Migration Review, 39*(1), 45–68.

Shinozaki, K. (2005). Making sense of contradictions: Examining negotiation strategies of "contradictory class mobility" in Filipina/Filipino domestic workers in Germany. In T. Geisen (Ed.), *Arbeitsmigration: WanderarbeiterInnen auf dem Weltmarkt für Arbeitskraft.* Beiträge zur Regional- und Migrationsforschung Band 5 (pp. 259–278). Frankfurt am Main/London: IKO-Verlag für Interkulturelle Kommunikation.

The Filipino Expats. (2005). *Special Issue,* May 2005, Vol. 1 Issue 008-05.

Wasserman, S., & Faust, K. (1994). *Social network analysis: Methods and applications.* Cambridge: Cambridge University Press.
Weekly, K. (2005). Filipina domestic workers in Hong Kong: Organisation and "Reintegration." In T. Geisen (Ed.), *Arbeitsmigration: WanderarbeiterInnen auf dem Weltmarkt für Arbeitskraft.* Beiträge zur Regional- und Migrationsforschung Band 5 (pp. 279–298). Frankfurt am Main/London: IKO-Verlag für Interkulturelle Kommunikation.
Weyland, P. (1997). Jeder hält doch nach einer grüneren Weide Ausschau! Philippinische Hausmädchen in Istanbul. *kea Zeitschrift für Kulturwissenschaften, 10,* 29–153.

Chapter 44
Ethnicized Youth Subcultures and "Informal Learning" in Transitions to Work

Vitor Sérgio Ferreira and Axel Pohl

Introduction

Young people who or whose parents have moved to another country are one of the key topics in debates surrounding educational achievement, labour market integration and integration into European societies at large. While one strand of research and public debate focuses on these groups under the angle of the assumed threat to social cohesion (Cheong et al. 2007) and regards primarily young males as potential perpetrators, other strands stress the continuing inequality facing racialized and ethnicized groups especially in the education system and labour market in particular (Geisen 2007). While the first perspective tends to interpret cultural or "ethnic" identities as a factor of self-exclusion (Terpstra 2006; Skrobanek 2007), the latter often tends to over-emphasize structural aspects where young people's ways of coping are seen as simple reflections of imposed disadvantageous situations. While much of the research relates these situations to young people's class background (Devadason 2006; Machado and Matias 2006), youth research often emphasizes the cultural heritage of migrants' descendants as a starting point for the explanation of subjective meaning-making (cf. Phoenix 2004).

Taking this phenomenon into account, the aim of this contribution is to use the notion of subculture to discuss the youth cultural orientations of young migrants and descendents from an *agency perspective* in order to observe what innovative potential is hidden in these social contexts, which are often only viewed under the angle of social deviation and/or reproduction of social inequality. As argued below, this view may well reveal subcultures as potential social contexts for agency and learning of young people with ethnic or migrant backgrounds, where we might observe closely their active process *to commit* to the demand for individualization,

V. S. Ferreira (✉)
Universidade de Lisboa, Av. Prof. Aníbal Bettencourt, n. 9, 1600-189, Lisboa, Portugal
e-mail: vitor.ferreira@ics.ul.pt

A. Pohl
Institute for Regional Innovation and Social Research (IRIS e.V.),
Fürststr. 3, 72072 Tübingen, Germany
email: axel.pohl@iris-egris.de

characteristic of late modern European society, and *to connect* with some kind of modern youth life world.

This contribution stems from the larger context of the EC-funded research project "UP2YOUTH—Youth: Actor of social change". The project was concerned with young people's agency in the context of social change. While their transitions to adulthood are structured by risk and uncertainty, young men and women develop coping strategies which in turn affect social structures, namely work, family, and citizenship which were the key topics of the UP2YOUTH project. However, whether these strategies contribute both to social integration and subjectively meaningful biographical perspectives depends on the scope of action provided by societal structures.

UP2YOUTH applied a methodological approach which could be labelled as a *qualitative meta-analysis*, combining country reports based on literature reviews and secondary analysis of mainly qualitative studies with explorative and evaluative workshops with policy-makers, practitioners and researchers from all fields concerned with transitions to adulthood. This chapter draws mainly from the discussions of the UP2YOUTH working group on "Transitions to work of young people from an ethnic minority or migrant background", consisting of research teams from Denmark, Spain, Germany, Finland, Romania, and Portugal (cf. Mørch et al. 2008).

Formal and Informal Structures of Transitions

In all the countries under analysis in this chapter,[1] the research finds that newcomers and descendents often have many problems with the education system, and evince higher school failure rates than their "native" counterparts (Mørch et al. 2008; Heath et al. 2008). The dominant trajectories or traditional pathways of young people with an immigrant or ethnic background through the education and training system—being African in Portugal, Latin American in Spain, or Turkish in Germany or in Denmark, for instance—are marked by massive and cumulative failure, as well as premature and unqualified drop out. At the same time, only the more unqualified segments of the labour market are open to them, in conditions of precariousness and/or underemployment (Heath et al. 2008).

Such weak school performances are not just because of poor language skills concerning the countries of residence, or the lack of familiarity with the school system and its formal culture. It is also because these young people very often experience the school as impermeable to their ethnic experiences, to their migrant history perspective, to their practices and forms of expression (Moldenhawer et al. 2009). Feeling neither identified nor supported or positively recognized by the school system, they experience discrimination and exclusion in the school territory (Downey 2008). Regarding the variable gender, all studies carried out in Portugal, for instance, point towards the fact that, in keeping with the pattern that has been consolidating itself in most developed countries, not only do girls have, on aver-

---

[1] This chapter was partially presented and discussed as a paper in the 4th Conference Young People & Societies in Europe and around the Mediterranean, Forlì, 26–28 March 2009.

age, a higher level of education than boys, but they also have lower failure rates (especially in terms of multiple repetition), achieving better school results than boys (Casa-Nova 2005; Martins 2005).

In this scenario, many young people search for positive challenges and identities in places other than school, work, or family. To be young, nowadays, is not just a time of transition to adulthood, dominated by family and school; it is also a social condition that has its own lifestyles and life worlds. As young people, with or without any kind of ethnic or migrant background, they find other particular worlds where they can *escape* from disciplinary and traditional controls of school and family, where they can find some social protection, recognition, and celebration, and where they can share a feeling of equality and reciprocity in social relations. Their distance from school, the labour market, and familiar cultures can be compensated by other meaningful social contexts, like *youth subcultures* or *youth scenes*.

As many studies have pointed out, many young people who have difficulties of integration into other formal social structures frequently participated in these microcultural contexts (Bennett 1999; Blackman 2005; Hesmondhalgh 2005; Muggleton 2002 [2000]). For those young people with an ethnic or migrant background, subcultures often function as a social support structure for those who, as a *newcomer* or *outsider,* feel alone or not "adapted" to the formal structures of the social world, not having many positive social references to construct their own identity and self-esteem, and/or are confronted daily with increasing social risks, insecurity, and hostility.

Considering gender, subcultures started as mainly male cultures, taking into account the relative marginality that girls have traditionally had within these social networks (Frønes 2001; McRobbie and Garber 1976). As noticed before, young migrant women and comparable native women use parallel forms of coping with school and the passage from school to work, much more committed with mainstream school life. They prefer to invest their strategies in more institutional spaces, such as schooling and training, trying to achieve higher competencies and skills for dealing with the double challenge of being a woman with an ethnic or a migrant background. However, some recent studies have noticed the increase in girls' presence in subcultural spaces, sometimes even creating particular forms of feminine subcultures as a strategy of social negotiation and emancipation of their female position in their life worlds, as happens with the movement of the RIOT GRRRLS— Revolution Girl Style Now (Gottleib and Wald 1994). The Latin Kings in Barcelona, for instance, have a girl as leader (Melody Jaramillo) since they acquired the status of legal cultural association. And they also have the Latin Queens, a segment for girls only inside the movement (Feixa et al. 2008). The hip hop culture, namely among rappers, currently has plenty of girls as members in Portugal as well, as in other national contexts (Guevara 1996; Simões and Nunes 2005).

Even if these micro-cultural youth contexts present themselves as authenticity enclaves, the scenes of young migrants or young people with an ethnic minority background frequently *(re)ethnicize* themselves (as a way of dealing with discrimination and with the challenges they are confronted with in late modernity) and are *(re)ethnicized* by others, many times in a stigmatic sense. The social image of these contexts is usually marked by stigma, much more produced, reproduced, and generalized by the media based on specific situations, than by interpretative and systematic ground knowledge. The fact is that false beliefs can produce real effects, many times perverse effects, such as discrimination, racism, and xenophobia. But the micro-cultural networks, or the *subcultural capital* (Thornton 1995) that these structures can provide, might also contextualize the transitions from school to work in an integrative or self-exclusion way, providing some skills, competencies, and even employment dreams, expectations, and opportunities.

Ethnicized Subculture Contexts and Agency

The transitions of young people of ethnic minority are, in fact, sometimes supported by marginalized social structures, locally and informally organized, created in the "streets"[2] (MacDonald and Shildrick 2007) and culturally oriented towards their own social interests and values. Despite being strongly criticized,[3] one can see this kind of structures as *subcultures*, a concept which stresses the power relations between socio-cultural forms. This concept has been seen by sociological tradition as minority and subaltern social affiliations (which might be based on age or generation) considering the hegemonic cultural model (which might be based on class or adulthood, for instance).

They correspond to underground youth networks, produced in a voluntary and informal way, more flexible and convivialist than the formal associative structures, without any kind of institutional frame or unidirectional ideological orientation. Their participants share a set of aesthetic and ethical affinities and emotional affectivities, representative of interests, which are more expressive than instrumental (Ferreira 2009). And they frequently present themselves as an alternative and dissident way of living youth life, considering the dominant patterns of youth life styles, which are more mainstreamed in the occidental consumer culture (Mørch and Andersen 2006).

Within those micro structures, cultural forms of reaction to the problems that their members are facing in everyday life are projected and elaborated, often as the result of structural tensions between minorities and hegemonic cultural forms. Considering the analytic tradition developed by the Centre for Contemporary Cultural Studies of Birmingham University, for instance, the youth subcultures that emerged after the Second World War were seen as *functional* answers towards transforma-

---

[2] The "street" designation corresponds to a metaphoric place constructed against institutional places such as "home" (ruled by parents) or the "class room" (ruled by professors). When the young people refer to the "street" usually they mean the exo-domiciliary and interstitial contexts where they live in their neighbourhoods or around.

[3] For a discussion about the heuristic validity and productivity of the subculture concept in contemporary society, see Redhead 1997; Bennett 1999; Muggleton 2002 (2000); Blackman 2005; Hesmondhalgh 2005.

tions and difficulties lived by young people (*age*) with working class background (*social class*) in this period (*generation*).[4] In this way, one can present these reactions as forms of *subcultural agency*, i.e. as a means of expressive and dissident action, characterized by a transforming intention and reflexivity, but socially localized far from the spheres of political decision making, intending to continue to reproduce this cultural and politically marginal localization.

Despite their importance, there are more variables involved on the basis of the social production of youth subcultures besides traditional *social class* and *age* or *generation*. Since their emergence, there have always been youth networks and subcultural forms produced on the basis of *migrant* and/or *ethnic background*.[5] These networks started to be mainly constituted, on the one hand, by young *newcomers* that did not take part of the decision-making process of migration, made by their parents and often an imposition that breaks primary socialization networks built up in the country of birth. Chicago sociologists witnessed within immigrant communities, as their young people came into contact with values and opportunities that differed radically from those experienced by their parents, how the organization of the city resulted in a tendency for the children of immigrants to escape parental control, with boy gangs acting as a substitute for morally effective institutions (Thomas 1909; Matthews 1977).

With the settlement of those communities, these networks started to also integrate young *descendents*, who were mainly born in their parents' country of residence, but who frequently felt like *outsiders*, as some studies show that they perceive themselves and their group as being discriminated against (Vala et al. 2003). Their poor and much territorialized socio-economic conditions, in association with their visible *ex-optic* phenotypes and particular looks and body performances—responsible for social "labels" that are usually used as stigmas and that are the basis of the negative social image constructed—lead to cultural, social, and institutional discrimination (Pais and Blass 2004).

On the other hand, subcultures were socially and even academically very connected with the *gang*, a social formation where some illicit and violent reactions (usually mugging and/or drugs trafficking) could be found. Even if these activities are not part of the core group activity, a negative social identity is built up in the public sphere, namely when media explore, give visibility and diffuse this kind of phenomena, producing some "moral panic" (Thompson 1998), leading to the negative evaluation of the subcultural capital with reference to the mainstream social capital. Subcultures are often seen as a factor of disturbance of the public order, and that kind of illicit behaviour is generalized to all young people recognized as members of the ethnicized group. Under the mask of the stigma, we find the creation of a stereotype, which can operate as a structural barrier to the development of a positive agency and identity within these micro and marginalized contexts.

---

[4] See Hall and Jefferson 1976; Mungham and Pearson 1976; Cohen and Taylor 1978; Hebdige 1986 (1979).

[5] See, for instance, the first research produced by the Chicago School, such as the studies of Thrasher (1963 [1926]) or Whyte (2005 [1943]).

However, if youth subcultures may sometimes be the stage for some cases of violence and illegal activities, they quite frequently function as a *crew*, an expressive and sociability structure where some young people can find emotional ties, friendship, commitment, positive identity, recognition, autonomy, creativity, and a sense of participating and being a protagonist in the social world, around some specific cultural practices, as producers and/or consumers. That is particularly true for those young people who feel culturally distant from the ethnic references of their parents and, at the same time, experience a sense of "otherness" in contact with the hegemonic culture of the country of residence. Some of them feel misfit in their own homes, in their schools, and in the labour market. Many of them find their own space in the public sphere during their leisure time. That is why these socio-cultural spaces of "youth subcultures" might indicate the dimension of social exclusion of many young people from the more normative trajectories and models of citizenship.

Even not knowing their parents' home countries, descendents can find in their ethnic roots relevant sources and resources (symbolic, material, and pragmatic) for the construction and expression of a positive sense of social and personal identity, as well as a sense of social agency and autonomy as young citizens. It is the case of resources such as music, dance, gastronomy, clothes, or even discursive language or slang, among others. The resources that they claim from their supposed origins, however, are not mobilized in their original "purity" or "authenticity". They are not just transmitted from one generation to another, but reinvented and rediscovered, in one word *(re)ethnicized* (Skrobanek 2007), by each generation, in its own context of production and reproduction.

(Re)ethnicization constitutes a strategy to emphasize or rather differentiate in-group specific—as opposed to out-group specific—cultural, social, or economic group properties and resources, to (re)gain social recognition or their valued group distinctiveness, i.e. (re)gain a positive social identity in comparison with the out-group they are discriminated against. The construction of ethnic identity can be considered a special form of social identity and allows a more or less clear differentiation between various groups, constituting a basis for comparison between groups. Furthermore, the subjective significance of ethnic identity for an individual appears within the scope of his/her evaluation of such an identity. The (re)ethnicization strategy affects both social and personal identity (closer to the group of origin) and sociabilities (the group boundaries are less permeable to others outside the ethnic group).

Data from many studies suggest that the tendency towards (re)ethnicization should not be interpreted as merely a lack of willingness to integrate. The (re)ethnicization strategy was used by groups such as the Turkish Power Boys in Germany (Tertilt 1996), as well as the Latin Kings in Spain (Feixa et al. 2008), or by the crews of the Hip Hop "black" movement in Portugal[6] (Contador and Ferreira 1997; Contador 2001; Fradique 2003; Raposo 2007), to react and to cope with the situation of socio-economic deprivation and feelings of marginality with reference to the dominant group. If these subcultures emerged and developed in restricted territories (the

---

[6] Crews of music rappers or DJs, break dancers, B-boys or painting writers/graffitists.

first in Germany, and the last ones in the USA), they are now transnational and deterritorialized, real, and virtually displaced and spread all over the world, acquiring hybrid specificities in each social and spatial context (Raposo 2007; Simões 2006).[7]

It is the case of rap culture in Portugal, for instance. Despite being an expressive form imported from the Bronx (United States), reproducing many of its rhythmic and linguistic mannerisms of origin, the fact that most of the rap produced in the streets of the degraded neighbourhoods of Lisbon is sang in Creole creates a specific social bond between their protagonists: it culturally localizes them in Portugal and gives them a strong power of social identification and connection ("it motivates more because it connects much more, it feels like it's done by us and for us") (Raposo 2006).

At the same time, it provides them with a sense of separation regarding the white Portuguese population: "I don't have to sing in Portuguese, they also didn't give me Portuguese nationality, although I was born in Portugal", says one of the protagonists of the documentary Nu Bai (Raposo 2006). Despite a Cape Verdean language system, the Creole brings together all young black people (and even some non black, also residents of the neighbourhoods and sharing the same youth hip hop scene[8]) with several ethnic and national backgrounds (Angolans, Cape Verdeans, Guineans, Mozambicans, etc.) under the umbrella of "blackness", "all blacks together".

On the other hand, even if the Creole is a cultural reference inherited from parents—who often try to avoid its reproduction to their children in order to promote the learning and use of Portuguese—the language system that those young people use in their lyrics and sociabilities is not exactly the one that those parents speak, which is emblematic of the continuities and changes between generations and the (re)ethnicization process. If the use of Creole shows the strength of the parents' cultural heritage, it also reveals a distinct appropriation from the adults' use. The Creole that young people use in their daily practices is a mix of words from American and Portuguese slang and "street neologisms" from everywhere in the world. In fact, the knowledge of the English language among these young people is very good, especially among those that sing rap. The need to understand the message of their favourite bands promotes the proficiency of English skills among young people even without much schooling.

---

[7] These specificities derive from the confrontation between triple cultural memberships: parental cultural background, dominant culture of the "host" society and global youth cultures.

[8] See Raposo 2007, pp. 93–94. As it happens in the case of the Latin Kings in Barcelona, whose members are mainly Latin American, in particular Ecuadorian, but with an important percentage of natives, or even members coming from non-Latin countries such as Morocco, Russia or Equatorial Guinea (Feixa et al. 2008, p. 66). The various expressions of hip hop are also very present among the Latin Kings, and since the beginning, Latin cultures were immersed in hip hop cultures (Flores 1994). More than a strict ethnic identity (in fact, it is nowadays a *trans-ethnic* phenomenon), their participants share a strong feeling of socio-economic deprivation and discrimination.

Subcultures as Arena of Civic Learning

Subculture networks create some solidarity among disadvantaged young people living in marginal neighbourhoods, often resulting in hostile rivalries between neighbourhoods. Even after compulsory re-housing, where long-standing socially structured bonds between residents are destroyed, rap, for instance, is able to "reunite what was dispersed, not allowing people's conscience to become divided" (Raposo 2006). It gives their members a feeling of ontological security and social comfort regarding the risks that they confront daily due to their public visibility: on the one hand, it provides them with a feeling of shared identity; on the other hand, the "group" can function as a *defensive community* (McDonald 1999, p. 203), in a context where the need for protection started to be real, considering the subcultural tension between some "neo tribes" (such as *rappers* and *skins*, or the Latin Kings and Ñetas y Maras, for instance) or even between groups of young people from different neighbourhoods.

At the same time, the subcultural memberships provide their participants with a sense of pride and respect about their own ethnic, socio-economic and territorial *difference*: being together, they can learn moral codes as resources and as references to build up a positive social identity, and find a support structure for mutual legitimation and recognition of their complex identities as (poor and discriminated) minorities. In these social contexts, young people with an ethnic background can construct and positively share their sense of "otherness" towards the dominant youth models and life styles. As Bouchet (1999) mentions regarding the Arabic or Palestinian youth in Denmark, they see themselves as "proud" of their origins and ethnic identity.

They mostly want to gain "respect" and positive social recognition. Therefore, the strategies of the "Arabic youth" seem to be formed as a mixture of attack at the outer world and a special form of self-defence or self-protection, which create an antagonistic identity. This also applies to the Turkish Power Boys, a German youth gang founded by young Turkish people of the Mainkur-Comprehensive school (Tertilt 1996); the principle of friendship, the Turkish concept of honour and the cultivation of "Turkish slang" are the main strategies to enhance a negative social identity.

In this perspective, youth subcultures may function for these young people as a *civic arena*, where they can find not only a large frame of aesthetic and expressive references, but also a large frame of ethical and intervention resources of action and reaction, of critique and reflexivity, in order to think about their social place in the world and how to be a protagonist in their "host" societies. These scenes project their participants in a symbolic and social scenario where they find themselves as active subjects of their own lives and trajectories, providing them with the opportunity of (re)inventing their own social and personal identity in a positive way, in subjective conditions of freedom, pride, respect and dignity.

In these subcultural contexts, young people with an ethnic background living in poor living conditions can find themselves more as *citizens* than as *victims*, more as *subjects of* their own biographies than *subject to* standard and pre-existing destinies. There they can find stimulus and recognition for their own creative initiatives, for their *agency* as actors of social change. The "street rap"[9] is perceived by its performers as a social intervention "weapon", as a way of "giving voice to people that never had a voice". Its purpose is to "transmit[ting] the power of the word" in the recovery of positive cultural and ethnic references (Raposo 2007, p. 164), as well as in the public criticism and denouncement of the degraded living conditions and discriminatory situations that their performers face in their daily life. Thus, it is a form of musical and literary expression characterized by a transforming reflexivity, to the extent that its purpose is to give visibility and vindicate to bring about change, to "make revolution" (Raposo 2007, p. 81). Through their expressions and performances, these young people feel that they hold some power over themselves, not letting others decide their own destiny.

These (re)ethnicized youth micro-cultures are not just contexts for cultural expression, but also for political and civic socialization and action. The resources that they provide are frequently used by young people to denounce, demonstrate and reclaim their specific perspectives on their spheres of life and identity, as well as on their current social problems.[10] We have to take into account that many of those young people are disaffected from and disenchanted with the formal political sphere, namely through voting. If some can vote, many cannot, not only because they are not old enough, but also because that they do not have the country's nationality or are illegal in the country.

Nevertheless, we should not forget that these ethnicized social networks are far from traditional governance, negotiating and decision-making powers, often ending up working as social networks relatively isolated from the world outside the degraded neighbourhoods, stigmatizing and classifying its residents and their social capital (for reflections on the convertibility of "subcultural capital", cf. Jensen 2006). The neighbourhood protects and provides its young people with a feeling of trust that is not found outside (the territory that rap Portuguese young people call "Babylon"), but at the same time might enclose their respective life world, since these are neighbourhoods that offer little employment, education, and leisure opportunities.

Subcultures and Skills

In a more pragmatic way, more than a stronger sense of positive identity, these micro-social structures might also give young people, despite their position of socio-economic disadvantage, conditions to develop confidence, specific skills, ambition for future career planning (which can involve re-engaging with school or some kind of training scheme) and even some opportunities for their transition to the labour market. Being underground networks, where deviation is the norm, their protagonists found some space to create inventive and original ways of dealing with the cultural resources and the aesthetical affinities that they share. Offering opportunities

---
[9] As opposed to "commercial rap", more elitized, whitened and "domesticated".
[10] Such as other micro-cultural youth styles not ethnicized. Cf. Pfaff, 2009.

to engage in a number of creative and performative activities, often these contexts feed the professional dreams of these young people, dreams that can sometimes turn into reality, in the form of professional projects that dribble pre-standard social trajectories: to become a musician, a show producer, a singer, a writer, a technician, a dancer, a sport player, a performer, a web designer, and so on.

Some studies present these social contexts as real *creative experimental laboratories* (Feixa et al. 2001, p. 298), or *cultural laboratories* (Melucci 1989), where young people can experience new visuals, new music forms, other new kinds of performative and communicative expressions and skills. The initiation of the younger ones in the music and lyrical forms of rap, for instance, takes place informally from a very young age, a mechanism of *inclusive socialization* (Drilling and Gautschin 2001, p. 313) carried out through osmosis and conviviality. The practical experimentation and observation are the main forms of apprenticeship in youth scenes, sometimes with the orientation of an older master. Following more formal pathways, training or workshops, for instance, might occur at a later stage, when the related expression is thought of as a potential career (Simões 2006, pp. 422–428).

In some neighbourhoods, youth associations and community rehearsal rooms, together with other services and amenities, are organized, bringing together MCs, writers, B-boys and DJs from several neighbourhoods, raising their awareness of and making them follow rules regarding work organization and planning, behaviour, schedules, etc., and, at the same time, providing them with the opportunity to come into contact with an assemblage of technology, knowledge, and people that, otherwise, would be very difficult for them to have access to. Some even have organized libraries, with books and films about their ethnic roots, information that often young people do not find in their schools (libraries and curriculum). These youth scenes can, therefore, not only provide some expression abilities, but also organizational, technical, historical, and collaborative skills that can change their life, being a way of integration that does not follow the traditional forms of parents' labour reproduction, so many times offered by traditional schemes of training for disadvantaged youth (carpentry, construction, and other low-qualified manual work).[11]

In some countries, some national and local organizations started to explore and to invest in these micro-cultural expressions as a way of intercultural communication, giving young people better conditions of production, development, and diffusion of their products and (informal) skills.[12] At the same time, some try to *seize* their

---

[11] About the social engagement of disadvantaged young people through artistic programmes and activities and its articulation with youth policy, see the research findings of Roeper and Savelsberg 2009.

[12] In Portugal, for instance, *Escolhas* [Choices], a national State programme, had a pioneer role in that task. In its first phase of implementation, which took place until December 2003, it primarily focused on Youth Criminal Prevention and Integration in the most problematic residence areas of the districts of Lisbon, Oporto and Setúbal. At the end of this period, and giving up on a discourse based on the threat of criminality, initially quite stigmatizing for the Programme's target audience, the new phase of *Escolhas* aims to promote the social inclusion of children and young people from the most deprived and problematic socio-economic contexts, giving support to youth collaborative projects and associations.

leaders or protagonists as cultural and/or social mediators, as a means of establishing contact between the formal world of institutions (school, migrant associations, unions, local, and national powers, etc.) and the "street world" of informal groups of young people.

This was the Danish case of the "Wild Street Workers" (Mørck 2006), which is about four ethnic young people who were given the possibility of working as street workers and helping their local community in Copenhagen, having their own embodied and biographical competences as street boys as main skills (*street wise*). But it was also, in a much larger scale, the case of the institutionalization of the Latin Kings and Queens in Barcelona as a legal cultural association, a task that was done with the collaboration of the City Council and Youth Council of Barcelona, among other institutional powers. This process entailed mainly giving positive visibility to the Latin population and their cultural expressions in that city and in the media, to have young interlocutors represented in decision-making processes of the local authorities concerning the Latin population living in Barcelona; and, at the same time, to have a formal platform close to this population, providing help and support (legal, counselling in school or labour affairs, competencies recognition or learning, etc.) to migrants (Feixa and Canelles 2007; Feixa 2008; Feixa et al. 2008).

Conclusions

As has been argued elsewhere (Pais and Pohl 2003), the world of labour increasingly depends on the capacity of its participants "to organise and structure their own working lives and to develop the personal and social competencies needed for this" (op. cit., p. 223). This development occurs at the same time as profound changes are affecting education and training systems. Due to the de-coupling of educational achievement and labour market integration, these systems are less and less capable of producing these competencies themselves, but depend on the outside world to provide young people with resources like meaning, subjectivity, and motivation (Pohl et al. 2006; Walther 2009).

Considering the scenario drawn, the increasing informal subcultural sociabilities reveal an extensive power of attraction and implication among young people—namely among young people with a migrant or ethnic background—being lived as social spaces of social participation and socialization on citizenship, learning, and work practices.

In this chapter, we have shown that (re)ethnicized youth subcultures are not a case of "ethnic revival", but a symbolic solution young people find to certain social situations marked by experiences of marginalization and exclusion (cf. Lang 2007, pp. 232–233). These solutions may constitute a case of coping with/idealization of their own marginal situation and hence contribute to processes of self-exclusion, which in certain constellations can become real "traps" (Spindler 2007). But, it can also be seen as a case of articulation and active self-positioning. The "objective" outcome of this strategy can only be determined empirically on a case-by-case examination.

Both academic and political institutions that deal with young people have given minor importance to the social role of these spaces on the margin of the established channels for political involvement and commitment, as well as, consequently, in adapting to proposals of social participation "from the ground", from the everyday dimension of life.

Both the sociological reflection on the action of young people in "public life", and the institutional political instances that outline and regulate this action, have been ignoring or demonizing some of the real contexts of social participation and citizenship practice of young people, thwarting the potential of social intervention that frequently misaligned and subterranean arenas provide them with.

"Youth subcultures", "youth tribes", or "youth scenes", whatever the theoretical paradigm under these concepts, function as a social support structure for those who feel alone or not "adapted" to the mainstream social world—as "newcomers" or "outsiders"—who do not have much more positive social references to construct their own identity and self-esteem, and/or who are confronted daily with more and more social risks, insecurity, and hostility.

The social image of these contexts is usually marked by stigma, much more under domination of criminological and moralistic stereotypes produced, reproduced, and generalized by the media from specific situations, than by interpretative and systematic ground knowledge. The fact is that false beliefs can produce real effects, many times perverse effects, such as discrimination, racism, xenophobia, and even physical violence.

But if youth subcultures may sometimes be the stage for some cases of violence and criminality, they quite frequently function as a defensive structure for those who feel insecure and frightened, and where some young people can find emotional ties, friendship, commitment, positive identity, recognition, liberty, autonomy, creativity, a sense of being an *agent* in the social world. In one sentence, subcultures may be social contexts where young people can find sources and resources to exercise their own agency as actors of social change.

Despite being micro-spaces, subcultures correspond to a global phenomenon, mainly urban, that usually emerges in social contexts defined by different forms of social exclusion (from school, work, citizenship, etc.) and discrimination (class, ethnicity, culture, "race", etc.), which they signal and reveal. The cultural practices and resources mobilized by young people in their scenes express a form of re-action on the part of those who early in life experience hostility and constraints from broader society and its formal structures. Through their social participation in subcultures, some young people can have a subjective way of exercising social power and trying to change their own living conditions.

It is in everyday life, particularly in interstitial social spaces where leisure and cultural production happens, that youth citizenship is often exercised, reinvented in its meanings, objectives and traditional modes of action. Actually, nowadays the institutional and organizational scale of youth citizenship cedes ever more to a micro scale, structured in micro-cultural networks, from which it emerges mainly as an expressive form of construction, exploration, recognition, and social preservation of personal and collective identities, namely (re-)ethnicized identities.

In many of these informal interaction networks, there arise effectively implicated cultural conflicts and claims, based on the sharing of specific distinct and distinctive forms of identity, providing their protagonists not only with a strong sense of inclusion and demarcation, but also of existence and intervention. These are social spaces where many disadvantaged young people feel like *someone*, *subjects of* their own biography more than *subject to* standard pathways.

However, the education systems in all countries of our study do not recognize these spaces and confine them to a kind of "outside world". A fact that is especially problematic for boys and young men. The practical examples show how non-formal education can be used and at the same time give some value to the life worlds of ethnic minority young people and their subjective self-positioning and to overcome the boundedness of subcultural social positioning.

This integration is also linked to the development of a fully reflexive education system in the sense of Giddens' "institutional reflexivity" (Giddens 1991, p. 35) that prioritizes not only formal competencies but also training in diversity as a key tool to avoid exclusion processes. Or, as one expert in an UP2YOUTH workshop put it: "You have to decide whether you want to be a German school—or a school in Germany" (quoted in Foitzik and Pohl 2009).

References

Bennett, A. (1999). Subcultures or neo-tribes? Rethinking the relationship between youth, style and musical taste. *Sociology, 33*(3), 599–617.
Blackman, S. (2005). Youth subcultural theory: A critical engagement with the concept, its origins and politics, from the Chicago School to postmodernism. *Journal of Youth Studies, 8*(1), 1–20.
Bouchet, D. (1999). *Det knuste spejl*, Afveje. Danmark: Odense Universitet.
Casa-Nova, M. J. (2005). (I)migrantes, diversidades e desigualdades no sistema educativo português: Balanço e perspectivas. *Ensaio, 13*(47), 181–215.
Cheong, P. H., Edwards, R., Goulbourne, H., & Solomos, J. (2007). Immigration, social cohesion and social capital: A critical review. *Critical Social Policy, 27*(1), 24–49.
Cohen, St. J., & Taylor, L. (1978). *Escape attempts: The theory and practise of resistance to everyday life*. London: Penguin.
Contador, A. (2001). *Cultura Juvenil Negra em Portugal*. Oeiras: Celta.
Contador, A., & Ferreira, E. (1997). *Ritmo e Poesia—Os Caminhos Do Rap*. Lisbon: Assírio e Alvim.
Devadason, R. (2006). Class, ethnicity and individualisation: Young adult narratives of transition in two European cities. *Journal of Education and Work, 19*(2), 153–169.
Downey, D. B. (2008). Black/white differences in school performance: The oppositional culture explanation. *Annual Review of Sociology, 34*(1), 107–126.
Drilling, M., & Gautschin, D. (2001). Youth cultures and adolescence: Limits to autonomous socialisation and demands on youth welfare. In A. Furlong & I. Guidikova (Eds.), *Transitions of youth citizenship in Europe: Culture, subculture and identity* (pp. 305–320). Strasbourg: Council of Europe.
Feixa, C. (2008). Generation Uno Punto Cinco. *Revista de Estudios de Juventud, 80*, 115–127.
Feixa, C., & Canelles, N. (2007). De bandas latinas a asociaciones juveniles: La experiencia de Barcelona. *Educação, 61*(1), 11–28.

Feixa, C., Costa, C., & Pallarés, J. (2001). From okupas to makineros: Citizenship and youth cultures in Spain. In A. Furlong & I. Guidikova (Eds.), *Transitions of youth citizenship in Europe: Culture, subculture and identity* (pp. 289–303). Strasbourg: Council of Europe.

Feixa, C., Canelles, N., Porzio, L., Recio, C., & Giliberti, L. (2008). Latin kings in Barcelona. In F. van Gemert, D. Peterson, & I.-L. Lien (Eds.), *Street gangs, migration and ethnicity* (pp. 63–78). Devon: Willan.

Ferreira, V. S. (2009). Youth scenes, body marks and bio-sociabilities. *Young, 17*(3), 285–306.

Flores, J. (1994). Puerto Rican and proud, boyee!: Rap, roots and amnesia. In A. Ross & T. Rose (Eds.), *Microphone fiends: Youth, music and culture* (pp. 89–98). New York: Routledge.

Foitzik, A., & Pohl, A. (2009). Das Lob der Haare in der Suppe: Selbstreflexivität interkultureller Öffnung. In W. Scharathow & R. Leiprecht (Eds.), *Rassismuskritik. Band 2: Rassismuskritische Bildungsarbeit* (pp. 61–76). Schwalbach: Wochenschau Verlag.

Fradique, T. (2003). *Fixar o Movimento: Representações da música rap em Portugal*. Lisbon: Publicações D. Quixote.

Frønes, I. (2001). Revolution without rebels: Gender, generation, and social change. In A. Furlong & I. Guidikova (Eds.), *Transitions of youth citizenship in Europe: Culture, subculture and identity* (pp. 217–234). Strasbourg: Council of Europe.

Geisen, T. (2007). Der Blick der Forschung auf Jugendliche mit Migrationshintergrund. In C. Riegel & T. Geisen (Eds.), *Jugend, Zugehörigkeit und Migration. Subjektpositionierung im Kontext von Jugendkultur, Ethnizitäts- und Geschlechterkonstruktionen* (pp. 27–59). Wiesbaden: VS Verlag.

Giddens, A. (1991). *Modernity and self-identity: Self and society in the late modern age*. Cambridge: Cambridge University Press.

Gottlieb, J., & Wald, G. (1994). Smells like teen spirit: Riot Grrrls, revolution and women in independent rock. In A. Ross & T. Rose (Eds.), *Microphone fiends: Youth music and youth culture* (pp. 250–273). London: Routledge.

Guevara, N. (1996). Women writin', rappin', breakin'. In W. E. Perkins (Ed.), *Droppin' science: Critical essays on rap music and hip hop culture* (pp. 49–62). Philadelphia: Temple University Press.

Hall, S., & Jefferson, T. (Eds.). (1976). *Resistance through rituals: Youth cultures in post-war Britain*. London: Hutchinson.

Heath, A. F., Rothon, C., & Kilpi, E. (2008). The second generation in Western Europe: Education, unemployment, and occupational attainment. *Annual Review of Sociology, 34*(1), 211–235.

Hebdige, D. (1986 [1979]). *Subculture. The meaning of style*. London: Methuen.

Hesmondhalgh, D. (2005). Subcultures, scenes or tribes?: None of the above. *Journal of Youth Studies, 8*(1), 21–40.

Jensen, S. Q. (2006). Rethinking subcultural capital. *Young, 14*(3), 257–276.

Lang, S. (2007). Interaktionen, Fremd- und Selbstrepräsentationen von Jugendlichen im Kontext von Migration. In T. Geisen & C. Riegel (Eds.), *Jugend, Partizipation und Migration: Orientierungen im Kontext von Integration und Ausgrenzung* (pp. 215–235). Wiesbaden: VS Verl. für Sozialwiss.

MacDonald, R., & Shildrick, T. (2007). Street corner society: Leisure careers, youth (sub)culture and social exclusion. *Leisure Studies, 26*(2), 339–355.

Machado, F. L., & Matias, A. R. (2006). *Jovens descendentes de imigrantes nas sociedades de acolhimento: Linhas de identificação sociológica*. CIES e-working paper. CIES.

Martins, J. L. (2005). *Jovens, Migrantes e a Sociedade da Informação e do Conhecimento: A escola perante a diversidade*, Observatório da Imigração, nº 16, ACIME.

Matthews, F. (1977). *Quest for an American sociology: Robert E. Park and the Chicago school*. Montreal: McGill-Queen's University Press.

McDonald, K. (1999). *Struggles for subjectivity: Identity, action and youth experience*. Cambridge: Cambridge University Press.

McRobbie, A., & Garber, J. (1976). Girls and subcultures: An exploration. In S. Hall & T. Jefferson (Eds.), *Resistance through rituals: Youth cultures in post-war Britain* (pp. 208–222). London: Hutchinson.

Melucci, A. (1989). *Nomads of the Present: Social Movements and Individual Needs in Contemporary Society*. Philadelphia: Temple University Press.

Moldenhawer, B., Miera, F., Kallstenius, J., Messing, V., & Schiff, C. (2009). *Comparative report on education: EDUMIGROM comparative papers.* Budapest. http://www.edumigrom.eu/sites/default/files/field_attachment/page/node1817/edumigromcomparativereporteducation.pdf. Accessed 3 January 2010.

Mørch, S., & Andersen, H. (2006). Individualisation and changing youth life. In C. Leccardi & E. Ruspini (Eds.), *A new youth? Young people, generations and family life*. Aldershot: Ashgate.

Mørch, S., Bechmann Jensen, T., Stokholm, M., Hansen, B., & Pohl, A. (Eds.). (2008). *Transitions to work of young people with an ethnic minority or migrant background: Thematic report of the UP2YOUTH project*. Tübingen: IRIS.

Mørck, L. L. (2006). *Grænsefællesskaber – læring og overskridelse af marginalisering*. København: Roskilde Universitets Forlag.

Muggleton, D. (2002 [2000]). *Inside Subculture. The Postmodern Meaning of Style*. Oxford: Berg.

Mungham, G., & Pearson, G. (Eds.). (1976). *Working class youth culture*. London: Routledge & Kegan Paul.

Pais, J. M., & da Silva Blass, L. (Eds.). (2004). *Tribos Urbanas: Produção Artística e Identidades*. Lisbon: Imprensa de Ciências Sociais.

Pais, J. M., & Pohl, A. (2003). Of roofs and knives: The dilemmas of recognising informal learning. In A. López Blasco, W. McNeish, & A. Walther (Eds.), *Young people and contradictions of inclusion: Towards integrated transition policies in Europe* (pp. 223–241). Bristol: Policy.

Pfaff, N. (2009). Youth culture as a context of political learning: How young people politicize amongst each other. *Young, 17*(2), 167–189.

Phoenix, A. (2004). Neoliberalism and masculinity: Racialization and the contradictions of Schooling for 11-to 14-Year-Olds. *Youth Society, 36*(2), 227–246.

Pohl, A., Du Bois-Reymond, M., & Burgess, P. (2006). Learning biographies: Case studies into dimensions and prerequisites of competence development. In A. Walther, M. Du Bois-Reymond, & A. Biggart (Eds.), *Participation in transition: Motivation of young adults in Europe for learning and working* (pp. 177–203). Frankfurt a. M.: Peter Lang.

Raposo, O. R. (2006). *Nubai: O rap negro de Lisboa [Nubai. The black rap of Lisbon]*, documentary directed by the anthropologist Otávio Raposo, edited by João Rosas.

Raposo, O. R. (2007). *Representa Red Eyes Gang: Das redes de amizade ao hip hop.* Dissertação de Mestrado em Antropologia Urbana. ISCTE—Instituto Universitário de Lisboa.

Redhead, St. (1997). *Subculture to clubcultures*. Oxford: Blackwell.

Roeper, J. de, & Savelsberg, H. J. (2009). Challenging the youth policy imperative: Engaging young people through the arts. *Journal of Youth Studies, 12*(2), 209–225.

Simões, J. A. (2006). *Entre o "real" e o "virtual": Representações e práticas culturais juvenis fora e dentro da internet: O caso do Hip Hop português*. Dissertação de Doutoramento em Sociologia. Faculdade de Ciências Sociais e Humanas. Universidade Nova de Lisboa.

Simões, J. A., & Nunes, P. (2005). Entre subculturas e neotribos: Propostas de análise dos circuitos culturais juvenis: O caso da música rap e do hip-hop em Portugal, *Fórum Sociológico*, (13/14), 171–189.

Skrobanek, J. (2007). Wahrgenommene Diskriminierung und (Re) Ethnisierung bei Jugendlichen mit türkischem Migrationshintergrund und jungen Aussiedlern. *Zeitschrift für Soziologie der Erziehung und Sozialisation (ZSE), 27*(3), 267–287.

Spindler, S. (2007). Eine andere Seite männlicher Gewalt: Männlichkeit und Herkunft als Orientierung und Falle. In C. Riegel & T. Geisen (Eds.), *Jugend, Zugehörigkeit und Migration: Subjektpositionierung im Kontext von Jugendkultur, Ethnizitäts- und Geschlechterkonstruktionen* (pp. 289–306). Wiesbaden: VS Verl. für Sozialwiss.

Terpstra, J. (2006). Youth subculture and social exclusion. *Young, 14*(2), 83–99.

Tertilt, H. (1996). *Turkish power boys*. Frankfurt a. M.: Suhrkamp.

Thomas, W. I. (Eds.). (1909). *Sourcebook for social origins*. Chicago: University of Chicago Press.

Thompson, K. (1998). *Moral panics*. London: Routledge.

Thornton, S. (1995). *Club cultures: Music, media, and subcultural capital*. Cambridge: Polity.

Thrasher, F. M. (1963). *The gang*. Chicago: University of Chicago Press.
Vala, J., Ferreira, V. S., Lima, M. E., & Lopes, D. (Eds.). (2003). *Simetrias e Identidades: Jovens Negros em Portugal*: Colecção Estudos sobre a Juventude, n° 8. Oeiras: Celta/IPJ.
Walther, A. (2009). It was not my choice, you know?: Young people's subjective views and decision-making processes in biographical transitions. In I. Schoon & R. Silbereisen (Eds.), *Transitions from school to work: Globalization, individualization, and patterns of diversity* (pp. 121–144). Cambridge: Cambridge University Press.
Whyte, W. F. (2005/1943). *Sociedade de Esquina: A estrutura social de uma área urbana pobre e degradada*. Rio de Janeiro: Jorge Zahar Editor.

Chapter 45
"I Am Illiterate. But I Am a Doctor of Capoeira": Integration of Marginalized Youth in Brazil

Karin E. Sauer

Introduction

So far, there is little research on the dimensions of social learning in Capoeira,[1] as most of the studies on Capoeira are mainly historically oriented (Vassallo 2008; Röhrig 2005; Lewis 1992) or give specialized information about individual Capoeira groups and their philosophies (Essien 2008; Vassallo 2003a).

Thus, there is an academic void concerning the question: Which strategies of social learning, given in Capoeira, are used by young people that are subject to social exclusion, in order to succeed in social ascension?

The article is based on preliminary considerations about networks of solidarity in marginalized social groups. Then, the political dimension of Capoeira is analyzed by means of a historical analysis, focusing on the social change in the Brazilian society from a colonialist to a democratic system. Up to the present, young people suffering from social exclusion associate Capoeira with the struggle for human rights and democracy. This is illustrated by examples from the research project *Trajectories of Integration in the Process of Education (TIE)* carried out in South Brazil in 2006 and 2007.[2] In spite of their disadvantaged social position, these young people follow successful trajectories of education. Among other factors, they refer to Capoeira as a meaningful orientation in their quest for social inclusion.

---

[1] For pedagogical questions in the context of Capoeira cf. e.g., Cordeiro 2007; Araújo 2004.

[2] This chapter is dedicated to Grupo Oxósse Capoeira Associação Preto Rico with Grão-Mestre Karcará, Mestre Ademir and Professor Predador, to Associação de Capoeira de Rua Berimbau with Mestre Militar and to Associação Ginga Sul Capoeira with Contra-Mestre Moa. Their company provided valuable insight into the universe of Capoeira.

K. E. Sauer (✉)
Fakultät für Sozialwesen, Baden-Wuerttemberg Cooperative State University, Duale Hochschule Baden-Württemberg, Schramberger Str. 26, 78054, Villingen-Schwenningen, Germany
e-mail: sauer@dhbw-vs.de

The findings are related to the psychological dimension of Capoeira. Its elements physical exercise, music, and song are described as potential resilience factors. These elements acquired by means of informal education, may promote identification with formal education and thus facilitate social ascension. Finally, processes of social ascension in heterogeneous societies are summarized, using the example of the doyen Mestre João Pequeno.

Context of the Project Trajectories of Integration in the Process of Education (TIE)

The study was realized in Rio Grande do Sul, in the area of Santa Cruz do Sul and Porto Alegre. The sample of interviewees consisted of ethnic and social minorities, including disabled young people, young Afro-Brazilians, German-Brazilians, and young people with other migration backgrounds, residents of peripheral and rural areas, like young farmers, descendants of Indian reservations, and Quilombos (settlements of escaped slaves).

In narrative interviews, the participants described their trajectories of education, focusing on what they found important for their educational success (cf. Sauer and Correa 2008a). Some of them had an affiliation to the Afro-Brazilian dance-fight Capoeira, which, according to them, had a positive impact on their careers.

Methodology

The methodological approach to the research question can be compared to Wacquant's (2004), combining the qualitative techniques of *interviews* and *participant observation* (cf. also Mayring 2002).

As the target group of young people from marginalized social groups with successful trajectories of education is rare and difficult to locate, the *snowball sampling* technique was used (Atkinson and Flint 2004). The process of acquisition was initiated by means of contact persons located in the field of parochial and community work in economically disadvantaged districts in both urban and rural areas of Rio Grande do Sul. In order to get a better understanding of the context of the interviewees' situation, five expert interviews were conducted with these contact persons, three of them being Afro-Brazilians (one female, two male), one white and one indigenous female, all of them having extensive experience in community work, and therefore knowing the specific difficulties of certain social groups.

Over the course of the study, the accumulation of referrals proceeded as the persons interviewed suggested other informants whom they happened to know and locate. Altogether, the sample represented the following diversification:

Sample	Afro-Brazilians	German-Brazilians	Indigenous	Persons with disabilities	Small-scale farmers	Persons from poor backgrounds	Persons with migration experience
Experts	1 female 2 male		1 female			1 female	
18–30-year-old youth	3 female 6 male	3 female 1 male	1 male	2 male	5 male	1 female 2 male	3 female 2 male

It should be noted that the assignment to one of the groups can only be one-dimensional. In a couple of cases, there is rather an intersection of characteristics, for example, looking at the case of a blind white man (disability) from a poor family, living in a predominantly Afro-Brazilian neighborhood.

Intersectionality (cf. Crenshaw 1991; Lutz and Wenning 2001) also applies to the Afro-Brazilian participants: All of them came from poor families and lived in either peripheral urban or rural areas. Five of the participants with an Afro-Brazilian background and one with migration experience practiced or made reference to Capoeira; two of the Afro-Brazilian experts were Capoeira teachers. Due to their intersectionality, which was even enhanced by their aspiration for a better social position, the participants were obliged to negotiate various questions of identity in a process of "positioning."

The effort of positioning implies a displacement from the interviewees' original environment by the process of education on a spatial and an intellectual level. The biographical approach provides an opportunity to concentrate on these negotiations in the interviewees' search for identity (cf. Marotzki 2006, p. 61). On the basis of the concept of "narrative identity" (cf. Holstein and Gubrium 2000), the *narrative interview* was chosen as the main methodological approach (cf. Lucius-Hoene and Deppermann 2004a).

> This approach proposes the use of "'positioning' for the empirical study of narrative identities using autobiographical narratives. Positioning is seen as an especially adequate way of conceiving of identities in narratives, because it allows for a reconstruction of discursive actions by which identities are accomplished, be it by description or by action. (…) Positioning analysis can offer valuable insights into the relations and tensions between varying conceptions of identity on different positional layers." (Lucius-Hoene and Deppermann 2004b, p. 166)

The interviewees' narratives were combined with *participant observation*, mainly in the field of Capoeira. Building on her experience as a Capoeirista in European Capoeira groups prior to the study, the author took part in Capoeira trainings, gatherings, and events of several Capoeira groups in Rio Grande do Sul. The findings gathered by means of observation as well as the interviews were analyzed by use of *qualitative content analysis* (cf. Mayring 2008).

In the next part, the results of the study shall be placed in the theoretical framework of *social ascension, solidarity,* and *networking*. The findings will also be located in the theoretical context of *recognition* and *empowerment*.

Networks of Solidarity Within Marginalized Social Groups

Reciprocity in "Social Projects"

Generally, diaspora, indigenous, and minority groups use formal and informal education to sustain cultural continuity while grappling with the influences and demands of wider globalizing, nationalizing, or other homogenizing and assimilatory forces (cf. Bekerman and Kopelowitz 2008). The young people who were interviewed were participating in solidarity groups, where they obtained informal education, such as spiritual, social, or cultural education. Many of them reported that this informal education helped them to aim at higher education, in order to find an economically and personally satisfying job, opening an access to more resources and, overall, social integration. Brecher et al. (2000) point out the reciprocity of the individual task and the one of the group which coincides in common activities.

> Seeing that other people share similar experiences, perceptions, and feelings opens a new set of possibilities. Perhaps collectively we can act in ways that have impacts isolated individuals could never dream of having alone. And if we feel this way, perhaps others do, too. This group formation process constructs new solidarities. Once a consciousness of the need for solidarity develops, it becomes impossible to say whether participants' motives are altruistic or selfish, because the interest of the individual and the collective interest are no longer in conflict; they are perceived as one. (Brecher et al. 2000, p. 20)

According to the Brazilian sociologist Velho (1999), this form of solidarity can be understood as a "social project": The possibility of individuals forming a group with a social project which encompasses, synthesizes, or incorporates the different individual projects, depends on the perception and experience of common interests which can be varied, such as social class, ethnic group, status group, family, religion, neighborhood, occupation, political party, etc. The projects constitute a dimension of culture. Being conscious and potentially public, they are directly linked to social organization and to processes of social change (cf. Velho 1999, pp. 33, 34).

For those involved in social projects, the importance of informal learning has two functions: Firstly, that they acknowledge informal learning as "part of who they are and how they interact with the world," secondly, that it is "not an inferior form of learning whose main purpose is to act as the precursor of the main business of formal learning. It is fundamental, necessary and valuable in its own right, at times directly relevant to employment" (cf. Coffield 2000, p. 8). Jean Lave also sees an intrinsic value in informal learning, as it enables individuals to make a contribution within the context of their own community (Lave 1996), which can lead to recognition and empowerment.

Recognition and Empowerment

The recognition that marginalized young people gain individually within their group of origin—or using Velho's term: their social project—at times leads to empowerment of the entire social group they are referred to. Thus, social movements are induced. In order to highlight the importance of recognition, two different approaches of analyzing social movements will be introduced. Charles Taylor writes:

> The demand for recognition ... is given urgency by the supposed links between recognition and identity, where this latter term designates something like a person's understanding of a human being. The thesis is that our identity is partly shaped by others, and so a person or group of people can suffer real damage, real distortion, if the people or society around them mirror back to them a confining or demeaning or contemptible picture of themselves. (Taylor 1992, p. 25, cit. by Singh Grewal 2008, p. 157)

Therefore, Taylor recommends both *politics of equal dignity* and *politics of difference*, asking for recognition of "the unique identity of this individual or group, their distinctness from everyone else" (Taylor 1992, p. 38, cit. by Singh Grewal 2008, p. 162 f.).

Yet, Axel Honneth points out the moral grammar of recognition, distinguishing "among three forms of mutual recognition: 'the emotional concern familiar from relationships of love and friendship', 'legal recognition', and the 'approval associated with solidarity', which are all 'particular ways of granting recognition'." (Honneth 1996, p. 95, cit. by Singh Grewal 2008, p. 159 f.)

The informal education given within the individual marginalized communities leads to an understanding of the structural disadvantages of the community regarding the access to the surrounding society and, consequently, to empowerment. In Latin America, this idea was put into action most prominently by Paulo Freire with his trailblazing "pedagogy of the oppressed" (2000, orig. 1968; cf. also McLaren and Leonard 2001). "Torres (1990, p. 129) in his study of the politics of nonformal education in Latin America similarly argues that many popular education programs have had a clear emphasis on social mobilization and political development. Churches, unions, and groups within social movements have been involved in such initiatives—and there has, in some at least, been a concern to resist unwarranted state intervention into civic life" (Smith 2001).

The mechanisms of recognition and empowerment can be found in solidarity groups, which are created due to suffering from unfair social structures. The next part focuses on the social conditions of slavery in Brazil and the solidarity groups emerging within this system in the form of resistance. These historical social movements still have an impact on the processes of identification and positioning of young Afro-Brazilians today (cf. also Almeida 2005).

Senzalas, Quilombos, and Capoeira—Resistance and Social Change

Slave trade was officially implemented in 1559 and lasted until 1888, when slavery was abolished. As slaves were regarded as goods, their human rights were not respected by their owners. To be able to defend themselves from the abusive practices of the slaveholders, slaves secretly exercised self-defense-strategies in the *senzalas*, cabins on the farmland they were forced to work on. In order to hide the purpose of their practice, they presented it as a ritual of African heritage, in the form of dance, accompanied by songs and music. This can be seen as one of the roots of Capoeira.

Another influence on the formation of Capoeira lies in the liberation movement started by the slaves, who had managed to escape from their owners. They built *Quilombos* (shelters) hidden in the scrubland. There, they succeeded in living in a parallel society, establishing a system of mutual support with a strong reference to African traditions. Living off the land, they maintained biodiversity and also used their ancestral knowledge of medical plants. The biggest Quilombo, which most successfully survived attacks of the persecutors, was Palmares, located in Alagoas, with their leader *Zumbi*. Soldiers killed him on November 20, 1695. Since Zumbi became the epitome of the Black Power movement in Brazil, this day is commemorated as the *Dia da Consciência Negra* (Day of Black Consciousness) since 1995. Consequently, Capoeira, as another survival strategy during slavery, places the roots of the Capoeira-movement in this context as well.

Both the Capoeira-movement of the senzalas and the liberation movement in the Quilombos, represent the above-mentioned formation of social networks. In 1988, the persistence of the Quilombolas led to the article 68 in the Brazilian Constitution, guaranteeing them property rights of the land they occupied (cf. Chagas 2001).

Yet, despite their legal rights, Quilombolas today are living under precarious conditions. One reason is the agricultural politics of Brazil, which is dominated by contracts with multinational enterprises which control most of the cultivation of the country. As independent small-scale farmers, Quilombolas have almost no chance to survive. Another reason lies in their secluded living conditions where it is hard to reach the institutions of formal education. Plus, the education provided does not match their way of life, but rather serves as a preparation to leave the land for the city. Overall, Quilombolas can be seen as some of the most disadvantaged in the process of globalization.

Nevertheless, there *are* young Quilombolas, who succeed in social ascension. Patrícia, who lives in a Quilombo, points out, how important the social recognition as a Quilombola was for both her personal educational success and for the integration of her community:

> I have lived here, since I was born. Many things have changed. In the beginning we weren't even recognized as vestiges of Quilombos. Before all that, in 2003, I completed the School of Rural Youth. There I got to know many people, made many friends. And from that time on I started, we started to integrate more. To get to know people, to try to achieve our dreams and try to realize them, fight for them. I am pretty motivated; I plan to go to college

still. And my family, my mother, motivates me a lot. She motivates all of us that we have to study, go to school, to strive for our goals. And to get somewhere in life.

Patrícia explains that one form of culture passed on in the Quilombos is Capoeira. As a symbol of the resistance against slavery it equates with the liberation from unequal social conditions. In the past as well as in the present Capoeira provides a framework of solidarity and informal education.

The Meaning of Capoeira for Marginalized Youth Today

The following examples explain the meaning of Capoeira for socially excluded youth today. To them, Capoeira represents values and orientation when reflecting existing social positions. This corresponds with the political/sociostructural dimension of social learning in Capoeira, as it allows individual positioning in the given social situation: All of the interviewees took the informal knowledge acquired in Capoeira to a level of formal knowledge that would help them achieve a better social position in the future.

As each of the interviewees reflects their personal conditions before training Capoeira and the positive change that occurred since practicing Capoeira, the psychological dimension of social learning in the context of Capoeira is shown. According to them, this is due to the personal relation between them and their Capoeira trainer (*professor/mestre*). The trainers offer help in difficult situations and—by means of Capoeira—teach coping strategies to solve everyday life problems of their students. The trainers also encourage them to continue formal education, in order to facilitate a better life in the future.

Fábio, Capoeira teacher, formulates the following:

> At the age of twelve I started having problems in school, in relationships, friendships. Capoeira and the project itself, my life with my professor, was what motivated me to practice Capoeira. He 'pulled my ears' for the first time, 'This is the way you need to follow. You need to look forward to stay on the right way. I don't want to see you, nor your fellows, now or later, in the middle of street corner gangs, with no good job in the future'. I always got by—I didn't always get it the way I wanted—but with Capoeira, working hard, I keep going and making it. So I leave a message, too: Let's not give up. You need to insist, persist for what you want. And study, too. That's what's most important. If you don't study, you won't get anywhere in life.

Fabíula's parents are separated; her father works as seasonal labor. Besides school, she works as a babysitter. As she is interested in biology and likes children, her professional aim is to become a biology teacher. She started training Capoeira as a child but had to pause after an injury until the age of 16:

> At the moment I just study and practice Capoeira. I know professor Moa pretty well. He remembered me the moment I returned. It was a neighbour of mine who invited me to participate in Capoeira again. Actually I didn't know that professor Moa was giving class. But when I went, it was him. It was very good for me. Actually, at home it is just me who participates in the Capoeira class.... I like practicing Capoeira a lot. It's making new discoveries.

Susana is the eighth child of a family from the interior. She left home early to live independently. She works as seasonal labor and studies whenever she can afford another semester. Besides that, she takes part in circus and dance performances. When she started training Capoeira 1 year ago, she felt that it was an integrate form of cultural expression:

> Capoeira is workout for the whole body and also workout for the mind. I always watched the people playing Capoeira, I thought it was beautiful...the fighting, the dance, people playing berimbau...Capoeira *called* me.

She also reports a strong emotional relation to her Capoeira group:

> My parents are in Arroio do Tigre. I am here alone. So I adopted Mestre Ademir and his wife as my parents. And my brothers and sisters in Capoeira as my siblings. I always want to go on. Who knows, maybe one day I'll be professor of Capoeira...maybe one day even mestra.

As the examples show, young marginalized people profit from both the political and the psychological dimension of social learning (as a combination of formal and informal learning) offered in Capoeira. As these qualities are strengthening their ability to cope with adverse situations, they are strengthening their *resilience*. The concept of resilience will be specified in the next part, where the elements of Capoeira practice are related to resilience research.

Capoeira and Social Learning: Resilience Factors Strengthened by Physical Exercise, Music, Song, and Play

In times of slavery Capoeira fulfilled criteria of coping strategies that nowadays are discussed in resilience research (Werner and Smith 2001; Welter-Enderlin and Hildenbrand 2006; Opp and Fingerle 2007). Resilience research deals with the dispositions which enable people to deal with difficult, dangerous, or traumatizing moments in life without focussing on the negative effects, but rather trying to make the best of these situations (cf. Huster et al. 2008, p. 29). This ability can be strengthened by the development of "resilience factors."

Firstly, the *sociostructural resilience* factor of the slaves in Brazil who practiced Capoeira was strengthened by its function of defending themselves, while at the same time defending their human rights (cf. Lewis 1992). Secondly, the *psychological resilience* factor was fortified by communicating their common African identity during the Capoeira game, which is accompanied by traditional African rhythms, originally used in religious rituals and songs, which tell various stories of their ancestry (cf. Merrell 2005).

The exercise of Capoeira offers several characteristics that can add up to the individual formation of resilience. Every Capoeira learner can benefit from its elements *physical exercise in a group, music, song, and play (the Capoeira game)*, which will be described in the following.

Physical Exercise in a Group

In the history and present of Capoeira the physical exercise in a group of Capoeiristas plays the most important part. The basic movement is called *Ginga*, a swinging movement of the body from one side to the other that connects every movement of defense or attack in a "dancing" manner. The constant motion of the Capoeirista when in Ginga serves as a form of tricking the opponent, as these supposedly dancing steps seem playful but may turn jeopardizing in an instant.

Capoeira uses frontal and circular motions on various levels of height, which is a reason why it is regarded as one of the most effective martial arts. To name some of the frontal kicks, there are *Benção* (mercy), *Martello* (hammer), *Queixada* (strike directed to the chin); some of the circular kicks are *Armada* (armada), *Meia Lua de Compasso* (half moon of the compass), or *Rabo de Arraia* (tail of the ray). In order to dodge the kicks, there are movements of defense like *Cocorinha* (squat) or *esquiva lateral* (lateral escape).

Capoeira also includes acrobatic elements, of which the most basic one is called *Aú* (cartwheel) that is also used as a way of transposition during a game of Capoeira. Of course, Capoeiristas who master acrobatic movements are given a lot of respect, not only by other Capoeiristas but also by the audience watching Capoeira. Yet there are other factors that add to real mastery of Capoeira, for example *mandinga* (wizardry), the fact of tricking and confusing the opponent.

Thus, the mere fact of practicing the movements regularly in a supportive Capoeira group and exposing oneself in public Capoeira events can consolidate the self-esteem of Capoeiristas, which indeed can resemble a resilience factor in uneasy situations.

All of these elements of physical exercise deal with the phenomenon of testing and extending one's own physical limits and the spatial limits given by the interaction with a partner. This moment of physically "taking up space" can also be transferred to a social level, as Capoeira was used as a strategy to "gain territory" in various periods of Brazilian history. Up-to-date motopedagogic findings prove the relevance of these interrelations, claiming that the exchange between self-perception and perception of others promotes the development of cognitive and emotional abilities, which may as well serve as resilience factors. Hence, the concept of the self, identity and self-awareness coincide with intersubjective relations and the acquisition of space to live (cf. Huster et al. 2008, p. 30).

Music

Capoeira often is characterized as a dance-fight, due to the use of musical accompaniment during the Capoeira practice. The instrumentation consists of very simple equipment that was easy to acquire even in the times of slavery: The characteristic instrument of Capoeira is the *berimbau*. The berimbau is a wooden bow (*verga*—traditionally made from *biriba* wood, which grows in Brazil), with a string (*arame*).

A gourd (*cabaça*) acts as a resonator. One strikes the arame with a stick (*vaqueta*) to produce the sound. A rattle (*caxixi*) accompanies the vaqueta. A coin or stone (*dobrão*) is moved back and forth from the arame to change the pitch produced by the berimbau. Although only three different sounds can be produced, there are many different rhythms.

Depending on the rhythm, the Capoeirista modifies the style of his or her play. The two most significant different rhythms and forms of Capoeira games are *Angola*, with a slow beat, and *Regional*, a faster, more vigorous style.

A complete *bateria* (rhythm section) consists of three differently tuned berimbaus (*viola, média, gunga*) and, additionally, one or two *pandeiros* (tambourines), one *atabaque* (a wooden handdrum), an *agogo* (agogo bells), and one *reco reco* (guiro). Who is not occupied playing one of the instruments will accompany the players by clapping their hands.

Although very simple, this instrumentation allows an esthetic experience and a form of communication by means of music. For the former slaves, this form of musical communication served as one strategy to cope with the deficits of personal development that were caused by the surrounding society, which practically blocked all their ways of self-fulfillment. When playing music in the community of like-minded Capoeiristas, they created a temporary social space where they felt a sense of belonging. This quality is nowadays referred to as resilience factor, generated by esthetic experience which includes prelinguistic thought, integrity of the senses and the feeling of participation in the community or the world (cf. Huster et al. 2008, p. 30).

Song

For the slaves, the conquest of a social space established by playing together was even amplified by singing together. The bateria is accompanied by collective singing, following the traditional African pattern of *call and response*, similar to the "field hollers" that the slaves sang on the plantations in order to put up with the strenuous work. The instrumentalists take turns singing the lead vocals, and everybody else joins the refrain. The lyrics often deal with Capoeira stories; they involve freedom songs as well as prayers to either African or Christian saints or gods and goddesses. Thus, within the social space conquered when singing and playing Capoeira music, a cultural and spiritual union is created. The message of the songs fulfils a bonding function between the group members. This solidarity framework among Capoeiristas can lead to a feeling of belonging and at the same time to a feeling of power to overcome the marginalized social conditions that their social group is subject to. This form of empowerment works in the solidarity group as well as for the identification process of each individual (see above: Brecher et al. 2000).

The following song explains the story of Capoeira as a survival strategy when being assaulted. At the same time it shows the elements of magic or religious rituals (with reference to the *Orixás*), which play an important role in terms of faith in a higher power that facilitates faith in oneself when—symbolically speaking— "the night is dark"[3]:

Era uma noite sem lua.	It was a night with no moon.
Era uma noite sem lua e eu tava sozinho.	It was a night with no moon and I was alone.
Fazendo do meu caminhar	Making of my wandering
o meu próprio caminho.	my own way.
Sentindo o aroma das rosas e a dor	Perceiving the scent of the roses and the pain
dos espinhos.	of the thorns.
De repente apesar do escuro eu pude saber,	Suddenly in spite of the dark I could tell
que havia alguém me espreitando sem	there was someone stalking me without
ter nem porque.	knowing why.
Era hora de luta e de morte,	It was the hour of death,
é matar ou morrer.	kill or be killed.
A navalha passou me cortando,	The blade passed cutting me,
era quase um carinho.	it was all but caress.
Meu sangue misturou-se ao pó e as	My blood mingled with the dust and the
pedras do caminho.	stones of the path.
Era hora de pedir o axé do meu Orixá.	It was time to beg for the spirit of my Orixá.
E partir para o jogo da morte.	And go for the game of death.
É perder ou ganhar.	It's lose or win.
Dei o bote certeiro da cobra,	I hit the mark with the cobra,
alguém me guiou	somebody guided me.
Meia lua bem dada é a morte,	Meia lua well done is death,
e a luta acabou.	and the fight is over.
Eu seguí pela noite sem lua,	I went on through the night with no moon,
histórias na algibeira.	histories in my pocket.
Não é fácil acabar com a sorte	It's hard to put up with the fortune
de um bom Capoeira.	of a good Capoeira.
Se você não acredita,	If you don't believe me,
me espere num outro caminho.	wait for me in another alley.
E prepara bem sua navalha,	And prepare your blade well,
eu não ando sozinho.	I don't walk alone.

Play—The Capoeira Game

The actual Capoeira game, played in a circle, the *roda*, unifies all of the elements above mentioned—dance, fight, acrobatics, music, song, magic (cf. also Browning

---

[3] On the importance of religion for marginalized youth in Brazil see also Sauer and Correa 2009.

1995). The most characteristic trait of the roda is improvisation. No matter how profound the knowledge or experience of the individual Capoeirista may be, and regardless of age, gender, intelligence, color of skin, disability, or class, each of them can play in the roda according to their capabilities (cf. e.g., Vassallo 2003a).

Two random players at a time will enter the roda and start playing, adjusting their individual bodily expression to the partner, the music and the energy displayed by the surrounding collective. They will always be procuring their space without being harmed or harming the opponent, nevertheless showing: "I could strike. But I will not" (i.e., "mandinga"). The roda can be seen as the essence of the definition of resilience, as the capability of "making the best of it."

Lewis (1992) describes the Capoeira game, taking into account Gadamer's reflections on play: "In one of the most penetrating discussions of the importance of play, Gadamer describes it as 'the to-and-fro movement which is not tied to any goal which would bring it to an end'" (1975, p. 93, cit. by Lewis 1992, p. 3). "He stresses the autonomy of play, not dependent on any particular subject or subjectivity, while at the same time emphasizing the fact that it can constitute, in its essential form, pure 'self-representation'" (1975, p. 95, cit. by Lewis 1992, p. 3). Lewis extends Gadamer's ideas, taking them to a level of social positioning by focussing on the exposure to an audience when playing in public:

> These ideas resonate immediately with the themes from Capoeira discourse, as when adepts experience the voice of the berimbau as 'calling' (chamando) them to come and play. But as play develops from childlike self-absorption to organized cultural expression, it opens itself out to an audience; it moves from mere self-representation to 'representation for someone'. (Lewis 1992, p. 3)

All of the factors that compose Capoeira, have now been explained both from an inside perspective of Capoeira practice and an outside perspective, analyzing the functions of Capoeira as coping strategies when exposed to social exclusion. It became clear that all aspects of Capoeira practice represent informal education and social learning, which, as the examples showed, can serve as incentives to social inclusion.

In the next part, processes of social learning will be focused, starting from informal education, as, for example, in the Capoeira group, leading to formal education, and consequently—using the terminology of Robert Putnam—from "bonding social capital" within the proper, marginalized social group to "bridging social capital" that provides access to other, more integrated social groups (cf. Putnam 2007; Sauer and Correa 2008b).

From Bonding to Bridging Social Capital by Identification with Education

A surprising finding of TIE was that for the ones who had shown resilience as to the fact of managing educational success in spite of difficulties, this success did not end in itself. Once having achieved their personal aim, the process of education was perpetuated. Even though they had struggled to overcome social barriers, many times distancing themselves from their original environment, in terms of space and also intellectually, they maintained a feeling of belonging to their origin. In various cases, the identification with their original social group continued until after having completed their education. As good examples, they motivated their companions in misfortune that social ascension *can* be realized by a process of education, be it formal or informal.

A parallel process of identification with education can also be found in the framework of Capoeira, where it is crucial that more experienced Capoeiristas hand down their knowledge to the less experienced ones (cf. Essien 2008). Quasi all Capoeira groups follow a graduation system that does not only include technical mastery of the Capoeira movements and the ability to sing and play but also the responsibility for teaching Capoeira. Teaching experience must be acquired under the direction of a *mestre de Capoeira* (master of Capoeira) during several years of giving Capoeira lessons.

The ones having reached the grade of *treinel, instrutor, professor, contra mestre,* or *mestre de Capoeira*, are not only responsible for promoting the Capoeiristic abilities of their students, but also they will have to be a role model for them in terms of behaving with integrity, personal and professional development as well as citizenship. By fulfilling this function as a role model, the advanced Capoeirista also acts politically beyond the setting of the Capoeira community. This leads to a transfer of the ethics of Capoeira to a larger social surrounding, broadening the horizon of every Capoeira learner. Thus, each Capoeirista can experience that it is possible to go for personal and professional goals, exemplified through the lives of their teachers (cf. Cordeiro 2007, p. 94). This is particularly important for the social ascension of marginalized young people, who need to go through an individual identification process, figuring out their own position within the framework of a society, which would normally exclude members of their own group of origin, especially regarding historically established structures of exclusion like racism (cf. Geisen and Riegel 2007 p. 13).

So far, the learning processes from within the framework of Capoeira have been highlighted. But one must also consider the learning processes related to Capoeira on the part of the surrounding society. Historically, Capoeira was an activity of the marginalized, the slaves, the outcast. Until the 1930 s Capoeira was officially forbidden in Brazil. Only in 1937 the President of the Republic at the time, Getúlio Vargas legalized the exercise of Capoeira and its institutionalization in the "Centro de Cultura Física e Capoeira Regional Baiana" of Mestre Bimba in Salvador. This legal recognition of Capoeira went along with a process of acknowledging that Brazil was a mestizo society, consisting of Luso-Brazilians of Portuguese descent and also of the Brazilian Indians and Afro-Brazilians, each of them shaping the society.[4]

---

[4] One of the most important representatives of this thought was Gilberto Freyre, who established a myth of ethnic democracy in Brazil in his works, most successfully in his book "The masters and the slaves" (1964, orig. 1933; cf. also Araújo 2004, p. 12).

From that time on, Capoeira became a fundamental part of Brazilian identity, representing its African part. The variant of *Capoeira de Angola* in particular emphasized its African roots, with its trailblazer Mestre Pastinha. Along with other prestigious Bahian intellectuals, like the sculptor and painter Carybé and the writer Jorge Amado, he managed to convey the Afro-Brazilian cultural heritage by means of the arts (cf. Vassallo 2003b). During these first years of mediation between Capoeira and the surrounding society, or between a former counter-culture and a dominant culture with a colonial past, African traditions blended with other influences of the Brazilian culture. Since then, the rituals and ethics of Capoeira themselves were continuously refined, depending on the actual time and place where they were practiced. In general, such cultural modifications in heterogeneous societies are referred to as hybridization (cf. Bronfen et al. 1997).[5]

By the dissemination of Capoeira throughout Brazil as "immaterial patrimony" (Vassallo 2008) or "cultural capital," it soon was to turn into "economic capital," bringing about material values. Tourism played an especially important part in this process. Thus, by being valued from the outside, Capoeira underwent a process of professionalization. The mestres were able to make a living teaching Capoeira, establishing their own academies, where today Capoeiristas from all over the world can be found.

Due to this recognition and the growing national and international reputation of Brazilian mestres, many of them emigrated to Europe or the USA, in the 1980s in particular. There, their knowledge was valued not only as cultural capital as a form of art, but also as intellectual capital.

Summary: Social Learning and Social Inclusion

Mestre João Pequeno, one of Mestre Pastinhas first disciples, can be stated as an example of social ascension by means of identification with education, as he made his way from a Salvadorian unskilled worker to a university professor. Currently in his nineties, he is the oldest active mestre of Capoeira, and he is recognized as one of the most important references of Capoeira in the world. During his career, he gained three doctorate degrees. Most recently he was recognized with an honorary doctorate from the Federal University of Bahia (UFBA) in 2008 (cf. FICA-DC 2008). The former president of Brazil, Luiz Inácio Lula da Silva, officially endowed him with the title of Cultural Commodore of the Republic[6]. Summarizing his trajectory, João Pequeno said: I am illiterate. But I am a doctor of Capoeira (*Eu sou analfabeto. Mas a Capoeira me fez doutor*).[7]

João Pequeno's expression highlights the value and appreciation of both "cultural" and "intellectual" education and their power to overcome social exclusion in

---

[5] A similar process can be detected in the history of Jazz in North America.

[6] Cf. http://www.capoeiraangolaacupe.org/grupoacupe/wp-content/uploads/2008/11/capoeira-trifold.doc

[7] Cf. CD: *João Pequeno de Pastinha* (2000: track 9).

general. The process of social inclusion takes place, when it comes to an exchange of different forms of capital, e.g., in associations, cultural clubs, trade unions, or universities. Based on their activities in these formal or informal settings of education, the individuals gain access to economic capital through qualified professional work, and also, in the terminology of Pierre Bourdieu, "symbolic capital," which generates from the other forms of capital mentioned above and finds expression in respect, trust, and power (Bourdieu 1993, p. 218).

The integration of subcultural movements, from the margins into the center of the society, can be explained with reference to the concept of "learning coping-strategies," which imply self-reflexive knowledge of transformation and action on various levels (Huster et al. 2008, p. 29). The ways of acquiring this kind of knowledge can be found in the movement of Capoeira, as it arose as resistance against existing social structures, but at the same time always kept up its "camouflage" as a merely cultural or even folkloric expression in the form of dance, music, and ritual. A camouflage that was deliberately maintained in order to keep the balance on a fine line between resistance and conformity, while at the same time influencing past residues of dominant forces by opening up new perspectives of (Capoeira-)learners and educators.

Beyond that, Capoeira generally can be seen as a reference point for marginalized young people, when negotiating their present and future social positions and cultural identities (cf. also Capoeira 2006). By means of strengthening individual and collective resilience, Capoeira proves a powerful tool for social change.

The analyses show that not only the excluded ones learn how to adapt or assimilate to the surrounding society, but also that the surrounding society learns and benefits from the social groups that initially were excluded. Looking into the future, social learning should always involve a dialogue between as many forms of cultural or intellectual knowledge as possible. In a knowledge-based global society, the value attached to heterogeneity should be the basis for negotiating fair social conditions on a universal level. Still, we cannot predict where such global networking will lead us. In the context of Capoeira, Mestre Pastinha put it like this: Wizardry of the slave in search of freedom—its origin has no method and its end is inconceivable even to the wisest Capoeirista.

Mandinga de escravo em ânsia de liberdade,
seu princípio não tem método e seu fim é inconcebível ao mais
sábio capoeirista.

Mestre Pastinha[8]

References

Almeida, M. V. de (2005). *An earth-colored sea: "Race", culture, and the politics of identity in the postcolonial Portuguese-speaking world*. New York: Berghahn Books.

---

[8] Retrieved from http://www.geocities.com/TheTropics/Cabana/9636/capoeira.html

Araújo, R. C. (2004). *Iê, viva meu mestre: A Capoeira Angola da 'escola pastiniana' como práxis educativa*. (Tese de Doutorado) São Paulo: Faculdade de Educação da Universidade de São Paulo.

Atkinson, R., & Flint, J. (2004). Snowball sampling. In M. Lewis-Beck, A. E. Bryman, & T. F. Liao (Eds.), *The Sage encyclopedia of social science research methods* (Vol. 1, pp. 1043–1044). Thousand Oaks: Sage.

Bekerman, Z., & Kopelowitz, E. (Eds.). (2008). Cultural education-cultural sustainability: Minority, diaspora, indigenous and ethno-religious groups in multicultural societies. New York: Routledge Education—LEA.

Bourdieu, Pierre (1993). *Sozialer Sinn: Kritik der theoretischen Vernunft* (5th ed.). Frankfurt a. M.: Suhrkamp.

Brecher, J., Costello, T., & Smith, B. (2000). *Globalization from below, the power of solidarity*. Cambridge: South End Press.

Bronfen, E., Marius, B., & Steffen, T. (Eds.). (1997). *Hybride Kulturen: Beiträge zur anglo-amerikanischen Multikulturalismusdebatte*. Tübingen: Stauffenburg.

Browning, B. (1995). *Samba: Resistance in motion*. Bloomington: Indiana University Press.

Capoeira, N. (2006). *A street-smart song: Capoeira philosophy and inner life*. Berkeley: Blue Snake Books.

Chagas, M. de F. (2001). A política do reconhecimento dos "remanescentes das comunidades dos quilombos". *Horizontes Antropológicos, 7*(15), 209–235.

Coffield, F. (Ed.). (2000). *The necessity of informal learning*. Bristol: Policy Press.

Cordeiro, Y. C. (2007). *Capoeira, identidade e adolescência*. Brasília: Editora do Autor.

Crenshaw, K. W. (1991). Mapping the margins: Intersectionality, identity politics, and violence against women of color. *Stanford Law Review, 43*(6), 1241–1299.

Essien, A. (2008). *Capoeira beyond Brazil: From a slave tradition to an international way of life*. Berkeley: Blue Snake Books.

FICA-DC Archives. (2008). Congratulations Mestre/Dr. João Pequeno. http://ficadc.blogspot.com/2008/04/congrautlations-mestre-dr-joo-pequeno.html. Accessed 18 April 2008.

Freire, P. (2000). *Pedagogy of the oppressed*. New York: Continuum.

Freyre, G. (1964). *The masters and the slaves: A study in the development of Brazilian civilization*. New York: Knopf.

Gadamer, H-G., Weinsheimer, J., & Marshall, D. G. (2006). *Truth and method* (3rd ed.). London: Continuum.

Geisen, T., & Riegel, C. (2007). Jugendliche MigrantInnen im Spannungsfeld von Partizipation und Ausgrenzung—eine Einführung. In T. Geisen & C. Riegel (Eds.), *Jugend, Partizipation und Migration: Orientierungen im Kontext von Integration und Ausgrenzung* (pp. 7–26). Wiesbaden: VS Verlag für Sozialwissenschaften.

Holstein, J. A., & Gubrium, J. F. (2000). *The self we live by: Narrative identity in a postmodern world*. New York: Oxford University Press.

Honneth, A. (1996). *The struggle for recognition: The moral grammar of social conflicts*. Cambridge: MIT Press.

Huster, E-E., Boeckh, J., & Mogge-Grotjahn, H. (2008). Armut und soziale Ausgrenzung: Ein multidisziplinäres Forschungsfeld. In E-U. Huster, J. Boeckh, & H. Mogge-Grotjahn (Eds.), *Handbuch Armut und Soziale Ausgrenzung* (pp. 13–35). Wiesbaden: VS-Verlag für Sozialwissenschaften.

Lave, J. (1996). Teaching, as learning, in practice. *Mind, Culture, and Activity, 3*(3), 149–164.

Lewis, J. L. (1992). *Ring of liberation: Deceptive discourse in Brazilian Capoeira*. Chicago: University of Chicago.

Lucius-Hoene, G., & Deppermann, A. (2004a). *Rekonstruktion narrativer Identität: Ein Arbeitsbuch zur Analyse narrativer Identität*. Wiesbaden: VS Verlag für Sozialwissenschaften.

Lucius-Hoene, G., & Deppermann, A. (2004b). Narrative Identität und Positionierung. Gesprächsforschung—Online-Zeitschrift zur verbalen Interaktion (pp. 166–183). http://www.gespraechsforschung-ozs.de/heft2004/ga-lucius.pdf. Accessed 7 Jan 2011.

Lutz, H., & Wenning, N. (Eds.). (2001). *Unterschiedlich verschieden: Differenz in der Erziehungswissenschaft.* Opladen: Leske+Budrich.
Marotzki, W. (2006). Bildungstheorie und Allgemeine Biographieforschung. In H-H. Krüger & W. Marotzki (Eds.), *Handbuch erziehungswissenschaftliche Biographieforschung.* (2nd ed., pp. 59–70) Wiesbaden: VS Verlag für Sozialwissenschaften.
Mayring, P. (2002). *Einführung in die Qualitative Sozialforschung: Eine Anleitung zu qualitativem Denken* (5th ed.). Weinheim: Beltz.
Mayring, P. (2008). *Qualitative Inhaltsanalyse: Grundlagen und Techniken* (10th ed.). Weinheim: Beltz.
McLaren, P., & Leonard, P. (Eds.). (2001). *Paulo Freire: A critical encounter* (5th ed.). New York: Routledge.
Merrell, F. (2005). *Capoeira and Candomblé: Conformity and resistance through Afro-Brazilian experience.* Princeton: Wiener.
Opp, G., & Fingerle, M. (Eds.). (2007). *Was Kinder stärkt* (2nd ed.). München: Reinhardt.
Pochmann, M. (2004). Juventude em busca de novos caminhos no Brasil. In R. Novaes & P. Vannicchi (Eds.), *Juventude e Sociedade* (pp. 217–241). São Paulo: Fundação Perseu Abramo.
Putnam, R. (2007). E Pluribus Unum: Diversity and community in the twenty-first century. *Scandinavian Political Studies, 30*(2), 137–174.
Röhrig Assunção, M. (2005). *Capoeira: The history of an Afro-Brazilian martial art.* New York: Routledge.
Sauer, K. E. (2008). "Ser alguém na vida" ou a importância de grupos solidários e formação informal para a ascensão social de jovens marginalizados. Pé na Terra. *Publicação Mensal da EJR e CPT Diocese de Santa Cruz do Sul, 2*(15), 7.
Sauer, K. E., & Correa, S. M. d. S. (2008a). To get somewhere in life—marginalized young people with successful trajectories of education in Rio Grande do Sul, Brazil. *Revista Electrónica Teoría de la Educación: Educación y Cultura en la Sociedad de la Información, 8*(2), 196–207. http://www.usal.es/~teoriaeducacion/rev_numero_09_02/n9_02_sauersouza.pdf. Accessed 7 Jan 2011.
Sauer, K. E., & Correa, Sílvio, M. d. S. (2008b). Capital Social, Diversidade Cultural e Juventude. In D. Cremonese & M. Baquero (Eds.), *Desenvolvimento Regional: Democracia Local e Capital Social* (pp. 249–268). Ijuí: Editora da Unijui.
Sauer, K. E., & Correa, S. M. d. S. (2009). Die Bedeutung der Religion für die Integration marginalisierter Jugendlicher in Südbrasilien. In K. E. Sauer & J. Held (Eds.), *Wege der Integration in heterogenen Gesellschaften. Vergleichende Studien* (pp. 104–117). Wiesbaden: VS Verlag für Sozialwissenschaften.
Singh Grewal, D. (2008). *Network power: The social dynamics of globalization.* New Haven: Yale University Press.
Smith, M. K. (2001). Informal and non-formal education, colonialism and development. *infed* (the informal education homepage and encyclopedia of informal education). http://www.infed.org/biblio/colonialism.htm. Accessed 7 Jan 2011.
Taylor, C. (1992). *Multiculturalism and the politics of recognition: An essay.* In A. Gutmann (Ed.). Princeton: Princeton University Press.
Torres, C. A. (1990). *The politics of nonformal education in Latin America.* New York: Praeger.
Vassallo, S. P. (2003a). Anarquismo, igualitarismo e libertação: A apropriação do jogo da capoeira por praticantes parisienses. Paper presented at the XXVII Encontro Anual da ANPOCS, October 2003, Caxambu. http://somaie.capu.vilabol.uol.com.br/capoeiraanarquista.html. Accessed 7 Jan 2011.
Vassallo, S. P. (2003b). Capoeiras e intelectuais: A construção coletiva da capoeira "autêntica". *Estudos Históricos 2*(32), 106–124.
Vassallo, S. P. (2008). A capoeira como patrimônio imaterial: Novos desafios simbólicos e políticos. Paper presented at the XXXII Encontro Anual da ANPOCS, October 2008, Caxambu. http://www.docstoc.com/docs/21727732/A_capoeira_como_patrimonio_imaterial_novos_desafios_simbolico_e_politicos-Simone_Vassalo. Accessed 7 Jan 2011.

Velho, G. (1999). *Projeto e Metamorfose: Antropologia das sociedades complexas* (2nd ed.). Rio de Janeiro: Jorge Zahar Ed.

Wacquant, L. J. D. (2004). *Body and soul: Notebooks of an apprentice boxer*. New York: Oxford University Press.

Welter-Enderlin, R., & Hildenbrand, B. (Eds.). (2006). *Resilienz – Gedeihen trotz widriger Umstände*. Heidelberg: Carl-Auer.

Werner, E. E., & Smith, R. S. (2001). *Journeys from childhood to midlife: Risk, resilience and recovery*. New York: Cornell University Press.

Chapter 46
Learning Insularity: Social Capital, Social Learning and Staying at Home Among European Youth

David Cairns and Katarzyna Growiec

This chapter examines the relationship between young people's residential situations and their intentions to be trans-nationally mobile in the future. We seek to explore the hypothesis that European youth are becoming insular in their life planning while living for prolonged periods in the parental home. More precisely, we contend that a process of informal social learning is taking place during this extended period of inter-generational co-residence which also involves being dependent upon family-generated social capital. With studies suggesting that the culture of prolonged home-staying may be becoming increasingly homogenous across Europe (Cherlin et al. 1997; Bendit et al. 1999; Billari et al. 2001; Aassve et al. 2002; Ford et al. 2002), this is a particularly pertinent discussion, with the possibility that learning insularity may now be the majority experience for European young people.

Families hence become active agents in migration, or rather non-migration. The parental homes which young people inhabit act as informal learning environments, wherein they learn to eschew geographical mobility in work and study. This phenomenon is not only interesting as an exemplar of social learning and increasing cultural heterogeneity in Europe, it also has Policy implications. Despite long-standing efforts by the European Commission to encourage youth mobility, particularly movement between European states (see, for example, European Commission 2001), the majority of European youth have preferred in the past not to accept this advice and instead choose not to be geographically mobile within their work and study trajectories. Neither is the assumption that young people are somehow "freer" to move and that they have a psychosocial cost in undertaking mobility proven (Fouarge and Ester 2007). We therefore need to examine the predispositions towards immobility held by these young people to determine if indeed there is a link between prolonged residence in the parental home and an aversion towards trans-national geographical mobility.

The group which provides our focus of investigation is European youth, in the present context, those predominantly from the 18–24-year-old age group who are

D. Cairns (✉)
Centre for Research and Studies in Sociology, ISCTE-Lisbon University Institute, Edifício ISCTE, Av. das Forças Armadas, Lisboa 1649-026, Portugal
e-mail: david.cairns@iscte.pt

still in full-time education. While many other authors have looked at the experiences of different minorities, based perhaps on ethnicity or nationality, looking at a specific section of the European population defined by their stage in the life course provides an alternate perspective, that is, this is a minority of a different kind. Through a better appreciation of immobility, specifically how and why young people do not wish to be trans-nationally mobile, we can learn more about the social and cultural influences which define migration for these individuals. This is somewhat akin to try to understand non-conformity to social norms through looking at those who do conform. However, when we consider the fact that all available statistical evidence points to the fact that most young Europeans, indeed most Europeans per se, are not geographical mobile, to look only at those who are or who are intending to be mobile would be to only concentrate upon outlying cases, from whom we might obtain a distorted impression of what shapes mobility orientations.

Theoretical Context

To explain immobility is possible more difficult than explaining mobility, not to mention a possibly more important issue considering that being sedentary is the norm for European youth. To help us explain how young people acquire their apparent aversion to trans-national mobility while they are living at home, we have adopted a theoretical framework utilising ideas from social capital and social learning theories. In regard to the former, resources embedded in *"relations among persons"* (Coleman 1988, p. 83; emphasis in original), particularly between parents and their children, are interpreted as embodiments or generators of social capital, while in respect to the latter, housing behaviours—leaving home and managing prolonged stays in the parental home—are discussed as being socially learnt.

In utilising social capital theoretical ideas, it is important to acknowledge the importance of key ideas derived from studies by Granovetter (1973), Burt (1995), Portes (1998), Woolcock (2001), Lin (2001) and Beugelsdijk and Smulders (2003) and also recognise the debt owed to Putnam's notion of "connections amongst individuals—social networks and the norms of reciprocity and trustworthiness that arise from them" —and use of the "bonding" and "bridging" social capital concepts: the former reinforce exclusive identities and the strength of homogeneous groups while the latter support more outward looking identities and enable the formation of effective relationships across social cleavages (Putnam 2000, pp. 19–22; see also Gittell and Vidal 1998). Bonding social capital thus denotes "ties between like people in similar situations, such as immediate family, close friends and neighbours", whereas bridging social capital refers to "more distinct ties of like persons, such as loose friendships and workmates" (Woolcock 2001, pp. 13–14).

Regarding the distinction between bonding and bridging social capital, we should refrain from being overly prescriptive: these are not "either-or" categories but rather "more or less" dimensions (Putnam 2000, p. 23); those who possess one variety of social capital may also be endowed with the other. It is also important to acknowledge that a substantial critique of social capital, and of Putnam's work, has emerged in recent years, such as the failure to adequately consider gender and other possible cultural biases (Arneil 2006). In his pioneering work on this theme, Bourdieu (1977, 1986) also places more emphasis upon the relationship between social capital and social class habitus. The present research hence takes into account social class, gender and the "complex and sophisticated agency and actions of young people" (Raffo and Reeves 2000, p. 148; see also Seaman and Sweeting 2004; Holland et al. 2007).

In explaining how young people learn specific housing behaviours, ideas associated with Bandura's social learning theory (see, for example, Bandura 1977) have been employed. This entails understanding both living independently and inter-generationally in terms of young people's need to attain competence in certain key areas, such as negotiating space in shared households (in both living with parents and peers), finding an affordable and appropriate home and forming peer networks to facilitate house-sharing. Although social learning theory has long been regarded as a powerful explanatory tool in such diverse fields as alcohol and drug abuse research (Akers et al. 1979; Niaura 2000), criminology (Akers 1990), domestic violence (Wofford Mihalic and Elliott 1997; Haj-Yahia and Dawud-Noursi 1998; Anderson and Kras 2005) and sexuality patterns (Hogben and Byrne 1998), our analysis represents perhaps the first attempt to relate social learning to youth housing behaviour. The theory itself states that:

> [...] social behavior is acquired both through direct conditioning and *imitation* or modeling of others' behavior. Behavior is strengthened through reward (positive reinforcement) and avoidance of punishment (negative reinforcement) or weakened by aversive stimuli (positive punishment) and loss of reward (negative punishment). Whether deviant or conforming behavior is acquired and persists depends on past and present rewards or punishments for the behavior and the rewards and punishments attached to alternative behavior—*differential reinforcement*. In addition, people learn in interaction with significant groups in their lives evaluative *definitions* (norms, attitudes, orientations) of the behavior attitudes, orientations) of the behavior as good or bad. These definitions are themselves verbal and cognitive behavior which can be directly reinforced and also act as cue (discriminative) stimuli for other behavior. (Akers et al. 1979, p. 638)

Peers and family are thus potentially major sources of reinforcement in youth housing behaviour, entailing punishment as well as exposure to models and normative definitions. "Rewards" in this context could be interpreted both literally in respect to economic benefits, or at least the avoidance of relative poverty, but also in terms of the sustaining of close emotional bonds and "ontological security" (Giddens 1991) should the correct or normative behaviour be adopted.

Research Context: European Youth at Home

Recent research has made clear that young people are living with their parents for increasingly protracted periods during the transition to adulthood (see, for example, Avery et al. 1992; Buck and Scott 1993; Wallace and Kovatcheva 1998; Cherlin et al. 1997; Galland 1997; Bendit et al. 1999; Billari et al. 2001; Aassve et al. 2002), amounting to the existence of a "nestling generation" (Nave-Herz 1997, p. 673). There is hence a growing cultural homogeneity in youth housing behaviour across Europe. We also know that as with youth migration decision-making (Cairns 2008, 2009; Cairns and Smyth 2011), youth housing behaviour tends to resist simple economic logic. Deciding to stay or leave home is "a complex process" (Rusconi 2004, p. 627), influenced by more than monetary concerns. For instance, research by Ford et al. (2002) shows that despite facing challenging circumstances, some young people still leave home at relatively early ages while others stay at home when material scarcities or other economic obstacles are not present.

Societal and regional norms and values—or "culturally usual and acceptable" (Iacovou 2002, pp. 67–68) housing behaviour—as transmitted through family relationships can help define youth housing behaviour. In Europe, youth home-staying has traditionally been most prevalent in southern Member States (European Observatory on the Social Situation 2006, pp. 36–37; see also Iacovou 2001) and research in these contexts points towards the importance of the family. In her study of young people in the Basque Country, Holdsworth reveals how "familism" and "family solidarity" act to postpone home-leaving (2005, p. 549). In Italy, studies by Sgritta (2001) and Santoro (2005) note that even when young people are in employment they may continue to live with their parents as part of a postponement syndrome. It is important to note that there is little or no consideration of formal education systems in mobility decision-making in these studies: young people receive their migration education at home and how to be, or not to be, mobile from their families. The results of these prior studies also make clear the significance of the physical assets of the parental home, alongside less tangible emotional resources, which range from access to a quiet place in which to study to use of the family car. Therefore, while more affluent parents may have the potential to subsidise their children's moves out of the parental home, their comfortable and spacious homes also provide their children with an opulent incentive to stay.

Research Contexts and Methodology

The original research upon which this chapter is based formed part of a research project entitled "Culture, Youth and Future Life Orientations". The aim of this project, conducted during 2005–2008 at the Institute of Social Sciences, University of Lisbon, was to examine the life plans of highly-skilled and well-qualified European young people in respect to geographical mobility and immobility. In the course of this research, young people were surveyed in two different geographical contexts: Northern Ireland and Portugal, specifically the Greater Belfast and Greater Lisbon regions. The choice of these two locations was inspired by prior research on education-to-work transitions, which revealed that in a study of nine different European regions, Portugal had the least geographically mobile young people and Northern Ireland some of the most, making for a potentially interesting contrast (Biggart and Cairns 2004; Cairns and Menz 2007). Both these regions also share a number of commonalities, such as strong historical traditions of migration and geographically peripheral positions within the European Union.

This project entailed undertaking both quantitative and qualitative investigation, although due to space restraints only the former is discussed in this chapter. In respect to trans-national mobility, while questions were asked regarding past travel experiences, the main emphasis was upon mobility intentions rather than studying migrants in their destination countries, due to the latter approach being too prone to incur bias due to "selectivity issues" (Fouarge and Ester 2007, p. 2). Samples were selected from third-level education systems. In the quantitative research phase, a questionnaire was administered to a total of 250 young people in Northern Ireland, all of whom studied at universities in and around the Belfast area, and 200 young people in Portugal, specifically those at university institutions in Lisbon. In both regions, respondents were sourced from four different academic areas: Arts and Humanities, Social Sciences, Science and Engineering. These samples were also balanced in terms of gender and inclusion from ethnic minorities, although a deliberate decision was taken not to include students from courses wherein geographical mobility is mandatory, such as languages, meaning that this is a study of "optional" movements (Findlay et al. 2006, p. 300).

Results

The following analysis explores the importance of social capital and social learning in mobility decision-making. Two key indices have been selected: intentions to be trans-nationally mobile and present residential status. These results are presented both with breakdowns between the two regions and within samples in respect to gender and social class.

Intentions to Live Outside Country of Origin

In respect to future educational and occupational planning, respondents in both areas were asked if they envisaged living outside their country of origin in the future. Unlike Eurobarometer surveys, there was no time limit as to when this anticipated mobility would take place or any indication of where they anticipated going.

Table 46.1 illustrates that 55% of those sampled in Northern Ireland and 32% in Portugal had intentions to live outside their countries of origin in the future. A gender breakdown is also included in Table 46.1, although the Pearson chi square level of significance indicates that differences between males and females are not of major importance. An important consideration in the analysis of migration orientations is the impact of socio-economic background as derived from parental occupation: do familial "affluence" or "poverty" have a stimulating effect or the potential to dissipate the desire to be geographically mobile?

Despite apparent differences within both sets of data, the contention that socio-economic background is related to a desire to be, or not to be, trans-nationally mobile

Table 46.1 Intention to live outside country of origin by region and gender

Region	Gender	Live outside country of origin? (%) Yes	No
Belfast	Male	60	40
	Female	51	49
	All	55	45
Lisbon	Male	35	65
	Female	30	70
	All	32	68

Pearson chi square level of significance = 0.170 (Belfast), 0.530 (Lisbon)

Table 46.2 Intention to live outside country of origin by region and socio-economic background

Region	Socio-economic background	Live outside country of origin (%) Yes	No
Belfast	Skilled non-manual	54	46
	Skilled manual	51	49
	Semi/Unskilled non-manual	69	31
	Semi/Unskilled manual	54	46
	Service	60	40
	All	54	46
Lisbon	Skilled non-manual	32	68
	Skilled manual	26	74
	Semi/Unskilled non-manual	38	62
	Semi/Unskilled manual	0	100
	Service	23	77
	All	29	70

Pearson chi square level of significance = 0.720 (Belfast), 0.477 (Lisbon)

in the future is not supported (see Table 46.2). In the Belfast sample, we can see that those from "non-manual" backgrounds are more likely to be considering mobility, while in the Lisbon sample, no one from the "semi/unskilled manual" group envisaged themselves living outside of Portugal in the future, but the Pearson chi square levels of significance tell us that these differences are not significant. The small size of some of these socio-economic sub-groups, particularly in the Lisbon sample, does however restrict what we can read into these results. Socio-economic status being unknown for 6% of the Belfast sample and 25% of those surveyed in Lisbon due to respondents having economically inactive parents is a further limitation.

Housing Mobility

One of the key findings of this research was that in both regions, almost three quarters of those sampled were found to be living in the parental home, somewhat more so in the Portuguese sample than in Northern Ireland (Table 46.3).

Table 46.3 Residential status by region and gender

Region	Gender	Residential status (%)	
		Living with parents	Independent
Belfast	Male	61	39
	Female	77	23
	All	70	30
Lisbon	Male	76	24
	Female	76	24
	All	76	24

Pearson chi square level of significance = 0.004 (Belfast), 0.884 (Lisbon)

As Table 46.3 illustrates, 70% of those sampled in Northern Ireland were presently residing at home with their parents, with the remaining 30% living in shared private or university-owned rental accommodation. It is evident that the female respondents in Belfast exhibit a stronger propensity to stay at home compared to their male peers in the same area. It may be the case that the parents of these young women are socialising their children in such a way that discourages them from leaving home while enhancing or being more indifferent towards males should they want to leave home (see Cairns and Growiec 2008). In terms of social learning, we can interpret this behaviour as indicative of the fact that for young women the family is a much stronger source of reinforcement and punishment, as well as being a source of behavioural models and normative definitions, the accepted parental normative definition of good behaviour in this case being "stay at home". Meanwhile, in the Portuguese sample, 76% of all those surveyed were found to be living at home, with no gender differential; the subsequent qualitative research also revealed that those living away from home were more likely to be residing with another relative or a partner rather than alone or with friends (see Cairns 2009).

Even though other recent work on student housing behaviour in Europe has suggested that staying at home has become more prevalent, at least in northern European contexts, the extent of this increase and the reasons for it may have been misunderstood. For instance, Holdsworth's study of youth housing transitions in Greater Merseyside found that only 23% of those surveyed were living at home, largely for financial reasons (Patiniotis and Holdsworth 2005, p. 88; Holdsworth 2006, p. 497). Alternatively, the trends we have uncovered in our research particularly in Northern Ireland may be of more recent origin, heralding the need for a serious rethink of this issue.

In regard to further analysis of housing transitions, Table 46.4 which follows presents a breakdown of residential status by region and socio-economic background of respondents. As was the case with the class breakdown of migration intentions (see Table 46.2), we can see that while there are differences between groups, they are not statistically significant.

For Portuguese youth, we can however see that contentment with living in the parental home is much greater, with 77% agreeing that it is a good idea to live with your par-

Table 46.4 Residential status by region and socio-economic background

Region	Socio-economic background	Living with parents	Independent
Belfast	Skilled non-manual	74	26
	Skilled manual	61	39
	Semi/Unskilled non-manual	75	25
	Semi/Unskilled manual	71	29
	Service	80	20
	All	70	30
Lisbon	Skilled non-manual	73	27
	Skilled manual	75	25
	Semi/Unskilled non-manual	65	35
	Semi/Unskilled manual	100	0
	Service	88	12
	All	75	25

Residential status (%)

Pearson chi square level of significance=0.404 (Belfast), 0.315 (Lisbon)

ents: 84% of home-stayers and 16% of home-leavers. Meanwhile, 71% of home-stayers in Belfast thought living at home was a good idea, as did 49% of home-leavers (Pearson Chi Square level of significance=0.001). That so many of those living at home are content with doing so leads us to conclude that these young people do not necessarily think of this as a negative condition but rather it is a normal part of growing up, a finding consistent with prior research on this theme (Jones and Wallace 1992, p. 93; Jones 1995, p. 1; Christie et al. 2002, p. 212). It may also be the case that there are reasons beyond enjoyment of inter-generational cohabitation accounting for this high level of satisfaction. Those living at home, for instance, were found to be significantly more likely to fear unemployment in the future: in Belfast, 55% of home-stayers and 39% of home-leavers had such concerns (Pearson chi square level of significance=0.021); in Lisbon, 79% of home-stayers and 21% of home-leavers had the same anxiety (Pearson chi square level of significance=0.064). This finding is particularly interesting, certainly in the context of Belfast, considering that the research time-frame was prior to the onset of the recent economic crisis in 2008.

Living Status and Migration Intentions

The next step in this analysis is to examine the possible relationship between living status and migration intentions, specifically whether or not we can establish a relationship (Table 46.5).

This relationship is statistically significant in both samples, although more so in the Lisbon sample, with those living in the parental home being much less likely to have migration intentions. In explaining this result, we might speculate that the strong economic and emotional grounding provided by continued close proximity to family of origin, coupled with the ability to maintain social ties with longstanding friends via residing in the same place where they grew up, assuming the family has

Table 46.5 Residential status and migration intentions by region

Region	Migration intentions	Residential status (%) Living with parents	Independent
Belfast	Yes	65	35
	No	77	23
	All	70	30
Lisbon	Yes	65	35
	No	81	19
	All	76	24

Pearson chi square level of significance=0.049 (Belfast), 0.015 (Lisbon)

Table 46.6 Statements on family life by residential status and region

Statement	Region	β	Exp (β)
Most of my family live near me	Belfast	1.083	2.955***
	Lisbon	2.250	9.489***
It's good to live at home with your parents	Belfast	0.970	2.639**
	Lisbon	1.288	3.616***
I would feel incomplete without my family	Belfast	0.009	1.009
	Lisbon	0.693	2.000
I need my family to support me	Belfast	0.146	1.157
	Lisbon	−0.347	0.707
Having a good family life is more important than having a good job	Belfast	−0.291	0.747
	Lisbon	0.176	1.193
My family need me to support them	Belfast	−0.339	0.713
	Lisbon	−0.614	0.541
My family would understand if I had to leave home to find a good job	Belfast	−0.675	0.509
	Lisbon	0.666	1.946
I have siblings who left home to live in other countries	Belfast	−0.376	0.686
	Lisbon	−0.974	0.378*
I have siblings who left home to live in other parts my country	Belfast	−0.535	0.585*
	Lisbon	−1.221	0.295**

Pearson chi square level of significance less than 0.050*/0.005**/=0.000***

not moved itself, inhibits these young people from imagining themselves undertaking trans-national mobility in future educational and occupational trajectories. This is a finding similar to that made by Holdsworth in Britain, who made the important point that while students who live at home may be "missing out" on campus life, they are also able to avoid the "sense of discontinuity" experienced by those who move away (2006, p. 508).

A further issue concerns the presence, or absence, of not only parents but also siblings. If brothers and sisters have also remained living at home, does this make respondents more likely to be home-stayers themselves? Furthermore, if there is a social learning dimension to home-leaving, do siblings who have departed provide a housing mobility role model? The impact of these relationships is further explored in Table 46.6, via a series of binary linear regression statistics, with residential status as dependent variable.

Table 46.7 Statements on peer relationships by residential status and region

Statement	Region	β	Exp (β)
Most of my friends live near me	Belfast	−0.126	0.882
	Lisbon	1.173	3.231**
I would feel incomplete without my friends	Belfast	0.198	1.219
	Lisbon	0.068	1.070
I have the same friends today as I had in childhood	Belfast	−0.157	0.855
	Lisbon	0.336	1.399
I expect to have the same friends in the future as I have today	Belfast	0.002	1.002
	Lisbon	0.009	1.009
My friends would understand if I have to leave home to live in another part of my country	Belfast	−0.448	0.639
	Lisbon	0.087	1.091
My friends would understand if I have to leave home to live in another country	Belfast	0.365	1.441
	Lisbon	−0.369	0.691
I have friends who live in other parts of the country	Belfast	−0.225	0.799
	Lisbon	−0.709	0.492
I have friends who live in other countries	Belfast	−0.335	0.715
	Lisbon	−0.082	0.921
Having good friends is more important than having a good job	Belfast	−0.656	0.519
	Lisbon	−0.010	0.990

Pearson chi square level of significance less than 0.050*/0.005**/=0.000***

Proximity to family and positive feelings regarding home-staying are important for young people living at home. For those who have left, to have siblings living outside the parental home or living outside country of origin is significant in both samples. Observing siblings living outside of the parental home can lead to imitation or housing behaviour modelled on this precedent. Exiting young people can also use their contacts with siblings as sources of information, for example where to look for accommodation to rent (Röper et al. 2009).

A final area of analysis concerns peer relationships. While we can see that siblings who have exited the parental home can act as mobility role models, who else might be having a decisive impact upon their future life plans (see Table 46.7)?

It is obvious from these outcomes that the quality and/or forms of friendship ties has little or no relationship with housing behaviour, with one solitary exception, that of those home-stayers in the Portuguese sample somewhat unsurprisingly being more likely to live near most of their friends. Clearly, in respect to housing behaviour, is it family and not friends who matter.

Discussion: Socially Learning Insularity?

In respect to youth housing behaviour, despite the association we might have between growing-up and wanting to live independently, for many young people in Europe today there is a seductive logic behind their prolonged home-staying if we consider the immediate absence of the expenses and inconveniences which would be incurred by leaving home. If we also take into account the fact that these home-stayers care more about maintaining their close relationships with family and long-standing friends than expanding their educational and occupational horizons through leaving home, then this choice makes sense. Furthermore, staying at home is not necessarily perceived as a negative condition, since parents may have positive attitudes towards their children's independence and will do much to enhance their lives. Parents today may also be better off than previous generations and be more tolerant and permissive, making prolonged home-staying a very comfortable situation (Biggart et al. 2004, p. 72).

Despite this apparently rosy picture, there may be unintended consequences for these young people such an acquired insularity, demonstrated in an aversion towards imagining a future outside of their countries of origin. The fact that European youth are learning to be immobile obviously means that they have little chance of using mobility as a resource in their transitions to adulthood and beyond. The relationship between immobility and mobility, or non-migration and migration, is one of the former replacing or negating the latter, that is, the failure to make the first move out of the parental home negates the probability of there being a second move out of their country of origin. This is not to mention the possible impact upon later housing market experience due to delaying the commencement of a housing career and losing the opportunity to learn independent living skills at a formative age. The gain from staying at home may therefore be short-term and actually prove to be a loss in the long-term should poor decisions or expensive mistakes be made about where and how to live. It is later in life when these young people have little or no choice but to enter the housing market that they may pay the price for not learning independent living skills or having availed of opportunities dependent upon geographical mobility.

Returning to the main theoretical theme of this chapter, we can see that it is possible to conceptualise tight social connections, particularly between parents and children and among siblings, as generators of social capital, specifically bonding social capital. Parents can reinforce the prolonged stays of their children at home, justifying or even rewarding such actions and giving them normative definitions. Siblings may also provide a mobility role model for those who wish to leave; however such actions are only pertinent to a minority of young people in our samples. In both respects, our research clearly shows the strength of family social ties and familial social norms.

The majority of young people sampled in both regions are also learning to be more geographically insular in terms of their reliance upon these family ties and the bonding social capital generated in these relationships. While there are a number of contrasts between the two regions covered, the similarities are more pronounced, both for those who stay and those who leave home, suggesting that youth housing behaviours may be shared experiences across contemporary European societies. This conclusion also implies a need for a better appreciation of the importance of local family cultures in discussing how trans-national population movements including migration are initiated or curtailed, as opposed to simplistic assumptions regarding young people as economic maximisers. And if European youth are to learn more about international opportunities, this may need to form part of their formal education since they are unlikely to obtain such knowledge at home.

References

Aassve, A., Billari, F. C., Mazzuco, S., & Ongaro, F. (2002). Leaving home: A comparative analysis of ECHP data. *Journal of European Social Policy, 12*, 259–275.
Akers, R. L. (1990). Rational choice, deterrence, and social learning theory in criminology: The path not taken. *The Journal of Criminal Law & Criminology, 81*(3), 653–676.
Akers, R. L., Krohn, M. D., Lanza-Kaduce, L., & Radosevich, M. (1979). Social learning theory and deviant behavior: A specific test of general theory. *American Sociological Review, 44*, 636–655.
Anderson, J. F., & Kras, K. (2005). Revisiting Albert Bandura's social learning theory to better understand and assist victims of intimate personal violence. *Women & Criminal Justice, 17*(1), 99–124.
Arneil, B. (2006). *Diverse communities: The problem with social capital.* Cambridge: Cambridge University Press.
Avery, R., Goldscheider, F., & Speare, A., Jr. (1992). Feathered nest/gilded cage: The effects of parental resources on young adults' leaving home. *Demography, 29*(3), 375–388.
Bandura, A. (1977). *Social learning theory.* Englewood Cliffs: Prentice-Hill.
Bendit, R., Gaiser, W., & Marbach, J. (1999). *Youth and housing in Germany and the European Union: Data trends on housing: Biographical, social and political aspects.* Opladen: Leske and Budrich.
Beugelsdijk, S., & Smulders, J. A. (2003). Bridging and bonding social capital: Which type is good for growth? In W. Arts, J. Hagenaars, & L. Halman (Eds.), *The cultural diversity of European unity: Findings, explanations and reflections from the European values study* (pp. 147–185). Leiden: Koninklijke Brill N.V.
Biggart, A., & Cairns, D. (2004). *Families and transitions in Europe: Comparative report.* Coleraine: University of Ulster.
Biggart, A., Bendit, R., Cairns, D., Hein, K., & Mørch, S. (2004). *Families and transitions in Europe—state of the art.* Brussels: European Commission.
Billari, F. C., Philipov, D., & Baizán, P. (2001). Leaving home in Europe: The experience of cohorts born around 1960. *International Journal of Population Geography, 7*, 339–356.
Boswell, C. (2008). Combining economics and sociology in migration theory. *Journal of Ethnic and Migration Studies, 34*(4), 549–566.
Bourdieu, P. (1977). *Outline of a theory of practice.* Cambridge: Cambridge University Press.
Bourdieu, P. (1986). The forms of capital. In J. E. Richardson (Ed.), *Handbook of theory for research in the sociology of education* (pp. 241–258). Westport: Greenwood Press.
Buck, N., & Scott, J. (1993). She's leaving home: But why? An analysis of young people leaving the parental home. *Journal of Marriage and the Family, 55*(4), 863–874.
Burt, R. S. (1995). *Structural holes: The social structure and competition.* Cambridge: Harvard University Press.
Cairns, D. (2008). Moving in transition: An exploration of Northern Ireland youth and geographical mobility. *Young, 16*(3), 227–249.
Cairns, D. (2009). The wrong Portuguese? Youth and geographical mobility intentions in Portugal. In H. Fassman, M. Haller, & D. Lane (Eds.), *Migration and mobility in Europe: Trends, patterns and control* (pp. 103–114). Aldershot: Edward Elgar.
Cairns, D., & Growiec, K. (2008). *I always need my mum:* Social capital and student housing transitions in Northern Ireland. Unpublished conference paper, BSA Youth Study Group/University of Teesside Youth Research Group: *Young people, place and class,* September 2008.

Cairns, D., & Menz, S. (2007). Youth on the move? Exploring youth migrations in Eastern Germany and Northern Ireland. In T. Geisen & C. Reigel (Eds.), *Youth and migration*. Frankfurt: IKO-Verlag.

Cairns, D., & Smyth, J. (2011). I don't know about living abroad: Exploring student mobility and immobility in Northern Ireland. *International Migration, 49*(2), 135–161.

Cherlin, A. J., Scabini, E., & Rossi, G. (1997). Still in the nest: Delayed home leaving in Europe and the United States. *Journal of Family Issues, 18*, 572–575.

Christie, H., Munro, M., & Rettig, H. (2002). Accommodating students. *Journal of Youth Studies, 5*(2), 209–235.

Coleman, J. S. (1988). Social capital in the creation of human capital. *American Journal of Sociology, 94*(supplement), 95–120.

European Commission. (2001). *European Commission White Paper. A New Impetus for Youth*. Brussels: Commission of the European Communities.

European Observatory on the Social Situation. (2006). *Demographic trends, socio-economic impacts and policy implications in the European Union*. Brussels: European Commission.

European Values Survey. (2006). *European values survey 1999/2000*. http://zacat.gesis.org/webview/index.jsp. Accessed Nov 2009.

Findlay, A., King, R., Stam, A., & Ruiz-Gellices, E. (2006). Ever reluctant Europeans: The changing geographies of UK students studying and working abroad. *European Urban and Regional Studies, 13*(4), 291–318.

Ford, J., Rugg, J., & Burrows, R. (2002). Conceptualising the contemporary role of housing in the transition to adult life in England. *Urban Studies, 39*(13), 2455–2467.

Fouarge, D., & Ester, P. (2007). *Factors determining international and regional migration in Europe*. Dublin: European Foundation for the Improvement of Living and Working Conditions.

Galland, O. (1997). Leaving home and family relations in France. *Journal of Family Issues, 18*(6), 645–670.

Giddens, A. (1991). *Modernity and self-identity*. Cambridge: Polity.

Gittell, R., & Vidal, A. (1998). *Community organising: Building social capital as a development strategy*. Thousand Oaks: Sage.

Granovetter, M. (1973). The strength of weak ties. *American Journal of Sociology, 78*, 1360–1380.

Haj-Yahia, M. M., & Dawud-Noursi, S. (1998). Predicting the use of different conflict tactics among Arab siblings in Israel: A study based on social learning theory. *Journal of Family Violence, 13*(1), 81–103.

Hogben, M., & Byrne, D. (1998). Using social learning theory to explain individual differences in human sexuality. *Journal of Sex Research, 35*(1), 58–71.

Holdsworth, C. (2005). When are the children going to leave home! Family culture and delayed transitions in Spain. *European Societies, 7*(4), 547–566.

Holdsworth, C. (2006). Don't you think you're missing out, living at home? Student experiences and residential transitions. *Sociological Review, 54*(3), 495–519.

Holland, J., Reynolds, T., & Weller, S. (2007). Transitions, networks and communities: The significance of social capital in the lives of children and young people. *Journal of Youth Studies, 10*(1), 97–116.

Iacovou, M. (2001). *Leaving home in the European Union. Working papers of the Institute for Social and Economic Research 2001–18*. Colchester: University of Essex.

Iacovou, M. (2002). Regional differences in the transition to adulthood. *Annals of the American Academy, 580*, 40–69.

Jones, G. (1995). *Leaving Home*. Buckingham: Open University Press.

Jones, G., & Wallace, C. (1992). *Youth, family and citizenship*. Buckingham: Open University Press.

Lin, N. (2001). *Social capital: A theory of social structure and action*. Cambridge: Cambridge University Press.

Nave-Herz, R. (1997). Still in the nest: The family and young adults in Germany. *Journal of Family Issues, 18*(6), 671–689.

Niaura, R. (2000). Cognitive social learning and related perspectives on drug craving. *Addiction, 95*(1), 155–163.

Portes, A. (1998). Social capital: Its origins and applications in modern sociology. *Annual Review of Sociology, 24,* 1–24.
Putnam, R. D. (2000). *Bowling alon: The collapse and revival of American community.* New York: Touchstone.
Raffo, C., & Reeves, M. (2000). Youth transitions and social exclusion: Developments in social capital theory. *Journal of Youth Studies, 3*(2), 147–166.
Röper, A., Völker, B., & Flap, H. (2009). Social networks and getting a home: Do contacts matter? *Social Networks, 31*(1), 40–51.
Rusconi, A. (2004). Different pathways out of the parental home: A comparison of West Germany and Italy. *Journal of Comparative Family Studies, 35*(4), 627–649.
Santoro, M. (2005). Living with parents: A research study on Italian young people and their mothers. In C. Leccardi & E. Ruspini (Eds.), *A new youth? Young people, generations and family life.* Ashgate: Aldershot.
Seaman, P., & Sweeting, H. (2004). Assisting young people's access to social capital in contemporary families: A qualitative study. *Journal of Youth Studies, 7*(2), 173–190.
Sgritta, G. (2001). Family and welfare systems in the transition to adulthood: An emblematic case study. *Working papers of the Institute for Social and Economic Research 2001–18.* Colchester: University of Essex.
Wallace, C., & Kovatcheva, S. (1998). *Youth in society: The construction and destruction of youth in East and West Europe.* Houndmills: Macmillan.
Wofford Mihalic, S., & Elliott, D. (1997). A social learning theory of marital violence. *Journal of Family Violence, 12*(1), 21–47.
Woolcock, M. (2001). The place of social capital in understanding social and economic outcomes. *Isuma: Canadian Journal of Policy Research, 2,* 1–17.

Chapter 47
Concluding Remarks

Zvi Bekerman and Thomas Geisen

In general, it could be said that there have been plenty of minority and migrant groups throughout history although they were not always referred to as such. With the genesis and rise of the nation-state in the nineteenth century, migrant and minority groups have become more relevant. The dichotomy of 'us' and 'them' seems to flourish within this rather modern political system for it helps establish that which is of utmost importance for nation-states—a strong feeling of belonging through the development of a sturdy 'national identity'. Migrants and minority groups became serviceable 'others' helpful in establishing through their alterity the 'us' nation states needed for its existence. In 'truth' not all migrant and minority groups have become an issue. The 'truth' is that some minority groups and immigrant groups are pretty successful while others are less so. Not all those 'successful' become an issue but all the 'unsuccessful' ones do. Even if the successful (the socially mobile) become an issue they always seem (and rightfully so) to be less of an issue than the unsuccessful. At times, certain individuals of a particular minority or migrant group are successful while others seem to inevitably fail. To be honest it is difficult to understand the differentiation made between minority and migrant groups. When unsuccessful both seem to suffer from similar ills and their location of origin inside or outside some imagined modern national borders seem, at the least, inconsequential to their suffering. Candidly, we need to acknowledge that the differentiations—diaspora, migrant, minority, indigenous—do feed academic turfs in an endless need to compartmentalize so as to survive and flourish, and yet they (the groups) all suffer.

These minority or migrant groups especially when they suffer are ethnicized (and by being ethnicized suffer). They are thought of as being imprisoned by cultures which prevent them from succeeding, adapting, making it in modern westernized contexts. It seems to be assumed that this cultural envelope to which they are

Z. Bekerman (✉)
School of Education, Melton Center, Hebrew University, Jerusalem 91905, Israel
e-mail: mszviman@mscc.huji.ac.il

T. Geisen
School of Social Work, University of Applied Sciences Northwestern Switzerland,
Riggenbachstrasse 16, 4600 Olten, Switzerland
e-mail: thomas.geisen@fhnw.ch

captive imbues them with mental qualities (intelligences, motivations, you have it) that prevent them individually from succeeding in the majority/new context. Yet we know many do succeed in the host context, which must mean that there is no such cultural/ethnic prison to which minority/migrants belong. Yet, again, this fact does not encourage us to ask; who are those in minority migrant groups which fail, when and how?

When we ask some questions about what can be done to better the lot of the marginalized we find it easy to point in the direction of education. Education seems to be the opium of modern states who offer it, in no little measure, free and compulsory. We know well that given the psychologized metaphors which dominate education pointing in the direction of education means for the most part pointing at the issues of minority and migrant groups as being problems in people's heads, malfunctioning in their qualities of mind. Thus, we know that if something has to be corrected it is the minority or migrant individuals themselves and or their families and or their cultures that are in need of advancement and development. 'US' in the educational system—the majority members—need to be respectful, considerate, sensitive, tolerant, inclusive, etc. to their (the groups) origins and if patient and responsive enough education will achieve the change. Other than the lack of good education nothing stands in the way of these groups to successfully join our host societies—or so we want to believe.

Clearly for many of us this reasoning is misguided at its best; evil if taken for what it is—a choice. The chapters in this volume are one more attempt to widen the discourse well knowing that education cannot all by itself do the magic but might still hold some openings to better, if only a bit, the world. Knowing as well, and trying not hide it, that good education can occur only after students' survival needs are met. The chapters in this edited volume have focused on the relation between different minority and migration groups and their position within society. They not only have discussed questions of dominance and marginalization but also issues of self-positioning and belonging. The chapters show, how education and learning interrelate with life processes for which individual and collective identifications are or are made to be highly relevant. This book is an invitation to confront complexity and to abandon individualized educational perspectives. To grasp complexity means much more than realizing the importance of accounting for the multiple social, political and economical contexts within which the marginalized are trying to survive. It means also to realize the centrality of historical evolving contexts to current social conditions; a historicity which belongs both to the minority migrant groups and to the host societies within which they live and try to flourish. And yet it is very interesting to notice, that the stories told about migrants and minority groups are often presented as 'their' stories and not as 'our' stories. National entities seem to need these groups disentangled and separated from what we call the 'majority' or 'dominant' society and yet in dialogue with it. This dialogue of negation is needed for it feeds and strengthens the dominant group's sense of togetherness without which a nation will not be. The histories of the marginalized are then always present in their absence and in their absence make 'us' present.

The belonging of the individual to one or more social groups and communities might indeed be a highly relevant 'fact', of no less importance so might be the positioning, the standing of his or her social group or community in the larger societal context. Resources, both material and symbolic, are allocated and made available differently to dominant and marginalized groups and individuals in these groups benefit from these resources differentially. The adopted or imposed belonging of an individual to a social/ethnic/cultural/national group affords and or limits his or her chances to benefit from the resources made available. Education, though not the only one, is an important resource which has the potential of affording participants access to other more important resources. In the case of immigrant and minority groups education can help make available resources other than the ones made available to or accumulated at present by the social group with which the participant is identified. The chapters in this volume have reveled in detail, the mechanisms put to work within educational settings which produce and help sustain present unequal access to societal resources thus depriving migrant minority participants from developing their 'individual' capacities and capabilities.

When cash, freedom, justice and solidarity are only shared by the few the great promise of the French revolution cannot be accomplished. The contributions in this volume show that marginalized and socially deprived individuals and social groups are often lacking not only solidarity in society, but freedom and justice as well. As long as there are individuals and social groups deprived of freedom, justice and solidarity, not only are the marginalized in danger but all of society is at risk too. We hope that the studies in this edited volume contribute not only to a better understanding of how migratory and minority groups become marginalized and what it means for these groups to be deprived but also that they offer valuable insights into possible openings to better their lot and with it that of us all.

Index

A
AB 540 legislation, 498, 505
Academic achievement, 232, 244, 286, 290, 391, 456, 480, 484, 485, 490–492, 551, 553, 556, 660, 663, 666, 668, 674
Academic success, 227, 232, 288, 290, 456, 480, 481, 490–493, 521, 599–601, 636, 659, 660, 673, 674
Achievement gap, 384, 390, 392, 394, 395
Acting, 28, 55, 69, 70, 153, 180, 430, 463, 580, 586, 617, 699
Adult education, 139
African immigrants, 153, 455–459, 479, 480, 486, 489, 492, 493, 659
African–American, 56, 324, 383–385, 389–394, 396, 397, 456, 457, 459, 479, 480, 482, 484–486, 488–490, 492, 493, 662, 664
Agency, 11, 24, 159, 160, 163, 165, 166, 190, 286, 325, 366, 367, 467, 522, 572, 586, 588, 589, 599, 635, 653, 674, 677, 680, 695, 696, 698–700, 703, 706, 731
Agency–structure interaction, 674
Ambivalences in educational, 333
Arendt, 10, 12, 36, 40, 41, 45, 113
Arjun Appadurai, 107, 108, 651, 652
Assimilation, 13, 41, 73, 91, 101, 121, 129, 133, 138, 165, 258, 323, 437, 446, 449, 517, 522, 643, 649, 653
Asylum, 16, 156, 159, 293
Attribution, 26, 59, 113, 340–344
Austro-Hungarian Monarchy, 255
Autonomy of migration, 70, 75

B
Balancing process, 23, 24
Bekerman, Zvi, 1, 10, 17, 35, 43, 45, 191, 193, 235, 237, 449, 464, 605, 607, 608, 611, 612, 617, 618, 714

Belonging, 10, 11, 25, 26, 275, 276, 367, 376, 377, 587, 601, 646, 627, 650–653, 655, 720, 744
Bhabha, 14, 27, 108, 111, 135, 269, 276, 277
Bilingual, 16, 121, 124, 126, 132, 169–182, 191, 193, 198, 219, 224, 225, 232, 235
Bilingual education, 169, 172, 219, 220, 224, 225, 301, 315
Biographical learning, 53
Biography, 30, 61, 701
Border patrol, 499, 500
Bourdieu, 14, 53, 103, 104, 106, 107, 136, 170, 192, 285, 286, 289, 325, 334, 491, 464, 597, 600, 725, 731
Brazil, 422, 445, 597, 711, 715, 716, 719, 723, 724
Bremen, 323, 324, 349–351, 355–360
British colonial period, 518, 554
Buenos Aires, 325, 326, 435, 442–449

C
California, 301, 430, 457, 498, 499
Canada, 1, 92, 169, 190, 192, 204, 213, 214, 223, 224, 232, 265–271, 273, 278, 279, 302, 303, 305, 306, 308, 309, 311, 322, 324, 327, 359, 365, 366, 369, 374, 375
cape Verdean origin, 421, 423–429
Capoeira, 600, 602, 711–713, 715–725
Case study, 192, 283, 287, 290–292, 295, 410, 415, 465, 519, 543, 550, 551, 556, 644, 663
Categorization, 101, 104, 192, 332, 343, 368, 407, 461, 464, 607, 608, 610, 663
Citizenship, 57, 63, 77, 94–98, 117, 119, 396, 505, 573
Class, 27, 139, 140, 164, 203, 204, 257, 260, 262, 272, 286, 332–334, 343, 367, 368, 441, 445, 584, 659, 661, 706
Classroom discussions, 507, 510, 645

Z. Bekerman, T. Geisen (eds.), *International Handbook of Migration, Minorities and Education,*
DOI 10.1007/978-94-007-1466-3, © Springer Science+Business Media B.V. 2012

Collectivistic Culture, 480, 485, 487, 489, 491, 492
Community, 2, 3, 10, 23, 29, 93, 94, 216, 218, 219, 221, 266, 431, 445, 499, 660
Community building, 96, 97
Community of learning, 325, 415
Community of practice, 180–182
Community schooling, 182, 215, 218, 599, 601, 645
Compensatory programs in education, 437, 438, 442
Complete network, 664
Conflict, 71, 101, 190, 192, 216, 218, 219, 222, 237, 238, 608
Constructing difference, 325, 435
Conversation, 190, 191, 214, 310, 322, 471, 472, 618
Co-operative learning, 309, 407
Coping, 28, 64, 71, 111, 153, 155, 399, 695–697, 705, 717, 718, 722, 725
Critical multiculturalism, 2, 598, 601, 606, 608, 617, 618
Critical psychology, 68, 70
Critical social science, 13, 80, 81
Croatia, 190, 192, 250, 252–262
Cultural capital, 14, 104–106, 192, 285, 286, 289, 295, 296, 334, 391, 602, 724
Cultural difference, 1, 4, 13, 15, 27, 28, 35, 104, 107, 113, 189, 208, 213, 226, 227, 255, 314, 327, 336, 339, 343, 376, 404–406, 408, 409, 423, 469, 480, 538, 597, 641, 643, 644, 652, 655
Cultural diversity, 107, 110, 162, 169–171, 191–193, 208, 249, 261–263, 285, 296, 325, 372, 397, 403, 437, 442, 443, 461, 687
Cultural homogeneity, 171, 410, 533, 646, 732
Cultural model, 191, 215–225, 580, 698
Cultural pluralism, 404, 410
Cultural repositioning, 25, 30
Cultural transmission, 192, 284, 286, 288–292, 294, 296, 582, 588
Culture, 1–3, 9–11, 17, 19, 23, 24, 28, 29, 105, 107, 225, 279, 303, 304, 313, 341, 367, 372, 374, 455, 465, 611, 613, 706, 732
Culture of migration, 679
Curriculum analysis, 610
Cyprus, 597, 598, 601, 605, 606, 608, 610–619

D
Decategorization, 407
Denmark, 599, 696, 702
Depression, 157, 384, 506–508, 599, 627, 641
Detention, 156–160, 162, 499, 648
Dharma, 525, 532, 581, 585, 589
Dialogue across differences, 302–304, 313
Diaspora, 62, 149, 190, 192, 254, 267, 271, 272, 274, 275, 425, 539, 579, 587, 680, 714, 743
Difference, 9, 11, 17, 61, 266, 342, 376, 652, 702, 715
Discourse analysis, 191, 193, 215, 216, 219, 222, 223, 304, 315, 598, 610, 611
Discrimination, 30, 56, 63, 117, 119, 153, 226, 233, 322, 352, 366, 369, 371, 396, 403, 406, 408, 409, 440, 441, 447, 448
Disparity, 103, 111, 207, 219, 221, 225, 521, 522, 547
Dispersal policy, 351, 353, 354, 357
Diversity, 14, 22, 103, 105, 113, 271, 328, 344, 376, 500, 571, 606
Doing difference, 331, 332, 341, 344
DREAM Act, 509, 511
Dubai, 597, 599, 602, 677, 678, 681, 683, 684, 686–691

E
Early childhood education, 16, 169–172, 174, 178, 179, 181, 182, 210, 385
Early childhood program, 393
East African immigrants, 492
Education, 3, 10, 41, 42, 88, 96, 98, 120, 124, 161, 165, 169–173, 178, 179, 231, 251, 323, 331, 354, 383, 435, 442, 444, 528, 566, 579, 584, 586, 608, 643, 682, 744, 745
Education strategies, political, 135
Education system, 106, 172, 192, 226, 249, 250, 260, 285, 313, 322, 323, 333, 334, 355, 536, 559, 562, 600, 601, 695, 696, 707, 732, 733
Effects of poverty, 21, 70, 385, 386, 436, 444, 501, 632, 636, 733
Ego-centric network, 664
Elementary education, 358, 560, 580, 631
Elementary school, 303, 393, 404, 408, 410, 415, 630, 631, 633, 634
Emancipation, 56, 256, 520, 521, 524, 528, 533, 536, 538, 539, 588, 697
Employment, 14, 21, 68, 109, 111, 112, 119, 284, 358, 359, 396, 480, 481, 547, 602, 647, 680–682, 685–687, 691, 692, 698, 703, 714, 732
Empowerment, 159, 160, 165, 166, 632, 714, 715, 720
English schools, 129, 544–547, 554

Equality, 9, 39, 57, 201, 254, 255, 257, 258, 262, 323, 327, 331, 333, 335–339, 342, 344, 383, 443, 447–449, 517, 559, 562–564, 570, 571, 697
ESL education, 305, 307, 308
ESL parent–teacher intercultural communication, 193, 305, 314, 315
Ethiopia, 156–158, 683
Ethnic diversity, 130, 198, 252, 254, 256, 259, 260, 287, 585
Ethnic groups, 12, 53, 55, 56, 60, 64, 192, 232, 250, 252–255, 258–260, 262, 383, 387, 388, 390, 392, 396, 526, 544–547, 580, 616, 628, 663, 678, 682, 691
Ethnic minorities, 109, 118, 119, 131, 165, 197–200, 232, 261, 357, 384, 388, 390, 394, 395, 397, 419, 489, 523, 530, 661, 733
Ethnicity, 2, 106, 149, 164, 251, 261, 271, 283, 285, 292, 325, 332, 333, 376, 388, 406, 448, 455, 587, 618, 706
Ethnicity and education, 13, 251
Ethnicized, 321, 324, 331, 334, 339, 366–369, 377, 683, 695, 698–700, 703, 743
EU, 14, 15, 73, 86, 91–93, 95, 96, 102, 108–111, 117–120, 124, 126, 131–133, 192, 195, 201–203, 283, 404, 422, 623, 733
European mixed families, 118
Europeanization, 110
Exclusion, 25, 26, 29, 41, 54, 57, 74, 80, 95, 98, 110, 164, 322, 338, 340–344, 365, 368, 369, 409, 537, 601, 610, 624, 629, 636, 696, 698, 705, 707, 723
Exclusion (excluded), 95, 98, 462

F
Family, 21, 29, 121, 126, 174, 177, 238, 375, 430, 526, 533, 599, 660, 674, 685, 696, 714
Family education strategies, 583
Finland, 204, 599, 696
Formal education system, 136, 732
Framework for diversity, 14, 102, 112
Francophone, 192, 224, 265–279
French, 57, 63, 77, 125, 129, 130, 156, 192, 259, 265–273, 275, 276, 278, 301, 374, 423, 443, 649, 745

G
Gender, 103, 271, 272, 325, 332, 333, 341, 343, 407, 457, 483, 488, 584, 588, 589, 696, 697, 722, 731, 733–735

Germany, 13, 20, 25, 26, 31, 61, 62, 68, 73, 77–79, 108, 169–172, 174, 178, 179, 182, 322, 324, 333, 334, 349, 351, 354–357, 359, 365, 366, 369, 422, 599, 684, 696, 700, 701, 707
Globalization, 9, 107, 153, 249, 267, 270, 334, 368, 462, 518, 651, 652, 716
Goal orientation, 480–482, 484, 485, 487, 488, 490, 491
Governmentality, 85, 86, 96, 166
Grammar of integration, 72, 73
Greece, 68, 79, 322, 403–405, 410, 412, 597, 598, 608, 610–613, 616, 624–630, 632, 634–637, 643–645, 649, 650, 652, 654
Greeks, 79, 108, 405, 612, 613, 616, 632, 634, 637, 650, 653

H
Hall S, 60, 61, 102, 106, 107, 135, 146, 265–267, 332, 464, 602, 641
Hanukkah, 135, 141–148
Hate climate, 511
Hate groups, 500, 504
Head Start, 324, 383–390, 392–397
Hegemony, 13, 36, 86, 93, 163, 323, 338, 343, 344, 442, 560, 605
Heterogeneous societies, 712, 724
Heteronormativity, 343, 368
Higher education, 3, 12, 43, 105, 239, 290, 351, 423, 440, 455, 456, 459, 485, 491, 493, 497, 507, 527, 530, 584, 585, 589, 654, 672, 714
Higher Education in the United States, 455–457
Hindu, 425, 519, 521, 525–527, 529, 531, 532, 538, 539, 579–589
Hindu identity, 521, 535, 539, 588
Hindu migration, 519, 520, 577, 578
Hindu schools, 520, 521, 523, 525, 528–539, 580
Hinduism, 425, 519–521, 524–527, 532, 534, 538, 539, 580, 582, 588
Hindus, 519, 525–527, 531, 534, 535, 538, 539, 544, 580, 581, 583–587
Hindutva, 539
History, 55, 140, 142–144, 196, 265, 267, 268, 271, 273, 277, 294, 326, 334, 373, 413, 464, 507, 528, 532, 553, 588, 598, 606, 610–617
Home, 15, 61, 62, 123, 175, 176, 199, 237, 241, 305, 427, 428, 589, 597, 602, 635, 730, 738–740

Home-staying, 729, 732, 738, 739
Homogenization, 2, 161, 197, 199, 254, 255, 323, 333–335, 420
Homophobia, 366, 369, 374–377
Hotel industry, 678, 687
Housing transitions, 735
Hybridity, 14, 108, 111, 112, 265, 270, 276, 277

I

"I Know, I Don't Forget and I Struggle", 606, 610, 614, 617
ICE/Immigration and Customs Enforcement, 499, 505, 507
Identification, 12, 13, 26, 58, 112, 132, 238, 260, 394, 410, 462–464, 470, 500, 505, 587, 602, 629, 635, 641, 645, 651, 653, 712, 715, 720, 722–724
Identities, 30, 61, 98, 107, 108, 112, 113, 135, 148, 149, 254, 277, 279, 366, 431, 449, 461, 466, 480, 573, 706, 730
Identity, 28, 39, 44, 224, 241, 266, 271, 273, 484, 485, 488, 534, 626
Identity and difference, 273, 461, 474, 475
Identity threat, 626, 628
Ideological ethos, 606, 617
Illegal immigrants, 77, 79, 507
Immigrant's children, 77, 117, 283, 284–289, 291, 292, 294, 296, 324, 326, 351–354, 356, 357, 419–421, 423, 430, 439, 441, 448, 634, 643, 699
Immigrant education, 356, 358, 359, 437, 442, 446
Immigrant perspective, 22, 23, 25, 71, 74
Immigrant students, 192, 283–296, 324, 326, 334, 336, 340, 354, 435–440, 442, 444–447, 449, 459, 463, 472, 659, 660
Immigrants, 22, 75–80, 87, 91, 136, 140–142, 145, 146, 148, 193, 249, 270, 284–287, 290, 291, 294, 295, 337, 356, 358–360, 403–405, 415, 422, 500, 597, 615
Immigration, 137, 147, 153, 267, 412, 442
Immigration history, 198, 350, 352
Inbetween/inbetweenness, 277
Inclusive approach, 178–182
Inclusive pedagogy, 462, 463
India, 421, 425, 472, 526, 527, 534, 535, 539, 577–582, 590, 591, 681, 687
Indian origin, 420, 421, 424–430
Indian women, 579, 580, 583, 588
Indigenous education, 213, 225–227
Individualistic culture, 480, 487, 491
Informal education, 136, 137, 520, 589, 712, 714, 715, 717, 722

Informal learning, 600–602, 678, 679, 691, 714, 729
Institutional actors, 509
Institutional agents, 457, 509, 667–669, 671
Integrated education, 88, 191, 192, 235, 243, 262, 440, 536, 576
Integration, 67, 68, 72–75, 77, 80, 87–89, 91, 93, 96, 97, 288, 394, 440, 520
Integration (policies), 14, 78, 85–97
Integration discourses, 21, 68
Integration regime, 75–79
Intercultural education, 294, 296, 325, 334, 343, 404, 405, 407–409, 411, 423, 437–439, 442, 448, 449, 610
Intersectional, 322–324, 365, 377
Intersectionality, 332, 344, 368, 713
Interviews, 15, 123, 124, 191–193, 222, 236, 270, 306, 307, 325, 331, 335, 411, 421, 457, 465, 502–504, 506, 551–553, 555, 578, 579, 588, 618, 665, 666, 712, 713
Inuit Qau-jimajatuqangit conversation, 191, 214, 222–227
Ireland, 73, 190, 192, 283–285, 289, 290–296, 521, 522, 559–561, 567, 568, 570, 573, 732–735
Islam, 63, 518, 526, 538, 539, 543–545, 548, 550, 553
Islamic schools, 518, 520, 524, 528–531, 545
Isolation, 166, 206, 217, 442, 506, 598
Israel, 15, 135–138, 140–144, 147, 148, 190, 191, 232–335, 238, 239, 408, 617

L

Labour, 19, 39, 41, 284, 526, 530, 602, 705
Language education policy, 169, 173, 178–180, 190, 195, 196, 269
Language policy, 196
Language revitalization, 190, 197, 203, 209, 210, 224
Language socialization, 147, 178
Language transmission, 120, 121, 123, 124, 127, 130–132
Large-scale immigration, 283, 296
Latin American, 73, 444, 696
Latin American immigrants, 435, 445
Latinos, 441, 458, 497–500, 508, 511, 613
Learning, 4, 10, 20, 23, 24, 38, 42, 44, 46, 47, 89, 148, 160, 161, 166, 405, 407, 458, 597, 702
Learning processes, 1, 3, 12, 22, 23, 30, 36–38, 41, 42, 44, 46, 112, 234, 517, 543, 678, 682, 723
Linguistic diversity, 171, 172, 205, 208, 209, 403–405

Literacy, 15, 136, 139, 140, 171, 172, 182, 256, 359, 393, 584, 643
Local knowledge, 599, 678, 679, 683–685, 687–692

M
Madrasah, 519, 543, 547–558
Madrasah curriculum, 543, 549–550
Madrid, 325, 435–442, 446, 447, 449
Mainstream culture, 449, 531
Mainstream multiculturalism, 606, 617
Malay Muslims, 518, 519, 543, 544, 554
Malay schools, 544–548, 554
Malta, 16, 153, 154, 156, 158, 166
Marginalized youth, 711, 717
Marriage, 15, 56, 59, 118, 119, 124, 374, 376, 425, 581, 582
Melbourne, 461–463, 465, 466, 598, 599, 601, 641–647, 649, 651–653, 655–656
Mergner, 4, 12, 23, 25, 30, 36–47, 68, 69, 390, 392
Migration, 2, 9–11, 15, 17, 19–22, 36–38, 46, 47, 74, 148, 155, 189, 267, 277, 322, 444, 448, 449, 480, 559, 577, 578, 583, 605, 652, 679–681, 688, 689, 699
Migration theory, 19–21, 31
Minorities, 1, 21, 26, 324, 393, 395, 397, 522, 524, 702, 730
Minority education, 132, 191, 195, 214, 226, 227, 254, 255, 256, 261, 302, 624
Minority education policy, 165, 203
Minority parents, 190, 191, 231, 232
Minutemen, 500
Mobility, 23, 70, 589, 730, 732
Modern Greek Language, 606, 610–612, 615, 617
Modernisation, 71, 234, 250
Monocultural habitus, 170, 171
Monolingual habitus, 171, 177, 334
Mother tongue, 126, 127, 196, 198, 220, 255, 257, 260, 266, 276, 289, 301, 352, 355–358, 410, 414, 423, 438, 549, 580, 587, 643, 644
Mother-tongue languages, 352, 355–357
Motivation, 38, 98, 172, 173, 210, 340, 438, 441, 459, 480–483, 489, 490, 492, 493, 501, 509, 553, 555, 628, 629, 661, 668, 673, 689, 705, 744
Mozambique, 422, 425, 430, 520, 577–579, 581–583, 588, 590, 591
Multicultural education, 252, 255, 439, 455, 462, 598, 605–607, 609, 610, 612, 617, 618, 643

Multiculturalism, 643, 648, 654, 655
Multiculturality, 254, 256, 259, 261
Multiethnic society, 625
Muslim community, 544, 546, 549, 553

N
Narratives, 13, 45, 146, 148, 154–156, 159, 160, 163–165, 267, 271, 277, 332, 343, 377, 410, 443, 608, 617, 618, 713
National curriculum, 371–373, 405, 411, 598, 606, 610, 617
Negotiation, 1, 4, 81, 190, 193, 215, 223, 313, 322, 327, 357, 412, 414, 439, 498, 519, 543, 546, 554, 556, 567, 672, 674, 713
Neo-liberal transformation, 13
Neo-liberalism, 90, 653–657
Netherlands, 1, 171, 520, 524–530, 533, 535–537, 539
Network theory, 21, 22
Newcastle-upon-Tyne, 323, 324, 349, 353
Non-formal education, 707
Northern Ireland, 732–735
Nunavut territory, 190, 214, 224, 226

O
Opportunity structure, 660, 668, 674, 678
Othering, 12, 163, 326, 331, 332, 337–341, 343–345, 365, 369, 376

P
Palestinians, 683
Parental involvement, 232, 234, 244, 393, 661
Parents expectations, 244
Parents' night, 193, 302, 304–309, 311, 312, 314
Participation, 2, 56–60, 63, 80, 87–90, 95, 104, 136, 181, 193, 234, 242, 244, 305, 309, 324, 327, 355, 383–385, 392, 396, 397, 410, 448, 458, 475, 507, 509, 535, 535, 627, 647, 654, 689
Peers, 440, 448, 501, 506, 589, 659, 660, 664, 667–670, 674, 731
Philippines, 677–680, 683, 686, 688–691
Pierre Bourdieu, 8, 104, 725
PISA, 334, 351, 352, 359, 360, 366, 403, 430
Place, 23, 28, 31, 139, 177, 266, 268, 271, 274, 277, 322, 328, 438, 470, 601, 623, 636, 651, 664, 725
Plural assimilation, 431
Pluralism, 95, 101, 112, 269, 270, 559, 563
Plurilingual, 17, 169, 170, 178–182
Policy on foreigners (Swiss), 92

Population, 55, 71, 73, 78, 79, 81, 86, 87, 96–98, 257, 445, 455, 501, 589, 705
Portugal, 124, 126–128, 132, 322, 352, 419–423, 425, 426, 430, 438, 519, 520, 577–579, 582, 583, 586, 587, 589–591, 599, 696, 697, 700, 701, 732–734
Positioning, 270, 377, 469, 470, 570, 707, 713, 715
Possible selves, 456, 457, 480–483, 485, 487–491
Postcolonial/postcolonialism, 108, 192, 265, 266, 269–271, 465
Postcolonialism, 279, 270, 462
Power, 4, 13, 70, 74, 80, 81, 85, 95, 96, 105, 111, 224, 226, 243, 270, 331, 332, 343, 344, 366, 406, 582, 600, 607, 627, 644, 646, 656
Prejudices, 334, 404, 406, 409, 415, 441
Privileged migrants, 117, 119
Process of socialization (Vergesellschaftung), 23
Producing and reproducing social categories, 42, 72, 122, 129, 131, 286, 297, 695
Professors, 459, 507, 509, 510
Project-based learning, 325, 403, 407, 412

R
Race, 117, 143, 164, 189, 193, 227, 271, 272, 279, 332, 367, 374, 455, 475, 486, 526, 608, 618, 661, 662, 706
Racial-ethnic identity, 484–490, 493
Racialization, 321, 325, 376, 662
Rawls, 563, 569–573
Recognition, 2, 11, 94, 163, 165, 209, 278, 323, 338, 344, 345, 409, 517, 518, 520, 521, 566, 697, 700, 706, 714, 715
Reconciliation, 304, 309, 517, 598, 610–612, 615, 617
Religion, 103, 117, 272, 283, 335, 341, 343, 372, 373, 449, 517, 520–525, 535, 556, 561, 583, 612, 651, 714
Resilience, 15, 160, 501, 600, 718, 722
Resources, 42, 56, 60–63, 88, 111, 112, 120, 161, 178, 219, 326, 552, 567, 635, 700, 705, 745
Right to diversity, 249, 257, 263
Risk policies or security, 97
Rituals, 129, 135, 142, 144, 145, 148, 447, 534, 583, 718, 720, 724
Rom, 598, 623–628, 630, 633, 635–637
Roma, 623, 625, 627, 629, 630, 633
Rushdie, 265, 267, 268, 273, 274, 277

S
Sacred spaces, 599, 647
School, 104, 126, 131, 177, 179, 206, 270, 294, 310, 325, 334, 335, 365, 414, 419, 421, 426, 441, 446, 465, 467, 506, 564, 566, 632, 634, 660, 661, 664, 671, 674, 697
School achievement, 301, 376, 419, 420, 428, 431, 440
School curriculum, 257, 259, 352, 463, 474, 518, 543, 554, 607, 678
School policies, 296, 311, 324, 365–367, 369, 376, 377
School segregation, 394, 395, 440, 445, 624, 636
Schooling, 68, 123, 169, 191, 192, 213, 221, 222, 259, 262, 291, 292, 335, 425, 427, 459, 504, 506, 508, 509, 519, 584, 589, 598, 644, 697, 701
Schools in Ireland, 560
Secularism, 560, 562, 567, 572–574
Separation, 263, 405, 520, 536, 537, 587, 632, 701
Sexuality, 103, 332, 314, 366–371, 373, 376, 377, 731
Singapore, 518, 519, 543–551, 554–557, 680
Social capital, 29, 111, 120, 121, 123, 126, 128, 286, 290, 292, 295, 296, 394, 498, 501, 505, 506, 522, 564, 568, 599, 600, 632, 659
Social class, 117, 119, 131, 154, 285, 286, 420, 445, 448, 583, 585, 586, 588, 661, 699, 714, 731, 733
Social cohesion, 3, 14, 109, 111, 112, 133, 249, 287, 297, 440, 442, 446, 518, 527, 536, 547, 605, 643, 695
Social difference, 10, 17, 37, 42, 189, 190, 193, 226, 227, 331–337, 340, 341, 343–345, 352, 543, 597
Social exclusion, 12, 37, 101, 109, 518, 600, 682, 700, 706, 711, 722, 724
Social heterogeneity, 323, 331–333, 335, 336, 338, 339, 345, 420
Social inequality, 1, 28–30, 233, 331, 332, 338, 343, 344, 518, 695
Social learning, 69, 288, 390, 600, 653, 711, 717, 718, 722, 724, 725, 730, 733, 735, 737
Social limits, 4, 31, 36–38, 41, 44, 47, 360, 384, 390, 392
Social mobility, 2, 11, 25, 28, 78, 120, 391, 518, 519, 527, 543, 549, 643, 671, 682
Social network, 22, 64, 117, 122, 126–128, 130–132, 164, 286, 291, 295, 444, 446, 463, 501, 519, 567, 579, 599, 659, 660, 663–666, 674, 678, 680, 687, 689, 690, 697, 730

Social relationships, 16, 21, 41, 106, 403, 659–661, 664, 666, 670, 674, 685, 688
Social security, 153, 160, 444
Social self-understanding, 13, 69, 80, 81
Society, 20, 24, 25, 29, 64, 72, 117, 119, 121, 127, 130, 161, 261, 336, 354, 383, 431, 570, 601, 629, 635, 720, 724, 725, 745
Socio-cultural criteria, 96
Socio-cultural theory, 16
Socio-economic, 96, 124, 547, 549, 584, 644, 661, 699, 700, 733, 734–736
Somali immigrant adolescents, 660, 662, 663
Somalia, 156–158
Spain, 108, 199, 322, 325, 422, 435–437, 441, 442, 444, 599, 623, 696, 700
Spatiality, 641, 642, 644–646, 651
Stigmatization, 165, 533, 579, 624, 627, 629, 631, 635–637
Stuart Hall, 60, 107
Student services, 459, 509
Students, 36, 190, 195, 203, 220, 292, 305, 307, 308, 310, 324, 334–337, 339, 341, 345, 447, 455, 463, 508, 509, 549, 644, 666
Subculture, 367, 599, 600, 695, 697–700, 702, 703, 706
Subjectivity, 13, 69, 70, 76, 81, 159, 328, 332, 376, 390, 464, 645, 705, 722
Surinam, 526, 527, 530, 535
Swann report, 352, 354, 355
Sweden, 61, 62, 136, 322, 324, 365, 366, 369, 371, 372
Systemic functional linguistics, 193, 302, 304

T

Teacher training, 203, 207, 295, 335, 344, 423, 437
Tertiary education, 3, 288, 550
Traffic checkpoints, 499
Transculturality, 2, 22

Translanguaging, 182
Transnationalism, 2, 22, 688
Transphobia, 369, 371, 374, 376

U

Undocumented immigrants, 499, 504, 505, 512
United Arab Emirates, 599, 677, 678, 681–683, 686, 689–691
University, 358, 498, 499, 502, 505, 672, 698
UP2YOUTH, 696, 707
Urban development, 109–111, 548
USA, 1, 56, 92, 110, 140, 169, 296, 322, 324, 383, 385, 408, 455–457, 461, 479–483, 485–493, 497–500, 503, 505, 597, 599–601, 663, 680, 724

V

Victimization, 60, 159
Voluntary, 56, 201, 203, 208, 209, 337, 480, 489, 560, 565, 570, 585, 610, 678, 698

W

Women, 9, 15, 59, 94, 370, 579, 585, 586, 588, 589, 648, 680, 688

Y

Young migrants, 11–14, 19, 20, 25–27, 30, 31, 35, 36–39, 41–47, 112, 327, 366, 369, 695, 697
Young people, 9–12, 36, 42, 46, 249, 278, 289, 321, 322, 325, 328, 366, 377, 430, 599, 647, 697, 703, 704, 706, 712, 723, 725
Youth, 19, 31, 68, 235, 271, 284, 324, 349, 356, 358, 366, 367, 370, 429, 600–602, 608, 636, 648, 654–656, 661, 697–707, 713, 717, 729, 731, 732, 735, 738, 739
Yugoslavia, kingdom of, 250, 256, 259
Yugoslavia, socialist, 257, 260